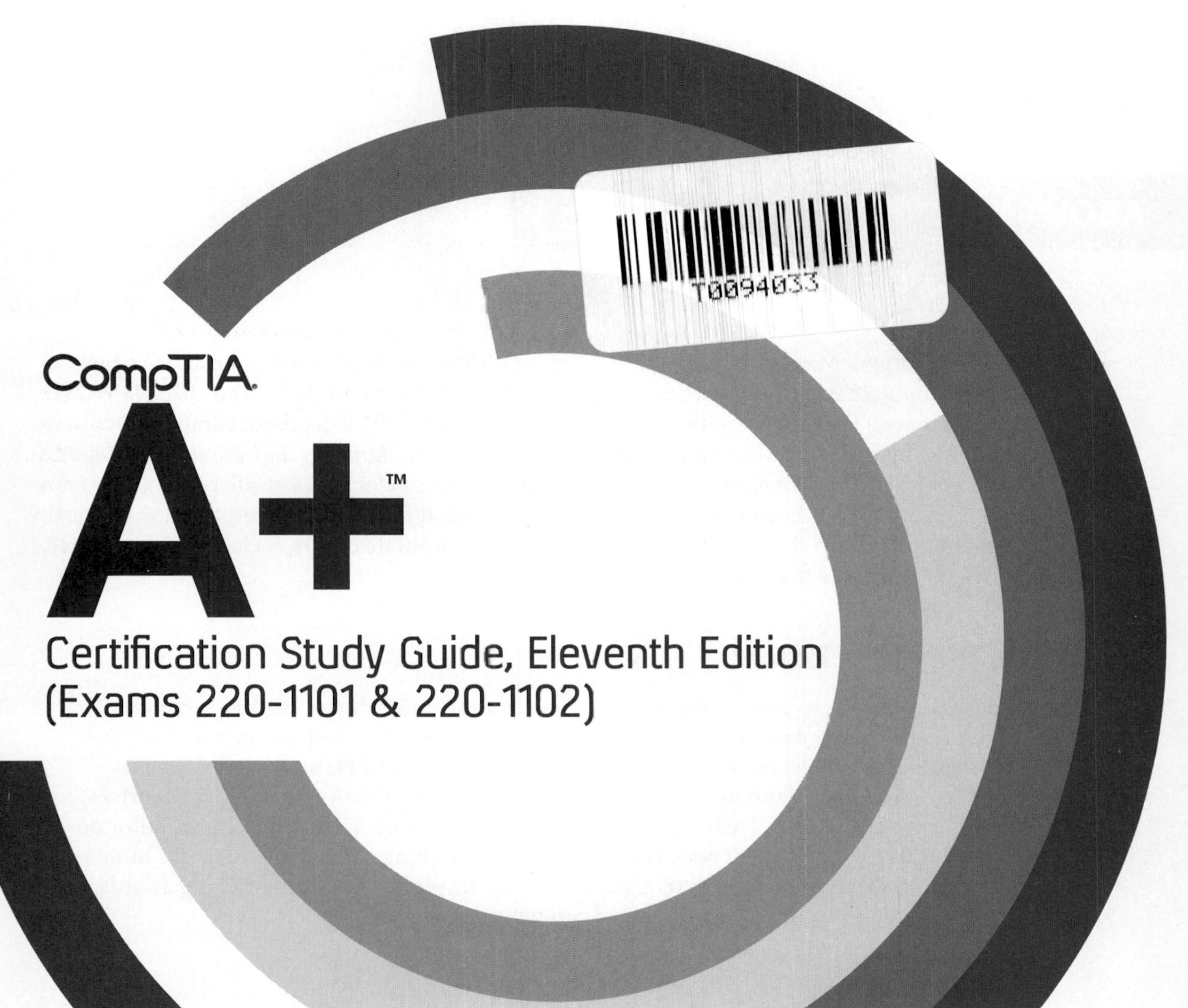

CompTIA

A+™

Certification Study Guide, Eleventh Edition (Exams 220-1101 & 220-1102)

ABOUT THE AUTHOR

Faithe Wempen, MA, CompTIA A+, MOS Master Instructor, has been writing and teaching about computers since 1993, with the release of her first book, *Abort, Retry, Fail: 101 MS-DOS Error Messages*. Faithe is the author/co-author of more than 150 books about computer hardware and software, including *Mike Meyers' CompTIA A+ Guide to Managing and Troubleshooting PCs Lab Manual, Fifth Edition,* as well as textbooks, magazine articles, and website content. For more than 20 years she has taught A+ certification prep classes at Indiana University/Purdue University at Indianapolis (IUPUI), and her free online classes for corporate clients, including Sony and HP, have educated more than a quarter of a million students.

About the Technical Editor

Chris Crayton is a technical consultant, trainer, author, and industry-leading technical editor. He has worked as a computer technology and networking instructor, information security director, network administrator, network engineer, and PC specialist. Chris has authored several print and online books on PC repair, CompTIA A+, CompTIA Security+, and Microsoft Windows. He has also served as technical editor and content contributor on numerous technical titles for several of the leading publishing companies. He holds numerous industry certifications, has been recognized with many professional and teaching awards, and has served as a state-level SkillsUSA final competition judge.

CompTIA A+™

Certification Study Guide, Eleventh Edition (Exams 220-1101 & 220-1102)

Faithe Wempen

New York Chicago San Francisco
Athens London Madrid Mexico City
Milan New Delhi Singapore Sydney Toronto

McGraw Hill books are available at special quantity discounts to use as premiums and sales promotions, or for use in corporate training programs. To contact a representative, please visit the Contact Us pages at www.mhprofessional.com.

CompTIA A+™ Certification Study Guide, Eleventh Edition (Exams 220-1101 & 220-1102)

1 2 3 4 5 6 7 8 9 LCR 26 25 24 23 22

Library of Congress Control Number: 2022939887

ISBN 978-1-264-62361-7
MHID 1-264-62361-5

Sponsoring Editor
Tim Green

Editorial Supervisor
Patty Mon

Project Manager
Revathi Viswanathan, KnowledgeWorks Global Ltd.

Acquisitions Coordinator
Caitlin Cromley-Linn

Technical Editor
Chris Crayton

Copy Editor
Lisa McCoy

Proofreader
Paul Tyler

Indexer
Ted Laux

Production Supervisor
Thomas Somers

Composition
KnowledgeWorks Global Ltd.

Illustration
KnowledgeWorks Global Ltd.

Art Director, Cover
Jeff Weeks

To Margaret, who makes it all possible.

—Faithe Wempen

CONTENTS AT A GLANCE

Part IV
Laptops and Mobile Devices

Part V
Networking

Part VI
Security

CONTENTS

Part IV
Laptops and Mobile Devices

Part V
Networking

PREFACE

The objective of this study guide is to help you prepare for and pass the required exams so you can begin to reap the career benefits of CompTIA A+ certification. Because the primary focus of this book is to help you pass the exams, we don't always cover every aspect of the related technology. Some aspects of the technology are only covered to the extent necessary to help you understand what you need to know to pass the exams.

In This Book

This book is organized in such a way as to serve as an in-depth review for the latest version of the CompTIA A+ exams, released in 2022: Exam 220-1101 (Core 1) and Exam 220-1102 (Core 2). Each chapter covers a major aspect of the exams, with an emphasis on the "why" as well as the "how to" of IT support in the areas of installation, configuration, and maintenance of devices, PCs, and software; networking and security/forensics; diagnosis, resolution, and documentation of common hardware and software issues; troubleshooting; Internet and cloud usage; virtualization; desktop imaging; and deployment.

In the Chapters

We've created a set of chapter components that call your attention to important items, reinforce important points, and provide helpful exam-taking hints. Take a look at what you'll find in every chapter:

- Every chapter begins with the **Certification Objectives**—what you need to know in order to pass the section on the exams dealing with the chapter topic. The Certification Objective headings identify the objectives within the chapter, so you'll always know an objective when you see it!
- **Exam Watch** notes call attention to information about, and potential pitfalls in, the exams. These helpful hints reinforce your learning and exam preparation.
- **Step-by-Step Exercises** are interspersed throughout the chapters. These hands-on exercises allow you to get a feel for the real-world experience you need in order to pass the exams. They help you master skills that are likely to be an area of focus on the exams. Don't just read through the exercises; they are hands-on practice that you

should be comfortable completing. Learning by doing is an effective way to increase your competency with a product.

- **On the Job** notes describe the issues that come up most often in real-world settings. They provide a valuable perspective on certification- and product-related topics. They point out common mistakes and address questions that have arisen from on-the-job discussions and experience.
- **Scenario & Solution** sections lay out problems and solutions in a quick-read format.
- The **Certification Summary** is a succinct review of the chapter and a restatement of salient points regarding the exams.

- The **Two-Minute Drill** at the end of every chapter is a checklist of the main points of the chapter. It can be used for last-minute review.

- The **Self Test** offers multiple-choice questions similar to those found on the certification exams. The answers to these questions, as well as explanations of the answers, can be found at the end of each chapter. By taking the Self Test after completing each chapter, you'll reinforce what you've learned from that chapter while becoming familiar with the structure of the multiple-choice exam questions. The book does not include other types of questions that you may encounter on the exams, such as performance-based questions.

Online Content

Included with this book is access to online practice exam software, videos, performance-based questions, and the glossary and an exam objective map viewable through your web browser. Please see the appendix for more information about accessing the online content.

Some Pointers

Once you've finished reading this book, set aside some time to do a thorough review. You might want to return to the book several times and make use of all the methods it offers for reviewing the material:

- *Re-read all the Two-Minute Drills,* or have someone quiz you. You also can use the drills as a way to do a quick cram before the exams.
- *Review all the Scenario & Solution* sections for quick problem solving.
- *Complete the Exercises.* Did you do the exercises when you read through each chapter? If not, do them! These exercises are designed to cover exam topics, and there's no better way to get to know this material than by practicing. Be sure you understand why you are performing each step in each exercise. If there is something you are not clear on, re-read that section in the chapter.

- *Retake the Self Tests.* Taking the tests right after you've read the chapter is a good idea, because the questions help reinforce what you've just learned. However, it's an even better idea to go back later and do all the questions in the book in one sitting. Pretend that you're taking a live exam. When you go through the questions the first time, you should mark your answers on a separate piece of paper. That way, you can run through the questions as many times as you need to until you feel comfortable with the material.

ACKNOWLEDGMENTS

Tim Green, executive editor, helped get the new edition off to a good start by managing the acquisitions process and provided helpful ideas and feedback along the way. Caitlin Cromley-Linn, editorial coordinator, expertly managed the technical editing and development phases of the project. Chris Crayton provided expert technical feedback and suggestions that ensured the accuracy of our manuscript. Revathi Viswanathan, project manager, oversaw the copyediting and layout processes and kept all the balls in the air, juggling multiple documents and details. Speaking of the copyediting, Lisa McCoy did an expert job ensuring that our language was as clear and consistent as possible. Patty Mon supervised the editorial process and cross-checked exam objectives and study questions. The professional staff of the production department at KnowledgeWorks Global Ltd. turned a plain manuscript into the beautiful book you hold in your hands (or read on your screen). Proofreader Paul Tyler made sure no minor mistakes slipped through the cracks, and Ted Laux indexed the book—which is no small feat for a book of this size, with hundreds of technical terms.

INTRODUCTION

Earning CompTIA A+ certification means that you have the knowledge and the technical skills necessary to be a successful entry-level IT professional in today's environment. The exam objectives test your knowledge and skills in all the areas that today's computing environment requires. Although the exams cover a broad range of computer software and hardware, they are not vendor specific.

Both the CompTIA A+ 220-1101 Exam (also called Core 1) and the CompTIA A+ 220-1102 Exam (also called Core 2) are required to achieve your CompTIA A+ certification. As stated by CompTIA, together, the 220-1101 and 220-1102 exams "measure necessary competencies for an entry-level IT professional.... Successful candidates will have the knowledge required to assemble components based on customer requirements; install, configure, and maintain devices, PCs, and software for end users; understand the basics of networking and security/forensics; properly and safely diagnose, resolve, and document common hardware and software issues; apply troubleshooting skills; provide appropriate customer support; and understand the basics of virtualization, desktop imaging, and deployment."

How to Take a CompTIA A+ Certification Exam

Pearson VUE provides proctored testing services for many companies, including CompTIA. In addition to administering the tests, Pearson VUE scores the exam and provides statistical feedback on each section of the exam to the companies and organizations that use their services.

Pearson VUE also offers OnVUE, an online proctored solution that enables certain candidates to take exams via a proctored online interface. You register for an online proctored exam the same way you register for the in-person kind, but after registration you receive a link to the online testing platform. Various checks are done to ensure the integrity and security of the online test-taking system, including artificial intelligence (AI) identification checking and validation of the test-taker's environment.

On Exams 220-1101 and 220-1102, unanswered questions count against you. Assuming you have time left when you finish the other questions, you can return to the marked questions for further evaluation.

The standard test also marks the questions that are incomplete with a letter "I" once you've finished all the questions. You'll see the whole list of questions after you complete the last question. This screen allows you to go back and finish incomplete items, finish unmarked items, and return to questions you flagged for review.

An interesting and useful characteristic of the standard test is that questions may be marked and returned to later. This helps you manage your time while taking the test so you don't spend too much time on any one question.

Question Types

The CompTIA A+ exams consist of several types of question formats, as described in a YouTube video on the test experience at https://www.youtube.com/watch?v=XVs-M3hValw. We strongly recommend that you take the time to watch this short video. Here is a brief overview of the question formats you may see on your exam.

Multiple-Choice Questions Many CompTIA A+ exam questions are of the multiple-choice variety. Below each question is a list of four or five possible answers. Use the available radio buttons to select the correct answer from the given choices.

Multiple-Response Questions A multiple-response question is a multiple-choice question with more than one correct answer, in which case, the number of correct answers required is clearly stated.

Fill-in-the-Blank Questions A fill-in-the-blank question prompts you to type a word or phrase. Be aware that answers may be case-sensitive.

Graphical Questions Some questions incorporate a graphical element or a video available via an Exhibit button to provide a visual representation of the problem or present the question itself. These questions are easy to identify because they refer to the exhibit in the question and there is an exhibit. An example of a graphical question might be to identify a component on a drawing of a motherboard. This is done in the multiple-choice format by having callouts labeled A, B, C, or D point to the selections. A drag-and-drop question is another form of graphical question in which you select a token, such as a graphic of a computer component, and drag and drop it to a designated area in response to the question.

Performance-Based Questions Performance-based questions include simulations and require the candidate to perform certain tasks based on multifaceted scenarios. When you encounter one of these questions, you will click a Simulation button and enter a simulated environment in which you must perform one or more tasks. Sample performance-based questions are included with the online content that accompanies this book (see the appendix for more details).

Study Strategies

There are different ways to study for the different types of questions you will see on the CompTIA A+ certification exams. The following section outlines some of the methods you can use to prepare for the different types of questions.

Knowledge-Based Questions

Knowledge-based questions require that you memorize facts. These questions may not cover material that you use on a daily basis, but they do cover material that CompTIA thinks an IT professional should be able to answer. Here are some keys to memorizing facts:

- **Repetition** The more times you expose your brain to a fact, the more it sinks in, and your ability to remember it increases.
- **Association** Connecting facts within a logical framework makes them easier to remember.
- **Motor association** Remembering something is easier if you write it down or perform another physical act, like clicking the practice exam answers.

Performance-Based Questions

The first step in preparing for performance-based questions is to absorb as many facts relating to the exam content areas as you can. Of course, actual hands-on experience will greatly help you in this area. For example, it really helps in knowing how to install a display adapter if you have actually done the procedure at least once. Some of the questions will place you in a scenario and ask for the best solution to the problem at hand. It is in these scenarios that having a good knowledge level and some experience will help you.

CompTIA A+ Certification Exam 220-1101

The CompTIA A+ Certification Exam 220-1101 (Core 1) consists of five domains (categories). CompTIA represents the relative importance of each domain within the body of knowledge required for an entry-level IT professional taking this exam.

1.0 Mobile Devices	15%
2.0 Networking	20%
3.0 Hardware	25%
4.0 Virtualization and Cloud Computing	11%
5.0 Hardware and Network Troubleshooting	29%

CompTIA A+ Certification Exam 220-1102

The CompTIA A+ Certification Exam 220-1102 (Core 2) consists of four domains (categories). CompTIA represents the relative importance of each domain within the body of knowledge required for an entry-level IT professional taking this exam.

1.0 Operating Systems	31%
3.0 Security	25%
4.0 Software Troubleshooting	22%
5.0 Operational Procedures	22%

Part I

Safety and Professionalism

CHAPTERS

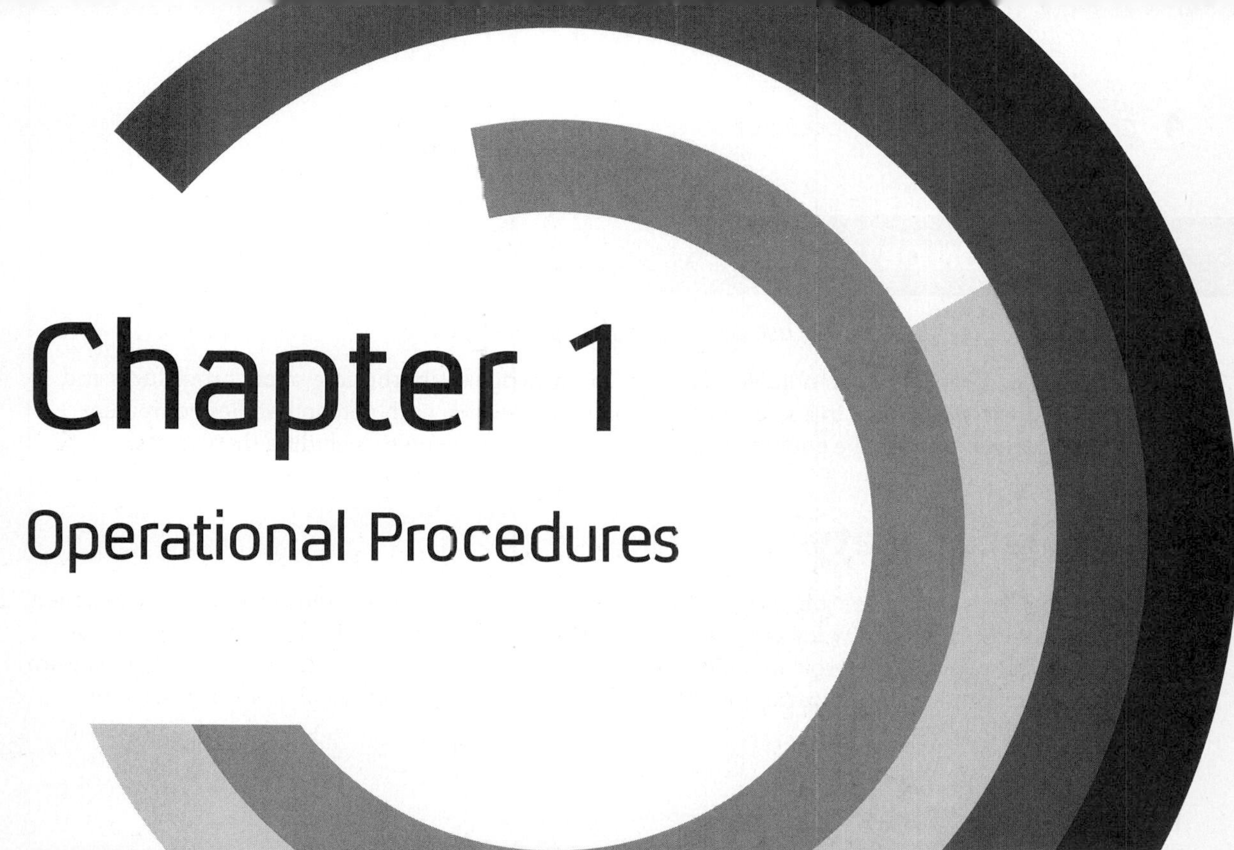

Chapter 1

Operational Procedures

CERTIFICATION OBJECTIVES

- **1102: 4.4** Given a scenario, use common safety procedures
- **1102: 4.5** Summarize environmental impacts and local environmental controls

✓ Two-Minute Drill

Q&A Self Test

Physicians take a Hippocratic Oath, in which they promise to "First, do no harm." It's essential that medical professionals, when working on such an important machine as the human body, not make things worse. This same concept applies to IT professionals as well. Even if you are not able to fix a device or solve a problem, at a minimum you should do no harm to the device, the user, the environment, or yourself. That's why this book begins with some basic IT safety training and environmental awareness.

CERTIFICATION OBJECTIVE

- *1102: 4.4 Given a scenario, use common safety procedures*

The CompTIA A+ candidate must prove knowledge of appropriate safety procedures and how to participate in a safe work environment in which each person handles equipment safely to protect the equipment and prevent injury to people (including themselves).

Workplace Safety

Safety is everyone's job, even in an organization in which designated employees are assigned direct responsibility for safety compliance and implementation. Everyone in an organization must play an active role in maintaining a safe work environment, which includes being aware of common safety hazards and acting to remove them to avoid accidents that can harm people and equipment.

Extinguishing Fires

If a fire should start, your first concern is safety for yourself and others. It is often better to escape a fire, trigger a fire alarm, and close doors behind you than to try to fight it. The following discussion will not fully prepare you to fight a fire, but it will make you aware of the dangers and the need for proper training.

The typical workplace has a variety of potential fire sources and fuels. Look around areas such as the break room, offices, work cubicles, the wiring closet, server room, and computer workbench and imagine how a fire could start and what would fuel the fire. One potential fire source is a faulty computer or peripheral power supply. The wiring in the wall, as well as in any equipment or appliance, could develop a short, resulting in heat that could spread to nearby fuels such as paper, solvents, or furniture. Fire extinguishers come in several classes based on the fuel feeding the fire. Following is a description of the most common fire extinguisher classes:

Class A	Use for fires involving ordinary combustible materials, such as wood, paper, cardboard, and most plastics.
Class B	Use on fires involving flammable or combustible liquids, including gasoline, kerosene, grease, and oil.
Class C	Use on fires involving electrical equipment, such as wiring, circuit breakers, outlets, computers, and appliances. The material in a Class C extinguisher is nonconductive to reduce the risk of shock that could result from using a conductive material.
Class D	Use on chemical fires involving magnesium, titanium, potassium, and sodium.
Class K	Use on fires involving cooking oils, trans fats, or other fats in cooking appliances. This type of extinguisher should be in commercial kitchens and restaurants.

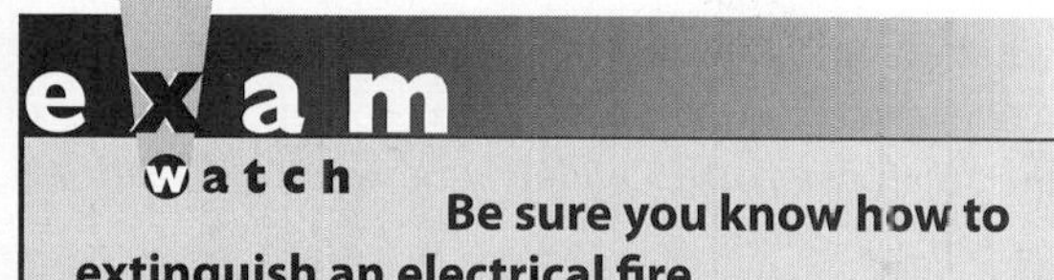

Be sure you know how to extinguish an electrical fire.

Keep at least one fire extinguisher of the appropriate class or classes handy by your desk or workbench, in the wiring closet, the server room, and other locations. In some locations, you may have air-pressurized water (APW) fire extinguishers. Only use these on fires involving ordinary combustibles (see Class A in the previous list).

Some fire extinguishers contain dry chemicals, which leave a residue that reduces the chance of the fire reigniting, and some dry chemical extinguishers are rated for more than one class, which is very handy for a multiple-fuel fire. For instance, a BC extinguisher can be used on Class B or Class C fires, but be aware that it will leave a residue that must be cleaned immediately because it is corrosive. An ABC fire extinguisher is rated for all three fire types, but it leaves a sticky residue that can damage computers and electrical appliances.

Some Class B and C extinguishers contain carbon dioxide (CO_2), a nonflammable gas. One advantage of a CO_2 extinguisher is that it does not leave a residue, but because a CO_2 extinguisher relies on high pressure, it may shoot out bits of dry ice. Never use a CO_2 extinguisher on a Class A fire because it may not smother the fire enough to fully extinguish it.

Another nonflammable gas sometimes used in Class B and C fire extinguishers is halon, with nitrogen as a propellant. Halon fire extinguishers are ideal for electronic equipment because they leave no residue; in addition, halon extinguishers are effective on Class A fires. However, halon was classified as an ozone-depleting chlorofluorocarbon (CFC) under the Clean Air Act, and production of halon ceased in 1994. There are no federal or state regulations prohibiting the buying, selling, or use of halon extinguishers, but once the existing supply of halon has been depleted, no more will be created.

Using the wrong type of fire extinguisher on a fire can spread the fire, and using water on an electrical fire could electrocute you.

Lifting Techniques When Moving Equipment

In the United States, lifting is the number-one cause of back injuries. When lifting and moving computer equipment or any objects, take the time to do it safely, protecting yourself and the equipment.

It is easy to injure your back when moving equipment. The weight of what you lift and how you lift it are important factors, which means that every instance of lifting and moving is different.

Lifting Weight Limits

There are no government regulations about what an employee can lift, and the Occupational Safety and Health Administration (OSHA) has no standards written for many specific workplace lifting situations. This is because the actual circumstances differ widely, and weight is just one consideration.

The National Institute for Occupational Safety and Health (NIOSH) publishes a lifting equation so that employers can evaluate the lifting tasks for employees and establish a recommended weight limit. This is a rather complicated equation requiring considerable effort to gather information about each situation. Government agencies and other organizations have created calculators based on this equation to help employees establish guidelines for lifting. Exercise 1-1 will help you research lifting guidelines.

EXERCISE 1-1

Research Lifting Guidelines

It is important to protect yourself from injury while lifting, so take some time to research the guidelines.

1. Use your favorite Internet search engine to search on the keywords "workplace safety lifting guide." Search through the results to find a guide that will help you with your own situation.

   The Ohio Bureau of Workers' Compensation site is one possible resource: https://www.bwc.ohio.gov/employer/programs/safety/liftguide/liftguide.aspx. If that URL doesn't work, go to their home page at https://www.bwc.ohio.gov and search for "lifting guidelines."
2. When you find a guide that allows you to enter criteria for a lift, make up a scenario, enter the data, and see the results it calculates.

Tips for Safe Lifting and Moving

The best protection is common sense and very careful lifting. So when lifting a heavy object, protect your back by following these tips:

- Plan the move and clear the path before beginning.
- Move as close to the item as possible.
- Check the weight of the equipment to see if you need assistance in lifting and moving it.
- Keep your back straight and vertical to the floor.

- Keep your head up and look straight ahead.
- Do not stoop, but bend your knees.
- Carry the item close to your body.
- Tighten the abdominal muscles to help your back.
- Use slow, smooth movements, and do not twist your back while lifting.
- Don't try to carry heavy items farther than a few feet without the aid of a utility cart.

Avoiding Touch Hazards

Whenever handling computer components, be careful of the sharp edges on sheet metal computer cases and in some peripherals. It is easy to cut yourself on these. Similarly, the backs of many circuit boards contain very sharp wire ends that can cause puncture wounds. Work gloves offer protection, even if they are a bit awkward to use while handling delicate computer equipment. If you cannot wear gloves, be cautious, checking each surface before positioning your hands.

Heat can also be a hazard. Some components, such as a central processing unit (CPU) heat sink and a laser printer's fuser, remain hot enough to burn you for several minutes after powering them down. Cautiously check for hot components by holding your hand near, but not on, computer components before you touch them.

Desktop PC power supplies and monitors are high-voltage equipment. Never open them, and never wear an antistatic strap while working with either of these components.

Avoiding Electric Shock

Both high voltage and low voltage can be dangerous, so be sure to follow precautions when working around high- and low-voltage devices and avoid contact with them. Leave servicing high-voltage peripherals such as monitors, laser printers, and power supplies to technicians trained in that area. Even when unplugged for an extended period, such devices can store enough voltage to cause severe injury or death from electrical shock. Never use an electrostatic discharge (ESD) wristband or other antistatic equipment (discussed later in this chapter) when working with high-voltage devices.

Working Safely with Printers

When working on printers, remove or constrain anything that might dangle down into the moving parts. This includes long hair, clothing, jewelry, long sleeves, scarves, and neckties. A necktie or scarf itself can also build up a static charge that it can pass to the component if it touches it. When wearing a tie or scarf, make sure you either tuck it into your shirt or use a clip or tie tack.

Do not try to operate a printer with the cover off, even if you don't have anything dangling. The cartridge in an inkjet printer and the print head in a dot matrix printer move rapidly back and forth across the page, and getting your hands or other objects caught is possible, damaging both you and the printer. The laser beam in a laser printer can cause eye damage. Most printers do not work when their covers are open anyway.

Working Safely with Power Supplies

The power stored in the capacitors in a computer's high-voltage power supply is enough to cause injury or death. Simply turning off the power switch is not enough. Even when turned off, the power supply in a computer or printer can provide electricity, and most motherboards continue to have power applied—a technology called soft power that we describe in Chapter 10. To be safe, unplug the power supply and never wear an ESD wrist strap (covered later in this chapter) when replacing or handling a power supply. Never open a power supply unless you are specially trained to do so because of the risk of electrocution; if a power supply or one of its fans isn't working, replace the entire unit.

exam watch

Before the introduction of the ATX motherboard design (1995), some technicians used to leave the power supply plugged in while they worked on the computer to allow static to bleed away from the computer into the wall outlet's ground wire. That worked because in those old AT motherboard systems, the motherboard received no power when the computer was off. In modern systems, the motherboard continues to receive power whenever the PC is plugged in, so there is a risk of electrical shock even when the computer is off. That's why today's technicians always unplug power before servicing a PC.

Working Safely with Display Devices

Although flat-panel displays have replaced cathode ray tube (CRT) monitors, there are still a few CRTs out in the field. Remember—like power supplies, CRT monitors are high-voltage equipment and can store a harmful electrical charge, even when unplugged. Never open a CRT case, and never wear an ESD wrist strap when handling a CRT. You do not want to provide a path to ground through your body for this charge. Flat panel monitors are less hazardous (especially when off), but you should not touch a liquid crystal display's (LCD's) inverter if the device is on. And be aware that traditional cold cathode fluorescent lamp (CCFL) backlights found in some LCD monitors carry several thousand volts.

Protecting Equipment

While personal safety is paramount, you are also responsible for protecting the equipment you handle to avoid repair and replacement costs.

Safely Transporting Equipment

If you are unsure of the proper way to move a computer or peripheral, check out the manufacturer's documentation. For instance, to protect fragile components, a scanner may have a transportation lock that you must engage before moving it. Some heavy devices, such as heavy-duty laser printers, may require two people to lift and carry.

Power down each piece of equipment and disconnect it from power outlets before moving it—even when moving it from one side of a desk to another. This includes laptops! Yes, they are portable devices, but if a laptop has a conventional hard disk drive (HDD), moving it around while it is actively running can potentially harm the hard drive. This warning doesn't apply to mobile devices with solid-state drive (SSD) storage only.

After the computer powers down, unplug the power cord before moving it. This precaution is not just about electrical power but also about a device not being physically tethered to a wall when it is on the move. A trip and fall or fumble can result in the power cord being forcibly disconnected at one end or the other, potentially causing damage.

Be especially careful when moving monitors. They can be fragile, and you must take care not to drop a monitor or put any pressure on its screen.

Protecting Components from Electrostatic Discharge

One of the most significant threats to a computer component is *electrostatic discharge (ESD),* also known as static electricity. Static electricity is all around us, especially when the humidity and temperature are both low. When putting on a jacket makes the hair on your arm stand up, you are encountering static electricity. When you slide your feet across a carpet and then touch a person, a doorknob, or a light switch and feel a jolt, you are experiencing a static discharge.

The Dangers of ESD

ESD happens when two objects of uneven electrical charge encounter one another. Electricity always travels from an area of higher charge to an area of lower charge, and the static shock that you feel is the result of electrons jumping from your skin to the other object. The same process can occur within a computer. If your body has a high electric potential, electrons will transfer to the first computer component that you touch.

ESD can cause irreparable damage to your computer's components and peripherals. Typical discharges range from 600 to 25,000 volts, although at tiny amperages. Damage to computer components can occur at as little as 30 volts—a charge you will not even detect because, under the right conditions, your body can withstand 25,000 volts.

These very low-voltage static charges, or "hidden ESD," can come from many sources, including dust buildup inside a computer. Dust and other foreign particles can hold an electric charge that slowly bleeds into nearby components, damaging them slowly over time.

exam watch

Most static discharges are well above 600 volts, but it takes a charge of only about 30 volts to weaken or destroy a computer component.

Protection from ESD Damage and Injury

There are many ways to prevent ESD from damaging computer equipment. Low humidity contributes to ESD, so when possible, keep computer equipment in a room in which the humidity is between 50 and 80 percent. Avoid cold and dry conditions, as that creates the ideal environment for ESD to occur. But do not allow the humidity to rise above 80 percent, or condensation could form on the equipment and cause it to short out.

on the job

The American Society of Heating, Refrigerating and Air-Conditioning Engineers (ASHRAE) recommends an acceptable operating temperature range of 64° to 81°F (18° to 27°C), with 50 percent humidity being ideal.

To prevent damage to the system, you must equalize the electrical charge between your body and the components inside your computer. Touching a grounded portion of your computer's chassis will work to some extent, but for complete safety, use an *ESD wrist strap* with a ground wire attached to the computer frame. See Figure 1-1 showing an ESD wrist strap with an alligator clip for attaching the ground wire to a grounded object. This will drain static charges from your body to ground. If a static charge has built up in the computer equipment, it will also bleed from the computer through your body to ground. This is true of any electrical flow, so you must never use an antistatic strap attached to your body when working around high-voltage devices.

Never use an ESD prevention device in a manner that puts your body between a power source and ground, such as when working around high-voltage devices.

Before you pick up a loose computer component, if you are not wearing or touching an antistatic device, discharge any static electricity on your body by touching something metal, such as a table leg or chair.

Many computer assembly and repair shops use an *ESD mat* that discharges static when you stand on it. An ESD mat on a bench table is a safe place to put expansion cards or other

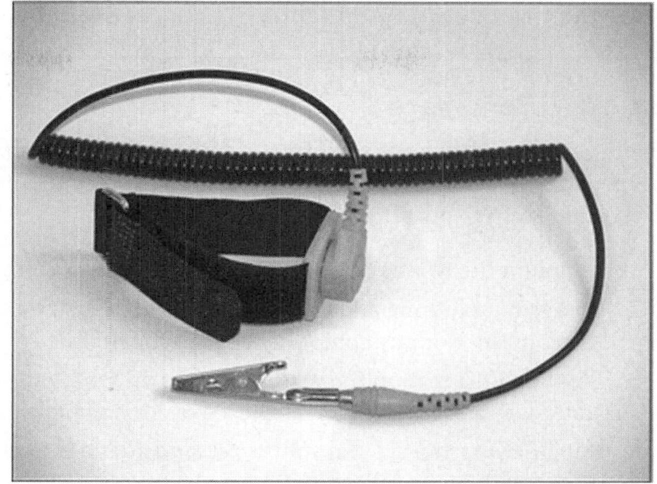

FIGURE 1-1

An ESD wrist strap with grounding wire and alligator clip

internal components that you have removed from the computer. An ESD mat looks like a vinyl placemat, but it has a wire lead and (usually) an alligator clip to connect it to ground. Equipment placed on the mat will discharge static through it.

ESD devices usually have cables that you must attach to a grounded metal object. Some have a single prong that you insert into the ground socket in a regular self-grounding wall outlet. In the United States and Canada, the ground socket is the single round socket offset from the two slender blade sockets. Other cables on ESD wrist or ankle straps or on ESD mats may use alligator clips for making this attachment.

Circuit boards may come in antistatic packaging, often an antistatic bag, and you should store used components in antistatic bags if their original packaging is not available. Do not remove the item from the packaging or bag until you are prepared to install it, and never place it on top of its antistatic packaging, since the outside does not offer any protection.

An antistatic bag provides no protection when used like a potholder to handle components. (Yes, we've seen people doing this.) There's no protection provided on the outside of the bag. ESD protection occurs only when the component is inside the bag. That's because the bag functions as a Faraday cage. (Google that if needed.)

In addition to the ESD/antistatic products mentioned in this section, there are others, including gloves, finger cots, labels, cleaners, bins, meters, and spray. Exercise 1-2 leads you through the process of protecting your workspace and computer from ESD damage using some of these products.

EXERCISE 1-2

ESD-Proofing Your Workspace

Whether your workspace is a cubicle or desk at which you do minor repairs, or a computer workbench where you do more extensive service on computers and peripherals, follow these simple steps to ESD-proof your workspace:

1. Maintain the room's humidity between 50 and 80 percent.
2. Spray your clothing and the work area with antistatic spray. Never spray directly on the computer or any components or peripherals.
3. Place an ESD mat on the workspace and attach its alligator clip to something stationary and metal, such as the leg of a metal table.
4. Put an ESD strap around your wrist, and attach the other end to a stationary metal object (if it has an alligator clip) or plug it into a wall outlet's ground socket (only if the grounding strap has an outlet prong).

SCENARIO & SOLUTION	
I just removed some RAM from a laptop PC; where is a safe place to store it?	To avoid damage from ESD, store RAM (random access memory) and other circuit boards inside antistatic bags.
Since a laptop is portable, is there any reason why I should not move it from desk to desk while it is operating?	A laptop's portability does not apply when it is up and running with the hard drive spinning. Before moving any PC, even a laptop, shut it down. After the computer turns off, unplug the power cord.
I have been assigned the task of buying fire extinguishers for a computer lab at a school. What kind should I get?	Make sure the extinguishers you buy are for Class C fires. You can also look for halon fire extinguishers, which work with all types of fires and leave no residue, but they might not be available.

CERTIFICATION OBJECTIVE

- ***1102: 4.5*** *Summarize environmental impacts and local environmental controls*

The CompTIA A+ candidate must prove knowledge of the dangers posed by inappropriate disposal of computer equipment and chemical solvents that contain materials hazardous to the environment. Similarly, the CompTIA A+ 1102 exam will test your knowledge of how to discover proper disposal methods in your community.

Environmental Concerns for IT Professionals

As an IT professional, you will be concerned with the environment of the workplace and its effect on the health of people and equipment. Earlier, we detailed the issues of safety in the workplace, which is just one part of addressing your workplace environment. Next, we will look at protecting people and equipment from the airborne particles generated by manufacturing or computer equipment, and then we will examine proper disposal of computer waste without causing a negative impact on the environment.

Protection from Dust, Debris, and Other Airborne Particles

You can use compressed air to clean dirt and dust out of computers, as described in "Cleaning Computer Components" in Chapter 12. When using canned compressed air to blow dust out of computers and peripherals, take care to keep the can upright while spraying and avoid tilting or turning the can upside down because the liquid gas that forces the air out may spill and cause freeze burns on your skin and/or damage components. Never use compressed air from an air compressor because the pressure is too high and it can damage delicate components.

When cleaning computer equipment with compressed air or a vacuum, you might stir up a cloud of dust, debris, or other particles that you don't want in your lungs. For example, toner (which is a blend of iron and plastic powder) can be hazardous to breathe in. The dust and debris that build up inside a PC case can also cause coughing and breathing difficulties if inhaled.

When cleaning dusty items with compressed air, wear an air filtration mask and safety goggles to keep all that dust and debris out of your eyes, nose, and mouth. Figure 1-2 shows these items.

FIGURE 1-2 A can of compressed air, eye protection, and a filter mask

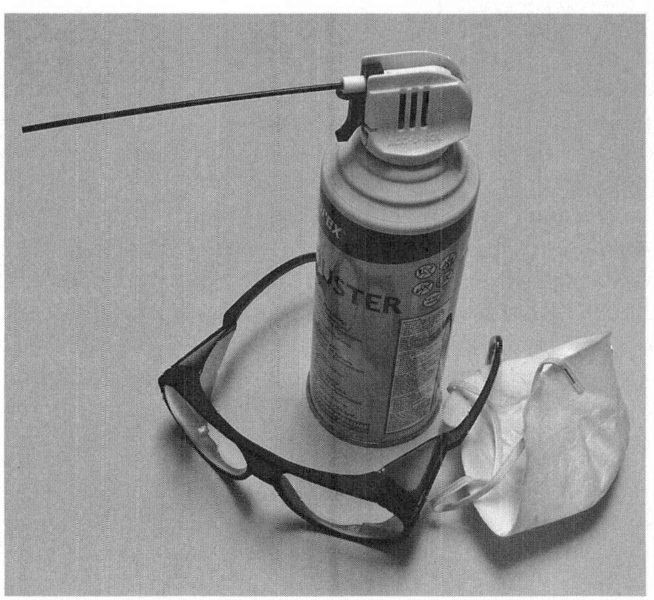

When using a vacuum to clean up spilled toner, make sure it is a model designed for electronics use, not a regular household vacuum. That's because the electronics vacuum has a finer filter on it; on a standard vacuum, the particles can pass right through the air filter and circulate out into the air you breathe. Household vacuums also generate static electricity, which is harmful to electronics.

Providing the Proper Temperature and Humidity

Extremes of heat and humidity are damaging to computers and peripherals. A rough guideline: if you are not comfortable, the PC is not either. A general recommended operating environment is in the range of 50°F to 90°F (10°C to 32°C) with relative humidity between 50 and 80 percent. The lower end of that temperature range is preferable for high-performance components because they tend to run hot. To find the specific temperature and humidity guidelines for a device, look in its manual. Dust buildup on a component can reduce the airflow to it, making it run hotter, so cleaning the dust out of a computer case regularly can help keep it cooler.

Make sure you understand the impact of location and equipment placement on a device's operational ability and lifespan.

The best operating environment for computers is a climate-controlled room with an air filtration system to reduce dust. However, since this is not always possible, consider an appropriate enclosure or case that will provide good ventilation and air filtration.

Providing Good Power

Matching power requirements for equipment with power distribution is important. Ensure that a power supply in a computer can handle the requirements of the components it supplies. Learn more in the discussion of power supplies, electrical terminology, and power requirements for PC components in Chapter 10, and learn about power requirements for laptops in Chapter 14.

When you consider a proper environment for computer equipment, you must also think of the power it receives. You should never plug critical equipment into a wall outlet without some provision to protect it from the vagaries of the power grid. While sags in power below the 120V U.S. standard can cause your computer to reboot or power off, a power surge can do significant damage. A *power surge* is a brief, potentially damaging increase in the amount of electrical power. A simple power strip offers no protection because it is nothing more than an extension cord with several power outlets. At a minimum, use a surge suppressor to protect all computer equipment, including modems and phone and cable lines.

Surge Suppressor

A *surge suppressor* (also called a *surge protector*) may look like an ordinary power strip, but it protects equipment from power surges. Your PC's power supply will also do this for small power fluctuations above the 115V U.S. standard, but it will eventually fail if it is the first line of defense. Therefore, plug your PC into a surge suppressor that has a protection rating of more than 800 joules. (A joule is a unit of energy.) Look for a surge suppressor that carries the Underwriters Laboratories (UL) label showing that it complies with UL standard 1449.

To distinguish a surge suppressor from a simple power strip, look for the UL label showing a protection rating of more than 800 joules.

Beyond Surge Suppressors

Do not just buy the minimum; buy the best power protection you can afford, which should include protection from power fluctuations, brownouts, and blackouts. *Power fluctuations* involve all sorts of inconsistencies in the delivery of electrical power—both too much (surges) and too little. A *brownout* is a period during which heavy demand or other problems cause a reduced flow of power, which can cause computers to behave erratically and suddenly power off. A *blackout* is a complete loss of power. The duration of a brownout or blackout depends on the cause and the ability of responsible parties, such as electrical utilities, to correct the problem. Blackouts can last hours or days, and your first concern related to a brownout or blackout is to have enough time to safely save your data and shut down your computer. The most common device that protects from power brownouts and blackouts while giving you time for these tasks is an *uninterruptible power supply (UPS)*. A UPS will also normally protect from power surges. A UPS is more expensive than a simple surge suppressor, but UPS prices have come down as more manufacturers have introduced consumer-level versions of these devices, such as the one shown in Figure 1-3. Notice the ports labeled Battery Backup and Surge Protection at the top and the ports labeled Surge Protection on the bottom. Plug your computer and display into the Battery Backup ports, and they will be doubly protected. Plug less critical equipment into the second type of port to protect it from surges only, not from power outages.

A power surge is a brief increase in power (voltage). Brownouts are partial power outages, while blackouts are total power outages.

To select a UPS, first determine the power requirements in watts for each device you will connect to the UPS and add them up. Then decide how much time you would require to save your data when main power fails.

A computer or other device plugged into a UPS battery backup port is truly isolated from line power because during normal operation, the device runs directly off the battery through

FIGURE 1-3 This type of UPS contains a battery backup that provides battery power for a limited period in the event of a power outage.

an inverter, which takes the direct current (DC) power stored in the battery and converts it to 110V, 60-cycle alternating current (AC) power. The battery is continually charging from line power, and when it loses line power, the battery continues to power the computer for a short period. The time the battery can power the computer is limited and varies by the capacity of the battery in the UPS and by how much power the computer draws. Unless line power comes back on quickly, you have a window of just minutes to save your data and to power down the computer. For this reason, a UPS device usually includes a data cable and software. Once the software is installed and the UPS senses a power outage, the software warns you to shut down. If no one is at the keyboard to respond, it will automatically save open data files, shut down the operating system, and power down the computer before the UPS itself runs out of battery power. A UPS is more expensive than a surge suppressor, but it gives excellent power protection.

In a real disaster, power can be off for days or weeks. Mission-critical systems in certain industries, like banking and hospitals, have backup power generators.

Disposing of Computer Waste

Lead, mercury (including the mercury in laptop backlights), cadmium, chromium, brominated flame retardants, polychlorinated biphenyls (PCBs)—what do they all have in common? They are toxic to the environment and to humans if mishandled. They are widely used in electronics, including computers, printers, and monitors, so you must dispose of or recycle these items in the proper manner. You should never discard them directly into the trash where they will end up in landfills and potentially pollute the groundwater.

In addition, electronics contain plastic, steel, aluminum, and precious metals—all of which are recoverable and recyclable. Provide containers in which to collect these components for proper sorting and disposal. Check with local agencies to ensure that you comply with local government regulations concerning disposal of all computer waste materials.

Batteries

Many batteries contain environmentally hazardous materials, such as lithium, mercury, or nickel and cadmium, so you cannot just put them in the trash where they will end up in a landfill. Many communities have special recycling depots that accept batteries so they do not introduce harmful elements into the environment; they may also periodically conduct hazardous material pickups in which you can hand over toxic materials, such as batteries and paint, for proper disposal.

Never store computer batteries for extended periods, and never leave batteries in equipment being stored for extended periods because battery casings are notorious for corroding, allowing the chemicals inside to leak or explode out. Leaking or exploding chemicals can create a mess, destroy nearby components, and cause skin burns if you touch them.

Laser Printer Toner Cartridges

Laser printer toner cartridges contain the *toner,* which is the print medium for laser printers, and they often contain other components important to the printing process, such as the photosensitive imaging drum. *Toner* is plastic powder combined with pigment and a small amount of iron. Although the chemical makeup of laser toner may not be harmful, the super-fine powder poses a hazard to your lungs. Be careful when cleaning up toner residue, using a damp cloth for any residue outside the printer and a filtered vacuum (antistatic, if possible) when cleaning up spilled toner inside a printer. Unplug the printer before using a vacuum inside it.

When working with laser printers and handling toner cartridges, avoid breathing in the toner powder.

The cartridges for some laser printers also contain the cylindrical photosensitive imaging drum, the cleaning blade, and other components that are also considered consumables because you normally replace the entire cartridge together with its contents once the toner is gone.

Laser printer toner cartridges provide a potential environmental hazard due in part to their large numbers and the space they can take up in a landfill. For this reason, you should not simply throw them away. Most toner cartridges have reusable components. Many companies will buy back used toner cartridges, refill and recondition them (if necessary), and then resell them. Learn more about the laser printing process in Chapter 13.

Ink Cartridges

The most common color printers found in homes and offices are inkjet printers that use wet ink that comes in cartridges. These cartridges are reusable, or you can recycle them for the plastic and other materials they contain. Many organizations accept used inkjet cartridges for recycling. Some, such as retailers, have collection containers for printer cartridges and other computer waste and will give you credit toward new or recharged cartridges.

Display Devices

Because CRT monitors are obsolete, your primary interaction with them will be to dispose of them. CRTs contain lead, which is toxic to the environment but is also a useful recyclable metal. Never throw CRTs in trash destined for a landfill. Always search for ways to recycle a CRT.

Flat-panel displays, including those in laptop computers, use fluorescent lamps that contain toxic material, so these displays must also be recycled. Call your local waste disposal organization and arrange to drop off monitors at its site. Many communities advertise locations and hours for these recycling services.

Circuit Boards

Circuit boards are mostly plastic, but the chips and transistors mounted to the boards are typically attached using lead solder, and lead can be bad for the environment. Circuit boards should be taken to recycling centers rather than put in the regular trash.

Cell Phones and Tablets

Even though they are small, cell phones and tablets are still computers and still contain many of the same materials that are bad for the environment, including lead solder in circuit boards and heavy metals such as lead, mercury, and cadmium in batteries. Therefore, you should not put them in the regular trash; always recycle them. Many companies will pay for used cell phones, whether working or not, so you may be able to make a few dollars. Recycling centers exist in most communities that will take these devices. For example, Call2Recycle.org provides a ZIP code lookup of electronics recycling drop-off locations.

Chemical Solvents and Cans

All chemical solvents are potentially hazardous to the environment, so you must dispose of them properly. If you are unsure of the proper handling or disposal procedures for a chemical, look for its *material safety data sheet (MSDS)*. An MSDS is a standardized document that contains general information, ingredients, and fire and explosion warnings, as well as health, disposal, and safe transportation information about a particular product. Any manufacturer that sells a potentially hazardous product must issue an MSDS for it.

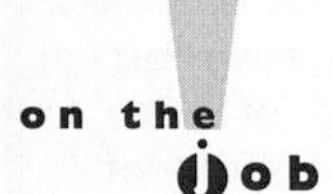

Industry terminology has recently changed, and MSDS is now more commonly referred to as safety data sheet (SDS). However, CompTIA still uses MSDS.

Be sure you know the purpose of an MSDS and how to obtain one.

If an MSDS did not come with a particular chemical, contact the manufacturer or search for it on the Internet. To find an MSDS on a particular product or type of product, use a search engine with appropriate keywords, including "MSDS" or "SDS" and terms associated with the product.

Many communities collect solvents and paints and make them available for recycling. Residents can go to the recycling center and obtain the solvents or paints for free or at a reduced cost. Those solvents and paints deemed unsafe for recycling are disposed of properly. Look for a hazardous material pickup or depot in your area.

Similarly, empty cans, including aerosol cans, should be disposed of in an appropriate manner. Contact your local waste disposal company for the proper handling and disposal of empty cans that once held solvents or other toxic materials. They may be as dangerous as their previous contents. Exercise 1-3 can help you get started researching the recycling options in your area.

EXERCISE 1-3

Researching Recycling Centers

Research the recycling options in your community.

1. First, look online for recycling centers in your area. List the center nearest your home here:_______________.
2. Call the center and determine if it accepts the following items: computer monitors, chemicals, empty paint and solvent cans, circuit boards, old computers, or batteries.
3. Find out the days and times when the center accepts these items for recycling and list them here:_______________.
4. Ask if the center has private home pick-up service for recycling, and ask how to arrange it.
5. Ask if the center has a business pick-up service for recycling, and ask how to arrange it.

SCENARIO & SOLUTION	
You work for a new small business that is planning to create an equipment room to house their network servers, network connection devices, and cabling. Describe the temperature and humidity ranges that are generally safe for this equipment.	The ASHRAE-recommended operating environment for computer equipment is in the range of 64°F to 81°F (18°C to 27°C) with a relative humidity of 50 percent.
What may happen to a computer when power to it sags below the 115V U.S. standard?	The computer may reboot or power off.
What documentation should a manufacturer provide that describes the proper disposal information for a chemical?	An SDS (or MSDS) is a standardized document that contains general information, ingredients, and fire and explosion warnings, as well as health, disposal, and safe transportation information, about a particular product.

CERTIFICATION SUMMARY

This chapter explored appropriate safety and environmental procedures to keep both people and equipment safe from harm. Safety in an organization is everyone's responsibility. Always be aware of potential safety hazards and practice safe equipment handling to protect both yourself and equipment. Always dispose of computer components properly. Handle components carefully when you store them. Keep them out of hot or damp places.

TWO-MINUTE DRILL

Here are some of the key points covered in Chapter 1.

Workplace Safety

- ❑ Learn about fire safety, including the types of possible fire fuels and the appropriate fire extinguisher to use for each.
- ❑ Protect your back when lifting and moving equipment by following published guidelines for what and how to safely lift.
- ❑ Turn off all equipment and disconnect the power cord before moving it, even laptops. Moving any computer while powered up could damage the hard drive(s).
- ❑ Avoid touching hot components, even after powering the equipment off.

- ❑ Do not try to service high-voltage peripherals, such as CRTs, laser printers, and power supplies.
- ❑ Do not use an ESD wristband when working with high-voltage devices.
- ❑ Both high-voltage and low-voltage devices can cause serious injury or death under certain circumstances.

Protecting Equipment

- ❑ ESD can cause damage to equipment, and low humidity contributes to ESD.
- ❑ Use ESD devices (wrist straps, mats, and antistatic bags) when working with and storing computer equipment, especially internal components.
- ❑ Once removed from a computer, a component is susceptible to damage unless it is properly stored to protect it from ESD and extremes of heat, cold, and humidity.
- ❑ Take extra precautions when working with a printer because long hair, loose clothing, and jewelry can catch in the moving parts or pass ESD to the printer.
- ❑ Do not try to operate a printer with the cover off.

Environmental Concerns for IT Professionals

- ❑ Be aware of the workplace environment and its effect on the health of people and equipment.
- ❑ Use compressed air to clean dirt and dust out of computers. Take care to blow the debris away from you and to clean up any mess.
- ❑ When cleaning dusty items with compressed air or a vacuum, wear an air filtration mask and safety goggles to keep all that dust and debris out of your eyes, nose, and mouth.
- ❑ Use a climate-controlled environment whenever possible for both people and equipment.
- ❑ If you cannot maintain a good working environment for equipment, consider using an appropriate enclosure or case that will provide better ventilation and filtration.
- ❑ Use a surge suppressor or a UPS to protect crucial components from power fluctuations. A surge suppressor with a rating of 800 joules or better is the least expensive protection from power surges.
- ❑ A UPS protects from power fluctuations, brownouts, and blackouts.
- ❑ Toxic metals and chemicals used in computers and peripherals include mercury, cadmium, chromium, brominated flame retardants, and PCBs.
- ❑ When a computer or component reaches the end of its useful life, dispose of it appropriately for proper handling of the toxic and reusable components.
- ❑ A safety data sheet (SDS), also called a material safety data sheet (MSDS), provides information about safe handling, usage, and storage of hazardous materials.

SELF TEST

The following questions will help you measure your understanding of the material presented in this chapter. Read all the choices carefully because there might be more than one correct answer. Choose all correct answers for each question.

Workplace Safety

1. Which of the following is the correct fire extinguisher class for an electrical fire?

A. A

B. B

C. C

D. D

2. You plan to replace the power supply in a computer. What is the most important safety measure you should take to protect yourself?

A. Wear an antistatic wristband.

B. Do *not* ground yourself.

C. Bend your knees when you lift it.

D. Buy a name-brand power supply.

3. A client has a large CRT monitor. It is malfunctioning, and none of the external buttons on the monitor help, nor can you fix it using the Properties settings in Windows. Although the monitor is quite old, the client likes it, and wants it to be repaired if possible. What should you do?

A. Open the CRT case and visually inspect for a loose connection.

B. Take it to a qualified repair center.

C. Tell the client the monitor is beyond repair and immediately discard it.

D. Find a service manual for it online and try to repair it yourself.

4. What should you do before moving any computer equipment?

A. Power down and disconnect the power cord.

B. Wear work gloves.

C. Put on a facemask.

D. Remove the power supply.

5. When should you wear an air filtration mask and goggles?
   A. When changing a toner cartridge
   B. When using compressed air to clean dust out of a PC case
   C. When installing RAM
   D. When disassembling a monitor
6. Which of these is *not* good advice for safe lifting and moving?
   A. Carry the item close to your body.
   B. Bend your knees.
   C. Use a fast, jerking movement to pick up a heavy object.
   D. Keep your back straight and vertical to the floor.

Protecting Equipment

7. Which statement is *not* true about ESD?
   A. ESD can kill a human.
   B. As little as 30 volts of ESD can damage a device.
   C. You can damage equipment via ESD without feeling any electrical shock yourself.
   D. Low humidity makes ESD more likely.
8. What can you use to protect a PC from power sags?
   A. Surge suppressor
   B. Power supply
   C. UPS
   D. APS
9. What is the ideal environment for ESD to occur?
   A. Hot and humid
   B. Cold and humid
   C. Hot and dry
   D. Cold and dry
10. You are getting ready to install a new component, a memory stick that came in its own antistatic bag. What is the correct way to handle this component and the bag?
    A. Remove the component from the bag and place it on top of the bag until ready to install.
    B. Remove the component from the bag and immediately discard the bag.
    C. Leave the component in the bag until you are ready to install it.
    D. Remove the component from the bag and turn the bag inside out before placing the component on the bag.

Environmental Concerns for IT Professionals

11. When cleaning dirty items with compressed air, what safety equipment should you wear?

A. Mouth/nose mask and gloves
B. Mouth/nose mask and goggles
C. An apron or protective jacket
D. Steel-toed shoes

12. In what way could compressed air harm a human body?

A. Alkaline burns
B. Acid burns
C. Heat burns
D. Freeze burns

13. When a computer system is no longer functioning and is not repairable, how should you dispose of it?

A. Put it in the trash.
B. Donate it to a charity.
C. Send it to a recycling center.
D. Send it to a landfill.

14. You do not know the proper handling of an old solvent previously used in your company, and now you need to discard it. How can you find out more about it?

A. Contact the manufacturer and ask for an MSDS.
B. Send it to a recycling center.
C. Transfer it to a glass jar for safe storage.
D. Call 911.

15. What should you do with a large number of used batteries accumulated in your office?

A. Dispose of them in the trash.
B. Find a recycling center that will accept them.
C. Send them back to the manufacturers.
D. Let them accumulate and dispose of them about once a year.

16. Which of the following protects against blackouts?

A. Power strip
B. Surge suppressor
C. Inverter
D. UPS

17. What unit of measurement describes a surge suppressor's ability to protect from power surges?

A. VA
B. Watts
C. ULs
D. Joules

18. Which of these is a metal that a battery might contain, requiring special disposition of it?
   A. Lithium
   B. Helium
   C. Hydrogen
   D. Calcium

19. What is it about a circuit board that makes it subject to special disposal procedures?
   A. Plastic
   B. Lead
   C. Aluminum
   D. Steel

20. What is the best way to recycle a cell phone?
   A. Hazardous waste collection facility
   B. Put in the regular trash
   C. Buy-back program
   D. Burn it

SELF TEST ANSWERS

Workplace Safety

1. ☑ **C.** Class C is the correct fire extinguisher class for an electrical fire.
☒ **A, B,** and **D** are incorrect because they are the classes for ordinary combustible materials, flammable or combustible liquids, and chemical fires, respectively.

2. ☑ **B.** The most important safety measure you should take to protect yourself is to not ground yourself, because you do not want to make your body a path for electricity to take to ground. Wearing an antistatic wristband, standing on a grounding mat, or touching something already grounded would do this and put you in danger.
☒ **A** is incorrect because this would expose you to possible electrical shock. **C** is incorrect because replacing a power supply should not require heavy lifting. **D** is incorrect because this is not a safety measure.

3. ☑ **B.** Take it to a qualified repair center.
☒ **A** is incorrect because it is dangerous to open a CRT, and only highly trained technicians should open a CRT case. **C** is incorrect because this is an extreme reaction until you know more about the nature of the problem and whether the CRT can be repaired. If it cannot, then recycle it, rather than "discard" it. **D** is also incorrect until you have more information about the problem and whether the CRT can be repaired. If you cannot get it repaired, then you will need to recycle it.

4. ☑ **A.** Power down and disconnect the power cord before moving any computer equipment.
☒ **B** is incorrect because you only need to wear gloves when you are moving something with sharp edges, and not all computer equipment has sharp edges. **C** is incorrect because a facemask is only needed if you expect to be exposed to airborne particles. **D** is incorrect because this is a very extreme and unnecessary action to take before moving computer equipment.

5. ☑ **B.** Compressed air is likely to stir up dust and other debris that could get in your eyes and lungs. Protect yourself with a mask and goggles.
☒ **A** is incorrect because changing a toner cartridge is not likely to release much toner into the air. **C** is incorrect because installing RAM is not likely to stir up any airborne contaminants. **D** is incorrect because disassembling a monitor would not likely stir up airborne contaminants (and you should not be disassembling a monitor anyway).

6. ☑ **C.** You should lift with a slow, smooth movement, not fast and jerking.
☒ **A** is incorrect because you should carry the item close to your body. **B** is incorrect because bending your knees is recommended to avoid stressing your back. **D** is incorrect because your back should be as straight and as vertical to the floor as possible.

Protecting Equipment

7. ☑ **A.** ESD may be high voltage, but due to the low amperage, it cannot kill a person, although it can startle.
☒ **B, C,** and **D** are incorrect because they are all true statements.

8. ☑ **C.** A UPS will protect a PC from power sags because it provides conditioned power, free from the surges, spikes, and sags coming from the power company.
☒ **A** is incorrect because a surge suppressor only protects from power surges, not from power sags. **B** is incorrect because a power supply does not protect a PC from power sags. **D** is incorrect because APS is not a standard acronym for a power protection device.

9. ☑ **D.** Cold and dry is the ideal environment for ESD to occur. This should be avoided because ESD can damage equipment.
☒ **A, B,** and **C** are incorrect because none of these is as ideal an environment for ESD as is a cold and dry environment.

10. ☑ **C.** Leave the component in the bag until you are ready to install it.
☒ **A** is incorrect because the outside of the bag may hold a static charge. **B** is incorrect because you may want to reuse the bag if you need to store this or another component at some time. **D** is incorrect because this procedure is not recommended and could expose the component to ESD.

Environmental Concerns for IT Professionals

11. ☑ **B.** A mouth/nose mask will keep you from breathing any debris or dust, and goggles will keep debris out of your eyes.
☒ **A** is incorrect because gloves are not important to wear for this task. **C** is incorrect because an apron or jacket would protect your clothing, but not your body. **D** is incorrect because steel-toed shoes would not be useful for protecting against dust and debris.

12. ☑ **D.** Compressed air gets very cold when released and could cause a freeze burn.
☒ **A** and **B** are incorrect because compressed air does not contain alkaline or acid. **C** is incorrect because compressed air does not generate heat when released.

13. ☑ **C.** Send it to a recycling center. Even a nonfunctioning computer has material in it that can and should be recycled.
☒ **A** is incorrect because something put into the trash will usually end up in a landfill (see response to **D**). **B** is incorrect because donating something that is beyond repair is not ethical and is passing on the responsibility for disposing of the computer. **D** is incorrect because computers contain components that can contaminate the environment and components that should be recycled.

14. ☑ **A.** Contact the manufacturer and ask for an MSDS (or SDS) because this document will contain instructions on safe handling and safe disposal of the chemical.
☒ **B** is incorrect, although this is what you may ultimately do. You first need to know how to safely handle the chemical. **C** is incorrect because no information is available to lead you to believe the original container is not adequate. **D** is incorrect because there is no emergency.

15. ☑ **B.** Find a recycling center that will accept batteries.
☒ **A** is incorrect because you should never throw batteries in the trash. They contain environmentally dangerous components and chemicals. **C** is incorrect in general. Some manufacturers may have a program for used batteries, but first locate a recycling center. **D** is incorrect because batteries stored for long periods can leak toxic chemicals.

16. ☑ **D.** A UPS is an online power protection device and protects against blackouts.
☒ **A** is incorrect because this provides no power protection whatsoever. **B** is incorrect because a surge suppressor only protects against power surges and is not an online power protection device in the way that a UPS is, providing full-time power from the battery. **C** is incorrect because an inverter takes low-voltage DC power and transforms it to 110V 60-cycle AC output.

17. ☑ **D.** Joules describes the protection level provided by a surge suppressor.
☒ **A** is incorrect because VA stands for volts/amps. It is a measure of the ability of a UPS to provide power. **B** is incorrect because wattage is a measurement of power consumption. **C** is incorrect because UL stands for Underwriters Laboratory, an agency that certifies electrical equipment's safety and performance.

18. ☑ **A.** Lithium batteries are common in mobile devices, and lithium requires recycling, not disposal in the regular trash.
☒ **B, C,** and **D** are incorrect because helium, hydrogen, and calcium are not metals, nor are they hazardous to the environment.

19. ☑ **B.** Lead is a soft metal that is used in the solder points on a circuit board. Lead can leach into soil in a landfill, unlike harder metals.
☒ **A** is incorrect because although plastic can harm the environment, it does not contaminate the soil it comes in contact with, as lead does. **C** and **D** are incorrect because aluminum and steel are not used in circuit boards, and they are also not environmentally hazardous.

20. ☑ **C.** A buy-back program is the best option because it will pay you for the phone.
☒ **A** is incorrect because although this is a responsible method of disposal, it pays nothing. **B** is incorrect because a phone should not be put in the regular trash because of the environmentally hazardous components in its battery and circuit boards. **D** is incorrect because burning plastic might generate toxic fumes and eliminates any possibility of recycling any of the parts.

Chapter 2

Planning and Professionalism

CERTIFICATION OBJECTIVES

- **1102: 4.1** Given a scenario, implement best practices associated with documentation and support systems information management
- **1102: 4.2** Explain basic change-management best practices
- **1102: 4.6** Explain the importance of prohibited content/activity and privacy, licensing, and policy concepts
- **1102: 4.7** Given a scenario, use proper communication techniques and professionalism

✓ Two-Minute Drill

Q&A Self Test

Having technical skills with hardware and software is only one part of what makes a good technician. You must also be able to communicate professionally in the workplace and practice good customer service when working with clients.

In the process of performing your duties at work, you may sometimes encounter content or behavior that is illegal or violates company policies. You must understand privacy, licensing, and policy concepts so that you can effectively identify and address prohibited materials and activities.

Another important administrative skill to have is documentation management. This can include establishing document management systems and processes, creating new documents, and managing existing ones. As procedures and situations change over time, you must also implement change management solutions that help everyone in the organization adapt.

Documentation systems often include databases that track assets and support activities as well. An asset management system is a critical part of ensuring that all company-owned IT equipment is accounted for, and a ticketing system ensures that support requests are promptly addressed and that no request is overlooked.

CERTIFICATION OBJECTIVE

- ***1102: 4.7*** *Given a scenario, use proper communication techniques and professionalism*

CompTIA requires an A+ candidate to demonstrate knowledge of appropriate interpersonal communication skills and professionalism in the workplace. Real communication between people consists of both the verbal and nonverbal behavior that results in exchanging thoughts, messages, or information. Not only must you say the right words, but your body language must convey the same message as your words. Professionalism includes your behavior in all interactions, as well as how you treat property belonging to your employer and customers.

Professionalism and Proper Communication

You show professionalism on the job in the way you dress and behave, as well as in how you communicate with customers and colleagues. In this section, we'll explore the intertwined topics of professionalism and proper communication. In short, it isn't just what you say—it's how you say it and what you do while you are saying it.

Professionalism

Professionalism is a set of behaviors that each of us should use whether we are being observed or not. Many occupations have a formal code of ethics that defines professionalism framed in the context of that occupation. In this section, we will explore a general definition of professionalism for an IT worker as it applies to behavior in dealing with others and in the treatment of property.

Professional Dress and Good Hygiene

Good grooming, cleanliness, and proper dress are part of professional behavior. Wear freshly laundered clothes appropriate for the tasks required and that fit into your work environment. If you support computers for a group of attorneys, you may need to wear pressed slacks, shirt, and even a jacket. Tank tops are not appropriate in any office; skimpy clothes and flip flops are for picnics and the beach, not for work. Wear closed-toe shoes with nonskid soles. Even if your employer allows blue jeans, consider upgrading yourself to neatly pressed slacks to look a bit more professional.

Respect Toward Others—Even the Difficult Customer

Professional behavior is respectful and ethical. This includes being pleasant, reasonable, and positive in the face of the variety of events that can occur in the work environment, such as dealing with difficult customers or situations. Ethics includes how you react to a wide variety of situations.

Unfortunately, any job in which you provide a service involves encounters with difficult customers, so expect some scenario-based questions on the exam involving your response to such situations.

Proper Language

Jargon is not necessarily bad—it is simply using words or acronyms, often technical and uncommon, that only people who share a common profession or interest understand. It is okay to use jargon when both parties understand it. It is not okay, or professional, to use jargon with people unfamiliar with it, such as the ordinary computer user you may encounter on the job or nontechnical customers and coworkers. Similarly, be very careful to avoid common or vulgar slang expressions.

Every profession has its own jargon. Because professions tend to be separate cultures, the use of jargon, abbreviations, acronyms, and slang among peers is generally acceptable, but do not let this spill over to your communications with people who are not part of your specific culture.

Actively Listen, Take Notes, and Do Not Interrupt

When a coworker or customer is explaining something to you—for example, when describing the symptoms of a problem—do not interrupt. Allow them to complete their statements. Do not jump to conclusions. If necessary, without interrupting, clarify customer statements by asking pertinent questions or restating your understanding in your own words. This shows that you are listening and helps you to avoid making incorrect assumptions.

Get Acknowledgment

Frequently confirm that the customer understands what you are saying by asking questions like, "Does that make sense?" "Does that sound okay to you?" "Would you like to go through those steps while I am here?" Think of the conversation as a train, with you as the engineer. The customer is a passenger waiting on the platform; if you do not stop or slow down, the customer cannot get on the train, and you will find yourself at the destination, but the customer will still be back at the station. Slow down and confirm that he is on board before you race ahead with a technical explanation that would please your coworkers but bewilder the customer.

Listening without interruption may be the most important communication skill you can develop, and you should expect scenario-based questions that test how well you embrace this idea.

Deal Appropriately with Customers' Confidential and Private Materials

When interacting with people, we learn things about one another; some of what we learn is personal and we should not share it with others. Being professional requires that you deal appropriately with confidential materials located on a customer's computer, desktop, printer, and so on. Whatever you may see as you interact with their computer is their property, and you don't reveal it to anyone.

Being professional includes knowing when to keep your mouth shut; this includes both company matters and someone's personal life. Being discreet shows respect for the privacy of others. Keeping such information to yourself helps you gain the trust of your coworkers and customers. Of course, being respectful of someone's privacy, you do not try to gain personal information, but sometimes you learn it inadvertently. However you learn such information, keep it to yourself.

Be Culturally Sensitive

In today's world, you may be dealing with people from around the globe. A smart-aleck comment that may be amusing in your own culture may be offensive to a person from another culture. Use professional titles such as Mr., Ms., Dr., or Professor when applicable; do not be overly familiar.

Be Cautious

Be careful with what you share with the customer. Sometimes technicians go too far in empathizing with the customer's plight and speak negatively about the equipment or software that the company pays you to support. The customer does not need to know that you think the printer the company bought for him is a poor one, or even that you dislike driving out to his office because of the terrible traffic conditions.

Avoid Arguing or Being Defensive

Avoid arguing with customers or coworkers, even if you feel the other person is being especially difficult. If you discover something that makes you angry, work to calm yourself before engaging about the problem. When others approach you angrily, stay calm and avoid becoming defensive. Resist falling into the payback trap of acting toward them the way they are acting toward you. These measured responses can defuse a potentially volatile situation.

Maintain a Positive Attitude and Project Confidence

Work to maintain a positive attitude and tone of voice. A positive attitude takes practice and discipline; everyone has personal problems and challenges in their lives, along with all the job issues such as politics, personalities, work goals, and more. You need to literally compartmentalize your life. Hold an image in your mind such that when you are at work the other parts of your life are behind doors. Try to keep the doors to these other parts of your life closed when you are at work and only open them at an appropriate time. When you become successful at this, you will find that you are more effective in all areas of your life, because you can give each area the full attention it deserves at the appropriate time.

Do Not Minimize Others' Concerns

Never minimize another person's problems and concerns. You are minimizing when you interrupt an explanation or show through body language, such as a dismissive wave of the hand, that his concern is not important to you. Do not tell the customer about someone else who has a worse predicament—that is irrelevant to him. Imagine how you would feel if you could not get some work completed on time due to a computer problem, and while trying to explain your plight to a technician, she minimized or dismissed your concern as being unimportant.

You must also strike a balance between not minimizing and assuring the customer that you have an easy fix for the problem. An easy fix just means that you can solve the problem soon; it does not mean the customer has no reason to mourn the lost time, lost deadline, or loss of productivity.

Avoid Judgmental Behavior

Avoid being judgmental and/or insulting to anyone. Never resort to name calling, which is damaging to any relationship and is completely unprofessional. For instance, if computer hardware and software fascinate you, you may find it difficult to be patient with those people who cannot seem to understand or even care how a computer works and who frequently need help with hardware or software. It is just a small baby step to behaving judgmentally toward the customer.

Avoid Distractions

Distractions reduce your productivity and value as an employee. Some jobs are filled with distractions—ringing phones, conversations, music, construction noise, traffic noise, and more. Many distractions are unavoidable, but you can control some distractions, and how you control them is a measure of your professionalism. Personal calls, personal interruptions, texting, using social media sites, and talking to coworkers while helping customers are distractions you must avoid because they show disrespect.

Taking Personal Calls Because you can only make personal calls such as calls to your doctor or child's school during normal business hours when medical offices and schools are open, if your workplace permits these, don't abuse the privilege. Keep them very short.

Talking to Coworkers A productive work environment normally involves a community of people who treat each other professionally and work as a team. Therefore, in most jobs, you will have frequent conversations with coworkers on both personal and professional topics. Personal discussion with coworkers should not occur within earshot of customers. When you are talking to a customer, he should have your full attention. The only excuse for a side conversation is if it concerns solving the customer's problem, and you should even do that outside the customer's hearing if possible. The best rule is not to talk to coworkers while interacting with customers.

Texting and Social Media Avoid carrying on text message side conversations while you are with a client unless the conversation is directly related to solving their problem; give them your full attention.

Do not share anything about the client or their case on social media; this is disrespectful of their privacy and can reflect badly both on you personally and on your employer.

Minimizing Personal Interruptions Personal interruptions come in many forms, such as personal calls, leaving the office during working hours for personal business, a family member or friend visiting the workplace, and attending to personal business in any way during work hours. Try especially hard to avoid these while helping a customer. Avoid personal interruptions as much as possible, and when such an interruption is necessary, be sure to minimize its impact on the customer by keeping it very brief, and don't extend its effect by sharing details of the interruption with the customer.

Set and Meet Expectations

Many things, both actual and perceived, influence a customer's expectations. Your company may set expectations by describing your department and/or job function and the services it will provide to customers. This expectation exists even before you answer the customer's call or walk into their office.

Beyond that, you control the expectations—either consciously or unconsciously. Be aware of ways in which you do this. If a customer makes an unreasonable demand, do not simply smile without comment. This sets the expectation that you will deliver according to her demand. If you must disappoint, do it as soon as possible, so a simple disappointment doesn't turn into the perception that you broke a commitment—perceived or otherwise.

Control expectations, beginning with the expectation that you will be on time. If delayed, be sure to contact the customer, apologize, and provide a reliable estimate of when you will arrive. Then, once you have determined what the problem is, be sure to give the customer your best and most honest estimate of the timeline for solving the problem. When possible, offer different repair or replacement options because they give the customer a sense of control of a situation.

At the conclusion of a service call or visit, provide the customer with proper documentation on the services you provided. Sit down with the customer and review all that you did. If appropriate, have her sign a receipt confirming the work you performed.

Follow up with each customer later to verify satisfaction. This is important because people don't always tell you when they are not happy, and a quick phone call or e-mail might alert you to their dissatisfaction and give you a chance to rectify the situation.

exam watch

Review 1102 exam Objective 4.7 carefully to make sure you understand all the prescribed professional behaviors listed there.

SCENARIO & SOLUTION

Scenario	Solution
How can I avoid a confrontation when someone else shows anger toward me?	Try to stay calm, avoid becoming defensive, and do not reciprocate the anger.
I try to put customers' concerns into perspective for them by telling them about others who are worse off. Is this a good practice?	No, this is not a good practice, because the customers will believe (rightly so) that you are minimizing their concerns.
If the company gives me a laptop to take home, do I have the right to use it for personal purposes?	No. Unless you have an unusual arrangement, you are to use the laptop given to you by the company for business purposes only. Using it for personal purposes is unprofessional.
I get very bored with talking to customers at the front counter, and I find that I can pick up my e-mail while listening to a customer's description of a problem. My boss has told me not to do this. Why is that?	This behavior is inappropriate for many reasons. Just one is that you are not showing the customer respect by letting him know that you are listening. And you may miss important information if you do not use active listening techniques.
I enjoy sharing information about office politics and unannounced changes in company policy. My boss has reprimanded me for this, but people seem to enjoy listening. Why is doing this a problem?	This behavior is inappropriate for many reasons. At the very least, revealing this information shows a lack of discretion and does not engender trust in you, even though people may seem to enjoy hearing the information.

CERTIFICATION OBJECTIVE

- ***1102: 4.6*** *Explain the importance of prohibited content/activity and privacy, licensing, and policy concepts*

The CompTIA A+ 220-1102 exam will test your knowledge of the general concepts surrounding prohibited content in the workplace and how you, as an IT professional, should handle the discovery of prohibited activity. You will also need to understand how privacy, licensing, and policies affect the proper handling of materials and dictate restrictions on procedures and behaviors.

Dealing with Prohibited Content and Prohibited Activities

Access to the Internet gives you access to the world with all its imperfections. Similarly, access to a corporate network gives you access to all types of content owned and managed by the corporation. As an IT professional, you need to be aware of issues related to the types of content available on the Internet and, on a smaller scale, on a corporate network and local computers. In the following sections, we will discuss prohibited content and activities and the government agencies and institutions that define and combat them. Then we will look at what you need to know about how you should respond on the job to discovery of prohibited content or activities.

Defining Prohibited Content and Behavior

Prohibited content is any content that an organization or government deems harmful to the institution in general and to all persons or a class of persons for which it is responsible. An example of a class of persons is children, who can be harmed by content deemed pornographic or violent. In the case of an organization, the persons for whom this content is defined may be their employees, customers, or members. For a government, it covers their citizens and anyone who enters the country or, in the case of the Internet, communicates over the Internet. Content may also be prohibited in certain situations because it exposes the company to potential legal liability or gives away trade secrets or demographic information that a competitor could exploit.

Some content or behavior may be prohibited to protect the privacy of customers, employees, or the organization itself. For example, companies that generate and store healthcare information are subject to the Health Insurance Portability and Accountability Act (HIPAA) and other federal laws designed to keep people's medical records private. IT professionals might be asked to monitor network communications to ensure that there is no "leakage" of private data through careless sharing.

A product's or company's licensing may also dictate that certain content or behavior be restricted to avoid legal problems. For example, making unauthorized copies of software to share with others is a violation of the software licensing agreement. An employee who puts installation files on a shared drive for the use of coworkers is engaging in prohibited behavior and exposing the company to legal liability.

As an IT professional, it is not usually your job to define what content should be prohibited in a particular environment; your job is to help enforce the guidelines or regulations that your employer provides by identifying, documenting, and reporting violations. Policy documentation is covered later in this chapter.

Responding to an Incident

So what should you do when you become aware of prohibited behavior? Perhaps you discover confidential patient information displayed on the screen of an unattended PC against company policy, or you find evidence of a coworker's access to a known pornographic website on their work PC. The answer is, "It all depends." Let's look at the three components of a first response to the two scenarios presented here.

Once you have clearly identified prohibited behavior, your first response will depend on the actual behavior, as well as the company's policies and procedures. The following sections explain the procedures to follow when identifying and reporting prohibited behavior.

Identify the Problem

Identify the problem by asking yourself if it is truly a case of inappropriate behavior. In the case of the unattended PC with confidential patient information, this is inappropriate behavior, but you may need to determine if any harm has been done, and how you react also depends on the urgency of the situation and if harm has actually been done. Are unauthorized persons within viewing range of the computer screen? If so, then do whatever you can to change the screen content to hide such information. Is the responsible employee nearby? If so, then call it to that person's attention and have it corrected. Once you have identified that inappropriate behavior has occurred, you need to comply with company policies and procedures to determine if you are required to report the problem.

Report Through Proper Channels

In the case of finding clear evidence of or upon witnessing a coworker's access to prohibited content, you are required as an IT professional to report the incident through proper channels as defined in the organization's policies and procedures documents. Reporting may include informing management or even law enforcement if necessary.

Document Your Findings

Accusing someone of breaking a law or violating company policies can have serious consequences, and you should not take it lightly. Therefore, you will need to document your observations that resulted in the accusation. This may require that you write a few simple statements, or it may require that you fill out forms. Whatever the case, when documenting any prohibited behavior, be sure to avoid expressing personal opinion and conjecture. Simply state what you observed.

Maintain Chain of Custody

Because such reporting can result in consequences to the employee, as an IT professional you will need to preserve and track evidence of the improper or even illegal behavior and present it to the proper person. It must be clear who has had access to the evidence, even digital evidence. This record of who has access or possession of evidence is called the *chain of custody,* and you will need to follow the procedures described in the policies and procedures documents. Someone—maybe you—must be responsible for tracking the evidence and documenting the entire process.

The chain of custody provides a record of the path evidence takes from acquisition to disposal. Make sure you understand the value of scrupulous care in maintaining the chain of custody.

Data/Device Preservation

Take steps to carefully preserve any data or device involved in the use of prohibited content; that includes capturing data that proves prohibited behavior. The steps you take will depend on the location of this data and/or device. If the data was stored on a local PC, you may need to remove the PC or make a copy of the hard drive (preserving data integrity) and store it in a secure location. If the incriminating data is stored on a network server, you may need to find a way to protect the data and leave it unaltered on the server, at the same time ensuring that no unauthorized person has access to it.

Incident response includes maintaining the chain of custody, communicating with management and law enforcement, maintaining data integrity and preservation, and documenting the incident thoroughly.

SCENARIO & SOLUTION	
You suspect that another employee is involved in prohibited activities. What should you do?	If all you have is a suspicion, you really cannot take action. Wait until you have proof.
You are unsure what is defined as prohibited content and prohibited behavior regarding the use of computer equipment in your organization. How can you learn more?	Go to a supervisor and tell them of your concern. Most organizations have manuals defining acceptable-use policy and also offer training to all employees.
Your company has a searchable policy document defining acceptable use. What term should you search to discover what actions you must take to file a claim against an employee for prohibited behavior?	Search on "incident report" or similar language in order to find to whom you report, what proof is needed, and the procedures required to file a claim.

Licensing, Privacy, and Regulations

Today's IT policies must address a complex set of responsibilities and expectations that may include governmental regulations, company-wide policies, licensing agreements, and protecting employees' and customers' privacy. The following sections outline some of the considerations behind IT policies that govern behavior and content in an organization.

Licensing, EULAs, and DRM

Software usually comes with a license agreement that you must accept in order to use the software. It may consist of fine print on the sleeve of a disc; opening the sleeve indicates that you accept the agreement. Or in the case of downloaded software, you may have to click your agreement to a page of legalese before you can download an application. This license is commonly referred to as the End User License Agreement (EULA).

The EULA specifies what you can and cannot do with the software. Most EULAs state that you do not actually "own" the software, but are buying (or acquiring for free) the right to use the software. They may also state that the software can be used for only certain purposes (for example, not for commercial activities) or in certain countries. They may state that you can install the software on only a limited number of devices or have a limited number of users accessing it.

As attorneys are fond of saying, "There is no right or wrong; there is only what's in the contract that you agreed to." A EULA is a type of contract. A software maker can stipulate any conditions they want in a license agreement, and your only choice is to use the software or not. If you use the software, you agree to be bound by that agreement, and they can pursue legal action against you if you violate the agreement. Therefore, as an IT professional, you must protect your employer (or clients, if you're the business owner) from legal liability by ensuring that the terms of the EULAs are followed for all software in use. The first step in doing so, of course, is to read the agreements and make sure that the company's IT policies enforce their requirements.

Open-Source vs. Commercial Licenses

Commercial software is software that is owned and controlled by a company or individual. The owner retains ownership of the software but allows other people to use it, subject to whatever conditions are placed in the license agreement. The owner keeps the source code private so other companies or individuals cannot easily create their own competing versions. Commercial software is sometimes free to use (for example, the Google Chrome browser), but more often the owner charges either a one-time fee for the license or offers a monthly or yearly subscription (for example, Microsoft Office or Microsoft 365).

With *open-source* software, the owner makes the source code available to the public so others can modify and improve it. The owner may still maintain the copyright for the original source code and may place restrictions in the license on how others can modify the code and distribute their versions. For example, they may stipulate that modified versions must be distributed for free. Perhaps the most famous example of open-source software is Linux. The Linux core is free, but companies may package it with other software and charge for the overall package. Other open-source programs include Apache Server, Firefox, and OpenOffice.

Public domain software takes open-source one step further. Not only does the author make the source code available but also relinquishes any right to the original code, placing it in the public domain without a license.

Software that is available without charge is sometimes called *freeware.* Freeware can be commercial, open-source, or public domain; you can't make assumptions about its license simply on the basis of its being free. Software that you can acquire for free initially and then pay for later if you decide to keep it is known as *shareware.* A shareware program may encourage users to pay by nagging them with reminders, by disabling certain features in the unpaid version, or by limiting the user to a certain number of days or uses.

A valid license is one that is of the correct type for the usage (for example, a corporate license for a business) and one that is not expired.

Personal vs. Enterprise Licenses

Some commercial software licenses allow the buyer to use the software on a small number of devices (in some cases, just one). These are *personal licenses* issued to an individual. For example, a productivity application license might allow for up to three to five devices per licensed copy of the software.

Businesses often need to make the same software available to dozens, hundreds, or even thousands of users, and for them an *enterprise license* may be a better value than individual personal licenses for everyone. Enterprise licenses offer a volume discount when purchasing the licenses to support many people. When you purchase an enterprise license, you do not typically get physical media (DVDs or USB thumb drives) for each user. Instead, you get a single copy of the setup file and permission to duplicate it as needed, up to the limit specified in the license.

There are several kinds of enterprise licenses, and they vary with each software company. For example, you can read about Microsoft's enterprise licenses here: https://www.microsoft.com/en-us/licensing/licensing-programs/licensing-programs.

Two common kinds of enterprise licenses are per seat and per user. *Per seat* gives permission for a certain number of devices. For example, suppose you have 100 desktop PCs and you have 200 employees working at them (on two shifts). You would need 100 licenses, one for each "seat" (that is, each device). *Per user* gives permission for a certain number of users. Each user may have more than one device. For example, suppose you have 200 employees, and each employee has both a desktop and a laptop. If you purchased per-seat licenses, you would need 400, but if you purchased per-user licenses, you would need only 200.

One benefit of a volume license is that you usually don't have to maintain separate product keys for each instance. You can use one master product key to activate many installations.

An OEM license refers to the license that a manufacturer installs on new devices. If this is your case, the product key isn't transferable, and you can't use it to activate another installation.

Digital Rights Management

Software owners don't just put the EULAs out there and expect people to adhere to them out of their personal sense of right and wrong. Often they "encourage" compliance by building restrictions into copyrighted digital works in the form of *digital rights management (DRM)*. For example, when you download music from certain online services, such as the iTunes Apple Store, DRM code embedded in the music files prevents you from copying the files to unauthorized devices, and when you install an application, it may prompt you for an installation key code that must be unique for each device on which you install it.

Hardware-based DRM is less common but does exist. For example, to access sensitive financial information for a business on a personal PC, the user might be required to connect a small authentication device (a *dongle*) to a port on the PC.

One common type of DRM is product activation, which you will learn about in "Registering and Activating Windows" in Chapter 4. Microsoft uses this for retail boxed versions of Windows and Office. When you install the software, you enter a product key, which is a lengthy string of numbers and letters. After a certain number of uses or number of days, you must activate the software in order to continue using it. Activation locks the product key to the specific device on which it is installed, so it can't be activated on any other device. Chapter 4 discusses the technical details of the activation process, as well as how to troubleshoot problems with it.

Regulated Data and Privacy

Privacy is important both to individuals and to the company as a whole. Customers are more willing to provide personal information if you can assure them that it will not be shared except as needed to complete the transaction at hand, and companies attract and retain workers more easily when worker privacy is respected. The company as a whole benefits from trade secrets, financial data, and other sensitive information being closely guarded.

The *Payment Card Industry Data Security Standard (PCI DSS)* is designed to reduce fraud and protect customer credit card information. It specifies rules for securely storing and handling customers' credit card data.

Personally identifiable information (PII) is information that can be used to trace an individual's identity. This type of data is a privacy concern to consumers because it includes information that criminals could use to stalk them or steal their identities, including Social Security number, mother's maiden name, biometric records, financial and employment information, phone numbers, home addresses, and so on.

Another type of sensitive data is *protected health information (PHI)*. It can include information about a person's medical conditions, medications prescribed, physical disabilities, and mental health, as well as hospitalization history. This data must be closely guarded by any institution that uses it because of the strict confidentiality requirements in HIPAA, a 1996 U.S. law that encourages the widespread use of electronic data interchange in the U.S. healthcare system and ensures the confidentiality of healthcare data.

exam watch **Make sure you can explain the various regulations governing data security, including HIPAA, PCI DSS, and GDPR. You should also know the difference between PHI and PII.**

Businesses operating in the United Kingdom (UK) must follow the rules specified in the General Data Protection Regulation (GDPR), a 2016 European Union (EU) regulation that requires anyone collecting personal data to disclose that fact and explain the purpose, timetable, and scope.

Some types of businesses have data retention requirements for certain data types. For example, some financial institutions are required to retain financial records for each account for a certain number of years. If the company you are working for has data retention requirements in place, that will affect the policies you must comply with when archiving and deleting files.

SCENARIO & SOLUTION	
Your company has 500 workers and about 750 devices between them, all of which need software licenses for a certain product. Which type of volume licensing would be the better choice: per seat or per user?	This is a tricky question, as it depends on the prices. It's often a better deal to buy per-user licenses when users have more than one device each, but a good price on a per-seat license could still be a better deal overall. You would need to price it both ways to see.
Your company is using Red Hat Linux for many of its servers. A manager questions the line item in the budget for operating system cost, claiming that Linux is free and you shouldn't be paying. How do you respond?	Red Hat is a Linux distribution that consists of the basic Linux OS (which is free) plus a variety of free and commercial add-ons that extend its functionality. Just because the Linux core is open source and free doesn't mean that every distribution is free.
You work for the IT department for a retail store. The company's database includes PII for thousands of customers. The manager claims that because you store PII on customers, the database is subject to HIPAA rules. How would you respond to that claim?	The manager is confusing PII with PHI, which is the purview of HIPAA. If your company does not store information about people's medical conditions and care, it is not subject to HIPAA. However, there may be other laws to comply with regarding general and financial privacy, depending on your location.

CERTIFICATION OBJECTIVE

- ***1102: 4.1*** *Given a scenario, implement best practices associated with documentation and support systems information management*

Information is an asset, just as much as hardware and software are. An important part of your job as an IT professional is to create and maintain documentation that will ensure that no data is lost if individual employees are no longer there to remember it. This objective tests your understanding of the various types of IT information that should be recorded and the best practices for doing so.

Documentation Management

As an IT professional, you will likely create and update many types of documentation for audiences ranging from end users, to executives, to outside auditors. This section looks at some of these documentation types and their importance to an IT department's successful operation.

General Documentation Best Practices

The following sections contain some tips and best practices for creating and managing IT documentation.

Document Structure

All your documentation should have the same standard structure, no matter what type of information is being delivered and no matter who the target audience is. Table 2-1 lists some standard information you will want to include at the beginning of every document.

Use the same structure and file format for all documents in your document library if possible. Choose a file format that everyone in your organization can access. PDF is a good choice because data originating from many different programs can be converted to PDF for publication. PDF format also discourages users from making changes to the documents and saving their own customized versions. HTML is also a good choice, particularly if your users will be accessing the documentation via a web browser. Some organizations use Microsoft Word or Rich Text Format documents, or even plaintext files.

File Naming Conventions

To keep your document management system orderly and well organized, assign each document a unique ID number or code, and refer to it on every page of the documentation and in the document's filename. Some people choose to include the date of the last modification in the filename too. For example, if the ID is SC295 revision A.1.2 and it is modified on 10/31/2023, the filename might be SC295A.1.2-103123.pdf. The details of your naming conventions are less important than the consistency with which you implement them.

TABLE 2-1 Information to Include in Documentation

Item	Explanation
Document ID	A unique ID assigned to the document
Version Number	A version number that increments with each edit
Version History	List of edits made, their dates, and a summary of their changes
Purpose	Summarizes the document's purpose or content
Summary	An outline of the headings or major topics
Created and Maintained By	Contact information for responsible person
Notes	Any pertinent extra information about the document itself
Body	The documentation itself

Document Audience

Documentation should be written for a specific audience, with the education level and technical proficiency of the audience taken into consideration. Don't try to use documentation written for system administrators to train nontechnical end users.

Document Writing Tips

Here are some tips for creating easy-to-understand documentation for any audience:

- Use headings to break up the material in long documents.
- Use bullet points to make lists easier to skim.
- If the documentation directs users to do something, make sure it explains in detail how to do it. Examples can be useful.
- Use numbered lists for steps that should be performed in a certain order.
- Don't assume knowledge, especially for less technical audiences. For example, don't assume the audience will know what acronyms mean; spell each one out the first time it's used in each document.

Store documentation in a central location where everyone can access it who needs it. Make sure your documentation is backed up frequently; automate the backup process if possible to ensure that the backups happen on schedule.

Next we'll look at some of the most common types of documentation that IT professionals may be called upon to create, edit, and/or manage.

Types of Documentation

The following sections briefly explain some of the most common documentation types that IT professionals may need to write, update, and/or maintain.

Acceptable-Use Policy

An *acceptable-use policy* (AUP) is an IT policy that explains what actions employees and contractors can take on data and computing resources. This includes but is not limited to storing, accessing, deleting, disseminating, and sharing that data through computers and networks. Such policy must comply with all applicable laws, as well as the policies and rules of the organization. An AUP normally defines how acceptable use is managed, ownership of data, what acceptable use is for various types of data and computing resources, and what incidental use of computing resources (e-mail, Internet access, fax machines, printers, copiers, etc.) is allowed for employees for personal use. The policy will define

- Who is responsible for defining and maintaining the policy, for training and educating employees about the policy, for establishing a formal review cycle for the policy, and for implementing the initiatives that result from it.
- An incident-report policy describing to whom employees should report any prohibited activity, what proof is needed to substantiate the claim, and what methods should be used to make a report.
- Classes of data. Confidential data is often organized into categories, such as patient medical data, patient/customer financial data, product data, research data, and many others.
- Who owns the data created and stored on the organization's computer systems.
- Which employees have the right to monitor and/or log all employee use of such data and access the data at any time without employee knowledge.
- The behavior of employees expected as part of acceptable use. This is usually a long list of requirements, as well as prohibited behaviors and reporting imperatives. For instance, it will require that employees report any indication of a problem with computer security to the appropriate support staff.
- A prohibition against users sharing their user accounts (network, e-mail, and others) and related passwords, personal identification numbers (PINs), smart cards and similar security tokens, and other means of accessing accounts. Some organizations define a separate e-mail policy for employees, while others may combine these policies to include all user accounts.
- A requirement that employee use of IT systems must not result in any direct cost, legal action against, or embarrassment to the organization, nor interfere with normal performance of the employee's job.

exam watch

Remember that your first response to prohibited behavior should be to identify the behavior, report through proper channels, and preserve the data (logs, etc.) or devices containing evidence of the prohibited behavior.

A *password policy* may be part of an AUP, or it may be a separate document. A password policy specifies the rules that users must follow when they create their passwords. For example, passwords might need to be a certain minimum length, to include both uppercase and lowercase letters, and/or to include numbers or symbols. Longer passphrases are also sometimes warranted, being even more difficult to crack. A password policy may also include an interval at which the password must be changed (because older passwords are more vulnerable to being discovered by unauthorized parties). It may also include information about how to get help resetting a lost password.

For the current NIST password guidelines, check out this article: https://auth0.com/blog/dont-pass-on-the-new-nist-password-guidelines/

Incident Documentation

Incident documentation is a written account about a problem and its resolution. The term "incident" is intentionally broad here and can refer to a security lapse, a hacker attack, inappropriate content found on a user's PC, a server crash that results in lost data, or any number of other IT situations.

Incidents are documented in order to capture knowledge about the incident while it is still fresh in the minds of everyone who was involved. The information may be passed up the management chain, reported to law enforcement authorities, shared as a "lesson learned" at staff meetings, or just filed away for later reference.

An *incident report* should contain the following information:

- Contact information for the person documenting the incident, including name, title, phone number, and e-mail address
- Contact information for everyone involved in the incident, particularly those who may have some input to contribute, such as witnesses or the person who discovered it
- A brief description of the incident in a factual, objective manner
- An assessment of the impact or potential impact to the organization, both short term and long term
- A description of what data was compromised and its level of sensitivity
- Who else has been notified (person and title)
- What steps have been taken so far
- The details of the incident, including
  - Date and time of discovery
  - Whether or not the incident has been resolved and things have returned to normal
  - The physical locations of the affected systems
  - The number of sites and users affected
  - Any customers or outside vendors affected by the incident

Network Topology Diagrams

Network administrators may need to create or modify *network topology diagrams,* which may also have written descriptions associated with them. *Topology* refers to the physical arrangement and location of network equipment. For example, a topology diagram for an office might include the physical locations, IP addresses, and/or ID numbers of each workstation, printer, switch, router, and so on.

Not all companies keep detailed diagrams that include information about every single workstation; some use diagrams only for the major components of the network, such as the servers and connecting devices.

Knowledge Base Articles and Help Systems

A *knowledge base* is a collection of articles on a particular subject. In an IT knowledge base, each article is written to explain a technology or feature, suggest best practices, or solve a problem. For example, Microsoft has a large, searchable knowledge base with articles that provide help and information about all Microsoft products.

As an IT professional, you might access a knowledge base as a consumer, looking for information that may help you solve a problem you are having. You might also access a knowledge base as a writer or editor, either creating new articles or adding/updating information to existing articles.

A *help system* is a searchable, browsable collection of information about a particular software or hardware product. Some manufacturers do not provide printed instruction manuals with their products at all, preferring instead to have users rely on their help systems for information. It is not common for IT workers to create or edit help systems, as this work is typically done by professional technical writers.

Standard Operating Procedures

Documentation should exist for all IT procedures that users are allowed to do, explaining what is allowed, under what circumstances, and how it should be accomplished. For example, there might be a *standard operating procedure (SOP)* for custom installation of software packages that certain employees or teams might need for their work.

User Account Management

Internal documentation should exist that tells IT staff how to set up the needed accounts for new employees, vendors, contractors, or others who are authorized to use the IT systems. There may be a list of accounts to create and permissions to grant for various job descriptions or departments, for example.

Even more importantly for security, there should be a similar checklist that guides IT staff in decommissioning a user account when the person leaves the company to ensure that former employees do not have access to sensitive information or important IT systems.

Make sure you understand best practices for incident reports, SOPs, new user setup, and end-user termination checklists.

Regulatory and Compliance Policy Documentation

As discussed earlier in the chapter, companies have a responsibility to make sure that employees, contractors, and in some cases customers comply with applicable regulations and policies. One way to help ensure compliance is to write clear, unambiguous documentation about the expected behavior and make sure it is distributed to everyone who needs it.

When writing documentation that explains rules to be followed, some of the important points to include are

- The descriptive title of the document
- A date and version number
- To whom it applies
- The purpose of the policy or regulation—in other words, what benefit the policy is designed to deliver
- An explanation of the rule using clear language that leaves no room for misinterpretation or loopholes
- An explanation of the consequences of not following the rule
- Contact information for someone who can answer questions about the policy or make corrections to the document

Some systems use a *splash screen* to pass compliance or usage information to users at sign-in. A splash screen is a box that pops up to convey the information over the top of the main interface. Depending on the configuration, users may be required to click a button to signify their agreement with the requirements in order to continue.

SCENARIO & SOLUTION

Scenario	Solution
Your company's IT documentation exists in a variety of formats, including Word, RTF, PDF, plaintext, PowerPoint, Excel, and XPS. You need to pick one format to standardize on. Which would you choose and why?	PDF is a good choice because most devices can read PDFs, because most applications can save documents in PDF format, and because PDF files format documents so they display consistently across platforms. Other answers are not wrong, but you should be able to justify your answer.
You are asked to devise a naming convention for product support documentation files. What elements should you make sure are included in the filenames?	Filenames should include a unique identifier such as an ID number, at a minimum. It is often helpful to also include other information such as a version number or modification date.
There have been problems lately with employees not following the rules regarding personal use of company-owned computers. You have been asked to write up a document that clarifies the expectations. What kind of document should you create?	An acceptable-use policy (AUP) defines what behavior is acceptable when working with IT systems and would be the right choice for this assignment.

Asset Management

IT professionals are often required to maintain computer hardware inventory information, including the specifications of each piece of equipment, its purchase date, its value, its physical location, and to whom it is assigned (if applicable).

Some of the tools and documentation that an IT department should maintain for asset management include the following:

- **An inventory database** The *inventory list* can be stored in a database application (for example, Microsoft Access for a small business, or some more robust database system for larger companies). For a very small company with a short list of IT assets, it could even be in a spreadsheet.
- **Asset tags and IDs** *Asset tags* are stickers or plates that you attach to devices with ID numbers on them that correspond to database entries. To make data entry easier, you can use *bar codes* on the asset tags and then use a hand-scanner to scan the bar codes.
- **Software licensing data** IT must maintain information about all the licensing that the company has paid for, for each application. For example, if the company has a site license for a certain number of users or seats, IT must be able to quickly retrieve that information when it is needed.
- **Warranties** IT must maintain information about the warranties on all hardware assets. For example, if a new laptop has a one-year warranty and the laptop comes to IT for repair, the technician must be able to look up whether or not the warranty has expired.
- **Assigned users** IT must be able to cross-reference devices and the users to which they have been assigned. This information must be kept up to date as hardware moves around to different locations or departments.

Ticketing Systems

A *ticketing system* is software that manages support requests from users. Ticketing systems are used in many professions, including customer service, but in this context we are thinking of them specifically for IT support. Your employer will provide a ticketing system; your job will be to use it appropriately and consistently.

Ticketing systems are essentially database management applications. They track all the information needed to make sure that each *ticket* (that is, each request) is received, reviewed, prioritized, and addressed in an appropriate order. To do this, a ticketing system collects the following information about each ticket:

- **User information** This can include name, job title, and contact information.
- **Device information** What device is having the problem? This information should include the device's asset tag number, which should cross-reference to the inventory database, and the current location of the device.

- **Description of problems** The user submitting the ticket will describe the problem initially, and the IT person responding to the ticket may have their own notes about what the problem turns out to be.
- **Categories** Categorizing tickets can help direct the appropriate IT staff to the problem. For example, there may be separate teams of support staff for Windows vs. macOS or for hardware vs. software.
- **Severity** Marking tickets according to severity can help prioritize them. For example, a departmental server outage should have a higher severity level than a bad keyboard on a user laptop because it affects more people.
- **Escalation levels** It is typical in an IT support system for there to be multiple tiers of support. When a user has a problem, a first-level support person tries to solve it. These are usually the less experienced people. If they are unable to solve the problem, the ticket is escalated to the next level of support personnel. The ticketing system should keep track of the ticket's current level of escalation.

Be sure you are familiar with best practices associated with documentation, including the types of documents, asset management, and ticketing systems.

When an IT professional works to solve a user's problem, it's important that they make clear, concise notes in the ticketing system that include the problem description (which may be different from the description that the user gave when submitting the request), the progress notes, and the problem resolution. Clearly documenting each problem and its resolution can not only help if the same device has a problem in the future, but it can also help IT management notice trends and make decisions about future hardware and software purchases.

CERTIFICATION OBJECTIVE

- ***1102: 4.2** Explain basic change-management best practices*

The CompTIA A+ 1102 exam may test your knowledge of the steps involved in planning and implementing an IT system change, from the initial concept through implementation and end-user acceptance.

Change Management

Change management is a disciplined approach to making system changes as fast, smooth, and problem-free as possible. Change management can apply to any kind of change in any type of organization—it's not specific to IT. However, in the context of the IT profession, change management most often refers to managing the upgrade or replacement of computer hardware or software. *Information Technology Infrastructure Library (ITIL) change management* is a collection of best practices for IT change management, and the CompTIA A+ objectives covering change management are based upon it.

For example, suppose your IT department plans to update all Windows PCs to Windows 11, including some PCs that run Windows 7. You haven't done it before because there are some concerns with some proprietary software that was created to run on earlier versions of Windows possibly not running well under Windows 11 and because some of the PCs are so old that Windows 11 might not install on them. You need to do it soon, though, because Microsoft has stopped releasing security patches for Windows 7, and machines running Windows 7 are at greater risk for malware and hacking. Using change management principles can help reduce the risk of work interruptions and data loss in making this change.

Changing Management Objectives

Change management, in a nutshell, goes something like this: "We think we want to make this change, and we want to make sure it's the right thing to do and that everyone is on board before we get started. We know there are some risks of business interruption, and we want to minimize those as much as possible. We also want to make the change happen as quickly and efficiently as we can and document the entire process well so that others coming behind us will know what we did." So that's the overall goal.

Let's break that goal down into more specific objectives. When making a change, we want to

- Make sure that management understands and approves the change before it happens
- Keep things running as normally as possible throughout the change and afterward
- Minimize the risks of any negative impact the change might bring with it
- Minimize the number of problems/incidents caused by the change
- Maintain good records/documentation about the change

There are many ways to organize a change management process, and you'll find lots of resources in books and online that outline structured processes. In the following sections we break it down according to the topics listed in the CompTIA A+ 1102 exam Objective 4.2 because that's what you're most likely to find on the exam, but keep in mind that there are other ways of looking at the same objectives.

Making Requests for Changes

Some kinds of IT changes are routine and simple, and any user can request them. For example, if a user needs a certain application to do their job but that application is not on the approved software list, that user might make a request to change the approved software list. The IT department may provide a request form that users can fill out to request minor IT changes.

On the other hand, big changes are typically requested by IT personnel, and the request is submitted to upper management. For big requests, it's customary to create a full proposal with documentation, rather than just filling out a form. The following sections describe some of the information that such a proposal might contain.

Describing the Purpose of the Change

Change always comes with a risk of failure (or at least inconvenience), so companies don't make IT changes willy-nilly. There must be a compelling reason to make a change: in other words, its *purpose*. A change management plan should begin with a clear statement of the purpose. In the aforementioned Windows upgrade example, the purpose would be "Upgrade all PCs to Windows 11 to provide better security protection." You would then elaborate on the benefits of that upgrade, explaining the details. Some changes may be driven by known problems or incidents; others may be proactive.

Defining the Type and Scope of the Change

The change management process varies depending on the type of change it is. A minor change may not require much planning at all, whereas a major change might require months of planning. Here are some ways to categorize change types:

- **Major** Changes that affect important systems or many users and radically change their processes and/or have a high risk of failure and business interruption. This type of change must be carefully planned and must go through an approval process.
- **Minor** Changes that are not likely to have a major impact or to cause problems. This type of change also requires planning and approval.
- **Standard** Preapproved changes that are low impact and low risk. They follow a standard procedure for implementation and don't usually require approval.
- **Emergency** Changes that need to be made to fix unexpected problems that affect essential systems. These changes do not usually go through the standard approval process because of their urgent nature; instead, the documentation is submitted for management review after the fact.

The *scope* of the change is a description of its reach. For example, will the change affect all PCs in the entire company or just certain ones? Will it affect mobile devices too or just Windows-based PCs?

Defining the Timetable

When should the change be made? Is this an "as soon as possible" thing, or is there a specific deadline to meet? For example, if the company needs to change to a different software package before the license agreement for the old one is expired, that needs to be stated in the proposal.

Analyzing the Risks and Impact

There's always risk when something changes. Make sure you can clearly and realistically assess the risks of your change proposal. In the Windows upgrade example, one of the risks is that software designed for earlier Windows versions may not work under Windows 11. Another risk is that older PCs may perform poorly under Windows 11 because they lack the recommended hardware configuration (such as not enough RAM or not a fast enough CPU). There may be other risks as well besides the obvious ones. For example, if specific computers that are important to business operations fail to restart normally after the upgrade, some revenue-generating operations could be interrupted, costing the company money. Another risk might be that employees will not immediately understand how to use Windows 11 and will not be productive until they receive training.

Formulating a Rollback Plan

If the change turns out to not be a good thing, how will the organization recover? A rollback plan explains how that will work. The *rollback plan* includes precautions to be taken, such as creating images of important storage devices before modifying them, having backup hardware available in the event of a hardware incompatibility or failure as a result of the change, and having extra IT personnel on call to quickly address any configuration problems.

Planning the Change

Next, you need a detailed plan that describes exactly how you will implement the change and who the *responsible staff member* will be. Include each step to be taken, in order, and the people and resources to be involved in each step. Indicate how long each step will take, what could go wrong, and how you will address any problems that occur. This planning process may take days, weeks, or even months to complete and may involve multiple people and departments. In addition to hearing from managers, make sure you get the input of the people who will be tasked with the ground-level work of rolling out the change; they may think of details that managers may not. Be sure to also involve any departments or managers whose budgets will be tapped to pay for the change.

Part of the plan may be to do *sandbox testing,* which means to test the change in a limited, controlled environment. For an application change, the staff might roll out new application software on a test server before pushing it out to all users.

Getting Approval and Implementing the Change

All the information from the last several sections is rolled into a *request for change proposal.* A request for change proposal is the tool you will use to "sell" the change to decision-makers. Someone from IT may be asked to present the information to management in a meeting, or there may be sign-off based on the document alone. There may be a *change board,* which is a group of senior managers and experts who approve or reject change proposals.

Once you get the approval to make a change, you start implementing the plan: acquiring the needed resources, scheduling the activities, and informing the affected parties.

Getting End-User Acceptance

The key to gaining end-user acceptance is communication. End users who will be affected by the change should be notified as far in advance as possible and then reminded of the change when it is imminent. There should be extra help-desk support available on the day the change happens so users do not get frustrated waiting for help if there is a problem. Training should be available to any end users who want help. In cases where the change results in a radically different end-user interface, training might even be mandatory.

Documenting the Changes

Documentation is an important step in change management. The guidelines for creating documentation that you learned earlier in this chapter apply here as well.

You will probably have a collection of documents for each change, beginning with the request for change proposal and continuing through the implementation and its aftermath.

As you document a change, make sure to include the following:

- Who approved the change and on what date?
- Who implemented the change and on what date?
- What specific actions were taken?
- What was the effect of those actions, both overall and on specific systems?

- What was the immediate or short-term impact of the change?
- Were there any problems that needed to be corrected? If so, describe them and their resolution in detail.
- What is the expected long-term effect of the change?

SCENARIO & SOLUTION	
You have been asked to create a request for change proposal for switching a large branch office over from nightly tape backups to an automated real-time backup appliance. Whose input would you solicit as you work on the proposal?	It would be helpful to have the input of many different people, but especially those who work directly with the current system and those who will work directly with the new system (if they are different people). Technical specialists should also be consulted, such as network administrators. If the money for the new system will come out of a certain manager's budget, then he or she should also be involved.
An important server has been crashing frequently, and each time it results in a 15-minute outage, during which time customers cannot place orders on your website. You have determined that the problem is being caused by a gradually failing power supply that was of inadequate wattage to begin with. Should you create a request for change (RFC) proposal for replacing it with a higher-wattage model? Why or why not?	No, you do not need an RFC. Because this problem is affecting the company's profitability, it can be considered an emergency change and can bypass the formal process of analysis and approval. Just change out the power supply and then let management know afterwards. Although you do not have to do a formal proposal, you should still go through the basic steps of thinking through the change beforehand and taking steps to minimize the impact of the downtime. For example, you might stand up a backup server to function as you are working on the main server.

CERTIFICATION SUMMARY

Candidates for a CompTIA A+ certificate must understand the communication skills required for success on the job. This includes listening and communicating clearly while employing tact and discretion with all interpersonal contacts. Be conscious of your body language to ensure that your words and actions are not sending conflicting messages.

You should understand what your organization and all applicable laws define as prohibited content and prohibited activity. Know how to respond to an instance of a use of prohibited content or prohibited activity, including how to report it through proper channels, how to preserve the data or devices involved, how to document it, and the proper chain of custody for the evidence.

Not only must your IT processes conform to company policies, but they must also align with governmental regulations and laws regarding licensing and privacy. Understand the types of software licenses and the ways that digital data and privacy are regulated.

An important part of performing IT work is to document your activities so that managers and other IT professionals will be able to understand the systems and their histories. Understand how to create consistent, professional IT documentation and how to organize and store it properly. Be familiar with a variety of documentation types.

Change management helps minimize the negative impact of any IT-related changes. Understand the overall objectives and strategies of change management, and be able to explain how to create a request for change proposal and how to plan, implement, and document changes.

TWO-MINUTE DRILL

Here are some of the key points covered in Chapter 2.

Professionalism and Proper Communication

- ❑ Professionalism is a set of behaviors that you should do whether you are being observed or not.
- ❑ Always practice tact and discretion in interactions with other people.
- ❑ Professional behavior is respectful and includes having a positive attitude, avoiding confrontation or having a judgmental attitude, and never minimizing others' concerns.
- ❑ When you are respectful, you are attentive and you respect confidentiality and privacy.

Dealing with Prohibited Content and Prohibited Activities

- ❑ Prohibited content is any content that an organization or government deems harmful to the institution in general and to all persons, or a certain class of persons, for which it is responsible.
- ❑ When prohibited content or behavior is discovered, be sure to document your findings, report the finding to the proper authorities, and maintain the chain of custody for any evidence.
- ❑ Governments have laws about prohibited content and behavior, and many organizations have documents defining how laws and the corporations' rules apply to employees and what employees must do to comply, published as policies and procedures and/or security policies.

Licensing, Privacy, and Regulations

- ❑ An End User License Agreement (EULA) specifies the terms under which software is licensed. The conditions of the EULA are specified by the software owner. You must either agree to the EULA or not use the software.
- ❑ Commercial software is controlled by a company or individual. Public-domain software is not owned or controlled by anyone. Open-source software makes the source code available to the public, but is not necessarily in the public domain.
- ❑ Personal software licenses are for individuals; enterprise licenses offer volume discounts for companies. Per-seat licensing requires a license for every device (seat); per-user licensing requires a license for every user.
- ❑ Digital rights management (DRM) forces users to comply with license agreement restrictions on the content's use. DRM can apply to both data files and applications. Activation is one type of DRM; another type is the copy restriction placed on some downloaded music and video files.

Documentation Management

- ❑ Documentation management includes not only creating and maintaining documents but also creating a consistent, coherent system of organization that includes consistently named files in a standardized format.
- ❑ Common types of IT documentation include acceptable-use policies, password policies, incident documentation, infrastructure diagrams, inventory management, knowledge base articles, and regulatory and compliance policy documents.
- ❑ An acceptable-use policy outlines expected employee behavior for ensuring the security, integrity, privacy, and availability of resources.

Change Management

- ❑ Change management is a disciplined approach to making system changes as fast, smooth, and problem-free as possible.
- ❑ The general objectives of change management are to approve changes before they happen, keep things running as normally as possible throughout the change, minimize the problems/incidents due to the change, have a back-out plan, and maintain good records.
- ❑ Planning for change includes defining its purpose and scope, identifying any potential risks, doing a cost/benefit analysis, and getting management approval. End-user approval and complete documentation are also important.

SELF TEST

The following questions will help you measure your understanding of the material presented in this chapter. Read all of the choices carefully because there might be more than one correct answer. Choose all correct answers for each question.

Professionalism and Proper Communication

1. When you are explaining something technical to a customer, which of the following is the best technique to use to confirm the customer understands your explanation?

A. As you explain, intersperse questions such as, "Does that make sense?"
B. After the explanation, give the customer a quiz.
C. Give the customer a printed explanation to read as you speak.
D. Maintain eye contact.

2. When someone has explained something to you, how can you make sure you heard and understood what she said?

A. Focus.
B. Repeat it back in your own words.
C. Imagine how you sound and appear to the other person.
D. Nod your head frequently.

3. Which of the following is a technique you would use to show respect to a customer? (Select all that apply.)

A. Be as clear as possible and correct any misunderstandings.
B. Show the customer your company's security policy.
C. Do not minimize the importance of what someone else tells you.
D. Treat others the way you like to be treated.

4. When a customer is explaining a problem, what is the single most important thing you must do?

A. Nod your head to show understanding.
B. Empathize.
C. Allow the customer to explain the problem without interruption.
D. Show respect.

5. What behavior shows a positive and professional attitude? (Select all that apply.)
   A. Avoiding confrontation
   B. Avoiding judgmental behavior
   C. Showing respect
   D. Minimizing another's concerns

Dealing with Prohibited Content and Prohibited Activities

6. You believe you have witnessed prohibited behavior, and you have clearly identified it by referring to company policies. What should you do next?
   A. Evaluate whether the policy is a good one and should be enforced.
   B. Report the incident through the proper channels.
   C. Minimize the importance of the violation by finding a rationale.
   D. Wait until you observe a second violation of the same policy.
7. Which of these is the best way to ensure that all employees are aware of an important security policy?
   A. Post a notice in a prominent place telling people to read the policy online.
   B. Post the policy in a prominent place.
   C. Require employees to sign and date a statement saying they have read the policy.
   D. Send the policy to all employees via SMS text message.
8. When investigating the finding of prohibited content on an employee's computer, it is important to:
   A. Express your personal opinion about the situation.
   B. Delete the prohibited content immediately from the computer.
   C. Use your own judgment and be flexible.
   D. Follow the company's policies about what to do.

Licensing, Privacy, and Regulations

9. What type of document specifies how many users or devices you can legally install a certain software product on?
   A. AUP
   B. EULA
   C. Source code
   D. Public-domain license
10. Which of these is *not* true of enterprise licensing?
   A. It provides one physical installation medium (such as a USB flash drive or DVD) for each user.
   B. It is a better value for high-volume purchases than personal licensing.
   C. It can be purchased on a per-seat basis.
   D. It can be purchased on a per-user basis.

11. Product activation is a form of:

A. AUP
B. DRM
C. EULA
D. RCP

12. Which of these is an EU regulation that requires anyone collecting personal data to disclose that they are doing so?

A. HIPAA
B. PHI
C. GDPR
D. PII

Documentation Management

13. Which of the following is a document that defines what actions can be taken on data and computing resources in a company?

A. Acceptable-use policy
B. Chain of custody
C. Statement of libel
D. User manual

14. Which of these does *not* need to be included in IT documentation?

A. A unique ID
B. The purpose of the document
C. Contact information for a responsible person
D. The names of the managers who approved the document

15. Where should documentation be stored?

A. In a protected location where nobody can access it
B. In a shared location where everyone authorized to access it can do so
C. On the hard drive of the author of it
D. On the hard drive of the manager responsible for keeping it updated

16. Which type of document would you create in order to record information about a security breach?

A. Incident documentation
B. Password policy
C. AUP
D. EULA

17. Which of these should *not* be included in an incident report?
   A. Contact information for everyone involved in the incident
   B. A detailed, objective description of the incident
   C. What steps have been taken so far
   D. Speculation about who is to blame for the incident

Change Management

18. Which of these is the best definition of change management?
   A. A policy document that specifies the rules for making changes to IT systems
   B. A disciplined approach to making system changes as smooth and problem-free as possible
   C. A way of making changes to a license agreement after purchasing hardware or software
   D. A schedule that specifies how often IT systems should be updated

19. Change management can help with which of the following objectives?
   A. Enforce penalties when end users do not comply with change-related policies
   B. Raise funds to pay for implementing a change
   C. Reduce the number and severity of problems that occur due to a change
   D. Shut down all IT functions while a change is occurring

20. Which of these is a document that describes a plan to implement an IT system change?
   A. EULA proposal
   B. PII proposal
   C. HIPAA proposal
   D. RFC proposal

SELF TEST ANSWERS

Professionalism and Proper Communication

1. ☑ **A.** As you explain, intersperse questions such as, "Does that make sense?" to confirm the customer's understanding.
   ☒ **B** is incorrect because giving a quiz is not the best technique and would probably make the customer angry. **C** is incorrect because this is not the best way to treat a customer. **D** is incorrect because although this should always be part of face-to-face interactions, eye contact is not the best technique to use to confirm understanding.

2. ☑ **B.** Repeat it back in your own words. This confirms that you heard and understand.
☒ **A** is incorrect, although focusing on the customer and the problem is an important thing to do. **C** is incorrect, although this is a good habit when you are the one doing the speaking. **D** is incorrect because although this tells the speaker that you are listening, nodding does not confirm that you heard and understood what she said.

3. ☑ **A, C,** and **D.** These are all correct techniques for showing respect.
☒ **B** is incorrect because although this is an important policy for an organization, this behavior does not directly show respect at the personal level.

4. ☑ **C.** Allowing the customer to explain the problem without interruption is the most important thing you must do when a customer is explaining a problem.
☒ **A, B,** and **D** are incorrect because although you should use all of these in your interactions with the customer, the most important thing to do in this case is to allow the customer to explain without interruption.

5. ☑ **A, B,** and **C.** These are all correct behaviors that show a positive and professional attitude.
☒ **D** is incorrect because this is negative and unprofessional behavior.

Dealing with Prohibited Content and Prohibited Activities

6. ☑ **B.** Report the incident through proper channels.
☒ **A, C,** and **D** are incorrect. It is not your job to evaluate the policy, minimize the importance of the violation, or wait for a second violation.

7. ☑ **C.** Having employees acknowledge reading the policy is the best way because it creates accountability.
☒ **A** and **B** are incorrect because there is no way to know who has received and read the policy. **D** is incorrect because there is no way of knowing whether the recipients read the policy and understand it and because distributing important documents via text messaging is a poor choice of medium.

8. ☑ **D.** Following the company's policies is essential; you protect both the company and yourself by doing so.
☒ **A** is incorrect because you should not express your personal opinion, only the facts. **B** is incorrect because you need to preserve the evidence. **C** is incorrect because using your own judgment can lead to going against company policy.

Licensing, Privacy, and Regulations

9. ☑ **B.** An End User License Agreement (EULA) is the license agreement for software; it specifies the rules for how you can use the product.
☒ **A** is incorrect because an acceptable-use policy (AUP) dictates the behaviors of employees for a company, not for a product. **C** is incorrect because source code is the uncompiled code of a program. **D** is incorrect because public-domain software, by definition, does not have a license.

10. ☑ **A.** Enterprise licensing typically does not provide installation media for each user; instead, it provides an executable setup file you can make your own copies of.
☒ **B, C,** and **D** are incorrect because they are all true statements about enterprise licensing.

11. ☑ **B.** Product activation is a form of digital rights management (DRM).
☒ **A** is incorrect because AUP is an acceptable-use policy, a document that dictates rules for employee behavior. **C** is incorrect because EULA is an End User License Agreement, a software license. **D** is incorrect because RCP is a request for change proposal, a document that proposes an IT change.

12. ☑ **C.** The General Data Protection Regulation (GDPR) is the regulation that specifies rules about collecting and disclosing personal information.
☒ **A** is incorrect because HIPAA is the Health Insurance Portability and Accountability Act, a U.S. law affecting healthcare data. **B** is incorrect because PHI stands for protected health information, the data that HIPAA protects. **D** is incorrect because PII stands for personally identifiable information, a general classification of information that can be used to trace an individual's identity; it is not a regulation.

Documentation Management

13. ☑ **A.** An acceptable-use policy defines what can be done with data and computing resources in a company in order to preserve the company's interests.
☒ **B** is incorrect because chain of custody refers to the disciplined documentation of who has ownership of an item at any given time. **C** is incorrect because a libelous statement is one that is false, malicious, and defamatory and appears in print. **D** is incorrect because a user manual would explain how to operate a certain piece of hardware or software but would not provide an overall policy for a company.

14. ☑ **D.** Documentation does not need to have the names of everyone who approved the document.
☒ **A, B,** and **C** are incorrect because all of these elements should be included in documentation.

15. ☑ **B.** Documentation needs to be always accessible by all those who need it.
☒ **A** is incorrect because protecting documentation is secondary; the main concern is that it be available. **C** and **D** are incorrect because if documentation is stored on a personal hard drive, its availability depends on that person having their computer up and running.

16. ☑ **A.** Incident documentation is a written account about a problem and its resolution.
☒ **B** is incorrect because a password policy dictates the rules for password usage. **C** is incorrect because AUP is an acceptable-use policy, which dictates rules for employee computer usage. **D** is incorrect because EULA is an End User License Agreement, which dictates how software may legally be used.

17. ☑ **D.** An incident report should not include speculation—only known, objective facts.
☒ **A, B,** and **C** are incorrect because all these things should be included.

Change Management

18. ☑ **B.** The term *change management* describes a process for ensuring the success of IT system changes.
☒ **A** is incorrect because change management is not a policy document. **C** is incorrect because change management has nothing to do with license agreements. **D** is incorrect because change management is not a schedule, although it may contain a project timetable.

19. ☑ **C.** Making a change happen with as few problems as possible is a primary objective of change management.
☒ **A** is incorrect because change management does not propose penalties for noncompliance. **B** is incorrect because change management does not raise funds for implementing a change. **D** is incorrect because change management tries to keep IT functions running as much as possible while a change is occurring.

20. ☑ **D.** A request for change (RFC) proposal presents a well-thought-out plan for making a change successfully; it is used to gain approval for the change from decision-makers within the company.
☒ **A** is incorrect because EULA is not a type of proposal; it is a license agreement. **B** is incorrect because PII is not a type of proposal; it stands for personally identifiable information. **C** is incorrect because HIPAA is healthcare-related legislation; it is not a type of proposal.

Part II

Operating Systems

CHAPTERS

Chapter 3

Operating System Fundamentals

CERTIFICATION OBJECTIVES

- **1102: 1.1** Identify basic features of Microsoft Windows editions
- **1102: 1.4** Given a scenario, use the appropriate Microsoft Windows 10 Control Panel utility
- **1102: 1.5** Given a scenario, use the appropriate Windows settings
- **1102: 1.8** Explain common OS types and their purposes
- **1102: 1.10** Identify common features and tools of the macOS/desktop OS

✓ Two-Minute Drill

Q&A Self Test

Like many people, you may have used Windows for much of your life, and you can competently do ordinary tasks, such as navigating folders, saving files, downloading files, and running programs. With such proficiency, you may wonder why you need to study the operating system any further. It's because you need a far different set of skills and knowledge to support Windows than you need to simply use it. Those skills include understanding it enough to competently install, configure, troubleshoot, and maintain it.

On the other hand, you do not need to be a programmer who understands the operating system's (OS's) source code. You only need a base of knowledge, a sharp mind, good powers of observation, and patience.

The coverage of Windows begins in this chapter with an overview of the ways that operating systems differ from one another. It then moves into a survey of the various Windows operating system versions included on the CompTIA A+ 220-1102 exam, including features that vary by version. It also looks at the macOS and Linux user interfaces and points out some of the features of those operating systems.

The discussion of Windows continues in the next several chapters. Each chapter covers a different aspect of supporting Windows, including installing and upgrading Windows—either into a virtual machine or, more conventionally, on a physical PC (Chapter 4), managing disks and files (Chapter 5), troubleshooting and maintaining Windows (Chapter 6), and working with Windows client virtualization (Chapter 7).

CERTIFICATION OBJECTIVE

- ***1102: 1.8*** *Explain common OS types and their purposes*

Introduction to Operating Systems

In this section, you will learn the purpose of operating systems on various types of devices, the characteristics of 32-bit versus 64-bit OSs, and the importance of updates. This section also discusses vendor-specific limitations such as end of life and update limitations on older operating systems and compatibility concerns between operating systems.

The Purpose of Operating Systems

The purpose of an *operating system* is to control all the interactions among the various system components, the human interactions with the computer, and the network operations for the computer system. An OS is not a single program, but a collection of programs that work together via a complex set of software layers that manage everything from the lowest level (the hardware) to the highest levels (user interactions).

The main functions of an OS are hardware control, file management, and providing a user interface. It also manages and directs the usage of memory and the central processing unit (CPU).

Hardware Control

An OS is aware of the hardware components of the computer, including any peripherals attached to it, and can communicate with each component. An important type of software that works closely with the OS is a *device driver*—program code that enables the OS to interact with and control a particular device. Many device drivers come with workstation (desktop/laptop) operating systems such as Windows, macOS, and Linux, and you can easily add others.

File Management

The OS is responsible for managing the computer's files in an organized manner and allowing the user to access data files. The OS keeps track of the functions of different files and brings them into memory as program code or data when needed. Furthermore, the OS is responsible for maintaining file associations so data files launch in the proper applications. The OS is also responsible for managing the computer's drives, keeping track of each drive's identification and controlling space usage.

User Interface

A *user interface (UI)* is both the visual portion of the operating system and the software components that enable the user to interact with the OS. A *graphical user interface (GUI)* is a user interface that enables the user to interact with the OS by manipulating graphic objects on the screen using a pointing device (such as a mouse or trackball).

Device Types and Architectures

Each class of computing device has a different kind of OS specifically tailored to its needs. For example, mobile devices such as cell phones and tablets need an OS that is compact and efficient (because storage space and memory are limited). A workstation PC needs a feature-rich OS that can manage many peripherals (including multiple monitors) and manage memory allocation for concurrently running applications. A server needs robust multitasking capabilities to handle input and output from multiple clients via network interfaces.

Within each general class of device are multiple competing operating systems. The most popular desktop/laptop operating systems are Microsoft Windows, Apple macOS, and Linux. The most popular mobile operating systems are Android and iOS.

CompTIA A+ 1102 exam Objective 1.8 also lists iPadOS as a separate topic from iOS under cell phone/tablet OS, but they are very similar. You do not need to study them separately; study whichever one you happen to have access to (iOS on a smartphone or iPadOS on an iPad).

Most mobile devices come with the OS preinstalled, and you can't change it. For example, when you buy an iPhone, you get the iOS operating system. Mobile operating systems are installed in a protected area of the device's storage so they can't be accidentally erased or corrupted. A system utility updates them when updates are available.

Android devices are more flexible than iOS devices in terms of being able to modify the OS, but it's not easy to do. That's a job for enthusiasts and experts; most users would not go to the time and trouble of hacking the OS, and that skill is not covered on the CompTIA A+ exams.

Most laptop and desktop PCs also come with an OS preinstalled, but you may be able to change it, depending on the system's architecture. A *computer architecture* (sometimes called the platform) is the basic design of a computer describing the data pathways and the methods the computer's CPU uses to access other components with the computer. In physical terms, the main components are the CPU, the firmware (such as BIOS or UEFI), and the chipset—all of which you will study in Chapter 8. Windows and Linux run on the same platform so you can switch between them, or even install both OSs on the same PC (each on a different volume) and choose which you want to boot to at startup.

For many years Apple's Mac computers had a proprietary architecture so you could only install macOS on them. In the last decade or so, however, Mac has switched to the same architecture as the others. That doesn't mean you can go out and buy a copy of macOS for your PC, though. Apple does not sell macOS separately from Mac hardware. What about the other direction—can you install Windows on Mac hardware? Yes, but you'll need to use the Mac's Boot Camp utility to set up dual-booting. I'll tell you more about this later in the chapter.

Servers run OSs that are optimized for server use and contain useful utilities for managing a server. Popular server OSs include Windows Server, certain Linux distributions, and Unix.

Objective 1.8 mentions one other workstation OS: Chrome OS. This is a simple OS designed for *thin clients*—that is, computers with minimal hardware resources. PCs that run Chrome OS are called Chromebooks, and they are used mainly to access network and Internet content. For example, someone who only uses cloud-based applications and the Web might find a Chromebook satisfactory for their needs. Some K–12 schools have invested in Chromebooks in an effort to inexpensively provide PCs to many students.

32-Bit vs. 64-Bit Operating Systems

Operating systems tie closely to the CPUs on which they can run. Therefore, we often use CPU terms to describe an operating system's abilities.

Most operating systems have 32-bit and 64-bit versions, and the correct version is factory-installed on new devices, depending on the CPU in the device. A 64-bit operating system requires a 64-bit CPU. A 32-bit OS can run on a system with either a 32-bit or 64-bit CPU.

Most versions of Linux and Windows (all the way back to Windows Vista) are available in both 32-bit and 64-bit versions. (Windows 11 bucks this trend and is only available as 64-bit.) The 32-bit version may be referred to as the x86 version, a tip of the hat to the ancient Intel CPUs that had names ending in 86 (286, 386, 486). The 64-bit version may be referred to as the x64 version.

Since most of workstation CPUs are 64-bit these days, you will probably want to go with the 64-bit version of your chosen OS. The biggest difference between the 32-bit and 64-bit versions of Windows is in the maximum amount of RAM it supports. The 32-bit version of Windows 10 supports a maximum of 4 GB of RAM; if the system has more RAM than that, it is ignored. The 64-bit versions of Windows 10 and 11 support up to 128 GB of RAM (in the Home edition) and up to 2 TB of RAM (in the Pro edition).

Some earlier Windows versions and editions supported less RAM, but you don't need to know those specs for the CompTIA A+ exams.

Applications can also be either 32-bit or 64-bit. Microsoft Office, for example, is available in both versions. If you have a 32-bit OS, it's important to check before purchasing an application to make sure it is 32-bit, because the 64-bit version won't install or run on that system. However, if you have a 64-bit OS, you can run either 32-bit or 64-bit applications. A 64-bit application is more desirable, all other factors being equal, because it can access more RAM and it's more efficient at communicating with the CPU.

End-of-Life (EOL) and Update Considerations

Old operating systems will theoretically keep running forever, but there are some reasons you might want to upgrade to newer versions as they become available.

One reason to upgrade is that the vendor has stopped supporting your current version, so security patches and updates are no longer developed for it. If a new security threat targets some vulnerable code in the OS, you can't count on the developer to provide a fix.

Microsoft, for example, has a standard ten-year support lifecycle for consumer versions of Windows. A *support lifecycle* defines the length of time the developer will support a product, as well as the support options.

Microsoft defines two service phases for product support: mainstream support phase and extended support phase. During mainstream support, a full array of support options are available. You can find out when mainstream support ends for an older version of Windows via a simple web search. For Windows 8.1, for example, mainstream support ended on January 9, 2018. When mainstream support has concluded, extended support is offered, and continues for ten years after the last update to it (excluding minor updates such as security patches). For Windows 8.1, extended support will end on January 10, 2023, and Windows 10 extended support will end in October 2025. Table 3-1 lists the Microsoft support phases.

Another reason to upgrade an OS is that the newer applications you need to use don't work well on the older operating system. Some applications are written for a specific OS version. Another way to solve this problem is by running the application in Compatibility Mode, discussed in Chapter 5.

TABLE 3-1 Microsoft Support Phases

Available Support	Mainstream Support Phase	Extended Support Phase
Paid support	X	X
Security update support	X	X
Nonsecurity hotfix support (to fix a specific problem)	X	*
No-charge incident support	X	
Warranty claims	X	
Design changes and feature requests	X	
Product-specific information available in the online Microsoft Knowledge Base	X	X
Product-specific information available by using the Support site at Microsoft Help and Support	X	X

*Extended support only available with an extended hotfix agreement purchased within 90 days of the end of mainstream support.

Be familiar with the various workstation OSs and cell phone/tablet OSs. Also understand what end-of-life (EOL) means, and consider update limitations as well as compatibility concerns between the various OSs.

CERTIFICATION OBJECTIVE

- ***1102: 1.1*** *Identify basic features of Microsoft Windows editions*

CompTIA A+ 1102 exam Objective 1.1 requires that you understand the differences among various editions of Windows. Be sure that you know the key features that distinguish the higher-priced versions like Pro and Enterprise from the lower-priced, consumer-level version (Home). Having this knowledge can help you advise customers as to which version they should purchase given their needs.

Windows Editions and Updates

Each Microsoft Windows *version* is a new level of the venerable operating system, with major changes to the core components of the operating system, as well as a distinctive and unifying look to the GUI. The CompTIA A+ 220-1102 exam covers only Windows 10 (and indirectly 11), so that makes it simple.

Server versions of Windows come in several editions for each version. However, no server versions are covered on the current CompTIA A+ exams, so you don't have to study them.

Windows 10 is the predominant OS on PCs purchased before November 2021. That was when Windows 11 began shipping on new PCs. Windows 10, shown in Figure 3-1, is a solid operating system that has been well received in the marketplace (unlike Windows 8 and 8.1, which were widely considered poorly designed and difficult to use).

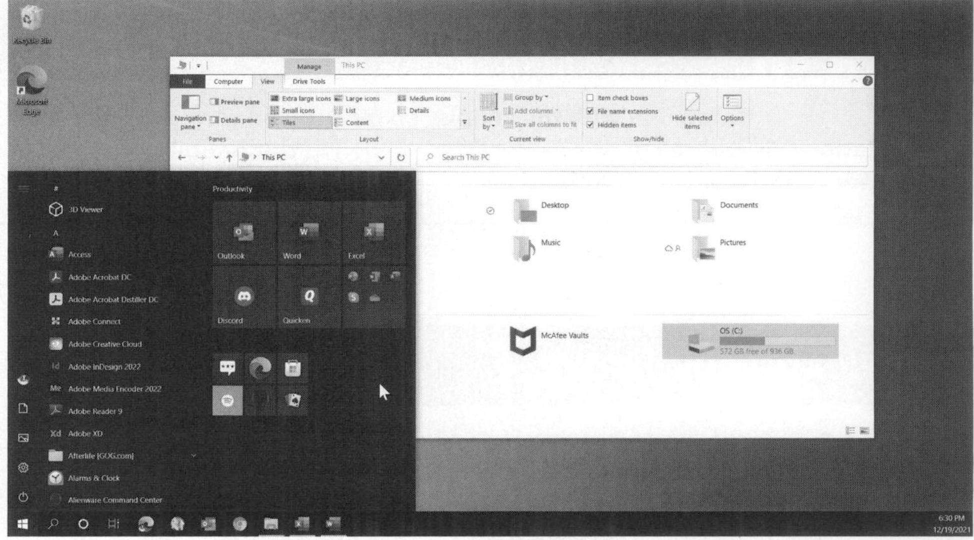

FIGURE 3-1 The Windows 10 desktop

exam watch **Although the current 1102 exam doesn't reference Windows 11 explicitly in any objectives, a note in the objectives' preface indicates that when an objective says Windows (without a version number), it is referring to both Windows 10 and Windows 11. Therefore as you study certain tasks, make sure you know how to perform them in both Windows 10 and Windows 11.**

Windows Editions

Each version of Windows is available in several different *editions,* each one with a customized mix of features for a certain audience. For the current CompTIA A+ exams, you only need to know about the Windows editions listed in Table 3-2. There are other editions of Windows, such as Education, but they aren't on the exam. (In case you're curious, the Education edition is most similar to the Enterprise edition but is missing a few features.) The editions in Table 3-2 are for Windows 10 and 11; earlier versions of Windows had some edition differences that you don't need to know about for the exam.

TABLE 3-2 Windows 10 and 11 Editions

Edition	Description	Where Available
Home	Consumer version for PCs and tablets. Does not include advanced security or domain network connectivity.	Retail, new PCs
Pro	All features of Home plus business features including Active Directory, BitLocker, Hyper-V, Remote Desktop, and Windows Defender Device Guard.	Retail, new PCs
Pro for Workstations	All features of Pro plus additional support for high-end processors and advanced types of memory and file storage.	Retail, new PCs
Enterprise	All features of Pro plus additional features for integration into large IT organizations, such as AppLocker, BranchCache, DirectAccess, and Microsoft Desktop Optimization Pack.	Volume license

Home Edition

The *Home edition* is the basic, inexpensive edition designed for home and small business users. It is missing many security and large-scale networking capabilities (discussed in the next section). Home editions are sold at retail stores and come preinstalled on new PCs.

Professional Editions

The Professional (Pro) editions contain all the features of the Home editions and add tools and capabilities useful to business users. The Pro editions are sold at retail stores and come preinstalled on new PCs.

There are two professional editions: a regular Pro edition for ordinary business use and a Pro for Workstations edition. Pro for Workstations is for users who need next-level processing power, such as computer-aided design (CAD) professionals, animators, and data scientists. It provides enhanced hardware support: up to 4 CPUs and up to 6 TB of memory, plus support for the Resilient File System (ReFS), nonvolatile memory modules (NVDIMM-N), and SMB Direct.

The Pro editions contain dozens of features and enhancements beyond the Home editions, but for the CompTIA A+ exams you only need to know about these:

- **Domain Access** The Pro editions enable connection to a network domain; Home users are limited to using peer-to-peer (workgroup) networking.
- **Remote Desktop Protocol (RDP)** This feature enables you to access the PC remotely from another PC connected via your local network or the Internet. See Chapter 17 to learn how to use it.

- **RAM support limitations** The 64-bit version of Pro supports up to 2 TB of RAM. (Some sources show 512 GB as the maximum but that is incorrect.) In contrast, the Home version supports only 128 GB—which is still far more RAM than any Windows PC you own in the next few years will probably have.
- **BitLocker** BitLocker is a full-drive encryption utility. The data on an encrypted volume cannot be read if it is removed from the PC in which it is installed. See Chapter 21 to learn more.
- **Gpedit.msc** This is the executable file for the Group Policy Editor, a utility that lets you establish and edit group policy settings within group policy objects. It's used primarily by administrators who need to modify settings for multiple computers and users at once. See Chapter 6 for more information.

Enterprise and Education Editions

Enterprise and Education editions are sold only through volume licensing to businesses and to schools, respectively. They contain some additional features that IT departments find useful for clients on large-scale networks to have. Windows' Education edition is very similar to the Enterprise edition, lacking only a few Enterprise-specific features.

The Enterprise edition contains many additional features over the Pro edition. You don't need to know any of these features by name for the exams; just know that Enterprise offers features that are useful on large networks.

Just for your own edification, here's a quick list of the features unique to Enterprise and Education editions: AppLocker, BranchCache, Credential Guard, Microsoft App-V, Microsoft Desktop Optimization Pack, Microsoft UE-V, start screen control with Group Policy, user experience control and lockdown, UWF, and DirectAccess.

Windows Updates and Builds

In Microsoft terminology, an *update* contains one or more software fixes or changes to the operating system. Some updates add abilities to the OS to support new hardware, and some resolve problems discovered with the operating system. This second type of update is often required to fix security problems. A *hotfix* or *patch* is a software fix for a single problem. However, Microsoft tends to call them all "updates" generically in newer Windows versions.

Windows Update downloads and installs updates automatically. In Windows 8.1 and earlier, users could easily turn off the automatic installation of updates, but Windows is insistent that you install updates as they become available and does not allow end users that control. IT professionals managing groups of client systems can still control the rollout of Windows updates using enterprise tools. Windows Update is configured in the Settings app in Windows. Open the Settings app and click Update & Security (see Figure 3-2).

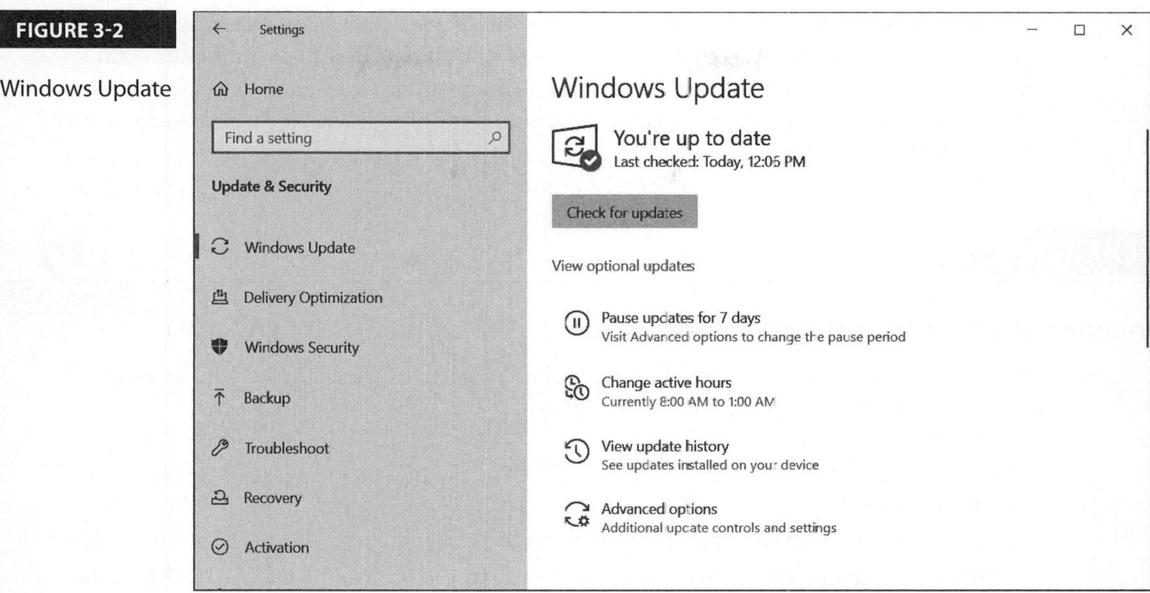

FIGURE 3-2 Windows Update

Here are a few things you can do from the Update & Security page.

- **Check For Updates** This connects to the Windows server online and starts downloading any available updates.
- **Pause Updates** You can click Pause Updates For 7 Days for a quick pause, or click Advanced Options to access the controls for pausing up to 35 days.
- **View Update History** Use this to check out a list of recent updates. From that screen you can click Uninstall Updates and remove any updates that might be causing a problem. (Not all updates can be removed.)
- **Advanced Options** Here you can access various update settings, such as choosing whether to receive updates for other Microsoft products.

Microsoft pushes out urgent updates about once a month—usually on the second Tuesday of the month (known as "Patch Tuesday"). These are important updates that apply security fixes and fix errors. Microsoft also pushes out major updates to Windows with new features and interface changes two times a year. There's one large update (usually in the fall) and one smaller one focused on reliability and performance. These major updates are assigned version numbers based on their release date. For example, the update pushed out in November 21 was called 21H2.

In addition to these major version changes, there are *builds*, which are like version numbers for each individual update instance. The build numbers become important when you are trying to troubleshoot problems that crop up immediately after installing a Windows update; you can look up the build number online to see if there are any known issues with it.

EXERCISE 3-1

Viewing the Windows Version and Edition

In this exercise, you will access the version and edition information for your copy of Windows 10 and check for Windows Updates.

1. Click the Start button and click Settings.
2. Click System.
3. Scroll down in the navigation pane on the left and click About.
4. In the Windows specifications section, read the information there. It shows the edition, version, and OS build. Write down the build number you see.
5. Click Home to return to the Home screen of the Settings app.
6. Click Update & Security.
7. Click Check For Updates.
8. If any prompts appear to download and install updates, click them to allow the install. Usually major updates that will interrupt your computing experience will request your permission, whereas simple updates will not ask.
9. If you installed any updates, check the build number again; it may have changed, depending on the type of update installed.

SCENARIO & SOLUTION

A worker has brought his Windows laptop from home but it won't connect to the network. What should you check first?	Check the edition. It may be a Home edition of Windows, which lacks domain support.
A user you support still has Windows 8.1 on his PC, and he likes it and wants to keep it. Will Microsoft continue to release any needed security updates for it via Windows Update?	January 10, 2023 is the date for the end of extended support for Windows 8.1. After that point, no security updates will be available, and that can put the PC and your network at security risk. Recommend strongly that he upgrades to Windows 10 or 11 before that date.

CERTIFICATION OBJECTIVES

- ***1102: 1.4*** *Given a scenario, use the appropriate Microsoft Windows 10 Control Panel utility*
- ***1102: 1.5*** *Given a scenario, use the appropriate Windows settings*

Configuring Windows Settings

Windows 10 and 11 have two different interfaces for viewing and modifying settings: the Control Panel and the Settings app. The Control Panel is the venerable old utility for this purpose, having been around for several decades in various Windows versions. The Settings app, first introduced in Windows 8.0, is the more modern interface and the wave of the future.

Microsoft has been gradually moving features and functionality from the Control Panel to the Settings app ever since Windows 8.0 was released. It seems like each time a new major update to Windows is released, some more settings are silently moved over. Some settings can be adjusted in either place; others are strictly in one utility or the other. And some commands have links in one of the utilities that takes you over to the other utility when you click it. Sounds confusing, doesn't it? And it is. This confusion will persist until Microsoft finally makes the migration complete and does away with the Control Panel completely—and who knows when that will be. It probably won't happen within the lifetime of Windows 10 or 11. In the meantime, two exam objectives deal with these utilities: 1102 exam Objective 1.4 is for the Control Panel and 1102 exam Objective 1.5 is for the Settings app.

Identifying Control Panel Applets

Applets are the little utility programs that are collected in the Control Panel interface. Each of the major sections of the Control Panel is actually a program of its own (with a .cpl extension). The Control Panel functions as a container that enables you to browse and access these applets in one place.

There are three ways to view the Control Panel's collection of applets. The default is by Category, where you start with eight categories (more or less) and drill down into them to find the applet you want (see Figure 3-3). The alternatives are Large Icons and Small Icons, which both show each applet as its own icon (see Figure 3-4). To switch between views, open the View By drop-down list in the upper-right corner of the Control Panel window. If you don't know which category a certain option is in, Large Icons or Small Icons is a good way of finding what you want alphabetically. You can also click in the Search Control Panel box at the top and type what you are looking for to quickly narrow down the listing.

There are a lot of applets, but not all of them are listed in the exam objectives. Table 3-3 summarizes the ones you need to know.

FIGURE 3-3

Control Panel, Category view

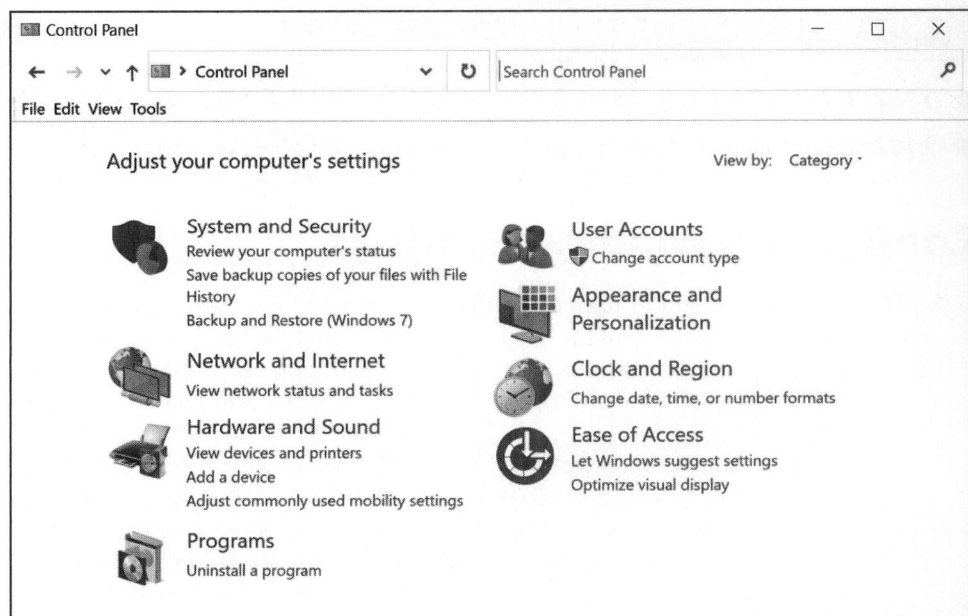

FIGURE 3-4

Control Panel, Small Icons view

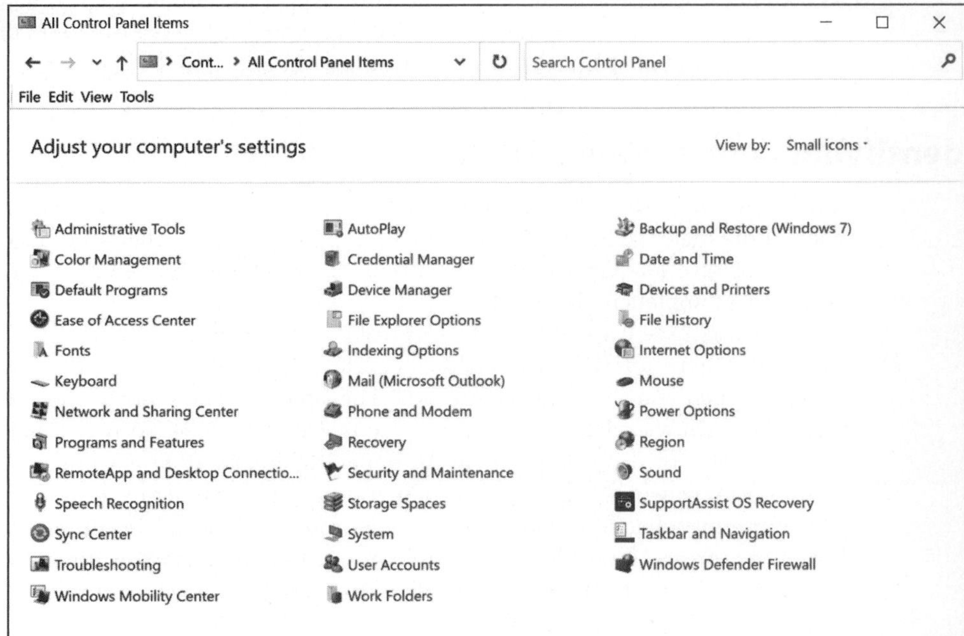

TABLE 3-3 Windows Control Panel Applets (*continued*)

Applet	Purpose	Notes	For More Information
Administrative Tools	Opens a folder containing shortcuts to many specialized applets for performing various system maintenance tasks.	You will learn about many of these in upcoming chapters when learning about system maintenance and troubleshooting. You can also access this applet from the Start menu, by choosing Windows Administrative Tools from the alphabetical list.	See Chapter 6
Device Manager	Opens an interface where you can browse all the installed hardware and view and modify the drivers used for each piece.	This applet is useful when a piece of hardware is malfunctioning and you are trying to determine why. You can also use it to temporarily disable a piece of hardware or to remove it and have Windows redetect it. You can also access this applet by right-clicking the Start button and choosing Device Manager.	See Chapters 9 and 12
Devices And Printers	Enables you to browse all the connected printers and several other kinds of peripherals and multimedia devices.	The most common use is to check a printer's configuration and status.	See Chapter 13
Ease Of Access Center	Set up accessibility features to make Windows easier to use for people with sight, hearing, and/or mobility challenges.	Accessibility settings normally apply only after the user signs in; if you need them to apply at sign-in, click Change Sign-In Settings on the left side of the screen.	Click the Get Recommendations To Make Your Computer Easier To Use hyperlink.
File Explorer Options	Opens the File Explorer Options dialog box, where you can control many settings for File Explorer.	This is the same dialog box as the one you see when you choose View | Options in File Explorer. Important exam-related options under the View tab include Show Hidden Files, Folders, and Drives and Hide Extensions For Known File Types.	See Chapter 5

TABLE 3-3 Windows Control Panel Applets (*continued*)

Applet	Purpose	Notes	For More Information
Indexing Options	Controls which locations will be indexed by File Explorer.	Indexing a location speeds up searches.	Click the How Does Indexing Affect Searches? hyperlink at the bottom of the Indexing Options dialog box.
Internet Options	Adjusts Internet-related settings.	Originally controlled settings for Internet Explorer (IE), which was Windows' default browser until Edge was introduced. Some of these settings affect Edge and/or Internet access in general; some only apply to IE.	See Chapter 18
Mail	Opens the Mail Setup dialog box for Outlook (assuming Outlook is installed on the PC). From here you can set up e-mail accounts, directories, data files, and profiles for using Outlook as an e-mail client.	These same settings can also be accessed from within the Outlook app. If Outlook is having a problem and won't open normally, you can sometimes fix it by using this applet to access its settings.	Browse or search the Help system in the Outlook app.
Network And Sharing Center	Shows your network connection status and provides options for configuring various aspects of network setup.	There are a few options here that aren't in the Settings app version, including Change Adapter Settings and Change Advanced Sharing Settings. The latter is useful for configuring file sharing options for a workgroup.	See Chapter 17

TABLE 3-3 Windows Control Panel Applets (*continued*)

Applet	Purpose	Notes	For More Information
Power Options	Enables you to choose or customize a power plan, which determines when the PC will put itself in low-power mode or turn itself off.	If you are working on a laptop, there are separate settings for the PC when plugged into alternating current (AC) power and when running on battery power. This is the same applet you see if you right-click the Power icon in the notification area and choose Power Options. The power options and settings you need to know for the exam are: ■ Hibernate ■ Power plans ■ Sleep/suspend ■ Standby ■ Choose what closing the lid does ■ Turn on fast startup ■ Universal Serial Bus (USB) ■ Selective suspend	See Chapter 14
Programs And Features	Shows installed applications and enables you to repair, modify, and uninstall them.	There is a direct equivalent to this in the Settings app under Apps; sometimes an installed app will appear in only one place or the other.	See Chapter 5
Sound	Opens the Sound dialog box, from which you can choose playback and recording devices and system sound schemes.	Sound schemes are sets that describe the sounds that should play when various Windows system events occur, such as startup, shutdown, and errors.	See Chapter 14
System	Displays information about your PC and your Windows version.	This section doesn't exist in the Control Panel anymore; it redirects to the About page of the Settings app.	See Chapter 6

TABLE 3-3 Windows Control Panel Applets

Applet	Purpose	Notes	For More Information
User Accounts	Enables you to create and remove user accounts and change account types and settings.	There are also links on this page for some advanced user configuration tasks, like managing credentials (saved passwords), changing environment variables, and setting up profile roaming.	See Chapter 20
Windows Defender Firewall	Configures the firewall software that comes with Windows.	If you have a third-party security suite installed, such as McAfee, you won't be able to adjust Windows Defender Firewall settings.	See Chapter 22

Be sure you are familiar with the Control Panel applets described in Table 3-3. Given a scenario, you may be asked how to access and configure settings using them.

Identifying Windows Settings

The Settings app was designed to eventually replace the Control Panel, offering a more seamless and integrated experience when customizing how Windows operates. As with the Control Panel, the Settings app has dozens of settings categories, and not all of them are tested on the CompTIA A+ exam. You should familiarize yourself with as many settings as possible just for practical purposes, but for your exam preparation, make sure you know the ones in Table 3-4.

TABLE 3-4 Windows Settings App Sections (*continued*)

Setting	Purpose	Notes	For More Information
Accounts	Enables you to set up new accounts, set sign-in options, and manage account permissions.	You must be signed into Windows with an Administrator account to manage user accounts other than your own.	See Chapter 20

TABLE 3-4 Windows Settings App Sections (*continued*)

Setting	Purpose	Notes	For More Information
Apps	Shows a list of installed applications. You can modify or uninstall them.	Click the buttons in the navigation bar on the left to access other things you can change about apps, including setting default apps and controlling which apps load at startup.	See Chapter 5
Devices	Provides controls for adjusting settings for peripherals such as mice, keyboards, printers, and scanners.	Click the buttons in the navigation bar to see settings for a certain type of peripheral, such as Printers & Scanners, Mouse, and Touchpad.	See Chapter 13
Gaming	Controls how Xbox Game Bar opens and recognizes a game.	The Xbox Game Bar can record game clips, enable in-game chatting, and receive game invites.	
Network and Internet	Shows the current network status and enables you to adjust its settings, as well as set up and manage other network connections.	Click the buttons in the navigation bar to see settings for specific network types and features, such as Wi-Fi, Ethernet, Dial-up, and VPN.	See Chapter 17
Personalization	Enables you to change appearance-related settings such as background, colors, fonts, and themes and to customize the Start menu and taskbar.	You can also get here by right-clicking the desktop and choosing Personalize.	
Privacy	Enables/disables features that perform useful functions but may compromise the user's privacy.	The navigation bar buttons are divided into two categories: Windows Permissions and App Permissions. The latter adjusts permissions for specific apps or specific types of activities.	See Chapter 22
System	Provides controls for adjusting how Windows interacts with system hardware.	Click the buttons in the navigation bar on the left to see settings for a certain type of device, such as Display, Sound, or Storage. You can change the display resolution here.	See Chapters 6, 9, and 10

TABLE 3-4 Windows Settings App Sections

Setting	Purpose	Notes	For More Information
Time And Language	Adjusts settings related to the real-time clock in Windows.	Click the buttons in the navigation bar to set Region, Language, and Speech options. Another way to get here is to right-click the clock in the notification area and choose Adjust Date/Time.	
Update & Security	Opens Windows Update, which keeps Windows fully patched and updated.		See "Windows Updates and Builds" earlier in this chapter

EXERCISE 3-2

Locating Windows Settings

Now that you know what the Control Panel and Settings app contain, try this scavenger hunt to see if you can find out where the following settings are located. For each configuration task, determine which utility it is in (and if the answer is both, then indicate that) and where in that utility (or in each utility) it is found.

- Change to a different mouse pointer style.
- Turn off the feature that automatically updates the date and time.
- Change the size of on-screen text and icons without changing the display resolution.
- Forget a saved wireless network's security key.
- Find out how much RAM is installed.
- Change the computer name.
- Change the Windows Hello PIN.
- Change the default audio output device.

CERTIFICATION OBJECTIVE

■ ***1102: 1.10*** *Identify common features and tools of the macOS/desktop OS*

As a CompTIA A+ certified technician, you probably won't spend a lot of time working on Macs, but when you do, you ought to be able to sit down at a Mac workstation and navigate with confidence. This section points out the specific macOS features listed under CompTIA A+ 1102 exam Objective 1.10. It's not a comprehensive list of important-to-know OS features, but it's a good start. We'll continue this topic in Chapter 5, when we look at OS utilities for maintaining a system. At that point we'll look at topics like backups, updates, and antimalware in a macOS context.

An Introduction to macOS

macOS is a GUI, as is Windows, so the principles of navigation are the same. It has a colorful background, icons, toolbars, menus, and windows. The key landmarks of the interface are the Dock, Finder, and Apple menu. Many of the features to be covered are shown in Figure 3-5.

FIGURE 3-5

The macOS desktop

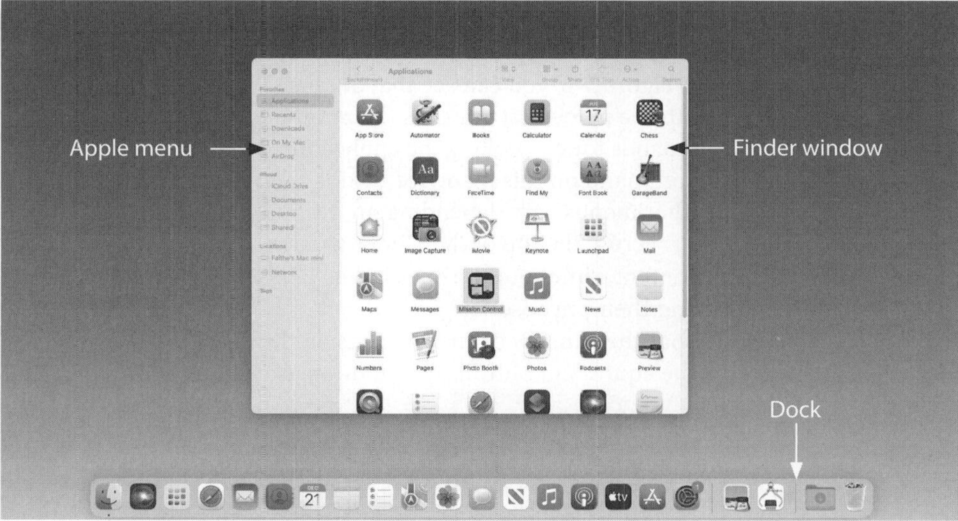

Dock

The *Dock* is the ribbon-like toolbar across the bottom of the screen in Figure 3-5. It's the equivalent of the taskbar in Windows. It's like a bulletin board where you can pin shortcuts to the things you use the most. It comes with some shortcuts already pinned to it, but you can customize it completely, adding and removing items as needed.

on the job

A black dot under an item on the Dock means it is running. In Figure 3-5, there is a black dot under the Finder icon (the leftmost icon).

To add an item to the Dock, drag and drop it onto the Dock in the desired position. To remove an item from the Dock, right-click its icon on the Dock, point to Options, and click Remove From Dock.

Finder

Finder (the open window in Figure 3-5) is the equivalent of File Explorer in Windows. It's your file management interface. If Finder isn't open, you can open it from the Dock by clicking the Finder icon (shown with the black dot under it in Figure 3-5).

Along the left side of the Finder window is a navigation pane containing shortcuts to commonly accessed locations. In Figure 3-5, the Applications shortcut has been selected, so the icons that appear are those of installed applications. You can start an application from here by choosing its icon.

In macOS, a menu system for the active application appears in the upper-left corner of the screen. In Figure 3-6, you can see that because Finder is open, a Finder menu appears. The menu with the name that matches the program name (in this case, the Finder menu) contains commands for controlling the application. Most applications (Finder is an exception) have a Quit command on this menu for exiting the application. There is also always a Help menu. The other menus vary depending on the application.

The buttons across the top of the Finder window help you navigate between locations and display content, similar to the ones in File Explorer in Windows. Figure 3-7 points out the buttons and their purposes.

A word about the window control buttons on the left side of Figure 3-7. They work mostly the same as the equivalent buttons in Windows, except for a few minor quirks:

- The Maximize button (green) maximizes the window such that you can't see the window controls anymore. Press ESC to un-maximize a window.
- The Minimize button (yellow) minimizes the running program or window to an icon on the right end of the Dock.

FIGURE 3-6 Menus appear for the active application.

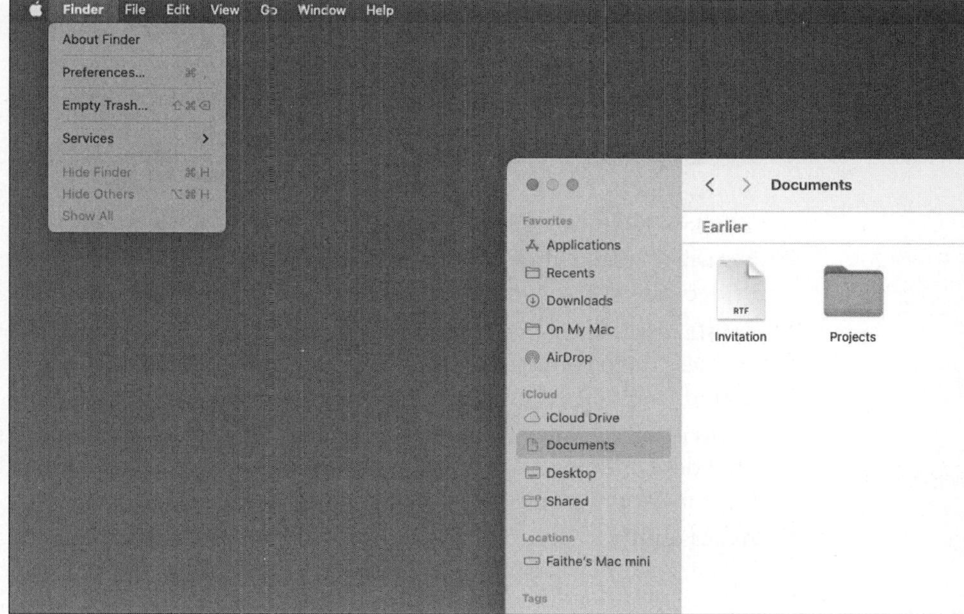

- The Close button (red) does not actually exit a running application; it just hides it. You can tell it's still running because its icon on the Dock appears with a black dot under it. If you want to exit a program, open its menu in the upper-left corner of the screen and choose Quit. (That doesn't work for Finder because Finder is not an ordinary application.)

One important thing to know about Finder is that it doesn't show you *all* the files the way File Explorer does in Windows. It keeps nontechnical users safe by showing only the files it thinks you want to see, like your data files and your applications. Everything else is hidden. (Stuff like this is why most newbies love Macs and most techies hate them.)

FIGURE 3-7 Finder buttons for controlling the display listing

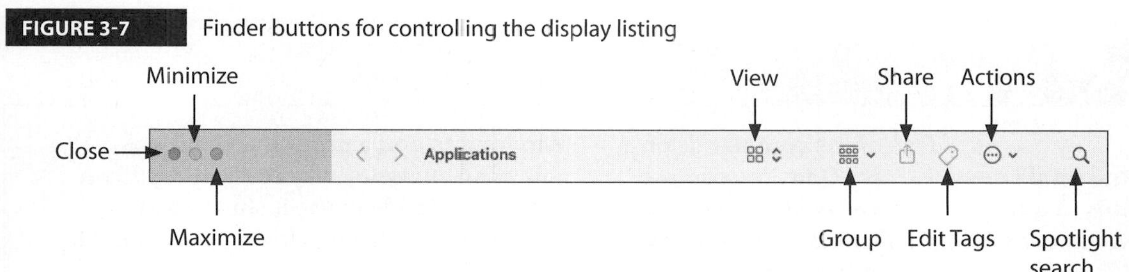

System Preferences

Selecting System Preferences from the Apple menu opens the System Preferences window. From here you can adjust a variety of system settings by clicking their icons, including:

- **Displays** Set the color profile, refresh rate, and rotation, and turn on Night Shift mode, which changes the tone of the color onscreen to one that does not cause as much eyestrain when working in a dark room.
- **Network** Shows the current connections (Wi-Fi, Ethernet, Bluetooth, Thunderbolt Bridge) and enables you to configure them.
- **Printers & Scanners** Displays the currently installed printers and scanners, and enables you to configure them. You can also add new printers and scanners here by clicking the Add (+) button.
- **Security & Privacy** Enables you to change your login password for the Mac, and provides controls for FileVault, Firewall, and a variety of privacy settings. You will learn more about FileVault in Chapter 5.
- **Accessibility** Turns various accessibility features on and off, such as VoiceOver, Zoom, and Spoken Content.
- **Time Machine** Configures the Time Machine feature, which is an automatic file backup system. When enabled, it can make hourly or daily backups of important fields, and can also save snapshots, which are full-disk backups. You will learn more about Time Machine in Chapter 21.

The settings listed above are the ones specifically mentioned in 1102 exam Objective 1.10. Make sure you can access and modify each of these settings.

Apple Menu

Click the apple symbol in the upper-left corner of the screen to open the Apple menu. From here you can shut down, log out, view system preferences, visit the App Store, and more (see Figure 3-8).

exam watch

One of the commands on the Apple menu is Force Quit. You can use this to quit an unresponsive app that results when the spinning pinwheel is displayed. It's similar to using the Task Manager in Windows to end a program. Don't use this as an everyday way of shutting down an application because it shuts down ungracefully, without closing any open files.

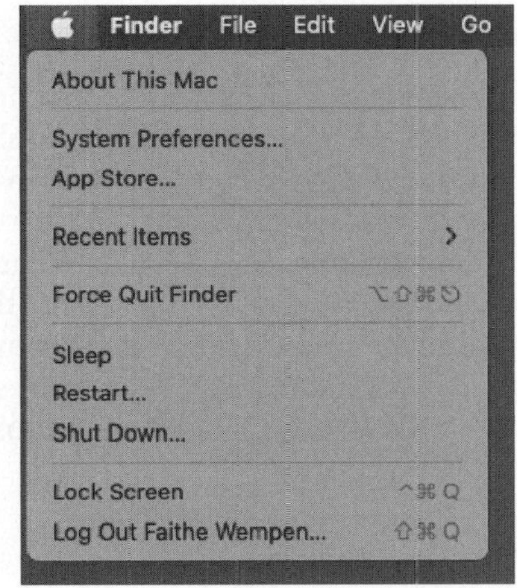

FIGURE 3-8 The Apple menu

macOS Versions

The macOS operating system names its versions differently than Windows does. It gives them both numbers and names, and most people refer to just the names. The current version at this writing is Monterey, also known as version 12. You can find the version of a system by clicking the Apple menu and clicking About This Mac.

As minor updates become available, they are assigned decimal places in the version number; for example, you might see a version number of 12.1.

Some other versions you may still find in use are Big Sur (11), Catalina (10.15), Mojave (10.14), High Sierra (10.13), and Sierra (10.12). That takes us back to 2016; if you need to go further back than that to reference a specific version, do a quick web search for *macOS version history*. The version number is sometimes an issue when you are troubleshooting why certain features don't work. For example, the optical drive sharing described later in the chapter requires Mojave (10.14) or earlier; it won't work on newer versions.

Running Applications

Clicking the Launchpad icon on the Dock opens Launchpad, a screen of icons for the installed programs. (You can point at each icon on the Dock to see its name.) Click an icon to run that program. Yes, many of these are the same as the ones on the Dock, but this is a more complete collection.

Another way to run an application is to open Finder and then click the Applications shortcut in the navigation bar. The resulting set of application icons is sorted somewhat differently than the ones in Launchpad, but you should be able to find them all here. If you don't see the application you want, begin typing its name in the Search box.

Using Multiple Desktops

macOS enables you to have multiple desktops running at once, each with different open applications. That way you can start with a clean slate without having to close running applications and windows. Microsoft Windows has a similar feature via Task View.

To access this feature, called Mission Control, run the Mission Control application from Launchpad or the Applications list in Finder. A bar appears across the top of the screen; this is your management interface. At the top are the current desktops; there may be just one (Desktop 1). Click the plus sign on the right end of this bar to create a new copy of the desktop, as shown in Figure 3-9. You can then switch back and forth between them by pressing CTRL-LEFT ARROW or CTRL-RIGHT ARROW.

Storing Passwords

The Keychain feature safely stores your Safari website user names and passwords, so you don't have to remember them or continually type them. It can also keep the accounts you use in Mail, Contacts, Calendar, and Messages up to date across all your Mac devices. When you set up a Mac initially, you are asked if you want to enable the Keychain feature. If you choose not to, you can do so later.

FIGURE 3-9 Mission Control enables you to have multiple desktops.

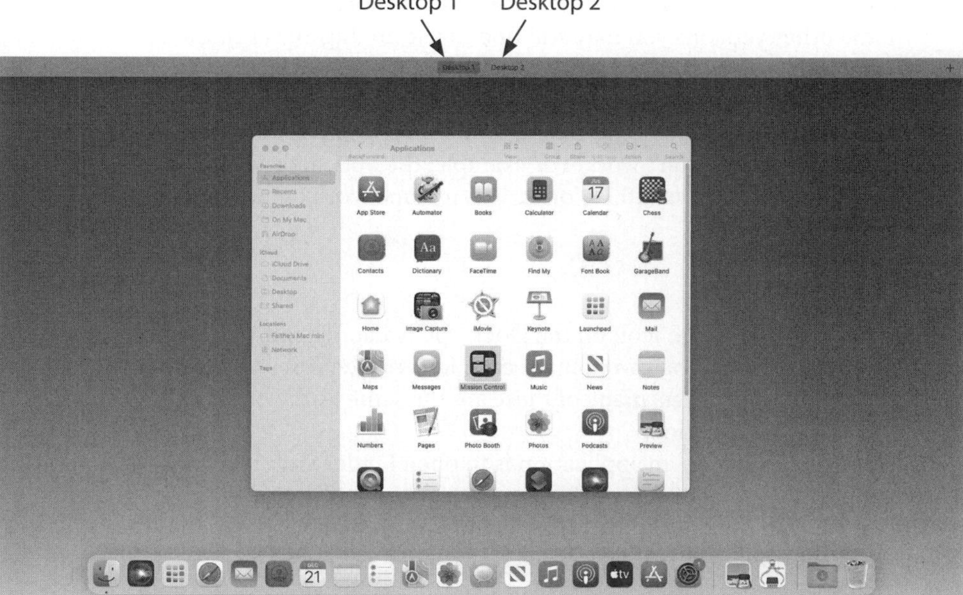

To enable Keychain, on the Apple menu, choose System Preferences | Apple ID | iCloud. If there is not a check mark next to Keychain, click to place one. Then work through the prompts.

Spotlight Searching

Click the magnifying glass icon in the upper-right corner of the Finder window to open Spotlight search. It searches the local system for files and applications, but it can also search the Internet for you.

Using Gestures

Gestures are navigation shortcuts that you can perform using a touchpad or touch screen, such as pinch, drag, zoom, and scroll. Here's a good way to learn about them: Open a web browser and navigate to https://support.apple.com/en-us/HT204895. You should know the basic gestures for the exam.

Accessing iCloud

iCloud is an online storage area free to Mac users, equivalent to OneDrive in Windows. To access iCloud, open Finder and, in the navigation pane, click iCloud Drive. You can drag and drop files to and from your iCloud drive (for example, from the desktop).

Dual-Booting with Windows

Boot Camp is a utility that helps you install Microsoft Windows on a Mac and then switch between the two operating systems. To use Boot Camp, make sure you have a Windows disk image (an ISO file). Then using Finder, click Applications | Utilities | Boot Camp Assistant. Work through the on-screen instructions to repartition the startup disk, download the needed drivers, and install Windows.

Using Another Computer's Optical Drive

Remote Disc provides a way for a Mac that doesn't have an optical drive, such as a Mac Mini, to borrow another Mac's optical drive via a network. This only works on systems with macOS 10.14 or earlier, though; it doesn't work on Catalina 10.15 or later.

Since the feature has been deprecated, you probably won't see a question about it on the 220-1102 exam, even though it persists in Objective 1.10 on the 220-1102.

To allow sharing, from the Mac that *does* have the optical drive, do the following: From the Apple menu click System Preferences | Sharing. Click DVD Or CD Sharing to place a check mark next to that feature. (If you don't have an optical drive, you won't see that option.)

Then to use the remote disc on the computer that does *not* have the optical drive, do the following: In Finder, if a computer on your local area network (LAN) is sharing an optical drive with you, that computer will appear as an icon in the navigation bar under Devices Or Locations. Double-click the icon to access the drive. To make the connection, you might need to click Ask To Use and then click Accept on the Mac that has the optical drive.

You can also share an optical disc from a Windows PC with your Mac, but you must download a utility to help with that. Go to https://support.apple.com/kb/DL112?locale=en_US to download the needed file on the Windows PC, and run the Setup program. Then open the Control Panel, open Hardware And Sound (in Category View), and click DVD Or CD Sharing Options. Click the check box to enable the feature.

An Introduction to Linux

The core part of Linux, its *kernel,* is open source. Companies and individuals add onto the kernel with extra utilities and shells (user interfaces) and then either give away or sell their customized versions, which are known as *distributions* or *distros*. There are distros customized for many different purposes, making Linux a very flexible OS. You can get desktop distros like Ubuntu, server distros like Red Hat, distros designed specifically for hacking and penetration testing like Kali, and so on. In Chapter 4 you'll learn how to download and install Ubuntu Linux, an easy-to-use, general-purpose client distro.

At its core, Linux is a command-line operating system, like Unix, and like the obsolete operating systems of old such as MS-DOS and CPM. If you use Linux as an everyday OS on a client PC, though, you will most likely use it in GUI mode, which resembles the Windows and Mac desktop interfaces. Many distros boot into the GUI by default, so casual users may not ever even realize there is a command-line world behind the GUI. To access the command prompt, you open a *terminal window,* which is a command-line environment (shell) within a window.

The exact appearance and behavior of the Linux GUI depend on which distro you are using; different distros come with different GUI shells. A *shell* is a user interface environment. The term *shell* is most often used when referring to the command-line interface but also applies to the graphical interface. Figure 3-10 shows the Ubuntu Linux desktop, which you will learn to install and configure in Chapter 4. I've opened a command-prompt window within the GUI so you can see what that looks like too.

The CompTIA A+ exams do not test your knowledge of specific aspects of the Linux GUI interface. How could it, since there are different interfaces, all of which are "Linux"? Instead, it tests you on your ability to use the command line to perform certain specific activities. In Chapter 5 you will learn some general Linux command-line activities for file management, and in Chapter 6 you'll discover how to troubleshoot using the Linux command line.

FIGURE 3-10 The Ubuntu Linux GUI desktop

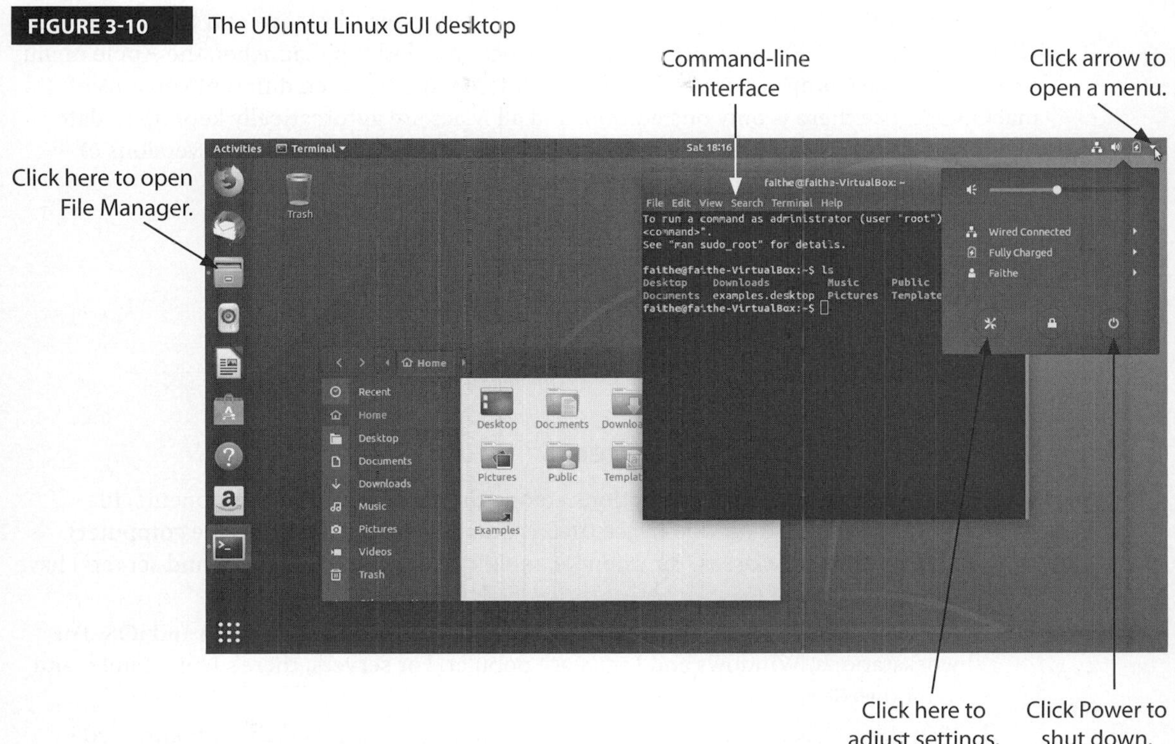
Command-line interface
Click arrow to open a menu.
Click here to open File Manager.
Click here to adjust settings.
Click Power to shut down.

CERTIFICATION SUMMARY

Before you can install and support computers, you must develop an understanding of the concepts beyond those required to simply use an OS. This begins with understanding the purpose of operating systems; knowing the differences among the major operating systems; and understanding versions, editions, and builds.

The CompTIA A+ 1102 exam objectives cover only Windows, macOS, and Linux operating systems in detail, but you should understand that there are different kinds of operating systems for desktops/laptops, mobile devices, and servers, and you should be able to identify the major OSs in each area.

You should also be proficient at using the Control Panel and the Settings app in Windows 10 and 11 to configure system settings. The Settings app is organized a bit differently between Windows 10 and 11; you should be able to navigate both versions with confidence. Make sure you can access and describe the purpose of all the settings listed in Objectives 1.4 and 1.5 on the 220-1102 exam.

macOS is the operating system for Apple Mac computers (desktops and laptops). It is a GUI, like Windows. The key features are the Dock, the desktop, Launcher, the Apple menu, and Finder. The CompTIA A+ exams do not differentiate between different versions of macOS because there is only one edition, and all Macs are automatically kept up to date with the latest version. However, keep in mind that Macs do have different versions of macOS, and sometimes features are added or removed.

TWO-MINUTE DRILL

Here are some of the key points covered in Chapter 3.

Introduction to Operating Systems

- ❑ An OS controls all the interactions among the various system components, file management, and user interface (that is, human interactions with the computer). Different device classes (for example, mobile devices, workstations, and servers) have different types of OSs.
- ❑ For mobile devices, the most popular operating systems are Android and iOS. For workstations, Windows and Linux are popular. For servers, there's Unix, Linux, and Windows Server.
- ❑ Windows 11 is the current version of Windows. It is not specifically mentioned in the current CompTIA A+ 220-1102 exam objectives, but a note in the objectives' preface states that wherever an objective doesn't mention a version number, assume that it applies to both Windows 10 and Windows 11.
- ❑ Windows 10 comes in different editions, such as Home, Pro, and Enterprise.
- ❑ Operating systems tie closely to the CPUs on which they run. Therefore, CPU terms such as 32-bit and 64-bit may also describe an OS. Most workstation operating systems are available in both 32-bit and 64-bit versions. The primary advantage of a 64-bit OS is the ability to use more RAM.
- ❑ An OS reaches the end of its life when its developer no longer provides updates for it; at that point, it becomes vulnerable to security threats. The Microsoft Support Lifecycle specifies the services available for different Microsoft products, such as Windows, during mainstream support and extended support periods. Microsoft ends extended support for a Windows version ten years after the last update to it.

Windows Editions and Updates

- ❑ A Windows version is a generation of the OS, such as Windows 10. An edition is a specific set of features for a particular version, such as Windows 10 Home or Windows 10 Pro. The Pro for Workstations version supports advanced hardware capabilities.

- ❑ Home editions are basic and inexpensive and are suitable for home and small business use. Professional editions include more security features and the ability to connect to a domain-based network. Enterprise editions are sold only via volume licenses to businesses and include extra utilities helpful for integrating with large networks.
- ❑ Some of the features available only with Pro or Enterprise include BitLocker, Remote Desktop Protocol (RDP) and Group Policy Editor (gpedit.msc).
- ❑ An upgrade path is a path from one version or edition of Windows to another. An in-place upgrade is one where you don't have to reinstall applications and data files.
- ❑ Generally speaking, you can upgrade in place from a lesser edition to a more feature-rich one, provided they are both the same number of bits (32 or 64). Microsoft defines allowed in-place upgrade paths; all other upgrades must be clean installs.
- ❑ Windows updates are software fixes to the operating system code to fix problems or enhance security. A patch is a fix for a single problem. Major updates are assigned version numbers based on their release date, such as 21H2. There are also builds, which are like version numbers, for each individual update instance.

Configuring Windows Settings

- ❑ Windows has two different interfaces for settings: the Control Panel and the Settings app. Microsoft is gradually migrating settings to the Settings app, but in the meantime you need to be able to use both.
- ❑ The Control Panel provides access to applets that enable you to adjust various settings. The important sections to know are Administrative Tools, Device Manager, Devices And Printers, Ease Of Access Center, File Explorer Options, Indexing Options, Internet Options, Mail, Network And Sharing Center, Power Options, Programs And Features, Sound, System, User Accounts, and Windows Defender Firewall.
- ❑ The Settings app is the newer interface for adjusting settings. Study the top-level categories in the Settings app: Accounts, Apps, Devices, Gaming, Network And Internet, Personalization, Privacy, System, Time And Language, and Update & Security.

An Introduction to macOS

- ❑ The current CompTIA A+ 1102 exam objectives expect you to know how to navigate a macOS system.
- ❑ The important features to understand involving everyday operation of macOS include the Dock, Finder, Mission Control, Apple menu, Keychain, Spotlight, iCloud, Gestures, Remote Disc, and Boot Camp.
- ❑ Chapter 5 will cover important macOS utilities you should know about.

An Introduction to Linux

- ❑ Linux's kernel is open source and free; some Linux distros are free, and some are for purchase. There are distros available for servers, for consumers, for power users, and for many other specialized purposes. Different distros contain different utilities and add-ons.
- ❑ Linux is a command-line OS, but you can optionally install GUI user interfaces to run on top of the command line. In most distros the GUI is installed and enabled by default. From the GUI, you can open a command-prompt window, also called a terminal window.
- ❑ This book uses Ubuntu Linux as its example distro since it is free and easy to use. You will learn how to install it in Chapter 4, and in Chapter 5 you will learn how to manage files with it. In Chapter 6 you will learn how to use Linux for troubleshooting.

SELF TEST

The following questions will help you measure your understanding of the material presented in this chapter. Read all the choices carefully because there might be more than one correct answer. Choose all correct answers for each question.

Introduction to Operating Systems

1. Which of these is *not* a responsibility of the operating system?

A. Managing files
B. Interacting with hardware
C. Providing a user interface
D. Performing the power-on self-test

2. Which of these is an OS for a mobile device?

A. macOS
B. Android
C. Windows 10
D. Unix

3. Which of these types of devices has a built-in OS that you can't change (only update)?
  A. Server
  B. Workstation
  C. Tablet
  D. Laptop

4. Which operating system(s) can run on a system with a 64-bit CPU?
  A. 32-bit only
  B. 64-bit only
  C. 32-bit or 64-bit
  D. 64-bit or 128-bit

5. What is the benefit of using a 64-bit version of Windows?
  A. Faster
  B. Supports more applications
  C. Supports more memory
  D. Supports larger hard drives

6. What Microsoft policy defines the length of time Microsoft will support a product, as well as the support options for that product?
  A. Software Assurance
  B. Support Lifecycle
  C. Upgrade Advisor
  D. Compatibility Wizard

Windows Editions and Updates

7. Windows 10 is a version; what is Windows 10 Enterprise?
  A. An OEM release
  B. An edition
  C. A patch
  D. An update

8. What feature is not available in the Home editions of Windows 10?
  A. BitLocker
  B. Control Panel
  C. Cortana
  D. Task View

9. What feature is available only in the Enterprise and Education editions of Windows?
   A. BitLocker
   B. BranchCache
   C. Ability to connect to a domain-based network
   D. Remote Desktop

10. Suppose you have a Windows 10 PC that can connect to a small workgroup network but not to a network domain. What should you do?
   A. Replace the network adapter
   B. Switch from a 32-bit to a 64-bit version of Windows
   C. Upgrade it to Windows 10 Professional or Enterprise
   D. Install Windows updates

Configuring Windows Settings

11. In which Control Panel applet will you find a collection of specialized applets for performing system maintenance tasks?
   A. Administrative Tools
   B. Device Manager
   C. Ease Of Access Center
   D. System

12. In which Control Panel applet can you find out the Windows version, edition, and build number?
   A. Programs And Features
   B. Windows Defender Firewall
   C. Device Manager
   D. System

13. In which section of the Settings app can you change the desktop background?
   A. Devices
   B. Update & Security
   C. Personalization
   D. System

14. In which section of the Settings app can you adjust the display resolution?
   A. Personalization
   B. Devices
   C. System
   D. Update & Security

15. From which app can you access the Network And Sharing Center?
    A. Control Panel
    B. Settings app
    C. Device Manager
    D. System
16. Where in the Control Panel can you go to manage credentials, change environment variables, and set up profile roaming?
    A. System
    B. Settings
    C. User Accounts
    D. Profile Manager

An Introduction to macOS

17. What is the name of the bar along the bottom of the screen in macOS?
    A. Finder
    B. Dock
    C. Launchpad
    D. Keychain
18. Which feature provides file system browsing on a Mac?
    A. Launchpad
    B. Notepad
    C. Finder
    D. Keychain
19. How do you shut down a Mac?
    A. Start | Shut Down
    B. Apple menu | Force Quit
    C. Finder menu
    D. Apple menu | Shut Down

An Introduction to Linux

20. The Linux _____ is open-source, but some ____ are commercial.
    A. distro, kernels
    B. kernel, distros
    C. shell, kernels
    D. GUI, VMs

SELF TEST ANSWERS

Introduction to Operating Systems

1. ☑ **D.** The power-on self-test (POST) occurs before the operating system loads.
☒ **A, B,** and **C** are incorrect because managing files, interacting with hardware, and providing a user interface are all OS responsibilities.

2. ☑ **B.** Android is a mobile device OS found on many smartphones and tablets.
☒ **A** is incorrect because macOS is a workstation OS for Mac computers. **C** is incorrect because Windows 10 is a workstation OS. **D** is incorrect because Unix is a server OS.

3. ☑ **C.** A tablet has a built-in OS; you can't change it.
☒ **A, B,** and **D** are incorrect because all these computer types can have their OS replaced with an entirely different OS.

4. ☑ **C.** A 64-bit CPU can run either a 64-bit or a 32-bit OS.
☒ **A** and **B** are incorrect because each can run, but is not the only one. **D** is incorrect because a CPU cannot run an OS with more bits than it has, so a 64-bit CPU could not run a 128-bit OS.

5. ☑ **C.** 64-bit versions can support more memory. A 32-bit version is limited to 4 GB of RAM.
☒ **A** is incorrect because the 64-bit version is not necessarily faster. **B** is incorrect because there are not more applications for 64-bit; if anything, there are more 32-bit applications. **D** is incorrect because 32-bit vs. 64-bit has no effect on the hard drive size limitations.

6. ☑ **B.** Support Lifecycle is the Microsoft policy that defines the length of time Microsoft will support a product.
☒ **A** is incorrect because this is Microsoft's software purchasing, volume licensing, and support plan for large organizations. **C** is incorrect because this is a utility for determining if an existing installation of Windows can be successfully upgraded to a newer version. **D** is incorrect because this is a Microsoft wizard for applying compatibility settings for the application program.

Windows Editions and Updates

7. ☑ **B.** Windows 10 Enterprise is an edition of the Windows 10 version.
☒ **A** is incorrect because an OEM release is a copy of Windows provided with a new PC. **C** and **D** are incorrect because patches and updates are downloaded corrections that fix or improve Windows.

8. ☑ **A.** BitLocker is one of the features that Home edition users do not have available.
☒ **B, C,** and **D** are incorrect because Control Panel, Cortana, and Task View are general features in Windows 10 (all editions).

9. ☑ **B.** BranchCache, a feature that caches data offline between branch offices for better performance, is available only in Enterprise and Education editions.
☒ **A, C,** and **D** are incorrect because BitLocker, the ability to connect to a domain, and Remote Desktop are all available in Pro, Enterprise, and Education editions.

10. ☑ **C.** Windows 10 Home cannot connect to a domain; Windows 10 Professional can.
☒ **A** is incorrect because if the network adapter were faulty, you could not connect to a workgroup either. **B** is incorrect because 32-bit vs. 64-bit does not matter in terms of connecting to a domain. **D** is incorrect because Windows updates should not make a difference in connecting to a domain or not.

Configuring Windows Settings

11. ☑ **A.** Administrative Tools opens a folder containing icons for many specialized system maintenance applets.
☒ **B** is incorrect because Device Manager opens a list of devices, not a list of applets. **C** is incorrect because the Ease Of Access Center sets up accessibility features. **D** is incorrect because System displays system information.

12. ☑ **D.** The version, edition, and build number can be looked up in the System applet.
☒ **A** is incorrect because Programs And Features does not provide information about Windows itself. **B** is incorrect because the Windows Defender Firewall provides information about firewall settings. **C** is incorrect because Device Manager provides information about devices.

13. ☑ **C.** Changing the desktop background is a type of personalization.
☒ **A** is incorrect because changing the desktop background is not a device. **B** is incorrect because changing the background is not an update or security setting. **D** is incorrect because the desktop background is not a system setting.

14. ☑ **B.** The display resolution is a device setting of the monitor.
☒ **A** is incorrect because even though display resolution might seem like a personalization issue, it is actually a device setting because it affects the way the device works. **C** is incorrect because the System section displays system information but does not make changes to it. **D** is incorrect because the display resolution does not affect Windows Update or security settings.

15. ☑ **A.** The Network And Sharing Center is available via the Control Panel.
☒ **B** is incorrect because although the Settings app provides some similar information, its equivalent section is not called Network And Sharing Center. **C** is incorrect because Device Manager does not display network information. **D** is incorrect because the System section does not contain network information.

16. ☑ **C.** The User Accounts section in the Control Panel has all these capabilities via links in the navigation bar.
☒ **A** is incorrect because the System section is for system information, not user account configuration. **B** is incorrect because Settings is not a section of the Control Panel; it is a separate utility. **D** is incorrect because there is no such section as Profile Manager in the Control Panel.

An Introduction to macOS

17. ☑ **B.** The bar along the bottom is the Dock; it is equivalent to the Windows taskbar.
☒ **A** is incorrect because Finder is the file management tool. **C** is incorrect because Launchpad opens a window of applications you can run; it is not a bar. **D** is incorrect because Keychain is a password management tool.

18. ☑ **C.** Finder is the file management utility in macOS.
☒ **A** is incorrect because Launchpad is an interface for running applications. **B** is incorrect because Notepad is a text editor in Windows. **D** is incorrect because Keychain is the password management feature in macOS.

19. ☑ **D.** To shut down a Mac, open the Apple menu and click Shut Down.
☒ **A** is incorrect because it is the Windows method of shutting down. **B** is incorrect because it is a means of shutting down an unresponsive application. **C** is incorrect because it does not contain a Shut Down command.

An Introduction to Linux

20. ☑ **B.** The Linux kernel is open-source, but some distros are commercial.
☒ **A** and **C** are incorrect because the Linux kernel is never commercial. **D** is incorrect because VM is a virtual machine and not a part of Linux (although Linux can be installed on a VM).

Chapter 4

Upgrading, Installing, and Configuring Operating Systems

CERTIFICATION OBJECTIVES

- **1102: 1.1** Identify basic features of Microsoft Windows editions
- **1102: 1.4** Given a scenario, use the appropriate Microsoft Windows 10 Control Panel utility
- **1102: 1.5** Given a scenario, use the appropriate Windows settings
- **1102: 1.9** Given a scenario, perform OS installations and upgrades in a diverse OS environment

✓ Two-Minute Drill

Q&A Self Test

In this chapter, you will learn how to install and configure Microsoft Windows. Whether you are upgrading from an older version of Windows or installing from scratch (a clean install), you must follow certain guidelines and procedures, including basic preparation and installation steps and post-installation tasks. Post-installation configuration involves many components, including network connections, registration and activation, updating applications and Windows components, installing devices, and configuring power management. We'll also look briefly at how to install and configure the macOS and Linux operating systems.

CERTIFICATION OBJECTIVES

- ***1102: 1.1*** *Identify basic features of Microsoft Windows editions*
- ***1102: 1.9*** *Given a scenario, perform OS installations and upgrades in a diverse OS environment*

CompTIA A+ 1102 exam Objective 1.9 asks you to determine the best way to install or upgrade Microsoft Windows on a PC, given a particular scenario. The following sections look at boot methods and types of installations, as well as file system choices and post-installation configuration processes like adjusting region and language settings and installing additional drivers and updates. First we'll look at upgrading, because that's a more common activity; then we'll turn our attention to clean installations. As part of the upgrade discussion, we'll consider valid upgrade paths as noted in Objective 1.1.

Considerations for Installing or Upgrading Windows

Unless you buy or build a custom computer, when you purchase a PC from a major manufacturer, it will come with the latest version of Windows installed. But what if you want to install the latest version on an existing PC? First, you need to see if your computer meets the recommended system requirements. Then you must determine if the new version is compatible with your existing hardware and applications. Finally, you need to know the upgrade paths to the new version to determine whether you will be able to upgrade (keeping your files and applications) or whether you will have to do a clean install.

System Requirements

Each version of an OS has specific minimum requirements for the type and speed of CPU, amount of memory, and amount of free hard disk space. To determine if it will run on your existing computer, check the *system requirements* listed on the package and published on the OS developer's website. The system requirements describe the minimum CPU, RAM, free hard disk space, and video adapter required. The system requirements for Windows 10 are listed in Table 4-1 and the requirements for Windows 11 in Table 4-2. These requirements are modest, and all new PCs sold today easily exceed them. Windows 11 has greater requirements, including requiring a Trusted Platform Module (TPM) 2.0 chip on the motherboard and Unified Extensible Firmware Interface (UEFI) firmware on the motherboard.

Even if a system meets all the CPU, memory, disk, and Internet requirements, it can't run Windows 11 without the TPM 2.0 chip and UEFI firmware. The setup program will check for all the requirements and not allow you to continue if they are not met.

TABLE 4-1 Windows 10 System Requirements (32-bit and 64-bit)

	Minimum Requirements
CPU	1 GHz (32-bit or 64-bit)
RAM	1 GB (32-bit) or 2 GB (64-bit)
Free Hard Disk Space	32 GB
Video Adapter	DirectX 9 adapter with WDDM 1.0 or higher device driver, at least 800 × 600 resolution
Internet	Internet connectivity and Microsoft account recommended

TABLE 4-2 Windows 11 System Requirements (64-bit only)

	Minimum Requirements
CPU	1 GHz with two or more cores
RAM	4 GB
Free Hard Disk Space	64 GB
Video Adapter	DirectX 12 adapter with WDDM 2.0 or higher device driver
Internet	Internet connectivity and Microsoft account required
Other	TPM 2.0 chip, UEFI firmware

Given information about a computer's CPU, RAM, and free hard disk space, make sure you can identify which versions of Windows would run well on that computer.

Another system requirement is the computer platform on which a given OS will run. Windows runs on the Microsoft/Intel platform, with a range of CPUs, BIOS/UEFI, and chipsets compatible with Microsoft OSs. Some call this the *Wintel* architecture. As you learned in Chapter 3, a 32-bit CPU can run only 32-bit operating systems, but a 64-bit CPU can run either 32-bit or 64-bit. Windows and Linux both are available in 32-bit and 64-bit versions.

You can install Windows on a system with only the minimum requirements, but applications won't run as well on it as on a system that meets the recommended configuration specifications. For a system that delivers top performance, double the requirements shown in Tables 4-1 and 4-2 for CPU and RAM.

Application and Hardware Compatibility

After Microsoft releases a new Windows version, there is a transition time during which many individuals and organizations choose to stay with the old version; some move to the new version right away, and others make the change gradually. Not everyone immediately embraces the new OS and replaces their old OS with the new one. There are many reasons for this.

System Requirements

Old hardware may be below the system requirements. Therefore, if the old operating system is functioning adequately, individual users, as well as businesses, will not simply reflexively upgrade to the new OS until they have a compelling reason to do so.

Hardware Compatibility

The firmware in an older PC may not support critical features of the new OS, and if the manufacturer does not offer a firmware upgrade, the computer will not support the new OS. An example of this is the TPM 2.0 requirement for installing Windows 11.

Hardware compatibility problems extend to peripherals when manufacturers do not create new device drivers for a new OS.

Software Compatibility

Some applications are written to take advantage of certain features (or weaknesses) in older versions of Windows. Large organizations have often delayed upgrading to a new OS until they could either find a way to make the critical old applications run in the new OS or find satisfactory replacements that would work in the new OS.

Clean Install vs. Upgrade

A clean install, as the name implies, wipes out the system drive's entire contents and starts fresh. The PC loses all data files, settings, and installed applications. You'll do a clean install on a new PC or when changing operating systems where there is no upgrade path from the old OS to the new OS. (See the next section for details about upgrade paths.)

on the job

Prior to Windows 8, sometimes a clean install was necessary to solve the thorniest OS problems. However, Windows 8 and all later versions include a Reset this PC feature as an alternative to doing a clean install for repair purposes. Reset has an advantage over a clean install, in that you can keep your files. (You'll still have to reinstall applications, though.) See "Recovery Options" in Chapter 6.

An upgrade of an operating system, also called an *in-place upgrade,* is an installation of a newer operating system directly over an existing installation. An upgrade has the benefit of saving you the trouble of reinstalling all your programs and creating all your preference settings. Windows Update may suggest an available version upgrade, and installing it may be as simple as clicking a button. Upgrades may not correct all previous system problems, however, and there is not always an upgrade path from the old to the new operating system.

During an in-place upgrade, Windows reads all the previous settings from the old registry (a database of all configuration settings in Windows), adapts them for the new registry, and transfers all hardware and software configuration information, thus saving you the trouble of reinstalling applications and reconfiguring your desktop the way you like it.

Upgrade Paths

The term *upgrade* can mean one of two things when referring to Windows: it can either mean moving from an older version to a newer one (for example, from Windows 8.1 to Windows 10 or 11), or it can mean moving from a lesser edition to a more feature-rich one (for example, from Windows 10 Home to Windows 10 Professional).

In order to do an upgrade installation, there must be a valid *upgrade path* from the old version to the new one. One global limitation is that you can't cross platforms (32-bit vs. 64-bit). Changing between those requires a clean install. Another limitation is that you can't upgrade if it would cause you to go backward edition-wise. For example, you can't upgrade Windows 8.1 Pro to Windows 10 Home, because you would be losing some features that might be in use (like BitLocker or connection to a network domain).

exam watch

Given any two Windows editions, you should be able to say whether or not an in-place upgrade path exists. It's not as hard as it sounds if you just remember these rules: you can't cross platforms (32-bit and 64-bit), you can't go backwards in version numbers (for example, Windows 11 to Windows 10), and you can't do edition downgrades (for example, Pro to Home).

exam watch

Windows 8.1 didn't have a Home edition per se, but the basic Windows 8.1 edition (sometimes referred to as the "Core" edition) was the equivalent of a Home edition. If you get a question about upgrading from Windows 8.1 to some version of Windows 10, assume that it's referring to a Home version of Windows 8.1.

An *in-place upgrade* is an upgrade where you don't have to reinstall your apps and re-copy your data back to the machine. You can do an in-place upgrade between Windows 10 editions, or between Windows 11 editions, when you go from a "lesser" edition to a more feature-rich one, but you can't go backwards. You also can't go backwards in versions (for example, from Windows 11 to Windows 10).

on the job

You can't do an in-place upgrade from Windows 7, 8, or 8.1 to Windows 11. If you really want an in-place upgrade, go from the earlier Windows version to Windows 10, and then from 10 to 11.

Tables 4-3 and 4-4 summarize the possible paths. For the combinations marked D, it's considered a downgrade. Personal data is maintained, but applications and settings are removed. For the ones marked No, you must do a clean install (wipe the drive and start over).

TABLE 4-3 In-Place Upgrade Paths Between Windows 8.1 and Windows 10

From	To Windows 10 Home	To Windows 10 Pro	To Windows 10 Pro Education	To Windows 10 Education	To Windows 10 Enterprise
Windows 8.1 Core or Connected	Yes	Yes	Yes	Yes	No
Windows 8.1 Pro, Pro Student, or Pro WMC	D	Yes	Yes	Yes	No
Enterprise	No	No	No	Yes	Yes

TABLE 4-4 Windows 10 and 11 In-Place Upgrade Paths Between Editions of the Same Version

	To Home	To Pro	To Pro Education	To Education	To Enterprise
From Home		Yes	Yes	Yes	No
From Pro	D		Yes	Yes	Yes
From Education	No	No	No	Yes	D
From Enterprise	No	No	No	Yes	Yes

There are different ways of doing in-place upgrades, including mobile device management (MDM), a provisioning package, a command-line tool, entering a product key, or purchasing a license. Not all those methods are available for every path. Here's an article that details each path and its available methods: https://docs.microsoft.com/en-us/windows/deployment/upgrade/windows-10-edition-upgrades. That's not on the exam.

SCENARIO & SOLUTION

A client wants to do an in-place upgrade from a 32-bit version of Windows to a 64-bit version. Is that possible?	No, changing between 32-bit and 64-bit versions requires a clean install.
A client has a Windows 8.1 PC and wants to know if he can upgrade to Windows 10 without adding any hardware. Can he?	Probably. Their system requirements are the same.
A client wants to upgrade from Windows 8.1 Enterprise to Windows 10 Home. Is that possible?	No, because you cannot downgrade in editions; Home is a downgrade from Enterprise.

Upgrading Windows

In this section, you learn what tasks to perform before an upgrade and how to perform the upgrade. The next section will detail how to do a clean install.

Pre-Upgrade Tasks

Before attempting an OS upgrade, check the requirements of the new version and verify compatibility with the existing system's hardware and software. Windows Update may do this work for you automatically and let you know that an upgrade is available if your system meets all requirements.

Then do whatever you can to clean up the existing system and safeguard its data, including backing up files, deleting unwanted files, and defragmenting the hard drive. The following sections explain these tasks in more detail.

Checking Requirements and Compatibility

When you run the Setup program for the new Windows version, the first step in the process will be to check the system for basic hardware requirements and for hardware and software compatibility issues. If any problems are found, you will need to abort the setup and find a way to correct the problem before continuing. For example, you might need an updated driver for some hardware, or you might need a new version of an old application (or you might need to abandon the old application entirely because it won't run on the new Windows version).

If an upgrade is available for an incompatible application program, obtain it and check with the manufacturer. Upgrade the application before upgrading the OS, unless advised otherwise by the manufacturer.

Remove any programs that will not run in the new OS from the computer before upgrading. There are also programs that interfere with the Windows Setup program but are compatible with the new Windows version after installation. This is sometimes true of antivirus software. The Setup program's initial compatibility check will list these and offer instructions.

If you have a critical app that is incompatible but you must use it in the new version of Windows, then use whatever compatibility options are available in the Windows upgrade after it is installed. See the section "Compatibility Issues with Older Applications" in Chapter 5 to learn how to set up Compatibility Mode for an application.

When it comes to hardware incompatibility, usually the device driver, not the hardware, is the source of incompatibility with an operating system. The Setup program will identify incompatibilities with your hardware. If any are found, contact the manufacturer to see if they have an updated driver that will work. If so, obtain the driver beforehand, and follow the manufacturer's instructions. You may need to wait to upgrade the device driver until after the Windows installation is completed.

If your research shows that a hardware incompatibility cannot be resolved, remove the hardware in question and replace it with a component that has a driver that works with the new OS.

Cleaning Up the Hard Drive

Before upgrading your computer to a new version of Windows, clean up the C: volume. This cleanup should include removing both unwanted programs and unnecessary files.

Removing Unwanted Programs The programs you should consider removing are those nifty programs you installed on a whim and now find you either dislike or never use. They are all taking up space on the hard drive.

Open Control Panel and use the Programs applet to find and remove the unwanted application. (You can also use the Apps section of the Settings app.)

Removing Unnecessary Files It's amazing how fast hard drive space fills up. One way it fills up is with large data files, especially music, video, and picture files. Another less obvious way hard drive space fills up is with temporary files, especially temporary Internet files that accumulate on the local hard drive while you are browsing the Internet. Windows has a nifty utility for cleaning up these files—Disk Cleanup. Exercise 4-1 walks you through the process of using the utility.

You may also want to defragment the hard drive after cleaning it up before upgrading the OS. See "Defragmenting a Hard Disk" in Chapter 6. Doing so physically relocates the existing files together on the hard disk, making it easier for the new files stored during the OS upgrade to be written contiguously. Windows may already have a scheduled task configured to defragment the drive on a regular basis. Defragmenting before upgrading the OS is useful only if the hard disk is the mechanical type (metal platters), not a solid-state drive, and only if it is fairly full.

EXERCISE 4-1

Using Disk Cleanup

In this exercise, you will use the Disk Cleanup utility to remove unnecessary files. You will need a PC with Windows installed. If at any point User Account Control (UAC) prompts you, click Continue to move past the warning.

1. Click File Explorer on the taskbar, and then, if needed, click This PC in the navigation bar to display a list of local drives.
2. Right-click the C: drive and click Properties.
3. On the General tab, click Disk Cleanup.
4. Click Clean Up System Files.

5. Select or clear check boxes as needed to fine-tune the cleanup. Then click OK to begin the cleanup.

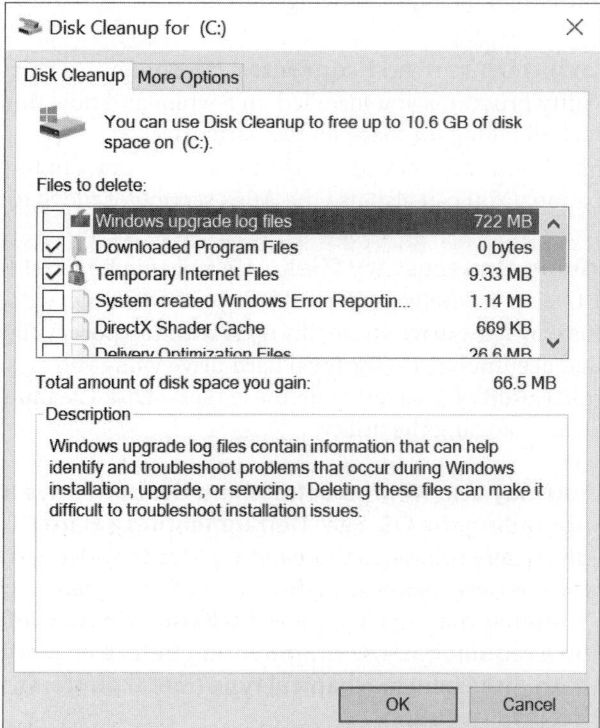

6. At the warning message, click Delete Files.
7. Wait for the cleanup to complete and its dialog box to close. Then click OK to close the Properties box.

Backing Up Data

Back up any data from the local hard drive. Installing a new OS should not put your data in danger, but you just never know. Upgrading makes many changes to your computer, replacing critical system files with those of the new OS. If your computer loses power at an inopportune time, it could become unusable. This is a rare but real danger, especially if the computer is very old. Besides, surely you need to back up your hard drive. Backing up can be as simple as copying the contents of your Documents folder onto an external hard drive or flash drive, or saving it to the OneDrive for the current user.

Upgrading to a Newer Version of Windows

The title of this section might be a bit confusing, but there is a difference between running an upgrade from earlier versions to new versions of Windows and running an upgrade from a less capable edition of a particular version to a more capable edition of the same version. This section describes an upgrade from an older version to a newer version. The next section discusses upgrading from one edition to another.

For any installation, you must decide if the installation will be unattended (run from a script) or attended. Unattended installations are usually done in large organizations to distribute software to many computers. We will discuss unattended installation later in this chapter. An *attended installation,* also called a *manual installation,* is an installation of Windows that is not automated, but rather requires someone be present to initiate it and respond to the prompts from the Setup program. And then we have attended clean installations (described later) and attended upgrades, described here.

One common attended upgrade scenario is via Windows Update. When you check for updates to the current version, you may see a message inviting you to upgrade to a newer Windows version. If you see that, just follow the prompts to make it happen.

You can also upgrade using a newer version of Windows on a USB flash drive or CD or DVD. Start the existing version of Windows and connect the USB flash drive or place the distribution DVD into the drive. Wait several seconds to see if the Setup program starts on its own. If it does not start, use File Explorer to browse to the drive and launch the Setup program. The Setup program will then detect the existing version of Windows. You can also upgrade from an ISO file that you download and then burn to a writeable DVD, or you can create a bootable USB flash drive from an ISO file.

Microsoft provides a free tool for making a bootable USB flash drive from an ISO file here: https://www.microsoft.com/en-us/download/windows-usb-dvd-download-tool.

If it is a version that you can directly upgrade, Upgrade will be an active option in the Setup program. If the OS cannot be upgraded, this option will be grayed out.

Click Next to continue with an upgrade, and Setup will continue in a manner similar to a clean installation (covered later in this chapter), but with fewer interruptions for information, and you will not be prompted to create a new partition for the OS (something we'll look at later in this chapter), since that would wipe out the installed OS and programs. You will need to provide a product key for any retail version, full or upgrade.

Upgrading to a Different Edition of the Same Windows Version

As discussed in Chapter 3, Windows versions each come in several editions. If you have a computer with a less capable edition, such as Home, and you discover it is lacking a feature you require, such as the ability to join your employer's corporate Microsoft domain, you can very easily upgrade without having to move to a new version at the same time.

You can upgrade to Windows 10 or 11 Pro from the Home edition by opening the Microsoft Store app and searching for Windows 10 Pro. A banner appears offering to upgrade to Windows 10/11 Pro. Select it and then follow the prompts. You cannot upgrade from Home or Pro to Enterprise or Education because those versions are volume-licensed by companies or schools.

Installing Windows

In this section we continue the coverage of CompTIA A+ 1102 exam Objective 1.9 with coverage of clean installations to individual computers and other installation options and types, such as installing from an image, from a recovery disc, and from a factory recovery partition.

Performing a clean install of a new operating system is not a one-step process—in fact, it occurs in three stages. In the first stage, you perform necessary tasks to prepare for the installation; in the second stage, you install the operating system; and in the third stage, you implement follow-up tasks. In this section, you will learn the necessary tasks for the first two stages when performing a clean installation of Windows.

Preparing to Install Windows

Prepare to install Windows by first ensuring the computer meets the minimum requirements. You should then verify hardware and software compatibility, understand the basics of disk preparation for installation as well as the choice of file systems (where appropriate), and finally, take steps to migrate data from a previous Windows installation to a new installation.

Hardware Requirements

Review the hardware requirements in Table 4-1 earlier in this chapter. Remember that minimums are just that: the lowest level of CPU, the minimum amount of RAM, and the minimum free hard disk space needed. You will need a more powerful computer in terms of CPU speed, hard drive space, and RAM to run a suite of office productivity tools or high-end graphics and video editing applications. The good news is that a basic consumer-grade computer today far surpasses the system minimums for Windows.

Verifying Hardware and Software Compatibility

Besides minimum system requirements, you must also consider the compatibility of the specific components installed in the PC. The Windows Setup program should check for incompatibilities automatically when it runs.

Don't forget about the issues of 32-bit versus 64-bit Windows and hardware and software compatibility. Most 32-bit Windows applications will run on the 64-bit version of Windows, but the reverse is not true; you cannot run 64-bit applications on a 32-bit version of Windows.

Locating Third-Party Drivers for Storage

Some storage devices, particularly those using redundant array of independent (or inexpensive) disks (RAID) or Small Computer System Interface (SCSI) controllers, aren't automatically recognized by Windows Setup. If you plan on installing Windows on a system where some sort of unconventional storage device must be accessed to complete the installation, make sure you have a Windows driver for that device ready to supply if needed. At some point during the beginning of the Setup process (the exact point varies depending on the Windows version), you might be prompted to press a key to load a third-party driver; after you do so, you'll be prompted for the location of that driver. It can be on a USB flash drive, an optical disc, or a hard disk drive that the Setup program recognizes.

Preparing a Storage Device

If you install Windows on an unpartitioned hard disk, the Setup program will automatically prompt you to create a partition, assign a drive letter, and format the partition. If you accept the defaults, it will create a partition of the maximum size available on the primary hard drive, assign the drive letter C: to the partition, and format it with the New Technology File System (NTFS) file system. After that, the actual installation of Windows will proceed.

We will take a few pages here to define partition tables (GPT versus MBR), partition types (primary versus extended), and file systems in the context of Windows Setup. In Chapter 5 you will work with Disk Management, the utility you use after Windows is installed to manage and maintain your storage devices.

Most of the time you will not need to change the defaults for partitioning and formatting during Windows Setup. However, in special situations where you need to override the defaults, it's important to understand what you are choosing and why.

Partitioning Before a basic disk can store data, it must be partitioned. *Partitioning* means dividing the disk into one or more areas that you can treat as separate logical drives, each of which can be assigned a different drive letter. Windows Setup can create a partition for you automatically, but it also includes an option that lets you fine-tune partition settings.

The partitions on a physical disk are managed by the disk's *partition table.* A partition table holds a record of the partition boundaries on a disk. A partition table can be one of two types: *master boot record (MBR)* or *GUID [globally unique identifier] partition table (GPT).* MBR is the older type, and is more universally accepted. GPT is newer and has two main advantages: it works with boot drives larger than 2 TB in capacity, and it allows up to 128 partitions per drive (as opposed to the usual limit of 4). The main requirement for booting from a GPT partition is having a motherboard with UEFI firmware (as opposed to BIOS firmware). You will learn about motherboard firmware in Chapter 8.

If the disk isn't larger than 2 TB and you don't need more than four partitions, go with MBR on a Windows system. That way if you ever need to move the drive to an older system that doesn't support GPT, it will still be bootable.

Most people think of a partition and a logical drive as roughly the same thing, and it's easy to make that assumption because a partition usually contains only one logical drive. However, a partition can be either primary or extended, and an extended partition can have multiple logical drives. It's therefore not always a one-to-one relationship.

- **Primary partitions** Each *primary partition* can have only one logical drive assigned to it encompassing the entire partition. Because a computer can only boot from a primary partition that is also marked as active, a Windows PC must have at least one primary partition.
- **Extended partitions** An *extended partition* is not bootable, but it can have more than one logical drive (each with a drive letter). The main advantage of an extended partition is that it can be divided up into any number of logical drives. If you're using a basic disk with MBR, the disk is limited to four partitions in total; if you need it to have more than four logical drives, you have to make one of the partitions extended.

Figure 4-1 shows two scenarios for a disk with MBR. The first one has four primary partitions, each of which has a single logical drive letter. The second one has three primary partitions and one extended partition, and the extended partition is divided up into three logical drives.

For Windows to boot from a partition, that partition must be a primary partition marked as active. This is because the startup procedure common to all PCs looks for an *active partition* on the first physical drive from which to start an OS. Installing Windows on a new unpartitioned hard drive creates a single primary partition and makes it active automatically.

When you partition a drive, the maximum partition size is the lesser of two values: the maximum partition size supported by the hardware or the maximum partition size supported by the file system. The older file systems that predated NTFS will be the limiting factors if you plan to format a partition with one of them. For instance, the FAT32 file system has a partition size limit of 2 TB. (A terabyte is 1 trillion bytes.)

If you use NTFS, which is the default file system when you install Windows, the hardware will be the limiting factor. The NTFS file system has a partition size limit of 16 EB (an exabyte is 1 billion, billion bytes) in modern Windows versions (7 and later). Now, this is obviously theoretical, because the hardware limit on a computer with a BIOS (versus UEFI firmware) is much smaller. Most modern BIOSs have a 2.2-TB limit. UEFI firmware breaks that limitation, but only if you use GPT rather than MBR as the partition table manager for the drive.

FIGURE 4-1

A disk with MBR partitioning allows for a maximum of four partitions.

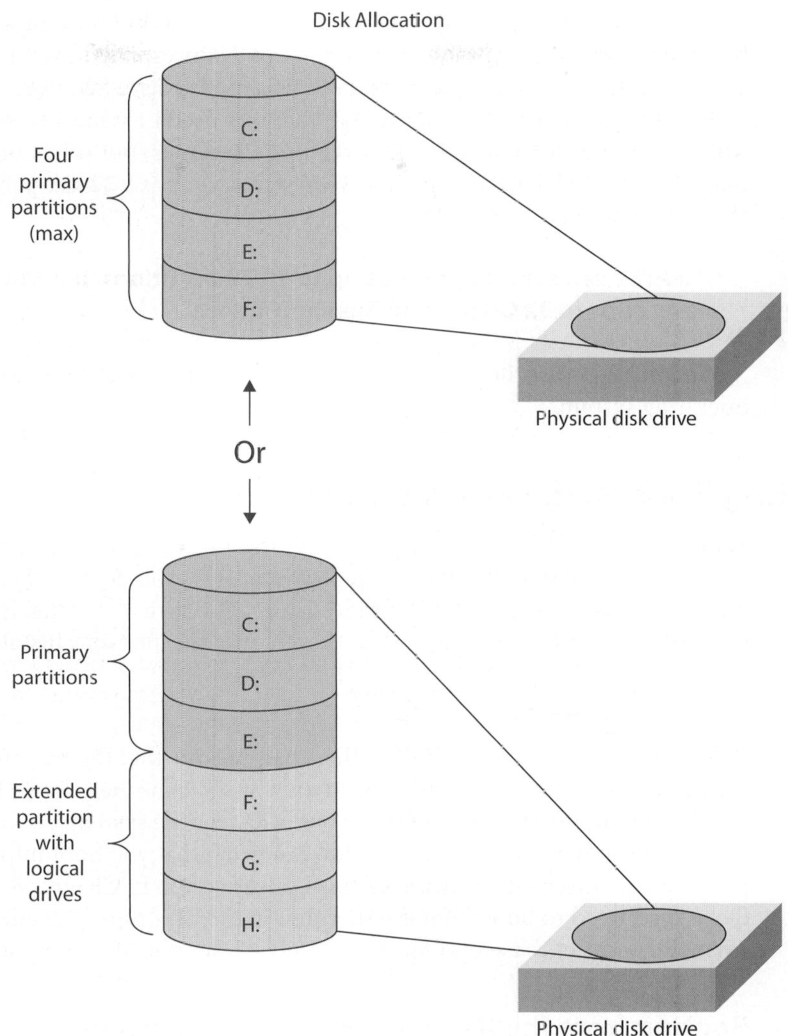

Selecting a File System for Windows After setting up a drive's partitions, you must format each logical drive with a *file system.* Windows Setup does this automatically if you stick with the defaults, but it also enables you to choose a different file system.

A *file system* is the means an operating system uses to organize information on disks. Windows Setup can format a hard disk with your choice of several file systems, including FAT32 and NTFS. Unless you have a special reason for selecting one of the older file systems, you should choose the NTFS file system during Windows installation.

NTFS is the default file system in Windows. It not only supports large partitions but also has many useful encryption and compression features, and in some Windows versions it allows you to set up disk quotas and other administrative features.

FAT32 is an older 32-bit file system that was used in Windows 95 through Windows Millennium Edition (ME). It supports long filenames, but it has many limitations that make it undesirable for use on modern systems, such as a 32-GB partition size limit on Windows systems.

FAT32 can actually support up to 16-TB partitions, but Microsoft limits FAT32 file systems to 32 GB per partition in Windows.

Chapter 5 covers file systems in greater detail, including file systems used in other operating systems.

Selecting Boot Media and Methods

When installing Windows on a new computer that does not have an OS on the hard drive, you will need to boot into the Setup program. How you do this depends on the computer, but your choices today include optical drive, USB device, external hard drive, and Preboot eXecution Environment (PXE) boot (for an over-the-network installation).

Modifying the Boot Order

If you want to boot from a device other than the one that the PC currently prefers (probably the hard disk or the optical drive), you must use the motherboard's firmware setup (BIOS or UEFI setup program) to change the boot order for the system.

Before you begin a clean installation requiring that you boot into the Windows Setup program, go into your firmware settings, as described in Chapter 8, and ensure that the device you need to boot from is either first in the list or not preceded by a bootable device. Then, for most of these options, you simply reboot and Windows Setup begins.

Booting from the Network (PXE Boot or NetBoot)

All modern network cards support the ability to start a computer over the network, without relying on a disk-based OS, using an Intel standard called *Preboot eXecution Environment (PXE),* or more simply *PXE Boot.* If network boot is selected in firmware setup, the network card will initiate the startup of the computer, downloading the initial bootup files from a network server. Then it is ready to perform a task, such as installing the new OS over the network or running centralized maintenance tests on the computer. However, someone must do the work of preparing a server running the Microsoft *Windows Deployment*

Services (WDS). This service responds to PXE Boot requests from network clients and supplies the environment needed to boot up. Then, usually through a script, the client computer is directed to connect to the network share containing the Windows installation files and run the Setup program over the network. On Macs, the equivalent technology is NetBoot, which enables Macs to boot from a network.

Over-the-Network Installation

A network installation can involve an image installation, an attended installation, or an unattended installation. Any of these network installation methods requires quite a bit of prep work, but what they have in common is the basic steps for preparing for the installation. Here, we will describe the steps required for either an attended or unattended network installation. Later, we will address an over-the-network image installation.

To prepare for an attended or unattended network installation, first copy the Windows source files into a shared folder on the server; second, configure the client computer to boot up and connect to the server; and third, start the Setup program itself. The actual steps for doing this are extensive, often requiring trained personnel and testing of the procedure.

CompTIA A+ 1102 exam Objective 1.9 requires only that you understand the differences among the various installation methods. You do not need in-depth, hands-on experience with the various methods.

Installing from a Factory Recovery Partition

A Windows PC may provide a factory recovery partition containing an image of the drive partition on which Windows is installed. The recovery partition itself is hidden and only accessible by a method the manufacturer provides for restoring the system to its fresh-from-the-factory state. Check the manufacturer's documentation long before you need to resort to installing from a factory recovery partition. In many cases, you enter the factory recovery partition utility by pressing a function key as the system starts up. If you install a new version of Windows on a computer with a recovery partition, the new OS may overwrite a critical part of the Windows partition containing information for calling up the recovery program, so check with the manufacturer before upgrading.

Attended Installation

Installing Windows requires inputting certain unique information for each computer. During an *attended installation* of Windows, also called a *manual installation,* you must pay attention throughout the entire process to provide information and to respond to messages. A Setup Wizard guides you through the process. The installation process takes about an hour, and you spend most of that time watching the screen. Most of the process is automated, with user interaction required only at the beginning and end. Feel free to walk away as the installation is taking place, because, if it needs input, the installation program will stop and wait until you click the correct buttons.

The following description is of a clean install, meaning the partitioning and formatting of the hard disk will occur during the installation. You would perform this type of installation on a new computer, or on an old computer when you want a complete new start. A clean install avoids the potential problems of upgrading, which we describe later in "Updating Windows."

Gathering Information

Before you begin an attended installation for a retail version of Windows, gather the specific information you need, which depends on whether you are installing a PC at home or in a business network. Either way, gather the appropriate information, including the following:

- The product ID code, such as one purchased online or provided by an employer or (less commonly these days) from a sticker on the envelope or jewel case of a Windows setup DVD.
- A 15-character (or less) name for the computer, which must be unique on the local network; you can make up a name yourself on a workgroup or home network. Some Windows versions create a name automatically during the installation.
- The name of the workgroup or domain the computer will join. You may need to get this information from a network administrator. Anyone can create and join a workgroup, but to join a domain, an administrator must create accounts in the domain for both you and your computer.
- If the computer will be joining a domain, the user name and password assigned to the user account need to be set up first on this PC.
- The necessary network configuration information. Ask your network administrator for this information, but the Windows default will configure the computer to receive an address automatically, which should work for you in a corporate setting, at home, and at school. Learn more about how a computer receives network addresses in Chapter 16.

In addition, gather the discs and/or setup files for any device drivers for the computer and its installed peripherals, especially the network adapters. (Everything else can be downloaded later, but the network card must be working in order to download anything.) You may need to download device drivers from manufacturers' websites. Windows may have appropriate drivers for all your devices, but if it does not, Windows Setup may prompt you to provide them. You can do that during Setup, or you can let Windows install minimal generic drivers during Setup and then install or update the drivers after Setup is complete.

Installing Interactively

Begin the attended Windows installation by booting into the Windows Setup program from one of the sources described earlier. In most cases, when installing to a single computer, you will begin by inserting the Windows distribution media and booting the computer. From there, just follow the prompts that appear.

All versions of Windows that we are studying here include an option to repair an existing installation early in the Setup process. Look for a *Repair Your Computer* link. You can use that instead of doing a clean install when a system is so badly damaged or corrupted that Windows won't start normally. Another possibility in such a situation is to refresh or restore the Windows installation, as explained in Chapter 6.

When you start up Windows from removable media containing Setup files, the *Windows Preinstallation Environment (Windows PE)* starts. This is a scaled-down Windows operating system with limited drivers for basic hardware. The Setup screens are similar between versions. The steps of the process include copying Windows files, expanding Windows files, installing features, installing updates, and completing installation.

If you're installing a volume licensed edition, Setup may ask you to specify which edition you are installing. Remember, you must choose the edition that matches the product key you have. You can't convert one edition to another just by choosing it from this menu. Windows Setup asks whether you want an upgrade or a clean install. If you're installing on an empty hard drive on a system with no other OS installed, both choices have the same result. Clean install may be phrased as Custom: Install Windows Only.

If you choose a clean install, Windows Setup displays a list of existing partitions and unpartitioned space. On most systems, this page will show a single disk, and you will simply click Next. Figure 4-2 shows this page. Although it is not obvious, in this case the disk is a virtual hard drive in a virtual machine, and the virtual hard drive is smaller than we would normally choose for a typical desktop, but otherwise, this is what you would expect to see.

If you accept the default, the disk will be partitioned using all available space, and it will be formatted with NTFS. If you need to load a third-party driver for the hard disk, click Load Driver. If you want to do anything different than the default, click Drive Options (Advanced). For instance, if the disk has enough space, you might want to create more than one partition or install Windows into a folder other than the default. We don't recommend straying from the defaults for most situations.

FIGURE 4-2

Change partitioning and choose a different volume if desired, or accept the default (most common).

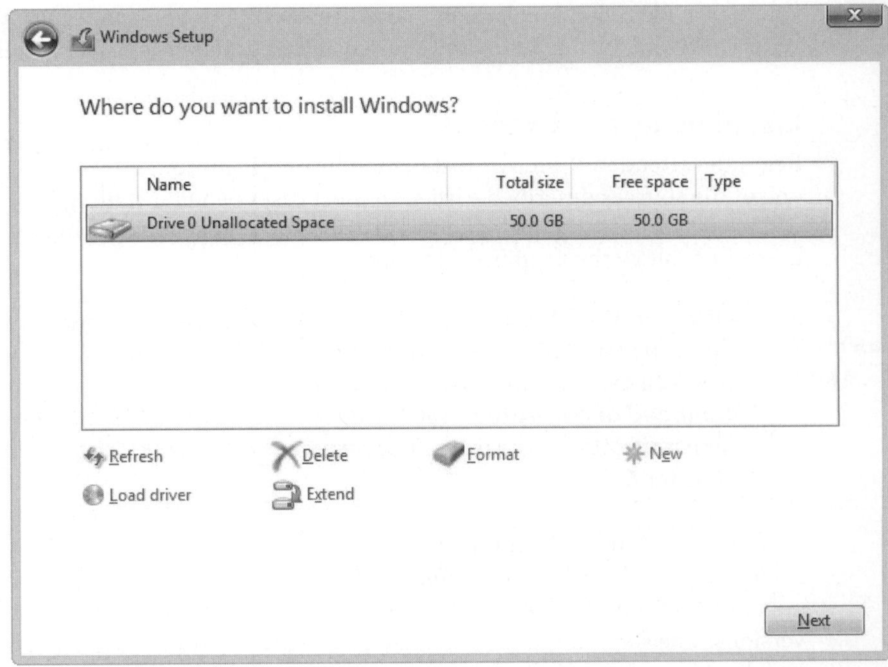

Setup copies files to the location you indicated or to the newly formatted partition. Unless you specify another location, Setup creates a folder named Windows in C:\, into which it installs the OS, creating appropriate subfolders below it. After it finishes copying the base set of files to this location, your computer reboots. At this point the PC reboots and returns to the graphical mode, usually at a higher screen resolution than before the restart because it is now using the newly installed drivers rather than the drivers used by PE. All versions of Windows Setup will restart multiple times during the Setup process.

Near the end of the Setup process, you will be asked some questions about the PC's configuration; follow the instructions on the screen, accepting the defaults when you are unsure.

If Setup detects a network card, the network components will install and configure with default settings. You may be prompted for a security key for connecting to a wireless router.

All versions give you a chance to personalize Windows by entering a user name and password (or signing in with a Microsoft account, or creating one), entering the computer name (in some versions), and joining a workgroup or connecting to a Windows domain (if applicable). The options available depend on the version and edition. We cover account creation and management later in this chapter. If asked about privacy settings, make choices you're comfortable with, or just go with the defaults.

EXERCISE 4-2

Performing an Attended Clean Install of Windows

In this exercise, you will do a clean installation of any edition of Windows 10. To complete this exercise, you will need Windows installation media (such as a USB flash drive or an ISO file) and the information listed earlier under "Gathering Information." Make sure you have the product key, in particular.

You can install on a separate PC, or you can use a virtual machine, covered in Chapter 7. For example, you can use VirtualBox and a Windows ISO file to perform the installation on your main PC and then delete the virtual machine afterward or keep it to perform additional lab experiments on in later chapters.

As an optional addition to this exercise, you can practice upgrading an OS. To do this, start by doing a clean install of Windows 10 (or an earlier Windows version) and then upgrade it to Windows 10 or 11. Do what you can with the Windows media you have available for use.

This exercise doesn't provide specific steps because there are so many variations in the Setup programs depending on both version and edition; refer to the general notes in the preceding section to guide you.

1. Insert or connect the installation media and then boot the computer. The Setup program should start automatically. If it doesn't, you may need to change the boot order in the BIOS/UEFI for the motherboard. See "Configuring a Motherboard" in Chapter 8 to do that.
2. Follow the prompts to install Windows. The steps and their order will depend on the Windows version you are installing. Make notes about the steps you took.

Unattended Installation

An *unattended installation* is one in which the installation process is automated. There are two general types of unattended installations:

- A scripted installation using *answer files* and *Uniqueness Database Files (UDFs),* which provide the data normally provided by a user during an attended installation
- An image installation, using either Microsoft software tools or a third-party tool

Scripting for Unattended Installations

A scripted installation uses scripts that someone has prepared ahead of time. Organizations with large numbers of desktop computers needing identical applications and desktop configurations use this. This type of installation normally requires trained people who plan and implement the installation using a variety of automation methods, including scripts and access to the Windows source files on a *distribution server.*

A typical scripted installation scenario involves placing the Windows source files from the distribution media onto a file share on a server, which is then called a *distribution share.* This assumes sufficient licenses for the number of installations from these source files. Then, each desktop computer boots up, either from the local hard drive or from another source, and runs a script that connects to the distribution server to begin the installation.

Although we place scripted installations under unattended installations here, the amount of interaction required ranges from none to as much as is required for an attended installation. In fact, certain software on the server side, such as Microsoft Endpoint Manager, can, with proper configuration of each client computer, push an installation down from the server with no one sitting at each desktop. This can include an automated installation of user applications on top of the newly installed Windows OS.

Drive Imaging

In organizations that want to install the same OS and all the same application software on many desktop PCs, drive imaging is often used. A *drive image,* or *disk image,* is an exact duplicate of an entire hard drive's contents, including the OS and all installed software, applied to one or more identically configured computers. CompTIA A+ 1102 exam Objective 1.9 calls this type of installation *image deployment.*

Microsoft has developed an entire suite of tools for deploying Windows to large numbers of desktop computers. These tools and sets of recommended procedures cover the planning, building (of the images), and deployment phases. Even an overview of these tools would take a great deal of time and space, and CompTIA A+ 1102 exam Objective 1.9 only requires that you understand the basics of image installations. Therefore, we will simply list and briefly describe the tools for the build and deployment phases.

- **Microsoft Deployment Toolkit** A technician uses this tool to create and manage both the distribution share and the various images. Plus, this tool will configure several deployment sources, including a single server, a deployment share, a DVD ISO image, or a directory that contains all the files needed for a customized deployment from a server running Microsoft Endpoint Manager software.
- **Windows System Image Manager** This tool allows a technician to create the components for automating custom installs using custom scripts.
- **ImageX** Use this tool to create the disk images.

- **Windows PE** PE is a bootable environment that gives operating system support during three types of operations: installing Windows, troubleshooting, and recovery.
- **User State Migration Tool (USMT)** Technicians use this tool for migrating files and settings to many desktop computers. It does not migrate programs, however, just data files, operating system settings, and settings from Microsoft applications.

Microsoft is not the only source for such tools: many third-party vendors offer an array of imaging and deployment tools. Learn more about these tools by searching on the Internet.

CERTIFICATION OBJECTIVES

- ***1102: 1.4*** *Given a scenario, use the appropriate Microsoft Windows 10 Control Panel utility*
- ***1102: 1.5*** *Given a scenario, use the appropriate Windows settings*

CompTIA A+ 1102 exam Objectives 1.4 and 1.5 both include accounts, and this section covers account creation and maintenance at a basic level. You should know how to manage accounts from both the Control Panel (1.4) and the Settings app (1.5). You'll learn more about accounts in Chapter 21.

Post-Installation Tasks

After installing Windows, you have a few post-installation and configuration tasks. They include verifying network access (assuming connection to a network exists), registering and activating Windows, installing any available Windows Updates, and installing applications and devices as needed. You may also want to migrate data from another device. The following sections cover several important post-installation tasks.

Checking for Internet Connectivity

Once you have completed the installation, verify that the computer can access the Internet. The Windows Setup program may have checked this for you already and established an Internet connection if one was available. If Windows Setup could not find a network, troubleshoot to find out why not. Internet connectivity is important because it allows you to use Windows Update to make sure you have the latest Windows patches and device drivers. See Chapter 19 for network troubleshooting help if needed.

Creating User Accounts

This section explains the basics of creating Windows user accounts. You'll learn about advanced user management in Chapter 21.

User Account Types

Users can sign into Windows with a Microsoft account or a local account. A *Microsoft account* (the default) is tied to a specific e-mail address, which is then registered with a Microsoft server. A *local account* exists only on the local PC. Microsoft accounts are generally a good thing. They can automatically transfer settings and appearance preferences between different PCs where the signed-in user is the same, and they enable you to access your OneDrive storage without having to sign in separately.

User accounts (of either type) can have either Administrator or Standard permissions. The first account you create on a new Windows install must have Administrator permissions so that there will be at least one account that is authorized to make all types of system changes. Therefore, the first account you configure using the Setup program is always set to the Administrator type.

Creating or Entering a User Account During Setup

Near the end of the Setup process, Windows prompts you to sign in with a Microsoft account or create a new Microsoft account.

Signing in with a Microsoft account links your stored settings and OneDrive files. If you are installing various Windows versions for study purposes and not for actual use, you may want to create a dummy Microsoft account using an e-mail address you don't use for anything else to avoid entangling your personal files and settings with the test machine.

If you can't sign in with an existing account, follow the prompts to create a new Microsoft account or to sign in with a local account.

Creating Additional User Accounts

Microsoft recommends that you not use an Administrator account on an everyday basis because of the risk of security breaches. If someone hacks into your system, they will be able to do more damage with an Administrator account than with a Standard one, so the less time you spend in an Administrator account, the better. Therefore, you will probably want to create one or more additional user accounts and assign Standard permissions to them. You may also want more user accounts so that each person using the PC can have individual personal file storage and settings.

In some Windows versions you can create "family member" accounts. Family member accounts can be set up as either adult or child accounts; child accounts can be configured so their ability to run certain applications or visit certain websites is limited. Family accounts aren't covered on the CompTIA A+ exams, so we don't get into them here.

While you can manage user accounts either from the Settings app or the Control Panel, you can only create new accounts via the Settings app. If you try to do it from the Control Panel, you are redirected to the Settings app for the activity. The following exercise shows how to create a new account in the Settings app.

EXERCISE 4-3

Video

Creating a New User Account with the Settings App

In this exercise, you will create a new user account with Standard permissions using the Settings app. You can either create a Microsoft account or a local account—your choice.

1. Activate Windows if your copy is not already activated. See the following section to learn how. You can't add more user accounts until you activate.
2. Make sure you are signed in with an account that has Administrative privileges.
3. Click Start | Settings | Accounts | Family & Other Users.
4. Click Add Someone Else To This PC.
5. Enter the e-mail address or phone number of the person you want to add. If there is an existing Microsoft account associated with that person, use the e-mail or phone number for that account. Then click Next, and then Finish, and you're done.

   –Or–

   If you don't have the person's sign-in information, you can create a new account for them. Click I Don't Have This Person's Sign-in Information and follow the prompts. Either fill out the form provided or click Add A User Without A Microsoft Account to create a local account and then follow the prompts to set that up.

There's a lot more you can do to configure user accounts on a Windows system, such as restricting user permissions and sign-in times, requiring users to change their passwords, and locking accounts after a certain number of password attempts; all of those activities are covered in Chapter 21.

Registering and Activating Windows

Many people confuse registration and activation. These are two separate operations. *Registration* informs the software manufacturer who the owner or user of the product is and provides contact information such as name, address, company, phone number, e-mail address, and so on about them. Registration of a Microsoft product is still entirely optional.

Activation, more formally called *Microsoft Product Activation (MPA),* is a method designed to combat software piracy, meaning that Microsoft wishes to ensure that only a single computer uses each license for Windows.

Activation is mandatory. Some versions/editions of Setup prompt you to do it during Setup; some don't. If prompted to activate during Setup, you can skip it. You have 30 days in which to activate Windows, during which time it will work normally (mostly—some features won't work until you activate, such as creating user accounts and personalizing desktop settings). If you don't activate it within that time frame, Windows will automatically disable itself at the end of the 30 days. Don't worry about forgetting, because once installed, Windows frequently reminds you to activate it. The messages even tell you how many days you have left.

Understanding activation is important because most Microsoft products require it, and Microsoft is not the only software vendor using an activation process. Software purchased with a volume license agreement does not require product activation.

Sometimes reactivation is required after major changes to a computer. To understand why, you need to understand how MPA creates the 50-digit value that identifies your hardware. MPA generates this hardware identifier value used during activation, called the "hardware hash," by applying a special mathematical algorithm to values assigned to certain types of hardware, such as adapters, RAM, processor (type and serial number), and drives.

MPA will occasionally recalculate the hardware hash and compare it to the one created during activation. When it detects a significant difference in the hardware hash, you will be required to reactivate, and you may need to contact Microsoft and explain the reason for the reactivation. This is Microsoft's way of ensuring that you did not install the product on another computer.

Updating Windows

Windows will automatically begin updating itself as part of Setup. The program that manages that, Windows Update, connects to Microsoft servers online and then downloads and installs any updates, patches, and other fixes that it finds.

After installing Windows, one of the first things you should do is manually check for updates to make sure the Setup program caught them all. Choose Start | Settings | Update & Security, and check the Update Status. Click Check For Updates, and follow the prompts to install any updates that are available. Windows automatically downloads and installs the updates.

Configuring Automatic Update Settings

Windows permits only very limited customization of the Windows Update process. You can't turn off updates altogether, as you could with earlier versions. Open the Settings app, click Update & Security (Windows 10) or Windows Update (Windows 11), and click Advanced Options to explore the available configuration options. Different editions have somewhat different choices.

In the Pause Updates section of the Advanced Options screen, you can temporarily pause updates for up to 35 days by selecting a date to resume. But when that date comes, you have to install any available updates before you can pause it again.

Corporate Policies That Prohibit Automatic Updating

In spite of the ease of updating Windows over the Internet, how you actually obtain updates will depend on the organization (school or business) that manages the computer, if it's not your own.

Updates can bring their own problems. Therefore, many organizations with IT support staff disable automatic updates, waiting until they have conducted their own internal tests before distributing them to users' desktops and laptops. In some organizations, the IT department may distribute updates intended for new installations on optical discs in order to install them before a computer ever connects to a network. Other organizations may make them available on a shared folder on the network, but many large organizations use a central management system for distributing and installing all desktop software—from the operating systems to applications and updates.

Uninstalling an Update

Sometimes an update will create new problems on specific PCs. If you experience problems with an update, you can remove the update via the Control Panel. Not all updates can be uninstalled; the newer the Windows version, the fewer updates are uninstallable.

From the Control Panel, navigate to Programs | Programs And Features, and then click View Installed Updates. Select the update you think is causing the problem and click Uninstall to remove it, just as you would remove any other software. If you can uninstall the update, the Uninstall link appears in the shaded bar at the top of the list when that update is selected. If you don't see Uninstall there, you can't uninstall it.

You can start the process from the Settings app, but it will redirect you to the Control Panel. From the Settings app, choose Update & Security | Windows Update and click View Update History. Then click Uninstall Updates to open the Control Panel to the Uninstall An Update page (same as if you had gone through the Control Panel directly).

SCENARIO & SOLUTION	
How do you boot into the Windows Setup program on a computer with an unpartitioned hard disk?	If the computer can boot from an optical drive, place the Windows distribution disc into the drive and start the computer. No optical drive? You can place the setup program on a USB flash drive and boot from that. You might need to change the boot order in BIOS/UEFI setup, though.
A client reports that Windows is prompting her to activate her upgrade of Windows, but she does not want to send personal information to Microsoft. Should she activate Windows?	Although the activation process is mandatory, it does not send personal information to Microsoft. Registration, which is optional, sends personal information.
You have hundreds of Windows 10 PCs that need to be updated to Windows 11. How can you do this as efficiently as possible?	Consider unattended network-based updates pushed out from a server rather than physically visiting and touching each device.

Installing and Upgrading macOS and Linux Operating Systems

The current CompTIA A+ exams do not require that you know how to install and upgrade Mac and Linux systems. However, CompTIA A+ 1102 exam Objective 1.10 requires you to know how to work with various features of both Mac and Linux systems, and in order to practice those skills, you are going to need a working macOS system and a working Linux environment. Therefore, a few words about installing and upgrading these systems are in order.

Upgrading macOS

Macs come with macOS preinstalled as the operating system. You can't buy the macOS operating system separately, so you will probably never do a clean install of macOS. Instead, you'll download and install an OS upgrade via the App Store. The process is mostly invisible and free of choices, so there's not much you need to learn about it.

It's technically possible to install macOS on a virtual machine under VirtualBox, but it's neither easy (i.e., there are lots of steps, and some of them involve manually editing command strings) nor legal. If you need to practice using a Mac, consider buying a used one that's a few years old, working with it as you study, and then reselling it.

File Systems for Linux and macOS

The native file system for macOS versions 10.13 and later is Apple File System (APFS). This file system features strong encryption, space for sharing snapshots, fast directory sizing, and improved file system fundamentals. The earlier file system, used on macOS versions prior to 10.13, was Hierarchical File System (HFS) Plus (HFS+).

It's unlikely that you will ever have to install MacOS on an empty system, so you will probably not ever have to make that choice, but it's important to know APFS and HFS+ for testing purposes.

When you are installing a Linux distro on an unpartitioned drive, you might be asked to make a choice of file systems: ext3 or ext4—or at least you might be able to select an advanced install option that permits you to make a choice.

Ext4, which was released in 2008, has these benefits over ext3:

- Larger maximum file size (16 TB versus 2 TB)
- Larger maximum partition size (1 EB versus 32 TB)
- Up to 64,000 subdirectories in a directory (up from 32,000 in ext3)
- Backward compatibility with ext3 file systems without upgrading them
- A multitude of features that improve performance

However, ext3 has one important benefit: you can share an ext3 partition with Windows. So if you multiboot your system (see the next section) and one of the drives must be accessed under both Windows and Linux, make sure that drive uses ext3.

Installing Linux

You'll need to study Linux in upcoming chapters as part of your exam prep, so take a few minutes now to acquire and install a copy of Linux on a virtual machine in Oracle VirtualBox on a Windows PC or directly onto the hard drive of any spare PC you happen to have around. (You can't do this for macOS, so if you want to practice on a Mac, you'll need an actual Mac computer.)

There are many distributions ("distros") of Linux, and some are easier to use than others. We recommend Ubuntu Desktop for the Linux activities in this book. Exercise 4-4 walks you through the process of downloading Ubuntu and creating a bootable DVD for it and then installing Ubuntu in VirtualBox (one of the hypervisors you will learn about in Chapter 7).

EXERCISE 4-4

Installing Ubuntu Linux

For this exercise you'll need a writeable DVD drive and a blank DV-R disc or a USB drive of at least 8 GB capacity with nothing on it that you want to keep. If you want to install on a virtual machine, you'll also need a hypervisor such as VirtualBox. If you are planning on using a virtual machine, skip ahead and read Chapter 7 first so you'll understand what that entails.

1. Download Ubuntu Desktop from www.ubuntu.com/download. The 64-bit version is better if your hardware will support it. (The host system's firmware should support virtualization if you're going with the 64-bit version. You will learn in Chapter 7 how to determine this.)
2. Do one of the following:
   a. If you are installing on a virtual machine, attach the ISO file as a virtual drive.
   b. If you are installing on a physical PC that contains an optical drive, use an ISO burning program to burn the downloaded .iso file to an optical disc. You must use a burning program that creates bootable discs; don't just copy the file over, or it won't be bootable. There are many good burning programs that will do this. Tuxboot is just one example (https://sourceforge.net/projects/tuxboot).
   c. If you are installing on a physical PC that does not contain an optical drive, use a utility that creates bootable USB flash drives and create one using the ISO file.
3. Do one of the following:
   a. If you are installing on a physical PC, boot the PC from the DVD or flash drive and follow the prompts to install Linux.
   b. If you are installing on a virtual machine, boot up the VM you created in Chapter 7, or create a new one for Ubuntu. Boot to the DVD or flash drive you created in Step 2, and follow the steps to install Ubuntu Linux. If offered the choices of Try Ubuntu and Install Ubuntu, go with Install, so you'll have it for upcoming chapters.

CERTIFICATION SUMMARY

You have many decisions to make before installing a new version of Windows. Will this be a clean installation or an upgrade? Will it be an upgrade or a clean install? What tasks should you perform before installing or upgrading Windows? What tasks should you perform after installing Windows?

The answers to all these questions are important to understand for passing the CompTIA A+ exam, and for doing your job.

TWO-MINUTE DRILL

Here are some of the key points covered in Chapter 4.

Considerations for Installing or Upgrading Windows

- ❑ The key considerations when planning a Windows installation or upgrade include the system requirements, application and hardware compatibility, and whether there is a valid upgrade path between the old and new version (if applicable).
- ❑ The basic rules of upgrade paths: you can't cross platforms, you can't go backward in version numbers, and you can't downgrade the edition.

Upgrading Windows

- ❑ An upgrade installs the new version of Windows directly on top of an existing installation, transferring all the settings from the old installation into the new one.
- ❑ Before upgrading, test for incompatible software and hardware and then resolve any incompatibilities.
- ❑ Before upgrading, back up all data and clean up the hard drive.

Installing Windows

- ❑ Installing Windows involves three stages: preparation, installation, and follow-up tasks.
- ❑ Preparation tasks include verifying the target computer meets the physical hardware requirements, as well as the hardware and software compatibility requirements.
- ❑ Windows 10 requires a 1-GHz CPU, 1 or 2 GB of RAM (32-bit or 64-bit, respectively), and 16 or 20 GB of free hard disk space (32-bit or 64-bit). When partitioning a disk, choose MBR or GPT. Choose a file system (probably NTFS). Plan the partitions on the disk if you are going to have more than one.
- ❑ When setting up a multiboot system, put each OS on its own partition, and install them in oldest to newest order.
- ❑ Setup can be started from a downloaded Setup file, an optical disc, a flash drive, an external hard drive, a network share, or a factory recovery partition.
- ❑ An attended installation requires the presence of a person who can respond to occasional prompts for information.
- ❑ Scripts that answer the Setup program's questions automate an unattended installation.
- ❑ A drive or disk image is an exact duplicate of an entire hard drive's contents, including the OS and all installed software.

Post-Installation Tasks

- ❑ After installation, test Internet connectivity and troubleshoot if needed.
- ❑ Activating Windows is mandatory, but registration is optional.
- ❑ Create additional user accounts if more than one person will be using the PC or if you wish to run a Standard account on a day-to-day basis for greater security. Accounts can either be Microsoft accounts or local and can either have Standard or Administrator permissions.
- ❑ Windows Update downloads and installs updates automatically.
- ❑ After completing a Windows installation and performing the most urgent configuration tasks, you should install and configure security programs and then install and configure other applications.

Installing and Upgrading macOS and Linux Operating Systems

- ❑ Macs come with the macOS preinstalled, and OS updates and new versions are provided via the App Store, so you will seldom need to install macOS.
- ❑ You can download a Linux distro for free, burn it to a DVD or flash drive, and then install it on an empty hard disk or a virtual machine.
- ❑ File systems for Linux are ext3 and ext4. Ext4 has several benefits, but ext3 offers the ability to share the partition with Windows. Macs use the APFS file system (or HFS+ on pre-macOS 10.13 systems).

SELF TEST

The following questions will help you measure your understanding of the material presented in this chapter. Read all of the choices carefully, because there might be more than one correct answer. Choose all correct answers for each question.

Considerations for Installing or Upgrading Windows

1. What is the minimum CPU speed required for Windows 10?

A. 800 MHz for 32-bit and 1 GHz for 64-bit

B. 1 GHz for 32-bit and 2 GHz for 64-bit

C. 1 GHz for both 32-bit and 64-bit

D. 2 GHz for both 32-bit and 64-bit

2. Which of the following is one of the system requirements Microsoft specifies for installing Windows?

A. Hard disk type (magnetic vs. solid state)

B. Amount of RAM

C. Form factor of case

D. Brand of sound card

3. Which of the following is *not* a valid in-place upgrade path?

A. Windows 8.1 Pro to Windows 10 Professional

B. Windows 10 Home to Windows 10 Professional

C. Windows 10 Education to Windows 10 Home

D. Windows 8.1 Enterprise to Windows 10 Enterprise

Upgrading Windows

4. Which of these is *not* a benefit of upgrading instead of doing a clean install?

A. An upgrade may install easily via Windows Update.

B. An upgrade may solve persistent system problems that a clean install cannot.

C. You can keep your old files and settings.

D. You don't have to reinstall all the applications.

5. What should you do before an upgrade if you discover incompatible software or hardware?

A. Nothing. The incompatibility will be resolved during the upgrade.

B. Buy a special version of Windows for incompatibility problems.

C. Resolve the incompatibility before beginning the upgrade.

D. Repartition and format the hard drive.

6. What Windows utility can be used to remove unnecessary files in preparation for a Windows upgrade?

A. Windows Update

B. Disk Defragmenter

C. Disk Cleanup

D. Check Disk

Installing Windows

7. Which of the following refers to the lowest level of CPU, the minimum amount of RAM, and the free hard disk space needed to install an OS?
   A. Hardware compatibility
   B. Software compatibility
   C. Hardware requirements
   D. Hardware optimizing
8. What is the preferred file system for Windows?
   A. NTFS
   B. FAT16
   C. FAT32
   D. ext3
9. Which of the following boot sources for Windows Setup is designed to initiate an over-the-network installation?
   A. eSATA
   B. PXE Boot
   C. Optical drive
   D. USB device
10. What type of installation requires a person's real-time response to prompts?
    A. Unattended
    B. Image
    C. Scripted
    D. Attended
11. What installation method places an exact copy of a hard drive containing a previously installed operating system and applications (from a reference computer) onto the hard drive of another computer?
    A. Attended
    B. Scripted
    C. Image
    D. Unattended
12. What are the two general types of unattended installations? (Select two.)
    A. Drive image
    B. Scripted
    C. Upgrade
    D. USMT

13. What is the minimum amount of RAM required for installing the 64-bit version of Windows 10?

A. 1 GB
B. 2 GB
C. 4 GB
D. 8 GB

14. Which of the following statements is true of the Windows Setup?

A. The computer will restart one or more times during Setup.
B. If the computer restarts during Setup, something has gone wrong.
C. The installation steps are identical to those for Linux.
D. You must install English as the primary/first language.

15. What bootable environment gives operating system support during three types of operations: installing Windows, troubleshooting, and recovery?

A. Safe Mode
B. USMT
C. NTFS
D. Windows PE

Post-Installation Tasks

16. What purpose does Microsoft Product Activation (MPA) serve?

A. Product compatibility
B. Prevention of software piracy
C. Product registration
D. Prevention of malware infection

17. What is the consequence of not completing the activation process for Windows within the required time period?

A. There is no consequence.
B. Windows will continue to work, but you do not receive updates.
C. Windows is disabled.
D. You will not receive e-mails about new products.

18. What app should you use to create an additional Windows account?

A. Registration
B. Programs
C. Settings
D. Sign-ins

Installing and Upgrading macOS and Linux Operating Systems

19. How do Macs receive OS updates?
   A. Users purchase retail DVD upgrades.
   B. Apple mails update DVDs to your registered address.
   C. They are downloaded from the App Store.
   D. Macs never need OS updates.

20. What is the least expensive way to acquire a desktop version of Linux?
   A. Purchase a download from an authorized website.
   B. Buy a used DVD on an auction site.
   C. Buy a retail box version.
   D. Download a distro and create a bootable USB flash drive.

SELF TEST ANSWERS

Considerations for Installing or Upgrading Windows

1. ☑ **C.** The minimum CPU speed for Windows 10 is 1 GHz, regardless of 32-bit or 64-bit.
☒ **A** is incorrect because Windows 10 will not run on an 800-MHz CPU. **B** is incorrect because Windows 10's requirements do not change for 32-bit vs. 64-bit. **D** is incorrect because the minimum is 1 GHz, not 2 GHz.

2. ☑ **B.** Amount of RAM is important in the system requirements for a Windows version.
☒ **A** is incorrect because the OS doesn't care what technology the hard disk uses. **C** is incorrect because this describes the dimensions of a hardware device, not the system requirements for an OS. **D** is incorrect because Windows can accept almost any sound card, provided the manufacturer supplies a driver.

3. ☑ **C.** You cannot upgrade from Windows 10 Education to Windows 10 Home because Home is a lesser edition than Enterprise.
☒ **A, B,** and **D** are incorrect because these are all valid upgrade paths.

Upgrading Windows

4. ☑ **B.** An upgrade may *not* solve persistent system problems that a clean install cannot. The opposite of that statement is actually correct; a clean install can solve problems that an upgrade may not fix.
☒ **A, C,** and **D** are incorrect because they are all true.

5. ☑ **C.** Resolving the incompatibility before beginning the upgrade is the correct action to take if you discover incompatible software or hardware.
☒ **A** is incorrect because the incompatibility will not be resolved during the upgrade. **B** is incorrect because there is no such version. **D** is incorrect because this will not solve the problem; it is extreme and will void the ability to install an upgrade.

6. ☑ **C.** Disk Cleanup can delete unnecessary files such as temporary files and setup files.
☒ **A** is incorrect because Windows Update looks for online updates; it does not affect files. **B** is incorrect because although Disk Defragmenter can help relocate files on a disk, it does not delete files. **D** is incorrect because Check Disk checks the file system for errors; it does not delete files.

Installing Windows

7. ☑ **C.** Hardware requirements are the CPU, minimum amount of RAM, and free hard disk space needed to install an OS.
☒ **A** is incorrect because hardware compatibility refers to the actual make and model of the hardware, not the level of CPU and quantity of RAM and free hard disk space. **B** is incorrect because software compatibility does not refer to the CPU, RAM, and free hard disk space. **D** is incorrect because hardware optimizing does not refer to the level of CPU and quantity of RAM and free hard disk space.

8. ☑ **A.** NTFS is the preferred file system for Windows.
☒ **B, C,** and **D** are incorrect because none of them is the preferred file system for Windows. FAT16 and FAT32 are obsolete versions of DOS and Windows file systems, and ext3 is for Linux systems.

9. ☑ **B.** PXE Boot uses a feature of a network card that will initiate the startup of the computer, downloading the initial bootup files from a network server, after which it is ready to perform a task, such as installing the new OS over the network or running centralized maintenance tests on the computer.
☒ **A, C,** and **D** are incorrect because while they are valid sources for starting an OS and going into Windows Setup, none of them was specifically designed for an over-the-network installation.

10. ☑ **D.** Attended installation is the type that requires a person's real-time response to prompts.
☒ **A** is incorrect because this type of installation does not require a person's real-time response to prompts. **B** is incorrect because this method replaces Setup altogether. **C** is incorrect because you could use this term to describe an unattended installation.

11. ☑ **C.** Image installation places an exact copy of the operating system and applications (from a reference computer) onto the hard drive of another computer.
☒ **A** is incorrect because attended installation does not place an exact copy of a hard drive onto another computer. **B** is incorrect because scripting is just part of an installation, not a method of installation. **D** is incorrect because this method may or may not include an image.

12. ☑ **A** and **B.** These are the two general types of unattended installations.
☒ **C** is incorrect because you can upgrade as either an attended or unattended installation. **D** is incorrect because USMT is a tool for migrating user settings and data.

13. ☑ **B.** 2 GB is the minimum amount specified by Microsoft.
☒ **A** is incorrect because this is the amount of RAM required for a 32-bit installation of Windows 10. **C** is incorrect because this is the amount of RAM required for installing Windows 11. **D** is incorrect because neither Windows 10 nor 11 requires this much RAM for installation.

14. ☑ **A.** The computer will restart one or more times during Setup. It is normal for this to occur and nothing to worry about.
☒ **B, C,** and **D** are incorrect because these statements are false.

15. ☑ **D.** Windows PE (Windows Preinstallation Environment) is a bootable environment that gives operating system support during three types of operations: installing Windows, troubleshooting, and recovery.
☒ **A** is incorrect because Safe Mode is a special limited functionality boot mode for troubleshooting. **B** is incorrect because USMT is a tool for migrating user settings and data. **C** is incorrect because NTFS is a file system.

Post-Installation Tasks

16. ☑ **B.** Prevention of software piracy is the purpose of Microsoft Product Activation.
☒ **A, C,** and **D** are incorrect because none of these is the purpose of MPA.

17. ☑ **C.** Windows being disabled is the immediate consequence of not completing the activation process for Windows within the required time.
☒ **A** is incorrect because there is a consequence. **B** is incorrect because Windows will not continue to work. **D** is incorrect because this may be a consequence of not registering.

18. ☑ **C.** Use the Settings app's Accounts section to create additional accounts.
☒ **A** is incorrect because there is no app named Registration. **B** is incorrect because there is no app named Programs. **D** is incorrect because there is no app named Sign-ins.

Installing and Upgrading macOS and Linux Operating Systems

19. ☑ **C.** Mac computers prompt the user to download an update from the App Store whenever one becomes available.

☒ **A** is incorrect because macOS is not available on retail DVDs. **B** is incorrect because you do not need to share your mailing address with Apple in order to receive an update. **D** is incorrect because Macs, like all operating systems, need updates periodically.

20. ☑ **D.** Downloading a distro and burning a bootable DVD costs nothing.

☒ **A, B,** and **C** are incorrect because most desktop distros of Linux are free. You should not have to pay anything to acquire one.

Chapter 5

Disk, File, and Application Management

CERTIFICATION OBJECTIVES

- **1102: 1.2** Given a scenario, use the appropriate Microsoft command-line tool
- **1102: 1.3** Given a scenario, use features and tools of the Microsoft Windows 10 operating system (OS)
- **1102: 1.4** Given a scenario, use the appropriate Microsoft Windows 10 Control Panel utility
- **1102: 1.7** Given a scenario, apply application installation and configuration concepts
- **1102: 1.8** Explain common OS types and their purposes
- **1102: 1.10** Identify common features and tools of the macOS/desktop OS
- **1102: 1.11** Identify common features and tools of the Linux client/desktop OS
- ✓ Two-Minute Drill
- **Q&A** Self Test

This chapter starts by covering disk management tools, both at the command line and in a graphical user interface (GUI). We focus mostly on Windows, but will also review some essential Mac disk management tools. We'll discuss file systems and attributes, contrasting Windows with Mac and Linux systems, and look at the tools and utilities each OS provides for file management. We wrap up by looking at installing, troubleshooting, and removing applications.

CERTIFICATION OBJECTIVES

- ***1102: 1.2*** *Given a scenario, use the appropriate Microsoft command-line tool*
- ***1102: 1.3*** *Given a scenario, use features and tools of the Microsoft Windows 10 operating system (OS)*
- ***1102: 1.10*** *Identify common features and tools of the macOS/desktop OS*

In Chapter 4 you learned about disk partitioning and file systems conceptually; now in this section you will learn how to manage disk partitions and file systems as a practical matter, using the actual GUI and command-line tools that you would use in the field. From CompTIA A+ 1102 exam Objective 1.3, you'll use the Disk Management tool. From 1102 exam Objective 1.2, you'll learn about the DISKPART command-line utility. From 1102 exam Objective 1.10, you'll learn about the Disk Utility in macOS.

exam watch

The CompTIA A+ 220-1102 exam does not cover dynamic disks, a Windows feature that enables you to create software RAIDs by foregoing traditional partitioning. Windows calls partitioned disks "basic disks" to differentiate them from dynamic disks. You don't need to study the alternative way dynamic disks work, so we don't cover them, but we do make passing mention to basic disks, meaning nondynamic ones.

Disk Management

PC technicians need to understand how to prepare a disk for use, a topic introduced in Chapter 4, which focused on OS installation. You learned in that chapter about master boot record (MBR) versus GUID partition table (GPT) partition management and commonly chosen file systems like New Technology File System (NTFS) for a Windows system.

The following sections expand on that knowledge via the Disk Management utility and some other tools in Windows, as well as equivalent tools in other operating systems.

Managing Disks in Windows

The main tool for managing disks in Windows is the Disk Management console, which lets you see disk drives as more than the drive letters, folders, and files you see in File Explorer. As with many Windows programs and features, there are several ways to launch Disk Management. For instance, it is a part of the Computer Management console, which you will find in Administrative Tools. You can also open the Disk Management console separately. Here are two ways to do that:

- Right-click the Start button and click Disk Management.
- Press WINDOWS KEY-R to open the Run dialog box, type **diskmgmt.msc**, and press ENTER.

Viewing a Disk

A basic disk has a single partition table that resides in the first physical sector. The partition table occupies a mere 64 bytes of the 512 bytes in the sector. This sector, called the MBR, also contains the initial boot program loaded by BIOS during startup. This program and the partition table are created or modified in this sector when someone partitions the disk. (Recall also that GPT is a more advanced alternative to MBR, available on some systems with Unified Extensible Firmware Interface [UEFI] firmware. Here, we are referring to both MBR and GPT generically as MBR for simplicity.)

Figure 5-1 shows Disk Management on a Windows computer with a single physical hard disk drive containing three volumes. Notice the volume information in the top pane displayed in labeled columns. The Status column shows the status for each volume. This

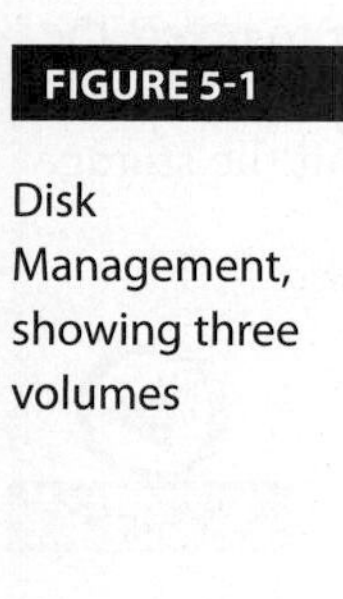

FIGURE 5-1 Disk Management, showing three volumes

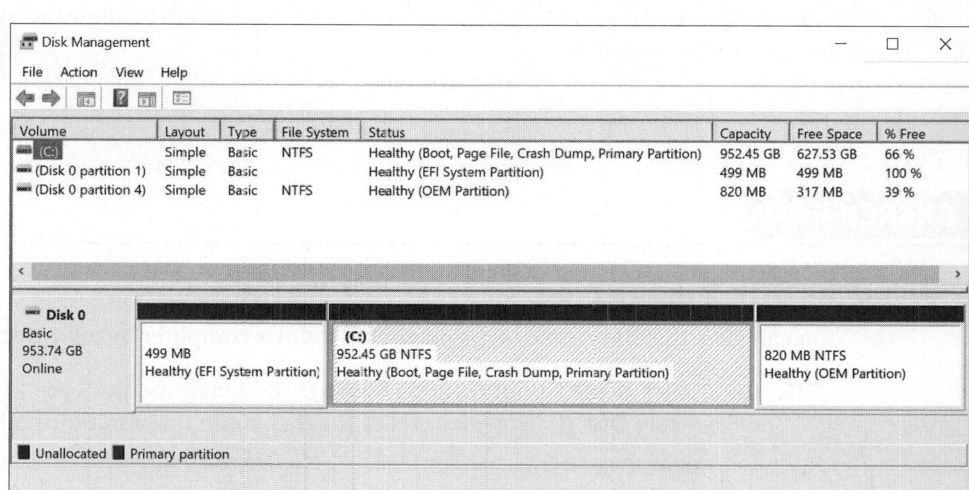

same information is displayed in the rectangle representing each volume in the graphical pane below the volume information. Information on the status of the physical disk (Disk 0) is on the left. If there were optical drives, they would appear on this list in the lower pane also, but this system doesn't have any. The status for the hard disk is Online.

If you have a Windows computer handy, open Disk Management and keep it open as you read through this section. You will have different disks and volumes, of course. You can easily simulate configurations that have multiple physical drives using a virtual machine such as VirtualBox (covered in Chapter 7).

Each volume of the basic disk in Figure 5-1 is shown with the Layout designation *simple*. A basic disk has a four-volume-per-disk limit (because, as you learned in Chapter 4, an MBR disk can be divided into no more than four primary partitions).

The CompTIA A+ 220-1102 exam objectives use the term "partition," as we did in Chapter 4. However, in Windows GUI tools such as Disk Management, you will see the terms *volume* and *partition* used loosely and interchangeably.

In Figure 5-1, the original volumes were probably created as an image by the manufacturer. The first volume is an EFI system partition. This type of partition is present only on systems that use the UEFI firmware interface. It holds some files needed for system startup, including boot loaders, device drivers for devices the firmware uses to boot, and some error logs. The second is the system volume, C:, where Windows was installed at the factory. The third is a recovery volume created by the computer manufacturer (Dell) to allow the user to revert the disk to a factory-installed state.

Exercise 5-1 walks you through opening Disk Management and checking out the storage type.

EXERCISE 5-1

Viewing the Disk Storage Type

You can view the disk storage type on your Windows computer by following these steps.

1. Right-click the Start button and choose Disk Management. There will be a short delay while Disk Management reads the disk configuration information.
2. In Disk Management, look for Disk 0. Disk 0 is normally your first internal hard disk drive, and usually the one from which Windows boots. Just below the words "Disk 0," you will see the storage type.

3. Determine the answers to these questions:
   - How many volumes are on Disk 0?
   - How many physical disks are in your computer?
   - What is the file system on the C: volume?
   - Are there any volumes that don't have letters assigned to them? What do you think they are for?
4. Leave Disk Management open.

Partitioning and Formatting

After installing a new hard disk (internal or external), look for it in Disk Management. It might already be partitioned and formatted, or it might be a blank slate ready for you to partition and format. In Figure 5-2, Disk 1 shows Unallocated, and there is no trace of it in the upper pane, where volumes are listed. That means you must partition and format it before you can use it. To get started with that, you can right-click it and choose New Simple Volume.

Exercise 5-2 walks you through creating a simple volume.

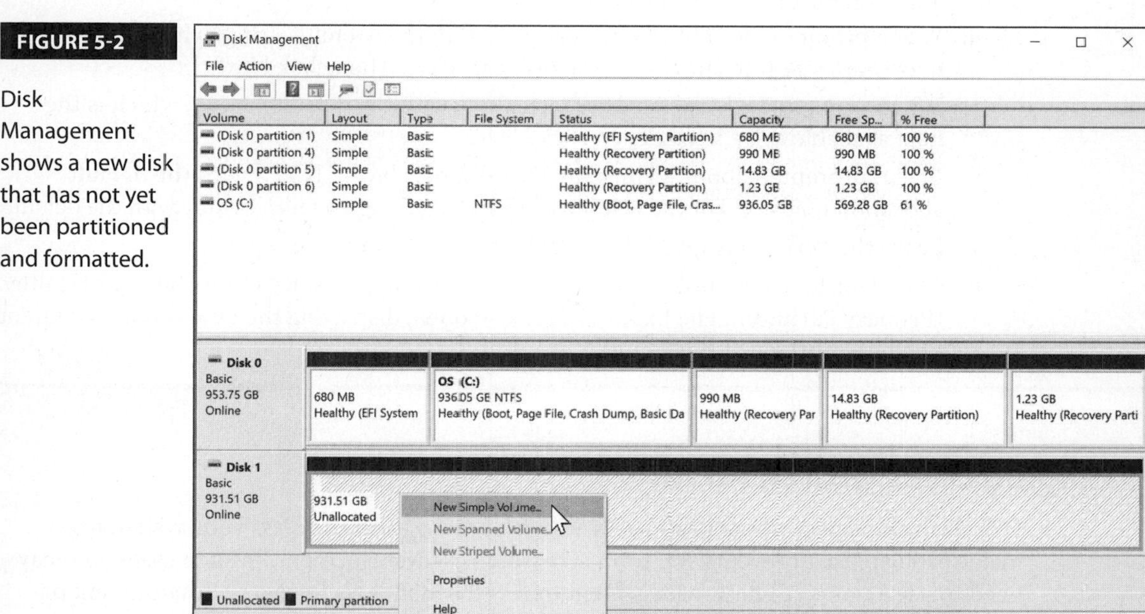

FIGURE 5-2 Disk Management shows a new disk that has not yet been partitioned and formatted.

EXERCISE 5-2

Creating a New Volume

In this exercise, you first remove any existing volumes from a disk, if needed, and then you create a new simple volume.

For this exercise you will need *one* of the following:

- A virtual machine running Windows configured for an additional virtual hard disk other than the one containing the OS.
- A PC running Windows that has an additional hard disk connected to it other than the one containing the OS and that either contains nothing you want to keep or already contains nothing.

1. From the Disk Management window, locate the disk you will be working with. Make sure it contains nothing you want to keep.
2. If a volume already appears in the lower portion of the Disk Management window (that is, if there is anything other than unallocated space on the extra disk), right-click the volume and click Delete Volume. Click Yes to confirm.
3. Right-click the unallocated space and click New Simple Volume. The New Simple Volume Wizard runs. Click Next.
4. When prompted for the volume size, stay with the default setting, which is the maximum size (the entire physical disk capacity). Then click Next.
5. When prompted to assign a drive letter, stay with the default setting, which is the next available drive letter. Then click Next.
6. When prompted about formatting the volume, choose NTFS with the default allocation unit size. For the volume label, use anything you like, or stay with the default.
7. Leave the Perform A Quick Format check box selected. Click Next.
8. Click Finish. After a brief pause, the new volume appears. Its status shows as Healthy (Primary Partition). File Explorer may also open, displaying the new volume's content (which is nothing at this point).

Managing Disks with DISKPART

Disk Management is where you usually will go to manage disks unless your system has a major problem that prevents you from accessing Disk Management. In such cases you may need to use a non-GUI disk management tool in the Windows Recovery Environment or Windows Safe Mode with Command Prompt. You will learn about those in Chapter 16. However, since we're working with disks in this chapter, we want to at least mention the utility available in those environments for managing disks: DISKPART.

DISKPART is an advanced utility for disk management. You can run it at a command prompt or use it in automated scripts. If you enter the command **diskpart** at a command prompt, it actually loads its own command interpreter with a prompt that looks like this: DISKPART>. At this prompt, you enter commands that DISKPART accepts with the correct syntax, and then you type **exit** to exit from DISKPART.

Once you get into DISKPART, you can type **help** for a list of commands that it accepts. However, DISKPART is not intuitive to use, and mistakes can be costly in terms of lost data, so we recommend you study an online reference for the command before attempting to use it for anything more than simply viewing current disk settings. Exercise 5-3 provides the most cursory of looks at the utility; don't go far beyond that without some study.

EXERCISE 5-3

Using DISKPART

In this exercise, you will use DISKPART to check out your system's volumes. You can use a virtual machine for this exercise if you like.

1. Open a command-prompt window with administrative privileges. One way to do this is to right-click the Start button and choose Command Prompt (Admin) or Windows PowerShell (Admin).
2. Type **diskpart** and press ENTER. Notice that the prompt changes to DISKPART>.
3. Type **help** and press ENTER. You see a list of commands. Notice that the list command displays a list of objects.
4. Type **list** and press ENTER. A list of valid parameters for that command appears.
5. Type **list disk** and press ENTER. A list of the physical disks on your system appears. This list is similar to the lower pane in Disk Management.
6. Type **list volume** and press ENTER. A list of volumes appears. This list is similar to the upper pane in Disk Management. Note the volume number for the volume you created in Exercise 5-2. (Ours is Volume 2.)
7. Type **select volume 2** (or whatever number you noted in Step 6) and press ENTER. Be careful; make sure you have selected the empty volume from Exercise 5-2, not your system volume, or you could be in real trouble.

```
DISKPART> list volume

  Volume ###  Ltr  Label        Fs     Type        Size     Status     Info
  ----------  ---  -----------  -----  ----------  -------  ---------  --------
  Volume 0         System Rese  NTFS   Partition    549 MB  Healthy    System
  Volume 1     C                NTFS   Partition     49 GB  Healthy    Boot
  Volume 2     D   New Volume   NTFS   Partition     49 GB  Healthy

DISKPART> _
```

8. Type **help format** and press ENTER. You see the syntax for formatting a volume.
9. Type **format fs=ntfs label="Ready" quick** and press ENTER.
10. Type **exit** and press ENTER.
11. Close the Command Prompt or Windows PowerShell window.
12. Open This PC and note the volume label on the empty drive (Ready).

Managing Disks in macOS

In macOS, the *Disk Utility* program is the equivalent of Disk Management in Windows. To access it, click the Launchpad icon on the Dock, then click the Other folder, and then click Disk Utility. The main screen is shown in Figure 5-3. The navigation pane on the left enables you to select physical disks (top level of the hierarchy) and logical volumes on them. In Figure 5-3 there is only one physical disk and only one volume on it.

As you can see, across the top of the window are seven icons:

- **Volume** Adjusts the partitions on a drive that uses Apple File System (APFS), which is the default file system for solid-state drives on newer versions of macOS.
- **First Aid** Diagnoses and fixes disk problems.
- **Partition** Allows you to view and adjust partitions, including creating new partitions and resizing existing ones. If this command isn't available, make sure you have selected a physical disk in the navigation pane.

FIGURE 5-3

The macOS Disk Utility

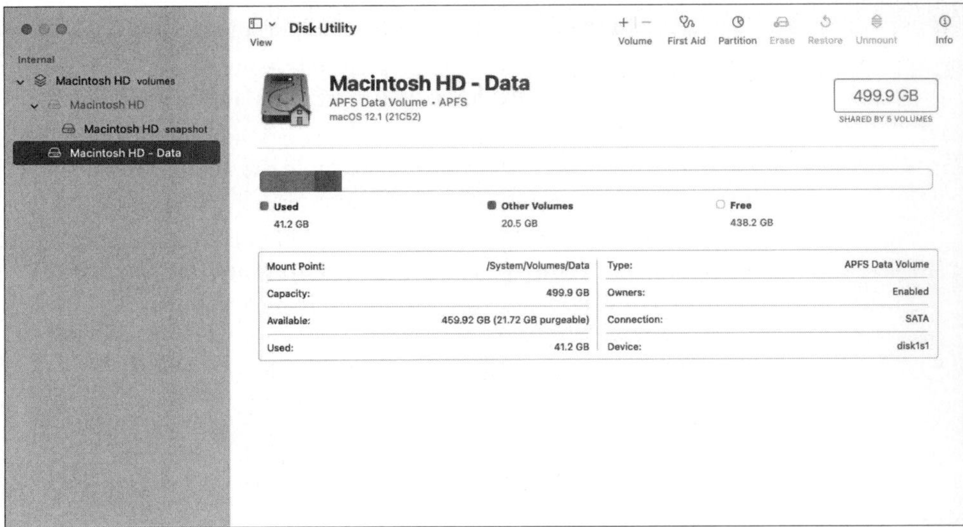

- **Erase** Wipes out existing data on a volume. This isn't available for the system volume, for safety reasons.
- **Restore** Restores the volume to a saved earlier snapshot of it.
- **Unmount** Disconnects the volume logically from the OS. This one also isn't available for the system volume.
- **Info** Provides information about the selected disk or volume.

Linux has a similar utility called Disks, but it is not covered on the current CompTIA A+ exams.

SCENARIO & SOLUTION	
How do you open Disk Management without going through Computer Management?	You can run the **diskmgmt.msc** command, or you can right-click the Start button and choose Disk Management.
You have added a new hard disk, but it doesn't show up in the Volume list in Disk Management. Why?	You must partition and format it first.
You need to manage the installed disks on a Mac. What utility should you use?	Use the Disk Utility application.

CERTIFICATION OBJECTIVE

- ***1102: 1.8*** *Explain common OS types and their purposes*

This section explores portions of CompTIA A+ 1102 exam Objective 1.8 relating to file systems. You'll learn about the features, limitations, and compatibility issues among all the file systems covered in the exam objectives, including FAT32, exFAT, NTFS, APFS, ext3, and etx4.

File Systems

File management begins with understanding the underlying file system that supports saving, retrieving, deleting, and other management tasks for files. Windows supports several file systems, so we will compare them. Although most file management tasks remain the same across all the file systems supported by Windows, you will learn about features that are not available in all of these file systems.

Windows fully supports several file systems, including NTFS, FAT16 (often simply called File Allocation Table, or FAT), and FAT32. The Format utility in Windows can format a drive in any of these file systems. Some drive types also permit additional file systems, such as exFAT for flash drives.

A partition can be formatted with only one file system at a time, and changing to a different file system generally requires reformatting, erasing all current content. The General tab of a drive's Properties dialog box will show which file system is on a drive.

Windows can use the FAT, FAT32, and NTFS file systems on any volume. Once you partition a disk, you may format it with any of these file systems.

General Characteristics of a File System

Before we look at individual file systems, let's review what differentiates one file system from another.

Number of Bits in the Table

Each file system maintains a table that tells what is stored in each physical location on the disk. Depending on the file system, this may be called the *file allocation table (FAT)* or the *master file table (MFT)*. Because the file system itself is also called FAT, sometimes this table is referred to redundantly as the *FAT table*. The table uses a certain number of binary digits to describe each addressable location on the disk. FAT16 is a 16-bit system, whereas FAT32 and NTFS are both 32-bit file systems. The more bits, the more addressable locations, and therefore the larger the maximum volume capacity.

Cluster Size

Cluster size is not covered on the current CompTIA A+ exams, but it is a practical consideration you may need to know about.

Each disk's storage is divided into sectors of 512 bytes each. However, if a file system were to address each sector individually, the file allocation table would run out of space quickly. For example, a 16-bit FAT would only be able to store information for about 33.5 MB (2^{16} bytes times 512 bytes). Therefore, sectors are grouped into *clusters,* also called *allocation units*. A cluster is the smallest individually addressable storage unit on the disk. Each entry in the FAT or MFT refers to the starting location of a different cluster.

When you format a disk, you can choose a cluster size, or you can accept the default cluster size, which is based on the volume size. For example, an NTFS drive with a volume size of up to 16 TB uses a default cluster size of 4 KB (eight sectors); higher volume sizes use larger clusters.

Why are there different cluster sizes? It's primarily a holdover from when disk capacity was more expensive and lesser than it is today. When the disk size is small, the default cluster size is small because that's preferable. A smaller cluster size means less wasted space on a volume. For example, suppose a file with a size of 7 KB is stored on a disk. On a disk with 4-KB clusters (that is, eight sectors per cluster), it occupies 8 KB. But on a disk with 64-KB clusters (that is, 128 sectors per cluster), it occupies 64 KB. If you store a lot of small files, this difference can really add up. However, as the volume size grows, the clusters must get larger to circumvent addressing limitations.

Special Features

Besides the raw storage capacity, a file system can also have special features, such as compression, error correction, and security encryption. NTFS is a much more feature-rich file system than either FAT or FAT32. We'll explain its features later in the chapter.

FAT

The *FAT file system* has been around for several decades and was the file system used in the original MS-DOS operating system. We have long been tempted to declare this file system dead or irrelevant, but it is still around, supported by almost any operating system you may encounter. That makes it great for compatibility across different platforms. It is also used on small storage devices because it takes up very little space on the disk for its own use (overhead) as compared to NTFS, which takes up a great deal of space, even while providing many benefits in exchange. We also include it in this discussion because FAT32 is listed in CompTIA A+ 1102 exam Objective 1.8, and FAT, FAT12, FAT16, and FAT32 are all in the Acronyms list for both exams.

FAT File System Components

When Windows formats a disk with the FAT file system, it places the FAT file system's three primary components on the disk. These components are the boot record, the FAT table, and the root directory. They reside at the very beginning of the disk, in an area called the *system area*. The space beyond the system area is the *data area*, which can hold files and subdirectories.

- **Boot record** The *boot record*, or *boot sector*, is the first physical sector on a FAT-formatted hard drive partition. The boot record contains information about the OS used to format the disk and other file system information. It also contains the boot code involved in the boot process, as described earlier.
- **FAT table** FAT is the file system component in which the OS creates a table that serves as a map of where files reside on disk.
- **Root directory** A *directory* (also commonly called a *folder*) is an organizing unit for file storage. The *root directory* is the top-level directory on the volume and the only

one created during formatting. The entries in a directory point to files and to the next level of directories. The root directory therefore contains information about any files stored at the top level of the volume and also about any folders stored at the top level.

FAT16

The *FAT16* file system, as implemented in the versions of Windows included in this book, is limited to 65,525 clusters (because of the 16-bit size of its file allocation table, as we discussed earlier). That means its maximum capacity per volume is 4 GB, which is inadequate for today's hard disks. You won't see FAT16 in use much anymore.

FAT32

The *FAT32* file system was introduced by Microsoft in a special release of Windows 95, over 23 years ago. This improved version of the FAT file system can format larger hard disk partitions (up to 2 TB) and allocates disk space more efficiently. A FAT32-formatted partition will have a FAT table and root directory, but the FAT table holds 32-bit entries, and there are changes in how it positions the root directory. The root directory on both FAT12 and FAT16 was a single point of failure since it could only reside in the system area. The FAT32 file system allows the OS to back up the root directory to the data portion of the disk and to use this backup in case the first copy fails.

NTFS

The primary file system used in Windows is *New Technology File System (NTFS)*. From its beginnings back in a 1993 version of Windows known as Windows NT, NTFS has been a much more advanced file system than any form of the FAT file system.

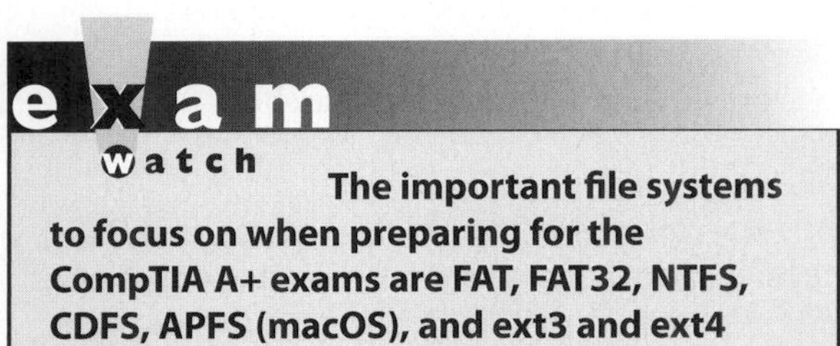

The important file systems to focus on when preparing for the CompTIA A+ exams are FAT, FAT32, NTFS, CDFS, APFS (macOS), and ext3 and ext4 (Linux).

Master File Table

In contrast to the FAT file system, NTFS has a far more sophisticated structure, using an expandable MFT. This makes the file system adaptable to future changes. NTFS uses the MFT to store a transaction-based database, with all file accesses treated as transactions, and if a transaction is not complete, NTFS will roll back to the last successful transaction, making the file system more stable.

Fault Tolerance

In another improved feature, NTFS also avoids saving files to physically damaged portions of a disk, called bad sectors. This is a form of fault tolerance.

NTFS on Small-Capacity Media

You may format a small hard disk partition with NTFS, but because of the overhead space requirements, the smallest recommended size is 10 MB. That's megabytes, not terabytes, so it is pretty much a nonissue today.

As much as we favor NTFS for all its advanced features, it is very much a Microsoft-only file system. FAT32, however, is supported by many operating systems, including macOS and variations of Unix and Linux. When we want to use an external hard drive or USB flash drive on our PC, as well as on our Apple iMac, we make sure to format it with FAT32.

NTFS Indexing

The indexing service is part of Windows and speeds up file searches on NTFS volumes. If this service is on, indexing of any folder that has the index attribute turned on will occur so that future searches of that folder will be faster.

NTFS Compression

NTFS supports *file and folder compression* to save disk space, using an algorithm to reduce the size of a file as it writes it to disk. You can turn it on for an individual file or for the entire contents of a folder, and this is a very nice feature if you are running low on disk space. However, the trade-off is that it takes Windows more time to write a file to disk when it has to compress it, and also more time to expand a compressed file as it brings it into memory when you open the file.

NTFS Security Features

NTFS offers encryption at the file and folder level in a feature called *Encrypting File System (EFS)*. *Encryption* is the conversion of data into a special format that cannot be read by anyone unless they have a software key to convert it back into its usable form. The encryption key for EFS is the user's authentication. Therefore, once a user encrypts a file or folder, only someone logged on with the same user account can access it.

Not all editions of Windows support EFS; look for it only in Windows Pro, Enterprise, and Education editions.

In addition, on NTFS volumes you can apply permissions to folders and files for added security. A *permission* is the authorization of a person or group to access a resource—in this case, a file or folder—and take certain actions, such as reading, changing, or deleting. This is one of the most important differences between NTFS and FAT file systems.

The Properties dialog box of each folder and file on a drive formatted with NTFS will have a Security tab showing the permissions assigned to that folder or file. Learn more about file and folder permissions in Chapter 21.

While Windows uses the term "folder" and shows a folder icon in the GUI, many of the dialog boxes and messages continue to use the old term "directory" for what we now know as a disk folder. People frequently use these two terms interchangeably. In this book, we generally use "folder" when working in the GUI and "directory" when working from the command line.

exFAT

Extended File Allocation Table (exFAT) is not intended for use on hard drives, but rather as a replacement for FAT32 on small solid-state storage devices such as USB flash drives and solid-state drive (SSD) cards. The Format utility in Windows makes it available as an option when you are formatting SSDs, but not when formatting regular hard drives.

The exFAT file system includes the following advantages over FAT32:

- A maximum volume size of 256 TB.
- A single folder/directory can hold up to 100 high-definition movies, 60 hours of high-definition audio, or 4,000 RAW images. A *RAW image* file contains unprocessed image data from a digital camera, image scanner, or digital movie scanner.
- Faster file saves so that solid-state devices can save at their full speed.
- Cross-platform interoperation with many operating systems; Apple added exFAT support to macOS beginning with Snow Leopard (10.6.5).
- The file system is extensible, meaning that manufacturers can customize it for new device characteristics.

Resilient File System

Resilient File System (ReFS) is a newer file system expected to replace the NTFS file system on Windows Server. It retains many of the features of the NTFS file system, but discards some features and adds many others for servers to support really large hard drives and RAID-style systems with very advanced performance and fault tolerance support.

You will not see questions concerning the Resilient File System on the CompTIA A+ 220-1101 or 220-1102 exam. In fact, you will not see this file system on desktop computers for a while since it is currently available only on Windows Server products. However, what appears on Windows Server products eventually trickles down to the desktop products, so you will eventually see it on the job.

Mac File Systems

For many years, macOS's native file system was Hierarchical File System Plus (HFS+). That's the file system that the system drive comes with on older Macs, with the OS preinstalled on it.

Newer Macs, especially those with solid-state drives, use a new file system called *Apple File System (APFS)*. It is optimized for SSDs and supports snapshots and encryption. It's available only on systems with macOS Sierra (10.12.4 and later).

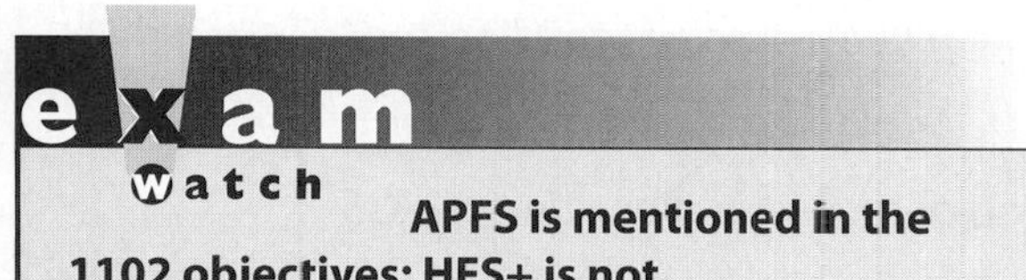

APFS is mentioned in the 1102 objectives; HFS+ is not.

macOS also supports FAT32 and exFAT (for flash drives). It reads NTFS file systems but can't write to them. macOS doesn't read any of the Linux file systems (ext2, ext3, or ext4)—which is ironic since macOS and Linux are based on the same core.

Linux File Systems

Linux's native file system is *third extended filesystem (ext3)* or *fourth extended filesystem (ext4)*. We reviewed the differences between ext3 and ext4 in Chapter 4 in the section "File Systems for Linux and macOS." Turn back there now if you need a reminder.

In addition, Linux can support ext2 (for older Linux system compatibility), FAT (for broad compatibility with nearly every kind of system), NTFS (for compatibility with modern Windows systems), and an encrypted version of ext4. It can also read and write HFS+ (but doesn't format disks using it). It doesn't read or write APFS unless you install a special driver.

SCENARIO & SOLUTION	
What is the preferred file system for Windows?	NTFS is the preferred Windows file system.
Which file system is best for an external drive that will be shared among Windows, macOS, and Linux computers?	FAT32 is the safest choice because they all accept that. macOS has only read-only support for NTFS and doesn't read ext3 or ext4, while Windows doesn't support HFS+ or APFS.
Which file system is best for a USB flash drive that will be used on both macOS and Windows systems?	exFAT is a good choice because both platforms read and write it natively for flash drives. FAT32 would also work, but exFAT has more features.
Why wouldn't you always use the smallest cluster size when formatting a disk?	A smaller cluster size may not allow for large enough volumes. For example, a FAT32 volume with 4-KB clusters can be a maximum of 8 GB. This is less of an issue on NTFS volumes; the limits are much higher.

CERTIFICATION OBJECTIVES

- ***1102: 1.2*** *Given a scenario, use the appropriate Microsoft command line-tool*
- ***1102: 1.4*** *Given a scenario, use the appropriate Microsoft Windows 10 Control Panel utility*
- ***1102: 1.11*** *Identify common features and tools of the Linux client/desktop OS*

This section starts out by explaining how to change File Explorer folder options, such as showing or hiding protected system files (from 1102 exam Objective 1.4). This section also covers working with the command-line interface, both in Windows (1102 exam Objective 1.2) and in Linux (1102 exam Objective 1.11).

File Management

File management is an end-user skill, so it's assumed background knowledge for technicians. Make sure you can move, copy, rename, delete, and restore files and folders, as well as create, delete, and rename folders. We aren't going to go into those skills in detail here. Instead, the following sections look at some specific file management topics mentioned on the 1102 exam.

Setting File Explorer Folder Options

File Explorer can be customized to display files and folders in different ways. The 1102 exam Objective 1.4 lists four important folder options that you should be able to access: View Hidden Files, Hide Extensions For Known File Types, General Options, and View Options:

- **View Hidden Files** This turns on/off the display of any files or folders that have the Hidden attribute set. This is a simple on/off, and you can set it directly from the File Explorer ribbon's View tab.
- **Hide Extensions For Known File Types** This turns on/off the display of file extensions if the particular extension is registered in Windows as a "known" type—that is, if Windows knows what program a data file belongs to or identifies it as an executable or a helper file for an executable. This setting can also be changed directly from the File Explorer ribbon.
- **General Options** You can open a Folder Options dialog box, and in it is a General tab. On the General tab you can control whether each folder is opened in the same window or its own window, whether you single-click or double-click to open an item, and whether or not frequently and recently used files are shown in Quick Access.
- **View Options** On the View tab of the Folder Options dialog box, you can adjust dozens of advanced settings that affect how File Explorer works in subtle ways. See Figure 5-4.

FIGURE 5-4

File Explorer's Properties box displaying the View tab.

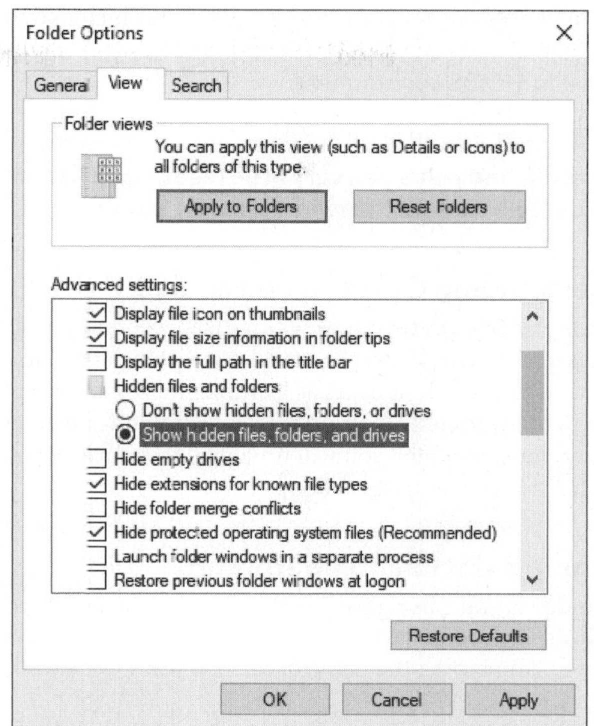

File Management at the Windows Command Prompt

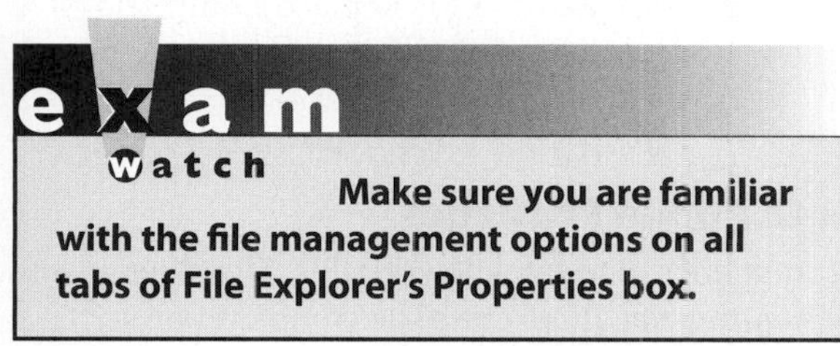

Make sure you are familiar with the file management options on all tabs of File Explorer's Properties box.

As we noted earlier, this chapter doesn't cover file management skills in the Windows GUI because we're assuming that by the time you get to the point where you are studying for a CompTIA A+ exam, you are already a competent Windows user with the requisite user skills. Being able to move, copy, rename, and delete files and folders in File Explorer is assumed.

However, the same cannot be said for file management at a command prompt. Many people who are otherwise Windows power users today lack this skill, simply because they have grown up in a computing environment where it wasn't needed. So let's spend some time reviewing command-line file management.

Why Use a Command Prompt?

Back in the days of MS-DOS, the command line was the only interface available for running programs and managing files. It persists today in the form of the Command

Prompt and Windows PowerShell applications included in Windows. Using one of these applications, you can issue commands in a text-prompt environment that is similar to that original MS-DOS environment.

Avoid doing routine file management from the command line. Text-mode commands give you very little feedback, and a minor typo can result in disaster. Use File Explorer instead whenever possible.

Understanding Cmd and PowerShell

A *command interpreter* is a program that accepts your typed commands. You have two choices of command interpreters when working at a command prompt. Cmd is the basic command prompt. It appears as Command Prompt on the Start button's right-click menu. Windows PowerShell is a more robust command-line interface with many additional features, most of which you will probably never use. Either one works equally well for the basic tasks we cover in this book.

Opening a Command Interpreter

In Windows, you can right-click the Start button and choose Command Prompt or Windows PowerShell, whichever one appears there. (If the one you want isn't the default, you can begin typing the name of the one you want and then select it from the search results.)

Changing the Default Command Interpreter

Here's how to change the default command interpreter in Windows 10: Right-click the taskbar and choose Taskbar Settings. Drag the slider to on or off for Replace Command Prompt with Windows PowerShell in the menu when I right-click the start button Or press Windows Key+X.

Elevating a Command Interpreter to Admin Privileges

Most of the time the regular command-prompt environment will work fine. However, if you see a message that *the requested operation requires elevation,* close the command prompt window and reopen it using administrator privileges. (That's most likely to occur when you are using network-related commands.) To open an elevated command prompt, right-click the Start button and click Command Prompt (Admin) or Windows PowerShell (Admin).

Managing Files at the Command Prompt

There are two commands for creating and deleting directories (folders) at a command prompt: md (Make Directory) and rmdir (Remove Directory). Use the dir (directory) command to view listings of files and directories. Move around the directory hierarchy at a command prompt using the **cd** (Change Directory) command. Use two dots together (..) to indicate the directory immediately above the current directory. You can use these in many command-line commands. For instance, if you only want to move up one level, type **cd ..** and press ENTER. (Commands are not case sensitive; most people use lowercase when typing them because it is easier.)

You can use wildcards from a command prompt. The most useful one is the asterisk (*). Use the asterisk to represent one or more characters in a filename or extension. For instance, enter the command **dir *.exe** to see a listing of all files in the current directory ending with "exe." Using *.* will select all files and directories. Use a question mark to indicate a single character.

When you are working at a command prompt, the previous commands and messages remain on the screen until they scroll off. To clear this information from the screen, use the cls (clear screen) command.

When you want to copy files, you have a choice of commands. The simplest is copy, which is a very, very old command that does not understand directories. To use this command on files in different directories, you must enter the path to the directory or directories in the command. It helps to first make either the source directory or the target directory current before using this command. We rarely use copy because of its limits. We prefer the **xcopy** command because it is a more advanced command that understands directories. In fact, you can tell xcopy to copy the contents of a directory simply by giving the directory name. The simple syntax for both commands is *<command>* *<from_source>* *<to_destination>*. Both copy and xcopy will accept either filenames or folder names in the source and destination arguments. For instance, the command **xcopy monday tuesday** can be entered to copy the contents of the folder Monday into the folder Tuesday.

A far more advanced command is *Robust File Copy,* which has the command name *robocopy*. It is a folder copier, meaning that you must enter folder names as the source and destination arguments. It will not accept filenames or wildcard characters in the source or destination arguments, although it copies all the files within the specified folder. In addition, robocopy has a list of advanced features, such as the ability to stop a copy operation that is interrupted by a disconnected network. It then resumes upon reconnection with the network. It also allows you to mirror two entire folder structures. This is a handy but tricky feature, because those files on the destination that are no longer present on the source will be deleted from the destination. There are many more robocopy features—all of which are accessed with the appropriate arguments. A simple example of a command that would mirror the DATA folder on two different drives is robocopy c:\data d:\data /mir.

Exercise 5-4 walks you through using various command-line commands for managing files and folders. One thing to notice as you complete this exercise is the /? switch, which gives you information about any command that you append it to at the command line.

EXERCISE 5-4

Managing Directories and Files at a Command Prompt

Practice working with directories and files from a command prompt.

1. Open a Command Prompt window, and note the location shown on the prompt. If you opened a standard-permissions command prompt, the active location is the user folder for the currently signed-in user, like this: C:\Users\Faithe. If you opened an elevated (admin) command prompt, it is C:\Windows\System32.
2. Type **help** and press ENTER. A list of all valid commands appears, but it scrolls by very quickly. Scroll the window upward so you can see the whole list, and then scroll down again to the prompt.
3. Type **dir /?** and press ENTER. An explanation of all the switches for the **dir** command appears. Note that one of them is /w for the wide list format.
4. Type **dir /w** and press ENTER. A listing of files and directories within the directory will display. The /w switch uses a compact, multicolumn listing.
5. Type the command again with the pause switch: **dir /p**. If prompted, press the SPACEBAR to advance the display one screen at a time to the end of the listing.
6. Type the clear screen command, **cls**, and press ENTER to clear the screen.
7. Type **cd ** and press ENTER to go to the root directory.
8. Type **cd %homepath%** and press ENTER to go to the home directory for the signed-in user.
9. Type **cd documents** and press ENTER to change to the Documents directory. Because it is a subdirectory of the current location, you can just use its name, rather than its full path.
10. Type **md testdata** and press ENTER. This creates a new directory in the Documents directory.
11. Type **copy nul > file.txt** and press ENTER. That creates a blank text file just to have a file to work with.
12. Type **copy file.txt testdata** and press ENTER. That copies the new file into the testdata directory.
13. Type **del file.txt** and press ENTER.
14. Type **rd testdata** and press ENTER. You get an error because only empty directories can be removed.
15. Type **del testdata*.*** and press ENTER.
16. Type **Y** and press ENTER to confirm.
17. Type **rd testdata** and press ENTER. This time it is removed.

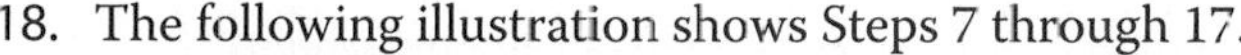

18. The following illustration shows Steps 7 through 17.

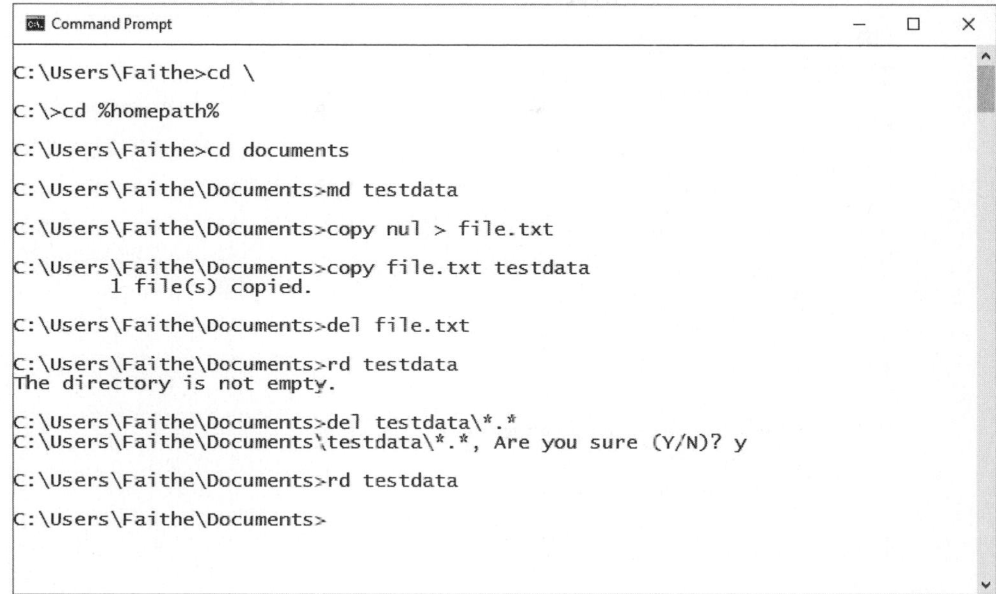

Command Prompt
C:\Users\Faithe>cd \
C:\>cd %homepath%
C:\Users\Faithe>cd documents
C:\Users\Faithe\Documents>md testdata
C:\Users\Faithe\Documents>copy nul > file.txt
C:\Users\Faithe\Documents>copy file.txt testdata
1 file(s) copied.
C:\Users\Faithe\Documents>del file.txt
C:\Users\Faithe\Documents>rd testdata
The directory is not empty.
C:\Users\Faithe\Documents>del testdata*.*
C:\Users\Faithe\Documents\testdata*.*, Are you sure (Y/N)? y
C:\Users\Faithe\Documents>rd testdata
C:\Users\Faithe\Documents>

19. Type **exit** and press ENTER to close the Command Prompt window.

Checking a Disk for Errors from a Command Prompt

The chkdsk (Check Disk) command is the text-mode version of the GUI Error Checking program you can access from the Tools page of the Properties dialog box for a disk. It checks disks for physical and logical errors. You must use an elevated command prompt to run this utility. Figure 5-5 shows a chkdsk operation in progress.

Running chkdsk without the /f parameter only analyzes the disk. It makes no corrections. If errors are found, rerun the command with the /f parameter and it will fix disk errors. Use the /r parameter together with the /f parameter, and chkdsk will both fix the disk errors and attempt to recover the data in the bad space by moving it.

If the volume is in use (as is always the case with drive C:), you might see a message asking if you would like to schedule the volume to be checked during the next system restart. Press Y and ENTER to schedule this. Be aware that chkdsk can take as much as an hour or more to check and repair a large hard drive.

FIGURE 5-5 A chkdsk check underway via an elevated Command Prompt window

```
Administrator: Command Prompt - chkdsk
Microsoft Windows [Version 10.0.10586]
(c) 2015 Microsoft Corporation. All rights reserved.

C:\WINDOWS\system32>chkdsk
The type of the file system is NTFS.
Volume label is OS.

WARNING!  /F parameter not specified.
Running CHKDSK in read-only mode.

Stage 1: Examining basic file system structure ...

  526592 file records processed.

File verification completed.

  15703 large file records processed.

  0 bad file records processed.

Stage 2: Examining file name linkage ...
Progress: 578967 of 663130 done; Stage: 87%; Total: 75%; ETA:   0:00:54 ...
```

Formatting a Disk from a Command-Line Interface

The **format** command enables you to format a hard drive or other media from a command prompt. Once again, the preferred way is to format from the GUI, where you are less likely to make an error when doing this. The choice of GUI tool is either the Disk Management console or File Explorer.

Figure 5-6 shows the command for formatting the D: drive using Windows PowerShell, a command-line environment. You can also use the standard command prompt (in Admin mode). Notice that it does not proceed until you press Y. Press N to cancel. This command

FIGURE 5-6

Press Y to continue with the formatting of the D: drive.

```
Administrator: Windows PowerShell
Windows PowerShell
Copyright (C) Microsoft Corporation. All rights reserved.

PS C:\WINDOWS\system32> format D:
The type of the file system is NTFS.
Enter current volume label for drive D: New Volume

WARNING, ALL DATA ON NON-REMOVABLE DISK
DRIVE D: WILL BE LOST!
Proceed with Format (Y/N)?
```

will wipe out the contents of the drive. Using the proper syntax, you can format a hard drive with any of the file systems supported by Windows for the target disk.

Checking System Files with sfc

System files have very privileged access to your computer. Therefore, malicious software (malware) targets system files so that it can have the same access. (More on malware when we describe security threats in Chapter 22.) At one time, system files were easy targets for such malware, but recent versions of Windows come with protections, both at the file system level (through assigned permissions) and using a service that protects system files.

Windows Resource Protection (WRP) is a Windows component that maintains a cache of protected files. If a file is somehow damaged, WRP will replace it with an undamaged copy from the cache. It also provides similar protection for registry keys. Learn more about the Windows registry in Chapter 6.

The *System File Checker (SFC)* is a handy utility that uses the WRP service to scan and verify the versions of all protected system files. The syntax for this program is as follows:

```
sfc [scannow] [scanonce] [scanboot] [revert] [purgecache] [cachesize=x]
```

When you run the **sfc** command with the /scannow parameter, you will see a message box showing a progress bar while it checks that all protected Windows files are intact and in their original versions. If SFC finds any files that do not comply, it will replace them with the correct signed file from the cache.

Using winver

The **winver** command is very simple: it displays the current Windows version. However, one thing you may not expect is that it doesn't display the information at the command prompt; it opens a GUI window with that information.

Using gpupdate and gpresult

IT professionals often use Microsoft's Group Policy Editor to make system or security changes to multiple networked PCs at the same time. Normally you would use the Local Group Policy Editor (gpedit.msc) via a Microsoft Management Console (MMC) snap-in, which is explained in Chapter 6. However, when that's not possible for some reason, you might need to make Group Policy changes via the command prompt. There are two commands you should know: gpupdate and gpresult.

The **gpupdate** command refreshes a Windows computer's policies. Use it at an Admin command line, and type **gpupdate /force**. This forces an update of policies, even if there is no expected change. It refreshes the policies on a machine. Reboot after running this command so the refreshed policies will take effect.

The **gpresult** command shows the active policies (official name: Resultant Set of Policy [RSoP]) based on the current Group Policy settings in effect. This is useful because sometimes there are multiple layers of policy, with one of them modifying or contradicting another. Many switches are available; type **gpresult** and press ENTER to see them. One basic switch to try out is /R, which provides a summary.

exam watch

Make sure you know how to elevate a command prompt and how to use these commands: chkdsk, diskpart, format, gpupdate, gpresult, sfc, shutdown, **and all the copying-related commands (xcopy, copy, and robocopy). You will learn about networking-related command-line commands in Chapters 16 and 17.**

Managing Files at the Linux or macOS Command Prompt

Linux is a command-line environment at its basic level; the friendly GUI shell you see on top of it in distros like Ubuntu is just a façade. It's no wonder, then, that Linux has a broad selection of commands to work with at a command prompt—a larger and more robust set than Windows provides.

The 1102 exam Objective 1.11 references a list of basic Linux command-line commands. We'll look here at the ones that pertain to file and folder management, and others we'll save for upcoming chapters on PC troubleshooting, maintenance, security, and networking. Because both macOS and Linux are based on Unix, macOS and Linux have the same Terminal window capabilities and accept the same Linux commands, so you can use either macOS or Linux to practice the commands covered in this section.

Windows 11 has a Terminal app (not the same as the Terminal app in the other operating systems) that provides a multi-tabbed interface for running command lines. Windows 10 users can download it from the Microsoft Store.

Remember that commands in the macOS and Linux command environments are case-sensitive; commands in the Windows command environment are not.

Opening Terminal in Ubuntu Linux or macOS

The command-line interface in Linux is called Terminal. Press CTRL-ALT-T to open it, or click the Ubuntu icon in the upper-left corner, type **terminal**, and click the Terminal application. In macOS, click Launchpad | Other | Terminal to open a Terminal window. See Figure 5-7.

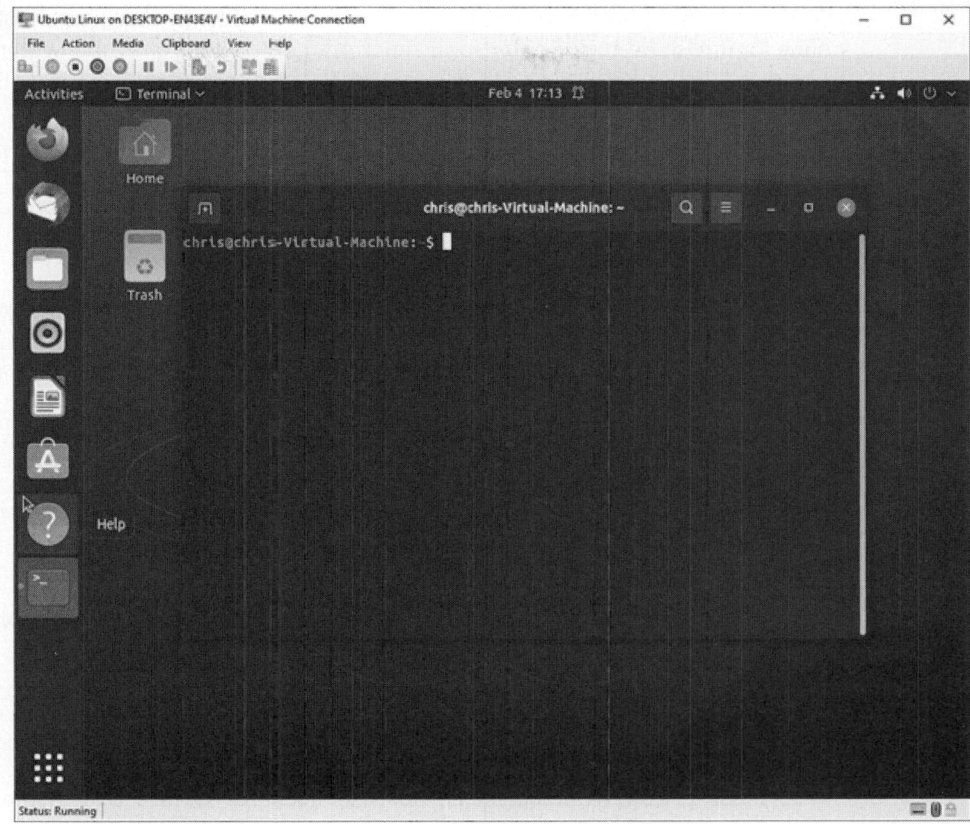

FIGURE 5-7 A Terminal window in Linux

Creating and Editing Files with the nano Editor

CompTIA A+ 1102 exam Objective 1.11 includes mention of the *nano* editor, which is a text editor designed to be used in the command-line environment in Linux or macOS. There is no modern equivalent for the Windows command prompt.

To enter the nano editor from a Terminal window, type **nano** and press ENTER.

To issue a command, hold down the CTRL key and type a letter. A status bar at the bottom of the nano window provides help for the most common activities. Here are a few:

- CTRL-X Exits
- CTRL-O Writes out (saves)
- CTRL-R Reads a file (opens it)
- CTRL-K Cuts the selected text
- CTRL-U Pastes the selected text

There isn't room in this book for a full discussion of nano, so check out a command reference online for it. Use Exercise 5-5 for some quick practice creating a text file with nano. You'll need to do this exercise, or create a file in some other way, to complete Exercise 5-6.

EXERCISE 5-5

Creating a Text File in nano

For this exercise you will need some version of Linux (such as Ubuntu) or macOS.

1. At the Linux desktop GUI, press CTRL-ALT-T. Or, at the macOS desktop, click Launchpad | Other | Terminal.
2. Type **nano** and press ENTER.
3. Type **I am typing this document.** and press ENTER twice.
4. Use the arrow keys on your keyboard to move the insertion point so it is positioned on the "d" in the word "document."
5. Type **excellent**. The word "document" moves over to make room.
6. Hold down the SHIFT key and press the LEFT ARROW key until the word "excellent" is selected.
7. Look in the navigation bar at the bottom. Notice that ^K is the shortcut for Cut Text. The ^ symbol represents the CTRL key.
8. Press CTRL-K to cut the word "excellent."
9. Press CTRL-O, which is the keyboard shortcut for Write Out, which means to save.
10. Type **excellent.txt** and press ENTER. This saves the file with that name.
11. Press CTRL-X to exit.

Using Basic File Management Commands in Linux or macOS

Linux does all the same file management tasks as Windows, but the commands and syntax are different. Table 5-1 compares the Windows and Linux commands. As you prepare for the 220-1102 exam, make sure you study each of the commands in the Linux column of this table, as well as its syntax. macOS is based on Unix (as is Linux), so its commands and syntax are the same as in Linux.

Make sure you know and can use the commands in Table 5-1.

TABLE 5-1

Comparison of Linux/macOS and Windows File Management Commands

Activity	Linux and macOS	Windows
List the content of the active location	ls	dir
Change to a different location on the same drive	cd	cd
Rename a file or folder	mv	ren
Delete a file	rm	del
Copy a file	cp	copy
Print current directory name	pwd	No equivalent command
Create a directory	mkdir	md or mkdir
Remove a directory	rmdir	rd or rmdir
Search for a file	find	dir -r
Search for a file that contains certain text	grep	findstr
Change security permission on a file or folder	chmod	No equivalent command
Change the owner of a file or folder	chown	No equivalent command
Concatenate files Display or print files	cat	type
Edit text	nano	No equivalent command
Display information about the file system	df	No equivalent command
Display the user manual (the help info) for a command	man	help
Display a real-time view of running processes and kernel-managed tasks	top	No equivalent command

EXERCISE 5-6

Managing Files at the Linux Terminal Window

This exercise begins where Exercise 5-5 ends and helps you explore many of the commands in Table 5-1. Complete Exercise 5-5 first so you have the file to work with for this exercise.

1. At the Linux desktop GUI, press CTRL-ALT-T to open a Terminal window. Or, on the macOS desktop, click Launchpad | Other | Terminal.
2. Type **ls** and press ENTER. Notice that excellent.txt is among the files listed from Exercise 5-5. The default location shown is the user folder for the currently logged-in

user. If you're working in Ubuntu Linux, the folder names are blue and the filenames are white.

3. Type **cp excellent.txt Documents** and press ENTER. This command copies the file into the Documents folder in your user folders.
4. Type **ls Documents**. A listing of the contents of the Documents folder appears. The copied file is there.
5. Type **cd Documents**. The active directory changes to that folder. Notice how the prompt changes to include /Documents.
6. Type **mv excellent.txt great.txt** and press ENTER. This renames the file.
7. Type **rm great.txt** and press ENTER. This deletes the file. Type **ls** and press ENTER to confirm that it is gone.
8. Type **mkdir Stuff** and press ENTER. This creates a new folder. Type **ls** and press ENTER to confirm that it exists.
9. Type **rmdir Stuff** and press ENTER. The new folder is deleted. Type **ls** and press ENTER to confirm it is gone.
10. Type **pwd** and press ENTER. The current folder's name appears. Its full path appears, not just the portion that was in the prompt.

The following illustration shows Steps 2–10.

```
faithe@Linux-Box: ~/Documents
faithe@Linux-Box:~$ ls
Desktop    Downloads          excellent.txt  Pictures  Templates
Documents  examples.desktop   Music          Public    Videos
faithe@Linux-Box:~$ cp excellent.txt Documents
faithe@Linux-Box:~$ ls Documents
excellent.txt  Private
faithe@Linux-Box:~$ cd Documents
faithe@Linux-Box:~/Documents$ mv excellent.txt great.txt
faithe@Linux-Box:~/Documents$ rm great.txt
faithe@Linux-Box:~/Documents$ ls
Private
faithe@Linux-Box:~/Documents$ mkdir Stuff
faithe@Linux-Box:~/Documents$ ls
Private  Stuff
faithe@Linux-Box:~/Documents$ rmdir Stuff
faithe@Linux-Box:~/Documents$ ls
Private
faithe@Linux-Box:~/Documents$ pwd
/home/faithe/Documents
```

11. Type **clear** and press ENTER. Notice that unlike in Windows, when the **cls** command actually cleared the screen, the **clear** command only scrolls the window down so you don't see your previous commands; you can scroll up to see them again if you like.
12. Type **cd** and press ENTER. You return to the top level of your user folders.
13. Type **find *.txt** and press ENTER. A list of files with that extension appears. (There is only one.)

14. Type **grep "excellent" *.txt** and press ENTER. The content of the excellent.txt file appears, showing the word *excellent* highlighted in red.
15. Close the Terminal window.

Using the Shutdown Command

Strictly speaking, the **shutdown** command is not a disk or file management tool, but rather a system management tool. It allows you to shut down the local computer or a remote computer using a command prompt, either immediately or after a certain delay you specify. Both Windows and Linux support this command (and so does macOS, since it's Linux based), although the syntax is different between the Linux/Mac and Windows versions.

Shutdown Command in Windows

The syntax and arguments for the **shutdown** command differ among Windows versions. Here's a good reference that explains the full syntax for each version: https://www.computerhope.com/shutdown.htm. In this section we'll provide a few basic switches that work in all versions.

To specify the kind of shutdown you want, use one of these switches:

- **/s** for a shutdown.
- **/r** for a restart.
- **/h** to hibernate.
- **/hybrid** to shut down and prepare the PC for fast startup. This option isn't available prior to Windows 8.

To specify a time delay, use **/t** and then provide a number of seconds. The default is 30. So, for example, to restart after 60 seconds, you would use this:

```
shutdown /r /t 60
```

You can also use shutdown to shut down a remote computer. To do this, use the **/m** switch, like this:

```
shutdown -s /m \\Server01
```

Since Windows has a perfectly good GUI shutdown method, why would you want to use a command-line shutdown? One reason is to create your own custom shutdown shortcuts on the desktop that have different settings. Right-click an empty area of the desktop and select New and then select Shortcut. In the Create Shortcut wizard, enter the string for the shutdown **command with the parameters you desire, then click Next and enter a name for the shortcut.**

Shutdown Command in Linux

In Linux, the command syntax uses dashes rather than slashes for the switches. Use this reference for a complete list of switches: https://www.computerhope.com/unix/ushutdow.htm. Here are a few of the most common ones.

To specify what happens during the shutdown, use one of these (case-sensitive) commands:

- **-P** for a shutdown and power down
- **-r** for a restart

To specify a time delay, use -**t** and then provide a number of seconds between sending processes the warning and the kill signal.

To specify a particular time of day, use the time argument. (It doesn't have a switch associated with it.) The time can be in hours and minutes, like 20:00, or in +m, where m is the number of minutes to wait. The word "now" is the same as +0. Here are some examples:

- To restart after 5 minutes: **shutdown -r +5**
- To shut down and power off immediately: **shutdown -P now**

CERTIFICATION OBJECTIVES

- ***1102: 1.7*** *Given a scenario, apply application installation and configuration concepts*
- ***1102: 1.10*** *Identify common features and tools of the macOS/desktop OS*

This section covers everything you need to know for CompTIA A+ 1102 exam Objective 1.7, which deals with installing and configuring applications within an operating system. It includes system and OS requirements, installation methods, local user permissions, and security considerations.

The objective does not mention any OS specifically, so this section includes information about installing applications on all three of the desktop platforms we have been looking at so far in this book: Windows, Linux, and macOS. Adding and removing apps under macOS is part of CompTIA A+ 1102 exam Objective 1.10.

Application Management

Many of the same principles for installing and configuring operating systems also apply to applications. For example, success depends on factors such as system requirements, hardware compatibility, user permissions, and security settings. The following sections outline some of the considerations to be aware of when installing and removing applications and configuring them to work properly on a given system.

Application System Requirements and OS Compatibility

If you buy a retail box application, you can read the application's system requirements on the outside of the box before purchase. When buying via download, you may have to look for the system requirements on the application's web page to ensure it will run on the system you plan to use it with.

As with OSs, an application's hardware requirements typically include CPU type or speed, RAM, and free disk space. However, with applications, there is sometimes a fourth requirement: display adapter. Some applications (notably games) even require you to have a display adapter chipset that's on an approved-compatible list, or may require a certain amount of video RAM or a dedicated graphics card (meaning one that's not integrated with the motherboard chipset). An application may also require certain hardware or sound support (if the application requires sound).

Some highly secure applications also require the presence of a *hardware token,* which is usually a card or key fob that contains a chip that authenticates the person possessing it. For example, a business's accounting or payroll software might require such authentication to prevent fraud and theft.

Applications are typically written for a specific operating system, such as Windows, Mac, or Linux. However, if you buy the product at retail, the installation media may contain versions for multiple OSs.

If you acquire an application from a Store app (Apple Store, Microsoft Store), you can be reasonably confident that the application will run on the computer from which you are accessing the store.

Some applications do not have any specific hardware requirements, but they require a certain version of a certain OS, and by doing so, they make some assumptions about your hardware. For example, any PC that is running a 64-bit version Windows 10 can be assumed to have at least 2 GB of RAM.

Methods of Installation and Deployment

A decade ago, nearly all software was acquired on some sort of physical media. Retail box products dominated for commercial software, and many shareware developers would mail you a disc if you paid for it. Nowadays that is far from the case. Retail box software is still available, of course, but nearly every boxed application can also be acquired online. You can download software from individual websites and acquire software from Store applications such as Microsoft Store (for Windows), Google Play (for Android), and Apple Store (for macOS and iOS).

Understanding the Types of Installations

The traditional type of Windows desktop software setup is sometimes referred to as an *MSI install.* MSI stands for Microsoft Installer; it's a standard process for installing desktop applications in Windows. It handles three important tasks: copying files to the hard drive, making registry changes to support the application, and creating a shortcut for the application on the Start menu. Applications you acquire on disc, and also many of the applications you download from websites, use MSI installers. To uninstall an application installed this way, you must use the Control Panel or Settings app. (More on that later in this chapter.)

Applications that come from OS-specific online stores download and install quickly with just a few clicks or taps in the Store app. In the past, this type of delivery was limited to small and simple apps, but more and more companies are choosing to release full-featured software via app stores. Open the Store app, browse for the application, and follow the prompts to download it.

Installing from Local Media

Local media means a disc you insert or device that you connect to your local PC physically.

When you insert a disc or connect a flash drive, Windows checks for an Autorun file, and if it finds one, it follows the instructions contained in that file. A typical instruction is to run a small app automatically that displays a welcome message and prompts you to click a button to begin the application's setup process.

You can choose what Windows does when you insert a disc. In Windows, choose Settings | Devices (or Bluetooth & Devices) | AutoPlay. In macOS, choose System Preferences | CDs & DVDs and set the disc type to Ignore.

You can also access the Setup utility by displaying the disc's content in the OS's file management utility (for example, File Explorer) then double-clicking the Setup file. It is typically named Setup but that's not always the case. Then follow the prompts to complete the installation. See "System Permissions for Managing Software" later in this chapter if you run into any security prompts.

Installing Downloaded Windows Applications

You can download MSI-type setup files for installing an application from the developer's website or from online retailers that the developer has made a distribution deal with, such as Amazon.com. If the application is shareware or freeware, you may also be able to download it from a general software repository such as Download.com. The default location for downloads on a Windows PC is the Downloads folder within the signed-in user's folder set (C:\Users*username*\Downloads).

When you acquire a commercial application by downloading (that is, one you pay for), you typically get a single file with an .exe extension. Double-clicking the file starts a Setup utility that performs all the tasks needed to install the application.

Smaller software publishers and those who distribute freeware or shareware sometimes make their downloads available in nonexecutable archive packages. An archive package is a bundled set of files in a certain compressed format. To install from this type of package, you would do the following:

1. Open the archive file. If it's a ZIP file, you can open it using File Explorer as if it were a folder; if it uses some other format, you may need a third-party utility.

Typical file extensions for archive files include .zip, .rar, .tar, .7zip, .7z, .gzip, .gz, and .jar. (Many of these are used mostly for Linux and Unix.) Some Linux archives also use the .scexe extension.

2. Extract the files within the archive to a new folder.
3. Double-click the Setup file in the new folder.

Some large application packages can also be downloaded as ISO files (Windows) or DMG files (macOS). These files contain an image of a DVD disc. To access an ISO file, use an optical disc-burning utility to save the file on a blank writeable disc or a USB flash drive, and then use that media to install the application. You can also mount an ISO file to a virtual drive or attach it to a virtual machine (see Chapter 7). In addition, there are third-party utilities that can view the content of an ISO in a file management window, enabling you to copy files out of the ISO without mounting it.

The next section covers what to do with a DMG file.

Installing Downloaded Mac Applications

One way to get Mac applications is via the Apple Store. Open the Apple Store app from any Apple device (macOS computer, iPadOS tablet, or iOS smartphone) and select the app you want. Follow the prompts to buy it (if it's not free) and install it. The purchase price will be charged to the credit card or other payment method associated with your Apple ID. (You need an Apple ID account to do almost everything on an Apple device.)

You can also download macOS-compatible apps from individual websites. Most non-Store Mac application downloads come in DMG, PKG, or APP format. Here's how to handle each one of them:

- **DMG** When you open a DMG file in Finder, macOS treats it like a mounted virtual hard drive. (Unlike with Windows, macOS mounts the file as a virtual drive automatically when you double-click it.) To install an app you've received as a DMG file, double-click the DMG file in Finder to open it, and you'll see an icon for the application package. Drag that icon to your Applications folder to install the software. You may want to unmount it in Finder when you're finished with it by clicking the Eject arrow next to its name in the navigation pane on the left.

A Mac application can be run from any location, not just the Applications folder. Storing them there is customary but not required.

- **PKG** A PKG file is similar to a Windows application setup file. Double-click the PKG file to open a setup program that installs the application. You can right-click or CTRL-click the package and choose Show Package Contents to see what's in the package before you open it.
- **APP** An APP file is a ready-to-run application package, similar to an executable EXE file in Windows. The package contains all the helper files needed to run the application. You can place an APP file anywhere and run it from your chosen location, but you should not remove files from the application package.

exam watch

For CompTIA A+ Exam 1101 Objective 1.10, focus on these file types for Linux app installations: dmg, pkg, and app. You should also be able to use the App Store and uninstall apps and understand corporate restrictions and the role of an Apple ID in installing macOS apps.

Acquiring New Linux Applications

There isn't a "Linux Store" per se, but there are some well-established software archives online that have most of the applications you may want. Linux calls application downloads *packages.* Most Linux packages are free, in keeping with the general philosophy of Linux itself. Linux is configured to access a certain online repository as its default (the repository varies depending on the distro), but you can change that default to use other sources.

The Linux configuration file to modify to change the repository is /etc/apt/sources.list.

To install Linux packages you will need superuser permissions, so you will precede the installation command with *sudo,* which is a prefix you add to individual commands to execute them with root privileges without actually switching to the root user.

One common way to acquire Linux software is with the **apt-get** command. That's short for Advanced Packaging Tool. It's the default for Debian, Ubuntu, and many other Linux distributions. The **apt-get** command downloads and installs not only the package you specify but also any helper applications or files it needs. The syntax is

```
sudo apt-get install [package_name]
```

If you don't know the package name, your best bet is to consult one of the thousands of websites that list useful Linux applications, such as https://linuxappfinder.com.

For Red Hat Linux, the primary tool for acquiring and managing Red Hat Enterprise Linux RPM software packages is the yum command. The syntax is

```
yum [options] <command> [<args>...]
```

There are also GUI-based front ends for installing Linux packages, such as Synaptic and Ubuntu Software Center. These front ends can search for new packages, install and remove packages, and upgrade packages.

Network Installation

Some applications can be installed over a corporate network. This can be very convenient in a business setting, where you have hundreds of PCs that all need the same application.

On a small network where you have just a few PCs, you could physically go to each individual PC and browse to a network location and run the Setup file from there. That's a minor time-saver over taking physical media to each computer. However, for large-scale installations, it may be more efficient to write an installation script and push it out to the network clients via your server infrastructure. Chapter 23 may be helpful in getting started on such a task.

System Permissions for Managing Software

To install software, the user account must have the appropriate permissions. These fall into two categories: permission to make system changes and access to specific folders.

Account Types and Permissions

As you learned in Chapter 4, Microsoft recommends that you work with Windows using a Standard user account on a daily basis, signing in with an Administrator account only when you need to perform actions that require the higher level of permission. Installing software is one such activity. Sign in with your Administrator account before installing or removing software. Or, to save time, you can run the Setup application using the Run As Administrator option. To do so, right-click the Setup file and choose Run As Administrator. When prompted, enter the password for the Administrator account to continue.

Access to Specific Folders

Obviously, to be able to run a Setup file, you must be able to access the folder where the file is stored. Administrator accounts in Windows can access most folders, even the personal folders of other local accounts. However, Standard accounts cannot access other users' folders. If the Setup utility you need to run is stored within someone else's personal folders (for example, their Downloads folder), you could ask them to move it into a common location for you, or you could sign in as an Administrator.

Security Considerations When Installing Applications

As an IT professional, you must be aware of the potential security impact when a user installs a new application. Applications that users find online can potentially contain viruses or other malware that can disable the individual PC and compromise network security. For this reason, many IT departments limit end users' ability to install new software. Users grumble about this, but they would complain even more if their systems became disabled because of some security disaster caused by untested software.

When a user wants to install a new application, ask for a copy of it and install it in a sandbox environment such as a standalone virtual machine, where it can't hurt anything. Test it for malware, as described in Chapter 22.

Also consider the effect the application may have on the network. For example, Spotify and YouTube are harmless applications, but as they operate they generate a lot of Internet traffic, downloading music and videos. That's fine if your company has bandwidth to spare, but if lots of people are doing it, the network could slow down and impair other users who are trying to work.

Compatibility Issues with Older Applications

Some older programs don't run well under newer Windows versions. It's usually because they were written to assume certain things about the host OS that are no longer true. For example, some applications require a certain display resolution that Windows no longer supports (like 640 × 480) or a certain way of handling sound, memory, or CPU usage. An older program may fail to install under the newer Windows version or may install but fail to run. You might or might not see an error message.

Fortunately, you can often trick an older program into installing and running in a newer version of Windows that it otherwise wouldn't accept by using *Compatibility Mode*. Compatibility Mode sets up a custom sandbox in which the application can run with the settings it needs. You can set up Compatibility Mode manually in the Properties box for the application's executable or shortcut, or you can run the Program Compatibility Troubleshooter via the Get Help app. The compatibility settings are saved for the executable or shortcut, so they apply whenever you run it. In Exercise 5-7, you will practice using Compatibility Mode by configuring it both automatically and manually.

If you always want the program to run with certain compatibility settings, set up Compatibility Mode for the executable. If you want the option of running different compatibility settings at different times, create shortcuts to the executable (for example, on the desktop) and configure Compatibility Mode separately for each shortcut.

Compatibility Mode does not set up MS-DOS applications to run in a DOS environment; it only works for certain older Windows versions. Windows 10 and 11 go back as far as Windows 95, but do not support any server versions.

Use Compatibility Mode only for old productivity applications (word processing, spreadsheet, and so on). Never use Compatibility Mode for antivirus programs, backup programs, or system programs (such as disk utilities and drivers) because these types of programs require more access to the disk and other resources than they will be allowed within Compatibility Mode.

EXERCISE 5-7

Exploring Compatibility Mode Settings

This exercise has two parts. In the first part you will learn how to automatically troubleshoot compatibility, and in the second part you will learn how to do so manually.

Part I: Troubleshooting Compatibility Automatically

One way to troubleshoot compatibility is to use the automated wizard.

1. Right-click the shortcut or executable file you want to set up for Compatibility Mode. This shortcut can be on the desktop, on the Start menu or Start screen, or in a Windows Explorer or File Explorer window.
2. Click Troubleshoot Compatibility.
3. In the Program Compatibility Troubleshooter window, click Try Recommended Settings.
4. Click Test The Program. Windows will attempt to run the program. Try out the program to make sure it works. Then return to the Program Compatibility Troubleshooter window, and click Next.
5. If the program worked okay, click Yes, Save These Settings For This Program. If it didn't, click No, Try Again Using Different Settings.
6. If you chose to try again, click to select the check boxes for the problems you found, and then click Next.
7. The screens that appear after this point depend on what you chose in Step 6, so follow along with the prompts to complete the process until the application is working.

Part II: Troubleshooting Compatibility Manually

If the automatic compatibility settings don't solve your problems, you can try adjusting the settings manually. (Actually, you might want to adjust the settings manually anyway if you think you know what's wrong.)

1. Right-click the shortcut or executable file you want to set up for Compatibility Mode.
2. Click Properties, and then click the Compatibility tab.

3. Click to place a check mark in the Run This Program In Compatibility Mode For check box, and then choose the desired Windows version from the drop-down list.
4. In the Settings area, click to place a check mark in any of the check boxes corresponding to options that you think might help correct the compatibility issues. You might need to experiment.
5. Click OK to apply the new settings, and then try running the application to see if your new settings helped. Repeat as needed.

Removing Applications

The process of removing an application is different depending on the OS on which it is installed and the installation type (for example, MSI vs. a Microsoft Store app).

Store apps are very easy to uninstall:

- On a Windows system, right-click the application on the Start menu and choose Uninstall. Click Uninstall to confirm, and you're done.
- On a macOS system, click the Launchpad icon in the Dock, and then press and hold the mouse button over the app's icon. Hold it until all icons begin to shake, and then click the app's Delete (X) button.

If it's a non-Store app, the process is just a bit more complex:

- On a Windows system, you can uninstall from the Control Panel or from the Settings app. The interfaces are similar, but not identical, between the two places, and occasionally an app will show up in one place but not the other.
  - **Control Panel method** In the Control Panel, navigate to Programs | Uninstall A Program. Select the program on the list and click Uninstall. Follow the prompts. Figure 5-8 shows an application ready to be uninstalled.
  - **Settings method** Open the Settings app and choose Apps. Select the program on the list and click Uninstall. Follow the prompts.
- On a macOS system, open the Applications folder, and locate the application's subfolder. Check for an uninstaller file. If you see one, double-click it and follow the instructions. If the app doesn't have an uninstaller or isn't in a folder, drag the app to the Trash can at the end of the Dock.

To remove a Linux application, you use the same tool you use to install one: apt-get. Instead of the install parameter, you use remove. Here's the syntax:

```
sudo apt-get remove [package_name]
```

You can also use a graphical front end to remove an application.

FIGURE 5-8

Look for an Uninstall, Change, or Repair button.

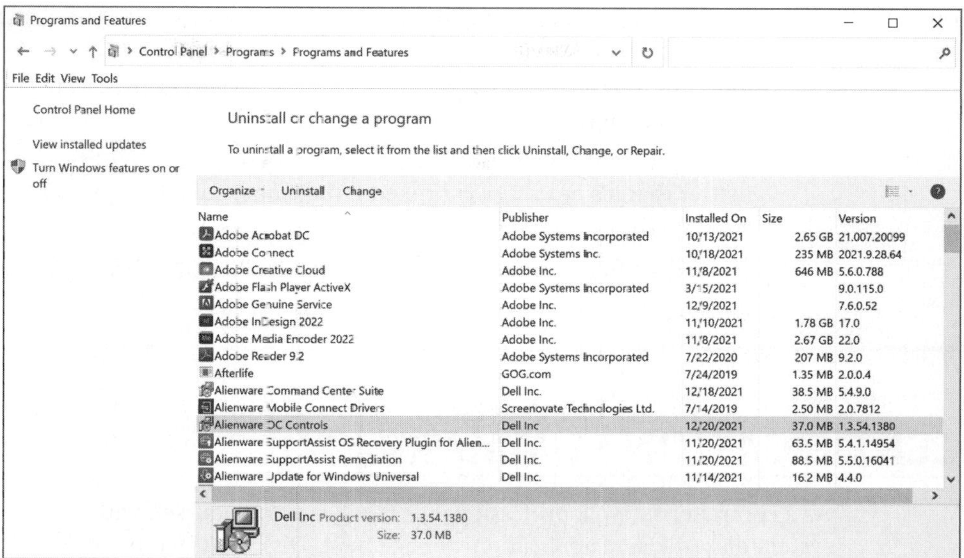

Repairing Applications

One way to repair a damaged application is to remove and reinstall it. However, there may be an easier and less time-consuming way. Some applications have a Repair functionality built into their Setup program. Many desktop applications installed via MSI have this feature, including Microsoft Office.

To see if a program has a Repair function, view the list of installed applications in Control Panel in Windows (Control Panel | Programs | Uninstall A Program). Select the application and then look in the shaded bar above the application list. If you see a Repair or Change button, there may be a way to repair the application without removing it. Click the button and follow the prompts. Sometimes a single button may have two functions, such as Uninstall/Change; you'll choose which you want after the Setup program launches.

Exercise 5-8 walks you through the steps for acquiring, installing, repairing, and removing an application.

EXERCISE 5-8

Working with Windows Applications

In this exercise you will practice installing and removing an application.

1. Sign in to Windows using an account with Administrator permissions.
2. Open a browser and navigate to https://download.cnet.com/games/windows. (We're using a game for this exercise rather than a more "serious" file because games are

less likely to make major system changes, and the last thing we want to do here is introduce an unexpected problem into your system.)

3. Pick a free game, and download and install it. Make notes of what you had to do to make that happen.
4. If the game has a Repair or Change feature, use it to repair the game. (It doesn't matter that it's not actually broken.) Make notes of the steps you took.
5. Remove the game. Make notes of the steps you took.
6. Open the Microsoft Store app. Download and install a Store app.
7. Remove the Store app.

CERTIFICATION SUMMARY

As a computer support professional, you need to arm yourself with knowledge of operating system disk, file, and application management. Disk management in Windows begins with understanding partitioning and formatting, including selecting an appropriate file system.

Most file management tasks remain the same across all the file systems supported by Windows. NTFS is the preferred file system for Windows, providing more advanced file storage features and file and folder security. You should perform file management from the GUI tools, but a technician should be familiar with command-line file management methods for certain troubleshooting scenarios. You should understand file-naming conventions, file attributes, file types, and text file editors and be able to organize files into folders. You should know the techniques and rules for moving and copying files in the GUI.

Application management includes installing and removing applications from Windows, macOS, and Linux systems. Applications can come from app stores, from web downloads, or from retail disc packages.

TWO-MINUTE DRILL

Here are some of the key points covered in Chapter 5.

Disk Management

- ❑ In Windows, the Disk Management tool is used to view and work with disks. Access it from the **diskmgmt.msc** command or through Computer Management.
- ❑ A disk can have up to four partitions. Either all four partitions can be primary, or the disk can have a combination of up to three primary partitions and one extended partition. Primary partitions are preferred.

- ❑ A PC with one or more disks must have at least one primary partition to boot Windows.
- ❑ Windows Setup creates a primary, active (bootable) partition and formats the partition with a file system.
- ❑ A quick format does not actually overwrite or test the entire volume but simply puts the file system components on the disk, refreshing the directory and allocation information so that the disk appears empty, whether it is or not. A full format overwrites all the data space, as well as the directory information.
- ❑ DISKPART is a command-line utility that performs many of the same operations as Disk Management.
- ❑ On a macOS system, the Disk Utility program is the equivalent of Disk Management in Windows. Its utilities include First Aid, Partition, Erase, Unmount, and Info.

File Systems

- ❑ Most file management tasks remain the same across all the file systems available in Windows: FAT12, FAT16, FAT32, and NTFS.
- ❑ The key characteristics of a file system include number of bits in the table (either FAT or MFT), cluster size, and special features like encryption and compression.
- ❑ Sectors are grouped into clusters to make addressable allocation units. Disks store files more efficiently with smaller cluster sizes, but to support large volumes, larger cluster sizes may be required.
- ❑ FAT systems include FAT16 and FAT32, with the numbers referring to the number of bits in the file allocation table.
- ❑ NTFS is the preferred file system for modern Windows systems because it works with larger hard drives, is more stable, and offers file and folder security and compression that is not available in the FAT file systems.
- ❑ exFAT is a file system designed for use on small solid-state storage devices such as USB flash drives and SSD cards.
- ❑ Resilient File System (ReFS) is a new file system expected to replace the NTFS file system on Windows Server.
- ❑ The native file system is HFS+ on older Macs and APFS on newer ones. The native file system on Linux is ext3 or ext4.

File Management

- ❑ File Explorer can be customized to display files and folders in different ways. Four important options you should be able to access are View Hidden Files, Hide Extensions For Known File Types, General Options, and View Options.
- ❑ You can manage files from a command-line interface within Windows using basic commands like **dir, copy, del, rename, xcopy, cd, rd,** and **md**. You should also understand gpupdate and gpresult.

- Use chkdsk to check a disk for errors at a command prompt. Use format to format a disk from a command prompt. Use sfc to check system files.
- macOS and Linux have the same underlying structure, so they have the same command-line commands and syntax. To open a Terminal window in Linux, press CTRL-ALT-T. In macOS, choose Launchpad | Other | Terminal.
- You should know how to use the nano editor to create and save text files from the Linux command prompt.
- The important Linux commands you need to know for the 220-1012 exam are ls, cd, mv, rm, cp, pwd, mkdir, rmdir, find, grep, chmod, chown, cat, df, and man. There are also some network-specific Linux commands you will learn about later in the book.
- Windows and Linux both have a shutdown command that enables you to shut down the PC from a command prompt, but they have different syntax.

Application Management

- Successful application installation and use depend on hardware and OS compatibility. You can check an application's requirements before purchase.
- A traditional Microsoft Installer (MSI) application is a setup program for a Windows desktop application. You can also install applications in Windows via the Microsoft Store.
- You can install an application from local media, such as a DVD or flash drive. Retail software often comes on a DVD in a box.
- You can download an application setup program from a website. This may be an executable file, a compressed archive, or an ISO file.
- Mac applications may come in a DMG file, which mounts in macOS as a virtual disk. Drag the application to the Applications folder. They may also come in a PKG file (equivalent to a Windows app Setup file) or APP file (equivalent to a Windows executable file).
- To install and remove Linux software, use apt-get. For apps on Red Hat Linux, you can also use the **yum** command.
- To install an application, you must use an Administrator account, and you must have access permission to the needed folders.
- When installing applications or allowing others to do so, think of the device's safety and the network's security and well-being.
- Compatibility issues with older applications can often be resolved in Windows using Compatibility Mode.
- To repair or remove a Windows application, use the Control Panel or the Settings app.

SELF TEST

The following questions will help you measure your understanding of the material presented in this chapter. Read all the choices carefully because there might be more than one correct answer. Choose all correct answers for each question.

Disk Management

1. Which of the following describes a partition from which Windows can boot?
   - A. Primary extended
   - B. Active extended
   - C. Primary active
   - D. Simple extended
2. Which GUI tool should you use to create a partition on a new drive?
   - A. My Computer
   - B. Device Manager
   - C. Disk Defragmenter
   - D. Disk Management
3. How many logical drives are on a primary partition?
   - A. 1
   - B. 2
   - C. 3
   - D. Up to 24
4. What utility can you use from a command prompt to manage partitions?
   - A. chkdsk
   - B. partition
   - C. diskmgt.msc
   - D. diskpart
5. What utility can you use in macOS to manage partitions?
   - A. Finder
   - B. Disk Utility
   - C. Disk Management
   - D. diskpart

File Systems

6. Which file system supports file compression and encryption?

A. FAT32

B. FAT12

C. FAT16

D. NTFS

7. Which feature of NTFS makes file searches faster?

A. Compression

B. Encryption

C. Indexing

D. MFT

8. What is the maximum capacity for a FAT16 volume?

A. 4 GB

B. 64 KB

C. 128 sectors

D. 32 GB

9. Instead of a file allocation table, what does an NTFS volume have?

A. MFT

B. Allocation units

C. Boot sector

D. Cluster

File Management

10. If file extensions appear for some, but not all, files, what can you assume about a file for which the extension does *not* appear?

A. It is a hidden file.

B. It is not a known file type.

C. It is a known file type.

D. It is a system file.

11. What disk error-checking program can you run from a command prompt to analyze the disk for physical and logical errors?

A. chkdsk

B. nano

C. format

D. grep

12. What command is used in both Linux and Windows to shut down the computer from a command prompt or script?

A. grep
B. shutdown
C. close
D. exit

13. Which two of the following are command interpreters for Windows 10?

A. Command prompt
B. PowerShell
C. Shell
D. Interpret

14. To switch command interpreters in Windows, open the settings for what Windows interface feature?

A. Recycle Bin
B. Start menu
C. Desktop
D. Taskbar

15. What is the purpose of opening an elevated command prompt?

A. More full-featured interface
B. Larger window
C. Greater security permission
D. Better help system

16. What is the purpose of the pwd command in Linux?

A. Set password
B. Show the active directory path
C. Find a text string in a file
D. List the contents of the active directory

17. What Windows command-line command scans and verifies the versions of protected system files?

A. chkdsk
B. defrag
C. scanboot
D. sfc

Application Management

18. A traditional desktop application Setup file uses a Microsoft Installer (MSI) that does all of the following *except* which one:

A. Makes registry entries

B. Creates an application shortcut on the Start menu

C. Connects to the Microsoft Store to activate the software

D. Copies the application files to the hard drive

19. If a downloaded application comes in a nonexecutable archive file, which of these would be a likely format for it?

A. .exe

B. .xlsx

C. .txt

D. .zip

20. What Windows feature might help if an older application won't run properly under Windows 10?

A. Device Manager

B. Compatibility Mode

C. Encryption

D. Archiving

SELF TEST ANSWERS

Disk Management

1. ☑ **C.** Primary active describes a partition from which Windows can boot.
☒ **A** is incorrect because it describes two different partition types. **B** is incorrect because you cannot mark an extended partition as active; only a primary partition can be marked as active. **D** is incorrect because Windows cannot boot from an extended partition (and "simple extended" is not a term that is normally used).

2. ☑ **D.** Disk Management is the GUI tool you should use for creating a partition on a new hard drive.
   ☒ **A** is incorrect because My Computer is not a tool for creating a partition. **B** is incorrect because Device Manager is for managing devices. **C** is incorrect because Disk Defragmenter is a tool for defragmenting files on a drive.

3. ☑ **A.** One, because it is the only number of logical drives that you can create on a primary partition. Only secondary partitions can have multiple logical drives.
   ☒ **B, C,** and **D** are incorrect because a primary partition can contain only one logical drive.

4. ☑ **D.** The application to use is diskpart.
   ☒ **A** is incorrect because chkdsk checks disks; it doesn't partition them. **B** is incorrect because there is no such command-line utility. **C** is incorrect because diskmgmt.msc opens the GUI Disk Management utility.

5. ☑ **B.** Disk Utility is the macOS tool for managing partitions.
   ☒ **A** is incorrect because Finder views and manages files but not partitions. **C** is incorrect because Disk Management is the tool in Windows for partition management. **D** is incorrect because diskpart is the Windows command-line utility for partition management.

File Systems

6. ☑ **D.** NTFS supports file compression and encryption.
   ☒ **A, B,** and **C** are incorrect because none of these file systems support compression or encryption.

7. ☑ **C.** Indexing, an NTFS feature, makes file searches faster.
   ☒ **A** and **B** are incorrect because although both compression and encryption are NTFS features, they do not make file searches faster. **D** is incorrect because although MFT is a core component of NTFS, it does not make file searches faster.

8. ☑ **A.** With a 64-bit cluster size, a FAT16 volume can support a 4-GB volume.
   ☒ **B** is incorrect because 64 KB is the cluster size, not the capacity. **C** is incorrect because number of sectors is not a capacity. **D** is incorrect because 32 GB is the maximum size for a FAT32 volume.

9. ☑ **A.** MFT, the master file table of NTFS, is the equivalent of the file allocation table, keeping track of volume contents.
   ☒ **B** and **D** are incorrect because they are synonyms that refer to a group of sectors. **C** is incorrect because the boot sector is the first sector on a disk, not strictly a part of a file system.

File Management

10. ☑ **C.** When Hide Extensions For Known File Types is enabled, some, but not all, files show with extensions. Known file types do not.
☒ **A** is incorrect because whether or not a file is hidden has no bearing on whether or not its extension displays. **B** is incorrect because unknown file types are the only ones that *do* show extensions when Hide Extensions For Known File Types is enabled. **D** is incorrect because whether or not a file is a system file has no bearing on whether or not its extension displays.

11. ☑ **A.** chkdsk is the disk error-checking program that you can run from a command prompt to do an analysis of the disk for physical and logical errors.
☒ **B** is incorrect because the nano command opens a text editor at a Linux command prompt. **C** is incorrect because the format command overwrites the contents of a drive with file-system components. **D** is incorrect because the grep command in Linux searches for files based on text strings in their contents.

12. ☑ **B.** The shutdown command serves this purpose in both Linux and Windows.
☒ **A** is incorrect because the grep command in Linux searches for files based on text strings in their contents. It is not present in Windows. **C** is incorrect because there is no close command in either Windows or Linux. **D** is incorrect because the exit command exits from some applications, such as DISKPART, but not from the OS itself.

13. ☑ **A** and **B.** Command prompt and PowerShell are the two command interpreter options for Windows.
☒ **C** is incorrect because shell is a generic term to describe a user interface. **D** is incorrect because there is no such command as Interpret in Windows.

14. ☑ **D.** Right-click the taskbar and choose Taskbar Settings to access the controls for choosing a command interpreter.
☒ **A** is incorrect because the Recycle Bin's properties have nothing to do with the command interpreter. **B** is incorrect because the Start menu's properties do not control the command interpreter—although logically it seems like it might because you start the command interpreter by right-clicking the Start button. **C** is incorrect because the desktop properties do not affect the command interpreter.

15. ☑ **C.** Greater security permission is the purpose of opening an elevated command prompt.
☒ **A, B,** and **D** are incorrect because there is no difference in any of those factors between a standard command prompt and an elevated command prompt.

16. ☑ **B.** Showing the active directory path is the purpose of pwd, which stands for print working directory.
☒ **A** is incorrect because the command for setting the password is passwd, not pwd. **C** is incorrect because it describes what the grep command does. **D** is incorrect because it describes what the ls command does.

17. ☑ **D.** The sfc command stands for System File Checker and is used to scan and verify the versions of protected system files.
☒ **A** is incorrect because chkdsk checks the entire disk for errors, not specifically the system files. **B** is incorrect because defrag defragments the volume. **C** is incorrect because scanboot is an argument you can use with sfc, not a separate command on its own.

Application Management

18. ☑ **C.** An MSI installer does not interact with the Microsoft Store.
☒ **A, B,** and **D** are incorrect because these are the three things that installing a desktop application does.

19. ☑ **D.** .zip is a common format for compressed archives and is nonexecutable.
☒ **A** is incorrect because .exe is an executable file. **B** is incorrect because .xlsx is an Excel data file. **C** is incorrect because .txt is a plaintext data file.

20. ☑ **B.** Compatibility Mode can help troubleshoot and fix problems with older applications not running under a newer Windows version.
☒ **A** is incorrect because Device Manager is for troubleshooting hardware, not software. **C** is incorrect because encryption is a security feature for files under NTFS. **D** is incorrect because archiving means to back up files.

Chapter 6

Operating System Troubleshooting and Maintenance

CERTIFICATION OBJECTIVES

- **1102: 1.3** Given a scenario, use features and tools of the Microsoft Windows 10 operating system (OS)
- **1102: 1.5** Given a scenario, use the appropriate Windows settings
- **1102: 1.9** Given a scenario, perform OS installations and upgrades in a diverse OS environment
- **1102: 1.10** Identify common features and tools of the macOS/desktop OS
- **1102: 1.11** Identify common features and tools of the Linux client/desktop OS
- **1102: 3.1** Given a scenario, troubleshoot common Windows OS problems

✓ Two-Minute Drill

Q&A Self Test

In this chapter, we turn our attention to troubleshooting operating systems (OSs), looking at problems large and small that might prevent an OS from functioning well. We focus mainly on Windows because it is the most popular OS, but we also provide some basic assistance for macOS and Linux to the extent dictated by the 220-1102 exam's objectives. We also look at some common preventive maintenance tasks that can help avoid problems down the road.

Quick Fixes

Perhaps you've heard of Occam's razor, aka the law of parsimony? Roughly paraphrased, it states that "among competing hypotheses, the one with the fewest assumptions should be selected." In other words, "try the simplest solution first." That applies very well to computer OS troubleshooting.

This chapter contains a lot of very detailed troubleshooting information and technique that you should know as a CompTIA A+ certified PC technician for very specific situations. However, in everyday tech work, the majority of the problems you face can be fixed by one of these general-purpose methods:

- **Reboot** Often a system restart is all that's required to clear up a problem.
- **Verify** Make sure the software or device you are attempting to install or troubleshoot is compatible with the hardware and software of the PC.
- **Repair** If the problem is with a specific application, repair it using the techniques you learned in the "Repairing Applications" section of Chapter 5. If the problem is with Windows itself, use a repair technique (dependent on Windows version) such as one of the techniques discussed later in this chapter.
- **Uninstall/reinstall** If the problem is with a specific device, remove it physically from the PC, and then remove its driver and all its software from the OS. Check for any updates for its driver or software online, and then reinstall.

CERTIFICATION OBJECTIVE

- ***1102: 1.3*** *Given a scenario, use features and tools of the Microsoft Windows 10 operating system (OS)*

This section mainly covers topics from CompTIA A+ 1102 exam Objective 1.3, including a variety of Windows features and tools used for troubleshooting.

Windows Troubleshooting Tools

In this section, you'll learn about the many Windows tools for troubleshooting operating system problems. We're assuming in this section that you are able to boot Windows normally to access these tools. If Windows won't boot normally, see the section "Troubleshooting Windows Startup Problems" later in this chapter.

Sometimes the solution to what seems like an OS problem is to modify a BIOS/UEFI setting. For example, enabling Virtualization support in BIOS/UEFI can fix performance problems with virtual machines (covered in Chapter 7). Review Chapter 8 for help entering BIOS/UEFI setup and making settings changes there.

Command Prompt/Terminal

Keep in mind that the Command Prompt window is always available from within the Windows graphical user interface (GUI), as you learned in Chapter 5. Many of the utilities we explain in upcoming sections run either from a command line or from the Run dialog box (WINDOWS KEY-R). Remember also from Chapter 5 that on Mac and Linux systems, the command prompt is known as Terminal.

Windows 11 also has a Terminal application that serves as a multi-tabbed command-line front end. Here's an article about that: https://devblogs.microsoft.com/commandline/windows-terminal-as-your-default-command-line-experience/.

The Windows Recovery Environment (Windows RE), explained later in this chapter, also has an option that enables you to work from a command prompt for system troubleshooting when the GUI doesn't start properly.

Troubleshooting Helpers

Windows includes many troubleshooting helpers (sometimes called *wizards*) that can walk you through fixing common problems. Each troubleshooter asks you questions and then offers to take action based on your answers.

To find them, open the Control Panel and search for *troubleshooting* using the Search box in the upper-right corner to open the Troubleshooting screen (see Figure 6-1). From there just click the button for the type of problem you are having and follow the prompts. You can also find troubleshooters by opening the Settings app and choosing Update & Security | Troubleshoot.

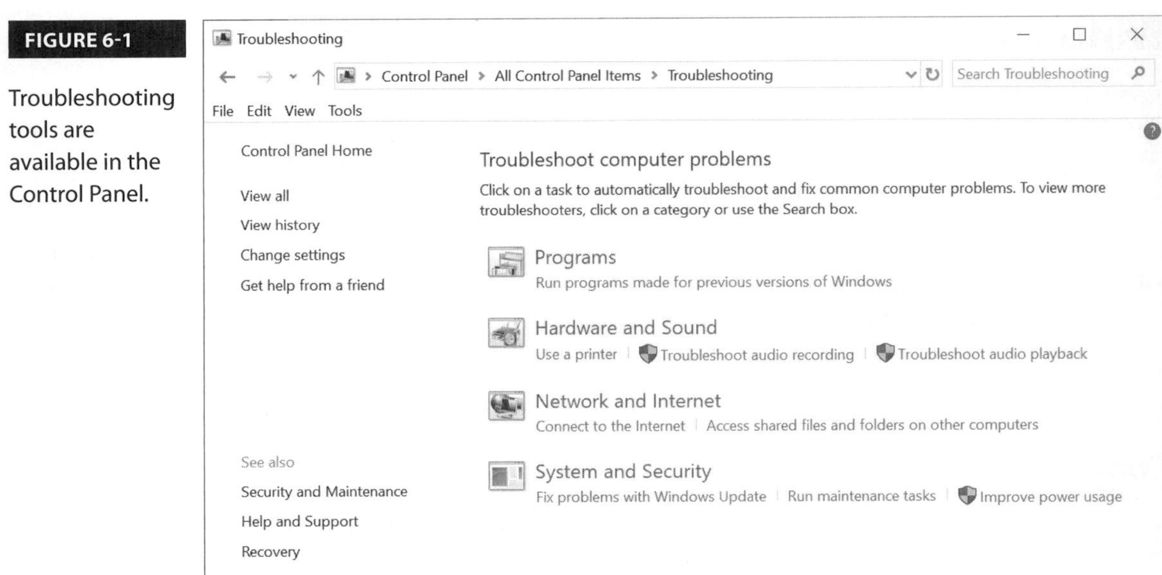

FIGURE 6-1 Troubleshooting tools are available in the Control Panel.

System Information (MSINFO32.EXE)

You sit down at a Windows computer you have never touched before. You know little about it, but you need to gather information to troubleshoot a problem. Where do you start? One of the first things you should do is learn as much as you can, as quickly as you can. What version, edition, and updates to Windows are installed? How much memory is installed? What CPU? This information and more is displayed as a summary of the hardware, operating system, and other installed software in *System Information*. You can access it through the GUI, or you can type its command (**msinfo32.exe**) from the Start menu or in the Run dialog box (WINDOWS KEY-R). Figure 6-2 shows this utility in Windows 10.

Registry

A basic knowledge of the registry is required of anyone supporting Windows. The Windows *registry* is a database of all Windows configuration settings for both hardware and software. As Windows starts up, it reads information in the registry that tells it what components to load into memory and how to configure them. After startup, the OS writes any changes into the registry and frequently reads additional settings as different programs load into memory. The registry includes settings for device drivers, services, installed applications, OS components, and user preferences.

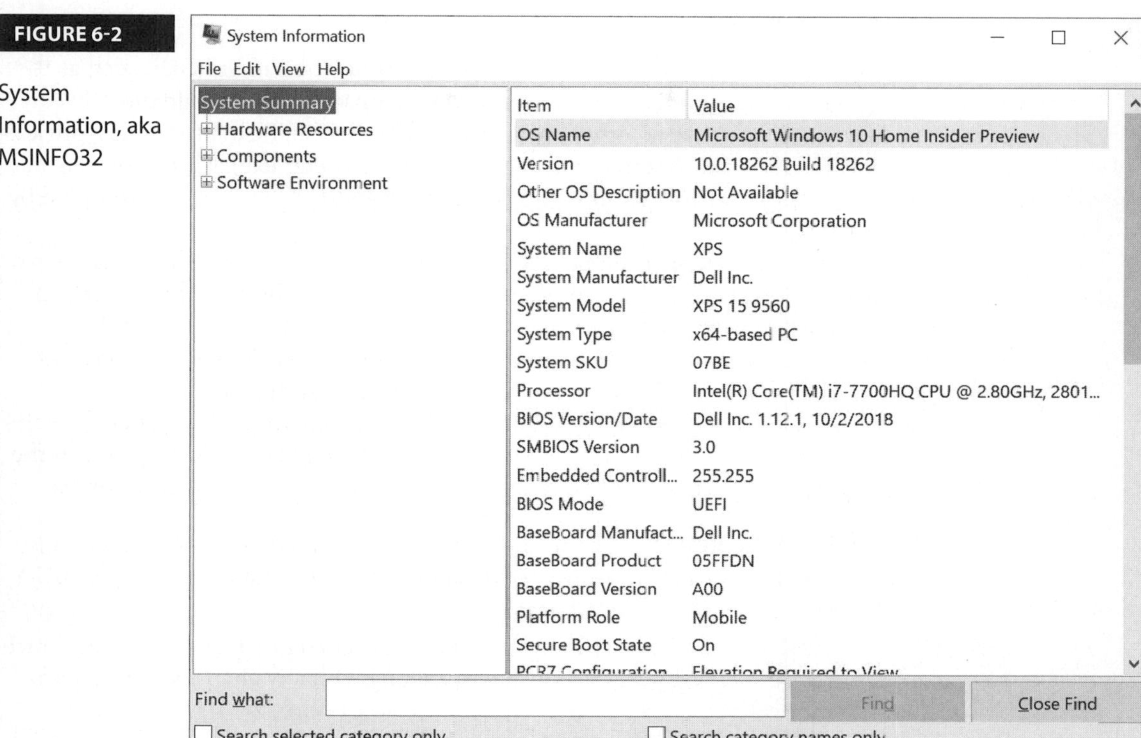

FIGURE 6-2 System Information, aka MSINFO32

Changing the Registry

The registry is created when Windows installs; however, configuring Windows and adding applications and devices continually modifies it. Here are the actions that cause registry changes:

- Windows starts up or shuts down
- Windows Setup runs
- Changes are made through a Control Panel applet
- Installing a new device
- Any changes made to the Windows configuration
- Any changes made to a user's desktop preferences
- Installing or modifying an app
- Any changes made to an app's user preferences

Using Registry Editor

The best way to change the registry is indirectly, using various tools in the GUI, such as the Control Panel applets, the Settings app, and some MMC consoles. You should directly edit the registry only when you have no other choice and you have specific instructions from a very reliable source. Then the tool to use is Registry Editor (regedit.exe), which you can start from the Run dialog box (WINDOWS KEY-R) by entering **regedit**. You might be prompted by UAC to allow access.

In Registry Editor, you can navigate the registry folders with your mouse in the same way you navigate disk folders. Each folder represents a *registry key*, an object that may contain one or more settings, as well as other keys, each of which is a *subkey* of its parent key. The top five folders, as seen in Figure 6-3, are *root keys*, often called *subtrees* in Microsoft documentation. Each of these subtrees is the top of a hierarchical structure.

A setting within a key is a *value entry*. When you click the folder for a key, it becomes the active key in Registry Editor. Its folder icon opens, and the contents of the key appear in the right pane, as shown in Figure 6-3. Here is an overview of each subtree and its contents:

- **HKEY_CLASSES_ROOT** The relationships (associations) between applications and file types. Shown as a root key, it is actually all the information located in HKEY_LOCAL_MACHINE\Software\Classes.
- **HKEY_CURRENT_USER** The user profile for the currently logged-on user, which consists of the NTUSER.DAT file for the user, along with any changes since logon.

FIGURE 6-3

Use Registry Editor (REGEDIT) to view the registry components.

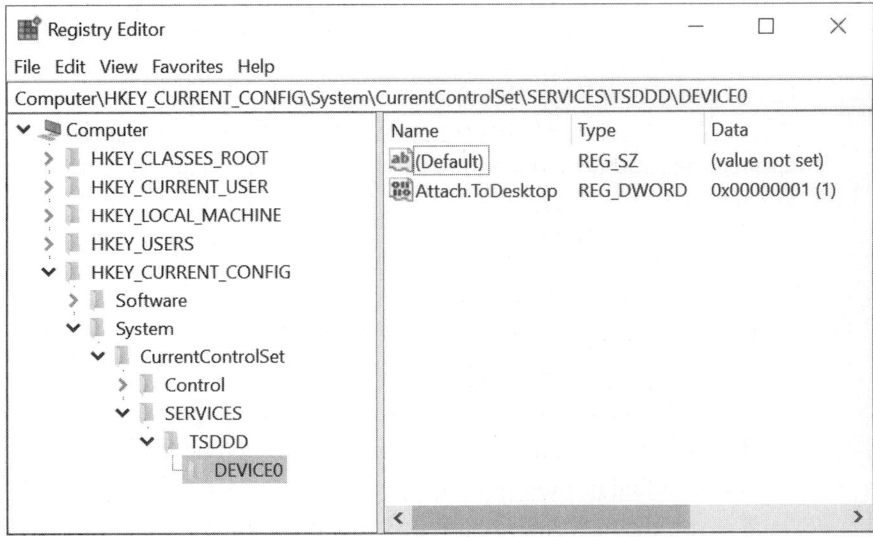

- **HKEY_LOCAL_MACHINE** Information about detected hardware and software, security settings, and the local security accounts database.
- **HKEY_USERS** All user profiles that are loaded in memory, including the profile of the currently logged-on user, the default profile, and profiles for special user accounts for running various services.
- **HKEY_CURRENT_CONFIG** Configuration information for the current hardware profile, which are settings defining the devices, the list of files associated with each device, and configuration settings for each. It also contains a set of changes to the standard configuration in the Software and System subkeys under HKEY_LOCAL_MACHINE.

Editing the registry is not difficult, but it can be dangerous if done improperly, causing system problems that can prevent Windows from starting or running properly. When you research a system problem online, you may find some recommended registry edits proposed as solutions. Be wary. Make registry edits with care, and only after making a backup of the registry or a particular section. Exercise 6-1 helps you make a backup of a registry key and then practice restoring a backup.

EXERCISE 6-1

Backing Up and Restoring the Registry

In this step-by-step exercise, you will back up a section of the Windows registry. You would do this before making a change to the registry as a safeguard. You could then restore the backup if the change you made caused system instability. You can back up the entire registry (although that creates a large file) or the individual key that you plan on editing.

1. Run REGEDIT to open Registry Editor. You can use the Run dialog box (WINDOWS KEY-R) or open the Start menu/screen and type **regedit**.
2. Click HKEY_CURRENT_USER to select that key.
3. Click File | Export. In the Export Registry File dialog box, change to a location where you can save temporary files (we use a folder called C:\Temp).
4. In the File Name box, type **HKEY_CURRENT_USER Backup** and today's date.
5. Click Save.
6. Click File | Import. In the Import Registry File dialog box, navigate to the folder you chose in Step 3.
7. Select the file you backed up.
8. If this were an actual import, you would click Open at this point, but instead click Cancel.

Microsoft Management Console

The *Microsoft Management Console (MMC)* is a user interface for Windows administration tools that is flexible and configurable. Most Control Panel applets and administrative applets that run within the Windows GUI open in an MMC window. *Computer Management* is a preconfigured version of the MMC with several common modules already loaded. You can access Computer Management by right-clicking the Start button and clicking Computer Management.

Figure 6-4 shows the Computer Management window. Notice the grouping of tools on the left. The tools (such as Task Scheduler and Device Manager) are all *snap-ins* to the Computer Management console, meaning they are MMC nodes that can be added to an MMC console.

An administrator can build their own custom consoles consisting of individual snap-ins. To do this, open the Start menu and type **mmc.exe** and then click mmc Run Command. This opens a blank console window on the desktop.

By choosing File | Add/Remove Snap-in, you can select one or more administrative snap-ins to create your custom console. Consoles have an .msc file extension, and you can call up your favorite tool directly by entering the correct filename and extension. For instance, to start Computer Management, shown in Figure 6-4, click the Start button or open the Start screen and then type **compmgmt.msc**.

Following are overviews of several MMC-based tools that are useful in both troubleshooting and preventing problems.

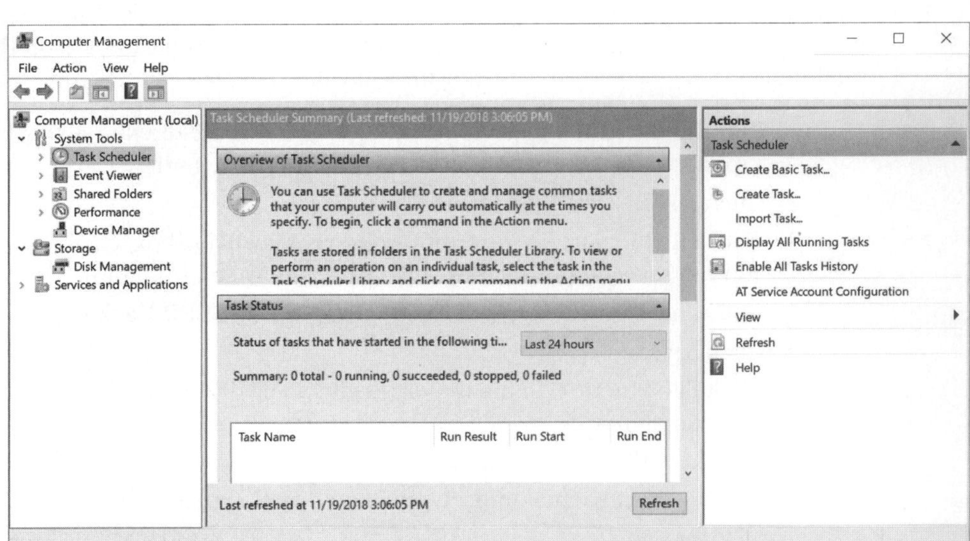

FIGURE 6-4 Computer Management console

Device Manager

Device Manager is an MMC snap-in that enables an administrator to view and change device properties, update device drivers (you normally will use the manufacturer's program to update a driver), configure device settings, roll back an updated driver that is causing problems, and uninstall devices. You can access Device Manager from the Control Panel. Alternatively, you can open the Run dialog box (WINDOWS KEY-R) and enter **devmgmt.msc**. This will open it into a separate MMC console window. You can also right-click the Start button and choose Device Manager. Chapter 12 covers Device Manager in detail.

Task Scheduler

Task Scheduler allows you to view and manage tasks that run automatically at preconfigured times. Use Task Scheduler to automate daily backups and updates. You can open Task Scheduler from the Run dialog box by entering **taskschd.msc**; then expand the Task Scheduler Library to see folders for the many categories of tasks. You will be surprised at the number of scheduled tasks. Most, if not all, of the tasks you will find there were not created by you directly, but were added to Task Scheduler when you installed a new app and configured it to automatically check for updates. We cover Task Scheduler in more detail later in the chapter, in the context of scheduling maintenance utilities to run automatically.

Performance Monitor

Network administrators use performance monitoring to watch for potential problems and to ensure quality of service. Desktop versions of Windows don't usually require monitoring, but they nevertheless come with several tools for monitoring performance and the overall health of the system.

The performance tool specifically mentioned in CompTIA A+ 1102 exam Objective 1.3 is Performance Monitor. You can run it via the Run dialog box (WINDOWS KEY-R) by typing **perfmon** or by searching for Performance Monitor. Performance Monitor tracks and gathers performance data for memory, disks, processors, networks, and more so that you can see if one of these items is showing performance problems.

Each item you can monitor, such as physical disks, memory, processor, and network interface, is an *object,* and it has one or more characteristics, called *counters,* that you may select for monitoring. Performance Monitor displays the data in real time in a report, line graph, or histogram (bar chart) format. Figure 6-5 shows Performance Monitor displaying processor performance information.

Event Viewer

Windows automatically saves most error messages in event logs for later viewing in Event Viewer. You can open Event Viewer from Administrative Tools or by typing its filename, **eventvwr.msc**, in the Run dialog box. Become familiar with Event Viewer before a problem

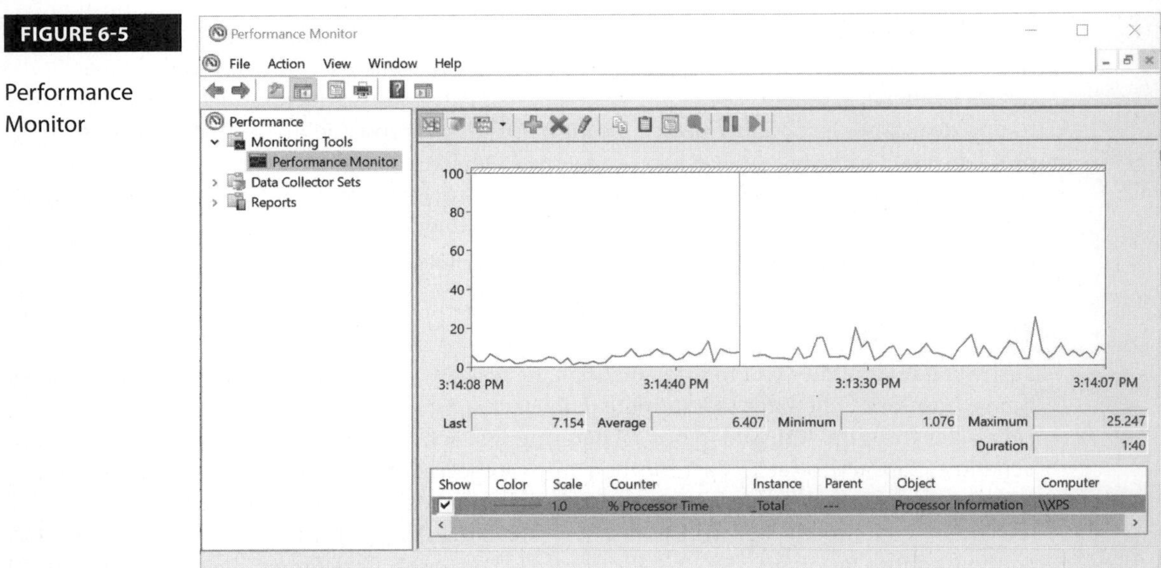

FIGURE 6-5 Performance Monitor

occurs so you will be comfortable using it to research a problem. Use Event Viewer to view logs of system, security, and application events, paying attention to the warning and error logs for messages you can use to solve problems.

Event Viewer has three standard categories of events: system, application, and security. Other event logs may exist, depending on the Windows configuration. For instance, Internet Explorer creates its own event log.

Event Viewer displays a list of Administrative events, which is a selection of events from all the log files that show a status of Warning or Error. This saves scrolling through all the Information events to find an event indicating a problem. To see the individual logs, select the Windows Logs folder in the left pane and select each event log in turn:

- The System log records events involving the Windows system components (drivers, services, and so on). The types of events range from normal events, such as startup and shutdown (called Information events), through warnings of situations that could lead to errors, to actual error events. Even the dreaded "Blue Screen of Death" error messages show up in the System log as STOP errors. The System log, shown in Figure 6-6, is the place to look for messages about components, such as a driver or service. Details for the selected event, including the actual message, display in the pane below the events list. The message itself may lead you to the solution. Each event also has an ID number. Search the Microsoft website for a solution, using either a portion of the error message or the event ID.

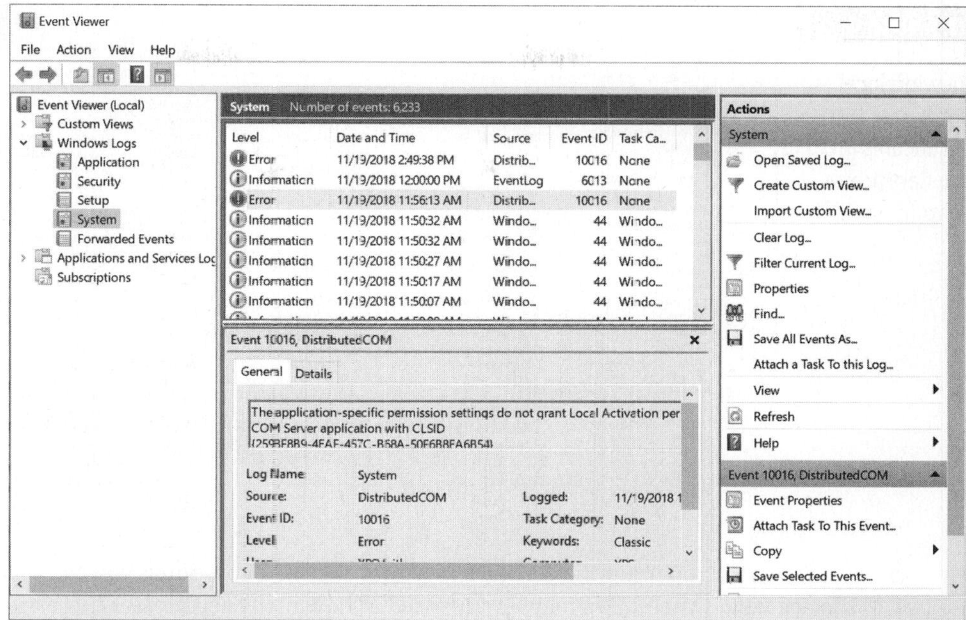

FIGURE 6-6 Windows 10 Event Viewer showing the System log

- The Application log shows events involving applications. These applications may be your Office suite of applications or Windows components that run in the GUI, such as Windows Explorer or Document Explorer. If you see an error on your screen that mentions an application, you will find the error listed in the Application log.
- The Security log will log events such as a successful or failed logon attempt. It will also log events relating to access to resources, such as files and folders. Several types of security events are logged by default, and an administrator can enable and disable logging of security events. See the section "Local Security Policy" in Chapter 21 to learn how to control what security messages are logged.

To learn more about Event Viewer, use the help command from within it.

Certificate Manager

Many secure services and clients use certificates to validate your (or your computer's) identity. You can view and manage these credentials using the *Certificate Manager* utility (certmgr.msc). When you add the Certificates snap-in to the MMC, you have a choice of choosing to view certificates for the local computer, the signed-in user, or specific services. If you run **certmgr** from outside of the MMC, you automatically get the local computer version.

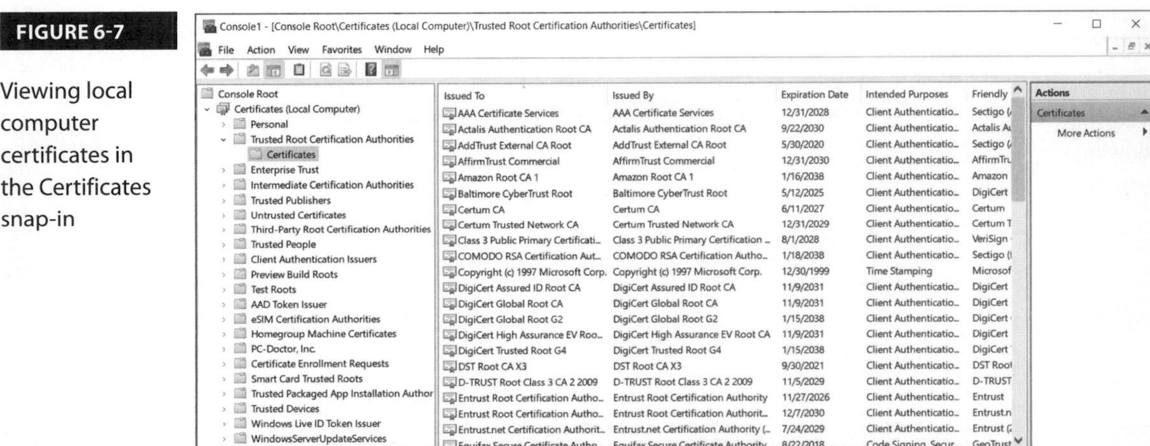

FIGURE 6-7 Viewing local computer certificates in the Certificates snap-in

Once you open up the certificates list for the local computer, you can browse its hierarchy to see what's there. You may be surprised at how many certificates there are on an average PC. For example, browse Certificates – Local Computer | Trusted Root Certification Authorities | Certificates. Figure 6-7 shows a screenful of examples. You can double-click a certificate to see its details, and right-click it and choose Delete to remove it.

Local Users and Groups

The recommended way of managing user accounts on a Windows PC is to use the Accounts tool in the Settings app or the User Accounts tool in the Control Panel. However, if you have Windows 10 Professional, Education, or Enterprise, you also have access to another tool (which is also an MMC snap-in): *Local Users and Groups* (lusrmgr.msc). It is also available via Computer Management and by typing the filename at the Start menu.

Some of the things you can do with this utility include enabling and disabling accounts (without deleting them entirely), enabling the Guest account, and creating/deleting accounts. You can also control some advanced settings for the accounts, such as whether the user can change their password and whether the password ever expires.

Group Policy Editor

Another utility that's for Windows Pro, Education, and Enterprise editions only is *Group Policy Editor* (gpedit.msc). It's also available from the Control Panel, in the Administrative Tools group, if you have one of the qualifying editions.

Its purpose is to enable users (and administrators) to configure user settings based on the group(s) that a user account is a member of. If you have ever used a work computer that didn't let you perform certain administrative tasks on a PC, that was the Group Policy Editor at work. Some of the things you can do with the Group Policy Editor include

- Prevent users from personalizing the Windows interface
- Prohibit external drives from being accessed
- Prohibit users from installing or removing applications
- Disable certain network protocols
- Control which Settings app and Control Panel utilities the user can make changes to
- Prevent users from accessing the Group Policy Editor utility, so they can't change the settings back

If you get a question about controlling what certain groups of users have permission to do on their Windows PCs, the correct answer probably involves the Group Policy Editor.

Resource Monitor

In Task Manager, on the Performance tab, you can access some real-time statistics about the PC's performance. You'll learn more about that later in this chapter. The *Resource Monitor* utility (resmon.exe) is an expanded version of that, providing more granularity.

One use for the Resource Monitor is to find bottlenecks in system performance. For example, suppose a PC is running apps sluggishly. Is the problem disk access time? Weak CPU? Too little memory? Bogged-down network? The Resource Monitor can show you moving graphs that illustrate how much of each resource is being used at any given moment. In Figure 6-8, for example, we can see that the CPU is having no problems at all but both Disk and Network are spiking.

Services

A *service* is a program that runs in the background, has no GUI, and supports other programs. For instance, there are specialized services associated with various devices, such as smart cards, printers, displays, digital tablets, and audio devices. Many services support networking and security, and the list goes on. Open the Services console by entering **services.msc** in the Run dialog box. The Services console, shown in Figure 6-9, lets you manage services.

You normally should not need to make any changes to services, but if you must make changes, use this tool rather than others. In the Services console, you can start, stop, pause, resume, and disable services. One common service you may need to restart is the Print Spooler, for example. This may be necessary if a printer's queue is not working.

FIGURE 6-8

The Resource Monitor utility

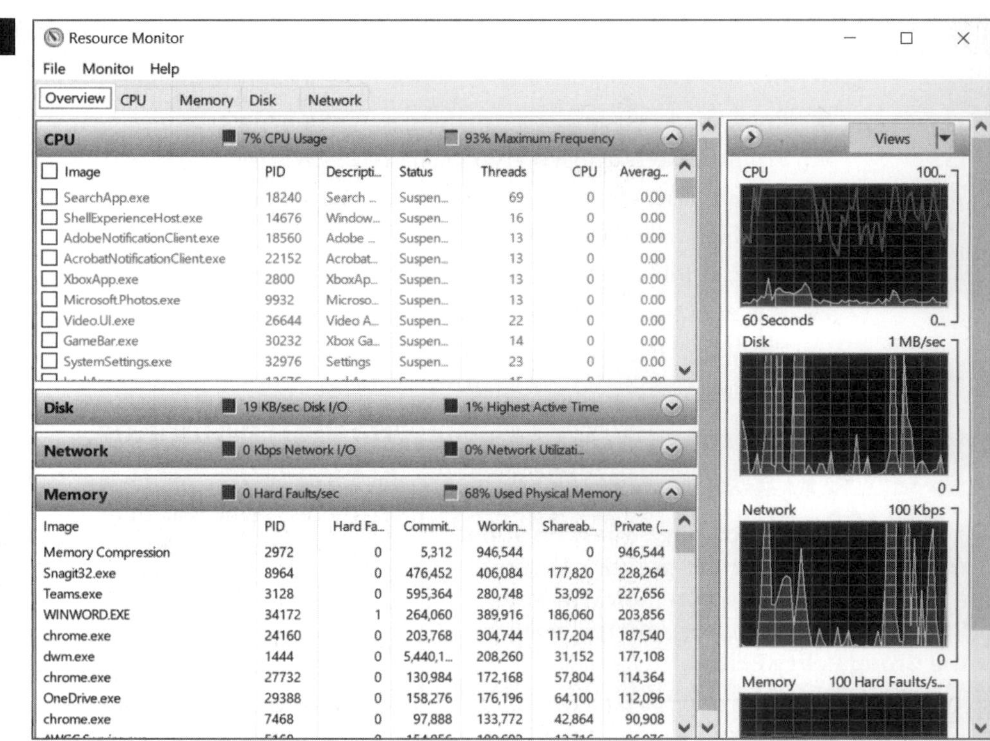

You can also configure the recovery options for what should occur when an individual service fails. To access that feature, you need to right-click a service in the Services console and select Properties. In the Properties dialog box for the service, click the Recovery tab, as shown in Figure 6-10. The recovery options include Take No Action, Restart The Service, Run A Program, and Restart The Computer.

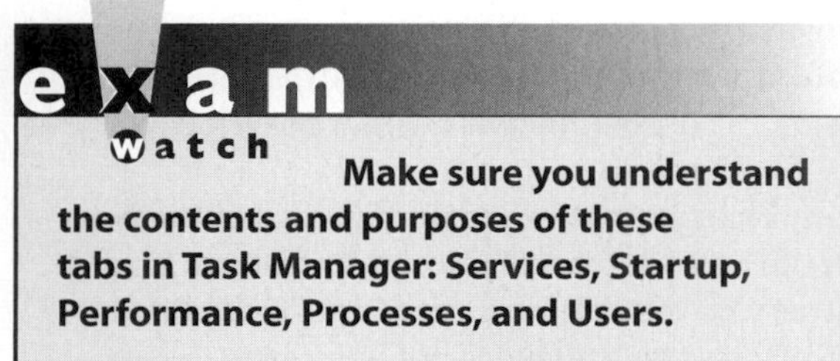

Make sure you understand the contents and purposes of these tabs in Task Manager: Services, Startup, Performance, Processes, and Users.

Task Manager

Task Manager is a utility for examining running processes and services and shutting them down if needed. The default Task Manager window is a simple, single window with no tabs, and you must click More Details to see the tabs.

To open Task Manager, press CTRL-SHIFT-ESC, or right-click an empty area of the taskbar and choose Task Manager or Start Task Manager.

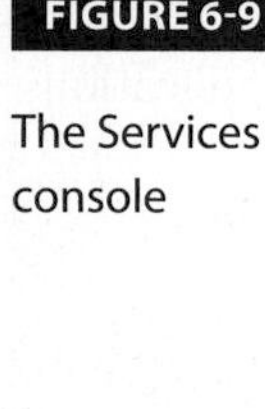

FIGURE 6-9

The Services console

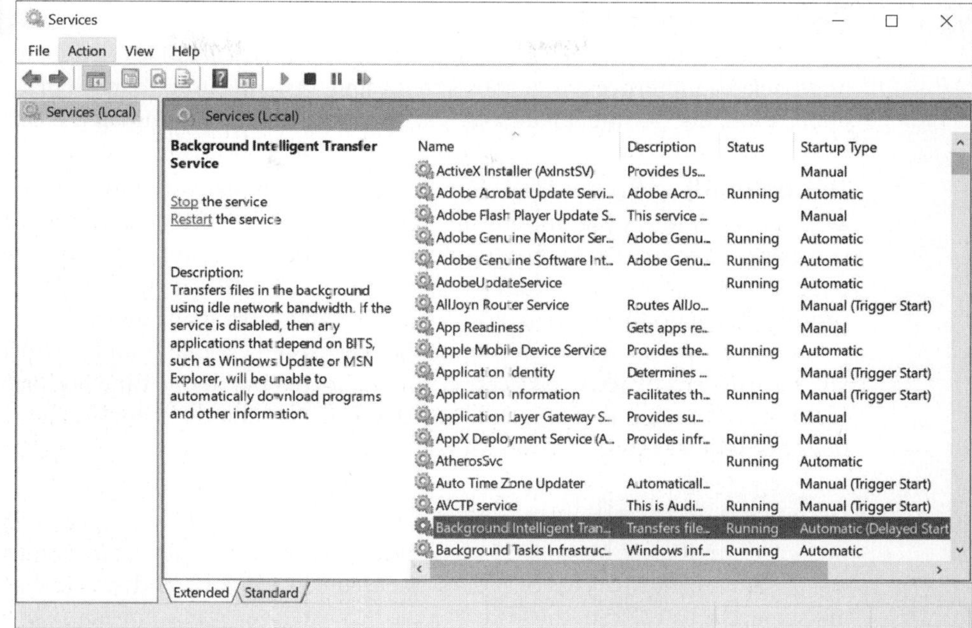

FIGURE 6-10

The Recovery tab on a service's Properties dialog box

Processes and Details Tabs

The Processes tab contains a simple list of processes, divided into two sections: Applications and Background Processes. It shows the system resource usage of each process or application, but not the full details. The process details are found on the Details tab.

Understanding Processes In case you aren't familiar with how processes work, here's a basic overview. A program runs in memory as one or more *processes*. A single process consists of memory space, program code, data, and the system resources required by the process. Each process has at least one *thread*, which is the program code executed by the process. An operating system has many active processes at any given time. Add to that the processes for such programs or applications as File Explorer and Microsoft Word, and you have dozens of active processes running in memory at one time performing various functions. A *background process* is one that runs "behind the scenes" and has a low priority, does not require input, and rarely creates output.

Viewing Process Priorities When a programmer creates a program, she gives it a *process priority level*, also called a *base priority level*, which determines the order in which the program code's process or processes execute in relation to other active processes. There are six levels, listed from the lowest to the highest: Low, Below Normal, Normal, Above Normal, High, and Real Time. A program that has a High priority level has the potential to tie up the processor, and one with a Real Time priority level can cause system crashes. The operating system can adjust these levels to some degree, and you can temporarily adjust the level of an active process by right-clicking it and selecting Set Priority. We do not recommend that you do this.

To view the priority level of active processes, first select the Details tab, and then right-click any column heading and choose Select Columns. In the dialog box that appears, click to place a check mark in the Base Priority box and click OK. This adds the Base Priority column.

Most of the processes will have a Base Priority level of Normal, with a few High priorities and perhaps one or two Below Normal. The High priority processes should be part of the operating system, such as csrss.exe, dwm.exe, or some (but not all) programs associated with a specialized device, such as a digital tablet. So how do you use this knowledge of processes in troubleshooting? If a system is slow, noting which processes are running with a High priority at the times of slow performance may tell you which ones are taking processing time away from others. Perhaps the answer is to evaluate the need for that app. If it is critical that you continue to use it and the software publisher does not have a solution, you may need to run it on a more powerful computer.

Performance Tab

The Performance tab is a "lite" version of Performance Monitor. Open this for a quick look at many different factors, including CPU, memory, disk, Ethernet, Wi-Fi, and GPU.

The most important object to check here is CPU. The graph measures the percentage of CPU usage in a separate window for each CPU or core. CPU usage usually bounces up and down as various processes execute. However, sustained usage above about 80 percent indicates that the CPU is inadequate for the task. This may indicate a problem with the CPU overheating or another cause, or it may simply mean it is time to upgrade the CPU or entire computer.

App History Tab

Whereas the Performance tab shows you current statistics about each running app, the App History tab shows you historical data. That's useful because you can't always catch a resource-hogging app in the act.

Startup Tab

The Startup tab lists all the applications and services that are set to load automatically at startup. It lists their names, publishers, status (enabled or disabled), and their startup impact (in other words, how long it delays the system startup when they are enabled to run at startup). This tab's functionality replaces that of the Startup tab in the System Configuration utility (MSCONFIG) in Windows 7 and earlier. You will learn more about the System Configuration utility later in this chapter. To enable or disable an item, select it and then click the Enable button or Disable button at the bottom of the Task Manager window.

It's important to note that the applications that appear on the Startup tab do not originate from Task Manager. They are set in the registry to load at startup. Disabling them from loading via Task Manager puts them on "pause," but it does not remove them from the registry; you can re-enable them at any point later. To remove the entry in the registry that causes them to be on this list, you must either remove the associated application or adjust the settings in that application to prevent it from loading things in the background.

Users Tab

The Users tab in Task Manager shows the currently logged-on users, including you, along with any users who are connected to a share on your computer over a network. When a network user is connected, their computer name will show up under the Client Name (or User) column. What will *not* show up are the various special user accounts that run services on your computer.

From this tab you can disconnect or log off a user. If it is a network user, you should click the Send Message button to send them a warning so that they can close any files they have open on your computer.

Services Tab

Click the Services tab to see the list of services loaded into Windows. If you look at the status in the Status column, you will see that not all of the listed processes are actually running. Many are stopped because they are only started when needed. Some processes and services are associated, and when you right-click a service that is running and select Go To Details, it will open the Details tab and highlight the associated process. However, if you do that on a running service and no process is highlighted, the process may be hidden and you will need to select Show Processes From All Users. You can learn more about the current services by clicking the Open Services hyperlink at the bottom of this screen. This will open the Services utility, which you learned about earlier in this chapter.

EXERCISE 6-2

Video

Exploring Task Manager

In this exercise you will start an application and then pretend that it has become unresponsive and shut it down manually using Task Manager. It's good practice for when an application actually does become unresponsive in Windows.

1. Start the Notepad app.
2. Right-click the taskbar and click Task Manager.
3. Click More Details or Fewer Details, whichever one appears, to toggle between the two display modes. When you're finished trying that out, end up with the tabs hidden (Fewer Details). Notice that only the running applications appear. Then click More Details. Notice that the applications appear on the Processes tab in an Apps section, and there is also a rather large Background Processes section with other processes.
4. Click the Memory column. The processes become sorted by the amount of memory they are using. If the largest amount doesn't appear at the top, click Memory again to reverse the sort. Then click the Name column to return the sort order to the default.
5. Click each of the other tabs to see what it contains.
6. Go back to the Processes tab and click Fewer Details.
7. Click Notepad, and click End Task.
8. Close the Task Manager window.

Virtual Memory

Windows allows you to *multitask*—that is, to have several programs open in memory at the same time. When you multitask with large program and data files, it is possible to run out of space in physical random access memory (RAM). When a Windows computer is running low on memory available for the operating system and any loaded applications, rather than limit your activities, it employs a technique called virtual memory.

Virtual memory or *virtual RAM* is the use of a portion of hard disk as a temporary storage space for data that would ordinarily be in the PC's RAM. This temporary storage space exists inside a special file called *PAGEFILE.SYS,* which is stored by default in the root directory of the C: drive. Virtual memory works by determining what data in RAM is the least likely to be needed soon (that is, has been least recently called for by the OS) and sending that data to the paging file for storage. It then creates a placeholder marker so the data can be found again later, and then makes that freed-up block of RAM available for other use. When a program calls for the paged data, it "swaps" the paged data back into actual RAM, moving whatever was in its place to the paging file. Because of this swapping of data into and out of RAM, a paging file is also called a *swap file*.

As a rule, Windows manages virtual memory just fine without intervention. We recommend that you don't change it unless you have a specific reason to. For 32-bit versions of Windows, the default paging file size is 1.5 times the amount of physical RAM. For 64-bit versions, Windows will dynamically adjust the paging file size as system usage dictates, within minimum and maximum values.

The general guideline for paging file size in Windows is three times the amount of physical RAM or 4 GB, whichever is larger. However, the optimal paging file size is not simple to calculate, and in most cases you're better off allowing Windows to perform that calculation for you by leaving the paging file set to a system-managed size.

In Exercise 6-3, you will view the virtual memory settings on your computer. The default location of the paging file is on drive C:. If you are running out of free disk space on drive C:—and if you have other internal hard drive volumes—consider moving the paging file to another drive that has more free space. In particular, if you have a solid-state drive that is not your primary hard drive and nowhere near being full, consider relocating the paging file to that drive, because it is likely to be your fastest drive and you'll get the best performance.

You can also have more than one paging file, but this is not normally necessary on a desktop or laptop computer. Never place the paging file on an external hard drive, because it may not be available during startup and this could prevent Windows from launching.

EXERCISE 6-3

Viewing the Virtual Memory Settings

This exercise shows you how to view the current virtual memory settings for a PC.

1. Open the System page of the Control Panel. To do so, open the Control Panel, click System And Security (in Category View), and then click System.
2. Click Advanced System Settings in the navigation bar at the left. The System Properties dialog box opens.

3. In the System Properties dialog box, select the Advanced tab.
4. Under Performance, click Settings.
5. In the Performance Options dialog box, select the Advanced tab.
6. Under Virtual Memory, click Change to view the virtual memory settings for all the hard drives on your computer.

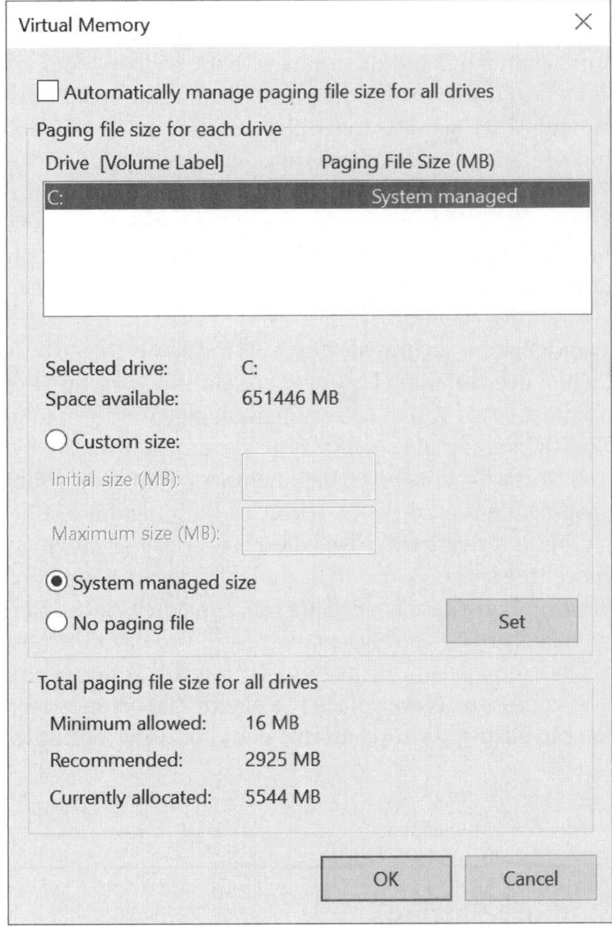

7. If you wanted to make changes, you would clear the Automatically Manage Paging File Size For All Drives check box (if marked) and then click Custom Size and enter a size value. However, for this exercise, just look and don't touch.
8. If you made no changes, click Cancel three times to close the three dialog boxes: Virtual Memory, Performance Options, and System Properties.

SCENARIO & SOLUTION	
You have researched a system problem on a client PC and have found a registry edit online that may help. Before performing the edit, what should you do?	Before performing a registry edit, especially one that's new and untried, you should back up the registry, or at least the root key that it pertains to.
You want to give several junior system administrators access to specific administrative tools. How can you build a custom set of tools for each person?	Use Microsoft Management Console (mmc.exe) to build a set of desired applications by loading snap-ins.

CERTIFICATION OBJECTIVES

- ***1102: 1.3*** *Given a scenario, use features and tools of the Microsoft Windows 10 operating system (OS)*
- ***1102: 1.9*** *Given a scenario, perform OS installations and upgrades in a diverse OS environment*
- ***1102: 3.1*** *Given a scenario, troubleshoot common Windows OS problems*

This section explains some ways to repair startup-related Windows problems. From CompTIA A+ 1102 exam Objective 1.3 it looks at System Configuration (aka MSCONFIG), and from 1.9 it covers the topics of recovery partitions and repair installations. Topics from 1102 exam Objective 3.1 include repairing Windows, restoring (from a System Restore point), and reimaging the OS.

Troubleshooting Windows Startup Problems

Startup problems can be especially frustrating and thorny to troubleshoot because some of the normal troubleshooting tools that you rely on may not be working properly (or at all). Fortunately Windows does not leave you bereft when serious system problems occur. In the following sections you'll learn about several tools and methods for restoring a damaged Windows installation to health.

Startup Settings Menu

The Startup Settings menu, shown in Figure 6-11, is a menu from which you can choose to put Windows in a special startup mode. This is useful if Windows isn't working correctly in its normal operating mode.

On systems that don't have Safe Boot enabled (a feature of UEFI firmware), you can press F8 at startup to access this menu. On systems with Safe Boot enabled by Unified Extensible Firmware Interface (UEFI) setup, which is common on systems with later Windows versions on them, you won't be able to use the F8 method.

To access the Startup Settings menu:

1. Open the Settings app and select Update & Security (Windows 10) or System | Recovery (Windows 11).
2. In Windows 10, click Recovery in the navigation bar. (This step is not needed in Windows 11.)
3. In the Advanced Startup section, click Restart Now to load the Windows Recovery Environment (RE).
4. Select Troubleshoot | Advanced Options | Startup Settings | Restart.

Startup Settings

Press a number to choose from the options below:

Use number keys or functions keys F1-F9.

1) Enable debugging
2) Enable boot logging
3) Enable low-resolution video
4) Enable Safe Mode
5) Enable Safe Mode with Networking
6) Enable Safe Mode with Command Prompt
7) Disable driver signature enforcement
8) Disable early launch anti-malware protection
9) Disable automatic restart after failure

Press F10 for more options
Press Enter to return to your operating system

FIGURE 6-11 The Startup Settings menu

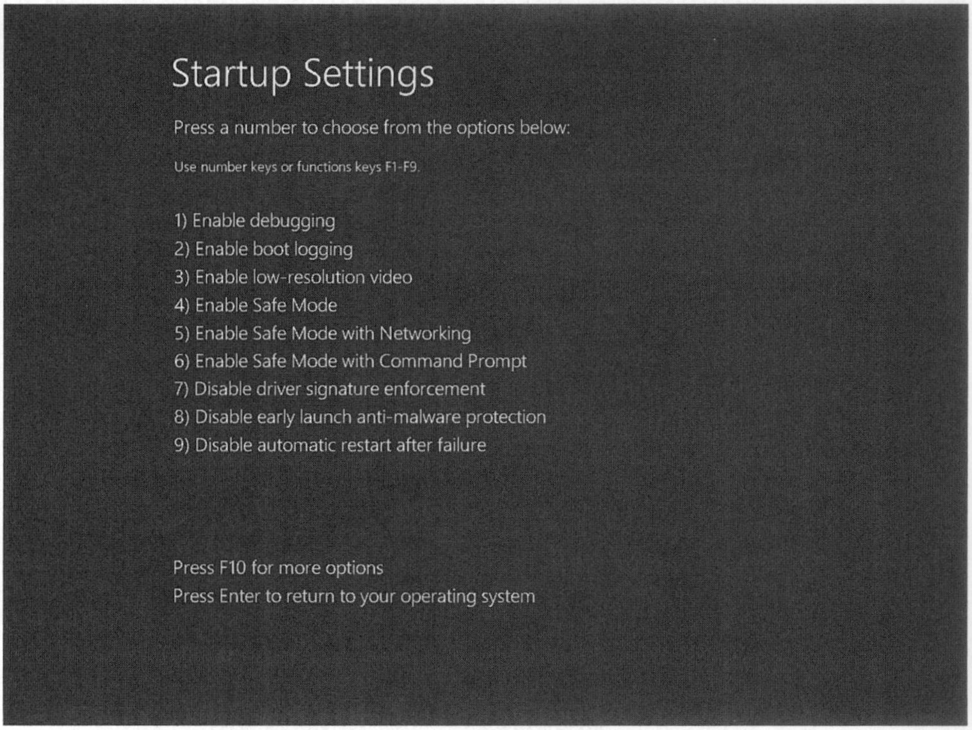

Here's a shortcut for Steps 1–3: from the Windows sign-in screen or from the open Start menu, hold down the SHIFT key and click the Power icon; on the menu that appears, select Restart.

Obviously if you can't start Windows at all, you can't follow these steps. There's a workaround, though: if you try unsuccessfully to restart Windows several times in a row, Windows boots automatically into the RE, which is where you end up after Step 3.

Following is a brief description of the startup options available from the Startup Settings menu.

Enable Debugging

Debugging Mode is a very advanced option in which Windows starts normally, and information about the activity (programs loaded and programs started) during Windows startup is sent over a cable to another computer that is running a special program called a debugger. This technique is more or less obsolete, but the option remains for backward compatibility.

Enable Boot Logging

Boot logging causes Windows to write a log of the activity (programs loaded into memory and programs started) during Windows startup in a file named ntbtlog.txt, and it saves it in the *systemroot* folder (usually C:\Windows). This log file contains an entry for each component in the order in which it loaded into memory. It also lists drivers that were not loaded, which alerts an administrator to a possible source of a problem.

Whereas boot logging occurs automatically with each of the three Safe Modes (described next), selecting Enable Boot Logging turns on boot logging and starts Windows normally.

Enable Safe Mode

Safe Mode is a startup mode for starting Windows with certain drivers and components disabled, but many troubleshooting and recovery tools do work in Safe Mode. If Windows will not start normally but starts just fine in Safe Mode, use Device Manager within Safe Mode to determine if the source of the problem is a faulty device. You can run System Restore while in Safe Mode and roll back the entire system to before the problem occurred. Safe Mode does not disable Windows security. You are required to log on in all three variants of Safe Mode, and you can only access those resources to which you have permissions.

Three Safe Mode variants are available: Enable Safe Mode, Enable Safe Mode With Networking, and Enable Safe Mode With Command Prompt.

- *Enable Safe Mode* starts up without using several drivers and components that it would normally start, including the network components. It loads only very basic, non-vendor-specific drivers for mouse, video (loading Windows' very basic VGA.sys driver), keyboard, mass storage, and system services.

- *Enable Safe Mode With Networking* is identical to plain Safe Mode, except that it also starts the networking components. Use the following debug sequence with Safe Mode With Networking:
  - If Windows will not start up normally but it starts fine in plain Safe Mode, restart and select Safe Mode With Networking.
  - If it fails to start in Safe Mode With Networking, the problem area is network drivers or components. Use Device Manager to disable the network adapter driver (the likely culprit), and then boot up normally. If Windows now works, replace your network driver.
  - If this problem appears immediately after upgrading a network driver, use Device Manager while in Safe Mode to roll back the updated driver. When an updated driver is available, install it.
- *Enable Safe Mode With Command Prompt* is Safe Mode with only a command prompt as a user interface. Windows would normally load your GUI desktop, but this depends on the program explorer.exe, the GUI shell to Windows. In place of this GUI shell, Safe Mode With Command Prompt loads a very limited GUI with a Command Prompt (cmd.exe) window. This is a handy option to remember if the desktop does not display at all. Once you have eliminated video drivers as the cause, corruption of the explorer.exe program itself may be the problem. From within the Command Prompt, you can delete the corrupted version of explorer.exe and copy an undamaged version. This requires knowledge of the command-line commands for navigating the directory structure, as well as knowledge of the location of the file that you are replacing. You can launch programs, such as the Event Viewer (eventvwr.msc), the Computer Management console (compmgmt.msc), or Device Manager (devmgmt.msc), from the Command Prompt.

Enable Low-Resolution Video

This option starts Windows normally, except that the video mode is changed to the lowest resolution (which varies depending on the Windows version), using the currently installed video driver. It does not switch to the basic Windows video driver. Select this option after making a video configuration change that the video adapter does not support and that prevents Windows from displaying properly.

Disable Early Launch Anti-Malware Protection

While it is a good thing to have your antimalware driver launch early so that it is ready to protect your computer, this very behavior may be tied to a startup problem. To eliminate this as the possible cause, select the *Disable Early Launch Anti-Malware Protection* option, which will apply to only one startup.

Disable Driver Signature Enforcement

If you are unable to install a driver because it has not been digitally signed and is being disabled by driver signing and you trust the manufacturer, select *Disable Driver Signature Enforcement,* which will start Windows normally, disabling driver signature enforcement just for one startup.

Disable Automatic Restart After Failure

The default setting for Windows is for it to restart after a system crash. However, depending on the problem, restarting may simply lead to another restart—in fact, you could find yourself faced with a continuous loop of restarts. If so, select *Disable Automatic Restart After Failure* (Windows 8 and later). Then Windows will attempt to start normally (just once for each time you select this option) and may stay open long enough for you to troubleshoot. Do not attempt to work with any data file after restarting with this option, because the system may be too unstable. If you are not able to solve the problem, you will need to restart in Safe Mode to troubleshoot.

Start Windows Normally

Press ENTER at the menu to return to your operating system, starting Windows normally.

EXERCISE 6-4

Working in Safe Mode

This exercise enables you to practice booting into Safe Mode.

1. From the Start menu, hold down SHIFT as you click the Power button and then click Restart. Wait for the Recovery Environment to load.
2. Select Troubleshoot | Advanced Options | Startup Settings | Restart.
3. Press 5 to choose Enable Safe Mode With Networking. Windows restarts.
4. Sign in as you normally would. Safe Mode loads with a black desktop background and the words "Safe Mode" in the corners of the screen.
5. Poke around in Windows to see what's different (and what's the same). When you finish exploring Safe Mode, restart Windows.
6. Repeat Steps 1–2.
7. Press 6 to choose Enable Safe Mode With Command Prompt. Windows restarts in command prompt mode.
8. If you know some command-line commands, try them out. For example, try typing **dir /w** and pressing ENTER.
9. Press CTRL-ALT-DELETE to open a menu.
10. Click the Power icon in the bottom-right corner of the screen and click Restart.

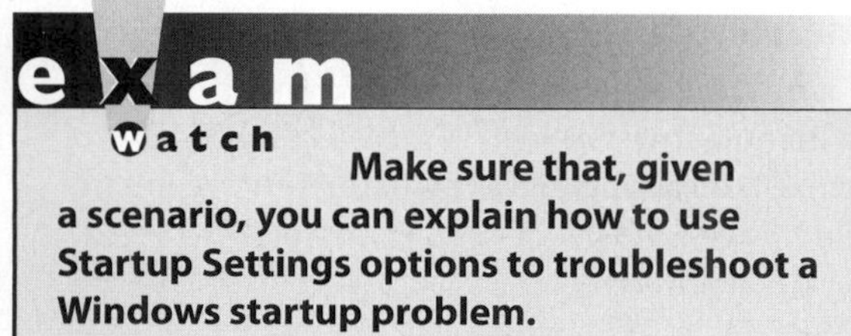

Make sure that, given a scenario, you can explain how to use Startup Settings options to troubleshoot a Windows startup problem.

System Configuration (MSCONFIG)

The *System Configuration,* also known as *MSCONFIG (*pronounced *M-S-config)* or msconfig.exe, has a number of useful capabilities for troubleshooting an ailing Windows system. It provides alternative ways of accessing the same boot modes as discussed in the preceding section, but it makes them "sticky" so that you continue to boot in that mode each time you reboot until you reenter System Configuration and change back to normal booting.

While you can call this program up from the GUI, the quick way to launch it from any version is by entering **msconfig** in the Run dialog box (WINDOWS KEY-R) or in the Search box on the taskbar.

General Tab

On the General tab you can choose from Normal Startup, Diagnostic Startup, or Selective Startup, as shown in Figure 6-12.

- *Normal Startup* is just what the name says: startup without any special options enabled.

FIGURE 6-12

The General tab of the System Configuration dialog box

- *Diagnostic Startup* is similar to Safe Mode, but not exactly the same. Whereas Safe Mode loads only a generic set of hardware drivers, Diagnostic Startup loads a basic set of drivers for the hardware that it detects you have. There may be cases where Diagnostic Startup will fail but Safe Mode startup will succeed, and that's why.
- *Selective Startup* enables you to exclude certain items from automatically loading at startup, so you can isolate the source of a startup problem. Once you determine what program or service is causing a problem, you can uninstall the program or permanently disable the service so it will not run when the computer boots.

Back in Windows 7 and earlier, the Startup tab in the System Configuration utility provided a list of applications and services that load at startup, and you could enable/disable each one individually to fine-tune exactly what loads at startup. However, starting with Windows 8 this functionality was moved to Task Manager. There is still a Startup tab in the System Configuration utility, but it's just an empty stub with a hyperlink to the new location in Task Manager.

The three check boxes under Selective Startup on the General tab are as follows:

- *Load System Services* enables the choices you make on the Startup tab (or in Task Manager) to take effect. If you clear this check box, none of the services listed there will load.
- *Load Startup Items* allows applications set to load at startup to do so. If you clear this check box, none of the applications chosen on the Startup tab (or in Task Manager) will load.
- *Use Original Boot Configuration* enables you to toggle back and forth between the original boot configuration and your modified one. If you haven't made any changes to the boot configuration on the Startup tab (or in Task Manager), this check box is unavailable.

Boot Tab

From the Boot tab (Figure 6-13), you can restart Windows in Safe Boot mode. After marking the Safe Boot check box, you can choose from one of four safe booting modes:

- **Minimal** This is the same as the Safe Mode you learned about earlier in this chapter. It loads only the most essential system services.
- **Alternate Shell** This boots you into the command-line interface. It's equivalent to Safe Mode With Command Prompt.
- **Active Directory Repair** This is equivalent to Directory Services Restore Mode. It allows Safe Mode to access hardware information so it can repair and refresh Active Directory information.
- **Network** This is equivalent to Safe Mode With Networking. It is just like Minimal, except it includes your network interface card's driver and networking services.

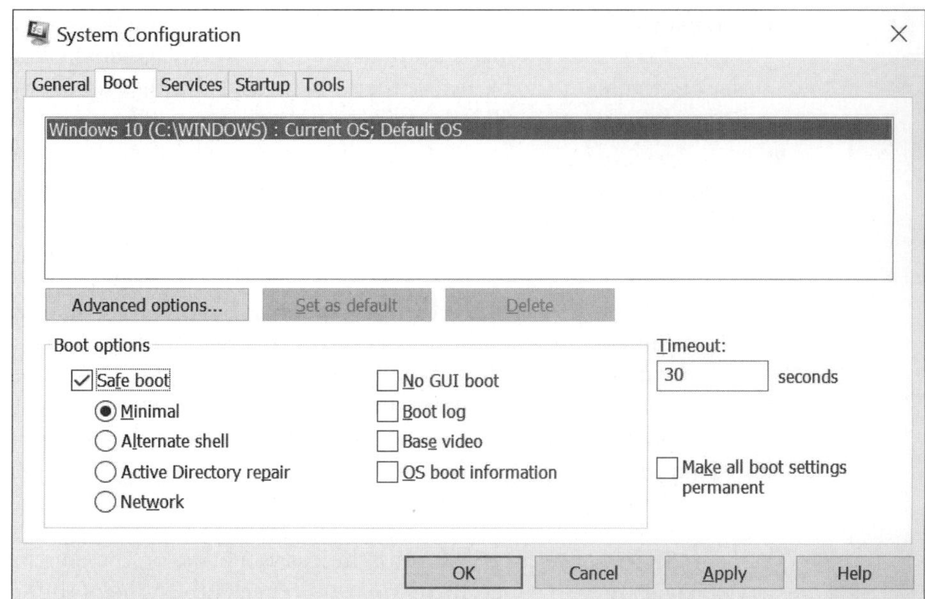

FIGURE 6-13 The System Configuration Boot tab

Do not experiment with the Active Directory Repair option. You may get locked out of Windows, where you face a blank opening screen with no sign-in prompt. If this happens, SHIFT-CLICK the Power icon and then choose Restart, and then choose Troubleshoot | Advanced Options | Startup Settings | Restart. When the Startup Settings menu appears, press 4 to enter Safe Mode. This will get you back to regular Safe Mode, and from there you can go back into System Configuration and disable Active Directory Repair on the Boot tab.

The check boxes to the right of the Safe Boot options enable you to further customize the boot. For example, if you want a Safe Mode With Networking boot and also an Alternate Shell boot, you could choose Network under the Safe Boot heading and then mark the No GUI Boot check box.

After you select a Safe Boot option and click OK, a message box displays, giving you the opportunity to either restart or exit without restarting. If you restart, you will be in Safe Mode, where you can continue your troubleshooting. When finished working in Safe Mode, open System Configuration again, clear the Safe Boot check box from the Boot page, return to the General page, and select Normal Startup. You will see the same prompt, where you will need to click the Restart button, and Windows will restart normally.

Services Tab

The System Configuration Services tab lets you select services to disable for a restart. This is one way to test if a certain service is causing a problem. Like the other tabs, when you click OK, you will be prompted to restart or cancel.

System Configuration is not the proper place to manage services on a routine basis. For that, use services.msc.

Startup Tab

There's nothing on the Startup tab except a link to the Startup tab in Task Manager, which is where you now go to choose what loads (and what doesn't) when in Selective Startup mode.

Customizing the list of automatically loading apps and services enables you to test "what-if" scenarios for startup. For instance, you can temporarily disable the startup of one or more programs, restart, and see if that eliminated the problem; if it did, make the change permanent so that the problem will not recur.

Tools Tab

The Tools tab contains a long list of troubleshooting and administrative tools, giving you yet another way to launch them. Select a tool in the list, and then click the Launch button.

EXERCISE 6-5

Exploring Boot Modes with System Configuration

In this exercise you will use System Configuration to restart Windows in several different boot modes. You can use any Windows version for this exercise.

1. Press WINDOWS KEY-R to open the Run box. Type **msconfig** and click OK.
2. On the Boot tab, mark the Safe Boot check box.
3. Select Minimal.
4. Click OK. When prompted, click Restart.
5. Repeat Steps 1 and 2. Then select Alternate Shell.
6. Click OK. When prompted, click Restart. Notice that the command prompt appears in an Administrator: cmd.exe window, on a black background, with Safe Mode in the corners.
7. Type **compmgmt.msc** and press ENTER. The Computer Management window opens. Notice that you can use GUI programs even without a desktop GUI.

8. Close the Computer Management window.
9. Type **exit**. Your command prompt is gone. Now you have effectively locked yourself out, and you will need to restart the system manually.
10. Restart the PC by pressing its hardware Power button. (Hold it down for five seconds so the machine turns off all the way, and then press it again.) If prompted to choose an action, choose Start Windows Normally. Windows reboots into the command prompt interface again.
11. Type **msconfig** and press ENTER. System Configuration reloads.
12. On the Boot tab, clear the Safe Boot check box.
13. On the General tab, select Normal Startup.
14. Click OK, and then click Restart.

System Restore

If you have ever added the latest software or new device to your Windows computer only to find that nothing seems to work right after this change, System Restore will come to your aid. If you can't access the GUI, you can access System Restore via the System Recovery Options menu, described later in this chapter under "Recovery Options."

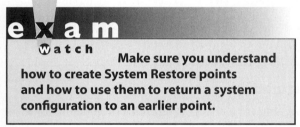

Make sure you understand how to create System Restore points and how to use them to return a system configuration to an earlier point.

System Restore creates *restore points,* which are snapshots of Windows, its configuration, and all installed components. Windows creates restore points automatically when you add or remove software or install Windows updates and during the normal shutdown of your computer. You can also choose to force creation of a restore point before making changes. If your computer has nonfatal problems after you have made a change, or if you believe it has a malware infection, you can use System Restore to roll it back to a restore point.

During the restore process, only settings and programs are changed—no data is lost. Your computer will include all programs and settings as of the restore date and time. This feature is invaluable for overworked administrators and consultants. A simple restore will fix many user-generated problems.

To open System Restore, open the Settings app, click System, and then scroll down to the Related Settings section (or Related Links in Windows 11) and click System Protection. That opens the System Properties dialog box to the System Protection tab. See Figure 6-14.

Click the System Restore button to start the System Restore Wizard, and then work through its steps. You will be prompted to select a restore point, as in Figure 6-15. Usually the most recent one is a good choice, unless you know specifically when the problem started and can choose a point right before that.

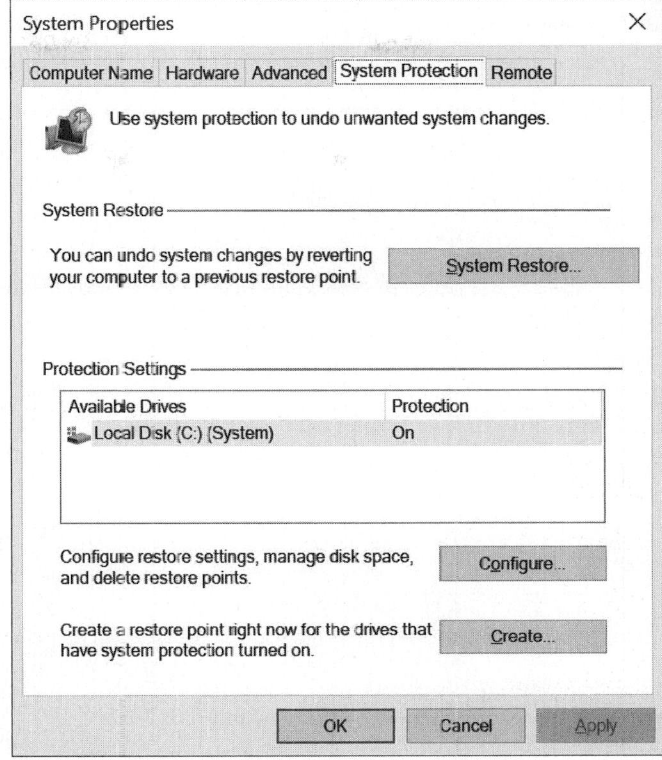

FIGURE 6-14 The System Protection tab of the System Properties dialog box

You don't have to just rely on the automatic creation of restore points. You can create a restore point at any time. From the System Protection tab in the System Properties dialog box (see Figure 6-14), click the Create button. Type a description for your restore point and then click Create. This is something to consider doing before making changes that might not trigger an automatic restore point, such as directly editing the registry.

System Restore is on by default and uses some of your disk space to save restore points each day. To turn System Restore off (disable) or change the disk space, click the Configure button on the System Protection tab of the System Properties dialog box (see Figure 6-14) and then choose Disable System Protection. You can also delete all restore points for the drive from here. You might want to turn off restore point creation to save disk space, or if you suspect that the system has a virus and you don't want anyone to be able to restore back to a point where the system files were infected.

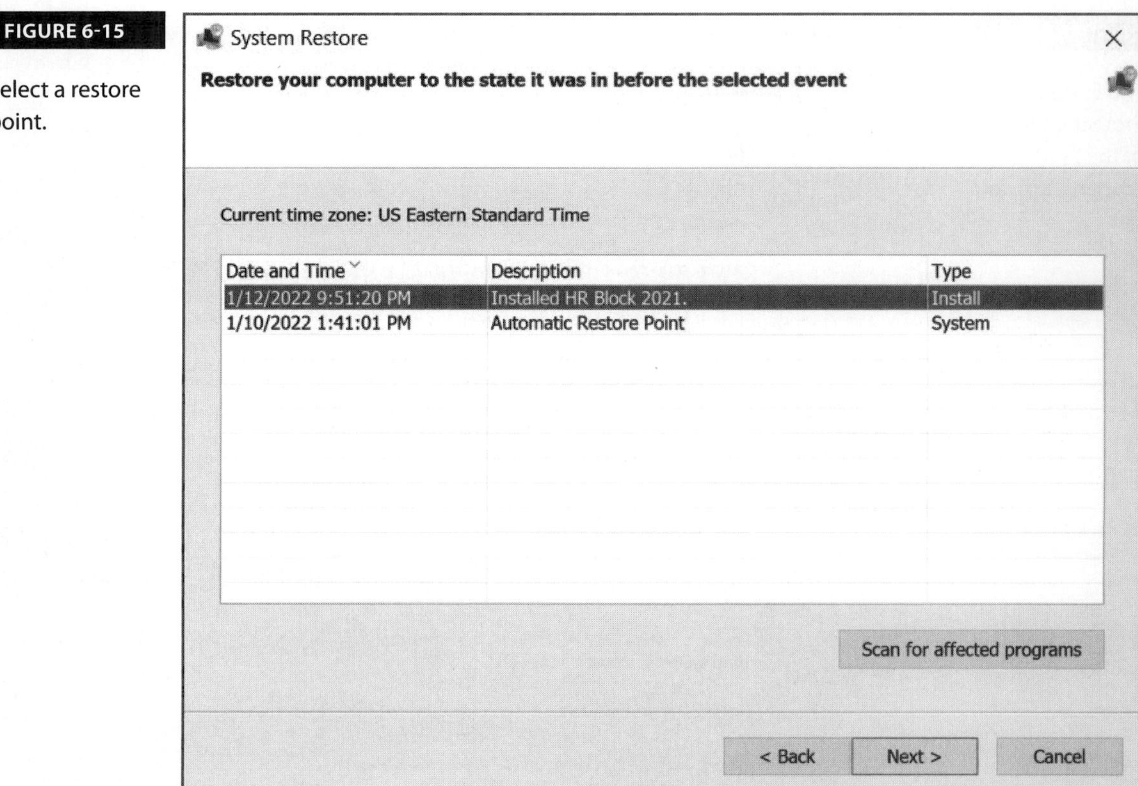

FIGURE 6-15 Select a restore point.

Recovery Options

When Windows won't start normally and you've exhausted the features described so far in this chapter (like System Restore and System Configuration), your next step is the recovery tools. These involve booting into a *preinstallation environment (PE)*. A PE is a special graphical environment designed to run diagnostic and troubleshooting tools on Windows itself and repair any problems found.

The Windows PE is a scaled-down Windows operating system with limited drivers for basic hardware and support for the NTFS file system, TCP/IP, certain chipsets, mass storage devices, and 32-bit and 64-bit programs. That description belies the power of this environment, because when needed, it supports a powerful group of diagnostics and repair tools called the *Windows Recovery Environment (Windows RE)*. Computer manufacturers have the option of adding their own repair tools to Windows RE.

Entering the Windows Recovery Environment

When a Windows computer fails to start a certain number of times in a row (which varies depending on the version), if the damage is not too extensive, Windows RE will start and load a recovery page, where you can choose Troubleshoot and then Advanced Options.

Another option is to start Windows RE by inserting the Windows media in the computer and restarting the computer. When prompted, press a key to start from disc. Select language, time and currency format, and keyboard or input method and click Next. On the following page, click Repair Your Computer. This brings up the Windows RE System Recovery Options dialog box. Select the operating system you want to repair and click Next, and the System Recovery Options menu appears.

If Windows came preinstalled on your computer, the manufacturer may have installed this menu as is or customized it, or they may have replaced it with their own recovery options.

If the Windows RE files are available on the local hard disk and you can boot into Windows (even if it's having problems), you can boot into Windows RE by holding down the SHIFT key as you click the Start button, click Power, and then click Restart. After the restart, choose Troubleshooting | Advanced Options.

Using the Windows Recovery Environment

Here are the tools available from the Windows RE:

- **Startup Repair** This tool replaces missing or damaged system files, scanning for such problems and attempting to fix them.
- **Startup Settings** This provides access to the Startup Settings menu, which you learned about earlier in the chapter.
- **Command Prompt** This tool provides a character-mode interface where you can use Command Prompt tools to resolve a problem, as explained in the following section.
- **Uninstall Updates** This command opens a menu from which you can choose to uninstall the latest quality update or the latest feature update.
- **UEFI Firmware Settings** This option boots into the motherboard's firmware configuration utility. (That's covered in Chapter 8.)
- **System Restore** This tool restores Windows using a restore point from when Windows was working normally. You learned about this tool earlier in this chapter.
- **System Image Recovery** If you previously created a complete PC image backup, this tool will enable you to restore it. You may need to click See More Recovery Options at the bottom of the screen to access this option.

Understanding the Windows RE Command Prompt

In the Windows RE Command Prompt, you can run some (but not all) commands you normally run within the Windows Command Prompt. The value of this command prompt is the ability to run such tools to repair the disk or boot configuration data (BCD) file when Windows will not start.

To see a list of Windows RE utilities, simply enter **help** at the prompt. To learn more about an individual command, enter the command name followed by /?. Here is a brief description of a few handy commands:

- **DISKPART** Performs disk partitioning
- **EXIT** Exits the recovery environment and restarts your computer
- **FIXBOOT** Writes a new partition table from the backup master file table on disk
- **FIXMBR** Repairs the master boot record (MBR)
- **HELP** Displays a Help screen
- **LOGON** Logs on to a selected Windows installation (if more than one is installed)
- **SYSTEMROOT** Sets the current directory to the location of the Windows system files—usually C:\Windows

You can also run a tool, BOOTREC, that is not available to you from within a normal Windows Command Prompt. Following are the BOOTREC commands you can run at the Windows RE Command Prompt for repairing a system partition:

- **bootrec /fixmbr** Repairs the MBR without overwriting the partitionable portion of the disk.
- **bootrec /fixboot** Overwrites the boot sector with one compatible with the Windows version installed.
- **bootrec /scanos** Scans all disks, looking for compatible Windows installations, and then displays the results.
- **bootrec /rebuildbcd** In addition to the scanning performed by /scanos, this option lets you select an installation to add to the BCD store. Do this if an installation on a multiboot system does not show as an option in the Boot Management menu.

Resetting Your PC

A last resort in Windows repair is to completely reset the PC by removing everything and reinstalling Windows from your original Windows installation media or recovery media that you have previously created. You lose all your applications and settings. You can choose whether or not to keep your data.

To access the Reset feature

- Open the Settings app (if you are able to access it) and do one of the following:
  - **Windows 10** Choose Update & Security | Recovery. Then under the Reset This PC heading, click Get Started.
  - **Windows 11** Choose System | Recovery. Then under the Recovery Options heading, click Reset PC.
- If you aren't able to access the Settings app, boot into the Windows RE (one way is to try to restart the computer a few times in a row) and choose Troubleshoot | Reset This PC.

SCENARIO & SOLUTION

You want to access the Advanced Boot Options menu at startup, but pressing the F8 key doesn't work. Why not, and how can you get to the menu?	The F8 method doesn't work on most modern systems (that is, those with UEFI firmware) because it poses security risks. Instead, you can go through the Settings app in Windows to access special boot modes.
You suspect that a user's problem with slow system performance is that there are too many background programs loading at startup. Where can you view what's being loaded and disable the unimportant items to see if that makes a difference?	You do this via the Startup tab in Task Manager. If you said to use System Configuration (msconfig), make a mental note that System Configuration doesn't work for this anymore as of Windows 8.

CERTIFICATION OBJECTIVE

- ***1102: 3.1*** *Given a scenario, troubleshoot common Windows OS problems*

This section details the possible solutions for the symptoms listed in CompTIA A+ 1102 exam Objective 3.1, along with appropriate tools for diagnosing and solving problems. Many of these solutions involve the tools you learned about earlier in this chapter. A few of this objective's topics are picked up in later chapters, such as the ones dealing with network issues (Chapter 19) and printing issues (Chapter 13).

Windows Symptoms and Solutions

Operating system failures occur for a variety of reasons, but just a few types—startup, device driver, and application failures—account for the majority. These often occur at startup. Operational problems are those that occur while Windows is running, as opposed to those that occur during startup. These may be instability problems, and they may involve OS components, including drivers, or application components. Regardless of the source of the problem, watching for error messages and familiarizing yourself with common error messages is important.

OS Instability Problems

What does OS instability look like? Instability includes a variety of symptoms, such as STOP errors, missing graphical interface, lockups of applications or the OS itself, and failure to open programs or files. The next several sections provide some guidance for various types of system instability situations.

The "Blue Screen of Death"

A fatal error is one that could cause too much instability to guarantee the integrity of the system. Therefore, when the operating system detects a fatal error, it will stop and display a text-mode screen with white letters on a blue background (Windows 10) or a black background (Windows 11). This screen is officially a STOP screen, but unofficially people call it the Blue Screen of Death (BSOD). There's a green-background version that appears sometimes when using certain Insider Preview versions. We will talk about it in Chapter 12 as well, because it is more often than not caused by hardware (or a hardware driver). It displays a message and multiple numbers that are the contents of the registers and other key memory locations. This information is usually not overly useful to a computer technician, but it can provide a great deal of information to developers and technical support professionals as to the nature of the failure. It is a good idea to capture that information before you contact customer support.

After capturing the information you need to troubleshoot, you must reboot (if the PC doesn't reboot itself automatically). Unlike most other Windows errors, this one requires a complete reboot; you can't recover any unsaved work in any applications.

If you are present when a STOP error occurs, read the first few lines on the screen for a clue. If the system reboots before you can read this information, you can view it in the System log after the reboot. Open Event Viewer and look in the System log for a STOP error.

For example, suppose the error message looks something like this: "STOP [several sets of numbers in the form 0x00000000] UNMOUNTABLE_BOOT_VOLUME." If you search www.microsoft.com using just the last part of this message (UNMOUNTABLE_BOOT_VOLUME), you may find sufficient information to determine the cause and the action to take by examining the values that preceded it. You can also go directly to Microsoft's online database of error messages at http://windows.com/stopcode.

FIGURE 6-16 A STOP error means your PC has crashed and needs to restart.

In the latest versions of Windows, the wording is friendlier, something along the lines of "Your PC ran into a problem and needs to restart." There is also a QR code (a type of bar code) that you can scan with a phone or other mobile device to look up the error online. See Figure 6-16.

Freezes and Spontaneous Shutdowns or Restarts

Sometimes the OS may stop responding to commands; this is called locking up or freezing. The mouse pointer may or may not still work depending on the nature of the underlying problem. If this happens once in a great while, don't worry about it; reboot and try again. But if it happens repeatedly (say, more than once a week), dig a little deeper.

First, assess whether this may be a problem with overheating or power. Overheating is the most common cause of system lockups, and it usually happens 15 to 30 minutes after the PC is started up. Check the CPU's heat sink and cooling fans for proper operation; you might need to install additional cooling methods. Spontaneous restarts and frequent shutdowns are almost always due to inadequate cooling or a failing power supply.

If cooling doesn't seem to be the problem, there are probably some corrupted system files. On a Windows system, try using the Windows RE covered earlier in the chapter to repair the Windows installation.

Improper shutdown can cause instability problems. All operating systems require a proper shutdown in order to close and save all open files. An improper shutdown can cause damage to open system and data files. Windows has controls built in that make this less likely to occur, such as the ability to configure the power button on your computer to not actually power down the computer but to send a shutdown command to the OS. Use the Power Options utility, described in Chapter 14, to configure your power button to shut down, hibernate, or put the computer to sleep.

USB Controller Resources Warnings

When plugging in a device to a USB 3.0 port, you might see an error "Not enough USB controller resources." This can happen when you have a lot of USB devices running at once. The reason is somewhat technical, involving EndPoint restrictions, and you don't really need to understand all that. Just know that the easy fix is to move devices that don't require USB 3.0 to a USB 2.0 port (if one is available) A more complex fix to try is to uninstall and reinstall the USB controllers from Device Manager.

You can also try running the USB Troubleshooter utility in Windows. Open an elevated command prompt window and run `msdt.exe -id DeviceDiagnostic` to start the Hardware and Devices Troubleshooter, click Advanced, and enable Apply Repairs Automatically. Then just let the troubleshooter do its job, and then restart the PC.

If the problem persists, a last resort is to downgrade the USB 3.0 ports to USB 2.0 level by going into BIOS/UEFI setup and disabling the XHCI Mode option by enabling the USB EHCI Debug option.

Time Drift

Time drift refers to the system's real-time clock getting out of sync with actual time. This can happen if Windows is not set up to automatically synch the real-time clock with online time servers. Here are some ways to troubleshoot this problem:

- In Windows' Date And Time Settings (in the Settings app), make sure that Set Time Automatically and Set Time Zone Automatically are both enabled. Click the Sync Now button to re-synchronize.
- Try a different time server. To do this, open up the Date And Time dialog box from the Control Panel (search for Date And Time), and on the Internet Time tab, click Change Settings. Choose a different server and click Update Now.
- Check the Windows Time Service in the Services app. Make sure it is set to start up automatically.
- Replace the motherboard's battery. The main purpose of the battery on a modern motherboard is to keep the real-time clock set to the correct time.

Slow or Sluggish Performance

Users often complain of slow system performance, such as interface delays (like having to wait a few seconds between clicking a command and something happening), sluggish startup, and lack of quick responsiveness when running multiple applications. Slowness can be due to many different causes, including malware infection, insufficient RAM or CPU for the tasks being performed, corrupted system files, malfunctioning cooling fans (causing the

The "Add resources" topic under 1102 exam Objective 3.1 refers to adding more RAM or hard disk space to improve system performance.

CPU to run hot and slow itself down to avoid overheating), and more. The following sections address some different types of slow performance and suggest some fixes.

Slow Bootup or Slow Profile Load

If a Windows PC takes a lot longer than normal to load (more than a couple of minutes), pay attention to which phase of the bootup process is taking all that time. If the delay occurs before the user sign-in prompt, it's likely a system problem. System Restore, System File Checker, and refreshing or repairing the Windows installation are all likely to help.

Slow profile load is common in enterprise environments where scripting is used to load roaming profiles. The fix often requires re-creating or rebuilding the user profile.

If the delay occurs *after* you enter the user account and password, the problem is likely with an individual account. Try rebuilding the user account, as described in "Rebuilding a User Account" in Chapter 20.

Sudden Slowdown of System Performance

Perhaps your system was zipping along nicely, and then after a restart, it suddenly slowed to a crawl. The root cause is probably the last thing you changed or installed. Use System Restore to go back to a previous restore point; this usually clears up the problem. If you have recently updated a driver, you might also try rolling back the driver in Device Manager.

Gradual Slowdown of System Performance

If your system gets slower gradually over time, you might have too much extraneous stuff running in the background. Check the Startup tab in Task Manager to see if there is anything loading that doesn't need to be loaded. You can also look in the Programs list in the Control Panel or the Settings app to see if there are any programs you can uninstall. This may help if one or more of the programs you are getting rid of is adware or if your hard disk is nearly full.

Slow performance can also be a symptom of malware infection. Make sure your antivirus program and definitions are up to date. Boot into Safe Mode with Networking and use your browser to do a system scan using a free service like Trend Micro or AVG Online.

Hard disk fullness can cause system slowdown because of the paging file (virtual memory). When the hard disk gets close to being full, Windows allocates less space to the paging file, so you have less virtual memory to work with. Consider moving the paging file to another drive, preferably a very fast one (such as a solid-state drive—but not a removable one, because the paging file must always be available).

Startup Error Messages

An IT professional must recognize and interpret common error messages and codes. These range from messages that appear during the early stages of a failed startup, through a variety of operational error messages. Once-fleeting messages that were not available after the fact are now logged in many cases, and a knowledgeable computer technician learns where to find them, as you will see in the sections that follow. Some of these refer to devices, services, or applications, but they appear at startup, rather than when those items are actually accessed.

When an OS fails in the early stages of startup, the problem often stems from corruption or loss of essential OS files. If this is the case, you may need to reinstall the OS, but before you take such a drastic step, consider other actions, such as the recovery options detailed earlier in this chapter.

Missing Graphical Interface/Fails to Load

The graphical interface is such an integral part of the OS that when it doesn't load, you know you've got some serious OS problems. Use the Windows RE to repair your Windows installation, as described earlier in the chapter.

Inaccessible Boot Device

This error may show as a STOP error, in which case the exact wording is Inaccessible Boot Device. This fatal error has several possible causes and solutions. Here are just a few:

- A boot-sector virus has infected the computer. Search for information about boot-sector viruses at https://support.microsoft.com.
- A resource conflict exists between the two disk controllers. This conflict is most likely to occur after the installation of an additional controller. In that case, remove the new controller and reboot. If Windows starts up normally, then troubleshoot the new controller for a configuration that conflicts with the boot controller.
- The boot volume is corrupt. If you have eliminated other causes, then remove the boot hard drive system and install it in another computer that has a working installation of the same version of Windows. Configure it as an additional drive, boot into the existing operating system, and then run CHKDSK (Check Disk, discussed later in this chapter) on the hard drive to diagnose and fix errors.

Missing Operating System

"Missing operating system" or "Operating system not found" may appear on a black screen when you start Windows. Then, because you cannot start up from the hard drive at all, you can try to boot from the Windows Setup disc and start the Recovery Environment.

At that point, if you see the message "Setup did not find any hard drives installed on your computer," the cause is most likely one of the following:

- BIOS/UEFI did not detect the hard drive.
- The hard drive is damaged. Run CHKDSK.
- The MBR (located in the first physical sector) or GUID partition table (GPT) is damaged.
- An incompatible partition is marked as Active.

To troubleshoot for this, restart the computer and access the BIOS/UEFI setup menu, as explained in Chapter 8. Check to see that the BIOS/UEFI recognizes the hard drive. If it is not recognized, check the computer or motherboard manufacturer's documentation to enable the BIOS/UEFI to recognize the hard drive and learn how to run diagnostics once the drive is recognized.

If the BIOS/UEFI still does not recognize the hard drive, power down, open the computer case, and check the data cable and power cable connections to the hard drive. If you find and correct a problem with the connectors, close the system up, restart and run the BIOS/UEFI setup again, and see if the drive is recognized. If it still fails, then the drive may be irreparable. But before you give up on the drive, restart again with the Windows Setup disc in the drive.

There are two useful utilities for this problem: CHKDSK and FIXMBR.

- CHKDSK will check for damage to the file system within the logical drive. Try it before trying FIXMBR. Run the CHKDSK command by entering **chkdsk c: /f /r**. The CHKDSK command can take hours to run, but we have been able to recover hard drives that seemed hopeless. After the command completes, restart the computer.
- If it boots into the operating system, you are good to go, but if not, repeat the steps to get back to the Command Prompt through the Recovery Options menu and then run FIXMBR. To run FIXMBR, it is best to specify the exact hard drive with the problem unless there is only one. If there is only one, you simply enter **fixmbr** at the command prompt, and the program will locate the backup copy of the master boot record and overwrite the damaged one. Hard disks are numbered beginning with zero (0). So if the disk is the second hard disk in the computer, run FIXMBR by entering **fixmbr \device\harddisk1**. If this fails to correct the problem, the disk may simply be too damaged to repair.

Service Has Failed to Start

If you see the error message "Service has failed to start" or a similar message, open the Services console (services.msc). In the contents pane, scroll down until you see the service that failed to start and right-click it. From the context menu, click Start. It may take several minutes for the service to start. If it starts normally, without any error messages, then do not take any further steps unless the problem recurs, in which case you will need to research the problem. Do this by searching the Microsoft site on the service name, adding the word "failed" to the search string.

Troubleshooting Applications

When an application that has opened before doesn't open, it's sometimes a system problem rather than an application problem. Restarting the OS is usually effective in clearing it up. If an application still doesn't open normally after a reboot, see the following sections for more guidance.

Inability to Open Any Applications

If programs or files won't run or open at all, that's a serious system problem. If you have already tried rebooting and that didn't help, repair your Windows installation. If programs appear at first not to run at all but are just painfully slow to open, see the earlier section, "Slow or Sluggish Performance."

Application Locks Up or Terminates Unexpectedly

If a particular application stops responding, you might be able to wait it out. Just let the PC sit for a few minutes, especially if the hard disk activity light is flashing vigorously on the PC. Things might come back to life again. If waiting it out (five minutes or so should be enough) doesn't do anything, terminate the unresponsive program with Task Manager. If the same application locks up again, investigate. Run the Repair function for that program in Programs in the Control Panel or Settings app, and try uninstalling and reinstalling the application. Make sure the display adapter's driver is up to date also (this is especially important for graphics-intensive games).

Individual Application Fails to Start

When an application won't start, a reboot will often solve the problem, because the problem is often a lack of available memory. Sometimes a program or process will claim memory and then fail to release it, leaving inadequate memory for other applications to run.

If a particular application still won't start after a reboot, repair or reinstall it. If multiple applications won't start, that's a system problem; repair Windows.

Application Compatibility Errors

Let's say you start an old application in a new version of Windows and it does not run correctly. Maybe the screen doesn't look quite right or perhaps the program frequently hangs up. To solve this problem, first check for program updates from the manufacturer and install those. If this does not help, try reinstalling the program. If that also does not work, then use the Program Compatibility Troubleshooter for the version of Windows you are running, as described in Chapter 5. You may also want to verify the system requirements for the application to make sure you are not trying to run it on a system that does not meet its minimum standards.

CERTIFICATION OBJECTIVES

- ***1102: 1.3*** *Given a scenario, use features and tools of the Microsoft Windows 10 operating system (OS)*
- ***1102: 1.5*** *Given a scenario, use the appropriate Windows settings*
- ***1102: 1.10*** *Identify common features and tools of the macOS/desktop systems*
- ***1102: 1.11*** *Identify common features and tools of the Linux client/desktop OS*

This section looks at some best practices for preventive maintenance for Windows, macOS, and Linux systems. Topics include defragmenting a disk (1102 exam Objective 1.3) and system updates and patch management for Windows (1102 exam Objective 1.5), macOS (1102 exam Objective 1.10), and Linux (1102 exam Objective 1.11).

OS Preventive Maintenance

Preventive maintenance for operating systems includes tasks that either prevent certain problems from occurring or guarantee that you can quickly recover from a problem or disaster with a minimum loss of time or data. The key activities in this area are running disk maintenance tools and keeping OS and driver files up to date.

Defragmenting a Hard Disk

Because of the way files are stored on a magnetic hard disk, the changes you make to a file may be written in a different spot on the disk than the original file. Such a file is fragmented. It takes longer to retrieve a fragmented file because the disk's read/write head must move multiple times to gather up the pieces. When lots of files are fragmented, disk read performance can suffer. (This doesn't apply to solid-state drives [SSDs] because the technology used to store files is different.)

Defragmenting a drive, also called *optimizing* a drive, relocates the pieces of each file so they are contiguous and relocates files as needed to create as much contiguous blank space as possible. Before upgrading Windows, it's a good idea to defragment the main hard drive to maximize the amount of contiguous blank space because then the newly installed OS files can be installed contiguously. You can also improve disk access times somewhat by defragmenting if the drive is severely fragmented.

Windows automatically defragments the system hard drive at regular intervals so it is not necessary to manually run it, but you can at any time using the Disk Defragment utility (dfrgui.exe).

Follow the steps in Exercise 6-6 to defragment a hard disk drive.

EXERCISE 6-6

Defragmenting a Disk Drive

In this exercise, you will use the Defragment and Optimize Drives utility in Windows to defragment a hard disk drive as a preparation for upgrading its operating system.

1. Open File Explorer and display a list of local drives in This PC.
2. Right-click the C: drive and click Properties.
3. On the Tools tab, click Optimize.
4. Select the desired volume if you have more than one. If the media type is Solid State, choose a different drive or stop here. (The utility may let you optimize an SSD, but it doesn't improve its performance, and repeated optimizing can shorten the life of an SSD.)
5. Click Optimize.
6. Wait for the defragmentation to complete. It may take up to several hours. You can continue to use the computer while the defragmentation is happening.
7. Click Close and then click Cancel to close the open dialog boxes.

Updates and Patch Management

As you learned in Chapter 4, an important part of OS maintenance is making sure that available updates are installed in a timely manner. Updates are sometimes called *patches* because they tend to fix problems. CompTIA A+ 1102 exam Objectives 1.10 and 1.11 refer to "updates/patches," and what they mean by this is the cumulative collection of all available updates, including OS, applications, drivers, and firmware.

Getting Updates and Patches in Windows

Windows has the Windows Update feature, previously introduced in the "Updating Windows" section in Chapter 4. Windows Update downloads updates for Windows itself, as well as for certain Microsoft applications. It can also download updates for some hardware drivers. However, it does not update most non-Microsoft applications or firmware; you must update them within the individual applications or by downloading and installing new versions manually.

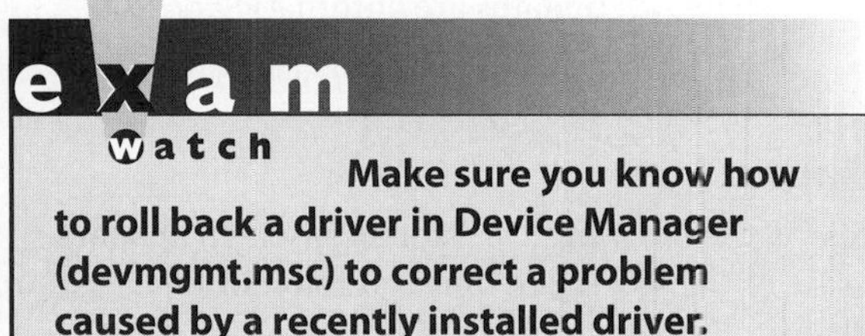

You can check for driver updates for most devices through Device Manager. Open the Properties dialog box for the device, click the Driver tab, and then click Update Driver and follow the prompts. See Figure 6-17.

If problems begin after updating a driver, you can roll back the driver update by selecting Roll Back Driver from the device's Properties box.

FIGURE 6-17 Update drivers from Device Manager.

Killer Wireless-n/a/ac 1535 Wireless Network Adapter Properties

Events | Resources | Power Management
General | Advanced | Driver | Details

Killer Wireless-n/a/ac 1535 Wireless Network Adapter

Driver Provider: Microsoft
Driver Date: 3/27/2018
Driver Version: 12.0.0.697
Digital Signer: Microsoft Windows

Driver Details — View details about the installed driver files.
Update Driver — Update the driver for this device.
Roll Back Driver — If the device fails after updating the driver, roll back to the previously installed driver.
Disable Device — Disable the device.
Uninstall Device — Uninstall the device from the system (Advanced).

OK | Cancel

Getting Updates and Patches in macOS

In macOS, you can manually check for system updates by opening System Preferences and clicking Software Update. The operating system handles all driver updates along with the OS updates, but you can adjust the update settings by clicking the Advanced button in the Software Update window. You can then enable or disable options such as Check For Updates, Download New Updates When Available, Install macOS Updates, Install App Updates From The App Store, and Install System Data Files And Security Updates. If you keep all these options enabled (which is the default), updates are automatic and you normally do not have to think about them.

Getting Updates and Patches in Linux

In Ubuntu Linux's GUI, you can get updates via the Software Updater app (which appears by default in the navigation bar on the left side of the screen). If a new version of Linux is available, it will let you know, and optionally install them automatically.

To set your update preferences, click Settings in this window to open the Software & Updates dialog box, shown in Figure 6-18. You can specify exactly which updates you want here, including Ubuntu software, other software, and additional drivers. This dialog box has multiple tabs, so make sure you have a look at all the tabs to see the full gamut of what you can control. (It's a lot more granular than either macOS or Windows update controls.)

From the command-line interface, you can also get updates with the apt-get command. Run **apt-get update** to update all package lists, and then run **apt-get upgrade** to update all installed software to the latest versions.

FIGURE 6-18

Configure updates of various types in Linux.

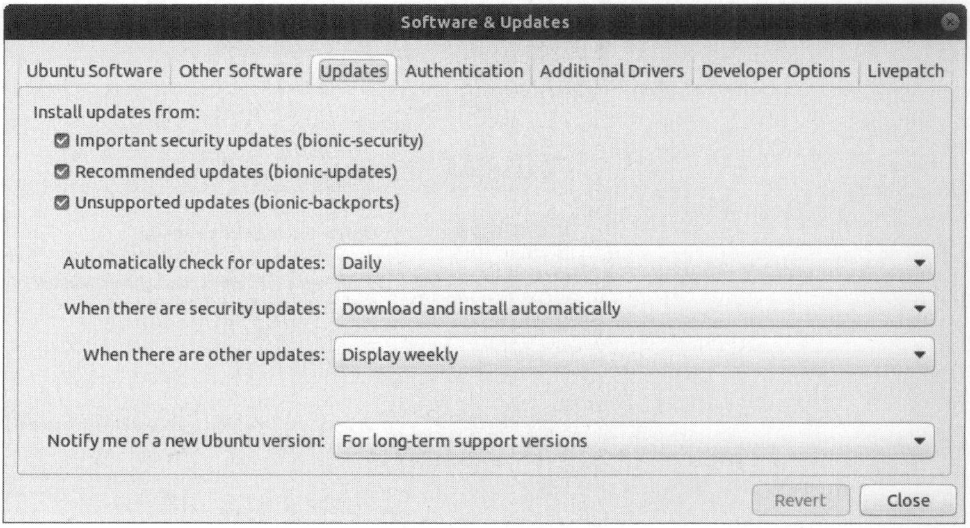

CERTIFICATION SUMMARY

As an IT professional, you must have a foundation of knowledge about operating systems in order to troubleshoot common problems, beginning with a few quick fixes to try before going any further in researching symptoms. Then, if the quick fixes don't work, attempt to pinpoint the problem's source to a single application or to the operating system in general. Ensure that a computer meets the minimum requirements for the installed OS and apps and has no known compatibility issues.

Familiarize yourself with the utilities and tools for troubleshooting. Begin with documentation resources available to you for troubleshooting and training yourself in using and supporting Windows and applications. Practice using Registry Editor, Device Manager, Task Manager, Task Scheduler, Performance Monitor, System Configuration (MSCONFIG), and Resource Monitor. Also practice modified startups using the various Safe Mode options. Ensure that you know the recovery options for Windows. Make sure you know the macOS and Linux equivalents of the Windows troubleshooting tools as well; you may need them in your work.

You should recognize common symptoms and understand the possible causes and solutions to these problems. Recognize common error messages and codes, and understand how to work with Event Viewer.

Practice preventive maintenance on Windows computers, including defragmenting hard drive volumes and ensuring automatic updates are enabled for both the operating system and applications. Make sure you know not only the Windows methods but the equivalent utilities and practices on Mac and Linux systems.

TWO-MINUTE DRILL

Here are some of the key points covered in Chapter 6.

Quick Fixes

- ❑ Try quick fixes such as rebooting before assuming that more in-depth troubleshooting is required.
- ❑ Verify that the software or device you are attempting to install or troubleshoot is compatible with the hardware and software of the PC.
- ❑ For application problems, use the Settings app's Apps section or Control Panel's Programs and Features applet to repair an application. If that doesn't work, uninstall and reinstall the application.

Windows Troubleshooting Tools

- ❑ Some BIOS/UEFI settings can affect OS functionality; check firmware setup for any settings that may be interfering with specific OS features.
- ❑ You can access a command-line interface in Windows, macOS, or Linux. In the latter two, it is called Terminal. You can run command-line commands there, or call the executable filenames for GUI programs. Windows 11 also comes with a Terminal app.
- ❑ Use the System Information utility (msinfo32.exe) to quickly learn about a system you must troubleshoot or support.
- ❑ The registry is a database of all Windows configuration settings that is best modified indirectly through many configuration tools, although administrators can use Registry Editor (regedit.exe) to view and directly edit it.
- ❑ The GUI for many Windows utilities is an MMC window. Some tools available in the MMC are Device Manager, Task Scheduler, Performance Monitor, Event Viewer, Component Services, and Services.
- ❑ Event Viewer (eventvwr.msc) enables you to examine error logs to determine when and how often problems are occurring.
- ❑ Use Task Manager to stop a program that has stopped responding and that cannot be stopped any other way. Be familiar with the Services, Startup, Performance, Processes, and Users tabs.
- ❑ Virtual memory or virtual RAM is enabled by default in Windows; it allows part of the hard disk to be used as a swap/paging area for memory so you can use more memory than you physically have. Manage it from the System settings in the Control Panel.

Troubleshooting Windows Startup Problems

- ❑ On an older, non-UEFI system, you can access the Windows Advanced Boot Options menu by pressing F8 as the computer is restarting. It contains many alternative ways to start Windows when you are troubleshooting startup problems. You can access it from the Settings app under Recovery or by holding down the SHIFT key as you restart the PC using Start | Power | Restart.
- ❑ Select from three Safe Mode options to troubleshoot and solve Windows problems. They are Enable Safe Mode, Enable Safe Mode With Networking, and Enable Safe Mode With Command Prompt.
- ❑ Use the System Configuration utility (msconfig.exe) to modify startup configuration settings without having to alter the settings directly. You can test startup settings without making them permanent until you are satisfied with the results.

- System Restore creates restore points, or snapshots, that Windows created automatically, including its configuration and all installed programs. If your computer has nonfatal problems after you make a change, you can use System Restore to roll it back to a restore point.
- To enter the Windows Recovery Environment (Windows RE), boot from Windows installation media or choose it from the Advanced Options menu. It might also load automatically after a startup failure.
- The Windows RE command prompt supports a subset of the normal command-line tools. One of these tools, BOOTREC, is not available except in Windows RE. It repairs the master boot record or boot sector and can rebuild the BCD store.

Windows Symptoms and Solutions

- OS instability problems include STOP errors, freezes and spontaneous restarts, booting into Safe Mode, missing graphical interface, and slow system performance.
- Slow system performance can mean insufficient memory, corrupt system files, a bad driver, or a virus. There are many possible causes. Try System Restore to go back to a time before performance degraded.
- Be familiar with command error messages and their possible solutions. Use Event Viewer to see error messages you missed.
- Sometimes if an application locks up, it will start working again if you wait a few minutes. If it does not, shut it down with Task Manager. Troubleshoot by repairing or reinstalling it, and check its compatibility with the installed Windows version.
- When an application fails to start but there are no other obvious symptoms, suspect that insufficient memory is the problem.

OS Preventive Maintenance

- Defragmenting a hard disk can improve the disk access times. Windows does it automatically at scheduled intervals, but you can also manually defragment. Windows 8 and later call the feature Optimize Disks, but the A+ objectives still call it defragmenting.
- Make sure the OS is configured to receive automatic system updates. Depending on the OS, there may be separate procedures for receiving driver, firmware, and application updates.

SELF TEST

The following questions will help you measure your understanding of the material presented in this chapter. Read all of the choices carefully because there might be more than one correct answer. Choose all correct answers for each question.

Quick Fixes

1. Which of the following is *not* a quick fix that you should at least consider before further investigation of a problem?
   A. Reboot the computer.
   B. Restore a system image.
   C. Uninstall a recently installed app.
   D. Uninstall a recently installed device.

Windows Troubleshooting Tools

2. What is the name of the executable file for System Information?
   A. MSINFO32
   B. MSCONFIG
   C. SYSINFO
   D. REGEDIT
3. Which of the following is a tool for making changes to the registry?
   A. MSINFO32
   B. MSCONFIG
   C. DISKMGMT
   D. REGEDIT
4. Computer Management is a preconfigured version of what utility?
   A. Compatibility Mode
   B. MSINFO32
   C. MSCONFIG
   D. MMC

5. What GUI tool do you use to stop an application that is not responding to mouse and keyboard commands?
   A. Startup disk
   B. Task Manager
   C. System Configuration Utility
   D. Device Manager
6. What application allows you to schedule system maintenance actions?
   A. Task Scheduler
   B. Task Manager
   C. System Configuration
   D. System File Checker
7. What is virtual memory?
   A. Physical memory that simulates hard disk storage
   B. Hard disk storage used as a swap area to augment physical memory capacity
   C. A USB flash drive that serves as extra system RAM
   D. Online memory accessed via the Internet
8. Where can you change which applications load at startup in Windows 10?
   A. Task Manager
   B. System Configuration
   C. Device Manager
   D. Computer Management

Troubleshooting Windows Startup Problems

9. How can you access advanced boot options at startup?
   A. Start menu
   B. Attempt unsuccessfully to boot normally several times in a row
   C. Control Panel
   D. System Properties
10. From what menu can you choose to start Windows in low-resolution video mode?
   A. Recovery
   B. Preinstallation Environment
   C. Control Panel
   D. Startup Settings

11. Which of these is a way of starting the Windows Recovery Environment?

A. Boot from Windows Setup media.

B. Restart the computer in Safe Mode.

C. Run Device Manager.

D. Press CTRL-ALT-DELETE.

12. What files does System Restore help you restore from previous saved versions?

A. Data

B. Applications

C. Favorites

D. System configuration

Windows Symptoms and Solutions

13. How do you recover after a STOP error?

A. Restart the computer.

B. Press ESC.

C. Open Event Viewer.

D. Use System Restore.

14. What should you suspect if Windows spontaneously reboots frequently?

A. Hard disk error

B. Corrupted registry

C. Failing power supply

D. Missing DLLs

15. If a system suddenly experiences a performance slowdown after installing new software, what is a possible fix?

A. Delete the paging file.

B. Defragment the hard disk.

C. Use System Restore.

D. Repair the MBR.

16. If you get an "Operating system not found" or "No OS found" error message at startup on a system that has previously booted fine, what is the first thing to check?

A. Flush the DNS cache.

B. Reinstall Windows on another drive.

C. Reformat the boot drive.

D. Check in BIOS/UEFI setup to see if the physical drive is recognized.

17. How can you recover from a BSOD error?
- A. Reboot.
- B. Sign out and back in again.
- C. Replace the motherboard.
- D. Reinstall Windows.

OS Preventive Maintenance

18. What does the Optimize command (on the Tools tab in the drive's Properties box) do to a drive in Windows 10?
- A. Defragments it
- B. Checks it for physical errors
- C. Fixes logical errors
- D. Deletes unwanted files

19. In which OS do you get system updates through the Software Update window?
- A. Windows
- B. macOS
- C. Linux
- D. All of the above

20. In which OS can you get system updates via apt-get update and apt-get upgrade?
- A. Windows
- B. macOS
- C. Linux
- D. All of the above

SELF TEST ANSWERS

Quick Fixes

1. ☑ **B.** Restore a system image is not a quick fix when compared to the other three options, which are quick fixes that would not have further impact. You would need much more investigation before you would restore a system image.
☒ **A, C,** and **D** are all incorrect because they are quick fixes, as opposed to restoring a system image.

Windows Troubleshooting Tools

2. ☑ **A.** MSINFO32 is the executable for System Information.
☒ **B** is incorrect because it is the executable for System Configuration. **C** is incorrect because it is not a valid command. **D** is incorrect because it is the executable for Registry Editor.

3. ☑ **D.** REGEDIT is a registry-editing tool.
☒ **A** is incorrect because MSINFO32 is a tool for viewing information about the hardware and software on a computer. **B** is incorrect because MSCONFIG is a utility for testing alternative startup settings. **C** is incorrect because DISKMGMT is the executable for running Disk Management.

4. ☑ **D.** Computer Management is a Microsoft Management Console (MMC) preloaded with several snap-ins.
☒ **A** is incorrect because Compatibility Mode is a method of running older programs on newer Windows versions. **B** is incorrect because MSINFO32 is the executable for the System Information utility. **C** is incorrect because MSCONFIG is the executable for the System Configuration utility.

5. ☑ **B.** Task Manager is the GUI tool used to stop an application that is not responding to mouse and keyboard commands.
☒ **A** is incorrect because this is neither a GUI tool nor the tool to use to stop a nonresponsive application. **C** and **D** are incorrect because neither is the correct GUI tool to use to stop a nonresponsive application.

6. ☑ **A.** Task Scheduler allows you to schedule system maintenance tasks.
☒ **B** is incorrect because Task Manager is a Windows utility that shows running tasks. **C** is incorrect because System Configuration manages system services and startup options. **D** is incorrect because SFC is the utility that checks and repairs system files.

7. ☑ **B.** Virtual memory is hard disk storage that serves as a swap file to augment physical memory.
☒ **A** is incorrect because this is the opposite of what virtual memory is. **C** is incorrect because virtual memory is not stored on a flash drive; this is the definition of ReadyBoost, another technology that was not covered in this chapter. **D** is incorrect because there is no such thing as online memory.

8. ☑ **A.** In Windows 10, startup programs are controlled from Task Manager.
☒ **B** is incorrect because System Configuration controls startup programs only in Windows 7. **C** is incorrect because Device Manager controls hardware, not software. **D** is incorrect because Computer Management does not include startup program control.

Troubleshooting Windows Startup Problems

9. ☑ **B.** Attempt unsuccessfully to boot normally several times in a row, and the Windows Recovery Environment loads automatically, from which you can access advanced boot options.
☒ **A, C,** and **D** are incorrect because these are all part of the Windows GUI, and the question asked how you do it at startup, before Windows fully loads.

10. ☑ **D.** Enable low-resolution video is an option on the Startup Settings menu.
☒ **A** is incorrect because Recovery is a section in the Settings app, not a menu. **B** is incorrect because Preinstallation Environment is not a menu; it is an environment in which Windows Recovery Environment runs. **C** is incorrect because Control Panel is not a menu; it is an interface from which you can access settings and utilities.

11. ☑ **A.** Boot from a Windows Setup disc and choose Repair to enter the Windows Recovery Environment.
☒ **B** is incorrect because Safe Mode is not connected to Windows RE. **C** is incorrect because Device Manager is a utility for analyzing installed hardware. **D** is incorrect because that key sequence opens a menu from which you can open Task Manager.

12. ☑ **D.** System Restore brings back old versions of system configuration files.
☒ **A, B,** and **C** are incorrect because System Restore does not restore any of these file or setting types.

Windows Symptoms and Solutions

13. ☑ **A.** Restart the computer. The computer must be restarted after a STOP error because it won't do anything until that happens.
☒ **B** is incorrect because the computer is locked up and ESC will do nothing. **C** is incorrect because you cannot run any programs until you restart. **D** is incorrect because you cannot run System Restore until you restart.

14. ☑ **C.** A failing power supply frequently causes spontaneous reboots.
☒ **A, B,** and **D** are incorrect because none of these things would cause spontaneous reboots.

15. ☑ **C.** Use System Restore to reverse any recent system changes that may be slowing down the system.
☒ **A** is incorrect because deleting the paging file will probably make the system run more slowly; you need the paging file for best performance. **B** is incorrect because defragmenting the hard disk is unlikely to cause a significant performance change. **D** is incorrect because you could not boot at all if the MBR needed repairing.

16. ☑ **D.** Before making any assumptions, check to see if the hardware is recognized.
☒ **A** is incorrect because a DNS cache is an Internet router feature and is not related to a local PC's booting. **B** is incorrect because it is premature to reinstall Windows at this point. **C** is incorrect because there is no need to reformat the hard drive until you have collected more information.

17. ☑ **A.** The only way to recover from a Blue Screen of Death (BSOD) error is to reboot.
☒ **B** is incorrect because you cannot sign in or out; the system is locked until you reboot. **C** is incorrect because replacing the motherboard is an extreme measure that is unlikely to help. **D** is incorrect because reinstalling Windows is an extreme measure that is unlikely to help.

OS Preventive Maintenance

18. ☑ **A.** Optimize and defragment refer to the same activity.
☒ **B** and **C** are incorrect because these are both functions of the Check Disk utility. **D** is incorrect because this is a function of the Disk Cleanup utility.

19. ☑ **B.** macOS updates are accessed via the Software Update window.
☒ **A** is incorrect because Windows gets its updates via Windows Update. **C** is incorrect because Linux gets its updates from Update Manager or apt-get. **D** is incorrect because A and C are incorrect.

20. ☑ **C.** Linux apps can be updated using apt-get.
☒ **A** is incorrect because Windows gets its updates via Windows Update. **B** is incorrect because macOS gets its updates via the App Store. **D** is incorrect because A and B are incorrect.

Chapter 7

Client-Side Virtualization

CERTIFICATION OBJECTIVES

- **1101: 4.1** Summarize cloud-computing concepts
- **1101: 4.2** Summarize aspects of client-side virtualization
- ✓ Two-Minute Drill
- **Q&A** Self Test

IT professionals who support desktop or server systems need to keep up to date on the newest operating systems (OSs) and applications. This can become expensive if they use dedicated computers for testing new software. But many do not. Instead, they use virtualization software to run the desktop or server OSs in a test environment, isolated from their organization's network. You can too once you learn how to work with the latest technologies in virtualization.

This chapter explains the big picture of virtualization, with examples of the different types. Then it compares server-side virtualization with client-side virtualization and provides more details on client-side virtualization to guide you through the hands-on experience of installing and configuring the software that supports desktop virtualization as an example of client-side virtualization. When you complete this chapter, you will not only understand virtualization conceptually, but you will know how to install and configure a hypervisor and set up a guest operating system.

CERTIFICATION OBJECTIVES

- ***1101: 4.1*** *Summarize cloud-computing concepts*
- ***1101: 4.2*** *Summarize aspects of client-side virtualization*

As you prepare for the CompTIA A+ certification exams, be ready to answer questions about the basics of client-side virtualization, including being able to define a hypervisor and install and use one. You should understand the purpose of virtual machines and be able to describe resource requirements for client-side virtualization, emulators, and networks, as well as the security requirements. In this chapter we go beyond the actual CompTIA A+ exam objectives to give you a broader understanding of client-side virtualization and some hands-on experience with it.

Although this section is not specifically about cloud computing (which is covered in Chapter 18), it does briefly cover one virtualization-related topic included in 1101 exam Objective 4.1: virtual desktop infrastructure (VDI).

Introduction to Virtualization

In this section, we detail the many purposes of virtualization and compare server-side virtualization to client-side virtualization. We will explore the types of client-side virtualization in preparation for the section that follows in which you will implement it.

Purposes of Virtualization

Virtualization is the creation of an environment that seems real but isn't. Virtualization is everywhere these days, and there are many types.

For example, you can explore a *virtual world,* such as Second Life or one of many massively multiplayer online games. Each of these virtual worlds contains a simulated environment within which participants create an online community. Within a virtual world a user often selects an *avatar,* an animated computer-generated human or animal image, to represent him or her. Virtual worlds are used in online training, in marketing of products, and in games because virtual worlds usually allow your avatar to interact with those of other people.

A *virtual classroom* is an e-learning tool for distance learning, usually provided as a service from an Internet-based source, such as eLecta Live (www.e-lecta.com) or Blackboard (www.blackboard.com). If you have taken online classes, you have probably experienced virtual classrooms used by instructors for presenting interactive lectures and even completion of coursework.

Many organizations use *storage virtualization* in which client computers can utilize many networked hard drives as though they are one drive or location. Network engineers work with *network virtualization* in which they create a network address space that exists within one or more physical networks. It is logically independent of the physical network structure, and users on computers accessing this virtual network are not aware of the underlying network. A *virtual network* can exist over a physical network, or one can be fully virtualized within a host computer.

Then there is *server virtualization*, in which a single computer hosts one or more server operating systems, each in a virtual machine and each performing tasks independently from the other virtual machines and from the host. Companies that provide low-cost web hosting services can create a separate virtual web server for each customer.

With only a small leap from server virtualization, we come to *desktop virtualization*. This is virtualization of a desktop computer into which you can install a desktop operating system, its unique configuration, and all the applications and data used by (normally) a single person. Each simulation of a machine is a *virtual machine (VM)*.

Today, desktop operating systems and their installed apps are clients to numerous services on private and public networks. The typical computer user seamlessly connects to a home network, corporate network, or the Internet to access services such as file and print sharing, e-mail, media streaming, social networking, and much more. For that reason, people often refer to desktop operating systems as clients, and it follows that when you create a virtual machine for Windows, it is called *Windows client virtualization*.

The purpose of a virtual machine is to simulate a real computer environment without requiring separate physical hardware.

Uses for Virtual Machines

IT professionals use virtual machines for a variety of functions, including these:

- **Sandboxes** When IT professionals make changes to systems, such as introducing new hardware or rolling out patches and updates to software, they need to test it in a no-risk environment where any problems that occur will not affect production systems. This is known as a *sandbox* environment. A virtual machine makes an ideal sandbox because it is isolated from other systems.

- **Test development** Developers use virtual machines to test new software as they are creating it, checking out how it works in a variety of simulated hardware environments. This is a tremendous time and cost saver because developers do not need to actually own all the different hardware configurations they wish to test on.
- **Application virtualization** IT professionals can virtualize applications, making them available to end users via virtual machines rather than directly installing them on user hardware. This has two main use cases:
  - **Legacy software/OS** If an application is old (that is, *legacy*), it may have been written for older hardware or an older OS version. A virtual machine enables that application to run on the hardware and software platform it was written for.
  - **Cross-platform virtualization** If a certain application needs to be available to users who have different systems (such as macOS, Windows, Linux, and so on), a virtual machine can make a single version of that application available to everyone, regardless of their OS or hardware.

1101 exam Objective 4.2 specifically mentions the three functions described here: sandboxes, test development, and application virtualization (and the use cases of legacy software/OS and cross-platform virtualization). Make sure you understand how each of those use cases is enabled by virtual machines.

Server-Side Virtualization vs. Client-Side Virtualization

A *client* is software that connects over a network to related server software. The term "client" can also refer to the operating system or to the computer hardware supporting the client software. Therefore, *client-side virtualization* is any virtualization that happens on the client side of a client-server relationship. When you install software that allows you to run different operating systems on a single PC in a virtual environment, that's client-side virtualization.

You can host one or more virtual machines on your PC if it meets the requirements for both the hypervisor and for each guest OS. Common examples of client-side virtualization of desktop environments include hypervisors that allow you to run Windows, Linux, Unix, and even DOS guest OSs in virtual machines on Windows, Linux, Unix, or macOS host OSs. For example, Figure 7-1 shows a Windows 11 desktop with a window open to a virtual machine that is running Ubuntu Linux. The hypervisor in this case is Oracle VM VirtualBox, a free and very capable hypervisor.

FIGURE 7-1 Ubuntu Linux running in a virtual machine on a Windows 11 PC

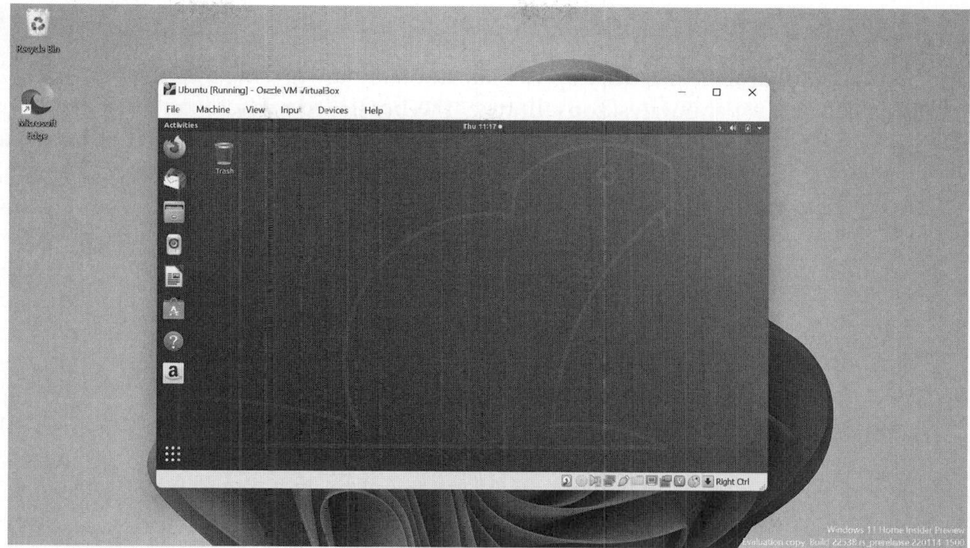

Virtual environments can also be hosted on specialized servers that clients connect to via network or Internet connections. This is *server-side virtualization*. For example, Microsoft's Windows 365 Cloud PC is a virtual version of Windows that displays on the user's screen as if the operating system were local. The value of this approach is that the local computer can be an older, less powerful computer because it only needs to run software to connect to the server, transfer video downstream to the thin client, and send mouse clicks and keystrokes upstream to the app on the server. It isn't doing the heavy lifting of processing; the server does that. This hosting of desktop environments and applications on servers centralizes all support tasks, simplifying the upgrading and patching of the operating system and applications in the virtual machines within the server or servers. This same centralization also gives IT more control over the security of the desktop.

exam watch

The term used today for hosting and managing multiple virtual desktops (often thousands) over a network is *virtual desktop infrastructure (VDI)*. The term is attributed to VMware in distinguishing its virtual desktop server products from the products offered by competitors, specifically Citrix and Microsoft. Today VDI applies to any server product that provides full virtual desktop support. 1101 exam Objective 4.1 mentions VDI, both on-premises and in the cloud.

Types of Client-Side Virtualization

While we will use desktop virtualization in our working examples, client-side virtualization is not just about desktops. In recent webcasts from Microsoft, they featured three types of client-side virtualization: desktop virtualization, application virtualization, and presentation virtualization. We have already defined desktop virtualization and will soon move into more details about that type. Here we will describe presentation virtualization and application virtualization.

In *presentation virtualization*, a user connects to a server from their desktop or laptop and accesses an application rather than an entire desktop environment. The application user interface (window) is "presented" on the user's desktop as if it were running locally, but it is actually running on the server. This allows the user to use an application that is incompatible with their local operating system or that cannot run on the local computer because the computer hardware is old or underpowered. Microsoft currently uses Windows Server running Remote Desktop Services for presentation virtualization. Notice that this is client-side virtualization, but it physically occurs on the server side and is presented on the client side, as shown in Figure 7-2. Specialized software sends the screens to the client computer and returns all input to the application on the server.

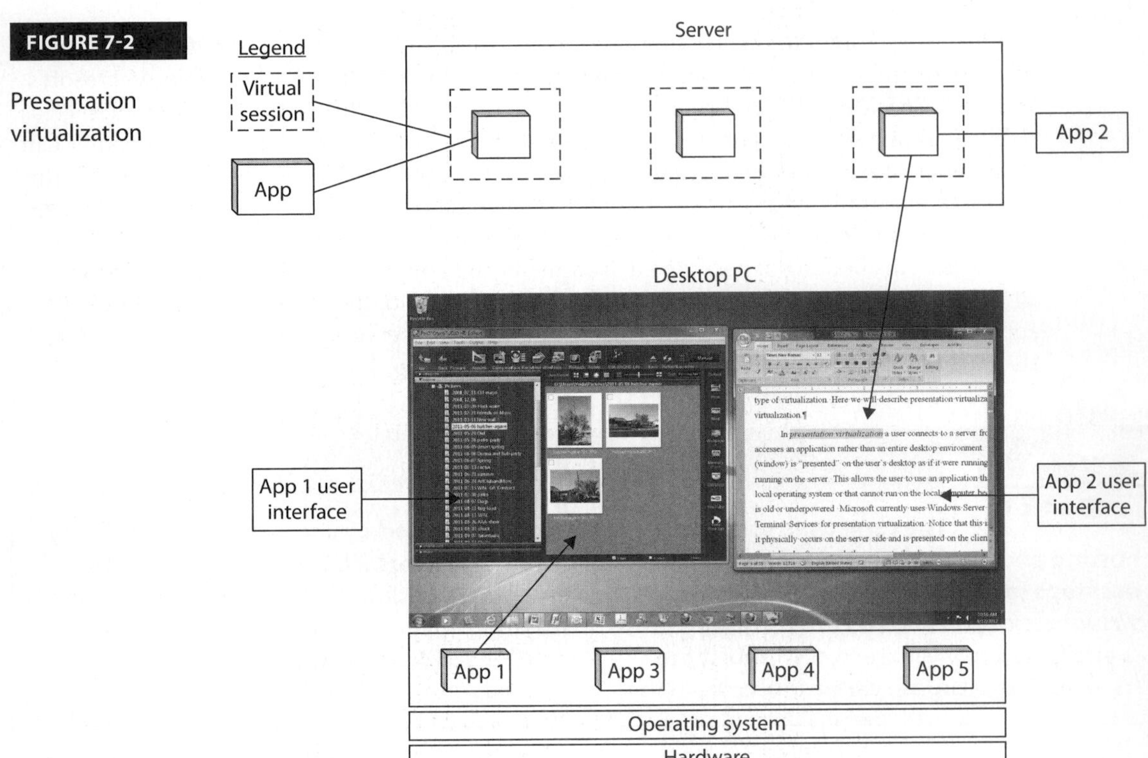

FIGURE 7-2 Presentation virtualization

FIGURE 7-3 Application virtualization

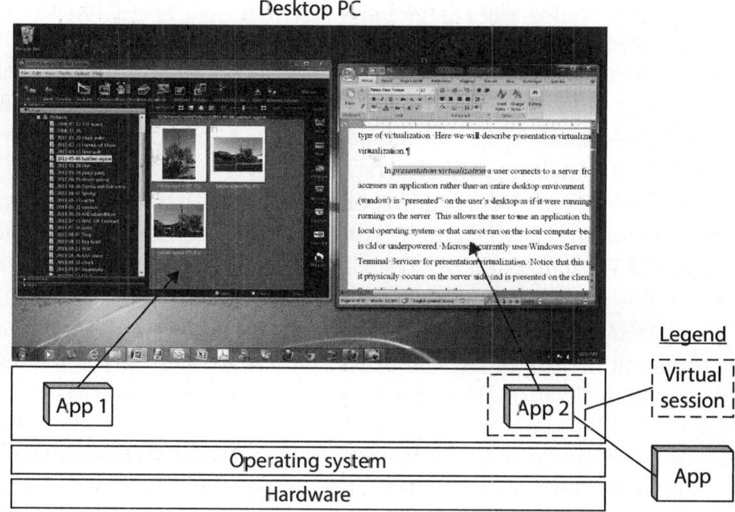

Another type of client-side virtualization is *application virtualization,* in which the application runs in a virtualized application environment on the local computer. The application is isolated from the surrounding system, interacting with the hardware (and user) through application virtualization software, a virtual machine with only the support required by the app (see Figure 7-3). This isolation of the application on the desktop computer requires a sufficiently powerful computer, but it has the advantage of being a compatibility solution when older, critical apps will not run on newer hardware or software. Another benefit is that a virtualized app is under IT control because they can install or update it over a network as a complete application without concern for the underlying system beyond the application virtualization software. Microsoft's current implementation of application virtualization is *Microsoft Application Virtualization (App-V).*

Implementing Client-Side Desktop Virtualization

This section begins by describing hypervisors, the software that supports desktop virtualization. Then it looks at specific hypervisors and their resource and network requirements. Finally, you will find out how to select and install a hypervisor on a desktop computer and create one or more virtual machines in preparation for installing an OS onto that virtual machine.

Hypervisors

To do desktop or server virtualization, you first need a hypervisor. A *hypervisor,* also called a *virtual machine manager (VMM),* is the software that creates a virtual machine, providing access to the necessary hardware on the host machine in isolation from other virtual machines and the host operating system, if present. This allows multiple operating systems to run simultaneously on a single physical computer, such as a network server or desktop computer. A hypervisor must create a virtual CPU compatible with that of the underlying machine—mainly either an Intel or an AMD CPU. This means that the installed OS must be capable of installing directly on the underlying computer.

Today's hypervisors require, or at least work best on, computers with *hardware-assisted virtualization (HAV)* features, either Intel Virtualization Technology for x86 (Intel VT-x) or AMD Virtualization (AMD-V). HAV supports and improves the performance of virtual machines on the host. Both Intel and AMD CPUs have supported HAV since 2006.

Virtual Machine Management Service, also known as VMMS or vmms.exe, is the main module in the Microsoft Windows operating system that controls all aspects of Hyper-V server virtualization. Hyper-V's hardware requirements are

- 64-bit processor with second-level address translation (SLAT)
- CPU support for VM Monitor Mode Extension (VT-x on Intel CPUs)
- 4 GB of RAM (at a minimum; more is better)

Having the right hardware is not enough, though; the right settings must also be enabled in the system BIOS/UEFI:

- Virtualization technology (the name may vary somewhat depending on the motherboard)
- Hardware-enforced data execution prevention (DEP)

Be sure you understand the resource requirements for virtualization using a hypervisor, including HAV.

Virtualization vs. Emulation

You may have heard the term *emulation* or mention of something called an *emulator.* At first glance, emulation and virtualization seem synonymous, but in computing, these terms are very different. Emulation differs very much from the virtualization of servers or desktops we discuss here. The key is compatibility. When we use a virtual machine, the hypervisor that creates and manages it must create a virtual machine compatible with the underlying virtual machine, even while isolating the virtual machine from the underlying hardware.

An *emulator,* on the other hand, is software that allows you to run an OS or device on hardware with which it is completely incompatible. This is done to run a critical application designed for an old type of computer system that is no longer available. In fact, in the early days of PCs many organizations used special adapter cards and software on PCs to emulate the old dumb terminals that connected to their large mini- or mainframe computer systems. Now we do this with terminal emulation software, such as the VT Series terminal emulators from Ericom (www.ericom.com) used to emulate physical terminal hardware systems by DEC, Compaq, and Hewlett-Packard. Vendors such as Ericom offer versions of their terminal emulation software that will run on Windows, macOS, or Linux operating systems. Today developers wanting to write apps for phones running the Android OS can use software that will emulate the underlying CPU and other hardware of an Android phone and run an Android OS—all on their desktop computer.

There are two types of hypervisors: Type I and Type II, as Figure 7-4 shows. A *Type I hypervisor*—sometimes called a *bare-metal hypervisor*—can run directly on a computer without an underlying host operating system and then manage one or more virtual machines. A *Type II hypervisor* requires a host operating system, such as Windows, macOS, or Linux. The Type II hypervisor runs as an app in that host operating system, putting more software layers between each virtual machine and the hardware.

Type I hypervisors first appeared on high-powered servers running server OSs in virtual machines. Examples of current Type I server hypervisors include VMware ESXI and Citrix XenServer. Type I hypervisors are very appealing because, when compared to an equivalent Type II hypervisor, a Type I hypervisor has a smaller layer of software between each *guest OS* running in a virtual machine and the underlying hardware.

The hypervisors we use in our examples and exercises in this chapter are all Type II hypervisors requiring an underlying operating system, the host OS, which is the operating system installed directly on the computer, and one or more guest OSs, which are the operating systems running within virtual machines.

You have several choices for Type II hypervisors for desktops. The major sources of hypervisors are VMware, Citrix, Parallels, Microsoft, and Oracle. There are many other players in the field, with virtualization topics appearing in the technical press every week. You can install a Type II hypervisor on your Linux, Windows, or macOS desktop and test another operating system without the expense of a separate computer.

FIGURE 7-4

Comparison of Type I and Type II hypervisors

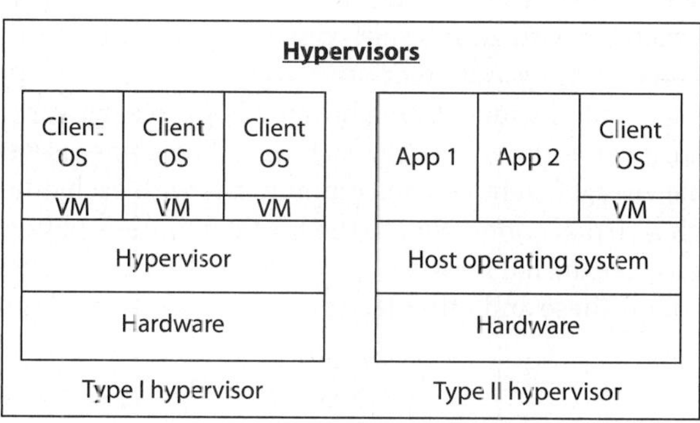

Planning a Desktop Virtualization Implementation

To implement desktop virtualization, you must first determine what desktop OS you will use as a guest OS. When it comes to selecting and installing a hypervisor, the general considerations and steps remain the same, whether you are planning server virtualization or desktop virtualization. For our purposes, we will focus on selecting and installing a Type II client hypervisor on a desktop computer for testing Windows and Linux operating systems.

Security for Virtual Machines

We cannot emphasize enough that you must keep your guest OS as secure as the host OS. At a minimum, you should create a strong password for the account used to log in to the guest OS and install security software in your guest OS. Chapters 20 and 21 give the bigger story of computer security, and you can flip forward to those chapters for details. However, there are many excellent free security suites from third parties, and Microsoft Windows comes with the free security tool Windows Defender.

Remember that you must treat a virtual machine as you would a physical machine and take the same security precautions, such as creating a strong password for the account used to log in to the guest OS and installing security software in your guest OS.

Networking Requirements

While it is possible to do desktop virtualization on a computer without an Internet connection, it would be very awkward for several reasons. First, the easiest way to obtain a hypervisor is over the Internet, and updates to the hypervisor, host OS, and guest OS are easily available with an Internet connection. Furthermore, if you create a virtual machine to test an operating system or other software for use in a normal environment, then you certainly should include testing how it works on a network. Therefore, the hypervisors we use simulate a network card within each virtual machine, as well as a network on the host, so that multiple virtual machines can communicate with each other and the underlying host. Then, through a virtual connection to the host computer's physical network adapter, each VM has access to an external network, and through that to the Internet, if available. Of course, you can turn off these and other features for a VM, if you desire.

Selecting a Guest OS for Desktop Virtualization

The selection of a guest OS for virtualization may be less selection and more necessity. Perhaps you need to learn Linux for a class you are taking, but you do not have a spare computer. Or maybe you would like to look at an older version of Windows without installing it on one of your PCs. Or maybe you just need to select an OS so that you can experiment with desktop virtualization. Whatever the reason, you will need a legal license to install it, just as you do on any computer. If you plan to install Linux, you will find many free versions online, and if you are testing a pre-release version of Windows, simply download it and save it as an ISO file.

Recall that while a network may not be required for a virtual machine, it is essential to have network access to easily update all the software and to create a real-world environment in which a computer is connected to a network.

If you are looking for an OS to install just for learning to work with virtualization, consider using an older version of Windows, if you happen to have an old disc around along with the product key. As you learned in Chapter 4, a *product key* is a string of alphanumeric characters, usually five groups of five each, printed on the packaging for retail editions of Microsoft software. You must provide this product key either during the installation or within 30 days, or the software will be disabled. This is Microsoft's protection against piracy. Ubuntu Linux is also a good choice for a guest OS because it is free and easy to obtain. It also has modest system requirements, so it runs well even on older PCs.

Selecting a Host OS for Desktop Virtualization

Deciding on the host OS and a host computer for desktop virtualization seems like the chicken and egg situation—which comes first? Well, it depends on what is available to you. However, since the CompTIA A+ exams focus mainly on the Windows OS, we will use the Windows OS as our host OS in the following exercises. But if you have a Linux or macOS system, there are hypervisors for them too.

Selecting a Host Computer for Desktop Virtualization

If possible, select a PC that supports HAV as the host computer. Not all hypervisors require it, but most will take advantage of the feature if it's available. Without HAV, some hypervisors will limit you to 32-bit installations of some operating systems.

How can you discover if your computer supports HAV? One of the BIOS/UEFI settings on a computer with HAV support will be virtualization and the ability to enable or disable it. If you are uncertain, skip ahead to Chapter 8's Exercise 8-5, "Viewing the Firmware Settings," to learn how to enter BIOS/UEFI settings and make sure virtualization is present and enabled.

Selecting a Type II Client Hypervisor

You have several options—both commercial and free—for running Linux or Windows on a Windows desktop computer. At this writing, you cannot run any version of macOS in a virtual machine on a PC, due more to licensing issues than technical issues. (Okay, technically there *are* ways to do it, but they require acquiring disk images illegally and then hacking them. The Internet will explain it.)

Of the non-Microsoft hypervisors, we selected Oracle VirtualBox to cover in this chapter. It's free, well designed, and mostly hassle free, and versions are available for Windows (all versions and editions), Linux, and macOS.

Hyper-V Manager is a hypervisor application that comes with the 64-bit Pro and Enterprise versions of Windows 8 and later. It's got some quirks and can be difficult to set up; frankly, we prefer VirtualBox and you probably will too, but it's good to have options. Hyper-V is available only in Pro and Enterprise versions of Windows.

There are other free hypervisors, most notably VMware Player, which doesn't have a version for macOS. The free VMware Player also has fewer features than the industry-leading hypervisor, VMware Workstation (the retail product), which also does not come in a version for macOS hosting. The entire suite of VMware products is very popular in large organizations, so you may want to download and install VMware Player on your own to become familiar with the VMware virtualization look and feel. All these hypervisors are downloadable from the Internet and they all work in a similar way, so working with one will teach you the basics of working with desktop virtualization.

This chapter would not be complete without some mention of Parallels Desktop for Mac, a very popular hypervisor for macOS hosts. It does not come in a free version, only a 14-day trial, which you may want to download from their website (www.parallels.com). While Parallels has versions for Windows and Linux hosts, their main efforts go to their product for macOS hosts, and the other versions are not kept as up to date. Therefore, since we work on both Windows and macOS hosts, we prefer to use Oracle VirtualBox on both platforms.

Installing and Configuring Oracle VirtualBox

Oracle VirtualBox will run on a variety of host operating systems, including Windows, Linux, and macOS. It is free, open-source software under the terms of the GNU General Public License (GPL) version 2. It will also run on hardware that does not support virtualization, but we strongly recommend you use a system with HAV when possible for the best performance.

The minimum requirements for VirtualBox include the following:

- **CPU** Any recent Intel or AMD CPU, but the more powerful the better. Streaming SIMD Extensions 2 (SSE2) support is required. Software-based virtualization is no longer supported as of version 6.1, so if you don't have HAV, you will need to download version 6.0 or earlier.
- **Disk space** At least 25 GB free space recommended.
- **Memory** At least 4 GB of RAM recommended.
- **Host OS** Windows, Linux, Solaris, or macOS.
- **Guest OS** Versions of Windows, Linux, Solaris, Open Solaris, OS/2, Open BSD, or DOS.

Learn more about VirtualBox at the VirtualBox website (www.virtualbox.org), where you will find the online user manual and a link to download the software.

Downloading VirtualBox

To complete Exercise 7-1, you will need to download VirtualBox. To do that, click the Downloads link on the home page. On the Download VirtualBox page, shown in Figure 7-5, locate the version for the host OS you plan to use and select it for download. In our case, we clicked the link for VirtualBox for Windows hosts. Once it completes downloading, you are ready to install it on your system. The screens and steps will vary depending on the version of VirtualBox and the host OS you use. For instance, the file downloaded to a macOS host (described on the VirtualBox download page as simply "OS X hosts") will have a .dmg extension.

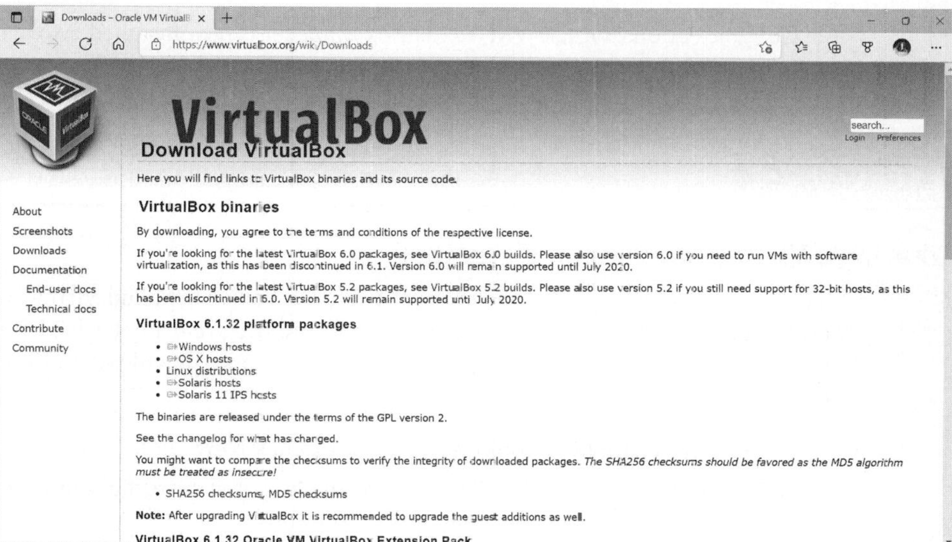

FIGURE 7-5 Select the correct download for your host OS.

Setting Up VirtualBox

Using the file you downloaded, run the VirtualBox installation wizard to install it on your Windows computer. To complete Exercise 7-1, you will need a system that meets the hardware and host OS requirements listed earlier. In addition, you will need the following:

- The user name and password of an administrator account for this computer
- A broadband Internet connection

After you install VirtualBox, you will need to create at least one VM in it, covered in Exercise 7-2.

EXERCISE 7-1

Installing Oracle VirtualBox

Follow these steps to install VirtualBox:

1. Locate and double-click the installation program. Your version will be newer than the one we used, called "VirtualBox-6.1.32--149290-Win.exe."
2. Run the downloaded file, following the prompts to install the application. If prompted with a warning about network interfaces, click Yes.
3. At the end of the setup process, click Finish.
4. If you see a prompt about having an old version of an extension pack, click Download and wait for the new one to be downloaded, and then click Install and wait for it to be installed.

Congratulations! Oracle VM VirtualBox Manager is now installed. Move on to Exercise 7-2.

EXERCISE 7-2

Creating a Virtual Machine in VirtualBox

This exercise picks up where Exercise 7-1 left off. You've installed VirtualBox, and now you'll create a new virtual machine. These steps assume you are using 64-bit Ubuntu Linux as the guest OS, which you can acquire from Ubuntu.com. Download an ISO, and then follow these steps.

1. On the VirtualBox application's toolbar, click New.
2. Type the name for the VM in the Name box. It is customary (and recommended) to include the guest OS name in the VM name.

3. Open the Type drop-down list and select the OS you plan to install, and then open the Version drop-down list and select the version. For this exercise, choose Linux as the type and Ubuntu (64-bit) as the version. Then click Next.
4. On the Memory Size page, if needed, drag the slider to 1 GB (1024 MB) and then click Next.
5. On the Hard Disk page, click Create A Virtual Hard Disk Now and click Create.
6. On the Hard Disk File Type page, select VDI (unless you have a reason to select something else) and click Next.
7. On the Storage On Physical Hard Disk Page, leave Dynamically Allocated selected and click Next.
8. On the File Location And Size Page, leave the default of 10 GB selected and click Create.
9. To start the VM, select it and click Start. A box will pop up asking you to choose the optical disc from which to install the OS. Point it to the ISO file or the physical optical drive and then follow the prompts.
10. If the VM you are installing is Ubuntu, you will see a Welcome screen with the choices Try Ubuntu and Install Ubuntu. We recommend Install because you will be using this VM for other chapters, and it will improve performance to have it installed. Make your selection and follow the prompts to complete the installation. Accept the defaults for any setting you are not sure about.
11. After Ubuntu restarts, you may see a message asking you to remove the ISO file as you are rebooting. To do that, open the Devices menu in VirtualBox, point to Optical Drives, and then select the Ubuntu ISO to remove the check mark next to its name. If you get a message that it can't be ejected, offering to let you do a force dismount, do that. With the ISO removed, you will be able to boot from the virtual hard disk where Ubuntu is installed.

Configuring VirtualBox

Your virtual machines appear in the left pane in the Oracle VM VirtualBox Manager window. You can click any VM and then click Settings on the toolbar to open its settings. In the Settings window, select a category on the left, and then select a tab across the top to view the pages of settings for that category (see Figure 7-6). Some settings may not be available when the VM is running.

Capturing and Releasing the Mouse and Keyboard in a Guest OS

Once you have a guest OS installed into a virtual machine, the guest OS and host OS are sharing the same physical hardware, but each physical device can serve only one master at a time.

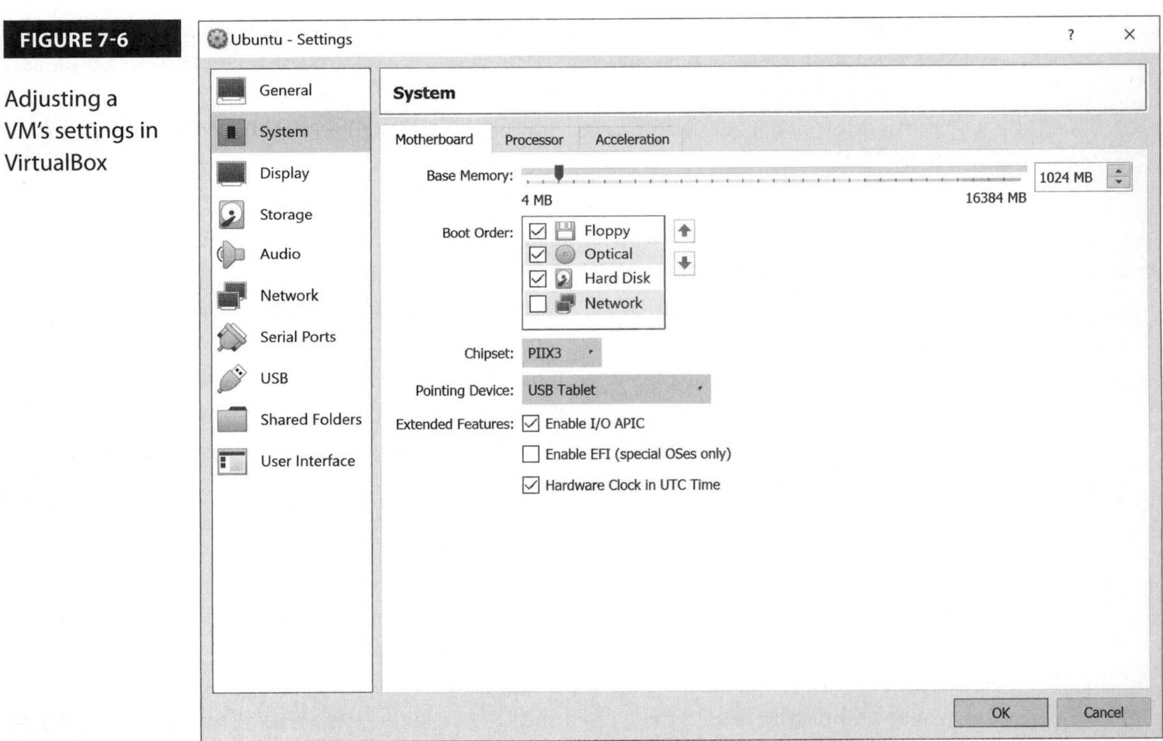

FIGURE 7-6 Adjusting a VM's settings in VirtualBox

Most hypervisors have extensions for most modern operating systems that allow control of the keyboard and mouse to pass seamlessly back and forth between the VM and the host system. (These are called *guest additions* in VirtualBox. You learn how to enable them in the next section.) When the VM window is active, the keyboard and mouse work within it. When the mouse moves outside the VM window and clicks, control returns to the host OS.

However, with some OSs, that smooth transfer doesn't happen automatically. In some cases you may be able to install extensions that enable the feature, but in other cases you may need to press a certain key sequence to release the mouse from the guest OS window each time you want to return to the host OS. This is called the *host key*.

The hypervisor assigns a host key. For instance, VirtualBox on a Windows computer uses the right CTRL key as the host key. VirtualBox on a macOS system uses the left COMMAND key.

Improving Guest OS Performance

After you install a guest OS into a guest VM, no matter which hypervisor you use, you may find that the screen and performance are not up to par, with only a low resolution available to you. Hypervisors usually have special software that you can install into the guest OS.

VirtualBox has special drivers and other software called collectively Guest Additions, and you install them after you install a guest OS. To do this, you start up your guest OS, and then access the VirtualBox menu system on the window containing your guest OS, and click the Devices menu. Click Install Guest Additions and follow the instructions to run the program.

If you don't see the Install Guest Additions command on the Devices menu, or if you see Insert Guest Additions CD Image, you might need to point it to the CD image. Choose Devices | Optical Drives | Choose Disc File to locate it. Look in C:\Program Files\Oracle\VirtualBox. The filename is VBoxGuestAdditions.iso. If prompted whether to run it, click Run.

When the Guest Additions are installed, you will be prompted to reboot the virtual machine. This is necessary before the changes take effect. Oracle VirtualBox configures your guest client to check for updates to the Guest Additions, so after you reboot the VM, if you are connected to the Internet through the host OS, you may see a message stating that there are updates—even if, as we did, you downloaded and installed VirtualBox on the same day.

Each hypervisor has its own set of drivers and other programs to improve the virtual machine performance, but they are all guest OS specific, and each vendor gives their group of guest OS drivers and programs a different name.

The result should be better performance overall, and you may find that Windows will have more resolution options for configuring your display.

SCENARIO & SOLUTION

Scenario	Solution
You want to set up a virtualization server specifically to make client OS environments available. Which type of hypervisor do you need?	A Type I hypervisor would be best in this case because you don't have the overhead of a host OS.
You want to set up a testing environment on the main desktop PC that you can use to test unstable pre-release versions of software your company is developing. What type of hypervisor do you need?	A Type II hypervisor is the best choice because it would enable you to run a separate OS space on your main PC while still using it for other tasks as well.
You want to install a 64-bit version of Ubuntu Linux on a virtual machine, but the hypervisor management software won't let you. What is the most likely reason?	You might not have HAV enabled in the system firmware, or the host OS might not be 64-bit.

CERTIFICATION SUMMARY

A technician should understand the basics of client-side virtualization; the purpose of virtual machines; and the various requirements, including resources on the host computer, emulator needs, security, and network. Also important is understanding what a hypervisor is and the types of hypervisors available.

TWO-MINUTE DRILL

Here are some of the key points covered in Chapter 7.

Introduction to Virtualization

- ❑ Virtualization is the creation of an environment that seems real but isn't.
- ❑ Virtualization is used for many purposes, such as a virtual world, a virtual classroom, storage virtualization, network virtualization, server virtualization, and desktop virtualization.
- ❑ Client-side virtualization occurs on the client side of a client-server arrangement.
- ❑ Server-side virtualization occurs on the server side of a client-server relationship.
- ❑ Virtual desktop infrastructure (VDI) is the hosting and managing of multiple virtual desktops on network servers.
- ❑ Examples of desktop virtualization include Windows, Unix, or Linux virtual machines running on Windows, macOS, or Linux systems.
- ❑ Examples of client-side virtualization include presentation virtualization, application virtualization, and desktop virtualization.

Implementing Client-Side Desktop Virtualization

- ❑ A hypervisor, also called a virtual machine manager (VMM), is the software that creates a virtual machine, providing access to the necessary hardware on the host machine in isolation from other virtual machines and from a host operating system, if present.
- ❑ Most hypervisors require, or at least work better with, hardware-assisted virtualization (HAV), features of Intel Virtualization Technology for x86 (Intel VT-x), or AMD Virtualization (AMD-V).
- ❑ In virtualization, the hypervisor must create a virtual machine compatible with that of the underlying machine, whereas emulation allows you to run an OS or device on hardware with which it is completely incompatible.
- ❑ Sometimes a virtual machine may emulate some piece of hardware that is either not present or not compatible in the underlying hardware.

- Internet access is important for working with virtual machines and keeping the hypervisor and its guest OSs up to date. A hypervisor will provide virtual network adapters, as well as a virtual network, on the host computer.
- The security requirements for a guest OS are the same as those for the host system. Therefore, immediately after installing a guest OS, install a security suite.
- Oracle VM VirtualBox Manager is a free hypervisor that runs on a variety of platforms and is easy to set up and use.

SELF TEST

The following questions will help you measure your understanding of the material presented in this chapter. Read all the choices carefully because there might be more than one correct answer. Choose all correct answers for each question.

Introduction to Virtualization

1. You may use one of these animated graphic objects to represent you in a virtual world.

A. Gadget
B. Guest
C. Avatar
D. Snap-in

2. What type of virtualization is used in distance learning for interactive presentations by instructors?

A. Server-side virtualization
B. Virtual classroom
C. Client-side virtualization
D. Application virtualization

3. This type of virtualization only provides support for an app's user interface and the user interface itself exists on a client computer, while the app runs on a server.

A. Application virtualization
B. Storage virtualization
C. Presentation virtualization
D. Server virtualization

4. In network virtualization, what portion of a network exists within one or more physical networks, creating a virtual network?
   A. Network adapters
   B. Network address space
   C. Switch
   D. Router
5. What acronym represents the term for hosting and managing multiple virtual desktops on a network?
   A. VMM
   B. HAV
   C. VDI
   D. App-V
6. In this type of client-side virtualization, a user runs an application in a virtualized application environment on the local computer, isolating the application.
   A. Storage virtualization
   B. Application virtualization
   C. Virtual world
   D. Thin client

Implementing Client-Side Desktop Virtualization

7. Which acronym is a generic term for virtualization support found in modern CPUs?
   A. VMM
   B. VDI
   C. HAV
   D. App-V
8. Which of the following terms is used in computers to describe the use of software that allows you to run an OS or device on hardware with which it is completely incompatible?
   A. Virtualization
   B. Hardware-assisted virtualization
   C. Emulation
   D. Linux
9. Which of the following is a free hypervisor by Oracle with versions for Linux, Windows, and macOS hosts?
   A. VirtualBox
   B. Parallels
   C. Player
   D. Hyper-V Manager

10. Which of the following does not require a host OS?
   A. Type II hypervisor
   B. Type I hypervisor
   C. Oracle VirtualBox
   D. Hyper-V Manager
11. Which of the following terms is synonymous with hypervisor?
   A. Type I
   B. Virtual machine manager (VMM)
   C. Type II
   D. Remote Desktop
12. Which hypervisor is available only in 64-bit Pro and Enterprise versions of Windows?
   A. Hyper-V Manager
   B. Parallels
   C. Windows Virtual PC
   D. VirtualBox
13. What legal issue must you consider when installing a guest OS in a virtual machine?
   A. Security
   B. Licensing
   C. Copyright
   D. Credentials
14. Which of the following will release the mouse and keyboard from control of a virtual machine?
   A. Host key
   B. Guest key
   C. Windows key
   D. Product key
15. In desktop virtualization, the OS installed directly on the hardware is the ______ and the OS installed in a virtual machine is the _____.
   A. Guest, host
   B. Host, guest
   C. Primary, secondary
   D. Secondary, primary
16. Put the following steps in order: (1) Install guest OS; (2) Install hypervisor; (3) Create virtual machine; (4) Install security software.
   A. 1, 2, 3, 4
   B. 1, 4, 3, 2
   C. 2, 3, 1, 4
   D. 4, 1, 3, 2

17. Which OS cannot legally be used as a guest OS in a Type II hypervisor?
A. Linux
B. Windows 7
C. macOS
D. Windows 10

18. Which of the following identifies Intel's CPUs with hardware-assisted virtualization technology?
A. HAV
B. App-V
C. VMM
D. VT-x

19. Which of the following describes a Type I hypervisor?
A. App-V
B. Guest OS
C. VDI
D. Bare-metal hypervisor

20. Which of these is a recommended way of securing a guest OS?
A. Not allowing additional monitors to be connected
B. Not allowing local access to the guest OS
C. Removing the password from the guest OS
D. Using a strong password to sign into the guest OS

SELF TEST ANSWERS

Introduction to Virtualization

1. ☑ **C.** An avatar is an animated, computer-generated human or animal image that represents a computer user in a virtual world.
☒ **A** is incorrect, as a gadget is a small program. **B** is incorrect because the only use of the term "guest" in this chapter is in the context of "guest OS," the OS running within a VM. **D** is incorrect because a snap-in is a utility module added to a Microsoft Management Console.

2. ☑ **B.** A virtual classroom is a type of virtualization used in distance learning for interactive presentations by instructors.
☒ **A** and **C** are both incorrect because these are simply terms for the hosting location of virtualization. **D** is incorrect because this is a type of client-side virtualization.

3. ☑ **C.** Presentation virtualization is a type of virtualization in which only support for an app's user interface, and the user interface itself, exist on a client computer, while the app itself runs on a server.
☒ **A** is incorrect because in this type of virtualization, the entire app is virtualized and the user interface is not separated from the app, but is isolated in a VM. **B** is incorrect because this type of virtualization allows client computers to utilize many networked hard drives as though they are one drive or location. **D** is incorrect because in server virtualization a single machine hosts one or more server operating systems, each in a virtual machine and each performing tasks independently from the other virtual machines and from the host.

4. ☑ **B.** Network address space exists within one or more physical networks, creating a virtual network.
☒ **A** is incorrect because it is the address space that is virtualized in network virtualization. **C** and **D** are incorrect because these are both types of network hardware not described in this chapter and are not used to create a virtual network.

5. ☑ **C.** VDI, virtual desktop infrastructure, describes the hosting and managing of multiple virtual desktops over a network.
☒ **A** is incorrect because virtual machine manager (VMM) is another term for hypervisor. **B** is incorrect because hardware-assisted virtualization (HAV) is hardware-level support for virtualization found in Intel and AMD CPUs. **D** is incorrect because Application Virtualization (App-V) is the term for Microsoft's application virtualization software.

6. ☑ **B.** Application virtualization is the type of client-side virtualization in which a user runs an application in a virtualized application environment on the local computer, isolating the application.
☒ **A** is incorrect because storage virtualization allows client computers to utilize many networked hard drives as though they are one. **C** is incorrect because a virtual world is an artificial environment that users can explore, often using an avatar. **D** is incorrect because a thin client is a low-cost PC that runs software to connect to a server, transfer video downstream to the thin client, and send mouse clicks and keystrokes upstream to the application on the server.

Implementing Client-Side Desktop Virtualization

7. ☑ **C.** HAV (hardware-assisted virtualization) is the generic term for virtualization support found in modern CPUs.
☒ **A** is incorrect because virtual machine manager (VMM) is simply another term for a hypervisor. **B** is incorrect because virtual desktop infrastructure (VDI) is a term for the creation and management of multiple virtual desktops. **D** is incorrect because App-V is a Microsoft term for their application virtualization software.

8. ☑ **C.** Emulation is the use of software that allows you to run an OS or device on hardware with which it is completely incompatible.
☒ **A** is incorrect, as virtualization is the creation of an environment that seems real but is not. While that is close to emulation, in the context of virtualization on computers, these terms are often kept separate. **B** is incorrect because hardware-assisted virtualization (HAV) is simply hardware support for virtualization built into modern CPUs. **D** is incorrect because Linux is simply an operating system.

9. ☑ **A.** VirtualBox is the free hypervisor by Oracle with versions for Linux, Windows, and macOS hosts.
☒ **B** is incorrect because Parallels is not by Oracle and is not free. **C** is incorrect because Player is by VMware, not Oracle, and it does not come in a version for macOS hosts. **D** is incorrect because Hyper-V Manager is by Microsoft, not Oracle, and it does not come in a version for macOS hosts.

10. ☑ **B.** A Type I hypervisor does not require a host OS.
☒ **A** is incorrect because a Type II hypervisor does require a host OS. **C** and **D** are incorrect because they are both Type II hypervisors that require a host OS.

11. ☑ **B.** Virtual machine manager (VMM) is synonymous with hypervisor.
☒ **A** and **C** are incorrect because while they are types of hypervisors, Type I and Type II are not synonymous with hypervisor. **D** is incorrect because Remote Desktop is a Windows feature that enables you to remotely access other systems; these are real systems, not virtual machines, and no hypervisor is involved.

12. ☑ **A.** Hyper-V Manager is available in 64-bit versions of Windows 8 and higher in Pro and Enterprise editions.
☒ **B** is incorrect because Parallels is primarily for the macOS and is not included in Windows. **C** is incorrect because Virtual PC is for Windows 7, not for later Windows versions. **D** is incorrect because VirtualBox is an Oracle product and is not included in any version of Windows.

13. ☑ **B.** Licensing of the guest OS is very important.
☒ **A** is incorrect because although security is very important for both the guest and host OSs, it is not, strictly speaking, a legal issue. **C** and **D** are incorrect because neither is a legal issue with a guest OS.

14. ☑ **A.** A host key is a special key or key combination that will release the mouse and keyboard from control of a virtual machine.
☒ **B** is incorrect because a guest key is not the key or key combination that will release the mouse and keyboard from control of a virtual machine. **C** is incorrect because the WINDOWS key (on the keyboard) works within Microsoft software on its own and in combination with other keys, and is many things other than a host key. **D** is incorrect, as the product key is not an actual key on the keyboard, but a string of characters used by Microsoft for piracy protection.

15. ☑ **B.** The OS installed on the hardware is the host, and the VM OS is the guest.
☒ **A** is incorrect because these answers are opposite of the correct ones. **C** and **D** are both incorrect because primary and secondary are terms used to describe hardware interfaces (as in primary IDE, secondary IDE); they are not applicable to virtualization.

16. ☑ **C.** (2) Install hypervisor; (3) Create virtual machine; (1) Install guest OS; (4) Install security software.
☒ **A, B,** and **D** are incorrect because they are not in the proper order as described in this chapter.

17. ☑ **C.** macOS cannot be used as a guest OS legally. It is available only preinstalled on Mac hardware.
☒ **A, B,** and **D** are incorrect because they all can be guest OSs in a hypervisor.

18. ☑ **D.** VT-x identifies Intel's CPUs with hardware-assisted virtualization technology.
☒ **A** is incorrect because HAV is simply the acronym for the generic term. **B** is incorrect because App-V is the abbreviation for Microsoft Application Virtualization. **C** is incorrect because VMM is the acronym for virtual machine manager, another term for hypervisor.

19. ☑ **D.** Bare-metal hypervisor describes a Type I hypervisor because it does not require a host OS between it and the hardware.
☒ **A** is incorrect because App-V is Microsoft's application virtualization technology. **B** is incorrect because the guest OS is the OS running within a virtual machine. **C** is incorrect because virtual desktop infrastructure (VDI) describes hosting and managing multiple virtual desktops (often thousands) over a network.

20. ☑ **D.** A strong password is an effective way to secure a guest OS.
☒ **A** is incorrect because the number of monitors does not affect security. **B** is incorrect because local access is the most common way to access a guest OS. **C** is incorrect because removing the password would be detrimental to security.

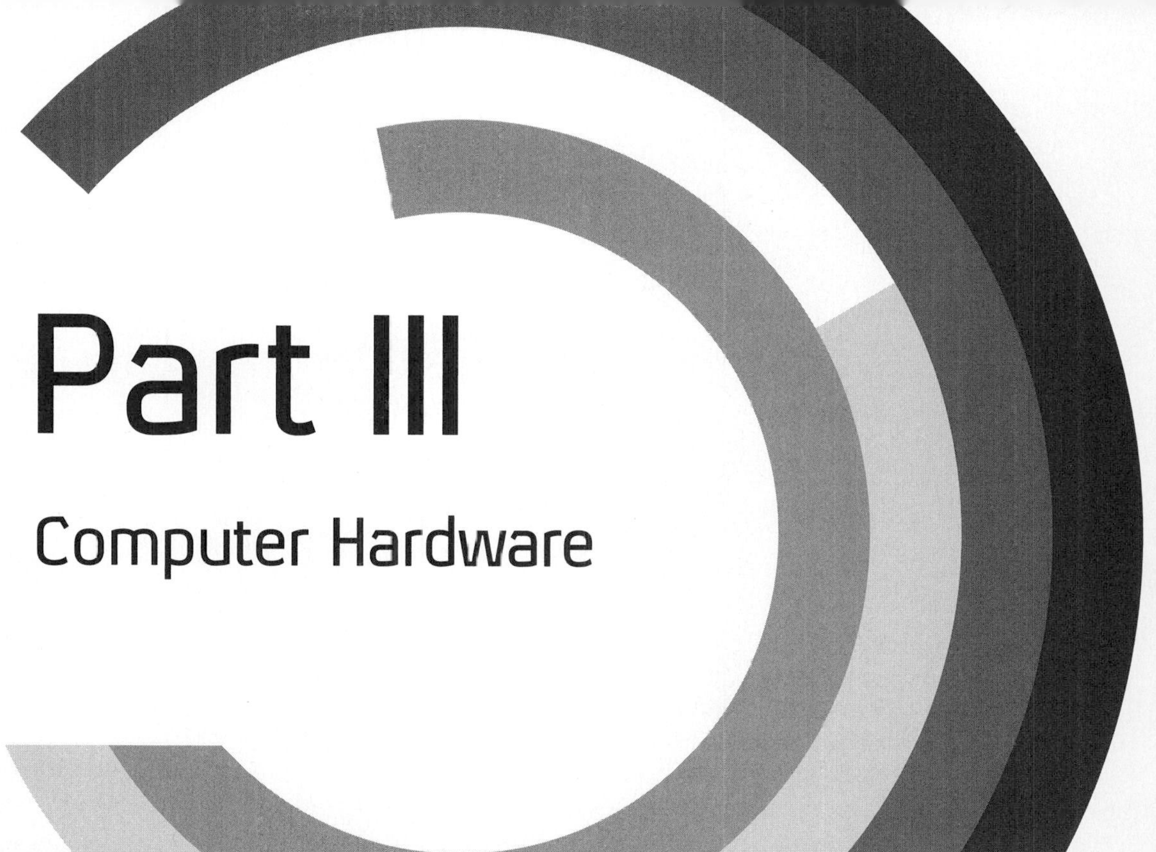

Part III

Computer Hardware

CHAPTERS

Chapter 8

Personal Computer Components: Motherboards and Processors

CERTIFICATION OBJECTIVE

- **1101: 3.4** Given a scenario, install and configure motherboards, central processing units (CPUs), and add-on cards

✓ Two-Minute Drill

Q&A Self Test

Together, this chapter and Chapters 9 and 10 introduce you to basic computer hardware concepts, including motherboards, CPUs, memory, adapters, storage devices, power supplies, display devices, and peripherals. These components comprise the basic set of hardware devices that you will work with over and over in your career as an A+ certified IT professional. This chapter begins the process by looking at the basic set of hand tools that a technician uses and by examining motherboards and CPUs—the components that empower and manage all the other components.

The hardware toolkit recommendations in this section include the tools outlined on CompTIA's A+ Proposed Hardware and Software List, as well as some additional tools you should know about. We will revisit many of these tools in scenarios in coming chapters. Chapter 17 covers the network-specific tools recommended in CompTIA A+ 1101 exam Objective 2.8.

The Hardware Toolkit

As a new PC technician, you might begin with a repair toolkit that is not very extensive: perhaps a small assortment of screwdrivers and nut drivers, a small flashlight, and an assortment of spare screws and nuts. You'll add tools as you need them for special jobs. You may decide to purchase a basic computer technician's toolkit or assemble the components yourself. Figure 8-1 shows some of the most basic tools a computer technician uses on the job, and following that is a more complete list of components you might want in your kit, depending on your responsibilities. Note that this list doesn't include network tools, which are covered at the beginning of Chapter 17.

- **Screwdrivers** You should have an assortment of Phillips head, flathead, and Torx screwdrivers, as well as varying sizes of nut drivers. For working on laptops, a very small Phillips head screwdriver is the single most important tool in your set. Flathead screws are seldom used in modern computer equipment, but you may need to use a flathead blade to pry something open at some point.
- **ESD protection** An *ESD wrist strap* helps prevent damage from static electricity when working on any component except the power supply, monitor, and laser printers. We discussed ESD wrist straps in Chapter 1. An *ESD mat* provides a static charge with a path to ground and is designed for the desktop or floor of a workspace. While this mat may not fit in your toolkit, it is something that should be available at any PC technician's workbench.

FIGURE 8-1

An assortment of basic tools

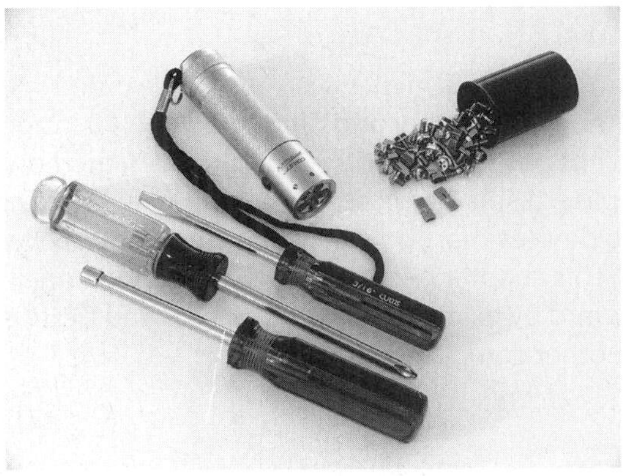

- **FRUs** *Field-replaceable units (FRUs)* should be included in your hardware toolkit. An FRU is any component that you can install into a system onsite. This includes such items as memory modules, heat sinks, motherboard batteries, various adapter cards, hard drives, optical drives, keyboards, mice, fans, AC adapters, spare cables and connectors, power supplies, and even spare motherboards. Of course, all of this depends on the scope of your job and how cost-effective it is to have these items on hand. If you support hundreds of computers that are all the same make and model, it may make sense to have spare parts; if you support a diverse fleet of devices, probably not.
- **Multimeter** A *multimeter* is indispensable in determining power problems from a power outlet or from the power supply. You'll use this handheld device to measure the resistance, voltage, and/or current in computer components (see Figure 8-2) using two probes (one negative, one positive) that you touch to power wires in the equipment you are testing. Multimeters can also be used for cable continuity testing, as described in Chapter 17.
- **Power supply tester** A *power supply tester* is a specialized device for testing a power supply unit and is a bit safer to use than a multimeter for this purpose. A power supply tester comes with connectors compatible with the output connectors on a standard power supply, rather than with just the simple probes of a multimeter. An LCD display or LEDs show the test results.
- **Camera** A digital camera or smartphone will enable you to document the condition of a computer before you begin troubleshooting. One important way we use a camera is to document the cabling and connections—both external and internal—before making any changes so that we can reconnect all components correctly. A camera is also handy for capturing low-level error messages that cannot be captured with a software screen capture utility and for capturing the model and serial number on a device.

FIGURE 8-2

A simple multimeter

- **Thermal paste** *Thermal paste* is an electrically insulating, heat-conductive paste that helps increase the transfer of heat between a hot chip and a heat-dissipating fan or heat sink. It is also called *thermal grease* or *heat sink compound.* You apply it in a thin layer between the components. Depending on the type, it may or not have adhesive properties; usually when it aids in adhesion, it is called *thermal adhesive.* When it comes in a solid pad that you place between the heat sink and the chip, it's called a *thermal pad.*
- **Drive adapter** A *SATA to USB connector* enables you to use an internal hard drive (using a serial ATA connector) as an external hard drive (using a Universal Serial Bus connector). It may be called a *drive enclosure* if it contains a plastic shell into which you can mount the drive to make it easier to handle and transport.

EXERCISE 8-1

What's in Your Toolkit?

In this exercise you will explore the tools used by PC technicians.

- If you are already working as a technician, gather your tools and compare them to the previously mentioned list. What would you add to the printed list? What is in the list that you would like to add to your toolkit?
- If you are not a technician, find one who will talk to you about the tools of the trade. You may find this person at work, at school, or even at a local PC repair business. Ask the technician to tell you which tools they use the most and what they recommend you have in a basic toolkit.

CERTIFICATION OBJECTIVE

- ***1101: 3.4*** *Given a scenario, install and configure motherboards, central processing units (CPUs), and add-on cards*

The motherboard is the real estate on which a PC is built; all PC components are directly or indirectly connected to this large printed circuit board (PCB). The rest of this chapter introduces many of the topics of CompTIA A+ 1101 exam Objective 3.4, including motherboard sizes (ATX and ITX), motherboard connector types, motherboard and CPU compatibility, CPU architecture, expansion cards, and cooling.

Motherboard Form Factors and Components

Each internal and external PC component connects, directly or indirectly, to a single circuit board. The *motherboard,* also referred to as the *mainboard,* the *system board,* or the *planar board,* is made of fiberglass, typically brown or green, and with a meshwork of copper lines, called *traces*. Power, data, and control signals travel to all connected components through these pathways. A group of these wires assigned to a set of functions is collectively called a *bus*.

Safety first! Hands-on experience is important for preparing for your CompTIA A+ exams, and as you study you will want to install and remove components on a PC system. Make sure you understand safety procedures, as detailed in Chapter 1.

In this section, we focus on types of motherboards, their typical integrated components, and the differences between the motherboard's communication busses and what components can connect to a motherboard through these various busses. Most of the specifications discussed in this section pertain more to desktop PCs than to laptops, but we will point out some differences where applicable. We will also address laptop hardware in more detail in Chapter 14.

If you work with experienced PC technicians, read trade publications, or visit technical websites, you'll probably see the slang term *mobo* used in place of motherboard.

Sizes/Form Factors

A motherboard *form factor* defines the type and location of components on the motherboard, the power supply that will work with it, the size of the motherboard, and the corresponding PC case that will accommodate both. There are several motherboard form factors, each with different layouts, components, and specifications. A motherboard will use only certain CPUs and types of memory. Therefore, if you decide to build a computer from components, you must ensure that the motherboard, power supply, CPU, memory, and case will all work together.

A motherboard's form factor does not tell you what CPUs and memory it is compatible with; there is little to no relationship there.

CompTIA A+ 1101 exam Objective 3.4 mentions two form factors: ATX and ITX. Be sure to pay attention to the differences between these form factors and know about their smaller-size variants. We discuss these form factors, as well as others that have some relevance to the exams, even if they are not listed in the objectives.

ATX

The *Advanced Technology eXtended (ATX)* motherboard standard was released by Intel Corporation in 1996 and has been updated many times over the years—both officially and through proprietary variations by manufacturers. Counting all the variations, it is the most commonly used form in PCs. The original ATX motherboard measures approximately 12" wide by 9.6" from front to back (305 mm × 244 mm).

Figure 8-3 shows an ATX motherboard in an older desktop.

Depending on the manufacturer and the intended market, today's ATX motherboard will contain memory slots for the latest RAM types and support for firmware-controlled power management, multimedia, Intel or AMD CPU sockets, disk drive connectors, and USB.

Besides the original full-size ATX motherboard, there are three smaller sizes: Micro-ATX, Flex-ATX, and Mini-ATX. Table 8-1 provides their dimensions.

Knowing the dimensions of the various motherboard sizes is useful if you are trying to determine what size a particular board is (so you can order a replacement, for example).

ITX

ITX, originally named EPIA, was developed by chipset-company VIA in 2001 for use in low-power CPUs (such as very small desktop PCs designed to be part of home entertainment systems) and chipsets in low-cost PCs but was never used in production. Subsequent

FIGURE 8-3

An ATX motherboard installed in a case with the CPU and some cables visible

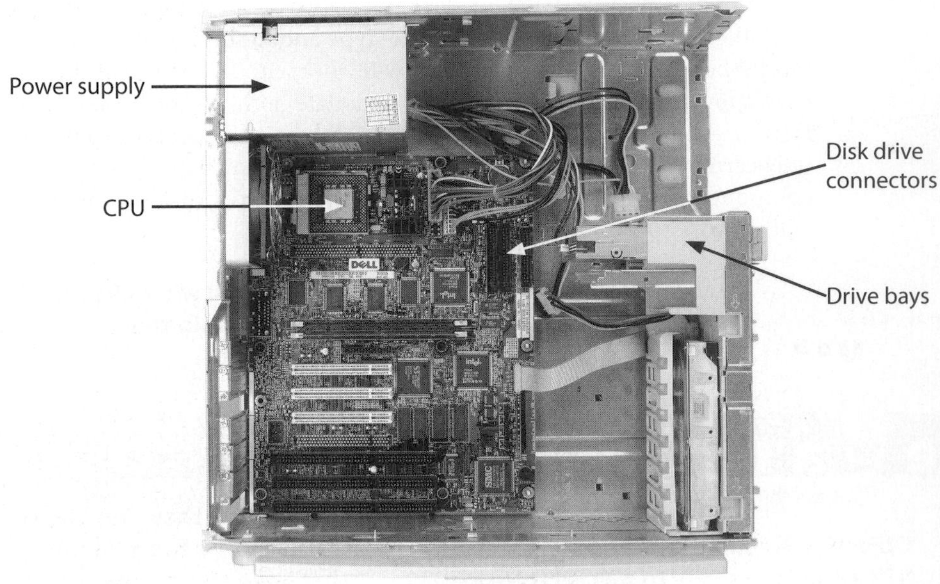

TABLE 8-1 Motherboard Approximate Size Comparison

Form Factor	Approximate Size
ATX	12" × 9.6" (305 mm × 244 mm)
Micro-ATX (mATX)	9.6" × 9.6" (244 mm × 244 mm)
Flex-ATX	9" × 7.5" (228.6 mm × 190.5 mm)
Mini-ATX	5.9" × 5.9" (150 mm × 150 mm)
ITX	8.5" × 7.5" (215 mm × 191 mm)
Mini-ITX (mITX)	6.7" × 6.7" (170 mm × 170 mm)
Nano-ITX	4.7" × 4.7" (120 mm × 120 mm)
Pico-ITX	3.9" × 2.8" (100 mm × 72 mm)
Mobile-ITX	2.9" × 1.77" (75 mm × 45 mm)

designs—the Mini-ITX, Nano-ITX, Pico-ITX, and Mobile-ITX—have been progressively smaller and targeted to embedded systems. See Table 8-1 for their specifications. The only one listed in the current CompTIA A+ 1101 exam objectives is the original ITX.

You would think that something named *micro* would be smaller than something named *mini* but that's not always the case. For example, Mini-ATX is smaller than Micro-ATX, as you can see in Table 8-1. Notice that the "m" in mATX stands for *micro*, whereas the "m" in mITX stands for *mini*. Figure 8-4 compares the various form factors of ATX and ITX visually.

FIGURE 8-4 A comparison of ATX and ITX sizes (Credit: VIA Gallery from Hsintien, Taiwan, CC BY 2.0 https://creativecommons.org/licenses/by/2.0, via Wikimedia Commons)

EXERCISE 8-2

Comparing Motherboards

In this exercise you will compare motherboard specifications and examine the motherboard on a desktop PC.

1. From a computer with an Internet connection, use your browser to search on the ATX and ITX form factors and their smaller variations.
2. Notice the locations of the CPU, expansion bus, and memory slots.
3. If possible, open a desktop PC, following the safety guidelines outlined in Chapter 1, and determine the form factor of the motherboard by measuring its dimensions and comparing them to those in Table 8-1. Do not disconnect or remove any components within the case.
4. Keep the computer open while you complete this chapter, locating as many of the components described as you can.
5. When you are finished, close the computer case, reconnect the computer, and make sure that it works as well as it did before you opened it.

Motherboard Components

The components built into a motherboard include sockets for various PC components, including the CPU and memory; expansion slots (such as PCIe and M.2); built-in components such as network, display, and sound adapters; hard drive controllers; support for various port types (such as USB); and the chipset. Following is an explanation of all of these, with the exception of hard drive controllers, which we will describe in Chapter 9 during the discussion of storage types.

RAM Slots

A motherboard has slots, or sockets, for system memory. Depending on the vintage and the manufacturer of a motherboard, special sockets accept one of the various types of RAM chips attached to small circuit boards called *memory modules* or, less formally, *memory sticks*. There have been many different types over the years, but the ones you need to know today are all some type of *Dual Inline Memory Module (DIMM)*. Different DIMMs include double data rate 3 (DDR3), DDR4, and DDR5 and small outline DIMM (SODIMM) versions of all of those. You'll learn about these in Chapter 9.

Some motherboards have paired RAM slots in a configuration called *dual-channel architecture* in order to improve RAM performance. In such motherboards, DIMMs must be installed in matched pairs in the slots with matching colors. For example, there might be two blue slots and two black ones. Dual-channel is a function of the motherboard, not the RAM itself; ordinary RAM is used in dual-channel slots. There are also *triple-channel* and *quad-channel architectures*. More about that in Chapter 9.

How do you find out what memory modules will work on a specific motherboard? You read the motherboard user guide. If you cannot find one for your computer, find the manufacturer's name and the model of the motherboard (or computer system) and query your favorite Internet search engine. You will often find the right manual in PDF format.

Bus Architecture

The term *bus* refers to pathways that power, data, or control signals use to travel from one component to another in the computer. Standards determine how the various bus designs use the wires. There are many types of busses on the motherboard, including the *memory bus* used by the processor to access memory. In addition, each PC has an *expansion bus* of one or more types. The most common types of expansion bus architectures are PCI, PCIe, and Mini PCIe, and we discuss these next. The following bus types are those that you can expect to see in PCs today.

The terms *bus, system bus,* and *expansion bus* are interchangeable. A bus refers to either a system bus or an expansion bus attached to the CPU.

PCI *Peripheral Component Interconnect (PCI)* is an expansion bus architecture released in 1993 but still around on some motherboards today for backward compatibility. In some documentation it is called *conventional PCI* to distinguish it from the more modern PCIe.

The PCI bus transfers data in parallel over a 32-bit or 64-bit data bus. (The 32-bit type is much more common.) Over the years several variants of the PCI standard were developed, and data transfer speeds vary depending on the variant and the bus width. The original 32-bit PCI bus ran at 33.33 MHz (megahertz) with a transfer rate of up to 133 megabytes per second (MBps).

PCI slots are 3" long and are typically white. PCI cards and slots are not compatible with those of other bus architectures. PCI was the assumed slot type for almost all expansion boards for various functions for many years, and motherboards typically had a lot of them. PCI was originally developed for video, back in the days when PCI was the fastest bus around, but few video cards are PCI anymore because there are faster alternatives. Nowadays a typical motherboard will have only one PCI slot, with the rest of them being PCIe.

PCIe *Peripheral Component Interconnect Express (PCIe)* differs from PCI in that it uses serial communications rather than parallel communications, as well as different bus connectors. Also called PCI Express and PCI-E, it has replaced PCI on modern systems and is incompatible with conventional PCI adapter cards.

Although PCIe programming is similar to PCI, the newer standard is not a true bus that transfers data in parallel, but rather a group of serial channels. The PCIe connector's naming scheme describes the number of serial channels each handles, with the designations x1, x4, and x16 indicating 1, 4, and 16 channels, respectively.

On the motherboard, a PCIe x1 connector is approximately 1½" long, whereas PCIe x4 is about 2" long, and PCIe x16 is close to 4" long. Figure 8-5 shows several PCIe slots and one conventional PCI slot.

The PCIe transfer rate depends on which version of the standard the bus installation supports. For instance, PCIe 1.0 supports data transfers at 250 MBps per channel, with a maximum of 16 channels. Therefore, the maximum transfer rate for 16-channel PCIe 1.0 is 4 GBps. PCIe 2.0, released in late 2007, added a signaling mode that doubled the rate to 500 MBps per channel. This rate was redoubled to 1 GBps per channel with the PCIe 3.0 (PCIe Gen 3) standard, which supports a signaling mode of 1 GBps per channel but is downward compatible with existing PCIe products. PCIe 4.0 (PCIe Gen 4) doubles it again, and PCIe 5.0 (PCIe Gen 5) doubles that.

FIGURE 8-5 From top to bottom: PCIe x4, x16, x1, and x16 and conventional PCI (Photo: https://commons.wikimedia.org/wiki/File:PCIExpress.jpg [Creative Commons license])

For the CompTIA A+ exam, you don't need to know the full specifications of standards such as PCI and PCIe, but you should understand the basics of each standard. For instance, know that PCI and PCIe are both expansion bus interfaces; remember that PCIe is the newer of the standards and is serial, whereas PCI is parallel. Be sure you can identify their physical differences on a motherboard.

Mini PCI and Mini PCI Express Mini PCI has a 32-bit data bus, like conventional PCI. The biggest difference is that Mini PCI is much smaller than PCI—both the card and the slot. If a laptop has an installed Mini PCI slot, it is usually accessible via a small removable panel on the bottom of the case. Mini PCI cards also come in three form factors: Type I, Type II, and Type III. Types I and II each have 100 pins in a stacking connector, whereas Type III cards have 124 pins on an edge connector.

Mini PCIe has replaced Mini PCI in modern laptops. (Depending on the manufacturer, this is also called *PCI Express Mini Card, Mini PCI Express, Mini PCIe,* or simply *MiniCard.*) This specification provides much faster throughput with a 64-bit data bus. At 30 mm × 26.8 mm, it is much smaller than a Mini PCI card and has a 52-pin edge connector. Figure 8-6 compares a Mini PCI card to a Mini PCI Express card.

FIGURE 8-6 Comparison of Mini PCI (left) and Mini PCI Express (right)

Although Mini PCI Express is more modern than PCI Express, it is still on the wane, thanks to a newer technology known as M.2, discussed next.

M.2

M.2 (pronounced *M dot 2*) is a modern connector type for mounting solid-state expansion cards and solid-state drives on a motherboard. It has replaced mSATA, an earlier way of mounting solid-state storage on a motherboard using the PCI Express Mini Card layout and connectors. We'll revisit M.2 in Chapter 9, when we talk about storage interfaces, but since M.2 is a multipurpose slot type, it warrants mention here as well.

M.2 can use the PCI Express (x4) bus, Serial ATA, and/or USB internally, depending on the M.2 module. Different types of M.2 connectors are keyed differently to ensure compatibility. On a motherboard, the M.2 slots will be labeled so you'll know which ones to use for each device. Figure 8-7 shows two different M.2 slots: one for an SSD (also called *M-key*) and one for a wireless network adapter (also called *E-key*). Notice the writing adjacent to the slots; the SSD one says PCIe SSD-2, and the Wi-Fi one says M.2 WLAN.

exam watch

There are multiple key IDs (A through M), each with certain pins notched on the connector. You don't need to know the specs on these different keys; just know that different keying exists and that you have to match the M.2 device with the right slot. If you're interested in the detailed specs on the different socket variants, there are plenty of Internet resources on it.

FIGURE 8-7 An SSD (left) and a Wi-Fi card (right) in two different kinds of M.2 slots

Motherboard Power Connectors

If you carefully examine a motherboard, you will see many connectors that range from tiny 3-pin connectors to long 24-pin connectors. These range from power connectors to connectors for onboard components, such as audio, I/O interfaces, and more. These will normally be labeled and well documented in the motherboard user's manual.

The main power connector for a modern desktop PC motherboard is a 24-pin connector with many different wire colors. In addition, look for one or more 4-pin or 6-pin connectors to the motherboard. The 4-pin variety is also called P4 or ATX 12V and delivers extra 12-volt power. This is necessary on many newer systems because they require more 12-volt power than the few 12-volt (yellow) wires in the 24-pin power supply connector can deliver. The 6-pin type is an auxiliary connector (AUX or ATX SYS), which supplies extra 3.3V and 5V current to the motherboard. You can distinguish it because it may have red, white, black, gray, and/or green wires but no yellow ones. Yellow is for 12V. Figure 8-8 shows one of each.

on the job

Older motherboards may have a 20-pin power connector. Some power supplies have a 24-pin connector where the last 4 pins snap off the end so the connector can be used on a 20-pin motherboard. This is called a 20+4 connector. Going the other direction, you can buy a 20-pin to 24-pin adapter that allows an older (20-pin) power supply to plug into a newer (24-pin) motherboard.

There may also be an additional 6-pin or 8-pin power connector on the power supply, called a PCIe power connector, designed to give PCIe cards a power boost. These are 12V connectors and will have yellow and black wires only. On some high-end (that is, power-hungry) systems you may see an 8-pin connector labeled EPS12V. (It is sometimes called EATX12V or ATX12V 2×4.) As the "12" in the name implies, it provides even more 12V power to the motherboard. Chapter 10 covers power supplies and power connectors in more detail.

FIGURE 8-8

A four-pin ATX 12V connector (left) and a six-pin AUX connector (right)

Laptop motherboards have different power connections than described here, but we aren't as concerned with them because of the way that power is supplied to a laptop. The connections are simpler, less configurable, and often proprietary. With a desktop, you can go out and buy a standardized power supply box to install in a desktop PC case. With a laptop, the power connectors and the motherboard's relationship to the incoming power vary among brands and models, and the technician does not normally need to make a lot of different power connections by hand.

Headers

Modern ATX motherboards have most of their ports built directly into the side of the board, so they are externally accessible via the back of the PC without having to run any cables between the motherboards and the ports. However, they don't always have every port built in directly; sometimes you may need to run a cable from a header to a port. That's particularly true when you need to connect to something on the front of the PC case. Another header that's difficult to overlook (because it's so large) is the main connector from the power supply to the motherboard, the P1.

A *header* is a set of pins on the motherboard to which you can connect a cable. A common kind of port to have a header on a motherboard is USB, but you may also see headers for other port types, depending on the motherboard design. Most motherboards have headers for connecting the power button and the CPU fan, as shown in Figure 8-9. Pay close attention to the labels near the ports, and do not get them confused. Consult the motherboard manual if the writing on the motherboard is unclear. Some headers have little plastic frames around them to protect the pins from getting bent; that's common with headers for connecting older parallel ATA (PATA) drives, as you will learn in Chapter 9, and also with headers for connecting USB 2.0 and 3.0 cables.

FIGURE 8-9 Headers for a power button (left) and a CPU fan (right)

USB 2.0 and USB 3.0 have separate kinds of headers; the USB 2.0 type is (usually) 9-pin, and the USB 3.0 type is 20-pin.

Firmware and Chipsets

Firmware refers to software instructions, usually stored on *read-only memory (ROM)* chips—special memory chips that retain their contents when the computer is powered off. Most PC components, such as video adapters, hard drives, network adapters, and printers, contain firmware. Firmware built into the motherboard controls the basic functions, capabilities, and configurability of a computer system. Firmware on the motherboard includes the chipset and system BIOS. You will learn how to configure a motherboard's firmware later in this chapter.

A critical component of the motherboard firmware is the *chipset*. When technicians talk about the chipset, they are usually referring to one or more chips designed to control and manage the data movement within the motherboard. It is the chipset that determines which CPUs and memory the motherboard will accept and how fast the various busses move data. Choosing a motherboard appropriate to the system you are building involves understanding the motherboard chipset's capabilities.

In past eras, it was common for a motherboard's chipset to be composed of two chips: the northbridge and the southbridge. Today, however, single-chip chipsets are common, such as the Platform Controller Hub (PCH) chip on some Intel motherboards, as shown in Figure 8-10. On some motherboards you might not be able to readily identify the chipset chip(s) because one or more may be covered with a heat sink and/or a fan.

FIGURE 8-10 A PCH chip on an Intel motherboard

SCENARIO & SOLUTION	
You have opened a PC, looking for the PCIe slots, and you see two sets of long slots in the expansion area; some are light in color, and others are dark in color and slightly longer than the others. Which is more likely to be a PCIe x16 slot?	The longer dark-colored slots are more likely to be PCIe x16. A PCIe x16 slot is the longest kind of slot found on a modern motherboard.
You need to replace the motherboard in a desktop PC but you do not know what form factor to shop for. How can you determine it?	Measure the motherboard and compare its dimensions to those listed in Table 8-1.

CPUs and Their Sockets

A personal computer is more than the sum of its parts. However, the most important part, without which it is not a computer, or even a useful tool, is the *central processing unit (CPU),* also called the *processor*. But a CPU may not be the only processor in a PC. Other components may include a processor for performing the intense work of the component. The most common example of this is the *graphics processing unit (GPU)* found on modern video adapters, used to render the graphics images for the display. GPUs were integrated onto system boards along with the video adapter, and now there is a trend of integrating the GPU into some CPUs. Wherever it is located, the GPU saves the CPU for other system-wide functions and improves system performance. The following is an overview of CPUs, their purposes and characteristics, manufacturers and models, technologies, and the motherboard sockets into which they fit.

In a PC, the CPU is the primary control device for the entire computer system. The CPU is simply a chip containing a set of components that manages all the activities and does much of the "heavy lifting" in a computer system. The CPU interfaces with, or connects to, all of the components such as memory, storage, and input/output (I/O) through busses. The CPU performs a number of individual or discrete functions that must work in harmony in order for the system to function. Additionally, the CPU is responsible for managing the activities of the entire system.

A CPU is printed in a single operation onto a silicon wafer, not assembled from discrete parts. Nevertheless, inside each CPU is a variety of component parts, each with a specific function. These include the control unit, the arithmetic logic unit (ALU), registers, busses, and memory caches. Each of these is explained in an upcoming section.

The Machine Cycle

The CPU's internal components perform four basic operations that are collectively known as a *machine cycle*. The machine cycle includes fetching an instruction, decoding the

FIGURE 8-11 The four-step machine cycle employs the control unit, ALU, and registers.

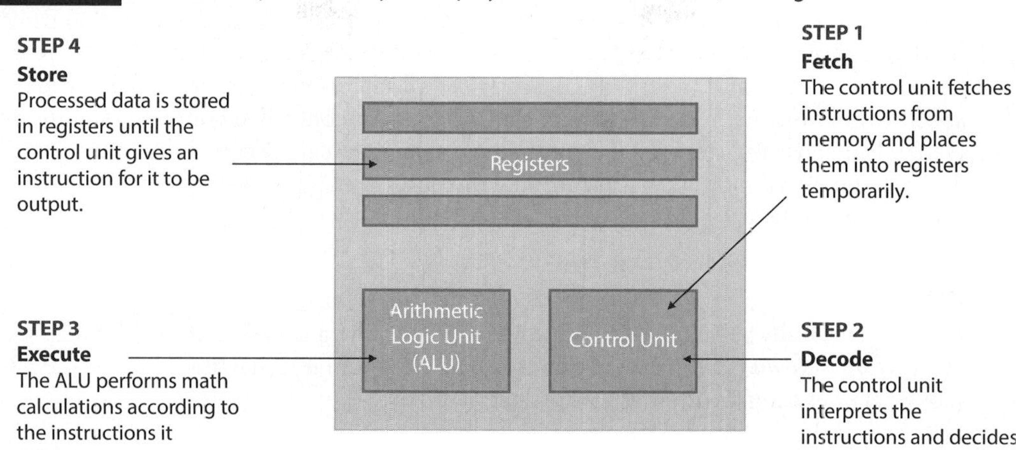
STEP 4
Store
Processed data is stored in registers until the control unit gives an instruction for it to be output.
Registers
STEP 1
Fetch
The control unit fetches instructions from memory and places them into registers temporarily.
STEP 3
Execute
The ALU performs math calculations according to the instructions it receives.
Arithmetic Logic Unit (ALU)
Control Unit
STEP 2
Decode
The control unit interprets the instructions and decides how to direct the ALU.

instruction, executing the instruction, and storing the result. Figure 8-11 provides an overview of this process. Understanding this process up-front will make the discussions of the individual components more relevant.

exam watch

The machine cycle isn't covered on the CompTIA A+ 1101 or 1102 exam, but understanding it can make it easier to grasp some other concepts that *are* covered, such as multiple cores, multithreading, and number of bits of processing.

Control Unit

The *control unit* is the "traffic cop" inside the CPU. It uses electrical signals to direct the CPU's overall operation. It signals to other parts of the computer system what they should do. The control unit interprets instructions and initiates the action needed to carry them out. First it *fetches,* which means it retrieves an instruction or data from memory. Then it *decodes,* which means it interprets or translates the instruction into strings of binary digits that the computer understands.

ALU

The *arithmetic logic unit (ALU)* is the part of the CPU that executes the instructions (Step 3 in Figure 8-11). It performs arithmetic operations on the data (add, subtract, multiply, and divide) and performs logical operations such as comparing two data strings and determining whether they are the same.

Registers

A *register* is a memory location inside the CPU, providing temporary storage that can be used as a scratch pad for calculations. Two types of registers are used in modern systems: dedicated registers and general-purpose registers. Dedicated registers are usually for specific functions such as maintaining status or system-controlled counting operations. General-purpose registers are for multiple purposes, typically when mathematical and comparison operations occur. Placing data into a register is the *storing* step of the machine cycle (Step 4 in Figure 8-11).

Busses

Busses, generically speaking, are pathways over which data travels. External busses, such as the *front-side bus,* carry data to and from the CPU, and internal busses in the CPU itself move data between its internal components.

Cache Memory

Because the CPU is so much faster than the computer's other components, it can potentially spend a lot of time idle, waiting for data to be delivered or picked up. The farther the data has to travel to get to the CPU, the longer the delay. To help minimize these delays, modern CPUs have multiple caches. A *cache* (pronounced "cash") is a pool of extremely fast memory that's stored close to the CPU and connected to it by a very fast pathway. Only when the needed data isn't found in any of the caches does the system have to fetch data from storage (for example, the main memory of the PC, or a hard drive).

When the CPU needs some data, it looks first in the L1 (level 1) cache, which is the one closest to the CPU. The L1 cache is an *on die cache;* that means when the CPU is stamped into the silicon wafer, the L1 cache is stamped into the same piece of silicon at the same time.

The L1 cache is quite small, so it can't hold everything the CPU has recently used or may need to use soon. If the data needed isn't found in the L1 cache, the system looks in the L2 cache. On older systems, the L2 cache was on the motherboard, but on modern systems, it's in the CPU package next to the silicon chip. If the data isn't in the L2 cache, the system checks the L3 cache, which is larger and slightly farther away from the CPU, although still within the ceramic chip that we call the CPU. On a multicore CPU (discussed later in this chapter), all of the cores share a common L3 cache.

CPU Technologies and Characteristics

A number of technologies are employed in a CPU, based on both standards and proprietary designs, which are constantly changing. This section describes common CPU technologies and characteristics you should know for the exam.

x64 and x86 Architecture

A CPU supports a certain *word size,* which is the size of the chunk of data that can enter and exit the CPU in one operation. This is also called the chip's *architecture,* and on modern PC CPUs it is either 32-bit (called *x86*) or 64-bit (called *x64*). The architecture is significant because it determines what version of the operating system the PC can use. On a 32-bit CPU, you are limited to the 32-bit version of Windows, which supports a maximum of 4 GB of RAM. A 64-bit CPU can handle either 64-bit or 32-bit Windows.

Remember that x64-based systems can access more than 4 GB of RAM. Also know that in a 64-bit version of Windows, 64-bit programs are stored in the C:\Program Files folder and 32-bit programs are stored in the C:\Program Files (x86) folder.

Advanced RISC Machine

Look back at Figure 8-11 and recall the machine cycle. The control unit fetches instructions and uses them to perform calculations. But what are these instructions? They are built-in functions that the CPU understands, like the functions in Excel and other spreadsheet programs. Some CPUs have a lot of instructions they can understand; these are called Complex Instruction Set Computers (CISCs).

The advantage of a complex instruction set is that the CPU can perform a wide variety of tasks efficiently. To further explore the spreadsheet metaphor, think about how a spreadsheet program contains hundreds of functions for doing math calculations. If you didn't have a function for something you wanted to do (for example, averaging a group of numbers), you would have to write out the math formula to do it, and that would be a much longer and more complicated programming instruction. Today's desktop and laptop CPUs are mostly CISC.

If you had a CPU that needed to do a smaller set of tasks but it needed to do them extremely quickly, one way to achieve that would be to reduce the instruction set and focus all the CPU's power on performing just a few functions. That's the idea behind a Reduced Instruction Set Computer (RISC).

Advanced RISC Machine (ARM) is one of the most common types of RISC CPUs. RISC CPUs are found in most mobile devices today, such as Android and Apple tablets and smartphones, and in gaming consoles. ARM's efficient architecture helps battery-powered devices last longer between charges. They are also found in some special-purpose computers that are dedicated to a narrow set of activities. In past decades they were also used on some low-cost desktop and laptop PCs, such as Chromebooks, and at the high end on some servers and supercomputers.

There is a special version of Windows called Windows on ARM that runs on some RISC CPUs designed for desktops and laptops. There are some limitations as to the apps that will run, but generally most Microsoft Store (aka Universal Windows Platform, or UWP) apps will run, as well as most 32-bit Windows apps. There are also some compatibility differences between Windows 10 and Windows 11 on ARM devices.

Clock Speed

The *clock speed* of a CPU is the speed at which it can potentially execute instructions. CPU clock speed is measured in billions of cycles per second, or gigahertz (GHz). A CPU of a certain type and model may be available in a range of clock speeds.

All other features being equal, the CPU with the faster clock speed will be more expensive. However, when comparing different models of CPUs, the faster clock speed alone will not determine the fastest CPU. Manufacturers use many technologies to speed up CPUs. For example, the number of clock cycles required for completing the same operation can vary among CPU models. To the end user, the perceived speed of a PC, or lack of it, may involve other aspects of the computer's total design, such as the cache size, the amount and speed of the RAM, the speed of the busses, and the speed of the hard drive.

Multithreading

A *thread,* or thread of execution, is a portion of a program that can run separately from other portions of the program. A thread can also run concurrently with other threads. *Multithreading,* also known as *hyperthreading* or *simultaneous multithreading (SMT),* is a CPU technology that allows two or more threads to execute at the same time within a single execution core. This is considered partially parallel execution. Intel introduced hyperthreading in the Pentium 4 Xeon CPU, referring to it as Hyper-Threading Technology (HT Technology). Multithreading is the more preferred term today and the one listed in Objective 3.4 on the 1101 exam.

Multicore

The most visible change in CPUs in recent years has been the introduction of *multicore CPUs* with more than one core on the same integrated circuit. Each *core* is essentially a CPU with its own set of control unit, ALU, and registers. The first of these were *dual-core* CPUs containing two CPU cores. Quad-core CPUs are commonly available, and manufacturers offer 6-core and more—even 128-core Superchip CPUs.

Server computers have long been available with multiple CPUs, so why not simply install two or more single-core CPUs on the same motherboard? Two cores on the same chip can communicate and cooperate much faster than two single-core processors sharing a motherboard can. A dual-core CPU can simultaneously process two threads in true parallel execution, and each core has its own L1 cache; triple-core CPUs can simultaneously process three threads, quad-core four threads, and so on. On top of the advantage of using multiple cores, the manufacturers have made other changes to the CPU architecture to make them faster and more energy efficient.

Make sure you understand how CPUs differ from one another in areas such as x64/x86, CISC vs. ARM, number of cores, multithreading, and virtualization support.

Virtualization Support

Remember in Chapter 7 when we talked about hardware-assisted virtualization (HAV) and its usefulness on machines that run VM hypervisors? Another name for HAV is *virtualization support.* Most modern CPUs include virtualization support—the ability to manage multiple operating systems running at once through virtual machines—enabled through BIOS/UEFI settings. In Intel CPUs, the name of the group of technologies involved is *Virtualization Technology (VT),* which may have an additional symbol or letter associated with a particular CPU model. AMD's virtualization technology is *AMD-V.* You used to have to consider HAV when shopping for a CPU, but today almost any new CPU is going to come with it.

CPU and Motherboard Brand and Model Compatibility

There are many CPU manufacturers, but the prevailing ones in the PC market today are *Intel Corporation* and *Advanced Micro Devices, Inc. (AMD).* Both companies manufacture more than CPUs, but their competition in the CPU market gets more attention in the trade and business press since AMD emerged as Intel's major competitor.

Fortunately, you don't have to memorize any names and characteristics of specific CPUs for the current CompTIA A+ exam. What is important for a tech to understand is that Intel and AMD are the two main players in the CPU market. A motherboard will support only AMD or only Intel—never both. Further, a motherboard will usually support only a very narrow band of specific models of CPUs from that one manufacturer, with a similar set of features. Each manufacturer makes dozens of CPU types and subtypes for nearly every type of device, from server to desktop to mobile hardware. There are *multisocket* motherboards for servers that accept multiple CPUs for increased processing power, CPU chips designed to be permanently mounted on mobile device motherboards (to save weight and space), and everything in between.

Cooling Mechanisms

The more powerful PCs become, the more heat they generate within the case. Heat is your PC's enemy, and it should be yours, too. An overheated CPU will fail. Rather than allow heat to cause damage, several techniques—both passive and active—are used to maintain an optimum operating temperature. Some components will even slow down so they produce less heat before any damage occurs. Manufacturers have struggled to keep ahead of the heat curve and provide sufficient cooling for the entire system. These methods involve fans, heat sinks, thermal compounds, and even liquid cooling systems.

CPU and Case Fans

Early PCs relied on the design of the PC case and the power supply fan to provide all the cooling for the computer's interior. During this era, the typical PC had vents in the front through which the power supply fan pulled cool air and in the back through which the heated air was exhausted. Today, we usually employ additional methods, but the power supply fan still plays an important part in cooling the PC. It is very common to see a fan mounted directly over the CPU, as shown in Figure 8-12.

One or more case fans may also supplement a power supply fan. A *case fan* is a fan mounted directly on the case, as opposed to a power supply fan, which is inside the power supply. Systems that do not come with a case fan may have mounting brackets for adding one or more case fans.

Heat Sinks and Fanless/Passive Cooling

Another device that works to cool hot components is a *heat sink*. This is usually a passive metal object with a flat surface attached to a component—a chip, for instance. The exposed side of a heat sink has an array of fins used to dissipate the heat. The heat sink shown in Figure 8-13 was made visible by removing the fan shown in Figure 8-12. This combination of heat sink and fan can be very effective; the heat sink absorbs the heat from the CPU and then the fan blows the heat away. In other systems the heat sink and fan are a single unit.

FIGURE 8-12

An open PC with the CPU fan visible

FIGURE 8-13 A heat sink attached to a CPU

Early CPUs used standard heat sinks for cooling, and they worked well enough for those CPUs because those CPUs didn't run very hot. On systems made in the last two decades, though, standard fanless (passive) heat sinks haven't cut it; powerful fans have been required to pull the heat away effectively. Motherboards still employ passive heat sinks for other chips besides the CPU, like the main chipset chips or the GPU, but not the CPU itself.

However, new generations of fanless cooling devices released lately have been challenging the assumption that a fan is always required for the CPU. These vary in their construction, but generally include copper heat pipes and a large stack of nickel-plated aluminum fins.

Thermal Compounds

As you learned earlier in the chapter, *thermal paste* is an electrically insulating, heat-conductive paste that helps increase the transfer of heat between a hot chip and a heat-dissipating fan or heat sink. It is also called *thermal grease, thermal pad,* or *heat sink compound.* You apply it in a thin layer between the components. Depending on the type, it may or may not have adhesive properties; usually when it aids in adhesion, it is called *thermal adhesive.*

Liquid Cooling Systems

Many of today's motherboards for sale on the Internet or at large electronics stores feature one or more *liquid cooling systems,* which range from sealed liquid cooling systems that transfer heat by conduction from several components to active systems that use tiny

Be sure you are familiar with the differences in cooling methods, including fans/heat sinks vs. liquid cooling, and know how to apply thermal paste/pads.

refrigeration units. Liquid cooling is generally more effective than standard cooling, so it is sometimes employed in overclocked systems (that is, systems that are rigged to run at higher clock speeds than the CPUs are rated for) to help keep the CPU cool enough to function at the higher speed. But it is also more expensive, is more difficult to install, and can cause serious system damage with short-circuiting in the event of a leak.

Case Design

The design of each case allows for maximum airflow over the components. Part of this design is the placement of vents, positioned to either bring in fresh air or to exhaust air. If this airflow is disturbed, even by additional openings, the system may overheat. Therefore, be sure that all the expansion slot openings on the back of the PC are covered. The expansion card's bracket covers each opening that lines up with an occupied expansion slot. A metal slot cover covers an empty slot in order to preserve the correct airflow.

EXERCISE 8-3

Checking Out Your Cooling System

If you have access to a PC with the conventional case-fan cooling system, check it out now.

1. Without opening the computer case, look for vents in the case.
2. If the computer is running, and if it is of a conventional design, you should hear a fan running in the power supply and see the vent from the power supply. You may hear another fan running and see a set of vents for that fan.
3. Are there vents that do not appear to have a case fan behind them?
4. Hold your hand by the vents you located and determine if airflow is going into or out of the computer case. Is the power supply fan blowing in or out? If you located a case fan, is it blowing in or out?
5. Make note of your findings and discuss with your classmates or coworkers.

SCENARIO & SOLUTION	
You have recently built a custom desktop PC for a user who complains that it overheats and shuts down after only a few minutes of operation. What might you have forgotten to do?	You might have forgotten to put thermal paste between the CPU and its cooling device, or you might have forgotten to connect the power to one or more fans.
You want to build a custom PC. Which would you choose first—the CPU or the motherboard? Why?	You would choose the CPU first, and then choose a motherboard it will fit into. You do this because the CPU will determine the performance level you get out of it; the motherboard is there to support the CPU.
A business executive asks you to install liquid cooling in his desktop PC. Is this a good idea? Why or why not?	Liquid cooling is generally appropriate only for PCs that require overclocking or extremely high CPU usage, and a business executive is unlikely to do those kinds of activities. You would want to question the user about his usage before performing this upgrade.

Configuring a Motherboard

After you physically install a motherboard and attach components to it, the next step is to configure the motherboard to perform optimally with the installed hardware. On very old motherboards, a few key settings are configured using jumpers. On modern motherboards, however, nearly all setup is done through a firmware (BIOS or UEFI) setup utility.

Understanding BIOS and UEFI

Each computing device has a chip on its main circuit board with some basic firmware that helps the device start up and communicate with the operating system and the other hardware. This firmware is traditionally known as the *basic input/output system (BIOS).* A PC's BIOS resides on the motherboard and is called the *system BIOS.* Each expansion card also has its own BIOS chip that, among other things, reports the device's plug and play settings to the motherboard's BIOS and to the OS.

The system BIOS is responsible for performing the *power-on self-test (POST),* a hardware test during startup, and informing the processor of the devices present and how to communicate with them. Whenever the processor makes a request of a component, the BIOS steps in and translates the request into instructions that the component can understand. That was true for many years and is true today, up to the point when an operating system loads, whereupon drivers loaded by the OS take over most of the BIOS functions.

The traditional PC system BIOS is a 16-bit program that requires x86-compliant hardware. However, newer systems that have large hard drives (more than 2.2 terabytes) bump up against a limitation there. Enter *Unified Extensible Firmware Interface (UEFI)*, which has taken the place of a traditional BIOS on most motherboards.

In simplistic terms, UEFI is a 32-bit or 64-bit BIOS alternative that adds some features and benefits. From an end-user and PC technician point of view, it's roughly equivalent to a BIOS. (A UEFI setup program is very similar to a BIOS setup program, for example.) The main advantages of UEFI are that it supports file systems that enable booting to large drives (2.2 terabytes and up), it supports 32-bit or 64-bit booting, and it's not dependent on x86 firmware. Many technicians use the term BIOS (or CMOS; see the next section) to refer to both BIOS and UEFI firmware.

A Brief History of the PC System BIOS

BIOS was originally stored on a ROM chip that was completely inaccessible for user changes. To get a BIOS update, you had to replace the BIOS chip on the motherboard. As you can imagine, that was a hardship, especially because back in those days, there was no plug and play. If your BIOS didn't recognize a certain type of drive or other hardware, you couldn't use it.

As a workaround, systems began offering BIOS written on *erasable programmable ROM (EPROM)* chips. These BIOS chips had a little clear window in the top. You could put the chip in a special machine that would flash a strong light into that window that erased the BIOS chip. Then the machine would reprogram the chip. That's how the name *flash BIOS* or *flash ROM* originated.

But even that was a pain. End users didn't have the needed machine, and many small repair shops didn't either. So the next evolutionary step was to make a BIOS chip that could be erased with a strong pulse of electricity, rather than light. This was known as *electrically erasable programmable ROM (EEPROM)*. An EEPROM update could be done in place on the motherboard using a software utility. Big improvement!

The problem with EPROM and EEPROM chips was that, except when using their special update procedures, you couldn't write changes to them. That meant that each time the PC turned on, it was a blank slate. The PC couldn't remember what drives or memory were installed, what user settings were desired, or even the current date and time. To get around this, motherboards had another chip, a *complementary metal-oxide semiconductor (CMOS)*. This was a special kind of dynamic RAM (DRAM) chip that stored the exceptions to the BIOS settings. First the BIOS would load its basic settings, and then the CMOS chip would load the changes to the defaults. The CMOS chip required electricity to hold its data, but it was a very small amount of electricity. Motherboard manufacturers supplied that electricity with a small battery on the motherboard.

As technology advanced, electrically rewriteable ROM chips became faster and less expensive, to the point where device makers were using them as a substitute for magnetic disk storage in systems. (USB flash drives and solid-state drives are two examples.) Motherboard makers began using this type of memory to hold the user customizations to the BIOS settings, rather than CMOS chips. Such chips don't require the motherboard's battery to retain their settings. So technically in modern motherboards there is no longer a CMOS chip. Motherboards still have a battery, but now it's just to maintain the real-time clock (RTC), which remembers the date and time when the PC is shut off.

The utility used to write the user changes to the chip was known as *CMOS setup* or *BIOS setup,* depending on the BIOS brand and model. Even though you won't find a CMOS chip on a motherboard anymore today, the term CMOS setup is still very common, referring to the firmware setup program. Sometimes a BIOS setup utility is even titled CMOS Setup in its interface.

Updating the Firmware

Motherboard manufacturers and PC makers periodically release firmware updates for their motherboards. These updates may correct bugs in the code and may add extra features, like support for a new type of device. Most PCs function just fine with the original firmware version they came with, but occasionally a problem can crop up that can be solved by updating the firmware to the latest version.

Updating the firmware involves running a program to "flash" the BIOS or UEFI. In modern terms, what that really means is to update the programming on the memory chip on the motherboard that holds the firmware. There's not really any flashing going on anymore, although the name persists. You can download a firmware update and accompanying utility for installing it (perhaps in a single executable) from the website of the motherboard or PC manufacturer.

It is very important to follow the directions given by the manufacturer when updating the firmware. A botched update can render the system inoperable and require a replacement chip from the manufacturer.

Configuring the Firmware

The most common way to optimize a motherboard is to modify the BIOS or UEFI setup configuration program, also called the *BIOS setup* or *CMOS setup*. Literally hundreds of settings are available in different computers; this section looks mainly at the ones that are specifically mentioned in Objective 3.4 of the CompTIA A+ 1101 exam. The choices available, and the methods for selecting them, may vary from one manufacturer to another. The best reference for using the firmware setup menus is the motherboard manual.

Accessing Firmware Settings

To access the computer's firmware settings, closely watch the computer screen at startup. Following the system hardware test, you may see a message indicating the proper key sequence you should use to enter the firmware setup program. It may simply say "Setup" followed by a key or key sequence name. This key or key combination varies among computers but is typically F2, DELETE, or CTRL-ALT-ESC. In most systems, the message will appear for only three to five seconds, and you must use the indicated key combination within that allotted time.

On newer systems, you probably won't see that prompt, though, and you'll need to go another route. On PCs with Windows 8 and higher and UEFI, if the Secure Boot feature is enabled in the firmware settings, you will not see a prompt as the PC starts telling you to press a key to enter setup. On such systems, there is an alternative method of getting into the setup program through the Settings app. See Exercise 8-4 for details.

EXERCISE 8-4

Booting into Firmware Setup

This exercise provides three different methods of entering firmware setup. Choose the method that is appropriate for the system you are working with.

Method 1: For BIOS-Based Motherboards Use this method if you see a message about a key to press at startup. Systems that provide this are typically older ones running Windows 7 or earlier and/or have a BIOS rather than UEFI firmware.

1. Reboot your PC, and as it reboots, watch the screen for a message telling you what key to press to enter Setup.
2. When you see that message, press the key as quickly as you can. If you see the Windows splash screen, you missed the window of opportunity; allow Windows to finish loading, and then restart and try again.

Method 2: For Windows 10 Use this method if you are running Windows 10 and don't see any message about a key to press at startup.

1. Click Start | Settings.
2. In the Settings app, click Update And Security. Then in the navigation bar, click Recovery.
3. Under the Advanced Startup heading, click Restart Now. Then at the Choose An Option screen, click Troubleshoot, and then click Advanced Options.
4. At the Advanced Options screen, click UEFI Firmware Settings and then click Restart. The PC reboots and opens the setup application.

Method 3: For Windows 11

Use this method if you are running Windows 11 and don't see any message about a key to press at startup.

1. Right-click the Start button and choose Settings.
2. In the Settings app, click System | Recovery.
3. In the Advanced Startup section, click Restart Now. Then at the Choose An Option screen, click Troubleshoot, and then click Advanced Options.
4. At the Advanced Options screen, click UEFI Firmware Settings and then click Restart. The PC reboots and opens the setup application.

Navigating in the Firmware Setup Program

Firmware setup programs differ widely. Some allow you to use the mouse, and some only the keyboard. The names of the settings might also vary slightly. Use the program's Help feature or on-screen prompts for information about how to navigate through the program and save or discard your changes. Usually, though, pressing the ESC key quits without saving, and pressing the F10 key quits and saves. The RIGHT and LEFT ARROW keys usually move between screens, the UP and DOWN ARROW keys move the highlight to select a different option, and pressing ENTER usually selects whatever option is highlighted.

EXERCISE 8-5

Viewing the Firmware Settings

In this exercise you will explore the firmware setup utility for a motherboard.

1. Enter the firmware setup program by completing Exercise 8-4.
2. Look at the bottom of the screen for navigation instructions, as well as how to access the Help utility (normally the F1 key). If it's a mouse-enabled program, there might not be navigation keys.
3. Browse through the screens carefully, and if you have a digital camera handy, take a picture of each screen. On a mouse-enabled system, there may be a navigation bar or a list of screens.
4. Locate the settings described in the following sections.
5. When you have finished, use the indicated key combination to exit *without* saving any changes.

Backing Up Firmware Settings

Make notes about the current firmware settings before you change them in case you need to change them back. A quick way is to use a digital camera, taking a picture of each screen or capturing a video that shows you paging through the screens without making any changes. Also, look for a firmware-settings backup utility in the firmware setup menus, sometimes located on a Tools menu, or check out the firmware manufacturer's website for backup instructions. Alternatively, look for a third-party firmware backup program.

Hardware Information

Usually the first screen you see is an informational one showing the system's hardware configuration. If you are ever in doubt about the system hardware, this screen provides a good reference point. Figure 8-14 shows an example.

Security Settings

Depending on the firmware make and version, you might have the option to configure up to three passwords in the Security section of firmware setup: Supervisor/Admin, User/System, and Hard Disk Drive (HDD). All are disabled by default.

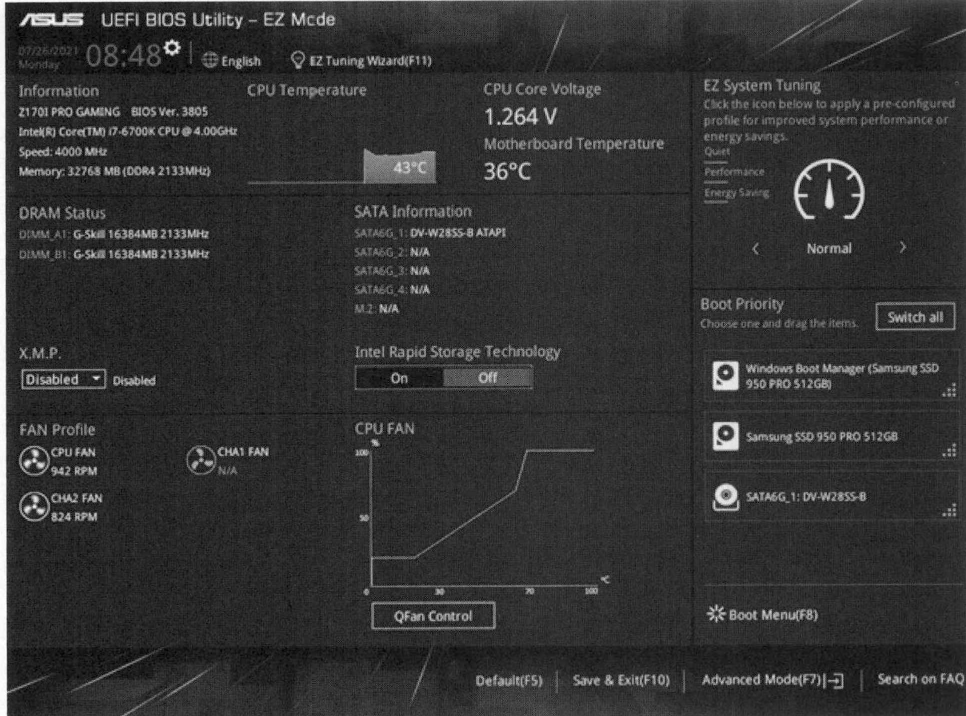

FIGURE 8-14

A UEFI BIOS utility's main screen showing basic hardware information

Except in special high-security situations, we don't recommend using the firmware-level passwords. It's too easy to forget that they're set when you pass along a PC to a new owner or to forget a password in times of distress, like when you need to get into the firmware setup to correct a problem in the middle of a tight deadline project.

The User or System password restricts booting the PC. A Supervisor or Admin password restricts access to the firmware-settings program itself or to change user passwords. Most firmware setup programs require that you first set a Supervisor/Admin password before it allows you to set a User/System password. Some systems also have an HDD password, which must be entered before a user can access the hard drive.

Some systems also have an option that allows you to enable the firmware interface to connect to a for-pay antitheft service. Enabling this option involves signing up for the service over the Internet and downloading additional software. Once you have enabled and subscribed to the service and connected the computer to the Internet, the software installed in your OS will contact the service's servers and check for a theft report, as well as transmit the system and GPS tracking information concerning the location of the computer. This service may have a product name attached to it, such as Computrace or LoJack.

Even formatting or replacing the existing hard drive will not bypass this security because it takes advantage of the built-in *Trusted Platform Module (TPM),* an embedded security chip that stores encrypted passwords, keys, and digital certificates. Various services can use the TPM chip. Even without a for-pay location service, when you combine the use of TPM with a firmware-level Administrator password and a User password required at power-on, the computer is virtually useless to a thief. In firmware setup, there may be a TPM On option, as well as options for controlling specific TPM settings. The TPM On option lets you control whether TPM is visible to the operating system; it does not change any TPM settings. There may also be a general Enable/Disable option for TPM that does turn TPM on/off completely.

exam watch

CompTIA A+ 1101 exam Objective 3.4 mentions encryption (separately from BIOS/UEFI settings), and under that, calls out TPM and Hardware Security Module (HSM). TPM and HSM are similar but not the same. TPM provides some basic encryption key storage services related to controlling access at the hardware level. You can view TPM information in Windows Pro and Enterprise editions, as shown in Figure 8-15. HSM is a more advanced technology that's an add-on to systems that need extra security, providing hardware-accelerated cryptography along with key storage.

FIGURE 8-15 TPM settings in Windows Pro

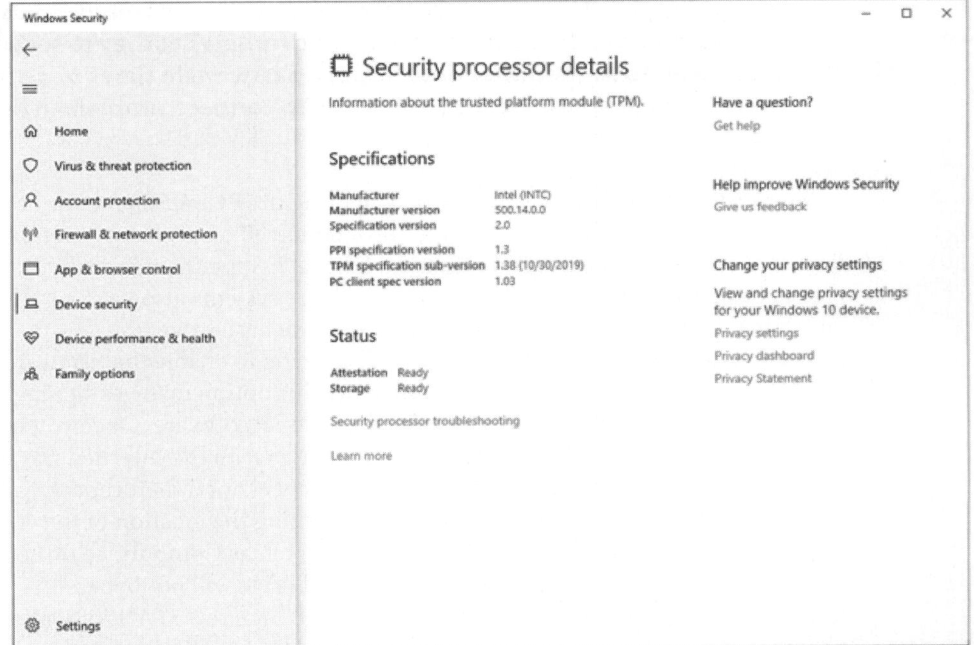

Considering how often users forget passwords, using the combination of TPM, Administrator password, and a required User password at power-on may make a computer useless to its authorized user! Use these security measures only where and when required, such as protecting mobile computers that contain sensitive information. See "Resetting the BIOS/UEFI" later in this chapter for help with a forgotten firmware password.

The *Secure Boot* feature is enabled/disabled in firmware setup, but also relies on the PC having Windows 8 or later and UEFI. Provided all three of those pieces are present, Secure Boot helps prevent malware (such as a rootkit replacing the Windows boot loader) and unauthorized OSs from loading during the system boot process. Secure Boot is enabled by default on systems where it is available. One drawback of it is that you can no longer press a key at startup to enter firmware; you have to go in through Windows, as in Exercise 8-4. The Secure Boot feature may be controlled from the Security section or the Boot section in firmware setup, depending on the firmware brand and version.

One way that a hacker might try to introduce malware into a system is by inserting a USB flash drive. Some firmware setup programs enable you to disable the USB ports on the system. This would normally not be a great idea, because you lose access to the ports, but for a highly secure system, it could be useful. If you ever needed to use a USB port, you would need to re-enter the setup program (presumably you would have an Admin password protecting access to it) and re-enable the port(s). There might be separate options governing whether the USB ports can be used at all and whether they can be booted from.

Another security issue involving USB ports is related to Intel Active Management Technology (AMT). AMT is a tool that enables system admins to remotely manage systems outside of Windows. In 2017 a remote exploit was discovered that allowed hackers to use AMT to bypass a system's password. If a system has an Enable USB Provision feature in the firmware setup, it should be enabled only if the managing organization requires it for USB-based AMT management.

Boot Sequence

Your system firmware will no doubt have a setting for selecting the order in which the system will search devices for an OS. You can normally select from among a variety of possible boot devices, including C: or hard disk, USB flash drive, and even the network. In the last case, the firmware will boot via your network interface card (NIC). All modern network cards support the ability to start a computer over the network, without relying on a disk-based OS, using an Intel standard called Preboot eXecution Environment (PXE).

If you plan to install a new OS on a system using a bootable external drive, you will need to go into the firmware setup program and change the boot order so that the optical drive precedes the hard drive. With this turned on, every time the system restarts with a bootable disc in the optical drive, you briefly see a message to press any key to boot from the external source. After installing a new OS, you might change the boot order back to start from the hard drive first. Then it only searches other drives at startup if it does not find an OS on the hard drive.

Fan Control

Many firmware setup programs provide a way of controlling the built-in fans in the system depending on your preferences. For example, you might choose cooler performance (more fan noise) or quieter performance (less cooling, but less fan noise). You might also be able to set the fan speed to Auto, allowing the firmware to choose a fan speed based on the internal temperature of the system. (Obviously that works only on systems with internal temperature sensors.)

Resetting the BIOS/UEFI

Older motherboards and other circuit boards sometimes have jumpers used to configure, enable, or disable a feature. A *jumper* is a small connector that slides down on a pair of pins jutting up from a circuit board, creating a connection between the two pins that changes the electrical flow through the motherboard, triggering a certain setting. Each possible jumper configuration is interpreted by the system firmware as a setting. Check the user manual that came with the motherboard or other circuit board to discover how to configure the settings you desire.

The one jumper remaining on nearly every modern motherboard is the one that resets the BIOS/UEFI in the event that you mangle its settings so badly that you can't boot into its setup program anymore, or you assign a firmware password and then forget it. To reset the BIOS/UEFI setup, consult the motherboard manual to locate the reset jumper and learn what position resets the motherboard. Move the jumper to that position and start the PC to perform the reset. The motherboard manual will explain the amount of time to wait. Then return the jumper to its original position and reboot. Another way to reset is to remove the motherboard's battery.

There might also be a setting in firmware setup that enables you to specify BIOS/UEFI recovery options. (You would need to do this ahead of time, when the system is working well.) For example, you might be able to set the firmware to permit BIOS/UEFI recovery from the hard drive, or automatic BIOS/UEFI recovery. You might also be able to tell the firmware to perform a firmware integrity check at every boot. There might also be a BIOS/UEFI Downgrade feature that enables you to go back to an earlier firmware version (for example, if a recent upgrade introduced a problem).

You can also clear TPM data from within Windows Pro or Enterprise, as shown in Figure 8-16.

FIGURE 8-16 Clearing TPM data from Windows

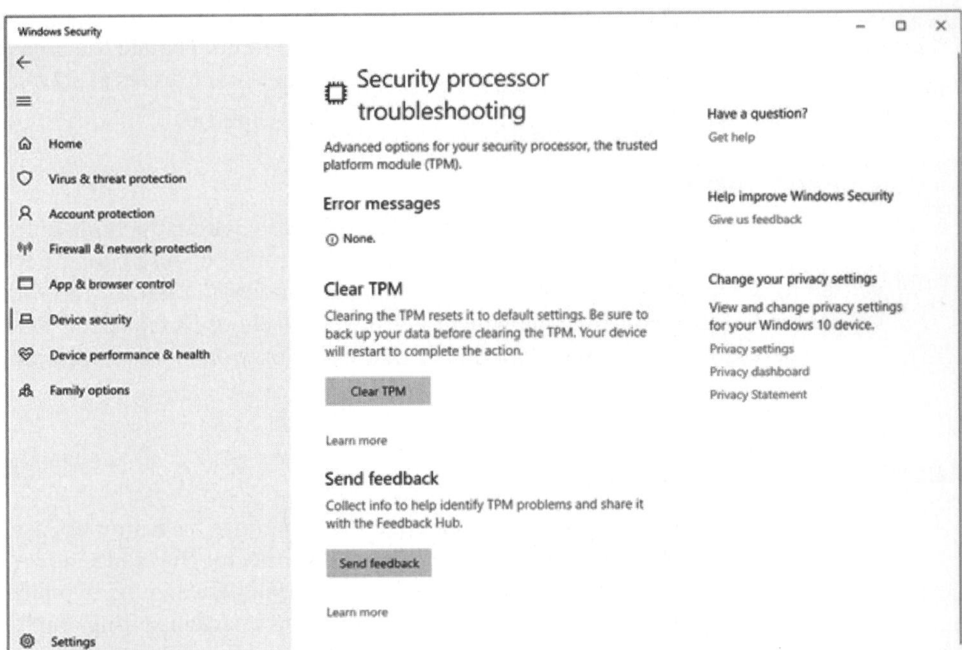

Motherboard Driver Software

Modern motherboards include a great many more devices and capabilities than older motherboards—often more than can be adequately supported by the motherboard firmware. In addition, some of the motherboard's features work differently when accessed via different operating systems or require drivers specific to an OS. Therefore, when you purchase a motherboard, it will often come with a driver disc containing utilities or support files to install in specific operating systems. If it's a retail-purchased PC (that is, if you didn't buy the motherboard as a separate item), you should be able to download motherboard driver software from the company's website. You will learn about installing and configuring motherboards and using a motherboard's driver setup utilities in Chapter 11.

SCENARIO & SOLUTION	
You need to access a PC's firmware setup program; in general terms, how will you do that?	If it's an older computer, restart it and watch carefully for a brief message that may say "Setup" followed by a key or key combination name. Press that key or combination to enter setup. If that doesn't work, follow the steps in Exercise 8-4, Method 2 or 3.
You need to boot a computer from an optical disc, but every time you try, it immediately boots from the hard drive and loads Windows. What can you do?	Go into the firmware setup and add the optical disc to the boot order, making sure it precedes the hard drive.
You want to prevent unauthorized persons from changing the firmware settings on a PC.	Set an Administrator password in the firmware setup utility. This will prevent unauthorized access to the setup utility but will allow the PC to boot normally otherwise.

CERTIFICATION SUMMARY

Common computer components include the processor, memory, storage devices, and input and output devices. All of these devices have specific functions, and your familiarity with them will help you to determine when to upgrade or replace a component.

This chapter described general characteristics of motherboards, installed motherboard components and form factors, and CPU technologies. You must use a motherboard that supports the selected CPU and RAM. Motherboards have many integrated functions. This chapter introduced several of the technologies that CompTIA A+ 1101 exam may test you on. A good knowledge of these concepts is also important when you are repairing or upgrading a computer system. Chapters 9 and 10 will continue with explanations of other important PC components, and Chapter 11 will describe how to install and upgrade PC components.

TWO-MINUTE DRILL

Here are some of the key points covered in Chapter 8.

The Hardware Toolkit

- Start out with a basic toolkit of an assortment of screwdrivers and nut drivers, a small flashlight, and an assortment of screws and nuts.
- In addition to a variety of tools and replacement parts, consider keeping a digital camera handy to document the physical condition of a computer before you begin troubleshooting and to capture low-level error messages that you cannot capture otherwise.

Motherboard Form Factors and Components

- All components, including external peripherals, connect directly or indirectly to the motherboard.
- A motherboard form factor defines the type and location of the components on the motherboard, the power supply that will work with that motherboard, and the PC case the components will fit into.
- ATX remains the standard for motherboards; several smaller-size versions are available, including mATX (Micro-ATX).
- ITX is a small-form-factor alternative to ATX and comes in several sizes as well, including mITX (Mini-ITX).
- Motherboard components include sockets for various PC components, including the CPU and memory, built-in components such as video and sound adapters, hard drive controllers, support for various port types, and the chipset.
- Memory slots can include DIMMs on motherboards for desktop systems and SODIMMs on laptop motherboards.
- Every motherboard contains at least one CPU socket, and the location varies, based on the form factor.
- The most common types of bus architectures are PCI (obsolete but still supported on some motherboards) and the current standard: PCIe. PCIe comes in several slot lengths, including x1, x4, and x16. Mini PCI and Mini PCI Express are versions of PCI and PCIe, respectively, in notebook PCs.
- M.2 is a modern connector type for mounting solid-state expansion cards and SSDs on a motherboard. Depending on the way the slot is keyed, M.2 devices can use PCI Express, Serial ATA, and/or USB busses internally.

- ❑ A variety of connectors attach to a desktop motherboard, including a large 24-pin connector from the power supply. Some internal cable connectors attach to headers, which are sets of pins on the motherboard.
- ❑ The chipset on the motherboard handles very low-level functions relating to the interactions between the CPU and other components.

CPUs and Their Sockets

- ❑ The CPU chip is the primary control device for a PC. A GPU is a processor on a video adapter dedicated to the rendering of display images.
- ❑ The CPU connects to all of the components, such as memory, storage, and input/output, through communication channels called busses.
- ❑ Some things that differentiate one CPU from another include architecture (x64 or x86), RISC vs. CISC, clock speed, multithreading, number of cores (single or multicore), and virtualization support.
- ❑ Intel Corporation and AMD (Advanced Micro Devices, Inc.) are the two top manufacturers of PC CPUs. You must match the motherboard to the CPU; they are not interchangeable.
- ❑ CPUs require cooling, as do some other hardworking chips, such as the graphics processor. Cooling is usually active (involving a fan), but can also be passive (with no moving parts, just a heat sink and thermal paste/pad). Liquid cooling is also an option for desktop systems that run hot.

Configuring a Motherboard

- ❑ The basic input/output system, or BIOS, is firmware that informs the processor of the hardware that is present and contains low-level software routines for communicating with and controlling the hardware. Configured through a BIOS setup program, you may also need to upgrade, or flash, an older BIOS.
- ❑ UEFI is the more modern replacement for BIOS. On a system with Windows 8, 8.1, 10, or 11 with UEFI, additional firmware features are available such as Secure Boot.
- ❑ To access firmware setup, press the key indicated on-screen at startup. To access UEFI firmware setup, you must go through the operating system.
- ❑ Follow the on-screen instructions to navigate in a firmware setup program.
- ❑ Firmware setup includes settings that control security features such as Secure Boot and TPM, boot sequence, and fan control.
- ❑ To reset the configurable settings of the firmware, you can use a jumper on the motherboard.

SELF TEST

The following questions will help you measure your understanding of the material presented in this chapter. Read all of the choices carefully because there might be more than one correct answer. Choose all correct answers for each question.

The Hardware Toolkit

1. What would you use to measure the resistance, voltage, and/or current in computer components using two probes?
   A. Multimeter
   B. FRU
   C. Cable tester
   D. Punchdown tool
2. Which of these is an example of an FRU?
   A. A cable tester
   B. Replacement parts such as extra memory modules
   C. An antistatic mat and wrist strap
   D. A parts grabber

Motherboard Form Factors and Components

3. Which is the most common type of RAM slot on modern desktop motherboards?
   A. RIMM
   B. SIMM
   C. SODIMM
   D. DIMM
4. Which of the following describes a motherboard form factor?
   A. The size and color of a motherboard
   B. The processor the motherboard supports
   C. The type and location of components and the power supply that will work with the motherboard, plus the dimensions of the motherboard
   D. Mid-tower

5. Which of these motherboards is the smallest?
A. mATX
B. ATX
C. ITX
D. mITX

6. Where is a PC's main chipset located?
A. In the CPU
B. One or more chips mounted on the motherboard, separate from the CPU and the BIOS or UEFI
C. In the hard disk drive
D. In the BIOS or UEFI chip

7. Which of the following describes a difference between PCI and PCIe?
A. PCIe is only used for graphics adapters; PCI is used by a variety of adapters.
B. PCI uses parallel data communications; PCIe uses serial communications.
C. PCIe uses parallel data communications; PCI uses serial communications.
D. PCIe is used by a variety of adapters; PCI is only used by video adapters.

8. What type of local bus connector is used for video cards on modern systems?
A. PCIe x16
B. PCIe x1
C. AGP
D. USB

9. Which of these busses is used to connect solid-state devices such as SSDs to the motherboard on a modern system?
A. PCIe x16
B. M.2
C. PCIe x1
D. USB 2.0

CPUs and Their Sockets

10. What is the purpose of the control unit in the machine cycle?
A. Performs math calculations
B. Evaluates logical statements
C. Fetches instructions or data from memory
D. Temporarily stores data to be processed

11. What is the purpose of the L1 cache?
   A. Holds data that the CPU is likely to need soon so it doesn't have to be retrieved from memory
   B. Holds applications loaded from the hard disk drive
   C. Swaps out data between main memory and the hard disk drive
   D. Performs the POST

12. What component in a CPU is responsible for all logical and mathematical operations?
   A. ALU
   B. Registers
   C. Control unit
   D. Processor bus

13. What CPU component temporarily stores data inside the CPU as it is being processed?
   A. Registers
   B. Processor
   C. Control unit
   D. Bus

14. What CPU technology allows two threads to execute at the same time within a single execution core?
   A. Multithreading
   B. Core
   C. Cache memory
   D. Microcode

15. Which of the following statements are true? (Choose two.)
   A. 32-bit systems can support 6 GB of RAM.
   B. 64-bit systems can support over 4 GB of RAM.
   C. In Windows, 64-bit programs are stored in the "C:\Program Files" folder and 32-bit programs are stored in the "C:\Program Files (x86)" folder.
   D. In Windows, 32-bit programs are stored in the "C:\Program Files" folder and 64-bit programs are stored in the "C:\Program Files (x86)" folder.

16. In a system with an integrated GPU, into what component is the GPU integrated?
   A. Motherboard
   B. CPU
   C. Memory
   D. L2 cache

17. Which of these is a company that makes CPUs for personal computers?
   A. Phoenix
   B. Microsoft
   C. AMD
   D. IBM

Configuring a Motherboard

18. What does an Admin or Supervisor password in firmware setup prevent unauthorized people from doing?

A. Booting the PC

B. Accessing BIOS/UEFI setup

C. Accessing the hard disk drive

D. Removing the hard disk drive

19. What is UEFI?

A. A type of RAM that the BIOS can automatically detect

B. An alternative to the traditional system BIOS

C. A motherboard driver on an optical disc

D. A POST routine

20. Which helps prevent malware (such as a rootkit replacing the Windows boot loader) and unauthorized OSs from loading during the system boot process?

A. Secure Boot

B. TPM

C. HSM

D. ARM

A SELF TEST ANSWERS

The Hardware Toolkit

1. ☑ **A.** A multimeter is the device you would use to measure the resistance, voltage, and/or current in computer components using two probes.

☒ **B** is incorrect because an FRU is a field-replaceable unit, or any component that you can install into a system onsite. **C** is incorrect because a cable tester is usually used for network cables to test if a cable can connect properly end to end. **D** is incorrect because a punchdown tool is a hand tool used for inserting various types of wire into appropriate wiring panels.

2. ☑ **B.** FRU is an acronym for field-replaceable units, aka replacement parts.
☒ **A** is incorrect because a cable tester is a machine, not an FRU. **C** is incorrect because antistatic protective equipment is not an FRU. **D** is incorrect because a parts grabber is a tool, not a replaceable unit.

Motherboard Form Factors and Components

3. ☑ **D.** DIMM RAM slots are the most common type of RAM slots on desktop motherboards.
☒ **A** and **B** are incorrect because they are old technologies not likely to be found on new desktop motherboards. **C** is incorrect because this type of RAM slot is usually found on laptops.

4. ☑ **C.** A motherboard form factor is the type and location of components and the power supply that will work with the motherboard, plus the dimensions of the motherboard.
☒ **A** is incorrect because while size may be part of a form factor, color has nothing to do with the form factor. **B** is incorrect because the processor the motherboard supports is not, by itself, a description of a form factor. **D** is incorrect because mid-tower is a case size, not a motherboard form factor.

5. ☑ **D.** The mITX motherboard is the smallest, at 6.7" square.
☒ **A** is incorrect because Micro-ATX (mATX) measures 9.6" × 9.6". **B** is incorrect because ATX measures 12" × 9.6". **C** is incorrect because ITX measures 8.5" × 7.5".

6. ☑ **B.** The chipset is mounted on the motherboard. It is not the same chip as the BIOS or UEFI chip.
☒ **A** is incorrect because the chipset is a feature of the motherboard, not the CPU. **C** is incorrect because the chipset is not a feature of the hard disk drive. **D** is incorrect because the motherboard's chipset is separate from its BIOS or UEFI chip.

7. ☑ **B.** PCI uses parallel data communications; PCIe uses serial communications.
☒ **A** and **D** are incorrect because both PCIe and PCI are used by a variety of expansion cards. **C** is incorrect because the very opposite is true. PCIe uses serial data communications, and PCI uses parallel data communications.

8. ☑ **A.** PCIe x16 is the fastest bus available on modern systems and is used by most video cards.
☒ **B** is incorrect because PCIe x1 is too small a bus to effectively handle video card traffic. **C** is incorrect because AGP is an old, obsolete expansion slot type for video cards. **D** is incorrect because USB is a peripheral bus, not a bus connector on the motherboard in which an expansion card is installed.

9. ☑ **B.** M.2 is designed to connect solid-state devices such as SSDs to the motherboard.
☒ **A** is incorrect because PCIe x16 is an interface for a video card. **C** is incorrect because PCIe x1 is too small a bus to effectively handle SSD traffic. **D** is incorrect because USB 2.0 is an external bus.

CPUs and Their Sockets

10. ☑ **C.** The control unit fetches instructions or data from memory.
☒ **A** is incorrect because it is a function of the arithmetic logic unit (ALU). **B** is incorrect because it is also a function of the ALU. **D** is incorrect because it is a function of the registers.

11. ☑ **A.** The function of the L1 cache is to hold data that the CPU is likely to need soon.
☒ **B** is incorrect because it is a function of the system's main memory, not the L1 cache. **C** is incorrect because it is a function of the paging file. **D** is incorrect because it is a function of the firmware.

12. ☑ **A.** The ALU is the CPU component that is responsible for all logical and mathematical operations.
☒ **B** is incorrect because the registers are just holding areas. **C** is incorrect because the control unit is the component responsible for directing activities in the computer and managing interactions between the other components and the CPU. **D** is incorrect because the processor bus is just a pathway among components in the CPU.

13. ☑ **A.** Registers temporarily hold data in the CPU.
☒ **B** is incorrect because processor is just another name for CPU. **C** is incorrect because the control unit does not store temporary data. **D** is incorrect because the bus is just a group of wires used to carry signals.

14. ☑ **A.** Multithreading is the CPU technology that allows two threads to execute at the same time within a single execution core.
☒ **B** is incorrect because a core is a CPU with its own cache, controller, and other CPU components. **C** is incorrect because cache memory is usually a relatively small amount of expensive, very fast memory used to compensate for speed differences between components. **D** is incorrect because microcode is the name for the low-level instructions built into a CPU.

15. ☑ **B** and **C.** 64-bit systems can support over 4 GB of RAM and in a 64-bit version of Windows; 64-bit programs are stored in the "C:\Program Files" folder, and 32-bit programs are stored in the "C:\Program Files (x86)" folder.
☒ **A** is incorrect because 32-bit systems can only support up to 4 GB of RAM. **D** is incorrect because the opposite is true. In Windows, 64-bit programs are stored in the "C:\Program Files" folder, and 32-bit programs are stored in the "C:\Program Files (x86)" folder.

16. ☑ **A.** An integrated GPU is built into the motherboard.
☒ **B** is incorrect because the GPU is not a part of the CPU. **C** is incorrect because a GPU is a processing chip, which could not be resident in memory. **D** is incorrect because the L2 cache is also a type of memory.

17. ☑ **C.** Advanced Micro Devices (AMD) is a manufacturer of CPUs; it is the major competitor to Intel, the world's largest CPU maker.
☒ **A** is incorrect because Phoenix makes BIOS/UEFI chips, not CPUs. **B** is incorrect because Microsoft makes software, not CPUs. **D** is incorrect because IBM makes computers, but not CPUs.

Configuring a Motherboard

18. ☑ **B.** An Admin or Supervisor password will prevent unauthorized people from accessing firmware setup.
☒ **A** is incorrect because it is what a User or System password will prevent. **C** is incorrect because it is what an HDD password will prevent. **D** is incorrect because there is no password that can prevent the HDD from being physically removed.

19. ☑ **B.** UEFI is a modern alternative to the traditional system BIOS.
☒ **A** is incorrect because UEFI is not RAM and because the motherboard can automatically detect all types of RAM anyway. **C** is incorrect because UEFI is built into the motherboard on a chip and is not a driver that would come on a disc. **D** is incorrect because a POST routine is a startup hardware check performed by the BIOS or UEFI at startup.

20. ☑ **A.** Secure Boot helps prevent malware (such as a rootkit replacing the Windows boot loader) and unauthorized OSs from loading during the system boot process.
☒ **B** is incorrect because a Trusted Platform Module (TPM) is an embedded security chip that stores encrypted passwords, keys, and digital certificates. **C** is incorrect because a Hardware Security Module (HSM) is an advanced technology that's an add-on to systems that need extra security, providing hardware-accelerated cryptography along with key storage. **D** is incorrect because Advanced RISC Machine (ARM) is one of the most common types of RISC CPUs. RISC CPUs are found in many mobile devices today, such as Android and Apple tablets and smartphones, and in gaming consoles.

Chapter 9

Personal Computer Components: Memory, Adapters, and Storage

CERTIFICATION OBJECTIVES

- **1101: 3.1** Explain basic cable types and their connectors, features, and purposes
- **1101: 3.2** Given a scenario, install the appropriate RAM
- **1101: 3.3** Given a scenario, select and install storage devices
- **1101: 3.4** Given a scenario, install and configure motherboards, central processing units (CPUs), and add-on cards

✓ Two-Minute Drill

Q&A Self Test

This chapter is a continuation of the survey of PC concepts and components begun in Chapter 8, which provided the purposes and technologies of PC motherboards, CPUs, and cases. We now will explore RAM memory, adapter cards, and storage devices. Further, we'll define the connection interfaces, connectors, and ports associated with the expansion cards and storage devices. Chapter 10 will continue this survey of PC concepts and components, and then in Chapter 11, we'll put it all together by installing components in a PC.

CERTIFICATION OBJECTIVE

- ***1101: 3.2*** *Given a scenario, install the appropriate RAM*

This section introduces most of the topics listed in CompTIA A+ 1101 exam Objective 3.2, including types of RAM (DDR3, DDR4, and DDR5); ECC; and single-channel versus dual-, triple-, and quad-channel. Virtual RAM was covered in Chapter 6, in the "Virtual Memory" section. Another topic in this objective, SODIMM, will be covered along with other laptop hardware in Chapter 14.

This chapter explains how to select the appropriate RAM, but it doesn't teach the physical installation; that's covered in Chapter 11.

Memory

In Chapter 8, you learned about a type of memory chip called read-only memory (ROM) and about the programs, called firmware, stored on those chips. However, when people discuss computer *memory,* they are usually referring to *random access memory (RAM),* so called because data and programs stored in RAM are accessible in any (random) order. Most of the memory in a PC is volatile RAM (also called *dynamic RAM,* or *DRAM*), meaning that when the computer is off and the RAM no longer receives power, the contents of this memory are lost. Computers use several types of RAM, each with a different function and different physical form. Chapter 8 described the various types of RAM memory slots used to connect RAM modules to motherboards, and we will complete that discussion in this chapter by describing how RAM and ROM are used and features and configurations of RAM chips and modules. But first we will define how we measure data quantities and the speeds of electronic components.

Capacity: From Bits to Exabytes

When we talk about storing data—whether it is in RAM or ROM or on storage devices like disk drives—we casually throw out terms describing the amount of data, or the amount of memory or storage capacity. These terms begin with the lowly *binary digit (bit).* Think of a single bit as being like a light switch: it can represent two states—either on or off. In computer storage, when a switch is on, it represents a one (1); when it is off, it represents a zero (0). This is the basis for binary numeric notation, and binary works well with computers because RAM, ROM, and storage devices all use binary, two-state methods of storing data. We won't go into just how they do this; just understand that they do.

In computing, we combine bits into groups to create a code or define memory or storage capacity. We call each group of bits a *byte.* Although a byte can be other sizes, it is usually a number divisible by 8. A single 8-bit byte may represent a character, like the letter A in a word processing document, or a very simple command, like the command to move down one line in a document. When we talk about memory and storage capacity, it is most commonly in terms of 8-bit bytes, and when you have 1024 bytes, you have 1 kilobyte (2 to the 10th power—"kilo" means 1000). Other terms we use represent larger quantities, which Table 9-1 shows. We tend to think about these values in round numbers, so a kilobyte is about a thousand, a megabyte is about a million, a gigabyte is about a billion, a terabyte is about a trillion, and so forth. However, this type of rounding can be deceptive, as you can see that a gigabyte is actually almost 74 million bytes larger than you may expect it to be.

Speed: From Hertz to Gigahertz

When we talk about the speed of electronics, such as RAM memory modules, we use the word *hertz (Hz),* a unit of measurement representing the number of electrical cycles or vibrations per second. One hertz is one cycle per second. Then, a *kilohertz (KHz)* is 1000 cycles per second, a *megahertz (MHz)* is 1 million cycles per second, and a *gigahertz (GHz)* is 1 billion cycles per second. Watch for these terms a little later when we discuss memory speeds.

TABLE 9-1

Common Values Used to Measure Data

	Calculation	Result in Bytes
One kilobyte (KB)	2^{10}	1024
One megabyte (MB)	2^{20}	1,048,576
One gigabyte (GB)	2^{30}	1,073,741,824
One terabyte (TB)	2^{40}	1,099,511,627,776
One petabyte (PB)	2^{50}	1,125,899,906,842,624
One exabyte (EB)	2^{60}	1,152,921,504,606,846,976

RAM and ROM

When a user makes a request, the CPU intercepts it and organizes the request into component-specific tasks. Many of these tasks must occur in a specific order, with each component reporting its results back to the processor before it can go on to complete the next task. The processor uses RAM to store these results until they can be compiled into the final results.

RAM also stores instructions about currently running applications. For example, when you start a computer game, a large set of the game's instructions (including how it works, how the screen should look, and which sounds must be generated) is loaded into memory. The processor can retrieve these instructions much faster from RAM than it can from the hard drive, where the game normally resides until you start to use it. Within certain limits, the more information stored in memory, the faster the computer will run. In fact, one of the most common computer upgrades is to increase the amount of RAM. The computer continually reads, changes, and removes the information in RAM, which is *volatile,* meaning that it cannot work without a steady supply of power, so when you turn your computer off, the information in RAM disappears.

Unlike RAM, ROM is read-only, meaning the processor can read the instructions it contains but cannot store new information in ROM. As described in Chapter 8, firmware is typically stored on ROM chips on circuit boards such as the motherboard and adapter cards. ROM has an important function; it is rarely changed or upgraded, and even then, instead of being physically replaced, it is more often "flashed," as described in Chapter 8, to change the information. So ROM typically warrants less attention by most computer users.

Features and Configurations of RAM Chips and Modules

When shopping for RAM, you need to understand the features and configurations of RAM chips and modules, such as the error-checking methods, single-sided versus double-sided, and single-channel versus multichannel. You should also understand the types of RAM and how to select among the various generations of double data rate (DDR) synchronous dynamic RAM (SDRAM), depending on the requirements and capabilities of a motherboard, which are described in a motherboard manual.

exam watch

Of these two (parity and ECC), only ECC is covered on the CompTIA A+ 1101 exam. Understanding parity helps you understand ECC, though, so it's useful to know about. The most important thing to remember is that ECC detects and corrects errors in RAM.

Memory Error Checking

Earlier you learned that RAM memory is volatile, so you should realize that memory can be error prone. Modern memory modules are very reliable, but you can build methods and technologies into RAM modules to check for errors. We'll look at two of these methods: parity and error-correcting code (ECC).

Parity In one type of memory error checking, called *parity,* every 8-bit byte of data is accompanied by a ninth bit (the parity bit), which is used to determine the presence of errors in the data. Of course, *non-parity* RAM does not use parity. There are two types of parity: odd and even.

In *odd parity,* the parity bit is used to ensure that the total number of 1s in the data stream is odd. For example, suppose a byte consists of the following data: 11010010. The number of 1s in this data is four, an even number. The ninth bit will then be a 1 to ensure that the total number of 1s is odd: 110100101.

Even parity is the opposite of odd parity; it ensures that the total number of 1s is even. For example, suppose a byte consists of the following data: 11001011. The ninth bit would then be a 1 to ensure that the total number of 1s is six, an even number.

Parity is not failure-proof. Suppose the preceding data stream contained two errors: 101100101. If the computer was using odd parity, the error would slip through (try it; count the 1s). However, creating parity is quick and does not inhibit memory access time the way a more sophisticated error-checking routine would.

A DIMM is 64-bits wide, but a parity-checking DIMM has 8 extra bits (1 parity bit for every 8-bit byte). Therefore, a DIMM with parity is 64 + 8 = 72 bits wide. Although parity is not often used in memory modules, there is an easy way to determine if a memory module is using parity—it will have an odd number of chips. A non-parity memory module will have an even number of chips. This is true even if the module only has two or three chips total.

If your system supports parity, you must use parity memory modules. You cannot use memory with parity if your system does not support it. The motherboard manual will define the memory requirements.

Modern PC motherboards do not support memory that uses parity. Other computing devices use parity, however. One example of parity use is in RAID 5 array controllers, mostly found in servers.

ECC *Error-correcting code (ECC)* is a more sophisticated method of error checking than parity, although like parity, it adds an extra bit per byte to a stick of RAM. Software in the system memory controller chip uses the extra bits to both detect and correct errors. Several algorithms are used in ECC. We call RAM that does not use this error checking and correcting method *non-ECC RAM.*

SRAM

Static RAM (SRAM) (pronounced "ess-ram") can hold its data without constant electrical stimulation. Although SRAM is very fast to access compared to DRAM, it is also very expensive. For this reason, PC manufacturers typically use SRAM only for caches. As you learned in Chapter 8, cache memory stores frequently accessed instructions or data for the CPU's use. On modern systems, the L1, L2, and L3 caches are all built into the CPU package.

DRAM

Dynamic RAM (DRAM) (pronounced "dee-ram") was developed to combat the high cost of SRAM. Although DRAM chips provide much slower access than SRAM chips, they are still much faster than accessing data from a hard drive. They can store multiple gigabytes of data on a single chip.

You can think of a DRAM chip as a tiny spreadsheet with billions of individual cells, arranged in rows and columns. The number of columns corresponds to the bus width of the RAM; a 64-bit chip has 64 columns. Every "cell" in a DRAM chip contains one transistor and one capacitor to store a single bit of information. This design makes it necessary for the DRAM chip to receive a constant power refresh from the computer to prevent the capacitors from losing their charge. This constant refresh makes DRAM slower than SRAM and causes a DRAM chip to draw more power from the computer than SRAM does.

Because of its low cost and high capacity, manufacturers use DRAM as "main" memory (system memory) in the computer. Modern DRAM operates at a speed dictated by the motherboard's system clock (aka system timer). Since it is synchronized with the system clock, it is known as synchronous DRAM, or SDRAM. Originally SDRAM operated at the same speed as the system clock, but more modern types operate at a multiple of that speed. The following sections explain the various types of DDR SDRAM.

Dual-, Triple-, and Quad-Channel Architecture One way of increasing the speed of the system RAM is to access it using two or more channels. With *dual-channel architecture,* the system alternates between reading two physically separate memory modules to read and write data twice as fast. With triple-channel, it alternates between three modules, and with quad-channel, it alternates between four.

Multichannel is a function of the motherboard, not of the RAM itself. Motherboards that support the SDRAM types you'll learn about in the next several sections also employ multichannel architecture to achieve speed improvements.

The important thing to remember about a multichannel-enabled motherboard is that the RAM must be installed in identical modules across a set of slots. For example, if you see two blue RAM slots and two black ones, the memory in the two blue slots must be identical in capacity, features, and all the other particulars, and the memory in the two black ones must be identical. The same goes for triple-channel and quad-channel, except there are three or four slots to identically match. That's because the motherboard treats these sets of slots as if they were a single slot logically.

exam watch

For the CompTIA A+ 1101 exam, be sure to understand the difference between single-, dual-, triple- and quad-channel architecture, especially how the RAM must be installed for it to work properly.

The following sections start out with DDR1 SDRAM and build up to DDR5, but only DDR3, 4, and 5 are listed in the CompTIA A+ 1101 exam objectives. We discuss DDR1 and 2 here because understanding their foundational principles will help you understand the newer types.

DDR1 SDRAM People often call any version of double data rate SDRAM simply "DDR RAM," but there are several versions. The first version, now called *DDR1 SDRAM,* doubled the speed at which standard SDRAM processed data by accessing the module twice per clock cycle. In addition, when you combine DDR memory with dual-channel or triple-channel architecture, you get even faster memory access. A stick of DDR SDRAM memory is an 184-pin DIMM with a notch on one end so it can only fit into the appropriate DIMM socket on a motherboard. It requires only a 2.5V power supply, compared to the previous 3.3V requirement for SDRAM.

DDR SDRAM may be marked with a code such as PC66, PC100, or PC133. Those numbers refer to the speed in MHz at which the memory operates, which should match the motherboard's clock speed.

DDR2 SDRAM *Double data rate 2 SDRAM (DDR2 SDRAM)* replaced the original DDR standard, now referred to as DDR1. Due to some improvements in electrical characteristics, DDR2 can handle faster clock rates than DDR1 can, beginning at 400 MHz, while using less power. DDR2 achieves much of its speed increase by clock-doubling the I/O circuits on the chips and adding buffers.

DDR2 modules may be marked with PC2- plus a number describing the speed (PC2-3200 to PC2-8500).

DDR2 sticks are compatible only with motherboards that use a 240-pin DIMM socket. The DDR2 DIMM stick notches are different from those in a DDR1 DIMM. A DDR2 DIMM only requires 1.8V compared to 2.5V for DDR1.

DDR3 SDRAM First appearing on new motherboards in 2007, *double data rate 3 SDRAM (DDR3 SDRAM)* chips use far less power than the previous SDRAM chips—1.5V versus DDR2's 1.8V—while providing almost twice the bandwidth, thanks to several technology improvements on the chips and modules. As with DDR2, the DDR3 DIMMs have 240 pins and they are the same size. However, they are electrically incompatible and come with a different key notch to prevent you from inserting the wrong modules into DDR3 sockets. DDR3 modules can take advantage of dual-channel architecture, and you will often see a pair of modules sold as a dual-channel kit. And it gets better—memory controller chips (MCCs) that support a triple-channel architecture (switching between three modules) are available, and DDR3 memory modules are sold in a set of three as a triple-channel set. DDR3 RAM is marked as PC3- plus a number describing the speed.

The low-voltage version of DDR3 is called *DDR3L*. It runs at 1.35V, in contrast to the 1.5V or 1.65V of standard DDR3. Low-voltage RAM is important in situations where there's a lot of RAM in the works, like in a datacenter or server farm. It runs cooler and decreases electricity usage. It doesn't make much difference in an individual desktop PC. The motherboard must support DDR3L for it to work, although it is slot-compatible with regular DDR3.

DDR4 SDRAM *Double data rate 4 (DDR4)* came out in 2014. As you might expect, it's faster, higher density, and lower voltage than DDR3. One big difference is that DDR4 changes how the channels are accessed, using a point-to-point architecture whereby each channel connects to a single module. This is a departure from the multichannel architectures of DDR1, DDR2, and DDR3. DDR4 comes on 288-pin DIMMs, so it's not compatible with slots that take earlier types. The voltage is 1.2, which is quite low. The maximum capacity for a DDR4 DIMM is 64 GB. DDR4 modules are 288 pin and are marked with PC4- followed by a speed. DDR4 DIMMs (and also DDR5 ones) are slightly taller in the center than at the ends, as shown in Figure 9-1.

DDR5 SDRAM *Double data rate 5 (DDR5)* became available in 2020. It doubles the bandwidth of DDR4 and also consumes less power. In addition, it bumps up the maximum capacity of a DIMM to 512 GB. There is a low-power version for laptops and smartphones, but standard DDR5 is already lower voltage than its predecessors, at 1.1V. Some DDR5 chips have on-die error correction code (ECC) built in. It comes on 288-pin DIMMs, but it is not compatible with 288-pin DDR4 motherboard slots. DDR5 modules are marked as PC5- followed by a speed. DDR5 DIMMs are usually enclosed in a plastic shell with heat sinks inside for better heat control. Whereas some older-technology RAM also had this, nearly all DDR5 RAM does.

exam watch **DIMMs include DDR 3 (240 pins), DDR 4 (288 pins), and DDR 5 (288 pins). RAM sticks are not backward compatible because they have different pin notching.**

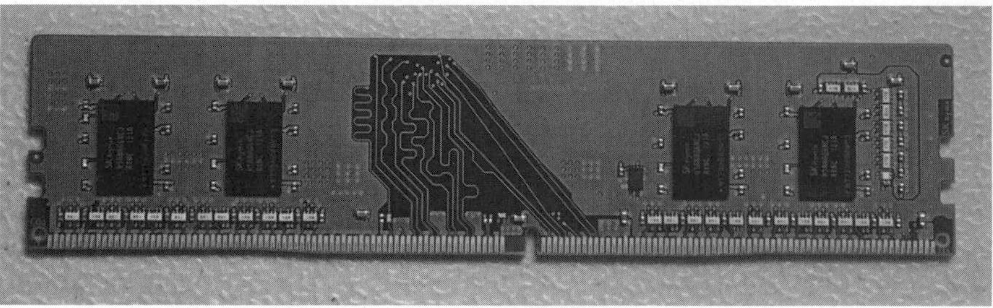

FIGURE 9-1

A DDR4 DIMM; notice the greater height in the center than at the ends.

RAM Compatibility

Before purchasing RAM modules for a computer, you should read the motherboard manual or other documentation from the manufacturer to determine what RAM is compatible with the motherboard. Normally, all RAM modules must match the features supported by the motherboard and chipset, including the features described in the following sections, as well as speed. The manual will describe any acceptable exceptions to this "perfect match" rule. Keep in mind that even if the motherboard and chipset support differences in RAM modules, such as different speeds, this will not be the optimum configuration, and it is fraught with potential for problems. It is best to have identical modules.

Many techs go to the manufacturers' sites to check memory compatibility and use memory checkers for upgrades. Examples: https://www.crucial.com/store/systemscanner and https://www.kingston.com/unitedstates/us/memory

SCENARIO & SOLUTION

You need to identify some RAM that you have found in storage. What are each of these?	Solution
288-pin DIMM that is slightly taller in the center than on the ends.	DDR4 or DDR5
240-pin DIMM labeled PC3-12800	DDR3
240-pin DIMM labeled 1.35V	DDR3L

CERTIFICATION OBJECTIVES

- ***1101: 3.1*** *Explain basic cable types and their connectors, features, and purposes*
- ***1101: 3.4*** *Given a scenario, install and configure motherboards, central processing units (CPUs), and add-on cards*

This section introduces the various types of adapter cards listed under CompTIA A+ 1101 exam Objective 3.4, including sound, video, capture cards, and network cards. In this section, we also examine various connection interfaces, including some of the cables and interfaces listed in 1101 exam Objective 3.1, notably USB and Thunderbolt. (Other connectors and cables mentioned in Objective 3.1 are covered later in this book.)

We save the actual installation and configuration of the components described in this section for Chapter 11.

Expansion Cards and Built-In Adapters

Traditionally, an *expansion card* or *adapter card* is a printed circuit board installed into an expansion slot in the motherboard to add functionality. However, in modern systems, many add-on devices do not fit that traditional description because they are external, connecting to a computer via an externally accessible port such as USB or built into the motherboard itself.

Examples of common adapter cards include display adapters, network interface cards (NICs), video capture cards, sound cards, and cards that add various types of ports, such as eSATA.

As you read about these types of devices, keep in mind that PC motherboards contain increasing numbers of these functions so they no longer need an adapter card added to the system. For example, a decade ago, most desktop PCs had adapter cards for display, sound, and network, but today most motherboards have these built in. Therefore, although the CompTIA A+ 1101 exam Objective 3.4 lists each of these as expansion cards, we will refer to them as *adapters,* which is what they are whether the device is on a separate circuit card or built into the motherboard. The functions, however, remain as described in the following sections that describe each of the most common adapters. The difference, of course, is in the necessity of physically installing expansion cards.

The term "adapter" has two meanings. One is as described in this section—display adapter, network adapter, and so on. The other meaning, as used in 220-1101 exam Objective 3.1, refers to a connector that converts one interface to another, such as a DVI-to-HDMI or USB-to-Ethernet converter.

Display Adapter

A *display adapter* (also called a *video adapter*) controls the output to the display device. This function may either be built into the motherboard of a PC or provided through an expansion card installed into the PCIe expansion bus (preferably the x16 slot, but not always; x4 and x1 adapters are also available). High-performance display adapters often require heat sinks or active cooling fans to keep within recommended operating temperatures.

You'll learn more about display adapters in Chapter 10 when we look at the various display technologies along with monitors that connect to the display adapters and the various connectors for attaching monitors to display adapters.

Sound Cards

A *sound card* (or *audio adapter*) converts digital information from computer programs into analog sounds that come out of your speakers. This is called a digital-to-analog converter (DAC). Sound cards convert in the other direction too, taking analog input from microphones and turning it into digital samples that can be stored on a PC. That's called an

TABLE 9-2 Sound Card Port Colors and Symbols

Color	Function	Connector	Symbol or Label
Pink	Analog microphone input	3.5 mm round	A microphone or MIC
Light blue	Analog line input	3.5 mm round	Arrow going into a circle or LINE IN
Light green	Analog speakers or headphones; if there are multiple speaker jacks, this one is for the front speakers	3.5 mm round	Headphones, or an arrow going out one side of a circle into a wave, or FRONT
Orange	Analog line output for center channel speaker and subwoofer	3.5 mm round	SUB/C/SL
Black	Analog line output for rear or surround speakers	3.5 mm round	REAR/SR

analog-to-digital converter (ADC). Sound cards can also process digital-to-digital input and output. Sound cards come in a full range of prices, based on the quality of the components and the number of features.

A typical configuration of sound card connectors consists of three or more audio ports, or "jacks." All of these are 3.5-mm mini jacks (small round holes). Sometimes they are color coded; other times they have symbols that tell their functions. Table 9-2 lists the commonly used colors and symbols.

Capture Cards

A *capture card* is a card (or external device) that converts data from an external video source to video files stored on a PC's local storage or an online storage location. In the past the most common use for a capture card was to digitize video from video cameras and VCRs. Today, the most common use is to convert gameplay signals from gaming consoles to videos that can be shared online. The capture card takes some of the processing burden off of the PC for converting the incoming data to a format that can be stored by video creation software.

Modern capture cards usually use an HDMI connection; previous-generation cards used VGA, S-Video, or RCA cables. Some popular brands include AVerMedia, Elgato, and Roxio. They typically come with capture software, or you can use third-party software.

External Port Adapters and Interfaces

PCs have evolved, and with the invention of more and more I/O devices, manufacturers have continued to integrate these new capabilities into the motherboard. While your PC has various I/O technologies built in, you may still wish to add an expansion card to give you additional ports.

Typically, the term *connector* refers to the plug at the end of a cable, and *port* refers to the socket where the cable attaches to the device or computer. Even though we refer to connectors and ports, remember the port is also a connector. The following sections contain descriptions of some common I/O interfaces and the connector types related to each.

USB

The *Universal Serial Bus (USB)* interface has become the interface of choice for PCs, making both parallel and serial ports obsolete and even replacing SCSI and FireWire/IEEE 1394 (discussed later in this chapter). All PCs manufactured in the last decade have at least one USB port, and many PCs literally bristle with USB connectors located conveniently on the front, as well as the back, of a desktop PC case, and on the sides and back of a laptop. So you are not likely to need to add a USB expansion card to a system. If you do need more USB ports, you can add a USB hub, a multiport connecting device for USB devices.

USB is an external bus that connects into the PC's PCI bus. With USB, you can theoretically connect up to 127 devices to your computer. There have been several versions of the USB standard; most notable are 1.0, 1.1, 2.0, and 3.0.

On some systems, there are different USB ports with different versions. They may be color-coded: black for USB 1.0/1.1, black or gray for USB 2.0, and blue for USB 3.0. If you look at the tab in the end of the cable's connector, it may be similarly color-coded; a cable designed for a USB 3.0 device will have a blue tab, for example. USB 2.0 and 3.0 ports might also have lettering on or near them indicating their speed.

exam watch

Make sure you can identify a USB port's version (for example, 2.0 vs. 3.0) based on physical cues such as port color and labels on or near the port. And given a physical port, make sure you can specify what type of USB connector plugs into it (for example, USB-C or USB-mini).

USB 1.0 and 1.1 The low-speed 1.0 and 1.1 versions transmit data up to 1.5 Mbps (megabits per second), whereas the full-speed 1.1 standard is rated at 12 Mbps. Communications are controlled by the host system and can flow in both directions, but not simultaneously. This one-way-at-a-time transmission is called *half-duplex communication.*

Hi-Speed USB 2.0 *Hi-Speed USB 2.0* transmits data at speeds up to 480 Mbps, which equals 60 MBps (megabytes per second), in half-duplex. You can attach a low-speed device

FIGURE 9-2

A SuperSpeed USB 3.0 port

like a mouse to a Hi-Speed port, but devices designed for Hi-Speed either require or run best when attached to a USB port that is up to the 2.0 standard. USB hubs and peripherals are downward compatible with hardware using the older standard, but when you plug an older device into a Hi-Speed USB port or connect a Hi-Speed USB device to a full-speed USB 1.1 port, the resulting speed will be at the lower rate, a maximum of 12 Mbps.

SuperSpeed USB 3.0 *SuperSpeed USB 3.0* operates at up to 5 Gbps (625 MBps), which is ten times the speed of USB 2.0. USB 3.0 also supports *full-duplex communication,* the ability to communicate in both directions at once. Figure 9-2 shows a SuperSpeed USB 3.0 port on a laptop with the familiar forked USB symbol and the letters "SS" indicating SuperSpeed. Manufacturers now integrate USB 3.0 into chipsets, so look for these fast ports on recently manufactured computers. Aside from physical marking on a USB 3.0 port, if you open the Universal Serial Bus Controllers node in Device Manager (as described in Exercise 9-2 a bit later), it may identify the USB level for the USB Host Controller and Root Hub as 2.0 or 3.0.

USB 3.1 USB 3.1 has a theoretical maximum speed of 10 Gbps (1.25 GBps), which is twice the speed of USB 3.0. It uses a different connector type, called a USB-C, shown in Figure 9-3. It is sometimes referred to as USB Type-C. Adapters are available that allow compatibility between USB 3.1 USB-C connectors and other port types, such as USB-C-to-DVI.

FIGURE 9-3

A USB 3.1 connector using a USB-C connector

USB-C provides both data and power to a device. Another nice feature is that it's the same in either direction, so there's no getting it upside-down. USB-C has been adopted by many high-end Android phones such as the Google Pixel 6 for charging and data transfer. USB-C offers not only faster data transfer but also faster charging.

The USB-C port can be used for different protocols. One of them is Thunderbolt, which is covered later in this chapter.

USB-C is a newer type of USB connector interface. To summarize, USB 3.1 generally refers to *the latest USB data transfer standard,* while USB-C is for a new USB connector type. A USB-C port is not necessary to support USB 3.1 data transfer.

exam watch

Make sure you can identify all the types of USB connectors on sight and determine whether a certain cable or connector can be used with a certain port or device.

USB 4.0 USB 4.0 (aka USB4) was released in August 2019. It requires USB-C connectors and cables. It can support up to 40 Gbps throughput. It's based on the Thunderbolt 3 specification and is required for Thunderbolt 4. USB4 is not covered on the current A+ exams.

Power for USB Devices USB was not originally designed to deliver much power to devices. Until USB 3.0, only low-power devices, such as flash drives, keyboards, and mice, could receive power through the USB bus, and some rechargeable devices could recharge via a USB 2.0 port. However, USB 2.0 could only output 500 milliamps. USB 3.0 outputs 900 milliamps, which permits faster charging and supports more power-hungry devices. And as you learned in the previous section, USB 3.1 can deliver a great deal of power to a device (up to 100 watts), effectively replacing the power cord on even large devices like monitors.

USB Ports, Connectors, and Cables Most computers and devices clearly identify USB ports with a trident (fork-shaped) symbol. Today's PCs can have two different physical USB port types: USB-A and USB-C.

USB-A is the older, traditional type of connector. It is rectangular and acts as a receiver for a USB type-A connector measuring 1/2" by 1/8" (look back at Figure 9-2). A plastic device in the port holds the four wires for USB 1.x or 2.0, and USB 3.0 has an additional five wires positioned behind the first four so that the connectors and ports from 3.0 are downward compatible with older ports and connectors. This, together with a similar plastic device in the connector, polarizes the connectors, which keeps the two from connecting incorrectly.

USB-C, shown in Figure 9-3, is the newer type and supports the USB 3.1 data transfer standard (as well as USB 4.0, which is not on the current exams).

USB-C cables are the same on both ends, but USB-A cables generally have the A connector on only one end. On the other end is a B connector. There are several sizes of USB-B

FIGURE 9-4

A USB cable showing the USB-B 2.0 connector on the left with a USB-A 2.0 connector on the right

connectors. Figure 9-4 shows a USB cable with a USB-A 2.0 connector on the right and a full-size, nearly square, USB-B 2.0 connector on the left. Notice that the two corners of the USB-B connector are beveled so that it cannot be inserted incorrectly. A USB-B 3.0 connector has a smaller connector containing the additional five wires mounted on top of what looks like a USB-B 2.0 connector.

There are also variations of small USB-A and USB-B connectors found on portable devices. The micro-B connector measures about 1/4" × 1/16". The mini-B connector is the same width as the micro-B connector, but it is twice as thick, measuring about 1/4" × 1/8". Figure 9-5 shows an example of a micro-B and mini-B connector.

The USB-C connector type is used for Thunderbolt 3, Thunderbolt 4, and USB 4.

Keep adapters on hand that convert between USB-C and older ports and devices that use USB-A/B. New computers in the next few years will increasingly come with more USB-C and fewer USB-A.

USB cables have a maximum length based on the version. For instance, USB 2.0 has a cable length limit of 4 meters, while USB 1.0 had a limit of 3 meters. The USB 3.0

FIGURE 9-5

USB-B connectors on two separate cables: the one on the left has a mini-B, and next to it is a micro-B.

specification does not give a maximum cable length, so it depends on the quality of the cable needed to maintain the speed of USB 3.0, which could limit the cable to as little as 3 meters. Further, a USB type-A connector has an additional pair of wires, but this type-A connector can still connect to a USB type-A port. USB 3.1 Gen 1 cables can be up to 2 meters, and USB 3.1 Gen 2 cables have a limit of 1 meter.

For Thunderbolt 3 and 4 cables (USB 4), the cable length limitation depends on the bandwidth. At a lower bandwidth (20 Gbps), the maximum is 2 meters; at a higher bandwidth (40 Gbps), the maximum is 0.8 meters. As the cable length becomes longer, bandwidth becomes lower.

USB 3.0 is downward compatible with USB 2.0, meaning that you can plug a USB 2.0 device and cable into a USB 3.0 port. You can also plug a USB-A 3.0 connector to a USB-A 2.0 computer port, even though the USB-A 3.0 connector has an additional pair of wires. The USB 3.0 device at the other end of this cable will only run at USB 2.0 speed. Further, you cannot use a USB 3.0 cable with an older USB device, and a USB 3.0 device cannot use a USB 2.0 cable. This is because the USB-B 3.0 connector that plugs into a device does not fit into the USB-B 2.0 port on a device.

USB hubs take you beyond these limits, but the connecting cables still must be within the prescribed limits. You can also find a USB cable that has a hub built in to extend the length, but this only works to connect one device to a computer.

Another type of USB cable is a simple extension cable that has a USB-A connector on one end and a receiving USB port connector on the other end. These come in varying lengths, and we keep several on hand. You never know when you might want to connect to a USB port on the back of a computer or on the front of a computer that is out of reach, such as under a table or in a cabinet. Plug in the extension cable and run it to your desk, where it is handy for plugging in your flash drives or other devices. Short extension cables also have their use. Many USB devices described in this book are very small and come without a cable. You simply connect the device to a USB port and it juts out from the computer, barely visible, but vulnerable. One wrong move and you can ruin the device or the port into which it is plugged. Our solution is to purchase and keep handy a couple of short (about 9") USB extension cables. Then the device sits on the desk, tethered to the port, and bumping it won't damage the device or the port.

EXERCISE 9-1

Researching USB Connectors

There are many variations of USB connectors. If you have a computer with an Internet connection, research USB connectors.

1. Open your favorite Internet search engine, such as Google or Bing.
2. Search on the keywords **usb connectors**.

3. Search the results for a site that gives you a range of connectors, as well as photos of each type.
4. Keep track of the number of variations you find, looking for the differences in the USB 2.0, USB 3.0, and USB 3.1 connectors.

EXERCISE 9-2

Exploring Your System's USB Ports

Follow these steps in Windows to check out your USB ports:

1. Open Device Manager. There are lots of ways to do this; you can go through the Control Panel, or you can right-click the Start button and choose Device Manager.
2. Double-click Universal Serial Bus Controllers to expand that category, and then double-click a USB Root Hub entry to open its Properties dialog box. (Or if you do not have USB Root Hub, try one of the other USB devices there, such as Generic USB.)
3. Examine the information on the tabs, and then close the Properties dialog box.
4. Repeat Steps 2 and 3 for several other devices under the USB Serial Bus controllers heading.
5. Check out the properties for items that appear under Universal Serial Bus Devices heading. Then close Device Manager.

USB Plug and Play USB supports *plug and play,* meaning the computer firmware and operating system recognize a USB device when you connect it, and the operating system automatically installs and configures a device driver (if available). Always check the documentation for a USB device, because many require that you install a device driver before you connect the device. USB ports also support *hot swapping,* which is the act of safely disconnecting and connecting devices while the computer is running, giving you instantly recognized and usable devices.

When Autoplay is enabled for removable drives, the system can be attacked if someone connects a USB device to it that contains malware. Because of this, many people choose to disable Autoplay for removable devices. Open the Settings app, and then navigate to Bluetooth & Devices | AutoPlay (in Windows 11) or Devices | AutoPlay (in Windows 10) and set the Removable Drive setting to Take No Action.

Adding More USB Hubs If a PC has too few USB ports for the number of USB devices a user wishes to connect, the easiest fix is to purchase an external USB hub and connect it to one of the PC's USB connectors. In fact, you can add other hubs and devices in this way. Although the USB standard allows for daisy-chaining of devices, manufacturers do not support this capability because they prefer to use hubs connected directly to the USB controller, which includes the root hub. There is a limit of five levels of hubs, counting the root hub. Each hub can accommodate several USB devices, possibly creating a lopsided tree. USB supports different speeds on each branch, so you can use devices of varying speeds. Figure 9-6 shows a PC with an internal root hub. Connected to this hub are a USB keyboard and another USB hub. Several devices connect to the first USB hub, including yet another hub, which in turn has several devices connected to it.

Thunderbolt

Thunderbolt is a high-speed interface that until recently was used primarily in Apple computers, but has started appearing on Windows PCs in the last several years. Dell Computers, for example, provides a Thunderbolt port on some of its XPS and Alienware laptops, and users can connect a port replicator/docking station using the Thunderbolt port.

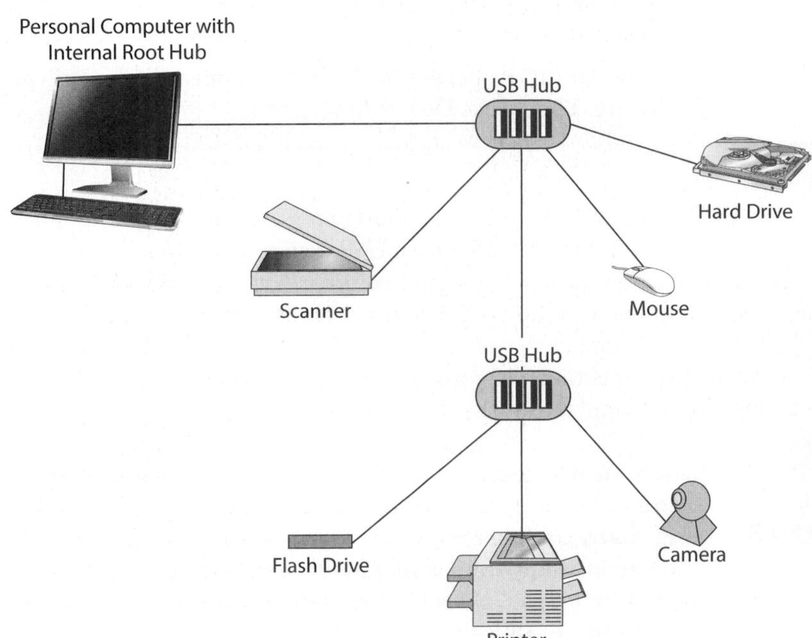

FIGURE 9-6 USB hubs can add more USB ports to a PC.

Thunderbolt 4 is a standardization of Thunderbolt 3. Their specifications are mostly the same.

Thunderbolt can carry DisplayPort data (for monitors) and also PCI Express and USB 3.1 data. The original Thunderbolt provided two separate channels on the same connector with 10 Gbps throughput in both directions. Thunderbolt 2, the next generation of Thunderbolt, increased that to 20 Gbps. This is 40 times faster than USB 2.0 and 4 times faster than USB 3.0. Thunderbolt 3 and 4 carry data at up to 40 Gbps.

It can also be used to daisy-chain multiple high-speed devices without using a hub or switch.

One cool additional feature is that you can purchase a Thunderbolt chassis, which is essentially an enclosure designed to hold PCIe cards, and connect that chassis to the main PC to access all the expansion slots within it.

What goes with thunder? Lightning, of course. Lightning is the connector/port used for both charging and data for iPhones and (older) iPads, as you will learn in Chapter 17. Newer iPads and Macs use USB-C.

DB-9 Serial Port

Serial cables had a variety of uses back in the days before USB; they were used to connect mice, modems, keyboards, printers, and many other peripherals before better, faster connectivity became possible for each of those device types. Very rarely will you find a computer old enough to have a serial port these days.

A serial port/cable, often referred to as legacy serial, uses a 9-pin D-sub connector (DB-9) and is often referred to as RS-232, which was the standard number for this port type. DB-9 serial ports have been replaced by faster, better ports such as USB on personal computers, but some specialized devices still use them, such as some point-of-sale systems and factory machinery.

A 9-pin D-sub connector is known as a DB-9 or DB9, and this is one of the connectors listed on 1101 Exam Objective 3.1. This objective also mentions Serial as a cable type. You should know that Serial and DB-9 both refer to the same port.

A *D-sub connector* is a connector that has either pins or holes with a protective D-shaped ring around it. Sub is short for *subminiature.* VGA monitor connectors also use this connector style. Another way to indicate a D-sub connector is DB, as in DB-9. The connector with pins is

FIGURE 9-7 A DB-9M connector on the back of a very old PC (Source: Duncan Lithgow [Public domain], from Wikimedia Commons: https://en.wikipedia.org/wiki/Serial_port#/media/File:Serial_port.jpg; image is public domain)

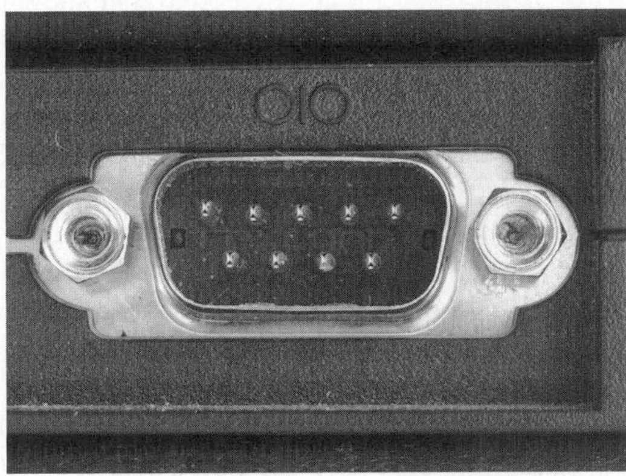

a male connector (DB-9M), and the corresponding connector with holes is a female connector (DB-9F). For a serial port, the connector on the PC itself is DB-9M. Figure 9-7 shows a DB-9M connector.

Communication Adapters

We have used the term "communication" many times in this and the preceding chapter, mostly in talking about communication between components within the PC. Now we will talk about the communication devices that connect a PC to a network, whether it is a local area network (LAN) or the Internet. Once again, the motherboards of most PCs now have these functions built in, and it is not usually necessary to add an adapter card to a computer for communications.

Network Adapters

A network adapter (or network card), often called a *network interface card (NIC),* connects a PC or other device to a type of network, such as a wired Ethernet network or a wireless Wi-Fi or cellular network. Most PCs and laptops contain an Ethernet NIC because most PC users require network communications and can usually connect to the Internet—directly or indirectly—through an Ethernet network. Many computers also include a wireless NIC—either Wi-Fi (the most common) or another wireless type, such as cellular, Bluetooth, or near field communication (NFC), all of which are covered in Chapter 16.

On the job, a typical desktop PC is connected to a LAN, which in turn may be connected to a larger private network and, ultimately, to the Internet. At home, you may connect two or more PCs via a LAN connection to share an Internet connection, such as a digital subscriber line (DSL) or cable modem Internet connection. The network adapter in the PC may be an Ethernet wired network adapter or a wireless adapter, depending on whether you wish to connect to a wired Ethernet LAN or a wireless LAN. We will save the larger discussion of networking for Chapters 17, 18, and 19, and in Chapter 14 we will describe the various types of wireless adapters found in laptops.

The most common connector for Ethernet NICs is RJ-45. A *registered jack (RJ)* connector is rectangular in shape and has a locking clip on one side. The number designation of an RJ connector refers to its size rather than to the number of wire connections within it. RJ-45 contains eight wires and most commonly attaches twisted-pair cables to Ethernet network cards. Figure 9-8 shows an RJ-45 port with the small notch to accommodate the locking clip on a cable connector labeled with a symbol representing a network.

Modem Adapters

A *modem,* so named for its combined functions of *mod*ulator/*dem*odulator, allows computers to communicate with one another over existing phone lines, a type of communication called dial-up that will be described in Chapter 17 when we look at how to connect to networks. A modem may be internal in the motherboard, or it may be an adapter card in the expansion bus. An external modem connects to a port on the computer, either serial or USB. Whether internal or external, a modem connects to a regular telephone wall jack using the same connector as a phone.

This type of modem is an *analog modem* as opposed to the data communication devices used to connect to a cable network or to phone lines for DSL service. "Modem" is actually a misnomer for the devices used on cable or DSL networks because the signals involved are all digital signals, and therefore, there is no modulating or demodulating of the signal. However, because they are physically between the computer and the network, much like a modem is, manufacturers use the term "modem."

An *RJ-11 port* is where you attach a phone cable to a modem (analog or other) and to a wall-mounted phone jack. It is similar to an RJ-45 port—only slightly smaller—and it

FIGURE 9-8 The RJ-45 Ethernet port on this laptop is labeled with a symbol resembling three computers connected to a network.

FIGURE 9-9 An analog modem adapter card with two RJ-11 connectors on the left side and a cable with an RJ-11 plug attached resting on top of the card

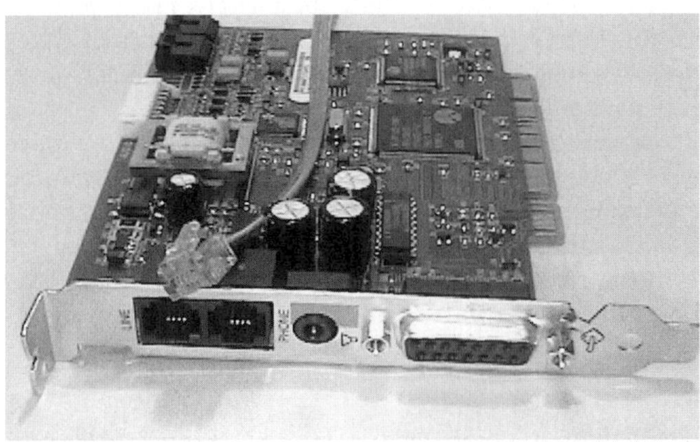

contains either two or four wires. Figure 9-9 shows two RJ-11 connectors on a modem adapter: one that connects to the wall jack, and the other that attaches to a phone set. A cable with an RJ-11 connector attached is resting on top of the card.

exam watch

Dial-up modems are not covered on the CompTIA A+ exams, but RJ-11 ports are, and modems are the primary kind of device that uses RJ-11. Be prepared to demonstrate that you understand the differences between RJ-11 and RJ-45 connectors. Remember their uses and the number of wires in each.

Adapters and Converters

For CompTIA A+ 1101 exam Objective 3.1, make sure you are aware of the various types of adapters (aka converters) that can be used in situations where you need to connect a device to a PC that doesn't have the right type of port. Converters are available for every combination of all the major types of display adapters, including DVI, HDMI, VGA (all covered in Chapter 10), and Thunderbolt. You can also convert USB to Ethernet and vice versa.

EXERCISE 9-3

Viewing Adapter Cards in Device Manager

Look at the list of installed adapters in Device Manager in Windows.

1. Right-click the Start button and click Device Manager.
2. In the list of devices in the Device Manager window, note those for adapters named in the previous section. This list will include but not be limited to display adapters, network adapters, and various controllers.
3. Close the Device Manager window.

SCENARIO & SOLUTION

Suppose you have a Thunderbolt docking station that you want to connect to a PC. Which type of port must it have?	USB-C
Which USB standard is represented by a blue inner tab in the connector?	USB 3.0
You have a sound card with six identically sized 3.5" round ports. How do you tell which is which?	They may be color-coded, or there may be labels etched into the backplate next to each port.

CERTIFICATION OBJECTIVES

- ***1101: 3.1*** *Explain basic cable types and their connectors, features, and purposes*
- ***1101: 3.3*** *Given a scenario, select and install storage devices*

This section introduces the storage types listed in CompTIA A+ 1101 exam Objective 3.3, magnetic hard disk drives (HDDs), optical drives, solid-state drives (SSDs), and flash drives. We'll also define special configurations of drives, called RAID, and the various media types and capacities of storage devices. Chapter 11 presents the actual installation and configuration of storage devices. This section also covers the interfaces related to storage devices from CompTIA A+ 1101 exam Objective 3.1, including SATA, IDE, SCSI, and eSATA.

Storage Devices and Interfaces

In computing, the function of a *mass storage device* is to hold, or store, a large amount of information, even when the computer's power is off. Unlike information in system RAM, files kept on a mass storage device remain there unless the user or the computer removes or alters them. In this section, we will first explore the types of interfaces for connecting storage devices to computers, and then we'll explore various types of storage devices in use today.

Drive Interfaces

Today, the dominant interface for internal drives is serial ATA (SATA). For external drives, external SATA (eSATA) is popular, along with USB, which you learned about earlier in the chapter. Most of the drives you install and configure will be SATA or eSATA.

Although SATA and eSATA are the drive interfaces you will use most often on the job, you might still encounter PATA and SCSI equipment, and parts of these technologies are included in CompTIA A+ 1101 exam Objectives 3.1 and 3.2. Therefore we will include sections on them in this chapter for reference purposes as well.

SATA

Serial ATA (SATA) is the dominant standard for connecting internal magnetic drives such as HDDs and optical drives. Some SSDs also connect to SATA, although more modern ones connect via M.2 (covered in Chapter 8).

A modern motherboard typically has at least four SATA connectors, like the ones shown in Figure 9-10. SATA cables (such as the one connected to the lower-left connector in Figure 9-10)

FIGURE 9-10 A cluster of four SATA connectors on a motherboard. The long, vertically oriented connector to their right is a PATA connector.

FIGURE 9-11 The SATA power and data ports on a hard drive. The power port is the long one on the right, and the data port is immediately to its left.

are thin and compact (compared to the bulky old ribbon cables of the past) and can be up to 39.4" long. Because each SATA device has a direct connection to the SATA controller, it does not have to share a bus with other devices, and therefore it provides greater throughput. Unlike PATA, SATA also supports hot swapping.

Even the first two SATA standards, SATA 1.5 Gbps (150 MBps) and SATA 3 Gbps (300 MBps), far exceeded the PATA speeds. The SATA 3.0 standard, or SATA 6 Gbps, released in May 2009, is fast enough for entry-level SSDs. SATA 3.1 includes support for SSDs in mobile devices, or *mSATA* (also called *Mini-SATA*), defining a scaled-down form factor.

Figure 9-11 shows the SATA ports on the back of an internal hard drive. The power port on the right has 15 contacts, while the SATA data port to the left of it has 7 contacts. Figure 9-12 shows the corresponding connectors on a power cable and a SATA data cable.

FIGURE 9-12 The power cable on the left connects to the power connector on a SATA drive, while the SATA data cable with its smaller connector is next to it.

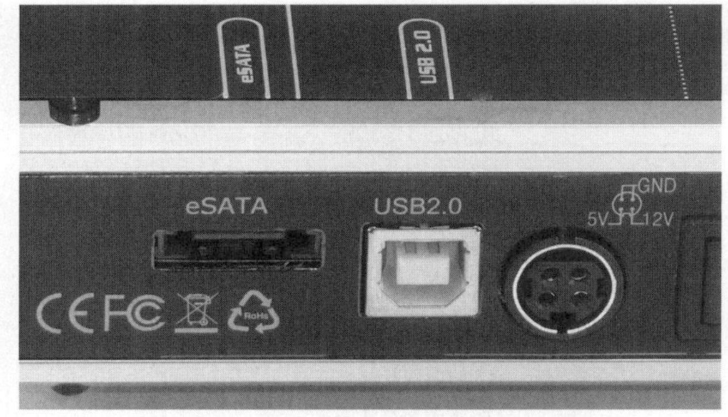

FIGURE 9-13 An eSATA port on an external hard drive enclosure

eSATA

External SATA (eSATA) is an extension of the SATA standard for external SATA devices with the same speeds as the SATA standard it supports, which at present is 300 MBps. Internal eSATA connectors are included in newer motherboards, in which case, cabling is required to connect them to an eSATA port on the PC case. Use eSATA adapter cards to add eSATA to older motherboards without built-in support. eSATA is replacing FireWire and at least competing with USB. Figure 9-13 shows an eSATA port on an external hard drive enclosure, and Figure 9-14 shows the connectors on either end of an eSATA cable.

Table 9-3 lists the characteristics of the various SATA types that you will need to know as part of 1101 exam Objective 3.1.

FIGURE 9-14 The eSATA connectors on either end of an eSATA cable

TABLE 9-3 Characteristics of SATA and eSATA

Interface	Used For	Max. Distance	Max. Speed	Connector
SATA1	Internal storage	1 meter	1.5 Gbps	SATA
SATA2	Internal storage	1 meter	3 Gbps	SATA
SATA3	Internal storage	1 meter	6 Gbps	SATA
SATA3 Revision 3.2	Internal storage	1 meter	16 Gbps	SATA, SATAe, mSATA, M.2
eSATA	External storage	2 meters	2.4 Gbps	eSATA

Interfaces for Mobile Devices

Overall the trend in storage is toward solid-state devices and away from magnetic hard drives. Mobile devices are leading the way, with most of them using solid-state. However, the interfaces that have traditionally been used for magnetic storage have proved inadequate for solid-state storage, especially as solid-state storage has gotten faster in the last several years.

mSATA has been used since 2009 in many small devices to connect small solid-state storage hardware. An mSATA storage card looks similar to a PCIe mini card, but it connects to the device's SATA controller, not its PCIe controller. Figure 9-15 compares an mSATA card to a 2.5" HDD typically used in a laptop computer.

New laptops (and some desktops) have increasingly been switching to a new interface that replaces mSATA, called *M.2*. M.2 is very flexible, allowing system designers to choose the desired bus interface to connect with (PCIe 3.0, SATA 3.0, USB 3.0/3.1, or USB4) and allowing devices to be different physical sizes. Figure 9-16 compares an mSATA SSD to an M.2 SSD. M.2 was also covered in Chapter 8.

Non-Volatile Memory Express (NVMe) is a logical interface specification that is designed to take advantage of the speed and parallel access capabilities of solid-state storage. It is designed to replace AHCI, which is the logical specification by which SATA host controllers interact with devices. It can be used with a variety of physical connectors, including mobile PCIe, SATA Express, and M.2.

Legacy Storage Interfaces

The CompTIA A+ 1101 exam objectives reference two legacy storage interfaces: IDE and SCSI. You will only occasionally run into these in the field, but we are including some basic information about them here both for study purposes and as a reference in case you ever have to work with them.

PATA and IDE *Parallel Advanced Technology Attachment (PATA)* was for many years the main way that hard drives connected to motherboards. Old systems might have two PATA connectors on the motherboard, each of which supports up to two devices. Modern

FIGURE 9-15 An mSATA card compared to a 2.5" HDD (Source: Vladsinger [CC BY-SA 3.0 (https://creativecommons.org/licenses/by-sa/3.0)], from Wikimedia Commons: https://commons.wikimedia.org/wiki/File:MSATA_SSD_vs._2.5%22_SATA_drive.JPG)

FIGURE 9-16 An mSATA SSD (left) and an M.2 SSD (right) (Source: Anand Lal Shimpi, anandtech.com [CC BY-SA 4.0 (https://creativecommons.org/licenses/by-sa/4.0)], via Wikimedia Commons: https://commons.wikimedia.org/wiki/File:M.2_and_mSATA_SSDs_comparison.jpg)

motherboards may have one PATA connector for backward compatibility in case you need to connect an IDE device.

Technicians tend to use the terms PATA, *Integrated Drive Electronics (IDE),* and *Enhanced IDE (EIDE)* interchangeably, but they are not exactly the same. IDE and EIDE both refer to a disk drive where the disk and the controlling electronics are inseparable (i.e., hard drives). Optical drives that use the PATA interface are technically not IDE because you can remove their discs. They are *Advanced Technology Attachment Packet Interface (ATAPI)* drives. However, the exam objectives use IDE generically to refer to the PATA interface.

The onboard drive controller of an IDE drive receives commands to the drive and controls the action of the drive itself. The technology allows one controller to take over the function of an additional drive, so you can have two drives per cable.

IDE connections use flat ribbon cables or (rarely) round cables. The round cables are more expensive, but they are superior to the 2"-wide flat cables because they allow better airflow in the case. Early PATA cables had just 40 wires, but newer cables have 80 wires, although they still have the same 40-pin connectors. The extra wires ensure better signal quality through grounding that shields against interference.

Both types of PATA cables normally come with three 40-pin connectors—one on each end and one in the middle. One end connects to the PATA channel connector on the motherboard, while the other two connectors plug into the drives. If the system has only one hard drive, attach it to the end of the ribbon cable. The red stripe along the length of the cable represents pin 1. Make sure this stripe aligns with pin 1 on both the hard drive and on the channel connector on the motherboard.

SCSI *Small Computer System Interface (SCSI),* pronounced "scuzzy," is a set of standards for interfacing computers and internal and external peripherals. For several years (two decades or so ago), SCSI was popular for high-end devices, such as hard drives, optical drives, and scanners; it was the disk controller of choice for many high-end servers and RAID arrays. However, today SATA and USB have pretty much replaced SCSI (SATA for drives and USB for everything else).

SCSI has several implementations with a variety of speeds. Until recently, SCSI systems all used a parallel interface to the computer. For the traditional parallel SCSI interface, there are four different connectors: 50-pin Centronics and three different sizes of D-sub connectors: 25-pin, 50-pin, and 68-pin. Internal SCSI cables are usually ribbon cables, like with PATA.

More recently, a serial interface has been used with SCSI—a marriage of SCSI and Serial ATA called *Serial Attached SCSI (SAS).* There are many types of SAS connectors, and they are much smaller than previous SCSI connectors—some are similar in size to USB and mini USB connectors—and the number of pins ranges from 26 to 36. SAS is used mainly on high-end systems, such as servers.

Some motherboards have SCSI support built in, and you can also add SCSI support via an adapter card. One of the advantages of SCSI is that you can daisy-chain multiple devices on a single SCSI controller. Depending on the controller, you might be able to attach 7, 15, 31, or more SCSI devices on a single chain. One of the disadvantages of chaining is that every SCSI device in the chain must participate in moving data through the chain so that means greater overhead for each device.

Each external SCSI device has two ports: one port receives the cable from the device before it in the chain, and one port attaches to the next device in the chain. An internal SCSI device may have only one port and require a special cable for daisy chaining with other internal devices. A SCSI adapter card typically has both an internal and an external connector so you can chain devices both inside and outside the case.

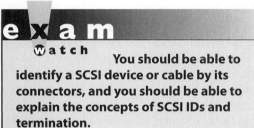

SCSI devices can be complicated to install. Each device in a SCSI chain requires a unique numeric identifier called a SCSI ID. (These aren't complicated IDs; they are simple integers starting with zero.) Newer SCSI devices may use plug and play to assign an available ID number. In addition, each SCSI chain must be physically terminated (with a terminator block connected to the "out" port on the last device or with jumpers or software) or the entire chain will not function.

You should be able to identify a SCSI device or cable by its connectors, and you should be able to explain the concepts of SCSI IDs and termination.

Mass Storage Devices

Many types of mass storage devices are available, including those that store data on magnetic media, devices that use optical technologies, and devices based on solid-state technology. Note that this list includes both removable and fixed (nonremovable) devices. Further, certain of these, depending on their interfaces, are hot-swappable devices, and many are considered backup media. Let's explore all these dimensions.

3.5" and 2.5" Magnetic Hard Drives

Magnetic mass storage devices used with computers store digital data on magnetized media, such as the metal platters in hard disk drives and magnetic tape used in tape drives (now obsolete). Unlike dynamic RAM, which loses its data when power to the device is off, this type of storage is *nonvolatile.* Read/write heads create magnetic patterns on the media that stay there until altered.

A *hard disk drive (HDD)* stores data using patterns of positive or negative magnetic polarity on metal platters. Hard drives are available in a wide range of capacities, and new hard drives now have a capacity between several hundred gigabytes and several terabytes.

Inside a hard disk casing is a stack of metal platters, spaced on a spindle so they do not touch. Each side of each platter has its own *read/write head* on an *actuator arm* that moves it in (toward the center of the platter) and out (toward the edge). The heads all move together as a single unit. The space between each platter and its read/write head is so small that even a tiny speck of dust could interfere with it; therefore, the components are encased in a sealed metal box assembled in a clean room. Each hard disk drive has a controller on a circuit board mounted on the outside of its casing; this controller communicates with the motherboard to read and write data. The original term for a drive with a built-in controller was Integrated Drive Electronics (IDE), and you may sometimes still see hard drives described as IDE or EIDE.

exam watch

Hard drives are often referred to according to the size of the platters: a 2.5" hard drive is for a laptop, and a 3.5" hard drive is for a desktop.

Figure 9-17 shows a 2-TB hard disk drive designed for internal installation. It has connectors for a SATA cable and for a connection to the PC's power supply. The hard drive shown in the figure is for a desktop and has 3.5" platters. A hard drive for a laptop is smaller and has 2.5" platters.

Hard drives designed for external use have a protective case around both the hard drive and its circuit board and usually require an external power cord and a USB, FireWire, or eSATA connector to an external port on the PC. You can buy a drive enclosure that converts an internal hard disk drive to an external one by adding a protective case and converting the data and power interfaces.

When buying a new computer or additional hard drive, look for the preferred interface (SATA or eSATA), the capacity, and the speed of the drive and try to buy the largest, fastest drive you can afford. The most common way to measure drive speed is the rate at which the platters spin—called *spindle speed*—measured in *revolutions per minute (rpm)*. Commonly available speeds in existing and new hard drives include 5400 rpm, 7200 rpm, 10,000 rpm,

FIGURE 9-17

An internal SATA hard drive

Make sure you can identify the speeds and form factors for HDDs and the communications interfaces and form factors for SSDs.

and 15,000 rpm. Data transfer rates tend to favor the higher rpms; prices vary accordingly.

Optical Disc Drives

An optical disc drive is a drive that can accept, read, and sometimes write to compact discs (CDs), digital versatile discs (DVDs), and/or Blu-ray discs. Note that the terminology differs slightly between optical and magnetic media; in magnetic media, it's disk (with a *k*) and in optical media, it's disc (with a *c*). Generally speaking, drives are backward compatible with earlier formats. For example, DVD drives can also read CDs, and Blu-ray drives can read all three types. Most drives sold today are *burners,* in that they can also write to blanks of the formats they support.

The standard CD, DVD, or Blu-ray disc is approximately 4.75" (12 cm) in diameter, but there are minidiscs that measure about 3.125" (8 cm). The surface is smooth and shiny with one labeled side and one plain side (unless it's a double-sided disc, in which case both sides are equally shiny). The data, music, or video is stored on the disc using microscopic depressed and raised areas called *pits* and *lands,* respectively, which are covered by a protective transparent layer. A laser beam and a light sensor are used to read the data from the disc. You can access data much faster from a hard drive than from an optical disc, but optical storage is more portable. Optical disc capacity is generally much smaller than commonly available hard drives.

Most new systems sold today do not include optical drives because of the move to USB technology and ISO images. They are often sold as external peripherals.

Solid-State Storage

Up to this point in the chapter, the storage devices we have looked at use magnetic or optical technologies. However, a growing category of storage devices use integrated circuits, which are much faster than these other technologies. Generically called *solid-state storage, solid-state drives (SSDs),* or *flash memory,* this technology has no moving parts and uses *nonvolatile memory,* meaning it does not require power to keep the stored data intact. These devices are more expensive on a per-gigabyte basis than conventional hard drives, but there are many uses for these very lightweight, quiet, and fast devices.

Many people assume that because this memory is able to be written and rewritten to and is nonvolatile, it is a type of SRAM. However, the memory in most solid-state storage is actually a variant of electrically erasable programmable read-only memory (EEPROM). Yes, it can be written to, but it is written in blocks, not written in bytes the way RAM is written. All that is invisible and irrelevant to the end user, of course.

SSDs come in a range of form factors. There are external and internal models. SSDs designed to replace HDDs in desktop or laptop PCs use the SATA interface and come in packages the same size and shape as the equivalent HDDs they replace (3.5" for desktops and 2.5" for laptops).

PCIe Storage It's not as common, but there are NVMe SDDs that come on circuit boards that fit into a PCIe slot on the motherboard. These fit into x4, x8, or x16 PCIe slots and come in handy on systems that need more internal storage but have no available SATA or M.2 slots available.

Flash Drives A *flash drive* is an inexpensive, highly portable type of external SSD, and is also called a *thumb drive, jump drive,* or *USB drive.* Flash drives can hold up to hundreds of gigabytes of data, with different capacities available to suit any budget, in a device about the size and shape of a human thumb. When plugged into your computer, it appears as an ordinary drive with a drive letter assigned to it.

Memory Cards Solid-state memory can also exist on tiny plastic wafers, called *memory cards,* that can be removed from their reading device (a *card reader*). Flash memory cards are commonly used in a variety of devices, such as in digital cameras, smartphones, and navigation devices. A prolific photographer will carry several memory cards, swapping out full cards for empty ones. Although many cameras come with software and cables for transferring the photos from the camera's memory card to a computer and/or printer, another method does not require either cable or software. In this method, you remove the card from the camera and insert it into a special slot on the PC or printer. Whether the card is in a camera or inserted directly into the computer's card reader, it is treated like a drive. There are many types of flash memory cards using various solid-state technologies, some with trademarked names. Figure 9-18 shows some of the most common sizes.

FIGURE 9-18 Common flash memory cards (Photo: https://commons.wikimedia.org/wiki/File: Flash_memory_cards_size_comparison_(composite).svg)

FIGURE 9-19 This computer is ready to read a variety of memory cards.

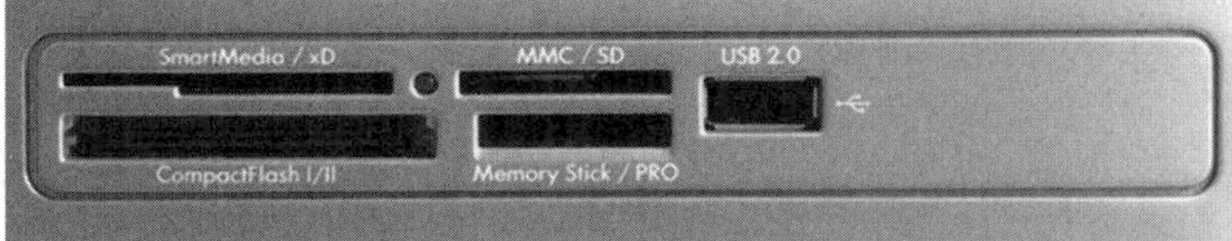

Because some of the sizes are so similar, card readers with multiple slots use labels to help you figure out which slot to use. Figure 9-19 shows the front panel of a PC with a variety of flash memory slots, including one labeled MMC/SD. If a card reader is not built into your PC and you require one, you can buy a bus card or an external USB card reader to add one to your PC.

EXERCISE 9-4

Identifying Your Storage Devices

Use Windows to view your connected storage devices.

1. Open File Explorer and view This PC. This will show you all the attached disk drives.
2. Identify the drives displayed. What kinds of drives do you have? For example, is there an optical drive? Does it have a disc in it? Is there more than one internal HDD or SSD? Are any removable drives connected, such as a USB flash drive?

RAID Arrays

Redundant array of independent (or inexpensive) disks (RAID) is a group of schemes designed to provide either better performance or fault-tolerant protection for data through the use of multiple hard drives. Often (but not always) RAID uses specialized hardware called a *RAID controller*. RAID can also be achieved using specialized software, but it always requires multiple drives configured to work together to use one of the RAID schemes. We call this set of disks collectively a *RAID array*. The drives should be of equal size, or you will waste space. We identify each RAID scheme by the word "RAID" followed by a number. Figure 9-20 shows a small RAID array for a home or small office.

Fault tolerance is the ability to survive a failure of a part of a system. When speaking of RAID arrays, fault tolerance is the ability to protect data from a failure. This is done through data redundancy or through a special algorithm. Only RAID 1 and RAID 10

FIGURE 9-20 A small RAID array

provide fault tolerance through data redundancy, and RAID 5 provides fault tolerance through the use of an algorithm. Learn how these different RAID levels work.

> **exam watch**
>
> **Although there are many RAID levels, only RAID 0, 1, 5, and 10 are listed under CompTIA A+ 1101 exam Objective 3.3, so be sure you understand these four RAID levels.**

RAID 0 *RAID 0* defines a simple striped set without parity. It gives improved drive read and write speeds. The operating system sees the separate physical drives in the array as a single hard drive, and each time data must be written to the drive array, the controller writes a portion of the data to each drive in the drive array, which is called a *stripe*. RAID 0 uses the total disk space in the array for data storage, without any fault-tolerant protection of the data from drive failure. If one of the drives in a RAID 0 array fails, all the data is lost.

RAID 1 *RAID 1,* also called *mirroring,* provides fault tolerance by writing all data simultaneously to the two drives in the *mirrored set*. If one of the drives should fail, the data still exists on the surviving drive. You may experience some improved performance on reads with RAID 1, depending on the operating system.

RAID 5 *RAID 5*, also called *striping with distributed parity* or *striping with interleaved parity*, requires at least three physical drives. As data is written to the striped set, it is written in blocks on each drive. In each stripe, the block written on just one of the drives (different with each write) is not the actual data, but the result of an algorithm performed on the data contained in the other blocks in the stripe. A single drive in a RAID 5 striped set can fail without a loss of data, because until the drive is replaced, the blocks in each stripe on the surviving drives are either the data itself (if the parity block was on the failed drive) or a parity block. Therefore, the controller uses the surviving data block and parity block in each set to reconstruct the data. Once the missing drive is replaced, the RAID controller will automatically rebuild the data as it existed on the failed drive, using the existing data and parity blocks. Also, until you replace the missing member of the set, the reads from the striped set are slower, due to the need to run the algorithm in order to produce the data.

exam watch **For RAID 0 and RAID 1, you need a minimum of two disks; for RAID 5 you need three, and for RAID 10 you need four, plus a hardware disk controller that supports it.**

RAID 10 A *RAID 10* array is a stripe of mirrors, requiring a minimum of four identical disks paired into two mirrored sets. Data is written in a stripe across the two mirrored sets as if they were simply two disks in a RAID 0 array. This gives you the fault tolerance of a mirror and the performance of RAID 0.

on the job **In most organizations, RAID is valued for the protection of data through redundancy, available with RAID levels 1, 5, and 10. Therefore, expect to encounter these types of RAID on the job, especially on servers. Outside IT departments, gamers are very savvy about RAID, but they lean toward RAID level 0, which gives performance gains without redundancy protection.**

SCENARIO & SOLUTION

Scenario	Solution
You are asked to recommend a computer to be a file and print server for a small business. What RAID configuration should you recommend to the small business owner to add data redundancy to the system?	RAID level 1; consider mirroring to give the server redundancy. RAID 5 could also be an option, as it, too, provides redundancy. You would not, however, recommend RAID 0.
You are shopping for an internal storage device for a desktop PC. What interface should you look for?	SATA or M.2, depending on what the motherboard supports.

CERTIFICATION SUMMARY

Identifying personal computer components and their functions is the first step in becoming a computer professional. While PC component technologies are ever-changing, understanding the basics of the components and their functions today will help you to understand newer technologies as they are introduced. This chapter described the important features of memory, expansion cards, and storage. It isn't enough to understand the technologies of these important components; you also need to understand the various connection interfaces related to them and the connectors and related cables, which were included in this chapter.

TWO-MINUTE DRILL

Here are some of the key points covered in Chapter 9.

Memory

- ❑ Data storage capacity is described in terms of bits, bytes, kilobytes, megabytes, gigabytes, and terabytes.
- ❑ The speed of electronics, such as RAM, is often described in terms of hertz (Hz), kilohertz (KHz), megahertz (MHz), and gigahertz (GHz).
- ❑ RAM is volatile and used to store active programs and data. ROM is nonvolatile and used to store firmware on motherboards and adapters.
- ❑ Most memory modules do not perform error checking. Some older memory modules use an error-checking method called parity, and others may use a more complex method called ECC.
- ❑ DIMMs come in both single-sided and double-sided versions.
- ❑ Some systems use multiple channels to improve RAM performance: dual-channel, triple-channel, or quad-channel. You must install RAM in matched sets in the correct slots to enable this.
- ❑ SRAM is very fast and very expensive, and is used for system cache in most systems.
- ❑ DRAM is slower than SRAM. It is less expensive, has a higher capacity, and is the main memory in the computer.
- ❑ DRAM technologies include SDRAM, DDR1 SDRAM, DDR2 SDRAM, DDR3 SDRAM, DDR4 SDRAM, and DDR5 SDRAM.
- ❑ To avoid compatibility problems, read the motherboard manual before buying and installing additional RAM modules in a computer.

Expansion Cards and Built-In Adapters

- ❑ Common expansion cards (adapters) include display adapters, network interface cards (NICs), sound cards, and cards that add various types of ports, such as eSATA or Thunderbolt. Most expansion cards are PCIe.
- ❑ The need for expansion cards has diminished as PC motherboards contain more functions.

Storage Devices and Interfaces

- ❑ SATA is the standard interface for internal mass storage. eSATA, USB, and Thunderbolt are all common interfaces for external storage devices.
- ❑ A mass storage device holds large amounts of information, even when the power is off.
- ❑ Mass storage devices come in three general categories: magnetic, optical, and solid-state storage.
- ❑ Hard disk drives and tape drives are examples of magnetic mass storage devices that store digital data on magnetized media.
- ❑ HDDs have different spindle rotation speeds; faster is better. Common speeds range from 5400 to 15,000 rpm.
- ❑ HDDs come in form factors of 2.5" or 3.5" for laptops or desktops, respectively. Those measurements refer to the sizes of the platters inside.
- ❑ Optical drives include CD, DVD, and Blu-ray drives, each of which has a variety of capacities and speeds.
- ❑ Solid-state storage, aka solid-state drives (SSDs), has no moving parts and uses large-capacity, nonvolatile memory, commonly called flash memory.
- ❑ M.2 is a common form factor for SSDs in both desktops and laptops today, replacing the older mSATA form factor.
- ❑ Hot-swappable drives can be connected or disconnected without shutting down the system. Some hard drive systems are hot-swappable, depending, in large part, on the interface.
- ❑ Hard drives with USB, SATA, or eSATA interfaces are usually hot-swappable, as is nearly any USB device.
- ❑ RAID, which stands for redundant array of independent (or inexpensive) disks, is a group of schemes designed to provide either better performance or improved data reliability through redundancy.
- ❑ RAID 0 defines a striped set without parity. It gives improved drive read and write speeds.
- ❑ RAID 1, also called mirroring, provides fault tolerance because all the data is written identically to the two drives in the mirrored set.
- ❑ RAID 5, also called striping with distributed parity or striping with interleaved parity, requires at least three physical drives.
- ❑ RAID 10 is a stripe of mirrors, requiring a minimum of four identical disks, paired into two mirrored sets, with data written in a stripe across the two mirrored sets.

SELF TEST

The following questions will help you measure your understanding of the material presented in this chapter. Read all of the choices carefully because there might be more than one correct answer. Choose all correct answers for each question.

Memory

1. This type of memory is volatile, is used as temporary workspace by the CPU, and loses its contents every time a computer is powered down.

A. ROM
B. DRAM
C. CMOS
D. Solid state

2. Cache memory uses which type of RAM chip because of its speed?

A. DRAM
B. VRAM
C. DIMM
D. SRAM

3. This type of SDRAM doubled the speed at which standard SDRAM processed data by accessing the module twice per clock cycle.

A. Dual-channel
B. Multichannel
C. Double-sided
D. DDR1

4. This type of RAM module uses a 240-pin DIMM socket.

A. DDR5 SDRAM
B. DDR4 SDRAM
C. DDR3 SDRAM
D. EEPROM

5. This specialized type of DDR3 runs at 1.35V, which decreases the electricity used.
   A. DDR4
   B. Dual-channel
   C. DDR3L
   D. Double-sided
6. What is ECC RAM's advantage over non-ECC RAM?
   A. Error correction
   B. Higher capacity
   C. Faster speed
   D. Less expensive
7. This chip manages the main memory on a motherboard.
   A. CMOS
   B. DRAM
   C. MCC
   D. DDR3

Expansion Cards and Built-In Adapters

8. Which of the following is *not* a technology for connecting external devices?
   A. Thunderbolt
   B. USB
   C. HDMI
   D. PCI
9. Name a common communications adapter card used to connect PCs to a LAN.
   A. NIC
   B. Modem
   C. USB
   D. Serial
10. What type of adapter would you install in order to connect an external hard drive via a fast interface?
    A. Network adapter
    B. Modem
    C. eSATA adapter
    D. Video adapter

Storage Devices and Interfaces

11. This is the component in a magnetic hard drive that reads and writes data.
  A. Spindle
  B. Head
  C. Platter
  D. Cable

12. Suppose you have an old EIDE hard drive you need to connect to a desktop PC to see what's on it. Which interface would you use?
  A. RS-232
  B. eSATA
  C. SATA
  D. PATA

13. Which of the following is an example of a magnetic mass storage device?
  A. SSD
  B. DVD drive
  C. HDD
  D. Flash drive

14. Name two common interfaces for external hard drives.
  A. PATA and SATA
  B. Serial and parallel
  C. USB and eSATA
  D. Modems and hubs

15. Which of these is *not* a connection for attaching storage to a PC?
  A. HDMI
  B. M.2
  C. SATA
  D. USB

16. Which type of RAID provides mirroring for fault tolerance but not striping for performance?
  A. RAID 5
  B. RAID 0
  C. RAID 1
  D. RAID 2

17. Which version of SATA allows a cable length of 2 meters and transfers data at up to 2.4 Gbps?
  A. SATA1
  B. SATA2
  C. SATA3
  D. eSATA

18. This feature indicates that a drive can be connected or disconnected without shutting down the system.
   A. External
   B. RAID
   C. USB
   D. Hot-swappable

19. How many drives are required to implement RAID 0?
   A. 1
   B. 2
   C. 3
   D. 4

20. This is a group of standards defining several schemes for using multiple identical hard drives, working together in an array with the goal of achieving either better performance or redundancy.
   A. RAID
   B. eSATA
   C. USB
   D. Serial

SELF TEST ANSWERS

Memory

1. ☑ **B.** Dynamic RAM (DRAM) is the type of volatile memory used by the CPU as workspace.
☒ **A** is incorrect because this type of memory is not volatile; its contents are not lost every time the PC is powered off. **C** is incorrect because it is special battery-powered support memory that holds basic system configuration information used by the computer as it powers up. **D** is incorrect because this is a type of storage device that is nonvolatile and is not used by the processor in the manner described.

2. ☑ **D.** SRAM is the type of RAM used for cache memory because of its speed.
☒ **A** is incorrect because this is slower than SRAM. **B** is incorrect because although it is fast, this type of RAM is used on video adapters. **C** is incorrect, as it is a RAM connector/slot type, not a type of RAM chip.

3. ☑ **D.** DDR1 SDRAM doubled the speed at which standard SDRAM processed data by accessing the module twice per clock cycle.
☒ **A** and **B** are incorrect because both are used to describe an architecture that speeds up memory access by having the MCC access each module on a different channel. **C** is incorrect because it describes a RAM module with chips populating both sides.

4. ☑ **C.** DDR3 SDRAM is the type of RAM module that uses a 240-pin DIMM socket.
☒ **A** is incorrect because it uses a 288-pin DIMM socket, not a 240-pin DIMM socket. **B** is incorrect because it uses a 288-pin socket, not a 240-pin socket. **D** is incorrect because it is ROM, not RAM.

5. ☑ **C.** DDR3L is correct, as this type of DDR3 is low-voltage.
☒ **A** is incorrect because DDR4 is not a type of DDR3 RAM. **B** is incorrect because dual-channel is a function of the motherboard, not of the RAM. **D** is incorrect because being single-sided or double-sided has no effect on voltage.

6. ☑ **A.** ECC stands for error-correcting code; this type of memory provides error correction.
☒ **B** is incorrect because ECC does not determine the RAM's capacity. **C** is incorrect because ECC is not faster than other RAM. **D** is incorrect because ECC memory is not less expensive.

7. ☑ **C.** MCC, or memory controller chip, controls the main memory on a motherboard.
☒ **A** is incorrect because the CMOS chip is a special battery-supported chip that retains the system settings. **B** is incorrect because DRAM is a type of RAM used for the main memory itself; it is not a memory controller. **D** is incorrect because DDR3 is a type of SDRAM, not a controller chip.

Expansion Cards and Built-In Adapters

8. ☑ **D.** PCI is an internal motherboard slot, not an external connection technology.
☒ **A, B,** and **C** are incorrect because they are external connection technologies.

9. ☑ **A.** A network interface card (NIC) is a common communications adapter card used to connect PCs to a LAN or to take advantage of a DSL or cable modem Internet connection.
☒ **B** is incorrect because although it is a communications adapter card, it is used for a dial-up connection, not for a LAN connection. **C** is incorrect because it is an I/O interface, not a communications adapter. **D** is incorrect because it is an I/O interface, not a communications adapter, although some external modems can connect to a serial port.

10. ☑ **C.** An eSATA card adds external SATA support to a PC for fast hard drive connectivity externally.
☒ **A** is incorrect because this type of adapter is used for network communications. **B** is incorrect because it is used for a dial-up connection. **D** is incorrect because it is used to drive a display device.

Storage Devices and Interfaces

11. ☑ **B.** The head is the component in a hard drive system that reads and writes data. There is one head for each platter side.
☒ **A** is incorrect because this rotating pole holds the platters in a hard drive. **C** is incorrect because this component holds the data. **D** is incorrect because a cable connects a device to a computer but does not read data from a hard drive.

12. ☑ **D.** An old EIDE hard drive is likely to require a PATA interface.
☒ **A** is incorrect because an RS-232 port is a legacy serial port and does not support hard drives. **B** is incorrect because eSATA is a modern interface for external hard drives and would not work with an old EIDE drive. **C** is incorrect because SATA is a modern interface for internal hard drives and would not work with an old EIDE drive.

13. ☑ **C.** A hard disk drive (HDD) is a magnetic storage device.
☒ **A** and **D** are incorrect because both are types of solid-state storage, not magnetic. **B** is incorrect because it provides optical storage.

14. ☑ **C.** USB and eSATA are two common interfaces for external hard drives.
☒ **A** is incorrect because these are interfaces for internal hard drives, not for external hard drives. **B** is incorrect because these are not interfaces for external hard drives. **D** is incorrect because these are not common interfaces for external hard drives.

15. ☑ **A.** HDMI is a video and sound interface.
☒ **B, C,** and **D** are incorrect because they are all common storage interfaces.

16. ☑ **C.** RAID 1 provides mirroring but not striping.
☒ **A** is incorrect because RAID 5 provides both mirroring and striping. **B** is incorrect because RAID 0 provides striping but not mirroring. **D** is incorrect because there is no such thing as RAID 2.

17. ☑ **D.** External SATA (eSATA) allows for a 2-meter cable length and 2.4-Gbps throughput.
☒ **A, B,** and **C** are incorrect because they all have a maximum cable length of 1 meter.

18. ☑ **D.** Hot-swappable is a feature that indicates that a drive can be connected or disconnected without shutting down the system.
☒ **A** is incorrect because while some external drives are also hot-swappable, the term "external" itself does not indicate that a drive has this feature. **B** is incorrect because although drives that are part of a RAID array may be hot-swappable, the term "RAID" itself does not indicate that a drive has this feature. **C** is incorrect because, although some hot-swappable drives use the USB interface, the term "USB" itself does not indicate that a drive has this feature.

19. ☑ **B.** RAID 0 requires 2 drives.
☒ **A, C,** and **D** are incorrect because those are not the required number of drives for RAID 0.

20. ☑ **A.** RAID is the acronym for redundant array of independent (or inexpensive) disks, a group of schemes designed to provide either better performance or improved data reliability through redundancy.
☒ **B** is incorrect because this is a standard for an external version of the serial ATA interface. **C** is incorrect because this is the Universal Serial Bus standard. **D** is incorrect because this is another interface, not a standard for disk arrays.

Chapter 10

Power Supplies, Display Devices, and Peripherals

CERTIFICATION OBJECTIVES

- ■ **1101: 1.2** Compare and contrast the display components of mobile devices
- ■ **1101: 3.1** Explain basic cable types and their connectors, features, and purposes
- ■ **1101: 3.5** Given a scenario, install or replace the appropriate power supply
- ✓ Two-Minute Drill
- **Q&A** Self Test

This chapter explores power supplies and display devices (both display adapters and displays), identifying the connector types and cables associated with these computer components.

CERTIFICATION OBJECTIVES

- ***1101: 3.1*** *Explain basic cable types and their connectors, features, and purposes*
- ***1101: 3.5*** *Given a scenario, install or replace the appropriate power supply*

This section describes power supply types and characteristics from CompTIA A+ 1101 exam Objective 3.5. You will learn about voltage, wattage, capacity, power supply fans, and form factors. Also included are descriptions of power cables and connectors. This section prepares you to select an appropriate power supply, remove an older power supply, and install a new one.

Power Supplies

A *power supply*, or *power supply unit (PSU)*, is the device that provides power for all other components on the motherboard and is internal to the PC case. Every PC has an easily identified power supply; it is typically located inside the computer case at the back, and parts of it are visible from the outside when looking at the back of the PC. On a desktop computer (PC or Mac), you will see the three-prong power socket. Most power supplies also have a label and sometimes a tiny switch to change voltages when used in different parts of the world.

Figure 10-1 shows the interior of a PC with a power supply on the upper left. Notice the bundle of cables coming out of the power supply. These cables supply power to the motherboard and all other internal components. Each component must receive the appropriate type and amount of power it requires, and the power supply itself has its own requirements. Therefore, you should understand some basic electrical terminology and apply it to the power supply's functions.

Electrical Terminology

Electricity is the flow of electrons (*current*) through a conductor, such as copper wire, and we use it in two forms: *direct current (DC)* and *alternating current (AC)*. In DC, the type of electrical current generated by a battery, the flow of negative electrons is in one direction around the closed loop of an electrical circuit. In AC, the flow of electrons around the electrical circuit reverses periodically and has alternating positive and negative values. AC is the kind of electricity that comes from a wall outlet.

A *volt (V)* is the unit of measurement of the pressure of electrons on a wire, or the electromotive force. A *watt (W)* is a unit of measurement of actual delivered power. An *ampere* (*A* or *amp*) is a unit of measurement for electrical current, or rate of flow of electrons, through a wire. When you know the wattage and amps needed or used, you calculate volts using the

FIGURE 10-1 The power supply, shown in the upper left, is usually located in the back of the computer case, with a three-prong power socket visible on the exterior of the PC.

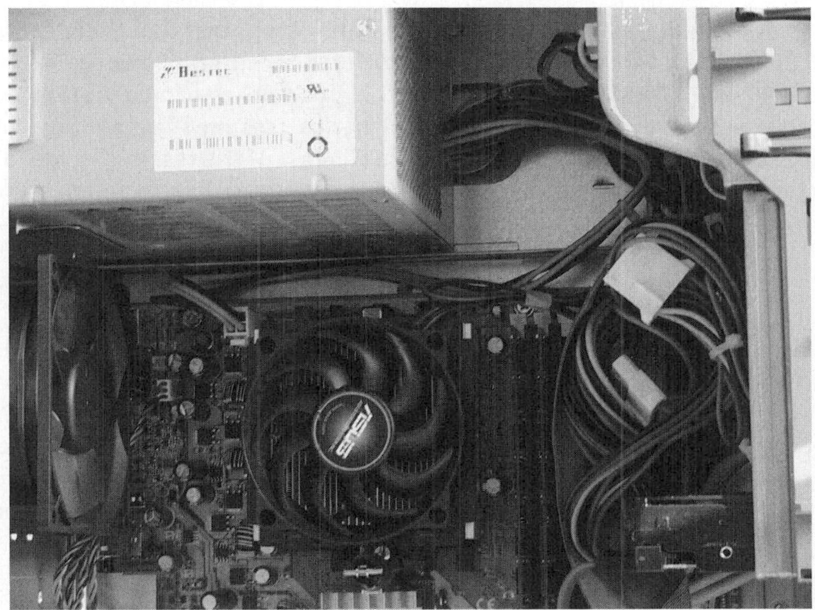

formula volts = watts / amps. When you know the voltage and amps, you can calculate wattage used or required with the formula watts = volts × amps. And if you need to know the amps but only know the wattage and voltage, use the formula amps = watts / volts. All these calculations are versions of Ohm's Law, which represents the fundamental relationship among current, voltage, and resistance.

Voltage

The power supply is responsible for converting the AC voltage from wall outlets into the DC voltage that the computer requires: ±12 VDC, ±5 VDC, or ±3.3 VDC (volts DC). The PC power supply accomplishes this task through a series of switching transistors, which gives rise to the term *switching-mode power supply.*

A device such as a laser printer that requires high voltage has its own *high-voltage power supply (HVPS).*

Typical North American wall outlets provide about 115 volts AC (VAC) at a frequency of 60 Hertz (Hz—cycles per second), which is also expressed as ~115 VAC at 60 Hz. The *frequency* is the number of times per second that alternating current reverses direction. Elsewhere in the world, standard power is 220 to 240 VAC at 50 Hz.

exam watch

CompTIA A+ 1101 exam Objective 3.5 specifically lists these as *Input 110-120 VAC vs. 220-240 VAC*. You may see voltages described elsewhere as specific numbers, like 115 or 230, but it refers to the same power system; the range simply recognizes that there are allowable differences among power grids. The main thing you need to know here is that North America uses the lower voltage and Europe (and most of the rest of the world) uses the higher voltage.

Power supplies manufactured for sale throughout the world are *dual voltage*, providing either the U.S. standard or the international standard. Dual-voltage options in power supplies come in two categories: power supplies that automatically switch and those that must be manually switched. An *auto-switching power supply* can detect the incoming voltage and switch to accept either North American or European power input, but a *fixed-input* power supply will have a switch on the back for selecting the correct input voltage setting. Figure 10-2 shows the back of a power supply with the *voltage selector switch* for selecting 115 VAC or 240 VAC. It is the tiny slide switch positioned below the power connector.

exam watch

Make sure you are familiar with the voltages required by computer components: 3.3V, 5V, and 12V. When you see these small voltages, you can assume they are DC current (VDC). When you see large voltages such as 115 or 230, you can assume they are AC current (VAC).

FIGURE 10-2 The back of a power supply, with the power connector socket and voltage selector switch below it

Wattage and Size

How big a power supply do you need? We are not talking about physical size, but the capacity or wattage a power supply can handle. A PC needs a power supply with a capacity that exceeds the total watts required by all the internal components, such as the motherboard, memory, drives, and various adapters. Figure 10-3 shows a label on a 700-watt power supply (as listed on the Total Power line). This is a rather basic power supply; a full-size desktop computer fully loaded with power-hungry components might have an 800- to 1500-watt power supply.

The total power is not the only factor to consider, however. How that power is allocated among multiple rails also matters. A *rail*, in power supply terms, is a pathway that delivers a specific voltage of power to a specific connection. Modern power supplies are designed for systems that need a lot of 12V power, far more than just the modest amount provided on the P1 connector (the big 24-pin connector to the motherboard). They provide one or more extra 12V connectors, as you learned in Chapter 8. Notice in Figure 10-3 that in the DC Output row four +12V rails are listed, each one with 18 amps allocated to it. The 12V Output Distribution List in the lower-left corner of the label explains how each of those rails is allocated.

Make sure you understand the wattage rating on a power supply and can read the power supply's label to determine its output capability. You should then be able to evaluate whether that power supply would be adequate in a particular system.

FIGURE 10-3

The maximum wattage supported by a power supply appears on the Total Power line.

Model No
XS700
AC Input
110-240 Vac ~ 10-5A 50 - 60Hz
DC Output
+3.3V
+5V
+12V1
+12V2
+12V3
+12V4
-12V
+5Vsb
Max Output Current
36A
30A
18A
18A
18A
18A
0.5A
3.0A
Max. Combined Power
155W
680W
20W
Total Power
700W
Total output current for this subject power supply is 70A
Maximum combined current for the 12V outputs shall be 50A
12V Output Distribution List
Output Voltage
Device
12V1
CPU1
12V2
PCI-E2/CPU2
12V3
M/B accessory
12V4
PCI-E1
WARNING! HAZARDOUS AREA
SAFETY INSTRUCTIONS:
DO NOT REMOVE THE COVER
NO SERVICEABLE COMPONENTS INSIDE.
REFER SERVICING TO QUALIFIED SERVICE PERSONNEL.
Tested To Comply With FCC Standards
FOR HOME OR OFFICE USE
CAUTION! HAZARDOUS AREA
SAFETY INSTRUCTIONS:
DO NOT REMOVE THE COVER
NO SERVICEABLE COMPONENTS INSIDE.
REFER SERVICING TO QUALIFIED SERVICE PERSONNEL.
CB
CE
224636
E243823

EXERCISE 10-1

Checking Out the Wattage on PCs and Other Devices

In this exercise you will determine the wattage and voltages for power supplies.

1. Look at the back of a desktop PC and find the power supply label. Record the wattage information. If wattage is not shown but the volts and amps are, multiply those two numbers to calculate the wattage.
2. Make a note of the voltages and watts for different rails, if that information is provided on the label.
3. Do the same on computer peripherals that are available to you, such as displays, printers, and scanners.
4. Similarly, check out the wattage on noncomputer devices in the classroom or at home.

Fans

Another function of a power supply is to dissipate the heat that it and other PC components generate. Heat buildup can cause computer components (including the power supply) to fail. Therefore, power supplies have a built-in exhaust fan that draws air through the computer case and cools the components inside. For more information on cooling, flip back and review the "Cooling Mechanisms" section in Chapter 8.

AC Adapters

Another form of power supply is an AC adapter used with portable computers and external peripherals. An *AC adapter* converts AC power to the voltage needed for a device. Like the power supply in a desktop PC, it converts AC power to DC power. Figure 10-4 shows an AC

FIGURE 10-4

An AC adapter for a laptop

adapter for a laptop with a coaxial connector on the right. On the far left is the cable that connects the adapter to a wall socket via a grounded plug. Notice the smaller three-prong plug that connects to the matching socket on the AC adapter. Not all of them are three-prong; some are two.

If you must replace an external power adapter, simply unplug it and attach a new one that matches the specifications and plug configuration of the adapter it is replacing.

Since AC adapters have different output voltages, only use an AC adapter with output voltage that exactly matches the input voltage for the laptop. Previously, laptop power supplies were *fixed-input power supplies* set to accept only one input power voltage. Now, many laptop AC adapters act as auto-switching power supplies, detecting the incoming voltage and switching to accept either 115 or 230 VAC. The part of the cord that plugs into the wall can be switched out depending on the country you are in.

Power Supply Form Factors and Connectors

When building a new computer, a power supply may come with the computer case, or you can purchase one separately, but you need to consider both wattage and form factor. Like motherboards and cases, computer power supplies come in a variety of form factors to match both the motherboard and case.

The most common power supply form factor for desktop PCs is referred to as the *ATX power supply,* used in most case desktop sizes, except the smallest low-profile cases and the largest, jumbo-sized full-tower cases. A smaller version of the ATX power supply is the *micro-ATX power supply,* which works in many of the smaller cases with the micro-ATX and similar motherboard form factors. There are many other form factors that are variations on the ATX PSU form factor. Whenever you need to match a power supply with a computer, start with the motherboard manual, and pay close attention to all the features required by the motherboard. Then consider the case and what will fit in it. In fact, when putting together a custom computer, a PSU will often come with the case.

In response to the demands of PC-based servers and gamers, power supply manufacturers have added proprietary features beyond those in any standards. You can find power supplies that offer special support for the newest Intel and AMD CPU requirements and greater efficiency, which saves on power usage and reduces heat output.

The form factor of the power supply determines the motherboard it works with and the type of connector used to supply power to the motherboard. Most motherboards use 24-pin connectors, called *P1 power connectors.* (Some are 20-pin in older systems.)

exam watch

A+ 1101 exam Objective 3.5 mentions 20-pin to 24-pin motherboard adapters. These are just what they sound like: adapters that enable you to use a power supply with a 20-pin P1 connector on a motherboard that requires a 24-pin P1, and vice versa. Some power supplies have a versatile type of P1 connector that enables you to snap off four of the connector pins on one end to convert the P1 to 20-pin.

The power supply will likely also offer some additional connectors to the motherboard. On most modern systems, a separate cable will connect to the motherboard with a 4-, 6-, or 8-pin connector. Under the *ATX 12V* standard, a 4-pin *P4 connector,* also called a *P4 12V connector,* supplies 12 volts in addition to that provided by the P1 connector or, based on the *ATX 12V 2.0* standard, a 24-pin main connector and a 4-pin secondary connector. Some motherboards require EPS12V connectors, which include a 24-pin main connector, an 8-pin secondary connector, and an optional 4-pin tertiary connector.

The *PCI Express (PCIe) power connector* comes in 6-pin or 8-pin configurations. A PCIe power connector attaches to a connector on a motherboard (if available) or to a connector on a specialized expansion card.

Some high-end non-ATX motherboards used in network servers and high-end workstations include a 4-pin or 8-pin connector to provide additional power to the CPU, which also derives power through its own motherboard socket.

exam watch

You don't need to know the details of all those smaller motherboard connectors for the exams, but you should understand that most modern motherboards require these extra power connectors in addition to the P1 connector, and you should be able to match up the connectors from the power supply to appropriate connectors on the motherboard.

Modern desktops and laptops include a power feature called *soft power,* which allows the computer to be turned on and off via software. A computer with soft power enabled has a pair of small wires leading from the physical power button on the case to the motherboard. Pressing the button shorts the connection between the two wires, sending an electrical signal to the motherboard to turn on. Most operating systems include controls for configuring soft power settings. In Windows, it's Power Options (via the Control Panel or the Settings app).

For safety's sake, you should always consider soft power as being on, because when you have enabled soft power, turning the power switch off means that although the computer appears to be off, the power supply is still supplying ±5 volts to the motherboard. This means you can never trust the power button to turn the computer completely off. Some PCs come equipped with two power switches. One is in the front, and you can consider it the soft on/off switch. The other is on the power supply itself, and this is the hardware on/off switch. Even so, the safest thing to do is to unplug the power cable from the wall outlet to ensure no power is coming to the motherboard before you start working inside a PC. If you're working on a PC with a battery, such as a laptop, you should also remove the battery (if it's removable) before servicing the inside of the unit.

Connecting Power to Peripherals

In addition to providing power to the motherboard, power supplies have connectors for providing power to internally installed peripherals—mainly various drives, but sometimes to expansion cards. Power supplies usually have cables (that is, small bundles of wires all connected to the same connector) that are permanently connected to the PSU, and they may have additional ports to which you can connect additional cables, allowing for expansion. (A power supply that lets you connect cables to it is called a *modular power supply*.) The cable connections on the peripheral end vary based on the type of device and power requirements.

Exam Watch ***Modular power supply*** **is a key term in 1101 exam Objective 3.5, and** ***Molex*** **is one of the connectors mentioned in 1101 exam Objective 3.1.**

Two traditional peripheral connectors are the 4-pin *Molex connector*, measuring about 7/8" wide, and the much smaller 4-pin *miniconnector* (often shortened as *mini*). The Molex and miniconnector each provide 5 and 12 volts to peripherals. Molex connectors traditionally connected to most parallel ATA (PATA) internal devices, while the miniconnector mainly connected to floppy drives and is now long-obsolete; most modern power supplies do not include it anymore. Figure 10-5 shows a mini and a Molex. Both are usually white.

On modern systems, most of the drives you will want to connect require a serial ATA (SATA) connector from the power supply, as shown in Figure 10-6. Look for a SATA power cable coming off the power supply with a 15-pin connector, usually black, for connecting to most optical or hard drives.

FIGURE 10-5 A miniconnector (left) and Molex connector (right) (Photo: https://commons.wikimedia.org/wiki/File:Molex1.jpg [Creative Commons license])

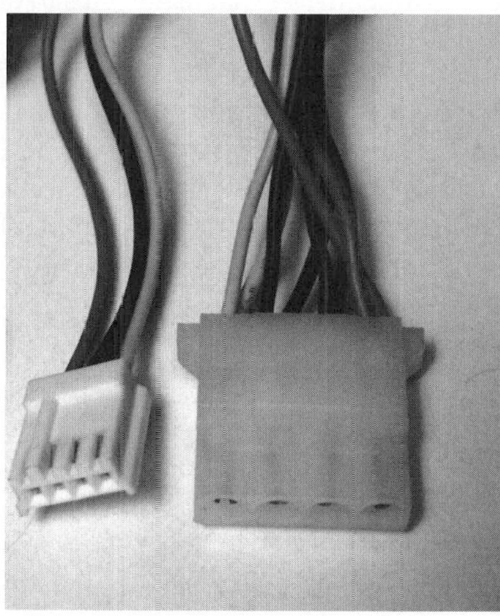

FIGURE 10-6 A SATA power connector to a drive (Photo: https://commons.wikimedia.org/wiki/File:SATA_Power_Cable_with_3.3_V.jpg [Creative Commons license])

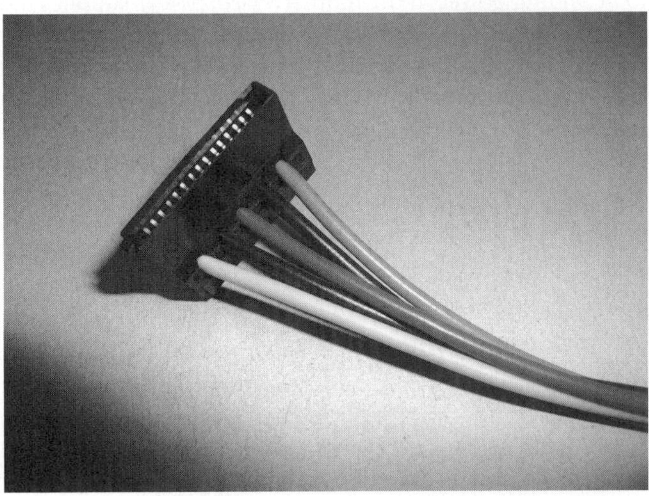

If an older power supply does not have this cable, use a Molex-to-SATA power connector adapter to connect the SATA power cable to a Molex connector from the power supply.

Small SATA storage devices have a tiny 15-pin micro SATA power connector. The pins in a SATA power connector supply different voltages for SATA devices, including 3.3V (orange), 5V (red), and 12V (yellow), and they support hot-swapping SATA devices. There is also a slimline version (found on portable computers) that has only 6 pins and delivers only 5V power, and a micro version used with 1.8" drives that uses 9 pins to deliver 3.3V and 5V power.

Some SATA connectors do not have the orange wire (they have only four wires) and do not supply 3.3V power. In addition, if you use an adapter to convert a Molex connector to a SATA one, you won't get the 3.3V rail. That's not a problem for most magnetic and optical drives, as they don't use the 3.3V power anyway. However, some solid-state drives and other specialty storage devices do require it, so check the power supply requirements for the drive if in doubt.

Energy Efficiency

Although not directly a power supply issue, energy efficiency in all PC components has become a very important feature and affects the selection of a power supply. We seem to need bigger and bigger power supplies to accommodate the increasing number and types of components we include in our PCs: more memory, larger hard drives, more powerful display adapters, and so on. The good news is that the power requirements have not grown proportionally with the performance improvements of these components, which are more energy efficient and have features that reduce their power consumption during idle times. Learn more about managing these energy-saving features in laptops in Chapter 14.

Removing a Power Supply/Installing a Power Supply

Whether you are purchasing a power supply for a new system or replacing an old one, you have the same set of concerns when selecting, installing, or removing a power supply. Power supplies in existing computers do fail from time to time, and you can replace them using the procedure outlined in Exercise 10-2, which provides basic steps for removing an old power supply and replacing a new one.

EXERCISE 10-2

Replacing a Power Supply

Do this exercise on a desktop PC.

1. Turn off the power and remove the power connector from the wall socket. Use appropriate electrostatic discharge (ESD) protective measures.
2. Disconnect the power connector(s) from the motherboard, grasping the plastic connectors, not the wires.
3. Disconnect the power connectors from all other components, including hard drives and optical drives.
4. Using an appropriately sized screwdriver, remove the screws that hold the power supply to the PC case. Do not remove the screws holding the power supply case together!
5. Slide or lift the power supply away from the computer.
6. Reverse these steps to install a new power supply.

Recall that power supplies can still hold a charge when turned off, especially if you use only the soft power switch. Before removing any power supply, even a failed one, be sure to unplug it from the wall outlet. To avoid the danger of electric shock, do not wear an antistatic wristband while working with power supplies.

You can test AC outlets with a receptacle tester, or even a multimeter. If using a multimeter, insert the black probe in the grounding hole (the round one) and the red probe in one of the other holes. Don't wear an antistatic wrist strap while doing this, and never insert the black probe anywhere in a power outlet except in the grounding hole.

You can test PC power supplies with a PSU tester, which tests 3.3V, 5V, and 12V. But remember to never open a PSU. It's a field-replaceable unit (FRU).

CERTIFICATION OBJECTIVES

- ***1101: 1.2*** *Compare and contrast the display components of mobile devices*
- ***1101: 3.1*** *Explain basic cable types and their connectors, features, and purposes*

This section explains the various types of display adapters and displays. It includes identifying and installing mobile device display components per CompTIA A+ 1101 exam Objective 1.2, as well as video cables per CompTIA A+ 1101 exam Objective 3.1.

Display Adapters and Displays

The quality of the image you see on a PC display depends on both the capabilities and configuration of the two most important video components: the display adapter and the display device (also called a monitor, when it is a separate unit). The technologies used in display adapters and displays have become more complex as we have transitioned from the old analog technologies to the digital technologies in use today.

Display Adapters

The display adapter controls the output from the PC to the display device. Although the display adapter contains all the logic and does most of the work, the quality of the resulting image depends on the modes supported by both the adapter and the display. If the adapter is capable of higher-quality output than the display, the display limits the result—and vice versa. In this section, we will explore video interface modes, screen resolution and color depth, the computer interfaces used by display adapters, and the connectors used to connect a display to the display adapter.

exam watch **Be able to identify on sight the various types of connectors and the video mode or technology associated with them: HDMI, DisplayPort, DVI, and VGA.**

Computer Interfaces

When purchasing a display adapter card, pay attention to the interface between the display adapter and the computer so that you select one you can install into your PC. The video cable connector types covered in the CompTIA A+ 220-1101 exam are VGA, HDMI, DisplayPort, and DVI.

VGA *Video Graphics Array (VGA)* is a display adapter standard introduced with the IBM PS/2 computers in the late 1980s. The VGA standard originally also specified a certain maximum display resolution (640 × 480 pixels with 16 colors), which is often referred to as *VGA mode*. However, connecting to a monitor via a VGA cable does not mean you are limited to the original VGA mode resolution and color depth; the connector is just a conduit for whatever resolutions and color depths the monitor and the display adapter can jointly support.

The VGA connector is more properly called DE-15 (or HD15 or VGA). It was the primary interface used on CRT monitors (now obsolete), which were analog only. VGA connectors are also found on some flat-panel LCD displays that have an analog input option.

VGA uses a cable that has a male DE-15 connector (a *VGA connector*) on each end, and the cable is often referred to as a *VGA cable*. It has three rows of five pins each, slightly staggered. The connector on both ends of the VGA monitor cable are male, whereas the connectors on the display adapter and the monitor are both female. Figure 10-7 shows a display adapter with a VGA connector on the right side. The other two connectors shown here are DVI-I Dual Link (left) and S-Video (center). Those latter two are rarely seen anymore, but DVI still remains as an exam objective.

FIGURE 10-7

DVI-I Dual Link, S-Video, and DE-15 connectors on a display adapter card

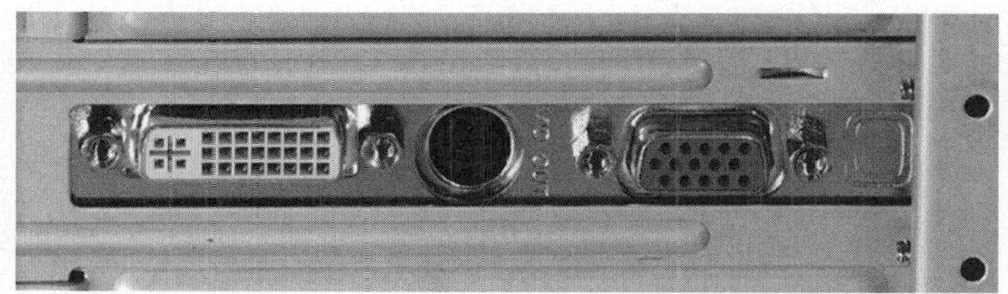

For nearly two decades, VGA was the only style of monitor cable/connection available, so there are still plenty of them in the field everywhere old computers are still in service.

While many sources incorrectly call a VGA connector DB-15, technically, a DB-15 connector has 15 pins in two rows of 7 and 8 and is not used for video. The correct terminology for the three-row 15-pin VGA connector is DE-15, HD-15, or VGA.

Perhaps you are wondering how a liquid crystal display (LCD) monitor, which is by nature a digital display, can accept input from an analog VGA connector. Although display adapters actually store information digitally in video random access memory (RAM), they have traditionally had to convert the digital signal to analog for analog monitors such as cathode ray tubes (CRTs). Therefore, LCD displays that connect to a PC via the DE-15 connector must include the ability to accept an analog signal and reconvert it back to digital for display. Such a monitor is called an *analog LCD display* (in spite of its digital nature).

Many LCD monitors have multiple connectors, so you have your choice of interfaces to use. If you have a choice between VGA, DVI, and HDMI, go with HDMI if possible, with DVI being the second choice. However, be aware that not all DVI is all-digital, as you'll learn in the upcoming "DVI" section. HDMI and DisplayPort, both covered following the "DVI" section, are all-digital by definition.

DVI Digital Video Interface (DVI) was the successor to VGA, and for several years was very popular. It is less popular now because of the widespread adoption of HDMI as a computer interface, but it is still found in the field.

DVI may be one term, but there are five variations of it, each with its own pin arrangement on the connectors and each transmitting a different kind of signal. All standard DVI type connectors measure 1" by 3/8" with a variety of pin configurations, including one or two grids of pins and a flat blade off to the side of the pin grid area.

You should be able to distinguish the five variations by looking at a connector. Figure 10-8 provides the layouts.

The digital mode of DVI, *DVI-D,* is partially compatible with HDMI (described in the next section). A DVI-D connector is digital only and comes in two varieties called Single Link and Dual Link. The DVI-D Single Link connector has two 3 × 3 grids of nine pins each, whereas the DVI-D Dual Link has a single 24-pin 3 × 8 grid. Dual Link doubles the bandwidth in the cable to support higher-resolution video modes.

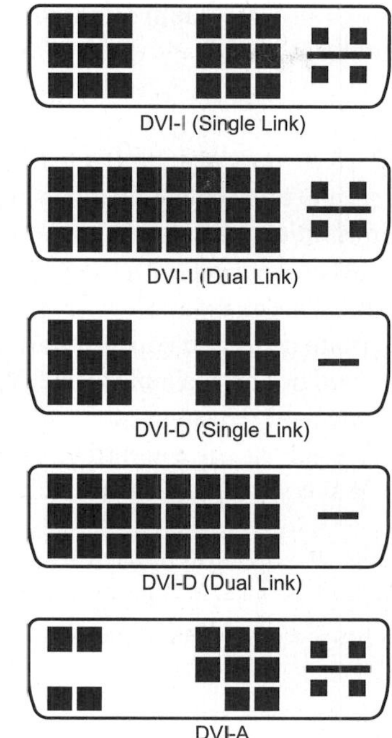

FIGURE 10-8 DVI connector pin layouts for DVI-I, DVI-D, and DVI-A

A *DVI-A* connector supports only analog signals, with four pins positioned around the blade to the side of the main pin grid area. It has two other groupings of pins: the first contains eight pins in a 3 × 3 grid (the ninth position is empty); the second group contains two sets of two pins with space between them.

DVI-I, or DVI-Integrated, supports both DVI-D and DVI-A signals and can control both digital and analog displays.

Be sure you recognize the pin compatibility issues with the various types of DVI connectors.

When connecting using any interface, you must match this type of display with an adapter card with the appropriate connector. However, in the case of DVI, you also need to match the pins, because several different configurations of DVI connectors look alike until you compare them closely.

DVI-I is interchangeable, supporting either analog or digital signals. It also comes in Single Link and Dual Link versions. Both versions resemble their DVI-D counterparts, with the addition of the four pins around the blade to support analog mode.

HDMI *High-Definition Multimedia Interface (HDMI)* is a relatively recent interface standard for use with computers, but it has been widely in use for quite a while with televisions and home theater equipment. It combines audio and video signals into an uncompressed signal and has a bandwidth of up to 10.2 Gbps. HDMI is integrated into many PCs, replacing DVI and VGA, and many home theater PCs (HTPCs) use this interface. Further, it supports a *digital rights management (DRM)* feature called *High-Bandwidth Digital Content Protection (HDCP)* to prevent illegal copying of Blu-ray discs. HDMI has added support for 4k and 8k video and dynamic HDR formats, as well as high-speed Ethernet communications.

HDMI is backward compatible with the DVI standard as implemented in PC display adapters and displays. Therefore, a DVI display adapter can control an HDMI monitor, provided an appropriate cable and converter are used. The audio and remote control features of HDMI, however, will not be available via a DVI display adapter, nor will 4k/8k resolution and Ethernet. One specially designed cable with an HDMI connector is all you need now between a compatible video device and the TV. Previously, several cables were required.

Five types of HDMI connectors are available:

- **Type A** The original and most widely used; this is the full-size HDMI connector used on most PCs, TVs, and gaming consoles.
- **Type B** This is a dual-link version developed for high-resolution displays; it was never used.
- **Type C** Also known as Mini HDMI, these connectors support the same features as the full-size Type A connectors. Some smaller devices such as tablets and digital cameras use this.
- **Type D** Also known as Micro HDMI, this is even smaller than the Mini HDMI; it is used on small mobile devices such as smartphones.
- **Type E** An automotive connection system for use with video systems installed in cars. The connector has a special locking mechanism to prevent it from working loose.

Figure 10-9 shows an HDMI socket for a Type A connector, and Figure 10-10 shows Type C Mini-HDMI connectors on a cable.

DisplayPort *DisplayPort,* a digital display interface standard developed by VESA, is the newest of the standards discussed here. Like HDMI, it supports both video and audio signals and contains HDCP copy protection. It is unique in that it is royalty-free to manufacturers and has some important proponents, such as Apple, Hewlett-Packard, AMD, Intel, and Dell. At first, industry experts observed that we did not need this standard after the wide

FIGURE 10-9

A Type A HDMI socket on a computer

FIGURE 10-10 Two Type C Mini-HDMI connectors on a cable

acceptance of HDMI, but that changed after DisplayPort received a huge boost in the fall of 2008 when Apple introduced new MacBooks with DisplayPort replacing DVI. DisplayPort 2.0, the latest version, supports a high bandwidth (77.37 Gbps) and up to 16k resolution (15360 × 8640) at 60 Hz. It also supports multiple monitors at high resolutions and frame rates. DisplayPort also includes copy protection for DVDs in the form of DisplayPort Content Protection (DPCP).

At less than 1/4" thick, a DisplayPort cable is slimmer than those of its predecessor, and the connectors are much smaller and do not require thumbscrews like those on DVI and VGA plugs. Some manufacturers include both DisplayPort and HDMI in the same devices, as evidenced by the presence of both connectors. DisplayPort comes in two sizes: standard and Mini DisplayPort. Figure 10-11 shows a Mini DisplayPort socket on a computer. Figure 10-12 shows a Mini DisplayPort connector on a cable end.

Display Types

The function of a PC video display device is to produce visual responses to user requests. Often called simply a *display* or *monitor,* it receives computer output from the display adapter, which controls its functioning. The display technology—which you have already learned about—must match the technology of the video card to which it attaches, so in this section we will explore types of displays and display settings.

FIGURE 10-11 A Mini DisplayPort socket

FIGURE 10-12 A Mini DisplayPort connector on a cable

CRTs

CRT monitors are obsolete, but you may still occasionally encounter them in the field, because many businesses keep old hardware in use until it breaks to save money.

A *CRT monitor* is a large boxy unit, approximately as deep as it is tall and wide. It is so bulky because of the large cathode ray tube it contains. A CRT uses an electron gun to activate phosphors behind the screen. Each pixel on the monitor has the ability to generate red, green, or blue, depending on the signals it receives. This combination of colors results in the display you see on the monitor. CRTs have extremely high-voltage capacitors inside, so do not open a CRT for any reason. If a CRT is malfunctioning, dispose of it properly by checking with local regulations for possible recycling.

Flat-Panel Displays

A *flat-panel display (FPD)* is a computer display that has a form that is very thin—many are thinner than 1/2" and take up far less desk space (at least front to back) than the traditional CRT displays. FPDs go beyond the standard two-dimensional images, offering *three-dimensional (3-D)* images with realistic depth that require HDMI display adapters. They also support high resolutions: 4k, 8k, and beyond. The following sections look at FPD technologies that are common to both computer displays (desktop monitors and laptop screens) and TVs. In Chapter 14 you will learn how to replace flat-panel displays and their associated components in a laptop PC.

LCD Displays An *LCD* and a *light-emitting diode (LED) display* are both actually types of LCDs because each has a layer of liquid crystal molecules, called subpixels, sandwiched between polarizing filters that are backlit when the display is powered on. The biggest difference between LCD and LED displays is the backlight source. In an LCD display, the source is one or more *cold cathode fluorescent lamps (CCFLs),* a type of lamp that provides a bright light but is energy efficient and long lasting. On the other hand, the light source in an LED panel is a grid of many tiny light bulbs called light-emitting diodes, positioned behind the glass enclosing the liquid crystals. When power is applied to the diodes, the bulbs glow.

In the following discussion, references to LCD will apply to both backlighting methods, unless we specify one or the other. When necessary to make the distinction, an LED backlit display will be referred to as an *LED-lit LCD*.

In a color LCD display, the individual molecules of liquid crystal are called *subpixels*. A see-through film in front of the crystal liquid consists of areas colored red, green, and blue. Each cluster of this trio of colors makes up a *physical pixel*. Images and colors are created by charging subpixels within the physical pixels.

An LCD display requires less than half the wattage of a comparably sized CRT. Add to this the power-saving features built into displays, such as the features defined by VESA's *Display Power-Management Signaling (DPMS)* standard. Rather than needing to turn off a display manually when you leave your desk or are not using the computer, DPMS-compliant displays automatically go into a lower power mode after a preconfigured amount of time without any activity.

LCD Technologies The most common technology for an LCD monitor is *twisted nematic (TN)*. This was the first type of LCD panel widely produced. LCD monitors are thin, clear, and inexpensive to produce and support higher refresh rates than IPS (discussed next), but they can suffer from uneven backlighting, motion blur, limited viewing angles, poor viewing in sunlight, and input lag.

In-plane switching (IPS) is a newer technology that improves viewing angles and color reproduction. The contrast ratio is also better, and the color accuracy is good. However, the response rate and maximum refresh rate are not as good as TN. Therefore, IPS monitors are more suitable for graphic design than for game playing.

A *vertical alignment (VA)* panel is a compromise between TN and IPS, offering advantages of both. VA panels support higher refresh rates, like TN panels, but support the higher color reproduction and better brightness and viewing angles of IPS.

exam watch

CompTIA A+ 1101 exam Objective 1.2 mentions LCD, IPS, TN, VA, and OLED. Make sure you are familiar with these acronyms and their associated monitor technologies.

OLED Yet another type of thin display technology uses *organic light-emitting diode (OLED)*, which does not require backlighting. OLED diodes use organic compounds for the electroluminescence. There are *passive-matrix OLED (PMOLED)* displays and *active-matrix OLED (AMOLED)* displays. A PMOLED display panel relies strictly on the electroluminescent layer to light the screen and does not use a *thin-film transistor (TFT)* backplane, as does an AMOLED. OLED screens are found in a wide range of devices from smartphones and tablets to computer displays and TVs. Presently, the organic materials in OLED displays degrade over time, making this technology more appropriate for devices that are not powered on for several hours a day, but are intermittently turned on instead, as with a smartphone or tablet.

SCENARIO & SOLUTION	
You need to connect an external monitor to a desktop PC. Both the PC and the monitor have DVI, VGA, and HDMI connectors. Which one should you use?	HDMI
A client wants a good-quality LCD monitor. Response time, brightness, and viewing angle are all important. Which technology would you recommend?	Vertical alignment (VA)

CERTIFICATION SUMMARY

This chapter wraps up the discussion of PC components begun in Chapter 8 and continued in Chapter 9, describing power supplies, display devices, and their associated connector types.

A power supply must deliver enough wattage to the device, but that's not all; it must also be able to supply enough of the correct voltages. You should be able to evaluate a power supply's output and a PC's power requirements to make sure they are compatible. You should also be able to remove and install desktop power supplies.

Display technologies have changed a great deal since the days of the analog CRT. The most recent developments include support for both video and audio through a single interface, connection, and cable. The physical form of the cable, and the connectors and ports used with a cable, depend on the purpose and design of the interface used and the device or devices that use the cable. Common cable types for displays include HDMI, DVI, DisplayPort, and VGA. Common LCD monitor technologies include IPS, TN, VA, and OLED.

TWO-MINUTE DRILL

Here are some of the key points covered in Chapter 10.

Power Supplies

- ❑ A power supply provides power for all components on the motherboard and those internal to the PC case.
- ❑ A volt is the unit of measurement of the pressure of electrons. A watt is a unit of measurement of actual delivered power. An ampere (amp) is a unit of measurement for electrical current or rate of flow of electrons through a wire.
- ❑ A power supply converts alternating current (AC) voltage into the direct current (DC) voltage required by the computer.
- ❑ Power supply capacity is measured in watts, with power supplies for desktop computers ranging up to about 1500 watts.

- An AC adapter is a form of power supply used with portable computers and external peripherals.
- Select a power supply that is of the correct form factor for both the motherboard and the case, and select one that has sufficient wattage for the internal components you expect to have.
- Most modern ATX motherboards use a 24-pin ATX (P1) connector to provide power. Some recent motherboards require two ATX 12V 2.0 connectors—one is a 24-pin main connector, and the other is a 4-pin secondary connector. Other newer motherboards require EPS12V connectors, which include a 24-pin main connector, an 8-pin secondary connector, and an optional 4-pin tertiary connector.

Display Adapters and Displays

- The display adapter controls the output from the PC to the display device. Display adapters support a variety of connections, including VGA (DE-15), DVI, HDMI, and DisplayPort.
- A display adapter may be built into the motherboard or may be a separate circuit board that plugs into a PCIe slot.
- Flat-panel displays (FPDs) have replaced CRT displays. The key technologies used in today's LCD displays are in-plane switching (IPS), twisted nematic (TN), vertical alignment (VA), and organic light-emitting diode (OLED).

SELF TEST

The following questions will help you measure your understanding of the material presented in this chapter. Read all of the choices carefully because there might be more than one correct answer. Choose all correct answers for each question.

Power Supplies

1. Which statement is true?
   A. A PC power supply converts wattage to voltage.
   B. A PC power supply converts voltage to wattage.
   C. A PC power supply converts AC to DC.
   D. A PC power supply converts DC to AC.

2. What is the name of the main power connector that goes between an ATX power supply and an ATX motherboard?
   A. P3
   B. P1
   C. P2
   D. P4
3. The capacity of a power supply is normally stated in these units.
   A. Volts
   B. Watts
   C. Amperes
   D. Ohms
4. What type of current is required by internal PC components?
   A. Alternating current (AC)
   B. Direct current (DC)
   C. DVI
   D. PSU
5. Which of these is *not* a common voltage that computer components require?
   A. 3.3 VDC
   B. 5 VDC
   C. 9 VDC
   D. 12 VDC
6. Which of the following calculations would you use to determine the capacity you require in a power supply?
   A. Add the voltage for all internal components.
   B. Add the wattage for all internal components.
   C. Add the voltage for all external components.
   D. Add the wattage for all external components.
7. This active component of a typical power supply dissipates heat.
   A. Heat sink
   B. P1 connector
   C. Fan
   D. AC adapter
8. What is a common term for a laptop power supply?
   A. PSU
   B. Heat sink
   C. AC adapter
   D. Thermal compound

9. Select all the items that should be considered when selecting a new power supply.
   A. Wattage
   B. CPU
   C. Form factor
   D. Power connectors
10. What equipment should you never use when working with a power supply?
   A. Screwdriver
   B. Connectors
   C. Motherboard
   D. Antistatic wrist strap
11. What does a Molex connector provide power to?
   A. PCIe cards
   B. PATA drives
   C. Motherboard
   D. SATA drives

Display Adapters and Displays

12. Which of these is the oldest type of display connector?
   A. DisplayPort
   B. HDMI
   C. DVI
   D. VGA
13. Which of the following video interface standards supports both analog and digital signals?
   A. DisplayPort
   B. HDMI
   C. DVI
   D. VGA
14. This video standard supports both digital video and digital audio and has the thinnest cable and the smallest connectors.
   A. DisplayPort
   B. HDMI
   C. DVI
   D. VGA

15. Cold cathode fluorescent lamps (CCFLs) are a feature of what kind of display?

A. CRT

B. LED

C. LCD

D. HDMI

16. This modern type of display device replaces an older technology that used more power and took up more desk space.

A. CRT

B. FPD

C. ATX

D. USB

17. Which of the following connectors is *not* used to connect a display to a digital video interface?

A. DVI

B. DE-15

C. HDMI

D. DisplayPort

18. Which of the following is *not* a DVI connector type?

A. DVI-A

B. DVI-B

C. DVI-I

D. DVI-D

19. Which types of video connectors include a digital rights management feature called HDCP? (Choose two.)

A. HDMI

B. DVI

C. VGA

D. DisplayPort

20. What is the primary drawback to OLED?

A. Requires an analog display adapter

B. Requires backlighting

C. Not as bright as LCD

D. The organic material degrades over time

A SELF TEST ANSWERS

Power Supplies

1. ☑ **C.** A PC power supply converts AC to DC.
☒ **A** and **B** are incorrect, because wattage equals volts times amps; wattage is a calculated value, not something that can be converted. **D** is incorrect because it does just the opposite.

2. ☑ **B.** P1 is the main power connector used between an ATX power supply and an ATX motherboard.
☒ **A** and **C** are incorrect because the chapter did not mention either a P3 or P2 connector. **D** is incorrect because a P4 is a four-wire 12V connector used in addition to the P1 connector.

3. ☑ **B.** The capacity of a power supply is stated in watts.
☒ **A** is incorrect because volts is a measurement of electrical potential. **C** is incorrect because amperes is a measurement of electrical current, or rate of flow of electrons through a wire. **D** is incorrect because ohms is a measurement of resistance.

4. ☑ **B.** Direct current (DC) is the type of current required by internal PC components.
☒ **A** is incorrect because alternating current (AC) is the type of current that is provided through the typical wall outlet. **C** is incorrect because DVI is a type of video connector. **D** is incorrect because PSU is an acronym for "power supply unit."

5. ☑ **C.** 9 VDC is not one of the voltages that computer components use.
☒ **A, B,** and **D** are incorrect because they are all commonly used voltages provided by the PC's power supply.

6. ☑ **B.** Add the wattage for all internal components to determine what capacity you require in a power supply.
☒ **A** is incorrect because this is not the correct measurement required. **C** and **D** are both incorrect because external components normally have their own power supplies and do not need to draw power from the computer's power supply.

7. ☑ **C.** The fan is the component in a typical power supply that dissipates heat.
☒ **A** is incorrect because a heat sink is something that draws heat off something and dissipates it in some passive manner, such as via metal fins. **B** is incorrect because the P1 connector is a power supply connector, not a part of a power supply that dissipates heat. **D** is incorrect because an AC adapter converts electrical power; it does not dissipate heat.

8. ☑ **C.** AC adapter is the common term for a laptop power supply.
☒ **A** is incorrect because PSU is an acronym for "power supply unit." **B** is incorrect because heat sinks dissipate heat. **D** is incorrect because thermal compound is used to increase the heat conductivity among components.

9. ☑ **A, C,** and **D.** You should consider wattage, form factor, and power connectors when selecting a new power supply.
☒ **B** is incorrect because although its wattage requirements are important, the CPU itself is not an issue when selecting a power supply.

10. ☑ **D.** You should never use an antistatic wrist strap when working with a power supply.
☒ **A** is incorrect because it may be necessary to remove the screws holding a power supply to the case. **B** is incorrect because you must work with the connectors from the power supply to the motherboard and other components. **C** is incorrect because you may need to work with the power supply connectors on the motherboard.

11. ☑ **B.** A Molex connector provides power to PATA drives.
☒ **A** is incorrect because PCIe slots and their cards get their power from the motherboard. **C** is incorrect because the motherboard receives power via the P1 connector and auxiliary connectors. **D** is incorrect because SATA drives use SATA power connectors.

Display Adapters and Displays

12. ☑ **D.** VGA is the oldest video interface standard still in use today.
☒ **A, B,** and **C** are incorrect because they are recent standards.

13. ☑ **C.** DVI is the video interface standard that supports both analog and digital signals.
☒ **A** and **B** are incorrect because DisplayPort and HDMI only support digital signals. **D** is incorrect because VGA is an analog video interface standard.

14. ☑ **A.** DisplayPort supports both digital video and audio and has the thinnest cable and the smallest connectors.
☒ **B** is incorrect because although HDMI supports both video and audio, it does not have the thinnest cable and smallest connectors. **C** is incorrect because DVI does not support both digital video and audio. **D** is incorrect because VGA only supports analog video.

15. ☑ **C.** LCD is the type of display that includes CCFLs.
☒ **A** is incorrect because a CRT monitor uses an electron gun. **B** is incorrect because an LED uses a light-emitting diode. **D** is incorrect because DVI is a connector type, not a monitor technology.

16. ☑ **B.** A flat-panel display (FPD) takes up less desk space and replaces an older (CRT) technology that uses more power.
☒ **A** is incorrect because a CRT takes up more desk space than a flat-panel display and uses more power. **C** is incorrect because ATX is a motherboard and power supply form factor, not a type of display. **D** is incorrect because USB is an I/O interface.

17. ☑ **B.** A DE-15 connector is not used to connect a display to a digital video interface.
☒ **A, C,** and **D** are incorrect because these connectors are all used to connect a display to a digital video interface of the same name.

18. ☑ **B.** DVI-B is not a DVI connector type.
☒ **A, C,** and **D** are incorrect because DVI-A, DVI-I, and DVI-D are all DVI connector types.

19. ☑ **A** and **D.** HDMI and DisplayPort both support HDCP.
☒ **B** and **C** are incorrect because DVI and VGA do not support HDCP.

20. ☑ **D.** The organic material in OLED degrades over time.
☒ **A** is incorrect because OLED does not require an analog display adapter. **B** is incorrect because OLED does not require backlighting. **C** is incorrect because OLEDs are not less bright than LCD.

Chapter 11

Installing and Upgrading PC Components

CERTIFICATION OBJECTIVES

- **1101: 3.2** Given a scenario, install the appropriate RAM
- **1101: 3.3** Given a scenario, select and install storage devices
- **1101: 3.4** Given a scenario, install and configure motherboards, central processing units (CPUs), and add-on cards

✓ Two-Minute Drill

Q&A Self Test

This chapter describes and demonstrates how to install and replace common PC components. With a little practice, you will be capable of performing these tasks on most personal computers, despite different layouts or new component designs. This chapter focuses mainly on desktop PC hardware; laptop PC skills are covered in Chapter 14.

CERTIFICATION OBJECTIVES

- ***1101: 3.2*** *Given a scenario, install the appropriate RAM*
- ***1101: 3.4*** *Given a scenario, install and configure motherboards, central processing units (CPUs), and add-on cards*

Chapters 8 and 9 looked at Objectives 3.2 and 3.4 of the CompTIA A+ 1101 exam from the conceptual angle; you learned about the various types of components and how they work together. However, what is the sense of understanding motherboards and their components, RAM, and CPUs if you don't know how to physically work with them? Therefore, in this section, you will look at how to install and configure these components.

Installing and Upgrading Motherboards and Onboard Components

Installing and upgrading a motherboard requires that you understand the CPU models that will work with the motherboard, as well as the appropriate type of memory compatible with both the CPU and motherboard and the amount of memory they can handle. Your best source for this information is the motherboard manual from the manufacturer.

Whenever you install or replace a computer component that involves opening the case, you must unplug power to the computer (and if it's a laptop, remove the battery if possible) and ensure that you follow the electrostatic discharge (ESD) procedures discussed in Chapter 1. All the exercises described in this book assume that you have taken steps to protect yourself, and the computer, from harm.

Replacing a Motherboard

Replacing a motherboard is not a common occurrence. If a motherboard fails while a computer is under warranty, it will be replaced as part of that coverage. Therefore, only if you work for a company that does such warranty work will motherboard replacement be a big part of your job. If a motherboard fails after the warranty period, you need to decide whether a suitable replacement is available and whether you will be able to use all your old components with a newer motherboard. In many cases it may make more sense to simply replace the entire computer.

Because most components attach physically to the motherboard, replacing it can be a very time-consuming task. If you are replacing one motherboard with another of the same brand and version, you should make notes about any firmware settings and jumper positions (if there are any jumpers) for the old motherboard in case you need to change them on the new board. You will use the firmware settings the first time you start up the computer after the installation, but make the physical jumper changes, if any, before securing the new motherboard in the case. The jumpers may not be as easy to reach after the motherboard is installed, especially if you don't do it until after you install other components. Once you have done this, you are ready for the real work.

When it comes to replacing a motherboard versus building an entirely new system from scratch, doing the latter may be easier, because you can buy all the pieces at once from one source and make sure that all the components will play nicely together.

Installing a Motherboard

When installing or replacing a motherboard, you should follow the instructions in the motherboard manual, your most important tool. In addition to listing the components supported, the typical motherboard manual includes instructions on installing the motherboard in a case and installing components, such as the CPU, memory, and power supply. The manual will explain how to set appropriate jumpers on the motherboard and how to attach all the various power and data cables. These include all the drive interface cables and connections to both front and back panel connectors for the various interfaces, such as Universal Serial Bus (USB); external SATA (eSATA); and even video, sound, and networking, if any of those components are built in.

Exercise 11-1 will guide you through the task of removing an old motherboard.

Before you open a computer case, be sure to unplug any power cords and turn off the power supply. Then, to prevent damage to the system, equalize the electrical charge between your body and the components inside your computer. If nothing else, touch a grounded portion of your computer's chassis. A better option is to place the computer on a grounded mat, which you touch before working on the PC. You could also wear an antistatic wrist strap.

EXERCISE 11-1

Removing an Old Motherboard

If possible, use a digital camera to record the steps, beginning with pictures of the unopened PC from all sides, then at each point before and after you make a change, such as opening the case and removing components. This can serve as your documentation for reassembling the computer.

1. If you haven't done this already, power down and unplug the PC's power cord.
2. Remove all expansion cards and cables from the motherboard.
3. If the drives and/or the drive bays interfere with access to the motherboard, remove them.
4. Remove any screws or fasteners attaching the motherboard to the case, lift the board out of the case, and put it aside. Be sure to carefully save any screws you remove.

The first three steps of Exercise 11-2 describe a recommended procedure for handling a motherboard, which applies to any circuit board. Remember to use proper handling precautions to avoid ESD damage to the board. The remainder of Exercise 11-2 includes general steps for installing a motherboard. Always check the instructions included with the motherboard or other component.

EXERCISE 11-2

Properly Handling and Installing a Motherboard

Complete this exercise to practice installing a motherboard while taking the appropriate safety measures.

1. Before unpacking a new motherboard, ensure that you have grounded your body properly. One method is to wear an antistatic safety wrist strap, as described in Chapter 1. Your work area should include a grounded antistatic mat.
2. Hold the board by its edges and avoid touching any contacts, integrated circuit (IC) chips, or other components on the surface.
3. Place the board on a grounded antistatic mat (described in Chapter 1).
4. Install the CPU and memory on the motherboard per the manufacturer's instructions.

5. Follow the motherboard manual's instructions for setting any jumpers on the motherboard, and pay attention to instructions for how to attach screws and standoffs, which keep the motherboard from touching the metal floor or wall of the case. Now you are ready to install the board.
6. To place the new motherboard in the computer, line it up properly on the chassis screw holes, and fix it into place.
7. Attach the power and drive connectors, as well as connectors to the correct ports on the case (both front panels and back panels).

Upgrading a CPU

Upgrading a CPU is uncommon anymore, but not unheard of. If your motherboard accepts multiple speeds of CPUs and your current one isn't at the top of that range, you might be able to switch out the CPU for a faster one. This might not provide the performance boost that you hope for, though. Motherboards typically accept CPUs in a rather narrow range of speeds. The performance difference between two CPUs in the same basic class (that is, two CPUs that would run on the same motherboard) is not likely to be a game-changer. You'll likely see much more dramatic performance increases when you add more RAM or install a better display adapter.

Be sure to consult the manufacturer's documentation for your motherboard to determine which processors and speeds it supports. In some cases, you might need to configure the board for the new speed or model using a set of jumpers, but most motherboards enable you to make such changes through BIOS/UEFI system setup. You can run a software test to see what CPU is installed. For instance, the free program CPU-Z will scan your computer and report on many onboard components, including the CPU, caches, the motherboard, memory, memory speed, and graphics.

When we mention free software in this book, we are only using it as an example; it's not an endorsement of that product. If you download and install such software, note that most of the websites offering free software also show links to download other software, and sometimes those links are positioned so that you might inadvertently download a program other than the one you intend. The installation program of the software you desire may also include installing add-ons to your browser. Watch for these, and do not install anything you do not explicitly want.

Removing a CPU

How you remove an installed CPU depends on the type of socket. Once again, read any manuals available for your motherboard or computer. You may need to consult the manufacturer for more information.

The existing CPU will have a heat sink and/or fan attached to it. If possible, remove the CPU without removing these attachments. However, if they interfere with the mechanism for releasing the processor, you may need to remove them.

There are two basic socket types: pin grid array (PGA) and land grid array (LGA). PGA sockets have a grid of holes in them to accommodate pins on the back of the CPU. LGA sockets have a grid of metal contacts, which connect with corresponding contacts on the back of the CPU. Both kinds of sockets have a lever on the side that you raise up to release the CPU and lower to secure it.

The main difference you will see between PGA and LGA sockets is that LGA sockets have a cover in addition to a lever. The cover holds the CPU firmly in place, while only the lever and the fit of the pins in the holes hold a CPU in a PGA socket. The steps for removing CPUs from both types of sockets are similar, with one important difference, as shown in Exercises 11-3 and 11-4. Both are *zero insertion force (ZIF)* sockets, meaning you do not have to apply any downward pressure to seat the CPU in the socket.

The processor will be very hot when you first turn off a PC. You can burn your fingers if you touch a hot CPU chip. Always allow at least five minutes for the chip to cool before you remove it.

EXERCISE 11-3

Removing a PGA Processor from Its Socket

Complete this exercise to practice removing a PGA processor.

1. First, ensure that you have an antistatic bag at hand.
2. Remove any cooling systems attached to the CPU.
3. Lift the socket lever. You might have to move it slightly to the side to clear it from a retaining tab.
4. Lift out the processor. Because this is a ZIF socket, you should encounter no resistance when you remove the CPU.
5. Place the CPU inside an antistatic bag. (Remember, putting it on top of the bag provides no protection.)

EXERCISE 11-4

Removing an LGA Processor from Its Socket

Complete this exercise to practice removing an LGA processor.

1. First, ensure that you have an antistatic bag at hand.
2. Remove any cooling systems attached to the CPU.
3. Lift the socket lever and cover.
4. Lift out the processor.
5. Place the CPU inside an antistatic bag.

Installing a CPU

The CPU socket on the motherboard will usually have a mechanism to make it easier to install the CPU without damaging any pins. As described earlier, CPUs designed for PGA and LGA sockets have levers, but the LGA sockets also have a cover.

When installing a CPU into a socket, raise the lever and position the CPU with all pins inserted in the matching socket holes. Then close the lever, which lets the socket contact each of the CPU's pins. Exercise 11-5 describes how to install a CPU in an LGA socket. In all cases, do not count on these simple instructions alone, but follow those provided in the manuals that come with the motherboard and CPU.

EXERCISE 11-5

Installing a Processor in an Empty LGA Socket

Complete this exercise to practice installing an LGA processor.

1. First, open the antistatic packaging containing the CPU, including any packing securing the CPU, but keep it within the packaging until you are ready to install it in the socket. Do not place the CPU on top of the packaging, because that will expose it to static.
2. Lift the socket lever and cover.
3. Align the CPU over the socket.
4. Position the cover over the CPU.
5. Press the lever down.
6. Apply thermal paste/pad and then install a cooling system such as a heat sink/fan combination.

When handling a CPU, grasp it by the sides—never touch the underside of a CPU, where the pins or contacts are.

Removing and Installing Cooling Systems

As a rule, the typical PC comes with a cooling system that is adequate for the standard components delivered with the PC. Once you start adding hard drives, memory, and additional expansion cards, you should give some thought to supplementing the existing cooling system. How far you go with this depends on just how much you add to the PC.

An overheated computer may slow down, thanks to built-in technology in some motherboards that senses the temperature of the motherboard and slows down the processor when the temperature exceeds a certain limit. This reduces the heat the processor puts out. In the extreme, overheating can damage PC components. The other side of this is that modern cooling systems also use heat sensors, and as temperatures rise, they will adjust their performance to keep the system cool. Newer power supply and case fans will change speed to match the temperature.

Common Sense First

Before you consider spending money on a new cooling system, check that the currently installed cooling system is not being impaired in any way. Maybe if you just corrected its problems, it would be adequate. Begin by ensuring that the PC case is closed during operation, that all slot covers are in place, that airflow around the case is not obstructed, and that the computer system is not installed in an unventilated space, such as an enclosed cabinet. Also, check to see if ribbon cables are blocking airflow inside the case. Use plastic ties to secure cables out of the way. Correct these problems before spending money supplementing the cooling system.

In addition, open the case and give the interior of the PC a good vacuuming before you spend money on upgrading the cooling system. Excessive dust and dirt on components will act as an insulator, keeping the heat from dissipating and causing a computer to overheat, which in turn can cause it to slow down, stop operating, or be permanently damaged. Learn more about vacuuming a PC and other maintenance tasks in Chapter 12.

Laptops are prone to overheating too because they have components crammed into such a tight space. Make sure that you do not block any fans on the bottom or sides of the laptop PC, and operate the laptop on a hard flat surface, not on your lap. A hot laptop PC sitting directly on your lap not only can overheat but can also burn your legs. If a laptop PC frequently overheats, consider disassembling it to clean out any dust or hair inside that may be interfering with airflow and fan operation.

Case Fan

New PCs often come with both a power supply fan and a separate case fan. Perhaps you can simply upgrade the present case fan. Also, check to see if the PC has an empty bay or bracket for a case fan. A case fan is a very inexpensive upgrade, cheaper than a latte and muffin at your favorite coffee shop. The only requirement is a bracket or bay in the case that will accommodate a case fan and the appropriate power connector.

When shopping for a case fan, you will need the dimensions of the fan bay (usually stated in millimeters), rated voltage, and power input. Features to compare are fan speed in revolutions per minute (rpm), airflow in cubic feet per minute (CFM), and noise level in decibels. A *decibel (dB)* is a commonly used measurement of sound. The fan speed and airflow reflect the fan's effectiveness for cooling. The noise level is an important consideration because fans and drives are the only moving parts in a PC and generate the most noise. Look for fans with a noise decibel rating in the 20s or below. In addition, check out the power connector on new case fans. Many come with a Molex connector that can connect directly to the power supply, and some have a special connector that must connect directly to the motherboard. Figure 11-1 shows a 100-mm-wide case fan with a Molex connector.

CPU Fans and Heat Sinks

If you are installing a CPU, then you will also need to install a cooling system for it. Today's processors typically require a fan/heat sink combination, which may also include some other cooling technology. Often, the cooling system and the CPU are packaged together, making the choice for you. Pay attention to the power connector for the fan, and locate the socket

FIGURE 11-1

A case fan

for this connector on the motherboard ahead of time. It is unlikely that you will replace an existing CPU fan and/or heat sink unless the CPU fan has failed.

When reinstalling a heat sink, keep in mind that thermal paste tends to degrade over time, so consider applying more before you reseat the heat sink. Thermal pads do not degrade as quickly, so an existing thermal pad is likely to still be usable.

Liquid Cooling Systems

As desktop systems continue to decline in popularity, even among gamers, liquid cooling has become less common. (Liquid cooling isn't a viable option for laptops, for obvious reasons.) Another factor in its waning popularity is that its primary purpose has traditionally been to cool overclocked systems, and overclocking in general has become less popular as CPU technology has improved and CPUs have become less performance-dependent on the clock speed.

If you do decide to investigate liquid cooling, do your homework because these systems have several issues. For one, they require special skills to install, and they take up considerable space inside a computer because they require specific tubing, reservoirs, fans, and power supplies to work effectively.

Removing a Cooling System

If a cooling system fails or is inadequate, you will need to remove it from the PC. In that case, properly shut down the computer and unplug its power cord, and ensure that you follow the ESD procedures. Then reverse the steps for installing the component, unplugging power and motherboard connectors, unscrewing mounting screws, and lifting it out of the case.

Installing and Configuring a Cooling System

When installing a new cooling system, be sure to read the documentation for the new components as well as for the motherboard, if appropriate. Assemble the components required, and follow good practices to avoid damaging the computer or injuring yourself. Turn the computer's power off, disconnect the power cord, and ensure that you follow the ESD procedures discussed in Chapter 1.

When installing a new case fan, affix the fan to the case in the appropriate bracket or bay, using the screws that came with either the case or the fan. Connect the power connector and any required motherboard connectors.

When installing a heat sink and/or fan on a CPU, be sure to apply thermal compound according to the instructions, and carefully connect the heat sink or fan using the clip provided. Plug the fan into the appropriate power socket on the motherboard.

SCENARIO & SOLUTION	
You are installing a motherboard in a desktop case, and you don't have any stand-offs. Is it okay to attach the motherboard directly to the case floor?	No. Stand-offs prevent the motherboard from touching the floor, thus preventing short-circuiting. Do not install a motherboard without them.
You have a motherboard that you know is good, because you just removed it from a working system. You install it in a different case, and it doesn't work anymore. Using a POST card reveals that the motherboard has been damaged and is dead now. What is the most likely cause of this damage?	The most likely cause of the damage is electrostatic discharge (ESD), or static electricity, due to sloppy handling practices either when removing or installing the motherboard.

Optimizing a System by Adding RAM

One function of RAM is to provide the processor with faster access to the information it needs. Within limits, the more memory a computer has, the faster it will run. One of the most common and effective computer upgrades is the installation of more system RAM.

The optimal amount of memory to install is best determined by considering the requirements of the operating system you are installing and how you will use the computer. On an existing system, you can run a software test that will scan your memory and report on what it finds, including the type and quantity of installed memory, the number of memory slots, and the number of available (empty) memory slots. It will then recommend upgrade requirements right down to the specifications you will need to select and purchase the correct RAM modules. One such software test is available at www.crucial.com. Exercise 11-6 will walk you through running the Crucial System Scanner.

on the job

Recall the earlier warning about downloading and installing free software. If you choose to use the Crucial System Scanner, be sure that you only download the scanner and that you do not agree to make any changes, such as an add-in to your web browser.

EXERCISE 11-6

Running a Memory Scanner

For this exercise, you will need a computer with Internet access. Depending on the browser and your security settings in the OS, the process for downloading the utility may vary slightly from what's described here.

1. Enter the URL **https://www.crucial.com/store/systemscanner** into the address box of your web browser. (If you are running macOS, you will be automatically redirected to a page from which you can download the Crucial Mac System Scanner.)
2. Click the I Agree To The Terms & Conditions check box (after reading the terms and conditions).
3. Click the Start Your Free Scan button.
4. If you are asked whether you want to save or run the file, choose Save. Save it in your Downloads folder or wherever you prefer.
5. In the Downloads folder, locate and click CrucialScan.exe.
6. If prompted by a User Account Control (UAC) dialog box, click the Yes button (if you are logged on as an administrator) or enter the administrator password if you are not logged on as an administrator.
7. A Scan In Progress message will appear followed by a page of results. Review the results.

Suppose that a scan of a laptop computer shows two slots, each of them containing one 8-GB SODIMM, and no empty slots, as in Figure 11-2. To upgrade a computer where all the RAM slots are full, you would need to replace at least one of the SODIMMs with a higher-capacity SODIMM. Before doing this, though, you would check the documentation for the computer to make sure the motherboard will accept 16-GB SODIMMs. (The one shown in Figure 11-2 will not. Under Maximum Memory, the utility correctly states that it's at its maximum already.)

You would also check the maximum amount of RAM the OS can support. Recall, for instance, that the 32-bit version of Windows 10 can use only 4 GB of RAM. If that were your OS, a RAM upgrade would be of no value until you moved to a different OS that supported more.

Installing and Removing DIMMs

Dual Inline Memory Module (DIMM) sockets are often dark in color with plastic clips at each end. DIMM sockets for PCs are 240-pin for DDR3 SDRAM sticks and 288-pin for DDR4 and DDR5 SDRAM. They are all keyed differently, and they are not interchangeable.

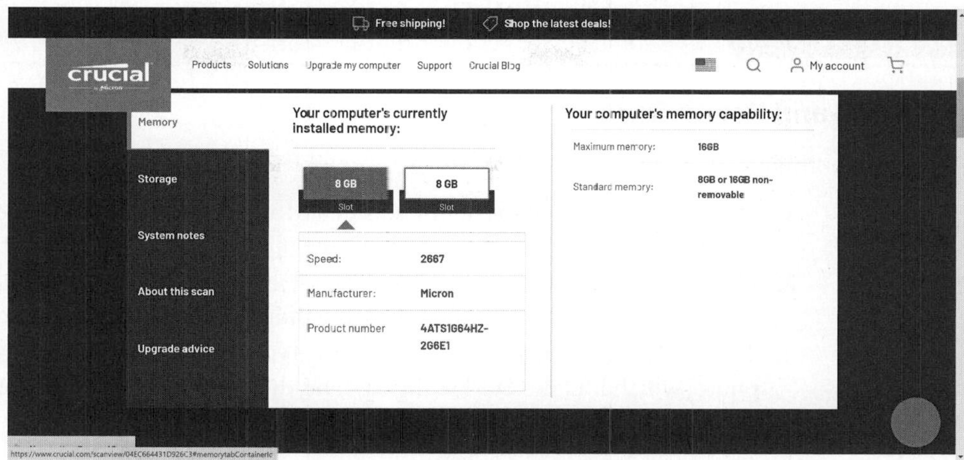

FIGURE 11-2 System scan results showing that this PC cannot accept more RAM.

You do not have to install DIMMs in pairs unless the motherboard is dual-channel (or triple-channel or quad-channel) architecture. If a motherboard has two different types of memory slots, such as four DIMM slots supporting DDR3 and two DIMM slots supporting DDR4, it is an either/or situation: you can install one or the other type of memory. If you install both, the system will not boot up.

Recall the descriptions of the various memory slots in Chapter 8 and memory sticks in Chapter 9. Be sure you remember that although some of the various memory sockets may seem similar, they are all keyed differently.

The technique for installing DIMMs is described in Exercise 11-7. A notch in each type of module is positioned to only fit in the appropriate type of memory socket, where a matching socket key will prevent you from installing the wrong type of module. So even if the number of pins is the same, you will not be able to install one type of module in the socket for another. When installing a memory module, pay attention to the location of the key on both the module and in the socket, and orient the module notch to line up with the socket key. Then open the retention clips on the socket and align the module vertically with the socket holding the module upright. Chapter 14 will detail how to install small outline DIMMs (SODIMMs) in laptops.

EXERCISE 11-7

Installing and Removing a DIMM

Complete this exercise to practice installing and removing RAM.

1. Open the retention clips on the socket and align the module with the slot, keeping it upright so the notches in the module line up with the tabs in the slot.
2. Gently press down on the module. The retention clips on the side should rotate into the locked position. You might need to guide them into place with your fingers.
3. To remove a DIMM, press the retention clips outward, as shown in the following photo, which lifts the DIMM slightly, and then grasp the DIMM by its circuit board (not by its chips) and lift it straight up.

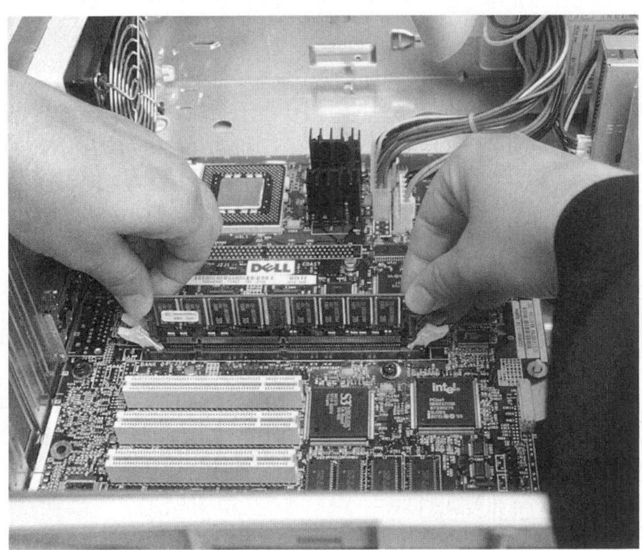

CERTIFICATION OBJECTIVE

- ***1101: 3.4*** *Given a scenario, install and configure motherboards, central processing units (CPUs), and add-on cards*

Chapter 9 described features and characteristics of the expansion cards listed in CompTIA A+ 1101 exam Objective 3.4. In this section, we will expand that discussion to describe the installation and configuration of expansion cards.

Installing Adapter Cards

Even with the large number of features built into PCs, technicians need to know how to add new adapter cards to PCs to add new functionality. Installing an adapter card requires that you open the case and install the card in an available expansion slot.

Before you buy an adapter card, consider the alternatives. Would you be able to achieve the same result (at the same performance level) from an external device using a USB or eSATA port? USB enables you to have multiple devices hanging off a single port.

In some cases, however, you can't avoid working with adapter cards. Anytime you want to add a component that transfers data at a higher bandwidth than the available external ports do, you should install an adapter card. That's not such an issue for USB 3.0 ports (4.8 Gbps), but USB 2.0 ports max out at 480 Mbps, so they're not fast enough for some things.

Removing an Adapter Card

Before removing an adapter card, be sure you have an antistatic bag in which to store the removed adapter card. Exercise 11-8 describes the general steps for removing an adapter card.

EXERCISE 11-8

Removing an Adapter Card

Complete this exercise to practice removing an adapter card from a desktop PC.

1. Properly shut down the computer, unplug its power cord, and ensure that you carry out proper ESD procedures, as described in Chapter 1.
2. Use a screwdriver to remove the screw fastening the card to the slot in the back of the computer case, or undo the retaining clip if the case style uses clips instead of screws.
3. Grasp the adapter card with both hands and pull straight up to remove it from the socket.
4. Place the card in an antistatic bag.

Installing and Configuring an Adapter Card

Once you have selected the adapter card that meets your needs, you will need to install it in the PC. Exercise 11-9 provides general steps for installing an adapter card. Although installing and configuring most adapter cards is straightforward, you must understand the card's purpose. Before you begin, check the documentation for both the adapter card and the motherboard, and note any variations from this general procedure. Check if the adapter card has any physical jumpers that you need to position. (Modern cards usually don't, as they are configured via their firmware or the operating system, but it doesn't hurt to check.) Look for any power connectors on the card that might indicate the need for supplemental power. Be sure to have the Uniform Resource Locator (URL) reference link handy where you can download any needed drivers and any related software after you install the adapter card; also, test the card after installing the driver and before securing the case cover, as described in the exercise.

EXERCISE 11-9

Installing an Adapter Card

Complete this exercise to practice installing an adapter card in a desktop PC.

1. Set any jumpers identified in the documentation for the card. Jumpers are uncommon on modern cards.
2. Properly shut down the computer, unplug its power cord, and ensure that you carry out proper ESD procedures, as described in Chapter 1.
3. Remove the slot cover for the appropriate expansion slot, removing whatever hardware is holding the slot cover in place.
4. Position the adapter card upright over the empty slot, aligning the card's slot cover with the opening behind that expansion slot.

5. Place your thumbs along the top edge of the card and push straight down.
6. Secure the card to the case using the existing screw holes.
7. After the board is installed but the case is still open, connect all necessary cables and start up the computer.
8. After the operating system starts up, install the device driver and test the device. (You learned about installing drivers in Windows in Chapter 4.) Once the device is working, turn the computer off and secure the case cover.
9. Restart the computer to ensure that replacing the case cover did not disturb any cables and connectors.

CERTIFICATION OBJECTIVE

- ***1101: 3.3*** *Given a scenario, select and install storage devices*

Chapter 9 introduced the various PC storage devices and media that are listed in CompTIA A+ 1101 exam Objective 3.3, but we delayed coverage of the installation and configuration of these devices for this chapter.

Installing Storage Devices

Replacing storage devices is a common task because those storage devices with moving parts tend to fail more than other components. Adding more storage space is also a common upgrade. Fortunately, because most drives are standardized, any PC can recognize them and they don't need special configuration.

New hard disk drives (and their SSD equivalents) must be partitioned and formatted before use. Some of them come prepartitioned and preformatted, especially external ones, but you can make changes. If you do want to change the drive's partitioning and formatting, the best time to do so is when the drive is new and contains no data. Chapter 5 explained partitioning and formatting procedures.

Removing an Internal Storage Device

To remove an internal storage device of any type, check the documentation for the device. Exercise 11-10 provides general steps that will work for most types of internal storage devices.

EXERCISE 11-10

Removing a Drive

Complete this exercise to practice removing a hard drive.

1. Remove the power supply and data cables from the back of the drive. Ensure that you grasp the plastic connector, not the wires themselves. If the connector doesn't come out easily, try gently rocking it lengthwise parallel to the socket from end to end (never side to side) while you pull it out.
2. Remove the screws that attach the drive to the drive bay, or push to release the retaining clips that hold the drive's rails into the bay. These are usually located on the sides of the drive. Be sure to carefully save any screws you remove. On some cases, before you can remove the screws on one side of a drive, you must remove the whole metal frame into which the drive is mounted.
3. Slide the drive out of the computer.
4. If the drive used rails to slide into the bay, remove the screws holding the rails to the drive.

You can usually install hard drives and other devices on their sides with no impact on operation or performance. Never install a magnetic hard drive upside-down, however. Solid-state storage can be installed at any orientation.

Installing Solid-State Storage

Solid-state storage is available for nearly every storage need. At the low end of the price scale, USB thumb drives provide a solution for someone needing ease of use and portability when transferring data among computers. Similarly, we use a variety of storage devices such as flash memory cards in smartphones and cameras, often connecting these devices, or their solid-state cards, to our PCs to transfer data. And SSDs are offered as a lighter-weight option compared to conventional hard drives in laptops because they add very little weight. At the high end, SSDs are available for large server systems at a higher price than comparably sized hard drive systems, but they offer better reliability and power savings over conventional hard drives. Low-end solid-state storage will plug into a PC's bus through a media reader or USB port, whereas high-end solid-state storage is more likely to come with the SATA, eSATA, or M.2 interface.

Exercise 11-11 walks you through the process of installing an M.2 SSD on a system with a built-in M.2 connector on the motherboard.

EXERCISE 11-11

Installing an M.2 SSD

Complete this exercise to practice installing a M.2 solid-state drive.

1. Check the motherboard manual to locate the M-keyed M.2 slots. Those are the ones for SSDs. If there is more than one, review the advice in the manual to determine which ones are for SSDs (vs. other device types, such as WLAN adapters). Review Chapter 8 to learn about M.2 slot keying types.
2. If there is more than one M-keyed M.2 slot available, review the motherboard manual's advice to determine which connector is optimal for your situation. (One may be better than another to use based on the number of other drives already installed.)
3. For each M.2 slot, there is a stand-off and screw on the motherboard that will eventually hold down the far end of the module (after it's installed). Look back at Figure 8-7 and notice the screws holding down the M.2 modules. There may be multiple screw holes at different positions from the slot to accommodate different lengths of M.2 SSD modules. Use the manual to locate the screw on the motherboard that you need to remove, and remove it. If needed, remove the stand-off and reposition it for the correct hole for the length of the SSD you are installing.
4. Insert the M.2 module in the slot at a 30-degree angle, wiggling it gently if needed to seat it in the slot.
5. Secure the end of the module by replacing the screw you removed in step 3 so that the module is flat against the motherboard.
6. Check the documentation for the M.2 module and the motherboard to see if the drive requires a heat sink. If so, install it according to the instructions. The heat sink may be a metal bar with an adhesive pad on it that fits onto the module.
7. Reconnect the power cable to the PC and start it up. If it doesn't recognize the new drive, boot into BIOS/UEFI and make sure the interface is enabled. Then locate the drive in Disk Management and partition and format it if needed.

Installing Drives on SATA Channels

Each SATA device has its own dedicated channel and does not require setting jumpers. Simply connect one end of the SATA data cable to a SATA channel and connect the other end to the drive's data connector.

FIGURE 11-3

A SATA data cable connector (left) next to a SATA power connector (right)

SSDs come in two different types: SATA and M.2. SATA SSDs are great for older systems that don't have M.2 connectors on the motherboard. HDDs (mechanical hard disk drives) always use SATA, unless they are really old and use the now-obsolete PATA interface.

Because the SATA data cable doesn't provide any power, SATA devices require a SATA power connector. You can use an adapter to convert a Molex connector to a SATA power connector if needed. Some older SATA devices may have two power connectors on the drive: one 4-pin Molex connector and one 15-pin SATA power connector. This is an "either-or" situation; use only one of these power connectors. If both are used, the drive will be damaged. Exercise 11-12 provides general instructions for installing an internal SATA drive. Be sure to follow the instructions in the manual for your motherboard and drive when installing a SATA drive. Figure 11-3 shows a SATA data cable alongside a SATA power cable.

EXERCISE 11-12

Installing a SATA Drive

Complete this exercise to practice installing a SATA drive.

1. Secure the drive in an available drive bay.
2. Locate an available SATA connector on the motherboard or on a SATA expansion card. Plug one end of the SATA cable into the motherboard and the other end to the drive. (The plugs on the ends of the cable are different so you will have no trouble plugging the cable in correctly.)

3. Locate a power connector coming from the power supply that matches the power connector on the SATA drive and connect it to the drive. The following photo shows an installed SATA drive connected to a SATA channel on the motherboard. Notice the three open SATA channel connectors at the bottom left, just above and to the right of the one into which the cable is connected.

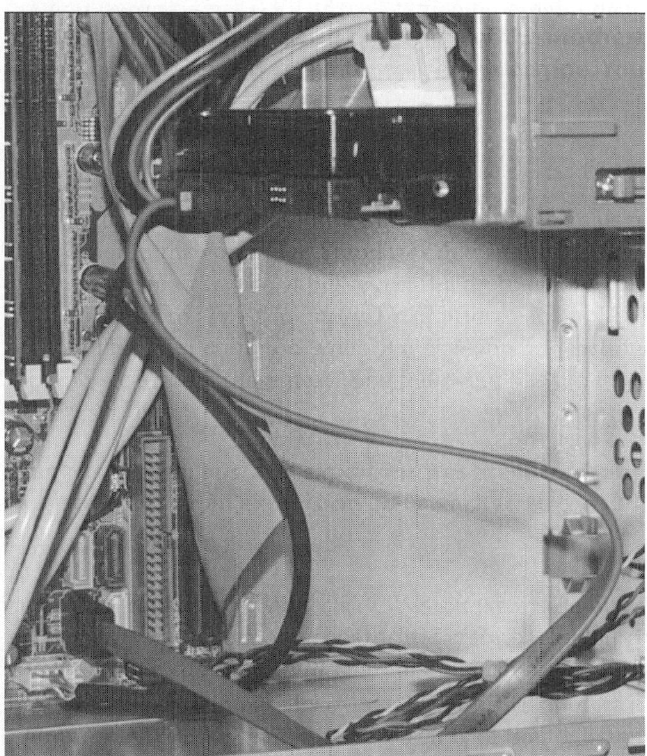

Installing RAID Arrays

Not too many years ago, if you wanted RAID, you had to add a special RAID controller adapter card to your computer. Today, many desktop and server motherboards come with a RAID controller built in. Therefore, if you need to create a RAID array on a recently manufactured computer, you will probably only need to add the appropriate number of hard drives. If this is not true of the computer you wish to add RAID to, then you will need to purchase an adapter and install it.

The physical installation of a RAID adapter is identical to installation of any other bus adapter. After installing it, you will need to install and connect each drive in the array to the controller, and then start the computer and run the RAID controller setup program.

The setup program will be similar whether the controller was integrated on the motherboard or on a separate controller card. You access it while starting up the machine. In the case of an integrated controller, the RAID setup program may be on the system BIOS/UEFI Setup menu, normally on an advanced menu. In the case of a separate RAID controller, watch during bootup for a prompt to press a key to enter the RAID setup. From there, you simply follow the menus and select the RAID level you desire.

Removing and Installing an External Storage Device

Today, the market is practically flooded with inexpensive external storage devices of all types and sizes, including USB flash drives, external optical drives, external HDDs, and external SSDs, as well as flash cards and their corresponding readers.

Most flash memory drives come with a USB interface, and external HDDs and SSDs have USB or eSATA. Newer computers come with eSATA ports for attaching external eSATA devices. An eSATA port connects to the motherboard's SATA bus. If you wish to connect an eSATA device to a computer without SATA support, you will need to add an adapter card.

Traditional external HDDs also come in a full range of sizes from hundreds of gigabytes to multiple terabytes. The tiny 2-inch format drives, like the thumb drives, do not need power supplies because they draw their power from the USB interface. The more conventionally sized drives require their own power supplies that plug into the wall outlet. All these drives are so simple to use that they hardly need instructions. Plug one in, and your OS will recognize the drive, assign it a drive letter, and include it in the drive list. You can then browse the contents of the drive and manage data on the drive using the Windows interface.

CERTIFICATION SUMMARY

This chapter led you through the processes required to install, upgrade, and configure PC components. You also learned the important issues for selecting each type of component, because whether you are building a system from scratch or just upgrading one or more components, you need to go through a selection process to ensure that the components will function well together. For this, use the knowledge gained in Chapters 8, 9, and 10 about the basic technologies and features of the components. Then, follow the appropriate step-by-step instructions from the manufacturer for the component you are installing. Never fail to read all the appropriate documentation for both a component and the PC or, specifically, the motherboard.

TWO-MINUTE DRILL

Here are some of the key points covered in Chapter 11.

Installing and Upgrading Motherboards and Onboard Components

- ❑ Select motherboard, CPU, and memory modules that are compatible with each other by researching the specifications of each.
- ❑ When installing a motherboard, follow the instructions in the motherboard manual.
- ❑ The ability to upgrade an existing CPU depends on the limits of the motherboard.
- ❑ One of the most common and most effective PC upgrades is the installation of more RAM.
- ❑ An overheated PC will slow down, stop functioning altogether, or become damaged.
- ❑ The typical PC comes with a cooling system adequate for the standard components delivered with it.
- ❑ Supplement the cooling system when adding hard drives, memory, and additional expansion cards or if the PC must function in a hot environment.

Installing Adapter Cards

- ❑ Select an adapter card that will add the functionality you need and that also fits an available expansion port on the motherboard.
- ❑ Read the documentation for the adapter card and the motherboard before installing the card.
- ❑ Physically install an adapter card; then restart the computer and install any necessary device driver and related software, and then test the adapter.

Installing Storage Devices

- ❑ Install an M.2 storage device on the motherboard, in an M-keyed M.2 slot. Insert it at a 30-degree angle. Look for a screw and stand-off on the motherboard to secure the other end of it.
- ❑ Only one SATA device connects to each SATA channel, so there are no configuration issues. Connect the SATA cable to the drive and the motherboard, and connect a SATA power connector to the drive.

- ❑ Newer PC firmware often supports at least one or two types of RAID arrays. Install the correct number of drives for the type of array, and configure the array through BIOS/UEFI setup.
- ❑ Various external storage devices, such as those with eSATA or USB connectors, are available today. These devices are truly plug and play, and once one is plugged in, the system recognizes it and assigns it a drive letter.

SELF TEST

The following questions will help you measure your understanding of the material presented in this chapter. Read all the choices carefully because there might be more than one correct answer. Choose all correct answers for each question.

Installing and Upgrading Motherboards and Onboard Components

1. How can you determine which CPU and memory modules to use with a certain motherboard?

A. All ATX motherboards accept all Intel and AMD CPUs and DIMMs.
B. Each motherboard is unique; check the manual.
C. Check the CPU documentation.
D. Check the RAM module documentation.

2. What type of CPU socket uses a lever for aligning the contacts and a cover for firmly securing a CPU?

A. PGA
B. LGA
C. HTPC
D. DIMM

3. How should you handle a motherboard?

A. Grasp the largest component on the board.
B. Grasp the handle.
C. Hold it by the edges.
D. Use a parts grabber.

4. Which of the following must you do when installing a DIMM?

A. Open the retention clips on the socket and tilt the DIMM at a 45-degree angle to the socket.
B. Open the retention clips on the socket and align the DIMM vertically with the socket.
C. Close the retention clips on the socket and tilt the DIMM at a 45-degree angle to the socket.
D. Close the retention clips on the socket and align the DIMM without tilting.

5. What prevents you from installing a DDR4 module into a DDR3 socket?

A. DDR3 installs at a 45-degree angle; DDR4 installs vertically.
B. The DIMMs are different thicknesses.
C. There is nothing to prevent this.
D. DDR3 and DDR4 have a different number of pins, even though they are the same length.

6. Suppose you replace the 8-GB DIMMs in your motherboard with 16-GB DIMMs, but now the system will not boot. What is the likely reason?

A. The motherboard does not support 16-GB DIMMs.
B. None of them are seated fully in their slots.
C. You have installed them backwards.
D. Installing the new RAM has created ESD, which has damaged the motherboard.

7. How do you know when a DIMM is fully seated in the motherboard?

A. Both ends are at the same height.
B. The retention clips lock into place.
C. The motherboard's speaker beeps once.
D. Gentle pressure on the top will not make it go any further.

8. What do modern PC cooling systems use to determine when to adjust the performance of the cooling system to keep the system cool?

A. CAM
B. Heat sensors
C. Case fan
D. Liquid cooling

9. Which of the following could impair the functioning of the installed cooling system? (Select all that apply.)

A. Keeping the case open during PC operation
B. Removing slot covers behind empty expansion slots
C. Vacuuming the interior
D. Dirt and dust

10. Adding this cooling component is an easy and inexpensive cooling system upgrade.

A. Liquid cooling system
B. Case fan
C. CPU heat sink
D. CPU fan

Installing Adapter Cards

11. You have just purchased a new device that requires USB 3.0, but your desktop's USB ports are only at USB 2.0. What is a good solution?

A. Buy a new computer.

B. Buy a converter for the device so it can use a parallel port.

C. Install a USB adapter card with USB 3.0 support.

D. Exchange the device for one with a parallel interface.

12. Before installing an adapter card in a computer, check the documentation and do one of the following, if necessary.

A. Set jumpers.

B. Install the driver.

C. Upgrade the card's firmware.

D. Partition the card.

Installing Storage Devices

13. To remove an internal HDD, which of these do you *not* need to do?

A. Run a utility to position the read/write heads in a safe location.

B. Release the drive from its bay, usually by removing screws.

C. Disconnect the power connector from the drive.

D. Disconnect the data connector from the drive.

14. At what angle should you insert an M.2 module into a slot on the motherboard?

A. Parallel to the motherboard

B. At a 30-degree angle to the motherboard

C. Perpendicular to the motherboard

D. At a 45-degree angle to the motherboard

15. Which of these is *not* solid-state storage?

A. Optical drive

B. M.2 drive

C. USB flash drive

D. Memory card

16. Which types of drives connect to the motherboard via a SATA data cable? (Select all that apply.)

A. USB flash drive

B. HDD

C. SSD

D. M.2 drive

17. How many SATA drives can be connected to a single data cable?

A. 1
B. 2
C. 3
D. 4

18. Which of these interfaces would not be used to connect external storage?

A. eSATA
B. USB 2.0
C. USB 3.0
D. PCIe

19. You have installed a new M.2 SSD in an existing system but Windows doesn't recognize it. What have you neglected to do?

A. Set its jumpers
B. Attach a heat sink
C. Connect power to it
D. Partition and format it

20. You might be able to configure a hardware RAID without installing a RAID controller card if the ______ supports RAID.

A. Motherboard
B. Video card
C. Network interface adapter
D. Sound card

SELF TEST ANSWERS

Installing and Upgrading Motherboards and Onboard Components

1. ☑ **B.** Each motherboard is unique; check the manual.
☒ **A** is incorrect because it states that all ATX motherboards accept all Intel and AMD CPUs and DIMMs. Each motherboard is unique in the components it will support. **C** is incorrect because checking the CPU documentation will not tell you if the motherboard itself will support this CPU. **D** is incorrect because checking the RAM module documentation will not tell you if the motherboard itself will support this module.

2. ☑ **B.** LGA (land grid array) is correct because this type of socket uses both a lever for aligning the contacts and a cover for firmly securing a CPU.
   ☒ **A** is incorrect, because while PGA uses a lever, it does not use a cover. **C** is incorrect because HTPC is the acronym for home theater PC. **D** is incorrect because DIMM is the acronym for Dual Inline Memory Module, a type of RAM.
3. ☑ **C.** Hold a motherboard by the edges.
   ☒ **A** is incorrect because you should never touch any components on the board. **B** is incorrect because circuit boards do not have handles. **D** is incorrect because you will not be able to remove or install a circuit board with a parts grabber.
4. ☑ **B.** Open the retention clips on the socket and align the DIMM vertically with the socket.
   ☒ **A** is incorrect because you must install DIMMs in an upright position. **C** is incorrect because you cannot insert a module if the clips are closed, and you do not insert a DIMM at an angle to the socket. **D** is incorrect only because you must open the clips first.
5. ☑ **D.** DDR3 and DDR4 have different numbers of pins and different lengths.
   ☒ **A** is incorrect because they both install vertically, aligned with the socket. **B** is incorrect because DIMM thickness is not a differentiating factor. **C** is incorrect because the number of pins and different notching prevent this.
6. ☑ **A.** Not all motherboards support higher denominations of RAM than they are originally equipped with. Check the motherboard manual.
   ☒ **B** is incorrect because although this is a possibility, it would be unlikely that all the DIMMs were not seated. **C** is incorrect because RAM is keyed so you can't install it backwards. **D** is incorrect because installing RAM is unlikely to create ESD.
7. ☑ **B.** The retention clips lock into place when RAM is fully seated. This is the surest way to tell.
   ☒ **A** is incorrect because both ends could be the same height because neither end is fully seated. **C** is incorrect because there is no power to the motherboard during RAM installation so there would be no beeping. **D** is incorrect because "gentle pressure" is subjective; the retention clips are the more reliable way to tell.
8. ☑ **B.** Heat sensors are used by modern cooling systems to detect when to adjust the performance of the cooling system to keep the system cool.
   ☒ **A** is incorrect because CAM is an acronym for computer-aided manufacturing. **C** is incorrect because a case fan is part of a cooling system, not something that would be used to detect a temperature problem. **D** is incorrect because liquid cooling is a type of cooling system, not something that would be used to detect a temperature problem.
9. ☑ **A, B,** and **D.** They are all actions that would impair the functioning of the cooling system. **A** and **B** disturb the airflow design for the case. **D** acts as insulation and reduces the cooling ability.
   ☒ **C** is incorrect because this will remove dirt and dust from components, improving the efficiency of cooling and not impairing it.

10. ☑ **B.** Adding a case fan is an easy and cheap cooling system upgrade if there is a place to mount the fan in the case and power is available.
☒ **A** is incorrect because a liquid cooling system is the most difficult and most expensive cooling system upgrade. **C** is incorrect because adding a heat sink would not be easy, although it may be cheap, unless the CPU is damaged in the process. **D** is incorrect because adding a CPU fan would not be easy, although it may be inexpensive, unless the CPU is damaged in the process.

Installing Adapter Cards

11. ☑ **C.** Installing a USB adapter card with USB 3.0 support is a good solution.
☒ **A** is incorrect because buying a new computer is not necessarily the solution to a single outdated component on a PC. **B** is incorrect because you do not know that this is even possible with the device or that the PC has a parallel port. **D** is incorrect because most devices have a USB interface, not parallel, and most PCs do not have parallel ports.

12. ☑ **A.** Set jumpers, if necessary, before installing an adapter card in a computer.
☒ **B** is incorrect because you will install the driver the first time you start the computer after installing the card. **C** is incorrect because you cannot update the card's firmware until after it is installed. **D** is incorrect because partitioning is not something you do to an adapter card.

Installing Storage Devices

13. ☑ **A.** You do not have to run any utility or set the read/write heads in any certain way before removing a drive.
☒ **B, C,** and **D** are incorrect because they represent the three things that you *do* need to do to remove a modern internal storage device. You must remove the drive from its bay and disconnect the power and data connectors.

14. ☑ **B.** Insert an M.2 module at a 30-degree angle, and then fasten it down to the motherboard with a retaining screw.
☒ **A, C,** and **D** are incorrect because they are not the correct angle. Although an M.2 module eventually ends up parallel to the motherboard after the retaining screw is connected, that is not how to install it initially.

15. ☑ **A.** An optical drive is not solid-state; it is a mechanical drive that relies on moving parts.
☒ **B** is incorrect because an M.2 drive is a solid-state drive. **C** is incorrect because USB flash drives are solid-state. **D** is incorrect because memory cards are solid-state.

16. ☑ **B** and **C.** Both HDD and SSD storage are available with a SATA interface.
☒ **A** is incorrect because a USB flash drive, by definition, uses a USB interface. **D** is incorrect because an M.2 drive, by definition, connects to an M.2 interface and does not use a cable.

17. ☑ **A.** Each SATA cable supports only one drive.
☒ **B, C,** and **D** are incorrect because SATA supports only one drive per cable, not two, three, or four. PATA drives (now obsolete) supported up to two drives per cable.

18. ☑ **D.** PCIe is an internal interface and would not support an external drive.
☒ **A, B,** and **C** are incorrect because eSATA, USB 2.0, and USB 3.0 are all common types of external storage connections.

19. ☑ **D.** SSDs, like all drives, must be partitioned and formatted.
☒ **A** is incorrect because SSDs do not have jumpers that need to be set for them to operate. **B** is incorrect because although some SSDs do have heat sinks, the lack of one would not be apparent until the module started to overheat. **C** is incorrect because M.2 modules do not require separate power connectors.

20. ☑ **A.** A motherboard can serve as a RAID controller if it includes that functionality.
☒ **B, C,** and **D** are incorrect because none of these adapter cards would include RAID functionality; they have nothing to do with storage.

Chapter 12

PC Hardware Troubleshooting and Maintenance

CERTIFICATION OBJECTIVES

- **1101: 5.1** Given a scenario, apply the best practice methodology to resolve problems
- **1101: 5.2** Given a scenario, troubleshoot problems related to motherboards, RAM, CPUs, and power
- **1101: 5.3** Given a scenario, troubleshoot and diagnose problems with storage drives and RAID arrays
- **1101: 5.4** Given a scenario, troubleshoot video, projector, and display issues
- **1102: 1.3** Given a scenario, use features and tools of the Microsoft Windows 10 operating system (OS)

✓ Two-Minute Drill

Q&A Self Test

The most common procedures you will perform as a computer technician are troubleshooting and resolving computer problems. The more familiar you are with a computer's components, the easier it will be for you to find the source of a problem and implement a solution. Build your comfort level by studying the previous chapters in this book and by gaining experience. In this chapter, you will first learn the best practice methodology to resolve problems and then you will progress to basic diagnostic procedures and troubleshooting techniques, practice isolating PC component issues, discover the appropriate troubleshooting tools, and become proactive using common preventive maintenance techniques.

This chapter covers all the 5.0 Network Troubleshooting domain objectives for the 1101 exam with three exceptions: mobile device troubleshooting (5.5) is covered in Chapter 13, printer troubleshooting (5.6) in Chapter 15, and network troubleshooting (5.7) in Chapter 19.

CERTIFICATION OBJECTIVES

- ***1101: 5.1*** *Given a scenario, apply the best practice methodology to resolve problems*
- ***1002: 1.3*** *Given a scenario, use features and tools of the Microsoft Windows 10 operating system (OS)*

For A+ 1101 exam Objective 5.1, CompTIA requires that you understand the best practice methodology, procedures, and techniques that this section details. This section also covers a single topic, Device Manager, from A+ 1102 exam Objective 1.3. (Device Manager is also listed in 1102 exam Objective 1.4.)

Preparing for Troubleshooting

Troubleshooting is the act of discovering the cause of a problem and correcting it. It sounds simple, and if you watch an experienced technician, it may appear to be. However, troubleshooting a PC requires patience, instinct, experience, and a methodical approach. In this section, we will explore a methodical approach to best practice methodology and techniques. You will need to acquire the experience on your own, and you will find that your experiences will hone your instincts.

Protecting Systems and Gathering Tools

When faced with a computer-related problem, resist the urge to jump right in and apply your favorite all-purpose solution. Rather, take time to do the following:

1. Make sure you understand the corporate policies and procedures relating to computer usage, and consider the larger impact of any changes you might make to a computer system. For example, if you need to take an important server offline to fix it, you ought to know what times of day the server is used the least so you can schedule the downtime accordingly.
2. Before you make any changes to a user's computer, verify that you have a recent set of backups of the user's data. If you find there isn't one, perform backups of data (at a minimum) and the entire system—providing the system is functional enough for these tasks. If backups are not available and there is no way to do a backup, inform the customer that they may lose all their data. Bad news is best served up immediately, but gently.
3. Always have a pad and pencil, tablet PC, smartphone, or other means to record your actions, findings, and outcomes. A digital camera or device with a camera built in is also handy for documenting the hardware before and after and at various stages of disassembly. Recording your actions will be critical to the documentation you create at the end of the entire process.
4. Assemble troubleshooting tools—both hardware and software tools. Check out the list in "The Hardware Toolkit" section in Chapter 8. Many software troubleshooting tools are built into Windows. Some of these were covered in Chapter 6, and we will describe others in this chapter.
5. Apply the best practice methodology, described next.

Troubleshooting Best Practice Methodology

Experienced IT professionals find that six procedures, taken in order, are important for solving most problems and for documenting the problems and solutions for future reference and training. CompTIA A+ 1101 exam Objective 5.1 lists the following procedures, and we describe each in more detail in the following paragraphs.

1. Identify the problem.
2. Establish a theory of probable cause (question the obvious).
3. Test the theory to determine the cause.
4. Establish a plan of action to resolve the problem and then implement the solution.
5. Verify full system functionality and, if applicable, implement preventative measures.
6. Document the findings, actions, and outcomes.

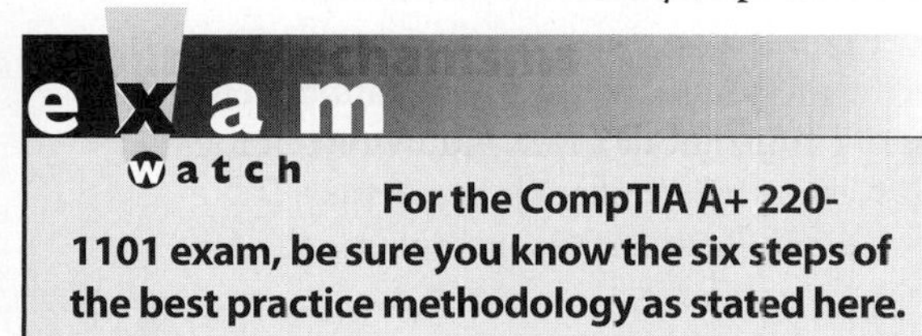

For the CompTIA A+ 220-1101 exam, be sure you know the six steps of the best practice methodology as stated here.

Identify the Problem

Clearly identify the problem. Always gather as much information as you can about the computer and its peripherals, applications, operating system, and history. Do this even when the solution seems obvious.

Examine the Environment Ideally, you will be able to go onsite and see the computer "patient" in its working environment so you can gather information from your own observations. Once onsite, you may notice a situation that contributed to the problem or that could cause other problems. If you cannot go onsite, you may be able to diagnose and correct software problems remotely, using Remote Assistance or Remote Desktop, methods you will explore in Chapter 18. Otherwise, you must depend solely on the user's observations. Whether onsite or remote, you are looking for the cause of the problem, which is often a result of some change, either in the environment or to the computer directly.

on the job

When troubleshooting a system that is not functioning properly, make it a practice to always perform a visual inspection of all cables and connectors, making sure all connections are proper before you invest any time in troubleshooting.

Question the User: What Has Happened? The best source for learning what happened leading up to a problem is the person who was using the computer when the problem occurred. Your first question to the user should be, "What happened?" This question will prompt the user to tell you about the problem—for example, "The printer will not work." Ask for a specific description of the events leading up to the failure and the symptoms the user experienced.

"Do other devices work?" This question will help you isolate the problem. If one or more other devices also do not work, you know you are dealing with a more serious, device-independent problem.

Ask about a problem device's history. "Did this device ever work?" If the user tells you that it is a newly installed device, you have a very different task ahead of you than if you learn that it has worked fine until just now. The former indicates a flawed installation, whereas the latter points to a possible failure of the device itself.

If the user mentions an error message, ask for as much detail about the error message as possible. If the user cannot remember, try to re-create the problem. Ask if this error message is new or old and if the computer's behavior changed after the error. For example, the computer might issue a warning that simply informs the user of some condition. If the error code points to a device, such as an optical drive, ask device-related questions.

The event logs in Windows save many error messages, so if the user cannot remember the error messages, check the event logs. Learn more about the Windows event logs in Chapter 6.

Sometimes customers are reluctant to give you all the details of the problem because they fear being embarrassed or held responsible. Treat the customer in a respectful manner that encourages trust and openness about what may have occurred. In Chapter 1, you learned how important good communication skills are and how to apply them every day.

Question the User: What Has Changed? You should also find out about any recent changes to the computer or the surroundings. Ask if a new component or application was recently installed. If so, ask if the computer has worked at all since then. The answer to this question could lead you to important information about application or device conflicts. For example, if the user tells you the audio has not worked since a particular game was loaded, you can surmise that the two events—the loading of the new game and the audio failure—are related. When troubleshooting, remove the software or any other upgrades installed shortly before the problem occurred.

Before making any changes, perform backups. And always remember to inquire regarding environmental or infrastructure changes.

Establish a Theory of Probable Cause

When you have determined the symptoms of a problem, try to replicate the problem and begin an analysis from which you will develop your theory of probable cause. Question the obvious. That is, if the user says the printer does not work, have him send another print job to the printer. Watch closely as he performs the task. Take note of any error messages or unusual computer activity that he may not have noticed. Observation will also give you a chance to see the process from beginning to end. Looking over the user's shoulder (so to speak) gives you a different perspective, and you may see a mistake, such as an incorrect printer selection or the absence of an entry in the Number of Copies to Print field, that caused the problem.

CompTIA A+ 1101 exam Objective 5.1 explicitly states "question the obvious." Be prepared for scenario-based questions in which the answer may not be exactly "question the obvious," but a choice that could be an example of doing that, as described here.

Vendor Documentation As you work to pinpoint the source of the problem, check out any vendor documentation for the software or hardware associated with the problem.

This may be in the form of hard copy or information posted on the vendor's website. For example, you might discover from the user forums on the website that there is a known incompatibility between a certain application and a certain brand of display adapter that can be resolved with a driver update. (That example is actually pretty common. Out-of-date display drivers can cause many problems that are not obviously display related.)

Hardware or Software From your observations and the information you gather from the user, try to pinpoint the cause of the problem. It may be obvious that a device failed if the device itself will not power up. If the source of the problem is not yet apparent, however, you need to narrow down the search even further by determining whether the problem is hardware or software related. We consider a hardware problem to include the device as well as its device drivers and configuration. Software problems include applications, operating systems, and utilities.

One of the quickest ways to determine if hardware or software is at fault is to use Windows *Device Manager*, a Windows GUI utility for viewing the status of devices and installing, removing, and updating devices. The list available to Device Manager, called the *hardware profile*, is a list in the registry of all devices that have been installed on Windows and not uninstalled (drivers have not been removed), even if the physical devices are removed or disabled. This gives Device Manager access to the listed hardware and their status. Device Manager will indicate any conflicting or "unknown" devices. But even if Device Manager offers no information about the problem, it does not mean it is not hardware related; it only means Windows has not recognized it. Exercise 12-1 shows you how to open Device Manager and look for problem devices, an important task when troubleshooting hardware.

EXERCISE 12-1

Troubleshooting with Device Manager

Complete this exercise to practice using Device Manager to troubleshoot hardware.

1. Open the Run dialog box (WINDOWS KEY-R), enter **devmgmt.msc**, and click OK. You can alternatively right-click the Start button and click Device Manager.

   In the Device Manager window, you will see the devices on your computer organized under types of hardware, such as Computer, Disk Drives, Display Adapters, and Human Interface Devices, as shown in the illustration on the following page.

   If Windows detects a problem with a device, it expands the device type to show the devices. In the case of a device with a configuration problem, you will see an exclamation mark on the device icon. When Windows recognizes a device but does not understand its type, it places the device under a type named Other Devices, and you will see a question mark.

2. If you see an exclamation mark or question mark on an icon, double-click the item to open its Properties dialog box. If not, double-click the Network Adapters category and then double-click any network adapter.
3. Look on the General tab in the Device Status box. It will either say *This device is working properly* or display an error message or code. You can look up error messages or codes online for further troubleshooting ideas.

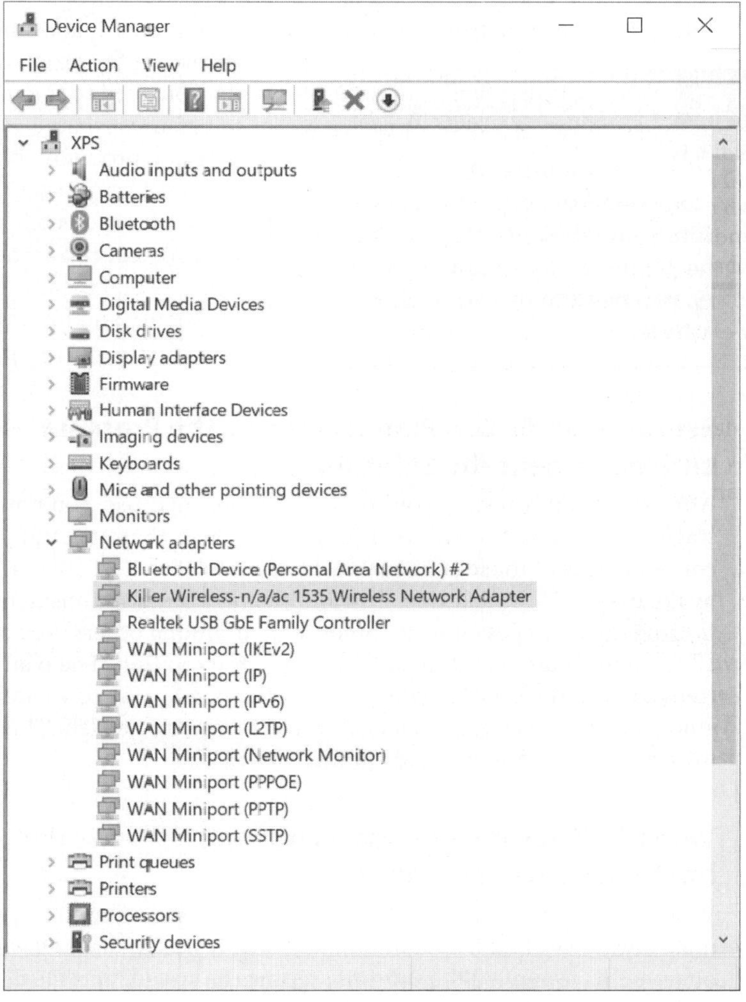

Probable Causes From your observations while conducting external or internal research based on symptoms, compile a list of probable causes, and if any of them has a simple solution, apply it first. If that does not solve the problem, then investigate the other items on your list.

Test the Theory to Determine the Actual Cause

After establishing a theory of probable cause, test the theory. You may need to do this on a test system, isolated from the rest of the network, or, if that is not an option, simply test the theory on the problem system. Whatever you do, you need to find a way to test your theory in a manner that does not endanger the user's data and productivity. Does this solution extend beyond a single user's desktop or beyond your scope of responsibility? If so, you must escalate the problem to another department, such as network administration. Once you have tested the theory and found it to be successful, you can move to the next step.

Remember that once a theory is confirmed during step 3, you need to determine the next steps to finally resolve the problem. If you can't confirm the theory, you need to re-establish a new one or escalate.

Establish an Action Plan to Resolve the Problem and Implement the Solution

After successfully testing your theory of probable cause, you now move on to the planning stage. Now you need to think through both the actions you must take and the possible consequences of those actions, involving people from all areas affected by the problem and by the effects of the solution. Possible business areas to consider include accounting, billing, manufacturing, sales, and customer service, among others. You also need to check with all IT support areas that must take part in the solution. The plan should then include the steps to take; the order in which to take them, referring to vendor instructions for possible guidance if necessary; and all testing and follow-up needed. This will include steps required to minimize any possible bad effects.

Verify Full System Functionality and, If Applicable, Implement Preventative Measures

Whether the problem and solution involve a single computer or an entire enterprise, you must always verify full system functionality. If you are dealing with a single desktop system, once you have applied the solution, restart the system and the device (if appropriate), and test to be sure everything works. If your solution seems to have negatively affected anything, take additional steps to correct the problem—you may find yourself back in the troubleshooting loop.

Once you have successfully tested a solution, have the user verify and confirm that your solution solved the problem. This verification should begin just like the user's workday begins: with the user restarting the computer and/or logging on and opening each application used in a typical day and then using all peripherals such as printers. Have the user confirm that everything is working.

This is a very important step to take, regardless of the scope of the problem and solution. Our experience has been that once you touch a problem system, even though you might solve the problem, the person in charge or individual user will associate you with the next thing that goes wrong. Then you will receive a call stating that "such and such" has not worked since you were there, even though "such and such" does not relate to any changes you made.

Therefore, once everything is working normally and both you and the client have tested for full system functionality, have them sign off on it to document the satisfactory results. If this last step is not an accepted procedure in your organization, you should suggest adopting it because it adds commitment to both sides of this transaction. You are committed to testing and confirming a successful solution, and the user is committed to acknowledging the solution worked.

Document the Findings, Actions, and Outcomes

Document all findings, actions, and outcomes! Take notes as you work, and once you have resolved the problem, review the notes and add any omissions. Sit down with the client and review what you did. This is your statement to the client that you made certain changes. You should be clear that you made no other changes to the system.

These notes, whether informal or formal, such as comments entered into a help-desk database, will be useful when you encounter identical or similar problems. It's a good idea to incorporate some of the lessons learned during troubleshooting into training for both end users and support personnel.

Training

Well-trained personnel are the best defense against problems. Therefore, an important troubleshooting technique is ongoing training for both end users and support personnel. The delivery methods and training materials should suit the environment, as many options are available for high-quality online training, starting with the help programs available in most operating systems and applications, user manuals, installation manuals, and Internet or intranet resources. All personnel involved should know how to access any training resources available. End users can often solve their own problems by checking out the help program or accessing an online training module, cutting down on the number of service calls and associated loss of productivity.

SCENARIO & SOLUTION	
You need to make some changes to a computer to test a theory of probable cause. What should you do before making the changes?	Verify there is a recent backup of all important files; if backups do not exist, perform a backup.
You think you know the cause of a problem by evaluating the symptoms. Should you question the user anyway?	Yes. You should learn what happened and what has changed and gather all the information before jumping to any conclusions about the solution.
You have found a solution, applied it, and successfully tested it. What is the final step you need to take?	Document the troubleshooting activities and outcomes.

CERTIFICATION OBJECTIVE

- ***1101: 5.2*** *Given a scenario, troubleshoot problems related to motherboards, RAM, CPUs, and power*

CompTIA A+ 1101 exam Objective 5.2 requires that you be able to explain and interpret common symptoms and, when faced with a scenario, know how to detect problems, troubleshoot, and repair or replace the essential computer components of RAM, CPUs, and power supplies. This section describes common symptoms and tools.

Troubleshooting Motherboards, RAM, CPUs, and Power

This section discusses procedures for troubleshooting common component problems, physical symptoms that can occur with various devices, power-on self-test (POST) audio and text error codes, and, for certain components, specific symptoms and solutions. For each component problem, we describe scenarios, probable causes, and solutions.

Procedures

When troubleshooting PC components, first do all that you can without opening the PC. If you do not find the source of the problem and a potential solution through nonintrusive methods, then you will have to open the PC. Follow these steps, which will take you from the least intrusive to the most intrusive:

1. Check for proper connections (external device).
2. Check for appropriate external components.

3. Check installation: drivers, driver settings, and physical settings.
4. Check proper seating of components (internal adapter card, memory, and so on).
5. Simplify the system by removing unneeded peripherals. If the problem goes away, then you must isolate the problem peripheral.

While the traditional PC cases—towers and desktop system units—are convenient to open for adding or replacing components, the same is not true of the newer all-in-ones, such as Apple iMacs. All the components normally found inside a computer case are inside the display case, and opening the case in most cases voids the warranty—and is very difficult to do without causing damage. This makes it even more imperative that you make every effort to troubleshoot using the least intrusive tactics.

Even the most knowledgeable technician cannot repair some problems with computers or components. That is why it is important to pay attention to warranties on equipment. In large organizations, warranties are managed through contracts with companies that provide the hardware and support it. In those cases, the contractor removes the failed equipment and replaces it. But if you, or your company or school, do not have such an arrangement, someone needs to be tracking the computer equipment as managed assets, and they must pay close attention to warranties—whether they are the basic warranty that comes with the item or a purchased extended warranty.

Manufacturers allow for returns of in-warranty equipment, but you need to contact the manufacturer and make arrangements, which will usually involve reporting the failure and receiving what amounts to permission to return the equipment. This permission is a *returned materials authorization (RMA)*, which now often comes by e-mail, and you must wait to receive this before packing up and returning the item. The RMA usually has a number that must be displayed somewhere on the packaging.

General Symptoms

Inspect a computer and its peripherals for physical symptoms. Several symptoms can apply to any of several components, such as excessive heat, loud noise, odors, status light indicators, and visible damage to the device itself or cabling. When one of these symptoms occurs, take appropriate action based on the symptom and the device.

Lockups, Shutdowns, and Crash Screens

There are many possible causes of system instability problems with symptoms like system lockups, spontaneous shutdowns, and OS-specific crash screens, like the Blue Screen of Death (BSOD) in Windows, which appears when a serious, system-stopping error occurs. (It's actually a black screen in Windows 11, but the nickname persists.) We tend to suspect software, especially device drivers, but these symptoms can and do occur after a failure of a motherboard component. We discussed troubleshooting software-caused problems in Chapter 6. However, if you see any of these symptoms, first do basic troubleshooting of your hardware, especially the motherboard and associated components. Here are descriptions of these system instability symptoms so that you recognize them:

- **System lockups** These appear as a screen that will not change or show any response to mouse movement. In some cases, the mouse pointer still moves but shows an hourglass, or whatever symbol it normally shows when the system or an app is busy and cannot respond to input.
- **System shutdowns/unexpected shutdowns** These are just what the terms imply: the system simply shuts down—usually without any warning. You may see an error message beforehand, but not necessarily.
- **OS-specific crashes** The BSOD, more conventionally called the *stop screen,* appears when the Windows operating system detects a critical error and literally stops the system so that the error doesn't cause loss of data (or further loss of data). All operating systems have some form of the stop screen, and the Windows stop screen displays an error message indicating what software component failed. You can use this information to troubleshoot the cause of the problem. Learn more about working with the BSOD error information in Chapter 6. On a Mac, instead of BSOD, you get the Pinwheel of Death, an endlessly spinning mouse pointer and failure to respond to keyboard or mouse input.

Excess Heat/Overheating/Burning Smell

If you observe a burning smell or smoke, or if wires or cables are hot, it's important to immediately unplug the computer to avoid an electrical fire. Leave the computer off and let it cool until you can safely replace it or otherwise solve the problem. Later in this chapter, we will discuss power supplies and cooling systems—components related to these symptoms.

Unusual Noises

Unusual noises may occur if a device has moving parts, such as a fan or printer. In these cases, a new or different noise usually means a component, such as a fan bearing, is failing. This will reduce the fan's effectiveness and cause an unusual noise.

Status Indicators

Many devices, such as printers and network adapters, have one or more *status light indicators*—usually a *light-emitting diode (LED),* a semiconductor resembling a tiny light bulb. These usually indicate a problem with the device by changing the color of the light, by blinking or remaining steady, or by a combination of both. Look for labels on the device itself defining the function of each light. For example, a network interface card (NIC) may have a light with a label of "ACT" for "activity," indicating the card is indeed transmitting data. A multispeed NIC might have a different colored light for each of its speeds. These same indicators are often duplicated as icons in the status area (also called the notification area) of the taskbar on the Windows desktop. The applet associated with the icon will issue alerts when a device malfunctions.

Other physical symptoms include damage to a device, such as an area of melted plastic on a case or cable, a broken cable or connector pin, or a socket device not getting the appropriate signals (often due to a loose connection). Of course, when inspection of a device or cabling shows physical damage, such as a break or the appearance of melted plastic, you need to determine the extent of the damage and the right solution for the problem, such as replacing the device or cable.

Black Screen/Only the Fan Works

If you can hear the power supply fan and/or a case fan but nothing else seems to work, including the display, then power the system off, open the case, and check out all power connectors between the power supply and the motherboard, reseating all of them. Also, look for some sort of debris that could be shorting out the motherboard and remove it. Something else that can cause the motherboard to short out is an incorrectly installed standoff—a washer-like part made of nonconductive material designed to keep the motherboard from coming in contact with the case. Yet another possible cause of this symptom is a failed CPU (although usually if the CPU doesn't work, the fan doesn't spin).

No Power

It's easy to assume that if you turn on the PC and nothing happens, the power supply is at fault. In actuality, though, a dead power supply is only one of several possible causes. A more likely cause is failure to supply AC power to the power supply; snug the power cord at both ends, and make sure that if it's plugged into a surge suppressor, the surge suppressor's on/off switch is in the On position. A faulty motherboard can also be the root cause, because the power coming from the power supply isn't being delivered via the motherboard to the other components.

Intermittent Shutdown/Device Failure

If one device fails periodically, there are several causes to investigate. First, there could be an incorrect BIOS/UEFI system setting or wrong device driver. Heat can cause such symptoms, in which case the device works fine until the system heats up. Because people use computers in all types of environments, we often forget that they work best in a low-to-moderate ambient temperature, around 60 to 75 degrees Fahrenheit. Of course, the internal temperature is higher than that, so the computer's own cooling system must work harder as the environment gets hotter. If you witness intermittent device failure that coincides with a rise in ambient temperature, take steps to cool the environment and/or to augment the internal cooling system, or replace the entire system with a more rugged system designed to survive the higher temperatures.

Another possible cause of intermittent device failure could be the power supply unit providing too little or too much power or not maintaining a constant supply to the system. Test the power supply, as described later in this chapter.

Troubleshooting Motherboard Problems

A properly configured motherboard will typically perform flawlessly for several years. Things that can change that happy state include power problems, actual component failure, and incorrect changes to the system. A major motherboard failure will prevent the computer from booting properly. However, if the firmware can run a POST, it might report a problem with the motherboard. In either case, consult the motherboard manual and the manufacturer's website for solutions to the problem.

POST Audio and Visual Errors

A faulty motherboard can cause many different symptoms and can even make it appear that a different component is at fault. This is because a motherboard problem might manifest in one particular area, such as a single circuit or port, causing the failure of a single device only. For example, if the video card's expansion slot on the motherboard stops working, it will appear that the display system has a problem. In this case, you are likely to discover the motherboard as the point of failure only after checking all other components in the video system.

In Chapter 8 we briefly described the POST that occurs when a PC starts up. The POST checks for the presence and status of existing components. A visual (text) error message on the screen or POST code beeps typically indicate errors found during the POST. A single beep at the end of the POST, or no beeps at all, normally means that it detected no errors and the system should continue booting into the operating system. A single beep is more common on an older PC; newer PCs do not usually beep at startup.

If you hear multiple beeps, or if the system does not continue the normal startup, consult the motherboard manufacturer's documentation. Different patterns of audible beeps can indicate different kinds of hardware problems on the motherboard and its components (like RAM, CPU, and built-in adapters).

On some systems, POST text error messages appear in the upper-left corner as white characters on a black screen and can point you in the right direction for troubleshooting an error at startup. For instance, if a firmware manufacturer uses the traditional codes 1*xx*, 2*xx*, and 3*xx* (where *xx* = a range of numbers from 00 to 99), they can indicate system board, memory, or keyboard failures, respectively. Similarly, the 17*xx* error codes may indicate a hard disk controller or hard drive problem. These are the original POST error codes. If you see numeric digits during a failed startup, check out the website of the firmware manufacturer to find a list of codes so that you can interpret them.

If you believe a motherboard component is failing but no type of error code displays, a POST card (one of the tools listed in the hardware toolkit in Chapter 8) will give you more information. Consider buying one if you support many computers with the same or similar motherboard. Install a POST card into a motherboard expansion slot, then power up the computer. A small two-character LED display will show hexadecimal codes for errors detected on startup, and the documentation that comes with the POST card will help you decipher the error codes. Then you will know what component is failing and you can decide how to fix it. If it is an embedded component that is not easily replaced, such as a problem with the chipset, you may need to replace the entire motherboard. You can usually remedy a problem with an embedded video adapter or drive controller by installing a replacement into an expansion slot.

Sometimes called PC analysis cards, POST cards come in a wide range of prices and with connectors for one or two types of expansion slots. Check out the specifications before purchasing, but an inexpensive card will usually suffice.

Physical Changes

Physical sources of motherboard problems can include jumper or switch settings, front panel connectors, back panel connectors, sockets, expansion slots, and memory slots. Because jumpers and switches are mechanical elements, they won't change unless someone has opened the system and fiddled with them. If you think someone has opened the system, double-check the jumper and switch settings and compare them with the manufacturer's documentation. If you are 100 percent sure that someone made a change that caused the present problems, determine the correct settings and then return the jumpers or switches to those settings. Jumpers are present mainly on old motherboards; newer ones use firmware settings instead to control board settings.

Another possible physical motherboard problem source is loose or improperly made connections. These could include improper insertion of adapter cards into expansion slots, or of memory sticks into memory slots, or of the cables connecting onboard I/O ports to front or back panel connectors.

Capacitor Swelling/Swollen Batteries

A physical inspection of the motherboard may show one or more capacitors that are distended (swollen) or have some sort of brownish residue on them. These capacitors are typically mounted on their ends, sitting perpendicular to the motherboard, as shown in Figure 12-1. Such a motherboard should be replaced even if it is currently exhibiting no problems. Electronics experts may attempt to change out the capacitors themselves (since the motherboard is going to have to be discarded otherwise), but most nonprofessionals will choose to replace the whole motherboard.

FIGURE 12-1 Swollen (distended) capacitors on a motherboard, with residue on the tops indicating physical failure (Photo: https://en.wikipedia.org/wiki/Capacitor_plague#/media/File:Al-Elko-bad-caps-Wiki-07-02-17.jpg [Creative Commons license])

A mobile device battery (such as the removable battery on a smartphone or tablet) can also become distended or swollen, indicating that it is failing. Do not use a mobile device if its battery appears physically abnormal; have the device serviced right away.

Inaccurate System Date Time/Firmware Problems

Motherboards come with a small coin-size battery, such as a 3-volt lithium battery. It keeps the real-time clock current. On older motherboards it also keeps the CMOS RAM powered to retain BIOS/UEFI settings. Since this battery supports the date and time tracking, the classic symptom of a failed battery is a system that does not keep the correct time after turning it off. If that occurs, open the case and remove the battery, much as you would remove a watch battery. Then find a replacement for it that matches the voltage and designation number of the old battery. On newer motherboards, settings are stored in nonvolatile memory, so a battery is required only to maintain the date/time. Exercise 12-2 walks you through the battery replacement process.

If the system repeatedly loses track of time when turned off, you probably need to replace the battery. This is usually a simple process, requiring opening the case and exchanging the old battery for a new one.

EXERCISE 12-2

Replacing the Motherboard Battery

For this exercise you will need a desktop system with a motherboard that has a battery.

1. Enter the computer's BIOS/UEFI setup program and make a backup copy of the current settings, using whatever method is available to you. You may want to take a digital picture with your camera, smartphone, or other device. You can also simply write down the settings.
2. Turn off the computer, unplug power, and remove the cover, ensuring you carry out the proper electrostatic discharge (ESD) prevention procedures.
3. Locate the battery on the motherboard.
4. Slide the battery out from under the retaining clip. The clip uses slight tension to hold the battery in place, so you do not need to remove the clip or bend it outward.
5. Note the battery's orientation when installed, and install the new battery the same way.
6. Restart the computer. Enter the system's setup program again and restore the BIOS/UEFI settings you recorded in Step 1.

If your system will not support a new device, you may need a firmware update. Before doing this, be sure to back up the firmware settings or make note of them in some way—such as photographing each screen with a digital camera. Then, using the manufacturer's utility, install the firmware update, either from a local drive or from a source over the Internet.

How is it possible to update something that is "read-only"? The answer is that you can change many modern ROMs, but only by special means. Today, that is normally a special program from the manufacturer. This is why reading the documentation before updating the firmware is important. We often call upgrading firmware *flashing the BIOS*. This applies to system-level firmware, as well as to the firmware on an individual adapter.

Become familiar with the firmware setup menu screens and practice navigating through these menus, as described in Exercises 8-4 and 8-5 in Chapter 8. This means booting the system and selecting the keyboard option after the POST that lets you access system setup. The first thing you should then do is look for the help hints, usually at the bottom or in a sidebar on every screen. Then find out how you can exit from the BIOS/UEFI without saving changes. Knowing this is important, because almost everyone who explores these menus gets confused about whether they have inadvertently made a change, and the best way to back out of that situation is to select Exit Without Saving, if it is available. If not, look for two exit methods. For instance, you might use the F10 function key for Save and Exit and the ESC key for exiting without saving.

Although the exact BIOS/UEFI menu organization varies by manufacturer, the main menu will have the most basic settings, such as system date and time, detected drives, and drive interfaces. An advanced menu will often have the settings for the CPU, the chipset, the onboard devices, the expansion bus configuration, and overclocking, an option that boosts CPU performance. You do not need to use overclocking on computers designated for simple office tasks, but people often use it for computers requiring higher CPU performance, such as for gaming and other tasks requiring maximum performance. (Overclocking may cause the CPU to overheat and may void the system warranty, so beware.) Other advanced BIOS/UEFI settings may involve configuring the PCIe bus and Universal Serial Bus (USB) settings.

Incorrect BIOS/UEFI settings can have many permutations because there are settings for a great variety of system elements, including the hard drives, the boot sequence, keyboard status, and parallel port settings. An incorrect setting will manifest as an error relating to that device or function, so pinpointing a specific source of a problem can be difficult. However, when you need to change or update firmware settings, enter the firmware setup program, as described in Exercise 8-4 in Chapter 8. Make the appropriate change(s), save the new setting(s), and restart the computer.

Troubleshooting RAM Problems

If you turn on the computer and it does not even complete the POST, or it does nothing at all, and you have eliminated power problems, the main memory might have a problem.

Sometimes the motherboard will emit multiple beeps at startup when memory is at fault. Check out a beep code reference online for the firmware brand you're working with, like the one at www.computerhope.com/beep.htm. Keep in mind that the firmware brand is different from the PC brand.

Windows offers the Windows Memory Diagnostic tool (Start | Run | mdsched), which you can use check your computer for memory problems. Many motherboard BIOS/UEFI utilities also have built-in hardware checkers that can report any faulty RAM.

The solution to a memory problem is to remove the offending component and replace it with a new one. If the error persists, the memory might be in a damaged slot or socket on the motherboard. In this case, replace the motherboard, or the entire PC.

One important thing to keep in mind is that the computer may not report some RAM errors at all. That is, if an entire memory module does not work, the computer might just ignore it and continue to function normally without it. At startup, watch the RAM count on the screen (if firmware configuration allows this) or check the reported memory amount in the OS to ensure the total amount available matches the capacity installed in the machine. If this amount comes up significantly short, you will probably have to replace a memory module.

There is also the possibility that the wrong kind of RAM has been installed or it has been installed improperly. Refer to Chapter 11, section "Optimizing a System by Adding RAM," for more information about properly installing and optimizing RAM.

Troubleshooting CPUs

In most cases, CPU problems are fatal, meaning the computer will not boot at all. These problems also closely relate to motherboard problems, such as CPU socket failure, so it can be difficult to pinpoint which component is at fault without having spare parts you can swap out or a POST card that provides a code.

If you turn on the computer and it does not complete the POST, or it does nothing at all, and you have eliminated power problems, you might discover the processor has a problem. A persistent error indicates a possible problem with the slot or socket that the processor connects to the motherboard with. In this case, you need to replace the motherboard. Check the system warranty before taking any action, because the warranty could cover motherboard failure. If you determine the problem is isolated to the CPU, then you will have to replace it, in which case you must replace it with an exact match for the motherboard, including the socket type, speed, number of cores, internal cache, power consumption, and other features. Use the motherboard documentation or information for the motherboard at the manufacturer's website to determine the exact requirements before purchasing a new CPU.

on the Job

Considering today's low PC prices, if you encounter a CPU or motherboard problem on a computer not covered by a warranty, consider replacing the entire system. First, however, check to see if it is a leased computer and what the lease agreement says about component failures, service, and replacement.

A computer that has become slower can be a symptom of overheating. The CPU may have reduced its clock speed in response to overheating, a practice called *throttling*. A processor that has activated thermal throttling will run slower. Why is the computer overheating? Perhaps because of dust, blocked vents, or a failed cooling fan. Check out these possibilities and remedy any that you find.

Troubleshooting Power Supplies

Power supplies can experience either total or partial failure, resulting in inconsistent or displaced symptoms. However, to pinpoint the problem, you can check a few common symptoms of power supply failure; we discuss those symptoms in the section "Symptoms Associated with Power Supply Problems" later in this chapter.

When the power supply fails, replace it. Never try to open or repair a power supply, because it can hold enough charge to injure you seriously, and the time spent on such a repair is more valuable than the replacement cost of a power supply.

When installing a new power supply in a PC, check the wattage and capacity, the availability and types of connectors, and the output voltage required by the computer components to ensure it will have sufficient power and the correct connections.

As suggested in Chapter 8, you can use either a multimeter or a power supply tester to make sure that a power supply is putting out the correct voltages. A multimeter requires more knowledge of electricity to use and is a more sophisticated instrument, measuring resistance, voltage, and/or current in computer components. Figure 12-2 shows a digital multimeter with a digital display. Analog multimeters exist (with a needle that swings to show values), but they are mostly obsolete.

To use a multimeter, you connect two probes (red and black) to the meter and set the meter to what you want to measure. For instance, set it to AC Volts to measure wall line voltage, DC Volts to measure the voltage coming from the power supply, or Ohms to measure resistance. Take a measurement by touching the ends of the probes to power wires in the equipment you are testing. For example, to check a yellow wire in a Molex connector coming from the power supply, you would insert the red (live) probe into one of the holes for the yellow wire and insert the black (ground) probe into the hole for a black wire in the same connector. If the multimeter is set for DC Volts and it reports a measurement of around +12V, you know that the yellow wire is doing its job.

FIGURE 12-2 A digital multimeter (Photo: https://commons.wikimedia.org/wiki/File:Digital_Multimeter_Aka.jpg [Creative Commons license])

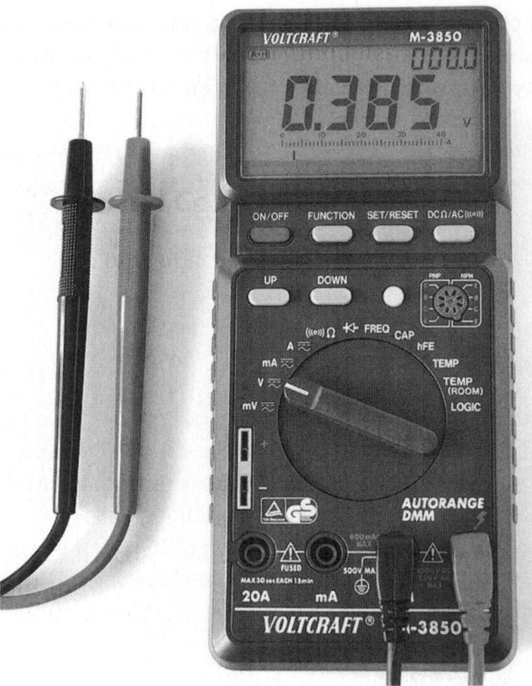

New technicians are sometimes intimidated by the prospect of probing live electrical connections, thinking they could be electrocuted. When checking voltages on a motherboard, though, the voltage is so low that there's no danger.

Some connectors can't be checked unless they are plugged in. For example, the P1 connector from the power supply to the motherboard must be connected to the motherboard for the power supply to operate, so you can't disconnect it and stick a probe down into one of the holes. In cases like that, you stick the probe down into the place where the wire enters the connector, from the back. This is called *back-probing* and is detailed in Exercise 12-3.

EXERCISE 12-3

Checking a P1 Connector

For this exercise you will need a desktop system and a multimeter. This exercise gives you plenty of experience with back-probing; by the time you've checked all the wires, you'll be confident about doing it.

1. Place the computer on its side so the motherboard is lying flat. Remove the computer's case cover so you can see the motherboard. Turn the computer on if it is not already on.
2. Set the multimeter to DC Volts.
3. Locate the P1 connector, the 20-pin or 24-pin connector that connects the power supply to the motherboard.
4. Carefully stick the tip of the red probe down as far as possible into the connector where a yellow wire enters the connector. If the probe tip is too wide to make contact with the bare wire, stick a steel pin (like you would use in sewing) or an open safety pin down to make contact, and then touch the probe to the pin.
5. Carefully stick the tip of the black probe down as far as possible into the connector where a black wire enters the connector.
6. Read the value shown on the multimeter. It should be +12V, plus or minus about 10 percent.
7. On another PC, do a Google Images search for "pin-out P1" to locate a chart that tells the expected voltages for the various wires on the P1 connector.
8. Check each of the remaining wires on the P1 connector and confirm that they are delivering the correct voltages. You don't have to move the black probe; just move the red probe from wire to wire.
9. Remove all probes from the connector, shut off the multimeter, and replace the computer's cover.

To measure resistance, you touch the probes to the circuit you want to measure. For example, to check a cable to make sure there are no broken wires, touch the red probe to a pin at one end, and touch the black probe to the corresponding pin at the other end. Consult a pin-out diagram for that cable as needed to determine which pins correspond.

To measure current, you must break the circuit so the electricity goes through the meter. Disconnect a connector, and then touch the red probe to a pin on the cable and the black probe to the corresponding pin or hole on the connector that the cable normally is plugged into. Most meters today are auto-ranging, meaning you don't have to choose a specific range; they change ranges on their own.

A power supply tester tests voltage output from a power supply unit and is much easier to use than a multimeter. Even an inexpensive power supply tester has several types of sockets to accommodate the variety of plugs available on power supplies. Simply connect the output connectors from a power supply to the matching socket, turn on the power supply, and a set of LEDs or a liquid crystal display (LCD) indicates whether the power supply is functioning correctly.

exam watch

For the exam, as well as for your own safety, remember that, like displays, power supplies can cause serious personal injury. Never open the case of a power supply!

Symptoms Associated with Power Supply Problems

Failed or failing power supplies have many symptoms. A failed power supply is dormant, and so is the entire computer, so the cause is not hard to determine once you have eliminated the simpler causes, such as the power button being in the off position or an unplugged power cord. A failing power supply will cause symptoms in other components, often leading you down the wrong troubleshooting path.

No Power/Nothing Happens when the Computer Is Turned On A few things can cause a total lack of activity at system startup. These include a bad processor (CPU) or memory, but the most likely suspect is the power supply.

First, check that the power supply connects properly to an electrical outlet. In addition, check the power selector (on the back of the computer near the power cord connection and the on/off switch) to ensure it has the right setting for your geographic region. Because you can switch many power supplies to use either North American or European voltages, verify that someone did not change the supply to the wrong voltage setting.

Make sure you remember that North America is 110 to 120 VAC at 60 Hz and Europe is 220 to 240 VAC at 50 Hz.

If the power supply's fan stops working, you must replace the entire power supply, not just the fan.

When the power supply stops working, so does the computer's fan, which is typically the first thing you hear (along with the hard drive) when you turn on the computer. Therefore, if you do not hear the power supply fan at startup (or any fan or hard drive noise), you should suspect a power supply problem and turn off the computer immediately. Some power supplies will shut down if the fan is not working.

on the Job

Be aware that the power supply fan may not work if the motherboard or CPU is dead, because the power supply requires a load (that is, power to be drawn from it) to operate. Therefore, don't assume that a lifeless-seeming power supply automatically means a dead power supply.

If only the power supply fan failed, then once the computer is off, try cleaning the fan from the outside of the case using an antistatic vacuum. Dust, lint, or hair can cause the fan to stop rotating. If cleaning does not resolve the problem, you must replace the entire power supply.

If the problem is not so easily isolated to the power supply fan because the system simply will not turn on, try removing all the power supply connections to internal components and turning the PC back on.

Also, check that the power cables attach properly to the motherboard and other necessary devices, including the computer's power button.

Memory Errors A memory error can be an indication of a failing power supply because it can provide inadequate power to the DIMMs and SODIMMs. If on each reboot, the memory error identifies a different location in memory, then it is more likely to be a power problem than a memory error. A real memory error would identify the same memory location on each reboot.

The Computer Reboots Itself, or Some Components Sporadically Stop Working

A computer with a bad power supply may continuously reboot itself without warning. If the power supply provides power only to some devices, the computer will behave irregularly; some devices will seem to work, whereas others will work only part of the time or not at all. Check that all power plugs connect properly.

Cooling Systems

Excessive heat can be a symptom of cooling system failure. Inadequate cooling will cause components to overheat, in which case they might work sometimes but not at other times, and very commonly, an overheated computer will simply shut down or spontaneously reboot. Try cleaning the power supply fan without opening the power supply itself by vacuuming the fan vents. If this does not solve the problem, replace the power supply or consider adding another case fan, if one will fit in your computer. Many cases come with brackets to add one or more case fans.

Missing Slot Covers

Believe it or not, the removable slot covers at the back of the computer are not there solely to tidy up the appearance of the computer. They keep dust and other foreign objects out of the computer, and if you leave the slot covers off, you run the risk of allowing dust to settle on the PC's internal components, especially the empty expansion slots (which are notoriously difficult to clean). Missing slot covers can also cause the computer to overheat. The design of the computer places the devices that generate the most heat in the fan's cooling airflow. Missing slot covers mean the cooling air's path through the computer could be changed or impeded, resulting in improper cooling of the components inside.

Noisy Fan/Grinding Noise

There are more cooling fans inside a computer than the one on the power supply. Today's computers have one (slot) or two cooling fans on the CPU. There can also be one or more strategically placed cooling fans inside the case.

When a fan begins to wear out, it usually makes a whining or grinding noise. When this happens, replace the fan, unless it is inside the power supply. In that instance, replace the entire power supply.

A grinding noise after the boot process starts can also originate from a mechanical HDD in which the bearings are going out or where the read/write head is scraping the surface of one or more platters.

CPU Cooling Issues

Considering the reliability of computer circuitry, you do not expect a CPU to fail, but modern CPUs generate a great deal of heat, and they can fail if adequate cooling aids are not properly installed. Proper installation requires applying thermal compound and attaching a heat sink and/or a CPU fan. Systems assembled in tightly controlled facilities by experienced technicians who practice excellent quality control methods should not fail due to overheating during normal operation. Normal computer operation usually means the CPU and/or busses are not overclocked or in an environment with temperature and humidity outside of the manufacturer's recommendations.

exam watch

Memory failures may not cause a system to appear to malfunction at all. Most modern systems will simply ignore a malfunctioning memory module, and normal operations will continue. The user may note performance loss, however, which is a key symptom of a memory module failure.

Adapter Cards

If you must replace or upgrade an adapter card in a motherboard, follow the steps to remove the old one in Exercise 11-8 in Chapter 11, and then follow the instructions for installing a new adapter card in Exercise 11-9. If the adapter card is a video card, ensure the replacement card has the correct interface.

SCENARIO & SOLUTION	
The computer does not maintain the date and time when powered on. What should I do?	Replace the motherboard's battery.
What should I do with a computer that keeps rebooting itself?	Test the power supply. You may need to replace it. Also suspect overheating issues (possibly due to fan failure) if the rebooting occurs after the PC has been running for 20 minutes or more.

CERTIFICATION OBJECTIVE

- ***1101: 5.3*** *Given a scenario, troubleshoot and diagnose problems with storage drives and RAID arrays*

This section looks at common symptoms of storage device problems, as described in 1101 exam Objective 5.3.

Troubleshooting Storage Devices

The steps you take when troubleshooting problems with storage devices vary based on the type of storage device. We will look at hard disk drives (HDDs), solid-state drives (SSDs), removable storage such as optical discs, and external storage such as USB flash drives.

Tools Required for Working with Drives

To work on internal storage devices, your single most important tool will be a Phillips-head screwdriver. You'll need this to open the computer's case (unless it has a latch or lever that opens it), and you'll need it to remove the drive from the case (unless the drive is on sliding rails that don't require screws to be removed).

When troubleshooting a drive, you might want to take it to another computer to see if it can be read there. If the other computer has an internal drive bay for it—great. But you might prefer to have a *drive enclosure* handy. A drive enclosure is basically a plastic box with drive connectors inside it. You can put an internal disk drive in there and then connect the plastic box to a USB port on any computer, turning an internal drive into an external one. Drive enclosures are designed for hard disks, but you can make one work in a pinch for an optical drive too, if you don't close the enclosure but just leave the drive dangling off its wires. (Not preferred, but it works for temporary use.)

Hard Disk Drives

Many things can go wrong with a hard drive, each of which can result in several different symptoms, so it can be difficult to determine the cause of the problem. You should replace a hard drive that begins corrupting data before all the information stored on it is lost. In Chapter 6, you learned about using specialized utilities to correct data problems on hard drives, including corrupted and fragmented files. We discuss the most common hard drive symptoms and problems in the sections that follow.

Computer Attempts to Boot to Incorrect Device

If a computer attempts to boot from the incorrect device and will not boot from the system drive (usually drive C:), the cause could be as simple as you inadvertently pressed a key as the system was starting up that the system interpreted as a command to boot in some special way, or it could be a more serious cause. Therefore, once this occurs, restart the system, taking care not to touch the keyboard until the system has completed the startup. We have even found that a messy desk can be the root cause if a book or a stack of papers rests on a key as the system boots up.

If the system still fails to boot up from the correct drive, then go into the BIOS/UEFI setup program and check out the boot order settings. Put the usual boot device first in the order and restart your computer.

If this still does not work, you may have a failed disk controller or hard drive, or the operating system might be corrupt. When the main hard disk doesn't appear to contain a usable operating system, the firmware skips it and tries the next-priority device, and that's probably what is happening. It might not appear to have a usable operating system because it doesn't work at all, or because the interface to which it is connected has failed, or because its content has become corrupted. Troubleshoot for the hardware problems first, reseating any existing connections, and try to boot once again. Chapter 6 describes how to recover from damage to the operating system. Try one of those methods before replacing the hard drive, which will require reinstalling or restoring the OS, your applications, and your data.

Bootable Device Not Found

If your computer fails to boot due to a hard drive or controller failure, you might receive a POST error message with an error code in the 1700 to 1799 range if your BIOS POST uses the traditional error codes. You could also get a message stating that there is no hard drive present. Typically, these errors are not fatal, and you can still boot the computer using some other bootable disk, such as a USB flash drive or optical disc.

This type of error means the computer does not recognize, or cannot communicate with, the hard drive. First, restart the computer and go into the firmware settings. In the firmware drive configuration, check that it has correctly detected the hard drive's model and capacity.

If the firmware settings are correct and the drive still will not work, or if the firmware cannot detect the hard drive, the system could have a cabling problem. Power the system off and check any connections to the disk in question; then replace any problem cables and reseat connectors. If there is another SATA connector available on the motherboard, try switching the drive's cable to that connector.

If the disk is recognized by the firmware but the OS does not start normally, check out the information in Chapter 6 on various Windows OS recovery options.

Exercise 12-4 walks through the steps in troubleshooting a nonworking hard disk drive.

EXERCISE 12-4

Troubleshooting a Drive Failure

Complete this exercise to practice troubleshooting a hard drive.

1. Reboot the computer, start the firmware system setup program (see Exercise 8-4 if needed), and check the settings for the drive and the interface (PATA, SATA, etc.), as appropriate. If you make any changes, restart and check to see if the problem is resolved. If it is not resolved, continue to the next step.
2. Shut down the system, unplug power to the computer, and open the case.
3. Ensure the connections are all secure. A serial ATA (SATA) drive does not require any jumper configuration, so settings should not be an issue.
4. Reboot the computer and see if the drive is now working.

If the drive is still not working, if possible, remove it from the PC and install it in a different, known-working PC to see if it will be recognized there. You can also use a drive enclosure to convert an internal hard drive to an external one that then can be connected to any PC via USB port.

Missing Drives in OS

When an OS doesn't see a drive that it previously saw, the first thing to check is the physical connectivity. Did any cables work themselves loose?

If physical connectivity is confirmed, the next place to look is in the BIOS/UEFI setup utility. If it sees the drive, then the drive has lost its partitioning/formatting somehow (perhaps the master file table [MFT] has become corrupted, for example). Try the drive in another system if possible to confirm that it's really the drive's fault and not something going on with the motherboard's control of it.

S.M.A.R.T. Failure

S.M.A.R.T. (yes, it's traditionally written like that, with the periods) stands for Self-Monitoring, Analysis and Reporting Technology. It's an interface between the BIOS/UEFI and a magnetic hard drive that allows the drive to alert you (via the BIOS/UEFI) when a failure is imminent so the user can pull off any critical data before that happens. The operating system *should* pass along any errors from S.M.A.R.T. to you, so no news is good news. However, you can also check S.M.A.R.T. anytime for your own peace of mind. S.M.A.R.T. is enabled/disabled via BIOS/UEFI setup.

Windows doesn't have a graphical interface for checking S.M.A.R.T. status, but you can download third-party utilities that will do it. You can also check a drive's status by entering the following commands at a command prompt:

```
wmic
diskdrive get status
exit
```

Read/Write Failure or Data Loss/Corruption

If you see a message containing the words "read/write failure," it means that the BIOS cannot find the information it needs in the first sector of the disk, where it expects to find information for either booting up from the disk or reading data from the disk. The possible causes can include a "head crash"—a collision that can occur in a magnetic hard drive between the disk drive's read/write heads and the platters containing the data. This is often unrecoverable if it occurs in a critical portion of the disk, such as in the first few sectors, but recoverable if it occurs elsewhere, depending on how extensive the damage is. If the read/write error message appears as you boot up, the error is most likely in a critical area, but if it occurs after the operating system is running and does not cause any other problem with the OS, it is in a less critical area and may present itself as a read/write error message within the OS. If you see that, you may be able to use a disk repair tool such as CHKDSK to find and fix the error, as explained in Chapter 6.

Slow/Sluggish Performance or Extended Read/Write Times

Sluggish performance can be a symptom that is difficult to quantify in a casual way because what may seem like a slow hard drive may be a slow system caused by overheating or other problems. One way to quantify read/write times is to run a utility that tests *input/output operations per second (IOPS).*

If you or a client perceives that the hard drive is slow and you have eliminated system performance as a symptom, then the problem is most likely with the file system. Try running a disk repair tool to find and fix storage errors that may be slowing down the system, or try using the Disk Defragmenter/Optimizer tool in Windows (the name varies depending on the OS version) to optimize file read/write performance.

Loud Clicking or Grinding Noise

A loud clicking noise is a very ominous symptom for a hard drive. If you can isolate this noise to your drive and the drive is not functioning, it is probably physically damaged beyond repair. The smartest thing to do if you cannot access any data on the drive is to replace it and restore your data from the latest backup.

OS Not Found

Once firmware finishes the POST, it looks for the presence of an OS on the hard drive. On an older drive using MBR (Master Boot Record), if the BIOS does not find a special OS pointer in the drive's master boot record, it assumes that no OS exists and it will display a message that the OS was not found. If you have not yet installed an OS, you must do so at this point. Chapter 4 describes how to install Windows. If an OS exists but is not accessible, refer to Chapter 6 for steps to take to recover from this situation.

SATA and eSATA Interfaces

The SATA and eSATA interfaces are pretty simple. They connect a single drive to the motherboard or controller board using a single cable per drive. There's no drive configuration required, so any problems can immediately be narrowed down to one of three things: the motherboard or controller, the cable, or the drive itself. Check all connections to make sure they are snug, and swap out components as you are able to isolate the source of the problem.

If you are connecting an external device, the eSATA cables must connect to an eSATA adapter card. Although it's possible to do so, you should not use SATA cables designed for internal use to connect a removable eSATA device. That's because the cables are not sturdy enough and won't hold up well with you constantly connecting and disconnecting them. eSATA cables and their connectors are designed for thousands of connection and removal cycles, but the SATA cables and connectors are designed for only about 50 such cycles. Fortunately, the cables are keyed differently, with the I-type eSATA cable plug having a

Knowing the features of the SATA and eSATA interfaces is important, especially such details as the L-type SATA connector versus the I-type eSATA connector.

simple narrow oblong connector and the L-type SATA connector having a notch in the female connector and a corresponding key on the cable plug.

RAID Arrays and Controllers

If a single drive in a RAID array fails, you will need to replace the drive with a comparable drive that will work in the array. After that, restart the computer and enter the RAID setup program, which may be part of the firmware system setup program or, as in the case of a RAID bus adapter, may be a program in the adapter's firmware that you can also enter during startup. Once in the RAID setup program, the steps you need to take depend on the level of RAID used.

If a drive in a RAID 0 array fails, you have lost the entire volume, because this type of RAID involves data written across the drives in the array, without any special algorithm for rebuilding the stripes in the array and recovering lost data should a drive fail. Therefore, once you replace a failed drive, run the RAID setup program, and re-create the array combining the drives into what appears to your operating system as a single logical drive. Then you must format the drive and restore your data from your latest backups. Chapter 5 discusses formatting disks and data backup.

If a drive in a RAID 1 array fails, the system will continue working, writing to the surviving member of the array mirror, but it will no longer mirror the data. This may result in an error message at the time of the failure and at each startup, or you might find a record of a RAID error event in one of the computer's log files. Once you determine that one of the drives in the mirror failed, do a full backup, replace the failed hard drive, and re-create the mirror using the RAID setup program.

If one drive in a RAID 5 or RAID 10 array fails, the RAID controller can rebuild the lost data. RAID 5 arrays have at least three drives, and RAID 10 arrays have at least four. In each case, all but one drive stripes data in every write operation; the remaining drive holds a parity bit (0 or 1). With each operation the drives take turns being the "parity bit" drive. When a drive fails, for each write where that drive was the parity drive, that parity bit isn't needed. For the writes where it contained data, the controller can combine the data from the other drives for that write operation plus the information the parity bit provides to reconstruct the missing data. A utility in the RAID controller's firmware should be able to rebuild the array once you've installed a replacement drive.

If you see a message such as "RAID not found," or if the entire RAID array stops working without a clear message and you cannot access the drives at all, then you need to do some serious hardware troubleshooting, beginning with checking the connections. Then, if it is software-level Windows RAID, open Disk Management and attempt to use it to determine if just one member of the array is failing and if you can replace it and re-create the array.

If it is hardware-level RAID, check the manufacturer's documentation to see if there is a diagnostics procedure you can follow, along with diagnostic utilities—sometimes this is built into the controller. Or test the array in another computer, which can be problematic if the RAID is hardware-level RAID built into the first computer. Then you will need to find an identical system to test the drives in. If the hardware-level RAID is based on a separate RAID card, test the card and the drives in another computer.

exam watch **When a RAID array fails with a RAID-specific error, troubleshoot the RAID controller or, if it is a Windows-based RAID, open Disk Management to see the status. Also remember to troubleshoot as you would any hard drive system.**

When a single drive in a RAID 5 array fails, an error message will appear, but the system will continue to write to the array in a stripe across the drives. The system will not be able to create a recovery block on one drive in each stripe, however, so you will have lost your fault tolerance, and reads will be slower as it re-creates the lost data on each read. Do a backup before replacing the failed drive and then restart the computer and run the RAID setup utility. The system will then rebuild the array without losing the data on the drive, re-creating the data on the replaced drive by using the data on the remaining drives and the algorithm block, when necessary.

Solid-State Storage Devices

When supporting SSDs, there are specific concerns for troubleshooting and caring for these devices. One is loss of data from incorrectly removing an external SSD from a computer. Other issues are exposure to dirt and grime and recovering lost data from SSDs.

Dirt and Grime

Solid-state storage seems indestructible, or at least considerably more stable than conventional hard drives, which are sensitive to movement or being dropped while operating. But with external SSDs, the very portability of these devices makes them vulnerable to dirt, dust, and magnetic interference. People often carry thumb drives on lanyards around their necks or on keychains, exposing them to a great deal of abuse—including food and beverage spills. Instruct your customers to always keep their solid-state storage devices protected. Thumb drives should always have a protected cap on when not connected to a computer. Each internal SSD has exposed connectors, and you should either install the SSD into a computer or portable device or keep it in the plastic case it came in. Cleaning up one of these devices involves carefully removing dirt and debris from the contacts on the device's connectors.

Recovering Lost Data from SSDs

If you are helping someone who lost data on a solid-state storage device, either from deleting the data or from mishandling the device, all may not be lost. Programs are available for recovering files from solid-state devices, such as CompactFlash, Memory Stick, Secure Digital Card, and MultiMedia Card. You must be able to access the device from your computer, and many of these utilities run in Windows.

exam watch

Understand the common symptoms involved in storage failure: LED status indicators, grinding or clicking noises, bootable devices not found, data loss/corruption, RAID failure, S.M.A.R.T. failure, extended read/write times, decreased IOPS, and missing drives in the OS.

SCENARIO & SOLUTION	
After moving a desktop PC to a new office, it fails to recognize the hard drive. What should you check first?	Look inside the case to make sure no cables have come loose from the jostling around involved in moving the PC.
When you try running your favorite game, you see an error message about a disk read error in Windows. What should you do?	Check the disk for errors with CHKDSK or some other disk utility. If the error persists, uninstall and reinstall the game.

CERTIFICATION OBJECTIVE

- ***1101: 5.4*** *Given a scenario, troubleshoot video, projector, and display issues*

CompTIA A+ 1101 exam Objective 5.4 lists several common symptoms of video and display problems, which we describe in this section. Problems with video adapters and displays can be frustrating because many of the symptoms leave you with no visual means to troubleshoot in the operating system, so we provide common solutions for these problems that will help you on the job, as well as in preparing for the exam.

Troubleshooting Displays

A computer's video system includes, at a minimum, the video adapter, one or more displays, and necessary cable and connectors. It may also include a video capture card or TV tuner, so diagnosing and resolving problems can be a bit tricky. Another difficulty in resolving video problems is that, without a working display, you cannot see the OS or firmware settings to remedy the problem. Flat-panel displays (FPDs) are now the norm for desktop PCs, and all laptops have this type of display.

PC technicians typically do not repair monitors without special training beyond that required for A+ certification. Monitors are so inexpensive today that just replacing them is the best course of action if you aren't trained in how to repair one. A new entry-level monitor costs less than a few hours of a trained technician's time.

Of course, the display is only part of a computer's video system, and therefore not the only source of problems. Therefore, we will talk about problems tied to all video components, including the device drivers, video adapters, displays, and cables and connectors. Following are some common video system symptoms and their most likely causes and solutions.

Black Screen at Startup

If, during the POST, the computer sounds the audio error code for a video problem and the display remains blank, the video adapter may not be connected to a display or the adapter may be damaged. First, check the connection between the display and the video adapter. Next, check the video card function. If the video adapter is not a motherboard-integrated adapter, and if you have a spare computer, install the adapter in another computer to determine whether it is functioning. If it does not work in another computer, install a new adapter into the problem computer.

If the video adapter is integrated into the motherboard—a common configuration today—check the motherboard documentation for how to disable it. You might be able to disable it in firmware setup, for example. Then, install a replacement video adapter card. If you cannot get the new adapter to work, you may need to replace the motherboard or the computer system itself, if it isn't cost-effective to replace the motherboard.

If the display shows no image at all at startup and the computer does not issue a beep code, check the video system components. Start with the display's connection to the power supply and ensure the display is on. Check the data cable and verify that none of the pins on the connector are bent; straighten them if necessary. Also, ensure the brightness is set at an adequate level.

You can determine if the display itself is at fault by swapping it with a known good one. If the new display works in the system, you can assume the original display is the problem. Again, because display costs have decreased so much in the last few years, it is less expensive to simply replace the display with a new one than to have a technician professionally repair it.

It seems counterintuitive, and you still must dispose of the old display appropriately, but that's today's reality. Chapter 1 describes proper disposal of PCs and their components.

If a problem continues after you have eliminated the display as a cause, and if the video adapter is a bus card, check for proper seating of the video card in the expansion slot. Some video cards do not seat easily, so press the card firmly (but not too hard) and listen for an audible click to tell you the card seats properly.

Screen Suddenly Shuts Down

If the screen seems to be functioning normally and then suddenly shuts down, the first thing you should do is move the mouse or press a key on the keyboard. This will reactivate the system if the screen is blank because of a screen saver or a power mode setting that causes it to go blank after a specified period. For any other component, we would have you check the connections first, but it takes so little effort to move the mouse or press a key, that it is the best first step in this case.

If moving the mouse or pressing a key does not solve the problem, the PC may have suddenly shut itself off due to power management settings. Windows may be set to put itself into Sleep or Hibernate mode automatically after a certain triggering event occurs, such as being idle for a certain amount of time or, in the case of a laptop or tablet, reaching a critical threshold in remaining battery charge. If the device has a battery, make sure the device is running on AC.

A sudden black screen can also mean that the monitor has overheated—perhaps due to a very hot environment. This is more common with older cathode-ray tube (CRT) monitors than with FPDs, which use less power. Do whatever you can to lower the temperature in the room where the computer resides.

If the ambient temperature is reasonable (around 65 to 70 degrees Fahrenheit), then troubleshoot for a problem with either the display or the video adapter. Check that the cable between them is snug on both ends. Switch out the monitor and see if the same problem occurs on a different display. If it does, then the video adapter is the source of the problem. If switching the display solves the problem, then the original display is damaged or defective and you should replace it, since displays are not user serviceable.

Screen Artifacts

Screen artifacts are tiny, pixel-size spots that randomly appear and disappear on the display screen. You can tell they are not physical, permanent spots because they come and go. Determine the software in use at the time, because the video adapter overheating can cause this symptom—in particular, the graphics processing unit (GPU) overheats when using software that is very video graphics intensive, such as photo-editing software. Test it by closing any photo-editing or other graphics-intensive software. If the artifacts disappear, then find a way to supplement the system's cooling system and/or replace the GPU or the entire video adapter with one designed for better cooling.

Burn-In

Burn-in is permanent discoloration of certain areas on a screen because of the screen displaying the same image for a very long time. You sometimes see this on old video arcade games, where the opening screen of the game can still be faintly seen as a ghost image even after the unit is turned off. Burn-in happens on obsolete phosphor-based displays (such as CRTs and plasma displays). This is not a common problem on most LCD monitors.

There isn't anything you can do to fix burn-in; it's permanent damage. However, you can prevent burn-in by not allowing the same image to display on the monitor for a long time. Screen savers—moving pictures that appear on a monitor when the computer is idle—were invented for this purpose. Set a display to either show a screen saver or turn off entirely after a certain period of idle time.

Fuzzy Display on FPD

An FPD looks good only at its maximum, native resolution. If the display doesn't appear crisp and clear, the first thing to check is whether the display resolution has been set for a lower setting than the maximum.

Flashing or Flickering Screen/Image

A flickering or flashing FPD display is a sign of a failing component within the display—either the backlight or the inverter. Both are reasons to replace the display, but before you go to that expense, perform a small experiment. Test a known good display on the computer. If the test display has the same problem, the video adapter is the cause—if the test display works just fine, then replace the flickering display. Only open an FPD display if you were trained on how to do it, because there is a serious risk of electrical shock if you do. The inverter supplies alternating current (AC) power at a high voltage, and to make it worse, an inverter may still retain a charge after you remove power—whether unplugging the power cord or, in the case of a laptop, both unplugging the power cord and removing the battery.

Screen Image Is Dim

Something as simple as a maladjusted brightness control on the display itself can cause a dim screen image. Most displays have buttons on the case in addition to the power button. Pressing one of these opens a hardware-level menu for adjusting the display. One of the many options on the menu is brightness. Related to this are the special keys on a laptop that control brightness on the display. Therefore, if your FPD on your desktop or laptop seems too dim, check these controls. And while you are at it, also use the display's controls to adjust contrast, which can also contribute to a perception that the display is dim.

On a laptop or tablet computer, the most common cause of a dim screen is that the computer is running on battery power and the OS's power management settings have been configured to dim the screen to save battery life.

A more serious case of a dim display is a bad inverter that simply isn't providing enough power to the display's light source. Once again, this may be justification for replacing the display. Recall the cautions in the previous section concerning attempting to open and repair an FPD.

Incorrect Data Source or Cabling Issues

When a monitor doesn't show an image, that usually means that there isn't a data source providing an image. The cable between monitor and PC may not be snug, or may be damaged, or the operating system may need to be told to start directing output to the port to which the monitor is connected.

On a laptop, there may be an FN key (that is, a key you press in conjunction with the FN key) that toggles between the various video outputs, including the internal display screen and any external monitor ports (such as VGA or HDMI). And in Windows, you can right-click the desktop and choose Display Settings to open the appropriate section of the Settings app for configuring multiple displays.

Dead and Stuck Pixels

LCD screens have special pixilation problems associated with the LCD or related technology. These screens have three transistors per pixel, one transistor each for red, green, and blue, called subpixels. The transistors turn on and off to create a combination of colors. When a transistor turns off permanently (not by design, but through failure), it shows as a dark spot on the screen called a *dead pixel*. Another, nearly opposite problem is a *lit pixel* (also called a *stuck pixel*). This occurs when a transistor is permanently turned on, causing the pixel to constantly show as red, green, or blue. When pixels contiguous to each other are all in this lit-pixel state, they show as the color derived from their combination.

Before you decide you have a defective FPD, be sure to wipe it clean with a soft, antistatic cloth, very slightly dampened with mild glass cleaner that does not contain ammonia.

You may have dead or lit pixels on your FPD without noticing it because the dead pixels are not visible when displaying an image with dark colors in the defective area, and lit pixels may not show when displaying an image showing the colors that result from the dark pixels. A few defective pixels are normal; it is nearly impossible to find an FPD without some. It only becomes a problem if many bad pixels are located together and cause the image to be distorted or unreadable. To test for dead or lit pixels, you need to configure the desktop with a plain white background, close all windows, and configure the taskbar so it hides. This will give you a completely empty, white screen. Now examine the screen, looking for nonwhite areas. These may appear as the tiniest dot, about the size of a mark made by a fine-point pen on paper. Black dots indicate dead pixels, whereas any other color indicates a lit pixel.

You will need to determine if the number you find is acceptable and what, if any, actions you will take. You cannot repair dead or stuck pixels.

Image Distortion or Incorrect Color Display

Improper display resolution or a driver issue can cause a distorted or discolored image. However, first check the display cable for damage or a bad connection. Check the manual settings on the display itself and reset it to the original settings (a common option). If this still doesn't resolve the problem, check the display resolution and refresh rate. If both appear to be at the recommended settings, check the manufacturer's website for a driver update. If an update is available, install and test the display with the update.

If the on-screen image doesn't appear to be a rectangle (for example, if one or both sides are bowed in or out, or the whole screen image is trapezoidal), the *screen geometry* may need to be adjusted. The monitor's built-in controls may be able to make a correction. Use the buttons on the front of the monitor to access a menu system, and then look for options that contain the word *shape* or *geometry*.

Projector Issues

In some ways, a digital projector is a lot like any other monitor. It connects to one of the computer's monitor ports, like HDMI or DVI. It has a maximum resolution at which it can display. It is subject to various types of image problems, such as fuzziness and dimness. The solutions for its problems are often different from the solutions for the same problems on a monitor or built-in computer screen, however. Table 12-1 lists some of the most common problems with digital projectors and some possible solutions.

TABLE 12-1 Common Projector Problems and Possible Solutions (*continued*)

Problem	Possible Solution
Nothing appears on the projection screen.	Make sure the projector is powered on and connected to the PC. Make sure you have removed the lens cap. Make sure the projector's lamp is installed properly and not burnt out.
The projector's startup screen displays briefly but not the computer image.	Make sure the connection is snug between the PC and the projector and that the cable is good. On a laptop, make sure the externally accessible monitor port is enabled. There may be an FN keyboard shortcut for this.
The projector shuts down intermittently.	Check fans to make sure they are operational, and make sure no air filters or vents are blocked; intermittent shutdown is often a symptom of overheating. Another possibility is that the projector is entering Standby mode after a period of inactivity or that the power connector is not snug.

TABLE 12-1 Common Projector Problems and Possible Solutions

Problem	Possible Solution
Projector's speakers are not outputting audio.	Not all projectors have speakers. If yours does and they're not working, first make sure you are connecting the PC to the printer using an HDMI cable (which carries both video and sound); a VGA connector carries only video. With VGA video, you'll need to connect an audio cable separately (usually a 3.5 mm type). On the software side, make sure that the PC's volume is not muted, is turned up, and the output port you are using for the projector is set up in the OS as an output source. The projector may also have a volume control; make sure it is not muted either.
Image is too dim.	Adjust the projector's brightness level. If the brightness level is already at maximum, replace the projector bulb/lamp (it may be failing or burned out) or move the projector closer to the screen so the image is smaller and more compact (which will also make it brighter).
Screen is truncated.	Make sure the display resolution in Windows is not set for a higher resolution than the projector can handle.
Image isn't centered on the display screen.	Reposition the projector. If the projector has horizontal or vertical position controls, adjust these.
Image is fuzzy.	Adjust the focus on the projector (usually a ring around the lens that you can turn). Move the projector toward or away from the projection screen.
Image is backward.	Check to make sure the projector is not operating in Rear Projection mode.
Image is upside down.	Check to make sure the projector is not operating in Ceiling mode.

CERTIFICATION SUMMARY

Understanding best practice methodology and taking a structured and disciplined approach will not only help you arrive at a solution but also help you quickly resolve similar problems in the future. If you determine that you have a software problem, check the application's configuration or try uninstalling and then reinstalling the program. If the problem is hardware related, identify the components that make up the failing subsystem. Starting with the most accessible component, check for power and that the component properly attaches to the computer. Check the device's configuration and the presence of a device driver. Finally, swap suspected bad components with known good ones.

Assemble the right tools for troubleshooting and maintenance before you need them. Take time to perform regular maintenance tasks on computers and peripherals to prevent future problems.

As a computer technician, you will be required to locate and resolve the source of computer problems. If you have a good knowledge of the functions of the computer's components, you will be able to quickly troubleshoot problems that occur.

However, there are other telltale signs of failed components. For example, you can use POST error codes to determine a problem's cause. Although the troubleshooting procedures differ from component to component, and even for different problems within the same component, many of the procedures involve cleaning the component, ensuring it is properly attached to the computer, or finally, replacing the component.

TWO-MINUTE DRILL

Here are some of the key points covered in Chapter 12.

Preparing for Troubleshooting

- ❑ Arm yourself with appropriate troubleshooting tools, including software and hardware tools.
- ❑ The six steps of the best practice methodology are (1) identify the problem; (2) establish a theory of probable cause (question the obvious); (3) test the theory to determine the cause; (4) establish a plan of action to resolve the problem and then implement the solution; (5) verify full system functionality and, if applicable, implement preventative measures; and finally, (6) document the findings, actions, and outcomes.
- ❑ Protect computers and data by performing backups of data and the operating system and always consider corporate policies, procedures, and impacts before making any changes to try to resolve problems.
- ❑ Ongoing user training can prevent many problems and ensure that users know how to respond to common problems.

Troubleshooting Motherboards, RAM, CPUs, and Power

- ❑ Procedures should move from least intrusive to most intrusive, checking proper connections, appropriate components, drivers, settings, and component seating for internal devices.
- ❑ General symptoms, such as excessive heat, noise, odors, and visible damage, can apply to any of several components.
- ❑ Various system instability problems are most likely to be software related, but they also may have a hardware-based cause. These include system lockups, system shutdowns, unexpected shutdowns, and OS-specific proprietary crash screens like BSOD/pinwheel.
- ❑ Never open a power supply because there is a danger of severe shock.
- ❑ POST error codes, such as 1*xx*, 2*xx*, and 3*xx*, can indicate system board, memory, or keyboard failures, respectively.

- ❑ Most CPU problems are fatal, which requires replacing the CPU or system. Check your warranty if you suspect a problem with the CPU because it may require replacing the motherboard.
- ❑ Incorrect firmware settings can affect a variety of system components. Check and correct these problems by running the system setup and changing the settings.
- ❑ Motherboard batteries last from two to ten years. A computer that does not maintain the correct date and time when powered off is a symptom of a failed battery.
- ❑ Most system board, processor, and memory errors are fatal, meaning the computer cannot properly boot up.
- ❑ Motherboard errors can be the most difficult to pinpoint and, due to the cost and effort involved in replacement, should be the last device you suspect when a subsystem or the entire computer fails.
- ❑ Be ready to troubleshoot problems such as black screens, no power, sluggish performance, overheating, burning smells, intermittent shutdowns, app crashes, grinding noise, and capacitor swelling.

Troubleshooting Storage Devices

- ❑ Replace a hard drive that begins to develop corrupted data before all the information stored on it is lost. S.M.A.R.T. technology may report an impending failure. A loud clicking noise also signals that the drive will fail soon.
- ❑ Failure to boot can be due to a bad drive, a loose connection, or corrupted or missing OS startup files.
- ❑ An L-type SATA connector is used for internal drives; it's bent like an L. An I-type eSATA connector is for external SATA and is straight.
- ❑ When a drive in a RAID fails, you can usually replace it without taking the RAID offline. The RAID controller can rebuild the data that was formerly on the missing disk on a new disk.
- ❑ One way to quantify read/write times is to run a utility that tests input/output operations per second (IOPS).
- ❑ A loud clicking noise means the drive is not functioning and probably physically damaged beyond repair. The best thing to do if you cannot access any data on the drive is to replace it and restore your data from the latest backup.

Troubleshooting Displays

- ❑ If no image appears on the screen, first check all connections and then check the video card functionality.
- ❑ Some displays automatically or even intermittently shut down when overheated. Check ambient temperature and cool it down, if possible. Switch displays to see if the problem is in the display or video adapter.

- ❑ Dead pixels are pixels that are off, creating dark spots on the screen. This is only a problem if bad pixels cause the image to be distorted or unusable.
- ❑ An overheating video adapter can cause screen artifacts that randomly appear and disappear—in particular, the GPU overheats when using software that is very video graphics intensive, such as photo-editing software. Find a way to supplement the system's cooling system and/or replace the GPU or the entire video adapter with one designed for better cooling.
- ❑ A fuzzy FPD display may indicate that the OS is running in a lower resolution than the device's maximum that is supported.
- ❑ Something as simple as a maladjusted brightness control on the display can cause a dim display image. Troubleshoot by adjusting the brightness control on a PC or laptop display. A more serious cause is a bad inverter, in which case, it may be wise to replace the display rather than try to repair it.
- ❑ A flickering FPD display is a sign of a failing component within the display—either the backlight or the inverter. Replace the display.
- ❑ Improper display resolution or a driver issue can cause a distorted image. You should first check the display cable for damage or a bad connection.
- ❑ Projector problems most commonly arise from lack of connectivity to the PC, projector positioning, burned-out lamp, and adjustment of projector controls such as focus.

SELF TEST

The following questions will help you measure your understanding of the material presented in this chapter. Read all the choices carefully because there might be more than one correct answer. Choose all correct answers for each question.

Preparing for Troubleshooting

1. Which of the following is a hardware diagnostics tool that you insert into an expansion slot in a motherboard?

A. POST card

B. Loopback plug

C. Video adapter

D. Nut driver

2. What should you do before making any changes to a computer?
   A. Turn off the computer.
   B. Use a grounding strap.
   C. Restore the most recent backup.
   D. If no recent backup of data and/or the operating system exists, perform a backup.
3. According to troubleshooting methodology, what should you do immediately after establishing a theory of probable cause?
   A. Identify the problem.
   B. Test the theory to determine the cause.
   C. Document the findings, actions, and outcomes.
   D. Establish a plan of action to resolve the problem.
4. When questioning a user to determine the cause of a problem, which of these is a respectfully phrased, useful question to ask?
   A. Did it ever work, or is this failure a recent change?
   B. What kind of CPU is installed?
   C. What did you do to it?
   D. What operating system is it?

Troubleshooting Motherboards, RAM, CPUs, and Power

5. Suppose a user says that her PC sounds different than it used to when it's on. You ask whether the sound is different all the time or only when accessing the HDD, and she reports that the sound is different all the time. What component is likely to be failing?
   A. RAM
   B. Case fan
   C. SDD
   D. HDD
6. Reorder the following troubleshooting steps from the least intrusive to the most intrusive.
   A. Check proper seating of internal components.
   B. Check for proper connections to external devices.
   C. Check installation: drivers, driver settings, and physical settings.
   D. Check for appropriate external components.
7. You first should narrow down the source of a problem to one of what two broad categories?
   A. Power or data
   B. Operating system or application
   C. Motherboard or component
   D. Hardware or software

8. How do you narrow down the problem to one hardware component?
   A. Remove the data cables.
   B. Run specialized diagnostics.
   C. Swap each suspect component with a known good one.
   D. Restart the computer.

9. After you apply and test a solution, what should you have the user do as part of evaluating the solution?
   A. Ground themselves using an antistatic wrist strap.
   B. Disconnect the problem component.
   C. Test the solution and all commonly used applications.
   D. Print out the user manual.

10. What should you do if you are unsure if a problem is limited to the single application that was in use at the time the problem occurred?
   A. Remove and reinstall the application.
   B. Upgrade the application.
   C. Use more than one application to perform the actions that resulted in the problem.
   D. Upgrade the driver.

11. A customer reports that the computer spontaneously reboots after being used for about 20 minutes and will not restart until it has sat idle for a few minutes. Furthermore, even when the computer does start, the fan does not make as much noise as before. What is the likely cause of these problems?
   A. The power supply
   B. The system board
   C. The processor
   D. The RAM

12. Which of the following is the safest and easiest device for measuring the voltage output from a power supply?
   A. Multimeter
   B. Power supply tester
   C. UPS
   D. Power Options

13. Your computer consistently loses its date and time settings. Which procedure will you use to solve the problem?
   A. Replace the motherboard battery.
   B. Flash the battery using a manufacturer-provided disk.
   C. Use the computer's AC adapter to recharge the battery.
   D. Access the firmware setting programs at startup and select the low-power option.

14. A user reports that when he turns on his PC, it beeps three times and nothing appears on the screen. What do you suspect about the problem?

A. The problem is with the motherboard, RAM, or a built-in component.

B. The problem is with a storage drive.

C. It's an operating system problem.

D. It's a problem with the external monitor.

15. Which of the following symptoms could *not* be caused by a RAM error?

A. The POST cannot be completed.

B. When you turn on the computer, nothing happens.

C. The system reports a No Operating System error.

D. The RAM count at startup does not match the capacity of the installed RAM.

Troubleshooting Storage Devices

16. Suppose you have a SATA drive that works in one PC, but when you move it to another PC, the new PC's UEFI does not recognize it. Cables are all snug. What should you try next?

A. Put the drive in an external enclosure and connect it to a USB port.

B. Reformat the drive on the original PC before moving it to the new PC.

C. Try using a PATA connector instead of a SATA.

D. Try a different SATA connector on the motherboard.

17. With which type of RAID array do you need to rerun the RAID setup program to re-create the array after replacing a faulty drive?

A. RAID 0

B. RAID 1

C. Both RAID 0 and RAID 1

D. Both RAID 1 and RAID 5

Troubleshooting Displays

18. Your video display is blank. Which of the following should you do first?

A. Swap the display with a known good one.

B. Replace the video adapter with a known good one.

C. Check the power and data cables.

D. Check the seating of the video adapter.

19. How do you repair a dead or stuck pixel on an LCD monitor?
    A. Update the display driver.
    B. Switch to a different display resolution.
    C. Power cycle the monitor several times.
    D. You cannot repair dead or stuck pixels.

20. Which of the following is a possible cause of a display suddenly shutting down?
    A. Overheating
    B. Incorrect resolution
    C. EMI
    D. Incorrect brightness setting

A SELF TEST ANSWERS

Preparing for Troubleshooting

1. ☑ **A.** A POST card is a hardware diagnostics tool that you install into an expansion slot. Then, when the computer boots up, the POST card performs diagnostics and reports an error code that you can look up to determine where the boot process is halting.
   ☒ **B** and **D** are incorrect because, although a loopback plug and a nut driver are examples of hardware tools, neither is insertable into an expansion slot. **C** is incorrect because a video adapter is not a hardware diagnostics tool, but a common PC component.

2. ☑ **D.** If no recent backup of data and/or the operating system exists, perform a backup. This is correct because you do not want to risk losing the user's data.
   ☒ **A** is incorrect because turning off the computer is rather irrelevant, although after taking care of the backup, you may want to restart the computer. **B** is incorrect because until you have narrowed down the cause, you do not know if using a ground strap will be necessary. You must do a backup before you reach this point. **C** is incorrect because you have no idea if restoring the most recent backup is even necessary at this point.

3. ☑ **B.** Test the theory to determine the cause.
   ☒ **A** is incorrect because you should identify the problem before you establish a theory of probable cause. **C** is incorrect because documenting the findings, actions, and outcomes is the very last procedure (sixth) of best practice methodology, while the procedure in question is the third procedure. **D** is incorrect because establishing a plan of action to resolve the problem comes after testing the theory to determine the cause.

4. ☑ **A.** Has this feature ever worked on this PC?
   ☒ **B** is incorrect because the user is not likely to know this, and it doesn't make a difference in most troubleshooting situations. **C** is incorrect because this phrasing is aggressive, putting the user on the defensive. **D** is incorrect because you can easily determine that for yourself.

Troubleshooting Motherboards, RAM, CPUs, and Power

5. ☑ **B.** Case fan.
   ☒ **A** and **C** are incorrect because these are both solid-state items that do not make noise as they operate. **D** is incorrect because an HDD might make different noises when reading or writing data if it were failing, but it would not make noise all the time.

6. ☑ **B, D, C, A** is the correct order.
   ☒ Any other order is incorrect.

7. ☑ **D.** Hardware and software are the two broad categories of problem sources.
   ☒ **A** is incorrect because although you may have problems in the power or data areas, they are not the two broad categories of problem sources. **B** is incorrect because an operating system and an application are both types of software, and software is just one of the two broad categories of problem sources. **C** is incorrect because a motherboard and a component are both types of hardware, and hardware is just one of the two categories of problem sources.

8. ☑ **C.** Swapping each suspect component with a known good one will narrow down a hardware problem to one component.
   ☒ **A** is incorrect because although cable removal may be part of removing a component, this alone will not help you narrow down the problem to one component. **B** is incorrect because specialized diagnostics lead to general areas, not specific components. **D** is incorrect because restarting will not indicate one component, although it might cause the problem to disappear.

9. ☑ **C.** The user should test the solution and all commonly used applications to confirm the fix works and to assure herself that the changes you made were not harmful.
   ☒ **A** is incorrect because grounding is something a technician would do when working inside a PC. **B** is incorrect because without the problem component connected, you cannot evaluate the solution. **D** is incorrect because printing the manual has little to do with evaluating the solution.

10. ☑ **C.** Use more than one application to perform the actions that resulted in the problem. If the problem only occurs in the one application, then focus on that application.
☒ **A** is incorrect because although removing and reinstalling the application may be a fix for the problem, you must first determine that the problem only occurs with that application before doing something so drastic. **B** is incorrect because although upgrading the application may be a fix for the problem, you must first narrow it down to the one application. **D** is incorrect because although this may be a solution, you must first narrow down the cause to specific hardware before upgrading the driver.

11. ☑ **A.** The power supply is the most likely cause of these symptoms. When a power supply begins to fail, it often manifests in several different, sporadic symptoms. If the power supply's fan stops working, the computer will overheat and spontaneously reboot itself. If the components are still excessively hot when the system restarts, the computer may not start at all.
☒ **B, C,** and **D** are incorrect because failure of any of these components does not cause the specific set of symptoms mentioned in the question. The system board does not include a fan, so would not affect fan noise, and if the system board were faulty, the PC would not boot at all. Although an overheated processor could cause the system to reboot, it would not be associated with the lack of noise from the power supply fan. A RAM failure will not cause the computer to reboot (unless all RAM fails).

12. ☑ **B.** A power supply tester is the safest and easiest device for measuring the voltage output from a power supply.
☒ **A** is incorrect because a multimeter requires much more knowledge of electricity to use and is a more complex device. **C** is incorrect because a UPS is not a device for measuring voltage output from a power supply, but an uninterruptible power supply device. **D** is incorrect because Power Options is a Windows Control Panel applet for managing the power-saving features of your computer.

13. ☑ **A.** You should replace the battery. When the computer "forgets" the time and date, it is most likely because the motherboard battery, which normally maintains these settings, is getting low on power and you must replace it.
☒ **B** is incorrect because it suggests flashing the battery. This procedure (flashing) applies to the upgrade of a firmware chip, not a battery. **C** is incorrect because it suggests recharging the battery with the computer's AC adapter. Although this procedure will work with a portable system battery, you cannot recharge motherboard batteries with an AC adapter. **D** is incorrect because it suggests selecting a "low-power" option in the firmware settings program. Any low-power setting in the firmware settings refers to the function of the computer itself, not to the battery. You cannot adjust the amount of power the firmware chip draws from its battery.

14. ☑ **A.** The problem is with the motherboard, RAM, or a built-in component.
☒ **B** is incorrect because a storage problem would not prevent a message from appearing onscreen reporting the error. **C** is incorrect because an OS problem would not cause multiple beeps. **D** is incorrect because a problem with an external monitor would not cause the multiple beeps.

15. ☑ **C.** The No Operating System error message is not associated with a memory error, but with a disk error on the system disk.
☒ **A, B,** and **D** are incorrect because these are all typical symptoms of bad memory. If the memory has totally failed, the firmware cannot conduct or complete the POST—it is also possible that the firmware might not even be able to initiate the processor. This problem might make it appear that the computer does absolutely nothing when turned on. A bad memory stick may not cause an error, but it will not work, and if you check the memory count in System Information, you may notice the count does not match the installed RAM.

Troubleshooting Storage Devices

16. ☑ **D.** Trying a different SATA connector is simple and quick, and may solve the problem.
☒ **A** is incorrect because that's a lot of work, so it should not be tried first. **B** is incorrect because reformatting the drive will not solve the problem. **C** is incorrect because a SATA drive cannot use a PATA connector.

17. ☑ **A.** A RAID 0 array stripes the data, so the RAID must be rebuilt after a drive replacement.
☒ **B** is incorrect because RAID 1 mirrors; it doesn't stripe. **C** and **D** are incorrect because each includes RAID 1, which doesn't stripe.

Troubleshooting Displays

18. ☑ **C.** Checking the power and data cables is correct because it is the least intrusive action. If this does not resolve the problem, check the brightness setting, and then continue to A, D, and B in that order.
☒ **A** is incorrect because swapping the display is more trouble than simply checking the cables. **B** and **D** are incorrect because replacing the video adapter with a known good one and checking the seating of the video adapter are both very intrusive actions and should not be attempted until you have performed less intrusive actions.

19. ☑ **D.** You cannot repair dead or stuck pixels; you can only decide whether or not to keep using the monitor as it is.
☒ **A, B,** and **C** are incorrect because none of these can repair a dead or stuck pixel.

20. ☑ **A.** Overheating can cause a display to suddenly shut down.
☒ **B** is incorrect because incorrect resolution would not cause the display to shut down. **C** is incorrect because although EMI can cause flickering problems with a CRT, it does not cause a display to shut down. **D** is incorrect because an incorrect brightness setting would only cause the display to appear too dim or too bright.

Chapter 13

Using and Supporting Printers

CERTIFICATION OBJECTIVES

- **1101: 3.6** Given a scenario, deploy and configure multifunction devices/printers and settings
- **1101: 3.7** Given a scenario, install and replace printer consumables
- **1101: 5.6** Given a scenario, troubleshoot and resolve printer issues
- **1102: 1.4** Given a scenario, use the appropriate Microsoft Windows 10 Control Panel utility
- ✓ Two-Minute Drill
- **Q&A** Self Test

In this chapter, you will examine printers to understand the types in use and the technologies, components, and consumables involved. You will learn about the typical issues involved with installing, configuring, and securing printers; the typical upgrading options; and preventive maintenance and troubleshooting.

CERTIFICATION OBJECTIVE

- ***1101: 3.7*** *Given a scenario, install and replace printer consumables*

CompTIA requires that A+ certification candidates recognize the various types of printers available for use with PCs and understand the differences among these device types so you can make purchasing decisions and determine the consumables required for each. These are listed in detail in 1101 exam Objective 3.7.

Printer Basics

Printers are among the most common peripherals used with PCs. Understanding such printer basics as printer types and their related technologies, paper-feeding technologies, printer components, and printer interfaces is important to your success on the exams and on the job.

Printer Types and Technologies

Printer types available today include impact, laser, inkjet, thermal, and 3-D. Laser and inkjet printers may be the most commonly used by the average home or business user, but the other types have their place in the world, and we will describe the characteristics of all types. Each has its own set of steps for taking output from your computer (or a scanned image) and printing it for you, called an *imaging process*.

Be sure you can distinguish among the types of printers listed in CompTIA A+ 1101 exam Objective 3.7: laser, inkjet, thermal, impact, and 3-D.

Impact

Impact printers were the original computer printers decades ago. An *impact printer* has a roller or platen the paper presses against and a *print head* that strikes an inked ribbon in front of the paper, thus transferring ink to the paper, like on a typewriter.

The only kind of impact printer still in use today is a dot matrix printer. The print head in a *dot matrix printer* uses a matrix of pins to create dots on the paper, thus forming alphanumeric characters and graphic images. Each pin is attached to an actuator, which, when activated, rapidly pushes the pin toward the paper. As the print head (containing the pins) moves across the page, different pins move forward to strike a printer ribbon against the paper, causing ink on the ribbon to adhere to the paper. Because they create printouts one character at a time, we call dot matrix printers *character printers*. The most common use for dot matrix impact printers today is for printing multiple-page receipts or forms that require an impact to make an impression on the second and third sheets of paper.

Impact printers have many disadvantages. The impact of the print head is often very loud, and the wear and tear of the repeated hammering makes these printers prone to mechanical failures. Impact printers do not provide very good resolution. Text and images appear grainy, and you can usually see each individual printed dot. Furthermore, impact printers are limited in their ability to use color, and they usually can only use one printer ribbon color (typically black, although you can substitute another color for that printer, if available). Even if you manage to find an impact printer that can use ribbons with up to four colors and/or up to four printer ribbons, it will not have as many color combinations as other printer types.

exam watch **For CompTIA A+ 1101 exam Objective 3.7, make sure you understand the terms *print head, ribbon,* and *tractor feed*. Tractor feed is covered later in this chapter under "Paper-Feeding Technologies."**

Laser

Most *laser printers* use a concentrated light beam (called a *laser beam* because a laser generates it) in the imaging process. Some less expensive ones use light-emitting diodes (LEDs) for this purpose. Laser printers are generally faster than other types of printers, provide the best-quality output, and have the most complex structure and process. Laser printers use very small particles of toner so they provide excellent resolution, and because of this and their speed, these are perhaps the most commonly used printers in business environments, especially for shared network printers. Figure 13-1 shows a typical laser printer for a home or small office.

FIGURE 13-1 A desktop laser printer with the manual tray open. The toner cartridge is hidden behind the panel above the paper feeder.

A laser printer is a nonimpact printer because it does not require any form of physical impact to transfer an image to a printout. Because it creates printouts one page at a time (rather than one character or line at a time), a laser printer is called a *page printer*.

Laser Printer Imaging Process Although some laser printers use a slightly different imaging process, we'll describe a typical order of events that occurs in the laser imaging process. Note that these events occur in repeating cycles, so it is not as important to know which step is first or last as it is the sequence of events. For example, some sources list charging as the first step, whereas others list cleaning as the first step.

exam watch

Make sure you are familiar with the laser printer imaging process. Especially, remember the order of the stages, what each stage accomplishes, and that the stages are in a cycle. The stages are processing, charging, exposing, developing, transferring, fusing, and cleaning.

In a laser printer, the *imaging drum* (the technical term is *electro-photosensitive drum*) is made of metal with an electro-photosensitive coating. The drum is actually more like a slender tube, with a typical circumference of less than an inch, so the imaging process must repeat several times per printout page. Both the drum and the primary corona wire are often contained within the toner cartridge. When printing a page, the feed mechanism moves the paper into the printer and the drum rotates. The steps that follow occur repeatedly while the paper is moving and the drum is turning, although even the processing step will need to repeat for large, multipage documents.

- **Processing** During the *processing* stage, the printer takes the file sent from a computer (or a scanned image) and creates a bit-mapped image (consisting of dots), called a *raster image*. Then it breaks this image up into its individual horizontal lines of dots, called *raster lines*, and the imaging process prints each raster line in turn until completing the page, processing each page in the document in turn.
- **Charging** In the *charging* step, the printer's high-voltage power supply (HVPS) conducts electricity to a *primary corona wire* that stretches across the printer's photosensitive drum (also called the *imaging drum*), not touching it, but very close to the drum's surface. The charge exists on the wire and in a corona (electrical field) around the length of the wire. The high voltage passes a strong negative charge to the drum. In more recent printers, a primary charge roller is used for this purpose.
- **Exposing** The surface of the imaging drum now has a very high negative charge. In the *exposing* (also called *writing*) stage, the printer's laser beam moves along the

drum, creating a negative of the image that will eventually appear on the printout. Because the imaging drum is photosensitive, each place that the laser beam touches loses most of its charge. By the end of the writing step, the image exists at a low voltage while the rest of the drum remains highly charged. The laser that generates this beam is normally located within the printer body itself, rather than in the toner cartridge.

- **Developing** In the *developing* stage, the "discharged" areas on the drum attract microscopic toner particles through the open cover on the printer's toner cartridge. By the end of this stage, the drum contains a toner-covered image in the shape of the final printout.
- **Transferring** During the *transferring* step, *pickup rollers* extract a single page of paper, and the paper moves through the printer close to the drum. The *transfer corona wire,* located within the body of the printer and very close to the paper, applies a small positive charge to the paper as it passes through on the *transfer roller.* This positive charge "pulls" the negatively charged toner from the drum onto the paper. At this point the only thing holding the toner to the paper is an electrical charge and gravity.
- **Fusing** As the paper leaves the printer, it enters the *fusing* stage, passing through a set of *fusing rollers* that press the toner onto the paper. These rollers are heated by a *fusing lamp.* The hot rollers cause the resin in the toner to melt, or fuse, to the paper, creating a permanent non-smearing image. These components, collectively called the *fuser assembly,* are normally located within the body of the printer rather than in the toner cartridge.
- **Cleaning** There are two parts to the *cleaning* stage. First, when the image on the drum transfers to the paper, a *cleaning blade* (normally located within the toner cartridge) removes residual toner, which drops into a small reservoir or returns to the toner cartridge. Next, one or more high-intensity *erasure lamps* (located within the body of the printer) shine on the imaging drum, removing any remaining charge on that portion of the drum. The drum continues to rotate, and the process continues.

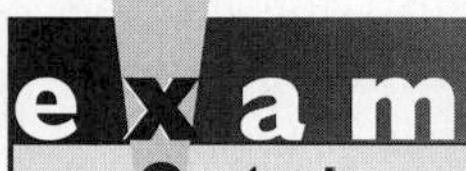

Make sure you can identify these parts of a laser printer: imaging drum, fuser assembly, transfer belt, transfer roller, pickup rollers, separation pads, and duplexing assembly.

Imaging Process Variations in Color Laser Printers Color laser printers can blend colors into practically any shade, typically using four toner cartridges. Therefore, the writing and developing stages take place four times (once for each color: black, cyan, magenta, and yellow) before the image transfers to the paper. Some color laser printers use a *transfer belt* to transfer colors from each cartridge to the final printed page.

Inkjet

The printers categorized as *inkjet* printers use several technologies to apply wet ink to paper to create text or graphic printouts. Inkjets use replaceable *ink cartridges*—one for each color. Some combine multiple ink reservoirs into a single cartridge, and other inkjet printers have a separate cartridge for each ink reservoir. An inkjet cartridge will only fit certain printer models. These printers provide much better resolution than impact printers, and many of them create wonderful color output because, unlike impact printers, inkjets can combine basic colors to produce a wide range of colors. Inkjet printers are very quiet compared to impact printers and even laser printers.

The *print head* in an inkjet ink cartridge is an assembly of components, including a tiny pump that forces ink out of the reservoir, through nozzles, and onto the page. There are many kinds of nozzles that make microscopic droplets, measured in picoliters (one-millionth of a millionth of a liter); a typical droplet measures 1.5 picoliters. Ink cartridges move back and forth across the page. They sit in a cartridge *carriage* mechanism driven by a *carriage belt* that allows the print heads to move over the paper. As in a laser printer, a feeder assembly feeds paper into the printer and a series of rollers moves the paper through.

When printing text, inkjet printers print a character at a time, so they are *character printers,* and their print mechanisms do not contact the page, making them nonimpact printers as well. The printers themselves are usually inexpensive, but the significant operating costs of these printers are the ink cartridges, which can cost between 10 and 25 cents per printed color page. Black and white pages are less expensive. So although these printers are inexpensive to buy, the cost of the consumables (ink) can be high.

Make sure you can identify these parts of an inkjet printer: ink cartridge, print head, roller, feed, duplexing assembly, and carriage belt.

Thermal

A *thermal printer* uses heat in the image transfer process. Thermal printers for PCs fall into two categories: direct thermal printers and thermal wax transfer printers.

In a *direct thermal printer,* a *heating element* heats a print head that burns dots into the surface of *thermochromic paper,* commonly called *thermal paper*. Early fax machines used this technology for printing, and direct thermal printers are commonly used as receipt printers in retail businesses. Thermal paper has a coating consisting of a dye and an acid in a suitable stable matrix. When the matrix heats above its melting point, the dye reacts with the acid and shifts to its colored form in the areas where it is heated, producing an image. Thermal printers are actually dot matrix printers, although no one calls them that. Thermal printers are roll-fed with a *feed assembly* that moves the paper appropriately past the print head.

exam watch

Make sure you know these parts of a thermal printer: feed assembly and heating element. Feed assemblies are covered later in this chapter, under "Paper-Feeding Technologies."

Thermal wax transfer printers use a film coated with colored wax that melts onto paper. Special paper is not required, but the film is somewhat expensive.

All-in-One Printers (Multifunction Devices)

Not many years ago, printers, scanners, copiers, and fax machines were each separate devices. Today, combination devices abound. These types of devices, often categorized as a *multifunction device (MFD)* or an *all-in-one printer*, combine the scanner, printer, and copier in one box, often with a built-in fax as well. Although an MFD can function like a copier or a fax machine (when you place an image to copy on the platen and the copied image comes out or a fax is sent over a phone line), there are significant differences between the old and the new. An MFD shines as a PC-connected device that provides all the functionality of a printer as well as a copier and scanner while using up the desk space of just one of these devices. The printing component of an all-in-one printer is usually either a laser printer or an inkjet printer. Figure 13-2 shows an MFD combining an inkjet printer, scanner, copier, and fax in one machine.

Multifunction devices are not mentioned in CompTIA A+ 1101 exam Objective 3.7, where printer technologies are discussed, but their installation and configuration are included in 1101 exam Objective 3.6, addressed later in this chapter.

3-D Printers

A *3-D printer* uses plastic filament (or sometimes another material, such as metal wire or ceramic powder) to create a 3-D object based on instructions from a 3-D modeling application. It's very different from the other printer technologies discussed so far, which all print two-dimensional images on paper.

FIGURE 13-2 An all-in-one inkjet printer that combines scanner, printer, fax, and copier in one machine

In the most common type of 3-D printing technology (fused deposition modeling), digitally controlled bars position the print nozzle (also called the extruder or the write head) and the writing platform in 3-D space, and then a *filament* is extruded from the print nozzle (extruder) onto the *print bed* in successive thin layers (as small as 100 microns per layer) to gradually build up the printed model from the bottom upward. There are several different methods for fusing the material:

- **Fused deposition modeling (FDM)** Plastic or metal wire filament is fed into the extrusion nozzle and melted, then pushed out onto the model.
- **Stereolithography (SLS)** Plastic, metal, plaster, or ceramic granules are applied and then fused to the previously applied layer.
- **Laminated** Each layer is cut from a paper, metal foil, or plastic sheet and then applied and fused to the previous layer.
- **Light polymer** There are two different methods. In the first, the printer starts with a vat of liquid polymer *resin,* to which it applies light in certain areas to harden the material. Then it drains off the excess to leave the object. In the second, photopolymer is sprayed onto the object and then hardened with light in certain areas to make it stick.

Depending on the technology, a 3-D printer might use either filament or resin as its material. FPM 3-D printers use filament, and light polymer printers use liquid resin.

3-D printer troubleshooting and maintenance vary greatly depending on the model and its underlying technology, so it is difficult to generalize here. Our best advice is to obtain a service manual for your 3-D printer model and follow its instructions closely. 3-D printer troubleshooting and maintenance is not covered on the current A+ exams, although understanding the technology and its consumables is.

Paper-Feeding Technologies

While each type of printer has unique qualities, each one has a set of components called the *feed assembly* that moves paper through the printer so that the image can be placed on it.

The two most common paper-feeding technologies are friction feed and tractor feed. A printer using *friction feed* prints on individual pieces of paper, moving the paper by grasping each piece of paper with rollers. *Tractor feed* requires *continuous form paper,* sheets of paper attached to each other at perforated joints, with perforations on the sides that fit over sprockets that turn, pulling the paper through the printer. Further, continuous-form paper has about a half-inch-wide border at each side that contains holes that accommodate the sprockets on the tractor feed mechanism, thus pulling the paper through the printer. These borders are removable. When using continuous form feed, you must disable the friction feed. Checks, receipts, and other forms, including multiple-part forms, use continuous form feed paper. Because these forms often have specific areas in which the information must print, a necessary step when inserting this paper into the printer is to register or align the perforation accurately between each form with a guide on the printer.

All the printer types discussed here can and usually do use friction feed to move paper through the printer. Some, especially laser printers, use more than one set of rollers to keep the page moving smoothly until ejecting it. Many laser printers use a *separation pad* to get proper feeding of a single sheet of paper. The pickup rollers press down on the paper to move it through the printer, while the separation pad keeps the next sheet from advancing. The separation pad is a replaceable item when paper stops feeding properly. Friction-fed printers usually have more than one paper source available: one tray that can hold a lot of paper and another that holds a smaller amount of paper. These trays can hold from a few pages up to several reams in the large paper feeders of high-end network printers.

Once in the printer, the path the paper takes during friction feed varies from printer model to printer model. Normally, *rollers* pick paper from the feed stack one sheet at a time and move it to the *feeder* mechanism that controls movement of the paper through the printer. The feeder moves the paper one line at a time either past a fixed point for printing or, in some printers, past a print head that moves back and forth printing each line.

Some friction feed assemblies are designed to allow selection of single-sided or double-sided printing. Some printers contain a *duplexing assembly* to print on both sides of the page, but many will require you to feed pages already printed back into the printer again to print on the other side of the page.

All printers eventually deposit the printed page in a tray where the user can retrieve it, and some support the *collating* of documents, placing them in page order—sometimes even for multiple copies.

Prevent paper jams and component wear and tear by using the proper paper for your printer. Read the documentation for the printer to determine the best paper for the results you desire.

Printer Components

The actual printer components vary, depending on the printing and paper-feed technology of the printer. However, regardless of the printing technology used, all printers have a certain set of components in common, which includes the system board, memory, driver and related software, firmware, and consumables.

System Board Each printer contains a system board that serves the same purpose as a PC's motherboard. Often referred to simply as a printer board, this circuit board contains a processor, read-only memory (ROM), and random access memory (RAM). The processor runs the code contained in the ROM, using the RAM memory as a workspace for composing the incoming print jobs (in most printers) and storing them while waiting to print them.

Firmware A printer, like a computer and most devices, has its own firmware code, including basic firmware that contains the low-level instructions for controlling it. Printer firmware is accessed by the driver, which is installed into the operating system. Another type of firmware code in printers is an interpreter for at least one printer language.

Driver A new printer comes packaged with a disc containing drivers, usually for several operating systems. Like drivers for other devices, a print driver allows you to control a printer through the operating system.

CERTIFICATION OBJECTIVES

- ***1101: 3.6*** *Given a scenario, deploy and configure multifunction devices/printers and settings*
- ***1101: 3.7*** *Given a scenario, install and replace printer consumables*
- ***1102: 1.4*** *Given a scenario, use the appropriate Microsoft Windows 10 Control Panel utility*

In this section we describe the use of the Windows Control Panel's Devices and Printers applet, listed in 1102 exam Objective 1.4. We thoroughly cover 1101 exam Objective 3.6, which requires that you understand printer drivers, print interfaces, and printer device sharing options and how to install a local printer versus a network printer, as well as how to install and use multifunction devices that include both printing and scanning. We also pick up the topic of calibration from 1101 exam Objective 3.7.

Installing and Configuring Printers

The plug and play nature of Windows, as well as of printers and scanners, makes installing and configuring these devices quite easy, even for the ordinary PC user. Before you install a printer, make sure that you have a print driver for that printer that will run in the version of Windows running on the computer. Not only must the version level be correct, but you must also match 32-bit Windows with 32-bit drivers and 64-bit Windows with 64-bit drivers. In this section, we will begin with unboxing a device. Then we'll move on to reviewing printer interfaces and then explore the issues related to installing and configuring printers.

Printer Interfaces

There are a number of interfaces for connecting a printer to a computer. For example, you can configure a printer so it attaches directly to a computer or indirectly through a network. You can also configure a printer so it is accessible to only one person or to an entire network of people. Printers use the common interfaces described in Chapter 9, and the following text describes usage of each of these interfaces with printers and scanners.

USB

Universal Serial Bus (USB) is the current dominant printer interface. As its name implies, data travels one bit at a time over the USB interface. However, as described in Chapter 9, USB is fast and requires only a very small connector on each end. Printers do not always come with a USB cable, and you may need to supply your own.

Because printers normally require more power than the small amount of electrical power a USB interface can provide from the PC, printers use an external power supply. To attach a USB device, simply plug it into a USB external socket or root hub.

Network Printing (Ethernet or Wi-Fi)

A printer connected to your PC for your own use is a *local printer*. A printer connected directly to the network is a *network printer*. However, this line blurs because it has long been common to share locally connected printers over a network or to connect one or more printers to a network-connected hardware print server. We will examine these three ways to connect a printer to a network.

- Use a *print server*, a hardware device connected to a network that controls the printing jobs to one or more printers, which are usually connected directly to the print server. Using the manufacturer's instructions, you configure this type of print server much as you do a wireless access point (WAP), by connecting your computer and the print servers with an Ethernet cable and entering its Internet Protocol (IP) address into a browser and configuring the device. As with a WAP or router, be sure to change the password.
- Use a true network printer that contains a network interface card (NIC) and that you configure in the same manner as any computer on the network. The printer acts as a print server, accepting print jobs over the network. If the printer is powered on and online, it is available to network users. The NIC may be an Ethernet NIC or a wireless NIC, or the printer may contain both types. Although this is not a hard-and-fast rule, high-end network printers most often have Ethernet NICs for use in businesses and large installations. The most common wireless printers use one of the 802.11*x* standards for Wi-Fi technology, although some may use Bluetooth. We describe Wi-Fi and Bluetooth in Chapter 14.
- A computer with a network connection can share a local printer attached to that computer's local interface (USB or other). This computer becomes the print server. In this case, you can only access the printer from the network if the computer attached to it is on and has network access.

You should be able to explain the mechanics of each of the preceding methods of making a printer available on a network, as well as its pros and cons.

Installing a Printer

Before installing any printer, you need to unpack it (if new) and test it. The actual steps you take to install it will depend on the individual printer and whether it is plug and play or non–plug and play. Any new printer today is plug and play, but on the job, you may run into some old printers that are not plug and play and be asked to install them on new computers.

Some Windows terminology is helpful at this point. To Windows, the *printer* is the software installed in Windows that controls a physical printer (or more, if other similar printers are available). To Windows, a physical printer is a *print device*. So when you install a printer into Windows, you are installing a software printer as well as the print driver. The printer uses the driver and spooler (queueing software) to process and send your print jobs to the print device. This explains why you can install multiple "printers" in Windows that all refer to the same physical device and configure different settings for each copy.

Properly Unboxing a Device

Follow the manufacturer's instructions to unpack a new printer, removing all the shipping material. You can download whatever drivers are needed from the Web if the OS doesn't automatically detect the device and set it up. There also may be media containing the printer driver (usually several for different operating systems) and additional software for working with the printer's features. Immediately check that you have a correct print driver for the operating system on the computer it will be connected to, or computers if it will be shared.

Know the appropriate print drivers for a given OS. Understand the difference between PCL and PostScript. PCL is used to print common office documents, while PostScript is used to print professional graphics.

Setup Location Considerations

When choosing an appropriate location for the device, consider the following:

- **Security** Don't put a printer that might print confidential or sensitive materials in an unmonitored, high-traffic location such as a hallway or break room; locate it in an area that only authorized people have access to.
- **Safety** Don't place the device on an unstable or flimsy table, and make sure the cords are oriented so that nobody will trip over them.

- **Environment** If possible, avoid locating devices in hot, humid, or dirty/dusty areas. Printers, like most electronics, work best in a clean, cool environment.
- **Connectivity** Choose a location that has reliable AC power and that is within range of the needed network connection (wired or wireless) if it's a network-enabled device.

After positioning the device in its new location, follow the instructions to install toner or ink cartridges and to load paper. You must power up some printers before you can install the ink or toner cartridges. Follow the manufacturer's instructions for printing a test page directly from the printer. Then move on to installing the printer in Windows.

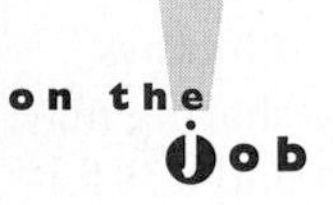

It is common to talk about installing a printer in Windows, but you are actually setting up a *driver* for the printer, not installing the printer itself. This differentiation is significant because you can have multiple instances of a printer set up in Windows, each with different settings, so you can use the same printer in different printing situations without changing its settings.

Choosing a Driver

Depending on the printer, there may be more than one driver available for it, each supporting a different printer language. Common printer languages include *PostScript, Hewlett-Packard Printer Control Language (PCL),* Windows graphics device interface (GDI), and other vendor-specific printer languages.

You might need to decide which driver to use for a printer from among the available choices. As a rule of thumb, PCL drivers are generally used for ordinary desktop printing, whereas PostScript drivers are commonly used for professional graphics printing.

Sometimes a problem with corrupted or garbled output from a printer can be solved by switching drivers.

Installing a Local Printer

You might not have to install a local printer in Windows. If it's connected via USB port, Windows should find the printer immediately after you connect it and offer to set it up automatically. If that fails for some reason, your next best recourse is to run the setup utility on the disc that came with the printer (or a downloaded equivalent of that). If that still doesn't work, the next thing to try is to ask Windows to look for new printers.

CompTIA A+ 1102 exam Objective 1.4 mentions Devices and Printers as a Control Panel utility. In Windows 10 it's still there, although portions of it redirect to the Settings app. However, in Windows 11 the Devices and Printers section of the Control Panel redirects to the Settings app's Printers & Scanners section.

To manually add a printer, do one of the following:

- **Windows 10 (Control Panel method)** Open the Control Panel and choose Hardware And Sound | Devices And Printers | Add A Printer.
- **Windows 10 (Settings method)** Open the Settings app and choose Devices | Printers & Scanners | Add A Printer Or Scanner.
- **Windows 11** Open the Settings app and choose Bluetooth & Devices | Printers & Scanners | Add Device.

As you set up a local printer (that is, one physically connected to the local PC), you might be asked whether you want to share it with others on your LAN. On a Windows system, this sharing will occur via the workgroup using TCP/IP. On a Mac, the sharing may occur via Bonjour or AirPrint. AirPrint is a protocol supported in both macOS and iOS for sharing printers via Wi-Fi. It requires a WAP. Bonjour is Apple's version of plug and play, discovering services and assigning technologies to them automatically.

Installing a Network Printer

When preparing to connect a printer directly to a network via the printer's built-in NIC, first unpack the printer, install ink or toner cartridges, load the paper, connect to a power source, and then connect the appropriate cable to a switch. If the printer has a Wi-Fi NIC, ensure that an appropriate wireless router is configured and within signal range of the printer. Then power up the printer and follow these general steps:

1. *Configure the IP address for the printer's network adapter.* Networks come with network protocols built in, including Transmission Control Protocol/Internet Protocol (TCP/IP). On a small office/home office (SOHO) LAN, if your router assigns IP addresses via Dynamic Host Configuration Protocol (DHCP), it may assign one to the printer automatically. On a corporate network, you will likely need to configure an IP address for the printer's NIC, because most business networks use reserved or static IP addresses for printers. (That's because you don't want the IP address of the printer to change.) You usually do this through a menu on the printer's control panel or via special software on a PC directly connected to one of the printer's ports, such as a USB port. The manufacturer's instructions will give you the details on the method, but you may want to talk to a network administrator to discover the correct IP address to assign to the printer's network adapter.
2. *Test the IP address.* Once you have assigned the IP address, test that you can reach the printer over the network. Testing will require going to a computer proven to be connected to the network and running the following command from a command line: **ping** ***<ip_address>***, where *<ip_address>* is the IP address assigned to the printer. IP addresses are described in Chapters 16 and 17. You might also be able to access the printer's configuration page via a web browser using its IP address, as shown with a SOHO router in Chapter 17.

3. *Prepare each network computer.* Install the printer driver and other utilities on each computer that will print to the printer. If the printer connected successfully to the LAN, the printer should be automatically detected when you run the Add Printer Wizard from Devices and Printers in the Control Panel.
4. *Adjust any data privacy and security settings.* You may be able to set up user authentication on the printer, for example, so that only certain users can print to it. You might also be able to control caching of print jobs for greater security.

Installing a Multifunction Device

When installing an all-in-one printer containing a scanner, copier, and fax, you will have a few additional tasks. When unpacking a new device, pay extra attention to the setup instructions because the scanner in the all-in-one may have a lock to secure the fragile internal components from damage during shipping. Release this lock once you have the device positioned properly on a clean surface. The setup program on the disc that comes with the device will have all the software for the various types of devices. You might already have software that will run some of the components. For example, Windows Fax and Scan will work with most multifunction devices to send and receive faxes and scan images.

If the all-in-one includes a fax and if you plan to use that feature, then you will need to connect a phone cable to the device's RJ-11 (landline phone) connector and connect this to a phone wall jack. Then follow the manufacturer's instructions for configuring the fax to send and receive fax messages.

Configuring a Printer

In Windows 10, after a printer is installed, it appears on the list of printers in the Control Panel (Hardware And Sound | Devices And Printers). If you right-click the printer's icon, a context menu appears, as shown in Figure 13-3.

The Windows 10 Control Panel method is referenced in the 1102 exam Objective 1.4 as Devices and Printers. The Settings app, covered next, is the more modern method and works in both Windows 10 and Windows 11.

There are three very similar commands to note on this menu: Properties, Printer Properties, and Printing Preferences. A few settings overlap between the dialog boxes that open when you select these commands, but generally the settings for each are very different. We'll look at those differences in the following sections. Your printer driver might not have

FIGURE 13-3 Right-clicking a printer's icon produces a menu with several similar-sounding commands on it.

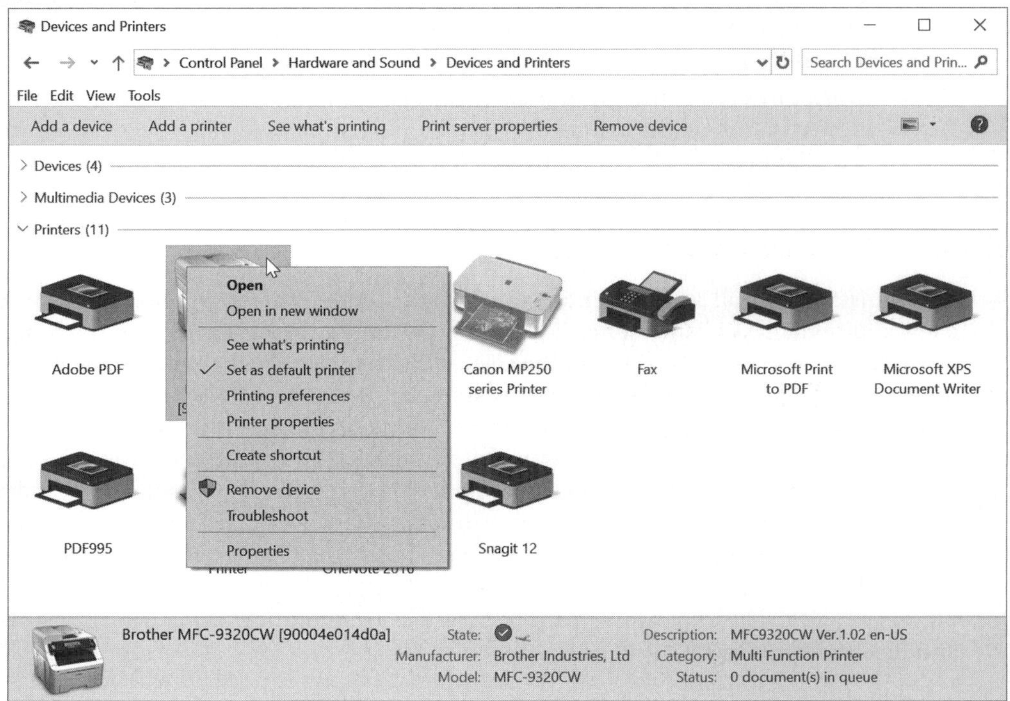

exactly the same dialog box features and tabs as the ones shown, as printer manufacturers tend to tweak the available settings based on the printer's features.

There is also an alternative method: using the Settings app:

- **Windows 10** Open the Settings app and choose Devices | Printers & Scanners, click the desired printer, and then click Manage.
- **Windows 11** Open the Settings app and choose Bluetooth & Devices and then click the desired printer.

On the page that appears (see Figure 13-4 for the Windows 10 version) are hyperlinks or commands that correspond to the context menu selections in Figure 13-3. (Hardware Properties is the equivalent of Properties; the other two commands have the same names as on the context menu.)

FIGURE 13-4 The Settings app in Windows 10 offers the same basic commands as the Control Panel's right-click menu method.

Properties

The dialog box that opens when you choose Properties (or Hardware Properties) is read-only; there are no settings you can change here. It focuses on the printer hardware, as shown in Figure 13-5.

On the Hardware tab there is a Properties button; if you click that, the Properties dialog box that opens is the same as the one that opens when you right-click the printer's icon in Device Manager and choose Properties.

Printer Properties

The dialog box that opens when you choose Printer Properties from the context menu, shown in Figure 13-6, gives you access to a variety of customizable settings for the printer, including sharing, ports, duplexing, and security. On the General tab (shown in Figure 13-6) you can change the printer's name and add a location and comment for it. This information may be useful if you share it with others on your LAN.

FIGURE 13-5

This dialog box appears when you choose Properties or Hardware Properties; it contains hardware and driver information for the printer.

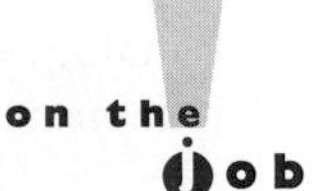

The actual tabs in the Printer Properties dialog box vary by printer and depend on the device driver, the Windows version, and, in some cases, certain Windows settings.

Some of the settings you may be able to adjust in this dialog box include the following, listed by tab:

- **Sharing** On this tab you can share the printer with other computers on your LAN. This option is available even if you access the printer via the LAN yourself, although it would be better for each of the clients to connect to the printer independently rather than go through your share.
- **Ports** On this tab you can specify which port the computer uses to connect to the printer. Various parallel (LPT) and serial (COM) ports are listed, but you can ignore those; they're for backward compatibility with very old printers. As long as the printer is working correctly, you should not have to change this setting.

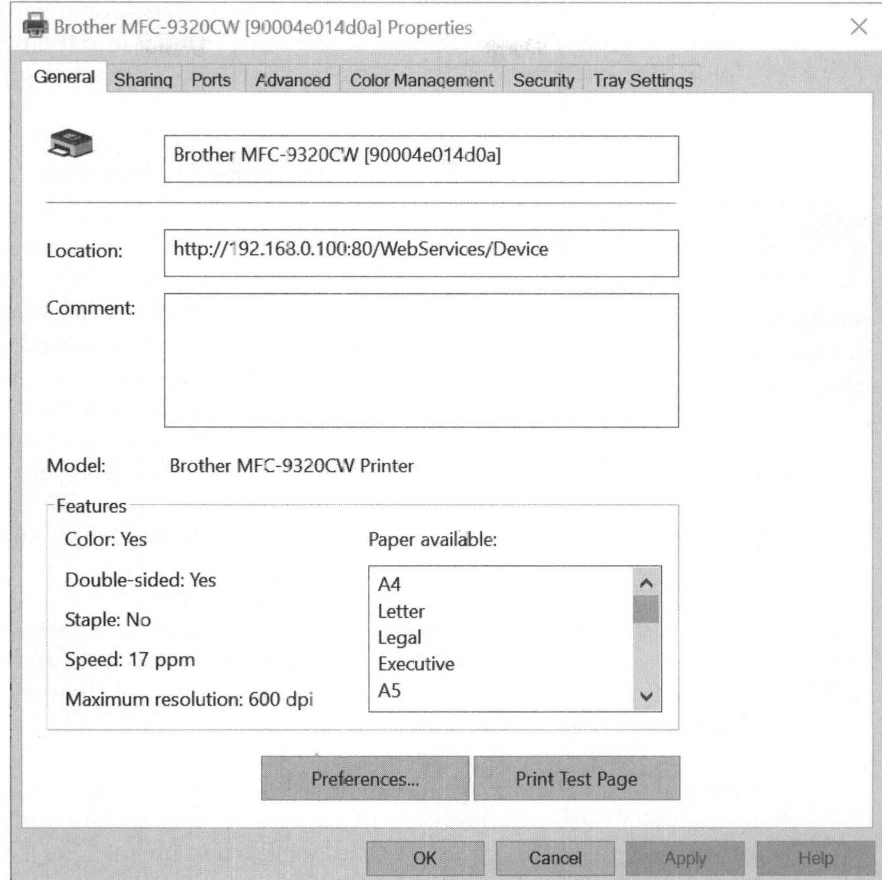

FIGURE 13-6 This dialog box appears when you choose Printer Properties; you can adjust many printer settings here.

- **Advanced** The Advanced tab, if present, may contain settings such as when to make a shared printer available on the network (a time range), whether to use the Windows print spooler (hint: use it), and whether to eject a blank separator page between each print job (wasteful, but useful in some situations).
- **Color Management** On a color printer, this tab may provide options for calibrating the colors or installing color profile files that help match up colors with a professional printing service.
- **Security** If present, this tab enables you to assign permissions to other accounts to use the printer.
- **Tray Settings** If present, this tab may contain a list of automatically adjusted settings and their current values, such as whether or not a duplexing unit or photo tray is installed or what size paper is in a particular paper tray.

Duplexing is the ability to print on both sides of the paper without the user manually flipping over the paper and reinserting it into the printer. If your printer has this feature, it may have a special hardware component that stores and flips pages.

Printing Preferences

The configuration settings explicitly mentioned in 1101 exam Objective 3.6 are duplex, orientation, tray settings, and quality.

If you select Printing Preferences, you get a dialog box containing settings that pertain to the way print jobs are processed. This dialog box varies greatly depending on the printer because this dialog box is generated from the printer's driver files, so its content comes from the printer manufacturer and not from Windows. Some printers have many more settings here than others. There may also be an Advanced button that opens a dialog box with more settings, as shown in Figure 13-7.

Somewhere among these settings you will find an Orientation command that lets you choose between Portrait and Landscape orientation.

It's better not to change to Landscape orientation here, because Landscape then becomes the default for all documents printed from all applications, and that's probably not what you want. Make orientation changes from within the individual applications that you print from.

There should also be settings that allow you to change the paper source (for example, choose between paper trays) and specify the type of paper you are using. This is significant on some photo-quality inkjet printers because if special photo paper is used, it can print at a higher resolution. There may also be a separate Quality setting where you can manually adjust the print resolution (such as Best, Better, or Draft). A lower-quality print mode might print more quickly or use less ink/toner.

In addition, there is probably going to be a Color setting where you can toggle between Black and White and Color (again, for *all* print jobs). We have used this setting to temporarily switch to black-and-white printing when the printer was out of colored ink or toner, for example.

A Collation option may be available for some printers. *Collation* refers to the order in which pages print when you print multiple copies of a multipage document. A collated document prints entire copies together, like pages 1, 2, 3, 1, 2, 3. An uncollated document prints all of one page, then all of the next page, like this: 1, 1, 2, 2, 3, 3.

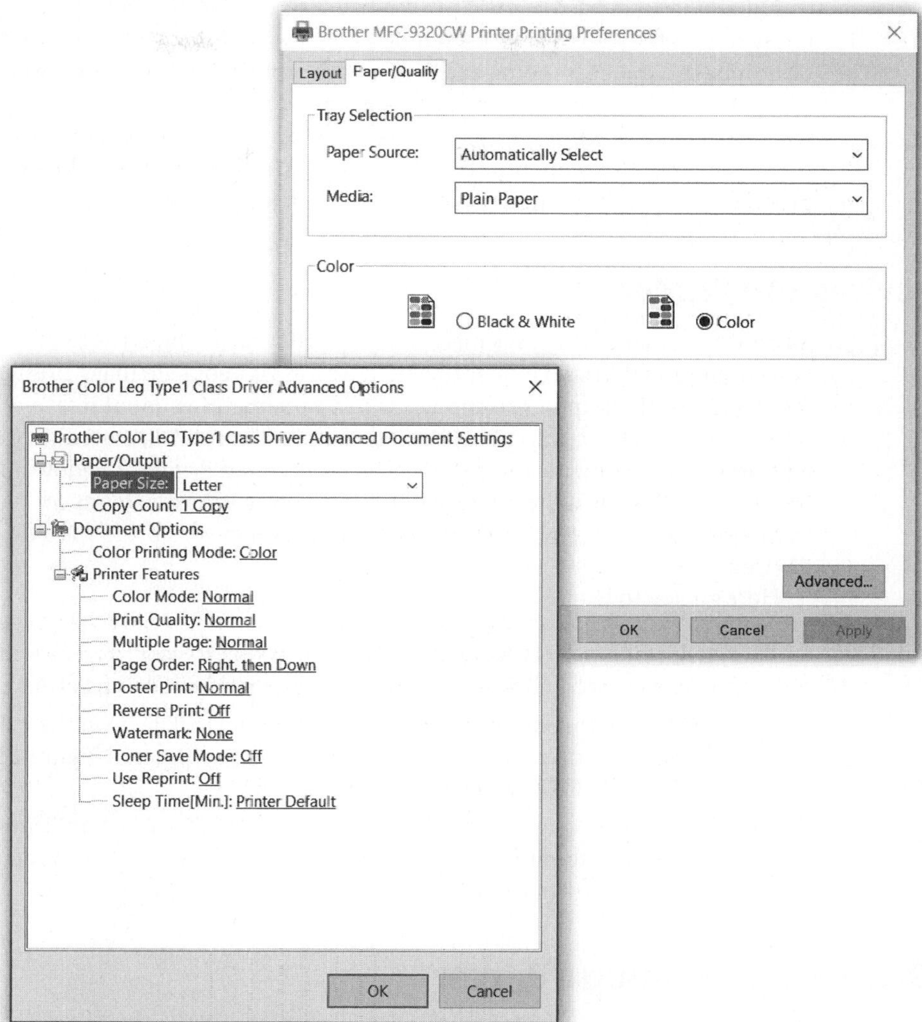

FIGURE 13-7 The available printing preferences will vary depending on the printer model.

Windows Print Processing

When you click Print to print your work in an application, your printer springs to life and you hear the hum of a busy printer. A few seconds later, you reach over and snatch the paper as it leaves the printer. However, there's more to the print story than a mouse click and an instant printout. Windows plays a big part in this frequent and ordinary transaction, doing some processing to prepare the job for the printer via the printer driver that controls how the document is prepared for the capabilities of the printer.

Once Windows has the print job ready to send, it doesn't leave the computer right away, but is sent to the *print spooler*, a Windows component that uses memory or disk to store print jobs in a queue, sending each one to the printer as it is ready to print. This feature is on by default, and is especially important when sending several jobs to a printer at once, whether to a local printer or to a network printer. Once a job is sent to the printer, additional processing is done by the printer before the document is printed. The extent of that processing depends on the printer, so we will look at printer types and technologies next.

Devices and Printers

Since Devices and Printers is mentioned in 1102 exam Objective 1.4, let's take a closer look at it. Even though it's no longer the main way most people manage printers (that honor now falls to the Settings app), you should still know something about it.

You saw the Devices and Printers interface in Figure 13-3, where we were checking out a printer's context menu commands. The Devices and Printers window might have several sections, but the one we're interested in right now is Printers. Icons for each printer appear in this section. (Remember, from Windows' perspective, a printer is a driver, not a physical device.)

Here's a key to what you see there:

- The default printer has a green check mark on its icon. You can change the default printer by right-clicking the desired printer and choosing Set As Default Printer.
- A printer with a dimmed icon or with a black clock face on the icon (depending on Windows version) is not currently available or offline. In Figure 13-3, for example, the Canon MP250 series Printer icon is dimmed.
- When you select a printer, the status bar in the Devices And Printers window shows information about that printer. In Figure 13-3, you see that the selected printer is a multifunction device with zero documents in the queue.

Sharing and Securing a Printer

If your computer is part of a workgroup or Microsoft Active Directory domain, you can share locally installed printers through the Sharing tab on the printer's Properties dialog box, shown in Figure 13-8. Click to place a check mark in the box labeled Share This Printer. If you have administrative rights and your computer is a member of a domain, there will be another check box labeled List In The Directory. Checking this will publish the printer in Active Directory, making it available to others in the domain to search Active Directory for your shared printer.

The Render Print Jobs On Client Computers option should be selected by default. If not, select it, because it moves the task of preparing a document for the printer to the client computer, saving your computer's processing power. Also, click Additional Drivers

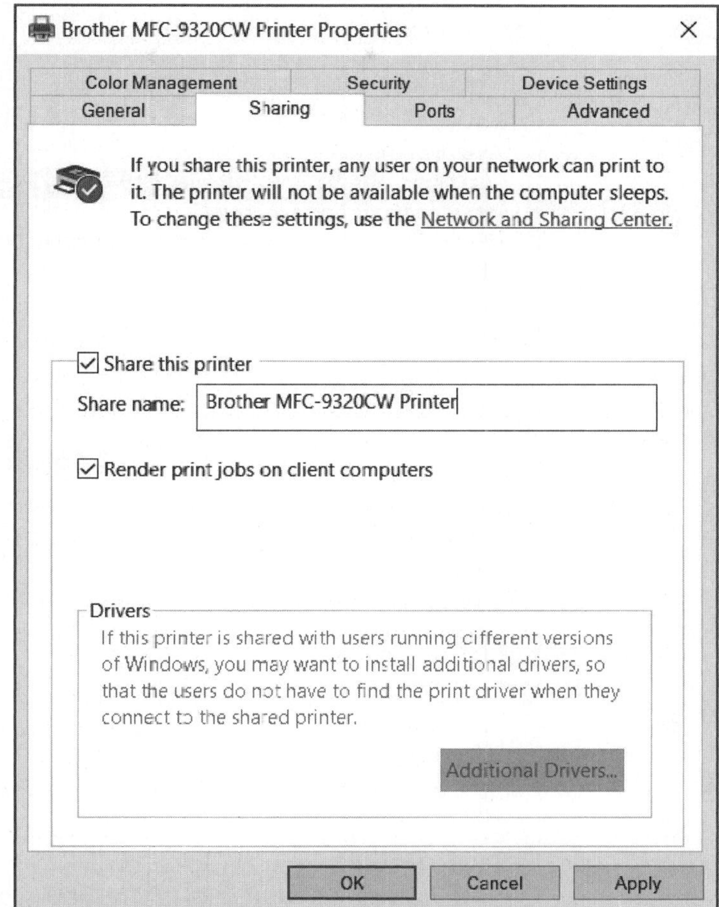

FIGURE 13-8 The Sharing tab in a printer's Properties dialog box

if computers that will be connecting to access the printer are running versions of Windows other than the one on this computer. Then select drivers for those printers, and when they connect, the correct driver will automatically be sent to their computer and installed.

Assigning Security Permissions to Access a Shared Printer

As with file sharing, when you share a printer in a workgroup or domain, you must assign permissions manually to the users connecting over the network, unless you leave the default permissions. In the case of a printer, the default permission gives the Everyone group Print permission, as shown on the Security tab in Figure 13-9.

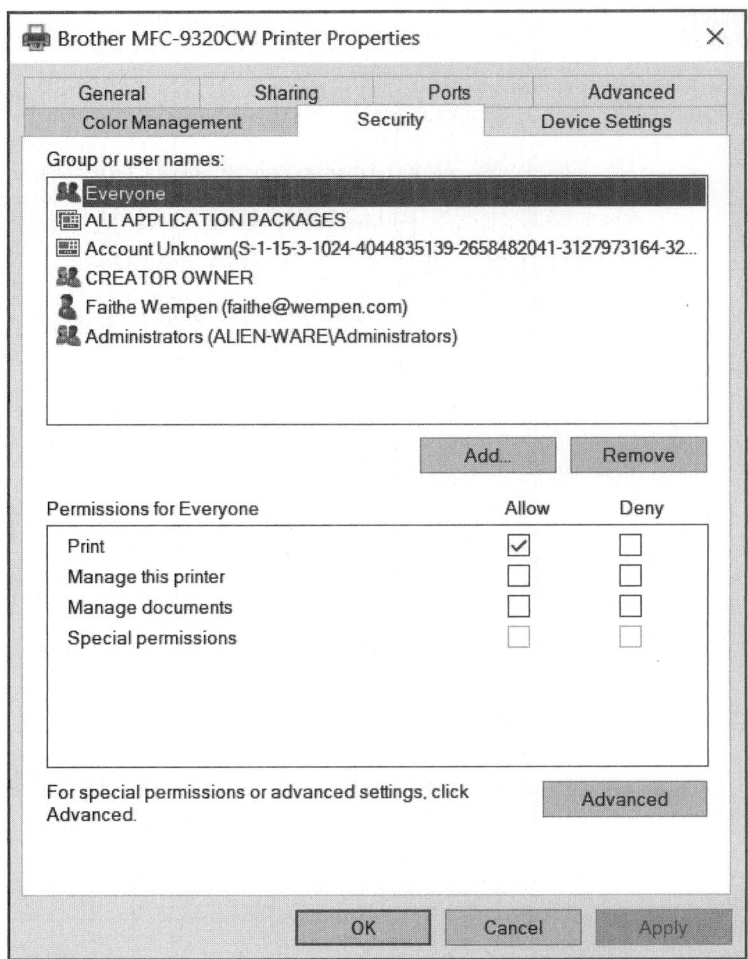

FIGURE 13-9 The Security tab in a printer's Properties dialog box

The four printer permissions are as follows:

- **Print** Allows a user to print, cancel, pause, and restart only the documents that the user sends to the printer.
- **Manage This Printer** Allows a user to rename, delete, share, and choose printer preferences. Also permits a user to assign printer permissions to other users and manage all print jobs on that printer.

FIGURE 13-10

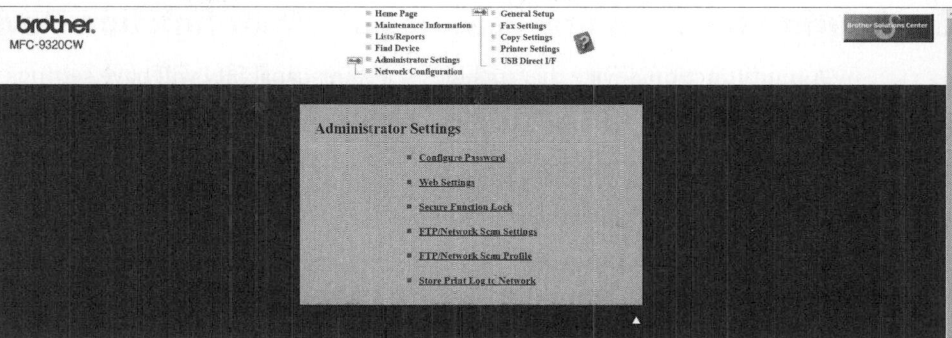

Network and security settings for a network-enabled MFD

- **Manage Documents** Allows a user to manage all jobs (for all users) in the printer's print queue.
- **Special Permissions** Primary use of special printers is by an administrator in order to change the printer owner. The person who installs a printer is the Creator Owner, who is automatically assigned the Manage Documents permission.

Configuring Security Settings on a Network-Enabled Printer or MFD

A network-enabled printer or MFD may have its own control panel or Settings app (usually network-accessible by entering the printer's IP address in a browser). In this app you should be able to restrict network access to the printer to certain users or certain IP addresses. Figure 13-10 shows an example. The settings will have different names and be arranged on different menus depending on the device make and model; consult the user manual for the printer or MFD for the specifics.

Some of the settings you may be able to control using the printer or MFD's built-in configuration and setup utility include the following:

- **Authentication** You may be able to authenticate users who are authorized to use the device. This authentication can be through IP addresses, user name and password/PIN, or badging. *Badging* refers to using a smartcard reader to authenticate users based on their possession of a physical badge.
- **Examine audit logs** There will probably be a section where you can view logs for the device's activities. These logs should show who accessed the device and what they did with it.
- **Secured prints** Some devices have a function lock that enables you to configure passwords for selected users and then grant access to some or all device functions using them. For example, you could restrict some users to black-and-white printing only or limit the number of pages they can print per day.

Configuring the Scanning Features of a Multifunction Device

A multifunction device that includes scanning capability will have settings you can adjust to control how the scanner operates.

Two areas specific to scanners are noted in 1101 exam Objective 3.6: automatic document feeder (ADF)/flatbed scanner and network scan services (e-mail, SMB, cloud services). You don't need to know the specifics of how these work, because the details are different for every make and model. However, you should know that the configuration options exist, and you should be able to suggest enabling them in specific scenarios.

Using a Flatbed vs. Automatic Document Feeder

Most scanners have a lid you can lift to manually position the item on a glass plate to scan it, like you would on a copier, and also an *automatic document feeder (ADF)*, which is like a paper tray you load multiple items into at once. Then the MFD pulls in each page, scans it, and then spits it back out into an exit tray.

When you load items into the document feeder, the MFD may detect their presence, so that when you press the Scan button on the front panel, the documents in the tray are scanned. There will also be a source option in the scanner's software that you access via the operating system. Figure 13-11 shows the scanner controls when scanning using an MFD via the Windows Fax & Scan utility, for example.

Network Scanning Services

A network-enabled MFD can be set up to save scans to a centrally accessible storage location automatically. The specified location can be a shared folder on the local network (via SMB), in a cloud storage location, or to an e-mail address (where the device would send an e-mail to a specified address containing each scanned file).

SMB uses network port 445. You'll need to know that for 1101 exam Objective 2.1, along with the numbers for many other ports.

SMB stands for *Server Message Block*. It's a protocol for sharing files on a network. It enables computer applications to read and write to network-stored files and request services from applications on a server. On MFDs that support it, you can set up the SMB Send feature and specify a network path to which to send scans.

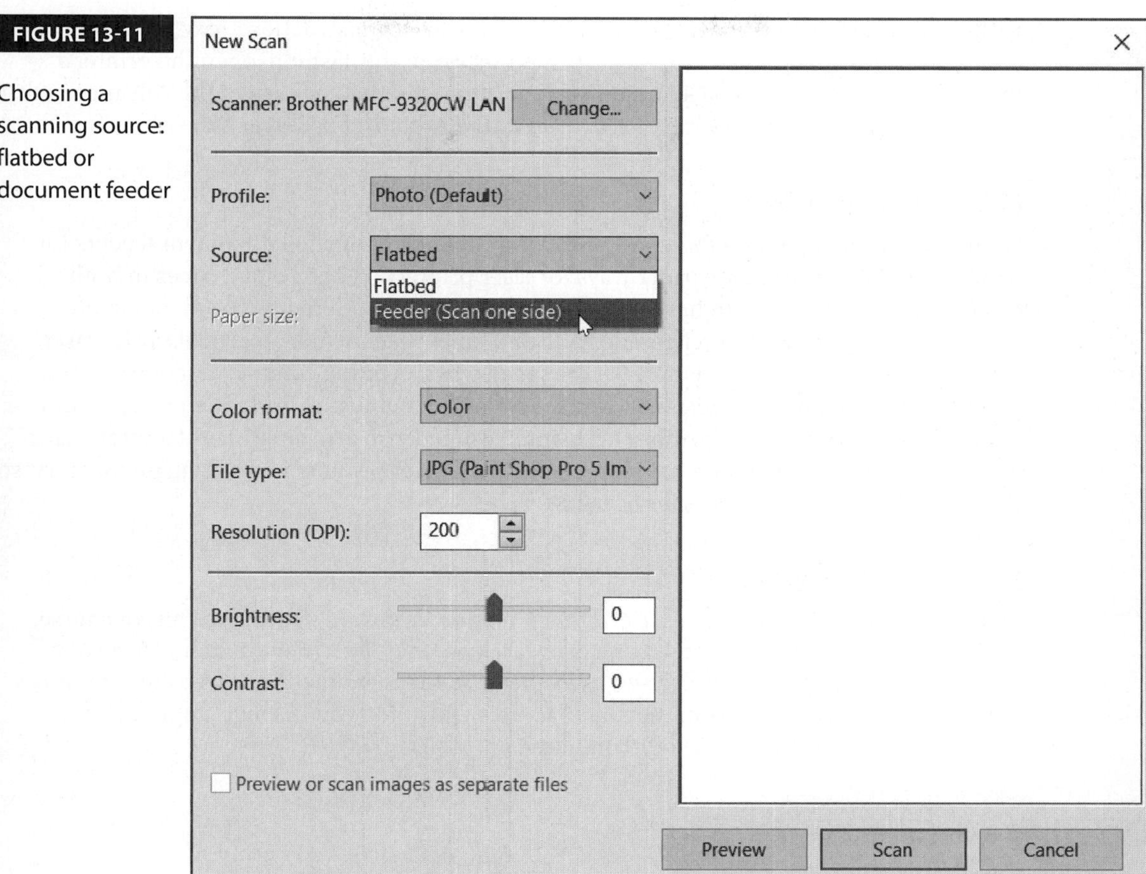

FIGURE 13-11 Choosing a scanning source: flatbed or document feeder

Printer Upgrades

Printers are somewhat limited in how you can upgrade them, but there are a few things you can do to enhance their performance. The following sections describe some possible software and hardware upgrades for printers.

Device Driver and Software Upgrades

Like other software, software associated with printers and scanners calls for occasional upgrades, with drivers being the most frequently upgraded. When an updated driver is available for your printer, follow the manufacturer's instructions to install it. If it comes with its own installation program, run it. Alternatively, the instructions may tell you to use the Update Drivers option. To update a printer driver in this fashion, open the printer's Properties dialog box (as you learned to do earlier in this chapter), select the Advanced tab, click New Driver, and follow the instructions in the Add Printer Driver Wizard.

Hardware Upgrades

Popular hardware upgrades for printers and scanners are automated document feeders for scanners and larger-capacity paper trays for laser printers. Higher-end devices in both categories are most likely to have upgrade options, usually offered by the manufacturer.

Another popular hardware upgrade has historically been memory, particularly for laser printers. Adding memory can increase the speed when printing complex documents or graphics. A search of the Internet will turn up many manufacturers of memory upgrades for laser printers. However, as memory has gotten less expensive, printer manufacturers have become less stingy when it comes to equipping new laser printers with adequate memory, so this upgrade is not as useful as it once was.

Firmware Upgrades

Some printers—in particular, laser printers—support firmware upgrades. This, of course, depends on the manufacturer releasing firmware upgrades. First, determine the firmware version currently in your printer and then check on the manufacturer's website for notices of upgrades. Instructions from the manufacturer will guide you through upgrading the firmware, which you do from your computer.

Deleting a Printer

When you no longer use a printer, you can delete it, either from the Control Panel or from the Settings app. You aren't really deleting the printer itself, of course, but rather its driver. (You are probably not actually deleting the printer's driver files from your hard drive, either; you're just de-registering it in the Windows registry. That's handy because if you ever want to re-add the printer to Windows, you won't have to re-download the needed driver.)

- **From the Control Panel** From the Devices And Printers section, right-click the printer and select Remove Device.
- **From the Settings app** From the Printers & Scanners section, click the printer and click Remove Device (Windows 10) or Remove (Windows 11).

SCENARIO & SOLUTION	
We need a printer that will print an image to multipart forms for retail receipts. What should we buy?	Buy an impact printer, which will be able to print to carbon-copy forms.
We need a printer that will print many pages quickly and not cost very much per page. What should we get?	A laser printer meets these criteria. It is a fast printing technology, and the per-page cost for a laser printer is much lower than for inkjet or thermal.
We need a printer that will print photographs on glossy photo-quality paper. What should we get?	Some—but not all—inkjet printers produce photographic-quality output that rivals photos printed at professional labs. Glossy paper is available specifically for this type of inkjet.

CERTIFICATION OBJECTIVE

■ ***1101: 3.7*** *Given a scenario, install and replace printer consumables*

This section covers printer maintenance tasks for the five types of printers covered on the CompTIA A+ 220-1101 exam that include maintenance topics in Objective 3.7: laser, thermal, impact, inkjet, and 3-D.

Printer Maintenance

Because of the frequency with which printers are used, they require almost constant maintenance. Fortunately, the maintenance procedures are usually easy—the most frequent tasks involve consumables. Consider scheduling regular maintenance, such as cleaning, based on the amount of usage for each printer and scanner. Manufacturers may provide a list of other maintenance tasks, such as vacuuming or replacing the ozone filter in laser printers, which should occur along with a regular cleaning, but not at the same frequency.

Maintenance Tools

The basic tool set that you use for maintaining a computer is appropriate for printers too. It includes using compressed air from pressurized cans for blowing out the paper dust and debris inside a printer and a small vacuum cleaner. Because the particles of toner in a laser printer are so small, it isn't a good idea to use a conventional vacuum because the toner can clog it up and because the filters may not be as fine on a regular vacuum, so toner particles might become airborne. Manufacturers do make special vacuums for laser printers, but they tend to be expensive. Laser printer manufacturers also make maintenance kits for replacing aging parts at predetermined intervals.

Replacing Consumables

The most common maintenance tasks involve replacing consumables. Printer consumables include the printer medium (such as ink or toner), some parts that wear out such as print heads and drums, and paper.

The *printer medium* provides the pigment for the image that a printer creates. The medium comes in a special form for the technology and is specific to the model of printer. The most common forms are ink ribbons, ink cartridges, and laser printer toner cartridges. If you are the one responsible for purchasing and storing these products, letting these supplies run out is bad for your career!

For the best results, use the manufacturer's recommended brand of consumables. In the case of the major printer manufacturers, their branded ink and toner products may only be available at premium prices. To save money, you can consider third-party sources, but be prepared to buy and test one set of the off-brand cartridges before ordering them in large quantities. Don't buy the cheapest replacements available, as they are more likely to leak, causing a huge mess inside the printer.

Shelf Life

The shelf life of both laser printer toner cartridges and inkjet cartridges is similar, and is usually two years from the production date or six months from when you first open the package or first put it into use. Even printer paper has a shelf life because paper for friction-feed printers must contain a certain range of moisture content to feed properly without causing jams. Old paper also may discolor unless it is of very high quality. Used printer consumables can negatively affect the environment and should be disposed of in a manner that is both legal and respectful of the environment, as described in Chapter 1.

Paper

All printers have the dreaded "paper out" light and Windows desktop error message (if connected to a computer). A printer in a cash register, a point-of-sale (PoS) printer, typically has an alarm.

With the exception of thermal printers and some impact printers that require tractor-feed paper, most printers can use standard-sized sheets of ordinary copier paper for drafts and everyday casual printing. For the best results, however, consult the printer documentation for the type and quality of paper to use. Paper should be stored in its packaging and in a cool, dry place. For instance, copier paper often comes in paper-wrapped one-ream (500-page) packages, but is also available in bulk boxes, in which the paper is not wrapped. Do not unwrap or remove paper from its container until ready to install in a printer. If you are using a tray to feed a friction-feed printer, simply pull out the appropriate paper tray. Gently riffle a stack of fresh paper and then insert it into the tray. If there is a lid for the tray, replace that before inserting the tray into the printer.

Tractor-feed impact printers printing multiple copies use either carbon paper or *impact paper* that contains encapsulated ink or dye on the back of each sheet except the last one so that the impact of the print head on the first sheet breaks the encapsulation on all sheets and causes a character image to appear on the subsequent sheets.

To replace paper in a tractor-feed printer, you will need to lift the printer lid, feed the first sheet of the new stack through the paper path, and line up the holes with the sprockets on the feed wheels. As this procedure varies from model to model, consult the manufacturer's documentation. Finally, stack the continuous form paper in a bin or next to the printer neatly so that it can easily feed into the printer.

When feeding card stock or sheets of labels through a printer, be sure to use the straightest paper path to avoid jams. Never feed a sheet of labels through a laser printer if one or more labels have been removed, because the "Teflon-like" material on the paper carrier will melt on the fusing roller and ruin it. A fusing roller is an expensive component to replace because you normally must replace the entire fusing assembly. And never use inkjet printer labels in a laser printer, because labels designed for inkjets may not be able to tolerate the heat inside a laser printer.

Adding paper to any printer should only take a few seconds because it does not involve turning off the printer's power. The error message should go away on its own. If you do not close or insert the tray properly, a Tray Open or Close Tray message may appear. If the printer uses an upright friction feed, follow the steps in Exercise 13-1 to add more paper.

EXERCISE 13-1

Adding Paper to an Upright Friction-Feed Tray

If you have access to a printer with an upright friction-feed tray, you can follow these instructions.

1. Release the tray lever at the back of the printer (if so equipped). This will cause the paper tray to drop away slightly from the friction rollers.
2. Place a small stack of paper in the tray, using the paper guides.

3. Engage the tray lever to bring the paper closer to the feed rollers.
4. The printer might automatically detect the paper and continue the print job. If not, look for and press the Paper Advance button on the printer. This instructs the printer to detect and try to feed the paper.

Multipart forms are not always available as continuous-feed paper, in which case, you need an impact printer capable of friction feed. Usually, this only requires removing the tractor feed assembly and making sure that the friction-feed mechanism is engaged (it is disengaged while tractor feed is in use).

Paper for a thermal printer comes in rolls. Perhaps the most common thermal printers are in cash registers; you have probably witnessed a cashier changing thermal paper while you waited in line with a shopping basket full of frozen food. To change the thermal paper roll, you first open the feed assembly compartment and remove the plastic or cardboard roll from the spent roll and remove any torn paper or debris in the compartment. Then place the new roll on the spindle, taking care to have the paper feed in the correct direction from the roll, and thread it through the assembly (look for directions mounted in the compartment or arrows on the components), making sure to thread the end of the roll outside. Close the door, give a gentle tug to the paper, and tear off the leading edge. Most thermal printers have a paper cutter where the paper exits.

Ink

The most common forms of ink for printers are ink ribbons for impact printers and ink cartridges for inkjet printers.

An impact printer uses a fabric ribbon embedded with ink. The ribbon is usually a closed loop on two spools (for unused and used ribbon) enclosed within a cartridge. This cartridge is either a movable cartridge mounted on the print head assembly or a stationary cartridge that stretches the ribbon the width of the paper, allowing the moving print head assembly to move back and forth. The used portion of the ribbon simply spools back into the ribbon cartridge. To install, follow the manufacturer's instructions, which will include carefully bringing the ribbon over the print head.

The medium for inkjet printers is ink contained in reservoirs. In the case of inkjet printers, this reservoir is part of a small cartridge that also may contain the print head that sprays the ink on the paper. Figure 13-12 shows an open inkjet printer with the cartridges exposed. You must turn this model on when you change the cartridges because when it is turned off, the cartridges are "parked" out of sight. Lights on each cartridge give the status of the cartridge: steady when there is adequate ink; blinking when ink is low.

If you search the documentation or the manufacturer's website, you can discover the expected yield of a cartridge. The yield of a typical inkjet cartridge is in the hundreds of pages and varies according to what you are printing and how much of the page is to

FIGURE 13-12

An open inkjet printer with the ink cartridges exposed

be covered. For example, one of our inkjet printers shows a black ink cartridge yield of 630 pages of text and 450 pages for graphic printouts that have 5 percent coverage. The same printer shows a color ink yield of 430 pages with 5 percent coverage per color. If your printouts use more ink per page, then the yield will be smaller.

Toner

Toner cartridges for a typical desktop laser printer run around $50 and up, and if you've got a color laser printer, you'll need four cartridges (cyan, magenta, yellow, and black). However, they last for several thousand pages, making these printers relatively inexpensive per page to use.

Several companies take used printer cartridges, recondition the drum and other components, refill the toner reservoir with fresh toner, and offer them at significantly lower cost than the manufacturer's fresh cartridges. We have had mixed experiences with these "refilled" cartridges. Some refilled/reconditioned cartridges have performed as well as the best brand-name new toner cartridges, whereas others have been very poor. Caveat emptor!

The brand-name cartridges from your printer's manufacturer will normally produce the highest quality and demand the highest price. New, off-brand cartridges are less expensive, and refilled/recycled off-brand cartridges are the cheapest (but also the most likely to produce poor-quality printouts). For business use, we recommend new cartridges only, because the additional cost of the cartridges is less than the labor cost to clean up problems that improperly filled used cartridges can cause.

The yield of a laser cartridge for a typical desktop monochrome black laser printer is several thousand pages. The actual number of pages depends on the coverage level—that is, the amount of each color used on each page. A page with a full-page, full-color graphic will use up a lot more toner than a business letter with a tiny full-color logo in the corner. Numbers such as 3000 to 8000 pages are common. The yield for a color laser printer generally runs over 1000 pages per cartridge. For instance, the documentation for one printer estimates the yield for a standard-capacity black toner cartridge at 4000 pages, whereas the estimate for each of the standard cyan, magenta, yellow, and black (CMYK) cartridges is 1500 pages. The high-capacity color toner cartridges show an expected yield of 4000 pages.

To replace a toner cartridge, turn off the printer and gently remove the old cartridge. Turning off the printer is not required for replacing the cartridge, but we recommend doing it because this is a good time to give the printer a quick cleaning, removing paper and toner debris, as described later in this chapter. After cleaning the printer, remove the new cartridge from its packaging and set it aside while you insert the old cartridge into the packaging for disposal. Then remove any tape or plastic components labeled to be removed before installing. Gently rock the cartridge from side to side, and then insert into the printer, per the manufacturer's instructions.

Cleaning a Printer

The best thing you can do to prolong the life of a printer and prevent problems from occurring is to clean it regularly. In all printers, whether laser, thermal, or impact, small particles of paper and other debris can be left behind and cause a potentially harmful buildup. This buildup can hold a static charge, which can, in turn, damage components through electrostatic discharge (ESD) or cause pages to stick together.

We do not recommend using any solvents to clean a printer, and you should never spray a liquid on or into a printer for any reason. Use a very dilute mixture of water and white vinegar to dampen a cloth, and thoroughly wring it out before wiping off the exterior of the printer. Do not use liquids inside the printer unless following the advice of the manufacturer.

Before opening up a printer for cleaning, power it down and unplug it. Do not touch the printer's power supply, and allow the fusing roller in a laser printer to cool down before you clean inside.

Removing the buildup will also keep the paper path clear, thus reducing paper jams and ensuring there is no inhibition of moving parts. You can remove dust and particle buildup using compressed air or a vacuum. As you clean the printer, be on the lookout for small paper corners left behind during the print process or after you cleared a paper jam.

In an inkjet printer, you should look for and remove ink from the inside of the printer. Ink can leak and cause smudges on the paper. As the ink dries, it can cause moving components or paper to stick.

Laser printers can accumulate toner. Remove excess toner using a paper towel or cotton swab, but beyond that, only clean laser printer internal components using the manufacturer's instructions, which may include using a *toner vacuum*, a vacuum with filters to protect you from inhaling the super-fine toner particles. This is essential if you support many laser printers.

You may have to replace the ribbon and the print head in an impact printer, and in a thermal printer you should clean the heating element. Figure 13-13 shows the interior of a color laser printer. The four bars across the center are the four toner cartridges.

Some manufacturers add a Maintenance tab to the Printer Properties dialog box for tasks such as those shown in Figure 13-14 for an inkjet printer. Notice the four buttons for cleaning various components, plus the buttons for Print Head Alignment and Nozzle Check.

exam watch

Make sure you can perform all the maintenance tasks for each type of printer listed in 1101 exam Objective 3.7:

Laser: Replace toner, apply maintenance kit, calibrate, clean
Inkjet: Clean heads, replace cartridges, calibrate, clear jams
Thermal: Replace paper, clean heating element, remove debris
Impact: Replace ribbon, replace print head, replace paper

There are no maintenance tasks listed for 3-D printers, only some parts to be aware of: filament, resin, and print bed.

FIGURE 13-13

A desktop laser printer opened and ready for cleaning

FIGURE 13-14 A Printer Properties dialog box showing maintenance options

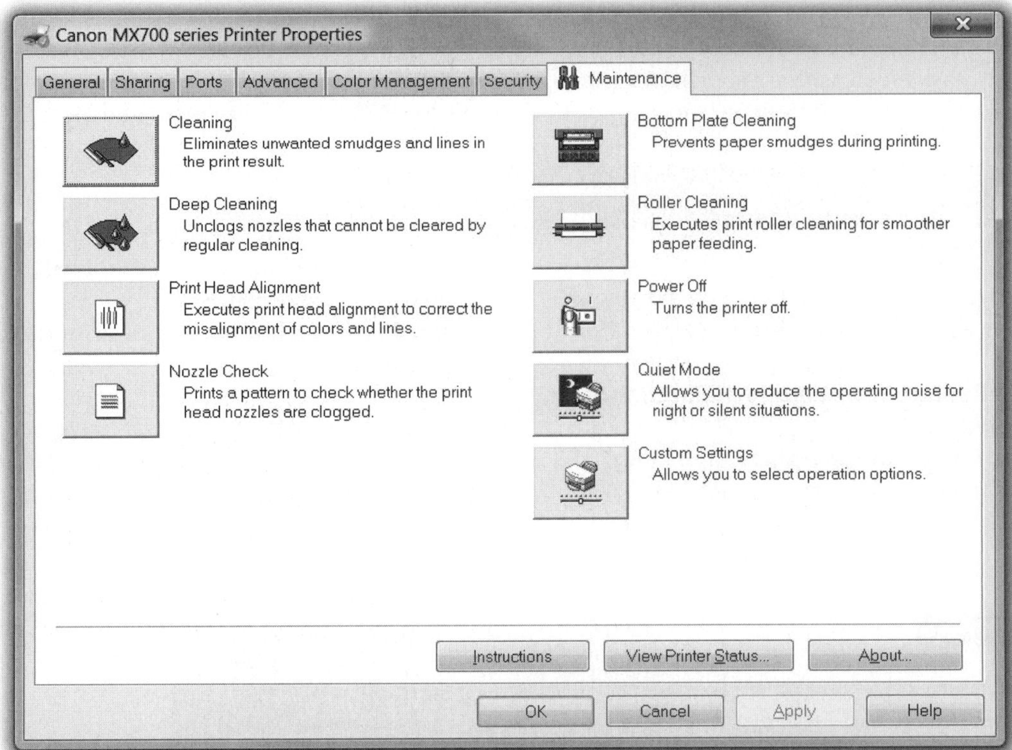

Replacing Print Heads

The print head is the hardest-working component in an impact printer, so be prepared to replace one if necessary. We will describe symptoms of problems with print heads later in "Troubleshooting Printers." If the solutions provided there do not eliminate the symptoms, then replace the print head. Contact the manufacturer for a replacement, and follow the instructions for removing the old print head and installing the new one.

The term "print head" can refer to different things depending on the printer type. On an impact printer, the print head is a big block of metal (usually aluminum) that travels across the paper and strikes the inked ribbon. On inkjet printers, the print head is the set of nozzles for a particular color that spray the ink onto the page. Laser printers don't have a print head.

Ozone Filters

The side effect of a laser printer's use of coronas in the imaging process is the creation of ozone (O_3), which can harm other printer parts, and if at sufficient levels in a closed area has the potential to be harmful to humans. Therefore, laser printers that produce ozone above certain levels have an *ozone filter* to remediate this, but others do not. If a printer has an ozone filter, your printer documentation will identify it. Ozone is only created when a printer is printing, and only some laser printers produce an amount of ozone requiring an ozone filter. Check with the manufacturer for recommendations for how to maintain the ozone filter. Some can be vacuumed, while others must be replaced at a specific interval.

Maintenance Kits and Page Counts

Some printers, mainly professional-quality and high-production laser printers, have "maintenance counts." The printer counts the number of pages printed over the lifetime of the printer, and when this page count reaches a certain number, called the maintenance count, a service message will appear on the printer's display. This message indicates that the printer has reached the end of the expected service life for some of its internal components, such as the various types of rollers, pads, and entire assemblies. When this occurs, you should install the manufacturer's maintenance kit of replacement parts, after which you must reset the page count so it can track the expected life of the parts in the new maintenance kit.

If you do not reset the page count, the printer will continue to issue the maintenance warning. Use the manufacturer's instructions for resetting the page count. In the rare instance when you must install a new maintenance kit before the page count reaches the maintenance count, on some models you must reset the maintenance count to match the page count. Then, when the next page is printed, you will receive the maintenance message and can proceed with the maintenance and reset the page count.

Calibration

Calibration is a process that matches colors seen on the screen to colors printed on paper. To get the best quality out of a color printer, look for a calibration tool in the Color Management tab of the printer's Properties dialog box. We opened the Color Management dialog box shown in Figure 13-15 by selecting the Color Management tab and then clicking the Color Management button. Notice the list in the box under ICC Profiles. These are sets of specifications used by your printer to print color per *International Color Consortium (ICC)* standards. ICC is a standards organization for color management systems. Find additional profiles on the All Profiles tab, which in this case contains *Windows Color System (WCS)* profiles. WCS is a color management system that Microsoft is promoting as a standard. You can select profiles from this list and add them to the printers list on the Devices page. Then print out samples and compare the screen image of each sample with

FIGURE 13-15 The Color Management dialog box

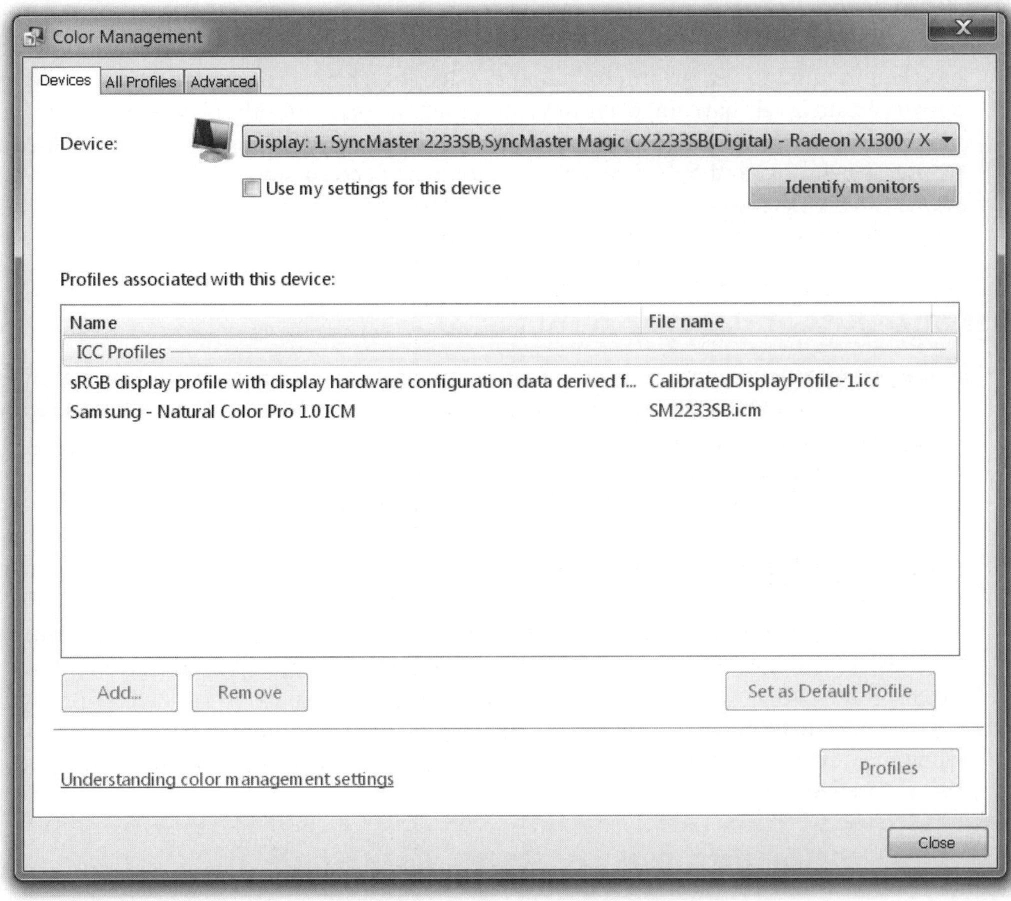

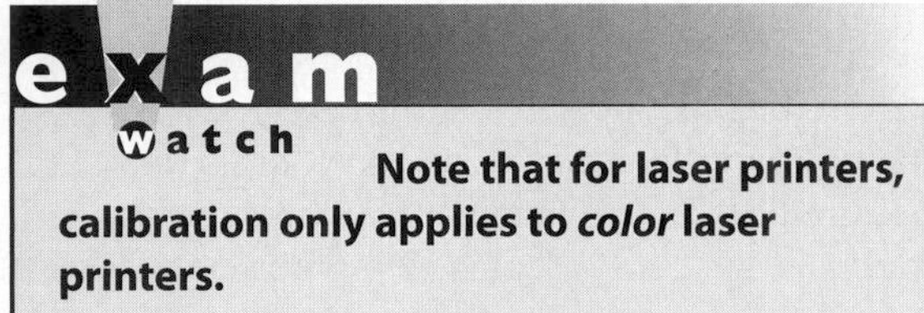

Note that for laser printers, calibration only applies to *color* laser printers.

the printed image. Using a utility like this, you are depending on your eyes to judge the correct settings. Of course, none of these profiles will work if your display's color is not right. So click the Advanced tab and click Calibrate Display. Follow the instructions for calibrating the display.

Ensuring a Suitable Environment

Prevent a myriad of problems with your printer by providing a suitable environment. Be sure the printer is on a level surface, close to the computer to which it is connected, and convenient for the user. Temperature extremes, dirt, and dust will negatively affect either type of device. Dirt and dust will affect the quality of scanned documents and, if they infiltrate the case, can cause heat buildup in any device.

CERTIFICATION OBJECTIVE

- ***1101: 5.6*** *Given a scenario, troubleshoot and resolve printer issues*

The following section covers all the topics in the 1101 exam Objective 5.6, which deals with the common printing problem symptoms and their fixes. It includes problems both with the printer hardware and with the OS being used to access it, as well as problems with the connectivity between the two.

Troubleshooting Printers

When troubleshooting printers, apply the same troubleshooting theory and procedures used with other computer components and use the same toolkit, as described in Chapter 8. When a printer needs a major repair, first evaluate the cost/benefit of the repair by finding out how much it would cost to replace the printer versus the cost of the repair. In this section, learn about common printer problems and their solutions.

Printers are one of the most commonly accessed network resources and are the cause of a majority of network-related trouble calls.

Paper Feed Problems

Common to all printers, paper feed problems have a variety of causes, and the symptoms are not just paper jamming and stopping the printing. Paper feed problems result in creased paper and paper simply not feeding at all because it never leaves the paper tray. Here are just a few possible causes and solutions:

- **Multipage misfeed** Too much paper can cause more than one page to feed through the printer at a time. The extra page can cause problems with the print process itself and jam within the printer. To avoid this, reduce the amount of paper you place in the tray.

- **Static electricity** If static builds up within the pages, it can cause the pages to stick together. Use your thumb to "riffle," or quickly separate, the pages before you load them into the paper tray. Riffling allows air between the pages and can reduce "static cling." Remove dust from the printer, as this can also cause static buildup.
- **Moisture in the paper** Moisture can cause pages to stick together or not feed properly. To protect paper from moisture changes, keep it in its packaging until needed. Store paper in a cool, dry place.
- **Worn-out friction-feed parts** Worn parts will fail to move the paper smoothly. Check feed rollers for wear. Feed rollers are often rubber or plastic, and you should replace them (depending on the cost of replacing parts vs. replacing the printer). You may also need to replace the separation pad.
- **The wrong paper** Use paper that is not too thin, not too thick, and that has a certain range of moisture content to avoid static buildup. Try using a different weight paper. Try feeding from an alternative (straight-through) paper path. Most printers have the option of a more direct paper path that can handle heavier-weight paper than the standard path.
- **Too few sheets in an upright paper tray** If the stack of paper in an upright paper tray is too small, the friction rollers might not be able to make good contact with the top page. Try putting a larger stack of paper in (without making it too large).
- **Broken parts in the paper path** Inspect for any broken parts in the paper path. If you find any, you will have to investigate repairing or replacing the printer. If necessary, clean the printer, and once you have finished clearing the jam, either resume the print job or send another print job. Most printers will not resume operation until you have completely cleared the jam. Many printers also require you to press the reset or clear button to restart the printer.
- **Misalignment of paper in tractor feed** Tractor feed has its own problems. These feed mechanisms are notorious for feeding paper incorrectly through the printer. Misalignment of the paper in the printer usually causes the problem. Tractor feeds require special continuous-form paper, in which each page of paper attaches to the one before it, much like a roll of paper towels. If the perforations between pages do not line up properly, the text for one page will print across two pages. When this happens, look for a Paper Advance button on the printer that will incrementally advance the paper until it is properly aligned. If you do not have the documentation for the printer, this task may take trial and error.
- **Friction feed not disabled for tractor feed** Another problem with tractor feeds occurs when the friction-feed mechanism is not disabled. The most obvious symptom of this problem will be torn paper if the tractor pulls faster than the friction feed moves, or bunched paper if the opposite condition exists.

Clearing a Paper Jam

Most paper jams will stop the current print job. If you suspect a paper jam, consult your printer documentation. In general, turn off and open the printer and carefully remove any paper jammed in the paper path, following the manufacturer's instructions. Some printers include levers that you can release to more easily remove jammed paper. Normally, you will need to gently pull the paper in the direction the paper normally moves through the printer. Pulling in the opposite direction could damage internal components, such as rollers. This is especially true of the fusion roller in a laser printer. Avoid tearing the paper. If it tears, be sure you locate and remove all pieces from the printer.

Paper-feed problem symptoms listed in CompTIA A+ 1101 exam Objective 5.6 include multipage misfeed, paper not feeding, and paper jams.

Multiple Pending Prints in Queue

Print spooler problems can cause a print job to not arrive at a printer or a job in progress to inexplicably stop. The print queue may be backed up because it is overwhelmed, or the print spooler service may have stopped. When this service stops, nothing prints until it is restarted. This is referred to as a "stalled print spooler."

You need to determine if the spooler is stalled. For this, you must have the Manage Documents permission to the printer. Assuming you logged on as a member of the Administrators group, which is automatically assigned this permission, do one of the following:

- **Settings app method** Open Printers And Scanners, click the printer, and click Open Queue.
- **Control Panel method** Open Devices And Printers and double-click the printer.

Doing this opens the user interface for the print queue from which you can manage the print jobs the print spooler is holding. Check the status of the print job. If the print job status is Paused, right-click it and select Restart. If this fails, attempt to cancel the print job. Sometimes canceling the first job in the queue will allow the other jobs to print.

If this does not help, then cancel each job in the queue. If you are not able to restart or cancel jobs in the queue, you will need to restart the Print Spooler service. Follow the steps in Exercise 13-2 to restart this service.

EXERCISE 13-2

Restarting the Print Spooler Service

Use the Services node in Computer Management to restart a stalled print spooler.

1. Right-click the Start button and click Computer Management.
2. In the Computer Management console, select Services And Applications, and then double-click Services.
3. In the contents pane, scroll down to Print Spooler.
4. Right-click Print Spooler and select Restart.

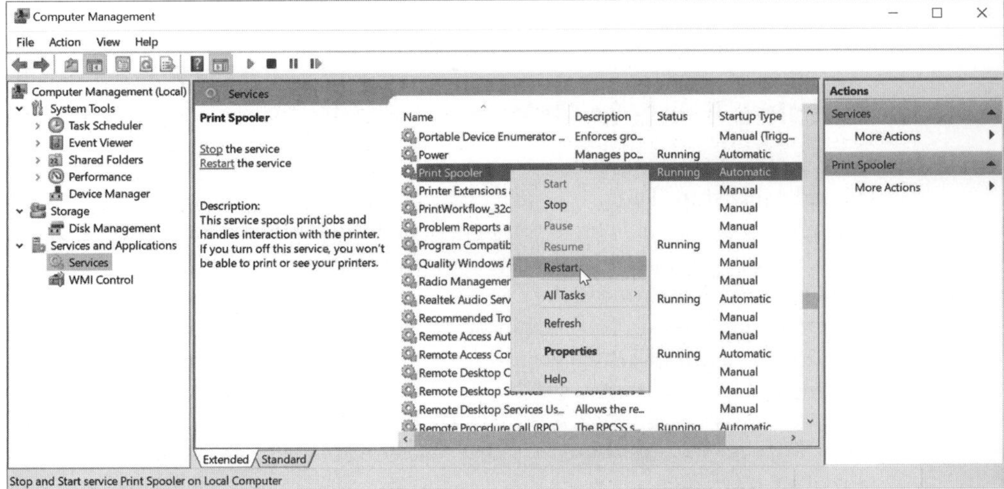

5. If restarting the service fails, then close all open windows and restart the computer. When Windows restarts, the Print Spooler service will restart.
6. Restart the printer.
7. Resend the print jobs to the printer.

Print Quality

Print quality problems are very common with all types of printers. In laser printers, print quality problems are most often (but not always) associated with a component in the toner cartridge. When troubleshooting a print quality problem on a laser printer, swapping the toner cartridge often solves many of the problems listed here. Following are several common print quality problems and their suggested solutions.

Faded Prints

Several things can cause faded prints from a laser printer. The toner in the cartridge could be low, the corona wire could be dirty and not passing the correct charge to the paper, or the drum could be dirty or defective. If the drum is part of the toner cartridge, replacing the cartridge could solve the problem. If the drum is separate from the toner cartridge, try replacing it. Most laser printers include a way to clean the corona wires. You must first power off the printer and disconnect the power cable. Then, using either a special felt-lined tool or a built-in slider, gently move the tool along the wire.

Faded prints on an impact printer are almost always due to ribbon problems. Replace the ribbon cartridge.

Printouts from thermal printers have a unique problem, especially since thermal printers are frequently used to print receipts. The paper darkens over time, and the image fades and becomes unreadable. There are several solutions to this, but thermal paper quality varies, so you may completely lose the image when you try some of these techniques. The best action to take is to immediately scan or copy all receipts before they fade. Then you either have a paper copy or an image of the receipt stored in your computer. Even this proactive technique has its risks, however, since the light from the copier can darken the thermal printout.

Another technique used after an image has faded is to copy or scan it after adjusting the contrast settings to try and recover the image. And yet another technique uses a laminating machine with the hope that the heat from the laminator will restore the image. None of these techniques is guaranteed to work.

Double/Echo Images on the Print

A double/echo image, also known as a ghost image, occurs when a faint image from a previous page appears on subsequent pages. This problem occurs only in laser printers and indicates a cleaning stage failure. The drum might have lost the ability to drop its charge in the presence of light. Replace the drum to resolve the problem. If the drum is not the cause, it could be either the cleaning blade or the erasure lamps. Because both the cleaning blade and drum are inside the toner cartridge in many laser printers, you can resolve this problem by replacing the toner cartridge. The erasure lamps are always (to our knowledge) in the printer itself, and they are not easy to replace. You will probably have to send the printer back to the manufacturer or to a specialized printer repair shop.

Toner Not Fusing to the Paper

If the toner is not sticking to the paper, the fusing roller is defective or the fusing lamp (inside the roller) is burned out and not heating the roller enough to melt the toner to the paper. Similarly, a scratched nonstick coating on the fusing roller or baked-on debris on it can cause smeared toner on the printout. Either way, replace the fusing lamp and/or the fusing roller to fix the problem.

Random Speckles, Smudging, Smearing, and Streaking

Ribbon ink, cartridge ink, and toner residue can be within the printer itself and transfer onto the paper. If any type of printer produces a page with speckles, smudging, smearing, or streaking of the ink or toner, try cleaning the printer. This includes manually cleaning it and/or using the printer software to instruct the printer to perform cleaning and other maintenance tasks. We described printer cleaning in this chapter in "Printer Maintenance."

If an impact printer produces a smudged, smeared, or streaked printout, check the pins on the print head. Stuck pins can cause printouts to have a smudged appearance as they continue to transfer ink to the page, even when they do not create a character or image. If this is the case, notify the manufacturer and replace the print head or the entire printer.

If the output from an inkjet printer appears smudged or smeared, the most likely cause is someone touching the printed page before the ink dries. The ink used in an inkjet printer must totally dry before it is touched, or it will smear. Most inkjet printers do not use permanent ink, and even after it has dried, these inks may smear if they become wet.

The heat and pressure of the fusion stage in a laser printer create a smudge-proof permanent printout. Smudged or streaked laser printouts could be caused by a dirty corona wire, but are usually the result of a failed fusing stage. Depending on the exact source of the problem, you may need to replace the fusing rollers, the halogen lamp, or the entire fuser assembly.

Repeated Pattern of Speckles or Blotches

A repeated but unintended pattern on a printout is another indication of ink or toner residue in the printer. Clean the printer, paying attention to the feed rollers in an inkjet and the transfer corona wire in a laser printer. If a repeated pattern is on the printout of a laser printer, suspect the drum. A small nick or flaw in the drum will cause toner to collect there, and it will transfer onto each page in a repetitive pattern. In addition, some drums lose their ability to drop their charge during the cleaning step. The drum has a very small diameter, so this same pattern will repeat several times down the length of the page. In either case, replacing the drum should solve the problem.

Incorrect Colors

Incorrect colors may be a problem with the ink or toner cartridges, or it may be a software problem of some sort. Modern color printers don't allow you to print if a cartridge is out of ink or toner, so we can usually rule out an empty color cartridge. However, open up the printer and take a look at the cartridges. Things have improved in this area, but if a color cartridge is low, some printers cannot produce the correct shades. To get the desired results in a printout, you may simply need to replace the cartridges.

Also, if the nozzles on an inkjet clog, the colors may come out "dirty" or might not appear at all. Follow the manufacturer's instructions for cleaning the nozzles.

Incorrect colors can be an application-related settings issue, and you should test a document using similar colors from another application. If the colors print out correctly from another app, there may be a problem with a setting in the first app.

Lines Down the Printed Pages

If vertical lines appear in a printout from an impact printer, the print head may have a malfunctioning pin, in which case, replace the print head. In any printer, parallel lines of print can indicate an incompatible driver, a problem you may solve by updating or replacing the driver. This symptom can also be a sign of a malfunction in the printer's electronics, so you need to repair or replace the printer, depending on its value and the cost of repair.

In a laser printer, a leaking toner cartridge or a dirty printer that has toner where the paper can pick it up as it passes through can cause vertical lines. Remove the toner cartridge, set it on a paper towel to see if it's leaking, clean it with a small vacuum cleaner, and then clean the interior of the printer until all the toner and paper dust are removed.

Garbled Print

Garbled output—often called "garbage"—usually indicates a communications problem between the computer and printer. The most common cause of this is an incorrect or corrupted print driver, but first check that the data cable is firmly and properly attached, and then try doing a power cycle (turning the printer off and then back on) because it may have simply experienced a temporary problem. Restarting the computer may also solve the problem.

If there are no connection problems and a power cycle of the printer and computer does not improve the printing, then check that the computer is using the correct printer driver. Look at the printer settings by opening the Devices and Printers folder and display the printer's Properties dialog box, as in Figure 13-5. Ensure that the physical printer matches the printer model shown in this dialog box. If the driver is not correct, uninstall it and reinstall the correct driver. If the driver appears to be correct, look at the manufacturer's site for an update and install the update. If the version of the driver is the most current, try reinstalling the driver.

Finally, this problem could be the result of insufficient printer memory. You can test this by trying to print a very small document. If it works, there is a chance that the original document was too large for the printer's memory. You can add more RAM. Check the documentation to find out how to check on the amount of memory, what type of memory to install, and how to install the memory.

Grinding or Clicking Noise

A grinding or clicking noise is caused by a physical problem with one of the moving parts. Some possibilities to investigate include

- Paper jam
- Foreign object in the printer, such as packing material
- An internal part has come loose inside the printer
- Failure to remove tape strip on new printer

- Incorrectly installed drum or toner cartridge (laser)
- Defective toner cartridge, particularly a defect in the gears on the side (laser)
- Drum gear drive assembly failure (laser)
- Ink cartridge not seated properly (inkjet)

If you are not sure if gear clicking is coming from the drum or the toner, remove the toner cartridge and see if that makes the clicking stop.

Incorrect Paper Size or Orientation

If the printer thinks you have a different size paper loaded than you actually do, it's probably an issue with the printer driver settings in the OS. You may need to adjust a setting there. Look for these settings:

- **Paper size** If this setting is present, make sure it is accurately set.
- **Resize document** If there is a setting that resizes the document to fit the printer page, set it to On (or turn it off if it's already on and it isn't working as expected).
- **Paper tray** Look for a paper tray tab or setting in the Printer Properties and make sure it is set correctly.

Less commonly, there may be a paper size adjustment button or switch on the paper tray that needs to be adjusted.

Incorrect orientation (landscape vs. portrait) usually occurs because someone has set Landscape in the printer's properties or printing preferences for a particular print job and then forgot they did it. Check all the dialog boxes in the OS related to the printer's settings.

Finishing Issues

Some business-class printers not only print, but they also finish the printed pages by adding staples and/or by punching holes for binding. Problems with these functions fall into consumables categories:

- Physical malfunctions with the equipment
- Consumables such as staples need to be loaded into the machine
- Printer driver settings are not correct for the output desired

Consult the manual for the printer to troubleshoot.

SCENARIO & SOLUTION	
The output from my laser printer is smeared. What should I do?	Clean the printer, especially the fusing roller. If this doesn't work, replace the drum. If the drum is in the toner cartridge, replace the toner cartridge. If none of this works, the problem may be with the fuser assembly, which will need replacing.
I am careful not to handle the wet printouts from my inkjet printer, but they are coming out with smudges. What can I do?	Check the paper path. Something may be contacting the page before the ink has had a chance to dry, or people may be handling the printout before it is dry.
Why do printouts from my color inkjet printer have the wrong colors?	The printer is probably low in one or more colors or has a clogged nozzle.

When an ink cartridge gets low, you should replace rather than refill it. By refilling an old cartridge, you are reusing old, possibly worn-out components.

CERTIFICATION SUMMARY

This chapter explored printer issues for IT professionals. The focus of this chapter was the components, procedures, troubleshooting, and maintenance procedures for common printer types. Impact printers provide the lowest quality, and today they mainly print multiple-part forms. Laser printers, the most expensive, can provide excellent printouts and are the most common type used in offices. For this reason, you are likely to deal with laser printers in businesses more frequently than with other printer types. Inkjet printers are extremely popular as inexpensive desktop color printers.

Before installing a printer, carefully read the manufacturer's instructions. When working with printer problems, apply the troubleshooting procedures learned in Chapter 12, and become familiar with the symptoms and problems common to the printer or scanner. Printers require maintenance to replenish paper and, less frequently, ink or toner. Clean printers regularly to ensure high-quality results and to avoid many problems that dirt, dust, and grime can create.

TWO-MINUTE DRILL

Here are some of the key points covered in Chapter 13.

Printer Basics

- ❑ Printers are the most common peripheral used with PCs.
- ❑ Impact printers are usually of low quality, use a ribbon, and move paper with friction feed or tractor feed, and their most common use is for printing multiple-part forms, such as retail receipts.
- ❑ Laser printers use laser light technology in the printing process. The stages of the laser printing imaging process are processing, charging, exposing, developing, transferring, fusing, and cleaning.
- ❑ The term "inkjet" refers to printers that use one of several technologies to apply wet ink to paper to create text or graphic printouts.
- ❑ Thermal printers use heat in the image transfer process.
- ❑ The two most common paper-feed technologies are friction feed and continuous form feed.
- ❑ The typical printer has a system board, ROM (containing firmware), and RAM memory, as well as various components related to the specific printing technology and paper-feed mechanism. Additional components include the device driver and related software and consumables in the form of paper, ink ribbons, ink cartridges, or toner cartridges.
- ❑ Manufacturers offer all-in-one printers, multifunction products that include a scanner, printer, copier, and fax integrated within the same case.
- ❑ Printer interfaces include USB, Ethernet, and wireless (Wi-Fi and Bluetooth).

Installing and Configuring Printers

- ❑ Before installing a printer, be sure to read the manufacturer's instructions.
- ❑ Installing a printer in Windows is a simple job, especially for plug and play printers. Even non–plug and play printers are easy to install using the Add Printer Wizard.
- ❑ After installing a printer, perform a test print.

- Configure a printer through the printer's Properties dialog box, the Printer Properties dialog box, and the Printing Preferences dialog box.
- There are a few common upgrades to printers, including device drivers and other software, document feeders, memory, and firmware.

Printer Maintenance

- Some laser printers track the number of pages printed in a page count and require that critical components be replaced using a maintenance kit. After installing the maintenance kit, you must reset the page count.
- Clean each printer according to the manufacturer's recommendations to avoid poor output and other problems.
- Provide a suitable environment for each printer to avoid problems that dirt and temperature extremes can cause in these devices.
- For the best results, use the recommended consumables in printers. This may require using the media and paper provided by the manufacturer or less expensive substitutes of equal quality from other sources.
- Laser printer maintenance includes replacing toner, applying maintenance kit, calibrating, and cleaning.
- Inkjet printer maintenance includes cleaning heads, replacing cartridges, calibrating, and clearing jams.
- For thermal printers, maintenance includes replacing paper, cleaning heating elements, and removing debris.
- Impact printer maintenance requires replacing ribbon, print head, and paper.
- 3-D printers use special filaments and resins and have a print bed.

Troubleshooting Printers

- The troubleshooting process for printers is identical to that used for computers.
- Common printer problems include those involving paper feed and print quality. Printer error messages on your computer screen or the printer display panel will alert you to common problems, such as paper out, I/O errors, and print spooler problems.

SELF TEST

The following questions will help you measure your understanding of the material presented in this chapter. Read all of the choices carefully, because there might be more than one correct answer. Choose all correct answers for each question.

Printer Basics

1. What is a common use for impact printers?
   A. High-quality color images
   B. High-speed network printers
   C. Multipart forms
   D. UPC code scanning
2. What type of printer is the most often used shared network printer in businesses?
   A. Laser
   B. Impact
   C. Thermal
   D. Inkjet
3. In what stage of the laser printing process does a laser beam place an image on the photosensitive drum?
   A. Cleaning
   B. Developing
   C. Charging
   D. Exposing
4. Which stage in the laser printing process is responsible for creating a permanent non-smearing image?
   A. Cleaning
   B. Fusing
   C. Transferring
   D. Exposing

5. What type of printer applies wet ink to paper?
   A. Laser
   B. Impact
   C. Thermal
   D. Inkjet
6. What is the unit of measure used to describe the size of droplets created by the nozzles in an inkjet printer?
   A. Millimeter
   B. Meter
   C. Picoliter
   D. Liter

Installing and Configuring Printers

7. When you select a printer in the Settings app and click Manage, several commands become available for managing the printer. Which of these would you choose if you wanted to share the printer on a LAN?
   A. Hardware Properties
   B. Printing Preferences
   C. Printer Properties
   D. Hardware Preferences
8. What important configuration task must you perform on a network printer before it will be recognized on the network?
   A. Install TCP/IP.
   B. Assign an IP address.
   C. Give it the address of each client.
   D. It must be detected by the clients.
9. Which of these would be the best location in which to install an Ethernet-enabled printer that multiple users in a legal department will access?
   A. In a centrally located hallway
   B. In a secure area that only department employees can access
   C. In the employee break room
   D. In one employee's office
10. If you set up a network-enabled MFD to save scans to a centrally accessible storage location on the local LAN, what protocol would be used for that file sharing?
    A. MFD
    B. Cloud
    C. IMAP
    D. SMB

Printer Maintenance

11. What should you do after installing a maintenance kit in a laser printer?

A. Reset the maintenance count.

B. Reset the page count.

C. Reset the printer.

D. Call the manufacturer.

12. What simple maintenance task for printers helps maintain high-quality results?

A. Performing a memory upgrade

B. Installing a maintenance kit

C. Replacing the fuser

D. Cleaning

13. For which type of printer would maintenance include replacing the print head and replacing the ribbon?

A. Impact

B. Laser

C. Inkjet

D. Thermal

Troubleshooting Printers

14. When multiple print jobs are backed up and not printing, check to see if this Windows service is running.

A. Printer

B. Spooler

C. Print driver

D. Print device

15. What can contribute to static buildup in a printer?

A. Dust

B. Ink

C. Overloaded paper tray

D. Paper jams

16. Which of these might be the cause of a grinding noise as the printer operates? (Choose two.)

A. Broken gear

B. Incorrect driver

C. Dried-up ink in ink cartridge

D. Incorrectly installed toner cartridge

17. What component on an inkjet printer may clog with ink?
A. Nozzles
B. Hammers
C. Friction-feed rollers
D. Tractor feeder

18. What component in a laser printer could be the source of a repeated pattern of speckles?
A. Fusion roller
B. Drum
C. Toner
D. Primary corona wire

19. When an echoed image from a previous page occurs on subsequent pages printed on a laser printer, what component is a probable source of the problem?
A. Fusion roller
B. Drum
C. Toner
D. Primary corona wire

20. Of all the possible solutions for garbled printing, which two are the first ones you should try?
A. Check for loose data cable.
B. Upgrade driver.
C. Power-cycle the printer and computer.
D. Uninstall and reinstall driver.

A SELF TEST ANSWERS

Printer Basics

1. ☑ **C.** Multipart form printing is a common use for impact printers.
☒ **A** is incorrect because impact printers do not create high-quality color images. **B** is incorrect because impact printers are not high-speed printers. **D** is incorrect because no standalone printer can scan UPC codes.

2. ☑ **A.** The laser printer is the most often used shared network printer in businesses.
☒ **B, C,** and **D** are incorrect because impact, thermal, and inkjet printers seldom are shared network printers in businesses.

3. ☑ **D.** Exposing is the laser printing stage in which the laser beam places an image on the photosensitive drum.
☒ **A** is incorrect because cleaning is the stage in which the drum is cleaned. **B** is incorrect because developing is the stage in which toner is attracted to the image on the drum. **C** is incorrect because charging is the stage in which a charge is applied to the drum.

4. ☑ **B.** Fusing is the stage in the laser printing process in which the image permanently fuses to the paper.
☒ **A, C,** and **D** are incorrect because none of these is the stage that creates a permanent non-smearing image.

5. ☑ **D.** Inkjet is the type of printer that applies wet ink to paper.
☒ **A** is incorrect because in a laser printer dry toner is fused to the paper. **B** is incorrect because an impact printer uses an ink ribbon. **C** is incorrect because a thermal printer uses heat to print an image.

6. ☑ **C.** Picoliter is the unit of measure used to describe the size of droplets created by the nozzles in an inkjet printer.
☒ **A** and **B** are incorrect because neither one is the unit of measure used for the size of droplets from the nozzles in an inkjet printer, which is a measurement of liquid volume. Both millimeter and meter are units of distance measure. **D** is incorrect because although liter is a measure of liquid volume, it is far too large a volume for such small drops.

Installing and Configuring Printers

7. ☑ **C.** Selecting Printer Properties opens the Printer Properties dialog box, where one of the tabs is Sharing.
☒ **A** is incorrect because Hardware Properties opens a read-only dialog box providing information about the printer at a hardware level. **B** is incorrect because Printing Preferences opens a dialog box specific to the printer where you can control settings such as orientation and paper/quality. **D** is incorrect because there is no such command.

8. ☑ **B.** Assigning an IP address is the important configuration task you must do on a network printer before it will be recognized on the network.
☒ **A** is incorrect because a network printer comes with TCP/IP installed. **C** is incorrect because the network printer does not need the address of each client; each client needs the address of the network printer. **D** is incorrect because the network printer must have an IP address before it can be recognized on the network.

9. ☑ **B.** A legal department is likely to print sensitive or confidential materials so the printer must be in a secure location.
☒ **A** and **C** are incorrect because these are both areas of high traffic where anyone could access the printouts. **D** is incorrect because while this might be a secure solution, the employee would be constantly interrupted by people coming to retrieve printouts.

10. ☑ **D.** Server Message Block (SMB) is a protocol for network file sharing.
☒ **A** and **B** are incorrect because these are not protocols. **C** is incorrect because IMAP is an e-mail protocol.

Printer Maintenance

11. ☑ **B.** Reset the page count of a laser printer after installing a maintenance kit.
☒ **A** is incorrect because resetting the maintenance count will set to zero pages the number at which the printer should receive maintenance. **C** is incorrect because resetting the printer will not turn the page count to zero, and the printer will display a maintenance warning. **D** is incorrect because calling the manufacturer is unnecessary when all you need to do is reset the page count.

12. ☑ **D.** Cleaning is the simple maintenance task for printers that helps maintain high-quality results.
☒ **A** is incorrect because upgrading memory is not a simple maintenance task, and it will not help maintain high-quality results. **B** is incorrect because installing a maintenance kit is not a simple maintenance task. **C** is incorrect because replacing the fuser is not a simple maintenance task but a complex repair task.

13. ☑ **A.** Only an impact printer uses a ribbon.
☒ **B, C,** and **D** are incorrect because none of them use a ribbon.

Troubleshooting Printers

14. ☑ **B.** Spooler is the Windows component that holds print jobs in its queue before sending them to the printer. The spooler can be stalled, preventing a job from printing.
☒ **A** is incorrect, although printer is the term for software in Windows that manages print jobs and sends them to print devices via the spooler. **C** is incorrect because this is a device driver for the printer. **D** is incorrect because the print device is the physical printer.

15. ☑ **A.** Dust can contribute to static buildup in a printer.
☒ **B** is incorrect because although ink residue may build up in a printer, it does not appreciably contribute to static buildup. **C** is incorrect because an overloaded paper tray is not a cause of static buildup in a printer. **D** is incorrect because although static buildup in a printer may occasionally cause a paper jam, it is not a primary cause.

16. ☑ **A** and **D.** Both are mechanical components with moving parts that can make noise when they are broken.
☒ **B** is incorrect because a driver is a software component and would not make noise. **C** is incorrect because dried-up ink in an ink cartridge would not make a noise.

17. ☑ **A.** Nozzles in an inkjet printer can become clogged with ink.
☒ **B, C,** and **D** are incorrect because these components do not become clogged with ink.

18. ☑ **B.** The drum could be the source of a repeated pattern of speckles on printouts from a laser printer.
☒ **A, C,** and **D** are incorrect because none of these is a probable source of a repeated pattern of speckles on printouts from a laser printer.

19. ☑ **B.** The drum is the probable source of an echo or ghost image printing on subsequent pages from a laser printer.
☒ **A, C,** and **D** are incorrect because none of these is a probable source of an echo/ghost image.

20. ☑ **A** and **C.** These are the first two solutions you should try for "garbage" printing because they are simple and easy to try.
☒ **B** and **D** are incorrect because they are not as simple and fast to try as the first two.

Part IV

Laptops and Mobile Devices

CHAPTERS

Chapter 14

Configuring and Using Laptops

CERTIFICATION OBJECTIVES

- **1101: 1.1** Given a scenario, install and configure laptop hardware and components
- **1101: 1.2** Compare and contrast the display components of mobile devices
- **1101: 1.3** Given a scenario, set up and configure accessories and ports of mobile devices
- **1101: 5.5** Given a scenario, troubleshoot common issues with mobile devices
- **1102: 1.4** Given a scenario, use the appropriate Microsoft Windows 10 Control Panel utility

✓ Two-Minute Drill

Q&A Self Test

Laptop sales surpassed the sales of desktop PCs in 2005, as the public demanded greater portability and convenience for their computing. Today's laptops are not much more expensive than desktop PCs and offer screen sizes, processor power, RAM configuration, and hard disk size and performance equivalent to desktops. Consequently, as a technician you may spend quite a bit of time configuring and servicing laptop PCs. You may also be frequently called upon to configure and troubleshoot smaller computing devices too, such as tablets and smartphones.

In Chapter 12 you learned about hardware troubleshooting and maintenance in general, but with a focus on desktop systems. This chapter extends this discussion to include laptops, looking at replacing some of the most common laptop components. It also explores Windows power option settings and laptop-related special features. Coming up in Chapter 15, we'll look at even smaller mobile devices, such as tablets and smartphones, and their unique challenges for use, maintenance, and troubleshooting.

CERTIFICATION OBJECTIVES

- ***1101: 1.1*** *Given a scenario, install and configure laptop hardware and components*
- ***1101: 1.2*** *Compare and contrast the display components of mobile devices*

In this section, we cover CompTIA A+ 1101 exam Objective 1.1, describing how to install and configure laptop components. This includes information about laptop-specific expansion slots; laptop devices; and how to replace those devices, including keyboards, HDD and SSD storage, RAM, wireless cards, and batteries. To prepare for CompTIA A+ 1101 exam Objective 1.2, be sure that you understand the components of a laptop display and how to replace a display and its associated parts, such as webcams and Wi-Fi antenna. (You also need to know the different technologies of laptop displays, which were covered in Chapter 10.)

Repairing, Upgrading, and Configuring Laptops

This section defines laptop computers, as distinguished from other portable computers, and then provides an overview of laptop disassembly and reassembly. Finally, it introduces you to some laptop-specific components and peripherals, describing installation and upgrading procedures where applicable. In all cases, when you consider installing a new component or replacing an old one, you should first check with the manufacturer for any firmware upgrades. If one is available, install it before you proceed.

What Is a Laptop?

A *portable computer* is any type of computer that you can easily transport and that has an all-in-one component layout. In addition to the size difference, portable computers differ from desktop computers in their physical layout and their use of battery power when not plugged into an alternating current (AC) outlet. Portable computers fall into two broad categories: laptops (by several different names) and handhelds, but they all are integral to mobile computing.

A *laptop* (also called a *notebook*) generally weighs less than seven pounds, fits easily into a tote bag or briefcase, and has roughly the same dimensions as a one- to two-inch-thick stack of magazines. The top contains the display, and the bottom contains the keyboard and the rest of the computer's internal components. A typical laptop uses a liquid crystal display (LCD) and requires small circuit cards that comply with modified versions of the bus standards found in full-size PCs.

Initially, people called most portable computers "laptops" because they could fit on the user's lap, although early laptops were a little heavy to do this comfortably. As technology improved, laptops became smaller and lighter, and the term "notebook" came into use to reflect this smaller size. As circuitry shrinks, we discover smaller and smaller portable computers and newer terms, such as *ultra-portable* for a laptop that weighs less than three pounds and gives up features to keep the weight down and maintain the highest battery life. A *two-in-one laptop,* also called a *convertible laptop,* is an ultra-portable laptop with a screen that rotates and folds backwards, covering the keyboard, so the device can be used as a tablet.

At the other extreme, many purchase laptops as full-featured desktop replacements in which performance is more important than battery life. These have large screens and weigh in at the top of the range.

Regardless of the size and type of portable computer, throughout this book we use the term "laptop" to encompass all these types to match the CompTIA A+ exam objectives' wording.

One key feature of laptops is the ability to run the same basic OS as their desktop counterparts. For example, a Windows laptop uses the same Windows product as a Windows desktop, and the same goes for Linux and Macintosh laptops. Some ultra-portable devices like tablets and smartphones use other operating systems or special scaled-down OS editions; these devices are covered in Chapter 15.

Opening a Laptop Case

Many laptop configuration and installation tasks are software or firmware based, but occasionally you'll need to do something that involves partially or fully disassembling a laptop, like upgrading the memory or replacing a screen or keyboard. If you do need to open the case, make sure you follow the safety precautions outlined in Chapter 1.

The tricky part about opening a laptop case is that there's not much standardization among brands and models. Components aren't located in standard places, and the disassembly procedures can vary widely. For example, on one model you might be able to access the hard disk drive from an access panel on the bottom of the laptop, whereas on another model you might have to remove the keyboard and touchpad to find it. Consequently, you should arm yourself with a service manual for the particular model before getting started. (Service manuals are typically available online for most laptops.) A service manual will show you where all the screws are and will tell you which ones you need to remove to replace specific components.

A laptop has two sources of power: the AC adapter and the battery. Therefore, for your own safety, ensure that there is no power to components. Always unplug the AC adapter and remove the battery (if possible) before opening the case in any way.

Use Appropriate Hand Tools

After reading the manufacturer's documentation and before beginning, assemble all the hand tools you expect to use. Refer to Chapter 8 for a list of tools. Most laptops use standard Phillips screws, although a few may use Torx or flathead.

Don't use magnetic screwdrivers when working on PCs, including laptops. If you have no choice, take care to keep the screwdriver tip well away from anything other than the screws.

Organize Parts

Have containers ready to temporarily hold the screws and other parts that you will remove (small pill bottles work well), and have antistatic bags handy for any circuit boards you remove. After you reassemble the laptop, you should not have any extra parts except for those that you replaced.

If there are multiple types of screws used in various spots, find a way to keep each type separate, and make notes about which type goes where. For example, there might be long screws holding parts of the case together and short screws that mount a disk drive.

Document and Label Cable and Screw Locations

This important step is also one that many people would rather skip. For internal component replacements, you will begin by removing screws from the body of the laptop. Before you open the laptop compartment, take photos with a digital camera or make a rough sketch of the exterior portion involved, and label cable and screw locations. You don't have to be an artist to do this—simple lines and shapes, carefully labeled, will suffice. Once you have removed any panels, photograph or sketch the inside, labeling any components and their cables so you will be able to reassemble the laptop after replacing or adding a part.

Replacing Laptop Components

Laptop components that distinguish one manufacturer's models from others are at least partially proprietary, but most manufacturers use at least some generic components, such as the CPU, memory, and hard drives. Therefore, if a laptop component fails, a carefully worded query in an Internet search engine should reveal sources for an appropriate replacement part or the name of a company that will replace the part for you. Both interior and exterior replacement parts are available, even plastic exterior components, such as the case, LCD lid, LCD bezels, palm rest, button panels, doors, and compartment covers for some popular laptop models. Always research whether replacing the part is more cost-effective than replacing the entire laptop.

Power and Electrical Input Devices

Laptops come with two sources of electrical input: an AC adapter for when AC power is available and a built-in battery for when external power is not available.

Battery When not plugged into a wall outlet, a laptop computer gets its power from a rechargeable battery. The typical laptop today has a *lithium ion (Li-Ion) battery*. These rechargeable batteries have a battery life between recharges in the range of five to eight hours. Previous generations of laptops used other types, such as nickel cadmium (NiCad).

Laptop batteries have only a few years of life, so expect to replace a laptop battery as it approaches two years of age. Purchase replacement batteries from the laptop manufacturer or other sources that specialize in laptop parts or batteries.

Removing a laptop's battery is a very basic skill that you'll need to do most of the other repairs outlined in this chapter. You should remove the battery before working inside the case because the laptop will automatically draw power from the battery when it is unplugged, even if it appears to be off. (For example, some low-power modes such as Sleep continue to draw a small amount of power from the battery.) Removing the battery will also prevent you from accidentally hitting the power button and powering on the system in the middle of a repair. Removing the battery can also perform a "hard off" on the hardware, which can sometimes fix problems related to not waking up from Sleep or Hibernate modes.

Battery removal differs greatly between models. On some models (mostly older ones) there is a battery compartment on the bottom of the laptop and an easy-to-operate button or switch that releases it. Lucky you if this is the case! On newer models, especially the small, thin ones, batteries are more difficult to access, and you may need to remove several screws and perhaps a plastic panel as well to access it. The battery shown in Figure 14-1 was under a cover secured with two screws, for example, and now that the cover is off, access is available to yet another screw that must be removed. There is a black plastic tab sticking out of the battery in Figure 14-1, which is designed to be used as a pull to lift the battery out. Check the laptop's user manual or service manual to find out the details for your model.

FIGURE 14-1

A battery on a large laptop

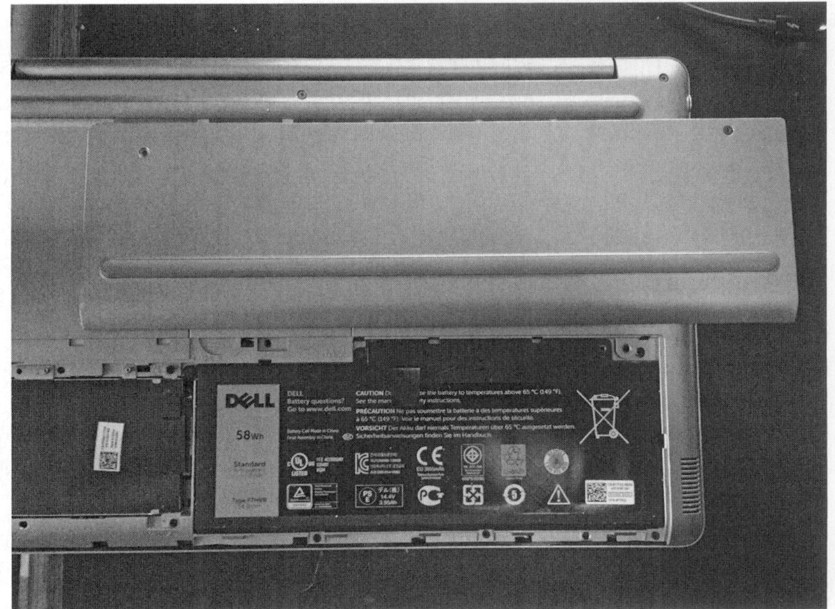

AC Adapter As described in Chapter 10, the AC adapter is your laptop's external power supply that you plug into an AC power source. Like the power supply in a desktop PC, it converts AC power to DC power. If you must replace an external adapter, simply unplug it and attach a new one that matches the specifications and plug configuration of the adapter it is replacing. Furthermore, AC adapters have different output wattages. An AC adapter will show its wattage on its label; if you are using an AC adapter other than the one that came with the laptop, read the label first and make sure it matches the wattage of the original AC adapter for that unit. An AC adapter with a lower wattage than the original may not work at all, or it may partially work but be lacking in some way (such as powering the laptop but not charging its battery).

There are different diameters to the round power plug that connects to the power jack on the laptop, depending on the wattage provided, and in some cases this prevents the wrong adapter from being used on a laptop (for example, if you have a workstation where several laptops are used at various times and different AC power cords for each of them). However, sometimes a power connector will physically fit into a laptop but not provide enough power to keep it charged. The laptop may be able to partially use the power from an incompatible adapter, but the battery won't charge, and the battery charge may gradually dwindle as it supplements the incoming AC with whatever extra is needed.

Wireless Cards

Laptop computers are designed for portability, so it is only natural that they should have built-in wireless communication. Wi-Fi is a given, of course, but most laptops also support Bluetooth, and some support less common wireless standards as well, such as WiMAX and/or cellular wireless (4G or 5G).

Most new laptops today come with a Wi-Fi adapter built in. For those laptops without built-in Wi-Fi, you can purchase Mini PCIe or USB add-ons. We will describe Wi-Fi in more detail in Chapter 17 and talk about configuring a Wi-Fi adapter in Chapter 18.

on the job

The switch to enable or disable a wireless adapter is often very easy to accidentally trigger, causing the wireless to turn off. If you support laptop users, educate yourself on the method used on each laptop so that you can help a client who accidentally disables the wireless adapter.

Some laptops come with a Bluetooth adapter built in. If not, you can purchase one—often along with one or more wireless devices that use the Bluetooth standard. A popular peripheral package is a Bluetooth keyboard and mouse bundled with a Bluetooth transmitter adapter using a USB interface. Many cell phones have Bluetooth built in for use with wireless headsets and for communicating with a Bluetooth-enabled computer to share the phonebook and other data stored in the phone.

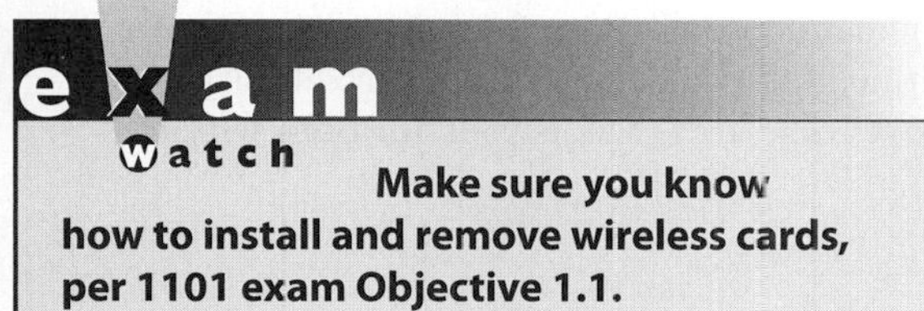

Make sure you know how to install and remove wireless cards, per 1101 exam Objective 1.1.

Some laptops have one or more expansion slots inside the case for installing add-on components. These are typically Mini PCIe or M.2. Unlike on a desktop system, these expansion slots have no connection to the outside of the computer, so you cannot use them to install components that add new ports to the system. Consequently, they are limited in purpose to components that are internal-only, such as wireless cards.

Mini PCIe Mini PCIe is based on the full-size PCIe expansion bus found in a desktop PC. They are both 64-bit interfaces; the Mini PCIe is just smaller. Depending on the manufacturer, this is also called *PCI Express Mini Card, Mini PCI Express, Mini PCI-E,* or simply *MiniCard.*

One of the most common uses for the Mini PCIe slot is for wireless network cards, such as Wi-Fi or Bluetooth. A cellular wireless card can also be Mini PCIe. Unlike on a desktop PCIe expansion card, there is no external access to a Mini PCIe card, so you can't use it to add new external ports. There is usually a cover on the bottom of the laptop that you can remove to expose the Mini PCIe slot. There may be just a single connection for a card, or it may accept multiple Mini PCIe cards. Power down the laptop and remove the battery. Then expose the slot, pull an installed card straight out of the slot, and insert a new one straight in, keeping in mind that the card typically sits parallel to the motherboard and the slot is perpendicular to that.

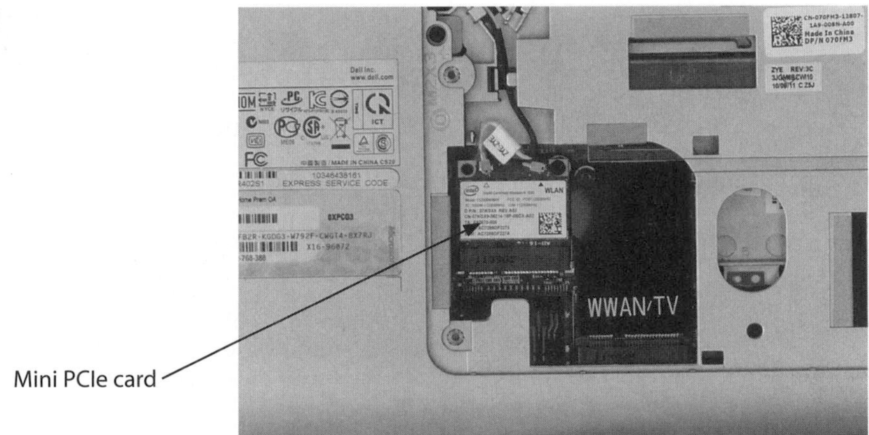

FIGURE 14-2

A Mini PCIe WLAN card installed in a laptop

Figure 14-2 shows a Wi-Fi wireless LAN adapter installed in a Mini PCIe slot. This particular adapter is actually two in one, as it is both a Wi-Fi adapter and a Bluetooth adapter. The antennas for this card run through the small black cable visible on the upper right of the card and running to the upper left. It leads up through the lid hinge into the lid behind the screen. If the antenna fails, it requires dismantling the screen of the laptop.

M.2 The M.2 interface, which you learned about in Chapter 8, is virtually the same on a laptop motherboard as on a desktop one. Refer to Chapter 8 to learn about its specifications and how to install and remove M.2 cards. M.2 is used for both wireless cards and solid-state storage.

Memory

Laptop memory modules come in small form factors. The most commonly used is *Small Outline DIMM (SODIMM),* which measures about 2-5/8", or about half the size of a Dual Inline Memory Module (DIMM). First-generation SODIMMs had 30 pins. That number of pins has been increasing steadily with every advance in technology, with DDR3 SODIMMs using 204 pins, DDR4 SODIMMs using 260 pins, and DDR5 SODIMMs using 262 pins.

As with DIMMs, SODIMMs have notches in them so that they only fit into the properly keyed SODIMM slots. When selecting SODIMMs for a system, as with desktop DIMMs, pay attention to the generation (for example, DDR3 vs. DDR4), the speed, and the capacity. If all those factors align with the laptop's needs, the compatibility should take care of itself.

Figure 14-3 shows a laptop with the battery removed and the access panel open to expose two 204-pin DDR3 SODIMMs, each populated with 4 GB of RAM. The top one (at bottom) has eight chips on it, and it covers up half of the module under it, showing only its top four chips. Visible near them are 102 of the top module's 204 pins, as well as the module notch. Also visible on the sides of each module are the clips used to secure them in place.

FIGURE 14-3

A laptop with access panel removed to expose the two DDR3 SODIMMs

MicroDIMM, a RAM module designed for smaller laptops, is half the size of a SODIMM and allows for higher-density storage.

You can add RAM to most laptops if there is a RAM slot available. If none is available, you must swap out the existing RAM module or modules for denser modules. Some systems include extra RAM slots within the chassis, which requires either opening the computer's case or removing the compartment cover and inserting the RAM module in an available slot. Exercise 14-1 describes the steps for installing memory in a laptop and for verifying that the system recognizes it.

EXERCISE 14-1

Installing SODIMM Memory

For this exercise, you will need a way to ground yourself and/or your work area. You will also need a new module of SODIMM memory appropriate for your laptop in an antistatic bag, the user's manual, a spare antistatic bag, and a small nonmagnetic screwdriver for opening the case. If you do not have a new module, simply remove an already installed module and reinstall it. In this case, you will just need an antistatic bag in which to place the module should you need to set it down.

1. Ground yourself using one of the methods described in Chapter 1.
2. Turn off the computer and all external devices.
3. Unplug power to the computer and disconnect all exterior cables and devices. Remove the laptop battery.
4. Following the instructions in the laptop user manual, open the compartment containing the SODIMM slots. Be careful, since the cover may have retaining tabs that break off easily.
5. Your laptop may have one or two memory slots. Look for numbers near any open slots and fill the lowest-numbered slot first.

6. If you are replacing memory, remove the module or modules you are replacing. To remove a module, press down on the retaining clips located on the sides, lift the edge of the module to a 45-degree angle, and gently pull it out of the slot, being careful to hold it by its edges without touching the contacts or chips.
7. Place the old module in an antistatic bag. Remove the new module from its antistatic bag, being careful to hold it by its edges without touching the contacts or chips.
8. Align the notch of the new memory module with that of the memory slot, as shown next, and gently insert the module into the slot at a 45-degree angle. Carefully rotate the module down flat until the clamps lock it in place.

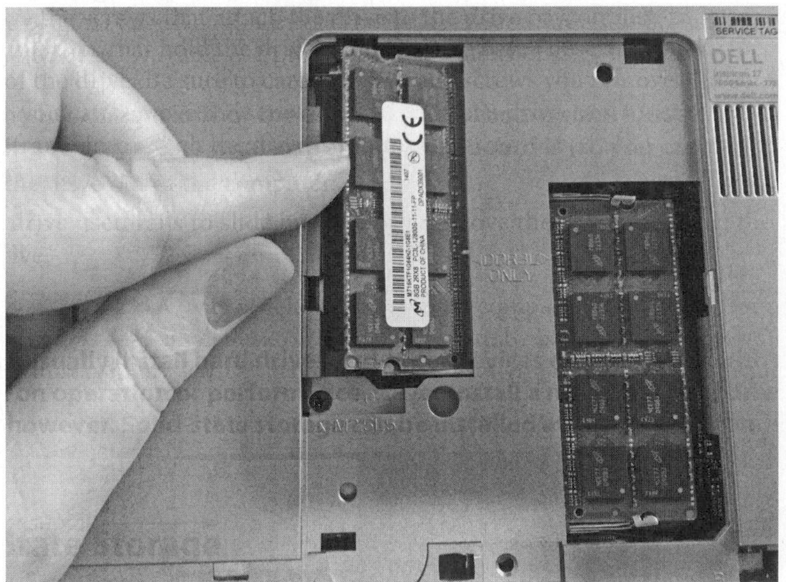

9. Close the memory compartment, reinstall the battery, and reconnect the power cable.
10. Power up the computer, and, if necessary (according to the user manual), configure memory in BIOS/UEFI setup, although this is not normally required.
11. Perform a normal startup in Windows, and check the Settings app's About screen to see if it recognized the new memory.

You may notice the memory amount reported does not add up to the total memory installed, which means your laptop may be using some of your system RAM for the video adapter, which often is the case with integrated video adapters if they do not have their own video RAM (VRAM). Main RAM memory used in this way is *shared video memory* and is not available to the operating system.

Make sure you know how to remove and install laptop RAM.

Storage Drives

The biggest change in laptop mass storage in the last several years has been large-capacity SSDs replacing hard disk drives (HDDs) at all price points of the newer ultra-portable models. SSDs in laptops are desirable because they are faster than HDDs, lighter, and less vulnerable to damage from impacts or excess motion. Today's laptops and other mobile devices may use a mass-storage interface designed for mobile devices called mSATA (or Mini-SATA), as described in Chapter 8. Introduced in 2009, the SATA 3.1 standard is a scaled-down form factor of the SATA mass storage interface with added support for SSDs in mobile devices. Alternatively they may use the newer M.2 interface, also described in Chapter 8. If they use the M.2 interface, the "hard drive" is actually a circuit board, as you saw in Figure 8-7.

Laptops that still use magnetic hard drives have small versions of them, typically with 2.5" or 1.8" platters, rather than the 3.5" hard drives used in desktop PCs. These connect to the SATA interface in the laptop, but not using the same type of cable and connector as in a desktop; the internal SATA interface on a laptop consists of a small flat or round cable. That cable may supply both power and data to the drive, even if it doesn't connect to the power connector on the drive itself. Figure 14-4 shows an example.

HDD/SSD Replacement After you power down the computer, use the same precautions you would use with a PC case before proceeding. Accessing an internal storage device may be as simple as removing a plastic access cover on the bottom or side of the laptop. In that case, simply slide the drive out and then replace it with a new drive and replace the cover. On the other hand, replacing a storage device may involve removing the keyboard or the entire bottom of the case. This is where the service manual comes in handy to find out where the hard drive is located and how to access it.

FIGURE 14-4

A 2.5" hard drive removed from a large laptop

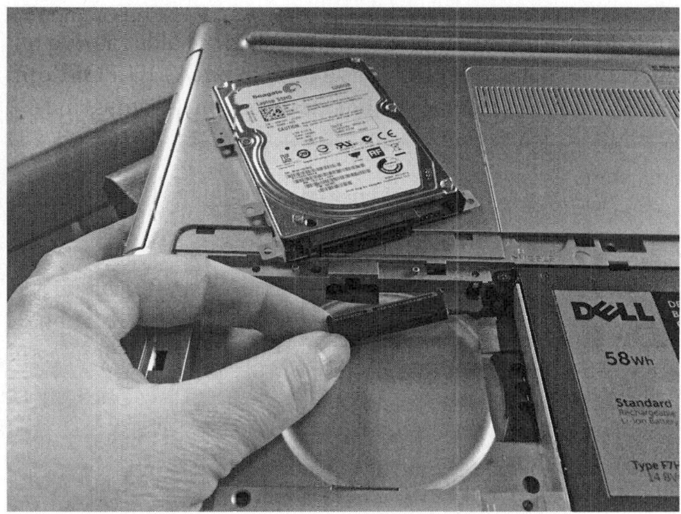

EXERCISE 14-2

Replacing a Hard Drive

For this exercise, you will need a way to ground yourself and/or your work area. You will also need a replacement hard drive (or you can remove and reinstall the same one if it's just for practice) and a small nonmagnetic screwdriver for opening the case.

1. Review the documentation or service manual for the laptop to learn how to access the hard drive. Depending on the model, it may be as simple as sliding a cartridge out from the side or as complicated as removing the keyboard and perhaps other components too.
2. Unplug power from the laptop and remove its battery. Again, consult the documentation or service manual to learn how to remove the battery. Some come out very easily; others not so much.
3. Prepare your work area. Lay down an antistatic mat if you have one, and have a small cup ready to hold screws.
4. Follow the service manual instructions to remove the screws and plastics necessary to access the hard disk drive. When you get to it, carefully note how it is connected.
5. Check for any screws holding the hard disk drive in place, and remove them. Then gently pull to disconnect the cable from the drive and lift it out. There might not be separate data and power cables, even if the drive has a connector for a separate power cable.
6. Insert the new hard drive, and reverse the process to secure it into the laptop and close things up.
7. Replace the battery, reconnect the power cord, and power up the unit to test it.

HDD/SSD Migration

Migration refers to moving the contents of a laptop's current hard drive to a new one so that the user will not lose their data and applications.

If you are migrating to a drive of the same or a larger size, you can use Windows' system imaging tool for this. You will create a system image in a temporary location, such as on an external hard drive or USB flash drive, and then install the new HDD or SSD in the laptop, and then use Windows' System Image Recovery to image the new drive. Here's an article that walks you through the process step-by-step: https://helpdeskgeek.com/windows-10/how-to-migrate-windows-10-to-a-new-hard-drive.

When migrating to a new storage device, you may run into a Windows activation issue, because Windows may interpret the hardware change as the copy of Windows being used in a different PC. Here's an article that explains how to resolve that: https://www.windowscentral.com/how-re-activate-windows-10-after-hardware-change.

Make sure you know how to perform HDD/SSD replacement and migration.

Display Screens and Associated Components

A laptop has a flat-panel display integrated into the "lid" of the case and connected to the integrated video adapter. A laptop display is usually some form of LCD display as described in Chapter 10—most often lit with *light-emitting diodes (LEDs)*. Many small-screen laptops or touch screen tablets have organic LED (OLED) or active-matrix OLED (AMOLED). An older LCD screen requires an internal *inverter* to convert the DC current from the power adapter or battery to the AC current the display requires. Newer LCDs use LEDs, which do not require an inverter. Some laptops also include a touch screen, so the screen functions as both an input device and an output device. The implementation of touch screen hardware depends on the model; use the service manual to get details.

Laptop display screens are rather delicate and often become damaged over the course of the laptop's life, so replacing a screen is a commonplace task for a technician. The procedure varies somewhat depending on the model, but the basics are the same.

The first step is to remove the bezel that holds the display panel in place. This is often the trickiest part of the whole process because it's not always obvious how the bezel is held on and how to get it loose without cracking the plastic. Refer to the service manual. A common way that laptops hide the display screws is to put rubber caps over the screw tops; these serve another purpose as well: providing a gap that protects the screen from directly touching the keyboard when the laptop is closed. Pry these caps off with your fingernails, and then glue them back in place afterwards if they don't stick anymore. Another common way a bezel is attached is via the hinges that connect the lid to the base. You might have to remove the hinge covers to expose screws or clips that hold the bezel in place. A service manual is your friend here!

If you are going to reglue the rubber caps over screws when reassembling, don't use a thick heavy glue that will interfere with the screw's usability later. Use a very thin coat of a very thin adhesive, such as a glue stick.

Once the bezel is removed, discover how the display is held in place (perhaps with additional screws, or perhaps there's a clasp) and carefully remove it. There may be multiple cables or connectors to the display, especially if it's a touch screen. Replace it with the new display, and then reverse the process to put things back together. As you are working, make sure you don't inadvertently dislodge any of the associated parts such as the webcam or Wi-Fi antenna connector.

When working with an unfamiliar laptop model, we find it helpful to watch YouTube videos that demonstrate how to perform specific tasks for that specific laptop model. YouTube is full of videos for performing nearly every repair task on every make and model.

exam watch

Replacing a display is no longer an exam objective, but a technician should still know how to replace one. In addition, several other components adjacent to the display are covered in 1101 exam Objective 1.2, including Wi-Fi antenna, microphone, and webcam, so you should still know your way around it.

EXERCISE 14-3

Replacing a Display Screen

This exercise carries with it the risk of cracking the plastic bezel on the laptop if you aren't careful, so don't do this exercise on your best machine (unless, of course, it actually needs its display replaced). For this exercise, you will need a way to ground yourself and/or your work area. You will also need a replacement display screen and a small nonmagnetic screwdriver for opening the case. You might also need a small flat-head screwdriver or a flat piece of metal for prying the display bezel away from the lid.

1. Review the documentation or service manual for the laptop to learn how to replace the display. The main challenge will be to get the bezel off without damaging it.
2. Unplug the laptop and remove its battery. Consult the documentation or service manual to learn how to remove the battery.
3. Prepare your work area. Lay down an antistatic mat if you have one, and have a small cup ready to hold screws.
4. Look in the upper corners of the display bezel for screws. They may be behind rubber caps. If you find screws, remove them. If you don't find any screws, consult the service manual to learn where and how to pry the bezel off without causing damage, and do so.
5. Examine the display to figure out how it is connected to the laptop. There is probably a small connector near the bottom of the screen. There may be multiple connectors, especially if it's a touch screen. Carefully disconnect them and lift out the display panel.
6. Insert the new display panel and reverse the process to secure the new display panel and replace the bezel. Don't forget to reattach the rubber caps if there are any. Their adhesive is usually strong enough to withstand being removed and replaced once.
7. Replace the battery and restart the laptop to check your work.

Replacing Other Parts Associated with the Display Several other components are also closely associated with the display due to their placement inside the laptop case. The Wi-Fi antenna, for example, is usually a wire that wraps around the edge of the display and is covered by the display bezel. The webcam, if present, is usually mounted in the plastic at the top of the display. The microphone may be built into the display lid as well. Replacing these components is usually a matter of prying off the bezel (gently) or removing the screens that hold it in place and then carefully removing and replacing the components behind it. Use the standard precautions for preventing electrostatic discharge (ESD), and make sure you keep your screws and other removed parts well-organized.

1101 exam Objective 1.2 asks that you be able to identify the following display components of mobile devices: Wi-Fi antenna connector/placement, camera/webcam, microphone, touch screen/digitizer, and inverter. All these parts are either built into or adjacent to the display on a laptop.

Keyboards

Due to size constraints, the built-in keyboard in a laptop has thinner keys that do not have the vertical travel that those on traditional keyboards do, so they do not give the same tactile feedback. If you often work in low-light environments, you may want a laptop with a *keyboard backlight,* a feature that gently lights the keyboard for ease of use. Just a few years ago, this feature was in only a few premium laptops, but in the last several years manufacturers have created more models with this feature or offer it as an upgrade option. If you choose a laptop with a backlit keyboard, accept the fact that using it will be yet another draw on the battery. (There may be an FN key combination you can press to toggle the backlighting on/off.) You can also purchase an external keyboard with this feature.

A laptop keyboard has the alphanumeric keys, ENTER key, function keys (F1, F2, ... F12), and some of the modifier keys (SHIFT, CTRL, ALT, and CAPS LOCK) in the same orientation to one another as on a full-size keyboard. But many of the special keys—the directional arrow keys and the INSERT, DELETE, PAGE UP, and PAGE DOWN keys—are in different locations.

The separate numeric keypad disappeared a long time ago from most laptops. (You'll still find them on large business laptops now and then.) On most laptops the keypad is completely absent or the function integrates into the alphanumeric keys, and small numbers on the sides of keys or in a different color on the top of each key indicate what number they are. Each alphanumeric key normally produces two characters—one when pressing the key alone and another when NUM LOCK is toggled on to enable the keypad. On many mobile keyboards an indicator light illuminates when NUM LOCK is on. On some laptops the keypad characters may be controlled by pressing the function-modifying FN key while pressing certain marked keys.

Like other laptop components, you can replace the built-in laptop keyboard if you can find a suitable replacement. If a laptop keyboard became damaged and you decide that you must replace it, and you have determined that it is cost-effective to do so, follow the manufacturer's instructions. Alternatively, you might just decide to use an external keyboard—a very inexpensive alternative since you simply plug it into a USB port.

Replacing a laptop keyboard is similar to replacing any other component (unfortunately), in that the procedure for doing so isn't standardized, so you must rely on the service manual to tell you how to access it. We've seen some keyboard replacements that were extremely easy (basically just pop it out by applying force with a flat screwdriver blade to a few specific areas around the keyboard), and some that were a huge pain in the neck, involving removing almost every other component in the system to get to it. Use standard safety precautions for ESD, keep your screws and tools organized, and follow the instructions.

Touch Screen/Digitizer

A *touch screen/digitizer* is a touch-sensitive input device that allows you to input data and commands using your finger or a stylus pen. If the laptop has a touch screen, the screen has a built-in digitizer. A touchpad is technically also a digitizer, although it isn't commonly lumped into that category.

A touch screen's digitizer hardware is a separate feature from the output component of the screen (that is, the display image). It's a transparent, built-in overlay on top of the screen. The digitizer could be broken while the screen is just fine, and vice versa. However, it's difficult to find them separated as replacement parts, so when one goes bad, you usually end up replacing the entire touch screen unit.

Multimedia Components

Laptops have much the same multimedia components as desktop PCs, although smaller, of course, and more difficult to get to if they must be replaced.

Camera/Webcam A built-in video camera, or *webcam,* typically appears at the top of the screen on a laptop, embedded in the bezel. Webcams have a variety of uses, including facial recognition, motion detection, and video chatting, depending on the software used with them.

The webcam may not be separable from the screen or from the lid of the laptop; you may need to replace the entire screen if the webcam isn't working or resort to using an external USB webcam replacement. Check the service manual for the laptop to determine how to access and replace the webcam if needed.

Microphone A laptop will have a built-in microphone, which the user can employ for voice pattern recognition security, speech recognition for data input, and audio recordings, among other things. The quality of the built-in microphone generally isn't very good, so power users of those features (especially those who convert speech to written text) may prefer to add an external microphone. An external microphone may plug into the Mic port on the laptop (if there is one) or to a USB port.

To access and replace the built-in microphone, consult the service manual for the laptop. It is probably located somewhere toward the front of the keyboard (that is, close to the person using the laptop), but designs vary greatly.

Physical Privacy and Security Components

Sign-ins with user names and passwords have traditionally been the primary user authentication method on mobile devices. However, many laptops and mobile devices now include hardware and software features that enable users to authenticate themselves based on who they are (biometrics) or what they have (a smartcard or other physical item).

The hardware for biometrics consists of some type of reader or camera that can scan body characteristics (like fingerprints, retinas, or facial features) and compare them to an internal database of allowed users. The hardware for a near-field communication (NFC) scanner consists of a type of radio transmitter that searches for nearby radio frequency ID (RFID) tags and interacts with them.

Both of those authentication types are covered in detail in Chapter 20, which looks at security.

SCENARIO & SOLUTION	
What important step in the disassembly of a laptop will help the most when you attempt to reassemble it?	Document and label cable and screw locations.
I need to completely remove power from a laptop before working on it, but I can't figure out how to remove its battery.	Review the service manual or other documentation for the laptop; different models vary greatly in how to remove the battery.
How can I replace a laptop's HDD with an SSD without completely reinstalling Windows and all the apps?	Migrate the contents of the HDD by either cloning it or using migration software. Then replace the HDD with the new SSD.

CERTIFICATION OBJECTIVE

- **1102: 1.4** *Given a scenario, use the appropriate Microsoft Windows 10 Control Panel utility*

CompTIA A+ 1102 exam Objective 1.4 contains a long list of Windows Control Panel utilities with a wide range of functionality. We discuss most of these in other chapters as appropriate, but here we will address an important subset for use on laptops: the Power Options. In this section you'll learn about Windows power management features that power down the screen and hard drive when it detects no activity and power-saving modes called Hibernate and Sleep (also called Suspend or Standby). You'll also learn about various power plans and options, as well as when and under what circumstances they are used.

Although this objective specifically references the Control Panel, Microsoft continues to move features from the Control Panel to the Settings app with each new update, so by the time you read this, some of the Control Panel features discussed may redirect to the Settings app, especially in Windows 11. Stay flexible, and make sure you know the current method of changing each setting.

Power Options

Nearly every component in a modern laptop has some sort of *power management* feature, a group of options in the hardware and the operating system that allows you to minimize the use of power—especially, but not exclusively—to conserve a laptop's battery life. In fact, even desktop computers come with power-saving features. Many devices, like the hard drive, will power down when not in use, and CPUs and other circuitry will draw less power when they have less demand for their services. Displays will power down after a configurable amount of time during which there was no activity from the mouse or keyboard. If a component is not drawing power, it is not creating heat, so power management and cooling go hand-in-hand.

Placing a PC in a Low-Power Mode

Depending on the power management settings (explained shortly), the PC may place itself in a lower power mode when certain conditions are met (such as a certain amount of idle time or a certain battery drain level). You can also manually place a PC in low power mode by clicking the Power icon on the Start menu in Windows and then choosing a power mode such as Sleep from the menu that appears. If one or more of the power modes you are expecting don't appear here, see the section "Displaying or Hiding Power Modes on the Power Menu" later in this chapter.

Configuring Power Management in Windows

Getting the most out of your laptop battery depends on how you manage the use of the battery's power. Using the Power Options Control Panel utility in Windows, you can configure the power management settings to minimize the power usage of laptop components.

On some versions of Windows that come preinstalled on the PCs, the PC manufacturer will add their own custom power options. For example, on a Dell laptop you might see a Dell power plan or a Dell Battery Meter application.

While the Power Options settings are available in Windows on all computers, you will find some differences in it when you compare Windows installations on desktops versus laptops. For example, a laptop will have separate settings for being on AC vs. battery power, and will enable you to control what happens when you shut the laptop lid. You will also see a battery meter that lets you know how much time is left on the battery's charge.

To access the power management options in Windows, open the Control Panel and navigate to Hardware And Sound | Power Options.

Power management can be configured in either the Control Panel or the Settings app, but because power options are covered under 1102 exam Objective 1.4, which explicitly references the Windows 10 Control Panel, that is the method we look at in this chapter.

Using Power-Saving Modes

Power-saving modes let you set the computer to use little or no power without shutting it down completely. The computer's current state (including all OS settings and open applications) is preserved so that when you resume work, the computer comes back up to full operation within seconds. You can configure these power modes via the Power Options applet in the Control Panel or from the Settings app.

Sleep Mode *Sleep mode* uses just enough power to keep the RAM powered on the computer and shuts down everything else (CPU, disk drives, display, and so on). The computer appears to be off, but it springs back to life, already booted up, when you press the power button. Sleep mode extends the length of the battery charge considerably, while keeping the machine state preserved so you don't have to close applications and shut down (and then restart everything later). You might use Sleep mode when packing up your work PC to go home if you plan on working when you get home, for example.

exam watch

1102 exam Objective 1.4 combines Sleep/Suspend in a single line, nodding to the fact that the terms are synonymous, but it lists Standby on a separate line, implying it is something different. It is not. Standby is another synonym for sleep that was used in some older versions of Windows (Windows XP and Windows 95, for example).

Sleep mode is good for short-term pausing (less than a day or so), but for longer stretches of time, if the PC is on battery power, the battery eventually runs out of power. What happens at that point depends on the power management settings configured in Windows. It could shut down (not optimal, because you lose any unsaved work), or it could switch over into Hibernate mode (described next). That automatic switchover is called *emergency hibernate.*

Hibernate Mode The *Hibernate* power-saving mode uses hard drive space to save all the programs and data that are in memory at the time you choose this mode. The computer then completely shuts down, using no power while it is hibernating. Like Sleep, Hibernate lets you stop work on your computer but quickly pick up where you left off. It takes slightly longer to go into and out of Hibernate than it does to go into and out of Sleep. Hibernate is a safer option if you aren't sure how long you'll be away from your computer, as it does not require any power since everything is saved to disk.

Choosing What Closing the Lid or Pressing the Power Button Does

On laptops, people are likely to be on the go, and they may quickly pack up their things by closing the laptop lid and placing it in a backpack or briefcase. Windows enables you to specify what happens when the lid closes (such as shutting down or entering Sleep or Hibernate) or the Power button is pressed, so users do not need to remember to issue a command before packing up.

To control the lid's behavior:

1. Open the Control Panel and navigate to Hardware And Sound | Power Options.
2. Click Choose What Closing The Lid Does (or click Choose What The Power Button Does—both commands lead to the same screen).
3. Open the When I Close The Lid drop-down list and click what you want to happen. Your choices are Do Nothing, Sleep, Hibernate, and Shut Down.

   On a laptop there will be separate settings for On Battery and Plugged In, as shown in Figure 14-5. On a desktop there will be only one setting. On a laptop with multiple buttons (for example, a Power button and a Sleep button), there will be separate controls for them.

FIGURE 14-5

Control the power button and lid behaviors.

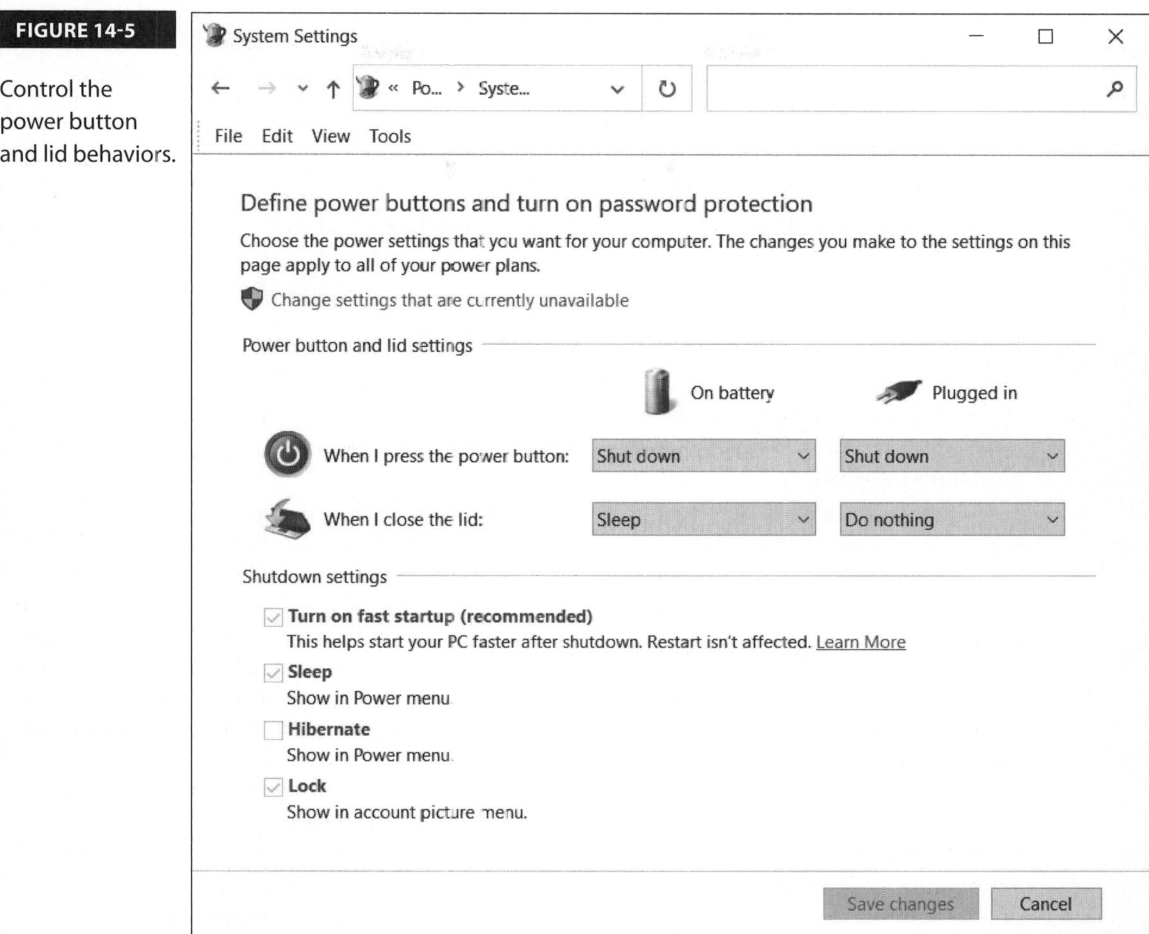

4. Open the When I Press The Power Button drop-down list and click what you want to happen. The choices are the same as in step 3.
5. Click Save Changes.

Enabling or Disabling Fast Startup

When you shut down a Windows computer using the Shut Down command, Windows uses a form of hibernation—not the entire saving-all-your-programs-and-data-to-disk hibernation, but a saving to disk of the Windows OS kernel as it appears in memory at the moment you shut down. This feature is called *Fast Startup*. As a result, Windows startup is very fast because it brings the Windows kernel out of hibernation, fully configured and ready to run.

To enable or disable Fast Startup:

1. Open the Control Panel and navigate to Hardware And Sound | Power Options.
2. Click Choose What The Power Button Does. See Figure 14-5.
3. Click Change Settings That Are Currently Unavailable. The check boxes under the Shutdown Settings heading become editable.
4. Clear or mark the Turn On Fast Startup check box.
5. Click Save Changes.

Displaying or Hiding Power Modes on the Power Menu

On some systems, Hibernate causes problems. The PC may not resume correctly from Hibernate, requiring a hard reboot, for example. On such systems, it's a good idea to hide the Hibernate command so the end user doesn't use it. On some systems, it is even disabled by default.

To hide Hibernate or Sleep on the Power icon's menu, follow the steps in the previous section for enabling or disabling Fast Startup, but instead of the Turn On Fast Startup check box in step 4, mark or clear the Hibernate check box.

Configuring Low-Battery Options

On a laptop, the Windows notification area of the taskbar displays a tiny battery icon that serves as an indicator of battery charge level. Hover the mouse pointer over this icon to see battery charge status.

Click the icon to display a pop-up panel (see Figure 14-6 for the Windows 10 version) that shows you the current power mode. From here you can click Battery Settings to open the Battery settings in the Settings app, and then adjust the Turn Battery Saver On Automatically At setting. (The default is 20%, meaning that when your battery has 20% or less power left, Battery Saver mode will activate automatically.) Battery Saver mode uses various power-saving techniques, such as lowering the screen brightness, turning off keyboard backlighting, and stopping HDDs from spinning when not in use.

Exploring Power Plans

Windows has preconfigured power settings, called *power plans*. Of the preconfigured plans, the Balanced power plan is a good bet for most laptop users because it balances power savings with performance. However, if better performance is more important to you than battery life, select the High Performance power plan. If you need every minute of battery power you can squeeze out of your laptop while away from the office, select the Power Saver plan.

Exercise 14-4 will guide you as you create a new plan.

EXERCISE 14-4

Video

Creating a Power Plan

For this exercise, you will need a computer with Windows 10 or 11 installed. It is not necessary to have a laptop for this, although there will be some differences. For instance, the screen brightness and lid-closing settings will not be available.

1. Open the Control Panel and click Hardware And Sound | Power Options.
2. Notice which plan is selected.
3. In the left pane, click Create A Power Plan.
4. In the Create A Power Plan window, select one of the default plans on which to base your new plan, and click Next.

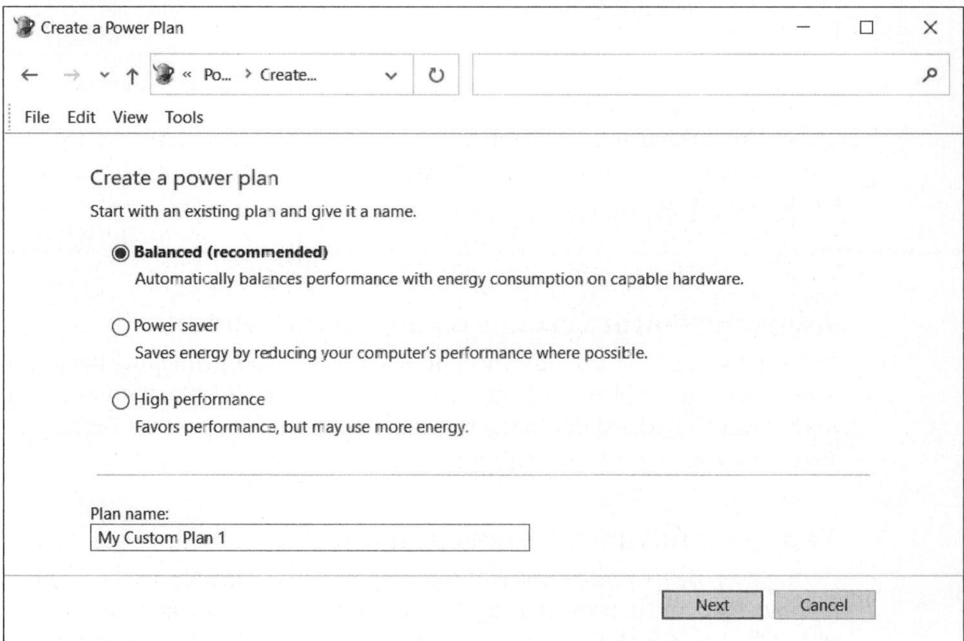
Create a Power Plan
« Po... › Create...
File Edit View Tools
Create a power plan
Start with an existing plan and give it a name.
Balanced (recommended)
Automatically balances performance with energy consumption on capable hardware.
Power saver
Saves energy by reducing your computer's performance where possible.
High performance
Favors performance, but may use more energy.
Plan name:
My Custom Plan 1
Next
Cancel

5. If you are using a laptop, notice the two groups of settings—one for when you're on battery and one for when the laptop is plugged in. If using a desktop, you'll see only one set of settings.

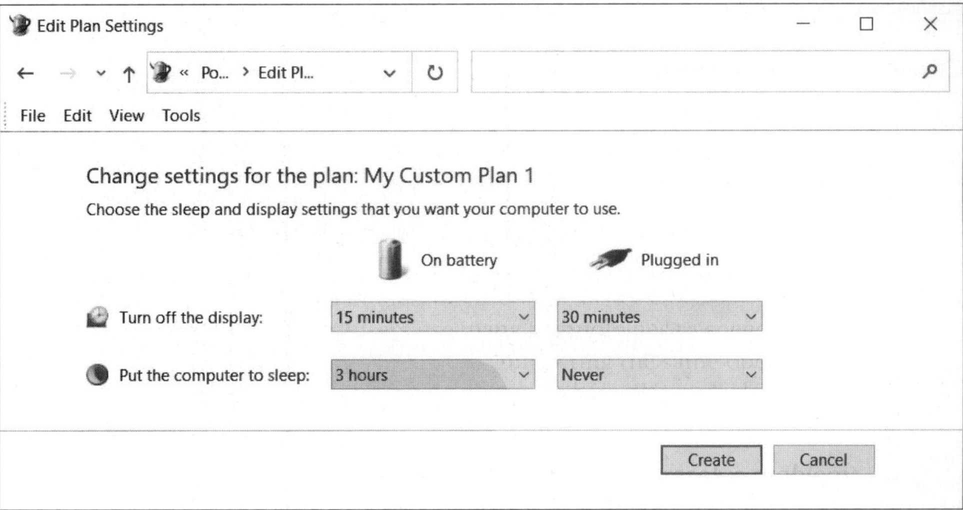

6. Make changes to the settings.
7. Click Create to save the new plan.
8. The new plan is now listed in Power Options.

Adjusting Power Settings on the Battery Meter

In Windows 10, you can quickly choose a power plan by dragging the slider on the battery meter. See Figure 14-6. To display the battery meter, click the battery icon in the notification area. Then drag the slider in the box that appears to choose Best Battery Life, Best Performance, or a middle setting between the two.

Changing Advanced Power Settings

To dig even deeper into power settings, open Power Options in the Control Panel, and click Change Plan Settings for the current power plan. Then, in the Edit Plan Settings window, click Change Advanced Power Settings. This will display the Advanced Settings tab of the Power Options dialog box, shown in Figure 14-7, where you can scroll through a long list of settings, each of which varies based on whether the computer is on battery or plugged in.

FIGURE 14-6

Switch power plans via the Battery meter.

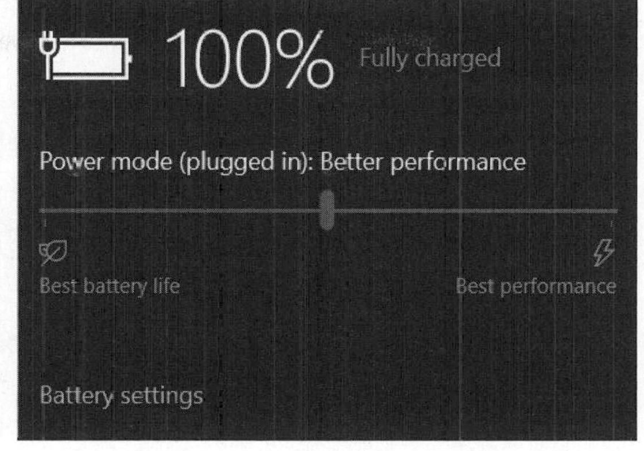

FIGURE 14-7

Fine-tune power settings.

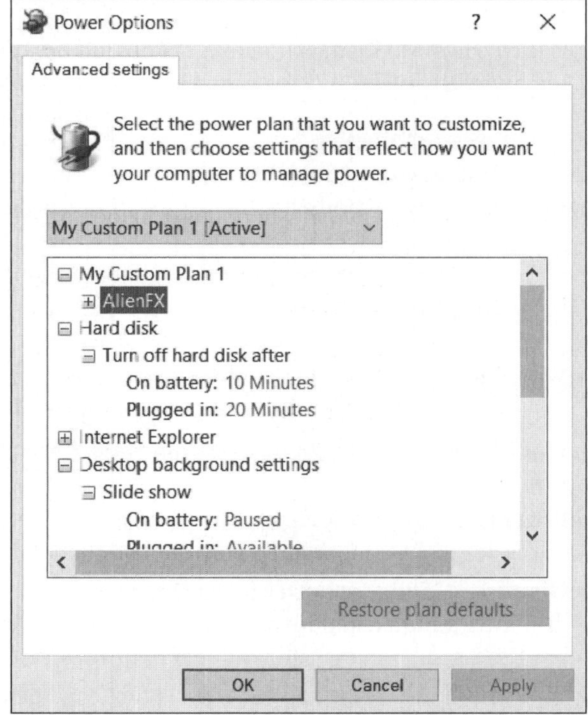

The actual items in this list may vary, based on the Windows version and on what hardware is present. Different Windows versions may list some of the options in a different order than listed here.

- **Hard Disk** Control how long the system waits after no activity before turning off the hard disk.
- **Internet Explorer** Select power management settings for when JavaScript is running in Internet Explorer. (Not that anyone still uses Internet Explorer. It's not even included in Windows 11.)
- **Desktop Background Settings** If the desktop background is a slideshow, this setting will control whether it is available or paused.
- **Wireless Adapter Settings** Save power by enabling the power-saving mode for the wireless adapter.
- **Sleep** Several settings control what length of inactive time will trigger sleep and which sleep mode is used (Sleep, Hybrid Sleep, or Hibernate). You can also configure wake timers.
- **USB Settings** Enable or disable USB Selective Suspend, a USB feature whereby a device driver can send a message to Windows requesting that the OS put the device into an idle (suspended) state. If this is disabled, Windows puts the device into suspend when the rest of the OS is suspended.

> **exam watch**
>
> **1101 exam Objective 1.4 specifically mentions USB Selective Suspend. Make sure you remember how to find and change it.**

- **Intel Graphics Settings** If present, select an Intel power plan for the Intel graphics adapter.
- **Power Buttons And Lid** Select what action will occur when (1) the lid is closed, (2) the power button is pressed, and (3) the sleep button (if physically present) is pressed.
- **PCI Express** Enable or disable Link State Power Management implementation of ASPM power plans.
- **Processor Power Management** Configure several power management settings for the system CPU.
- **Display** Configure power management settings for the display to control when the display is dimmed and by how much. Also enable or disable automatic (adaptive) brightness on systems with ambient light sensors.
- **Multimedia Settings** Control power management under two sets of circumstances: (1) when an external device is playing media shared from this computer and (2) when this computer is playing video.

- **Battery** Define what constitutes critical and low battery levels, the actions taken when the critical level is reached, and the notification settings for when a low battery level exists. Also, set the level at which the battery will go into reserve power mode. A smart configuration will issue a warning sound for both low and critical and place the computer into Sleep or Hibernate (better choice) when the critical level is reached.

on the Job

Power management isn't just for laptops, although some features, such as battery management, only apply to laptops. However, minimizing power usage of desktop computers is important to both individuals and big organizations. Therefore, you will want to apply what you learn here to the desktop computers that you support.

SCENARIO & SOLUTION	
I use my laptop at work, carrying it with me from meeting to meeting to take notes. How can I avoid the hassle of waiting for it to power up at the beginning of each meeting?	Select Sleep from the shutdown options.
When traveling, I would like to save all my work and the desktop when I shut down and have the laptop start up with my work state exactly as it was when I stopped. How do I achieve this, plus conserve as much battery life as possible?	Enable Hibernate in the Power Options applet in Control Panel, and then, when you are ready, select Hibernate from the shutdown options.
How do I configure a different set of behaviors for when my laptop is on battery as opposed to when it is plugged in?	Open the Power Options applet and click Change Plan Settings for the current plan. In the Edit Plan Settings dialog box, you can configure one group of settings for when the laptop is on battery and another set for when it is plugged in.

CERTIFICATION OBJECTIVE

- ***1101: 1.3*** *Given a scenario, set up and configure accessories and ports of mobile devices*

In this section, we review some ports and accessories common to laptops, per 1101 exam Objective 1.3. Some of these are also relevant to other mobile devices such as smartphones and tablets, which are covered in Chapter 15.

Laptop Connection Methods and Accessories

This section looks at two important topics: the various ports and technologies for connecting laptops to other devices and networks and the accessories you might want to connect to them.

Connection Methods

Laptops have a variety of ways that they connect with peripherals and accessories and with networks such as local area networks (LANs) and the Internet. Many of these you may already be familiar with from Chapter 9, but here's a quick round-up of the interfaces you need to be able to identify and use:

- **USB** As you learned in Chapter 9, there are various types of USB. Most laptops have at least one USB-A connector, and some have USB-C (Thunderbolt) connectors too. Some smaller mobile devices (like smartphones and tablets) may also have Mini-USB or Micro-USB connectors for data transfer and/or charging.
- **Lightning** Lightning is not a common interface on Windows PCs; it's mainly found on older Apple mobile devices, like tables and iPhones, for data transfer and charging. Newer iPads and Macs use USB-C instead.
- **Serial interfaces** Very few laptops have a serial interface anymore; it's odd that serial interfaces are still listed in 1101 exam Objective 1.3. Refer to the "DB-9 Serial Port" section in Chapter 9.
- **Near-field communication (NFC)** This technology, covered in Chapter 16, creates an ad hoc wireless network on-the-fly for devices in close proximity to one another. It's used in point-of-sale terminals to create chip-based credit cards, for instance, and some mobile devices can use NFC to share files with one another.
- **Wi-Fi** This is the most popular connection type for a laptop to access a LAN or the Internet. As you will learn in Chapter 16, it uses radio frequency (RF) signals to communicate with an access point.
- **Bluetooth** Also covered in Chapter 16, Bluetooth is another short-range wireless networking technology for connections between individual devices. Laptops may use Bluetooth for connecting peripherals such as headphones, printers, wireless keyboards and mice, and so on.
- **Hotspots** A hotspot is a Wi-Fi access point, as you will learn in Chapter 16. Most laptops contain Wi-Fi adapters that enable you to connect to a hotspot to access the Internet or other networks.

exam watch **Make sure you can physically identify each of these connections (except for the wireless ones, of course) and explain how a laptop might use them. If one of them isn't working on a laptop, you should be able to suggest some troubleshooting procedures for it.**

Port Replicators and Docking Stations

The laptop owner who uses a laptop while traveling but also as a desktop replacement usually has a "base of operations" office. This office is where the owner will use external devices such as a keyboard, printer, display, mouse, and external hard drive storage. The user must connect and disconnect the laptop from these components every time he or she returns to or leaves the office with the laptop. The solution to that inconvenience is a port replicator or docking station.

A *port replicator,* a device that remains on the desktop with external devices connected to its ports, can make this task less time consuming by providing a single connection to the laptop and permanent connection to these external devices.

A more advanced (and more expensive) alternative to the port replicator is a *docking station*. In addition to the ports normally found on a port replicator, a docking station may include full-size expansion slots and various drives. In the past, port replicators and docking stations were always proprietary—often only fitting one model of laptop. If the manufacturer did not make one of these devices to fit your laptop, you had no options. Now you can easily find an inexpensive "universal" port replicator or docking station that interfaces with a laptop via a Thunderbolt or USB port. Whether you have a proprietary device that fits your laptop or one that uses a generic connector, be sure to read the documentation that comes with the docking station or port replicator and follow the instructions for connecting and disconnecting the device.

Laptop Accessories

You can expand a laptop's capabilities and versatility with a variety of accessories. 1101 exam Objective 1.3 explicitly lists several such accessories, which you should be able to set up and configure. The installation for each of these typically involves connecting it to the laptop via a wired or wireless port and then running its setup software. (Some devices don't need the setup software to function; the OS detects them automatically.)

- **Touch pen** A *touch pen* is sometimes used with a touch screen for more precise selection and movement. There are active touch pens that have buttons on them you can press to issue commands or access special functions, and there are passive touch pens that are basically just soft-tipped styluses.
- **Headset** A *headset* is a combination of headphones and a microphone; people who spend a lot of time talking on the phone (or the computer equivalent of that) use headsets to keep their hands free for typing. Because a headset is a combination input (mic) and output (speakers) device, the operating system sees it as two separate components in some cases. Most headsets work at a basic level immediately when you connect them to the PC, but advanced features may require software setup.
- **Speakers** A laptop typically has a built-in *speaker* (or multiple speakers); you can also connect external ones. Some external speakers connect via USB; others connect to the 3.5" round jack on the laptop that doubles for both audio input and audio output. Speakers do not require any special setup to function, but their setup software or driver properties may enable you to configure a speaker set in different ways. For example, a Dolby 5.1 set of speakers may let you choose which speakers are front vs. back.
- **Webcam** Many laptops have a built-in *webcam,* but you can also add an external webcam (usually via USB port). Most webcams do not require software setup.
- **Trackpad** Most laptops have a built-in *trackpad* (also called a touchpad) that you can use as a pointing device, moving your finger across it to move the on-screen pointer. External trackpads are also available, usually connecting via USB.
- **Drawing pad** A *drawing pad* uses the same basic technology as a trackpad, except that instead of moving the on-screen pointer, a drawing pad enables you to use a touch pen or stylus to "draw" on the pad surface to create artwork on the computer screen. Drawing pads may require special software setup to enable all their features, and may require a special drawing application that supports the drawing pad hardware.

Touchpad Configuration

Most laptop touchpads (called trackpads in 1101 exam Objective 1.3) do not require configuration to operate; they work as a pointing device automatically. However, there are several options you can set to fine-tune touchpad behavior.

There are two types of touchpads: standard (normal) and precision. Precision touchpads have more adjustable options, including sensitivity settings. To find out which type a PC has and to access the touchpad controls, complete the following exercise.

EXERCISE 14-5

Exploring Touchpad Settings

1. Select Start | Settings | Devices | Touchpad.
2. Look at the top of the window, under the Touchpad heading. If you see *Your PC has a precision touchpad,* as in the following illustration, then you have one. If you don't see that message, you don't.

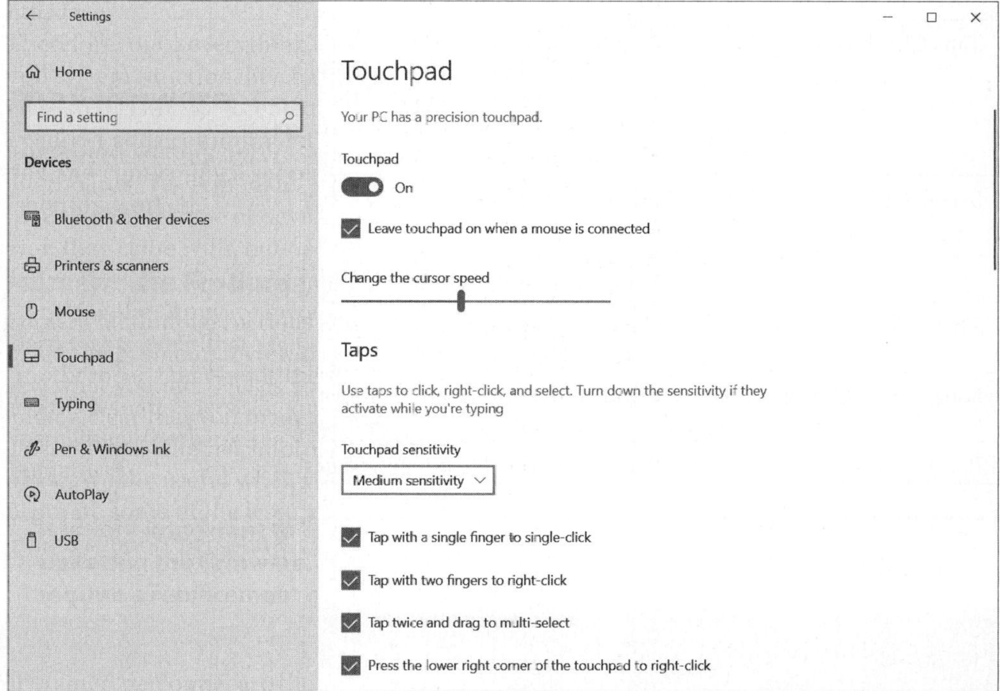

3. Adjust any settings as desired, as explained in the next sections.

From the Touchpad screen in the Settings app, choose Most Sensitive, High Sensitivity, Medium Sensitivity, or Low Sensitivity. Sensitivity is the only option available on a standard touchpad.

If you have a precision touchpad, you can also adjust the settings described in the following table.

Setting	Description
Touchpad (On/Off)	Enables or disables the touchpad.
Leave Touchpad On When A Mouse Is Connected	Turns off the touchpad if there is another pointing device in use.
Change The Cursor Speed	Adjusts the amount the on-screen pointer moves for a movement of your finger on the touchpad.
Taps Check Boxes	Enable/disable specific tap operations: ■ Tap with a single finger to single-click ■ Tap with two fingers to right-click ■ Tap twice and drag to multi-select ■ Press the lower-right corner of the touchpad to right-click
Scroll And Zoom	Enable/disable the following check boxes: ■ Drag Two Fingers To Scroll ■ Pinch To Zoom You can also set a scrolling direction here.
Three-Finger Gestures	Control what swiping with three fingers does in each of four directions and what tapping with three fingers does.
Four-Finger Gestures	Control what swiping with four fingers does in each of four directions and what tapping with four fingers does.
Reset	Resets the default settings and gestures.

SCENARIO & SOLUTION

I plug my laptop into an external display, printer, and keyboard every time I return to the office. Is there an easier way to do this?	Yes. Plug each of these devices into a port replicator and leave them there. To access the devices, simply attach your laptop to the port replicator.
I use an external mouse, but I keep accidentally touching the touchpad on my laptop. Can I disable it?	Yes. Follow the steps in Exercise 14-5 to access the touchpad settings and set the Touchpad slider to Off.

CERTIFICATION OBJECTIVE

■ **1101:5.5** *Given a scenario, troubleshoot common issues with mobile devices*

This section addresses some of the common problems and symptoms of malfunctioning mobile devices covered in CompTIA A+ 1101 exam Objective 5.5. In this objective, we assume that the term "mobile device" refers generically to laptops, tablets, and smartphones, the full gamut of portable devices. We assume this because some of the topics can reasonably be assumed to refer only to laptops (such as sticking keys, since tablets and phones don't have hardware keys for the most part). Some of these topics are also covered in Chapter 15 in the context of smartphones and tablets.

Troubleshooting Laptop Problems

Laptops live in that gray area between desktops and mobile devices. They have many of the same problems as desktop PCs, which you learned about in Chapter 12, along with many of the same problems as tablets and smartphones, which are coming up in Chapter 15. This section touches on some of the most common laptop problems you may encounter, overlapping somewhat with those other two chapters' coverage but also hitting some unique topics.

Broken Parts

Physical damage to a laptop is not so much a troubleshooting issue as it is an evaluation of whether the damage can be economically repaired to bring the device back into full functionality versus recycling and replacing it. Some of the most common types of physical damage include broken screens and physically damaged ports. Broken plastic parts are also common.

Broken plastic parts are sometimes not essential to the laptop's operation. You may be able to tape or glue them back into place, or just leave them off.

The important thing to remember about repairing physical damage is to consult the service manual for the device to find out how each part should be removed and replaced. There are many different laptop designs, each one with its own unique design and disassembly procedure.

Liquid Damage

Another type of physical damage comes from liquids, such as a beverage, spilled on a keyboard or a laptop being dropped into a body of water (bathtubs, fountains, lakes…it happens more than you might think). Water and electronics don't mix, because water is a very good conductor of electricity, and when a component gets wet, the electricity stops traveling through its normal pathways and jumps through the liquid instead, creating short-circuits that can damage circuit boards.

The first thing to do is to get the power off to the device immediately when water comes into the picture to stop further damage.

After that, the next step is to take the device apart (if possible) and let it dry. If the device cannot be disassembled, put it into a bag with some dry rice, which can help absorb the moisture.

You may need to clean some parts if the liquid had any sugar in it. Alcohol works best, but when cleaning up a sticky or dirty liquid, a mild soap and water can also be used as long as you make sure everything is bone-dry before you try to power it on. A hair dryer (on low heat only) can speed the drying process. If relying on air drying, give it at least 72 hours. Then reassemble the device and power it up to assess whether there is any permanent damage.

Touchpad and Mouse Troubleshooting

A malfunctioning touchpad is usually the result of a missing, corrupted, or out-of-date driver or improper configuration settings. If the touchpad is properly installed, it's fairly foolproof.

First, confirm that the touchpad appears in Device Manager and there are no problems with it. Try updating its driver from the Driver tab in its Properties box. The touchpad may be listed under Mice And Other Pointing Devices or under Human Interface Devices, and it may appear either as an entry with the word *touchpad* in its name or as HID-compliant mouse.

If that doesn't work, try uninstalling it in Device Manager and then refreshing the hardware list or restarting the PC. Also check out the touchpad in the Settings app (see Exercise 14-5) and make sure that the Touchpad setting is On.

If that doesn't work, you might try using the generic driver for the touchpad in Windows. To do that, in Device Manager, right-click your touchpad driver and choose Update Driver | Browse My Computer For Drivers | Let Me Pick From A List Of Available Drivers On My Computer. Select HID Compliant Mouse, select Next, and follow the prompts.

Cursor drift or *ghost cursor* describes the condition where the on-screen pointer seems to move all by itself. In very rare cases, this can indicate malware infection (i.e., someone is remotely controlling the computer), but it's much more likely that the touchpad sensitivity is set too high and the user's hands are brushing against it when typing. It also may need calibration, explained in the next section. Another common cause for this is conflicting device drivers. Try removing any custom drivers for external pointing devices and sticking with the general Windows-provided drivers to see if that solves it.

Touch Screen/Digitizer Troubleshooting

If a touch screen is completely nonresponsive, try using the keyboard and mouse. If they don't work either, the device is locked up. If they work okay, try rebooting. You'd be amazed (or maybe you already know) how often that fixes whatever problem you're having. Still no luck? Make sure the connections inside the laptop to the monitor are snug. There may be two separate cables connecting the display to the motherboard—one for the touch screen and one for the display output.

1101 exam Objective 5.5 lists touch screen problems as "digitizer issues." A digitizer is a transparent touch-sensitive sheet of film over a display screen that senses touch activity.

Calibration is also occasionally an issue. If where you touch and where the touch is registered don't match up, you might need to calibrate the screen. This is more common on tablets and phones than on laptops but you can still use the calibration utility on a touch screen laptop. The main reason you might calibrate a laptop touch screen is because you've just replaced it.

In Windows 10, open the Settings app, and in the Find A Setting search box, type **calibrate**. Then click Calibrate The Screen For Pen Or Touch Input. This opens the Tablet PC Settings dialog box. (If you don't see that option, the PC doesn't have a touch screen.) From there, click the Calibrate button to run the Digitizer Calibration Tool utility. Follow the prompts from there, which involve touching various spots on the screen marked by a crosshair.

Keyboard Troubleshooting

If you press one key and the character for another appears instead, the keyboard map has gotten confused. Rebooting should fix the problem. If it doesn't, try using compressed air to blow out the space under the keys, if you can get to it.

If a key is physically sticking and you can't get access to the space under the key without tearing up the keyboard, consider replacing the keyboard. Laptop keyboards are not very expensive (under $50 usually).

Here's a less obvious fix for keyboard issues that we stumbled upon a few years ago by accident. We had a laptop keyboard where the period key stopped working. All other keys were fine. The solution we finally found was to do a hard reboot on the machine by holding down the hardware Power button for five seconds so Windows booted from scratch (not just into and out of Fast Startup's hibernation mode). Problem solved.

Another common problem (well, not really a problem but an annoyance) that users have with keyboards is the Num Lock indicator being stuck on or off. Many laptop keyboards don't have a NUM LOCK key that you can easily press to toggle it. Look for an FN key combination that operates the NUM LOCK. You might also find a BIOS/UEFI firmware setup setting that controls the initial state of the num LOCK KEY at startup.

Display Troubleshooting

If you don't see anything on the display screen, try rebooting. Do you see anything at all, like a hardware startup logo, when it first starts booting? If so, the display is fine and the OS is to blame. If not, the display may be defective or its connector to the motherboard may have come loose. Try plugging in an external monitor; if it works, the display screen hardware is at fault.

Here are some other display issues you may need to troubleshoot:

- **Dim display** A dim display could be the result of defective hardware, but it is more likely caused by a setting that is telling the device to conserve battery power by placing the display in a low-power-consumption mode. Check the device's power management settings, and do a hard reboot (power completely off and then back on again) before you assume that your display is defective. When a battery gets below a certain charge level, the OS may dim the display automatically.
- **Flickering display** A severely flickering display on a laptop device is probably experiencing a hardware issue. Try rebooting the device. The display may need to be replaced if that doesn't work. If it's just flickering slightly, try increasing the display refresh rate.
- **Can't project to external monitor** If you can't project to an external monitor, first make sure that Windows recognizes the external monitor. Open the Display settings in the Settings app or Control Panel and click Identify to see which monitors Windows sees. Try clicking Detect to detect additional monitors. Then press WINDOWS KEY-P to open the Project task panel, and click Extend to extend the display onto the external monitor.

Sound Troubleshooting

If you aren't hearing any sound from your laptop's speakers, here are some possibilities to look at:

- Right-click the speaker icon in the notification area and choose Open Sound Settings. Make sure your speakers are chosen under Choose Your Output Device.
- Make sure the Master Volume is not set to Mute. Click Troubleshoot under the Master Volume slider in the Sound section of the Settings app.
- Check in Device Manager that the sound support's drivers are correctly installed. Reinstall or update them if needed.
- If you're using external speakers, make sure they are plugged in and turned on.

Overheating

Just like with a desktop PC, a laptop can overheat when its cooling fans and other cooling mechanisms (like heat sinks and air vents) aren't adequate. The first line of troubleshooting overheating in a laptop is to clean all the air vents; often over time they become clogged with dust and debris. Next, make sure all the fans are working, and make sure the heat sink(s) on the CPU, GPU, and other major chips on the motherboard have not become detached as the thermal paste dries out and degrades over time.

Check in BIOS/UEFI setup to see if there is a setting that controls the fan speed or the cooling mode. You may be able to control how often and how loudly the internal fans operate by selecting Cool mode or Quiet mode in the setup utility. If a laptop is overheating, setting it to Cool mode will force the fans to work harder and more consistently.

Battery Health

If the battery isn't charging, the battery may be worn out and unable to hold a charge. There are free battery testing utilities you can use to check that out. However, the most common reason a laptop battery doesn't charge is that the wrong AC adapter is being used, generally one with not enough wattage, or the AC adapter is faulty. You might see a system message letting you know that the system cannot identify the AC adapter, or the battery simply might not charge.

If the laptop won't start up at all (no power), the battery could be completely drained and the laptop isn't receiving AC power. Another reason you might not see anything when you press the Power button is that the laptop has gotten hung up in Sleep or Hibernate mode. Hold down the Power button for five seconds or more and then release it to do a hard shutdown that clears out any sleep or hibernation.

Occasionally when a battery goes bad physically, it becomes swollen or distended, sometimes even making the plastic on its cover bulge. Remove a swollen battery immediately and dispose of it, recycling it if possible.

CERTIFICATION SUMMARY

Most PC technicians will need to understand laptop technologies and how to replace components in them, since use of these portable computers remains widespread in both the workplace and the home—even as the sales of newer tablet computers cut into the number of laptops sold each year. Laptops come in many sizes, from the very lightweight ultra-portables or netbooks to desktop replacements.

Although laptops are basically compatible with standard PC operating systems like Windows, macOS, and Linux, they use smaller integrated components that, for the most part, do not conform in either form or size with the standard PC components.

A technician should know how to disassemble a laptop and replace its components as needed. Often this knowledge comes from a review of the laptop's service manual. Some of the key components you may need to replace include memory, storage devices, keyboards, wireless cards, and digitizers. You may also need to troubleshoot to determine whether a problem has a hardware or software origin and to narrow down the cause and perform the fix.

TWO-MINUTE DRILL

Here are some of the key points covered in Chapter 14.

Repairing, Upgrading, and Configuring Laptops

- ❑ A laptop is a portable computer that can run the same operating systems as a desktop PC, with a keyboard in the base and a display in a hinged top.
- ❑ Internal and integrated laptop hardware, such as the display, keyboard, pointing device, motherboard, memory, hard drives, and expansion bus, has special scaled-down form factors, but a laptop can use most standard external PC peripherals.
- ❑ Your laptop disassembly and reassembly processes should include consulting the manufacturer's documentation, using appropriate hand tools, organizing parts, and documenting and labeling cable and screw locations.
- ❑ Although laptop components are at least partially proprietary, you can find replacement parts from the original manufacturer or from other sources. Always research the cost-effectiveness of replacing parts rather than replacing the entire laptop.
- ❑ Internal expansion slots include Mini PCIe, mSATA, and M.2.
- ❑ You add memory to a laptop in the form of SODIMMs installed into slots inside the case.
- ❑ Most older laptops use 2.5" HDDs, but some smaller models use 1.8" hard drives. Drives can be either magnetic or solid state. Newer laptops often use SSDs, often connecting with the mSATA or M.2 interface.
- ❑ The flat-panel display built into a laptop is likely some form of LCD, backlit with LEDs or CCFL, or organic LED (OLED). To extend the display to an external monitor, use the appropriate FN key combination or a command in the OS or press WINDOWS KEY-P and choose Extend.

- ❑ Laptops have many of the same I/O ports and adapters that desktops have, including one or more display ports (such as HDMI), multiple USB ports, and audio ports.
- ❑ Laptops often come with built-in communications adapters—including Wi-Fi and Ethernet for LAN connections, Bluetooth for short-distance wireless communications, and cellular adapters for connecting to cellular networks.
- ❑ A laptop comes with two sources of electrical power: a rechargeable battery and an AC adapter.
- ❑ A laptop will usually have a built-in microphone and one or more built-in speakers. There will be ports for external sound input and output as well.

Power Options

- ❑ You can use the Windows Power Options utility to configure power management settings in laptops that comply with power management standards through the operating system to shut down the display, the hard drive, and even the entire system after a period of inactivity and/or when the battery is low.
- ❑ Hibernate is a Windows state that uses hard drive space to save all the programs and data that are in memory at the time you choose this mode. The computer then completely shuts down and requires no power while it is hibernating.
- ❑ Sleep is a state that conserves power while saving your desktop in RAM memory in a work state; it requires a minimum amount of power.

Laptop Connection Methods and Accessories

- ❑ Laptop connection methods include USB, Lightning, Serial, NFC, Bluetooth, and Wi-Fi.
- ❑ Port replicators and docking stations provide permanent connections for external devices used in the laptop user's office. Universal docking stations and port replicators have USB interfaces and therefore connect in the same manner as other USB devices.
- ❑ Laptop accessories you should be able to install and configure include touch pen, headset, speakers, webcam, trackpad, and drawing pad.

Troubleshooting Laptop Problems

- ❑ Touchpad problems are most often the result of a missing, corrupted, or out-of-date driver or improper configuration settings.
- ❑ Broken parts should be physically replaced when practical (and when it is not cheaper to replace the entire device). Refer to the service manual for disassembly instructions.
- ❑ In the event of liquid damage, power off the device immediately and let it dry for at least 72 hours.

- ❑ If the pointer appears to move by itself (cursor drift), try turning off the touchpad; your hands may be activating the touchpad by accident as you type.
- ❑ Touch screens may occasionally need to be calibrated using the Digitizer Calibration Tool utility in Windows.
- ❑ Keyboard problems are often solved by rebooting. Keyboard replacement is not uncommon on a laptop and not expensive.
- ❑ A dim display may result from improper brightness settings; rebooting can also sometimes fix it. For no-display problems, try an external monitor to help diagnose.
- ❑ Sound problems may result from driver problems or the sound being accidentally muted in the operating system.
- ❑ Overheating is usually caused by blocked vents, dead fans, and firmware settings that prefer quiet operation over cool operation.
- ❑ If a battery isn't charging, it may be worn out, or you may be using the wrong AC adapter for the laptop's wattage needs.

SELF TEST

The following questions will help you measure your understanding of the material presented in this chapter. Read all the choices carefully because there might be more than one correct answer. Choose all correct answers for each question.

Repairing, Upgrading, and Configuring Laptops

1. How many pins does a DDR4 SODIMM have?

A. 102

B. 200 or 204

C. 260

D. 262

2. What is the name for system memory used by the video adapter and therefore unavailable to the operating system?
   A. VRAM
   B. SODIMM memory
   C. Shared video memory
   D. SRAM
3. What type of battery is most common on a modern laptop?
   A. Coin-style
   B. 9-volt
   C. Nickel-cadmium
   D. Lithium-ion
4. Which types of expansion slots are common on modern laptops? (Choose two.)
   A. Mini PCIe
   B. M.2
   C. PCI
   D. VGA
5. Which of the following is a laptop component used to convert the DC power from the power adapter or battery to the AC power required by the LCD display?
   A. Inverter
   B. Converter
   C. Power switch
   D. Generator
6. What is the most common laptop memory module?
   A. SORIMM
   B. MicroDIMM
   C. SODIMM
   D. DIMM
7. Which is a common size for a laptop hard disk drive (HDD)?
   A. 2.5"
   B. 5"
   C. 3.5"
   D. 1"
8. Which of the following allows you to attach nearly any type of desktop component to a laptop?
   A. Port replicator
   B. Enhanced port replicator
   C. Extended port replicator
   D. Docking station

9. What utility in Windows could you use to migrate an HDD to a new SSD in Windows?
   A. Activation
   B. System Image Recovery
   C. Windows Preinstallation Environment
   D. System Restore
10. How is a Mini PCIe card in a laptop different from a PCIe card on a desktop?
    A. Larger card
    B. 64-bit data bus
    C. Not an externally accessible card
    D. All of the above
11. Where is the hard disk located on a laptop?
    A. Under the keyboard
    B. On the side, in a removable slot
    C. On the underside, next to the battery
    D. Varies depending on the model
12. Which wireless communications standard is used between a laptop and nearby devices and is limited to devices within a few meters of the computer?
    A. Cellular
    B. Wi-Fi
    C. Bluetooth
    D. Wired Ethernet
13. On a touch screen, what component allows the screen to function as an input device?
    A. Video adapter
    B. Shared memory
    C. Digitizer
    D. Touchpad

Power Options

14. How can you manually place a PC in Sleep mode?
    A. Power icon on Start menu
    B. ALT-F4 keyboard shortcut
    C. CTRL-S keyboard shortcut
    D. BIOS/UEFI setup

15. What Windows utility can you use to configure low-battery options for a laptop?
   A. Power Options
   B. System Properties
   C. Battery Options
   D. BIOS/UEFI setup

16. Which low-power mode uses the least amount of electricity?
   A. Sleep
   B. Suspend
   C. Hibernate
   D. Jumpstart

17. Which of these is not one of the actions you can assign to the act of closing a laptop's lid?
   A. Sleep
   B. Hibernate
   C. Do nothing
   D. Restart

Laptop Connection Methods and Accessories

18. Which of these is *not* a common connection interface for a modern laptop?
   A. USB
   B. Wi-Fi
   C. Bluetooth
   D. Serial

Troubleshooting Laptop Problems

19. What is the most urgent concern when a laptop comes in contact with water?
   A. Clean off any sticky parts with alcohol.
   B. Disconnect external peripherals.
   C. Dry out the circuit boards.
   D. Cut the power to the laptop.

20. How can you clear a laptop out of Sleep mode if it gets stuck in sleep and won't wake up?
   A. Press CTRL-ALT-DELETE.
   B. Press and hold the Power button for five seconds or more.
   C. Press CTRL-ALT-INSERT.
   D. Shake the laptop vigorously.

A SELF TEST ANSWERS

Repairing, Upgrading, and Configuring Laptops

1. ☑ **C.** A DDR4 SODIMM has 260 pins.
☒ **A** is incorrect because at this writing, this is not a valid number for pins on any SODIMM. **B** is incorrect because 200 or 204 is the number of pins for a DDR3 SODIMM. **D** is incorrect because 262 is the number of pins for a DDR5 SODIMM.

2. ☑ **C.** Shared video memory is the name for system memory used by the video adapter and therefore is unavailable to the operating system.
☒ **A** is incorrect because volatile RAM (VRAM) is the type of memory used on a video adapter. A video adapter with VRAM installed does not need to use system memory. **B** is incorrect because although a SODIMM is the physical memory module used in most laptops, the name for the portion of this memory used by the video adapter is what the question asks for. **D** is incorrect because SRAM (static RAM) is simply a type of very high-speed RAM.

3. ☑ **D.** Modern laptops use mostly lithium-ion batteries.
☒ **A** is incorrect because a coin-style battery is common on desktop motherboards. **B** is incorrect because 9-volt batteries are not used in modern computers. **C** is incorrect because nickel-cadmium batteries were used in earlier generations of laptops.

4. ☑ **A** and **B.** Mini PCIe and M.2 are both common expansion slot types on modern laptops.
☒ **C** is incorrect because PCI is a much older type of expansion slot. **D** is incorrect because VGA is a video connector.

5. ☑ **A.** An inverter converts DC power to the AC power required by an LCD panel.
☒ **B** is incorrect because a converter does just the opposite, converting AC power to DC power. **C** is incorrect because the power switch simply turns the main power to the laptop on and off. **D** is incorrect because this is not a component of a laptop. A generator generates power using an engine powered by fuel such as gasoline or diesel.

6. ☑ **C.** SODIMM is the most common laptop memory module. It is a scaled-down version of the DIMM memory module used in desktops.
☒ **A** is incorrect because SORIMM is a now-obsolete memory module form not discussed in the book. **B** is incorrect because the MicroDIMM module is half the size of SODIMM and is used in handheld computers and, less often, in laptops. **D** is incorrect because DIMM is a full-size memory module for desktop PCs.

7. ☑ **A.** 2.5" is the most common size of a laptop hard disk drive (HDD).
☒ **B** is incorrect because 5" is a very large size not used in laptops. **C** is incorrect because 3.5" is also a large size that is not used in laptops but is common in desktop PCs. **D** is incorrect (at this writing) because 1" is not a size commonly used in laptops.

8. ☑ **D.** A docking station allows you to attach nearly any type of desktop component to a laptop. The docking station can remain on the desk with all the desired devices installed or connected to it. To access these devices, simply plug the laptop into the docking station.
☒ **A** and **B** are incorrect because neither a port replicator nor an enhanced port replicator allows access to the number and variety of devices that a docking station does. **C** is incorrect because an extended port replicator is not a real type of portable system component.

9. ☑ **B.** You can use System Image Recovery to copy a saved system image of the old drive onto the new one.
☒ **A** is incorrect because activation is an anti-piracy check when installing an application. **C** is incorrect because Windows PE is the setup program used to install or repair Windows. **D** is incorrect because System Restore is a Windows utility that restores backups of system files only.

10. ☑ **C.** Mini PCIe is not externally accessible, unlike the desktop PCIe version.
☒ **A** is incorrect because Mini PCIe in laptops is smaller than PCIe used in desktops. **B** is incorrect because they are both 64-bit. **D** is incorrect because A and B are incorrect.

11. ☑ **D.** Hard disk placement varies depending on the model. It can be in any of the locations listed or in a different place.
☒ **A, B,** and **C** are incorrect because although they are all possible locations, there is no guarantee. You must consult the service manual to find the correct location or, if the manual is not available, disassemble the laptop and locate the hard drive visually.

12. ☑ **C.** Bluetooth is for short-range communications only. The others listed have longer ranges.
☒ **A** is incorrect because cellular technology can be used to connect a laptop to the Internet from cell towers several miles away. **B** is incorrect because Wi-Fi connects a laptop to a wireless local area network (WLAN) at distances of several hundred feet. **D** is incorrect because wired Ethernet requires a cable.

13. ☑ **C.** The digitizer is the part of the display that is touch sensitive and enables touch input.
☒ **A** is incorrect because a video adapter allows the screen to function as an *output* device. **B** is incorrect because shared memory is system RAM, not an input device. **D** is incorrect because although a touchpad is an input device, it has no connection with the touch screen.

Power Options

14. ☑ **A.** Click the Power icon on the Start menu and then click Sleep.
☒ **B** and **C** are incorrect because there are no keyboard shortcuts in Windows for placing the PC in Sleep mode. **D** is incorrect because BIOS/UEFI setup cannot be used to put the PC in Sleep mode.

15. ☑ **A.** Power Options is the utility where you can configure low-battery options for a laptop.
☒ **B** is incorrect because you cannot configure low-battery options in System Properties. **C** is incorrect because there is no such utility as Battery Options in Windows. **D** is incorrect because BIOS/UEFI setup is not in Windows, but at the system level of the computer.

16. ☑ **C.** Hibernate uses no power at all when in use.
☒ **A** and **B** are incorrect because they both refer to the same Sleep mode, which keeps memory and the CPU active by using a small amount of electricity. **D** is incorrect because Jumpstart is not a term discussed in this book.

17. ☑ **D.** Restart is not an action to be performed when shutting the lid; that would be counterproductive.
☒ **A, B,** and **C** are incorrect because these are all actions you can assign to that act.

Laptop Connection Methods and Accessories

18. ☑ **D.** Serial is an obsolete type of connection that is seldom found on laptops today.
☒ **A, B,** and **C** are incorrect because they are all common connection interfaces on a modern laptop.

Troubleshooting Laptop Problems

19. ☑ **D.** Cutting the power is the most urgent step because water conducts electricity and could cause a short-circuit.
☒ **A** is incorrect because cleaning sticky parts quickly will cause no damage. **B** is incorrect because not disconnecting peripherals quickly will cause no damage. **C** is incorrect because although drying is necessary before using the device, it is not urgent.

20. ☑ **B.** Holding down the Power button clears out any low-power-state modes the laptop might be holding in.
☒ **A** and **C** are incorrect because no keyboard keypresses can be recognized while the computer is in a low-power or off state. **D** is incorrect because shaking a laptop is not an effective solution for any problem and can damage it.

Chapter 15

Supporting Mobile Devices

CERTIFICATION OBJECTIVES

- **1101: 1.3** Given a scenario, set up and configure accessories and ports of mobile devices
- **1101: 1.4** Given a scenario, configure basic mobile-device network connectivity and application support
- **1101: 5.5** Given a scenario, troubleshoot common issues with mobile devices
- **1102: 2.7** Explain common methods for securing mobile and embedded devices
- **1102: 3.4** Given a scenario, troubleshoot common mobile OS and application issues
- **1102: 3.5** Given a scenario, troubleshoot common mobile OS and application security issues

✓ Two-Minute Drill

Q&A Self Test

Mobile computing was once solely the territory of the business traveler with laptop in tow, resting what was sometimes a hefty computer on knees in waiting rooms and on trays on airliners. Today that model of mobile computing seems quaint as more and more ordinary people are doing mobile computing with smaller, faster devices in more places—many of them not far from home. Tablets are issued to schoolchildren of all ages for delivering courseware content. And let's not even begin to talk about the use of smartphones among even the youngest of children.

In this chapter we explore mobile devices from the CompTIA A+ technician's perspective, focusing on device support and troubleshooting. You will learn how to configure network connectivity and application support in iOS and Android devices and how to synchronize data between a mobile device and a desktop or laptop PC. We'll also look at some common methods for securing mobile and embedded devices and troubleshooting mobile OS and application issues.

CERTIFICATION OBJECTIVES

- ***1101: 1.3*** *Given a scenario, set up and configure accessories and ports of mobile devices*
- ***1101: 1.4*** *Given a scenario, configure basic mobile-device network connectivity and application support*
- ***1102: 2.7*** *Explain common methods for securing mobile and embedded devices*

To prepare for CompTIA A+ 1101 exam Objective 1.4, this section details how to enable or disable Wi-Fi or cellular connections and how to configure them. It also describes how to enable Bluetooth for pairing with another device or computer, including the use of a PIN code for some devices, and how to test the connectivity. For 1101 exam Objective 1.4, you need to know the options for mobile device synchronization, including the software requirements to install synchronization apps on a PC, the connection types for synchronization, and the types of data to synchronize. Creating a mobile hotspot (tethering), also covered in this section, is listed under two different 1101 exam Objectives: 1.3 and 1.4. Finally, this section covers two topics from 1102 exam Objective 2.7: OS updates and remote backup applications.

Configuring and Using Mobile Device Connections

In this section we will describe how to connect your mobile device to three types of wireless networks: cellular, Wi-Fi, and Bluetooth. We also examine some useful tasks that rely on connectivity, including configuring e-mail, creating a hotspot, and data synchronization.

Connecting to Wireless Networks

As described earlier, smartphones and tablets come with network adapters for cellular data networks, Wi-Fi networks, or both. They also have Bluetooth connections for connecting to nearby devices. Now learn how to connect to these wireless networks.

Connecting to Cellular Networks

When you buy a smartphone or a tablet with cellular data capability, you make the choice at the point of sale concerning the cellular network to which you will subscribe, and you normally sign a contract for a certain level of service before you gain possession of the device (whether in person or over the Internet). Therefore, the actual configuration is done in the store; or in the case of a purchase over the Internet, all you need to do is enter credentials received from the cellular provider on the first use.

Connecting to Wi-Fi Networks

To connect to a Wi-Fi network for the first time, open the Settings app on your device. Then select the option for Wireless (or Wi-Fi) and turn on Wi-Fi, if necessary. In the list of available cellular networks, displayed by SSID, select one and enter the required password. Windows will remember this network, maintaining a list of Wi-Fi networks it has successfully connected to, as shown in Figure 15-1, and providing the password whenever it detects a network. If you travel, you will need to do this for each new Wi-Fi network you connect to.

exam watch

All radio frequency (RF) signals coming from mobile devices must be turned off when you fly on a commercial airliner. Therefore, smartphones and tablets have a mode called *airplane mode* that does just that, allowing you to continue using your device for access to locally stored data, while complying with the regulations. Look for it in the Settings app.

Creating a Mobile Hotspot (Tethering)

You can use a smartphone's cellular network connection to access the Internet when no Wi-Fi is available. Furthermore, you can share that cellular connection to the Internet with other nearby devices. For example, you can share your phone's Internet connection with your laptop when you are somewhere that cell service is available but Wi-Fi is not.

FIGURE 15-1 Turn on Wi-Fi and then connect to a detected network.

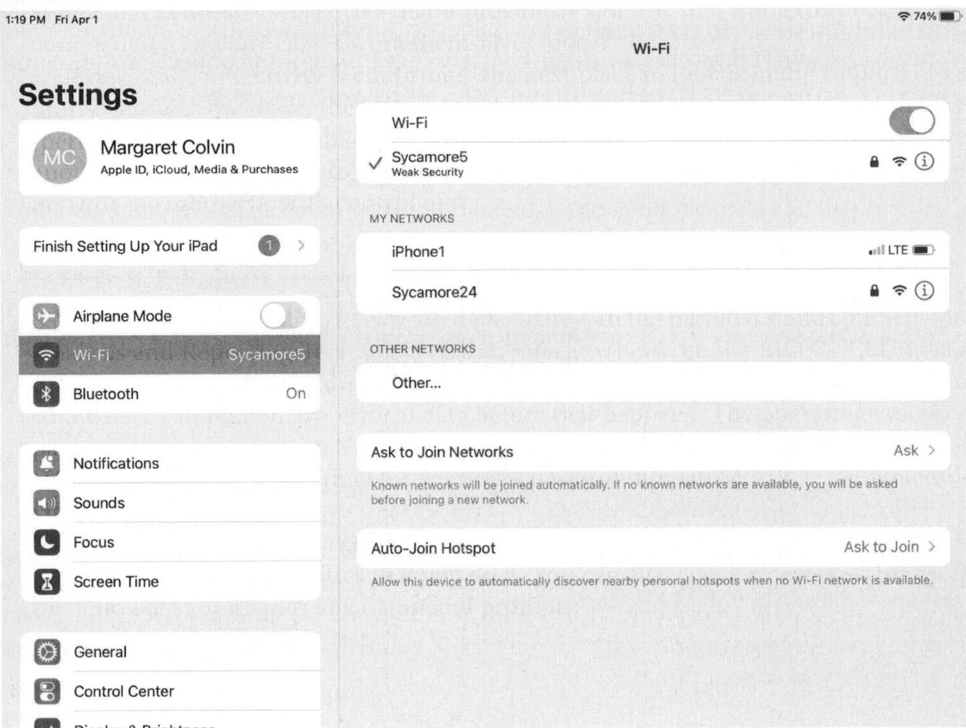

The phone becomes a *mobile hotspot*. This is also known as *tethering*. (Some people use the term *tethering* only when referring to a situation where you physically connect a smartphone to a computer via cable, but Android's OS settings use the term for a Wi-Fi hotspot too, and so do we.) You assign a PIN or password to the connection so that only authorized devices may access the connection.

In iOS, from the Home screen, tap Settings | Personal Hotspot and drag the slider to On. In Android, tap Settings, and in the Wireless Network section, tap More | Tethering & Portable Hotspot. In Windows Phone, tap Settings and then scroll down and tap Internet Sharing. Drag the slider to On.

Remember that creating a mobile hotspot means that other devices are going to be using up your cell plan's data allotment. Make sure you are aware of any potential overage charges you may incur. Even if you have unlimited data, you might still want to monitor and restrict usage because after a certain amount of data is used, some carriers reduce your data speed (known as *throttling*).

Connecting to Bluetooth Devices

Bluetooth, described in Chapter 14, is a wireless standard used for communicating over very short distances. You might want to use Bluetooth to connect a Bluetooth keyboard to your mobile device or to connect a mobile device to a PC or Mac to synchronize data. Bluetooth consumes battery power, so it is disabled by default. When you want to use Bluetooth, you first need to go into the Settings app on your mobile device and enable Bluetooth. Then enable it on your computer or Bluetooth device with which you wish to connect to so that they can discover (find) each other, which they will attempt to do as soon as Bluetooth is enabled. A connection between two Bluetooth devices is called a *pairing.* When both devices have discovered each other, go to the Settings screen on each one and select the other device for pairing. After a short pause, a message will display with a pairing code (also called a PIN code).

When connecting a keyboard, you will need to enter the code using the keyboard. When pairing a computer with a mobile device, you may simply need to confirm that the same pairing code shows on the screen for both devices. Finally, test connectivity between the devices. We have found that just entering the pairing code on a keyboard is not enough confirmation that the connection is working. You wouldn't want to set up a Bluetooth connection for a client and then find out after you leave that it didn't work for them. So in the case of a keyboard, open an app, such as an Internet browser, click in a box requiring text (such as an address box), and then start typing on the keyboard. If it does not work, you may not have confirmed the pairing on both sides (not always necessary). Although we have found that a failure to connect is often a case of impatience, if you have a problem with the pairing, disable Bluetooth on both devices and start over again. Refer to the section "Bluetooth Connectivity Issues" later in this chapter for more help.

CompTIA A+ 1101 exam Objective 1.4 lists steps in this order for setting up Bluetooth: enable Bluetooth, enable pairing, find device for pairing, enter the appropriate PIN code, and test connectivity. The objective does not make it clear that these are ordered steps, but they are.

E-mail Configuration

If you would like to use your mobile device to access your e-mail, you begin by adding the account, which requires first that you select the type of account.

Web-Based E-mail Accounts

For recognized web-based e-mail accounts, such as Microsoft 365, Outlook.com, Gmail (Google Workspace), iCloud, or Yahoo! mail, you do not have to specify a sending and receiving server. All you need to enter is your user name and password. That's because your mobile OS already knows the incoming and outgoing mail server addresses and ports for these commonly used systems. Just select the provider from the list and follow the prompts to complete the setup.

POP3 and IMAP Accounts

If you want to use an account type other than a web-based e-mail service, you will need server addresses obtained from your e-mail server administrator. To receive mail, you will need an address for either a Post Office Protocol 3 (POP3) server or Internet Message Access Protocol (IMAP) server that receives your incoming mail and forwards it to you. An e-mail client uses one or the other of these. To send mail, you usually need the address of your Simple Mail Transfer Protocol (SMTP) server that accepts your outgoing mail and forwards it to an e-mail server.

Although POP3 and IMAP e-mail setup on a mobile device is no longer an exam objective, you should still know how to configure them.

The addresses for these servers are not numeric. A POP3 address will simply be the name of a mail server in an Internet domain and may resemble this: pop.domainname.com. The address for an IMAP server might look something like this: imap.domainname.com. The SMTP address might look like this: smtp.domainname.com. These are just examples, so you need to get the actual addresses for these servers from your e-mail administrator. Some Internet service providers (ISPs) use mail server names that don't have anything to do with the actual domain name; for example, one uses pop.secureserver.net, imap.secureserver.net, and smtp-out.secureserver.net for all the thousands of domain names that it hosts.

Armed with the needed information, locate the e-mail settings on your mobile device and carefully enter the information. On an iPad open the Settings app and tap Mail. Then, in the right pane, tap Accounts | Add Account. Is the type of e-mail account you need to use listed? If it is, tap it and continue. If not, tap Other at the bottom of the list and then tap Add Mail Account. The New Account dialog box will display, along with the virtual keyboard (unless you have an external keyboard connected). Enter your name (not a user account name), e-mail address, password for that e-mail account, and a description for the e-mail account that will identify it for you in the list of accounts. Tap Next and follow the instructions, using the addresses you obtained from your e-mail server administrator, as shown in Figure 15-2. If you need to change the security settings for the account, edit the account's properties and choose Advanced to reach those settings.

On an Android device, you will have a Google account for accessing Google services, as well as a required Gmail account. In fact, the Email icon opens to Gmail. To configure another type of account in Android, open Settings, select Accounts, and then select Add Account. This opens the Setup Accounts screen that lists a variety of account types, not just e-mail accounts also but social networking sites, photo sharing sites, data backup sites, and other accounts added as you install certain apps.

FIGURE 15-2 Configuring a POP3 e-mail account

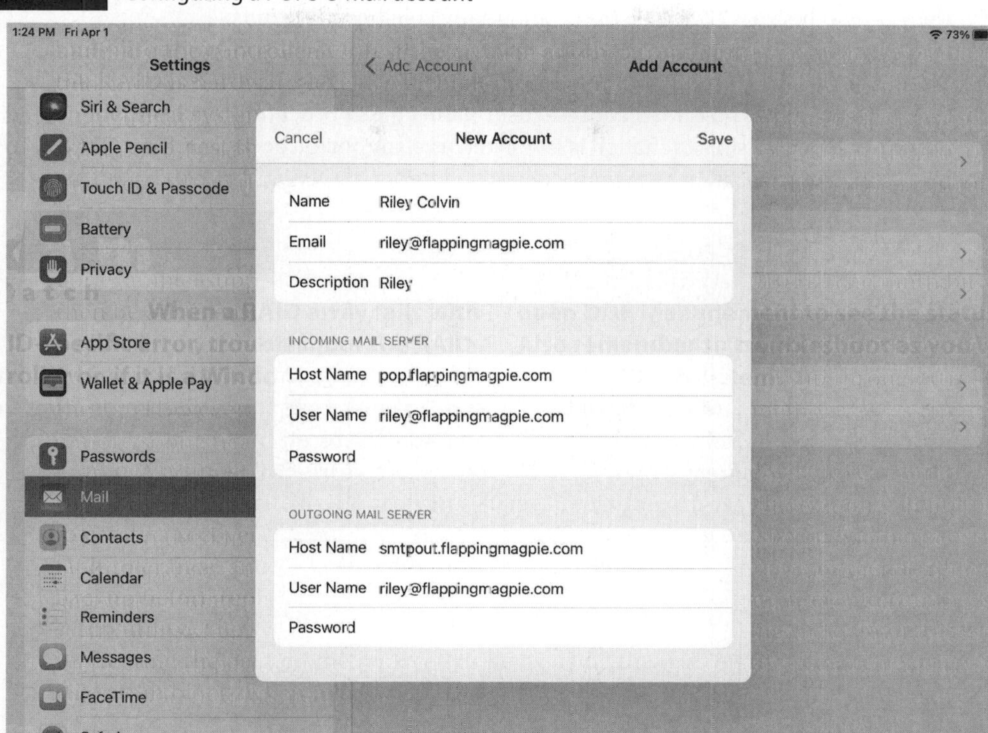

Tap Email and enter the account information described earlier. If your administrator indicates that your account requires a different port setting or needs a special Secure Sockets Layer (SSL) setting, tap Advanced Settings at the bottom of the Outgoing Server page. This will bring up a page for the port settings, as well as the security settings. The default port is 25 for outgoing e-mail. This page shows settings for Transport Layer Security (TLS), which is a protocol based on SSL. Do not change these settings unless your administrator requires it.

Configuring an Exchange/Office 365 Client

Many organizations use internally maintained Microsoft Exchange e-mail servers for employee e-mail accounts and for sending e-mail within the organization, as well as over the Internet. Organizations that contract with Microsoft for the Office 365 suite of applications may also have Exchange-based e-mail services included in that. Also, many hosting services for Internet domain names offer Exchange e-mail services to their clients. Exchange gives the organization full administrative control, while providing users with a central location for their e-mail history, contacts, tasks, and many collaborative tools.

If you need to connect your device to an Exchange server, first open Accounts from Settings and see if your device lists Microsoft Exchange as an account type. If it does, select it and enter the e-mail address, user name, password, and a description for the list of accounts. If Microsoft Exchange is not listed as a supported account type, you will need to manually configure it, as previously described under "POP3 and IMAP Accounts."

exam watch

All Exchange accounts stored in one Exchange accounts database are centrally managed by and belong to the organization owning the Exchange server and domain, such as a business or university. The same is true of corporate-managed Google Workspace accounts. In contrast, the individual accounts stored in iCloud, Gmail, and Outlook.com are centrally maintained and administered by Apple, Google, and Microsoft, respectively.

OS Updates

Installing OS updates can correct system problems, add more features, enhance security, and in some cases even change the user interface. The process of updating the OS is somewhat like that of updating the BIOS/UEFI on a PC motherboard in that it is stored in read-only memory and updates are "flashed" to it.

When an update is available for a smartphone, you might see an on-screen message alerting you and inviting you to tap a button to allow the update to proceed. On the other hand, you might have to go looking for an update in the Settings app to see whether one is available. In iOS, choose Settings | General | Software Update, for example. Just follow the prompts to install the update after making sure that the device has sufficient battery charge left (at least 50 percent) or is plugged into alternating current (AC) power. An OS update may take a half-hour or more, so be prepared to be without the use of your phone for that time.

Trouble with the OS update? See the section "OS Fails to Update" later in this chapter.

Synchronization

When you have multiple computing devices, who knows which device you might be using at any given moment? Desktop…tablet…cell phone—they're all in constant rotation. You might send an e-mail or create a document on any one of them and then want to refer to it later on another. To make that possible, you need to *synchronize,* or *sync,* certain data.

When data is synchronized between two devices or locations, the files are examined and newer files replace the older files—sometimes, but not always, in both directions. Synching data can also be a backup, an insurance policy against losing your data if a mobile device is lost or stolen.

What kind of data can/should you sync? CompTIA A+ 1101 exam Objective 1.4 recommends this list:

- Mail
- Photos
- Calendar
- Contacts

You can synchronize either to another device, such as a desktop PC, or to a cloud service, such as iCloud. Many synchronization programs offer you the opportunity to choose between those two options and to specify an exact location in each one.

If you synchronize with a computer, you can do it either with a cable (usually USB) or in some cases wirelessly, via a Wi-Fi connection. Syncing to a cloud-based service occurs through an Internet connection—whether it is via a Wi-Fi connection or through a cellular connection.

Depending on the device and OS, a specific cloud service may be the recommended default. For example, for Apple devices, iCloud is the default service. Synchronizing with iCloud has many advantages, such as being able to restore your data and personal information easily if your device locks up and must be reset to factory settings.

You don't necessarily have to choose between local and cloud synchronization. You can do both. Alternatively, you can set up both devices to synchronize to the same account on the same cloud service so they keep each other synchronized that way.

Connecting Mobile Devices for Syncing

You can sync your smartphone or tablet with your computer, either locally with a USB cable or over the Internet using a cloud-based service. For the local option, use the USB cable that came with the smartphone, usually attached to an AC adapter for charging. Disconnect it from the AC adapter. Connect the end previously connected to the power supply (usually a standard USB connector) to the computer and connect the other end to the device. On Android smartphones, this will usually be a micro USB connector; on an iPad or iPhone and some other tablets, it is a Lightning or USB-C connector. On some devices, this connection will cause two programs to run on the computer—one from your cell provider (if the device has cellular service) for configuring your online account (if you already have one, you simply log in) and a second one that is device specific and aids in transferring files.

Some newer automobiles may also enable you to sync your smartphone to their internal computer, either via USB cable or Bluetooth. The instructions for doing so can be found in the automobile's owner's manual.

exam watch

CompTIA A+ 1101 exam Objective 1.4, mobile device synchronization section, asks you to be able to configure synchronization via account setup for three specific types of accounts: Microsoft 365, Google Workspace, and iCloud. As a study aid, do a web search for each of those account types plus "synchronization setup" to locate instructions and videos that show you how to set up each of those account types for synchronization.

Syncing iPhones and iPads

You can use Apple iTunes for syncing an iPhone and iPad with a Mac or PC. iTunes comes with all Apple computers and is a free download for Windows PCs. Although it is best known as a music player, it also has the side use of being a synchronization utility for Apple devices.

You may also want to explore the iCloud desktop app for Windows or Mac. This app enables you to configure your cloud-based storage. You can specify what kinds of data should be synced in the cloud (Photos, Contacts, Bookmarks) and how it is stored. See Figure 15-3.

exam watch

CompTIA A+ 1101 exam Objective 1.4 includes "Recognizing data caps." This refers to being aware of any limitations on the amount of data that can be transferred in a certain time period (such as a monthly limit on cellular data). It can also refer to any limits that an Exchange server's administrators may place on individual user accounts. Normally synchronization of business data would not push an account over a limit, but synchronizing very large files like videos and music clips might.

FIGURE 15-3 Use the iCloud desktop app to configure cloud-based storage.

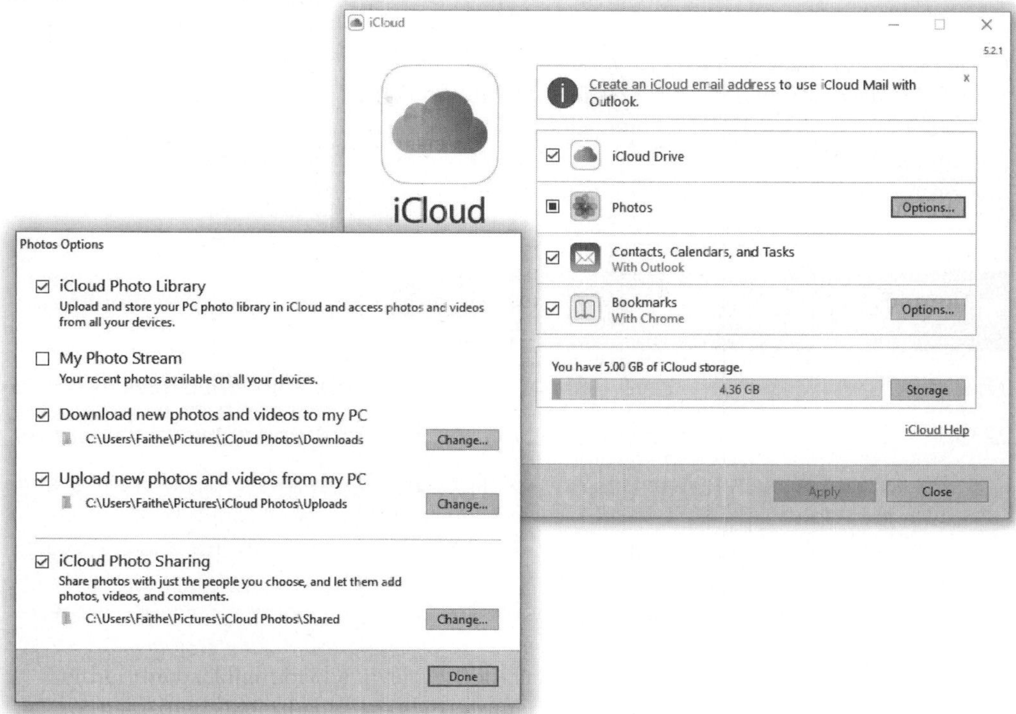

Another option that is more of a backup than a syncing option is iCloud. This data is available to all devices from any location with Internet access.

Syncing Android Devices

When you connect an Android device to your computer, it is treated like an external drive, and you can copy files back and forth. Strictly speaking, this isn't syncing. There are individual solutions for various types of data. For instance, when you create a contact in Android, it asks you to pick an account to store (or back up) the contact information. The choices are Google or one provided by your cellular carrier. Select Google, and your contacts will be automatically backed up and synced to Google over the Internet, either through a cell connection or via Wi-Fi. After all, who do you expect to have the longest relationship with, Google or your cell provider? We use Google to back up our contacts because it will be available to use if we cancel the contract with the cell provider.

Using a Different Cloud Sync/Backup Service

Phone OSs make it painless and easy to back up using their preferred provider, but you can also use other cloud backup providers, regardless of your phone model.

For example, Google Sync works with iOS devices to synchronize them with a Google Workspace or Gmail account. This can be useful if your phone is Apple but you prefer Google's cloud as your backup location. Android devices don't require Google Sync. Similarly, there are OneDrive synchronization apps for Android and iOS. iCloud is available on Android via a synchronization app as well.

CERTIFICATION OBJECTIVES

- ***1102: 2.7*** *Explain common methods for securing mobile and embedded devices*
- ***1102: 3.5*** *Given a scenario, troubleshoot common mobile OS and application security issues*

This section covers the many methods of hardware- and software-based security and user authentication available on mobile devices, including the list of topics from CompTIA A+ 1102 exam Objective 2.7, such as screen locks, antivirus/antimalware, and corporate policies and procedures that promote good security. It also looks at OS and application security issues covered in A+ 1102 exam Objective 3.5. The balance of that objective is covered later, in Chapter 22.

Securing Mobile Devices

Mobile devices have become a security issue in many organizations for the very reason that mobile devices are part of the CompTIA A+ 220-1101 and 220-1102 exams: they have become ubiquitous and have come into the workplace, both by invitation when required for work and as party crashers when users bring their favorite mobile devices to work, even connecting them to the corporate intranet. The act of bringing your own device from home to a workplace or organization is known as *bring your own device (BYOD).* System administrators have much less control over BYOD devices than they do corporate-owned devices.

One way that businesses combat the potential security problems from BYOD is with firm *policies and procedures* that dictate how personal devices should be configured and should connect to the company network. As you learned in Chapter 2, such a policy is often called an *acceptable-use policy (AUP),* and employees may have to sign it as a condition of employment. For example, an AUP might specify that employees cannot use mobile devices that have been "cracked," meaning the devices have been modified to allow them to run untrusted applications from nonstandard app stores. Such applications can make the device (and the network) more vulnerable to malware. An AUP might also have *profile security requirements,* such as requiring a complex password rather than a simple four-digit passcode.

To meet the challenges of supporting mobile devices in the workplace, you need to know about the hardware and software tools and features available for making mobile devices more secure, thereby protecting not only the devices but also the valuable (and perhaps confidential) data that they can access.

Mobile Security Risks

There are several risks in using a mobile device, including unauthorized device access, spying, unauthorized use of the cellular data plan to access the Internet (on smartphones and tablets with cellular service), and malware. Let's look at each of those risks in more detail.

Unauthorized Device and Account Access

Unauthorized device access occurs when someone other than the owner is able to physically gain access to the device without permission. This can happen if there is no lock password on the device or if the person is able to circumvent or guess the password. Unauthorized account access occurs when the intruder is able to gain access to the owner's personal accounts or data as a result of gaining physical access to the device. The intruder is then able to snoop personal documents and notes and even sign into online services where data is stored.

The best way to prevent unauthorized device access is with a strong screen lock authentication. See "Sign-in Authentication," later in this chapter, to learn about the available options.

exam watch **Make sure you understand the risks involved in using root access/jailbreak to make changes to system files.**

Root Access/Jailbreak On an Android device, it is possible for an intruder to gain *root access,* which allows the user to access the Android operating system itself to make changes to system files. This can result in malware being installed or the OS not working properly. This is called *rooting,* and it usually requires specialized rooting software. On an iOS-based device such as an iPhone, this process is called jailbreaking, although it's more difficult to do.

on the job **By default, Android devices don't allow root access. However, some users choose to "root their phones" to install unauthorized applications or to remove preinstalled applications put there by the wireless carrier. This can wreak havoc with security and should be strongly discouraged.**

Location Services If a device is missing, you can use *location services* to locate it (if location services is enabled), initiate a loud alarm on the device, and/or do a *remote wipe* (deleting all contents) of your device, making it effectively unusable by anyone who steals or finds it. Location services use the device's GPS capabilities and/or cellular location services like the ones that emergency services use to locate a device's last known location based on what cellular towers they accessed.

However, location services can also present a privacy or security risk. Someone gaining unauthorized access to a device may surreptitiously enable location-tracking software that can send data back to the hacker remotely to track the location of the device owner without his or her knowledge. Turning off location services can also prevent people from broadcasting their location when posting pictures or status updates to social media.

exam watch **Make sure you know how to turn location services on and off on both Android and iOS smartphones.**

Android Package (APK) Source On Android devices, you can choose to acquire applications from unofficial sources in addition to getting them from the Play Store. CompTIA A+ 1102 exam Objective 3.5 calls this concern *Android package (APK) source.* If you don't know the source of the application you are installing, you can't be sure it is safe. When you use an untrusted source, you run the risk of introducing malware into your system or installing poorly written apps that crash.

exam watch **Make sure you understand the importance of knowing the source of an APK and what can happen if you install an untrusted app.**

Developer Mode Another way that Android phones can be compromised is via *Developer mode.* The Developer options menu on an Android device is hidden by default, but anyone who knows how can unhide it and then activate it to gain access to advanced features that can lessen security. The exact process depends on the version of the OS, but one method is Settings | About Device (or About Phone) and then scroll down and tap Build Number seven times. This places a Developer options menu on the Settings menu.

Antivirus/Antimalware Software

Because Android devices allow users to install apps from untrusted sources, these sources place the device at risk for *malware.* Some applications function as Trojan horses, appearing to do something useful but also compromising or infecting the system. Antivirus software can help detect this, but the best policy is to only install apps from official/trusted sources.

Bootleg/malicious applications sometimes trick unsuspecting users into revealing their sign-in credentials via *application spoofing,* which means to mimic a legitimate app. For example, a malware app might appear to be the app from a bank.

Malware creators historically haven't paid much attention to mobile OSs, and in fact Apple doesn't even recommend antivirus software for iOS. However, malware is still a threat, especially on Android devices, and can result in the same kinds of problems as on a desktop computer, including power drain, performance slowdown, and slow data speeds. Malware (including the symptoms of malware infection on mobile devices, per 1102 exam Objective 3.5) is covered in detail in Chapter 22.

Spying

Spying can take many forms. The simplest kind is ordinary *shoulder surfing,* where someone watches you as you use your device. It's harder to spy on a smartphone or tablet screen from a distance because it's smaller than a desktop or laptop screen, but it still happens.

Spying can also include unauthorized *location tracking,* as mentioned in the previous section. Someone who has had physical access to your device can install a tracking device or tracking software on it. With certain spyware installed on your device without your knowledge, the hacker can also access your microphone and camera to spy on you visually or aurally.

Unauthorized Wi-Fi or Bluetooth Connection

If your smartphone includes a tethering/mobile hotspot feature, you can share your Internet connection with others. The downside of that is someone could guess or hack the password for that connection and use your phone as a hotspot without your permission. This might result in data overages for you, as well as slow application performance as your phone's processor handles the increased processing load (high resource utilization).

A hacker could also potentially connect his or her device to yours via Wi-Fi or Bluetooth without your permission to transfer files, install malware, or collect personal information. One way to secure your device against such threats is to turn off Wi-Fi and Bluetooth connectivity when you are not using them.

Mobile Security Tools

Now that you're aware of the security risks, let's look at how those risks can be mitigated.

Sign-in Authentication

When a mobile device is at rest, a lock screen appears, usually with some picture of your choice and the current date and time. When you swipe or tap, the device wakes up. This is called a *swipe lock.* A swipe lock provides no security; it just keeps you from butt-dialing people.

Mobile devices usually have a setting for a passcode lock. A *passcode lock* restricts access to a device by requiring a login to the device using a pattern (screen gestures you choose), a *PIN code,* or password after swiping to wake the device up. On Android devices look for Set Up Screen Lock Settings under Location And Security Settings.

You should require a login for access to your mobile device. On an iOS device, you can make your login more secure by using a complex password, rather than the standard simple passcode. Note that the Auto-Lock option only sets the amount of time of inactivity before a device locks, but this does not, on its own, require a passcode. If you don't require a passcode, you simply use a swipe to close the lock screen and access the device.

Some devices also employ *biometric authentication* as an option. Biometric authentication verifies the user's identity by examining some part of their body. For example, some iPhones include a *fingerprint scanner* on the Home button, and newer iPhones and Android phones use the built-in camera to do facial recognition for authentication, also called a *face lock* or *facial recognition.*

When a device requires more than one authentication method, it's known as *multifactor authentication*. For example, a device might ask for both a passcode and facial recognition for extra security. Most devices don't offer multifactor authentication in the OS, but you can install *authenticator applications* that enable that option.

Restrictions for Failed Login Attempts

Some devices put restrictions (or consequences) on multiple consecutive failed password attempts. For example, you can set up a smartphone so that there is a lockout period of several minutes after a certain number of failed password attempts. This prevents someone from repeatedly guessing the password quickly. Eventually guessing it is still possible, but it will take the hacker much longer. Some devices also enable you to turn on a feature that will erase the data on the device after a certain number of failed login attempts.

Security Software

Many security programs are available for mobile devices with such features as antivirus, antispam, browsing protection, *firewalls,* and privacy features that will alert you if an app attempts to access your private information (e.g., location, contacts, and messages). These inexpensive security suites also include backup features and missing device features. Apple devices are less prone to viruses because of the closed nature of their application delivery system; the Apple Store vets all apps before they are released to the public. However, this does not stop Apple devices from being prone to other threats, such as spam, visits to websites containing malware, and invasion of privacy from phishing and other threats outlined in Chapter 22.

Device Encryption

Device encryption encrypts all the data on the phone so that it cannot be booted except by someone with the PIN code or password. On some devices, encryption is synonymous with the lock screen passcode that you learned about earlier in this chapter. On other devices, notably some Android devices, you can choose to encrypt your data separately from setting a passcode. You still use the same passcode to gain entry, but if you don't know the passcode, it's harder to hack into the device to get at the data than if encryption is not enabled. Some versions of Android also let you set a separate encryption password.

Why would you set a separate encryption password from the lock screen password? It's primarily to balance security with convenience. The encryption password is required only when rebooting, so you can use a stronger, more complex password for it. You can leave the lock screen passcode as a simple number for quick availability.

Be aware when you are using your mobile device on a Wi-Fi network, especially when using a public access point that is not password protected. All the devices connected to the same router are effectively on a LAN together. Do not send and receive sensitive information on an unsecure network, no matter what kind of device you are using.

Recovering After a Device Is Lost or Stolen

All the major mobile device OSs include features that help you when your device is lost or stolen, so don't panic. These are the major tools in the arsenal:

- Locators, which can use Internet and cell tower usage to determine your device's location
- *Remote wipe features,* which can erase all the data on the device remotely the next time it connects to the Internet
- Information utilities that enable you to send a message to your lost device so that whoever has it will see it and be able to contact you (if it was lost, rather than stolen)

If it's an Android device and is signed into a Google account, you can use the Android Device Manager (on any device with a web browser) to show your device's location. For this to work, the device must have a Wi-Fi connection or mobile data connection and an active SIM card. In other words, it doesn't work for devices where the finder doesn't want it to be located. The Android Device Manager also allows you to remotely contact, lock, or erase the device.

On an iOS device, sign into iCloud using a web browser and select Find iPhone. Then click All Devices and select the desired device. The next step depends on whether you think you lost the iOS device or it was stolen. If you think you lost it and that someone has found it and the person who has it might want to return it to you, click Lost Mode. Lost Mode locks the device with a passcode (if you didn't already have one set) so that others can't access your personal information. It also displays a custom message on the screen, such as how to contact you. If you think your device was stolen and you want to delete all the data on it, click Erase iPhone to perform a remote wipe.

CERTIFICATION OBJECTIVES

- ***1101: 5.5*** *Given a scenario, troubleshoot common issues with mobile devices*
- ***1102: 3.4*** *Given a scenario, troubleshoot common mobile OS and application issues*
- ***1102: 3.5*** *Given a scenario, troubleshoot common mobile OS and application security issues*

This section covers parts of three major objectives, all having to do with mobile troubleshooting. CompTIA A+ 1101 exam Objective 5.5 looks at hardware issues with mobile devices, such as overheating, poor battery health, and digitizer issues, and the procedures used to remediate those issues. Some of these were also covered in Chapter 14 in the context of laptops, and the problems and solutions are similar here.

CompTIA A+ 1102 exam Objective 3.4 contains software troubleshooting topics like applications failing to launch and connectivity issues. Also covered are common symptoms listed in 1102 exam Objective 3.5, such as high network traffic, limited or no Internet connectivity, and fake security warnings. These objectives have a lot of topics in common, so you'll see quite a bit of overlap.

Troubleshooting Mobile Device Problems

To round out this chapter, we will next look at some of the many things that can go wrong with mobile devices and how to fix them.

Hardware Issues

Hardware issues include problems with the hardware components on the device, such as the touch screen and the battery. Be aware, however, that sometimes software issues will manifest themselves as problems with hardware. For example, background-running applications might be the underlying cause of short battery life.

Digitizer/Touch Screen Issues

If the touch screen doesn't produce any response in the OS, the device is probably locked up. Use hardware buttons to do a soft reset (reboot). If it still has no response after the reboot, try a hard reset (a factory reset). If that doesn't work, the device will need to be professionally serviced by a technician trained in mobile devices.

Keep in mind that most touch screens are *capacitive,* which means they respond to the electrical charge in a person's finger. They don't respond very well to gloved fingers or styluses not specifically designed for touch screen use. So first, make sure you are using a clean, dry finger on the screen.

Next, make sure the screen is clean and accessible. Wipe it with a soft, slightly damp, lint-free cloth. If you are using a screen protector on the device, remove it.

Restart the device. If it won't restart normally, force-stop it and restart it, as explained later in this chapter. After you restart the device, if the touch screen fails its startup diagnostic, you likely have a hardware problem. You can attempt to replace the touch screen yourself, but if you're not familiar with disassembly and assembly of mobile devices, you could easily break something; it's better to enlist the help of someone who repairs mobile devices for a living.

You can also employ diagnostics tools to check the screen. On an Android phone, you can use the Device Diagnostics Tool, for example. For more information about this tool, check out online resources.

If you touch one spot and your touch registers in another spot, that's a screen calibration issue, which is a disparity of positions between the display part of the screen and the touch-sensitive input part of the screen. Lack of calibration should not be a problem on capacitive screens because of their technology, so this is not an issue on devices that have capacitive screens (like most modern iPhones, for example). Check in the Settings app for a calibration utility. If there isn't one, your screen is probably capacitive.

It's easy to say that calibration shouldn't be an issue, of course, but what if it is anyway? If you experience calibration problems and you don't have access to a calibration utility, try doing a hard reset on the device or take it to a repair shop to have them replace the digitizer.

Overheating

Does your mobile device get hot? This used to be a bigger problem than it is today, back when phone batteries were bigger and bulkier. On some models overheating may still occur today, however, especially on devices with removable batteries. A few years ago, the Samsung Galaxy Note 7 had an issue with overheating and catching fire, for example, and a massive recall was issued.

First, where is your device getting hot? If it's on the back, it might be a problem with the battery. Try a different battery (if the battery is removable, which used to be more common than it is today). If it gets hot on the bottom and only when plugged into AC power, there may be an issue with the charger. Try a different charger if possible. If it gets hot above the battery compartment (if there is one), the device itself is probably overheating. This is also true if the device heats up near the speaker (where you put your ear when talking if it's a phone) or if the heat is coming from the screen.

Overheating can occur when you have many applications open simultaneously because this puts a strain on the CPU to run continuously, generating heat. Watching downloaded movies or streaming video on a device can also cause it to overheat because of the constant activity of the screen, memory, and CPU. Give your device time to rest and cool off. Carrying your phone in a pocket or other enclosed area can also contribute to overheating, as can using a tight case that doesn't allow for any ventilation.

Disabling unneeded background applications and features can also help keep the device cool. For example, if you aren't using Bluetooth or Wi-Fi, turn them off in the Settings app.

Do not put a mobile device into a refrigerator or freezer to cool it off. Moisture can condense on the circuitry, causing a short-circuit.

Frozen System

If your phone suddenly seizes up when you are using it, there could be a number of different root causes. If the screen goes dark, you have probably run out of battery. Try connecting it to AC power.

If power wasn't the issue, try a soft reset. If that doesn't work, try a hard reset. See "Resetting a Mobile Device," later in this chapter.

Power Drain/Short Battery Life/Battery Not Charging

Devices are designed to put themselves into a low-power mode after a few minutes of inactivity. If they're on constantly, the battery gets drained fairly quickly. Make sure that the device's Lock Timeout setting is set as low as you can tolerate without finding it annoying for maximum battery life.

If the device appears completely lifeless, its battery is probably drained. If charging the battery does not solve the problem, the display hardware may have failed or the device may need a soft or hard reset. See "Resetting a Mobile Device" later in this chapter.

exam watch

Battery problems on mobile devices are listed in two different objectives: 1101 exam Objective 5.5 calls it "Poor battery health" (referring to physical issues with the battery) and 1102 exam Objective 3.4 calls it "Battery life issues" (referring to software problems that result in poor battery life).

A battery that just plain drains quickly may be in need of replacement. On a device with a replaceable battery, just buy the kind you need and swap them out. On a device with a built-in battery, battery replacement can be complicated and can void the warranty, so consider using an authorized repair shop or an Apple Store. Before you replace the battery, though, try restarting the device; occasionally a device will get an application that is "stuck" running, and that application's activity will cause the battery to drain quickly. Restarting can shake that off.

It's rare these days to have a swollen or leaking battery, but it does happen, mainly on older cell phones and tablets. The battery compartment may appear bulging, and the battery may leak or have crystalized residue on the outside. Avoid touching the battery and get help from a professional trained to service mobile device hardware.

Poor/No Connectivity

In this section we look at problems involving data and connectivity, including cell service, Bluetooth, and Wi-Fi.

exam watch

Mobile device connectivity is covered in several objectives. This isn't unnecessary duplication, though, because each instance refers to a specific context. 1101 exam Objective 5.5 calls it "Poor/ no connectivity," referring to hardware problems. 1102 exam Objective 3.4 calls it "Connectivity issues" and lists four specific types of connectivity: Bluetooth, Wi-Fi, NFC, and AirDrop, each of which can be enabled/configured via software. 1102 exam Objective 3.5 lists "Limited Internet connectivity" and "No internet connectivity" under the "Common symptoms" heading, referring to issues caused by security breaches.

Wi-Fi Connectivity Issues

Using cellular data to surf the Internet on a wireless device can eat up your data plan allotment quickly, so you will want to connect to a Wi-Fi network whenever it is available. When a wireless network is in range that you have already connected to, it may reconnect automatically. If you aren't getting a wireless connection, however, check these things:

- Make sure there is a wireless access point (WAP) or router nearby that is offering Wi-Fi service. If you have another Wi-Fi–enabled device, connect to that access point with it if you can.
- Make sure Wi-Fi is enabled on your device. Sometimes you might turn it off to save battery life when you don't need it and then forget you have done so.
- Verify that you have the right password for the router or WAP.

Intermittent Wi-Fi access can be the result of the same sort of problems that you might face on a desktop or laptop computer that has Wi-Fi. Check the following:

- Check the distance from the WAP or router. Get closer to it if possible.
- Do a soft reset of the device.
- Reset the router or WAP if you can access it.

Bluetooth Connectivity Issues

Bluetooth can be turned on and off in the device's Settings app; don't forget to check that setting if Bluetooth isn't working. Refer to "Connecting to Bluetooth Devices" earlier in this chapter for pairing directions.

If your Bluetooth adapter is working but you can't pair with devices, here are some tips:

- Determine what pairing process the device uses. The process can vary. Sometimes you can enter a code; other times you just touch the device to the accessory you want to pair it with or hold down a button.
- Move away from nearby Wi-Fi routers and USB 3.0 ports, both of which may generate interference.
- Make sure the devices you are trying to pair can connect with each other.
- Make sure your device's Bluetooth is set to be discoverable.
- Make sure the two devices are close enough to one another.
- Power-cycle each device.
- Power down any devices that may be interfering with the pairing, such as other Bluetooth devices in the area.
- If the device has been paired in the past but won't pair now, delete its information from your device and rediscover it.
- Investigate whether you need to install a driver for the accessory.
- Investigate whether a firmware update is available for either device.

NFC Connectivity Issues

Near-field communication (NFC) enables some mobile devices to connect to nearby devices wirelessly. One common use for NFC with smartphones is to connect a smartphone to a payment processing terminal to pay for purchases via credit card in a digital wallet (as with Apple Pay on an iPhone).

If the NFC function isn't working, do the following:

- Make sure the device supports NFC; older ones may not. (For example, iPhones must be version 7 or later with iOS version 11 or later.)
- Make sure your device has an NFC reader app installed, if one is needed for that model. (Check the documentation.) You should be able to get a free NFC reader app from the appropriate store for your OS.
- Adjust NFC in the device's settings if needed.
  - On Android, go to Settings | Connected Devices | Connection Preferences | NFC Options.
  - On an iPhone, go to Settings | General | AirDrop to control NFC file transfer, or Settings | Wallet & Apple Pay to control NFC for payments.

On iPhones, certain models have an NFC tag reader that you can enable from Settings | Control Center so that it appears in the Control Center. Other models (notably newer ones) have a background tag reader capability that automatically detects NFC connection opportunities without having to activate the tag reader from the Control Center.

AirDrop Connectivity Issues

AirDrop is an Apple iOS feature that enables you to transfer files (such as pictures, videos, and contact information) between nearby iPhones. If it isn't working, try the following:

- Toggle Wi-Fi and Bluetooth off and back on again. AirDrop uses Wi-Fi and Bluetooth to transfer files, so if either isn't working, it won't function.
- Make sure the other device you are trying to connect with is compatible with AirDrop. (Most iPhones and iPads are compatible, provided they run iOS 7 or later.)
- If you are trying to connect with a device where the user isn't in your contacts list, change the AirDrop setting (Settings | General | AirDrop) to Everyone temporarily. (It's set by default to Contacts Only.)
- Reboot both devices. See "Resetting a Mobile Device" later in this chapter.
- Check to see if an OS update is available (Settings | General | Software Update) and if so, install it.
- Reset networks (Settings | General | Reset | Reset Network Settings).

Make sure you know how to troubleshoot NFC and AirDrop connectivity issues on both iOS and Android devices.

Unintended Wi-Fi Connection or Bluetooth Pairing

If you have established a Wi-Fi connection with a WAP or router in the past, it may connect automatically when the device is within range, even if you don't intend it to. To prevent this, go into Settings and disconnect manually from the access point. To be extra sure it won't happen again, turn off Wi-Fi.

The same goes for Bluetooth. A previous pairing may repeat itself automatically. Disconnect it manually in Settings. Turn off Bluetooth for extra assurance that it won't connect.

Application Issues

Issues with individual apps may manifest as applications not loading at all, performing poorly, locking up, or using more system resources than they should.

If an application won't launch, fails to close, or crashes, rebooting the device (soft reset) is likely to help. If not, try reinstalling the application or perhaps just giving up on it and trying a different application. When an application malfunctions, it may run slowly, or it may use more than its allotted share of memory, making other concurrently running applications run slowly. This problem is usually caused by an error in the application's code. If it's an error in the copy of the application on your device, you might be able to fix it by uninstalling and reinstalling the application. If it's a bug in the application itself, there's not much you can do other than search for a newer version of it. The same goes for an application that runs poorly (slowly in general or starting and stopping). There may be clues in the Application log as to what is happening as well.

When an application fails to update, it's usually because the newer version of the app is not compatible with the operating system version. Try updating the OS and then retrying the application update.

OS Fails to Update

An OS update failure can have several possible root causes:

- If it's an older device, the new OS version may not be compatible with it. Check the documentation for the new OS version to make sure your device is on the supported list.
- Some large OS updates may require that the battery charge be above a certain level (such as 50%) to avoid problems that might occur should the device lose battery power during the update.
- Some large OS updates may require the device to be connected to Wi-Fi.
- An OS update may require a download to your device's local storage, and if there's not enough room, the update may not be possible. Free up some storage space by transferring some photos, music, or videos.
- Try re-downloading the update. It is possible that a glitch during the original download corrupted the setup file.

Screen Does Not Auto-Rotate

When you tilt a mobile device on its side, the screen should rotate if the app you are using supports it. (Not all apps do.) Check to see if other apps (or the Home screen) will auto-rotate to determine whether the problem is with a specific app. If it is, try stopping and restarting that app. You can also try rebooting the device.

If auto-rotation isn't working at all, the auto-rotation feature may be turned off in the OS. Try toggling the auto-rotation feature in the device's settings. On an Android, it's System | Display | Auto-Rotate Screen.

On an iPhone, Portrait orientation can be locked on. On an iPad, either Portrait or Landscape orientation can be locked on. To check, open the Control Center (swipe down from the upper-right corner) and make sure that Portrait Orientation Lock (or Landscape Orientation Lock if using an iPad) is not activated. Tap its button to turn it off if needed.

Random Reboots

Hardware damage is a possible cause of a mobile device that restarts for no apparent reason. Was the device dropped or did it suffer water damage? Is it overheating?

After hardware has been ruled out, next consider the OS. A recent OS update may have introduced a bug that is causing the reboots. On the other end of the spectrum, a device that needs an OS update may also reboot spontaneously, and installing the latest OS version may fix the problem.

Apps may also cause reboots. A poorly written app can cause the whole device to reboot. On an Android device, you can disable certain system apps, and if another app relies on one of those, trying to access that app may cause a reboot.

To completely rule out software problems, a factory reset may be needed.

Be sure you are familiar with troubleshooting common mobile OS and application issues. Exam 1102 Objective 3.4 specifically wants you to know how to handle apps failing to launch, closing/crashing, and failing to update, as well as random reboots and screens not auto-rotating.

Closing, Uninstalling, and Reinstalling Mobile Applications

If you suspect a problem with an application, uninstall it. The process for doing so depends on the OS. You can then reinstall a clean copy of it from a trusted source.

If an application is running, you might not be able to remove it until you shut it down completely. One way is to reboot the device. Another way is simply to close the application.

Quitting an app on iOS is easy. On a model with a Home button, double-press the Home button, swipe to the app you want to force-quit, and then swipe it up to close it. On a model without a Home button, swipe up to see the open apps, and then swipe right or left to select the one to close, and then swipe up again to close it.

On Android devices there is an option called *Force Stop* that enables you to shut down an application completely so it can be removed. If you attempt to remove an application but its Uninstall or Remove button is unavailable, use the Force Stop button to shut it down and then remove it. If both the Uninstall and Force Stop buttons are unavailable, it's a system app and you cannot uninstall it.

Resetting a Mobile Device

There are two kinds of resets. A *soft reset,* also called a *force-restart,* is basically just a reboot. Sometimes when a device locks up or starts acting squirrelly, a soft reset will do the trick. A *hard reset* (also called a *factory reset* or *clean install*) wipes out everything on the device and takes it back to its original factory settings. (You want to avoid doing that if possible because you lose everything you've stored.)

Sometimes a hard reset is the fastest and easiest way to ensure that your device doesn't have any virus or other security-compromising malware on it. Some may say a hard reset is overkill, but if your device is experiencing puzzling symptoms, a hard reset beats spending weeks of trying various fixes and hoping for the best.

Resetting a Device

To reset an Android device, you will want to access the Factory Data Reset screen. The tricky part is that different phone brands and models access this screen differently. Look up the exact steps for your model online. On one of our phones, for example, with it powered off, you can hold down Volume Down and Power together. When you see the brand logo, you release the Power button only, and then immediately press it again, and then you release both buttons when the Factory Reset Data screen appears. If that sounds as awkward as a game of Twister…it is. It's difficult on purpose, so you don't do it accidentally.

To reset an iOS device, you need a computer with iTunes installed. Connect the device to the computer and open iTunes. Then do one of the following:

- **iPhone 8 and newer** Press and hold Volume Up while you press and release Volume Down. Then press and hold the top button until the phone restarts in recovery mode.
- **iPhone 7** Press and hold the top button (or right button in some cases) and the Volume Down button. Release the buttons when the phone restarts in recovery mode.
- **iPhone 6 and earlier** Press and hold the Home button and the top (or right) button. Release the buttons when the phone restarts in recovery mode.

In each of these cases, do *not* release the buttons when you see the regular Apple logo; keep holding them until you see the Recovery Mode screen.

A message appears in iTunes that there's a problem with the device that requires it to be updated or restored. Click Update and wait for iTunes to fix the device. iTunes will attempt to repair the OS without deleting your data and apps. If this doesn't work, you can do a hard reset by repeating the process, but click Restore instead of Update at the end.

Getting Your Data Back After a Hard Reset

If you're lucky enough to have backed up or synched the device's settings before the disaster occurred, you can restore them as follows.

On an Android device, after a hard reset, you are prompted to walk through a setup process. As part of it, you're prompted to sign in to Google. When you do so with the same Gmail account you used for synching, your data is automatically restored to the device.

On an iOS device, when the device comes back up after a hard reset, the Setup Assistant runs. Go to Set Up Your Device, tap Restore From a Backup, and sign in to iCloud. Tap Choose Backup, and then select the backup you want to use and follow the prompts.

CERTIFICATION SUMMARY

Because mobile devices have come into all areas of our daily life and are used more and more at work (officially and unofficially), a CompTIA A+ certification candidate needs to be prepared to support users of these small but useful devices. Understand their hardware features and the sources of apps for the most popular devices, which run the Apple iOS or Android OS.

The primary purpose of a mobile device is to communicate with networks and other devices, so you will need to know how to enable and configure various types of connections, including Wi-Fi, Bluetooth, NFC, and AirDrop. You should be able to create a mobile hotspot and synchronize data between devices.

There are many options for securing mobile devices, from security apps for Android devices to a variety of security settings on both Android and iOS devices. You should know about both hardware- and software-based security and authentication, including antimalware software, authentication, and corporate policies and procedures that promote good security.

Mobile devices, because of their on-chip OS, don't get easily corrupted. However, they do get confused sometimes and need to be reset, either with a soft or hard reset. Settings can also be misadjusted, resulting in certain components not appearing to work. Know where the basic settings are located for various types of mobile devices and how to reset them. Familiarize yourself with troubleshooting procedures for both hardware and software, and be able to identify and correct common problems with digitizers, batteries, overheating, and connectivity.

TWO-MINUTE DRILL

Here are some of the key points covered in Chapter 15.

Configuring and Using Mobile Device Connections

- ❑ A smartphone typically comes with several types of wireless connectivity, including cellular, Wi-Fi, Bluetooth, and NFC. Apple iPhones also come with AirDrop. These are all disabled when you put the device in airplane mode.
- ❑ Tethering, or creating a mobile hotspot, enables a smartphone to serve as a wireless access point for other devices.
- ❑ To set up a Bluetooth pairing, first you enable Bluetooth, have the devices discover each other, then enable pairing, then either enter a PIN code on one side or confirm that the same code displays on both devices, and finally test connectivity.
- ❑ To configure e-mail on a mobile device, you need certain information that you may have to obtain from an e-mail administrator if you do not already have it. For connection to popular web-based e-mail systems like Gmail, you only need the e-mail address and password. For other e-mail connections, you may also need server addresses for POP3 or IMAP and SMTP, as well as port and TLS/SSL settings.
- ❑ Install OS updates to make sure a mobile device has all the latest patches and security features. Use the Settings app.
- ❑ You can synchronize devices by connecting the device to a computer or over an Internet connection to a cloud-based service. Data you can sync includes contacts, programs, e-mail, photos, calendar, and contacts.

Securing Mobile Devices

- ❑ Mobile security concerns and risks include APK source, developer mode, bootleg/malicious apps, app spoofing, unauthorized device access, unauthorized account access, malware, spying, and unauthorized use of Internet access.
- ❑ Mobile security begins with sign-on authentication, such as a passcode lock/PIN, biometric authentication, and restrictions for failed login attempts. Most devices don't offer multifactor authentication in the OS, but you can install authenticator apps that enable that option.

- ❑ To avoid malware and crashing applications, acquire applications only from trusted sources. Do not jailbreak/root a device to disable built-in security features. Doing so may void warranties and cause other issues.
- ❑ To protect data stored on a device, consider full device encryption, strong authentication, and frequent data backup via synchronization.
- ❑ Before a device is lost or stolen, enable remote backups and be prepared to do a remote wipe. For iOS devices, keep data synced to iCloud, and use its remote-wipe feature on the lost or stolen device. On an Android device, install a security suite that includes remote wipe. You can also use Android Device Manager to remotely erase the device.
- ❑ If you enable locator features, you can use a locator app to find your lost or stolen mobile device using a map on another device or computer.
- ❑ If the device is stolen, use a remote wipe to prevent the thief from having access to your data.

Troubleshooting Mobile Device Problems

- ❑ A nonresponsive touch screen can sometimes be corrected with a reboot. Also make sure the screen is clean and dry. Some types of screens may need calibration.
- ❑ Apps that fail to launch, crash, or are slow to respond may need to be removed and reinstalled.
- ❑ If the OS fails to update, the update may be incompatible with the hardware. If an app fails to update, the app may be incompatible with the OS version.
- ❑ Overheating can occur from a defective battery, charger, or motherboard. Let the device breathe; don't store it in a pocket or an unventilated case.
- ❑ Connectivity issues can often be resolved by enabling the connection in the app's settings or by moving nearer the source (for example, a wireless access point or peripheral).
- ❑ A soft reset keeps all data and settings. A hard reset should be used only if all else fails; it wipes all data and settings.
- ❑ For lack of wireless connectivity, make sure the interface is enabled in Settings. For intermittent or slow wireless, check location and interference.
- ❑ For application issues, uninstall and reinstall.
- ❑ To get your data back after a hard reset, use your backup created with synchronization.

SELF TEST

The following questions will help you measure your understanding of the material presented in this chapter. Read all the choices carefully because there might be more than one correct answer. Choose all correct answers for each question.

Configuring and Using Mobile Device Connections

1. When you purchase a smartphone, it has this type of connection configured for you.
A. Wi-Fi
B. Cellular
C. Bluetooth
D. Tethered

2. _______ means sharing your phone's Internet connection with another Wi-Fi–enabled device.
A. Airplane mode
B. Pairing
C. Near-field communication
D. Tethering

3. ________ means connecting a Bluetooth-enabled accessory to a smartphone, tablet, or other mobile device.
A. Airplane mode
B. Pairing
C. Near-field communication
D. Tethering

4. What mode on mobile devices turns off all RF broadcasts?
A. Pairing
B. Airplane
C. Tethering
D. Wi-Fi

5. What information do you need to configure your mobile device to connect to a Gmail account?
A. Server addresses for IMAP and POP3
B. URL of the web-based e-mail interface
C. E-mail address and password
D. Port numbers

6. What type of e-mail service is internally maintained for an organization's employees, with all accounts centrally administered by the organization's e-mail administrator?

A. Gmail

B. Outlook

C. Microsoft Exchange

D. POP3

7. How might you perform a cloud synchronization on a mobile device?

A. USB cable

B. AirDrop

C. Wi-Fi

D. NFC

Securing Mobile Devices

8. What security feature requires you to enter a PIN for access to a device?

A. Remote wipe

B. Failed login attempts restrictions

C. Multi-touch

D. Passcode lock

9. Which of these is an example of a profile security requirement?

A. Password complexity

B. NFC

C. Multi-touch

D. Remote wipe

10. Which of these is a method of circumventing the built-in iOS protections against getting root access to a mobile device's system files?

A. Location services

B. Jailbreaking

C. Malware

D. Swipe lock

11. Which of these is a biometric authentication feature?

A. PIN

B. Password

C. Facial recognition

D. Jailbreaking

12. To ensure that you do not install malware on an Android device, what do you need to make sure you know?

A. APK source

B. OS version number

C. Bluetooth type

D. Rooting method

13. Which of these would you *not* use after your mobile device is lost?

A. Locator

B. Remote wipe

C. Disable Wi-Fi and Bluetooth remotely

D. Configure a passcode lock remotely

Troubleshooting Mobile Device Problems

14. Which of these would *not* be a likely cause of overheating?

A. Tight case with no ventilation

B. Too many applications open at once

C. Wi-Fi disabled

D. Defective battery

15. Which problem would a soft reset *not* fix?

A. Touch screen not responding

B. Dim screen

C. Frozen system

D. System lockout due to forgotten passcode

16. When you are outdoors in a rural area and have a weak cell signal, what is likely the problem?

A. Destructive interference

B. Distance from a cell tower

C. No nearby WAP

D. Constructive interference

17. Which of these would *not* help a problem with slow or intermittent Wi-Fi?

A. Soft reset of the mobile device

B. Reset the router

C. Reduce 2.4-GHz band interference

D. Calibrate screen

18. When two nearby Bluetooth-enabled devices don't recognize each other, what is likely the problem?
   A. The devices need to be touching.
   B. One of the devices isn't set to be discoverable.
   C. Wi-Fi is not enabled.
   D. Interference exists from a nearby cordless landline phone.

19. When an app crashes, what solution should you try first?
   A. Turn off Bluetooth.
   B. Turn off Wi-Fi.
   C. Remove and reinstall the app.
   D. Reboot the device.

20. How can you do a hard reset on an Android phone that is not responding to commands?
   A. Access the Factory Data Reset screen from the Settings app.
   B. Press buttons on the device in the sequence specified in the device's manual.
   C. Tap the Settings app repeatedly on the Home screen.
   D. Completely drain the battery and then completely recharge it.

SELF TEST ANSWERS

Configuring and Using Mobile Device Connections

1. ☑ **B.** When you purchase a smartphone, it has a configured cell connection.
☒ **A, C,** and **D** are incorrect because you need to configure Wi-Fi, Bluetooth, and a tethered connection separately.

2. ☑ **D.** Tethering means sharing your phone's cellular Internet connection via Wi-Fi.
☒ **A** is incorrect because airplane mode turns off all wireless services on the device. **B** is incorrect because pairing means to connect two devices via Bluetooth. **C** is incorrect because near-field communication (NFC) is a very-short-range kind of wireless connectivity used for credit card terminals and payment systems.

3. ☑ **B.** Pairing means to connect two devices via Bluetooth.
☒ **A** is incorrect because airplane mode turns off all wireless services on the device. **C** is incorrect because near-field communication (NFC) is a very-short-range kind of wireless connectivity used for credit card terminals and payment systems. **D** is incorrect because tethering means to share your phone's cellular Internet connection via Wi-Fi.

4. ☑ **B.** Airplane mode turns off all RF broadcasts.
☒ **A** is incorrect because pairing is done between two Bluetooth devices. **C** is incorrect because tethering describes a cable connection between a mobile device and a computer. **D** is incorrect because Wi-Fi describes a wireless network using one of the 802.11 standards.

5. ☑ **C.** The e-mail address and password are all you need to configure your mobile device to connect to a Gmail account.
☒ **A** is incorrect because that address information is needed only for IMAP or POP3 accounts. **B** is incorrect because you connect to web-based e-mail accounts via your mail app on a mobile device. **D** is incorrect because port numbers are not required when configuring a Gmail account.

6. ☑ **C.** Microsoft Exchange is a type of e-mail service that is internally maintained for an organization's employees, and all accounts are centrally administered by the organization's e-mail administrator.
☒ **A** is incorrect because Gmail is not maintained internally, nor is it centrally administered by anyone other than Google. **B** is incorrect because Outlook is an e-mail client. Outlook.com is also a mail service, but it is not centrally maintained for an organization. Microsoft administers it. **D** is incorrect because POP3 is a type of e-mail account used for privately owned domains and is maintained and configured by the owner.

7. ☑ **C.** A Wi-Fi connection to the Internet enables you to synchronize with the cloud.
☒ **A** is incorrect because a cable would be used for a local synchronization to a PC. **B** is incorrect because AirDrop is a method of transferring data between two nearby Apple devices. **D** is incorrect because NFC is an extremely short-range communication method.

Securing Mobile Devices

8. ☑ **D.** Passcode lock is a security feature that requires you to enter a PIN for access.
☒ **A** is incorrect because remote wipe does not restrict access by requiring a login. **B** is incorrect because this is simply a setting for consequences of entering the wrong password too many times. **C** is incorrect because multi-touch just describes a feature of a touch screen.

9. ☑ **A.** A password complexity rule is a type of profile security requirement.
☒ **B** is incorrect because NFC is a technology for short-range wireless communication. **C** is incorrect because multi-touch describes a feature of a touch screen. **D** is incorrect because remote wipe is a feature that enables a stolen device to be wiped clean of personal information remotely.

10. ☑ **B.** Jailbreaking is a way of gaining root access to the operating system. Jailbreaking applies to Apple iOS. Rooting is similar, but is used to access Android-based operating system files.
☒ **A** is incorrect because location services provide a method of locating a device physically. **C** is incorrect because malware is harmful software designed to compromise a system or do damage to it. **D** is incorrect because swipe lock refers to waking up a device by swiping or tapping.

11. ☑ **C.** Facial recognition is a type of biometric authentication.
☒ **A** and **B** are incorrect because PINs and passwords are authentication methods that require the user to know something, whereas biometric authentication relies on what the user is, rather than what they know. **D** is incorrect because jailbreaking is a means of obtaining root access to a mobile device's operating system.

12. ☑ **A.** Knowing the APK source (in other words, the source of the application installation package) can help protect against malware disguised as useful apps.
☒ **B** is incorrect because the OS version number will not help in avoiding malware. **C** is incorrect because Bluetooth plays no role in installing apps. **D** is incorrect because rooting (called jailbreaking in iOS) is a means of circumventing security on an Android-based device, not enforcing it.

13. ☑ **C.** You would not disable Wi-Fi and Bluetooth remotely after a device has been lost.
☒ **A** is incorrect because a locator service might be used to locate the lost device. **B** is incorrect because remote wipe might be used to prevent a privacy breach. **D** is incorrect because configuring a passcode lock remotely can be done on some mobile OSs, such as in Lost Mode for iOS.

Troubleshooting Mobile Device Problems

14. ☑ **C.** Wi-Fi being disabled would not be a cause of overheating. Turning off a feature would not generate more heat.
☒ **A, B,** and **D** are incorrect because these are all possible causes of overheating.

15. ☑ **D.** Only a hard reset can fix system lockout.
☒ **A, B,** and **C** are incorrect because a nonresponsive touch screen, a dim screen, and a frozen system can all likely be fixed by a soft reset.

16. ☑ **B.** Distance from a cell tower is the most likely cause of a weak cell signal.
☒ **A** is incorrect because destructive interference is likely to occur in crowded urban areas with many cell towers. **C** is incorrect because cell service doesn't come from a WAP. **D** is incorrect because there is no such thing as constructive interference.

17. ☑ **D.** Calibrating the screen would have no effect on Wi-Fi.
☒ **A, B,** and **C** are incorrect because a soft reset of the mobile device, resetting the router, and reducing 2.4-GHz band interference could all potentially help with slow or intermittent Wi-Fi.

18. ☑ **B.** Both devices must be discoverable for a pairing to work.
☒ **A** is incorrect because Bluetooth devices do not need to touch; this would apply more to near-field communication (NFC). **C** is incorrect because Bluetooth is not dependent on Wi-Fi. **D** is incorrect because interference from a cordless landline phone is an issue with some Wi-Fi standards, not with Bluetooth.

19. ☑ **D.** Rebooting the device is the least work and will likely fix the problem.
☒ **A** and **B** are incorrect because turning off wireless services is not likely to help fix an app crash. **C** is incorrect because although this may solve the problem, it is more work than rebooting, which should be tried first.

20. ☑ **B.** The device manual will specify which buttons to press to perform a hard reset.
☒ **A** and **C** are incorrect because the question specified that the device is not responding, so neither if these actions would be possible. **D** is incorrect because the battery's charge has no relationship to performing a hard reset.

Part V

Networking

CHAPTERS

Chapter 16

Network Basics

CERTIFICATION OBJECTIVES

- **1101: 2.1** Compare and contrast Transmission Control Protocol (TCP) and User Datagram Protocol (UDP) ports, protocols, and their purposes
- **1101: 2.2** Compare and contrast common networking hardware
- **1101: 2.3** Compare and contrast protocols for wireless networking
- **1101: 2.6** Compare and contrast common network configuration concepts
- **1101: 2.7** Compare and contrast Internet connection types, network types, and their features
- **1101: 3.1** Explain basic cable types and their connectors, features, and purposes

✓ Two-Minute Drill

Q&A Self Test

Computer networks provide users with the ability to share files, printers, resources, and e-mail globally. Networks have become so important that they provide the basis for nearly all business transactions.

Obviously, a discussion of the full spectrum of network details and specifications is too broad in scope to be contained in this book. However, as a computer technician, you should be aware of basic networking concepts so you can troubleshoot minor problems on established networks. This chapter focuses on basic concepts of physical networks; Chapter 17 guides you through simple small office/home office (SOHO) network installation, and Chapter 19 provides the basis for troubleshooting common network problems.

CERTIFICATION OBJECTIVE

- ***1101: 2.7** Compare and contrast Internet connection types, network types, and their features*

This section describes the types of networks based on how they are connected (topology) and based on the area they service (LAN, WAN, PAN, MAN), as required by CompTIA A+ 1101 exam Objective 2.7.

Network Classifications

For a computer professional working with PCs, the networked computer is the norm, not the exception. A computer not connected to a network has become a nearly extinct species as more and more PCs network together—even within homes.

To understand networks, you must first be familiar with basic network performance and classifications, which describe networks by speed, geography, and scale, beginning with the smallest networks up to globe-spanning ones.

We classify networks by geographic area types, and specific technologies are designed for each of them. Network builders select these technologies for the capabilities that match the distance needs of the network.

For the CompTIA A+ 220-1101 exam Objective 2.7, be sure that you understand the distinctions between the various location-based network types, including PAN, LAN, MAN, and WAN.

Personal Area Network

You may have your own *personal area network (PAN)* if you have devices such as smartphones, tablets, or printers that communicate with each other and/or your desktop computer. A PAN may use a wired connection, such as Universal Serial Bus (USB) or FireWire, or it may communicate wirelessly using one of the standards developed for short-range communications, such as Bluetooth.

As you learned in Chapter 14, Bluetooth uses radio waves, which do not require line-of-sight, but the signal can be disrupted by physical barriers as well as interference from other signals. The Bluetooth standard describes three classes, with power requirements and distance limits. The Bluetooth standard commonly used with computer peripherals and mobile devices is Class 3, limited to a distance of 1 meter, or Class 2, limited to about 10 meters.

Local Area Network

A *local area network (LAN)* is a network that covers a much larger area than a PAN, such as a building, home, office, or campus. Typically, distances measure in hundreds of meters. A LAN may share resources such as printers, files, or other items. LANs operate very rapidly, with speeds measured in megabits or gigabits per second, and have become extremely cost-effective. While there are many LAN technologies, the two most widely used in SOHO network installations are Ethernet and Wi-Fi.

Metropolitan Area Network

A *metropolitan area network (MAN)* is a network that covers a metropolitan area, connecting various networks together using a shared community network and often providing WAN connections to the Internet. A MAN usually runs over high-speed fiber-optic cable operating in the gigabits-per-second range. Although people tend to be less aware of MANs, they nonetheless exist. In fact, a MAN may well be somewhere between you and the Internet.

Wide Area Network

A *wide area network (WAN)* can cover the largest geographic area. A *WAN connection* is the connection between two networks over a long distance (miles). The term WAN is used to describe a wired WAN connection versus a *wireless wide area network (WWAN),* a wireless connection between two networks over a long distance.

Storage Area Network

A *storage area network (SAN)* is not the same kind of network as the other types covered so far. It's a data network created for one purpose: to connect and manage large-scale storage devices, such as file servers, and make that storage capacity available to users who need it. Users do not directly access the storage on a SAN; they access a SAN server, which facilitates usage of the storage, making the actual location and configuration of the storage devices invisible to the end users. The server operating system maintains its own file system, and that file system is what user PCs interact with.

A SAN has its own hardware and software protocols and layers, but you don't need to understand them in detail. Just make sure you know what a SAN is and what its benefits are.

Companies that have large-scale storage needs often implement SANs because they can aggregate the storage available from hundreds of different locations and load-balance the traffic among them, while the user sees the entire network as a single location.

CERTIFICATION OBJECTIVE

- ***1101: 2.7** Compare and contrast Internet connection types, network types, and their features*

This section describes Internet connection types, as required by CompTIA A+ 1101 exam Objective 2.7.

Internet Connection Types

Next we'll review the Internet connection types. They fall into two broad categories: wired and wireless. The wired ones are fiber, cable, and DSL, and the wireless ones are satellite, long-range fixed wireless, and cellular. Although satellite is technically "wireless" in that it receives and sends via a satellite dish rather than via cables, that satellite dish is wired to the location receiving the service, so although it is wireless, it isn't mobile.

Make sure you understand how each Internet connection type works, its benefits/drawbacks, and in what situations it is the best choice.

Each of these Internet connection types (except cellular) can easily be shared within the service location by connecting it to a router, which also serves as a switch that connects the computers in that location as a LAN. The router shares the Internet connection with the entire LAN. In contrast, cellular is usually a one-device connection, such as a smartphone or cellular-enabled tablet. However, cellular devices can be set to serve as a mobile hotspot, and multiple devices can be tethered to it (usually wirelessly) to share its Internet connection. You learned about that in Chapter 15, and they're also covered later in this chapter.

Understanding Bandwidth and Latency

When evaluating different Internet connection options, two important factors to consider are bandwidth and latency. *Bandwidth* is the amount of data that can travel over a network within a given time. It's often used rather loosely to mean speed, but it's more a measure of the amount of data that can be sent during a specific timeframe (1 second). It may be expressed in megabits per second (Mbps) or gigabits per second (Gbps)—that is, millions of bits per second or billions of bits per second. In this book we don't provide specific bandwidth ratings for the different connection types because these are constantly in flux, with providers finding new ways to bump up their bandwidth almost weekly. In addition, most providers offer a variety of connection packages at different prices and bandwidths. In general, though, the following sections list the connection types from fastest to slowest.

Another network characteristic related to bandwidth is latency. *Latency* is the delay between sending a network request and the arrival of that request at its destination. In some cases, latency is determined by measuring the time it takes for a packet to make a round trip between two points. This can be a more important measurement, as it does not measure the speed at which the packets travel, but the length of time it takes a packet to get from point A to point B. It is like measuring the actual time it takes you to travel by car from Los Angeles to San Francisco. The actual time of travel varies by the amount of traffic you encounter and the interchanges you pass through. The same is true for a packet on a network.

Fiber Internet

Fiber-optic service (often abbreviated as just "fiber") is an extremely high-bandwidth Internet service that uses fiber-optic cable to send and receive data using pulses of light. Many providers deploy fiber-optic cables all the way up to the subscriber address, making it possible to deliver Internet upload and download rates of 1 Gbps or more. This is sometimes referred to as *pure fiber.* Other providers use fiber to go into a neighborhood, but then use copper cables for the "last mile" of the connection to individual buildings. Fiber-optic cables are discussed in more detail later in this chapter. The main drawback of fiber is limited availability outside of major cities.

Cable Internet

Cable and fiber-optic providers battle back and forth for the title of highest-bandwidth Internet service, and their highest-rate plans are usually comparable. However, the actual rate of cable Internet is seldom as high as its theoretical capability, because whereas fiber and DSL services are point-to-point from the client to the ISP, a cable client shares the network with their neighboring cable clients. It is like when multiple PCs in your home share an Internet connection and several PCs are streaming high-definition video at once. The rate degrades as more locations share the local cable network.

Cable networks use coaxial cable to connect a cable modem to the network. They use the same cable to provide both Internet and cable TV, with a splitter used to connect both the broadband modem and the TV to the same wall jack if needed.

DSL Internet

Digital subscriber line (DSL) uses existing copper telephone wire for the communications circuit. A DSL modem splits the existing phone line into two bands to accomplish this: one for voice, the other for data. Voice phone calls happen normally, and the data connection is always on and available.

DSL service is available through phone companies, which offer a large variety of DSL services. Some services, such as *asymmetric DSL (ADSL),* offer asymmetric service in that the download rate is higher than the upload. Other, more expensive services aimed at business offer higher rates. *Symmetric DSL (SDSL)* offers matching upload and download rates.

Because DSL relies on standard copper wire phone lines, it can't match the bandwidth of fiber. Its main advantage is broader availability; most urban and suburban areas have robust phone systems that can carry DSL data. Not every location that has telephone service can support DSL, though; the location must be within 18,000 feet of a *central office (CO).* The closer to the CO, the faster the speed available. At a certain point, the distance becomes too great to offer satisfactory DSL speed.

Many providers that have offered DSL in the past, such as AT&T and Verizon, are switching to fiber service instead, which offers much higher speeds. DSL, even the fastest versions of it, is increasingly becoming "old technology."

Satellite Internet

Satellite Internet offers relatively high-speed Internet service to areas where fiber, cable, and DSL are not available. It uses a satellite dish for receiving and a transmitter mounted to the dish for sending. Both the dish and the transmitter connect to a terminal adapter that functions much like a cable or DSL modem.

Early satellite communications systems were very expensive to maintain and operate. Today, however, a number of companies offer decent Internet speeds at affordable prices. As with TV satellite service, you must have a place to mount the dish antenna with a clear view of the southern sky.

The problem with satellite service is not so much the raw speed, but the latency. Because the signal must travel into space and back, there is an unavoidable delay each time your computer requests data, which makes satellite service seem slower than raw speed tests would have you believe.

Long-Range Fixed Wireless

Long-range fixed wireless is a relatively new entry into the Internet service provider market. Like satellite, it connects locations with Internet service without having to run cables. But instead of connecting to an orbiting satellite, its antenna communicates with a transmitter/receiver on a land-based tower, like the towers used for cellular service. Its latency is much less than that of satellite.

The most common use for this technology is by *wireless Internet service providers (WISPs),* which provide wireless Internet access in rural and underserved areas via unlicensed frequencies. This brings high-speed Internet to people and locations that do not have access to fiber, cable, or DSL. The antennas installed at the service locations must have a line-of-sight to the tower.

The Federal Communications Commission (FCC) licenses most of the radio frequency (RF) spectrum to certain users, such as radio and TV providers. They pay a fee for exclusive rights to broadcast on a certain frequency in a certain geographic area. There are also unlicensed frequencies, but it's a fairly small bandwidth. Anyone can broadcast on those frequencies, but if someone else is also broadcasting in the same area at the same time, it can cause conflicts.

To avoid a "Wild West" situation in the unlicensed spectrum, the FCC imposes regulatory limitations on the amount of broadcast power antennas can use, which in turn limits the distance that the antenna can be from the tower. These power regulations keep things orderly, but they prevent some locations from receiving service that might be able to take advantage of it if the broadcast power were increased.

Long-range fixed wireless is a new addition to the 1101 exam. Make sure you understand who can benefit from long-range fixed wireless and how WISPs provide Internet service using unlicensed bandwidth. You should also understand the relationship between broadcast power and the maximum distance between the antenna and the tower.

Cellular Internet

Long used mainly for voice, the cell networks provide cellular WAN Internet data connections, also referred to as WWAN. These data services have a range of broadband speeds, depending on the cellular provider and the level of service you have purchased.

Different technology generations are in use on different cellular networks. Third generation (3G) is considered old technology today, and 4G is on the wane; 5G is the current standard. 5G is superior to earlier generations in several ways, including higher speed, lower latency, and greater bandwidth.

EXERCISE 16-1

Testing Broadband Speeds

Regardless of the broadband service you use, they all vary in the actual speeds they provide from moment to moment. Connect to one of the many broadband speed-testing sites on the Internet and test yours now.

1. Open your favorite search engine and enter a search string that will locate an Internet speed testing website. We used **network speed test**.
2. From the results listed in the search engine, select a site (we chose www.speedtest.net). Often sites suggest downloading and running other software to test your computer, so be careful to only select the speed test and not to download or run programs you do not want.
3. Follow the instructions for testing your connection. Some sites test as soon as you connect, and some test sites ask you to select a city near you. The test may take several minutes.
4. View the results. Are the results congruent with the service you expect from your broadband connection?
5. Time permitting, try this at another time, or even on another day, and compare your results.

SCENARIO & SOLUTION

I want the fastest possible Internet service at home. What should I choose?	Fiber and cable are the fastest at this writing, with the advantage shifting to one or the other as each technology develops some new edge. Either would provide ample speed for home use.
I like to play online games. I have heard satellite Internet is no good for games. Is that true?	Satellite Internet isn't good for games where quick reaction time is important because it inherently has quite a bit of latency. However, for turn-based games, satellite is fine.

CERTIFICATION OBJECTIVES

- ***1101: 2.1*** *Compare and contrast Transmission Control Protocol (TCP) and User Datagram Protocol (UDP) ports, protocols, and their purposes*
- ***1101: 2.3*** *Compare and contrast protocols for wireless networking*
- ***1101: 2.6*** *Compare and contrast common network configuration concepts*

This section details the topics required for CompTIA A+ 1101 exam Objective 2.6. DNS and DHCP coverage of CompTIA A+ 1101 exam Objective 2.1 is also included in this section because it is part of the TCP/IP story. It includes an explanation of both TCP and UDP protocols, as well as other TCP and UDP protocols and related services, and the ports used by TCP and UDP. This section also reviews the various IEEE 802.11 Wi-Fi standards, per CompTIA A+ 1101 exam Objective 2.3.

Network Software and Protocols

The software on a network is what gives us the network that we know and use. This is the logical network that rides on top of the physical network. In this section, we'll explore several aspects of networking that are controlled by software, including the network roles, protocol suites, and network addressing of the logical network.

Network Roles

You can describe a network by the types of roles played by the computers on it. The two general computer roles in a network are *clients,* the computers that request services, and *servers,* the computers that provide services.

Peer-to-Peer Networks

In a *peer-to-peer network,* each computer system in the network may play both roles: client and server. They have equal capabilities and responsibilities; each computer user is responsible for controlling access, sharing resources, and storing data on their computer. In Figure 16-1, each of the computers can share its files, and the computer connected to the printer can share the printer. Peer-to-peer networks work best in a very small LAN environment, such as a small business office, with fewer than a dozen computers and users. Microsoft calls a peer-to-peer network a *workgroup,* and each workgroup must have a unique name, as must each computer.

FIGURE 16-1 A peer-to-peer network

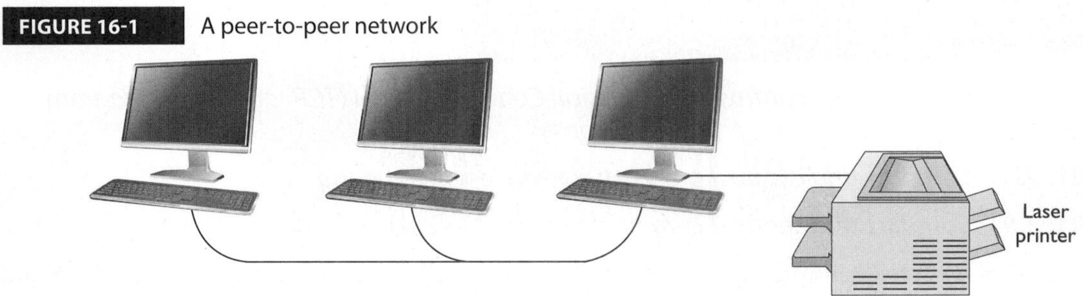

Client/Server-Based Networks

A *client/server-based network* uses dedicated computers called *servers* to store data and provide print services or other capabilities. Servers are generally more powerful computer systems with more capacity than a typical workstation. Client/server-based models also allow for centralized administration and security. These types of networks are scalable in that they can grow very large without adding administrative complexity to the network. A large private internetwork for a globe-spanning corporation is an example of a client/server-based network. When configuring the network, the network administrator can establish a single model for security, access, and file sharing. Although this configuration may remain unchanged as the network grows, the administrator can make changes, if needed, from a central point. Microsoft calls a client/server network with Microsoft servers a *domain*. The domain must have a unique name, and each client or server computer must have a unique name.

Organizations use client/server environments extensively in situations that need a centralized administration system. Servers can be multipurpose, performing a number of functions, or dedicated, as in the case of a web or e-mail server. Figure 16-2 shows a network with servers used for e-mail and printing. Notice in this example that each of the servers is dedicated to the task assigned to it.

TCP/IP

Every computer network consists of physical and logical components controlled by software. Standards, also often called *protocols,* describe the rules for how hardware and software work and interact together.

These protocols control the addressing and naming of computers on the network, among other tasks. They combine into suites that include a group of protocols built around the same set of rules, with each protocol describing a small portion of the tasks required to prepare, send, and receive network data.

FIGURE 16-2 A client/server environment where dedicated servers perform assigned functions

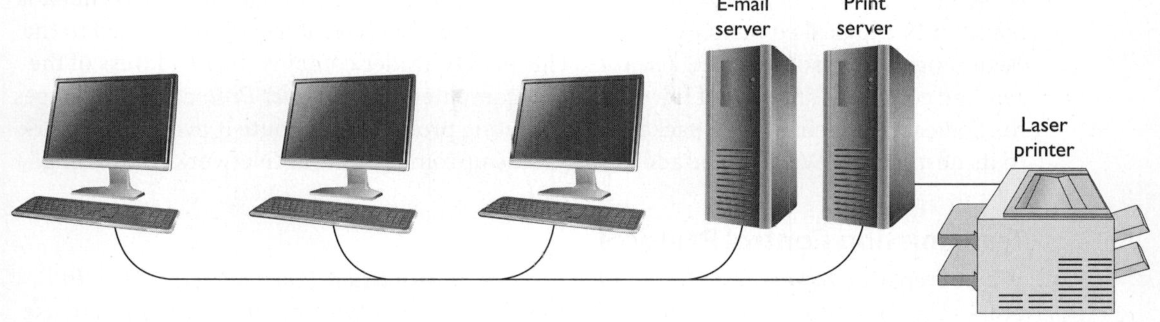

The CompTIA 220-1101 exam requires that A+ candidates understand the basics of the *TCP/IP* protocol suite because it is the most common protocol suite used on LANs and WANs, as well as on the Internet. It involves several protocols and other software components, and together, we call these a protocol stack or a protocol suite.

Transmission Control Protocol/Internet Protocol (TCP/IP) is by far the most common protocol suite on both internal LANs and public networks. It is the Internet's protocol suite. TCP/IP requires some configuration, but it is robust, usable on very large networks, and routable (a term that refers to the ability to send data to other networks). At each junction of two networks is a router that uses special router protocols to send each packet on its way toward its destination.

TCP/IP allows for cross-platform communication, meaning that computers using different OSs (such as Windows and Linux) can send data back and forth, provided they are both using TCP/IP.

Although the TCP/IP suite has several protocols, the two main ones are the Transmission Control Protocol (TCP) and the Internet Protocol (IP). We now briefly describe these two cornerstone protocols of the TCP/IP suite.

The CompTIA A+ 220-1101 exam expects you to understand the basics of TCP/IP, the difference between TCP and UDP, and the purpose of the various protocols and their associated ports.

Internet Protocol

Messages sent over a network are broken up into smaller chunks of data, and each chunk is placed into a logical container called a *packet*. Each packet has information attached to the beginning of the packet, called a *header*. This packet header contains the IP address of the sending computer and that of the destination computer. The *Internet Protocol (IP)* manages this logical addressing of the packet so that routing protocols can route it over the network to its destination. We describe addressing in the upcoming section "Network Addressing."

Transmission Control Protocol

When preparing to send data over a network, the *Transmission Control Protocol (TCP)* breaks the data into chunks, called datagrams. Each *datagram* contains information to use on the receiving end to reassemble the chunks of data into the original message. TCP places this information, both a byte-count value and a datagram sequence, into the datagram header before giving it to the IP protocol, which encapsulates the datagrams into packets with addressing information.

When receiving data from a network, TCP uses the information in this header to reassemble the data. If TCP is able to reassemble the message, it sends an *acknowledgment (ACK)* message to the sending address. The sender can then discard datagrams that it saved while waiting for an acknowledgment. If pieces are missing, TCP sends a *non-acknowledgment (NAK)* message back to the sending address, whereupon TCP resends the missing pieces.

An excellent 13-minute movie describing how TCP/IP works in an amusing and interesting fashion is available for viewing at www.warriorsofthe.net and is well worth watching.

Network Addressing

Identifying each computer or device directly connected to a network is important. We do this at two levels: the hardware level, in which the network adapter in each computer or network device has an address, and the logical level, in which a logical address is assigned to each network adapter.

Hardware Addressing

Every network interface card (NIC), and every device connected to a network, has a unique address placed in ROM by the manufacturer. This address, usually permanent, is called by many names, including *Media Access Control (MAC) address,* physical address, and NIC address.

A physical address is 48 bits long and usually expressed in hexadecimal. You can view the physical address of a NIC in several ways. It is usually, but not always, written on a label attached to the NIC. Figure 16-3 shows the label on a wireless USB NIC. The words "MAC Address" appear above the physical address. The actual address on this NIC is six 2-digit

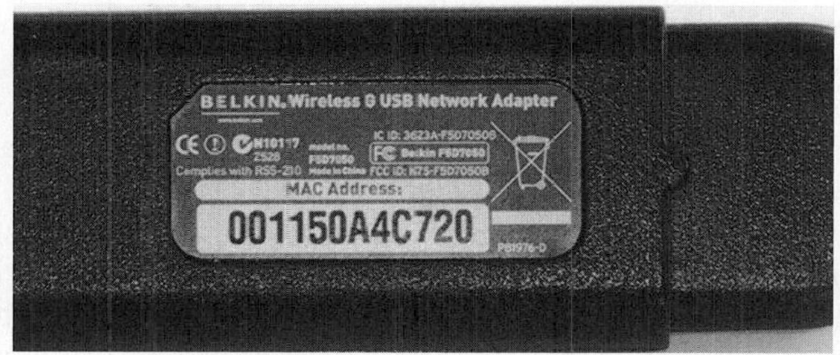

FIGURE 16-3

The physical address of a NIC, labeled "MAC Address," and shown on the NIC

hexadecimal numbers, but on this label, the numbers are not separated. It is easier to read these numbers if separated by a dash, period, or space, like this: 00-11-50-A4-C7-20.

Locating the physical address is not always so easy. You can also discover the address of a NIC through Windows. Use the *IPCONFIG* command-line utility that is installed on a Windows computer with the TCP/IP protocol suite. This command lets you view the IP configuration of a network connection and perform certain administrative functions. To see the physical address as well as the rest of the IP configuration for a connection, simply open a Command Prompt window (as described in Chapter 5) and type the **ipconfig /all** command. The physical address is in the middle of the listing. Notice that it shows six 2-digit hexadecimal numbers, each separated by a dash.

This physical address identifies a computer located in a segment of a network. However, you use logical addresses to locate a computer that is beyond the local network segment.

Logical Addressing/IP Addressing

In addition to the hardware address, a computer in a TCP/IP network must have a logical address that identifies both the computer and the network. This address comes under the purview of the IP protocol. Internet Protocol version 4 (IPv4) and its addressing scheme have been in use for over the past three decades. It offers almost 4.3 billion possible IP addresses, but the way they have been allocated throughout the world reduces that number. The Internet is currently transitioning to Internet Protocol version 6 (IPv6) with a new addressing scheme that provides many more addresses.

An IP address identifies both a computer, a *host* in Internet terms, and the logical network on which the computer resides. This address allows messages to move from one network to another on the Internet. At the connecting point between networks, a special network device called a *router* uses its routing protocols to determine the route to the destination address before sending each packet along to the next router closer to the destination network. Each computer and network device that directly attach to the Internet must have a globally unique IP address. Both versions of IP have this much and more in common. Following are explanations of these addressing schemes to help you distinguish between them.

IPv4 Addresses An IPv4 address is 32 bits long, usually shown as four decimal numbers, 0 to 255, each separated by a period—for example, 192.168.1.41. Called *dotted-decimal notation,* this format is what you see in the user interface. However, the IPv4 protocol works with addresses in binary form, in which the preceding address looks like this: 11000000.10101000.00000001.00101001.

IPv4 addresses are routable because an IP address contains within it both the address of the host, called the *host ID,* and the address of the network on which that host resides, called the *network ID (netID).* A mask of 1s and 0s separates the two parts. When you put the mask over an address, the 1s cover up the first part, or network ID, and the 0s cover up the remaining part, or host ID. The address portion that falls under the 1s is the network address, and the address portion that falls under the 0s is the host address. In the preceding example, with a mask of 11111111.11111111.11111111.00000000, or 255.255.255.0, the network ID is 11000000.10101000.00000001.00000000 and the host ID is 00101001 (see Figure 16-4).

In dotted-decimal form, the network ID is 192.168.1.0 and the host ID is 41. Often called a *subnet mask,* this mask is an important component in a proper IP configuration. After all, the IP address of a host does not make any sense until masked into its two IDs. When you enter the subnet mask into the Windows user interface in the Properties dialog box of the NIC, you will enter it in dotted-decimal notation, but we commonly use a shorthand notation when talking about the subnet mask, and you will see this notation in some user interfaces. For instance, a subnet mask of 255.255.255.0 is easily represented as /24. Therefore, using our example address from earlier, rather than saying the IP address is 192.168.1.41 with a subnet mask of 255.255.255.0, you can put it together as 192.168.1.41/24.

exam watch

Be sure you understand how the subnet mask divides the host ID and network ID of an IP address. Also make sure that you understand the purpose of the following addresses as used in an IP configuration: default gateway, DNS server, and DHCP server.

FIGURE 16-4

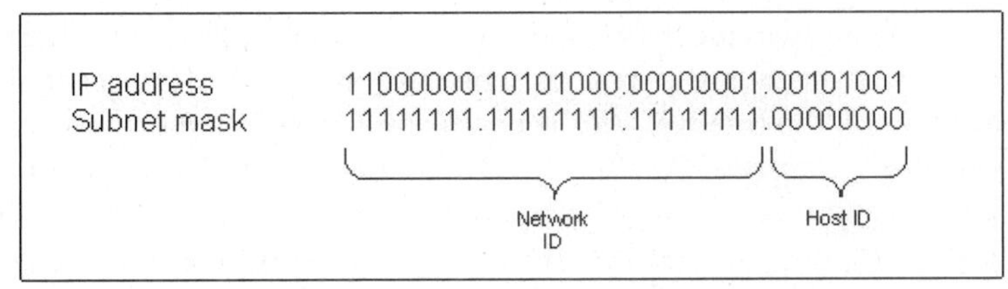

The subnet mask defines the network ID and host ID portions of an IP address.

IPv6 Addresses In preparation for the day when ISPs and the Internet routers are fully IPv6-ready, all modern Windows versions support both IPv6 and IPv4, as do most new network devices. In fact, some high-speed internetworks already use IPv6. IPv6 has 128-bit addressing, which theoretically supports a huge number of unique addresses—340,282,366,920,938,463,463,374,607,431,768,211,456 to be exact.

An IPv6 address is shown in eight groups of hexadecimal numbers separated by colons, such as this: 2002:470:B8F9:1:20C:29FF:FE53:45CA. Sometimes the address will contain a double colon (::)—for example, 2002:470:B8F9::29FF:FE53:45CA. This means there are consecutive groups of all 0s, so :: might be shorthand for :0000:0000:0000. *Global unicast* addresses, the public IPv6 addresses, have a prefix of 001.

IPv6 addresses use a network mask the same way IPv4 addresses do—to distinguish which portion of the address identifies the network. As is often done with IPv4, the mask is expressed with a front slash (/) and the number of bits in the mask; for example, 2002:470:B8F9:1:20C:29FF:FE53:45CA/64 implies a 64-bit network mask.

You can see both IPv4 and IPv6 data by using IPCONFIG at a command prompt or from a GUI interface. In Windows 10, click Start | Settings | Network & Internet | Status, and then scroll down in the right pane to the Change Your Network Settings section and click View Your Network Properties. See Figure 16-5. In Windows 11, click Start | Settings | Network & Internet | Properties.

Addresses for IP Configuration

When you view the IP configuration for the NIC on your PC, you may be surprised to see other IP addresses besides that of the NIC. These include addresses labeled Default Gateway, DHCP Servers, and DNS Servers.

Default Gateway When your IP protocol has a packet ready to send, it examines the destination IP address and determines if it is on the same IP network (in the earlier example, this is 192.168.1.0) as your computer. If it is, then it can send the packet directly to that computer (host ID 41 in the example). If the destination IP address is on another IP network, then your computer sends it to the IP address identified as the *default gateway*. This address is on your network (same IP network ID), and it belongs to a router that will send the packet on to the next router in its journey to its destination. Without a default gateway, your computer does not know what to do with packets that have a destination address beyond your IP network. IPv6 also requires a default gateway setting to route packets to remote networks. This can be configured manually or delivered via a Dynamic Host Configuration Protocol (DHCP) device that supports IPv6.

DNS Server A *DNS client* uses the DNS server IP address for name resolution. The *Domain Name System (DNS)* manages access to Internet domain names, like mcgraw-hill.com. The server-side service maintains a database of domain names and responds to

FIGURE 16-5 Viewing your network's properties in the Settings app in Windows 10

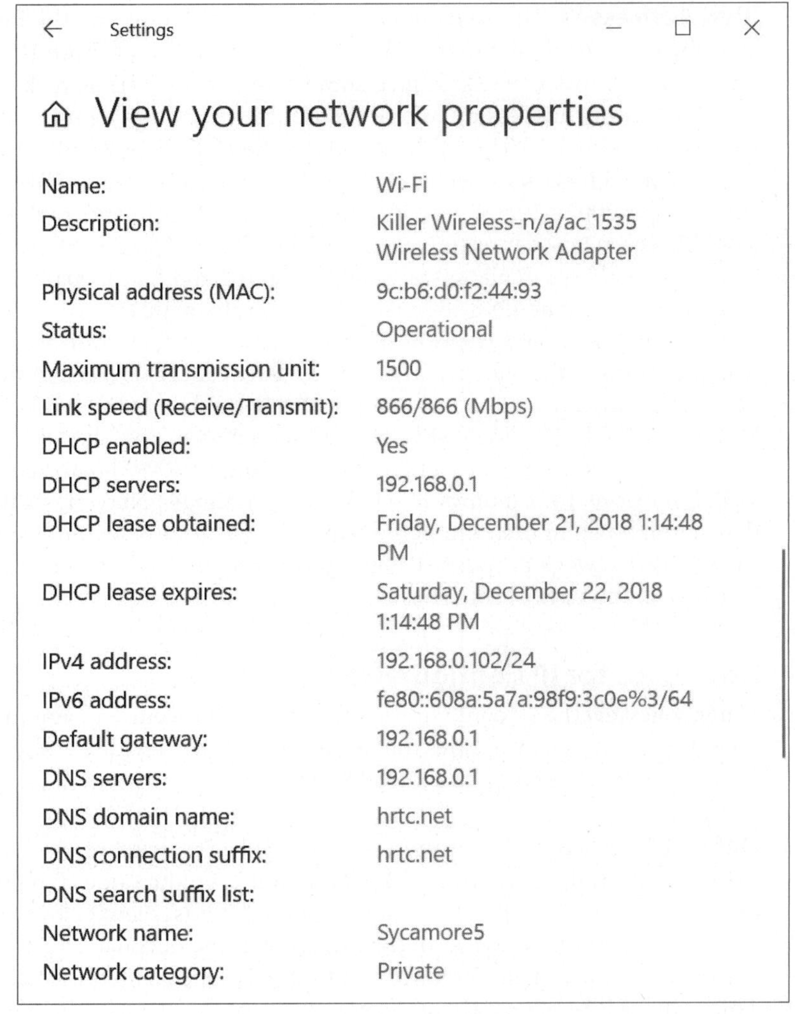

queries from DNS clients (called resolvers) that request resolution of Internet names to IP addresses. A client will do this before sending data over the Internet, when all it knows is the domain name. For instance, if you wish to connect to a McGraw Hill web server, you might enter **www.mheducation.com** in the address bar of your browser. Then, your computer's DNS client (the resolver) sends a request to a DNS server, asking it to resolve the name to an IP address.

Once the DNS server has the answer (which it most likely had to request from another DNS server), it sends a response to your computer. The IP protocol on your computer now attaches the address to the packets your computer sends requesting a web page.

IPv4 clients query a DNS server for "A" records, which map to an IPv4 address. IPv6 clients query an IPv6 DNS server for "AAAA" (quad A) records to resolve names to IP addresses. Note that an IPv6 address (128 bits) is four times longer than an IPv4 address (32 bits)!

1101 exam Objective 2.6 lists A, AAAA, MX, and TXT as DNS configuration components. Make sure you understand the purpose of each.

DNS also uses other records. For example, a *mail exchange (MX) record* is used to route e-mail messages to a mail server using Simple Mail Transfer Protocol (SMTP).

Spam Management with DNS Another type of DNS record is Text (TXT). *TXT records* are used to send human-readable information about a server or network. 1101 Objective 2.6 lists only one use for TXT records: spam management. You add TXT records to your DNS server to help protect PCs against spamming, phishing, and other threats. Here are the specific record types the exam objective mentions:

- **Domain Keys Identified Mail (DKIM)** Signs messages with encryption to prevent your e-mail address from being spoofed by someone trying to send messages posing as you. It attaches a digital signature to your outgoing mail, which the receiving server can verify.
- **Sender Policy Framework (SPF)** Prevents attackers from using your domain to send spam by specifying which servers and domains are allowed to send e-mail.
- **Domain-based Message Authentication, Reporting, and Conformance (DMARC)** Provides instructions to receiving servers about how to handle messages that appear to come from your domain but don't pass SPF or DKIM tests.

To add TXT records for your domain, sign into the site where you host your domain and use the administrative configuration tools there. The details will depend on the admin interface your host provides.

Assigning IP Addresses to NICs There are two ways to assign an IP address to a network host: manually (or statically) and automatically (or dynamically). We will discuss assigning an address manually here and automatically in the next section when we discuss DHCP. When you assign an address manually in Windows, you must open the Properties dialog box for the NIC and enter the exact IP address (obtained from your network administrator), subnet mask, and other configuration information, which includes the addresses for the default gateway and DNS server. An IP address configured in this manner is a *static address.* This address is not permanent, because an administrator can easily change it, but some documentation uses the term permanent rather than static.

DHCP Server When you install any non-server version of Windows, the Setup program installs the TCP/IP protocol suite and configures the computer (or its network card, to be more specific) as a *DHCP client,* meaning it configures it to obtain an IP address automatically from a DHCP server. A NIC configured as a DHCP client will send a request out on the network when Windows starts.

Now, you would think that a client computer without an IP address would not be able to communicate on the network, but it can in a very limited way. Using a special protocol called *BOOTP,* the computer sends a very small message that a *Dynamic Host Configuration Protocol (DHCP)* server can read. It cannot communicate with other types of servers until it has an IP address. A properly configured *DHCP server* will respond by sending the DHCP client an IP address and subnet mask (also using BOOTP). This configuration is the minimum it will assign to the client computer. In most cases, the server will provide the other IP configuration addresses, including the default gateway and DNS server.

A DHCP server does not permanently assign an IP address to a client. It leases it. *Lease* is the term used, even though no money changes hands in this transaction between a DHCP client and a DHCP server. When one half of the leased time for an IP address (and its associated configuration) has expired, the client tries to contact the DHCP server in order to renew the lease. As long as the DHCP server has an adequate number of unassigned IP addresses, it will continue to reassign the same address to the same client each session. In fact, this happens every day for a computer that is turned off at the end of the workday, at which point the DHCP client will release the IP address, giving up the lease.

The *scope* of a DHCP server is the range of addresses it can assign to clients on a certain subnet. Certain addresses may be reserved for certain devices, but outside of those *reservations,* clients requesting an IP address are assigned one from the available pool of addresses—and it may not be the same address each time.

Make sure you understand how a DHCP server leases IP addresses that are within its defined scope, honoring any address reservations that are configured in it.

Exercise 16-2 walks you through using a command that displays the physical address and IP address for your network card.

EXERCISE 16-2

Viewing the Physical and IP Addresses of a NIC

To view the physical and IP addresses of a NIC, follow these steps:

1. Open a command prompt.
2. In the Command Prompt window, enter the command **ipconfig /all** and press ENTER.
3. The result should look something like the following illustration, only with different addresses.

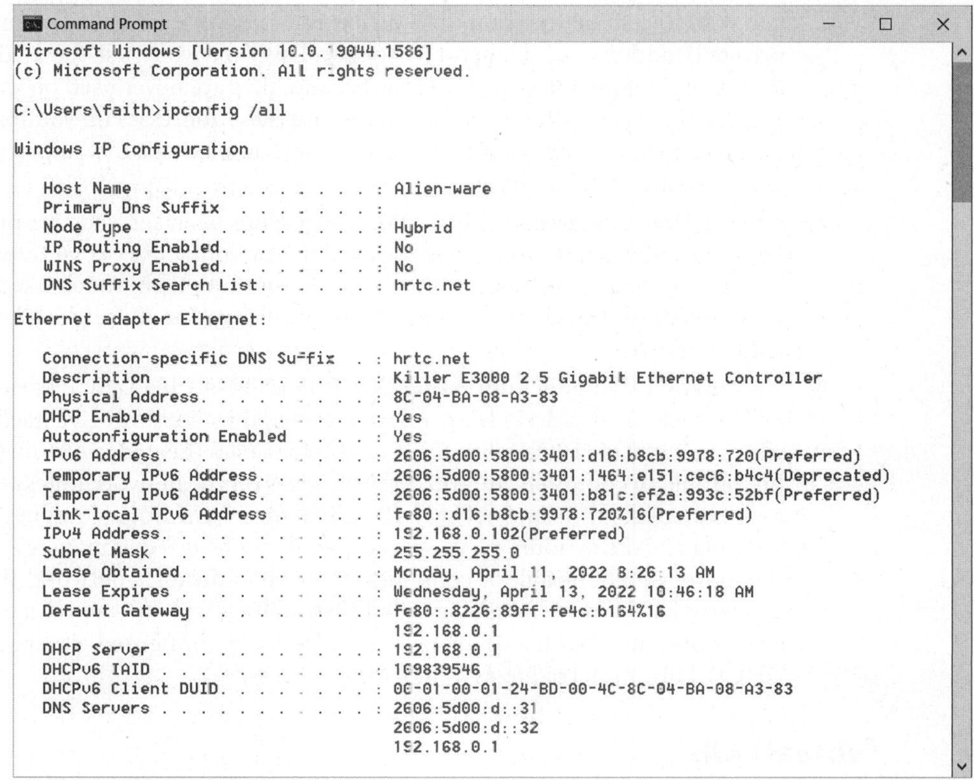

Command Prompt
Microsoft Windows [Version 10.0.19044.1586]
(c) Microsoft Corporation. All rights reserved.
C:\Users\faith>ipconfig /all
Windows IP Configuration
Host Name . . . . : Alien-ware
Primary Dns Suffix . . . . :
Node Type . . . . : Hybrid
IP Routing Enabled. . . . . : No
WINS Proxy Enabled. . . . . : No
DNS Suffix Search List. . . . . . : hrtc.net
Ethernet adapter Ethernet:
Connection-specific DNS Suffix . : hrtc.net
Description . . . . : Killer E3000 2.5 Gigabit Ethernet Controller
Physical Address. . . . . : 8C-04-BA-08-A3-83
DHCP Enabled. . . . . : Yes
Autoconfiguration Enabled . . . . : Yes
IPv6 Address. . . . . : 2606:5d00:5800:3401:d16:b8cb:9978:720(Preferred)
Temporary IPv6 Address. . . . . . : 2606:5d00:5800:3401:1464:e151:cec6:b4c4(Deprecated)
Temporary IPv6 Address. . . . . . : 2606:5d00:5800:3401:b81c:ef2a:993c:52bf(Preferred)
Link-local IPv6 Address . . . . . : fe80::d16:b8cb:9978:720%16(Preferred)
IPv4 Address. . . . . : 192.168.0.102(Preferred)
Subnet Mask . . . . : 255.255.255.0
Lease Obtained. . . . . : Monday, April 11, 2022 8:26:13 AM
Lease Expires . . . . : Wednesday, April 13, 2022 10:46:18 AM
Default Gateway . . . . : fe80::8226:89ff:fe4c:b164%16
192.168.0.1
DHCP Server . . . . : 192.168.0.1
DHCPv6 IAID . . . . : 109839546
DHCPv6 Client DUID. . . . . : 00-01-00-01-24-BD-00-4C-8C-04-BA-08-A3-83
DNS Servers . . . . : 2606:5d00:d::31
2606:5d00:d::32
192.168.0.1

4. The address of the NIC is labeled Physical Address. Notice that the physical address is six pairs of hexadecimal numbers separated by hyphens.
5. Three lines below that is the NIC's IPv6 address, and four lines below that is the IPv4 address.
6. Locate the other addresses discussed in the preceding text, including those of the default gateway, DNS servers, and DHCP server (if present).

Special IP Addresses You use public IP addresses on the Internet, and each address is globally unique. But there are some special IP addresses that are never allowed for computers and devices connected directly to the Internet. They are as follows:

- **Loopback addresses** Although it is generally believed that the address 127.0.0.1 is the IPv4 loopback address, any Class A address with a network ID of 127 is a loopback address, used to test network configurations. If you send a packet to a loopback address, it will not leave your NIC. Sounds like a useless address, but you will use it for testing and troubleshooting in Chapters 17 and 19. Also, note that the IPv6 loopback address is ::1 (0:0:0:0:0:0:0:1).
- **Private IPv4 addresses** If a network is not directly connected to the Internet, or if you wish to conceal the computers on a private network from the Internet, you use private IP addresses. Millions of locations all over the world use these addresses, and they are therefore not globally unique because they are never used on the Internet. In Chapter 17, we will describe how you can use these addresses on your private network, yet still access resources on the Internet, thanks to methods that hide your address when you are on the Internet.
- **Private IPv6 addresses** The FC00::/7 range has been set aside for private IPv6 network addressing. These addresses will not be routable by IPv6 Internet routers, but internal routers within an organization can route them much like they do IPv4 private addresses. The proper term for this type of address is a Unique Local Address (ULA).
- **Automatic Private IP Addressing (APIPA) address** If a DHCP client computer fails to receive an address from a DHCP server, the client will give itself an address with the 169.254 /16 network ID. If a computer uses this range of addresses, it will not be able to communicate with other devices on the network unless they also have addresses using the same network ID, which means the other computers must also be using an APIPA address. These clients will not have a default gateway address and therefore will not be able to communicate beyond the local network. IPv6 behaves similarly, except that the self-assigned IPv6 address will have a prefix of FE80 and is always present, even if a routable IPv6 address was configured either statically or via DHCP. This is referred to as a "link local address."

Virtual LANs

Sometimes you might wish that physically separate LANs were all part of the same LAN, so you would operate on them as a group as a network administrator. A *virtual LAN (VLAN)* allows you to do just that. It enables devices from multiple wired and wireless networks to exist as a single logical network so you can administer them as a group.

To create a VLAN, all the routers and switches involved must support VLAN configuration. You'll find VLAN controls in the router's browser-based setup. The entire router or switch does not have to be on the same VLAN; you can set up individual ports on a switch to be part of a specific VLAN.

You don't have to know the details of setting up a VLAN, but you should at least be able to explain what a VLAN is and why you would want one.

Common Ports

It isn't enough for a packet to simply reach the correct IP address; each packet has additional destination information, called a *port,* which identifies the exact service it is targeting. For instance, when you want to open a web page in your browser, the packet requesting access to the web page includes both the IP address (resolved through DNS) and the port number of the service. In this case, it would be HTTP for many web pages and HTTPS for a secure web page where you must enter confidential information. All the services you access on the Internet have port numbers. These include the two services just mentioned, plus FTP, POP3, SMTP, Telnet, SSH, and many more. Each port is also associated with a protocol. The most common protocols for communicating with Internet applications are TCP and UDP. TCP is used for communications that are connection oriented, which is true of most services you are aware of using, whereas *Universal Datagram Protocol (UDP)* is used for connectionless communications, in which each packet is sent without establishing a connection. Therefore, in Table 16-1, we identify the protocol along with the port number for common TCP/IP services.

exam watch

Make sure you understand that TCP is connection-oriented, whereas UDP is connectionless. DHCP can use either one. TFTP is an example of a port that always uses UDP, and HTTPS and SSH are examples of ports that always use TCP.

For the CompTIA A+ 220-1101 exam Objective 2.1, be sure you understand the common TCP and UDP ports and protocols mentioned in this section.

TABLE 16-1 Protocol and Port Numbers for Common Internet Services

Service	Port	Descriptions
Domain Name System (DNS)	UDP 53	Used by DNS clients to perform DNS queries against DNS servers
Dynamic Host Configuration Protocol (DHCP)	TCP/UDP 67/68	Used for assigning IP addresses to clients; can be used with either TCP or UDP
File Transfer Protocol (FTP)	TCP 20/21	Transfers files between an FTP client and FTP server
Hypertext Transfer Protocol (HTTP)	TCP 80	Web page transmission to web browser (not secure)
HTTP over Secure Sockets Layer/ Transport Layer Security (HTTPS)	TCP 443	Secure transmission of web pages
Internet Message Access Protocol Version 4 (IMAP4)	TCP 143	Retrieves e-mail; advanced features beyond POP3, such as folder synchronization
Lightweight Directory Access Protocol (LDAP)	TCP 389	A standard method of accessing a network database; often used for authenticating user accounts during user logon
NetBIOS/NetBIOS over TCP/IP (NetBT)	TCP 137/139	Supports older applications that use the NetBIOS protocol
Post Office Protocol Version 3 (POP3)	TCP 110	Retrieves e-mail from a POP3 mail server
Remote Desktop Protocol (RDP)	TCP 3389	Used to remotely access a Windows desktop
Secure Shell (SSH)	TCP 22	Secure (encrypted) terminal emulation that replaces Telnet
Server Message Block (SMB)/ Common Internet File System (CIFS)	TCP 445	Windows file and print sharing service
Simple Mail Transfer Protocol (SMTP)	TCP 25	Sending e-mail
Simple Network Management Protocol (SNMP)	UDP 161/162	Queries network devices for status and statistics
Telnet	TCP 23	Terminal emulation; all data sent in clear text (not secure)
Trivial File Transfer Protocol (TFTP)	UDP 69	Differs from FTP in that there is no option for authentication

exam watch

CompTIA A+ 220-1102 exam Objective 1.11 mentions Samba for Linux machines. Samba is an application suite that uses the SMB protocol to enable Linux machines to make network connections to Windows machines. You don't need to know how to configure Samba, but you should know its purpose and be able to suggest it as a method of making such connections.

SCENARIO & SOLUTION

Scenario	Solution
Is it better to assign IP addresses to individual workstations through static addressing or dynamic addressing?	Dynamic addressing is better because it prevents most IP address conflicts.
When would I use an IPv6 address?	Most of the Internet still runs on IPv4 at this writing, but most larger Internet providers also support using IPv6, so you should follow the lead of your provider.
My PC has an automatically assigned IP address of 169.254.2.1. Why?	That's an APIPA address, and you have it because your router's DHCP server failed to assign the PC an address. Investigate the router settings.

CERTIFICATION OBJECTIVES

- ***1101: 2.2*** *Compare and contrast common networking hardware*
- ***1101: 2.3*** *Compare and contrast protocols for wireless networking*
- ***1101: 3.1*** *Explain basic cable types and their connectors, features, and purposes*

In this section we will survey the various hardware devices used on networks—some of them for connecting networks to each other, and some for allowing client computers and devices to access networks. Knowledge of these is required for CompTIA A+ 1101 exam Objective 2.2. This discussion will also venture into the Wi-Fi networking standards implemented in wireless networking hardware, covered in CompTIA A+ 1101 exam Objective 2.3.

This section also covers the features and characteristics of network cabling, including fiber-optic, twisted-pair, and coaxial cabling, as well as their connectors, as required by CompTIA A+ 1101 exam Objective 3.1.

Network Hardware

Network hardware includes many network connection devices that are part of the infrastructure of small networks, as well as large internetworks, and of the largest internetwork, the Internet itself. We limit the hardware we describe in this section to the network adapters used in PCs, the medium that connects these adapters to the network, the devices that connect networks to one another, and a few miscellaneous devices included in the CompTIA A+ 220-1101 exam objectives.

Network Adapters

While we previously mentioned network interface cards (NICs) in this chapter, we now focus on this particular type of network hardware device. Each computer on a network must have a connection to the network provided by a NIC, also called a *network adapter,* and some form of network medium that makes the connection between the NIC and the network. NICs are identified by the network technology used (Ethernet or Wi-Fi) and the type of interface used between the NIC and the PC, such as the PCIe interface introduced in Chapter 8 or the USB interface defined in Chapter 9.

Most Ethernet NICs come with status indicators as lights on the card itself and/or software that displays the status on the notification area of the taskbar. You can use these when troubleshooting, as described in Chapter 19.

Transmission Media

The transmission medium for a network carries the signals. These signals may be electrical signals carried over copper-wire cabling, light pulses carried over fiber-optic cabling, or radio waves transmitted through the atmosphere. In these examples, the copper wire, fiber-optic cable, and atmosphere are the media. In this section, after an overview of cable in general, we'll look at the basics of twisted-pair, coaxial, and fiber-optic cabling. We also look at Wi-Fi networking standards for wireless data transmission.

Cable Basics: What's Inside a Cable?

A wide variety of cables physically connect computer components and networks. These cables carry electronic signals for power, control of devices, and data. But what's inside these cables? The basic cable types you will encounter are twisted-pair (shielded and unshielded), fiber-optic, and coaxial. All of these except fiber-optic are classified as *copper cable.*

> **Copper cable includes unshielded twisted-pair categories (Cat 5, 5e, 6, and 6a), shielded twisted-pair, and coaxial.**

A *straight-pair cable* consists of one or more metal wires surrounded by a plastic insulating sheath. A *twisted-pair cable* consists of two sheathed metal wires twisted around each other along the entire length of the cable to avoid electrical interference, with a plastic covering sheath surrounding it. A *multicore twisted-pair cable* has multiple pairs of twisted wires, but in practice even the multicore twisted-pair is simply called "twisted-pair."

A *coaxial cable* contains a single copper wire, surrounded by at least one insulating layer, a woven wire shield that provides both physical and electrical protection, and an outer jacket.

A *fiber-optic cable* has a core made of one or more optical fiber strands surrounded by a protective cladding, which is in turn reinforced by strength fibers; all of this is enclosed in an outer jacket. Fiber-optic cable carries light pulses rather than electrical signals, so it is not susceptible to electromagnetic interference (EMI).

Figure 16-6 displays these five basic cable types. We will revisit the use of various cables in future chapters.

FIGURE 16-6 Common cable types used to connect computer components and networks

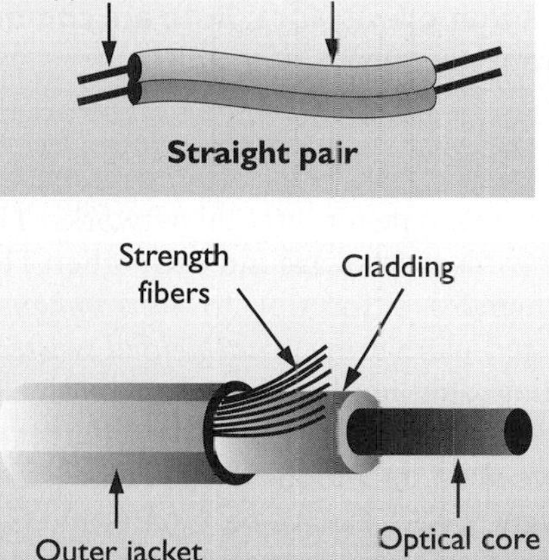

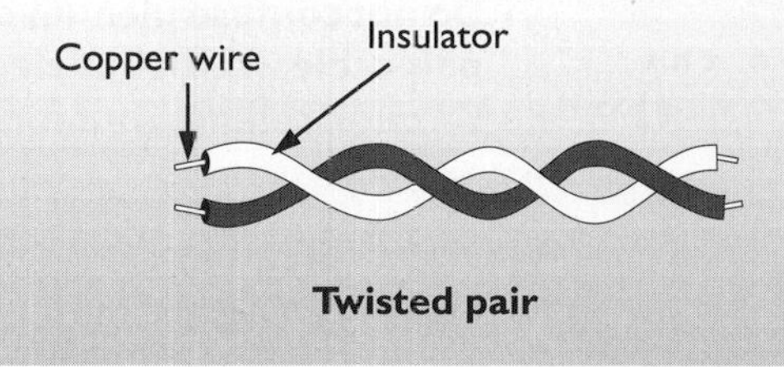

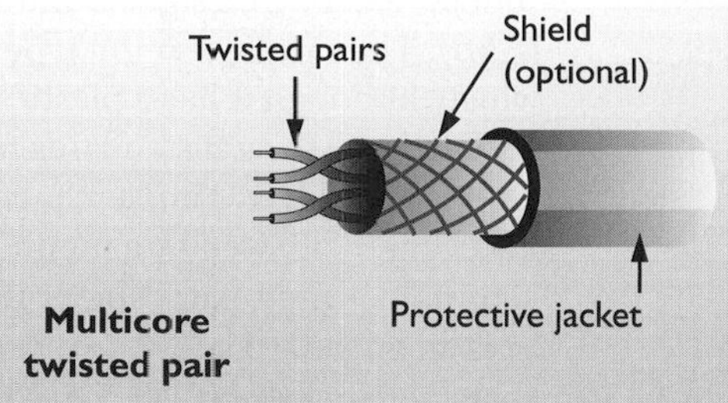

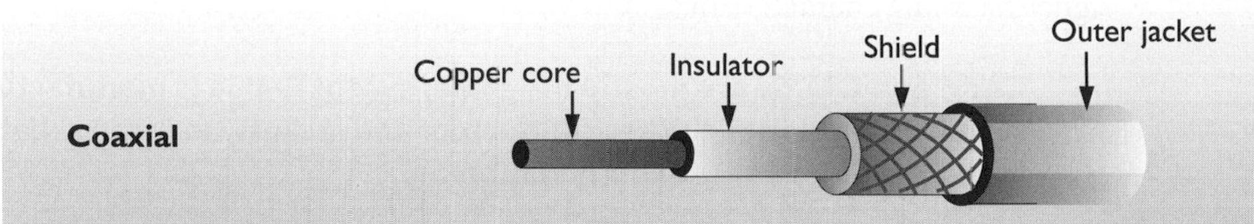

Direct Burial Cable

Direct burial cable is cable that is buried underground outdoors, such as when running fiber-optic or coaxial cable from the street to a residence. Direct burial cable is extra sturdy, crush-resistant, and water-resistant, so it won't degrade over time from the moisture and temperature fluctuations. Shielded twisted-pair and coaxial cable both come in direct burial versions.

Remember that direct burial wire is required when running cables underground.

Plenum vs. PVC

Many commonly used network cables use a *polyvinyl chloride (PVC)* outer sheath to protect the cable. PVC is not fire resistant, and, by code, you cannot use it in overhead or *plenum* areas in offices—those spaces in a building through which air conditioning and heating ducts run. *Plenum cable* uses a special fire-resistant outer sheath that will not burn as quickly as PVC. Plenum cable frequently costs more, but most areas require it. Most of the standard cables discussed in this chapter are available in plenum-grade ratings.

Do not confuse plenum cable, which has fire resistance, with shielded twisted-pair cable, which has electromagnetic resistance. Both are commonly run through ceilings, but for different reasons.

Twisted-Pair

Twisted-pair cable is the most popular cable type for internal networks. The term "twisted-pair" indicates that it contains pairs of wires twisted around each other. These twists help "boost" each wire's signals and make them less susceptible to *electromagnetic interference (EMI).* The most common type of twisted-pair wiring is *unshielded twisted-pair (UTP),* which, although it has a plastic sheathing, does not have actual metal shielding.

There are several standards for twisted-pair cables, each with a different number of wires, certified speed, and implementation. We often refer to these standards as CAT (short for "category") followed by a number. Currently, CAT 5, CAT 5e, CAT 6, and CAT 6a are the most common twisted-pair cable types. Table 16-2 summarizes twisted-pair cable standards. CAT 5e is an enhanced and more stringently tested version of CAT 5 that offers better transmission characteristics than CAT 5. CAT 6 and CAT 7 cable offer even higher bandwidth and improved signal-handling characteristics.

CAT 6 and CAT 6a are mostly the same, except Cat 6a is manufactured to tighter standards and uses thicker conductors and jackets, so it can reliably transmit at high speeds across greater distances.

TABLE 16-2

Cable Categories

Type	Speed
CAT 5	100 Mbps
CAT 5e	1 Gbps
CAT 6	10 Gbps at up to 165 feet
CAT 6a	10 Gbps at up to 328 feet
CAT 7	10 Gbps
CAT 8	25 Gbps or 40 Gbps

The telecommunications standards organization, *Telecommunication Industry Association/Electronics Industry Alliance (TIA/EIA),* developed the *TIA/EIA 568* standards for telecommunications cabling. TIA/EIA standards are now labeled per the standards group, the American National Standards Institute (ANSI), with an ANSI prefix. A portion of these standards, now called the *ANSI/TIA/EIA-568-B* standard, includes pin assignments for connecting eight-wire cabling to Ethernet connectors. One pin assignment is called *T568A,* and the other is *T568B.* Technically, as long as you standardize on one pin assignment, either is fine. However, T568B is recommended, and the use of T568A is only recommended if you want to create a cross-over cable, which you can accomplish by using the T568A standard on one end and the T568B standard on the other, as the main difference is in the assignment of the two wires that these two standards reverse.

According to the ANSI/TIA/EIA standard for CAT 5e copper cable (TIA/EIA 568-5-A), the maximum length for a structured wiring cable segment is 100 meters (328 feet) without need for a switch or a hub (repeater). With a repeater, you can run up to five segments for 10BaseT. For 100BaseT, you can use two hubs for a cable run of up to 200 meters (656 feet). Using modern switches with 100M and Gigabit LANs raises these limits. Consult the switch vendor's specifications for details.

Twisted-pair cable is also available as *shielded twisted-pair (STP),* with an extra insulating layer that helps prevent data loss and blocks EMI. However, due to the expense of STP, UTP is more commonly used.

You can identify a twisted-pair cable by its use of RJ-45 connectors, which look like regular RJ-11 phone connectors but are slightly larger, as they contain eight wires, whereas RJ-11 connectors contain four wires.

The oldest cabling you should normally encounter in a business is CAT 5e, although it is certainly possible to find very old installations of CAT 5 or even CAT 3 cabling (used for regular analog telephone service), neither of which is adequate for modern networks.

Coaxial Cable

The type of cabling used to connect a cable modem to a cable network is coaxial cable, which consists of a central copper wire surrounded by an insulating layer, which is itself surrounded by a braided metal shield that protects the signals traveling on the central wire from outside interference. A plastic jacket encases all of this. Refer back to Figure 16-6.

Coaxial cable used for standard cable television and high-definition TV (HDTV), as well as cable-modem Internet access, is usually RG-6 cable with a 75-ohm rating. Theoretically, signals can travel up to 300 meters at 500 Mbps over RG-6 coax cables, but the practical limit is 50 Mbps, which still makes this medium very popular for broadband Internet connections. The specific distance and speed vary, depending on the type of signal and the devices generating the signal.

Expect an RG-6 cable to connect to the cable wall jack and cable modem with *F-type connectors* that you must securely screw on.

A *splitter* is a box that allows two cables to join to a single cable. Splitters are most common on coaxial cable, such as when splitting the incoming signal from a cable TV/ Internet provider into two branches: one for the TV and one for the cable modem. Splitters do affect signal strength, so don't use them unnecessarily. If you think that splitting may be degrading the signal to the point where errors are occurring, ask a service technician from the cable company to check the lines.

Splitters are also available for UTP cable, but you probably don't want one. If you want to share a single incoming network signal with multiple devices, use a switch or router.

Fiber-Optic Cable and Connectors

Fiber-optic cable (*fiber* for short) has commonly been used to join separate networks over long distances, but until recently, LANs seldom used fiber-optic cable. Increasingly, however, many new homes, apartments, and businesses have both fiber and copper wiring installed when being built. Also, some phone companies are using fiber to connect directly to homes and businesses.

Fiber transmits light rather than electrical signals, so it is not susceptible to EMI. It is capable of faster transmission than other types of cable, but it is also the most expensive cable.

A single light wave passing down fiber cabling is a *mode*. Two variants of fiber used in fiber-optic cables are *single-mode fiber (SMF)* and *multimode fiber (MMF)*. SMF allows only a single light wave to pass down the cable but supports faster transmission rates over longer distances. MMF allows multiple light waves to pass simultaneously and is usually larger in diameter than SMF; each wave uses a certain portion of the fiber cable for transmission. There are many Ethernet standards for fiber-optic cabling, with a wide range of maximum speeds and distances. MMF is used most often in LANs with speeds up to 1 Gbps and a maximum range of 1000 meters, whereas SMF has a range of dozens of miles with speeds in the terabits per second range.

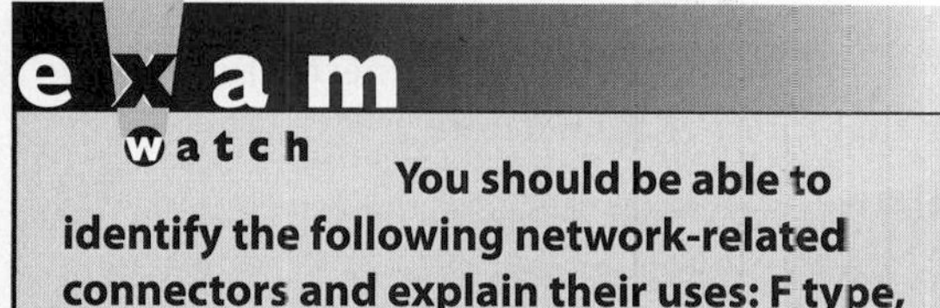

You should be able to identify the following network-related connectors and explain their uses: F type, RJ11, RJ45, ST, SC, and LC.

Fiber-optic data transmission requires two cables: one to send and another to receive. Connectors enable fiber-optic cable to connect to transmitters, receivers, or other devices. Over the years, the various standards for connectors have continued to evolve, moving toward smaller connectors. Here are brief descriptions of three types of connectors used with fiber-optic cable:

- **Straight-tip (ST)** A straight, round connector used to connect fiber to a network device. It has a twist-type coupling.
- **Subscriber connector (SC)** A square snap coupling, about 2.5 mm wide, used for cable-to-cable connections or to connect cables to network devices. It latches with a push-pull action similar to audio and video jacks.
- **Lucent connector (LC)** Also called *local connector,* it has a snap coupling and, at 1.25 mm, is half the size of the SC connector.

Figure 16-7 shows ST and SC connectors.

Wireless Networking Standards

Wireless LAN (WLAN) communication (local area networking using *radio frequency,* or *RF*) is very popular. The most common wireless LAN implementations are based on the IEEE 802.11 group of standards, also called *Wireless Fidelity (Wi-Fi).* There are several 802.11 standards in use, and more have been proposed. These wireless standards use either 2.4-GHz or 5-GHz frequencies to communicate between systems. The range on these systems is relatively short, but they offer the advantage of not requiring cable for network connections.

Many public places, such as libraries, restaurants, and other businesses, offer free or pay access to Wi-Fi networks that connect to broadband Internet services. Such a point of connection to the Internet through a Wi-Fi network is called a *hotspot.* On an interesting twist on this concept, cellular providers and manufacturers of cellular-enabled mobile devices have cooperated to provide a newer type of service called a *mobile hotspot.* You

FIGURE 16-7 The ST and SC connectors used with fiber-optic cable

can create a mobile hotspot (also called *tethering*) by connecting to the Internet with your smartphone's cellular service and then using the smartphone's Wi-Fi connectivity to allow other nearby Wi-Fi–enabled devices to share that Internet connection.

1101 exam Objective 2.3 lists all the 802.11 standards: a, b, g, n, ac (Wi-Fi 5), and ax (Wi-Fi 6). Make sure you can put them in order of oldest (slowest) to newest (fastest) and identify their maximum bandwidths and ranges.

Here is a brief description of several 802.11 standards and their features:

- **802.11a** The *802.11a* standard was developed by the IEEE at the same time as the slower 802.11b standard, but the "a" standard was more expensive to implement. Manufacturers therefore tended to make 802.11b devices. 802.11a uses the 5-GHz band, which makes 802.11a devices incompatible with 802.11b and the subsequent 802.11g devices. Because 802.11a devices do not provide downward compatibility with existing equipment using the 802.11b or newer 802.11g standards, they are seldom used. An 802.11a network has speeds up to 54 Mbps with a range of up to 150 feet.
- **802.11b** The *802.11b* standard was the first widely popular version of Wi-Fi, with a speed of 11 Mbps and a range of up to 300 feet. Operating in the 2.4-GHz band that is also used by other noncomputer devices such as cordless phones and household appliances, these devices are vulnerable to interference if positioned near another device using the same portion of the radio spectrum.
- **802.11g** *802.11g* replaced 802.11b. With a speed of up to 54 Mbps and a range of up to 300 feet, it also uses the 2.4-GHz radio band. 802.11g devices are normally downward compatible with 802.11b devices, although the reverse is not true.
- **802.11n** The *802.11n* standard has speeds of up to 100+ Mbps and a maximum range of up to 600 feet. The standard defines speeds of up to 600 Mbps, which actual implementations do not achieve. *MIMO (multiple input/multiple output)* makes 802.11n speeds possible using multiple antennas to send and receive digital data in simultaneous radio streams that increase performance.
- **802.11ac** The *802.11ac* standard has multistation throughput of 1 Gbps and a single-link throughput of 500 Mbps. It accomplishes these higher speeds by using a wider RF bandwidth than 802.11n, more MIMO streams (up to eight), and high-density modulation. It can operate in both the 2.4-GHz and 5-GHz ranges, which allows for more available channels. It is also called Wi-Fi 5.
- **802.11ax** The *802.11ax* standard operates only in the 5-GHz range. It combines some advanced wireless techniques to achieve bandwidth improvements of up to 3.5 Gbps for a single stream (14 Gbps with four streams combined), while still maintaining backward compatibility with 802.11n and 802.11ac. It is also called Wi-Fi 6.

Although it's not on the current exams, Wi-Fi 6e is now available, which uses the 6-GHz spectrum.

A frequency band such as 2.4 GHz is logically segmented into *channels.* A device will be configured to use a particular channel. You'll learn more about channels in Chapter 17.

In 1101 exam Objective 2.3, channels 1 to 11 are referenced; those are the channels commonly used for the 2.4-GHz band.

When considering a wireless network, determining its speed and range can be nebulous at best. In spite of the maximums defined by the standards, many factors affect both speed and range. First, there is the limit of the standard, and then there is the distance between the wireless-enabled computer and the *wireless access point (WAP),* a network connection device at the core of a wireless network. Finally, there is the issue of interference, which can result from other wireless device signals operating in the same band or from physical barriers to the signals. In Chapter 17, you will learn about installing a WLAN to avoid interference and devices that will extend the range of the signals. You will also learn about the configuration options for wireless networks, including the use of identifiers for the wireless devices, secure encryption settings, and settings for keeping intruders out.

Be sure you understand that Wi-Fi alone does not give you a connection to the Internet, because it is a LAN technology. The reason people are able to connect to the Internet through a Wi-Fi connection is that the Wi-Fi network connects to a broadband connection through a device called a *wireless router*, a combination WAP and router.

Devices for Connecting to LANs and the Internet

Most LANs now connect to other LANs or through WAN connections to internetworks, such as the Internet. A variety of network connection devices connect networks. Each serves a special purpose, and a single device may contain two or more of these functions.

Repeater

A *repeater* is a device used to extend the range of a network by taking the signals it receives from one port and regenerating (repeating) those signals to another port. Repeaters are available for various networks. For instance, on an Ethernet network, you would use an Ethernet repeater, and on a Wi-Fi network you would use a wireless repeater (often called a signal booster) to boost the signal between wireless networks. In both cases, the repeater must be at the appropriate level and speed for the network.

Bridge

A *bridge* is a device used to connect two networks, and it passes traffic between them using the physical address of the destination device. Bridges segment large networks into smaller networks and only forward network traffic to the segment where the recipient station resides. A bridge is specific to the hardware technology in use. For instance, an Ethernet bridge looks at physical Ethernet addresses (MAC addresses) and forwards Ethernet frames with destination addresses that are not on the local network. Bridges are now seldom used, since a switch functions as both a bridge and a hub.

Optical Network Terminal

An *optical network terminal (ONT)* is a type of bridge that converts data from an optical network into a format that can be delivered using standard Ethernet cable. For a fiber to the home Internet installation, the ONT is typically mounted on the side of the home or in the garage. It may have a battery backup connected to it. An Ethernet cable then runs from the ONT to a wall jack in the home, to which you would connect your router.

Hub

A *hub* is a device that is the central connecting point of a classic Ethernet LAN. It is little more than a multiport repeater, because it takes a signal received on one port and repeats it on all other ports. An *active hub* will regenerate the signal and send it on to all devices connected to the network. A *passive hub* is simply a wiring panel or punchdown block for connecting or disconnecting devices.

Switch

After the introduction of 100BaseT, the *switch* replaced the classic hub. This is a more intelligent device that takes an incoming signal and sends it only to the destination port. This type of switch is both a bridge and a hub. At one time switches were very expensive, but now small eight-port switches are inexpensive and commonly used, even in very small LANs.

As always, each computer or other device in a network attaches to a switch of the type appropriate for the type of LAN. For example, computers using Ethernet cards must connect to an Ethernet switch; wireless devices attach wirelessly to a wireless hub, more often called a WAP or wireless router. Devices may combine these functions, as in the case of a WAP or wireless router that includes an Ethernet switch (look for one or more RJ-45 connectors). This last scenario is very common.

Switches can be either managed or unmanaged. An *unmanaged switch* has no configuration options and no interface with which to configure them. *Managed switches* enable you to control them by logging into them with a browser or some other method, such as an SNMP agent or a Telnet or Secure Shell (SSH) connection. There are two subclasses of managed switches. Smart switches (intelligent switches) have only a limited feature set and are used in small networks. Enterprise-managed switches have more options and are used in large business environments.

Router

Connections between networks usually require some form of routing capability. In the case of a connection to the Internet, each computer or device connected to the network requires a TCP/IP address. In order to reach a computer on another network, the originating computer must have a means of sending information to the other computer. To accomplish this, routes are established, and a *router*, a device that sits at the connection between networks, stores information about destinations.

You should be able to identify and compare common network hardware, including routers, switches, and access points, and explain how they perform different functions than Internet connection boxes such as cable and DSL modems.

Patch Panels

In corporate networks with many clients, the sheer number of individual Ethernet cables running from individual PCs to routers is staggering. A *patch panel* can help keep the cable connections orderly by providing a central point into which the cables for many workstations can connect (see Figure 16-8). Some high-capacity switches also serve as patch panels, physically organizing a large number of cables, as well as distributing local network data.

Power over Ethernet

Power over Ethernet (PoE) passes electrical power through twisted-pair Ethernet cabling. It allows one cable to serve as both data and electrical conduit to a device. It allows you to set up network devices in locations where there is no AC outlet and power them via the same Ethernet cable that connects them to the network. PoE is popular for use with security cameras, paging systems, wall clocks that get the time from the network, and routers placed in out-of-the-way locations.

FIGURE 16-8 A patch panel (Photo: https://commons.wikimedia.org/wiki/File:In_Floor_Patch_Panel_Fiber.jpg [Creative Commons license])

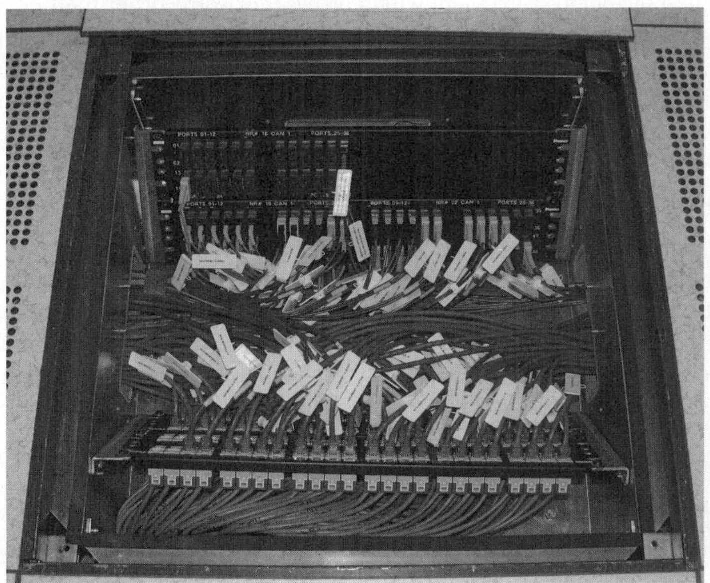

A switch that supports PoE has *power injection* built in. In other words, it injects power into the cables that run to the PoE devices. A device called a *midspan injector* (or *PoE injector*) can be used to add PoE capability to regular non-PoE network switches and routers.

Wireless Access Point

A *wireless access point,* also called a WAP, allows wireless clients to connect to a wired network. Most access points also have built-in routing capability and, as such, are called *wireless routers*. Modern access points are configurable in "isolation mode," which isolates wireless clients from one another, usually for security or privacy purposes.

Cable or DSL Modem

A *cable modem* (or *DSL modem*) is a communication box that sends/receives data between a cable or DSL ISP and a client's local PC or network. Customers sometimes may buy their own boxes, but they are typically rented from the ISP and are swapped out for newer models as technology advances every few years to allow greater speeds.

Depending on the technology used for the Internet connection, there might or might not be translation between analog and digital, so technically these boxes may not be modems using the strictest definition of the term. Some people call them *terminal adapters* instead, which they insist is more accurate. Nevertheless, the terms cable modem and DSL modem are widely used.

Firewall

A *firewall* restricts or allows the flow of network traffic based on a set of rules. A firewall can be a hardware device or it can be software. Hardware firewalls run on network devices such as dedicated firewall appliances or routers or on a dedicated computer. Software firewalls run within an operating system and apply *IP packet filtering,* a service that inspects (or filters) each packet that enters or leaves the network; apply a set of security rules defined by a network administrator; and do not allow packets that fail inspection to pass between networks. When you change the rules to allow a certain type of traffic through a firewall, you are making an *exception.* To allow or deny traffic, you can base a firewall rule on many attributes, including

- **Type of packet** Defined by port; TCP 80 (HTTP website) or TCP 443 (HTTPS website) traffic might be allowed, whereas TCP 25 (SMTP outbound e-mail) traffic might be denied.
- **Source/destination** SMTP traffic to a specific host might be allowed, but all other destination SMTP hosts could be denied.

Firewalls are also covered in Chapter 22.

EXERCISE 16-3

Identifying Network Hardware

See what network hardware you can identify in your home, office, or school.

1. If you have a PC in your home and it has a connection to the Internet, locate and identify the network components.
2. If you use a dial-up connection, look for the modem, the telephone cable between the modem and the phone jack on the wall, and the RJ-11 connectors at either end of the telephone cable.
3. If you have a DSL connection, look for the Ethernet cable that runs between your computer and the hub/switch or modem. Examine the RJ-45 connectors on either end of the cable. The cable may connect to a single box that performs all of these functions.

4. If you have cable Internet service, look for an Ethernet cable between your computer and the cable modem, and then look for a coaxial cable between the modem and the wall connector.
5. At school or work, all you may find is an Ethernet cable connecting your computer to a wall jack that connects to the cable in the walls that connects to the network. Ask the network administrator to describe how you connect to the Internet through the network.

Software-Defined Networking

As Internet connectivity becomes faster and more reliable, some companies are turning to software-defined networking (SDN), a cloud-based solution for networking. It pushes much of the network routing and management functions to cloud services to enable secure connectivity between branch offices and buildings more inexpensively and reliably than a business could set up using their own hardware. Nearly any network function that can be achieved via local hardware can be done using SDN. Chapter 18 looks at cloud services in more detail.

exam watch

A+ 1101 exam Objective 2.2 includes the term *software-defined networking*. Make sure you understand that some aspects of a network can be managed via software as an alternative to local hardware systems.

SCENARIO & SOLUTION	
I need to set up some security cameras in locations where there is no power outlet. How can I power them?	Power them with Power over Ethernet (PoE). Use PoE injectors if needed to inject power into the connections provided by your existing switches, or use switches with PoE capability.
What good does it do me to memorize TCP port numbers?	You can allow or block access to certain ports in your firewall program, and you can understand security reports that show certain ports being used. It will also help you pass the CompTIA A+ 220-1101 exam.
What's the difference between a switch and a router?	A switch handles only local network traffic; a router provides a path out of the local network to another network such as the Internet.

CERTIFICATION SUMMARY

IT professionals preparing for the CompTIA A+ 220-1101 and 220-1102 exams must understand the basic concepts of computer networks. More in-depth knowledge is required for other exams, such as the CompTIA Network+, Security+, and Server+ exams. Basic concepts include network topologies—the geographic classifications of networks into PANs, LANs, MANs, and WANs. You must also understand Internet connection methods, such as fiber, cable, DSL, and satellite. Be able to identify the most common cabling types, connectors, and common network adapters used in PCs.

Understand that TCP/IP is a protocol suite designed for the Internet and now used on most LANs and interconnected networks. Understand network-addressing concepts, including physical addresses assigned to network adapters and logical addresses assigned and used through the network protocols.

Understand the various addresses that are part of an IP configuration and their roles. These include the IP address and subnet mask of the network adapter, default gateway, and DNS server and DHCP server addresses and functions.

Be prepared to distinguish between various network hardware, including adapters, the transmission medium, network-to-network connection devices, and devices for connecting computers to a network (hubs and switches).

TWO-MINUTE DRILL

Here are some of the key points covered in Chapter 16.

Network Classifications

- ❑ Networks fall into several classifications, including PAN, LAN, MAN, WAN, and SAN.
- ❑ PAN technologies include the use of standards for wireless transmissions over very short distances. These include infrared (IR/IrDA), limited to about 1 meter, and Bluetooth, which has a range of up to 10 meters.
- ❑ A LAN is a network that covers a building, home, office, or campus. Common LAN technologies include Ethernet in wired LANs and Wi-Fi in wireless LANs.
- ❑ A MAN covers a metropolitan area and generally uses fiber-optic cable.
- ❑ A WAN covers a large geographic area, connecting networks across long distances. A WWAN is a wireless WAN.
- ❑ A SAN is a data network that connects and manages large-scale storage devices.
- ❑ Dial-up WAN connections are the slowest and require initiation of the connection every time a user wishes to connect to a remote resource.

Internet Connection Types

- Bandwidth and latency are two important evaluative factors for Internet and network connections.
- Fiber is fast and reliable but is not available in all areas.
- Cable Internet is also fast, but you have to share the bandwidth with your neighbors.
- DSL is an older technology, not as fast, that uses copper telephone lines.
- Satellite Internet is available almost anywhere but has high latency and tends to be more expensive than other options.

Network Software and Protocols

- The roles played by the computer on the network describe the network. The two most general roles are those of clients and servers.
- A network in which any computer can be both a client and a server is a peer-to-peer network. A client/server network is one in which most desktop computers are clients and dedicated computers act as servers.
- A protocol suite is a group of related protocols that work together to support the functioning of a network. TCP/IP is the dominant protocol suite, as well as the protocol suite of the Internet.
- TCP/IP is a suite of protocols used for most networks today, including the Internet. Its two main protocols are TCP and IP.
- TCP is a connection-oriented protocol used for transmissions where receipt must be verified. UDP is a connectionless protocol used for transmission where no verification of receipt is required.
- Network addressing occurs at both the physical level and the logical level. Every Ethernet network adapter from every Ethernet NIC manufacturer in the world has a unique physical address, also called a MAC address, which is 48 bits long and is usually shown in hexadecimal notation.
- Internet Protocol is concerned with logical addresses. An IPv4 address is 32 bits long and is usually shown in dotted-decimal notation, as in 192.168.1.41. IPv6 has 128-bit addressing, which theoretically supports a huge number of unique addresses.
- An IPv4 and IPv6 address configuration includes a subnet mask, which determines the host ID and network ID portions of the address. In addition, the IP configuration may include addresses for a default gateway, DNS server, and DHCP server.
- Items that have IP addresses assigned to them include the NIC, default gateway, DHCP server, and DNS servers. IP addresses can be assigned in a static or dynamic way.
- DNS servers store information in records. A records map to IPv4 addresses, and AAAA records map to IPv6 addresses. MX records route e-mail messages. DNS server records can be used for spam management via DKIM, SPF, and DMARC.

- ❑ A DHCP server dynamically assigns IP addresses. It leases an address to a device, within its defined scope, honoring any address reservations.
- ❑ Special IP addresses include loopback, private addresses, and APIPA addresses. APIPA addresses are assigned if the client computer fails to receive an address from a DHCP server.
- ❑ A virtual LAN enables devices from multiple networks to exist as a single logical network.
- ❑ In addition to an IP address, a packet will contain a port number identifying the service on the target computer that should receive the packet's contents. You should be familiar with the port numbers for common networking services.

Network Hardware

- ❑ A network adapter provides the connection to the network medium. Network adapters (network interface cards) are available for the various networking technologies, such as Ethernet and Wi-Fi.
- ❑ Physical transmission media include twisted-pair, fiber-optic, and coaxial cable. UTP cable is categorized (CAT 5e, CAT 6, and so on). TIA/EIA T568A and T568B are wiring standards for twisted-pair cable.
- ❑ Coaxial cable is usually RG-6, with an F type connector. Fiber-optic cable can be single-mode or multimode, and can use an ST, SC, or LC connector.
- ❑ Special-purpose cables include direct burial and plenum.
- ❑ Wireless networking standards are governed by IEEE 802.11. Common standards within that specification are 802.11a, b, g, n, ac, and ax.
- ❑ A repeater is a device used to extend the range of a network by taking the signals it receives from one port and regenerating (repeating) those signals to another port.
- ❑ A bridge is a device used to connect two networks and pass traffic between them based on the physical address of the destination device. An ONT is a bridge used to connect a fiber network to a copper wire network.
- ❑ A hub is a device that is the central connecting point of an old LAN, with all network devices on a LAN connecting to one or more hubs. More intelligent devices called switches or switching hubs now replace hubs on Ethernet networks. These take an incoming signal and send it only to the destination port.
- ❑ A router sits between networks and routes packets according to their IP addresses. Many routers combine routing and bridging and connect multiple network technologies, such as a LAN and a WAN.
- ❑ A patch panel is like a switchboard for networking connections, helping to organize cables.
- ❑ Power over Ethernet (PoE) enables you to deliver power to devices through the same network cable that carries its data. A midspan injector can add PoE capability to non-PoE equipment.

- ❑ A wireless access point (WAP) is a wireless switch.
- ❑ A cable or DSL modem is a box that communicates between an ISP and the client's local network or PC.
- ❑ A firewall is hardware or software that restricts the flow of network traffic based on a set of rules.
- ❑ Software-defined networking (SDN) uses cloud services to handle network routing and management functions.

SELF TEST

The following questions will help you measure your understanding of the material presented in this chapter. Read all the choices carefully because there might be more than one correct answer. Choose all correct answers for each question.

Network Classifications

1. Which type of network enables two laptops in the same room to share files?

A. PAN
B. LAN
C. MAN
D. WAN

2. Which of the following statements is true about a LAN versus a WAN?

A. A LAN spans a greater distance than a WAN.
B. A WAN spans a greater distance than a LAN.
C. A LAN is generally slower than a WAN.
D. A WAN is used within a home or within a small business.

3. Which of the following is a PAN technology?

A. Ethernet
B. Satellite
C. Bluetooth
D. 802.11

4. What is the type of network that connects many private networks in one metropolitan community?
   A. PAN
   B. MAN
   C. WAN
   D. LAN

Internet Connection Types

5. Which of the following uses copper telephone lines for Internet service?
   A. Fiber
   B. DSL
   C. Cable
   D. Satellite
6. Which of the following Internet connection methods uses light rather than electricity to send and receive data?
   A. Fiber
   B. DSL
   C. Cable
   D. Satellite
7. Which of the following Internet connection types uses a network originally created for television transmissions?
   A. DSL
   B. Cellular
   C. Cable
   D. Fiber
8. Which of the following is a term that describes the amount of data that can travel over a network within a given time?
   A. Bandwidth
   B. Kilobits
   C. Latency
   D. IPv4
9. Which of the following is a term that describes the amount of time it takes a packet to travel from one point to another?
   A. Bandwidth
   B. Mbps
   C. Latency
   D. UDP

Network Software and Protocols

10. Which statement describing IPv4 versus IPv6 differences is correct?
    A. IPv6 uses a subnet mask, while IPv4 uses 128-bit addressing.
    B. IPv4 uses 128-bit addressing, while IPv6 uses 32-bit addressing.
    C. IPv4 uses 32-bit addressing, while IPv6 uses 128-bit addressing.
    D. IPv4 uses double colons to indicate consecutive groups of 0s.
11. Which port is the correct one for Hypertext Transfer Protocol (HTTP) and web page transmission to a browser?
    A. TCP 80
    B. UDP 53
    C. TCP 443
    D. TCP 110
12. What protocol used on the Internet is concerned with the logical addressing of hosts?
    A. TCP
    B. IP
    C. UDP
    D. MAC
13. What protocol adds the old Microsoft naming system to TCP/IP?
    A. Fiber
    B. NetBIOS
    C. DHCP
    D. DNS
14. What divides an IP address into its host ID and network ID components?
    A. Default gateway
    B. DNS server
    C. DHCP server
    D. Subnet mask
15. A NIC has this type of a permanent address assigned to it by the manufacturer.
    A. IP address
    B. Physical address
    C. Host ID
    D. Automatic address

16. A packet with a destination address not on the local network will be sent to the address identified by which label in the IP configuration?
   A. Default gateway
   B. DNS server
   C. DHCP server
   D. Subnet mask

Network Hardware

17. Which of the following statements is correct?
   A. CAT 5 cable can transmit 1 Gbps.
   B. CAT 6 cable can transmit 10 Gbps.
   C. CAT 5, CAT 5e, and CAT 6 segments can all be a maximum of 200 meters long.
   D. CAT 5e cable can transmit 10 Gbps.
18. Which of the following is not a network medium?
   A. Plenum
   B. Twisted-pair cable
   C. Fiber-optic cable
   D. Atmosphere
19. Which type of cable uses ST, SC, or LC connectors?
   A. STP
   B. UTP
   C. Fiber-optic
   D. Coaxial
20. Thousands of this type of device exist on the Internet between networks, direct the traffic of the Internet using the destination IP address of each packet, and pass the packets to their destinations along the interconnected networks of the Internet.
   A. Router
   B. Modem
   C. NIC
   D. Hub

SELF TEST ANSWERS

Network Classifications

1. ☑ **B.** A local area network (LAN) enables devices in the same building or room to share files.
☒ **A** is incorrect because a PAN is used to connect peripherals to computers wirelessly at very short range. **C** is incorrect because a MAN is a network within a city or metro area. **D** is incorrect because a WAN is a network with a large geographical area.

2. ☑ **B.** A WAN spans a greater distance than a LAN.
☒ **A, C,** and **D** are incorrect because they are not true.

3. ☑ **C.** Bluetooth is a personal area network (PAN) technology used to connect devices and computers over very short distances.
☒ **A, B,** and **D** are incorrect because none of these is a PAN technology. Ethernet is a wired LAN technology, satellite is a WAN technology, and 802.11 is a set of WLAN standards.

4. ☑ **B.** MAN, a metropolitan area network, is the type of network that connects many private networks in one community.
☒ **A** is incorrect because a PAN is a personal area network that only connects devices in a very small area (usually a few meters). **C** is incorrect because a wide area network connects over long distances. **D** is incorrect because a local area network is limited to a distance of hundreds of meters and would not span an entire metropolitan community.

Internet Connection Types

5. ☑ **B.** DSL uses copper telephone lines.
☒ **A** is incorrect because fiber uses fiber-optic cable. **C** is incorrect because cable uses coaxial cable shared with TV cable service. **D** is incorrect because satellite uses a satellite dish with a transmitter.

6. ☑ **A.** Fiber uses fiber-optic cable, which transmits data via light.
☒ **B** and **C** are incorrect because DSL and cable both use copper wire. **D** is incorrect because satellite transfers data wirelessly.

7. ☑ **C.** Cable Internet uses the same coaxial cable used for television transmissions.
☒ **A** is incorrect because DSL uses the same twisted-pair cable used for telephone. **B** is incorrect because cellular Internet uses cell phone towers. **D** is incorrect because fiber uses fiber-optic data lines.

8. ☑ **A.** Bandwidth is the amount of data that can travel over a network within a given time.
☒ **B** is incorrect because kilobits is a measurement of thousands of bits. **C** is incorrect because latency describes the amount of travel time for a packet. **D** is incorrect because IPv4 is the standard governing IP addressing.

9. ☑ **C.** Latency is the term for the time it takes a packet to travel from one point to another.
☒ **A** is incorrect because bandwidth is the amount of data that can travel over a network within a given time. **B** is incorrect because Mbps is a measurement of millions of bits per second. **D** is incorrect because UDP is a type of connectionless protocol.

Network Software and Protocols

10. ☑ **C.** IPv4 uses 32-bit addressing, while IPv6 uses 128-bit addressing.
☒ **A** is incorrect because IPv4 uses 32-bit addressing. IPv6 can use a subnet mask also. **B** is incorrect because it is just the opposite. **D** is incorrect because it is IPv6 that uses the double colons to indicate consecutive groups of 0s.

11. ☑ **A.** TCP 80 is the correct port number for HTTP and web page transmission to a web browser.
☒ **B** is incorrect because UDP 53 is the port for Domain Name System used by clients to perform DNS queries against DNS servers. **C** is incorrect because TCP 443 is the port used by HTTPS for secure web page transmission. **D** is incorrect because TCP 110 is the port for Post Office Protocol that retrieves e-mail from a POP3 mail server.

12. ☑ **B.** IP is the protocol used on the Internet that is concerned with the logical addressing of hosts.
☒ **A, C,** and **D** are incorrect because these are not concerned with the logical addressing of hosts.

13. ☑ **B.** NetBIOS is the protocol that adds the old Microsoft naming system to TCP/IP.
☒ **A** is incorrect because fiber is a cable type. **C** is incorrect because DHCP is the protocol used for automatically allocating IP addresses. **D** is incorrect because DNS is the protocol that supports Internet-style names.

14. ☑ **D.** A subnet mask divides an IP address into its host ID and network ID components.
☒ **A** is incorrect because the default gateway is the name of the router address to which a computer directs packets with destinations beyond the local network. **B** is incorrect because the DNS server is where a network client sends queries to resolve DNS names into IP addresses. **C** is incorrect because the DHCP server is what automatically assigns IP addresses to DHCP client computers.

15. ☑ **B.** The physical address is the type of permanent address assigned to a NIC by the manufacturer.
☒ **A** is incorrect because an IP address is not a permanent address, but a logical address not permanently assigned to a NIC. **C** is incorrect because the host ID is the portion of an IP address that identifies the host. **D** is incorrect because an automatic address usually refers to an IP address assigned to a PC by a DHCP server.

16. ☑ **A.** The default gateway is the address to which the router sends packets that have addresses not on the local network.
☒ **B** is incorrect because this server resolves DNS names. **C** is incorrect because the DHCP server assigns IP addresses automatically. **D** is incorrect because a subnet mask is not an address, but a mask used to divide an IP address into its host ID and network ID components.

Network Hardware

17. ☑ **B.** CAT 6 can indeed transmit 10 Gbps.
☒ **A** is incorrect because CAT 5 can only transmit 100 Mbps. **C** is incorrect because each of these cable categories requires a repeater or a switch at 100 meters. **D** is incorrect because CAT 5e can only transmit 1 Gbps.

18. ☑ **A.** Plenum is not a network medium, but rather a characteristic of certain network media (cables), indicating the cable sheath is fire resistant and appropriate to run in plenum space.
☒ **B, C,** and **D** are incorrect because all are networking media.

19. ☑ **C.** Fiber-optic cable uses ST, SC, or LC connectors.
☒ **A, B,** and **D** are incorrect because they do not use ST, SC, or LC connectors.

20. ☑ **A.** A router is the device that exists on the Internet and passes IP packets from many sources to destinations along the Internet.
☒ **B** is incorrect because a modem does not pass packets along the Internet, although it is a beginning point for a single computer to send packets. **C** is incorrect because a network interface card (NIC) is simply a device for connecting a single computer to a network. **D** is incorrect because a hub is an older device used at the heart of a LAN, but not an Internet device.

Chapter 17

Installing a Small Office/Home Office (SOHO) Network

CERTIFICATION OBJECTIVES

- **1101: 2.3** Compare and contrast protocols for wireless networking
- **1101: 2.5** Given a scenario, install and configure basic wired/wireless small office/home office (SOHO) networks
- **1101: 2.6** Compare and contrast common network configuration concepts
- **1101: 2.8** Given a scenario, use networking tools
- **1101: 5.7** Given a scenario, troubleshoot problems with wired and wireless networks
- **1102: 1.4** Given a scenario, use the appropriate Microsoft Windows 10 Control Panel utility
- **1102: 1.5** Given a scenario, use the appropriate Windows settings
- **1102: 1.6** Given a scenario, configure Microsoft Windows networking features on a client/desktop

- **1102: 2.2** Compare and contrast wireless security protocols and authentication methods
- **1102: 2.9** Given a scenario, configure appropriate security settings on small office/home office (SOHO) wireless and wired networks
- **1102: 4.9** Given a scenario, use remote access technologies

✓ Two-Minute Drill

Q&A Self Test

In this chapter, you will learn the tasks required to install and configure client computer access to a local area network (LAN) or wireless local area network (WLAN), focusing mainly on a small network, such as you would find in a small office or home office (SOHO).

CERTIFICATION OBJECTIVE

- ***1101: 2.8** Given a scenario, use networking tools*

We start out this chapter by reviewing the hardware tools for creating and maintaining networks covered in CompTIA A+ 1101 exam Objective 2.8. Some of these tools were also mentioned in Chapter 8 in the section "The Hardware Toolkit," but in the following section they get full coverage.

Using Networking Tools

Networking tools—at least the hardware ones—are mainly required to make wired connections and test those connections. As you read through the descriptions for using these tools and the discussion in the next section on connecting a wired NIC to a network, recall the information in Chapter 16 in the section titled "Cable Basics: What's Inside a Cable?"

Crimper and Cable Stripper

To create your own unshielded twisted-pair (UTP) network cables, you will need bulk UTP cabling, RJ-45 connectors, and a crimper. A *crimper,* also called a crimp tool, resembles a pair of pliers, but is used to terminate a multistranded cable into a connector.

To terminate a Cat-5/6 Ethernet cable, for example, use a *cable stripper,* also called a *wire stripper,* on each end of the cable to strip off the insulation and expose the four wire pairs. Ensure the wires are in the correct order and place them into an RJ-45 connector. Insert the RJ-45 connector into the crimper and squeeze the crimper handles, clamping each wire in place. The RJ-45 connector has eight small metal probes or needles, each of which will pierce one of the eight wires. Figure 17-1 shows a crimper with a crimped network cable.

Punchdown Tool

Network installers have the responsibility of running network cables through walls and creating RJ-45 wall outlets in offices. This is done by hard-wiring the cable to the wall outlet at one end and to a patch panel in the wiring closet at the other end.

First, a network installer runs cable through the walls of the building, with one end terminating in the wiring closet and the other end poking out of a small hole in the office receiving the wall outlet. Then at the office end, the installer uses a *punchdown tool* (see Figure 17-2) to insert each of the bare wires into the back of a port mounted in a wall plate and then attaches that plate to the wall. A punchdown tool has a screwdriver-type handle and one or more specialized blades for inserting various types of wiring into appropriate wiring panels.

Next, the installer goes to the wiring closet and uses the wire stripper and punchdown tool again to connect the wires inside the cable to the back of an RJ-45 port on a patch panel. Now the cable has been hard-wired from the wall outlet to the wiring panel. Next, the installer uses a short cable to connect the newly wired RJ-45 port on the wiring panel to a switch or router, being careful to label the short cable to describe the location of the office being connected.

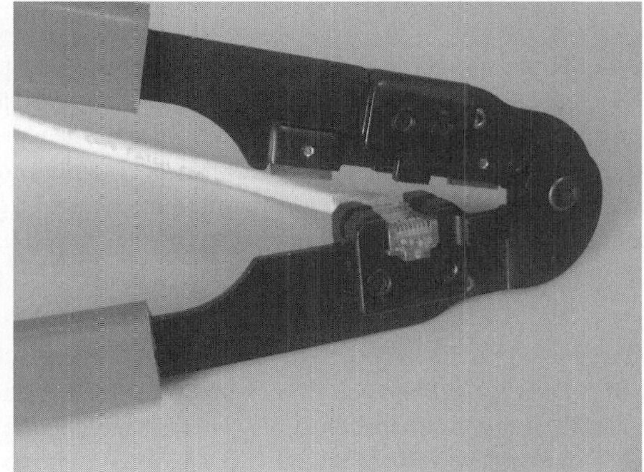

FIGURE 17-1

Using a wire-crimping tool to attach an RJ-45 connector to a UTP cable

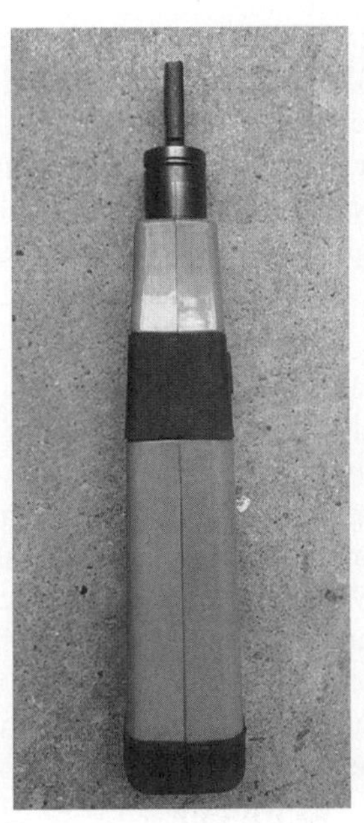

FIGURE 17-2 A punchdown tool helps insert bare wires into connectors. (Photo: https://commons.wikimedia.org/wiki/File:Ideal_punchdown_tool,_side.jpg [Creative Commons license])

Why not just directly hard-wire the cable into the switch or router? You can probably guess the answer. If you need to replace the switch or router, you don't want to have to rewire dozens of ports.

Toner Probe

Wiring rooms can sometimes look like a packrat's nest—complete and utter chaos. To determine exactly which cable in the wiring room maps to a network jack in another room, use a tone generator and probe. A tone generator and *toner probe* work together as a pair. The tone generator connects to a cable or network jack and sends a tone along the cable. As you pass the toner probe near the cable carrying the tone, the probe gets louder. This helps you isolate a specific cable in a cable bunch.

Cable Tester

Sometimes network cables look fine, but some wires inside may be bent and broken. Testing STP and UTP network cable continuity is easy with a *cable tester,* a machine that detects if a cable can correctly carry a signal. It has two RJ-45 ports where you plug in each end of the cable. Indicator lights tell you whether wires inside the cable are intact. You can test some kinds of cable with a multimeter by checking each wire individually, but a cable tester is much quicker because it tests all the pins/wires at once. Several types of cable testers are available, such as those for copper Ethernet and phone cables, fiber-optic cable testers, and coaxial cable testers. See Figure 17-3.

Loopback Plug

A *loopback plug* is a plug wired to send signals back to a specific port type or device, such as a USB port or Ethernet adapter, as a test of the device. It reroutes the sending pins from the port or device to the receiving pins, thus allowing you to test the ability to send and receive without connecting to an external device or network. It's employed along with software that sends and receives the signal through the port and interprets the results.

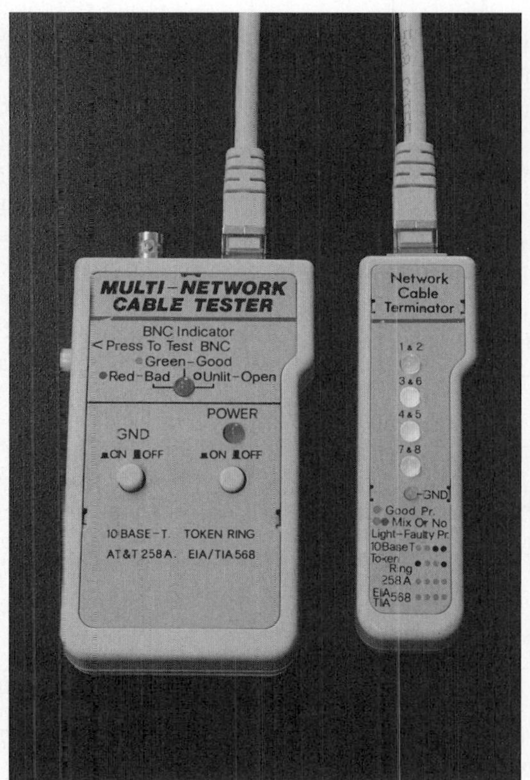

FIGURE 17-3

A network cable tester (Photo: Rainer Knäpper; Free Art License, http://artlibre.org/licence/lal/en/)

Wi-Fi Analyzer

A *Wi-Fi analyzer* is an electronic device that lets you know what wireless networks are within range and some basic information about them, such as the Service Set Identifier (SSID), channel, signal strength, encryption type, geographical coordinates (working in conjunction with GPS), and many other details. Used often during wireless site surveys to detect nearby WLANs and their channels, the tool can also be used during a security audit to test WLAN visibility, distance, and security. A wireless locator can be a specialized handheld device or software installed on a smartphone, tablet, laptop, or PC. Fluke is one popular brand of Wi-Fi analyzer for professional use.

A tablet or smartphone can be used as a basic wireless locator without any special software. Just pull up the settings screen, where you choose a wireless network, and watch the list of available networks as you move around.

Network Tap

Tap is an acronym for *test access point*. It's a device that you insert in the network traffic flow that copies packets for use in security analysis and network monitoring. There are different kinds of taps, including passive (listen-only), active (with additional functions, like regeneration and filtering), and virtual (which support monitoring traffic into and out of virtual environments like containers and virtual machines).

A *network tap* is used to get greater visibility into a network's operation. After collecting the network traffic data, you can then use it to analyze the network activity or to find security holes.

The CompTIA A+ 1101 exam may present a scenario where you need to implement the appropriate networking tool. Be sure you are familiar with all the tools covered in this section.

CERTIFICATION OBJECTIVES

- ***1101: 2.3*** *Compare and contrast protocols for wireless networking*
- ***1101: 2.5*** *Given a scenario, install and configure basic wired/wireless small office/home office (SOHO) networks*
- ***1101: 5.7*** *Given a scenario, troubleshoot problems with wired and wireless networks*
- ***1102: 1.6*** *Given a scenario, configure Microsoft Windows networking features on a client/desktop*

- ***1102: 2.2*** *Compare and contrast wireless security protocols and authentication methods*
- ***1102: 2.9*** *Given a scenario, configure appropriate security settings on small office/home office (SOHO) wireless and wired networks*

A CompTIA A+ certification candidate must know how to connect desktop and laptop computers to a LAN. This requires understanding how to install and configure common network hardware.

In this section we cover the wireless encryption types listed in CompTIA A+ 1102 exam Objective 2.2 and channel and frequency selection from 1101 exam Objective 2.3. This section also covers WAP and router security settings from 1102 exam Objective 2.9. We also hit a few troubleshooting topics from 1101 exam Objective 5.7 that can be avoided by making good decisions when setting up the network initially.

Installing and Configuring SOHO Networks

A *small office/home office (SOHO)* is an office consisting of a single computer or just a few computers. The location may be in a home or in a commercial office. Computers in a SOHO environment need to connect to the Internet, requiring the same steps you would take in a larger environment. A connection to a LAN requires a network adapter for each computer—whether it is a wired NIC (Ethernet) or a Wi-Fi NIC. Therefore, the first step in connecting a computer to a network is to install a NIC appropriate for the type of network—wired or wireless. Once you've installed the NIC and driver, you need to configure the NIC with an appropriate IP configuration, along with any other settings appropriate to the type of network. In this section, we describe the software tools and settings required for installing and configuring a network and then describe the steps for configuring a typical SOHO network.

Installing a Network Adapter

Most computers have a built-in wired Ethernet adapter, but add-on adapters are also available. A network adapter can be internal (using a PCIe card) or external (using a USB port or ExpressCard slot). You learned in Chapter 9 how to install an internal expansion card. If your network adapter is built into the motherboard, you can enable or disable it via the motherboard BIOS/UEFI and perhaps adjust some of its settings there too. You learned how to access that in Chapter 8.

To connect a computer to a LAN, plug one end of an Ethernet cable into the network adapter on the computer and plug the other end into a switch or router. Use UTP cable of no more than 100 meters that conforms to at least the Cat 5e standard. Connect the other computers in the network to the same switch or router, and voila, you have a LAN. Most switches and routers have at least four wired Ethernet ports on them (in addition to any wireless device connection capabilities they might have), as shown in Figure 17-4.

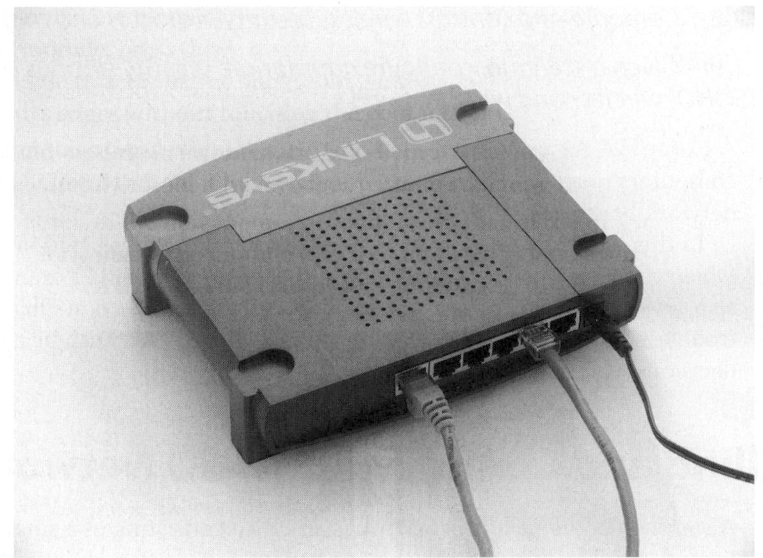

FIGURE 17-4

This SOHO router acts as a switch for the LAN and provides a connection to a cable or DSL modem.

Connecting a Network Adapter to a Switch or Router

The next step is to make a physical connection between the network adapter and the switch or router. Most SOHO switches are also *broadband routers,* meaning they are designed to allow several computers to share an Internet (broadband) connection. You connect an Ethernet cable from the broadband modem (or from the fiber connection jack) to the router via a specially labeled port on the router (usually something like WAN or Internet).

Older routers may have an uplink port in addition to the WAN or Internet port. An uplink port is a reverse-wired port, designed to be used with a cross-over cable to connect two routers. Don't confuse this with the WAN port, which is what you plug the Internet cable into.

Creating a Wi-Fi Network

Before you install a wireless network, you must consider some special issues for selecting and positioning wireless hardware. These issues include obstacles between the computers and the WLAN, the distances involved, any possible interference, the standards supported by the devices on the Wi-Fi network, and the wireless mode for your WLAN. Then you should take steps to update the firmware on the wireless access point (WAP), if necessary.

External Interference and Obstacles

Certain devices emit radio signals that can interfere with Wi-Fi networks. These devices include microwave ovens and cordless telephones that use the 2.4-GHz radio band, as well as other nearby WAPs. WAPs normally support channel selection. Therefore, if you have a 2.4-GHz cordless landline phone that supports channel selection, configure the phone to use one channel (channel 1, for instance) and the WAP and each wireless NIC to use another channel, like channel 11. In addition, metal furniture and appliances, metal-based ultraviolet (UV) tint on windows, and metal construction materials within walls can all block or reduce Wi-Fi signals.

on the job

When a computer or other physical device connects to a network, it is called a *node*.

Certain businesses and organizations require a professional wireless site survey, a set of procedures to determine the location of obstacles and interference that would disrupt wireless signals. WAP placement is then determined from this site survey. Although a professional site survey is too costly for a small business or home owner, you can use the site survey feature of your wireless NIC to discover which channel nearby wireless networks are using. The name of the site survey feature may simply be Available Networks, which shows a list of wireless networks. Clicking a network in the list reveals the channel in use and other important information. Alternatively, use a wireless locator, described earlier in this chapter.

For 2.4-GHz mode, channels 1, 6, and 11 are all good, because they don't overlap each other. For 5-GHz mode, there are plenty of channels without overlap so channel selection is less of an issue.

Distances and Speeds

A huge issue with wireless networks is the signal range of the communicating devices. All the Wi-Fi standards give maximum outdoor signal ranges of 75 to 125 meters, but that is for a signal uninterrupted by barriers, such as walls that may contain signal-stopping materials like metal lath. Position a WAP in a central location within easy range of all devices, NICs, and access points.

The farther a wireless NIC is from a WAP, the more the signal degrades and the greater the chance of slowing down the connection speed. Actual ranges for these devices once in place vary greatly. For devices that use multiple bands to achieve their throughput, like 802.11ac, a WAP will be described in its marketing with the number of streams it supports. The theoretical maximum for 802.11ac is eight streams, but most SOHO routers support either two or three.

exam watch

Make sure you understand how a standard's operating frequency, data rate, and range factor into deciding when and how to use it.

The ranges for the various standards are shown in Table 17-1.

TABLE 17-1 Summary of Common Wi-Fi 802.11 Standards

IEEE Standard	Operating Frequency	Typical Data Rate	Maximum Data Rate	Indoor Range	Outdoor Range
802.11b	2.4 GHz	6.5 Mbps	11 Mbps	~35 meters	~100 meters
802.11g	2.4 GHz	25 Mbps	54 Mbps	~25 meters	~75 meters
802.11n	2.4 GHz or 5 GHz	200 Mbps	540 Mbps	~50 meters	~125 meters
802.11ac (Wi-Fi 5)	5 GHz	866 Mbps per stream	3.5 Gbps	~50 meters	~125 meters
802.11ax (Wi-Fi 6)	2.4 GHz or 5 GHz	1.2 Gbps per stream	9.6 Gbps	~70 meters	~240 meters

Using a USB Wi-Fi network adapter is fine, but if it's not connected to a USB 3.0 port or better and you have an extremely fast Internet connection, you might lose out on some speed. Recall that USB 2.0's top speed is 480 Mbps, which is slower than the maximum speed of 802.11ax routers (1.2 Gbps per stream).

When a wireless network spans buildings, you encounter special problems. For instance, the material in the building's walls may interfere with the signal. Now you need to get creative. For instance, consider a wireless NIC with a directional dish antenna that you can position in a window and point directly toward the WAP. Another option is a wireless range extender—a device that resembles a WAP but is designed to boost the signals from a WAP and extend its coverage distance.

Once you find the ideal location for each WAP, you may discover that you do not have a power connection available to each one, but you do have a nearby run of Ethernet cabling to tap into so that the WAP/router can connect to an Ethernet network. It requires the correct Ethernet cable and *PoE splitter*. (You may recall Power over Ethernet, PoE, from Chapter 16.) The Ethernet cable from the network plugs into the splitter, which splits the signal and sends it to two connectors: an Ethernet jack and a power connector. You then connect the WAP by Ethernet cable to the jack and by power cable to the power connector.

In addition to WAPs and wireless routers, all types of networked devices, such as security cameras, IP phones, and Ethernet switches, use PoE.

Compatibility

Another issue is the standard supported by each device. If possible, for each wireless network installation, select NICs and WAPs that comply with the exact same Wi-Fi standard. A single device that supports only a lower standard on a higher-standard

WAP will slow down the entire WLAN. For example, while an 802.11g or 802.11n NIC can communicate with an 802.11ac WAP, all other traffic on that router will suffer in performance as long as it is connected.

In addition, use devices from the same manufacturer when possible, because some manufacturers build in special proprietary features—support for higher speeds or greater range—that are only available in their device. However, this rule is difficult to enforce in practice, especially when you add a laptop with a built-in wireless NIC to your network.

Setting Up a WAP

SOHO WAPs also typically include routing capabilities for Internet connection sharing and are referred to as *wireless routers*. The one pictured in Figure 17-5 includes a dedicated Ethernet port for connecting to a broadband modem, plus a four-port Ethernet switch. The wireless nodes (including the WAP) communicating together in infrastructure mode make up a *Basic Service Set (BSS)*.

The WAP in Figure 17-5 has only one antenna, but many WAPs have more than one. Where there are two antennas, one is generally for transmission and one for reception. On WAPs that support multiple input/multiple output (MIMO), like 802.11ac and ax models, there may be one or two separate antennas for each stream. Some WAPs have internal antennas, though, so you can't rely on an antenna count to know how many streams a WAP supports.

FIGURE 17-5

A wireless access point

Position a WAP in the center of all the computers that will participate in the wireless network. If there are barriers to the wireless signals, you will need to determine if you can overcome them with the use of an enhanced antenna on the WAP or a wireless signal booster to reach computers that are beyond the WAP's range.

To configure a new WAP, you normally connect to it using an Ethernet cable between a computer with an Ethernet NIC and the WAP. Check the documentation that comes with the WAP in case you need to use a special cable. Direct connection via the Ethernet port is required only for initial setup of the WAP. Once it is up and running, you can connect from any computer on the network, wired or wirelessly, and modify the configuration.

It only takes a few minutes to set up a WAP physically and then to configure it to create your wireless LAN. You will need a WAP and its user manual, a computer with an Ethernet NIC, two Ethernet cables (one may have come with the WAP), and the WAP's IP address, obtained from the user manual. If you will be using the WAP to share an Internet connection, you will need the Internet connection device (such as a broadband modem or terminal adapter) already set up and ready to go. With all the materials assembled, follow these general instructions. The actual steps required to configure a WAP may vary from these steps. These general instructions work for most WAPs we have used.

1. Connect one end of an Ethernet cable to the WAN port of the WAP, and connect the other end of the cable to the broadband modem. If you have a broadband modem that also functions as a router, you won't be able to do this step, obviously, because they're already joined.
2. Connect another network cable to your computer's Ethernet NIC and to one of the Ethernet ports on the WAP.
3. If the broadband modem isn't powered on, power it on and wait for the lights on it to settle down (generally about three to five minutes).
4. Turn the WAP's power on by connecting the power cable that came with the WAP, first to the WAP and then to an electrical outlet. If the WAP has a power switch, turn it on now.
5. Turn the computer's power on.
6. Now look at the WAP and verify that the indicator lights for the WAN and WLAN ports light up. Ensure that the indicator light for the LAN port to which the computer connects is lit as well.

Once you have completed these steps, you can test the connection to the WAP, and if all works well, you can configure the WAP settings. Exercise 17-1, later in the chapter, will walk you through testing the WAP connection and then using your web browser to connect and configure the WAP settings.

Status messages will appear over your notification area when a wireless connection is first established and when a wireless connection fails. These messages only display briefly, so most NICs also change the appearance of the icon, showing perhaps a blue or green icon when the NIC is connected and a red icon or an icon with an *x* over it when the NIC is disconnected. A laptop with an integrated wireless adapter will usually have a hardware switch to enable or disable the wireless connection. Be sure you have this turned on.

Accessing a Configuration Utility

Several of the upcoming sections refer to changes you can make in the WAP's configuration utility, so before you go any further, you should learn how to access this utility. (This is the same for routers and wired switches as well.)

Depending on the WAP, you initially might have to access the configuration utility via a wired Ethernet connection rather than wirelessly. Let's assume that is the case for now. Connect an Ethernet cable from a desktop or laptop PC's Ethernet port to any of the Ethernet ports on the back of the WAP (except one of the special ones like WAN or Uplink).

Consult the documentation for the WAP to find out its default IP address. It probably starts with 192.168. Then open a web browser, and in the address bar, type the IP address. You're in! Figure 17-6 shows the configuration utility for a LinkSys Wi-Fi router. The layout and look vary dramatically between makes and models.

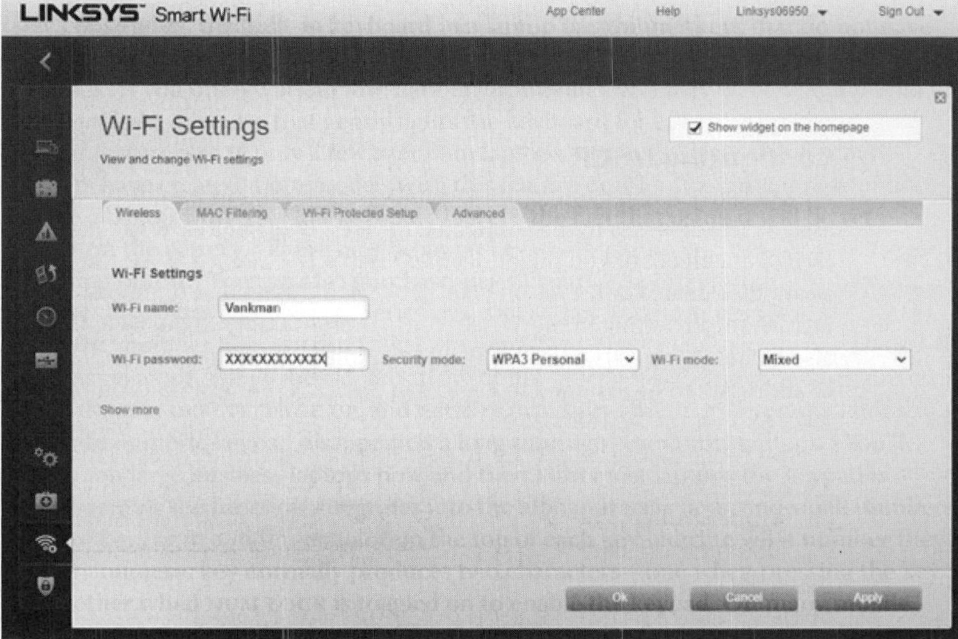

FIGURE 17-6 An example configuration utility; yours may look very different.

You might see a prompt for a user name and password, either initially or when you try to change certain settings. Consult the manufacturer's documentation for the WAP to find out the default user name and password, and enter these. Then change them. Use the configuration utility in the web browser to configure various settings on the WAP, such as the ones described in the following sections.

on the job

If the WAP is also a cable/DSL modem, you may see settings for the Internet connectivity in the configuration utility. Leave those settings alone unless directed by a qualified cable/DSL technician.

Updating Firmware

A WAP has its own firmware (BIOS) that holds its low-level settings. Before you spend a lot of time configuring it, you might want to check to make sure the firmware is up to date, because installing a firmware update may wipe out any custom settings, returning the WAP to factory defaults. (Whether or not this happens depends on the brand and model.) Updated firmware may correct problems, add more features or more compatibility with newer devices, and be less vulnerable to hacking and malware.

To check the firmware version, find the System Information (or similar) page in the configuration utility, and note the Firmware or Software Version setting. Then go online to the support website for the make and model of the WAP and see whether a firmware update is available for download. Compare its version number to the one you have, and if the downloadable one is newer, go ahead and get it. Follow the instructions on the support website for downloading and installing it.

Configuring DHCP

As you learned in Chapter 16, a Dynamic Host Configuration Protocol (DHCP) server assigns IP addresses to the connected devices. By default, a WAP or wireless router has DHCP enabled, but you might need to disable DHCP on a WAP for some reason (such as another device or server on your network fulfilling that function). You should find the DHCP on/off setting in the WAP's configuration utility in the DHCP section. You should also be able to specify the DHCPv4 Start Address and Stop Address, which defines the range of addresses to be assigned to devices in the LAN. For example, on my WAP, the range is 192.168.1.64 to 192.168.1.253.

You can also reserve certain IP addresses for certain devices to make sure that the right address is always available even when the device is offline for a while. This can also prevent an intruder from claiming a certain IP address using a different machine.

If you turn off DHCP and no other DHCP server is operating on the LAN, you will need to manually assign static IP addresses to each device. That skill is covered later in this chapter in the section "Assigning Static IP Addresses at the Router."

For the CompTIA A+ 220-1101 and 220-1102 exams, be aware that most of the topics discussed next under "Securing a Wireless Network" apply to both wired and wireless networks. Those that apply only to a wireless network include changing the SSID, disabling SSID broadcasts, and the wireless standards discussed under the topic "Wireless Encryption." You can apply much of what you learn here to configure a router/firewall on a wired network, although the examples given here and in Exercise 17-1 are of a wireless network.

Securing a Wireless Network

There are several techniques for protecting a wireless network—both through maintaining physical security and through the configuration utility for a WAP or wireless router. Even devices designed for the consumer market have sophisticated security technologies, and any technology or feature that applies rules to control access between networks is a firewall technology. On top of that, many of these devices automatically and securely configure themselves while walking you through the process.

We will review important tasks for securing a wireless network next, and in the upcoming Exercise 17-1, you will see the steps required to configure settings for most of these.

Physical Security

Ensure that you physically protect the heart of the wireless network, the WAP or wireless router, both from theft and from harmful conditions. Then consider the physical security of the computers and devices that connect to the network; because many of them are small mobile devices, those two characteristics make them vulnerable to theft. Therefore, consider taking steps to protect those devices and the data on them. For instance, using Apple's iCloud service, you can configure an iPad so that if it is lost or stolen, you can see its location via the Internet and the use of GPS. You can remotely lock it or erase it. You learned about mobile devices in Chapter 15.

Wireless Encryption

Wireless transmissions are vulnerable because they travel over radio waves, which are easy for anyone with the right equipment to pick up and read the data. Therefore, you should take steps to encrypt any data sent over a wireless network. There are two current sets of standards for this: WPA2 and WPA3. (WPA and WEP are older, obsolete standards.)

Wireless encryption (as well as other encryption methods) depends on the use of a code called an *encryption key* (also simply called a *key*) that is issued automatically by the encryption software. The key is used by other devices or users for decrypting the encrypted data. The types of keys and how they are used is one of the features that distinguishes the standards.

Wi-Fi Protected Access (WPA) is a data encryption standard based on the IEEE 802.11i security standard for wireless networks. There have been three versions of it: WPA, WPA2, and WPA3. They all issue keys per user and per session and include encryption key integrity checking. The original WPA uses a *Temporal Key Integrity Protocol (TKIP)* with a 128-bit encryption key for authentication. It is now obsolete because hackers have broken the TKIP encryption key.

At this time, both *Wi-Fi Protected Access 2 (WPA2)* and *Wi-Fi Protected Access 3 (WPA3)* are in use. Both offer secure authentication and encryption, thus providing true end-to-end data encryption with authentication.

WPA2 uses *Extensible Authentication Protocol (EAP),* which defines a type of wrapper for a variety of authentication methods. A *wrapper* is program code that acts as a logical container for other code or data. Wireless devices generally use *EAP with Personal Shared Key (EAP-PSK),* which involves using a string of characters (a shared key) that both communicating devices know. WPA2 uses an encryption standard approved by the U.S. government—*Advanced Encryption Standard (AES).*

When preparing for the CompTIA A+ 220-1102 exam, make sure you remember that WEP and WPA are obsolete and should not be used and that both WPA2 and WPA3 are acceptable to use today.

WPA3 has two encryption modes: personal (128-bit encryption) and enterprise (192-bit encryption). Instead of using the EAP-PSK, it uses *Simultaneous Authentication of Equals (SAE),* which makes the initial key exchange more secure.

Each computer that connects must have a wireless NIC that is compatible with the version of wireless encryption in use on the WAP/router and will be required to enter a password. Normally, you can configure your wireless NIC to remember the password and use it every time it connects to that Wi-Fi network. Learn how to do this a bit later in Exercise 17-1, "Configuring a WAP or Wireless Router."

Changing SSID and Disabling SSID Broadcast

A *Service Set Identifier (SSID)* is a network name used to identify a wireless network. Consisting of up to 32 characters, the SSID travels with the messages on the wireless network, and all the wireless devices on a WLAN must use the same SSID in order to communicate. Therefore, assigning an SSID is part of setting up a wireless network. A WAP or wireless router comes from the manufacturer with a preconfigured SSID name. You must change this name in the WAP; in fact, some configuration programs assign a random new name for you every time you run the configuration utility but allow you the option to provide a different name if you wish. You can also disable SSID broadcast through the configuration menus on a WAP or wireless router. This means that before any clients can connect, someone must manually enter the WLAN name into the configuration for that client's NIC.

Changing Default Administrator User Name and Password

WAPs and wireless routers come with a default administrator user name and password, which you must change immediately so that no one can easily log on to the WAP and change its configuration. Here again, the configuration program in many wireless routers will prompt you to do this.

Disabling Ports

Recall the section in Chapter 16 titled "Common Ports" and the description of the services that use each port. A wireless broadband router limits incoming traffic from the Internet that was not initiated from inside the wireless network. It does this by disabling incoming ports in the router's settings. By default, most wireless broadband routers have all incoming ports disabled, requiring a request from the local wireless network to open a port. For instance, when you browse to web pages on the Internet, the router recognizes that the website is responding to your requests.

Firewall Settings

We mention firewall settings as a separate topic here mainly because A+ 1101 exam Objective 2.5 calls it out separately, but firewall settings are not one simple, well-contained feature. *Firewall* describes a whole class of features and options.

A firewall blocks unauthorized port usage. A firewall can be a separate hardware device, software utility running in the OS (like Windows Defender Firewall), or a collection of settings on the router or WAP. The configuration utility for your WAP or router may contain a Firewall section, and in it you may find settings for packet filtering and NAT, both of which are covered in upcoming sections.

One of the most commonly configured firewall settings on a WAP or router is Hosted Applications. People who play multiuser games have the option in some games of hosting a game on their computer to which other players connect via the Internet. A firewall would normally prevent such connections, but you can configure the WAP or router to allow them. Our WAP, for example, has a list of services we can choose to allow past its firewall, as shown in Figure 17-7.

Port Forwarding/Mapping

If you have a server on your private network that you would like to receive traffic from the Internet, then you will need to enable *port forwarding,* which you do through the router's settings, mapping the port to the IP address of the server (a static IP address). Then outsiders

FIGURE 17-7 This WAP allows you to specify certain games that should be allowed to circumvent the firewall settings.

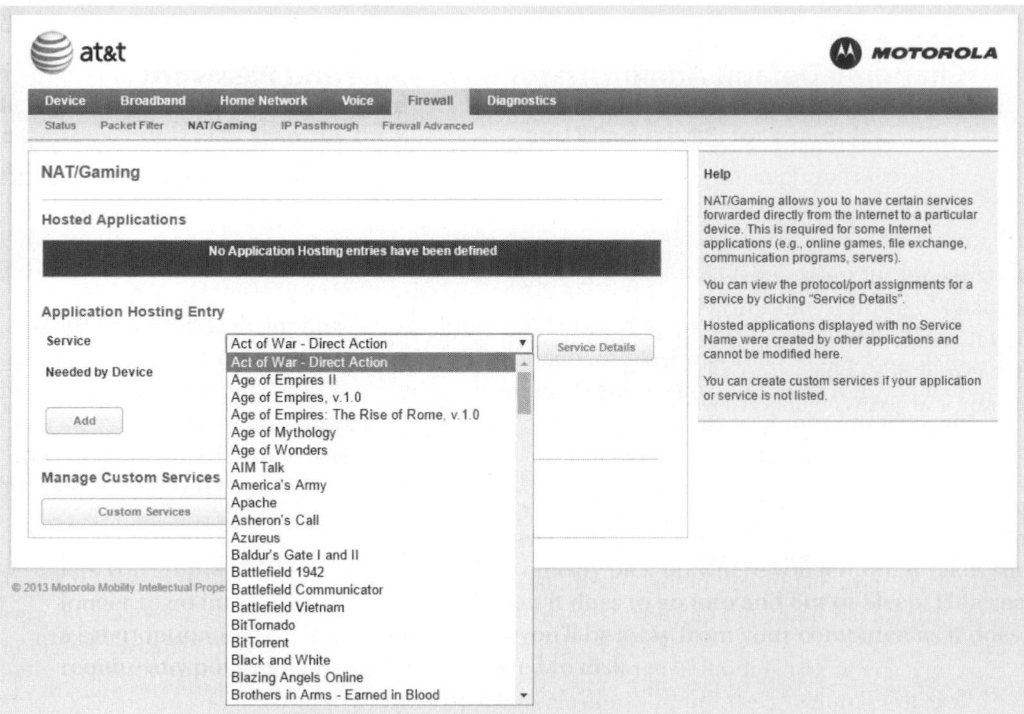

can access that server. The technique involved in doing port forwarding is called *destination network address translation (DNAT)*. A situation in which you may need to enable port forwarding that does not involve what you normally think of as a server is when you want to allow Remote Desktop Protocol (RDP) access from a computer beyond the router to an internal host. Upcoming Exercise 17-1 includes instructions for configuring this on the router.

Port Triggering

While port forwarding requires that the host within the private network have a static address, you can use *port triggering* to allow incoming traffic to reach a host that receives its address via DHCP and is behind a NAT router (true of wireless broadband routers). To enable port triggering, you specify a range of outgoing ports, and when an interior host makes an outgoing connection through a port in that range, a specified incoming port will open for a brief period. Exercise 17-1 shows an example of port triggering to enable Internet Relay Chat (IRC), which is an online chat system.

Universal Plug and Play

Universal Plug and Play (UPnP) uses Internet and web protocols to help various types of devices connect to a network and automatically know about each other. It's an extension of the plug and play technology in individual PCs that allows a PC to identify new hardware components as they are installed. With UPnP, a new device connecting to a network can configure itself, acquire an IP address, and let other devices on the network know about its existence. For example, when you connect a new computer to an existing network, UPnP would allow that computer to discover the available printers on the network and install drivers for them automatically.

If your router or WAP supports UPnP, there will be a setting for it in the configuration utility. When it's enabled, it allows applications running on PCs to open inbound ports to receive information from other network devices. Some security experts warn that UPnP increases a network's vulnerability to worm and malware attacks, and they recommend configuring port forwarding manually instead. However, for a SOHO network, you may decide that the convenience outweighs any risks.

You can also enable or disable UPnP in Windows itself for individual PCs, although the feature has a different name in Windows. From the Network and Sharing Center, click Change Advanced Sharing Settings. In the Network Discovery section, choose to turn network discovery on or off.

Screened Subnets

A standard firewall feature is support for something called a *screened subnet,* also called a *demilitarized zone (DMZ).* This is essentially a network between firewalls. One firewall is at the gateway between an internal network and the Internet, and another firewall is at the connecting point between the first internal network and another internal network. You place servers you want accessible from the Internet on the first network, the DMZ, and you open ports on the external firewall for the services on these servers. Then, on the internal firewall, you close those ports. An inexpensive broadband router (wireless or wired) will have a DMZ feature that opens ports just for certain MAC addresses on the internal network.

Assigning Static IP Addresses at the Router

Any NIC accessing a Wi-Fi network must be assigned an IP address with the same network ID as the Wi-Fi network. The DHCP server on most WAPs and wireless routers will do this by default. However, you can configure static addresses—either through the WAP's or router's DHCP settings or in the settings for the NIC in each computer's OS.

The section "Using a Static IP Address" later in this chapter specifically addresses how to assign static IP addresses in Windows. (That's the most common way of doing it.)

If you assign a static address through the DHCP settings on the WAP or router, you will need the MAC address for each NIC you wish to allow to connect to the network. Sometimes the WAP or router helps in this regard, displaying the MACs of detected NICs, and you can then associate a static IP address to the NIC. Technically, this isn't a static address, since it is assigned through DHCP, but it has the same result, in that the same address is always given to the same MAC address (which DHCP tries to do anyway), but it also keeps a NIC with a different MAC address from connecting.

exam watch

The best way to prepare for the networking objectives in both CompTIA A+ 220-1101 and 220-1102 exams is to get as much hands-on experience connecting wired and wireless computers to a network as you can. Also, if you have access to any type of router, access it remotely, as shown in the upcoming Exercise 17-1, and browse through the settings. If you are concerned about the stability of the network, do not change any settings. If you are permitted, go directly to Step 12, back up the existing settings, and then experiment with modifying settings described in the exercise.

Enabling IP Filtering

IP filtering is a firewall feature that enables you to control what IP addresses will be able to come into and go out of your local network. You can filter the traffic by individual IP addresses (or blocks of IP addresses) by setting up the allowed addresses in an Allow Access (or similar) section in your router setup.

Enabling Content Filtering

Some (but not all) SOHO routers include content filtering, which can block certain websites at the network level. This obviates the need for each individual client PC to have filtering software installed on it. It's only useful for blocking or allowing a few specific sites that you enter, though; it won't block all adult sites or sites by a particular topic or category. The few routers that do provide a real filtering solution have special filtering software built in, which usually requires you to sign up (and pay) for the service.

Another option if you want to implement content filtering throughout your network is to use a DNS-based filtering solution, such as OpenDNS. It doesn't require any special hardware or software on your network. All you must do is change the DNS server addresses on your router to addresses that point to a filtering DNS service.

Individual users can bypass DNS filtering by setting a different DNS address on their individual devices. However, you can thwart them by setting the port filtering feature on the router to block users from accessing port 53 to all IP addresses except the IP addresses of the DNS-based filtering solution you are using. Users are effectively blocked from using any other DNS servers besides the one you specify.

Guest Access

Some routers enable you to create a separate wireless network for visitors, so people can use your access point without having access to your local LAN. You might have a different password for this network, or even no password at all for it. This is better than giving everyone complete access, of course, but it still poses a security risk. You can enable, configure, and disable guest access in your router/WAP setup.

EXERCISE 17-1

Configuring a WAP or Wireless Router

You will need to obtain the IP address for the WAP and then use the ping command to test the connection between the computer and the WAP. Once you determine that the connection works, you can connect and configure the WAP.

1. Open a Command Prompt window in Windows.
2. Test the connection using the ping command. Type **ping *ip_address_of_WAP*,** where *ip_address_of_WAP* is the IP address of the wireless access point. A successful test will show results similar to those in the following illustration.

```
Command Prompt
Microsoft Windows [Version 10.0.19044.1645]
(c) Microsoft Corporation. All rights reserved.

C:\Users\faith>ping 192.168.0.1

Pinging 192.168.0.1 with 32 bytes of data:
Reply from 192.168.0.1: bytes=32 time<1ms TTL=64
Reply from 192.168.0.1: bytes=32 time<1ms TTL=64
Reply from 192.168.0.1: bytes=32 time<1ms TTL=64
Reply from 192.168.0.1: bytes=32 time=1ms TTL=64

Ping statistics for 192.168.0.1:
    Packets: Sent = 4, Received = 4, Lost = 0 (0% loss),
Approximate round trip times in milli-seconds:
    Minimum = 0ms, Maximum = 1ms, Average = 0ms

C:\Users\faith>
```

3. Open a web browser, and in the address box, enter the address you successfully tested in Step 2.
4. If prompted for a user name and password, use the one provided in the WAP's user manual. At your first opportunity, change this user name, as well as the password, so no one else familiar with the default settings can connect and change them. (If you're doing this in a classroom or with someone else's router or WAP, make sure you document the change.)
5. The next screen might be a setup utility for the WAP. If you see setup questions, follow the instructions and provide the type of Internet access, using information from your Internet service provider (ISP). Perform other steps appropriate to your type of Internet access, and if needed, provide the user name and password required for Internet access so the router can connect to the Internet.
6. There should also be a LAN IP Address setting where you can specify the router's/WAP's local IP address. Make sure the first three numbers are the same as all the other devices on the LAN (usually 192.168.0). Locate this setting in your utility. It may be under a Network section.
7. Most WAPs, by default, act as DHCP servers, running the DHCP service and giving out private IP addresses to computers on the internal WLAN and LAN (if appropriate). If there is no other DHCP server on your network, leave this as the default. If there is a DHCP server for your LAN, disable DHCP for the LAN (all Ethernet connections) but leave it enabled for the WLAN (all wireless connections). It may be under an Internet section. You may also be able to specify a DHCP address range to control what IP addresses are assigned to devices.

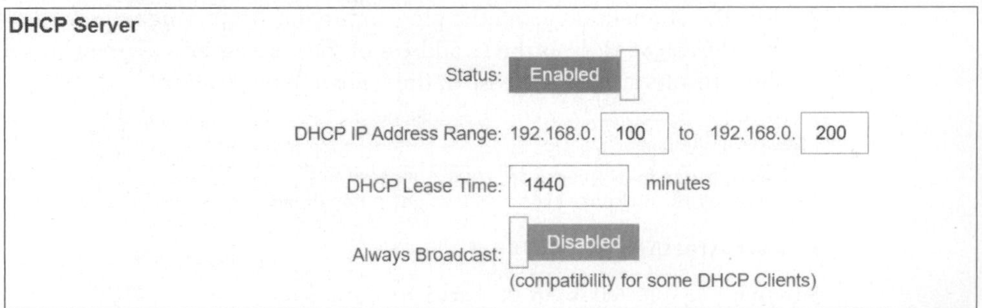

8. There should be a screen in which you can configure wireless settings. The look of the screen and the settings available will vary widely. It may be under a Wireless section. There will probably be multiple tabs, and perhaps multiple levels of tabs, within each major section. Look for an 802.11 Mode setting, which enables you to specify which standards can be used to connect. Allowing a or b standards may slow down the network, but disallowing them may prevent older devices from connecting. Locate this setting in your utility.

9. Look for the SSID setting, and change it from the default name to a unique name; for additional security, consider disabling SSID broadcast by changing the Visibility Status (or equivalent). Locate this setting in your utility.
10. Configure wireless encryption. In the following figure we've chosen WPA-Personal and entered a passphrase of P@$$w0rd. If WPA2 or WPA3 is available, use one of those.

5GHz

Status: Enabled

Wi-Fi Name (SSID): Sycamore5

Password: P@$$w0rd

Advanced Settings...

Security Mode: WPA-Personal

802.11 Mode: Mixed 802.11a/n/ac

Wi-Fi Channel: Auto

Transmission Power: High

Channel Width: Auto 20/40/80 MHz

Visibility Status: Visible

Schedule: Always Enable

11. Locate the port forwarding controls in your utility. For example, here we see a port-forward configuration allowing RDP access to an internal host (192.168.0.2) on port 3389. By default, the wireless router does not allow inbound traffic to internal hosts.

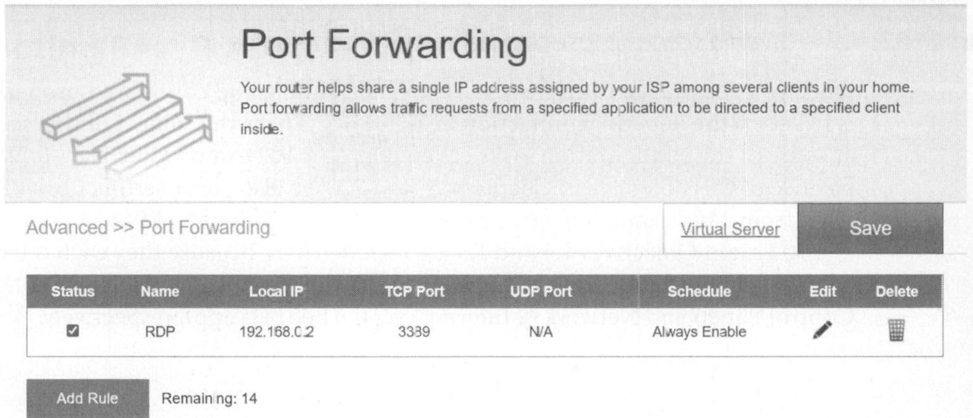

12. After completing the configuration, save your settings, and then log out of the utility.

SCENARIO & SOLUTION

You need to connect an Ethernet port on a PC to a broadband router. What kind of cable should you use?	Use at least Cat-6 cable, or better if available.
You need to connect a SOHO router to a cable modem. Which port should you plug the cable into on the router?	Use the WAN port (or Internet port).
Which Wi-Fi standard offers the maximum range?	802.11n and 802.11ac both have an indoor range of about 50 meters, and 802.11ax has an indoor range of about 70 meters.
You need to access a wireless router's configuration utility. How can you do this?	Through a web browser by entering its IP address in the address bar. Look up its IP address in its manual if needed.

CERTIFICATION OBJECTIVES

- ***1101: 2.6*** *Compare and contrast common network configuration concepts*
- ***1102: 1.4*** *Given a scenario, use the appropriate Microsoft Windows 10 Control Panel utility*
- ***1102: 1.5*** *Given a scenario, use the appropriate Windows settings*
- ***1102: 1.6*** *Given a scenario, configure Microsoft Windows networking features on a client/desktop*
- ***1102: 4.9*** *Given a scenario, use remote access technologies*

Once you get your network hardware up and running and configured properly, the next step is to set up the network connection in Windows. That's the subject of this section, looking at some of the configuration tasks covered in A+ 1102 exam Objective 1.6. We will cover the balance of this objective in Chapters 21 and 22. We also cover setting up a VPN connection here, from 1101 exam Objective 2.6 and 1102 exam Objective 4.9.

1102 exam Objectives 1.4 and 1.5 are included here because they each reference a method of accessing the networking settings in Windows: Network and Sharing Center (via the Control Panel) and Network & Internet (via the Settings app), respectively.

Configuring a Network on a Windows PC

There are two ways to access network settings in Windows 10 and 11: the Control Panel and the Settings app. You will use these apps in the following sections and also in upcoming chapters to configure various network-related Windows settings.

The *Network and Sharing Center* is a Control Panel app that provides links to a variety of networking configuration activities. Open it from the Control Panel (Network And Internet | Network And Sharing Center). You can also access network settings from the Settings app; right-click the networking icon in the notification area and choose Open Network & Internet Settings.

From the Network and Sharing Center you can see the active networks, change adapter settings, and control media streaming options. You can also access a network troubleshooter. See Figure 17-8.

The Network and Sharing Center is mentioned in 1102 exam Objective 1.4. You should be able to open it, and you should understand what each of the commands/settings in it does.

FIGURE 17-8 The Network and Sharing Center

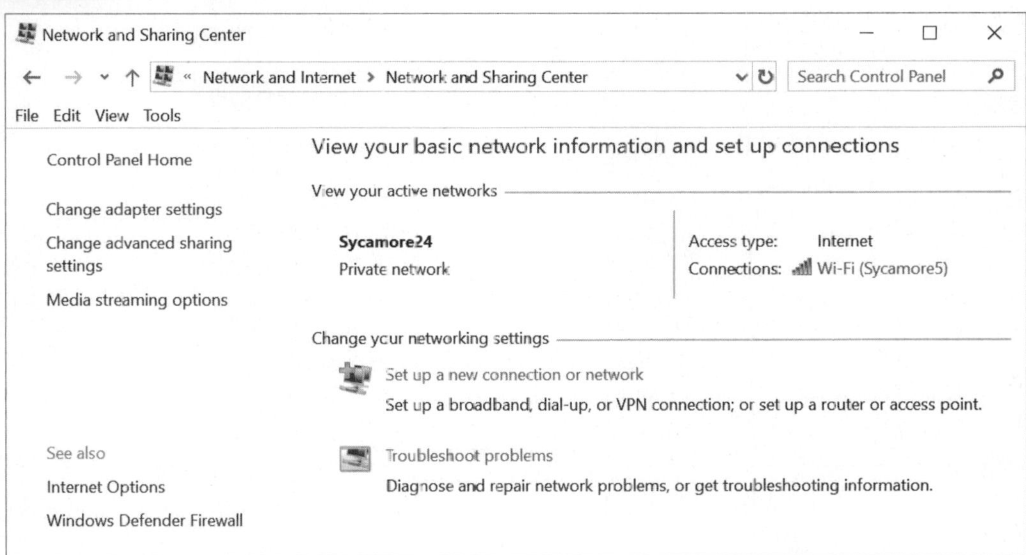

Network and Internet is a section in the Settings app that contains most of the same settings as the Network and Sharing Center. Because eventually the Control Panel will be going away in Windows, it's useful to know how to configure network settings in the Settings app. See Figure 17-9.

This chapter deals with Windows settings only, but you should also study the equivalent settings in macOS. To work with network properties, open the Apple menu and choose System Preferences | Networks.

FIGURE 17-9 The Network & Internet section of the Settings app

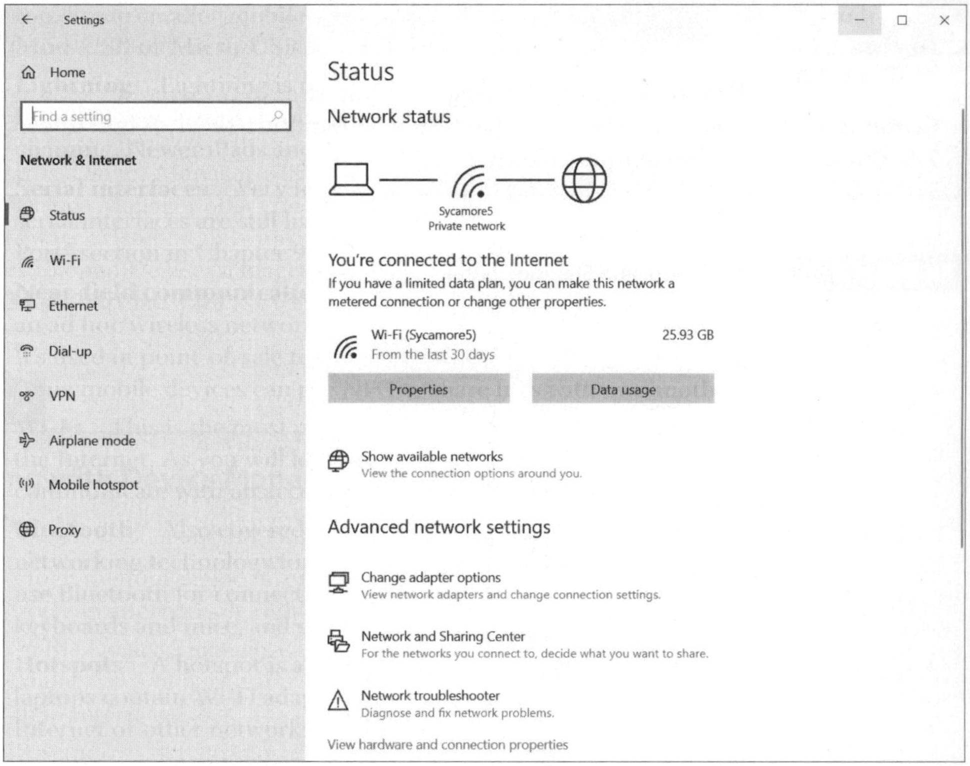

Settings
Home
Find a setting
Network & Internet
Status
Wi-Fi
Ethernet
Dial-up
VPN
Airplane mode
Mobile hotspot
Proxy

Status
Network status
Sycamore5
Private network
You're connected to the Internet
If you have a limited data plan, you can make this network a metered connection or change other properties.
Wi-Fi (Sycamore5) 25.93 GB
From the last 30 days
Properties
Data usage
Show available networks
View the connection options around you.
Advanced network settings
Change adapter options
View network adapters and change connection settings.
Network and Sharing Center
For the networks you connect to, decide what you want to share.
Network troubleshooter
Diagnose and fix network problems.
View hardware and connection properties

Connecting to a Hidden Wireless Network

To connect to a wireless network where the SSID is visible, click the network icon in the notification area and then do the following:

- **Windows 10** Click the desired network and click Connect.
- **Windows 11** Click the Manage Wi-Fi connections arrow, and then click the desired network and click Connect.

That's old news; you've probably done that hundreds of times. But what if the SSID isn't visible? What if it's been hidden for security reasons? In that case, do the following instead:

1. Open the Network and Sharing Center in the Control Panel and click Set Up A New Connection Or Network.
2. Click Manually Connect To A Wireless Network and then click Next.
3. Fill out the form to specify the network name (the SSID), security type, encryption type, and security key, and set any options desired.
4. Follow the prompts to complete the setup.

Using a Metered Connection

A *metered connection* is one that limits the amount of data you can transfer and then either cuts you off, slows you down, or charges you extra for it. Cellular networks often limit your data, for example.

When using a metered connection, you may want to configure the connection so that Windows is aware that it's metered and can help minimize the amount of data used.

To set a connection to be metered in Windows:

1. Open the Settings app and click Network & Internet | Wi-Fi | Manage Known Networks.
2. Click the network that should be set to be metered.
3. Click Properties (Windows 10 only).
4. Set the Metered Connection (or Set As Metered Connection) slider to On.

Using a Static IP Address

By default, Windows assumes that each network connection will receive an IP address automatically via a DHCP server on your network. This is true of connections made via an Ethernet NIC, as well as through a wireless NIC.

You may need to set up a computer on a LAN in which all the computers are assigned static IP addresses. In that case, you will obtain the configuration information from a LAN

TABLE 17-2

Sample IP Configuration Settings

IP Configuration Setting	Setting Value
IP address	192.168.227.138
Subnet mask	255.255.255.0
Default gateway	192.168.227.2
DNS server	192.168.227.3
WINS server (rarely used)	192.168.227.4

administrator and then manually enter an IP configuration into Windows. This information should include the IP configuration addresses described in Chapter 16. The list will resemble Table 17-2, although the actual addresses will be unique to your network. Notice that these are private IP addresses.

You'll need to know how to configure IP addressing, subnet masks, DNS servers, and default gateways in Windows. If you don't know what these are, look back at the thorough conceptual coverage of them in Chapter 16. If you just want to know how to configure them, follow along with the upcoming Exercise 17-2.

If you need to manually configure IP settings, make a list like that in Table 17-2, showing the required settings that you received from your network administrator. Then open the IP configuration dialog for your network adapter. Exercise 17-2 describes how to do this in Windows via the Network and Sharing Center.

EXERCISE 17-2

Configuring a Static IP Address

The following steps will guide you through entering IP configuration settings in Windows.

1. Open the Network and Sharing Center (Control Panel | Network And Internet | Network And Sharing Center).
2. In the navigation pane at the left, select Change Adapter Settings.
3. Right-click the icon for the network connection you wish to configure and select Properties from the context menu.

4. Locate the list of items used by the connection, and double-click Internet Protocol Version 4 (TCP/IPv4) to open the Properties dialog box. Click the radio button labeled Use The Following IP Address.
5. Enter the IP Address, Subnet Mask, and Default Gateway settings.
6. If you have a DNS server address to use, click the radio button labeled Use The Following DNS Server Addresses and enter the Preferred DNS Server. If you have an address for the Alternate DNS Server, enter that address, too.
7. The Internet Protocol Version 4 (TCP/IPv4) Properties dialog box should resemble the following illustration. Check the numbers you entered, click OK to accept these settings, and then click the Close button in the Properties dialog box for the connection.

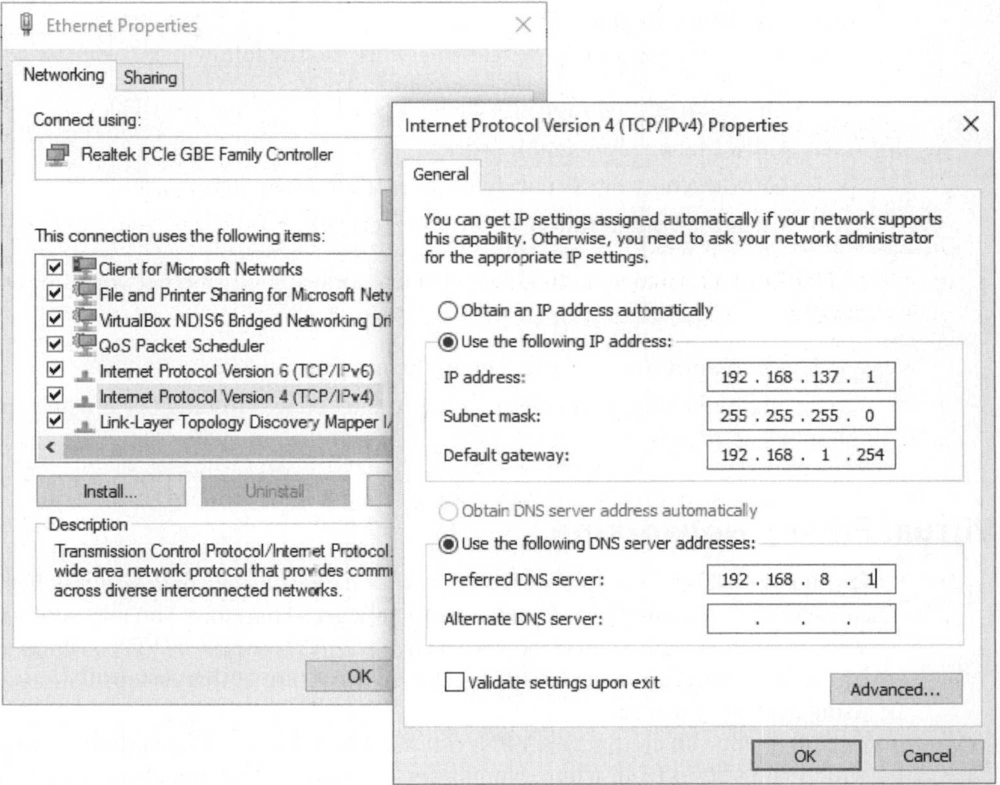

8. To test your settings, open a Command Prompt window and ping the gateway address to ensure your computer can communicate on the LAN. If your configuration is correct and if the gateway router is functioning, you should see four replies.

Another way to set a connection's IP address is via the Settings app. From the Network & Internet section, click either Wi-Fi or Ethernet depending on what kind of connection it is. Then click the Properties button for the connection, and in the IP Settings section, click Edit and choose Manual.

Forgetting a Wireless Network

For your convenience, Windows remembers the passphrase for every secure wireless network you successfully connect to, so you don't have to retype it in the future. If you travel a lot, you might end up with hundreds of remembered Wi-Fi access points in Windows. You can clear some of these out if you like by telling Windows to "forget" them. You might also sometimes need for Windows to forget a connection as part of a troubleshooting process, so you can reconnect to it afresh.

To have Windows forget a wireless network, do the following:

1. Open the Settings app and click Network & Internet | Wi-Fi.
2. Click Manage Known Networks.
3. Click the network you want to forget (Windows 10 only).
4. Click the Forget button next to the network.

Here's an alternative method, which works only on wireless networks that are currently in range:

1. Right-click the Network icon in the notification area.
2. Right-click the network to forget. It must be within range or it won't appear.
3. Click Forget.

Virtual Private Networking

If you connect over the Internet to your work network, your data is at risk because your messages are traveling over an unsecured network. Therefore, you and your employer will want to protect that connection with a *virtual private network (VPN)*, which was briefly introduced in Chapter 16. A VPN creates a virtual tunnel that encapsulates your traffic using special protocols.

Before you can configure a VPN, you must have the specific configuration information, which you obtain from whomever is providing the VPN connection. You need the host name or IP address of the VPN, a valid user name and password, and any custom technical configuration details that may be required.

In Windows, open the Network and Sharing Center from the Control Panel (Network And Internet | Network And Sharing Center), and click Set Up A New Connection Or Network.

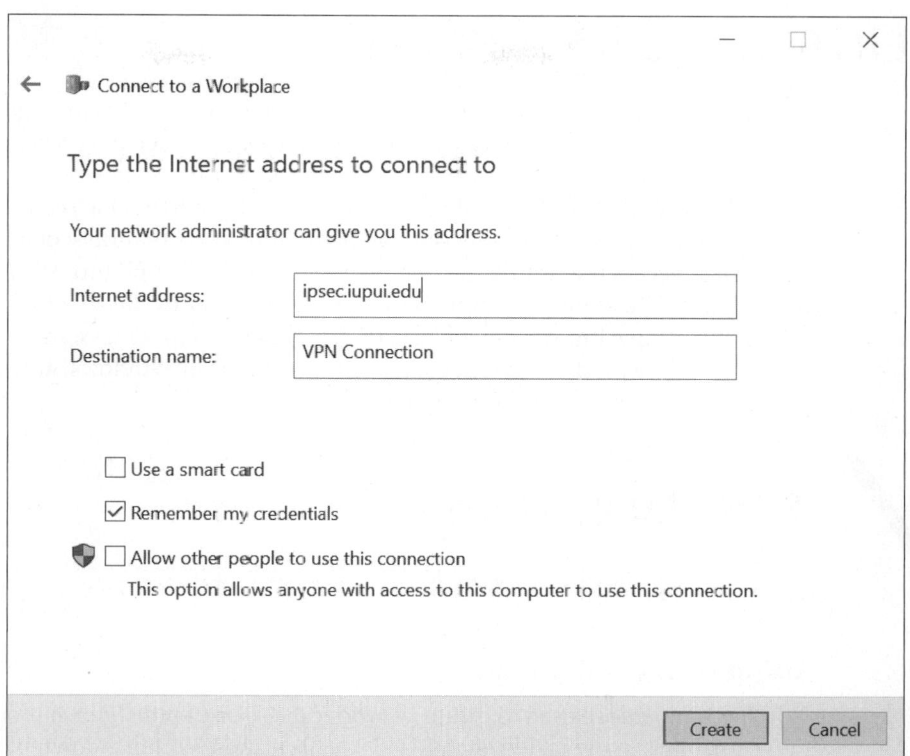

FIGURE 17-10 Setting up a VPN connection

Then click Connect To A Workplace, click Next, and click Use My Internet Connection (VPN). Fill in the details of the connection in the boxes provided (see Figure 17-10), and then click Create.

SCENARIO & SOLUTION

Scenario	Solution
My company wants me to use VPN to work from home. How do I set that up?	From the Network and Sharing Center, click Set Up A New Connection Or Network, and then choose Connect To A Workplace.
I'm trying to connect to a Wi-Fi router that I previously connected to, but now I'm getting errors. How can I clear the settings and start over with this router?	Use the Manage Known Networks section in the Network and Sharing Center (Windows 10) or the Settings app (Windows 11) to find and "forget" the network.

CERTIFICATION SUMMARY

Be able to identify basic network tools and describe their use, including crimper, cable stripper, punchdown tool, toner probe, cable tester, loopback plug, wireless (Wi-Fi) analyzer, and network tap.

Understand the steps in setting up and configuring a SOHO wired or wireless network, including configuring the many settings in the configuration utility of a SOHO router or wireless access point. In particular, make sure you can configure Wi-Fi encryption and differentiate among the available encryption standards. Be able to establish static IP addresses for specific Windows client PCs, including subnet mask and default gateway.

Be familiar with the network configuration options in Windows, accessed both through the Control Panel and the Settings app.

TWO-MINUTE DRILL

Here are some of the key points covered in Chapter 17.

Using Networking Tools

- ❑ Crimpers are used to create network cables. Use a punchdown tool to connect network cabling to the inside of an RJ-45 wall jack and to a punchdown block. Use a cable stripper to prepare the wires to be punched down.
- ❑ Cable testers test for broken wires inside network cables. A toner probe helps identify cable ends by sending a signal through the cable that the probe can pick up.
- ❑ A loopback plug reverses the receive and transmit wires on a port so you can test if the port is functional. A Wi-Fi analyzer provides information about wireless networks within range.
- ❑ A network tap is a device inserted into the network traffic flow that copies packets for use in security analysis and network monitoring.

Installing and Configuring SOHO Networks

- ❑ Each computer on a network requires a network interface card (NIC) in order to connect. The NIC may be Ethernet (wired) or Wi-Fi (wireless).
- ❑ Decide how a NIC should interface with your computer (bus, USB, or other interface), and select a NIC for the type of network you require.

- ❑ When installing a NIC, you will connect the NIC to the port or slot, connect the NIC to the network, and then start the computer and let Windows recognize the NIC. When prompted, provide the location of driver files.
- ❑ When connecting to a wired Ethernet network, use Cat 5e/6 or greater UTP cabling with an RJ-45 connector. Connect one end to the NIC and the other to the wall jack or directly to a hub or switch.
- ❑ When creating a Wi-Fi network, check for possible obstacles and interference sources that can block the signal. Signals degrade over distance, causing slower data speeds, so verify that the distances between the wireless devices are well within the published signal range for the devices.
- ❑ A Service Set Identifier (SSID) is a network name used to identify a wireless network. All of the wireless devices on a WLAN must use the same one.
- ❑ To connect a wireless network directly to another network, you need to use a wireless access point (WAP) for all nodes on the network.
- ❑ You normally do the initial setup of a WAP with a directly wired Ethernet connection between a PC and the WAP. You can make subsequent changes over the wireless network.
- ❑ Most WAPs run the DHCP service to give out IP addresses on the WLAN. Most can also do the same over their Ethernet port or ports.
- ❑ Change the default SSID of a WAP to a unique name, change the default user name and password to ones that will not be easily guessed, enable MAC address filtering and wireless encryption, and set other security options as appropriate for your WLAN. Use WPA3 encryption when available, with WPA2 as a fallback option.
- ❑ Port forwarding allows external stations to connect through a wireless router to internal network services such as Remote Desktop.
- ❑ Port triggering dynamically opens inbound ports when certain outbound port traffic is detected.
- ❑ Once a NIC connects to the network and the drivers are installed, configure the TCP/IP properties. If your network has a DHCP server, you can leave these settings at their default, and your computer will acquire an IP address automatically from the DHCP server.
- ❑ If you do not use a DHCP server and wish to communicate beyond a single network, you must configure IP settings manually (static IP), including IP address, subnet mask, default gateway, and DNS server.
- ❑ Other switch/router options you can enable include IP filtering, content filtering, screened subnets, and guest access.

Configuring a Network on a Windows PC

- You can configure most network settings in Windows via either the Control Panel's Network and Sharing Center or the Setting app's Network & Internet section.
- To connect to a hidden wireless network, open the Network and Sharing Center and click Set Up A New Connection Or Network | Manually Connect To A Wireless Network.
- To set a connection to be metered so Windows minimizes the amount of data used, click Settings | Network & Internet | Wi-Fi | Manage Known Networks and alter the properties of the network that should be set as metered.
- To use a static IP address, open the Network and Sharing Center and click Change Adapter Settings. Right-click the network connection and click Properties. In the list of items used by the connection, open Internet Protocol Version 4 and enter a static IP address.
- To forget a wireless network so Windows will re-prompt for its credentials, or to reset a problematic connection, choose Settings app | Network & Internet | Wi-Fi | Manage Known Networks. Click the network to forget and click the Forget button.
- Virtual private networking creates a secure tunnel on the Internet. To set up a VPN connection, open the Network and Sharing Center and click Set Up A New Connection Or Network | Connect To A Workplace | Next | Use My Internet Connection (VPN).

SELF TEST

The following questions will help you measure your understanding of the material presented in this chapter. Read all the choices carefully because there might be more than one correct answer. Choose all correct answers for each question.

Using Networking Tools

1. What tool would you use to connect a Cat-6 cable to a patch panel?
   A. Crimper
   B. Punchdown tool
   C. Loopback plug
   D. Network tap

2. What tool would you use to determine which cable in a wiring room maps to a certain network jack?
   A. Wi-Fi analyzer
   B. Patch panel
   C. Loopback plug
   D. Toner probe

Installing and Configuring SOHO Networks

3. Which of these is a SOHO network?
   A. Two hundred computer workstations in a client/server network
   B. A customer connecting to the Amazon.com website
   C. A broadband router in a coffee shop that provides free Internet access to customers
   D. All of the above
4. What kind of cable connects a NIC to a switch in a SOHO network?
   A. Fiber-optic
   B. Coaxial
   C. Cat 45
   D. Cat 6
5. Which Wi-Fi standard has the highest maximum data rate?
   A. 802.11ac
   B. 802.11ax
   C. 802.11g
   D. 802.11n
6. Which of the following is the acronym for the name that identifies a wireless network?
   A. VPN
   B. DHCP
   C. SSID
   D. WAP
7. What radio band does 802.11ac use?
   A. 2.4 GHz
   B. 10 GHz
   C. 5 GHz
   D. 7 GHz

8. What happens as you move a wireless NIC and host computer farther away from a WAP?
   A. Signal increases
   B. Connection speed increases
   C. No change
   D. Connection speed decreases

9. How do you access the configuration utility of a WAP?
   A. FTP
   B. Web browser
   C. E-mail
   D. NetBIOS

10. What should you update on a WAP to ensure it has all available updates and fixes?
   A. OS
   B. Applications
   C. Firmware
   D. Administrator account

11. What wireless encryption is the most secure and the one you should use when available?
   A. WEP
   B. WPS
   C. WPA
   D. WPA3

12. What routing feature hides the IP addresses on a private network from hosts beyond the router?
   A. DHCP
   B. NAT
   C. DNS
   D. DMZ

13. Which of these is the best description of a screened subnet?
   A. A type of firmware
   B. A WPA3 subnet
   C. A DHCP server
   D. A network between firewalls

14. Which of these do you specify when configuring a static IP address? (Select all that apply.)
   A. DMZ server
   B. DHCP server
   C. Default gateway
   D. Subnet mask

Configuring a Network on a Windows PC

15. From what utility do you access the Network and Sharing Center?

A. Control Panel

B. Settings app

C. Computer Management

D. Network Management

16. How can you connect to a Wi-Fi network with a hidden SSID?

A. Right-click the network icon in the notification area and choose Manual Setup.

B. Click the network icon in the notification area and choose Wi-Fi.

C. From the Network and Sharing Center, click Set Up A New Connection Or Network.

D. Any of the above will work.

17. How can you set a network to metered status?

A. Network And Sharing Center | Change Adapter Settings

B. Settings | Network & Internet | Wi-Fi | Manage Known Networks

C. Settings | Network & Internet | Mobile Hotspot

D. Network and Sharing Center | Proxy

18. How can you assign a static IP address to a connection? (Choose two methods.)

A. In the adapter's Properties dialog box, select Internet Protocol Version 4 and make the change to the protocol's properties.

B. In the Settings app, under Network & Internet, click Static IP Address.

C. In the Settings app, view the Properties for the connection, and under IP settings, click Edit | Manual.

D. In the Control Panel, click Network And Internet | Static IP Addresses.

19. How can you tell Windows to forget a wireless network? (Choose two methods.)

A. From the Settings app click Network & Internet | Wi-Fi | Manage Known Networks | *select the network* | Forget.

B. From the Control Panel, click Network And Internet | Delete Browsing History And Cookies.

C. In the Control Panel, click Network And Internet | View Network Computers And Devices, and then click a device and click Forget.

D. Right-click the network icon in the notification area, right-click a network, and click Forget.

20. How can you set up a VPN connection from the Control Panel?

A. Network And Internet | Network And Sharing Center | Set Up A New Connection Or Network | Connect To A Workplace

B. Network And Internet | Connect To A Network

C. Network And Internet | Set Up A VPN

D. Network And Internet | Network And Sharing Center | VPN

SELF TEST ANSWERS

Using Networking Tools

1. ☑ **B.** Use a punchdown tool to connect a cable to a patch panel.
   ☒ **A** is incorrect because a crimper attaches an RJ-45 connector to a Cat-6 cable. **C** is incorrect because a loopback plug is used in testing a port. **D** is incorrect because a network tap is used to get greater visibility into a network's operation. After collecting the network traffic data, you can then use it to analyze the network activity or to find security holes.

2. ☑ **D.** Use a toner probe to send a signal on a cable that will be received at its other end.
   ☒ **A** is incorrect because a Wi-Fi analyzer is used to locate Wi-Fi access points. **B** is incorrect because a patch panel is a panel of ports. **C** is incorrect because a loopback plug is a tester for checking internal functionality of a port.

Installing and Configuring SOHO Networks

3. ☑ **C.** A SOHO network is a network in a small office or home office, and a coffee shop meets the criteria for being a small office.
   ☒ **A** is incorrect because a client/server network with 200 computers is a much larger network than a SOHO network. **B** is incorrect because it is an example of a wide area network (WAN). **D** is incorrect because A and B are incorrect.

4. ☑ **D.** Cat 6 is an eight-wire UTP cable suitable for connecting a NIC to a switch.
   ☒ **A** is incorrect because fiber-optic cable is costly and difficult to install and is used only in high-traffic network areas. **B** is incorrect because coaxial is the kind of cable used to deliver cable and satellite TV and Internet signal to a modem. **C** is incorrect because there is no such thing as Cat-45 cable.

5. ☑ **B.** 802.11ax has the highest maximum data rate of the standards listed at 1.2 Gbps per stream.
   ☒ **A** is incorrect because 802.11ac has a maximum data rate of 866 Mbps per stream. **C** is incorrect because 802.11g has a maximum data rate of 54 Mbps. **D** is incorrect because 802.11n has a maximum data rate of 540 Mbps.

6. ☑ **C.** SSID, or Service Set Identifier, is the term that describes a name that identifies a wireless network.
   ☒ **A** is incorrect because a VPN is a virtual private network, a private tunnel across a public network such as the Internet. **B** is incorrect because DHCP is a service that assigns IP addresses to connected devices. **D** is incorrect because a wireless access point (WAP) is a hub for a wireless network.

7. ☑ **C.** 5 GHz is the band used by 802.11ac.
☒ **A** is incorrect because 2.4 GHz is used by some Wi-Fi standards, but not by 802.11ac. **B** and **D** are incorrect because none of the Wi-Fi wireless standards use these radio bands.

8. ☑ **D.** Connection speed decreases as you move a wireless NIC and host computer farther away from a WAP.
☒ **A** and **B** are incorrect because in both cases the opposite happens as you move a wireless NIC and host computer farther away from a WAP. **C** is incorrect because connection speed decreases because the signal degrades as distance increases.

9. ☑ **B.** You use a web browser to access the configuration utility of a WAP via its IP address.
☒ **A** is incorrect because FTP is a protocol for sending and receiving files. **C** is incorrect because the configuration utility cannot be accessed via e-mail. **D** is incorrect because NetBIOS is an alternative network-addressing method used on some older LANs.

10. ☑ **C.** Firmware, the low-level software settings stored on a chip in the device, may need to be updated on a wireless access point to make sure it is up to date.
☒ **A** is incorrect because WAPs do not have OSs, at least not in the traditional sense. **B** is incorrect because WAPs do not have applications. **D** is incorrect because an Administrator account would not need a downloaded update.

11. ☑ **D.** Wi-Fi Protected Access 3 (WPA3) is the most secure of the methods listed.
☒ **A** is incorrect because Wired Equivalent Privacy (WEP) is a very old encryption standard and not very secure. **B** is incorrect because Wi-Fi Protected Setup (WPS) is a method of configuring security between a WAP and a device by pressing a button. **C** is incorrect because WPA is an older and less secure version of WPA2.

12. ☑ **B.** Network address translation (NAT) hides the IP addresses from external hosts to keep them secure.
☒ **A** is incorrect because Dynamic Host Configuration Protocol (DHCP) is a means of dynamic IP address assignment. **C** is incorrect because Domain Name System (DNS) is a means of translating addresses between IP addresses and domain names on the Internet. **D** is incorrect because a DMZ is a network between firewalls.

13. ☑ **D.** A screened subnet, also called a DMZ, is a network between firewalls.
☒ **A** is incorrect because a screened subnet is not a type of firmware. **B** is incorrect because WPA3 is a wireless encryption standard. **C** is incorrect because a DHCP server assigns IP addresses; it is not a subnet.

14. ☑ **C** and **D.** When setting up a static IP address, you must specify the default gateway and subnet mask.
☒ **A** is incorrect because there is no such thing as a DMZ server. **B** is incorrect because a DHCP server assigns dynamic IP addresses, not static addresses.

Configuring a Network on a Windows PC

15. ☑ **A.** The Network and Sharing Center is accessed from the Control Panel.
☒ **B** is incorrect the Settings app does not include the Network and Sharing Center. **C** is incorrect because Computer Management does not include the Network and Sharing Center. **D** is incorrect because there is no such utility as Network Management.

16. ☑ **C.** To connect to a hidden network, you need to set up a new connection.
☒ **A** is incorrect because there is no Manual Setup command on the network icon's menu. **B** is incorrect because doing this will display existing connections; it will not set up new ones. **D** is incorrect because not all the other options will work.

17. ☑ **B.** To modify a network to be metered, you need to manage known networks.
☒ **A** is incorrect because metering is not an adapter setting. **C** is incorrect because metering is not a mobile hotspot setting. **D** is incorrect because metering is not a proxy setting.

18. ☑ **A** and **C.** Either of these methods will take you to interfaces where you can set a static IP address.
☒ **B** and **D** are incorrect because neither of those commands exist.

19. ☑ **A** and **D.** Either of these methods will help you forget a network.
☒ **B** is incorrect because there is no such command. **C** is incorrect because there is no Forget command when you select a device this way.

20. ☑ **A.** To set up a VPN connection, you set up a workplace connection.
☒ **B, C,** and **D** are incorrect because none of those commands exist.

Chapter 18

Internet, Cloud, and Remote Access

CERTIFICATION OBJECTIVES

- **1101: 2.1** Compare and contrast Transmission Control Protocol (TCP) and User Datagram Protocol (UDP) ports, protocols, and their purposes
- **1101: 2.4** Summarize services provided by networked hosts
- **1101: 4.1** Summarize cloud-computing concepts
- **1102: 1.4** Given a scenario, use the appropriate Microsoft Windows 10 Control Panel utility
- **1102: 1.6** Given a scenario, configure Microsoft Windows networking features on a client/desktop
- **1102: 2.10** Given a scenario, install and configure browsers and relevant security settings
- **1102: 4.9** Given a scenario, use remote access technologies

✓ Two-Minute Drill

Q&A Self Test

In this chapter, you will learn about the services, protocols, and applications that comprise the world's largest network: the Internet. You'll learn how the Internet addresses clients and servers, what protocols make activities like the Web and e-mail possible, and what kinds of servers businesses and organizations make available online to provide the services that people rely on in their daily lives. You'll also learn what cloud computing entails and the levels of services that cloud providers offer. You will also learn several ways of remotely accessing other computers.

CERTIFICATION OBJECTIVES

- ***1101: 2.1*** *Compare and contrast Transmission Control Protocol (TCP) and User Datagram Protocol (UDP) ports, protocols, and their purposes*
- ***1101: 2.4*** *Summarize services provided by networked hosts*
- ***1102: 4.9*** *Given a scenario, use remote access technologies*

This section examines the nuts and bolts of the Internet, including some of the common protocols and services listed in CompTIA A+ 1101 exam Objective 2.1. It also looks at the roles of various types of servers listed in 1101 exam Objective 2.4, including web servers, file servers, mail servers, proxy servers, and so on. This section also covers legacy/embedded systems and Internet of Things (IoT) devices, also listed in 1101 exam Objective 2.4. One of the remote access technologies from 1102 exam Objective 4.9 is also briefly covered: Secure Shell (SSH).

Internet Concepts

You probably use the Internet every day as a consumer, using one of the connection types discussed in Chapter 16, but there's a lot more to it than meets the eye. In this section you'll learn about the physical structure of the Internet; how service providers make a living while helping people connect; and how domain names, IP addresses, protocols, and services create a balanced online ecosystem. You'll also learn about the types of Internet-based servers and about embedded systems and IoT appliances.

How the Internet Is Structured

The Internet is a huge, global wide area network (WAN) with the hardware provided collaboratively by businesses all over the world. No one company "owns" the Internet because it is a joint venture. Physically the Internet's layout resembles a mesh of routers, with many alternative paths available between any two points. This redundancy makes the Internet a fairly reliable and stable network, because even if many pathways are blocked at once, there is nearly always a way for a packet to reach its destination.

The group of main routes of the Internet, its super-highway system, is referred to as the *backbone*. This backbone is composed of high-speed fiber-optic networks that join together at connections called network access points. A small number of companies own these high-speed backbone networks; those companies are called Tier 1 providers. Tier 1 providers work cooperatively; they do not charge each other fees to connect to one another. You probably don't know the names of these Tier 1 providers because they don't sell anything directly to the public so they don't advertise where you would be likely to see it.

Tier 1 providers make their money from Tier 2 providers, who own smaller regional Internet segments. The big-name companies in this arena, like Earthlink and Comcast, are Tier 2 providers. Tier 2 providers manage their own small segments of the Internet, and they rent the use of their segments to individuals on a monthly basis, functioning as *Internet service providers (ISPs)*. They also sell connectivity to smaller providers, Tier 3 providers, who are even smaller and more localized.

The lesson from that overview of the tier system is simply that you can't connect to the Internet directly all by yourself. You have to contract with an ISP, which is either a Tier 2 or Tier 3 provider and which grants you the right to connect into their little segment of the Internet and from there gain access to the rest of the world.

Internet Service Providers

As we mentioned in the preceding section, an ISP is a company in the business of providing Internet access to users. When you connect to the Internet from your home or office, you connect through your ISP. While you are on the Internet, your ISP relays all data transfers to and from locations on the Internet. Traditionally, ISPs were phone companies, but now ISPs include cable companies and organizations that lease phone or cable network usage.

The ISP you select will depend on the type of connection available to you. For instance, a cellular provider will be your ISP if you choose to connect to the Internet via the cellular network, and a cable company will be your ISP if you connect over the cable network. As for DSL, at first local phone companies mainly offered this service, but eventually many other companies offered DSL using the telephone network, and some telephone companies are now offering Internet access via their fiber-optic networks. Meanwhile, some ISPs specialize in satellite Internet access. See Chapter 16 for in-depth discussions of connectivity types.

In addition to Internet connection services, ISPs now provide a number of other services. Some of these services, such as e-mail, are free, and the cost of others, such as hosting web servers, is based on the complexity of the web services provided. For example, an e-commerce site in which you sell products and maintain customer lists is a service that would come at additional cost. You also are not limited to purchasing Internet services from your ISP. There are now a huge variety of sources for all these services.

Domain Names, IP Addresses, and DNS Servers

Whenever you visit a website, you enter or select the Uniform Resource Locator (URL) of the website you want to visit—in other words, its web address. A URL consists of a domain name, such as microsoft.com, plus additional information that points to a particular folder and page on that website, like this:

https://www.microsoft.com/en-us/windows

Let's break down that URL into its component parts. A URL starts with the protocol, which is https in the example. HTTPS is a secure form of Hypertext Transfer Protocol, the main protocol used for web pages.

The next part, www.microsoft.com, is known as a *fully qualified domain name (FQDN)*. It's called that because it contains both a host name (www) and a domain (microsoft.com). Let's look at these parts separately:

- The *host name* is the name of the server or service within the domain. Some small websites have only one host, and it's usually www (traditional for websites). However, larger sites may have several hosts, representing different services. For example, Microsoft has support.microsoft.com and www.microsoft.com, to name only two of many.
- The domain includes a *top-level domain*, or TLD (in this case, com), and a *second-level domain*, or SLD (in this case, microsoft). The top-level domain describes the general category of domain; com is short for "commercial," for example. There are several dozen top-level domains with names like edu (for education), gov (for government), mil (for military), and org (for organization), as well as individual country codes like ca (for Canada) and uk (for United Kingdom).
- The ending part of the address is the file path of the host's server—in this case, en-us/windows. Just like in local file paths, slashes separate directories. On the host server, there is a folder called en-us, and within that is a folder called windows.

If you leave off the host name when typing a URL into a browser, the browser will usually assume www as the host name.

exam watch **Make sure you understand the purpose of a DNS server and that you can explain the concepts of top-level domain and fully qualified domain name. Remember also that DNS uses port 53.**

The irony of all these text-based names is that the Internet, as a computer network, doesn't actually use any of them. They are a figment of our collective imagination. The real addresses on the Internet are IP addresses, assigned by the Internet Assigned Numbers Authority (IANA). So how do the IP addresses and domain names connect to one another? They do so through a series of servers called *Domain Name System (DNS)* servers.

A DNS server receives a domain name and looks it up in a giant table it maintains to find its IP address match. Then it provides that IP address to the requesting computer. That's all it does, millions of times a minute, 24/7. There are thousands of DNS servers all over the world performing this task, all at once.

Maintaining a complete table of every IP address and domain name would be nearly impossible for any single DNS server, no matter how capable, and looking up addresses would take too long. Therefore, the work of DNS servers is split up according to top-level domains. One DNS server only parses between top-level domains, routing a request to the appropriate server. For example, a server says "microsoft.com, that's a dot-com, so I'll send it to the dot-com DNS server." Then another server receives the request that has a table of only the dot-com IP addresses and domains. It looks up the IP address for the requested domain and sends it back to the requesting computer.

Remember that if you can ping by IP address but not by host name or FQDN, there's a problem with a DNS server.

Internet Services and Protocols

There are many Internet services, enabling activities like web browsing, mail delivery, and instant messaging. In this section, we will describe a few of these services. Some of them have been covered elsewhere in the book, but we provide them here for easy study reference, all being related to Internet usage.

Not all of the protocols in this section are listed in any specific exam objective, but they appear in CompTIA's A+ Acronyms list. At a minimum, you should know what each acronym stands for and what kind of activity it describes.

Simple Mail Transfer Protocol

Simple Mail Transfer Protocol (SMTP) transfers e-mail messages between mail servers (discussed later in this chapter). Clients also use this protocol to send e-mail to mail servers. When configuring a computer to access Internet e-mail, you will need the address or name of an SMTP server to which your mail client software will send mail. SMTP uses port 25.

Post Office Protocol

Post Office Protocol (POP) is the protocol used to allow client computers to pick up (receive) e-mail from mail servers. The current version is POP3. POP3 uses port 110.

Internet Message Access Protocol

Internet Message Access Protocol (IMAP) is a protocol used by e-mail clients for communicating with e-mail servers. IMAP allows users to connect to e-mail servers and not only retrieve e-mail but also manage their stored messages without removing them from the server. The current version is *IMAP4.* IMAP uses port 143.

Hypertext Markup Language

Hypertext Markup Language (HTML) is the language of web pages. Web designers use the HTML language to create web page code, which your web browser converts into the pages you view on your screen. HTML doesn't have a port number because it's not a communication protocol; it is more similar to a programming language.

Hypertext Transfer Protocol

The *World Wide Web (WWW)* is the graphical Internet consisting of a vast array of documents located on millions of specialized servers worldwide. The *Hypertext Transfer Protocol (HTTP)* is the information transfer protocol of the Web. Included in HTTP are the commands web browsers use to request web pages from web servers and then display them on the screen of the local computer. HTTP uses port 80, which is insecure, and has been mostly replaced by HTTPS over port 443.

Hypertext Transfer Protocol Secure

Hypertext Transfer Protocol over Secure Sockets Layer (HTTPS) is a protocol that encrypts and decrypts each user page request, as well as the pages downloaded to the user's computer. Most websites use HTTPS nowadays due to its increased security. It uses port 443.

Secure Sockets Layer

The *Secure Sockets Layer (SSL)* is a protocol for securing data for transmission by encrypting it. Encryption is the transformation of data into a code that no one can read unless they have a software key or password to convert it back to its usable form (decrypt it). When you buy merchandise online, you go to a special page where you enter your personal and credit card information. These web merchants almost universally use some form of SSL encryption to protect the sensitive data you enter on this page. When you send your personal information over the Internet, it is encrypted and only the merchant site has the key to decrypt it. As with most computing technologies, there are improvements to SSL, and a newer encryption technology, *Transport Layer Security (TLS),* for secure transmission over the Internet. SSL doesn't have a port number because it's an encryption protocol, not a transfer protocol.

TLS has replaced SSL. However, SSL is still mentioned throughout the industry and typically appears as SSL/TLS or TLS/SSL.

Telnet

At one time, all access to mainframes or minicomputers was through specialized network equipment called *terminals*. At first, a terminal was not much more than a display, a keyboard, and the minimal circuitry for connecting to the mainframe. People called it a "dumb terminal." With the growing popularity of PCs in the 1980s, it wasn't unusual to see both a terminal and a PC on a user's desktop, taking up a great deal of space. Eventually, by adding both software and hardware to a PC, the PC could emulate a terminal, and the user would switch it between terminal mode and PC mode.

The *Telnet* utility provides remote terminal emulation for connecting to computers and network devices running responsive server software, and it works without concern for the actual operating system running on either system. The original Telnet client was character based, and it was a popular tool for network administrators who needed to access and manage certain network equipment, such as the routers used to connect networks. Very occasionally you may encounter an old device that can be configured with Telnet via a serial cable connection, but this is no longer common. Telnet uses port 23.

exam watch **Telnet is insecure and has been replaced by SSH, but it still appears as a port number to know in 1101 exam Objective 2.1.**

Secure Shell

Although Telnet supports the use of credentials for a terminal emulation session, it sends those credentials in clear text that many methods can pick up, such as a device that connects to the network and collects the traffic. To overcome that limit, the *SSH* service has replaced Telnet because it secures all traffic using a tunneling technique similar to a VPN (described in Chapter 17). It is used to connect to terminal servers that require sophisticated security protocols. SSH uses port 22.

File Transfer Protocol

File Transfer Protocol (FTP) is a protocol for computer-to-computer (called host-to-host) file transfer over a TCP/IP network. The two computers do not need to run the same operating system; they only need to run the FTP service on the server computer and the FTP client utility on the client computer. FTP supports the use of user names and passwords for access by the FTP client to the server. FTP uses port 20 or 21.

For decades FTP was widely used on the Internet for making files available for download to clients. However, it is an insecure protocol because it transfers the data as plaintext, so it's vulnerable to various types of network attacks. Today most FTP software supports some form of encryption, such as SSL/TLS or SFTP, covered next.

Secure Copy and SFTP

Another file transfer method is *secure copy (SCP),* which uses SSH for encrypting data. SCP lacks the file management capabilities of other methods, such as Secure FTP (SFTP). Therefore, SFTP, which also uses SSH, is often preferred.

Challenge-Response Protocols

Often, when you create a new account of almost any type on the Internet, after you have created your user name (often an e-mail address) and password, you may encounter a challenge test—a test that a human can easily pass but a computer cannot. You enter a response to continue. A popular type of challenge-response is *Completely Automated Public Turing test to tell Computers and Humans Apart (CAPTCHA).* A CAPTCHA usually consists of an image of one or two hard-to-read words, or at least a string of characters. To pass the test and proceed with creating your new account, you must enter the characters you see into a box. This ensures that a computer program is not attempting to automatically create accounts for nefarious reasons, such as for sending spam. To learn more about CAPTCHA, point your browser to www.captcha.net.

SCP, SFTP, and CAPTCHA are only in the CompTIA official Acronyms list; they're not in any of the 1101/1102 exam objectives.

Server Types

Servers are essential to Internet operation. Different kinds of servers perform different important roles in your Internet experience, and you probably don't even notice what kind of server is serving you at any given moment. For example, the DNS server (discussed earlier in the "Domain Names, IP Addresses, and DNS Servers" section) makes it possible for you to visit websites by typing user-friendly, text-based domain names instead of having to remember an IP address consisting of a long string of numbers.

Make sure you understand the role of each of these server types. We cover them here in the Internet chapter because most of them pertain to the Internet, but several of these could be part of any network, not necessarily an Internet-enabled one.

Web Server

While the World Wide Web (the Web) is just one of the many services that exist on the Internet, it alone is responsible for most of the huge growth in Internet use that began after the Web's introduction in the 1990s. Web technologies changed the look of Internet content from all text to rich and colorful graphics. A *web server* provides the graphical content, called web pages, that we access by web browsers. There are many choices of web server software, but the most popular may be *Apache HTTP Server*, open source software that runs on a wide range of operating systems, including Windows and several versions each of Linux and Unix.

Microsoft's web server software, *Internet Information Services (IIS)*, runs only on Windows and supports the traditional HTML content as well as the transfer services HTTP and HTTPS. It also supports other services, such as FTP and SMTP.

File Server/Fileshare

A *file server*, as the name implies, makes files available to users. There are file servers on business networks that deliver private files to employees, and there are file servers on the Internet that provide the same service to the public or to users who have the appropriate credentials with which to log in.

File servers are listed as fileshare in 1101 exam Objective 2.4.

One common type of file server uses the FTP protocol and is referred to as an *FTP server*. An FTP server can be open to the public to log into via an anonymous connection, or it can require a user name and password. As you learned in Chapter 17 and previously in this chapter, FTP is not particularly robust in security, so some FTP servers use SFTP instead.

Users can access an FTP server via most web browsers, although the interface may be somewhat awkward. Most people who use FTP servers frequently use special FTP software, such as the free program FileZilla.

Print Server

A print server manages multiple printers that connect to it and makes those printers available to users. *Print servers* are much more common on business networks than on the Internet. Part of a print server's job is to hold the incoming print jobs in memory until they can be parsed out to the available printers. A print server can be a full-fledged computer with printers attached to it, or it can be a network appliance that's basically just a box with a network connection and some printer ports. In the latter case, you would configure the print server by talking to it via a web browser using its IP address.

DHCP Server

As you learned in Chapter 17, a *DHCP server* assigns IP addresses to clients that request them. Your ISP may have a DHCP server that it uses to assign IP addresses to its customers, providing dynamic IP addressing for Internet usage. That's the norm because it is most efficient. Unused IP addresses can be dynamically assigned to other customers whenever they become available. An alternative is a static IP address assignment, which you would want if you were hosting your own web server. Most ISPs charge more if you want that.

DNS Server

We talked about *DNS servers* earlier in this chapter; recall that they translate between IP addresses and domain names. There are DNS servers all over the Internet publicly available for use. The use of a DNS server is invisible to the end user.

Mail Server

A *mail server* manages e-mail accounts. A company might have its own e-mail server, for example, that stores incoming messages for each user and then forwards them to the individual client PC whenever that user's e-mail application connects to the server. (That's called a *store-and-forward system*.) Similarly, your ISP has its own mail servers that receive mail on your behalf and then deliver it to you when you open your e-mail program and connect. Some ISPs have a single mail server for both incoming and outgoing mail; others have two separate servers (more common).

When you configure an e-mail application, you might need to enter the addresses of your mail server(s). These are usually three-part names with the parts separated by periods, like this: pop.mymail.com. The incoming mail servers are usually either POP3 or IMAP, and the outgoing mail server is usually SMTP. You learned about these and other protocols earlier in this chapter, in "Internet Services and Protocols."

Authentication Server

An *authentication server* is in charge of logging users in to and out of a secure system. Corporate networks use authentication servers to allow users to access networked computers on a domain; if you sign into your company's network each morning at work, you can thank an authentication server. The Internet also has authentication servers. For example, if you sign into your account at an online store like Amazon.com, an authentication server checks your credentials and grants you access. Chapter 20 covers authentication servers in greater detail.

Proxy Server

In many instances, an Internet connection includes a *proxy server,* a network service that handles the requests for Internet services, such as web pages, files on an FTP server, or mail for a proxy client, without exposing that client's IP address to the Internet. There is specific proxy server and client software for each type of service. Most proxy servers combine these services and accept requests for HTTP, FTP, POP3, SMTP, and other types of services. The proxy server will often cache a copy of the requested resource in memory, making it available for subsequent requests from clients without having to go back to the Internet.

1101 exam Objective 2.4 mentions AAA, which stands for Authentication, Authorization, and Accounting. You will learn more about that in Chapter 20.

A client PC can be configured to use a specific proxy server. Some content filtering programs do that, for example—they set the PC to go through a proxy server online that only allows "clean" content through, according to the rules of the filtering. Some ISPs also recommend you use their proxy server for better performance. Satellite Internet providers sometimes provide a proxy server on which commonly accessed pages are cached. To learn how to configure a Windows client to use a proxy server, see "Proxy Servers," later in this chapter.

The 1101 exam Objective 2.4 lists *syslog* as a server role even though it is not a type of server in the same sense as the others. Syslog is short for *system log*. System administrators can designate a certain file to be used to store system event logging, and the same file can be used for multiple servers to consolidate information for convenience. A typical syslog consists of a facility code (which specifies the type of program logging the message), a severity level, and a message.

Legacy and Embedded Systems

CompTIA A+ 1101 exam Objective 2.4 lists legacy/embedded systems. While it's not clear what CompTIA may be referring to here, we surmise that they want you to be aware that there are embedded systems nearly everywhere you look around you, such as in IoT-enabled devices, and that there are servers all over the world that talk to them. Most people think of the typical desktop or laptop PC when they picture an Internet connection, or perhaps a smartphone or tablet connection. All those are great for single-user Internet connectivity, of course, but a wide variety of devices connect to the Internet that you might not think of, from street lights and traffic signals to wristwatches and refrigerators. These computing components are called *embedded systems*. Believe it or not, it is estimated that 98 percent of all microprocessors manufactured today are for embedded systems, not for personal computers. For example, there's probably a microprocessor in your car that can report error codes to a technician, and in some cases can even upload those error codes to a server.

One such embedded system is *SCADA*, which stands for *Supervisory Control and Data Acquisition*. It is a hardware and software system used in industrial environments to control machinery and to monitor and process data about the manufacturing process. SCADA systems can interact with hardware such as motors, valves, and sensors via software and can retain a record of all events.

The "legacy" part may refer to the fact that these systems typically stay in service for many years, long past their technology being state-of-the-art. One of the dangers of a legacy system is that it may be more subject to hacking because it lacks the latest security precautions. For example, an ATM running on Windows XP is (theoretically) more easily hacked than one running Windows 11, because support for Windows XP ended in 2014 and Microsoft has not released any new security patches for it.

Internet Appliances

Internet appliances are a class of server applications and services designed to protect servers (and thereby protect users). While as a PC technician you will not be called upon to set up or configure such services, you should understand what they are and what they do. The objectives specifically refer to four kinds of Internet appliance: spam gateways, unified threat management (UTM), load balancers, and proxy servers.

- A gateway is like a portal that everything passes through, like the gates of a walled city. A *spam gateway* is an application that e-mail passes through as it is being sent and received. The gateway filters e-mail to eliminate the majority of the spam received.
- *Unified threat management (UTM)* is the principle of creating a unified package of appliances that work together to reduce the threat of harm from attacks. A UTM solution might include intrusion detection systems (IDSs), intrusion prevention systems (IPSs), virtual private networks (VPNs), firewalls, antimalware applications, and other tools.
- A *load balancer* is a device that helps spread out the load (that is, the network traffic) across multiple servers to keep data flowing without bottlenecks. It works by performing calculations that determine the optimal order in which waiting traffic should pass through a certain point and which servers or devices that traffic should be handled by.
- You learned about *proxy servers* earlier in the chapter. They serve as a gateway between the users and the Internet, which adds a layer of protection.

Internet of Things Devices

IoT is another type of networked host mentioned in 1101 exam Objective 2.4. The IoT refers to the computing/networking capabilities of everyday objects like household appliances, lights, locks, security systems, and so on, which all have some type of electronically controlled hardware, along with some software for configuring that control, and some wireless networking capability for operating that software remotely.

Installing and configuring *IoT devices* is difficult to generalize about because they are all so different and come with specific instructions. They also don't always use standard wireless networking types. Some do use Wi-Fi and can connect to your household network,

You do not need to know how to configure IoT devices; just be aware of their general functionality and how to keep them secure.

but others use Bluetooth (so you need to have your smartphone or tablet near the device to control it). Others use less common wireless network types such as Z-wave and Zigbee.

Like other network devices, IoT devices need to be secured. Some ways you can make your IoT devices less vulnerable to intrusion include the following:

- Modify the device's default network settings, such as its access password.
- Require strong passwords to connect.
- Update the device's software and firmware regularly.
- Disable features you don't need.
- If possible, do not connect the device to public Wi-Fi.

CERTIFICATION OBJECTIVES

- ***1102: 1.4*** *Given a scenario, use the appropriate Microsoft Windows 10 Control Panel utility*
- ***1102: 1.6*** *Given a scenario, configure Microsoft Windows networking features on a client/desktop*
- ***1102: 2.10*** *Given a scenario, install and configure browsers and relevant security settings*

This section covers the browser installation and configuration topics from 1102 exam Objective 2.10, which are mostly related to security. That's because security is of prime concern whenever you're dealing with outside networks, and the Internet is the biggest, wildest-west outside network of them all. You will learn more about network security in Chapter 22, but here we confine our discussion to settings specifically related to browsers.

This section also looks briefly at the Internet options topic listed under CompTIA A+ 1102 exam Objective 1.4. This topic refers to the Internet Options controls in the Control Panel. One of the settings in that dialog box deals with using a proxy server, so we use that opportunity to cover the proxy settings topic listed under 1102 exam Objective 1.6.

Configuring Browser and Internet Settings

In this section we run down the list of topics from Objective 2.10, which is all about installing and configuring browsers and their relevant security settings. Because each browser has different configuration options and procedures, it isn't possible to provide exact steps here, so instead we look at the topics conceptually.

Browser Download and Installation

When acquiring a third-party browser, it's important to make sure that you are downloading from a trusted source. The most trusted source for a browser is the official website of its maker. For example, here are the official download sites for several popular browsers:

- **Google Chrome** https://www.google.com/chrome/downloads/
- **Firefox** https://www.mozilla.org/en-US/firefox/
- **Safari** https://www.apple.com/safari/
- **Opera** https://www.opera.com/

When downloading from less trusted sources, the possibility exists of receiving a download that has been altered and contains malware. Running a malware-infected browser can have serious consequences, because nothing you do with that browser is secure or private. Sites that use HTTP rather than HTTPS for downloads are particularly at risk.

Because of the security risk of downloading from an untrusted site, you may wish to verify the integrity of a download using *hashing*. A *hash* is a code generated by passing the file through an encryption algorithm. The resulting code is unreadable, but reproducible if the same input is used. So if the hash generated by the file you downloaded is identical to the hash that the file provider posts on their website for comparison, you know the file has not been altered. Hashing is usually done using one of these algorithms: MD5, SHA1, SHA256, and CRC32B.

exam watch **Make sure you understand the differences between trusted and untrusted sources and the purpose of hashing in verifying a download's integrity.**

Extensions and Plug-Ins

Most browsers support the use of small add-on applications called *plug-ins* or *extensions*. The naming depends on the browser. These apps add functionality to the browser beyond its native capabilities. For example, there are extensions for finding coupon codes while shopping, for blocking pop-ups, and for checking websites you visit for malware.

Extensions can be useful, but untrusted extensions can also bring with them a risk of malware. For that reason, you must make sure that extensions come from trusted sources too, just like the browsers themselves.

If a browser provides a Manage Extensions utility (or similar), that's usually a good source for trusted extensions you can install with confidence. Avoid installing extensions from websites that are outside the browser's own listings or databases, particularly those from untrusted websites.

Password Managers

One very handy browser extension you might install is a *password manager*. Password managers keep a record of your login credentials for various websites and fill in the information automatically whenever you visit each saved site.

Password managers help enhance user security because they free the user from having to remember many different passwords. People tend to use the same short passwords on multiple websites because it's less they have to remember, but password reuse can result in security problems because when one site's password database is stolen, the thieves can try that same user name and password combination at other websites too. A password manager makes it easy for users to have strong passwords that are unique for each website without unduly taxing their memory.

When selecting and installing a password manager, it's critical to acquire it from a trusted source. As you can imagine, a rogue password manager that contains malware could be disastrous, exposing your credentials for hundreds of websites. Some popular password managers include Firefox Password Manager, Sticky Password, Roboform, Apple Keychain, and TrueKey by McAfee.

Secure Connections and Sites

A decade ago, nearly all websites used the unsecure HTTP protocol. With today's level of hacking sophistication, an HTTP site is an invitation to hackers to create spoofed pages, redirects, and all manner of deceit that you'll learn about in Chapter 22. That's why most websites today instead use the HTTPS protocol, which classifies them as *secure websites*.

Secure websites operate by sending security challenges and responses between the client and the server that require the server to prove its identity—in other words, to prove that it hasn't been compromised or redirected to a look-alike rogue site. They do this with *security certificates* issued by a *certificate authority (CA)*.

When a web client (a user PC, for example) contacts a web server that uses the HTTPS protocol, it requests the server's SSL/TLS certificate. The browser then contacts the certificate authority company to verify that the certificate is valid. If everything checks out, the client begins a secure communication session with the server. This verification process is nearly instantaneous, and you don't see it happening.

The only time you *do* see any evidence of this security check is when you see a message that there is something wrong with the certificate. Maybe it's invalid, or maybe it's expired. When you see such a message, you must use your best judgment as to whether or not to continue to that website.

In cases where you are not exchanging sensitive data (such as signing in with a password), it is often okay to accept a certificate that has a recently expired date on it. You should contact the website owner to let them know you had a problem with their certificate, though. Do not enter any personal or sensitive information at a website where there is a certificate problem.

Most browsers have an option that lets you view the certificates and publishers you have chosen to trust. You can also clear the SSL/TLS state so that any security that is currently in effect must be reauthenticated. This is done at the browser level.

Proxy Servers

You learned about proxy servers earlier in this chapter. If your network has a proxy server, you can configure your browser to send requests to the proxy server, which will forward and handle all requests.

You can configure a proxy server in an individual browser's settings, and it will apply only when using that browser. However, if you set up the proxy server from the Internet Properties dialog box (from the Control Panel) in Windows, the resulting setting will apply to the entire Internet connection for that PC, across all browsers.

exam watch

CompTIA A+ exam 1102 Objective 1.4 lists Internet Options as a topic of interest. The Internet Options (or Internet Properties) dialog box mostly deals with Internet Explorer settings (now obsolete), but some of its settings do apply to Windows itself, and its Proxy Server setting is one of them.

Windows provides options for four types of proxy servers: HTTP, Secure (HTTPS), FTP, and Socks. You should already be familiar with the first three of those. Socks is a proxy server protocol. If you have a proxy server for other services not supported by Windows, you will need to install a proxy client provided by the vendor of the server software.

EXERCISE 18-1

Configuring a Proxy Server

To configure Windows to use a proxy server via Internet Options, follow these steps:

1. Open the Control Panel and click Network And Internet | Internet Options. The Internet Properties dialog box opens.
2. On the Connections tab, click the LAN Settings button to open the Local Area Network (LAN) Settings dialog box.
3. Under Proxy Server, click to place a check mark in the box labeled Use A Proxy Server For Your LAN (These Settings Will Not Apply To Dial-Up Or VPN Connections).

4. Enter the IP address in the Address box and the port number (obtained from your network administrator or from the documentation for the proxy server) in the Port box. Click Advanced if you need to add more addresses and ports for other services.
5. Click OK twice to close all open dialog boxes, or click only once to keep the Internet Options dialog box open for the next section.

Browser Security and Privacy Settings

Each individual browser has its own security and privacy settings. By and large, these are not configured at the Windows-wide level, although there are a few exceptions (such as the proxy server settings you learned about in the previous section).

Security in a browser context means the ability to prevent your computer from being harmed by malware. When you crank up the security settings to a high level, you minimize the chance that visiting a website with malicious code will infect your computer and cause problems. High security settings may prevent some websites from performing as intended, though; for example, some shopping sites won't work with security settings at their highest levels. *Privacy* in a browser context means the ability to limit the amount of your personal information that gets shared with others. This can include your browsing history, your location, and any information stored in cookies.

The A+ exams will not ask you for the step-by-step processes for configuring security and privacy settings for a browser, but will test you on your conceptual understanding of these settings and ability to identify situations where adjusting those settings would solve a specific problem.

Internet Options and Internet Explorer

CompTIA A+ 1101 exam Objective 1.4 refers to Internet Options, which is a command in the Control Panel, as you saw in the previous section. This command opens an Internet Properties dialog box, from which you can adjust various Internet-related settings. Nearly all the settings in this dialog box apply only to Internet Explorer, the now mostly obsolete browser that came with earlier versions of Windows. However, you still need to be able to navigate this dialog box and locate settings there.

To access the Internet Properties dialog box, you can use either of these methods:

- Open the Control Panel and choose Network And Internet | Internet Options.
- Open the Internet Explorer browser (if you're using a version of Windows that includes it) and then choose Tools | Internet Options.

The dialog box has a different title depending on the method you choose for opening it. When opening through Internet Explorer, it's Internet Options; when opening through the Control Panel, it's Internet Properties. The dialog box content is the same either way.

Controlling Cookies

A *cookie* is a small text file stored on your computer that remembers your settings for a particular website. If you ever revisit a website where you've previously signed in and the page greets you by name, that's a cookie at work.

Cookies come from two different sources. A *first-party cookie* comes from the website you are actually visiting. First-party cookies can actually be helpful. A *third-party cookie* comes from another source, such as an advertisement on the web page. Third-party cookies have no benefit to you as a user.

A browser's cookies settings enable you to choose how to handle first-party and third-party cookies. Your choices are to allow them, block them, or prompt each time one tries to write to your hard disk. You can also choose certain websites to always allow or always block from using cookies.

Blocking Pop-Ups

A *pop-up blocker* is a browser feature or extension that stops websites from automatically opening additional windows (usually to display ads or otherwise annoy you). Most of the time turning off pop-ups is good, but if a website isn't working properly, sometimes enabling pop-ups can allow it to do what it needs to do. For example, some websites open a new window when you are placing a secure order or requesting a chat session with a customer service person.

Private Browsing

Most browsers have a *private browsing* mode, which may be called InPrivate (Internet Explorer and Edge), Incognito (Chrome), or some other similarly themed name. You might use it when visiting a website that you don't trust, for example, or one that you don't want any record to be made of your having visited. By default this mode disables all toolbars and extensions. However, if there's an app on the website that requires a certain extension to be loaded, you might need to allow toolbars and applications.

Sign-In/Browser Data Synchronization

Some browsers (such as Chrome) enable you to create an account with their servers and sign into the browser. Doing so *synchronizes* your bookmarks/favorites and toolbar shortcuts so that they appear on whatever computer you are using at the moment. This can be handy if you use that browser on multiple devices. It can also enable you to sign into/out of different accounts on the same browser to see different sets of bookmarks.

Ad Blockers

Ad blockers do just what the name says: they prevent some ads from appearing on web pages. We say "some" because it only works on certain kinds of ads. Some browsers have a basic ad blocker built in, and you can also install robust third-party ad blockers as extensions.

Because websites don't make any money from ad revenue when you block their ads, some sites now include code that checks for an ad blocker and displays a nag screen or error message when one is detected. You may have to temporarily disable your ad blocker to continue at such sites. This is significant from a technician's viewpoint because end users may complain that web pages aren't displaying properly and may need to be educated about the consequences of using an ad blocker and how to disable it if needed.

Clearing the Cache and Browsing Data

The *cache* is a repository of temporary files that the browser generates as it operates. It may save static versions of recently or frequently visited web pages, for example, so they will load more quickly. It also may save temporary copies of downloads or other content.

Hackers (and ordinary snoops) trying to get information about a person or system may search through the PC's cached files and recent browsing history. You can circumvent that by regularly clearing the browsing history and the cache.

Another reason you might clear a cache is to resolve performance problems with certain websites. For example, if a certain online order form or web app doesn't work correctly in a certain browser (but it works in another browser), sometimes clearing the cache is the fix.

All browsers have a cache-clearing command, which may be part of a larger command that deletes many different kinds of historical data. You can choose which types of data you want to clear. For example, you can clear your browser history without deleting saved passwords.

SCENARIO & SOLUTION	
A user is concerned about keeping their browsing habits private. What do you recommend they do?	They could clear their browser history regularly to remove recently saved history, or they could use private-mode browsing to prevent a record of the session from being recorded at all.
A user wants to install a browser extension that offers to save his passwords for him. What advice can you give him about choosing the right extension?	Choose a well-known, popular password manager extension and download it from its official (trusted) site or from the browser's library of available extensions.
A user is getting a certificate error when accessing a web site that he has successfully accessed in the past. What should he do?	If it is an expired certificate, he should assess the risk of proceeding and continue only if he is not going to be entering any private data. He should contact the site owner to inform them of the error. If it is an error that suggests that the certificate is invalid for some other reason than being expired, he should avoid using the site altogether.

CERTIFICATION OBJECTIVE

- *1101: 4.1 Summarize cloud-computing concepts*

This section covers all the topics from CompTIA A+ 1101 exam Objective 4.1, which deals with cloud computing. These topics include characteristics of a cloud environment, types of cloud services, and types of cloud deployment. For the CompTIA A+ exams you don't need to know how to actually implement cloud services, but you should be able to describe how clouds work and recommend different types of clouds and cloud services in certain scenarios.

Cloud Concepts

A *cloud* is an online location that offers one or more types of computing services to users. For example, a cloud-based file storage system like OneDrive or Dropbox enables people to store, access, and share files from any Internet-connected computing device. A cloud-based application might allow users to perform tasks online that normally are accomplished on a local PC, like editing a business document, or to interact with an online application to place orders or collaborate with others. In the following sections we'll look at some key cloud-related terms you should understand.

Characteristics of a Cloud Environment

The National Institute of Standards and Technology (NIST) defines cloud computing as having five key characteristics. The original characteristics of cloud computing were defined in NIST SP 800-145, "The NIST Definition of Cloud Computing." CompTIA A+ exam 1101 Objective 4.1 rewords and tweaks them a bit. The following characteristics are the A+ exam set:

- **Shared resources** The provider's computing resources are pooled to serve multiple consumers using a multitenant model, with different physical and virtual resources dynamically assigned and reassigned according to consumer demand. There is a sense of location independence, in that the customer generally has no control over or knowledge of the exact location of the provided resources, but may be able to specify location at a higher level of abstraction (e.g., country, state, or datacenter). Examples of resources include storage, processing, memory, and network bandwidth.
- **Rapid elasticity** Capabilities can be elastically provisioned and released, in some cases automatically, to scale rapidly outward and inward commensurate with demand. To the consumer, the capabilities available for provisioning often appear unlimited and can be appropriated in any quantity at any time.

- **Metered utilization** Cloud systems automatically control and optimize resource use by leveraging a metering capability at some level of abstraction appropriate to the type of service (e.g., storage, processing, bandwidth, and active user accounts). Resource usage can be monitored, controlled, and reported, providing transparency for both the provider and consumer of the utilized service.
- **High availability** Cloud systems are supported by robust, reliable commercial server farms with high reliability ratings, so cloud services are almost never unavailable.
- **File synchronization** Cloud systems can synchronize data across systems, including between end users' local devices and the centralized cloud storage system.

Make sure you can explain these characteristics of a cloud environment, and use them as criteria to determine whether or not an environment is cloud-based.

For more information about NIST publication SP 800-145, see https://csrc.nist.gov/publications/detail/sp/800-145/final.

Cloud Service Models

Three basic cloud service models are defined in NIST SP 800-145, based on what is being provided. An organization can choose among these to find the best fit for the services they wish to implement.

Software as a Service (SaaS) enables users to run software from the cloud's server, rather than downloading and installing it on their own individual computers. For example, Microsoft 365 is SaaS.

Platform as a Service (PaaS) provides developers a cloud-based environment on which to deploy their own applications that they can in turn offer to consumers in a cloud environment. For example, if a company wanted to provide a human resources application to their employees that could be accessed online, they might use PaaS to develop it.

Infrastructure as a Service (IaaS) allows companies and developers to create and control their own platform. They can provision servers, storage, networks, and virtual machines as needed to create PaaS and SaaS to offer to consumers. For example, a company might create their own fully immersive suite of tools online, including a nonstandard user interface.

Deployment Models

Another way that NIST SP 800-145 classifies clouds is according to where the hardware and software running the cloud are located or hosted.

A *private cloud* is operated on a network that only one company or organization has access to. It may be managed either internally within the company or by a contractor, but the key feature here is that the server or virtual machine being used is for internal use only. It's hosted at the company's own datacenter, where all the data is protected behind a firewall. A private cloud scores high on control and security, but it can be expensive to maintain.

exam watch

An *intranet* is an internal network that uses web software and protocols to share information internally within a company. That sounds like the definition of a private cloud, doesn't it? Cloud computing uses some more advanced designs and services than simple web technology, but a private cloud can basically be thought of as a fancy intranet.

A *community cloud* is a cloud where several companies or organizations have agreed to cooperate to share a private cloud. It's the equivalent of a co-op of friends buying a house together. It cuts down on costs, but there is more administration involved because the parties must agree on its management.

A *public cloud* operates on a network open for public use, such as the Internet. The cloud content is hosted at the vendor's datacenter, and the vendor is responsible for server management and security. Even though you don't manage the server's security, your data remains separate from that of other customers, and you can still require people using your cloud services to sign in securely.

A *hybrid cloud* is a conjunction of two or more of these cloud types. They remain separate clouds, but they are connected in some way. For example, a business might have two clouds: a private one for sensitive internal data, and a public one for interacting with customers. Those two clouds could be joined together to provide employees seamless access to both kinds of data.

Cloud Services and Functions

Here are some of the most common things that companies and individuals do with their cloud services:

- **Shared resources** Cloud services can share almost any type of hardware or software resource. You can print to a cloud-connected printer, for example, or mirror your screen to a cloud-connected projector or monitor. Resources can be either internal (that is, owned and managed by your company) or external (owned and managed by some other company).

- **Offsite e-mail applications** Rather than maintaining your own mail server onsite, you can use a mail server on a cloud platform to provide e-mail services to your users. This can save quite a bit in hardware management labor.
- **Cloud file storage** This is the most common use of a cloud system, to store and share files. This not only minimizes the need for local storage but also provides a safer environment because someone else is managing the integrity and physical security of the data storage. *Synchronization apps* can be used to keep the cloud storage synchronized with local storage, making the cloud storage into a secure backup.
- **Virtual application streaming and cloud-based applications** Applications no longer must be stored on the local devices on which they run; applications can be cloud-hosted and accessed via custom interfaces or standard web browsers on cell phones, tablets, laptops, and desktops.
- **Desktop virtualization** Users can connect to desktops on a cloud platform that mimic local operating system desktops; this can be useful to enable users to run applications that may not be available locally, for example, and can further free up local system resources by not having to support multiple full-featured operating systems on each device. Desktop virtualization is enabled by virtual desktop infrastructure (VDI), which can be hosted either on-premises (that is, the company can host it on their own private servers) or in the cloud.

CERTIFICATION OBJECTIVE

- ***1102: 4.9*** *Given a scenario, use remote access technologies*

This section covers all the remote access technologies outlined in 1102 exam Objective 4.9 (except VPN, which was covered in Chapter 17).

Remote Access Technologies

Remote access technologies enable you to access another computer remotely via a network or the Internet. Remote access can be very useful in performing technical support troubleshooting, for example, and for running applications on one computer as you are physically sitting at another computer. This section explains the basic technologies and applications behind remote access capability.

Remote Desktop Protocol (RDP) is Microsoft's protocol for providing remote access. It has two parts to it. The computer to which you want to connect must run RDP server services, and the computer(s) that want to connect to it must run RDP client software. Windows includes RDP server functionality in the Pro, Pro for Workstations, Education, and Enterprise editions (but not in the Home and basic editions). It includes client functionality, called *Remote Desktop Connection (RDC),* in all editions, for which the executable file is mstsc.exe. That stands for Microsoft Terminal Services Client, which was an earlier name for the feature.

Another technology for remote access is *virtual network computing (VNC).* This is a different protocol from RDP and has its own pros and cons.

- RDP has traditionally been proprietary to Microsoft (although that's changing); VNC is platform-independent.
- With RDP, when someone takes remote control of a computer, the computer can't be locally controlled until that control is terminated. With VNC, on the other hand, users at both ends of the process can see the screen at the same time, so that makes it handy for training sessions and remote support.
- RDP is faster and more efficient and results in better performance, so it's often preferred when visibility at both ends is not important.

Establishing a Remote Desktop Connection in Windows

To access one Windows computer from another Windows computer across your LAN, first set up the sharing computer to allow desktop connections. This PC must have a Pro, Pro for Workstations, Enterprise, or Education edition of Windows installed. Follow the steps in Exercise 18-2 to set it up.

EXERCISE 18-2

Allowing Remote Desktop Connections

These steps will work in Windows 10 or 11 Pro, Enterprise, or Education edition.

1. Open the Control Panel and navigate to System And Security | System | Remote Settings. The System Properties dialog box opens to the Remote tab.

2. In the Remote Desktop section, select Allow Remote Connections To This Computer, as shown in the following illustration.

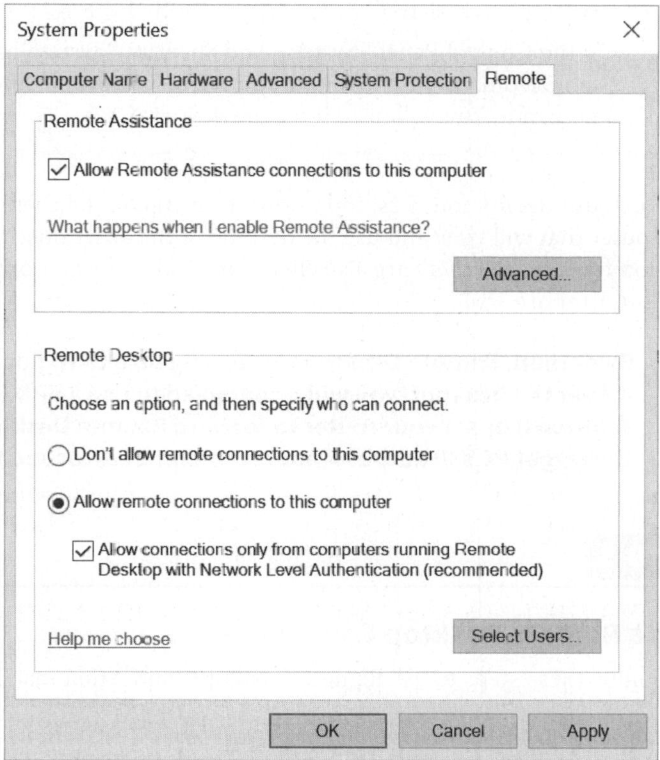

3. Click Select Users to open the Remote Desktop Users dialog box.

   See the information about restricting logins in the section "Security Considerations for Remote Access" later in this chapter.

4. Click Add to set up a new user. Then enter or select a user in the Enter The Object Names To Select box.

   If you are on a domain-based network, you will be able to choose other users from Active Directory. If you are on a peer-to-peer network, you'll need to set up local user accounts on this PC with the e-mail addresses of the people you want to be able to connect to it and then set them up here.

5. Click Check Names to make sure the users you enter are valid. Then click OK.
6. Click OK to close the Remote Desktop Users dialog box.
7. Click OK to close the System Properties dialog box.
8. On the Control Panel | System And Security | System page, look in the Computer Name, Domain, And Workgroup Settings section for the computer name, and make a note of it. You will need it for the next exercise.

Next, use the Remote Desktop Connection app on the client computer—that is, the computer that will view and use the desktop of the other one. You can use any Windows edition for this, and there are also clients available for other operating systems. Follow the steps in Exercise 18-3.

By default, Remote Desktop works only on a LAN, not over the Internet. To use it over the Internet, you will either need to use a VPN (the better of the two solutions) or set your router to forward Remote Desktop traffic (TCP port 3389) to the target PC's IP address (not recommended, for security vulnerability reasons).

EXERCISE 18-3

Establishing a Remote Desktop Connection

Follow these steps to use Remote Desktop Connection in Windows 10 or 11.

1. On the client PC, click in the Search box on the taskbar, type **mstsc**, and click Remote Desktop Connection in the search results.
2. In the Computer box, type the name of the PC from Step 8 of Exercise 18-2.

3. Click Connect.
4. When prompted for your password, type the password for your account on the remote PC. Or if you have a different user name on the remote PC, click More Choices and then click Use A Different Account to enter those credentials.

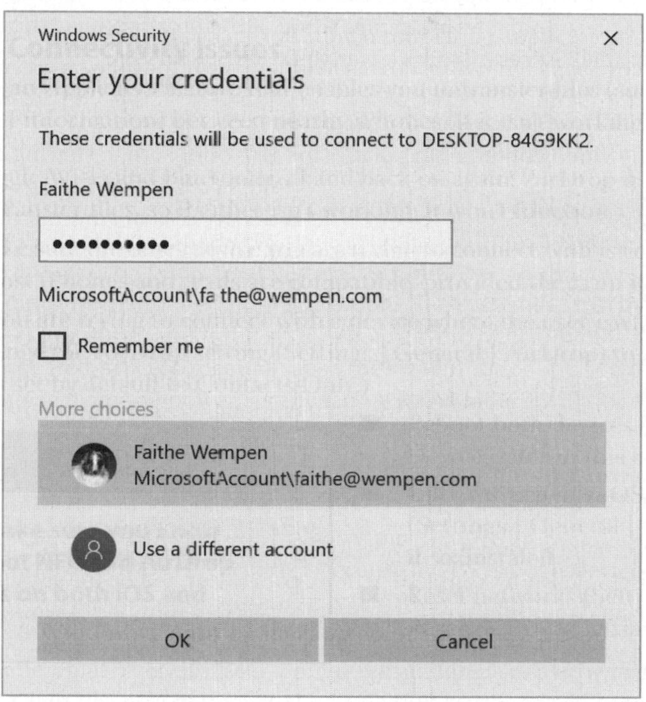

5. If you see a warning that the identity of the remote computer cannot be verified, click Yes.
6. Wait for the connection to be established. When it is, the remote system's desktop appears full-screen on your display. A blue bar at the top enables you to minimize the connection window or restore it down to a resizable (non-full-screen) window if desired.
7. When you are done using the remote system, click the Close button in the blue bar at the top of the screen to close the connection, and then click OK to confirm.

Using Third-Party Remote Desktop Tools

Windows Remote Desktop Connection is handy and readily available, but there are many other client and server systems you can use for remote connectivity. If you work for a business's help desk, you may be provided remote access software to assist users who call you for technical support, for example. Some of the most popular third-party tools include AnyDesk, Parallels Access, TeamViewer, Splashtop, RealVNC, LogMeIn, and GoToMyPC. These third-party tools may include a screen-share feature (where you can share control of the desktop GUI), a file transfer feature (where you can access files on the remote system), or both. Many video conferencing platforms also offer screen sharing capabilities.

1102 exam Objective 4.9 refers to desktop management software, which is a more generic way of referring to an RMM system.

Remote Monitoring and Management (RMM) is the process of administrators monitoring and controlling remote systems via software designed for that purpose. The IT departments at large companies often use enterprise-level RMM software to provide troubleshooting assistance, roll out updates, and monitor systems for compliance with company policies.

Security Considerations for Remote Access

Any time you make a computer accessible from another PC, you run the risk of that permission being used by someone who is not authorized or for activities that you have not authorized. You can minimize the vulnerabilities in a number of ways, including these:

- Restrict who can sign in using Remote Desktop. By default all Administrator accounts on the server PC can sign in remotely. You can make the change in Local Security Policy. Remove the Administrators group, but leave the Remote Desktop Users group in place. Then add the users into the Remote Desktop Users group by entering them as in Exercise 18-2, Steps 3–6.
- Use your firewall settings to restrict access to port TCP 3389, which is the remote desktop listening port.
- Do not configure Remote Desktop servers to permit connections without Network Level Authentication (NLA) unless you are connecting using client platforms that do not support NLA. (Note the check box for it in the illustration in Exercise 18-2.) It should be enabled by default. You can check and change it in Group Policy Editor.

Beyond the scope of this book, there are some additional things you can do to further secure remote access. A quick web search will turn up details about these ideas: use RDP gateways, change the RDP listening port, and tunnel connections through IPSec or SSH.

Using Remote Assistance

Microsoft Remote Assistance (MSRA) is a feature of the Windows help system that allows users to send assistance requests to others via e-mail or hyperlink. The recipient of an assistance request can then click it to gain access to the requester's PC without needing to have Remote Desktop client or server services or software running. It's a simplified version of some more robust third-party technical support applications; its advantage is that it comes free with all Windows editions.

To send a Remote Assistance request in Windows, open the Start menu and search for **Remote Assistance** or **MSRA**. Click Remote Assistance in the search results to run the Windows Remote Assistance Wizard. Then click Invite Someone You Trust To Help You, and follow the prompts to send the request. For this to work, the computer that is requesting help must be configured to allow remote assistance connections. You can set this up in the System Properties dialog box on the Remote tab.

If you are the recipient of a request, you can click the invitation request file in the e-mail that you received to open Windows Remote Assistance. Or if you have saved the invitation attachment to your local storage, open Windows Remote Assistance on your PC, then click Help Someone Who Has Invited You, and then click Use An Invitation File to browse for the invitation file.

CERTIFICATION SUMMARY

Be able to explain how the Internet is structured, including domain names, IP addresses, and DNS servers. Make sure you can identify the protocols and services involved in Internet usage, including those for web, mail, file transfer, and authentication.

Be able to explain the functions of the many kinds of servers in use on the Internet, including web, file, print, DHCP, DNS, mail, authentication, and proxy, and understand the presence and purpose of legacy and embedded systems, Internet appliances, and IoT devices.

Understand how to maintain security and privacy standards when installing and using web browsers.

Make sure you understand the cloud concepts outlined in the publication NIST SP 800-145, including the characteristics of cloud computing; the differences among SaaS, PaaS, and IaaS; and various common deployment models, such as private, community, public, and hybrid. Be sure you are familiar with cloud characteristics such as shared resources, metered utilization, rapid elasticity, high availability, and file synchronization.

Be able to explain and, given a scenario, implement the various types of remote access such as RDP, VPN, VNC, SSH, and MSRA. Know how to set them up and use them. Be familiar with the various remote access third-party tools. Be aware of the security concerns involved in remote access.

TWO-MINUTE DRILL

Here are some of the key points covered in Chapter 18.

Internet Concepts

- ❑ The Internet is a huge, global WAN. No one company owns it. Its major pathways collectively are called the backbone.
- ❑ Backbone networks are owned by Tier 1 providers. Tier 2 providers are large ISPs that purchase access from Tier 1 providers. Tier 3 providers are small ISPs and individual companies.
- ❑ Which ISP you should select depends on the type of connection you want. Some ISPs provide only one kind of connection; others offer a choice, such as DSL versus fiber.
- ❑ A website's address is its Uniform Resource Locator (URL). In a URL, the first part is the protocol, such as http. The next part is the host name, such as www. The domain name consists of a top-level domain like .com and a second-level domain like microsoft. Forward slashes (/) separate the parts of the page's path on the host.
- ❑ A domain name that includes a host name as well as a top-level domain and a second-level domain is a fully qualified domain name (FQDN).
- ❑ Domain Name System (DNS) servers translate between domain names and IP addresses.
- ❑ Protocols for mail delivery include SMTP (port 25), POP3 (port 110), and IMAP (port 143).
- ❑ HTML is the language of web pages. HTTP is the protocol used to display web pages.
- ❑ HTTPS (port 443) is the secure version of HTTP (port 80). Secure web pages use SSL or TLS to encrypt the data for transmission, and use HTTPS as the protocol to display the pages.
- ❑ Telnet (port 23) is a very old and insecure protocol used to emulate a terminal environment. SSH (port 22) is a secure remote administration protocol/tool that has replaced Telnet.
- ❑ FTP (File Transfer Protocol, ports 20/21) is employed by many online file servers. Secure Copy (SCP) uses SSH for encrypting data. SFTP is a secure version of FTP.
- ❑ CAPTCHA is a challenge-response service used to create a test that only a human can pass, such as finding text in a graphical image, so online users can prove they are not a machine.

- ❑ Types of server roles you should know about include DNS, DHCP, file (fileshare), print, web, mail, syslog, and authentication.
- ❑ A proxy server points Internet requests for data to an alternative server that manages the requests, such as directing them to cached copies or declining to display certain content.
- ❑ A legacy system is one with old hardware or software. An embedded system is a computer that is inside an object that is not primarily a computer, like a microwave oven or a clock/radio.
- ❑ Internet appliance is a class of server applications and services designed to protect Internet servers. Common types include spam gateways, unified threat management (UTM), load balancers, and proxy servers.
- ❑ UTM is the principle of creating a unified package of appliances that work together to reduce the threat of harm from attacks.
- ❑ Internet of Things (IoT) refers to the computing/networking capabilities of everyday objects like appliances, lights, and security systems.

Configuring Browser and Internet Settings

- ❑ When downloading a browser or an extension, it's important to acquire them from trusted sources.
- ❑ When acquiring downloads from an untrusted source, hashing may be useful in validating the download.
- ❑ Extensions add capabilities to a browser. Some common extensions include password managers and pop-up blockers.
- ❑ A password manager keeps a record of login credentials for various websites; it's critical to acquire password management software from trusted sources only.
- ❑ Websites that use secure HTTPS connections rely on certificates to validate them. If you see a certificate error, evaluate it closely and do not trust the website until you understand why the certificate is in error.
- ❑ To configure a proxy server in Windows, use the Internet Options applet in the Control Panel, which opens the Internet Properties dialog box. Set it up on the Connections tab.
- ❑ Security and privacy settings in a browser that you may need to work with include cookies, pop-ups, private browsing, browser data synchronization, ad blockers, and cache/history clearing.

Cloud Concepts

- The five characteristics of a cloud environment are shared resources, rapid elasticity, metered utilization, high availability, and file synchronization.
- Software as a Service (SaaS) allows users to run software from the cloud's server.
- Platform as a Service (PaaS) provides developers a cloud-based environment on which to deploy their own applications.
- Infrastructure as a Service (IaaS) allows companies to create and control their own platform.
- A private cloud is hosted on a private server inside a company's firewall.
- A community cloud is a cloud where several companies share a private cloud.
- A public cloud operates on an open network, such as the Internet. Even though the network itself is public, you can still require users to sign into your cloud.
- A hybrid cloud is a joining of two or more other cloud types.
- Some of the services that can be cloud-shared include hardware resources, e-mail, file storage, applications, and virtual desktops.

Remote Access Technologies

- Remote Desktop Protocol (RDP) is a Microsoft protocol for remote access, operating by default on TCP port 3389. The Windows client for creating a remote connection is Remote Desktop Connection.
- Virtual network computing (VNC) is a platform-independent protocol for remote access that is often used in remote assistance applications because it allows screen viewing on both ends.
- To allow remote desktop connections on a Windows PC running a Pro, Pro for Workstations, Enterprise, or Education edition, open the System Properties dialog box and on the Remote tab, choose Allow Remote Connections To This Computer.
- To make a remote connection from Windows (any version) to a server PC, run Remote Desktop Connection (mstsc.exe).
- Many third-party applications are available for remote desktop access, including professional products used for help desks.
- Use Microsoft Remote Assistance (MSRA) to request help from someone remotely, using the Windows Remote Assistance Wizard. Doing so generates an e-mail with an attached invitation.

SELF TEST

The following questions will help you measure your understanding of the material presented in this chapter. Read all the choices carefully because there might be more than one correct answer. Choose all correct answers for each question.

Internet Concepts

1. Which type of companies own and control the Internet backbone?

A. Tier A

B. Tier B

C. Tier 1

D. Tier 2

2. Which of these is an FQDN?

A. http

B. www

C. sycamoreknoll.com

D. www.sycamoreknoll.com

3. Which of these is a host name?

A. http

B. www

C. sycamoreknoll.com

D. www.sycamoreknoll.com

4. What kind of server translates between IP addresses and domain names?

A. DHCP

B. ISP

C. DNS

D. FQDN

5. Which of these is a mail protocol?

A. HTML

B. IMAP

C. Telnet

D. FTP

6. Which of these is the protocol for a secure web page?
   A. SFTP
   B. HTTPS
   C. SSH
   D. POP3
7. What kind of server would use FTP?
   A. Web
   B. File
   C. Mail
   D. Authentication
8. What kind of server assigns IP addresses to clients?
   A. Web
   B. DNS
   C. File
   D. DHCP
9. What kind of server handles requests for Internet services for a client without exposing the client's IP address to the Internet?
   A. DNS
   B. Proxy
   C. Mail
   D. Authentication
10. Which is the best description of SCADA?
   A. Industrial system to control and monitor machinery
   B. IoT device
   C. Proxy server
   D. Secure web server

Configuring Browser and Internet Settings

11. When downloading browsers, the most important security consideration is:
   A. Using a proxy server
   B. Not installing multiple browsers on the same device
   C. Choosing a browser with robust security features
   D. Downloading from a trusted source

12. If your browser doesn't come with a password manager, how can you add that feature to it?
   A. Pop-up
   B. Extension
   C. Cookie
   D. Private mode browsing
13. What kind of cookie comes from the website you are visiting?
   A. First-party
   B. Second-party
   C. Third-party
   D. Fourth-party
14. Which of these problems can clearing a browser's cache sometimes solve?
   A. Recall forgotten passwords
   B. Prevent saved passwords from being automatically filled in
   C. Resolve performance problems with certain websites
   D. Delete cookies that may be causing page loading problems
15. HTTP, HTTPS, FTP, and Socks are four types of what?
   A. DHCP servers
   B. Websites
   C. LANs
   D. Proxy servers

Cloud Concepts

16. Which of these is *not* one of the five characteristics of cloud computing?
   A. Rapid elasticity
   B. Shared resources
   C. Metered utilization
   D. Private server
17. Which of these refers to users running applications from a cloud's server, rather than downloading the application?
   A. Infrastructure as a Service
   B. Platform as a Service
   C. Software as a Service
   D. Hardware as a Service

18. A cloud that operates via the Internet is a __________ cloud.

A. Hybrid
B. Community
C. Public
D. Private

Remote Access Technologies

19. What is mstsc.exe?

A. The executable file for Local Security Policy
B. The executable file for the Group Policy Editor
C. The server application for allowing a Remote Desktop connection
D. The client application for creating a Remote Desktop connection

20. If you wanted to help someone fix their Windows computer remotely but they didn't have a Pro, Enterprise, or Education edition of Windows, what tool would you use?

A. Remote Assistance
B. Remote Desktop
C. Network Level Authentication
D. None of the above would work

A SELF TEST ANSWERS

Internet Concepts

1. ☑ **C.** Tier 1 providers own and control the backbone.
☒ **A** and **B** are incorrect because tiers are numbered, not lettered. **D** is incorrect because Tier 2 refers to large ISPs.

2. ☑ **D.** A fully qualified domain name (FQDN) includes both a host and a domain.
☒ **A** is incorrect because it is a protocol. **B** is incorrect because it is a host name. **C** is incorrect because it is a domain name but it lacks a host name.

3. ☑ **B.** www is a host name.
☒ **A** is incorrect because it is a protocol. **C** is incorrect because it is a domain name but it lacks a host name. **D** is incorrect because it is an FQDN.

4. ☑ **C.** A Domain Name System (DNS) server translates between IP addresses and domain names.
☒ A is incorrect because a DHCP server dynamically assigns IP addresses to clients. **B** is incorrect because ISP refers to an Internet service provider, a company that provides Internet service. **D** is incorrect because FQDN describes a web address that includes a host name.

5. ☑ **B.** IMAP, Internet Mail Access Protocol, is a mail protocol.
☒ **A** is incorrect because HTML is the language used to create web pages. **C** is incorrect because Telnet is a terminal emulation protocol. **D** is incorrect because FTP is a protocol for transferring files.

6. ☑ **B.** HTTPS is a secure form of HTTP, a web protocol.
☒ **A** is incorrect because SFTP is a protocol for secure file transfer. **C** is incorrect because SSH is for secure terminal emulation or file transfer. **D** is incorrect because POP3 is a mail protocol.

7. ☑ **B.** A file server would be used for FTP, which is a file-transferring protocol.
☒ **A** is incorrect because a web server delivers web pages. **C** is incorrect because a mail server is used for e-mail. **D** is incorrect because an authentication server verifies user identities.

8. ☑ **D.** A Dynamic Host Configuration Protocol (DHCP) server assigns IP addresses.
☒ **A** is incorrect because a web server delivers web pages. **B** is incorrect because a DNS server translates between IP addresses and domain names. **C** is incorrect because a file server allows users to upload and download files.

9. ☑ **B.** A proxy server protects the client's IP address from the Internet, among its other benefits.
☒ **A** is incorrect because a DNS server translates between IP addresses and domain names. **C** is incorrect because a mail server sends and receives e-mail. **D** is incorrect because an authentication server verifies user identities.

10. ☑ **A.** SCADA is an industrial control system used in factories.
☒ **B** is incorrect because an Internet of Things (IoT) device is a network-connected home appliance or system. **C** is incorrect because a proxy server is a network service that handles Internet requests without exposing a client's IP address. **D** is incorrect because a secure web server responds to requests from web client browsers.

Configuring Browser and Internet Settings

11. ☑ **D.** Downloading from a trusted source is critical.
☒ **A** is incorrect because a proxy server is only needed in certain situations. **B** is incorrect because having multiple browsers installed has no impact on security. **C** is incorrect because although robust security features are useful, they are not as important as downloading from a trusted source.

12. ☑ **B.** Extensions add new functions to a browser, such as a password manager.
☒ **A** is incorrect because a pop-up is an automatically opening extra browser window. **C** is incorrect because a cookie is a small text file that retains a setting needed for a website. **D** is incorrect because private mode browsing is browsing without leaving any record of the activity.

13. ☑ **A.** A first-party cookie comes from the website you are visiting.
☒ **B** and **D** are incorrect because there is no such thing as second-party or fourth-party cookies in cookie classification. **C** is incorrect because a third-party cookie is a cookie from an advertiser.

14. ☑ **C.** Clearing a browser's cache is a common solution for resolving performance problems with certain websites.
☒ **A** is incorrect because clearing a cache will not recall a forgotten password. **B** is incorrect because passwords are not saved in the cache. **D** is incorrect because cookies are not saved in the cache.

15. ☑ **D.** HTTP, HTTPS, FTP, and Socks are four types of proxy servers.
☒ **A, B,** and **C** are incorrect because HTTP, HTTPS, FTP, and Socks are not types of these items. HTTP and HTTPS are protocols for delivering web pages, and FTP is a file-transferring protocol.

Cloud Concepts

16. ☑ **D.** Private server is not one of the five characteristics.
☒ **A, B,** and **C** are incorrect because each is one of the five characteristics of cloud computing.

17. ☑ **C.** Software as a Service (SaaS) is the term for running an application from the cloud.
☒ **A** is incorrect because IaaS refers to creating an entire infrastructure environment in the cloud. **B** is incorrect because PaaS refers to having developers create their own cloud applications on a supplied platform. **D** is incorrect because Hardware as a Service is not a recognized cloud service model.

18. ☑ **C.** A public cloud is one that operates via a public network such as the Internet.
☒ **A** is incorrect because a hybrid cloud joins two or more other types of clouds. **B** is incorrect because a community cloud is a deployment in which several organizations share a private cloud. **D** is incorrect because a private cloud is a deployment where the company running it also controls and manages the server and network.

Remote Access Technologies

19. ☑ **D.** The file mstsc.exe is the client executable for Remote Desktop Connection. Its name comes from Microsoft Terminal Services Connection, an old name for the feature.
☒ **A** is incorrect because Local Security Policy is secpol.msc. **B** is incorrect because the Group Policy Editor is gpedit.msc. **C** is incorrect because there is no application for the server hosting a remote connection; it is enabled via the Control Panel.

20. ☑ **A.** Microsoft Remote Assistance (MSRA) enables any Windows edition to accept remote connections for troubleshooting purposes.
☒ **B** is incorrect because Remote Desktop doesn't allow a Windows PC to accept incoming connections unless it has a Pro, Enterprise, or Education edition. **C** is incorrect because NLA is an authentication method for Remote Desktop Protocol. **D** is incorrect because Remote Assistance will work.

Chapter 19

Troubleshooting Networks

CERTIFICATION OBJECTIVES

- **1101: 5.7** Given a scenario, troubleshoot problems with wired and wireless networks
- **1102: 1.2** Given a scenario, use the appropriate Microsoft command-line tool
- **1102: 1.10** Identify common features and tools of the macOS/desktop OS
- **1102: 1.11** Identify common features and tools of the Linux client/desktop OS
- **1102: 4.5** Summarize environmental impacts and local environmental controls

✓ Two-Minute Drill

Q&A Self Test

Although there are many network problems only a trained network specialist can resolve, there are also many common and simple network problems that you will be able to resolve without extensive training and experience. You can also run certain tests that will give you important information to pass on to more highly trained network specialists, such as those in a large corporation or at your local Internet service provider (ISP).

In this chapter, you will explore the tools and techniques for troubleshooting common network problems. You will also learn about preventive maintenance tasks for networks.

CERTIFICATION OBJECTIVES

- ***1101: 5.7*** *Given a scenario, troubleshoot problems with wired and wireless networks*
- ***1102: 1.2*** *Given a scenario, use appropriate Microsoft command-line tool*
- ***1102: 1.10*** *Identify common features and tools of the macOS/desktop OS*
- ***1102: 1.11*** *Identify common features and tools of the Linux client/desktop OS*

This section covers topics from multiple exam objectives that involve network troubleshooting. For CompTIA A+ 1101 exam Objective 5.7, be prepared to identify common symptoms of network malfunction and their causes. Practice and review troubleshooting techniques for networks. For CompTIA A+ 1102 exam Objective 1.2, familiarize yourself with command-line tools for network management, such as ipconfig, ping, tracert, and so on, and for 1102 exam Objectives 1.10 and 1.11, know how to open a Terminal window in both macOS and Linux and how to use common network-related commands in Linux.

Troubleshooting Common Network Problems

To troubleshoot networks, a PC professional must call on all the skills required for hardware and software support, applying a structured approach to determining the problem, applying solutions, and testing. However, keep in mind that if you make all the connections properly and all the hardware is working properly, the most common problems will involve the TCP/IP configuration of network interface cards (NICs).

The tools you will use for network troubleshooting include both hardware and software tools. The hardware tools and some software tools were described in Chapter 17 as tools needed to create a network, but you also need them to troubleshoot network problems.

In this chapter, as we visit troubleshooting problems, we will describe which of those tools to use and how to use them.

Be sure you also know how each of the following hardware tools is used for troubleshooting networks: cable tester, toner probe, loopback plug, punchdown tool, cable stripper, crimper, and network tap. Refer back to Chapter 17 to review these.

Opening a Command Prompt or Terminal Window

To work at a command prompt within a GUI operating system, you need to open up a command prompt window. The process is different for each of the operating systems we study for the CompTIA A+ certification:

- **Windows** Right-click the Start button and click Command Prompt, or Command Prompt (Admin) if you need admin privileges. Windows 11 also includes a Windows Terminal command prompt window, which you can access the same way.
- **macOS** Open the Applications folder, open Utilities, and double-click Terminal. Alternatively, click Launchpad in the Dock, search for Terminal, and then select it.
- **Linux** In its native form, Linux's shell *is* a command prompt. The process for opening one within a GUI shell depends on the distro, but in most distros you can press CTRL-ALT-T.

Command-Line Tools for Network Troubleshooting

When the TCP/IP protocol suite installs into Windows, **it also installs a variety of command-line tools, such as ipconfig, ping, tracert, netstat, and nslookup**. These are the handiest and least expensive tools you can use for network troubleshooting or a variety of problems—those both local to and far removed from the computer, such as Domain Name System (DNS) and Dynamic Host Configuration Protocol (DHCP) problems.

Each utility provides different information and is most valuable when used appropriately. For instance, on a Windows system, you should first view the IP configuration using the *ipconfig* utility and verify that the configuration is correct for the network to which you are connected. If you discover any obvious problems when you view the IP configuration, correct them before proceeding. Then, select the tool that will help you diagnose and—in some instances—resolve the problem.

CompTIA A+ 1102 exam Objective 1.2 mentions two other command-line tools: hostname **and** winver**. These commands report back simple information: the name of the host computer (as configured in Windows) and the Windows version number, respectively. Make sure you can recall these commands and use them to collect those pieces of information from a command line.**

At a Linux Terminal window, you can type **/usr/bin/hostname** to display the name of the current host system. Only users with root user authority can set the host name.

Most of these utilities have many optional parameters you can enter at the command line to change the command's behavior. In this book, we provide the simplest and/or most often used syntax. If you would like to learn more about each command, in Windows, simply open a Command Prompt window and enter the command name followed by a space, a slash, and a question mark, and then press ENTER. For the **ipconfig** command, for example, enter the following: **ipconfig /?**.

A *parameter* is a string of characters entered at the command line along with the command. Some parameters are data, such as the IP address you enter with the **ping** command, and other parameters are switches, which alter the behavior of the command, such as the "/?" switch that requests help information about a command. Most command-prompt commands will accept either a hyphen (-) or a slash (/) character as part of a switch. When entering commands at the command line, separate the command name, such as "ipconfig," from any parameters with a space. In the case of **ipconfig /?**, the slash and question mark together comprise a parameter, which is separated from the command name with a space. Do not insert a space between the slash or hyphen and what follows, such as "?" or "all." If additional parameters must be used, separate each parameter with a space.

On the macOS and Linux side of things, the modern command is **ip**. Earlier versions still work: ifconfig for wired networks and iwconfig for wireless ones.

The syntax for the **ip** command is as follows:

```
ip [ OPTIONS ] OBJECT { COMMAND | help }
```

Some of the available OBJECTs you can use include

- **link (l)** Display and modify network interfaces
- **address (a)** Display and modify IP addresses
- **route (r)** Display and alter the routing table
- **neigh (n)** Display and manipulate neighbor objects (ARP table)

The ip command receives only passing mention in the CompTIA A+ 220-1102 exam objectives, but you should at least be able to state that it is associated with Linux and macOS and to use it to examine your network's IP addresses.

Now that you understand some of the basics of command-line tools, we will look at some common network problems. Some require hardware tools, but most require that you use command-line tools—both to test for a problem and to resolve a problem. As we go through the various types of problems in this chapter, we will cover all the network-related command-line tools listed in 1102 exam Objective 1.2.

Connectivity Problems

Connectivity problems are more obvious because the user simply fails to connect to a computer and usually receives an error message. For the PC technician troubleshooting connectivity problems involving the Internet, there are literally worlds of possible locations for the problems. When you suspect that a computer does not have network connectivity, check the network hardware, and use a variety of utilities to determine the cause, as described in the following sections. Learn how to pinpoint the location of a connection problem, from the local computer to Internet routers.

Checking Network Hardware

When there is a connectivity problem, first check the hardware. Check the NIC, cables (for a wired network), hub, switch, wireless access point (WAP), and router. Check the NIC by examining the status indicator lights on it, if available. On a bus NIC, the lights are on the card's bracket adjacent to the RJ-45 connector. Status indicator lights typically indicate link (a connection to a network), activity, and speed. Since most NICs receive power from the PC, any light is a good indication that the NIC's connection to the PC is working (or at least the power lines are). Look closer to check the connection. The Link light (usually green), when steady, indicates the connection to the network is live, and it will usually blink when sending or receiving. Multispeed NICs may have a separate Link light for each speed the NIC supports, and the lights may be labeled 100M for 100 Mbps and 1000M for 1000 Mbps (1 Gbps). If a Link light is off, there is either no power to the NIC or the connection is broken, which may be caused by a broken connector or cable.

Status indicators for network hardware include light-emitting diode (LED) lights on the physical device itself and/or software installed along with the device driver. With a quick glance at the lights on a device or at the icons and messages on your computer screen, you will know that the device is powered up, that it is receiving and transmitting data, and (in the case of wireless devices) the strength of the signal. Many NICs have at least an *activity (ACT)* light that blinks to indicate network activity. These lights also indicate problems when they flash or change color. Read the device's documentation so you understand what these lights mean when troubleshooting.

Most NICs—both Ethernet and Wi-Fi—install with a configuration utility that can be opened from an icon in the taskbar's system tray. A balloon message may appear over the notification area when the status of one of these devices changes. The icon may also change to indicate the device's current status, and you can pause your mouse over one of these icons to display the status of the devices. For example, you might see a message such as "A network cable is unplugged," and the icon might have a red X over it.

In addition, some wireless NICs have five LEDs that indicate signal strength, much like the bars on a cell phone. One lit light indicates a poor connection, and five lit lights indicate an excellent connection.

With many Ethernet and wireless NICs now built into computers, you often do not have physical status lights but must rely on status information provided in Windows. Check the notification area on the taskbar for an icon for the NIC.

If you have determined that a NIC has power but there is no evidence of a connection (Link lights or status icon), take steps to correct this. In the case of a wired Ethernet NIC, check for a loose or damaged cable and examine the RJ-45 connectors for damage. Follow the cable to the hub or switch. We recommend the use of a cable tester since broken wires inside the cable are not revealed by visual inspection.

If the cable tests okay, check that the hub, switch, WAP, and router are functioning. Check for power to each device. These devices also have status lights similar to those of NICs. If all the lights are off, check the power supply. In the case of an Ethernet hub or switch, if it has power, look at the status light for each Ethernet connection on the device. If the light is out for the port to which the computer connects, swap the cable with a known good cable, and recheck the status. Also check the cable standard that is in use. You may still find Cat 5 cabling in use. Upgrade the cabling to, at a minimum, Cat 5e, and preferably Cat 6 or 7. Remember that network devices such as switches and WAPs are computers. So, for example, if all users connected to the same WAP have the same network problem, consider restarting the WAP.

Check for any source of electrical interference affecting the cabling. Unshielded twisted-pair (UTP) cabling does not have shielding from interference, relying instead on the twists in the cable pairs to resist electromagnetic interference (EMI). Many things can cause EMI. Heavy power cables running parallel to network cabling emit signals that can cause interference, especially if there are intermittent loads on the power cable, such as when a large electric motor starts and stops. *Radio frequency interference (RFI)* can also affect networks if a source of RFI, such as a poorly shielded electronic device, is located near network cabling. If you find such a situation, take steps to move the cabling or the source of the interference.

If you cannot find any physical problems with the NIC, cabling, hub, switch, or WAP and cannot find a source of interference, check the status of the NIC in Network Connections (in the Control Panel, choose Network And Internet | Network And Sharing Center | Change Adapter Settings and double-click the name of the NIC).

Figure 19-1 shows the Status dialog box from a Windows 10 computer with no connectivity. We could click the Diagnose button at the bottom of the dialog box to run Windows Network Diagnostics, which may be able to identify the problem. If there were connectivity, *Internet* would appear next to either IPv4 Connectivity or IPv6 Connectivity.

A lack of error doesn't necessarily mean there is absolutely no problem with the NIC, but when you are first troubleshooting a network problem, accept this opinion at least temporarily and perform other tests before doing anything drastic, like replacing the NIC.

You can also check the status of the network connection in Windows via the Settings app. Open Settings and click Network & Internet to see whether or not you are connected to the network and the Internet. You don't get any of the details this way, but you can access the same details as in Figure 19-1 from here by clicking Change Adapter Options (Windows 10) or Advanced Network Settings | More Network Adapter Options (Windows 11) and then double-clicking the adapter's icon.

FIGURE 19-1

Check the status of the NIC.

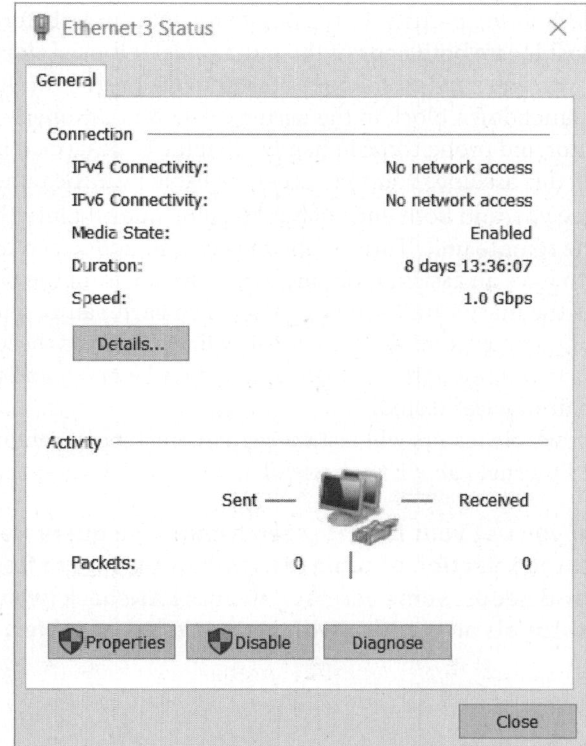

FIGURE 19-2

A cable-testing tool

Testing a Cable To test for a broken cable, use a cable tester, such as the one shown in Figure 19-2. Notice that there are two separate components: a master unit and a smaller remote terminator. This makes it possible to connect to each end of a cable when those ends are in separate rooms or even on separate floors, in which case, you will need a troubleshooting partner on the other end. Of course, before you can test for a broken cable, you must locate both ends of the same cable. If the far end is connected to a punchdown block, you will need to connect a tester to the correct RJ-45 socket, which can be a challenge if the punchdown block in the wiring closet is not properly labeled. That is where a tone generator and probe come in handy. Chapter 17 described how to use a toner probe. Of course, this assumes you can access the cable near the punchdown block.

Once you find both ends of a cable, plug one end into the master unit and the other end into the remote unit. Turn on the master unit and watch the lights on the remote unit. (It helps to have an assistant on one end.) The LEDs on the remote terminator will light up in turn as the master unit sends signals down each pair of wires. If the cable wiring is intact, the LEDs corresponding to each pair will be green. If there is damage to the cable wiring, the LEDs will not light up at all, or may first be green and then turn red. This is true for each pair of wires tested.

Some cable testers will test more than one type of cabling, but in most LANs, being able to test Ethernet cable is very useful and may be all you need.

If you use your favorite search engine to query "cable tester," you will find a large selection of cable testers. You are sure to find one that fits your budget and needs. Some vendors, such as LANshack (www.lanshack.com), publish free tutorials on working with various types of cables.

If you find problems with a cable, you may need to run a new cable, which also means getting out the punchdown tool for attaching cable to a punchdown block and going into your supply of spare RJ-45 connectors and crimping new ones onto the ends of cables before connecting the ends to the hubs/switches and NICs.

Testing Network Ports Loopback plugs test whether or not a physical port, such as an RJ-45 port on a switch or the RJ-45 port in a wall jack, are working. Some variations of this device are essentially a single plastic RJ-45 connector with two very short internal looped wires—one connecting pin 1 to pin 3, and the second wire connecting pin 2 to pin 6, all within the same RJ-45 connector. Indicator lights may be present to let you know if the connection is good or not.

Troubleshooting Wireless Connectivity

When you encounter connectivity problems on an existing wireless network that involve more than one computer, try the easier fix: restart the WAP/broadband router. In our home offices, this is an almost guaranteed solution. If this is a new wireless network, wireless connectivity problems may be the result of too great a distance between the wireless NICs and a WAP, or it could be interference problems. The farther a Wi-Fi NIC is from a WAP, the lower the radio frequency (RF) signals. This translates to slower network speeds. But what if you are within a reasonable distance that had a much better signal before? The three most likely suspects are changes to the environment, new signal-impeding obstructions, or interference. Snow storms in the winter and thick foliage in the summer can affect your signal. Higher-gain antennae on the WAP and the Wi-Fi clients (if feasible) can help.

Using an *RF spectrum analyzer*, a generally expensive hardware device, you can do an RF spectrum analysis to discover interference from other nearby devices using the same frequency range, be they wireless local area networks (WLANs), cordless phones, microwave ovens, and so on. Assuming you don't have the budget for an RF spectrum analyzer, there are many inexpensive or free wireless analyzers (defined in Chapter 17) that only detect Wi-Fi networks. Figure 19-3 shows the result of using a wireless locator application called inSSIDer (www.metageek.com). It discovered six wireless networks and displays information it detected by analyzing the signals from each network. Because a software wireless locator like inSSIDer depends on your Wi-Fi adapter to detect signals, it will not detect the broad range an RF spectrum analyzer can, but it will detect nearby Wi-Fi networks.

Once you run one of these tools, the solution here is to configure the WAP to use a channel as far away from the interfering frequencies as possible. Each channel uses a different frequency, although adjacent channels—for example, channels 2 and 3—are so close together that changing from channel 2 to 3 will not make a difference.

Another common problem with Wi-Fi is that the expected SSID is not found. Users want to connect to your Wi-Fi network, but as far as they can tell, it doesn't exist. This happens when the WAP isn't broadcasting the SSID, which may be for any number of valid reasons.

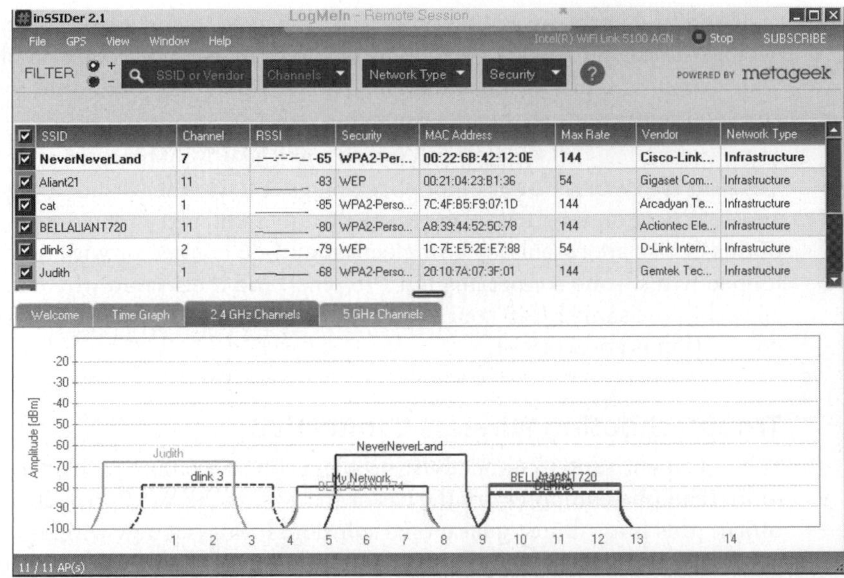

FIGURE 19-3 Scanning for wireless networks using inSSIDer

For example, perhaps you turned it off to increase security. Users can find the network by setting it up manually in their OS. For example, in Windows, open the Network And Sharing Center and click Set Up A New Connection Or Network, and then choose Manually Connect To A Wireless Network. This starts a wizard that walks you through the prompts to establish a connection with an access point by manually entering its SSID. If you set up this connection to automatically reconnect, you shouldn't have to reconfigure it again after that initial setup.

Troubleshooting Limited Connectivity

Limited connectivity should mean that you only have a local LAN or WLAN connection, but a router of some sort is present and you cannot communicate beyond the LAN.

Sometimes limited local connectivity means an IPv4 address could not be acquired via DHCP but there is a local IPv6 address (prefix of FE80). In this case, open the Properties dialog box for the NIC involved and deselect Internet Protocol Version 6 (TCP/IPv6). Click OK to accept that change and then open a Command Prompt window. Then, in the Command Prompt window, type **ipconfig /release** followed by **ipconfig /renew**. This command forces the DHCP client to release any IP address it may have and request a new IP address. It may take several seconds before you see a response, but it should receive a new address if it is able to reach the DHCP server. The output from the command will make it clear whether the computer receives an address. Remember this command because it is very useful, and we will recommend this command as a solution at least two more times in this chapter.

There are other possible causes for "limited or no connectivity" messages, and we will review some scenarios and possible solutions:

- For encrypted wireless networks, ensure your wireless NIC supports the encryption method. For example, perhaps your card only supports Wired Equivalent Privacy (WEP) but the wireless network is using Wireless Protected Access 3 (WPA3). Check the configuration on both ends of the wireless connection. You may need to upgrade your NIC. If they both are using the same encryption method, ensure you have correctly entered the wireless encryption passphrase.
- From the Command Prompt, type **ipconfig**. If the NIC's IP address begins with 169.254, this means it issued itself an *Automatic Private Internet Protocol Addressing (APIPA)* address because it did not reach a DHCP server to receive a valid IP configuration. If other stations are experiencing the same issue, consider restarting the DHCP server—bear in mind, however, that the DHCP server might be your wireless router. If only this station is having problems, type **ipconfig /release** and then type **ipconfig /renew**.

exam watch

The Linux/macOS IP command doesn't have a direct equivalent to the ipconfig /release **and** ipconfig /renew **commands. Instead, you use the dhclient command. The equivalent of** ipconfig /release **is** dhclient –r eth0**, where eth0 is the network interface. (eth0 stands for Ethernet 0, the first Ethernet connection; wlan0 would represent the first wireless connection.) The equivalent of** ipconfig /renew **is** dhclient eth0**.**

- Ensure you have the latest stable driver for your wireless NIC and that Device Manager is not reporting a problem. Consider uninstalling and reinstalling the driver.
- Use **ipconfig /all** to ensure you have a valid default gateway and DNS server configured.
- If your computer has more than one NIC (for example, a wired NIC and a wireless NIC), consider enabling one at a time and testing network connectivity individually.
- Reset the NIC. Open Network Connections in the Control Panel, right-click the name of the NIC, select Disable in the Status dialog box (refer to Figure 19-1), and when that completes, right-click again and select Enable. Wait a few minutes before testing connectivity.
- If disabling and enabling the network adapter does not resolve the problem, then run diagnostics. From the Network Connections screen in the Control Panel, right-click the NIC and select Diagnose. In both cases, Windows will attempt to detect and repair the problem.

- On a wireless network, interference usually causes intermittent connectivity problems. Try configuring the wireless router to use a different channel.
- Check that the configuration of installed antimalware or firewall programs is not interfering with network operations.
- Check the router to see if Media Access Control (MAC) address filtering is preventing WLAN connections.

As the Internet and the world in general move to IPv6, you will want to learn more about working with it. Some of the traditional command-line commands work with IPv6—and some these require special parameters. For instance, to release and renew an IPv6 DHCP address, the commands to enter are ipconfig /release6 **and** ipconfig /renew6**. Use** ipconfig /? **for more IPv6 options.**

Testing IP Configuration and Connectivity

If you have eliminated obvious and easy-to-check connectivity issues, use ipconfig to first check that the IP configuration is correct and then use ping to test connectivity. To test for slow communications over a routed network, use the **tracert** command, and use the **netstat** command to troubleshoot some connection errors.

Verifying IP Configuration with ipconfig When you are troubleshooting network connectivity problems on an IP network, after eliminating an obviously disconnected or failed NIC, use the **ipconfig** command to verify the IP configuration. Ensure that the IP address is within the correct range and has the appropriate subnet mask and DNS settings. If you completed Exercise 16-2 in Chapter 16, you already saw what this command can do, but you will now learn how to use the information.

Remember that IP addresses must be unique on a subnet. DHCP servers are smart enough to only assign unused IP addresses to clients, but it is possible for somebody to manually configure an IP address already in use on the network—Windows is not shy about telling you there is an IP address conflict. When you see this message, first check the IP configuration on the computer reporting that problem. If it has a static address and there is no good reason for that, change it to automatic (DHCP) and use the command **ipconfig /release** followed by **ipconfig /renew**. If that does not solve the problem, check the IP addresses in use on the DHCP server (or in your WAP or router). If you have more than a handful of computers on the network, this can be a tedious task.

When you open a Command Prompt and enter **ipconfig /all**, it will display the IP configuration of all network interfaces on the local computer, even those that receive their addresses and configuration through DHCP. In fact, if your NIC is a DHCP client, this is the best way to see the resulting IP configuration quickly in all versions of Windows. You can only view this information for one connection at a time, so techs still like to use **ipconfig /all** to see information about all connections at once. Figure 19-4 shows an example of running the **ipconfig /all** command on a computer with multiple network adapters.

When the output from the **ipconfig** command shows an IP address other than 0.0.0.0, you know that the IP settings have been successfully bound to your network adapter. “Bound” means that there is a linking relationship, called a “binding,” between the network protocol and the adapter. A binding establishes the order in which each network component handles network communications.

The Linux/macOS equivalent of ipconfig /all **is** ip -a**. It doesn’t show all the same information, but it’s similar, showing all network interfaces.**

FIGURE 19-4

The result of running the **ipconfig /all** command

```
Administrator: Command Prompt
Microsoft Windows [Version 10.0.19044.1645]
(c) Microsoft Corporation. All rights reserved.

C:\WINDOWS\system32>ipconfig /all

Windows IP Configuration

   Host Name . . . . . . . . . . . . : Alien-ware
   Primary Dns Suffix  . . . . . . . :
   Node Type . . . . . . . . . . . . : Hybrid
   IP Routing Enabled. . . . . . . . : No
   WINS Proxy Enabled. . . . . . . . : No
   DNS Suffix Search List. . . . . . : hrtc.net

Ethernet adapter Ethernet:

   Media State . . . . . . . . . . . : Media disconnected
   Connection-specific DNS Suffix  . : hrtc.net
   Description . . . . . . . . . . . : Killer E3000 2.5 Gigabit Ethernet Controller
   Physical Address. . . . . . . . . : 0E-CD-2A-58-5E-CF
   DHCP Enabled. . . . . . . . . . . : Yes
   Autoconfiguration Enabled . . . . : Yes

Ethernet adapter Ethernet 2:

   Connection-specific DNS Suffix  . : hrtc.net
   Description . . . . . . . . . . . : Realtek USB GbE Family Controller
   Physical Address. . . . . . . . . : D4-81-D7-C6-CF-24
   DHCP Enabled. . . . . . . . . . . : Yes
   Autoconfiguration Enabled . . . . : Yes
   IPv6 Address. . . . . . . . . . . : 2606:5d00:5800:3401:2c69:1579:2d97:ddb4(Preferred)
   Temporary IPv6 Address. . . . . . : 2606:5d00:5800:3401:75c0:6ba9:65b0:469d(Preferred)
   Link-local IPv6 Address . . . . . : fe80::2c69:1579:2d97:ddb4%15(Preferred)
   IPv4 Address. . . . . . . . . . . : 192.168.0.127(Preferred)
   Subnet Mask . . . . . . . . . . . : 255.255.255.0
   Lease Obtained. . . . . . . . . . : Friday, April 29, 2022 8:28:51 AM
   Lease Expires . . . . . . . . . . : Saturday, April 30, 2022 8:28:47 AM
   Default Gateway . . . . . . . . . : fe80::8226:89ff:fe4c:b164%15
                                       192.168.0.1
   DHCP Server . . . . . . . . . . . : 192.168.0.1
   DHCPv6 IAID . . . . . . . . . . . : 265585111
   DHCPv6 Client DUID. . . . . . . . : 00-01-00-01-29-F2-70-57-0E-CD-2A-58-5E-CF
   DNS Servers . . . . . . . . . . . : 2606:5d00:d::31
```

In addition, when viewing the IP configuration information, verify that each item is correct for the IP network segment on which the NIC is connected. There are three rules to keep in mind when evaluating an IP configuration:

- The network ID and the subnet mask of each host on an IP segment must match.
- The default gateway address must be the IP address of a router on the same subnet.
- Each host on an IP segment must have a unique host ID.

Therefore, if there are other hosts on the same subnet, run ipconfig on each of them to determine if all the hosts comply with these rules. If not, correct the problem.

Finally, if the computer in question has an IP address that begins with 169.254, this is an APIPA address—an address that a DHCP client can assign to itself when it cannot reach a DHCP server. If this is a very small network of just a few computers in which all the computers use APIPA, this may be okay, but in most cases, consider this address a sign of a failure. If possible, check to see if the DHCP server is available. For a large network, you will need to contact a network administrator.

In a small office or home office (SOHO) network, the DHCP server may be part of a broadband router. In that case, reset the router. If you wait long enough, the DHCP server should assign an address to the DHCP client computer, and if you wish to take control of the process, use the command **ipconfig /release** followed by **ipconfig /renew**.

Troubleshooting Connection Errors with the ping Command The *ping* command is useful for testing communications between two hosts. The name of this command is an acronym for Packet Internet Groper. We prefer to think (as many do) that it was named after the action of underwater sonar. Instead of bouncing sound waves off surfaces, the **ping** command uses data packets, sending them to specific IP addresses and requesting a response (hence, the idea of pinging). Then, ping listens for a reply.

If you completed Exercise 17-1 or 17-2 in Chapter 17, you know the simplest syntax of the **ping** command, which is **ping *target-IP-address*.** However, you do not always need to know a target's IP address. You can also ping a domain name, such as mcgraw-hill.com, and on a network running Windows computers, you can ping the computer name. Use the **ping** command to test a new network connection and, for troubleshooting, a connection failure. The following is a suggested order for doing this:

1. Ping the local NIC using the command **ping localhost**. The standard host name *localhost* is assigned by the IP protocol to the loopback network interface, and no packets will leave the NIC; if it is functioning, it will send the normal response back. Recall the discussion of loopback in Chapter 17. If the ping results in four responses, move on to the next step. If this fails, troubleshoot the NIC as you would any hardware component. If you have another identical NIC known to work, swap it with the current NIC. If the replacement NIC works, replace the original NIC.

2. Ping the IP address of the default gateway. If this does not work, verify that the gateway address is correct. If there are other computers on the network, compare the IP configuration settings. If the address for the default gateway matches those of other hosts on the network, ping the default gateway address from another computer.
3. Ping the IP address or DNS name of a computer beyond the default gateway.

This order tests, first, if the NIC is working. It also tests that the address works within your LAN, because the default gateway address is on the LAN and has the same network ID as the local NIC. Finally, successfully pinging an address beyond the gateway confirms at least two things: the router works, and the NIC of the target host is functioning and can respond to ping requests. If you cannot ping any computer beyond the router, the problem may be in the router itself.

The **ping** command has several switches. Use the **-t** switch when you want to ping an address repeatedly. The default is to ping an address four times. It will continue until you stop it. Pressing the CTRL-BREAK key combination will cause it to display statistics and then continue. To stop this command, press the CTRL-C key combination. Figure 19-5 shows the output from **ping** with this switch.

Another default of the **ping** command is the size (or length) of the data it uses. The default size is 32 bytes, which is not a very heavy load for any connection. Therefore, administrators sometimes test a connection by sending more data. Do this with the **-l** switch followed by a space and the size, such as 1024. For instance, type the command **ping 192.168.0.1 -l 1024**. A connection that can easily handle the 32-byte size with zero percent loss of data may show some data loss with the 1024-byte size.

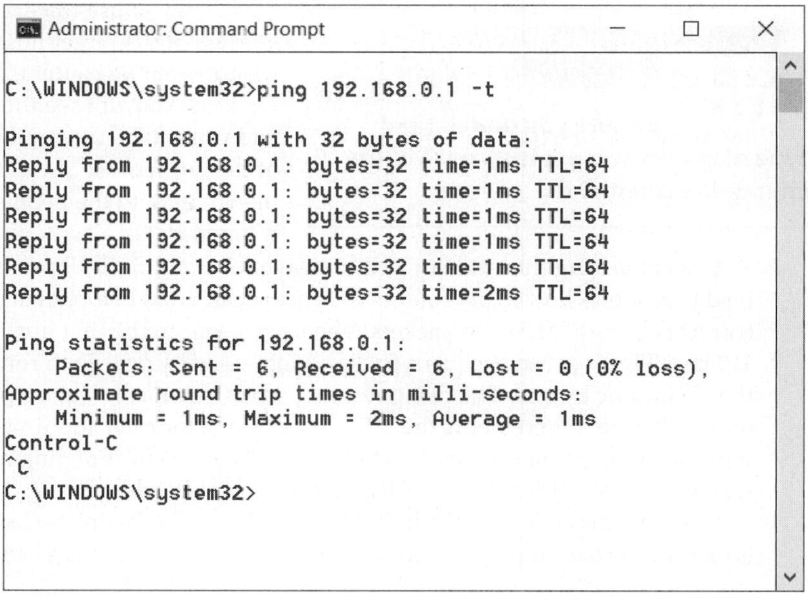

FIGURE 19-5

Using the **ping** command with the **-t** parameter

```
Administrator: Command Prompt

C:\WINDOWS\system32>ping 192.168.0.1 -t

Pinging 192.168.0.1 with 32 bytes of data:
Reply from 192.168.0.1: bytes=32 time=1ms TTL=64
Reply from 192.168.0.1: bytes=32 time=1ms TTL=64
Reply from 192.168.0.1: bytes=32 time=1ms TTL=64
Reply from 192.168.0.1: bytes=32 time=1ms TTL=64
Reply from 192.168.0.1: bytes=32 time=1ms TTL=64
Reply from 192.168.0.1: bytes=32 time=2ms TTL=64

Ping statistics for 192.168.0.1:
    Packets: Sent = 6, Received = 6, Lost = 0 (0% loss),
Approximate round trip times in milli-seconds:
    Minimum = 1ms, Maximum = 2ms, Average = 1ms
Control-C
^C
C:\WINDOWS\system32>
```

Now for some technical information about **ping** and related commands. The **ping** command uses a subprotocol of IP called the *Internet Control Message Protocol (ICMP)*. This little protocol has a big job in a TCP/IP internetwork. It detects problems that can cause errors. Such problems include congestion and downed routers. When ICMP detects these problems, it notifies other protocols and services in the TCP/IP suite, resulting in routing of packets around the problem area.

When you use ping, it sends *ICMP echo packets* to the target node. An echo packet contains a request to respond. Once the target node receives the packets, it sends out one response packet for each echo packet it receives. You see information about the received packets in the lines that begin with "Reply from." Pay attention to the time information on this line. It should be below 200 ms; if the time is greater than 500 ms, there is a connectivity issue between the two hosts. Of course, a little common sense may tell you that it will take a longer time to receive a response from the other side of the world.

Practice working with these command-line tools before your network has a problem. Then you will be more comfortable with the tools and their screen output.

Using tracert and pathping to Troubleshoot Slow Communications You may have situations in which you can connect to a website or other remote resource, but the connection is very slow. If this connection is critical to business, you will want to gather information so a network administrator or ISP can troubleshoot the source of the bottleneck. You can use the **tracert** command to gather this information. *tracert* is a command-line utility that traces the route taken by packets to a destination.

Be sure you understand the type of results you get from each of the command-line commands.

When you use tracert with the name or IP address of the target host, it will ping each of the intervening routers, from the nearest to the farthest. You will see the delay at each router, and you will be able to determine the location of the bottleneck. You can then provide this information to the people who will troubleshoot it for you.

Understanding *time to live (TTL)* is also important. Each IP packet header has a TTL field that shows how many routers the packet can cross before being discarded. Like **ping**, tracert creates ICMP echo packets. The packet sent to the first host or router has a TTL of 1. The TTL of each subsequent packet is increased by one. Each router, in turn, decreases the TTL value by one. The computer that sends the tracert waits a predetermined amount of time before it increments the TTL value by one for each additional packet. This repeats until the destination is reached. This process has the effect of pinging each router along the way, without needing to know each router's actual IP address.

Consider a scenario in which your connection to the Google website (www.google.com) is extremely slow. You are working from a small office that has a cable modem connection to the Internet, and you are accustomed to very fast responses when you browse the Web. You have connected in the last few minutes to other websites without significant delay, so you believe there is a bottleneck between you and Google.

The **tracert** command will reveal the address of the router that is the bottleneck between you and a target host. Normally, the first and last numbered lines in the output represent the source IP address and the target IP address. Every line in between is a router located between your computer and the target. You can verify that the last line is the target by matching the IP address to the one you entered at the command line. If you entered a DNS name at the command line, the IP address will display below the command line.

An alternative to tracert is the **pathping** command. It is similar in functionality, and in some ways even better suited to the task of testing for network connectivity and name resolution issues. It combines the functions of ping and tracert in a single command.

The **pathping** command sends echo requests to each router and evaluates the speed at which the packets are returned. It also reports the packet losses for each router. You can use that information to find routers with network issues.

EXERCISE 19-1

Using tracert and pathping

In this exercise, we use Facebook as the target, but you can substitute another domain name or IP address. This exercise compares the output from the two commands.

1. Open a Command Prompt window.
2. Type **tracert www.facebook.com** and press ENTER.
3. In the following illustration, one of the routers shows a value that is much greater than the others, but it is not greater than 500 ms, so there is a bottleneck relative to the others, but it is not a serious one.

```
Administrator: Command Prompt

C:\WINDOWS\system32>tracert www.facebook.com

Tracing route to star-mini.c10r.facebook.com [2a03:2880:f127:283:face:b00c:0:25de]
over a maximum of 30 hops:

  1     1 ms     1 ms     1 ms  2606:5d00:5800:3401:8226:89ff:fe4c:b164
  2    13 ms    10 ms    28 ms  2606:5d00:5001:2::1
  3    12 ms    12 ms     9 ms  ::ffff:10.102.3.5
  4   439 ms    10 ms     7 ms  ::ffff:10.102.3.4
  5    17 ms    14 ms     9 ms  9006.mcvl.ninestarconnect.com [2606:5d00::3]
  6     *        *        *     Request timed out.
  7    30 ms    17 ms    15 ms  100ge5-1.core1.chi1.he.net [2001:470:0:580::1]
  8     *        *        *     Request timed out.
  9    12 ms    16 ms    19 ms  po121.asw01.ord3.tfbnw.net [2620:0:1cff:dead:beef::8f2]
 10    17 ms    18 ms    17 ms  po216.psw02.ord2.tfbnw.net [2620:0:1cff:dead:beef::1ba8]
 11    19 ms    19 ms    19 ms  po2.msw1ap.02.ort2.tfbnw.net [2a03:2880:f027:ffff::53]
 12    17 ms    17 ms    18 ms  edge-star-mini6-shv-02-ort2.facebook.com [2a03:2880:f127:283:face:b00c:0:25de]

Trace complete.

C:\WINDOWS\system32>_
```

4. Type **pathping www.facebook.com** and press ENTER. Then wait for the results to appear. It may take a few minutes.

```
Administrator: Command Prompt
C:\WINDOWS\system32>pathping www.facebook.com

Tracing route to star-mini.c10r.facebook.com [2a03:2880:f127:283:face:b00c:0:25de]
over a maximum of 30 hops:
  0  Alien-ware.hrtc.net [2606:5d00:5800:3401:75c0:6ba9:65b0:469d]
  1  2606:5d00:5800:3401:8226:89ff:fe4c:b164
  2  2606:5d00:5001:2::1
  3  ::ffff:10.102.3.5
  4  ::ffff:10.102.3.4
  5  9006.mcvl.ninestarconnect.com [2606:5d00::3]
  6     *        *        *
Computing statistics for 125 seconds...
            Source to Here   This Node/Link
Hop  RTT    Lost/Sent = Pct  Lost/Sent = Pct  Address
  0                                           Alien-ware.hrtc.net [2606:5d00:5800:3401:75c0:6ba9:65b0:469d]
                                0/ 100 =  0%   |
  1    1ms     0/ 100 =  0%     0/ 100 =  0%  2606:5d00:5800:3401:8226:89ff:fe4c:b164
                                1/ 100 =  1%   |
  2   14ms     1/ 100 =  1%     0/ 100 =  0%  2606:5d00:5001:2::1
                                0/ 100 =  0%   |
  3  ---     100/ 100 =100%    99/ 100 = 99%  ::ffff:10.102.3.5
                                0/ 100 =  0%   |
  4  ---     100/ 100 =100%    99/ 100 = 99%  ::ffff:10.102.3.4
                                0/ 100 =  0%   |
  5   16ms     1/ 100 =  1%     0/ 100 =  0%  9006.mcvl.ninestarconnect.com [2606:5d00::3]

Trace complete.

C:\WINDOWS\system32>
```

5. Compare the results from the two commands.

Using netstat to Troubleshoot Connection Errors The *netstat* command will give you statistical information about the TCP/IP protocols and network connections involving your computer, depending on the parameters you use when you enter the command. Although netstat has many options, there are a few you should remember. For instance, running **netstat** without any parameters, as shown in Figure 19-6, will show the current connections by protocol and port number. The **netstat** command by itself can show you a connection that is not working—perhaps because an application has failed. Running **netstat -s** displays statistics on outgoing and incoming traffic on your computer. If this test shows there is no traffic in one direction, you may have a bad cable.

Troubleshooting with the net Command

The Windows *net* command is a command-prompt utility that can be used to perform a variety of administrative and troubleshooting tasks. We have even used this command to create scripts for automating the creation of user accounts in a Windows domain—an advanced task. You can use the **net** command to start and stop network services. To learn more about the net command, enter **net help** to display a list of subcommands. You can then learn more about a single subcommand. For instance, the command for starting

FIGURE 19-6

The **netstat** command shows current connections.

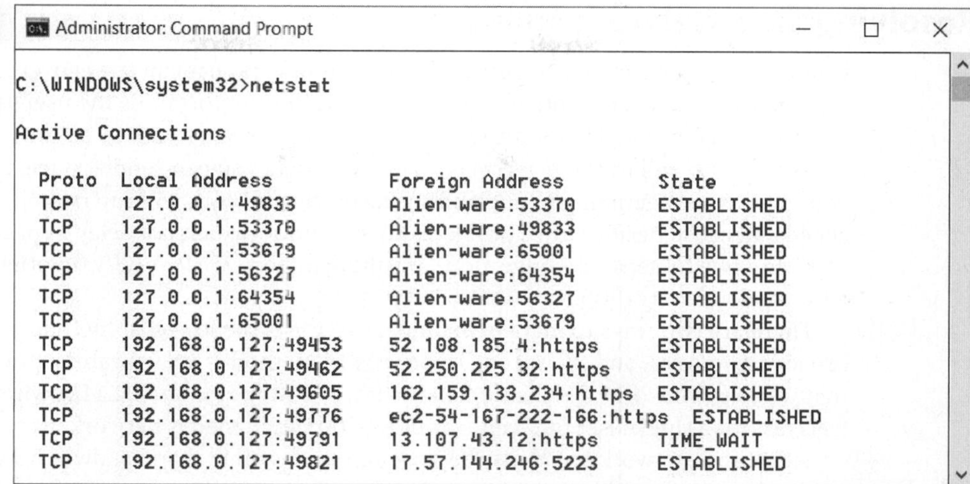

network services is **net start service**, where *service* is the name of the network service you wish to start. Enter **net stop service** to stop a service. To see a list of the services you can start, enter this command: **net help start**. To see a list of the services you can stop, enter this command: **net help stop**. You will see fewer services listed for the stop command because some services cannot be stopped.

Administrator: Command Prompt
C:\WINDOWS\system32>netstat
Active Connections
Proto Local Address Foreign Address State
TCP 127.0.0.1:49833 Alien-ware:53370 ESTABLISHED
TCP 127.0.0.1:53370 Alien-ware:49833 ESTABLISHED
TCP 127.0.0.1:53679 Alien-ware:65001 ESTABLISHED
TCP 127.0.0.1:56327 Alien-ware:64354 ESTABLISHED
TCP 127.0.0.1:64354 Alien-ware:56327 ESTABLISHED
TCP 127.0.0.1:65001 Alien-ware:53679 ESTABLISHED
TCP 192.168.0.127:49453 52.108.185.4:https ESTABLISHED
TCP 192.168.0.127:49462 52.250.225.32:https ESTABLISHED
TCP 192.168.0.127:49605 162.159.133.234:https ESTABLISHED
TCP 192.168.0.127:49776 ec2-54-167-222-166:https ESTABLISHED
TCP 192.168.0.127:49791 13.107.43.12:https TIME_WAIT
TCP 192.168.0.127:49821 17.57.144.246:5223 ESTABLISHED

CompTIA A+ 220-1102 exam Objective 1.2 includes the net use **and** net user **commands. These are both subcommands of the net command with specific functions. The net use command displays information about shared resources and enables you to connect and disconnect to resources from a command line. The** net user **command adds, deletes, and manages users on a computer.**

Use the **net** command with the *use* subcommand to connect to a network share. A *network share* is a resource, such as a file folder or printer, that is available to you over the network. For instance, to connect to a shared folder named data on the computer named Wickenburg, enter **net use \\Wickenburg\data**. Use this command if you have determined that you can ping another computer but are not able to access a shared folder on that computer.

At the command line, you can enter net /? **to view information about the net command. However, this version is really a condensed version of** net help **and gives you less information. So, remember** net /? **for the exam, but use** net help **on the job.**

Resolving Slow Network Speed

Chapter 16 described *bandwidth* as the amount of data that can travel over a network at a given time. That is deceptively simple when what is important is the user's perception of network slowness. Therefore, when a user perceives a network to be slow, increasing the bandwidth will improve its speed. The more data you can send at once, the faster data will move from beginning to end and the faster the network will run overall. Slow network speed can cause performance problems such as *jitter* (which is a delay in packet sending and receiving due to network congestion), resulting in poor *VoIP quality* (in other words, poor audio and video quality).

There are two ways to increase bandwidth. One is the low-cost method of reducing the broadcast sources, and the second, more costly, method is a hardware upgrade. Remember that wireless networks are shared bandwidth; 800 Mbps for an 802.11ac wireless network feels fast for a single user but feels slower for 100 simultaneous network users.

Sometimes network speed may be slow for reasons other than bandwidth. For example, a network that seems like it would have plenty of bandwidth might suffer from *high latency,* especially if the data has to travel a long distance between points. For example, satellite Internet is prone to high latency because the signal has to travel all the way to an orbiting satellite.

Make sure you can explain the root cause and symptoms of the performance problems listed in CompTIA A+ 1101 exam Objective 5.7: intermittent wireless connectivity, slow network speeds, limited connectivity, jitter, poor VoIP quality, port flapping (covered on the next page), high latency, and external interference.

Reducing Sources of Network Broadcasts

Most protocol suites have at least a few subprotocols that rely on network broadcasts. A *broadcast* is a transmission of packets addressed to all nodes on a network.

Broadcast traffic is, to some extent, unavoidable within a network segment, but too much of it takes up bandwidth needed for other traffic. Although broadcasts do not cross routers, they still persist within the network segments between routers, thus taking up valuable bandwidth. Reduce these sources by searching for the unnecessary protocol suites, and then look within the suites that are necessary and reduce the amount of broadcasting within them.

Why do unnecessary protocols exist on a network? First, more than one protocol suite can be active on a Windows computer, but that is rarely necessary anymore. If you have a TCP/IP network and you find another protocol suite on a computer and there is no good reason to have it, remove it.

Of course, as you learned in Chapter 17, you can turn off the Service Set Identifier (SSID) broadcast from a WAP. This is not only more secure—it also reduces broadcasts. However, when it comes to the use of excess protocol suites, the most common offenders are not usually computers, but old print servers, which may have come with several protocol suites enabled. Whether a print server is a separate box or integrated into a network printer, find out how to access the print server configuration. In the case of a separate print server box, you will normally enter the print server's IP address into a web browser's address box and access it remotely. You will need the administrative user name and password to access it. For a print server integrated into a printer, it all depends on its design. The documentation for the printer will give instructions on how to access its configuration—usually through a web browser or through a control panel on the printer. In both instances, look for protocols and remove protocol suites that are not required on your network.

on the job

Unnecessary streaming can also hamper performance. Today's Internet users enjoy streaming audio and video, which means that users listening to Internet radio or Internet TV can have a negative impact on network throughput for others. This is a serious problem in a working environment because, aside from the ethical problem of spending work time for personal activities, using shared network bandwidth for downloading and uploading questionable content such as movies and music using a BitTorrent client can also seriously degrade network performance.

Bad network cables can result in *port flapping* (which is the repeated starting and stopping of data transmission at the switch's physical interface, usually due to a bad or unsupported type of cable). If you are experiencing network performance that's much slower than it ought to be given the installed hardware, an inexpensive thing to try is to swap out the cables.

After you've verified that the cables and equipment are functioning, consider increasing a network's baseline bandwidth by upgrading the network's hardware. If the network has any Ethernet hubs, replace them with switches. Recall that a hub takes a signal received on one port and repeats it on all other ports. This consumes bandwidth. A switch, on the other hand, is a more intelligent device, which takes an incoming signal and only sends it to the destination port. This saves bandwidth. If the network already has switches, then consider upgrading to faster equipment. For example, a LAN with Fast Ethernet (100 Mbps) equipment can be upgraded to Gigabit Ethernet (1 to 10 Gbps).

Be sure that when you upgrade to increase bandwidth, the upgrade is thorough. That is, *all* the NICs, switches, and routers must support the new, higher speed. Although the faster equipment is downward compatible with the slower equipment, the network will only be as fast as its slowest hardware component. Also, on an Ethernet network, do not forget to upgrade the cabling to the grade required for the network speed you want to achieve. So if you want to achieve Gigabit Ethernet speeds, you need a Gigabit Ethernet NIC, cable, and switch.

Similarly, to upgrade a wireless network, replace slower equipment with newer, faster equipment. Increase signal strength with proper placement of the wireless antenna, and install signal boosters, if necessary. For example, if you have a home network with an 802.11n router and several PCs with 802.11ax network adapters and your home Internet service is fiber, you are not going to get maximum Internet speed on your PCs. Upgrading to an 802.11ax router will help a lot. Newer wireless equipment will also have better security (WPA3, for example).

Troubleshooting DNS Problems

DNS problems show themselves as messages such as "Server not found." These messages can appear in your web browser, your e-mail client, or any software that attempts to connect to a server. How do you know it is a DNS problem? You do not know this until you eliminate other problems, such as a failed NIC, a broken connection, a typo, or an incorrect IP configuration. But once you have eliminated these problems, use the following tests to troubleshoot DNS problems.

Using ping to Troubleshoot DNS Problems

Notice that in the steps provided for using both the **ping** and **tracert** commands in the previous sections, you can use either the IP address or the DNS name. When you use the DNS name with either of these commands, you are also testing DNS. For instance, if you open a Command Prompt window and enter the command **ping www.mcgraw-hill.com**, before the **ping** command can send packets to the target, www.mcgraw-hill.com, the DNS client must resolve the DNS name to an IP address. This is exactly what happens when you enter a Uniform Resource Locator (URL) in the address box of a web browser. The DNS client resolves the name to an IP address before the browser can send a request to view the page.

When pinging a DNS name is successful, you know several things: your DNS client is working, your DNS server is responding and working, and the target DNS name has been found on the Internet. Now, notice that the name we used (www.mcgraw-hill.com) has three parts to it. Reading from right to left, "com" is the *top-level domain (TLD)* name, and mcgraw-hill is the *second-level domain (SLD)* name within the com TLD. Both of these together are usually referred to as a domain name. So what is "www"? The owner of the second-level domain name defines everything else you see in the URL.

For instance, www.mcgraw-hill.com is listed in DNS servers that are probably under the control of McGraw-Hill or its ISP. The entry points to a server, named "www," where web pages can be found. So to the left of the second-level domain name are the names of servers or child domains of mcgraw-hill.com. This allows McGraw Hill to organize their portion of the DNS name space and help client computers locate resources on these servers. Another example is support.microsoft.com that points to the Microsoft Support website.

And what about all those letters, numbers, slashes, and other characters to the right of the TLD? They point to specific documents on the servers. Simple? To the casual observer, yes, because DNS hides the complexity of the organization and the locations of servers and documents. Understanding this much will help you to work with DNS and perform basic troubleshooting.

So the next time you cannot connect to a website from your browser, first double-check your spelling. If you entered the URL correctly, then open up a Command Prompt window and ping the portion of the URL that contains the TLD and SLD. In our first example, you would open a Command Prompt window and type **ping mcgraw-hill.com**. If the ping is not successful, you should immediately ping another domain name and/or try connecting to another URL through your browser. If you are successful pinging another location, then the problem may be with a router in the path to the first location. Use tracert, described earlier, to pinpoint the problem router.

Using ipconfig to Flush the DNS Cache

Before a DNS client queries a DNS server for a specific name, it checks a little chunk of memory, the *DNS cache,* where it retains a list of previously resolved DNS names and IP addresses. If the DNS client finds the name in the cache, it does not query the DNS server. However, if the server address has changed since it was recorded in the DNS cache, the DNS client will return an error and you will not be able to connect to the server. So if you recently were able to connect to a server through your browser but have a "server not found" error, an easy solution to try is to flush the DNS cache so that the client will query the DNS server rather than use the address in the cache. To do this, open a Command Prompt window and enter this command: **ipconfig /flushdns**. Then open your browser and attempt to connect to the server again.

There isn't a direct equivalent in the macOS/Linux ip command to flush the DNS cache. Instead, you would restart the nscd daemon to flush the cache. In a Linux Terminal window, type /etc/rc.d/init.d/nscd restart**. In macOS, type** dscacheutil –flushcache **in a Terminal window.**

Using nslookup to Troubleshoot DNS Problems

To further troubleshoot DNS problems, use the *nslookup* command, which lets you troubleshoot DNS problems by allowing you to query DNS name servers and see the result of the queries. In using nslookup, you are looking for problems such as a DNS server not responding to clients, DNS servers not resolving names correctly, or other general name resolution problems. nslookup bypasses the client DNS cache and talks directly to the DNS server and is thus more reliable than ping for DNS troubleshooting. nslookup has two modes:

- **Interactive mode** In interactive mode, nslookup has its own command prompt, a greater-than sign (>) within the system Command Prompt. You enter this mode by typing **nslookup** without any parameters, or **nslookup** followed by a space, a hyphen, and the name of a name server. In the first instance, it will use your default name server, and in the second instance, it will use the name server you specify. While in interactive mode, enter commands at the nslookup prompt, and type **exit** to end interactive mode and return to the system Command Prompt.
- **Noninteractive mode** In noninteractive mode, you enter the **nslookup** command plus a command parameter for using one or more nslookup subcommands. The response is sent to the screen, and you are returned to the Command Prompt. Exercise 19-2 uses noninteractive mode.

EXERCISE 19-2

Video

Using nslookup to Troubleshoot DNS

In this exercise you will use nslookup to resolve an Internet domain name to an IP address.

Open a Command Prompt window, and enter the following command: **nslookup mcgraw-hill.com**. If the name server is working, the result will resemble the following illustration.

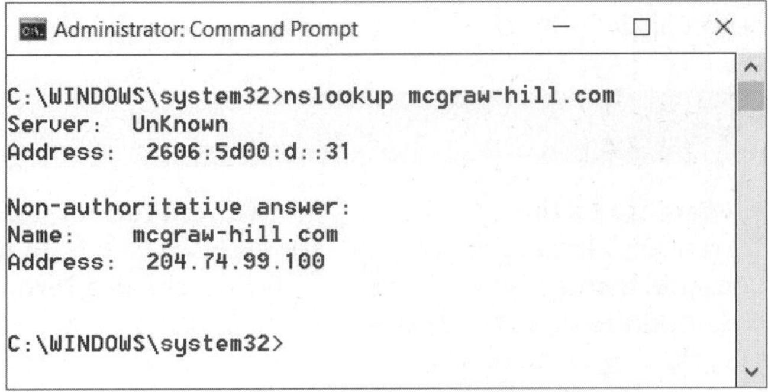
Administrator: Command Prompt
C:\WINDOWS\system32>nslookup mcgraw-hill.com
Server: UnKnown
Address: 2606:5d00:d::31
Non-authoritative answer:
Name: mcgraw-hill.com
Address: 204.74.99.100
C:\WINDOWS\system32>

- The server and address in the first and second lines of the output are the name and IP address of the DNS server that responded to your request. This will be the name server used by your ISP or your company.
- The name in the Server line may show as Unknown if you don't have a reverse DNS (rDNS) zone set up for your network/subnet (so it doesn't return a reverse lookup for its name); this is not an error and does not cause any problems.

- The second group of lines shows the result of the query. It is called a non-authoritative answer because the name server queried had to query other name servers to find the name.

The results in this illustration show that DNS name resolution is working. Therefore, if you are unable to connect to a server in this domain, the server may be offline or a critical link or router between it and the Internet has failed. If you were troubleshooting a connection problem to this domain, you would pass this information on to a network administrator or ISP.

Using the Linux dig Command to Troubleshoot DNS

The **dig** command in Linux (short for *Domain Information Groper*) provides DNS information. Most Linux distros include it. To see if you have it, type

```
dig -v
```

If the command isn't there, install it with this command in Debian or Ubuntu:

```
sudo apt-get install dnsutils
```

or this command in RedHat or CentOS:

```
sudo yum install bind-utils
```

These commands are all examples of CompTIA A+ 1102 exam Objective 1.11 topics in action!

The most common use for dig is for DNS lookup. For example, the following command finds the IP address for mcgraw-hill.com:

```
dig mcgraw-hill.com
```

The IP address appears in the ANSWER SECTION area of the results.

If you don't want to wade through a page of results to find the IP address, add the **+short** argument:

```
dig mcgraw-hill.com +short
```

You can also use dig to trace a route, similar to the **tracert** command in Windows:

```
dig mcgraw-hill +trace
```

There's a lot more to the **dig** command than can be covered here, but that gives you enough for exam purposes. You may want to explore this command on your own if you work with Linux systems.

SCENARIO & SOLUTION	
My network has a DHCP server. I need to see if the NIC was assigned an IP address, but when I look at the properties of the Local Area Connection, the IP address is empty. What can I do?	Open a Command Prompt window and enter the following command: **ipconfig /all**. This will display the IP configuration.
I have connected to a certain website many times, but today the connection to this one website is very slow. I would like to talk to my ISP about this, but I need more information. How can I tell where the problem is?	Because other websites do not seem as slow, use the tracert command to trace the route to the website and determine where the bottleneck may be.

CERTIFICATION OBJECTIVE

- ***1102: 4.5*** *Summarize environmental impacts and local environmental controls*

This section briefly revisits some of the environment-related topics from CompTIA A+ 1102 exam Objective 4.5, this time in the context of servers and other networking equipment.

Preventive Maintenance for Networks

It is always better to prevent problems than to spend your time solving them. In this section, you will learn the basic maintenance tasks specific to networks, which include maintaining all the equipment directly attached to the network and the media over which the signals travel. However, the value and usability of a network also depend on proper functioning of the attached computers (clients and servers), as well as other shared devices, such as printers. In Chapter 12, you learned preventive maintenance for computers. Preventive maintenance for network devices, such as NICs, hubs, switches, WAPs, and routers, is identical to that for computers.

A network also depends on the maintenance of an appropriate and secure environment for both the equipment and data. Chapters 20 and 21 explore security issues for computers and networks, and Chapter 1 presented safety and environmental issues.

Therefore, although this chapter presents some network-specific maintenance tasks, keep in mind that a computer professional must look beyond the components and software that are specific to a network and approach network maintenance holistically.

Maintaining Equipment

Network equipment, from the NICs in the computers to the bridging and routing devices that connect networks together, all have similar requirements. For instance, they all require sufficient ventilation and cooling systems to maintain the appropriate operating environment.

Reliable Power

All computer and network components must have electrical power. Providing reliable power begins with the power company supplying the power, but your responsibility begins at the meter. Do not assume that the power will always be reliable. Most of us have experienced power outages and can understand how disrupting they are. However, bad power, in the form of surges, spikes, and voltage sags, can do a great deal of damage. Prevent damage and disruption from these events by using uninterruptible power supply (UPS) devices or other protective devices. Versions of these power protection devices come in a form factor for mounting in equipment racks. Equipment racks are discussed in the following section.

Be aware of the number and location of circuits in the building and the total power requirements of the equipment you have on each circuit. If you have network equipment unprotected by a UPS, be sure this equipment is not sharing a circuit with a device that has high demands, such as a laser printer or photocopier.

Consider using a dedicated circuit for the most critical equipment. A dedicated circuit has only either one or very few outlets.

Housing Servers and Network Devices

Servers and network devices such as switches and routers should be in a physically secure room or closet with proper climate controls. The humidity should be at or near 40 percent, and the temperature should be no higher than 70 degrees. Provide adequate spacing around the equipment for proper ventilation. When dealing with more than a few servers plus network equipment, use rack-mounted servers that fit into the specially designed equipment racks for holding servers and other devices, such as UPSs, routers, and switches. These take up less space and, unlike tables and desks, allow more air to flow around the equipment.

Dedicate the room or closet to the equipment. Do not make this a multipurpose room for storage or office space, because that is inviting disaster, especially if the space is readily accessible by people who have no professional reason to be in contact with the servers or network equipment. The unintended consequences of such an arrangement can damage the equipment.

Techs should keep informed of the evolving Ashrae standards for temperature and humidity: https://www.ashrae.org.

Securing and Protecting Network Cabling

Regardless of the size of the network, keep network cabling neat and labeled. In the equipment room or closet, use patch panels. A *patch panel* is a rack-mounted panel containing multiple network ports. Cables running from various locations in the building connect to ports on the back of the patch panel. Then shorter cables, called *patch cables,* connect each port to switches and routers in the closet or equipment room. This keeps cables organized and even allows for labeling the ports. This will help prevent damaged cables and confusion when troubleshooting a cable run.

Secure and protect network cabling to avoid damage from mishandling or mischief, and ensure that it is well labeled so that it is easier to add new equipment and to troubleshoot.

Horizontal runs of cabling often must run through suspended ceilings. Resist the urge to simply lay the cabling on the top of the ceiling tiles. This arrangement may be okay for a very small number of cables, but it only takes a few cables to make a tangle. Further, running additional cables into this space can be very difficult. Therefore, bundle cables together and run them through channels where possible. If the budget allows, specialized cable management systems are worth the investment. Use cable trays for running cables in the ceiling. A *cable tray* is a lightweight, bridge-like structure for containing the cables in a building.

CERTIFICATION SUMMARY

This chapter explored the tools and techniques for troubleshooting networks and preventive maintenance for networks. You also learned strategies for using commands to analyze network problems.

Analyze network connectivity problems based on error messages or other symptoms. If you see no obvious source for the problem, check the hardware, beginning with the NIC, cables, hubs, switches, WAPs, and routers. Check for any source of EMI. If you detect no physical source of a problem, check the IP configuration of the NIC and correct any errors you find.

Use command-prompt utilities to reveal the IP configuration, test connectivity, locate a bottleneck on the Internet, reveal statistics about the TCP/IP protocols and network connections involving the local computer, and detect DNS problems.

Most preventive maintenance for network devices is identical to that for computers. There are some special considerations for the servers, network devices, and cabling, for which preventive maintenance begins with providing a proper and secure environment and carefully organizing the cabling and the cable runs through ceilings and walls.

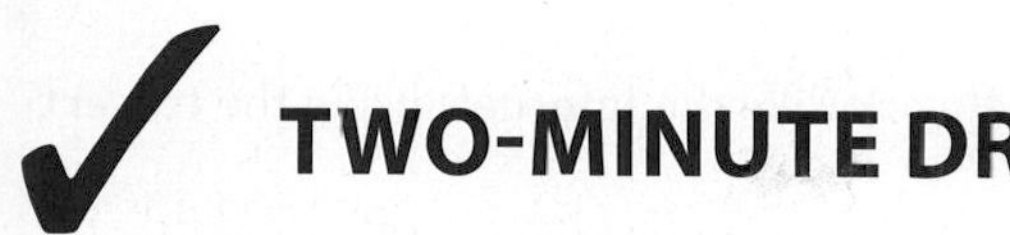

TWO-MINUTE DRILL

Here are some of the key points covered in Chapter 19.

Troubleshooting Common Network Problems

- ❑ A group of command-prompt utilities installs with the TCP/IP protocol suite. Among them are ipconfig, ping, tracert, pathping, netstat, and nslookup.
- ❑ The macOS/Linux version of ipconfig is ip.
- ❑ Use the /? switch with any command-prompt utility to learn about the variety of subcommands and parameters that alter the behavior of the utility.
- ❑ Status indicators for network hardware include LED lights on physical devices and/or status information from software installed along with the driver.
- ❑ A quick glance at indicator lights on a device or icons and messages on the computer screen reveals valuable information.
- ❑ The typical NIC installs with a configuration utility that you can open from an icon in the notification area of the taskbar. A change in status or hovering your mouse over this icon will cause a message to appear over the notification area.
- ❑ A cable tester connects to the ends of a cable and sends a signal down the cable in order to detect breaks in it.
- ❑ You can use a wireless locator to identify the source of wireless interference and to optimize WAP configuration.
- ❑ Sometimes simply restarting the WAP/broadband router solves connectivity issues.
- ❑ Media Access Control (MAC) address filtering might be preventing WLAN connections.
- ❑ Wireless encryption settings and passphrases must match on both the WAP and the wireless client.
- ❑ Make sure you are using the correct updated wireless NIC driver.
- ❑ A degraded wireless signal could be due to interference in the same frequency range, atmospheric conditions, or physical obstructions.
- ❑ Some antimalware and firewall programs can cause problems with wireless connections—check their configuration.
- ❑ Use the **ipconfig** command to check the IP configuration.
- ❑ Use the **ping** command to test for connectivity to another host.

- ❑ Find a network bottleneck on a routed network (like the Internet) using the **tracert** or **pathping** command.
- ❑ Use the **netstat** command to view statistics about connections to the local computer.
- ❑ The **net** command performs a variety of tasks, such as starting and stopping services.
- ❑ Troubleshoot DNS problems with ping and nslookup, as well as ipconfig.
- ❑ One way to increase network bandwidth is to remove unnecessary protocol suites from the network. Check computers for unneeded protocol suites and other network devices, such as print servers, which may come with several protocols enabled.
- ❑ One way to increase network bandwidth is to upgrade hardware. Consider changing all the network hardware (NICs, switches, cabling, etc.) to hardware capable of higher speeds than the existing equipment.
- ❑ When troubleshooting network connectivity problems, physically check the local network hardware. Next, check the status of the NIC driver in the Properties dialog box for the NIC.
- ❑ When only certain resources are unavailable, try using Windows troubleshooters to identify the problem, and check sharing permissions.
- ❑ Power-cycling a broadband modem can sometimes correct problems related to lack of Internet access.

Preventive Maintenance for Networks

- ❑ Preventive maintenance for network devices, such as NICs, hubs, switches, WAPs, and routers, is identical to what we described in Chapter 12 for computers.
- ❑ Do not overload circuits, and provide reliable power using power protection devices, as described in Chapter 1. Consider using a dedicated circuit for the most critical equipment.
- ❑ Locate servers and network devices in a dedicated space, such as a room or closet. Make sure the environment in this space is appropriate, and restrict access to the equipment.
- ❑ Secure, protect, and organize network cabling by using patch panels in the closet or room housing the network devices and by using cable management systems, such as cable trays for horizontal runs through ceilings.

SELF TEST

The following questions will help you measure your understanding of the material presented in this chapter. Read all the choices carefully because there might be more than one correct answer. Choose all correct answers for each question.

Troubleshooting Common Network Problems

1. You need to find out the Windows version number of a customer's system. Which command-line tool should you use?
   A. hostname
   B. vernum
   C. ip
   D. winver
2. You are testing network connectivity and need a tool that sends echo requests to each router and evaluates the speed at which the packets are returned. What tool should you use?
   A. net user
   B. pathping
   C. dig
   D. sudo
3. Which of the following is a command-line utility you would use to release a DHCP-allocated IP address from a local NIC?
   A. net user
   B. ping
   C. ipconfig
   D. nslookup
4. What tool would you use if you suspected that a cable contained broken wires?
   A. Cable ping
   B. Cable tester
   C. Status indicator
   D. Loopback plug

5. Which of the following is a delay in packet sending and receiving due to network congestion often resulting in poor VoIP quality?
   A. Jitter
   B. Port flapping
   C. Binding
   D. TTL
6. What should you look for first on a network that seems to have a bandwidth problem?
   A. Unnecessary protocol suites
   B. Unnecessary servers
   C. Unnecessary network printers
   D. Unnecessary print servers
7. How can you quickly view the IP configuration information for all the network adapters in your computer?
   A. Open the Network and Sharing Center.
   B. Run **netstat**.
   C. Run **ipconfig /renew**.
   D. Run **ipconfig /all**.
8. Which of the following devices reduces network traffic within an Ethernet LAN?
   A. Hub
   B. Switch
   C. Router
   D. NIC
9. How would you check the signal strength received by a wireless NIC? (Select all that apply.)
   A. Check indicator lights on the wireless NIC.
   B. Check indicator lights on the WAP.
   C. Open the NIC's program from the notification area.
   D. Run **ipconfig**.
10. Which tool will show you the status of nearby Wi-Fi networks?
   A. Punchdown tool
   B. netstat
   C. Toner probe
   D. Wi-Fi analyzer

11. What is the effect when an older-technology NIC connects to a newer-technology switch?

A. The communication between the NIC and the switch is at the speed of the NIC, but other connections to that switch are not affected.

B. The communication between the switch and all connected devices occurs at the speed of the slowest NIC.

C. The communication between the switch and all connected devices occurs at the switch's maximum speed.

D. The communication between the NIC and the switch is at the speed of the switch.

12. The distance between a WAP and one group of wireless hosts causes the signal to degrade so badly that the transmissions are too slow and users are complaining. What can you do?

A. Install a signal booster.

B. Upgrade all the wireless devices to a faster speed.

C. Install an Ethernet network.

D. Install a router.

13. Which type of server automatically assigns IP addresses to hosts?

A. DHCP

B. PING

C. DNS

D. APIPA

14. What command can you use to force a DHCP client to request an IP address assignment?

A. **ping localhost**

B. **ipconfig /renew**

C. **ipconfig /all**

D. **tracert**

15. A user complains that an Internet connection to a website she needs to access for her work is extremely slow. Which of the following commands will you use first to analyze the problem?

A. netstat

B. ipconfig

C. tracert

D. nslookup

16. Which of the following command-line utilities would *not* help when troubleshooting a possible DNS problem?

A. net use

B. ping

C. ipconfig

D. nslookup

17. How do you stop the output from a **ping** command in which you used the -t switch?

A. Type **exit**.

B. Press the CTRL-C key combination.

C. Type **pause**.

D. Press the CTRL-BREAK key combination.

18. When you ping this name, you are pinging the loopback network interface as a test of the local NIC to see if it is functioning.

A. server

B. echo

C. localhost

D. gateway

Preventive Maintenance for Networks

19. Which of the following is the preferred environment for network equipment and servers in a law office?

A. A broom closet

B. A reception desk

C. A dedicated, climate-controlled room

D. A conference room

20. You need to run a group of wires through a suspended ceiling. What should you use to keep the wires organized within the ceiling area?

A. An equipment rack

B. A UPS

C. Cable wraps

D. Cable trays

A SELF TEST ANSWERS

Troubleshooting Common Network Problems

1. ☑ **D.** You should use winver command from the command line to display the Windows version number of the customer's system.
☒ **A** is incorrect because the hostname command will display the name of the client's computer (as configured in Windows). **B** is incorrect because vernum is not a recognized command-line command. **C** is incorrect because the **ip** command is used in macOS and Linux to display IP address and other network interface information.

2. ☑ **B.** An alternative to tracert is the **pathping** command. It sends echo requests to each router and evaluates the speed at which the packets are returned. It also reports the packet losses for each router.
☒ **A** is incorrect because the **net user** command adds, deletes, and manages users on a computer. **C** is incorrect because the **dig** command in Linux (short for Domain Information Groper) provides DNS information. **D** is incorrect because the **sudo** command in Linux permits a regular user to execute a command or program as the superuser (aka root user) or another user.

3. ☑ **C.** Use ipconfig to release a DHCP-allocated IP address from a NIC (**ipconfig /release**, which you would normally follow with **ipconfig /renew** to renew the address).
☒ **A** is incorrect because net user lets you manage user accounts on Windows PCs, but it does not release an IP address. **B** is incorrect because ping tests a connection between two hosts. **D** is incorrect because nslookup tests for DNS problems.

4. ☑ **B.** You would use a cable tester if you suspected that a cable had broken wires.
☒ **A** is incorrect because a cable ping was not even mentioned and may not exist. **C** is incorrect because status indicator is not a tool you would use if you suspected that a cable was bad. **D** is incorrect because a loopback plug tests a port, not a cable.

5. ☑ **A.** Slow network speed can cause performance problems such as jitter (which is a delay in packet sending and receiving due to network congestion), resulting in poor VoIP quality (in other words, poor audio and video quality).
☒ **B** is incorrect because port flapping is the repeated starting and stopping of data transmission through a cable, usually due to a bad cable. **C** is incorrect because "bound" means that there is a linking relationship, called a "binding," between the network protocol and the adapter. A binding establishes the order in which each network component handles network communications. **D** is incorrect because each IP packet header has a time to live (TTL) field that shows how many routers the packet can cross before being discarded.

6. ☑ **A.** Unnecessary protocol suites are what you should look for first in a network that seems to have a bandwidth problem.
   ☒ **B, C,** and **D** are incorrect because none of these contribute to bandwidth as much as unnecessary protocol suites.

7. ☑ **D.** Run **ipconfig /all** to quickly see the IP configuration information for all the network adapters in a computer.
   ☒ **A** is incorrect because the Network and Sharing Center shows only information for the PC on which you are viewing it. **B** is incorrect because running **netstat** displays information on the open connections by protocol and port number. **C** is incorrect because running **ipconfig /renew** forces a DHCP client to send an IP address renewal request to a DHCP server.

8. ☑ **B.** A switch is the device that reduces network broadcasts in an Ethernet network.
   ☒ **A** is incorrect because a hub sends a packet to every port, which increases traffic, whereas a switch only sends packets to the destination port. **C** is incorrect because a router connects LANs, whereas a switch is within a LAN. It is true that a router will keep broadcast traffic from traveling between LANs. **D** is incorrect because a NIC is a network adapter, which is not a device that reduces network traffic.

9. ☑ **A** and **C.** The indicator lights on the wireless NIC and the NIC's program, available from the notification area, are both places where you could look for the signal strength received by a wireless NIC.
   ☒ **B** is incorrect because since the WAP is the source of the signals, indicator lights on the WAP do not indicate the strength of the signal received by a wireless NIC. **D** is incorrect because running **ipconfig** is not how you check the signal strength received by a wireless NIC.

10. ☑ **D.** A Wi-Fi analyzer will show you the status of nearby Wi-Fi networks.
    ☒ **A** is incorrect because a punchdown tool is used to connect cabling to a punchdown block. **B** is incorrect because netstat is a command-line utility that provides statistical information about the TCP/IP protocols and network connections. **C** is incorrect because a toner probe is a hardware tool for locating both ends of a cable.

11. ☑ **B.** The switch can operate no faster than the maximum speed of the slowest device connected to it.
    ☒ **A** is incorrect because all connected devices' speeds are affected by its presence. **C** and **D** are incorrect because communication can be no faster than the NIC's speed.

12. ☑ **A.** The solution to the degraded signal due to distance is to install a signal booster.
    ☒ **B** is incorrect because the question does not mention the standard of the device in use, and it may be at the highest level available. **C** is incorrect because a wireless network is often installed where it is not possible or practical to install a wired network. **D** is incorrect because installing a router would not solve the problem of the weak signal within the wireless LAN.

13. ☑ **A.** DHCP is the type of server that automatically assigns IP addresses to hosts.
☒ **B** is incorrect because **ping** is a command, not a type of server. **C** is incorrect because the DNS server resolves Internet domain names to IP addresses. **D** is incorrect because APIPA does not describe a server, but an IP address (beginning with 169.254) that a DHCP client can assign to itself if it does not get a response from a DHCP server.

14. ☑ **B.** You use the **ipconfig /renew** command to force a DHCP client to request an IP address assignment.
☒ **A** is incorrect because **ping localhost** is used to ping the local NIC. **C** is incorrect because **ipconfig /all** is used to look at the TCP/IP configuration. **D** is incorrect because **tracert** displays a trace of the route taken by packets to the destination.

15. ☑ **C. tracert** is the command to use to analyze the problem of a slow connection to a website.
☒ **A, B,** and **D** are incorrect because none of these is the correct command to analyze the problem described.

16. ☑ **A.** net use would not help when troubleshooting a possible DNS problem, because net use is for viewing and managing network devices.
☒ **B, C,** and **D** are incorrect because these are all useful when troubleshooting a possible DNS problem.

17. ☑ **B.** Pressing CTRL-C will stop the command and return you to the prompt.
☒ **A, C,** and **D** are incorrect because none of these will stop the command output.

18. ☑ **C.** localhost is the name of the loopback network interface, and pinging it tests the NIC.
☒ **A, B,** and **D** are incorrect because none of them is the name of the loopback network interface.

Preventive Maintenance for Networks

19. ☑ **C.** A dedicated, climate-controlled room is the preferred environment for network equipment and servers in any organization.
☒ **A, B,** and **D** are incorrect; they are unsuitable locations because they do not restrict access to the equipment and do not provide the correct climate-controlled environment.

20. ☑ **D.** You should use cable trays to keep the wires organized within the ceiling area.
☒ **A** is incorrect because an equipment rack is not used within ceiling areas. **B** is incorrect because a UPS is a power protection device, not something for organizing cables. **C** is incorrect because although you could use cable wraps to organize cables, they are not the best solution for organizing cables within the ceiling (nor are they mentioned in the chapter).

Part VI

Security

CHAPTERS

Chapter 20

Physical Security and User Authentication

CERTIFICATION OBJECTIVES

- **1101: 2.4** Summarize services provided by networked hosts
- **1102: 1.4** Given a scenario, use the appropriate Microsoft Windows 10 Control panel utility
- **1102: 1.5** Given a scenario, use the appropriate Windows settings
- **1102: 1.10** Identify common features and tools of the macOS/desktop OS
- **1102: 2.1** Summarize various security measures and their purposes
- **1102: 2.2** Compare and contrast wireless security protocols and authentication methods
- **1102: 2.4** Explain common social-engineering attacks, threats, and vulnerabilities
- **1102: 2.5** Given a scenario, manage and configure basic security settings in the Microsoft Windows OS
- **1102: 2.6** Given a scenario, configure a workstation to meet best practices for security

- **1102: 2.7** Explain common methods for securing mobile and embedded devices
- **1102: 2.8** Given a scenario, use common data destruction and disposal methods
- **1102: 3.1** Given a scenario, troubleshoot common Windows OS problems
- ✓ Two-Minute Drill
- **Q&A** Self Test

This chapter covers two important facets of IT security: physical security measures and methods of user authentication and authorization. We review many types of physical protections you can implement to keep intruders away from your valuable hardware and data. We also cover the proper physical disposal of unwanted data storage hardware to prevent its data from falling into the wrong hands. You will also learn about both local and domain-based user accounts and how to create, delete, and manage them.

Security Threats: An Overview

You need to understand security threats in order to put security concepts, technologies, and features into context and then to implement strategies for protecting against those threats. Security concerns can be divided into these broad categories:

- **Physical security** Controlling who has physical access to computer resources and ensuring that hardware is not stolen, damaged, or compromised.
- **User authentication** Controlling who can sign in to secured computing and network resources with verified credentials and preventing unauthorized access. This topic encompasses various types of account management and authorization, including passwords and biometrics.
- **Data protection** Ensuring that data is accessible only to authorized users and that data is not destroyed, corrupted, or manipulated, either accidentally or intentionally. Data protection also includes data backup, setting file sharing and security permissions, version management, and disaster recovery planning. These topics are covered in Chapter 21.

- **Malware and social engineering** Ensuring that unauthorized persons or software are not able to access protected hardware, applications, or data. This topic is covered in Chapter 21.

CERTIFICATION OBJECTIVES

- ***1102: 2.1*** *Summarize various security measures and their purposes*
- ***1102: 2.4*** *Explain common social-engineering attacks, threats, and vulnerabilities*
- ***1102: 2.7*** *Explain common methods for securing mobile and embedded devices*

The following section addresses many types of safeguards against physical intrusion, outlined in CompTIA A+ 1102 exam Objective 2.1, including barriers such as door locks and equipment locks and entry authorization methods such as badge readers. This section also looks at a few physically based social engineering threats from A+ 1102 exam Objective 2.4: shoulder surfing, tailgating, and dumpster diving. We also pick up IoT device security here, from A+ 1102 exam Objective 2.7.

Securing the Local Physical Environment

Physical security begins when an individual approaches the entrance to a building or campus. The level of security and the lengths to which an organization will go to secure an area depend on what they are protecting.

Many organizations do not require any type of authentication until an employee is logging on to their computer—which is digital security. Others secure only small areas of their buildings, while some require authentication before you can access a campus or larger geographic area. Think of a government installation, manufacturing facility, or research institute. In this section we will look at some methods used to prevent unauthorized physical access to areas ranging in size from a computer closet to an army base.

If an unauthorized person manages to gain access to one of these areas, how do they secure the documents? We will discuss the methods for securing digitally stored documents later in this chapter, but what about the data visible on screens and on paper documents? That is another facet of physical security, and we will address that in this section as we examine methods to secure access to paper documents and on-screen data.

Physical control of assets also means not letting them get stolen. Thieves steal an astounding number of computers, especially laptops, tablets, and other mobile devices, each year from businesses, homes, and automobiles. The result is loss of important tools and valuable data files—and perhaps even a loss of identity, not to mention the downtime until equipment is replaced and programs and data are restored. At one time, most computer equipment thieves simply wanted to sell the hardware quickly for cash—at a fraction of the value of your computer and data to you or your business. Today, thieves realize the value of the data itself, so the data may be their main objective in stealing hardware; they will go through your hard drive looking for bank account, credit card, and other financial data so they can steal your identity.

Physical Barriers

Locked doors and physically secured computers are the best protection from computer hardware theft. You can achieve locked doors against unauthorized access with low-tech methods ranging from limiting distribution of *keys* to the physical locks to other methods such as human guards at entrances examining conventional badges as people enter and leave, to high-tech solutions for authentication at entrances using smart cards, radio frequency identification (RFID) badges, key fobs, RSA tokens, or biometric authentication, all of which are discussed later in this chapter. You can secure special equipment such as switches, routers, and servers inside locked areas, but the typical desktop computer or laptop cannot always be physically secured. There are devices for physically securing computers, such as kiosk enclosures, but you rarely see them in use except in high-risk environments, such as schools and public buildings.

For ultra-high-security areas, an *access control vestibule* (also called a mantrap) may be implemented. An access control vestibule is a set of two locked doors where the first door must close before the second door can be opened. In an automatic vestibule, ID may be required to open each door, or possibly two different kinds of ID, like a proximity smart card and a PIN typed on a keypad.

Two other physical security measures also mentioned in the exam objectives are fences and bollards. Fences are fairly self-explanatory; secure facilities often have fences around them. You've probably seen bollards before, but you might not have known what they were called. *Bollards* are short posts on a pedestrian walkway that prevent vehicles from driving on it.

Security Policies

As you learned in Chapter 2, establishing and enforcing user access policies can be effective in making end users part of the security solution through acceptable-use policies, password policies, and incident documentation.

One policy, for example, might be to keep a list of allowed users on an *access control list (ACL)* for accessing a protected area, such as a server room. It can be as simple as a paper roster with a guard that ensures that every person entering the area is authorized, or it can be an electronic record that documents the badge number or credentials of each person who uses an electronic system of authentication. Human security guards can also be posted and a video camera system deployed.

Another policy that can be helpful in protecting users and systems is a *mobile device management (MDM)* policy, which specifies rules for mobile device usage on company networks. An MDM policy is closely related to a *bring your own device (BYOD)* policy, in that both can help prevent lax security settings on users' private mobile devices from adversely affecting the company's network. A *mobile application management (MAM)* policy is also similar, being a policy that controls what applications are installed on corporate devices.

exam watch

1101 exam Objective 1.4 asks you to be aware of three aspects of MDM and MAM: corporate e-mail configuration, two-factor authentication, and corporate applications. Careful management and monitoring of these three factors can greatly enhance security. You don't need to know step-by-step configuration techniques for these, but you should understand the value of each one and be able to identify situations where they might be needed.

Securing IoT Devices

Many devices that are not computers, strictly speaking, nevertheless have some computing components in them. Internet of Things (IoT) devices are a prime example of this. They not only contain software that helps the device function, but they also have network connectivity. This network connectivity makes them vulnerable, because if someone can connect to your network via one of these devices, they may be able to shift laterally to other devices, and from there gain access to more important data.

Here are some basics for securing IoT devices:

- Maintain physical control of the device. For example, if you have a water filtration system with IoT capability and it's installed in an out building, keep that building locked.
- Engage security features. If the device has any security features, such as password protection, enable it.
- Store gathered information remotely. For example, if you have an outdoor IoT security camera, set it to transfer the stored video footage to an indoor, secure computer.
- Dispose of old devices properly. If you are planning to sell or give away an IoT device, make sure any personal data is wiped from it first.
- Keep IoT firmware updated to make sure you have the latest security features.

Preventing Piggybacking and Tailgating

Piggybacking is when someone follows an authorized person into a secure area with their consent. When someone does the same thing without the authorized person's consent, perhaps slipping into a door behind the authorized person, it is *tailgating*. Campuses and buildings with restricted areas need to guard against piggybacking and tailgating practices. If using guards, an organization must train them to not allow this. Authorized employees must agree not to participate in piggybacking (bringing in unauthorized people) and to watch out for people following them closely in the hopes of tailgating. Using surveillance video may be necessary, along with having personnel monitor the video and taking action, watching both who comes in and who leaves.

Using Equipment Locks

You can secure both desktops and laptops to a hard point such as a bolted-down desk or an eyebolt in a wall using a locking cable/*equipment lock*. While a determined thief can get around this, given time and privacy, use of a locking cable dramatically cuts down on hardware "walking away." When locking down a desktop PC, make sure the cable passes through the metal frame of the case and is not simply bolted to the outside of the case. Otherwise, a thief could remove the case cover and take the PC chassis.

Many laptops have a special hole or socket in the side of the case designed to work with a cable lock. Kensington makes one very popular kind of lock, and the corresponding hole in many laptops is called a K-slot.

Monitoring Access

Intrusion alert systems can provide a second layer of defense, behind the physical security. Some common monitoring types include

- **Video surveillance** Video cameras can monitor important areas; these cameras can be computer-enabled and can send data to a PC via wired or wireless technologies.
- **Alarm systems** Certain areas can be set up to set off alarms if activity/motion is detected or if certain doors or cabinets open.

Intruders can hide in the dark and shadows, so many companies deploy 24/7 lighting around important buildings and in access hallways to important assets. These lighting systems can also serve as intrusion detection systems when they are set to turn on when motion is detected.

CompTIA A+ 1102 exam Objective 2.1 mentions lighting, video surveillance, alarm systems, and motion sensors as physical security devices. Be aware of their usefulness in physically securing an area and understand how they can be tied into a computer-based monitoring system.

Preventing Dumpster Diving

Private individuals and organizations combined generate many tons of waste paper each year. Much of that is in the form of documents holding confidential information of some sort, from credit card information on receipts, to individual health status information, to corporate secrets. When thieves target exploitable information in waste paper, it is called *dumpster diving*. It is usually done as part of a larger social engineering campaign, to be discussed in Chapter 21.

The main way to prevent dumpster diving is to educate users about what information can be safely put in the regular trash versus shredded. Providing each department with its own paper shredder can help, as well as conducting data disposal training classes. Depending on the business type and the level of data sensitivity, shredded documents may need to be burned.

Requiring Badges

A simple paper or plastic ID badge, with photo, is a traditional method for gaining access to areas with security guards at entrances. But unless the badge also contains some digital technology, such as a smart card or RFID, it is not very good security, especially in a large facility where the guards may not recognize individuals well enough to challenge badge holders. See the section "Device-Based Authentication: What You Have" later in this chapter to learn about some technologies that make badges more useful for security.

Detecting Weapons at Key Entry Points

Magnetometers are often deployed at key access points to a secure facility to ensure that not only are entrants authorized but that they don't bring in weapons that could be used to forcibly take sensitive data or expensive hardware. A magnetometer uses an electromagnetic field to scan a person or object (such as a backpack or suitcase) for metal objects. Magnetometers are similar to metal detectors, and some people use the terms interchangeably, but the internal technology is somewhat different.

exam watch

Know the term *magnetometer* and its purpose in securing a facility. You do not need to understand the technology behind it.

Preventing Unauthorized Physical Access to Information

Securing physical access to data can begin with the access to a building or area, as just described, requiring some form of authentication with a password or one of the authentication devices. In addition, there are methods for guarding against data loss by preventing shoulder surfing, securing documents in locked storage, shredding documents, and disposing of used equipment after removing all data and then following environmentally safe disposal methods.

Preventing Shoulder Surfing

One method people use to gain access to your bank account, computer and corporate network, and secure physical areas is by *shoulder surfing* to steal your security code, passcode, or other security credentials as you enter them, or even as you write them on a form. The most primitive example is someone peering over your shoulder to see the keystrokes you enter at the checkout counter, ATM cash machine, or entrance to a secure building. The thief may literally be standing at your shoulder or may be at a distance using binoculars. More sophisticated implementations include using cameras or devices attached to the security keypad itself to log the keystrokes and either save the information for later retrieval or transmit it wirelessly to the thief.

exam watch **Be sure you understand how thieves use shoulder surfing to steal security credentials.**

When sitting at your desk, your computer screen may also be a target of shoulder surfing, and the methods are the same as those used on ATM terminals.

The low-tech way to guard against shoulder surfing is to attach a *privacy filter* to any screen that may be targeted, including ATMs, desktop PCs, and laptops. Privacy filters narrow the screen's viewing angle, which ensures that only the person sitting directly in front of the system can view the screen contents.

Using Locked Storage for Documents

Confidential documents should be in a secure area or in locked containers. You should also control access to these areas with the methods discussed earlier. Some storage devices themselves can also be locked. For example, some USB flash drives can be password-protected for access. You can also password-protect a document server, either at the operating system or BIOS level.

Using BIOS/UEFI Passwords

As described in Chapter 8, you can set one or more passwords in the system firmware setup program to help secure a local workstation. For example, the motherboard's firmware may support three types of passwords: one type restricts access to the computer itself; another type restricts access to the BIOS/UEFI setup; and a third, less common type restricts access to hard drives, a feature called "DriveLock" on HP computers. As a further enhancement, an embedded Trusted Platform Module (TPM) chip restricts access to hard drives, providing more advanced security.

One feature of UEFI is Secure Boot, a security standard that helps ensure that a device boots only trusted software. When the PC starts, UEFI checks the signature of each piece of boot software, including the UEFI firmware drivers, EFI applications, and the operating system, for valid signatures.

BIOS/UEFI Passwords for Setup and Startup

Many BIOSs and UEFIs (let's call them *firmware* here generically for simplicity) allow you to set a password that must be given before anyone can change firmware settings, and many allow you to set a separate password required to start up the computer. The first is reasonable if a computer is in an environment where people may tend to tamper with the firmware settings. An example would be in a student lab. The second is a bit extreme unless security requirements dictate this.

To set a firmware password for setup or startup, check the manual for the motherboard, and then go into the firmware setup program and navigate to the correct setting; it may simply be called "Set Password." Selecting this option will open a password dialog box, in which you enter the new password. On another screen, you configure the password requirement for setup and/or startup.

Some manufacturers provide a firmware feature (HP calls theirs DriveLock) that allows you to set a password that you must provide at startup. This password is stored on the hard drive, which means that even if you move the drive to another computer, it will be inaccessible.

TPM

A more sophisticated method is to store the cryptographic keys for encrypting and decrypting disk volumes in an embedded TPM chip, as described in Chapter 8. With TPM enabled, the user might optionally have to enter a PIN at bootup. If the PIN is correct, TPM decrypts the disk volume and allows the bootup to continue. If the drive is removed from the computer and installed into another computer, it will not be accessible unless the encryption data was transferred from the original TPM chip to the new TPM-enabled computer. TPM can also verify that the hardware boot sequence has not been tampered with.

The Windows BitLocker Drive Encryption feature (described in Chapter 21) works with TPM to secure drive contents, although this is just an option, and you can choose to use a password or smart card for unlocking the drive. The Windows BitLocker To Go feature that encrypts flash drives does not use TPM, but lets you configure it to use either a password or smart card to store the password.

exam watch

Make sure you don't confuse BitLocker with Microsoft's Encrypting File System (EFS); EFS encrypts specified files and folders on NTFS disk partitions, whereas BitLocker encrypts entire disk drives. For the utmost data storage security, consider using both.

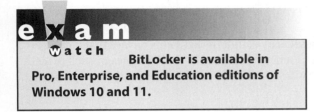

BitLocker is available in Pro, Enterprise, and Education editions of Windows 10 and 11.

When you install an edition of Windows that includes BitLocker support on a computer with a TPM 1.2 or newer chip on the motherboard, Windows Setup will automatically enable BitLocker and install the BitLocker applet in Control Panel.

Locking a Computer with Windows

Another way to physically secure a workstation is to lock it using Windows. Use the Lock Computer option to secure your desktop quickly, while leaving all your programs and files open. It is very simple to do. Before leaving your computer unattended, simply press WINDOWS KEY-L. This will lock the computer; the desktop will disappear, replaced by a screen with a message that the computer is locked. When you return to your desk, simply enter your password and your desktop appears. Use this when you must leave your desk for a little while, like when you go to lunch.

SCENARIO & SOLUTION

I am preparing a new computer for a computer lab. How can I configure the computer so students will not be able to access the system setup and change the BIOS/UEFI settings, making the computer unusable?	Check out the manufacturer's documentation on the computer's system settings and look for the password settings. Set the password for accessing the BIOS/UEFI Settings menu only. Do not set the password to be required for system startup unless the security policy for the computer lab requires this.
How can I prevent laptops from being stolen out of conference rooms?	Consider using a cable lock to attach the laptop to a hard point such as a metal loop attached to some heavy furniture or a wall. Many laptops have a K-slot designed specifically for inserting a certain type of cable lock.
Our employees' computers are in a public area where customers and others can easily wander in and out. Employees must frequently leave their computers unattended during the workday for brief periods. How can they keep their desktops secure without shutting down their applications and Windows?	We suggest you show the employees how to use the Windows Lock Computer option (WINDOWS KEY-L). For physical security, invest in cable locks that work with the K-slots in the laptop chassis.

CERTIFICATION OBJECTIVE

- ***1102: 2.8*** *Given a scenario, use common data destruction and disposal methods*

CompTIA A+ 1102 exam Objective 2.8 includes tasks required to destroy the data on a computer when you no longer need that computer, primarily to prevent unauthorized individuals from accessing any leftover stored data. Whether you are giving it away to be used again, moving it to another user's desk in your organization, or disposing of the equipment, you need to ensure that you are not giving away personal or organizational data. This objective includes both the physical destruction of the storage device and the use of software in the form of formatting, overwriting, and drive wiping.

Securely Disposing of Data Storage Hardware

How does your organization dispose of old computer equipment? This is a topic described in Chapter 1 with regard to keeping discarded computer equipment out of the waste stream, recycling components, and disposing of hazardous waste contained in computers and related equipment. When storage devices are no longer needed, you might choose to recycle them, repurpose them, or donate them to charity, but before you can do any of that, you need to make sure that the data on them cannot be read. Otherwise, you are creating a security risk for your company (or for your own personal privacy, if it's your own drive).

The level of data destruction to employ depends on how sensitive the data is—that is, how bad would it be if someone were able to read it? This can range from mildly bad (like someone could read a bunch of boring internal memos), to really bad (like someone could see customer mailing addresses), to unbelievably bad (like your customers' credit card data is sold to a criminal syndicate).

You can handle the secure disposition of storage hardware yourself, or you can turn to a third-party vendor (aka *outsourcing*). Either way, you need to know the options and their pros and cons.

Wiping a Storage Device

Ordinary deletion of the files in Windows will not completely delete files, even if you reformat the hard drives. Therefore, you should use a program that will truly erase all the data from the hard drives so it is not recoverable, even with very sophisticated tools. This process is called *drive sanitation*.

Described on the next page are some of the ways you can destroy data that you won't want others to access, listed from least to most effective.

- **Deleting files** This is the quickest and least secure method of clearing a disk. Just select the files in File Explorer and press DELETE and then empty the Recycle Bin.
- **Reformatting** You can use the Format utility in the OS to perform a format. This erases the master file table (or file allocation table). The data is still on the disk, but there is no easy way of retrieving it. Someone would have to use a special disk repair utility or investigate the drive sector by sector to piece it together. The A+ 1102 exam Objective 2.8 calls this *standard formatting.*
- **Repartitioning** You can use a utility like Disk Management in Windows or GParted for Linux to delete the existing partitions on the drive, create a new partition, and format it. Deleting and re-creating the partitions adds another degree of difficulty for the person trying to restore data.
- **Low-level formatting (disk wiping)** What people call "low-level formatting" in the context of security is not really low-level formatting (at least not in the sense that it's done at the factory), but rather high-level formatting plus zero-filling all sectors of the hard drive. You can do this with a third-party drive utility, or in Linux you can do it from a command prompt with the **dd** command, like this:

```
dd if=/dev/zero of=/dev/<target device>
```

There are different security standards for different levels of disk wiping. For example, the U.S. military standard (DoD 5220.22-M) overwrites the entire hard drive six times, through a series of wiping passes, so if you need to wipe to a certain standard, make sure the wiping software you are using conforms to this.

Physically Destroying a Storage Device

If you do not have the option of using a software tool to destroy data on old equipment, then you have other options for physically destroying the data, depending on your budget. A hand power drill is something everyone can buy from a hardware store, and unless your drives contain government secrets or data that is worth millions (or at least hundreds of thousands) of dollars, aggressively attacking a hard drive (or SSD storage) with a power drill will render the data irretrievable. Of course, the *drilling* method will cause metal bits and pieces to fly out of the target, so it does pose some risks to the individual doing it. Wear safety glasses, gloves, and protective clothing.

Yet another tactic is to use an electromagnetic device such as a *degaussing tool* to remove storage from hard drive platters. These devices are costly, running from several hundred for a simple handheld wand to several thousand dollars for a powerful device into which you insert a hard drive or tape drive; it first erases the data through degaussing and then physically crushes the storage device. Obviously this doesn't work on solid-state drives because they don't store data magnetically.

Incineration (burning) is another destruction option. There are security management companies that specialize in the thorough destruction by fire of sensitive data documents and hardware, and a company can also operate its own incinerator for documents and magnetic media (like tape and disks).

In some high-security situations, you might need to have documentation that sensitive records or equipment has been destroyed: a *certificate of destruction*. The destruction management company you work with can provide this, or if you are doing your own destruction, you can document it by maintaining careful records and taking photos of destroyed equipment.

SCENARIO & SOLUTION	
Is there a way to make an old hard drive physically inaccessible without spending a fortune on professional data destruction?	Yes! Drill a few holes in it with an ordinary electric drill. This makes the platters unusable without having to crack open the case and remove them and without paying a data disposal company.

CERTIFICATION OBJECTIVES

- ***1101: 2.4*** *Summarize services provided by network hosts*
- ***1102: 1.4*** *Given a scenario, use the appropriate Microsoft Windows 10 Control Panel utility*
- ***1102: 1.5*** *Given a scenario, use the appropriate Windows settings*
- ***1102: 1.10*** *Identify common features and tools of the macOS/desktop OS*
- ***1102: 2.1*** *Summarize various security measures and their purposes*
- ***1102: 2.2*** *Compare and contrast wireless security protocols and authentication methods*
- ***1102: 2.5*** *Given a scenario, manage and configure basic security settings in the Microsoft Windows OS*
- ***1102: 2.6*** *Given a scenario, configure a workstation to meet best practices for security*
- ***1102: 3.1*** *Given a scenario, troubleshoot common Windows OS problems*

Authenticating users is a common thread across many areas of computing, and the wide range of exam objectives covered in this section reflects that.

This section is all about user accounts and how they are used for authentication, authorization, and accounting (AAA), a topic mentioned in CompTIA A+ 1101 exam Objective 2.4. We cover the User Accounts topic from CompTIA A+ 1102 exam Objectives 1.4 and 1.5, and from A+ 1102 exam Objective 1.10, we pick up a single topic: Apple ID and corporate restrictions. We look at several of the account-based topics from A+ 1102 exam Objectives 2.1 and 2.2, including authentication, user education, user authentication (single and multifactor), strong passwords, and the principle of least privilege.

From A+ 1102 exam Objective 2.5, we cover user account types (such as Administrator and Standard) and what privileges they confer. From A+ 1102 exam Objective 2.6, we describe best practices to create a password and secure a workstation, as well as how to perform basic Active Directory functions. We also mention one topic from 1102 exam Objective 3.1: rebuilding Windows user profiles.

Working with User Accounts

Good user management practices are essential for protecting systems from unauthorized use and exploitation. In this section, you will learn how to implement the various methods of authenticating and managing user accounts, including creating, securing, and deleting them and establishing limits on their use.

Access control to resources on a local computer or over a network involves *authentication* (verifying a user's identity) and *authorization* (determining the level of access an authenticated user has to a resource). A third factor is often included with these, *accounting* (keeping a record of what has occurred), and the three are abbreviated as *AAA*. Keep an eye out for these terms as we discuss user accounts and data access in this chapter and also the next one.

exam watch

For CompTIA A+ 1101 exam Objective 2.4, make sure you can identify the "three A's" and explain the role of each of them in security—authentication, authorization, and accounting (AAA)—covered in Chapter 16. Don't confuse this with the "four A's" involved in DNS, per 1101 exam Objective 2.6: An AAAA DNS record matches a domain name to an IPv6 IP address.

Authentication Factors

The information or device used for authentication verification is an *authentication factor.* There are four categories of authentication factors: something you know, something you have, something you are, and somewhere you are. An example of something you *know* is a user name and password or a personal identification number (PIN). Something you *have* might be a smart card, and something you *are* might be a measurement of a physical or behavioral characteristic (a biometric), such as a fingerprint or retina scan. *Somewhere you are* would be a specific geographical area or boundary. Authentication involves one or more of these factors, so you can have one-factor, two-factor, or three-factor authentication. When two or more factors are used, it is called *multifactor authentication (MFA).*

You should be able to identify and explain the categories of authentication factors in MFA: something you know, something you have, and something you are. The fourth factor, somewhere you are, isn't in the exam objectives but you should still be aware of it.

The following sections explain some of the ways that users can be authenticated and authorized.

Passwords: What You Know

A *password* is a string of characters that a user enters, along with an identifier, such as a user name, in order for authentication to take place. This security tool is an important one for anyone who uses a computer, especially one connected to any network, including the Internet.

In the vast majority of cases, especially in a small office/home office (SOHO) environment, people are authenticated to computers and networks with a user name and password. This does not require any special hardware, as the user name and password can be entered using the keyboard. We discuss passwords in depth in the section "Best Practices to Secure a Workstation" later in this chapter.

Device-Based Authentication: What You Have

Organizations requiring more stringent authentication practices for protecting digital access than simple password-based systems can provide will use specialized technologies, such as smart cards, RFID badges, key fobs, biometric scanners, hard tokens, and soft tokens. All these technologies provide more secure authentication at an additional cost, but the costs are decreasing, and the technologies are becoming more widespread.

Smart Cards A *smart card* is a plastic card, often the size of a credit card, that contains a microchip. The microchip can store information and perform various functions, depending on the type of smart card. Some smart cards only store data, whereas others may have a variety of functions, including security cards for gaining physical access to facilities or logging on to computers and networks. If configuration of the Windows domain and local Windows computers allows acceptance of smart card logons, users may use this method of presenting credentials and logging on. The domain controllers require certain software security components, and the local computer must have a special piece of hardware called a *smart card reader* or card terminal. When the user inserts the card into the reader, the reader sends commands to the card in order to complete the authentication process. As is true of a bank cash card, the user may also need to enter a PIN into the keyboard in conjunction with the smart card. The two together comprise two-factor authentication.

Smart card setup requires you to install a special service called *Certificate Services* on the domain controllers for the Windows domain. Once you have installed the reader and configured the domain controllers to support Certificate Services, users can log on to the computer. Inserting the card into the reader has the same effect as pressing the CTRL-ALT-DELETE key combination, which is normally required on a Windows computer logging on to a domain. Either action constitutes a *secure attention sequence (SAS)* that clears memory of certain types of viruses that may be lurking and waiting to capture a user name and password. Smart cards are a very secure and tamper-resistant method of authentication.

Modern debit and credit chip cards are smart cards. These are considered safer than the magnetic-strip cards, which only require a signature.

RFID Cards and Badge Readers Another variation of smart card authentication includes *radio frequency identification (RFID) badges*. These cards contain an RFID chip (also called an RFID tag) with a radio antenna that can be carried by employees to allow access to secured facilities or computer systems and that can also be used to track user activity and location. These badges work wirelessly within a few meters and do not depend on line-of-sight communication—this tends to be more convenient than swipe cards. More important, no physical contact with the authenticating device is required as long as the RFID badge is within range of the device. You can also tie RFID badge authentication to the user network account to simplify multifactor authentication.

exam watch

CompTIA A+ 1101 exam Objective 1.1 includes a mention of near-field scanner features. Since near-field scanners are measurement devices to determine special distribution of electricity and don't have anything to do with computer security, we presume that this is a reference to near-field communication (NFC), which is used in badge readers to read data from an RFID chip. You learned about NFC in Chapters 14 and 16.

Key Fobs and Tokens Much like a smart card, a *key fob* is a small device containing a microchip, and you can use it to gain access to a secure facility or to log on to a computer or a network. Also called a *security token,* it has a form factor that suggests something you might attach to a key chain, as its name implies. A common procedure for using a key fob is to enter the PIN, which identifies the user as the owner of the key fob. Then, the key fob displays a string of characters, and the user enters the string into a keypad terminal or computer to gain access. This string is a *one-time password (OTP).* The key fob generates a different password at a prespecified interval, and this guarantees that the user has a unique, strong password protected from the vulnerabilities of ordinary user-generated passwords, which may be too easy to guess or which the user may write down somewhere to avoid having to memorize them.

Examples of key fobs are the RSA SecurID hardware security tokens from RSA Security, referred to in CompTIA A+ 1102 exam Objective 2.1 as *hard tokens.* These are very popular for authenticating to virtual private networks (VPNs), although you can also use them to authenticate to e-mail, your Windows desktop, and so on. To authenticate to a server, the user enters their PIN, and the device generates a numeric value every 60 seconds that corresponds to a server-side numeric value.

Installing support for a key fob involves installing an agent that runs on the local computer and a service on the domain controller, such as Active Directory. The agent acts as a front end to the authentication process, passing encrypted authentication information to the domain controller that responded to the authentication request. On the domain controller, the service decrypts the password and provides the password and the user name to the security components for authentication. If the password and user name match a domain user account, the user is allowed access to the resources that she has been granted permissions and rights to.

exam watch **Be sure you understand the differences between key fobs and smart cards.**

Soft Tokens One popular type of multifactor authentication is to require a *soft token* (software token) to be stored on a second device, such as a smartphone or tablet. When the user attempts to sign in, first the user name and password are verified, and then a request is sent via the Internet to the secondary device, asking for verification that this is a valid login attempt. An app on the secondary device manages the request, the user taps a prompt to confirm, and the sign-in completes on the original device. Popular software to manage this process includes Duo and RSA SecurID.

exam watch **Software tokens can be placed on a variety of general-purpose electronic devices. In contrast, hardware tokens require the credentials to be stored on a specific, dedicated hardware device, such as a USB key designed for that purpose.**

Authenticating with a Smartphone or Other Device "What you have" can not only include devices and objects but also what you have access to—another device that is known to be under your control. For example, if you use a smartphone to provide additional authentication, the authentication system might send a request to your smartphone in one of these ways:

- **Authenticator app** You might have an app installed that responds to an Internet or network ping by generating a code that you must type into another device (like a PC) or by prompting you to click a box to confirm that you are logging in on some other device.
- **E-mail message** You might receive an e-mail message that provides a code.
- **Short Message Service (SMS) message** You might receive a text message that provides a code or asks for a confirmation.
- **Voice call** You might receive a voice call that provides a code or asks for a confirmation.

Biometric Authentication: What You Are

Users can easily forget passwords or PINs and lose authentication devices such as key fobs. But each person can be uniquely identified by measurements of a physical or behavioral characteristic—a *biometric.* Biometrics are used both for physical access to buildings or areas and for logging on to computer networks. A logon based on one of these measurements is a *biometric logon.* Commonly used biometrics include fingerprints, *palmprints,* and *retinal scans* (a scan of the retina in a person's eye). A hardware device, such as a *retina scanner* or *fingerprint scanner* (also called a *fingertip scanner*), performs that scan. A fingerprint scanner is the least expensive of the biometric devices. The built-in fingerprint scanners are the size of a Universal Serial Bus (USB) port, with a slender scanning slot. External USB fingerprint scanners are available from several vendors.

Biometric scanners require both drivers and software to integrate with the computer's or network's security system to send the scanned information to the security components for processing. If the computer is a member of a domain, you must install special software on the domain controller servers. The software will update the domain accounts database with the biometric information for each user account for which this type of logon is enabled.

Anyone traveling with a laptop with sensitive data should look into purchasing a laptop with a built-in fingerprint scanner. Follow the manufacturer's instructions for installing the software and hardware. After installing the software, configure it to recognize your fingerprint and associate it with your user account. To do this, you will need to provide a user name and password. If your computer is a member of a workgroup, you will need to provide either the computer name or the workgroup name. If your computer is a member of a domain, you must provide the domain name and your user name and password in the domain. When the configuration utility is ready to scan your fingertip and associate it with your user account, it will prompt you. To do this, swipe your finger across the scanner's sensor. You can scan one or more fingers and use any one of them for login. In most cases, the scanner's associated software will also save passwords for applications and websites and associate them with your profile.

RADIUS and TACACS

Here are a couple of protocols that aren't directly applicable to supporting desktop PCs, but you should know about them in case you happen to get a question about one of them.

Remote Authentication Dial-In User Service (RADIUS) is a protocol set commonly used for network-access *authentication, authorization, and accounting (AAA)*. It carries authentication traffic from the network device to the authentication server. It operates on UDP ports 1812 and 1813 or 1645 and 1646. It performs both authentication and authorization in each transaction; the two are not separate. Its primary use is network access; many ISPs use it to manage user authentication when connecting subscribers to the Internet via their servers.

TACACS stands for Terminal Access Controller Access-Control System. It is a protocol set that was originally developed for communicating with Unix terminals. Cisco released their version of it, called TACACS+, in the early 1990s. The main benefit of TACACS+ over the older RADIUS protocol set is its ability to separate the three A's. That's useful because you might need to authenticate (when you initially connect) far less frequently than you authorize (perhaps with every command issued). It operates on TCP port 49. Its primary use is device administration.

Apple IDs and Corporate Accounts

Some companies (primarily those with a mostly Mac-centric workplace) created managed *Apple IDs* for employees to use for business purposes. These IDs are managed separately from the employees' personal Apple IDs, but may be associated with the same e-mail address and phone number as their personal IDs. The company can impose restrictions on these *corporate accounts,* blocking them from services such as Apple Pay and Wallet, for example.

Managing Local User and Group Accounts in Windows

Each Windows user must have an account. In a Windows network, the account can be a local account (existing only on the individual PC) or a centralized domain account (also called an Active Directory account). Of course, whenever possible, use centralized accounts so each user only needs to sign in to the centralized database for authentication, after which, as he or she attempts to access resources on other computers in the domain, the system performs authorization to verify the user's level of access to the resource.

Each installation of Windows for desktop PCs, laptops, and tablets maintains a local accounts database containing *local user accounts* and *local group accounts.* A user account represents a single person, whereas a local group account can contain multiple users and other groups. When the computer is a member of a Windows domain, a local group may contain domain users or domain group accounts to give domain users and groups access to resources on the local computer. Logging on with a local account gives you access only to the resources on that computer, although you may have access to other resources on your network through relationships.

Windows 8 and later versions enable you to sign in with a *Microsoft account,* which is an e-mail address and password combination that serves as your credentials to an account with one of Microsoft's online services, such as Xbox Live or OneDrive. You are still signing on with a local account because the Microsoft account is associated with the local account. The benefit is that you have access to local resources as well as all online resources granted to the Microsoft account.

When any user logs on to a Windows computer for the first time, a local user profile is created for that user, as well as a set of personal folders for that user's data. A *user profile* includes registry settings for all personal settings for that user.

Each version of Windows surveyed in this book has several graphical user interface (GUI) tools for administering local accounts. There's at least one (two in some Windows versions) that is very simplified and hides many accounts and the complexity from you. There's another that lets you see all local user and group accounts. As you read this section, you may want to open some or all of these tools.

The simple account management tool is User Accounts, accessed from the Control Panel. The Windows 10 version is shown in Figure 20-1. The pane on the right contains links to enable you to make changes to your account. Because the logged-on user is an administrator,

FIGURE 20-1 Managing Windows 10 user accounts from the Control Panel

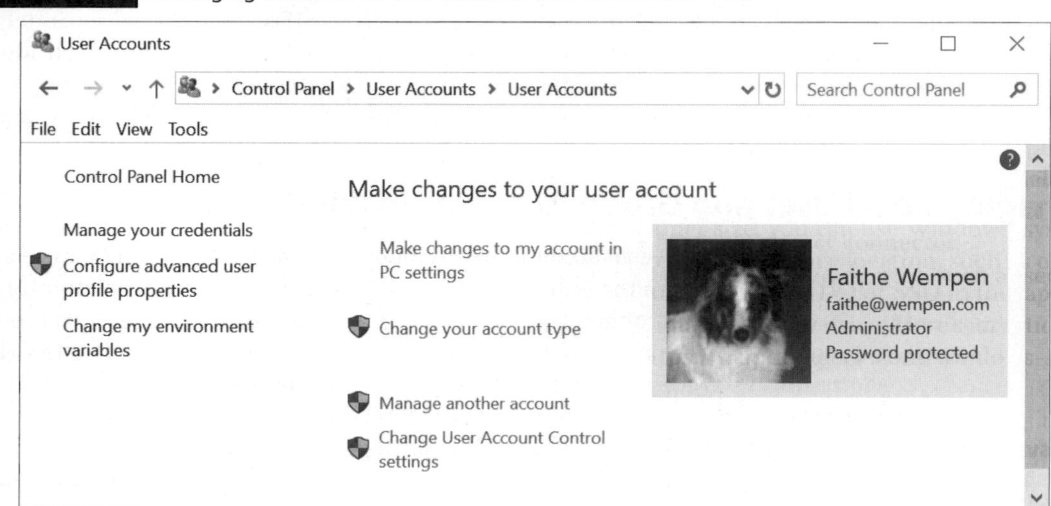

the contents pane also includes two links that only an administrator can use: Manage Another Account and Change User Account Control Settings. (You'll learn about User Account Control Settings later in this chapter.) The task pane on the left contains links to more tasks.

There is an even simpler alternative: the Family & Other Users page of the Settings app. In Windows 10 (shown in Figure 20-2), the path to it is Settings | Accounts | Family & Other Users. As you can see in Figure 20-2, you can select an account to manage from among the local accounts on this PC, and you can create new accounts.

In all Windows versions, the more complex tool has remained much the same, and it is the Local Users and Groups node of the Computer Management console, shown in Figure 20-3. To open this, right-click the Start button and choose Computer Management. This tool is available only in the Pro, Enterprise, and Education editions.

Built-In Accounts

Windows has several built-in user and group accounts, plus the installation of certain services and applications automatically creates some users and groups needed for the service or program, but not necessarily directly used by a human user. Notice in Figure 20-3 that there are several built-in accounts, including Administrator, DefaultAccount, Guest, and WDAGUtilityAccount.

FIGURE 20-2 Managing Windows 10 user accounts from the Settings app

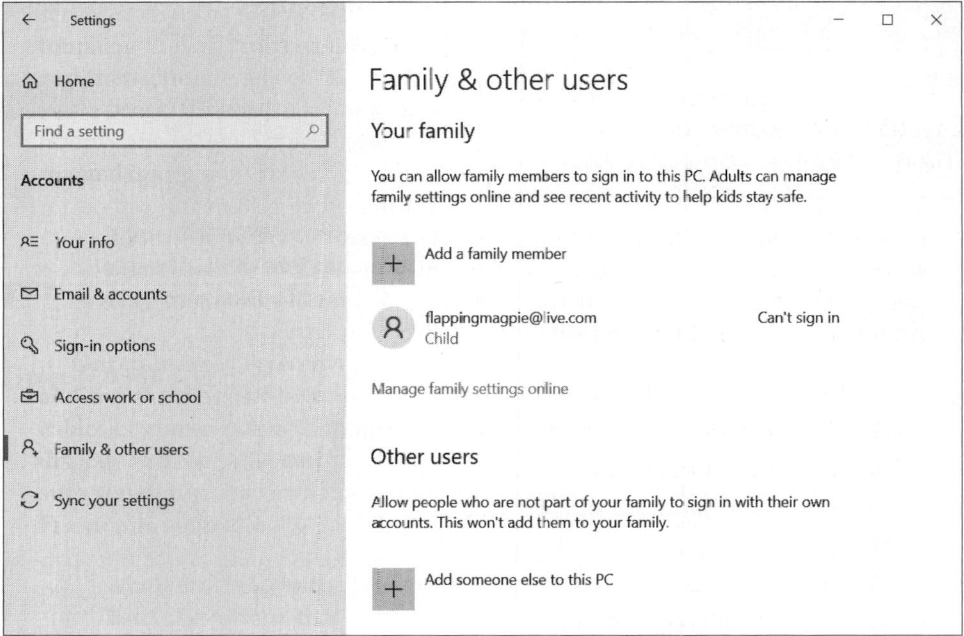

FIGURE 20-3 The Computer Management console showing the local users

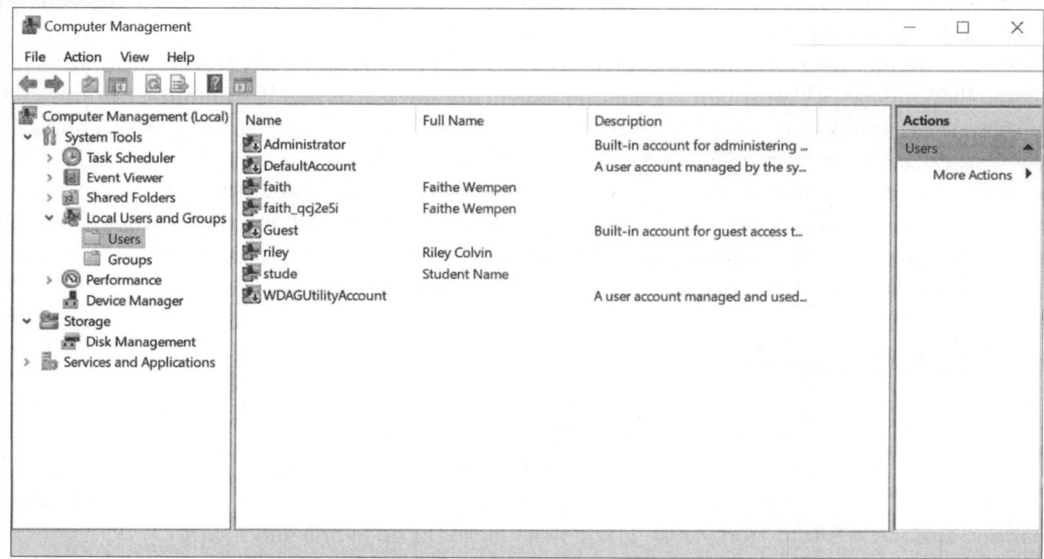

> **exam watch**
>
> **The four groups described in this section are the ones specified in CompTIA A+ 1102 exam Objective 2.5.**

Built-In Groups

There are also many built-in groups, as shown in Figure 20-4. The important group accounts to understand are Administrators, Users, Guests, and Power Users.

The *Administrators* group has full control over the entire system and can perform all tasks on a computer, from installing a device driver to creating other security accounts. Any account added to this group gains those permissions. *Administrator* is a built-in account that is a member of the Administrators group. It cannot be renamed, disabled, or deleted. Administrators can do the following:

- Create any type of local user account
- Change permissions for any local user account
- Modify any local user account
- Install new hardware and software
- Run any program
- Modify all system settings
- Upgrade and repair Windows

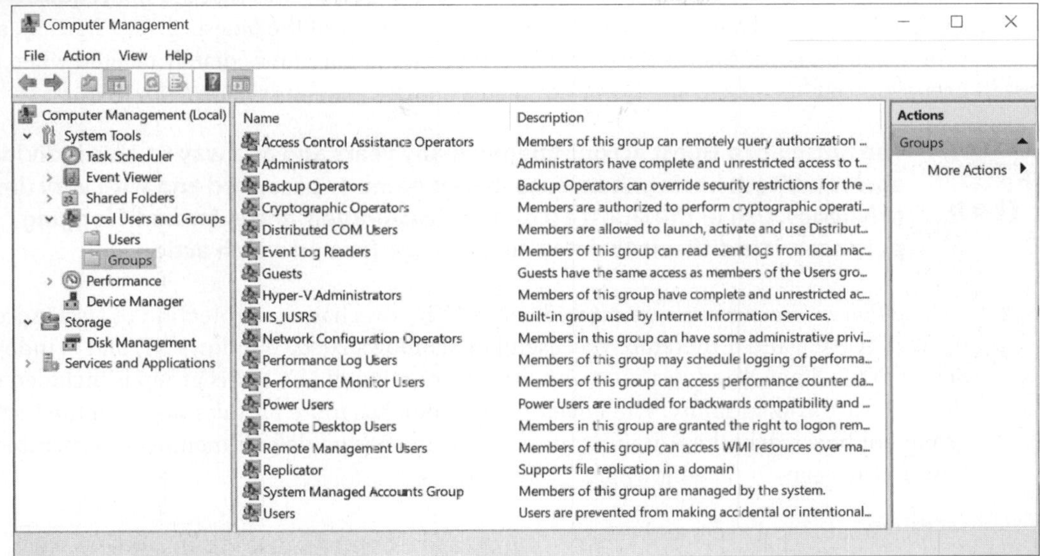

FIGURE 20-4 The Computer Management console showing the local groups

- Back up and restore Windows system files and user data files
- Take ownership of any other local user's files
- Manage security and auditing logs

To allow multiple users to perform administrative functions on a computer (or network), rather than use the built-in Administrator account, make each individual account a member of the Administrators group. Then, if you ever need to find out who performed a certain administrative action (most are automatically logged), they will be identified in the logs by user name.

Do not confuse the Administrator account (that is, the account with the user name of Administrator, shown in Figure 20-3) with an account that belongs to the Administrators group (shown in Figure 20-4).

The built-in *Users* group has limited permissions, preventing members of this group from making system-wide changes, although they can run most applications that do not change system settings.

The *Guests* group has the same limited permissions of the Users group, but the default member of this group, the built-in *Guest* account, is further restricted to have fewer privileges than those granted by the Guests group and is disabled by default. You cannot delete the

Guest account, but you can rename and disable it. Another name for this type of account is *anonymous,* as used with older File Transfer Protocol (FTP) sites that did not require a user to sign in to upload and download files. When a member of the Guests group signs in, a user profile and personal folders are created for that user but are immediately deleted when the user signs out.

The notion of a Guest account began many years ago as a way to give individuals access without having them enter a user name or password and with very limited privileges. Use of the Guest account is discouraged, since, for audit logging purposes, it is difficult to determine who performed which action.

The *Power Users* group was created before Windows had the protection of User Account Control (UAC), and it therefore was useful in Windows 2000, Windows XP, and Windows Server 2003. Since Windows Vista and the introduction of UAC, this group is included only for backward compatibility. The Power Users group has more permissions than the Users group but fewer than the Administrators group and has no default members. A member of Power Users can do the following:

- Create local users and groups
- Modify local user and group accounts created by that power user
- Remove users from the Power Users, Users, and Guests groups
- Install most applications
- Create, manage, and delete local printers
- Create and delete file shares

Windows Account Types

When you set up a new account, you choose an account type for it. In this context, *type* refers to the permissions granted to the account—in other words, the groups into which it is granted membership by default.

A *Standard user account* is appropriate for an "ordinary" user without Administrator status. This account is a member of the local Users group. A user signed in with a Standard account can change her password and other personal settings but cannot change computer settings, install or remove software and hardware, or perform other system-wide tasks. In contrast, a user signed in with an account that is an *Administrator account* type can perform system-wide tasks.

When you create new accounts using the PC Settings app, the account is automatically a Standard one. However, after creation, you can edit the account to change it to Administrator, as shown in Figure 20-5. You can also edit account types and groups from the Local Users and Groups settings in Computer Management.

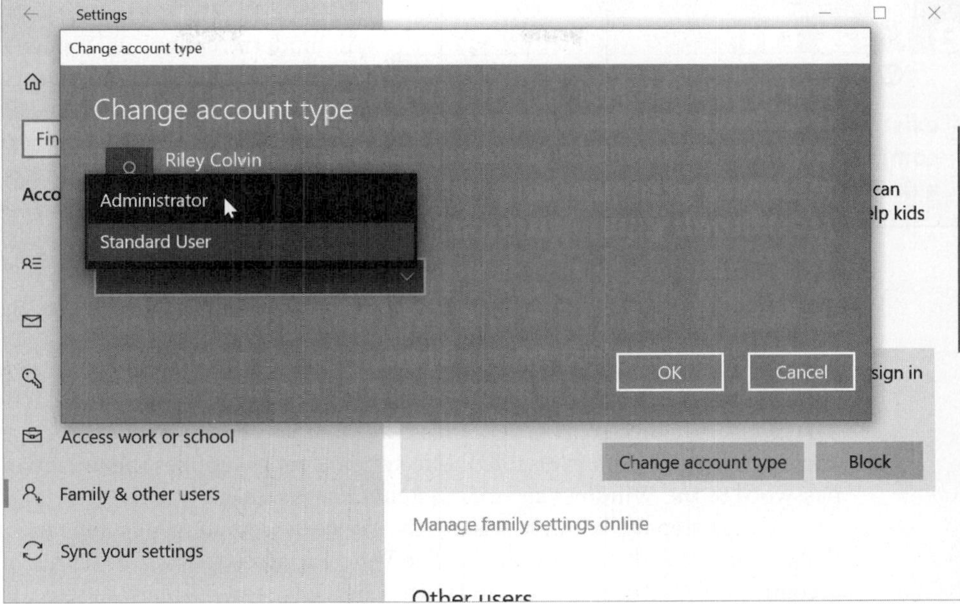

FIGURE 20-5 Change a user's account type from Standard User to Administrator if needed.

Microsoft has long recommended not using the Administrator account as a day-to-day account. This is because prior to the introduction of UAC in Windows Vista, if you signed in with an account belonging to the Administrators group (the Administrator account or other account), a program could install without your knowledge and run with full administrative rights to your computer. That is how a lot of malware infected Windows. The User Account Control feature alerts the user—even an administrator—when a program attempts to install or make other unauthorized changes to Windows. Later in this chapter, you will learn more about UAC, including how it works and how to configure it.

When you initially install Windows, the Setup application walks you through creating a user account. This account is a member of the Administrators group. That's necessary because it's important to have at least one account with Administrator privileges on a PC. Other accounts you create can have Standard or Administrator privileges, as you prefer.

Special Groups

Special groups are groups created by the Windows security system, and no user can create or modify these groups. The membership of a special group is predefined, and the group is available to you only when you assign permissions or rights. A few important special groups are *Creator Owner* (membership consists of the user who created a file or folder), *System* (the operating system), and the *Everyone* group, which includes all users on a network, even those who have not been authenticated.

Local accounts always exist on Windows computers, whether the computer is a member of a workgroup or in a domain.

Windows Sign-In

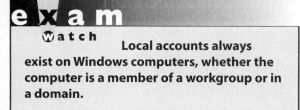

All modern versions of Windows require a sign-in, meaning you must provide a user name and password that are verified against a security database, either local or on a server on the network. Even your home computer that perhaps boots up right to the Windows desktop without asking for a user name or password is actually performing a sign-in.

If your computer is not a member of a Windows domain, but rather a member of a workgroup, and you are only signing in to the local computer, then it is possible to configure it to start up right to the desktop without a password prompt or account selection. This scenario occurs when there is only one user account on a computer and it does not have a password assigned to it—a very unsecure situation, but typical for a home computer—and the Guest account is disabled. The system simply supplies the user name and blank password to the Windows security system during sign-in.

The next step up, security-wise, is the Welcome screen, which appears on computers that are not on a Windows domain. The Welcome screen shows the names of all the local user accounts (except Administrator and Guest) and only requires that you select the user name and enter the password. When you start up a Windows PC, a Lock screen appears with a graphic and the current date and time. Press any key to move past that to the Welcome screen. Then click the icon for the desired user account and type the password. If you don't sign in within a short time (a minute or so), the Lock screen reappears.

The last sign-in method is the Security dialog box. If a computer is a member of a domain, it uses the Security dialog box by default, and another level of security requires the user to press the CTRL-ALT-DELETE key combination before this dialog box will appear. To sign in, you enter your user name, password, and (when appropriate) domain name into this dialog box.

exam Watch

In CompTIA A+ 1102 exam Objective 2.6, the "Use timeout/screen lock" topic refers to Windows' ability to revert to the Lock screen if you don't sign in quickly after pressing a key to clear the Lock screen or pressing CTRL-ALT-DELETE (if on a domain). When you use the Lock Computer feature, described in the next section, the Lock screen reappears.

Rebuilding a User Account

Sometimes user accounts get corrupted and the user cannot sign in, or can sign in but the Start menu doesn't work. Another possible symptom of a corrupted user account is that all the Microsoft Store apps fail to run.

Before trying to rebuild a user account, first salvage as much of its data and settings as you can. Sign in using an Administrator privileges account, browse to the profile's folder in the C:\Users folder, and copy out everything you can. You can then copy it back again after rebuilding the user account.

If it's a roaming account profile (that is, an Active Directory profile), the system administrator must remove or rename the roaming profile, and the local copy of the profile must be deleted.

If it's a local user account, sign in as a different user who has Administrator rights. Open the Control Panel and navigate to System And Security | System. Click Advanced System Settings in the navigation pane at the left, opening the System Properties dialog box. On the Advanced tab, in the User Profiles section, click Settings. Select the account that you need to rebuild and click Copy To to copy it to another location for backup. Then click Delete to remove it. When you reboot, you'll still see that account as available to sign in to. When you sign in to it, you get a fresh copy of the profile.

Best Practices to Secure a Workstation

This section covers many of the best practices for securing a workstation listed under 1102 exam Objective 2.6.

Require and Set Strong Passwords

Require and use passwords wherever possible. A *strong password* is one that meets certain criteria that make it difficult to crack. Passwords that do not meet these criteria are weak and ineffective and provide negligible security.

The criteria for a strong password have changed over time, as people with malicious intent (hackers) create more and more techniques and tools for discovering passwords. One definition of a strong password is one that contains at least eight characters; includes a combination of letters, numbers, and other symbols (such as _, -, $, and so on); and is easy for you to remember but difficult for others to guess.

For instance, some people take a song title or part of the lyrics from a favorite song, remove the spaces, and substitute numbers for some of the letters. For instance, the lyrics "Dance while the music goes on" (from the ABBA song "Dance") would turn into the password "dan2ewh1lethemu3i2g0es0n." The longer the better, and if nonalphanumeric characters are permitted, throw in a few of them, too, to make it even stronger.

Use strong passwords for the following account types:

- Banks, investments, credit cards, and online payment providers
- E-mail
- Work-related
- Online auction sites and retailers
- Sites where you have to provide personal information

Be sure you remember that passwords are case sensitive but user names are not.

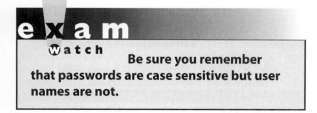

Every account should have a unique user name (if possible) and a unique password (always). Many websites require your e-mail address as the user name, so these will not be unique.

The Windows authentication system does not require case sensitivity for user names, but it does for passwords. So as long as you enter the correct characters for your user name, case does not matter. Case is very important for passwords, which is why Windows login will warn you when the CAPS LOCK key is turned on.

Windows includes other sign-in variations such as Picture Password (which consists of tapping or clicking certain spots on a photo), facial recognition (through a feature called Windows Hello Face), fingerprint recognition (through Windows Hello Fingerprint), and entering a PIN (Windows Hello PIN). Each user must have a user name and password as the main sign-in method, however; all those others are optional local alternatives.

All the local sign-in alternative methods are actually very secure, even though some of them might be easier to crack than a regular password (a four-digit PIN, for example). That's because they are set up only for local sign-in, not network access. Therefore, anyone wanting to hack the system using them must have physical access to the machine.

Lock the PC or Sign Out

To prevent unauthorized local users from sitting down at an unoccupied workstation, users who are stepping away from their computer for a few minutes should lock it. On a Windows PC you can click Start | *username* | Lock or press CTRL-ALT-DELETE and then click Lock. Locking does not close any open applications or data files.

If a user is going to be gone for a longer time (such as overnight), they should sign out. Signing out closes open applications and data files, so even if someone were able to unlock the PC, they still would not have ready access to what was being worked on.

Enable Screen Saver Lock

If you have sensitive data on your computer or available to your user account over a network and you use a screen saver, be sure to require that you must sign in again to resume. You should also shorten the wait period if you are using your screen saver rather than locking your computer (in our view, Lock Computer is a better practice). Then if you walk away from your computer and the screen saver turns on, it will require a password to return to the desktop. Otherwise, anyone passing by your desk can simply touch the mouse and keyboard and then access everything on your local computer and network that you can access.

To enable the screen saver password, open Control Panel and type **screen saver** in the Search box. In the results list, select Change Screen Saver. This will open the Screen Saver Settings dialog box shown in Figure 20-6. Click to place a check in the check box in the middle of the dialog box labeled On Resume, Display Logon Screen.

FIGURE 20-6

Display the logon screen after resuming from screen saver use.

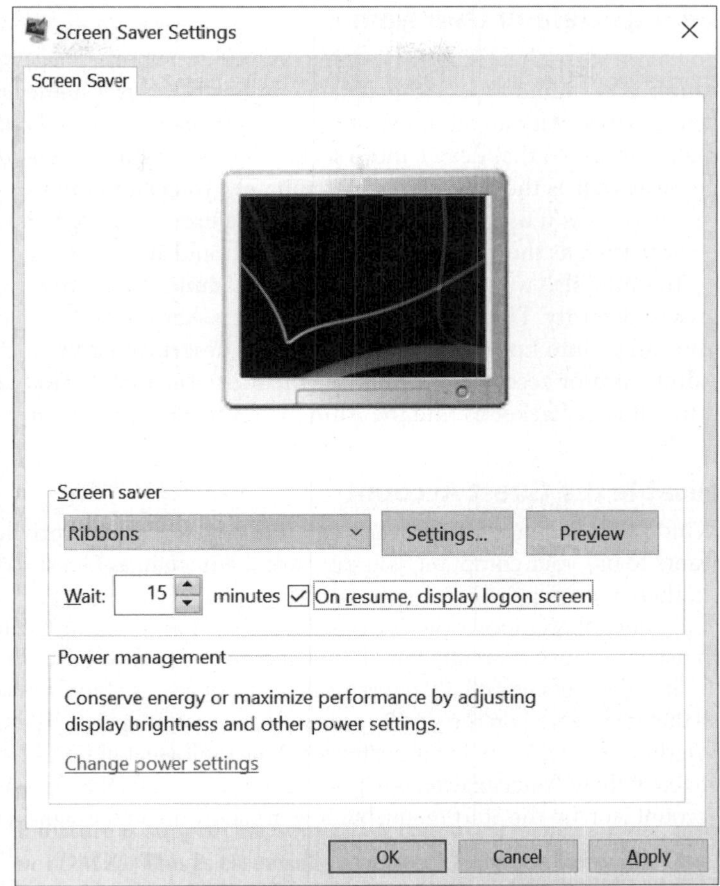

Lock Computer is a better practice than enabling the password for the screen saver, even though "Use screensaver locks" is listed as a best practice in CompTIA A+ 1102 exam Objective 2.6.

Restrict User Permissions

Users are often tempted when sharing files and printers to grant full access to these resources to everyone, but that can make for vulnerable "Swiss cheese" security—that is, full of holes. In Chapter 21 you will learn how to apply permissions more selectively, giving each person or group just the level of permission they need to accomplish their work without giving them too much. This is the *principle of least privilege,* and it is a key factor in creating a robust security system.

Change Default User Names

You learned in Chapter 17 that when configuring a wireless access point (WAP) or broadband router, you should change the default administrator user name and password. These devices usually come with an administrator user name of Admin, and changing it and the password makes access to that device more secure because someone would need to guess the user name as well as the password. Unfortunately, you cannot do this on the many websites that require that you use your e-mail address as a user name, but you do have this option on devices such as those mentioned, and you should always change such default user names.

You may also want to change the default admin user account and password as well for greater security. The default admin account is Administrator, and it is disabled by default. You can go into Local Users and Groups, as described earlier in this chapter, right-click the Administrator account, and choose Rename to rename it. This can make it a little more difficult for a hacker to find the Administrator account and target it for exploitation.

Disable the Guest Account

Windows has a built-in Guest account that has very limited privileges. If an untrusted person wants to use your computer, you can have them log in as Guest so they can't cause any trouble (in theory, anyway).

By default, Windows disables the local Guest account, and Microsoft encourages you not to use it because it's really not all that secure and gives a false sense of security

In earlier versions of Windows, you could actually use the Guest account by configuring it so that it appeared on the sign-in screen as an account option. The Guest account still exists in Windows 10 and 11, but you can't use it. You'll still see it in Local Users and Groups, and you can enable it there. You can even see it on the list of accounts that appears when you click your user account icon on the Start menu, but it won't show up on the sign-in screen, and you can't sign in to it. However, you can create your own limited-privileges account in Windows. Just create a new account and then assign it to the Guests group in Local Users and Groups. Because Guest is a reserved name, you can't call it Guest; call it something similar, like Visitor or Tourist.

Set Password Expiration

An old password is less secure than a newly set one because nobody will have had time to snoop or guess it. For this reason, you may want to set user account passwords to expire after a certain amount of time. For example, some organizations set an expiration period of six months to one year. This type of group policy is typically set at the domain level, rather than for individual workstations.

Restrict Login Times

You can also set restrictions on when users can log in to a system. This prevents people from coming in during off-hours to access systems for which they are not authorized. If your authentication processes are robust, this is unlikely to occur, but for systems containing sensitive data, it adds an extra layer of security. For example, if the company is closed on Sundays, you could set a group policy to prevent Standard users from signing in on Sundays. This kind of restriction is controlled via the Local Security Policy editor or Group Policy Editor.

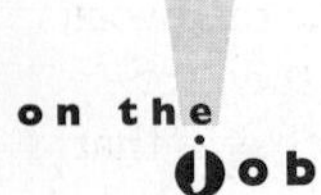

Be cautious when setting a sign-in time restriction, because there's always going to be that exceptional user who needs in the system when nobody else is there, and if he can't get in, you're going to get an irate phone call over the weekend.

Failed Attempts Lockout

To prevent hackers from repeatedly trying to guess the password on an account, you can implement a failed attempts lockout policy using the Local Security Policy editor or Group Policy Editor. (See the upcoming Exercise 20-1 to try it out.) You can set an account to be locked after a certain number of failed guesses, either permanently (until an administrator resets it) or for a certain number of minutes.

Disable Autorun/AutoPlay

The *AutoPlay* feature (called *Autorun* in some earlier Windows versions) enables Windows to automatically find and run the content on removable media when it connects to a computer. The AutoPlay applet in Control Panel displays a long list of media and content types, and you can choose exactly how each is treated when it is placed in your computers. Beware, however, that AutoPlay can make you vulnerable to malware infections, because removable media is a vector for malware. The safest thing to do is to disable AutoPlay and simply choose the action you want each time you place removable media in your computer. Figure 20-7 shows the Windows AutoPlay Control Panel applet; clear the Use AutoPlay For All Media And Devices check box to disable the feature. There is also a simplified version of these controls in the Settings app.

Adjusting User Account Control Settings

UAC is a Windows feature that protects against programs making unwanted changes to system operation without your consent. Its primary function is to prevent certain types of malware from installing new programs and changing system files.

UAC prevents Standard users from making system changes that affect more than just their own account. For example, it blocks them from installing most new software and accessing certain Control Panel settings. If you examine the options in the Control Panel, you'll notice that some of them have a little blue and yellow shield next to them. These options cannot be used by Standard users. However, there's a workaround, in case you are logged into a Standard account by choice and you also have an Administrator account. When you try to access one of these options as a Standard user, you are prompted to enter the sign-in credentials of an Administrator, and if you're able to do that, the operation continues apace, without your having to switch accounts.

FIGURE 20-7 To turn off AutoPlay, clear the check box labeled Use AutoPlay For All Media And Devices.

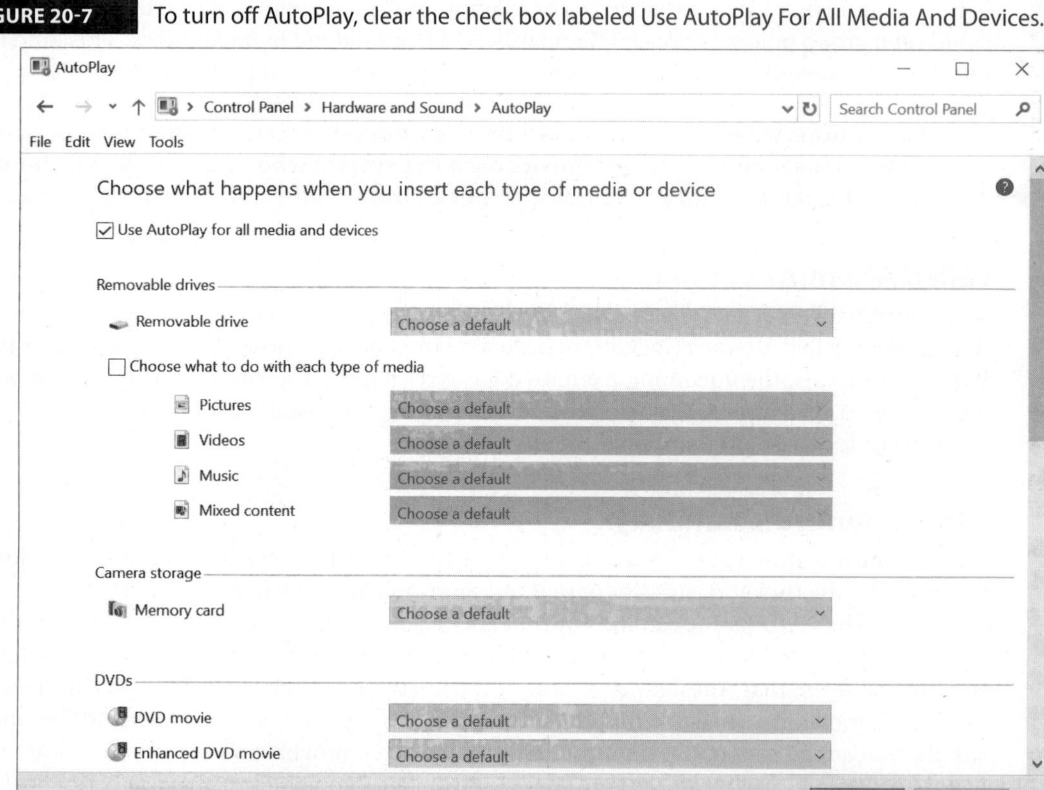

In the User Access Control Settings in the Control Panel, you can adjust UAC's level of sensitivity—that is, when UAC will interrupt your work to ask if a certain change is okay to make. There are four possible UAC settings. Finding the right UAC setting is a matter of compromise between convenience and security. A low setting never interrupts what you are doing but provides little benefit. A high setting provides the greatest security, but you may have to click additional prompts when you want to make any system changes that affect more than just the active user.

To access User Account Control, make sure you are signed in with an account that has Administrator account privileges, and then open the Control Panel and follow this path: User Accounts | User Accounts | Change User Account Control Settings. In the User Account Control Settings dialog box (Figure 20-8), drag the slider up or down to adjust the setting. You can read about each setting to the right of the slider as you select it. For most PCs, the next-to-highest setting (the default) is appropriate.

FIGURE 20-8 Adjust the User Account Control settings.

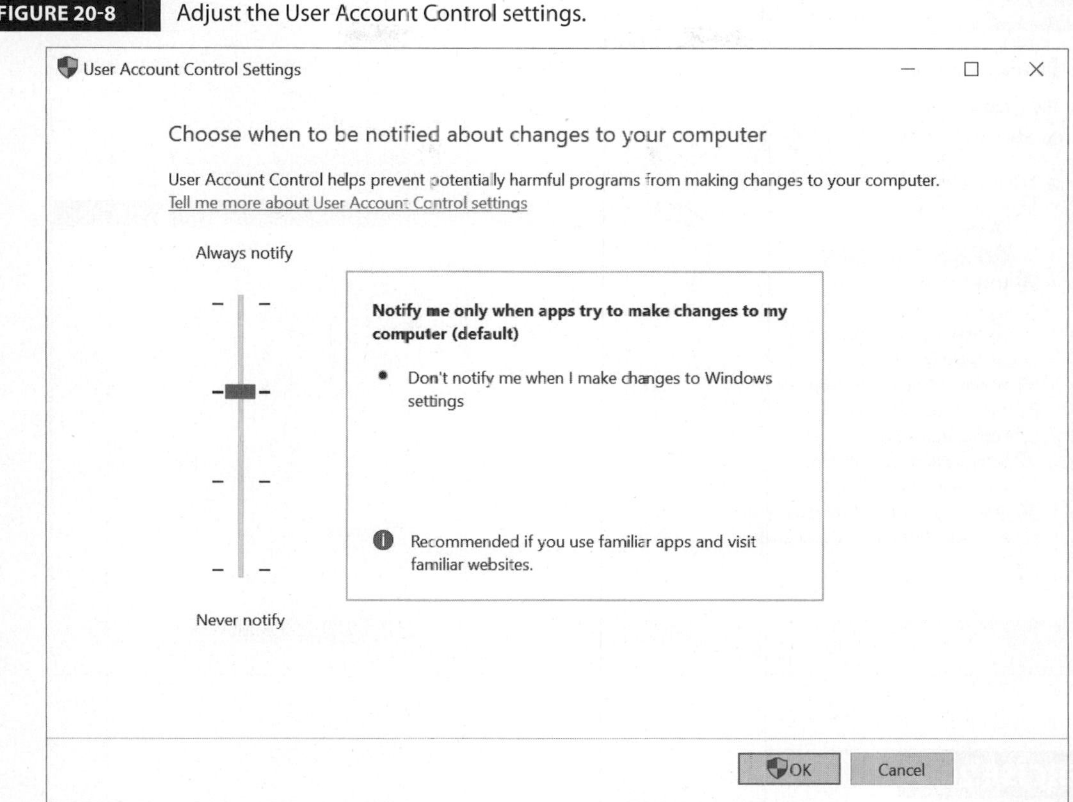

Setting Local Security Policies

The Local Security Policy app enables you to fine-tune various security settings. Be careful with this, because experimenting willy-nilly can result in frustrating, difficult-to-troubleshoot access problems. It can be accessed as an MMC snap-in or by searching for Local Security Policy using the taskbar's Search box. It is available only in Pro, Enterprise, and Education editions.

Because this chapter is focused on user accounts, let's look at the policies related to that. As you can see in Figure 20-9, the Account Policies section (selected in the left pane) contains two groups of policies: Password Policy and Account Lockout Policy. You might set an account lockout policy to prevent brute-force password guessing by hackers, for example. Exercise 20-1 walks you through configuring an account lockout policy.

While you're in the Local Security Policy app, take a look at Local Policies | Security Options to get a feel for the breadth of settings you can adjust. For example, notice that you can rename the Administrator account or the Guest account, restrict CD-ROM access to locally logged-on users only, and prevent users from installing printer drivers, to name only a few.

FIGURE 20-9 Edit security policies via the Local Security Policy app.

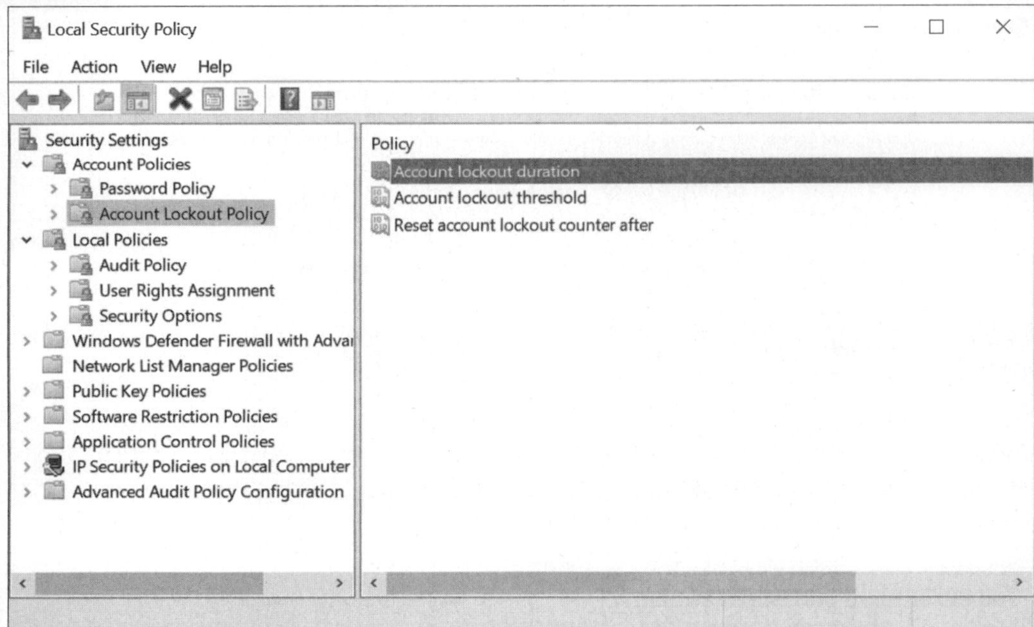

EXERCISE 20-1

Using the Local Security Policy Editor

In this exercise, you set up an account lockout policy so that people cannot repeatedly try to guess an account's password on the local machine.

1. Click Start and then type **Local Security**. Click Local Security Policy in the search results.
2. In the left pane, expand Account Policies if needed, and click Account Lockout Policy.
3. In the right pane, double-click Account Lockout Threshold, opening the Account Lockout Threshold Properties dialog box.
4. Increment the counter on the Local Security Setting tab to 7, and click OK. A Suggested Value Changes dialog box opens, suggesting an Account Lockout Duration and Reset Account Lockout Counter After values.
5. Click OK to accept the suggested values.
6. Close the Local Security Policy window, or if desired, change the Account Lockout Threshold back to its original value first.

Using Windows Credential Manager

Windows allows you to store credentials to automatically sign in to servers, websites, and certain applications. These are stored in local folders, called *vaults*. The user of these locally stored credentials provides a *single sign-on (SSO)*, meaning that a user only need provide credentials (usually user name and password) once and have access to multiple resources. The *Credential Manager* applet in the Control Panel enables you to directly manage your credentials. Figure 20-10 shows the Windows 10 Credential Manager. We expanded one of the credentials—for connecting to a computer named INSPIRON17—so that you can see the links to edit or remove these credentials. The Edit option allows you to change the user name and password.

Credential Manager in Windows allows you to securely store login credentials, including user names and passwords. macOS has a similar tool called Keychain which can store passwords and certificates.

FIGURE 20-10 Credential Manager in Windows 10

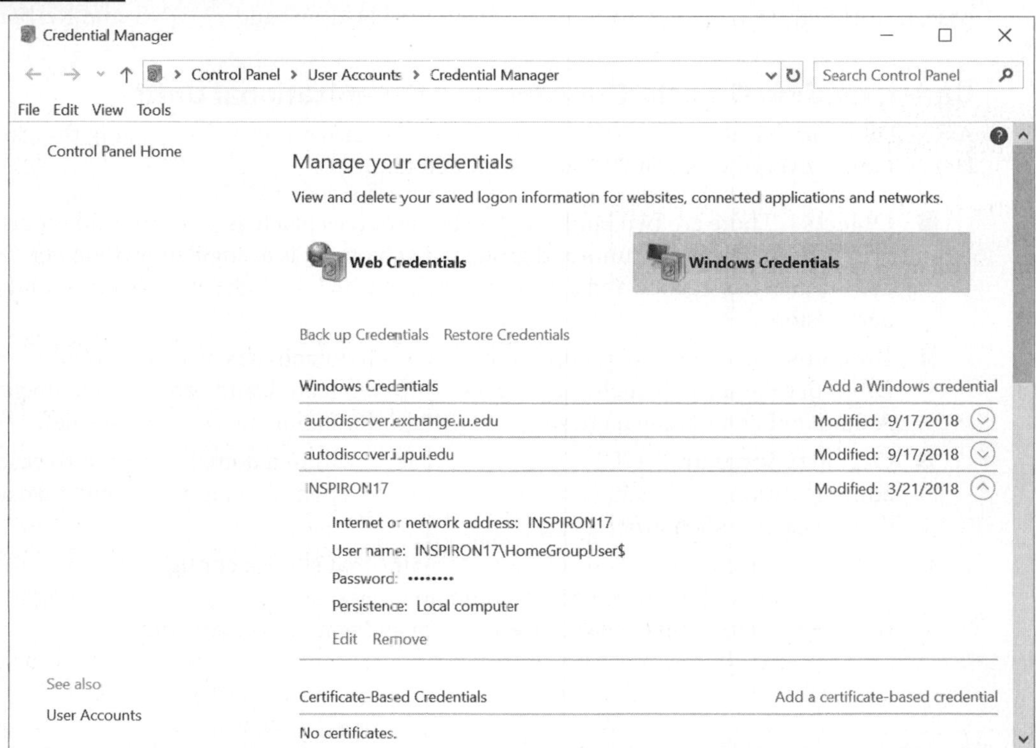

With single sign-on (SSO) a user can log in to multiple apps during a session while only authenticating one time.

Managing Domain User Accounts

Most people who use Active Directory have some formal training in server management, and you'll need some if you are expected to serve as a network administrator. There are entire courses devoted to this subject that reach far beyond the CompTIA A+ exam objectives. However, because CompTIA has chosen to add some Active Directory topics to the latest A+ 220-1102 exam, we'll briefly address those topics here.

What Is Active Directory?

In a nutshell, Active Directory is the software that runs on a Windows domain controller. All user names and passwords are stored in its database for ease of management and also physical security, since presumably the domain controller hardware is in a more secure location than the various clients that connect to it. Active Directory Domain Services (AD DS) authenticates users and authorizes them for certain permissions, depending on the policies configured on the server.

Active Directory is more than just a user authentication and authorization service, however. It also provides a framework for other services, such as certificate management, rights management, BitLocker, Remote Desktop Services, and SharePoint Server. Protocol-wise, it uses Lightweight Directory Access Protocol (LDAP) v2 and v3, DNS, and Kerberos.

Understanding Objects, Domains, and Organizational Units

Active Directory has its own unique set of vocabulary for naming and managing things. Here's a quick overview of some terms you should know:

- **Objects** There are two kinds of objects: resources (such as printers) and security principles (such as accounts and groups). Each object is a single user or object. Each object has a name and a set of attributes, which includes its properties and its permissions.
- **Domains** Domains are groups of objects. Each domain has its own Active Directory database (which can be backed up, replicated, and otherwise managed). A domain has a unique namespace, much like domain names on the Internet.
- **Organizational unit (OU)** A group of objects within a domain, created to ease its administration. For example, within the office.xyz.com domain you might have an OU for each branch office.
- **Tree** A tree consists of one or more domains that share a contiguous namespace—in other words, they share part of a domain namespace. For example, you might have two domains in a single tree: office.xyz.com and warehouse.xyz.com.

- **Forest** A forest is a collection of trees that share certain top-level features, such as logical structure, directory scheme, and a common global catalog.
- **Security group** A security group is just what it sounds like: a group of users who have certain security permissions.

Of the terms just introduced, the three that are directly referenced in an exam objective (1102: 2.1) are domain, organizational unit, and security group. The others are useful to know because they help make sense of those three.

Understanding Kerberos

Kerberos is a centralized authentication system that mutually authenticates servers and users. It runs as a Key Distribution Center (KDC) server. It has three components:

- The authentication server (AS) performs the authentication and decides who gets a ticket (via the ticket granting server) for access to the network.
- The database contains a list of valid users and their permissions; the AS uses this when determining who should have access.
- The ticket-granting server (TGS) issues the ticket that allows network access.

You do not need to know the inner workings of Kerberos, but you should know that it is a user authentication system used on Active Directory networks.

Creating an Active Directory User Account

There are many ways to set up users in Active Directory, depending on the server version and your preferences. For example, you can create individual user accounts manually, either in a GUI or at a command prompt, or you can write scripts to automate the process of creating or importing multiple accounts at once.

Here is a basic process you can follow: Open Microsoft Active Directory Users and Computers (Start | Programs | Administrative Tools | Active Directory Users And Computers). Your existing client accounts appear, arranged by OU. Right-click the desired OU, point to New, and click User. Fill in the fields in the dialog box that appears.

You can create new users via a command prompt:

```
New-ADUser -Name username
```

However, because you will probably want to set multiple properties when creating the new account, you might find it easier to use the GUI.

Disabling or Deleting an Account

Deleting an account removes it permanently; do this if you are sure the user isn't coming back. You might disable a user account (rather than delete it) if an employee is going on hiatus but will eventually come back.

To delete a user account, open Active Directory Users and Computers, and click Users in the console tree (under the appropriate domain if there is more than one). Right-click the desired user and choose Delete from the context menu. Click Yes to confirm.

Some people recommend that you not delete an Active Directory account, but instead disable it so it can be resurrected in the future if any historical information needs to be retrieved from it. If someone new is being hired to replace the former worker, you could also rename the account with the new person's name so the account history is preserved.

To enable or disable a user via the Windows interface, open Active Directory Users and Computers, and in the console tree, under the appropriate domain node, click Users. Then right-click the user and choose Disable Account. Repeat this process, choosing Enable Account, to enable an account.

To use the PowerShell command line to delete an account, type

```
Remove-ADUser -identity UserDN
```

where *UserDN* is the name of the user to be deleted.

To use the PowerShell command line to disable or enable an account, type

```
dsmod user UserDN -disabled {yes|no}
```

where *UserDN* is the name of the user to be disabled or enabled. Don't use the curly brackets around yes or no; just type one or the other of those. For example, to disable the account TommyX:

```
dsmod user TommyX -disabled yes
```

Resetting a Password

Users are always forgetting their passwords, it seems. Some networks have a self-service password reset enabled, but in case yours doesn't, you can reset a password manually.

To enable or disable a user via the Windows interface, open Active Directory Users and Computers, and in the console tree, under the appropriate domain node, click Users. Then right-click the user and choose Reset Password. Then type and confirm the password.

The password you specify can be either permanent (inform the user what it is) or temporary. If you set the User Must Change Password at Next Login option, the user will be prompted to change the password to one of his or her choice.

To use the PowerShell command line, type

```
dsmod user UserDN -pwd newpassword -mustchpwd {yes|no}
```

where *UserDN* is the name of the user and *newpassword* is the new password. Again, don't use the curly brackets around yes or no; just type one or the other of those. For example, to reset the password for the account TommyX to PleaseChangeMe so the user must change the password at the next login, type the following:

```
dsmod user TommyX -pwd PleaseChangeMe -mustchpwd yes
```

Assigning a Home Folder

A *home folder* is a starting point for a signed-in user, much like the Documents folder is a default save location for local Windows PC users for saving data files. By specifying home folders, you can simplify Active Directory administration by collecting the user's files in a single location. If you don't assign a home folder to a user account, the default local home folder is used, such as the Documents folder.

To assign a home folder to a user, from Active Directory Users and Computers, right-click the user account and click Properties. In the Properties dialog box, click Profile. To assign a home folder on a network server, click Connect and then specify a drive letter. In the To box, type a path (such as \\server\users\myname). Click OK.

You can also assign a home folder from a command prompt using the net user command:

```
net user myname /homedir:\\server\myname$
```

Understanding Folder Redirection

Folder redirection is a way of configuring Active Directory accounts so that whichever PC a user signs in to, it seems like his private folders are following him and appear on his local machine as if they were actually local. You can set up folder redirection via Group Policy Objects (GPO). Folder redirection works by copying user profile data from the server to the local PC when the user signs on and then copies any changes made to it back to the server when the user logs off. To set it up, you create a security group for folder redirection using Server Manager and then create a file share for redirected folders (again from Server Manager). Then you create a Group Policy Object for folder redirection via Group Policy Management. For more detailed instructions, see https://docs.microsoft.com/en-us/windows-server/storage/folder-redirection/deploy-folder-redirection.

exam watch

Setting up folder redirection can be somewhat complicated, as you'll see if you follow the hyperlink in the preceding paragraph. You don't need to know the details of how to do it for the CompTIA A+ exams. However, you should know what it is and why you would do it, and you should know that it's done via a group policy.

Understanding Login Scripts

A *login script* runs when an Active Directory user signs in, taking multiple actions to prepare the user environment. This can include setting system environment variables, mapping network drives, folder redirection, running programs and commands, and calling other scripts. Login scripts are usually stored in the Netlogon share on the domain controller (%systemroot%\System32\Repl\Imports\Scripts). You just place the script in this location and it replicates to all domain controllers in the domain. They are plaintext files you can edit with PowerShell or Notepad and can include operating system commands (like in batch files) or VBScript or Jscript commands. Chapter 23 covers basic script writing, which will be useful if you need to write login scripts yourself.

To create a login script, expand Local Users and Groups in the console tree and select Users. Then in the right pane, right-click the user account and click Properties. On the Profile tab, in the Logon script box, type the file name (and the relative path if necessary) of the logon script.

Managing Group Policies in Active Directory

It is often better administratively (not to mention easier) to apply permissions and parameters to entire groups of users rather than individuals in Active Directory. To do this, you work with the Group Policy Management Console (GPMC) to create and manage GPOs. You can then change settings there or in the Group Policy Object Editor (gpedit.msc) console.

To create a new group policy, open GPMC on the domain controller and select the location in the left pane. Then right-click the Group Policy Objects container and choose New. Enter the name of the new GPO and click OK.

To edit a group policy and view its settings, right-click the Group Policy Objects container and select an object. In the right pane, click the Settings tab and click Show All. To configure the policy settings, right-click in the right pane and click Edit. Then set up the configuration in the Group Policy Object Editor.

SCENARIO & SOLUTION	
We are getting ready to order ten laptops for traveling auditors who will have sensitive data on the hard drives. We are looking for a secure authentication method beyond a simple user name and password for basic interactive sign-in to a Windows domain. What do you recommend?	Since you are in the process of purchasing the laptops, check out biometric devices, such as fingerprint scanners. These are more secure than the basic interactive sign-in and work with a Windows domain.

CERTIFICATION SUMMARY

There are no easy answers or quick fixes when it comes to computer security. Security threats go beyond simple computer invasions to inflict damage to threats against your very identity. Therefore, computer security must be multifaceted to protect computers, data, and users.

Physical security means safeguarding hardware and making sure it can be accessed only by authorized persons. This can include security policies, locking doors, using cable locks, and requiring badges, as well as password-protecting a PC at the local firmware level and teaching users how to lock workstations when they are away from them.

Also, old hardware should be disposed of in a way that is environmentally sound (described in Chapter 1), but before disposing of old hardware, remove sensitive data previously stored on hard drives and other storage devices.

One way to protect computer systems and networks at the local level is to make sure effective user authentication and authorization policies are implemented, including choosing Standard accounts over Administrator ones where possible, using password policies that make systems more hacking-resistant, and implementing local security policies. Managing user accounts at the domain level involves working through Active Directory to create, delete, and disable/enable accounts; change their passwords; and perform other administrative activities there.

TWO-MINUTE DRILL

Here are some of the key points covered in Chapter 20.

Security Threats: An Overview

- ❑ Effective security includes managing physical security, user authentication, data protection, and malware/social engineering protection.

Securing the Local Physical Environment

- ❑ Keeping important hardware in a locked room helps keep it away from unauthorized users. Depending on the sensitivity and value of the data it holds, special physical protection may be appropriate for an area, such as an access control vestibule, a human guard, security cameras, or smart card badges.
- ❑ Prevent hardware theft from offices and conference rooms with cable locks.

- Shred important papers to prevent dumpster diving.
- Use screen filters to minimize shoulder surfing, and use locked storage for paper documents. Some electronic storage can also be locked, such as a protected USB flash drive.
- Two types of BIOS/UEFI passwords can be set—one that must be entered at startup before an operating system is loaded, and another that is required for access to the firmware system settings (also known as CMOS settings).
- When a user needs to walk away from a PC for short periods, the Lock Computer option will hide the desktop until the user returns and enters his or her account password.
- Fences are fairly self-explanatory; secure facilities often have fences around them. Bollards are short posts on a pedestrian walkway that prevent vehicles from driving on it.
- A mobile device management (MDM) policy specifies rules for mobile device usage on company networks. A mobile application management (MAM) policy controls what applications are installed on corporate devices.
- Internet of Things (IoT) devices contain software that helps them function, but they also have network connectivity, which makes them vulnerable. Remember to maintain physical control of the device, engage security features, store gathered information remotely, and update firmware.
- A magnetometer uses an electromagnetic field to scan a person or object for metal objects. Magnetometers are similar to metal detectors.
- EFS encrypts specified files and folders on NTFS disk partitions, whereas BitLocker encrypts entire disk drives.

Securely Disposing of Data Storage Hardware

- Erase data on a disk before recycling, repurposing, or donating it.
- Deleting the files and reformatting is not very secure, but it is better than nothing. Repartitioning requires somewhat better security, but for the best security, use a disk-wiping utility that does multiple passes to wipe to the standard required for the industry.
- To physically destroy a storage device, you can drill holes in it, use a degaussing tool, or burn it. You may need a certificate of destruction, depending on the sensitivity of the data it once contained.

Working with User Accounts

- ❑ Access control to resources on a computer or network begins with authentication (verifying a user's identity) and authorization (determining the level of access an authenticated user has to a resource).
- ❑ Authentication factors include what you know (passwords), what you have (device or key), and what you are (biometrics).
- ❑ Use the local Group Policy Editor to manage built-in accounts, change account types, enable and disable the Guest account, and create special groups.
- ❑ Local security policies can be used to fine-tune the security of accounts.
- ❑ Windows Credential Manager can store user names, passwords, and certificates in the Windows Vault to automate logging on to various network services. macOS has a similar tool called Keychain which can store passwords and certificates.
- ❑ Manage domain accounts via Active Directory Users and Computers. From there you can create, delete, enable, and disable accounts, as well as reset passwords and redirect folders.
- ❑ Software tokens can be placed on a variety of general-purpose electronic devices. In contrast, hardware tokens require the credentials to be stored on a specific, dedicated hardware device, such as a USB key designed for that purpose.
- ❑ An authentication system might send a request to your smartphone using an authenticator app, e-mail message, Short Message Service (SMS) message, or voice call.
- ❑ Remote Authentication Dial-In User Service (RADIUS) is a protocol set commonly used for network-access authentication, authorization, and accounting (AAA). It carries authentication traffic from the network device to the authentication server. It operates on UDP ports 1812 and 1813.
- ❑ The main benefit of TACACS+ over RADIUS is its ability to separate the three A's. That's useful because you might need to authenticate (when you initially connect) far less frequently than you authorize (perhaps with every command issued). It operates on TCP port 49. Its primary use is device administration.
- ❑ With single sign-on (SSO) a user can log in to multiple apps during a session while only authenticating one time.
- ❑ A security group is just what it sounds like: a group of users who have certain security permissions.
- ❑ Kerberos is a centralized authentication system that mutually authenticates servers and users. It runs as a Key Distribution Center (KDC) server.

SELF TEST

The following questions will help you measure your understanding of the material presented in this chapter. Read all of the choices carefully because there might be more than one correct answer. Choose all correct answers for each question.

Security Threats: An Overview

1. ______ security is when you ensure that hardware is not damaged or compromised.
A. Physical
B. Authorization
C. Data
D. Social engineering

Securing the Local Physical Environment

2. Which of the following uses an electromagnetic field to scan a person or object for metal objects?
A. Bollard
B. Magnetometer
C. MDM
D. MAM

3. Which of the following is a simple physical-security device for protecting on-screen data from prying eyes?
A. Privacy filter
B. Shredding
C. Key fob
D. Degaussing

4. What is it called when someone follows an authorized person into a secure area without their consent?
A. Piggybacking
B. Tailgating
C. Vestibule
D. Dumpster diving

5. What should you set to prevent someone from changing the boot order on a PC?
   A. Guest password
   B. Screen saver password
   C. Windows sign-in password
   D. Firmware settings password
6. Before walking away from your computer, press WINDOWS KEY-L to enable this security feature.
   A. Secure Boot
   B. Lock Computer
   C. Screen Saver
   D. TPM

Securely Disposing of Data Storage Hardware

7. Which is the most secure way of deleting data from a hard disk before recycling it?
   A. Repartitioning
   B. Disk wiping
   C. Deleting files
   D. Reformatting

Working with User Accounts

8. Which of the following is a centralized authentication system that runs as a KDC server and mutually authenticates servers and users?
   A. SSO
   B. RADIUS
   C. TACACS+
   D. Kerberos
9. Microsoft recommends that you use a(n) ____________ user account for everyday use to minimize the risk of malware modifications to system files.
   A. Standard
   B. Administrator
   C. Guest
   D. Normal
10. When you use a smart card with a PIN, this is an example of which of the following?
    A. RFID
    B. One-factor authentication
    C. TPM
    D. Multifactor authentication

11. Which of the following is a best practice to apply to passwords?
   A. Short passwords
   B. Memorable passwords
   C. Strong passwords
   D. Blank passwords

12. This local built-in Windows account, disabled by default, is restricted in what it can do if enabled.
   A. Administrator
   B. Guest
   C. Anonymous
   D. Power User

13. This Windows feature protects against programs running in the background, changing settings, and installing malware when a logged-on user is a member of the Administrators group.
   A. UEFI
   B. TPM
   C. UAC
   D. Autorun

14. What Windows utility stores and manages local passwords?
   A. TPM
   B. Credential Manager
   C. BitLocker
   D. Secure Boot

15. How can you prevent hackers from trying repeatedly to guess a password?
   A. Disable Guest account
   B. Password expiration
   C. Disable AutoPlay
   D. Failed attempts lockout

16. Which type of Windows account is the most resistant to malware attacks?
   A. Null
   B. Power User
   C. Administrator
   D. Standard

17. How do you rebuild a corrupted local Windows user account?
   A. Delete it from the System Properties dialog box, and it will be re-created the next time you sign in to it
   B. Rebuild it by using the Rebuild option in the System Properties dialog box
   C. Run Windows Defender and rebuild it from there
   D. Restore the entire PC to factory settings with the Reset utility

18. What is the most common reason why you might not be able to access the Group Policy Editor on a user's PC?

A. Corrupt user profile
B. Home edition of Windows
C. Malware
D. It has been deleted

19. How do you create Active Directory user accounts?

A. Create them online using Microsoft's website
B. Create them on the local PC and then join them to the domain
C. Create them in the Active Directory Users and Computers app on the domain controller
D. Create them using Linux

20. What PowerShell command can you use to enable or disable an Active Directory account?

A. dsmod
B. new-aduser
C. remove-aduser
D. net user

SELF TEST ANSWERS

Security Threats: An Overview

1. ☑ **A.** Physical security consists of protecting the physical hardware and people's access to it.
☒ **B** is incorrect because authorization security deals with user accounts and what permissions they have logically. **C** is incorrect because data security is about protecting information, not hardware. **D** is incorrect because social engineering security helps prevent users from being tricked into divulging private information.

Securing the Local Physical Environment

2. ☑ **B.** A magnetometer uses an electromagnetic field to scan a person or object for metal objects.
☒ **A** is incorrect because bollards are short posts on a pedestrian walkway that prevent vehicles from driving on it. **C** is incorrect because a mobile device management (MDM) policy specifies rules for mobile device usage on company networks. **D** is incorrect because a mobile application management (MAM) policy controls what applications are installed on corporate devices.

3. ☑ **A.** A privacy filter is a simple device that fits over a screen and prevents unauthorized screen viewing.
☒ **B** is incorrect because shredding is the destruction of paper documents. **C** is incorrect because a key fob is a device for gaining physical access to a building or logging on to a computer. **D** is incorrect because degaussing is the electromagnetic erasure of magnetically stored data.

4. ☑ **B.** Tailgating occurs when an intruder follows an authorized person into a secure area without their permission.
☒ **A** is incorrect because piggybacking occurs with the authorized person's permission. **C** is incorrect because a vestibule (that is, an access control vestibule) is a system of double doors designed to trap an intruder. **D** is incorrect because dumpster diving refers to looking through trash to find information that can be helpful in hacking.

5. ☑ **D.** A firmware settings password will prevent someone from changing the boot order, which is a firmware setting.
☒ **A** is incorrect because the Guest account has no password. **B** is incorrect because the screen saver password is the same as the user's regular password for signing in to Windows; it does not protect firmware settings. **C** is incorrect because, like the screen saver password, the Windows sign-in password does not protect firmware settings.

6. ☑ **B.** Lock Computer is enabled when you press WINDOWS KEY-L, requiring authentication before anyone can access your computer.
☒ **A** is incorrect because Secure Boot is a feature of the UEFI firmware that locks access to hard drives. **C** is incorrect because WINDOWS KEY-L does not enable the screen saver. **D** is incorrect because TPM (Trusted Platform Module) is a chip that can store passwords or keys for accessing a computer's hard drive.

Securely Disposing of Data Storage Hardware

7. ☑ **B.** Disk wiping is the most secure of the listed methods.
☒ **A** is incorrect because repartitioning is more secure than C or D but not the most secure. **C** is incorrect because deleting files is the least secure. **D** is incorrect because reformatting is the second-least secure.

Working with User Accounts

8. ☑ **D.** Kerberos is a centralized authentication system that mutually authenticates servers and users. It runs as a Key Distribution Center (KDC) server.
☒ **A** is incorrect because with single sign-on (SSO) a user can log in to multiple apps during a session while only authenticating one time. **B** and **C** are incorrect because remote RADIUS and TACACS+ are protocol sets commonly used for network-access authentication, authorization, and accounting (AAA).

9. ☑ **A.** Standard user accounts are suitable for everyday use because they cannot modify system settings.
☒ **B** is incorrect because Administrator is a type of account that has full permission to modify system settings and so is dangerous to use on a daily basis. **C** is incorrect because Guest is a type of account that is so limited that it is not suitable for daily use. **D** is incorrect because Normal is not one of the account types.

10. ☑ **D.** Multifactor authentication. In this case, you are using something you have (the smart card) and something you know (the PIN).
☒ **A** is incorrect because radio frequency ID does not require entering a PIN, or even touching a computer or keypad. **B** is incorrect because it depends on only one factor, which could be a password. **C** is incorrect because TPM (Trusted Platform Module) is a chip that can be used to store passwords or keys.

11. ☑ **C.** Strong passwords are a best practice for passwords. This means a password should be both long and complex, with numbers, letters, and symbols.
☒ **A, B,** and **D** are incorrect because none of them is a best practice, and you could call blank passwords a worst practice.

12. ☑ **B.** The Guest account is built in, disabled by default, and restricted in what it can do.
☒ **A** is incorrect because the Administrator account is not disabled and is not restricted. **C** is incorrect because Anonymous is not a Windows account. **D** is incorrect because there is no built-in Power User account, although there is a built-in Power Users group.

13. ☑ **C.** UAC (User Account Control) prevents programs from running in the background, changing settings, and installing malware when a logged-on user is a member of the Administrators group.
☒ **A** is incorrect because UEFI is a type of motherboard firmware. **B** is incorrect because TPM (Trusted Platform Module) is a chip that can store passwords or keys. **D** is incorrect because the Autorun feature (AutoPlay in newer versions) enables Windows to automatically find and run the content on removable media when it connects to a computer.

14. ☑ **B.** Credential Manager stores and manages local passwords.
☒ **A** is incorrect because TPM stands for Trusted Platform Module and is the technology for encrypting volumes using BitLocker. **C** is incorrect because BitLocker is a whole-disk encryption utility. **D** is incorrect because Secure Boot is a feature of UEFI firmware that locks access to hard drives.

15. ☑ **D.** Failed attempts lockout prevents password guessing by locking out sign-in after a certain number of failures.
☒ **A** is incorrect because disabling the Guest account will not prevent hacking. **B** is incorrect because password expiration will make passwords change frequently but will not prevent repeated attempts. **C** is incorrect because AutoPlay has no effect on password security.

16. ☑ **D.** A Standard account is most resistant to malware because it has few privileges for making system changes.
☒ **A** is incorrect because there is no such account type as Null. **B** is incorrect because Power User is a group, not an account type. **C** is incorrect because Administrator is an account type with full privileges, so it can do anything, and is therefore vulnerable to malware making it do things that are harmful.

17. ☑ **A.** Deleting an account from the System Properties box forces it to be re-created the next time you sign in to it.
☒ **B** is incorrect because there is no such option in the System Properties dialog box. **C** is incorrect because there is no option for rebuilding profiles in Windows Defender. **D** is incorrect because using Reset is a drastic measure meant to correct the most serious system problems—not a good fix for a corrupted user account.

18. ☑ **B.** The most common reason Group Policy Editor is not present is that the user has an edition of Windows installed that does not include it.
☒ **A** is incorrect because a corrupt user profile would not cause this app to be unavailable. **C** is incorrect because malware is unlikely to make this app unavailable. **D** is incorrect because it is possible it might have been deleted, but very unlikely, as it is not stored in an easily accessed location where you could delete it accidentally.

19. ☑ **C.** Use the Active Directory Users and Computers app to manage domain accounts.
☒ **A** is incorrect because you could create a local Microsoft account on Microsoft's website, but not a domain account. **B** is incorrect because a local account cannot morph into a domain account without server setup. **D** is incorrect because Active Directory is a Windows service, not Linux.

20. ☑ **A.** The dsmod command is used to enable or disable domain accounts.
☒ **B** is incorrect because new-aduser creates a new account. **C** is incorrect because remove-aduser deletes an account. **D** is incorrect because net user can be used to change a user's password.

Chapter 21

Protecting and Managing Data

CERTIFICATION OBJECTIVES

- **1102: 1.6** Given a scenario, configure Microsoft Windows networking features on a client/desktop
- **1102: 1.10** Identify common features and tools of the macOS/desktop OS
- **1102: 1.11** Identify common features and tools of the Linux client/desktop OS
- **1102: 2.1** Summarize various security measures and their purposes
- **1102: 2.5** Given a scenario, manage and configure basic security settings in the Microsoft Windows OS
- **1102: 2.6** Given a scenario, configure a workstation to meet best practices for security
- **1102: 3.1** Given a scenario, troubleshoot common Windows OS problems

- **1102: 4.3** Given a scenario, implement workstation backup and recovery methods
- **1102: 4.5** Summarize environmental impacts and local environmental controls

✓ Two-Minute Drill

Q&A Self Test

At work, at school, and at home, computer users depend on client software components to accomplish work—whether they are doing research over the Internet, playing an Internet game, using e-mail, or transferring files from a server to the desktop computer. Making files and devices available to network users has led to the need for securing those resources, possibly the most important set of tasks on a network.

This chapter continues the discussion of authentication, authorization, and accounting (AAA) begun in Chapter 20 where we described methods for authenticating access to buildings and campuses. Here we look at *authorization* for access to computer and network storage. We will explain how to configure Windows clients for file and printer sharing; then we look at how to apply permissions on NTFS volumes for both local and network users and how to apply share permissions, which combine with NTFS permissions for network users. You will also learn about file and folder encryption on NTFS volumes and BitLocker drive encryption.

CERTIFICATION OBJECTIVE

- ***1102: 1.6*** *Given a scenario, configure Microsoft Windows networking features on a client/desktop*

In this section you'll learn how to configure Windows clients for file and printer sharing, using the two methods listed in CompTIA A+ 1102 exam Objective 1.6: workgroup and domain.

Configuring Windows Clients for Sharing

In this section we explain the difference between the public and private network options that Windows prompts for when you connect to a network and how they affect security settings such as network discovery, file sharing, and the Windows Defender Firewall.

We will examine two methods for sharing files and printers from a Windows client computer: workgroups and domains. Workgroups are appropriate for a home or small office network that does not require a great deal of security. The alternative is for the Windows client to join a Windows domain, which is a common method used in medium-to-large organizations and small organizations with a greater need for security and better in-house services.

Public vs. Private Networks

When you connect to a network, Windows prompts you to choose the location: either Private or Public. This setting has an impact on your ability to use the file and printer sharing methods we discuss in this chapter. You can adjust this setting via the Settings app in the network's properties.

Private Network

Choose Private as your location when you trust all the computers on your network, as you would at home or in a small office environment. When you choose this, the *Network Discovery* feature is turned on, your computer will be visible to other users on the network, and you will see other computers on the network.

To manually turn Network Discovery on or off, open the Network and Sharing Center (Control Panel | Network And Internet | Network And Sharing Center) and select Change Advanced Sharing Settings. Expand the current network profile if needed. Then click Turn On Network Discovery or Turn Off Network Discovery.

Public Network

The Public network location is the right choice for untrusted locations, such as public waiting rooms and coffee shops. (It is listed as *Guest or Public* in the network settings in the Control Panel.) It is also the preferred choice if you are using a mobile broadband connection or if your computer connects directly to the Internet without going through a router. You will not be visible to other computers on the network because Network Discovery is automatically turned off. This is also the safest choice if you do not want to share your local files or printers with others on your network.

Be sure you understand that Windows will configure Windows Firewall settings based on the network location and that the Public network setting is the safest. Network Discovery is turned on for Private networks and turned off for Public networks.

Private vs. Public is a factor only for workgroups (covered next). You cannot change the network location setting if the computer is joined to a domain.

EXERCISE 21-1

Changing Between Private and Public Settings

Complete this exercise to learn how to change the location between private and public.

1. Open the Settings app and select Network & Internet. For the current connection, click Properties.
2. Under the Network Profile Type heading, click Public Network (Recommended) or Private Network.

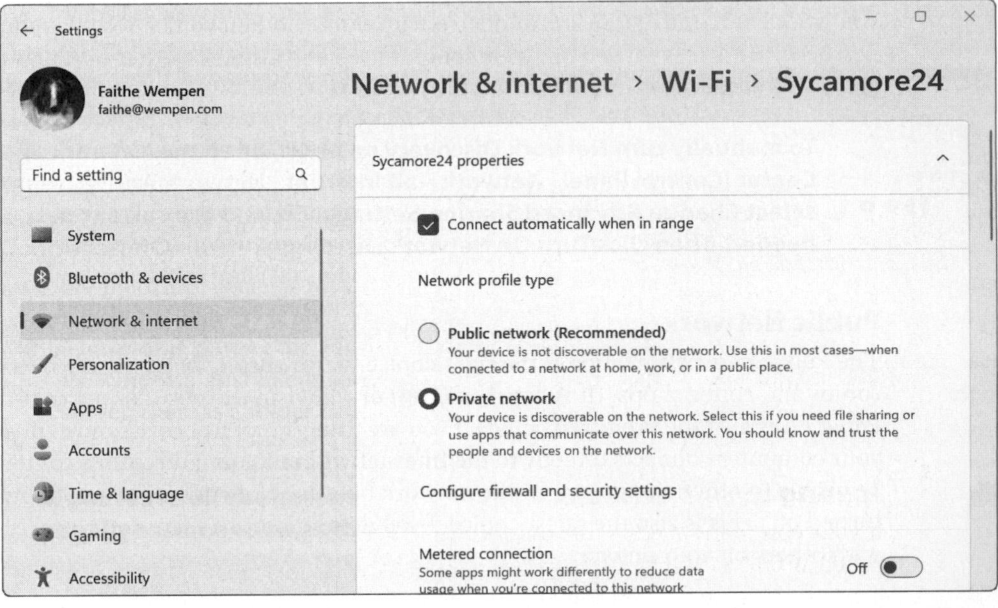

Workgroups

A *workgroup* is a uniquely named collection of networked computers participating in file and print sharing but with no central administration. Small groups of computers band together, creating a peer-to-peer network, to share resources without relying on a server.

FIGURE 21-1 View and change the workgroup name.

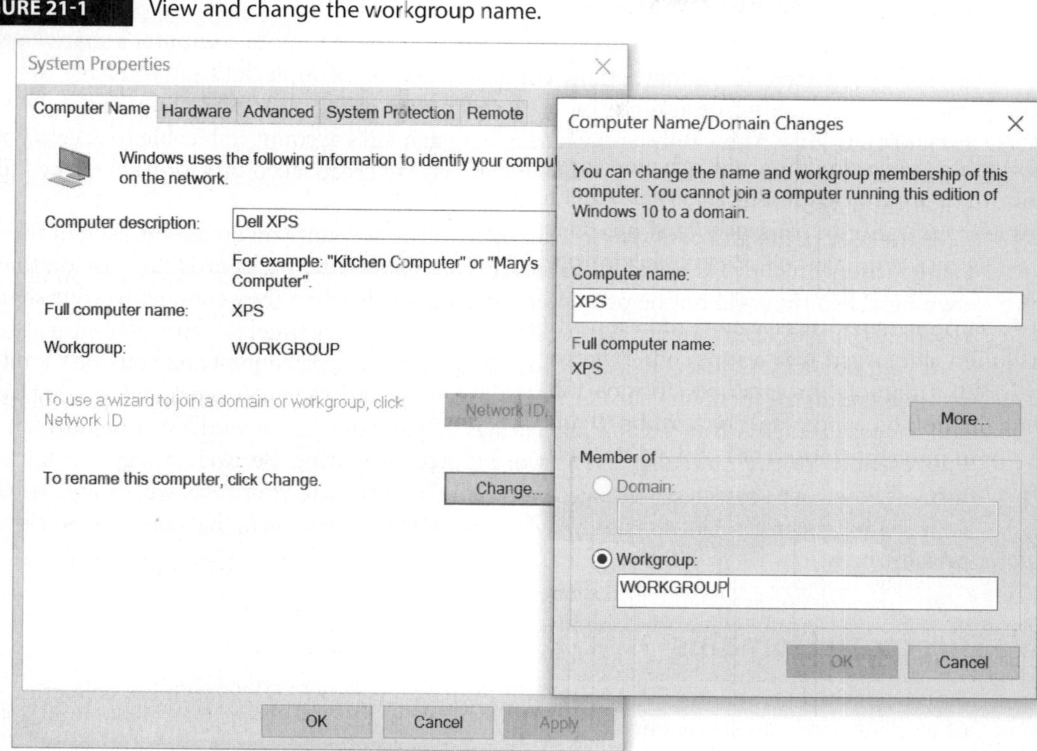

The simple peer-to-peer network you learned how to create in Chapter 17 with a small office/home office (SOHO) router is a workgroup.

Joining a Workgroup

If your computer is not a member of a domain, it is automatically a member of a workgroup called WORKGROUP. You can join a different workgroup (or create one) by changing the workgroup name in Windows.

To change a workgroup name, open Control Panel. In the Search box type **computer name**. In the results list select Rename This Computer to open the System Properties dialog box. On the Computer Name tab, click the Change button. In the Workgroup field of the dialog box that opens (see Figure 21-1), change the workgroup name and then click OK. Follow the prompts to restart your PC to make the name change take effect.

Workgroup Administration

In a workgroup situation, each user who wants to access a remote computer's shared assets must have an account on that remote computer. So, for example, let's say you have two computers in your home and one of those computers has three user accounts on it, one for each of your kids: Abby, Billy, and Charlie. For each kid's account to be able to access your PC's shared resources over the LAN, you will need to create accounts for each of the kids on your computer.

If the user name and password credentials for the account you create for each of those remote users on your PC are identical to the user names and passwords they use on their own local PC, they will not be prompted for credentials when they connect to your shared resources. If they aren't identical, they'll be prompted every time.

If you want all LAN users to be able to access certain shared content and you don't want to set up accounts for them on your PC, there's a workaround. Open Network and Sharing Center, and choose Change Advanced Sharing Settings. Expand the All Networks section, turn on Public Folder Sharing, and turn off Password Protected Sharing. Be aware, though, that if you turn off Password Protected Sharing, anyone who has access to your LAN will be able to use your shared resources. Unless your LAN is very tightly locked down, that could be a serious privacy threat.

Active Directory Domains

As you learned in Chapter 20, a Microsoft *Active Directory (AD) domain* is a collection of workstations and servers under single administrative control. The security accounts database is much more sophisticated than that on local Windows computers and resides on at least one special Windows Server computer called a domain controller. The security accounts database, or directory, is replicated across all domain controllers in the domain, allowing for more efficient access to the domain controllers from many locations. A medium-size organization might consist of a single AD domain, whereas a large multinational firm might consist of many AD domains.

Joining a Client PC to a Domain

For a client PC to be able to connect to a domain, you must join it to the domain. You can do this with any valid AD user account. From then on, each time Windows starts up, it connects to the domain, and instead of showing a local user sign-in prompt, it shows a domain-based sign-in. The user signing in is validated by Active Directory, rather than the local PC's user accounts, and the signed-in user has access to any network-shared resources for which the AD user account has authorization to access.

To join a computer to a domain, open Control Panel. In the Search box, type **computer name**. In the results list select Rename This Computer to open the System Properties dialog box. On the Computer Name tab, click the Change button. Click the Domain button, and then specify the domain name in the Domain text box. Click OK. Follow the prompts to restart. Refer to Figure 21-1; it's the same dialog box, just a different use for it.

Only Pro, Enterprise, and Education editions of Windows can join a domain. If the Domain option is unavailable, check your Windows edition.

Benefits of Joining a Domain

Here are some benefits of joining a domain:

- You can log on to the computer using any valid user account that exists in Active Directory or any local account.
- You will not be asked to authenticate again to resources to which you have permissions in the domain.
- The domain administrator can create centralized *Group Policy settings* for both your domain user account and your local computer that apply every time you log on (in the case of user settings) and every time the computer logs on (in the case of computer settings).
- The AD Domain Admins group is automatically added to the local computer Administrators group. This means members of Domain Admins have full control over every computer joined to the domain.

Users of non-domain-joined computers can still access network resources in an AD environment if they have valid AD credentials. The AD credentials of mobile laptop users will be cached locally (no expiration) so that these users can use the same credentials to authenticate to the laptop whether they are connected to the network or not. When signing in to a domain-joined computer, you can specify either a local user name and password or an AD user name and password. Remember that only passwords are case-sensitive.

Domain-joined computers can share folders and printers in the same way that workgroup computers do. (Sharing is covered in the next section.) The only difference shows up when selecting the users and groups to which you are granting share permissions; you can select local users and groups, or you can select users and groups that exist in the AD domain.

SCENARIO & SOLUTION	
You need to set up a SOHO for a customer with ten computers and printer. Should you use a workgroup or a domain?	You should use a workgroup. Workgroups work well in small networks of ten computers or fewer.
What Windows editions allow you to join an Active Directory (AD) domain?	The Pro, Enterprise, and Education editions allow you to join a domain.

CERTIFICATION OBJECTIVES

- ***1102: 1.6*** *Given a scenario, configure Microsoft Windows networking features on a client/desktop*
- ***1102: 2.1*** *Summarize various security measures and their purposes*
- ***1102: 2.5*** *Given a scenario, manage and configure basic security settings in the Microsoft Windows OS*
- ***1102: 2.6*** *Given a scenario, configure a workstation to meet best practices for security*

This section's focus is CompTIA A+ 1102 exam Objective 2.5. We describe how to create network shares and map network drives, how NTFS and share permissions interact, and how permission inheritance works. We will also look at BitLocker.

In addition, this section picks up a few specific topics from several other objectives. From 1102 exam Objective 1.6, we look at drive mapping and also printer sharing versus network printer mapping. From A+ 1102 exam Objective 2.1, we cover access control lists. And from 1102 exam Objective 2.6, we cover data-at-rest encryption (which is also mentioned in Objective 2.5 as Encrypting File System, or EFS).

Implementing File Sharing and Security

In this section we will look at the file- and folder-level permissions you can set on an NTFS volume and how they apply to both local users and users connecting over a network. We will detail how to share and map resources and then how to apply NTFS file and folder encryption as compared to BitLocker drive encryption. We will also look at Local Security Policy and how it affects user permissions.

NTFS Permissions

NTFS permissions apply not only to the local user sitting at the computer but also to someone accessing a file or folder over a network. You need to understand permissions and how to apply them.

on the job

You should set NTFS permissions at the most restrictive level that will enable users to accomplish their work. This is an application of the principle of least privilege described in Chapter 20.

The NTFS file system in Windows supports file and folder permissions through *discretionary access control (DAC)*, in which the creator of each file or folder is the owner and can control access. Additionally, NTFS permissions can be controlled by any account that is a member of the Administrators group.

NTFS permissions should be assigned based on the principle of least privilege, using an *access control list (ACL)* on each file and folder. This list is a table containing at least one *access control entry (ACE),* which in turn is a record containing just one user or group account name and the permissions assigned to that account. Administrators, the owner, or anyone with permission to create ACEs for that file or folder can create them. You manage permissions using the Security page in the Properties dialog box of a file or folder (right-click the file or folder, choose Properties, and click the Security tab).

Allow and Deny

Each NTFS permission can be allowed or denied. Permissions explicitly denied always override allowed permissions. For example, if the Sales group is given the List Folder Contents NTFS permission to D:\Reports and Bob is a member of Sales, Bob can list the contents of D:\Reports. If we deny Bob (or any group of which he is a member) the List Folder Contents permission for D:\Reports, Bob cannot list the contents of D:\Reports even though he is a member of a group that can.

Use Deny very sparingly, as it can create some difficult-to-troubleshoot permission difficulties when someone belongs to multiple groups that have different permissions assigned. To deny permission, it's better to just clear the Allow check box.

Permission Inheritance

When folder permissions and the permissions on the files within the folder are combined, the least restrictive permissions apply. But we also need to address the issue of *permission inheritance* throughout the folder hierarchy. When you create a new folder or file, it inherits the permissions of the parent folder, unless you choose to block permission inheritance.

When you view permissions on a file or folder, the permissions inherited from the parent will be grayed out, and you will not be able to modify those permissions at the child (inherited) level. You can assign new permissions, but you cannot alter inherited permissions unless you modify them in the folder in which they originated. You can block inheritance on a folder or file to which you wish to assign different (usually more restrictive) permissions.

Further, you can bypass inheritance with Allow and Deny settings for a file or folder. For instance, if you explicitly allow one of the standard permissions, such as Full Control, the user will have full control over the file or folder, even if inheritance would have given the user a lesser permission. If you explicitly deny a permission, the user will be denied that permission even if it was granted to the user at a higher level in the folder hierarchy or through membership in a group. When a conflict occurs, Deny overrides Allow, and Deny creates the one exception to the rule that when NTFS folder and file permissions, including all inherited permissions, are combined, the least restrictive permission applies.

Permissions and Moving and Copying

When a file or folder is created on an NTFS volume, it inherits permissions from its parent folder; this is also true when a file or folder is copied or moved to a folder on an NTFS volume. There is one important exception to this rule that occurs when you move a file or folder to a different folder on the same NTFS volume: in this case, the file or folder takes its permissions with it.

Make sure you understand what happens to the permissions when you move and copy files and folders to or from an NTFS volume.

Permissions on System Files and Personal Folders

Windows assigns permissions automatically to certain files and folders. They include system files and each user's personal folders.

System Files and Folders Windows assigns restrictive permission on the folders in which the system files and other critical files are stored. In addition, the default setting in File Explorer is to hide these files and folders. You learned how to control the display of hidden and system files in Chapter 5.

System files are designated as such by the System flag (attribute) assigned to the file. You cannot assign or remove the System flag on a file from within Windows, but you can do it from a command prompt using the **attrib** command: **attrib +S *filename*** to add the System flag, and **attrib -S *filename*** to remove it.

Personal Folders When a user signs in to a computer for the first time, Windows creates personal folders on the local hard drive for that user. Windows will assign a default set of permissions to those folders designed to keep other users out. The user has full control over their personal folders, as does the Administrators group and SYSTEM (the Windows operating system). No other user has permissions to these folders, nor can they view their contents. The default location for personal folders is in the C:\Users folder, in a subfolder for the user name.

Use Exercise 21-2 to view permissions on your personal folders on a Windows PC.

EXERCISE 21-2

Viewing Folder Permissions in Windows

In this exercise, you will view the permissions on your personal folders.

1. Open File Explorer and browse to C:\Users. Notice the folders. There should be one for each user who has signed in, plus one titled "Public." There might also be a Default.migrated folder if an upgrade was performed.

2. Open the folder with the user name that you used when you signed in. View the contents of this folder. These folders make up the user profile for your user account on this computer. Click Back to return to C:\Users.
3. Right-click the folder with the user name that you used to sign in. Select Properties, and then select the Security tab. Examine the list of users and groups that have permissions to the folder.
4. The following illustration shows this dialog box with the user Faithe Wempen highlighted in the list of user names and the permissions for that user listed below. These permissions amount to full control, which is also true for the Administrators group and SYSTEM. No other user or group has full control permissions to access these folders. Close the window when you are finished.

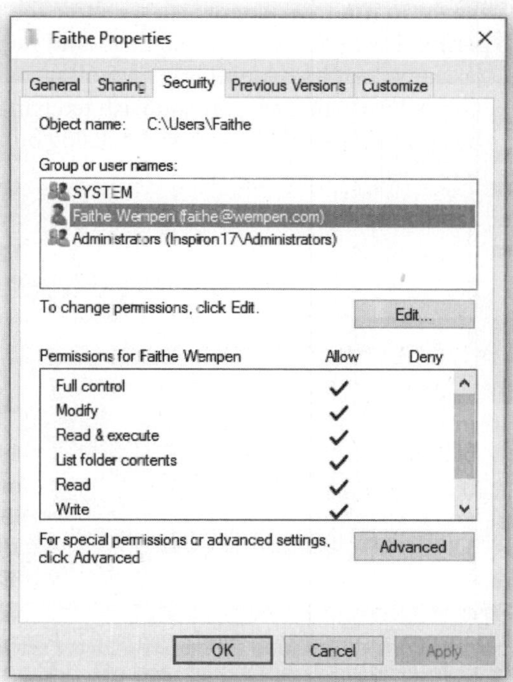

Applying Share Permissions

While we use the term "file sharing," sharing is actually done at the folder level. A *share* is a folder or printer that is available to network users. *Share permissions* are permissions set on a share, and they only apply to network users. If a shared folder is on an NTFS volume, a network user is affected by both share and NTFS permissions, but local users are only affected by NTFS permissions. When preparing to share a folder with network users, the recommended order is as follows:

1. Create the folder.
2. Set the appropriate NTFS permissions on the folder and individual files (if needed).
3. Create the share.
4. Set the share permissions.

To create a file share on your PC, browse to a folder you wish to share, right-click that folder, and select Properties. Click the Sharing tab in the folder's Properties dialog box. From the Sharing tab, click the Advanced Sharing button, and then mark the Share This Folder check box, as shown in Figure 21-2 in which we share the Blueprints folder.

A share has three permissions—Full Control, Change, and Read—and each permission has an explicit Allow or Deny permission level. The default permissions on a share give the Read permissions to the Everyone group. If you wish to change the default permission, click the Permissions button to access the Permissions dialog box for the share, as shown in Figure 21-3.

FIGURE 21-2

In the Advanced Sharing dialog, click to place a check mark by Share This Folder.

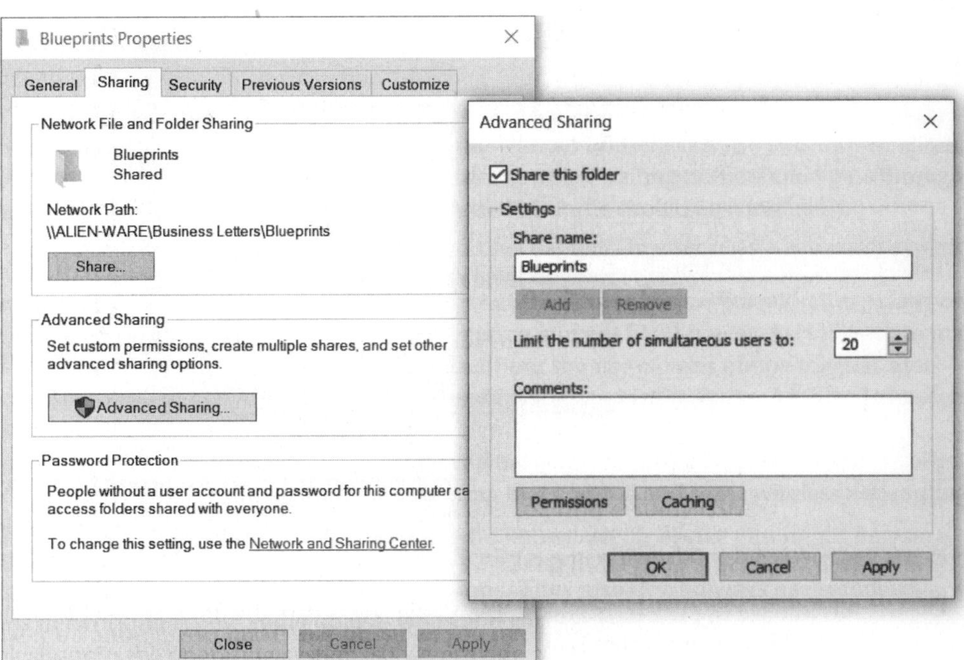

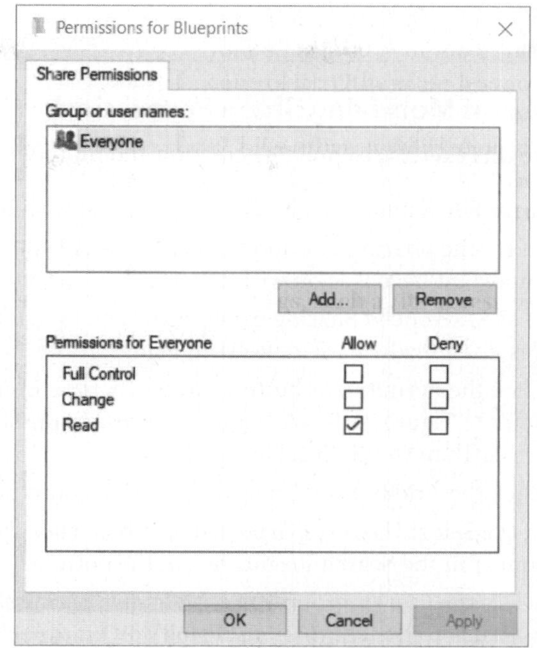

FIGURE 21-3

The default permission on a shared folder gives the Everyone group only the Read permission.

Advanced sharing is simply a term for managing shares the old-fashioned way—one share at a time—turning on sharing for a folder or printer and giving users access to that share.

Now consider what happens when a user connects to files through a share. First, the NTFS file and folder permissions (inherited and otherwise) are combined with the resulting least-restrictive permission applying at the NTFS level, and then the resulting effective NTFS permission is combined with the share-level permission and the most restrictive permission is applied.

Because you are depending on the NTFS permissions to provide file security to a shared folder and you know that when NTFS and share permissions are combined, the most restrictive permission applies, it follows that the default Everyone Read Only permissions on a share will be both too permissive ("everyone" can read the contents) and yet too restrictive if you wish to allow network users to modify files in the shared folder. Exercise 21-3 walks through the steps to modify the share permissions so only the users or groups you wish to give access to have the Full Control permission and the Everyone group is completely removed from the share. Modifying the permission simplifies your administrative tasks by allowing you to assign the specific permission at the NTFS level.

EXERCISE 21-3

Creating a Share and Modifying Share Permissions

Complete this exercise to practice creating and modifying a share.

1. From File Explorer, right-click a folder you wish to share and select Properties.
2. Select the Sharing tab, and then click the Advanced Sharing button. This step is important because you wish to modify the permissions on the share you will create.
3. In the Advanced Sharing dialog box, click to mark the Share This Folder check box if it is not already marked. Refer to Figure 21-2.
4. Click the Permissions button. Notice that the Everyone group has Read permissions. Refer to Figure 21-3. We want to assign permissions to specific users or groups rather than to the Everyone group.
5. Click the Add button. Then click the Advanced button.
6. In the Select Users Or Groups dialog box, click Find Now, and the local accounts will appear in the Search Results box at the bottom.
7. Select the user or group you wish to give permissions to the share. Click OK twice to return to the Permissions dialog box for the selected folder. The name or group should now be included.
8. In the Group Or User Names section at the top of the Permissions dialog box, select the added user or group, and then click the Allow check box for Full Control.
9. Once you have assigned the desired permission, select the Everyone group and click the Remove button.
10. Click OK twice and then click Close to close the Properties dialog box.

Administrative Shares

Windows has special hidden administrative shares that it creates automatically and uses when administrators, programs, and services connect to a computer over a network to perform special tasks that are mainly for use in a Microsoft domain network. You cannot modify the permissions on an administrative share.

An administrative share has a special name that ends in the $ character, which marks the share as being hidden as well as being administrative. You can create a hidden share by appending the dollar sign to its name, but only the operating system can create administrative shares. These are the administrative shares:

- **Root partitions or volumes** Only internal storage is shared, no removable drives (optical, USB flash drives, etc.). The administrative share for drive C: is C$. The complete network path to this share is *computername*\C$, which is a Universal Naming Convention (UNC) path, described later in the section titled "Connecting with a UNC Path."

- **System root folder** This share points to the folder in which Windows was installed, which usually is C:\Windows. The UNC path to this share is *\\computername\admin$*.
- **FAX$ share** This share points to a shared fax server.
- **IPC$ share** This share is used for temporary connections for remotely administering a computer.
- **PRINT$ share** This share is used for remote administration of shared printers.

Connecting to a Shared Folder

There are three ways to connect to a shared folder: browse to it for one-time use, map a drive letter to it, or connect using the UNC path.

Browsing for One-Time Use

Browsing to a share is simple—you open File Explorer and first navigate to the computer and then to the share, open it, and access files.

Mapping a Drive Letter

Mapping a drive letter requires that you associate a local, unused drive letter with the share on another computer. This can be automated in a logon script or through settings in Group Policy, or it can be done manually. In the latter case, you can do it in the GUI or from the command line.

To map a network drive from a GUI:

1. Browse your network via File Explorer and right-click the folder you want to map to a drive letter.
2. Click Map Network Drive.
3. Select the desired drive letter, and set any options, such as Reconnect At Sign-In. See Figure 21-4.
4. Click Finish.

Mapping a drive from the command line is done using **net use**:

```
net use z: \\192.168.1.102\Blueprints /persistent:yes
```

You can use either the IP address or the host name. The **/persistent:yes** parameter ensures that drive S: is mapped each time the user logs on. Take note that

```
net use * \\192.168.1.102\Shared_Files
```

would consume the next available drive letter.

FIGURE 21-4 Mapping a drive letter to a shared folder in the GUI

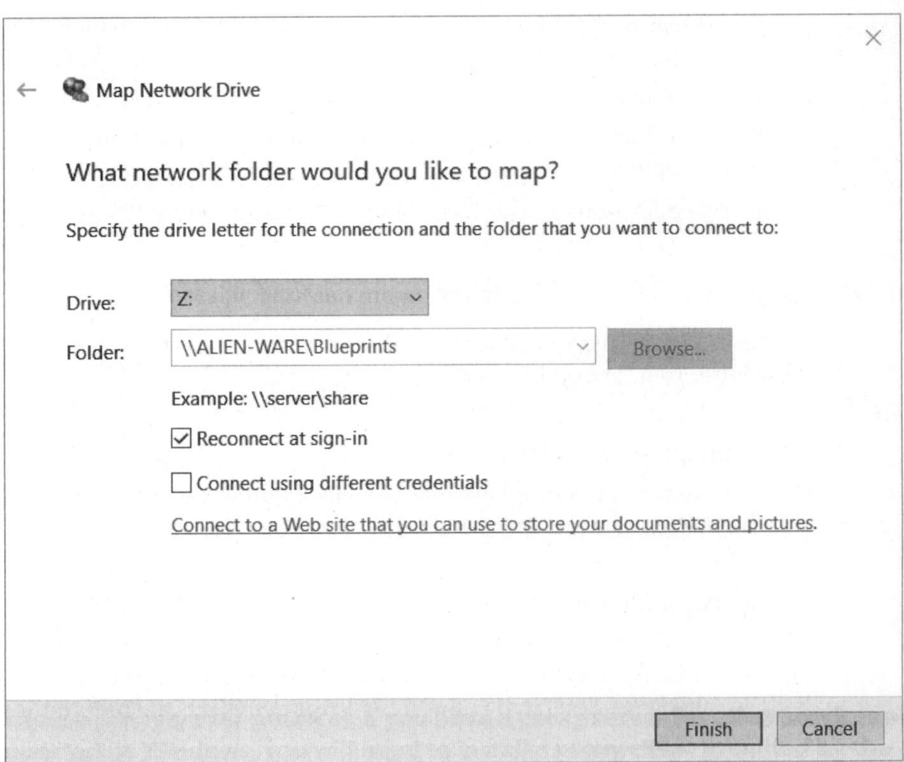
Map Network Drive
What network folder would you like to map?
Specify the drive letter for the connection and the folder that you want to connect to:
Drive:
Z:
Folder:
\\ALIEN-WARE\Blueprints
Browse...
Example: \\server\share
Reconnect at sign-in
Connect using different credentials
Connect to a Web site that you can use to store your documents and pictures.
Finish
Cancel

Connecting with a UNC Path

You can also map to a network share using a UNC path. *Universal Naming Convention (UNC)* is a method for pointing to shares on a network that begins with two backslashes (\\) followed by the name or IP address of the server, followed by a single backslash and the name of the share on the server. Do this in the Windows GUI by opening File Explorer, clicking in the address/navigation bar, and entering the UNC path. For instance, you would type **\\INSPIRON17\research** to create a mapping to the research folder on the computer named INSPIRON17. This method does not consume a local drive letter. In a workgroup, you will be prompted for credentials unless the target computer has the same user name and password you are currently using.

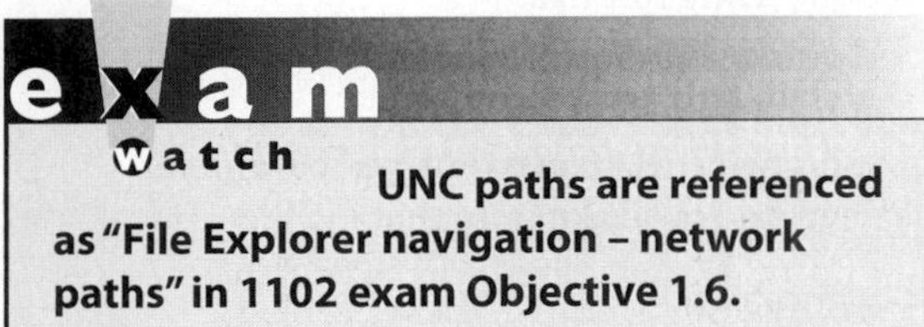
exam
watch

UNC paths are referenced as "File Explorer navigation – network paths" in 1102 exam Objective 1.6.

Applying NTFS File and Folder Encryption

Encrypting a folder using the Encrypting File System (EFS) on a Windows NTFS volume does not encrypt the folder itself—it encrypts the files within the folder. Any new files saved in the folder later will be automatically encrypted as well.

NTFS encryption applies to files only when they are saved in the encrypted folder and when they are moved or copied into unencrypted folders on NTFS volumes that support encryption. This is true even if the folder to which the files are moved does not have encryption turned on. The files are not encrypted if they are copied to non-NTFS volumes or if they are e-mailed to someone.

CompTIA A+ 1102 exam Objective 2.6 refers to data encryption as *data-at-rest encryption*. That's referring to the fact that the data is encrypted in its storage system: it is at rest. It's not being actively used or transferred.

To encrypt a folder, open the Properties dialog box of the folder and click Advanced on the General tab. In the Advanced Attributes dialog box, click Encrypt Contents To Secure Data and then click OK.

You can decrypt a file only when logged on with the account used to encrypt it. Knowing this is important. Then decryption is transparent; simply open the file using the usual application for that file type. Both normal permissions and a special authorization to decrypt are applied. Even when logged on with another account with Full Control permissions to the file, you will not be able to decrypt the file and will not be able to use it in any way.

EFS in Windows has the following features:

- A user can share encrypted files with other users.
- A user may encrypt offline files, which are files that are stored on a network server but cached in local memory when the local computer is disconnected from the server.

The only person who can decrypt a file or folder is the person who encrypted it or an EFS Recovery Agent. By default, only the local or Active Directory Administrator account is an EFS Recovery Agent.

BitLocker

BitLocker, briefly described in Chapter 3, will encrypt your entire boot volume. It requires that the boot volume be separate from the system volume; when you install Windows on a blank hard disk, Windows Setup creates two volumes in case you later decide to enable BitLocker. BitLocker is supported in the Windows Pro, Enterprise, and Education editions.

The macOS equivalent of BitLocker is FileVault, which is mentioned in CompTIA A+ 1102 exam Objective 1.10. To enable FileVault, open the Apple menu and choose System Preferences | Security & Privacy | FileVault. Enter an administrator name and password and click Turn On FileVault.

BitLocker and Partitions

The system volume is the active primary partition containing the boot loader accessed by the system firmware during startup. Traditionally, the system and boot volumes are the same, but they must be separate because BitLocker cannot encrypt the system volume. The BIOS/UEFI must be able to access the system volume at startup, and it cannot access an encrypted drive. Therefore, when you install Windows on an unpartitioned hard drive, the Setup program creates a small system partition and a second partition containing the balance of the drive space as the boot partition, as shown in Figure 21-5. Disk 0 contains a 499 MB NTFS volume identified as System and a 952.45 GB partition identified as Boot, Page File, Crash Dump, and Primary. The boot volume is drive C:. This configuration enables BitLocker to store the encryption key on the hard drive.

Encryption Keys

You can configure BitLocker to install the encryption key in one of several locations, including a Universal Serial Bus (USB) drive, a Trusted Platform Module (TPM) chip, or on the system volume. If storing encryption keys on a USB drive, this USB drive must be

FIGURE 21-5 The system volume and boot volume are separate on Disk 0.

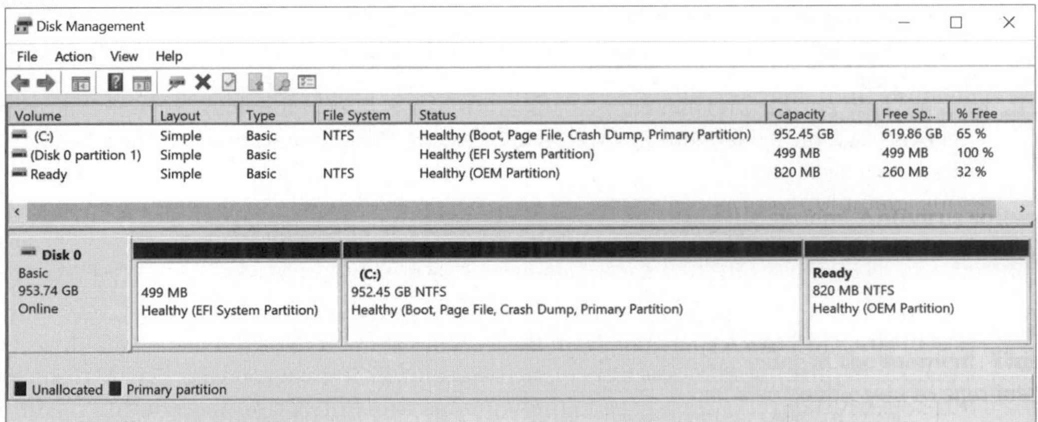

plugged in during computer startup for decryption to succeed. To turn on BitLocker, open File Explorer and right-click the drive. Then select BitLocker, which opens the BitLocker Drive Encryption Wizard. Select how you want to unlock the drive, and then click Next and follow the instructions.

You can also store keys in Active Directory if you're on a domain. The user boots up, and a reference code is displayed on the screen. That code is given to an AD administrator, who looks up the user's computer in AD and gives the BitLocker password code to the user.

BitLocker To Go

Windows also has a feature called *BitLocker To Go,* which encrypts external hard drives and flash drives. To encrypt a removable drive, locate it in File Explorer and right-click the drive. Then select Turn On BitLocker; after it encrypts the drive, in the dialog box that appears, choose how you want to unlock the drive.

BitLocker is a full disk encryption feature included with Microsoft Windows operating systems that uses the Advanced Encryption Standard (AES) to protect data by encrypting entire volumes. With BitLocker To Go you can encrypt external hard drives and flash drives.

File Attributes

While not strictly part of security, file attributes, as you learned in Chapter 5, can affect your access to files on both File Allocation Table (FAT) and NTFS volumes. The use of hidden and system attributes is the closest thing to file security you have on a FAT volume. Attributes can be viewed, and in some cases set, by right-clicking a file or folder and choosing Properties (for advanced attributes, click the Advanced button).

As you saw earlier in the chapter when discussing system files, using the **attrib** command is the command-line method for setting file attributes. You can turn attributes on and off by using + or – along with the letter that represents the attribute. For example, to make a file hidden and read-only, use **+h** and **+r**, respectively, like this:

```
attrib +h +r c:\budgets\budget2022.xls
```

The most common attributes are listed in Table 21-1. (We haven't listed all of them here because some are obscure and rarely used.) For a complete list, type **attrib /?** at the command prompt.

TABLE 21-1 Common Attributes You Can Set with attrib

Attribute	Meaning
h	Hidden
r	Read-only
a	Archive
s	System
o	Offline

SCENARIO & SOLUTION

How would you connect to a shared folder in Windows?	There are three ways to connect to a shared folder: browse to it for one-time use, map a drive letter to it, or connect using the UNC path.
You need to encrypt the contents of an entire USB drive. What Windows Pro edition tool would you use?	Use BitLocker To Go, which encrypts external hard drives and flash drives.

CERTIFICATION OBJECTIVES

- ***1102: 1.10*** *Identify common features and tools of the macOS/desktop OS*
- ***1102: 1.11*** *Identify common features and tools of the Linux client/desktop OS*
- ***1102: 3.1*** *Given a scenario, troubleshoot common Windows OS problems*
- ***1102: 4.3*** *Given a scenario, implement workstation backup and recovery methods*

This section covers all the topics in CompTIA A+ 1102 exam Objective 4.3, which deals with disaster prevention and recovery. This includes backups of various types.

We also look at some Mac and Linux backup tools from A+ 1102 exam Objectives 1.10 and 1.11. From CompTIA A+ 1102 exam Objective 3.1, we cover reimaging a drive, which was also covered in Chapter 6.

Backing Up Data

In this section we look at developing and implementing a plan to back up data, keeping it safe against disasters, cyberattacks, and human error. A written backup plan that includes specific procedures and processes should be a part of your IT documentation. It should include the following topics.

Scheduled vs. Real-Time Backups

Most corporate backups are file-based rather than image-based because image files can be very large, and it can be wasteful of both time and storage space to back up an entire image frequently when only a few files on the volume have changed. In addition, many companies use virtual desktops for their client desktops, so if something happens, they can simply reload an image of it. We will address image-based backups later in this chapter; let's focus for now on file backups.

There are two main types of file backups: scheduled and real-time. A *scheduled backup* is an activity that occurs at certain times or intervals to copy files to a backup location. When triggered, backup software determines which files should be backed up (according to rules the administrator sets up) and then copies them to a backup device. This is the traditional type of backup. The Backup and Restore utility included in Windows 7 did this type of backup. It is included in Windows 10 via the Control Panel, but Microsoft recommends using it only to restore old backups, not to create new ones.

A *real-time backup* system automatically backs up (mirrors) all files immediately as they are created or changed. With this type of system, you do not have to worry about "making backups" because backing up is part of ordinary file operations. Real-time backup systems require continuous, reliable, high-bandwidth connectivity between the original location(s) and the backup media. A large business might set up all their computers (or some of them) to automatically be backed up to a cloud storage service, for example. On a much smaller scale, Microsoft OneDrive can automatically synchronize (mirror) files between an individual user's cloud-based OneDrive storage location and the OneDrive folder on the local hard drive. The macOS equivalent is iCloud.

Backup Software and Technologies

The best backup system to use depends heavily on the size of the data pool to be backed up. What's right for an individual user PC in a home office is obviously not what's right for a large company with many servers.

Windows 10 comes with the Windows 7 Backup and Restore utility (via the Control Panel) to allow people to restore from previous backups. Microsoft has gone back and forth in allowing this app to make new backups; it is currently allowed but discouraged.

The Windows 7 Backup and Restore utility is cumbersome and difficult to manage. It creates a backup set that compresses and stores multiple files in a single large backup file. The backup file requires decrypting with the same Backup program if the backups must be restored. The advantage of this is the compression; the backup data can fit in less storage space than it could if the files were uncompressed. The disadvantage, obviously, is convenience. You can't just browse the backup and pick out the file you want to restore.

You can buy third-party backup utilities that back up to external hard drives or optical media and that are marginally better than the Backup and Restore program in Windows, but that type of backup is rather outdated. Backup utilities have fallen out of favor as other backup solutions have become more desirable. Nowadays the best bet for an individual user's backup is to mirror important files on a cloud system such as OneDrive or to subscribe to an inexpensive cloud-based backup service.

Backup utilities like the ones that come with Windows and Mac operating systems are very basic, small-potatoes programs. Large companies don't use them; instead, they either use real-time backup or they have dedicated backup servers and software that perform scheduled backups using the company's network during off-hours.

Backup Storage Locations

Storage of the backup media should also be part of your disaster recovery policy. The main decision to be made is whether backups will be stored in the cloud or on a local network-connected server. Using the cloud exposes your data to a third party (who presumably will take good care of it), which can be a security concern for some organizations, but it's ultra-convenient and generally considered safe and secure to outsource your backup storage to a reputable company. Storing your own backups locally ensures your privacy but also makes you responsible for their physical safety.

If you store your own backups, remember that the backup storage location should not be in the same location as the original systems you are backing up. This is in case there is some other disaster that wipes out the whole building. In the past it was common for scheduled backups to be stored on magnetic tape reels because this was the most cost-effective way of storing a lot of data at the time. Digital storage was very expensive per megabyte back then, and most companies could not afford enough digital storage to back up everything they wanted to preserve. Each night after the backup process was complete, someone would take the tapes to an offsite location. Today, however, most companies use high-speed data networks to transfer the data to be backed up to the offsite storage location.

exam watch **Make sure you can explain the 3-2-1 rule and its benefits.**

To protect data from loss with greater confidence in the system, some companies adopt what's known as the *3-2-1 rule* when it comes to choosing backup media and its storage location(s):

- **3** You should always have three copies of your data: one primary backup and two additional copies.
- **2** You should save backups on two different types of media, such as on local storage and in the cloud.
- **1** You should keep at least one backup offsite.

Backup Testing

Backup files and storage systems should be tested periodically to ensure that they are working properly and that data can actually be restored from them. A disaster recovery plan should specify either a schedule for backup testing or an interval (frequency) at which testing should be performed.

You need to be careful when test-restoring a backup, because if the backup is even minutes old and you have made changes to files since the backup, you will end up restoring on top of the changed files and lose your new work. Therefore, if possible, test your backups by restoring to another identically configured computer—perhaps one you use for testing or training purposes.

Backup Rotation Schemes

The same media is commonly used for backups over and over, with the backup sets being rotated so that the oldest set's media is reused for the new set each time. That's called *first-in first-out (FIFO).* There are various backup rotation schemes you can use to create a disciplined, regular schedule.

A *full backup,* as the name implies, backs up everything in a data set. It makes restoring easy, but it takes a long time to make each backup and uses a lot of media storage space. To economize without losing access to any data, two systems are often used.

An *incremental backup* backs up only what has changed since the last backup (including other incremental backups). So, for example, suppose you do a full backup on Monday, and on Tuesday you back up only what has changed since Monday. Then on Wednesday you back up only what has changed since Tuesday. You go through the whole week that way, until you get to Monday again, when you do another full backup. This method results in shorter backup durations because less data needs to be backed up each day. However, it requires you to hold onto seven backup sets at any given time. And if you ever need to restore, you must restore from up to seven sets.

A *differential backup* backs up only what has changed since the last full backup. So, suppose you do a full backup on Monday. On Tuesday you back up what has changed since Monday. But here's where it gets different: On Wednesday, you back up what has changed since *Monday.* On Thursday you do the same, and so on. So at any given time, you have only two backup sets: the Monday full backup and the last day's differential backup.

A *synthetic backup* is an odd duck, but it can be effective in some situations. It generates a file from a complete copy of an old version and one or more incremental copies of that file. It's called synthetic because it's restoring a file that doesn't exist (at least not in that form) on any backup media. In other words, it's *synthesizing* the copies.

One way to plan your backup rotation is the *grandfather-father-son* scheme. In this scheme there are three backup cycles: daily, weekly, and monthly. Each cycle is rotated separately. For example, the daily backup media is reused only for newer daily backups, the weekly only for weekly, and so on. Some of the backups may be removed offsite for safe-keeping.

CompTIA A+ 1102 exam Objective 4.3 lists Backup and Recovery as a major topic, including the types of backup rotations you can perform (full, incremental, differential, and synthetic). It also includes the grandfather-father-son scheme.

Using Backup Tools in macOS

macOS uses a real-time backup utility called *Time Machine*. You can connect an external drive to your Mac, and as you work, your files will be backed up hourly. Time Machine keeps hourly backups for the past 24 hours, daily backups for the past month, and weekly backups for all previous months. When the backup disk becomes full, the oldest backups are deleted. While cloud-based real-time backup services have made Time Machine less desirable than it once may have been, it's still very handy for those who don't always have reliable Internet access.

To enable Time Machine, connect an external drive to your Mac. Then open System Preferences (cog icon in the Dock) and click Time Machine. Click Select Disk to choose the disk to use, and then drag the Time Machine slider to On if it doesn't set itself that way automatically. See Figure 21-6. You might be prompted to erase the disk if its current file system is incompatible with macOS.

To access your backups, on the Dock click Launchpad. Click the Other folder, and click Time Machine. Scroll through the available backups with the up and down arrow buttons, and then select the file(s) to restore and click Restore.

You can also do a complete system image reinstallation or restore a backup from Time Machine using macOS Recovery, which is the built-in recovery system in macOS. To start macOS Recovery, turn on the Mac and press and hold COMMAND-R until you see the Apple logo or spinning globe. A macOS Utilities window opens. Make your selection from the menu, as shown in Figure 21-7.

CompTIA A+ 1102 exam Objectives 1.10 and 1.11 mention backups as a best practice for macOS and Linux, respectively.

Using Backup Tools in Linux

Different Linux distros have different backup tools. In Ubuntu, there's a utility called Déjà Dup

FIGURE 21-6 Time Machine backs up every hour automatically.

that you can access in the GUI. Click System Settings and then click Backups. This simple utility enables you to choose which folders to save and which to ignore, where to store the backups, and on what schedule to do the backing up. You can choose to back up once a day or once a week (not hourly as on the Mac).

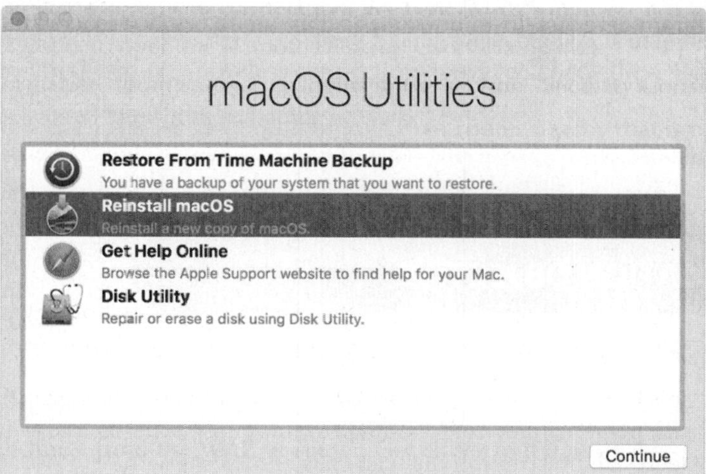

FIGURE 21-7 Restore a macOS computer from the macOS Utilities app.

Creating System Images

A *system image* (or *recovery image*) is a complete backup of an entire storage volume. You might create a system image to preserve a certain point in time, such as when you have a brand-new PC and everything is working great on it. You could then restore from that image later if something goes wrong, such as malware infection.

There are many third-party tools that you can use to create a system image. You can create an image backup on a hard disk, one or more DVDs, or a network location. There is also a utility for creating a system image in Windows, although it's difficult to find if you don't know it's there. Open the Control Panel, switch to Large Icons view, and then click Backup and Restore (Windows 7). There's a link to the left: Create A System Image. Click that to run the Create a System Image wizard.

For system images in Linux, you can use the **dd** command. Here's an article explaining how that works: https://www.thegeekdiary.com/how-to-backup-linux-os-using-dd-command. The **dd** command is not covered on the current CompTIA A+ exams.

exam watch **System image is referred to as *reimage* in CompTIA A+ 1102 exam Objective 3.1.**

SCENARIO & SOLUTION

A home computer user is concerned about keeping his personal documents safely backed up. What do you recommend?	Cloud-based backup solutions such as OneDrive are inexpensive (or free), reliable, and automatic.
A business backs up their server every night to an offsite backup server using a rotating incremental backup system. Are they following the 3-2-1 rule?	No. It doesn't sound like they have three copies of their data, and they are only backing up to one kind of media.
You need to make an exact copy of a hard drive onto another hard drive. What's the best way to do this?	You need to create a system image. You can use a third-party tool or the Create a System Image wizard in Windows.

CERTIFICATION OBJECTIVE

■ ***1102: 4.5*** *Summarize environmental impacts and local environmental controls*

This brief section covers the part of CompTIA A+ 1102 exam Objective 4.5 that deals with power surges, undervoltage events, and power outages—in other words, the types of electrical interruption that can cause problems with data storage.

Protecting Storage from Electrical Interruption

Electrical devices rely on the power coming from the wall outlet to maintain a certain well-defined voltage range (around 100 to 120 volts). However, the actual range may differ from this because of problems with the local electricity provider, wiring in the home or office, or environmental conditions. Sometimes there are outages, power surges or spikes, and sags, all of which can interfere with data storage. Too much or too little voltage occurring as a file is being written or changed can cause the file to become corrupted.

Make sure you understand the problems caused by power surges, undervoltage events, and power outages and can explain how to avoid those problems.

A surge and a spike are basically the same thing: too much voltage. The term *spike* refers to a more dramatic surge. A sag is an undervoltage event, also sometimes called a brownout. A blackout is a complete power outage, which could last anywhere from a few seconds to many days. External devices can help compensate for the various failings of household and office electricity. This section will review some of these devices and explain why you might want them.

Surge Suppressor

A *surge suppressor* (also called a *surge protector*) is basically an extension cord, but inside it is a metal oxide variable resistor (varistor), sometimes abbreviated MOV, that can absorb any excess power during a surge or spike, preventing it from reaching the plugged-in devices. An occasional power surge can be the result of poor electrical service, but the really damaging power spikes almost always come from lightning strikes.

The varistor works by depleting its own ability to resist, so over time a surge suppressor loses its effectiveness in protecting the device from power overage. With an inexpensive model there is no way of gauging the hits that it has taken or the remaining effectiveness. Some of the better models have lights that indicate the surge suppressor's "ready" status.

A surge suppressor does nothing to help with power sags or outages; for that you need a UPS, described in the next section.

Uninterruptible Power Supply

An *uninterruptible power supply (UPS)* is a combination of a surge suppressor and a battery backup. It handles power surges in the same way that a surge suppressor does, but it has the added bonus of being able to power the device for a few minutes when a power outage occurs. This is very useful because it helps avoid glitches that happen when the power goes off unexpectedly in the middle of a file writing operation. In most cases a UPS includes power conditioning, so it protects against undervoltage situations as well as complete power failures.

CompTIA A+ 1102 exam Objective 4.5 refers to a UPS as "battery backup."

Most UPSs have some rudimentary firmware programming that can communicate the UPS's status to a connected PC (usually via USB cable), letting you know the battery's status and other helpful facts. This connection can also be used to shut down any connected PCs (certain operating systems only) if the battery is almost depleted to at least allow the device to shut down gracefully.

There are two types of UPS devices. An *online UPS* always runs the connected devices off its battery. The power comes into the battery and charges it continuously, and the devices draw their power from the battery. If the power stops coming from the wall outlet, the devices simply continue running on the battery as long as they can. This type of UPS is expensive. Some call it a "true" UPS.

The other type is a *standby UPS.* It works as a surge suppressor most of the time, passing the wall outlet current straight through to the devices connected to it. The battery stays charged, but it is not in the main loop. When the wall outlet stops providing power, the UPS quickly switches the devices over to the battery. There is a momentary skip when the power changes over, but it is so brief that most devices will continue working without interruption. This type of UPS is the model that local computer stores typically carry for sale and is much more affordable. However, some experts argue that it is not a real UPS, but a standby power supply.

exam watch

Don't confuse a UPS with a *redundant power supply*, mentioned in CompTIA A+ 1101 exam Objective 3.5. A *redundant power supply* is a duplicate power supply that serves as an in-device backup. For example, a critical server might have two power supplies, with the second one operating only when the first one fails. It's the same principle as a UPS, but it is hardware-based. In other words, it kicks in due to hardware failure, not due to the failure of the local electrical system to supply power.

CERTIFICATION SUMMARY

Make sure you understand the differences between workgroups and Microsoft Active Directory domains and how to configure Windows clients in each of these resource-sharing models. You should also know the differences and features of NTFS permissions, including how NTFS permissions apply to resources for the local user as well as network users.

Another important topic is NTFS permission inheritance. Be able to compare NTFS and share permissions, and be sure you understand how both share permissions and NTFS permissions are combined to apply to network users. Practice and understand methods for creating shares on the server side and for mapping shares from the client side.

Encryption is also a topic of interest here. Understand the differences between NTFS Encrypted File System (EFS) as a file encryption tool and BitLocker and BitLocker To Go as disk encryption tools.

Understand and be able to explain various ways of protecting data, including developing a backup plan, creating system images, and using backup tools. You should also be able to distinguish between surge suppressors and battery backups (UPSs) and explain how they help prevent problems due to power surges, undervoltage events, and power failures.

TWO-MINUTE DRILL

Here are some of the key points covered in Chapter 21.

Configuring Windows Clients for Sharing

- ❑ Workgroups are a peer-to-peer file and print sharing option, with decentralized administration, requiring creating both shares and user accounts on each computer in the workgroup that will share resources.
- ❑ A Microsoft Active Directory (AD) domain is a collection of workstations and servers under single administrative control, meaning that access to all computers and other resources in the domain is centrally managed.
- ❑ Windows Professional, Enterprise, and Education editions can join a domain.

Implementing File Sharing and Security

- ❑ NTFS permissions apply not only to local users but also to those accessing resources over a network. Share permissions apply only to network users.
- ❑ Permissions that are explicitly denied always take precedence over any allowed permissions.
- ❑ To connect to a shared folder, browse the Network in Windows Explorer/File Explorer. UNC paths and drive letter mappings can be used to access shared folders.
- ❑ Use EFS encryption on the most sensitive data files. BitLocker encrypts entire volumes and is supported in the Pro, Enterprise, and Education editions of Windows.
- ❑ Windows includes BitLocker for encrypting desktop hard drives and BitLocker To Go for encrypting removable hard disks or flash drives. The macOS equivalent is FileVault.
- ❑ File attributes are not strictly part of security, but the use of hidden and system attributes is the closest thing to file security available on a FAT32 volume.

Backing Up Data

- ❑ Backup systems can be either real-time or scheduled. A real-time backup system backs up files continuously as they change to an outside server or a cloud storage location.
- ❑ A disaster recovery plan should include a backup plan that specifies the type of backup, where the backups are stored, which files will be backed up, and how frequently files will be backed up.
- ❑ A system image is a complete backup of an entire storage volume.
- ❑ Time Machine is the primary backup tool in macOS; it keeps automatic backups at specified intervals, such as hourly backups for the past 24 hours and daily backups for the past month.
- ❑ To restore from a macOS image or Time Machine backup, hold down COMMAND-R as the Mac boots to access a macOS Recovery menu.

Protecting Storage from Electrical Interruption

- ❑ A surge suppressor is an extension cord that can absorb power surges or spikes to protect the hardware attached to it.
- ❑ An uninterruptible power supply (UPS) functions as a surge protector and has a battery backup to supplement power when undervoltage events and power outages occur.

SELF TEST

The following questions will help you measure your understanding of the material presented in this chapter. Read all the choices carefully because there might be more than one correct answer. Choose all correct answers for each question.

Configuring Windows Clients for Sharing

1. If you want your PC to be visible to other PCs browsing your local network, set the network type to what?

A. Private

B. Enterprise

C. Public

D. Workgroup

2. From which Windows Control Panel dialog box can you choose a different workgroup or domain?
   A. Network Manager
   B. System Configuration
   C. System Properties
   D. Disk Management
3. What should you disable if you want people who don't have an account on your local PC to be able to access your shared folders?
   A. NTFS sharing
   B. Password-protected sharing
   C. Workgroup sharing
   D. Active Directory
4. A tax auditor is at your office for the next three days. She requires access to resources stored on servers in your AD domain. What should you do to grant her access to those resources she needs?
   A. Join her computer to the domain.
   B. Provide domain administrative credentials to her.
   C. Enable the AD Guest account.
   D. Create an AD account for her, grant permissions, and set the account expiration date to four days in the future.
5. Which of these Windows editions cannot join an AD domain?
   A. Home
   B. Pro
   C. Enterprise
   D. Education

Implementing File Sharing and Security

6. What strategy should you use when setting NTFS permissions?
   A. Set the least restrictive level for all users.
   B. Set the most restrictive level that still allows users to accomplish their work.
   C. Give the Everyone group Read permissions.
   D. Use Allow or Deny on every permission.
7. What setting, applied directly to a file, defeats permission inheritance?
   A. Deny
   B. Allow
   C. Full Control
   D. Modify

8. What rule does Windows apply to inherited NTFS permissions to determine effective permissions?
   A. Most restrictive applies.
   B. Least restrictive applies.
   C. Full Control is calculated first.
   D. Read is calculated first.
9. What is the recommended order of tasks for creating shares and applying permissions?
   A. Create the share, apply NTFS permissions, and apply share-level permissions.
   B. Give Everyone Read access, apply NTFS permissions, apply share-level permissions, and create the share.
   C. Apply NTFS permissions, create the share, and apply share-level permissions.
   D. Apply NTFS permissions, apply share-level permissions, and create the share.
10. When a user connects over a network to a file share, how are the effective NTFS permissions and the share permissions combined for that user?
    A. Most restrictive applies.
    B. Least restrictive applies.
    C. Full Control is calculated first.
    D. Read is calculated first.
11. If an encrypted file is moved or copied into an unencrypted folder on an NTFS volume, which of the following will occur?
    A. It will be decrypted.
    B. It will remain encrypted.
    C. It will be read-only.
    D. Encrypted files cannot be moved or copied.
12. Which encryption feature comes with Windows 10 and 11 Pro, Enterprise, and Education and encrypts an entire volume?
    A. NTFS encryption
    B. WPA3
    C. FileVault
    D. BitLocker
13. Where are personal folders stored in Windows?
    A. C:\Windows
    B. C:\Program Files
    C. C:\Personal Folders
    D. C:\Users

14. Which of the following identifies the administrative share that points to the system root folder?

A. C$

B. IPC$

C. *computername**admin$*

D. PRINT$

15. Which of the following commands will map G: to the root of drive C: on a laptop called PC424?

A. NET USE C: \\G:\PC424

B. NET USE G: \\PC424\C$

C. NET USE G: \\PC424\C:

D. NET USE G: \\PC424\C:$

Backing Up Data

16. Which of these is a real-time backup method you might use on a Windows system?

A. The Backup and Restore utility in Windows

B. Synchronizing (mirroring) local files to OneDrive

C. Time Machine

D. Using a third-party backup utility that performs an incremental backup each night to a network location

17. For what does the 3-2-1 rule provide guidelines?

A. Deciding between real-time and scheduled backups

B. Deciding between full and incremental backups

C. Determining what backup rotation to use

D. Choosing and storing backup media

18. Which of these is a backup rotation type that backs up only what has changed since the last full backup?

A. Differential

B. Incremental

C. Synthetic

D. Scheduled

19. Which of these is a backup utility included in Ubuntu Linux?

A. Time Machine

B. Backup and Restore

C. Disk Management

D. Déjà Dup

Protecting Storage from Electrical Interruption

20. What kind of device can protect a file server against file writing errors caused by power sags?
   A. Router
   B. RAID controller
   C. UPS
   D. Surge suppressor

SELF TEST ANSWERS

Configuring Windows Clients for Sharing

1. ☑ **A.** The Private network type, when configured in Windows settings, turns on Network Discovery.
☒ **B** is incorrect because Enterprise is not one of the choices of network type in Windows. **C** is incorrect because Public turns off Network Discovery. **D** is incorrect because Workgroup is a peer-to-peer network; it has nothing to do with sharing permissions.

2. ☑ **C.** The Computer Name tab in the System Properties dialog box controls those settings.
☒ **A** is incorrect because there is no such dialog box. **B** is incorrect because the System Configuration utility configures Windows startup settings. **D** is incorrect because Disk Management is a console where you can manage the partitioning and formatting of storage devices.

3. ☑ **B.** Disabling password-protected sharing enables remote users who do not have a user name and password to connect and access your shared folders.
☒ **A** is incorrect because NTFS sharing is local sharing. **C** is incorrect because if workgroup sharing is disabled, remote users on your LAN cannot connect at all. **D** is incorrect because disabling Active Directory would not enable other users to connect.

4. ☑ **D.** When accessing domain resources, the tax auditor will be prompted for domain credentials, which she will supply to get access to network resources.
☒ **A** is incorrect because her computer does not have to be in the domain. **B** is incorrect because you should never give somebody more access than they require to perform a task. **C** is incorrect because enabling the AD Guest account makes audit tracking difficult and thus is not recommended.

5. ☑ **A.** Home editions cannot join a domain.
☒ **B, C,** and **D** are incorrect because all these editions can join a domain.

Implementing File Sharing and Security

6. ☑ **B.** When setting NTFS permissions, set the most restrictive level that still allows users to accomplish their work.
☒ **A** is incorrect because setting the least restrictive level for all users would expose data to unauthorized users. **C** is incorrect because giving the Everyone group Read permissions would often be too permissive. **D** is incorrect because using Allow or Deny on every permission defeats inheritance, which is not a good strategy.

7. ☑ **A.** Deny explicitly defeats an inherited permission when applied directly to a file.
☒ **B** is incorrect because Allow defeats all inherited permissions except Deny. **C** and **D** are incorrect because Full Control and Modify are defeated if they are explicitly set to Deny.

8. ☑ **B.** Least restrictive applies is the rule Windows uses for determining effective permissions on a file or folder on NTFS.
☒ **A** is incorrect because this is not the rule used. **C** and **D** are incorrect because permissions are not based on which is calculated first.

9. ☑ **C.** Apply NTFS permissions, create the share, and apply share-level permissions is the recommended order of tasks for creating shares and applying permissions.
☒ **A** is incorrect because if you create the share before applying NTFS permissions, the share-level default permissions will leave the shared files and folders too vulnerable. **B** is incorrect for two reasons: Everyone Read is too open for most situations, and you cannot apply share-level permissions before you create a share. **D** is incorrect because you cannot apply share-level permissions before you create the share.

10. ☑ **A.** Most restrictive is how effective NTFS permissions and share permissions combine for a user.
☒ **B** is incorrect, although this is how the effective NTFS permissions are applied. **C** and **D** are incorrect because permissions are not based on which is calculated first.

11. ☑ **B.** The file will remain encrypted if moved or copied into an unencrypted folder on an NTFS volume.
☒ **A** is incorrect because if the move or copy is not performed as a drag-and-drop operation, an encrypted file will remain encrypted. **C** is incorrect because this is not the result of moving or copying an encrypted file into an unencrypted folder on an NTFS volume. **D** is incorrect because encrypted files can be moved or copied.

12. ☑ **D.** BitLocker is the encryption that comes with the OS and protects an entire volume on a computer running Windows 10 or 11 Pro, Enterprise, or Education edition.
☒ **A** is incorrect because NTFS encryption only encrypts at the folder level on an NTFS volume. **B** is incorrect because WPA3 is a Wi-Fi encryption standard. **C** is incorrect because FileVault is an encryption technology for macOS.

13. ☑ **D.** Personal folders are stored in C:\Users in subfolders for each user.
☒ **A** is incorrect because C:\Windows is used for storing Windows files. **B** is incorrect because C:\Program Files is used for storing programs. **C** is incorrect because this is not a system-created location.

14. ☑ **C.** *\\computername\admin$* identifies the system root folder administrative share.
☒ **A, B,** and **D** are incorrect because although all are administrative shares, they do not point to the system root folder.

15. ☑ **B.** Drive C: is a hidden share (suffixed with a $). The correct syntax is the drive letter to assign, two slashes, the computer name, a slash, the letter of the drive to be mapped, and a dollar sign.
☒ **A, C,** and **D** are incorrect because they do not follow this pattern.

Backing Up Data

16. ☑ **B.** Synchronizing to OneDrive is a real-time backup method available in Windows.
☒ **A** is incorrect because the Backup and Restore utility in Windows is not a real-time backup system. **C** is incorrect because Time Machine is the real-time backup utility for macOS. **D** is incorrect because this method is a scheduled backup, not a real-time one.

17. ☑ **D.** The 3-2-1 rule provides guidance for choosing and storing backup media in multiple formats and places for maximum safety.
☒ **A, B,** and **C** are incorrect because the 3-2-1 rule does not involve these decisions.

18. ☑ **A.** A differential backup backs up only what has changed since the last full backup.
☒ **B** is incorrect because an incremental backup backs up only what has changed since the last backup of any type (including incremental). **C** is incorrect because a synthetic backup can restore a file by piecing together different versions of the file to create a restored copy that is different from all the reference copies used. **D** is incorrect because a scheduled backup is any backup that does not occur in real time.

19. ☑ **D.** Déjà Dup is a backup utility for Linux.
☒ **A** is incorrect because Time Machine is a backup utility for macOS. **B** is incorrect because Backup and Restore is a backup utility for old versions of Windows (7 and earlier). **C** is incorrect because Disk Management is a Windows utility for partitioning and formatting storage.

Protecting Storage from Electrical Interruption

20. ☑ **C.** A UPS has a battery that supplements sagging power.
☒ **A** is incorrect because a router does not provide power conditioning of any kind. **B** is incorrect because a RAID controller functions as a drive; it does not provide or supplement power. **D** is incorrect because a surge suppressor only protects against power surges and spikes, not sags.

Chapter 22

Defending Against Malware and Social Engineering

CERTIFICATION OBJECTIVES

- **1101: 5.5** Given a scenario, troubleshoot common issues with mobile devices
- **1102: 1.4** Given a scenario, use the appropriate Microsoft Windows 10 Control Panel utility
- **1102: 1.6** Given a scenario, configure Microsoft Windows networking features on a client/desktop
- **1102: 1.10** Identify common features and tools of the macOS/desktop OS
- **1102: 1.11** Identify common features and tools of the Linux client/desktop OS
- **1102: 2.3** Given a scenario, detect, remove, and prevent malware using the appropriate tools and methods
- **1102: 2.4** Explain common social-engineering attacks, threats, and vulnerabilities
- **1102: 2.5** Given a scenario, manage and configure basic security settings in the Microsoft Windows OS

- **1102: 3.2** Given a scenario, troubleshoot common personal computer (PC) security issues
- **1102: 3.3** Given a scenario, use best practice procedures for malware removal
- **1102: 3.5** Given a scenario, troubleshoot common mobile OS and application security issues

✓ Two-Minute Drill

Q&A Self Test

Windows and other modern operating systems have a long list of security features. That's good because it's a dangerous world out there. Malware, worms, exploits, phishing, social engineering … it seems like there is a criminal lurking around every corner, just waiting to sabotage your computer or steal your private information. It's not paranoia if everyone really *is* out to get you.

In this second and final chapter on security, we discuss various types of malware and security threats and the symptoms of their presence. Then we look at ways to protect computers against them, such as antivirus/antimalware tools, keeping the OS and applications patched, being careful about responding to suspicious e-mails, and using firewalls.

CERTIFICATION OBJECTIVES

- ***1102: 2.3*** *Given a scenario, detect, remove, and prevent malware using the appropriate tools and methods*
- ***1102: 2.4*** *Explain common social-engineering attacks, threats, and vulnerabilities*

This section covers the malware types listed in CompTIA A+ 1102 exam Objective 2.3 under the Malware heading. It also defines each of the many threats, vulnerabilities, and social engineering attacks listed for A+ 1102 exam Objective 2.4.

Security Threats

In this section, you'll learn about malicious software attacks and the long list of vectors (methods) they use to infect our computers and then consider a list of threats that may do damage, make data inaccessible, and/or cause inconvenience. Finally, we'll consider the various methods that hackers use to gain access or gather information.

Malicious Software Attacks

Malicious software (*malware*) attacks are, sadly, now common on both private and public networks. The cybercriminals who launch these attacks make an avocation or vocation out of creating ways to invade computers and networks. The following are some of the most common types of malware.

Make sure you can explain the basic characteristics of each of the types of malware presented in CompTIA A+ exam Objective 2.3. They are all covered in the following sections.

Viruses

A *virus* is executable code that hides inside executable files. When that executable file is run, the virus is copied into memory, along with the regular executable code, and from there it copies itself to other executable files when they are also run. Like a living virus that infects humans, a computer virus can result in a wide range of symptoms and outcomes. Loss of data, damage to or complete failure of an operating system, and theft of personal and financial information are just a few of the results of viruses infecting an individual computer. If you extend the range of a virus to a corporate or government network or portions of the Internet, the results can be devastating and costly in terms of lost productivity, lost data, lost revenue, and more.

A *boot sector virus* is a virus that hides in a drive's boot sector. When someone boots from that drive, the virus is read into memory as part of the boot process, and once it's in memory, it proceeds to copy itself into as many of the files that the computer runs as possible.

Denial-of-Service Attacks

A *denial-of-service (DoS) attack* occurs when someone sends a large number of requests to a server, overwhelming it so it stops functioning on the network, making it unavailable to legitimate users. A *distributed denial-of-service (DDoS) attack* occurs when a massive number (as many as hundreds of thousands) of computers are infected with malware that forces them to unwittingly participate in a DDoS attack on a server.

Know the difference between DoS and DDoS. A DDoS attack is launched from multiple infected systems instead of a single system.

Rootkits

A *rootkit* is malware that hides itself from detection by antimalware programs by concealing itself within the operating system (OS) code or any other program running on the computer. Someone with administrator (root) access to the computer first installs a rootkit; then the rootkit is used as a vector to install any type of malware to quietly carry out its mission.

For CompTIA A+ 1102 exam Objective 2.3, be sure you know that a rootkit hides within the OS code.

Ransomware

Some malware makes money for its owner by locking down an infected system and demanding that a ransom be paid to unlock it. This is known as *ransomware*. It might include dire warnings about having a certain limited amount of time to comply before the computer's contents will be deleted. Some ransomware purports to be from an official government agency and accuses the computer user of having illegal content on their computer, such as child pornography.

Cryptomining

With the rise of bitcoin and other cryptocurrencies, "mining" for cryptocurrency has become profitable enough that malware creators are looking for ways to hijack people's computers to use their processing power for mining operations. *Cryptomining* malware uses the victim computer's CPU, so it inhibits the computer's ability to do everything else. Users may experience slow performance, crashes, or other symptoms of high usage.

Malware Vectors

A *vector* is any method by which malware gains access to a computer or network. While some malware may use just a single vector, multi-vector malware uses an array of methods to infect computers and networks. Sometimes it is difficult to separate the vector from the malware's attack (that is, the type of damage it does), but we'll try. Let's look at a few well-known vectors.

"Vector" is not a term you will see in the objectives for the CompTIA A+ 220-1101 and 220-1102 exams, but it is part of what you need to understand about how computers become infected so that you can work to educate yourself and others. There's a difference between the vector (how the malware gets in) and the attack (what damage it does).

Trojan Horse

A *Trojan horse,* often simply called a Trojan, is both a type of malware and a vector. The modern-day Trojan horse program gains access to computers much like the ancient Greek warriors who, in Homer's famous tale *The Iliad,* gained access to the city of Troy by hiding in a large wooden horse presented as a gift to the city (a Trojan horse). A Trojan horse program installs and activates on a computer by appearing to be a harmless program that the user innocently installs. It may appear as just a useful free program that a user downloads and installs, but it is a common way for malware to infect your system.

On-Path Attack

With an *on-path attack,* the attacking software (or person) secretly inserts itself between two parties in a secure conversation, gathering data from each. For example, one party might send an authentication code, and the other party might respond with the correct code to indicate its identity. If someone is spying on that conversation, they now know both codes and can thwart their mutual authentication or can allow the authentication to take place and continue to spy on the conversation to collect additional sensitive data. This type of attack is sometimes called *man-in-the-middle.*

E-mail

Some malware infects computers via e-mail—mainly when the recipient opens an attachment or clicks a link. You may have believed it was always safe to open e-mail as long as you didn't open attachments, but that's no longer the case. Some malware can infect a computer just by reading the message, depending on the software you are using to read it.

The e-mail vector often depends on convincing you that it is in your interest to click a link, perhaps by stating that Microsoft or another software publisher is sending you an update. Don't fall for this; Microsoft never sends out updates through e-mail!

Websites Containing Malicious Code

Some malware infects computers by lurking in hidden code on websites. When an unsuspecting user browses to that site and clicks a link, it launches and installs malware on her computer without her knowledge. Clicking the link gives the program permission to run.

In addition to shady or fraudulent websites created by people who want to spread malware, there can be threats from legitimate websites that have been compromised by those people. These websites may be owned and operated by innocent victims whose only crime was to not have adequate security on their site administration.

Browser Hijacking

We received a call the other day from Dave, a finance officer at a large farm-implement company. Every time he opened his web browser, the home page pointed to a site advertising adware removal software. This is an example of *browser hijacking* (which A+ 1102 exam Objective 3.2 calls *redirection*), a practice that has been growing. Browser hijacker malware infected his Internet browser, changing or redirecting the home page. It is not always about selling you adware removal software; there can be many reasons for browser hijacking. Sometimes the hijackers do it so that a website will register more visitors and the owners of the site can raise their rates to advertisers.

Dave was able to reverse this by changing the default page in his browser settings, but it was very annoying. He was lucky; sometimes hijackers make it very difficult to defeat the hijack by modifying the registry so that every time you restart Windows or your browser, the hijack reinstates. Chapter 18 provides some suggestions for recovering from this.

Vulnerabilities and Exploits

When an application or operating system has a security flaw that exposes it to potential compromise by malware, that's called a *vulnerability.* When such an attack actually occurs, it's called an *exploit.*

Computer criminals are constantly on the lookout for holes in OS and application software that can be exploited, and of course, the makers of those software products are constantly looking too so they can issue fixes before some malicious person finds the vulnerability. When the hacker discovers and exploits a vulnerability before the software vendor is aware that the vulnerability exists, it's called a *zero-day attack* because the vendor has zero days to patch the vulnerability before the attack.

CompTIA A+ 1102 exam Objective 2.4 calls these vulnerable systems *unpatched systems.* An unpatched computer can serve as an open door to malware and hacking. All it takes is for some malware that searches for computers with security flaws to notice that it is vulnerable. The malware takes advantage of the flaws to install itself on the computer and then uses that computer to gain access throughout a private network.

In most large networks, there are policies for keeping computers up to date and keeping security settings consistent across all PCs and departments. For example, an IT department might require all PCs on the network to run a certain kind of antivirus/antimalware software or to disable automatic updating of the OS in favor of updates implemented on a precise schedule. When a PC on the network has changed settings that do not comply with the corporate policies, it is known as a *noncompliant system.*

An *end-of-life (EOL) operating system (OS)* is one that is so old that the maker has stopped supporting it with updates. Windows 7 is an example of such an OS; Microsoft has discontinued its support, so any flaws in it will not be patched. This makes Windows 7 an inherently insecure OS, so it should no longer be used.

When a new computer joins the network, such as a laptop someone has brought from home, it's a *bring your own device (BYOD)* situation. If it doesn't usually have the security policies and settings specified by the IT department (and it usually doesn't), it is known as a *rogue system.* Both noncompliant and rogue systems pose a security risk, not only because they can bring malware into the network but also because they may violate security best practices that the IT professionals have worked hard to implement and standardize.

exam watch

Per CompTIA A+ 1102 exam Objective 2.4, make sure you understand the vulnerabilities of EOL OSs and noncompliant, unpatched, unprotected (missing antivirus/firewall software), and rogue BYOD systems and that you know how to remedy those conditions.

Spyware and Adware

Spyware is a category of software that runs surreptitiously on a user's computer in order to gather information without his or her permission and then sends that information to the people who requested it. Internet-based spyware, sometimes called "tracking software" or "spybots," may be installed on a computer by one of many means of secretly installing software. A company may use spyware to trace users' surfing patterns in order to improve its marketing efforts. Some individuals use it for industrial espionage. With appropriate legal permissions, law enforcement officers use it to find sexual predators and other criminals. Governments use forms of spyware to investigate terrorism.

Adware, which also installs on a computer without permission, collects information about a user in order to display targeted advertisements, either in the form of inline banners or pop-ups. Inline banners are advertisements that run within the context of the current page, just taking up screen real estate. Pop-ups are a greater annoyance, because each ad runs in a separate browser window that you must close before you can continue with your task. Clicking an offer presented on an inline banner or pop-up may trigger a pop-up download that can install a virus or worm.

How spyware and adware get installed on your computer is yet another issue. Users have a hard time believing that their actions invite in malicious programs, but that is how it happens. Perhaps you installed a wonderful free program. You may be very happy with the program itself, but you may have also installed spyware, adware, or worse along with the program.

The most insidious method used to install spyware and adware on your computer comes in the form of a pop-up window resembling a Windows alert. These bogus messages may warn you that spyware was installed on your computer and you must take some action, such as clicking OK in the pop-up window. By clicking OK, you supposedly start downloading software from Microsoft or another credible source to install on your computer to rid you of the threat. In reality, it is only a disguised method for installing spyware or adware.

Fighting these threats begins with being very careful about how you respond to messages in pop-up windows and what you install on your computer while browsing the Web. If you are unsure of a message, do not click any buttons or links within the window, but do close your browser. Be aware that you can infect your computer by simply viewing a website without clicking anything.

Spam and Spim

Spam is unsolicited e-mail. This includes e-mail from a legitimate source selling a real service or product, but if you did not give the source permission to send such information to you, it is spam. Too often spam involves some form of scam—a bogus offer to sell a service or product that does not exist or that tries to include you in a complicated money-making deal. If it sounds too good to be true, it is! We call spam perpetrators *spammers,* and spam is illegal in many places. Some corporate network administrators report that as much as 60 percent of the incoming e-mail traffic is spam. Most often, spam is a vector for social engineering, but it can also be used to deliver malware to your computer. Spam accounts for a huge amount of traffic on the Internet and private networks, as well as a great loss in productivity as administrators work to protect their users from spam and individuals sort through and eliminate spam.

Spim is an acronym for *sp*am over *i*nstant *m*essaging, and the perpetrators are spimmers. Small programs, called *bots* (short for robot, a program that runs automatically) and sent out over the Internet to collect information, often collect instant messaging screen names. The spimbot then sends unsolicited instant messages to the screen names. A typical spim message may contain a link to a website, where, like spam, the recipient will find products or services for sale, legitimate or otherwise.

Methods for Gaining Access and Obtaining Information

People can gain access to computers and networks through a variety of techniques that include both physical access and malicious software. Here are just a few methods.

Insider Threats

Employees and other trusted people have access to sensitive information in an organization and may have accounts with high levels of access permissions. If just one of these people can be enticed to turn against the company and give up their sign-in credentials to a hacker, the whole organization can be at risk. An *insider threat* can be a disgruntled employee or even a well-meaning employee who is unaware of company security policies and procedures.

Password Theft and Password Crackers

People use a huge number of programs and techniques to steal passwords, and once they have one password, they have access to at least one source of information or money, and maybe more. We will explain a few of those techniques.

A huge number of programs and techniques are available to people who want to discover passwords. In addition to invading an unsecured website, another technique is to use a *password cracker*, a program used to discover a password. Some password crackers fall into the *brute-force* category, which simply means the program tries a huge number of permutations of possible passwords. Because most people tend to use simple passwords such as their initials, birthdates, addresses, pets' names, and so on, the brute-force method often works. Other password crackers use more sophisticated statistical or mathematical methods to discover passwords. A *dictionary attack* is a password-cracking attempt that systematically tries every word in a dictionary as the password. (It is surprising and disappointing how often this works, as many people don't use strong passwords.)

If you enter the words "password cracker" into your favorite search engine, you will discover that there are password crackers for every operating system, every type of computing device, and all the social networking services in use today.

Keyloggers

A *keylogger* (also called a *keystroke logger*) is either a hardware device or a program that monitors and records a user's every keystroke, usually without their knowledge. In the case of a hardware logger, the person desiring the keystroke log must physically install it on the computer before recording keystrokes and must then remove it afterward in order to collect the stored log of keystrokes. Some keyloggers transmit pressed keystroke data in real time wirelessly to a receiver unit. A software keylogger program may not require physical access to the target computer, but simply a method for downloading and installing it on the computer. Any one of several methods—for instance, a pop-up downloader or drive-by downloader (see the preceding sections)—can be used to install a keystroke logger. A keylogger can send the collected information over a network to the person desiring the log.

Some parents install keyloggers to monitor their children's Internet activity, but such programs have the potential for abuse by people with less benign motives, including stalking, identity theft, and more.

SQL Injection and Cross-Site Scripting

If a website's forms are not securely designed, a hacker can inject Structured Query Language (SQL) code into the database by filling out the form using SQL commands that instruct the database to display or send information. The information the hacker gains from such a query can be used to find valid user names for the system, which can then be used to gain system access.

Cross-site scripting (XSS) is a similar type of attack. An attacker injects a script into a trusted website's code, usually by using social engineering to convince someone to click a malicious link to sign into a website they trust. From there, the attacker can steal the user's session cookie and communicate with that website as if they were the victim.

The best defense against both SQL injection and XSS is using secure design practices when constructing website code that collects form data. For example, form designers should validate user input, encode output, and have their form checked by a penetration tester to make sure it can't be compromised. A *penetration tester* is a hacking specialist who works cooperatively with a company to test its defenses.

Social Engineering

Social engineering encompasses a variety of persuasion techniques used for many purposes—both good and bad. People with malicious intent use social engineering to persuade someone to reveal confidential information or give something else of value to the perpetrator. The information sought may be confidential corporate data, personal identifying or financial information, user names and passwords, or anything you can imagine that could be of value to another person.

There are many social engineering techniques, all of which depend on the natural trusting behavior of the targeted people. Once you understand the forms of social engineering threats, you are less likely to become a victim.

The best response to any form of social engineering is to not respond and/or not reveal any information. And you should never send money in response to a communication from a stranger, no matter how enticing the offer may be.

Impersonation (Fraud) *Impersonation* is the use of a false identity to persuade someone to hand over money or valuables. It is often associated with identity theft because the perpetrator will falsely pose as the owner of the victim's credit cards and other personal and financial information.

Phishing and Spoofing *Phishing* is a fraudulent method of obtaining personal and financial information through pop-ups, e-mail, and even letters mailed via the Postal Service that purport to be from a legitimate organization, such as a bank, credit card company, retailer, and so on. They often (falsely) appear to be from well-known organizations and websites, such as various banks and credit card institutions, eBay, PayPal, Microsoft, Target, or Walmart. As such, the typical phishing attack relies on a *hoax*, meaning that it uses deception and lies to gain your confidence.

In a typical phishing scenario, the message will contain authentic-looking logos, and an e-mail may even link to the actual site, but the link specified for supplying personal financial information will take recipients to a "spoofed" web page that asks them to enter their personal data. The web page may look exactly like the company's real web page, but it's not the legitimate site. A common practice is for a phisher to use the credit card information to make purchases over the Internet, choosing items that are easy to resell and having them delivered to an address unconnected to the phisher, such as a vacant house to which he has access.

When an attack is directed at one person in particular, it's called *spear phishing.* When an attack is directed at a high-level individual or a group of high-level individuals (such as senior technical administrators or executives), it's called *whaling.*

Hackers can be very clever and can involve the forgery of data packets so that a transmission appears to have originated from a legitimate source. This type of forgery is called *spoofing.* Spoofing can involve IP addresses, Address Resolution Protocol (ARP) or a DNS server, or lower-tech trickery such as making phone calls to try to trick the person into giving up sensitive information that can be used for hacking. (The latter is called *vishing.*)

exam watch **Make sure you understand the terms phishing, whaling, and spoofing.**

Be very suspicious of e-mails requesting personal financial information, such as access codes, Social Security numbers, or passwords. Legitimate businesses will never ask you for personal financial information in an e-mail.

To learn more about phishing and to see the latest examples, point your web browser to www.antiphishing.org, the website of the Anti-Phishing Working Group (APWG), which reports that every possible measurement of phishing activity shows huge increases. For instance, in December 2021, the APWG noted 316,747 attacks, the highest monthly total in reporting history. You can report phishing attacks at this site.

Would you recognize a phishing e-mail? There are websites that work to educate people to recognize a phishing scam when they receive it in e-mail or other communications. Exercise 22-1 describes how to use just one of these sites.

EXERCISE 22-1

What Is Your Phishing IQ?

You can test your phishing IQ and learn to identify phishing scams.

1. Use your web browser to connect to the Phishing IQ test at https://www.sonicwall.com/en-us/phishing-iq-test.
2. You will see ten e-mails, one at a time. You must decide whether each is legitimate or phish.
3. When you finish, you can review the correct answers, along with a detailed explanation as to why each is either legitimate or phish.

If you completed Exercise 22-1, you will have noticed that phishing e-mails look very official, but in some cases, careful scrutiny reveals problems. Although the signs identified in these messages are not the full extent of the problems you can find in a phishing e-mail, this type of test helps to educate people so they do not become victims of phishing.

Although not all phishing e-mails have the same characteristics, the following lists just a few problems detected in phishing e-mails:

- The "To:" field is not your address, even though it appeared in your inbox.
- There is no greeting, or the greeting omits your name.
- The message text shows bad grammar or punctuation.
- When you click a link, the Uniform Resource Locator (URL) you are directed to does not match what appears in the e-mail.
- A link does not use Hypertext Transfer Protocol Secure (HTTPS).
- The title bar reveals that a foreign character set (e.g., Cyrillic) is used.
- What appears to be a protected account number (revealing only the last four digits) is not your number at all.
- What appears to be an account expiration date is not the correct expiration date for your account.

- A URL has a slightly misspelled domain name that resembles the legitimate domain name.
- There is no additional contact information, such as a toll-free phone number and a name and title of a contact person.

Now to make things more confusing, some legitimate e-mails may show some of these problems or practices, and not all phishing e-mails have all of these negative characteristics.

A safer way to include a URL in a legitimate e-mail is not to make it a link, but to include it in the e-mail as unformatted text, with instructions to cut and paste it into a web browser. This way, malware cannot redirect you to a bogus website, but you must still be diligent and examine the URL before using it.

For the exam, be sure you recognize the signs we listed of a phishing e-mail.

Vishing

As briefly mentioned previously, *vishing* (voice phishing) is another form of phishing. In order to gain the intended victim's confidence, a phishing e-mail will urge the reader to call a phone number to verify information, at which point the person on the phone will ask the victim to reveal the valuable information.

What makes this so compelling to the user is that phone phishing often involves a very authentic-sounding professional interactive voice response (IVR) menu system, just like a legitimate financial institute would have. It may ask the user to enter his password or personal identifying number (PIN). To ensure that the system captures the correct password or PIN, the system may even ask the victim to repeat it. Some systems then have the victim talk to a "representative" who gathers more information.

Keep yourself up to date on the latest threats. Microsoft, Norton, Trend Micro, and other software vendors, particularly those who specialize in security products, offer a wealth of information on their websites. You can also subscribe to newsletters from these same organizations. You can also find information about common vulnerabilities and exposures (CVEs) at https://cve.mitre.org.

Enticements to Open Attachments

Social engineering is also involved in the enticements—called "gimmes" in e-mails, either in the subject line or the body of the e-mail—to open the attachments. Opening the attachment then executes and infects the local computer with some form of malware. A huge number of methods are used. Sadly, enticements often appeal to basic characteristics in people, such as greed (an offer too good to be true), vanity (physical enhancements), or simple curiosity. Some bogus enticements appeal to people's sympathy and compassion by way of a nonexistent charity, or the author of the e-mail will pose as a legitimate charity—anything to get you to open the attachment.

Evil Twin Attacks

An *evil twin* is a fake Wi-Fi hotspot that a hacker might set up in a public place, hoping that someone will try to connect to it to get free Internet access. When they do, they get Internet access, but the hacker collects all the data that they send and receive, and can often glean passwords, credit card numbers, and other sensitive information from that data flow. This type of attack is sometimes called a *rogue hotspot.*

SCENARIO & SOLUTION

Scenario	Solution
Some of your end users have been using common dictionary words as passwords. Why is this a bad idea?	Password-cracking programs use dictionary lists to guess passwords; if your password is in the dictionary, it'll be quickly guessed by such a program.
A user has received an e-mail that seems to be from his bank, prompting him to sign in from a link provided. How can he tell if this is a legitimate message?	Banks do not send out requests for information via e-mail. Any such request you receive is phishing.
Several of your users have been putting off installing Windows updates. Why should you insist that they install updates promptly?	OSs can contain security vulnerabilities, and if a hacker finds them before the vendor does, the hacker can develop exploits and launch a zero-day attack. Installing OS updates ensures that all available security patches are applied, minimizing the risk of attack from exploits. In addition, if the OS has reached the end of its life (EOL), it is not receiving security patches anymore.

CERTIFICATION OBJECTIVES

- ***1102: 3.2*** *Given a scenario, troubleshoot common personal computer (PC) security issues*
- ***1102: 3.5*** *Given a scenario, troubleshoot common mobile OS and application security issues.*

This section covers many of the symptoms of malware infection or hacker intrusion listed in CompTIA A+ 1102 exam Objectives 3.2 (for desktop and laptop PCs) and 3.5 (for mobile devices).

Identifying the Symptoms of Malware Infection

Sometimes it can be difficult to distinguish the symptoms of a security problem from the symptoms of other types of system problems. For example, slow performance—is it because of system file corruption, or because the PC has been commandeered by a botnet program and is being used in a DDoS attack? Or OS update failure: Has some malware disabled your ability to update your system, or is it just an incompatibility issue between your hardware and the latest Microsoft Windows patch? Often the initial symptoms are just an alert, and you'll need to do significant diagnosis and troubleshooting to find the root cause of a problem.

In this section we review many types of PC issues that can sometimes signify security breaches or malware. These are just warnings and alerts, and you'll need to follow them up using your own experience and common sense.

Internet Connectivity and Browser Behavior

Let's start off with a few problems with Internet service and browser usage that can sometimes be caused by security breaches or malware.

Internet Connectivity Issues

Internet connectivity issues are more likely to be from the causes described in Chapter 17 than from a malware infection. Troubleshoot using the methods described in that chapter, and if you cannot find the cause and solution, boot the computer to Safe Mode, described in Chapter 6, and run a complete antivirus/antimalware scan.

Pop-Ups and Redirection

A sudden increase in the number of browser pop-up windows can indicate that adware may be present. Another symptom is a home page that redirects to a page you did not choose, especially if the page comes back after you reset it to your own favorite.

Certificate Warnings

If you see an invalid certificate error when browsing the Web, it doesn't usually mean you have been infected with anything—yet. It just means that the certificate that this supposedly secure website is offering up was not issued by a trusted authority. If you see this kind of warning, click the Back button; do not proceed to that site. If you absolutely must proceed, do so in a high-security browsing mode such as InPrivate browsing in Edge or Incognito in Chrome.

Operating System Problems

Many different system problems can be signs of malware infection. Here are some of the most common things to look for.

Disabled Antivirus Program

One of the most common symptoms of malware infection is that your antivirus/antimalware software is disabled and cannot be re-enabled. Look for a change to the program's icon in the notification area, perhaps with a red X on its icon to indicate it is turned off. Uninstalling and reinstalling the application will not usually solve the problem. In such cases you can turn to an online, real-time scanner to determine which malware has infected the system and then do a web search to determine how to remove it.

Desktop Alerts

Windows will usually display security alerts when it detects a security problem. You can view these via the Security and Maintenance area of the Control Panel (called Action Center in some Windows versions) or via the Notifications task pane. Some common messages you might see include warnings about no antivirus or spyware protection being detected or a disabled Windows Defender Firewall. Respond to the message, for instance, by installing antivirus and antispyware software. In the case of a no-firewall message, open Security and Maintenance (or Windows Action Center) and enable Windows Defender Firewall, or, if you have another firewall installed, select the option that informs Windows of this.

Third-party firewalls can disable Windows Defender Firewall, and that's expected and okay. Having two software-based firewalls running at the same time would cause confusion and conflicts.

Unwanted Notifications in the OS

Some desktop alerts are useful, in that they let you know that there's a problem with your system. However, malware can also produce fake notifications that misdirect you to sites where more malware can infect your system.

Slow Performance

Slow performance can have several causes, depending on what there is about the computer that is actually slow. Chapter 12 described this symptom and solutions related to hard drives; Chapter 6 described slow system performance and some solutions. Chapter 19 described slow network transfer speeds and some solutions. After eliminating other causes for slow performance, follow the instructions under the sections "2. Quarantine Infected Systems," "4. Remediate the Infected Systems," and "6. Enable System Restore and Create a Restore Point in Windows," later in this chapter.

OS Update Failure

Update failures can be a sign of a malware infection because they often disable the OS updates so that your computer will not become more secure through security updates.

When an update failure occurs, read the message and research the cause. It may have been a network connection problem or an incompatibility issue. If it is not clearly a network connection problem, use the error message to do an Internet search for a solution. Look at solutions from both the OS maker's site and other technical sites that you trust.

False Antivirus Alerts and Rogue Antivirus Software

Malware or malicious websites can display false antivirus alerts, trying to trick you into thinking your system is infected and then offering to "sell" you a solution. The antivirus solution they sell you is often itself infected with malware in the form of a rogue antivirus.

Earlier in this chapter we described one example of a rogue antivirus when we discussed Trojan horses. A rogue antivirus is a Trojan horse masquerading as an antivirus program. Education and prevention are the best defenses because rogue antiviruses look like the real thing, and we know several people who installed the malware. Again, the best solution is to boot the computer to Safe Mode, described in Chapter 6, and run a complete antivirus scan.

Renamed System Files

Renamed system files are less of a threat because malware can simply infect the system files themselves. Both renaming the system files and directly infecting system files are less likely with many of the protections built into Windows. You can solve this by booting the computer to Safe Mode, described in Chapter 6, and running a complete antivirus scan. If removal of the virus leaves your system unbootable, then run the System Recovery Options menu from a Windows installation media.

Missing Files

Disappearing files is a malware symptom, but before you assume malware has caused it, look at how it was discovered and what you or the client was doing at the time the files disappeared. Sometimes, we just forget where we stored files. However, it never hurts to run a security scan, even from Safe Mode. If you discover malware, remove it and restore your files from the latest backup.

File Permission Changes and Access Denied

File permission changes are also not as likely to happen in the newer versions of Windows because of User Account Control (UAC). If you notice that permissions have changed, change them back (if your permissions allow), then boot the computer to Safe Mode, described in Chapter 6, and run a complete antivirus/antimalware scan.

If access is denied to a resource a user previously was able to access, first reboot to ensure that it's not a temporary OS glitch, such as a memory error. Then troubleshoot it as a file permission change.

System/Application Log Errors

If you look in Event Viewer, do you see any unusual messages that you can't account for? This can be a symptom of malware infection or hacker intrusion. The Event Viewer is a good place to look if you suspect that things are going on behind the scenes on a client PC.

You should be able to identify common symptoms of malware infection, including inability to access the network, desktop alerts, false alerts regarding antivirus protection, altered system or personal files, unwanted notifications, and OS update failures.

Unexpected E-mail Behavior

E-mail becomes a routine, reliable part of people's daily lives, so when the e-mail client doesn't work as usual or when the mail volume and type change, users are likely to notice. Here are some e-mail behaviors that can indicate malware or a hacked system.

Spam

If you experience a sudden increase in the amount of spam you receive, your e-mail address may have been sold to a spamming company. Other than changing to a different e-mail address, there is not much you can do about that. Once it's in the system, it's forever exposed.

Although you can't reduce the amount of spam that gets sent your way, there are a number of ways to reduce the amount of it that actually reaches your inbox. You can turn on *e-mail filtering* at the ISP level (and, in fact, many ISPs have that enabled automatically). You can also enable e-mail filtering in your e-mail application, and you can install additional third-party spam filtering programs.

Hijacked E-mail

If your friends and family start receiving odd messages from your account that you didn't send, your e-mail may have been hijacked. Another symptom is automated replies from servers saying that a message could not be delivered—a message that you don't recall sending.

In the event of a hijacked e-mail, you should do three things: immediately change your password, change your security question and answer, and verify that you are the owner of your alternative e-mail address (most e-mail accounts ask you to provide an alternative e-mail address). Hopefully the people you e-mail know that you're not stranded in Ireland and need money to get home, or whatever message the hijacker sent out from your account.

You should probably send everyone an e-mail telling them what happened, reminding them not to click anything and to delete anything strange coming from your address.

Sometimes the hijacker changes your password and locks you out. In that case, contact the e-mail provider for help in resolving the problem.

Symptoms of Infection on a Mobile Device

Many of the symptoms of malware infection you see on a mobile device are the same as those on a desktop or laptop. These include a greater-than-normal number of ads when using a browser, fake security warnings, leaked personal/data files, and sluggish response time (usually due to high network traffic). One symptom that is unique to devices that get Internet via cellular service is an unexpected data-usage limit notification, indicating you have used up all your data for the billing period. This can be caused by malware that transfers data to or from your device without your knowledge.

CompTIA A+ 1102 exam Objective 3.5 lists many symptoms of mobile device malware infection, including high network traffic, sluggish response time, data-usage limit notification, high number of ads, fake security warnings, unexpected application behavior, and leaked personal files/data.

CERTIFICATION OBJECTIVES

- ***1102: 1.4*** *Given a scenario, use the appropriate Microsoft Windows 10 Control Panel utility*
- ***1102: 1.6*** *Given a scenario, configure Microsoft Windows networking features on a client/desktop*
- ***1102: 1.10*** *Identify common features and tools of the macOS/desktop OS*
- ***1102: 1.11*** *Identify common features and tools of the Linux client/desktop OS*
- ***1102: 2.3*** *Given a scenario, detect, remove, and prevent malware using the appropriate tools and methods*
- ***1102: 2.5*** *Given a scenario, manage and configure basic security settings in the Microsoft Windows OS*
- ***1102: 3.3*** *Given a scenario, use best practice procedures for malware removal*

In this section we will continue the coverage of topics on the CompTIA A+ 1102 exam, including antivirus/antimalware, firewalls, and e-mail filtering.

Malware protection is mentioned in many different objectives, as you can tell by the preceding list. These entries are mostly duplicates, though. For example, firewall use and configuration is a topic in CompTIA A+ 1102 exam Objectives 1.4, 1.6, and 2.5. Antivirus/antimalware tools are also listed in multiple objectives, including CompTIA A+ 1102 exam Objectives 1.10, 1.11, 2.3, and 3.3.

Implementing a Defense Against Malware

There are many small building blocks to an effective defense against malicious software. It begins with educating yourself about threats and defenses and setting up a foundation of secure authentication and data protection techniques, and continues with placing a firewall and related technologies at the junction between a private network and the Internet. Then each computer in the private network must use a group of technologies, such as software firewalls and programs that detect and remove all types of malware, to protect it from attacks.

Make sure you keep an eye out for the symptoms listed in the preceding section that may indicate a security problem or malware infection.

User Education

Research malware types, symptoms, and solutions to keep yourself informed. Check out the many *virus encyclopedias* on the Internet sponsored by many different organizations, including security software manufacturers such as Trend Micro, Kaspersky, and Norton. Despite the use of the word "virus," these lists contain all types of known threats and are always up to date. Threat Encyclopedia is the title of the list maintained by Trend Micro, a security software manufacturer. Also look for antivirus support forums, which include information about threats other than viruses.

Such resources categorize the malware by type and describe symptoms and solutions. The website www.av-comparatives.org contains lists of antivirus support forums and virus encyclopedias. The U.S. government maintains excellent general information on all types of threats to computers at the United States Computer Emergency Readiness Team (US-CERT) website at www.us-cert.gov/ncas/tips/.

User Account Control

Malware often runs in the background without user consent, making system changes and installing itself. To prevent this, Microsoft added UAC in Windows. You learned about it in Chapter 20 in "Adjusting User Account Control Settings," but now let's look at it in the context of malware prophylaxis.

on the job

UAC does not negate the need for antimalware tools.

UAC can prompt the user when an application tries to change system settings or run other programs to prevent malicious code from running unknown in the background. With UAC enabled, you can expect two scenarios. In the first, a user logged on with a name and password that is a member of the Administrators group only has the privileges of a Standard account (member of the Users group) until the user (or a malicious program) attempts to do something that requires higher privileges. At that point, UAC makes itself known, graying out (dimming) the desktop and displaying the *consent prompt* with a message concerning the action. Click Continue or Yes (depending on the message) to allow the action. You can choose to cancel the action by clicking No. If you click Yes, the task runs with your administrative privileges, and you return to working with standard privileges in other programs.

In the second scenario, a user logs on with the privileges of a Standard user and attempts to do something that requires administrative privileges. In this case, UAC displays the *credentials prompt* requiring the user name and password of an account with administrative privileges. If you provide these, the program or task will run with these elevated privileges, but you will return to the Standard user privileges for all other activities. In either case, if you do not respond in a short period of time, UAC will time out, cancel the operation, and return control of the desktop to you. By default, UAC is turned on.

Even with UAC turned off, you will not be allowed to perform all tasks and will see a message such as "The requested operation requires elevation" when you attempt to perform certain functions. As you learned in Chapter 20, you can modify User Account Control settings in the Control Panel (User Accounts | User Accounts | Change User Account Control Settings).

System Protection

One way to recover in the event of a recent malware infection or unwanted system settings change is to restore the system files back to an earlier checkpoint. This is done using System Protection.

As you learned in Chapter 6, System Protection is the feature we most often call System Restore, although it also includes Shadow Copy. From the System applet of the Control Panel, select System Protection from the task list, which opens the System Properties dialog box to the System Protection tab. From this tab, you can start System Restore and undo recent system changes. You can also configure System Restore settings and create a new restore point.

Software Firewalls

In Chapter 17, you learned that a firewall is a hardware device or software that uses several technologies to prevent unwanted traffic from entering a network. If your computer is behind a well-configured hardware firewall, it will be protected against attacks coming from outside the private network. However, many attacks come from within a private network. Therefore, whether your computer is behind an expensive, well-managed hardware firewall or an inexpensive small office/home office (SOHO) broadband router, you still need to install and configure a software firewall on every Windows computer. The best strategy is to start with the most restrictive settings and then make exceptions to allow the required traffic to pass through the firewall. Since one of the main jobs of a firewall is to maintain port security, exceptions are in the form of port numbers and can even include specific IP addresses or domain names associated with port numbers.

Windows Defender Firewall

Windows Defender Firewall (called Windows Firewall prior to Windows 10) is on by default, and you can open the Windows Defender Firewall dialog box through its Control Panel applet or by finding it by typing **Firewall** at the Start menu.

Figure 22-1 shows the Windows Defender Firewall page in Windows 10. It contains simple status information and has links if you need to make any changes to the firewall.

FIGURE 22-1 Windows Defender Firewall

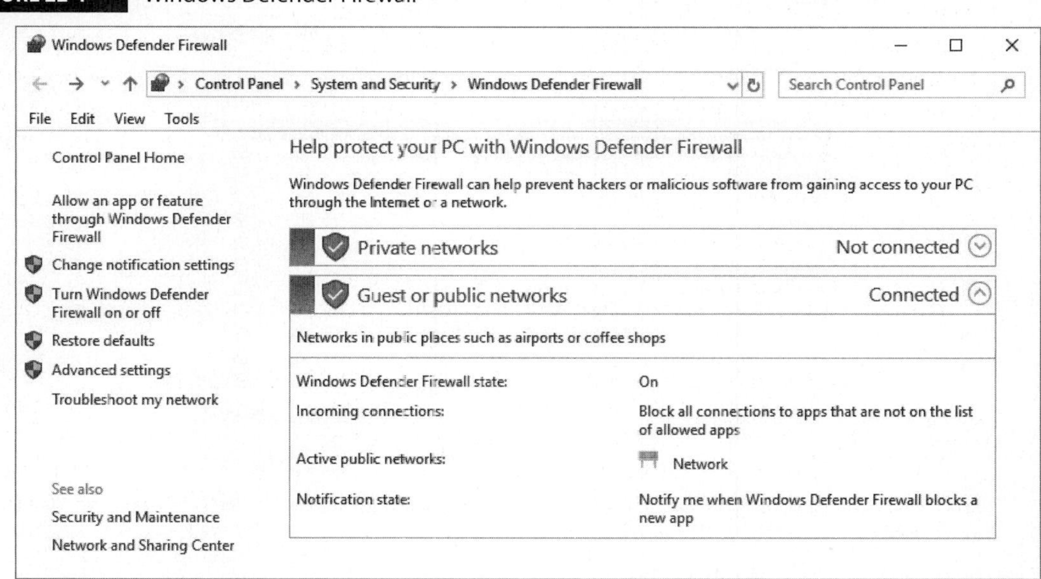

Clicking the link labeled Allow An App Or Feature Through Windows Defender Firewall will open a new page, shown in Figure 22-2. Then click the Change Settings button at the top of the page. You will need to do this to allow traffic for certain apps or services in.

on the job

If a certain application that uses the Internet seems to be working okay but isn't connecting to its online resources, suspect a firewall issue. Make sure that the application is allowed through the firewall in the list shown in Figure 22-2.

For situations where you need even more control over firewall settings, Windows offers an alternative Windows Defender Firewall interface called Windows Defender Firewall with Advanced Security. You can get to it by clicking Advanced Settings in the navigation pane on the left at the Windows Defender Firewall screen (refer to Figure 22-1). This window works more like an MMC snap-in, with three panes, as you can see in Figure 22-3. You can create inbound and outbound rules from here, as well as set up connection security rules and monitoring.

FIGURE 22-2 Windows Defender Firewall Allowed Apps page

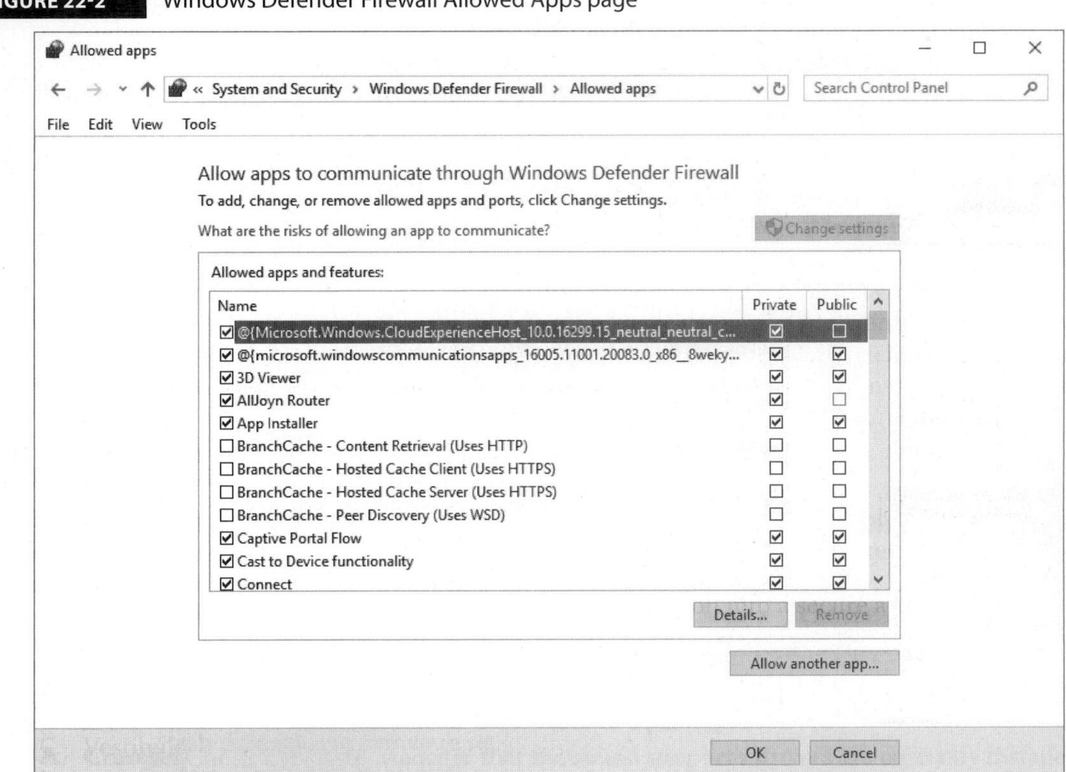

FIGURE 22-3 Windows Defender Firewall with Advanced Security

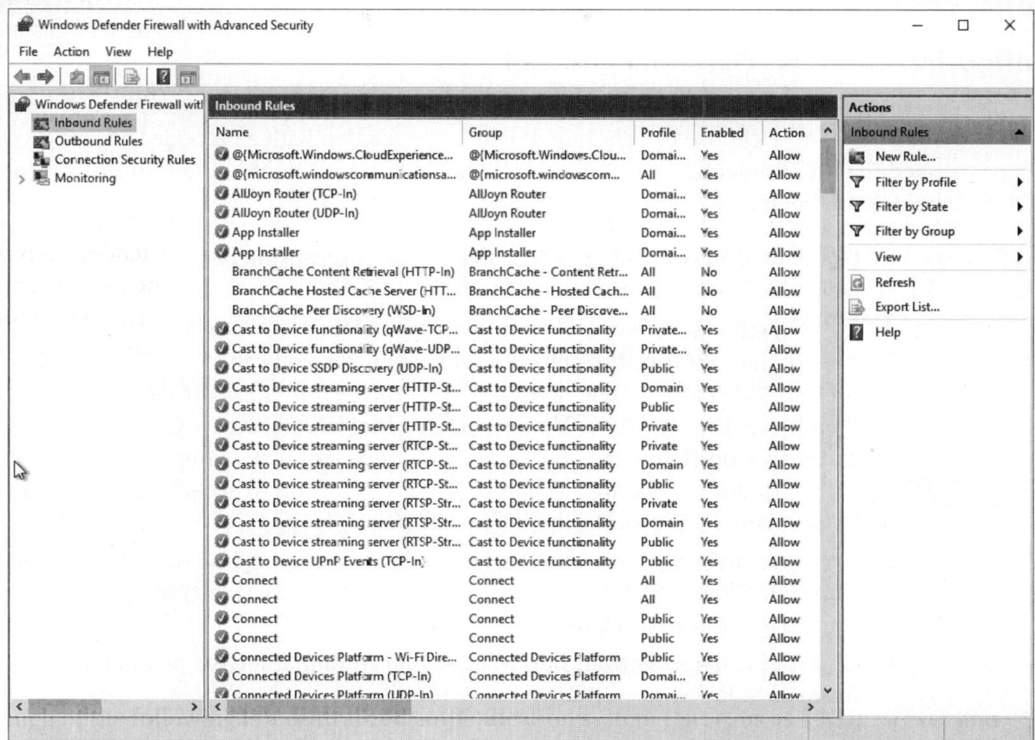

Exercise 22-2 will help you learn more about Windows Defender Firewall. You must be signed in with an account that has administrative privileges to work with Windows Defender Firewall (and to complete this exercise). If you installed a third-party firewall, you should turn off Windows Defender Firewall (if it's not off already), because multiple firewalls on the same computer do not cooperate. Therefore, when you do Exercise 22-2, if you find that Windows Defender Firewall is turned off, do not turn it on unless you are sure that no other firewall is installed. Exercise 22-3 will provide practice in creating a new firewall rule with Windows Defender Firewall with Advanced Security.

exam watch

Make sure you understand the purpose of a firewall and that you know how to block ports in Windows Defender Firewall.

EXERCISE 22-2

Configuring Windows Defender Firewall

In this exercise, you may encounter UAC prompts. If you are logged on with an Administrator account, simply choose to continue. If you are logged on with a Standard account, you will need to enter credentials to continue, in which case, you should obtain these credentials before you begin.

1. Open the Control Panel and type **fire** in the Control Panel Search box. Select Windows Defender Firewall from the results.
2. If the Windows Defender Firewall is on, as in Figure 22-1, proceed to Step 3. If it is not on, find out why. If you have another firewall, you can look at the settings for that firewall. If Windows Defender Firewall is turned off but no other firewall is enabled, then locate the link Turn Windows Defender Firewall On Or Off in the task pane and turn it on. There may be more than one location showing, so be sure you have it turned on for all locations. Then click the OK button to accept the change and return to the main Windows Defender Firewall page.
3. On the main Windows Defender Firewall page, select Allow An App Or Feature Through Windows Defender Firewall (a task item on the left) to open the Allowed Apps page, shown in Figure 22-2.
4. Click the Change Settings button to enable editing. If a UAC prompt appears, respond to it.
5. Select or deselect programs to allow through the firewall, and click Details to look at details that describe the program and the protocols it uses.
6. If you need to add another program/app, click Allow Another App, and then follow the prompts. We do not recommend adding a program unless you are confident that this exception is required and will not cause harm. If you need to remove an app from the list, use the Remove button.
7. When you have finished with the Allowed Apps (or Allowed Programs) page, if you have made changes, click OK. If you have not made any changes or wish to discard your changes, click Cancel. This will bring you back to the main Windows Defender Firewall page. Leave this window open for the next exercise.

EXERCISE 22-3

Creating a Firewall Rule

Complete this exercise to practice creating a firewall rule.

1. In the Windows Defender Firewall screen in the Control Panel, in the navigation pane on the left, click Advanced Settings. The Windows Defender Firewall with Advanced Security app opens (see Figure 22-3).
2. Click Inbound Rules in the navigation pane on the left. Then browse to see the various rules in effect.
3. Click Outbound Rules to see the outbound rules.
4. Click Monitoring to see a summary.
5. Click Inbound Rules again, and then in the Actions pane on the right, click new Rule. The New Inbound Rule Wizard runs.
6. Click Predefined and then open the drop-down list and choose one of the predefined rules. For a harmless example, choose Windows Media Player.
7. Click Program, and then click Next.
8. Click This Program Path. Then enter the path to an application. You can use any application for this exercise. Browse for it if you need to. For a simple example, choose something like Notepad. Then click Next.
9. Confirm that Allow The Connection is selected, and then click Next.
10. Leave all three check boxes selected, and click Next.
11. Type a name for the rule (for example, **Notepad Test**) and then click Finish.
12. Return to the Windows Defender Firewall with Advanced Security window. Locate and select the rule you just created. (It may be at the top of the list rather than in its alphabetical place.)
13. In the Actions pane, click Delete to remove the rule you created. Click Yes to confirm.
14. Close all open windows.

Firewall Settings in the Settings App

The Control Panel firewall settings have been the mainstay of firewall configuration in Windows for many years, but the Settings app also contains some firewall settings you can adjust. You should know about these because they're referenced in CompTIA A+ 1102 exam Objective 2.5.

The fastest way to get to these settings is to open the Settings app and search for Firewall, and then click Firewall & Network Protection. (That works in Windows 10 and 11.) See Figure 22-4 for the Windows 11 version.

From there, you can view the firewall status of your networks, and you can access various firewall-related settings:

- **Allow an app through firewall** This directs you to the same Control Panel interface that you learned about earlier for this task.
- **Firewall notification settings** Here you can change the apps and services that protect your devices and manage the notifications you receive.
- **Advanced settings** This opens Windows Defender Firewall with Advanced Security, which you learned about earlier.
- **Restore firewalls to default** On this screen you can click Restore Defaults to reset all custom settings.

Firewall Settings in macOS

In macOS, you can access the settings for the built-in firewall via Apple menu | System Preferences | Security & Privacy | Firewall. There you will find many of the same configuration options as in Windows Defender Firewall.

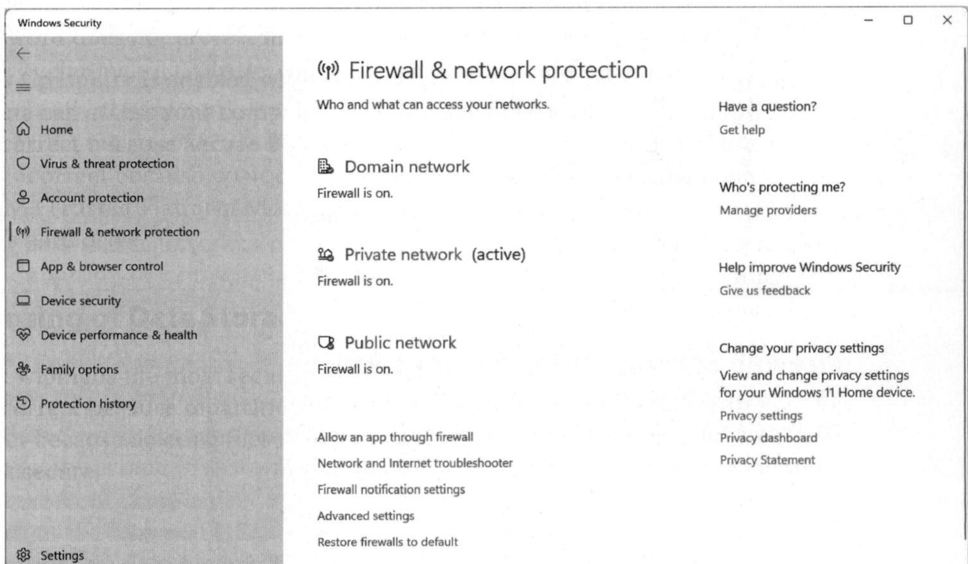

FIGURE 22-4 Firewall settings accessed via the Settings app

Firewall Settings in Linux

Linux has a built-in firewall called Netfilter. You can use the **iptables** command at a Terminal window to configure it. For example, to start, stop, or restart the iptables service:

```
service iptables start
service iptables stop
service iptables restart
```

To open the iptables file:

```
gedit /etc/sysconfig/iptables
```

A complete discussion of the syntax of the **iptables** command is beyond the scope of this book; here's a good additional reference: https://www.geeksforgeeks.org/iptables-command-in-linux-with-examples.

Third-Party Software Firewalls

There are many inexpensive third-party software firewalls—some commercial and some free. Examples of personal firewalls are ZoneAlarm Extreme Security by Check Point and McAfee Personal Firewall. Each of these is available as a separate product or as part of a security software bundle.

Antivirus and Antimalware Software

An antivirus program can examine the contents of a drive and random access memory (RAM), looking for hidden viruses and files that may act as hosts for virus code. Effective products not only detect viruses in incoming files before they can infect your system but also remove existing viruses and help you recover data that has been lost because of a virus.

An antimalware program is similar but provides a broader base of coverage, looking not only for viruses but for other kinds of malware too, including spyware and adware.

To keep an antivirus/antimalware program up to date, always enable the update option (which should be enabled by default). Configure it (if needed) to connect automatically to the manufacturer's website, check for updates, and install them.

An antivirus/antimalware program will update at least two components: the detection engine (the main program) and a set of patterns of recognized threats, usually contained in files called definition files. Some manufacturers of commercial programs may charge an annual subscription fee. There are also excellent free services for home users. Even the commercial vendors who do not offer a completely free product often allow you to try their product for a period, usually 30 days.

As you learned earlier in this chapter, spyware and adware are types of programs that install on your computer and perform functions on behalf of others. The intent of spyware can be very malicious, including identity theft, whereas the intent of adware is generally less malicious, even if the people responsible for the adware hope to profit by advertising their products.

Many free and commercial programs are available that effectively block various forms of spyware and adware, especially pop-ups. These are the easiest to block, and the most annoying, because a pop-up advertisement appears in its own window and must be closed or moved before you can see the content you were seeking. Such a blocking program is a *pop-up blocker*. Configure a pop-up blocker so it will block pop-ups quietly. You can also opt to configure it to make a sound and/or display a message, allowing you to decide whether to block each pop-up. Pop-up blockers are commonly available as add-ons (plug-ins) for all the popular browsers, and most browsers have a basic pop-up blocker built in.

Windows and macOS both come with built-in malware protection utilities, discussed next. In contrast, most Linux distros do not include built-in antivirus utilities. Some people will tell you that you don't need it, because viruses that affect Linux are very rare, or because Linux is more secure by design. Nevertheless, third-party antivirus tools for Linux are available. Some popular and reliable tools are ClamAV, Sophos, ESET NOD32 Antivirus for Linux, and Bitdefender GravityZone Business Security.

Windows Defender

To activate/deactivate Windows Defender's antivirus protection, you can access its settings via the Settings app. Open the Settings app, search for antivirus, and click Virus & Threat Protection. See Figure 22-5 for the Windows 11 version.

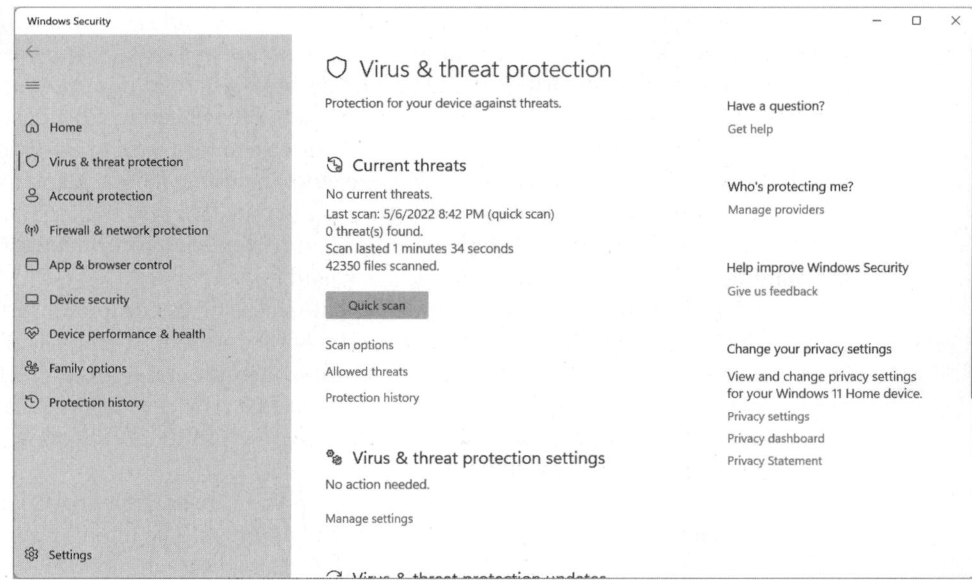

FIGURE 22-5 Windows Defender's virus and threat protection configuration options in the Settings app

From here you can

- Click Quick Scan, or click Scan Options and choose a different type of scan, to scan for malware.
- Click Manage Settings to turn protection on and off, access cloud-delivered protection or not, and adjust other settings.

You do not have to manually update the virus definitions because they are delivered automatically via Windows Update. Triggering a manual Windows Update action will look for new definitions and install any that it finds.

macOS XProtect

macOS includes XProtect, an antivirus application. Its virus definitions are updated daily via automatic updates, provided you are connected to the Internet. Its main job is to scan files looking for malware in files or applications; if it finds any, it notifies you. There is also a built-in Mac Malware Removal Tool that scans the PC regularly and removes any malware it finds.

Mac systems are less vulnerable to malware than Windows PCs because of the design of the operating system; features such as Execute Disable (XD), System Integrity Protection (SIP), and Address Space Layout Randomization (ASLR) run in the background, preventing most malware from making changes to system files. Apple also maintains tighter control on what apps can be installed by making most apps available only via the Apple Store.

Identifying Trusted Software Resources

One way that malware can enter a computer is through an untrusted download. If you are in charge of a group of individual users, who knows what trouble they may get into online, going to shady websites over their lunch breaks? It's important to set acceptable-use policies (AUPs) about software sources that restrict users from downloading files except from trusted sources.

Which sites can be trusted? It depends on how draconian your company wants to be. The stricter the policy, the more you will impede users from doing what they perhaps legitimately need to do, but the fewer malware infections you will have to deal with. In general, we would trust sites such as the official websites for well-known hardware and software (like https://support.microsoft.com) and government sites (with domain names that end in .gov).

Implementing Security Suites

Today's security software is very different from a decade ago because today's threats are more diverse than a decade ago. Therefore, you are not as likely to install a simple antivirus program, but rather an entire security suite, so we'll talk in terms of a multifunction security suite. Norton, Trend Micro, and many other software manufacturers offer such suites, which normally offer a full range of security products, including antivirus, antispyware, phishing filters, and even firewalls. Installing a security suite will normally disable any Windows components that provide equivalent functionality; for example, a suite that includes antimalware will disable Windows Defender, and a suite that includes a firewall will disable Windows Defender Firewall. That's good, because running two utilities that duplicate each other's functionality can cause problems.

Part of the installation of a security suite is a thorough scan of your computer, including memory contents and all portions of all storage devices, examining all types of files, and the parts of the disk where viruses can hide, such as the boot sector or boot block. Also, as part of the installation, you can choose to turn on automatic scans (the normal default) and the frequency of those scans. Even when you configure automatic scans, you can choose to initiate a scan when you detect possible malware symptoms. In this case, boot the computer to Safe Mode or the Windows Recovery Environment, as described in Chapter 6, and run a complete antivirus scan, then follow the instructions described in the upcoming section "Removing Malware."

You do not always have obvious symptoms of malware infections, because some malware is not detectable under normal computer operation. These infections are often, but not always, ones that occurred before a system was adequately protected. They can also occur if you have not kept up to date with updates—both to the operating system and to the security programs. If you suspect that a computer is infected but a normal scan from within Windows does not detect malware, then you should try a special technique for detecting and removing malware. For such a scenario, the top security programs have a special Safe Mode Scan that runs in Windows Safe Mode. To do this, restart Windows in Safe Mode, and then locate the security program and have it run a full scan. If it detects malware, have it quarantine or remove it, and then restart the computer and see if the symptoms have gone away.

Although the top security programs claim to protect against all types of malware, including boot sector viruses, these are rather difficult viruses to detect and remove once they have infected a computer. Therefore, security software will, by default, scan all removable media upon insertion, not allowing access to it or programs to run from it until the scan is complete. Never disable this option.

If you suspect a boot sector virus, use the System Recovery Options menu described in Chapter 6.

Removing Malware

When malware is detected, you must remediate the infected systems, removing the malware and repairing any damage it may have done. The following sections outline the seven-step best practices procedure for malware removal, as listed in CompTIA A+ 1102 exam Objective 3.3.

1. Investigate and Verify Malware Symptoms

Malware symptoms range from no symptoms to overt—but not too obvious—symptoms, such as sudden slowness, unusual cursor movements, and unusual network activity (indicated by status lights or messages) when you are not actively accessing the network. In some cases, it is a true symptom of a security problem or actual malware infection. Other symptoms can have other causes that you will need to eliminate before taking direct action against malware. You must investigate and verify malware symptoms.

2. Quarantine Infected Systems

When you suspect a computer is infected with malware, remove it from the network in order to quarantine it and keep other computers from being infected. In addition, your security program may quarantine the malware file or remove it entirely. It all depends on the security software configuration. A quarantined file is disabled but not removed from the computer. Some security software talks about the malware being in a "vault," which is the same as quarantining. Since security software can make mistakes and identify critical and uninfected files as malware, consider configuring your security program to quarantine detected malware so that you have the opportunity to review the file and decide what action to take.

3. Disable System Restore in Windows

Because System Restore (covered in Chapter 6) keeps snapshots of your computer configuration and system files, the malware can be included in those files, and your computer would be reinfected when you restored from a restore point. Only after you have removed malware should you re-enable System Restore and create a new restore point.

4. Remediate the Infected Systems

Next, remove the infection. To do this you will probably need to boot into Safe Mode (or Safe Mode with Networking). Update your existing antimalware program if you can, and run a complete scan with it. Or use a real-time scanner such as Malwarebytes if your regular antivirus program isn't working. (Some malware shuts down any installed antivirus software.)

Depending on when the infection occurred and how often you do backups, it may be possible to restore the system back to an earlier point before the infection occurred. If it's a really problematic infection, you might need to boot into the Windows Preinstallation Environment and do a repair (see Chapter 6). Boot back into Windows normally and run your antivirus software scan again to confirm the infection is gone. Use a real-time online scanner to confirm if there is any question about whether your antivirus software is giving you reliable results.

CompTIA A+ 1102 exam Objective 2.3 mentions the Recovery Console, but this is outdated wording referring back to the preinstallation environment in Windows XP. The modern equivalent to that is to boot from the Windows installation media and use the Windows Recovery Environment (RE) repair tools. It also mentions OS reinstallation as a solution for malware infection, but this is a last resort to fall back on only when all other measures have failed.

5. Schedule Scans and Run Updates

To cut down on the chance of the infection recurring, make sure your antimalware application is up to date. Download any available updates. Then make sure it is set for real-time scanning and also to do a full system scan at certain intervals.

6. Enable System Restore and Create a Restore Point in Windows

When the system is back in order and your antimalware program is updated and working, re-enable System Restore and create a new restore point representing the new, clean system state.

7. Educate the End User

Finally, if you know how the system got infected, use that information to educate yourself and everyone else who uses the PC so it won't happen again. For example, did you click a download link on a shady-looking website? Did you open an e-mail attachment from an unknown sender? Trace back to the origin of the infection and learn from it.

SCENARIO & SOLUTION	
I support computers in a large organization that uses Cisco routers and firewalls at all connections to the Internet. Why should we use personal firewalls on all our Windows computers?	A properly configured hardware firewall will protect against invasions to the network, but it will not protect each computer from invasion from within the private network.
Now that I have antimalware software enabled in Windows, do I need to be on the watch for phishing?	Yes, you still must watch for phishing attempts, because they come from social engineering. Educate yourself on the techniques phishers use to obtain your personal financial information.

CERTIFICATION SUMMARY

A computer professional must understand the threats to people, computers, and networks. These include malicious software, social engineering tactics, and many others. To that end, this chapter began with an overview of the various threats.

TWO-MINUTE DRILL

Here are some of the key points covered in Chapter 22.

Security Threats

- ❑ Malicious software attacks are common on both private and public networks. Some forms include viruses, DoS and DDoS attacks, zero-day attacks, ransomware, cryptomining, and rootkits.
- ❑ Many malware vectors exist, including Trojan horses, on-path attacks, e-mail, hidden malware installation code on websites, and browser hijacking.
- ❑ An un-updated system is at risk for exploits that target vulnerabilities in the OS. On a business network, a noncompliant system that is not fully updated and protected, such as a machine an employee brings from home, may represent a violation of the company's security best practices. An end-of-life (EOL) OS is one that is so old that the maker has stopped supporting and updating it.
- ❑ Perpetrators use a variety of methods to gain access and obtain information. Some common methods include insider threats, password theft, keyloggers, SQL injection, cross-site scripting (XSS), social engineering, vishing, and evil twin attacks.
- ❑ Password theft occurs via brute-force and dictionary attacks (password crackers), unsecured websites, and keystroke loggers.
- ❑ Social engineering involves a variety of techniques used to persuade someone to reveal confidential information or give something else of value to the perpetrator. Phishing, phone phishing, hoaxes, and enticements to open attachments all employ persuasive social engineering tactics.

Identifying the Symptoms of Malware Infection

- ❑ Malware infection may show itself as you are working online as Internet connectivity problems, pop-ups, redirection, and invalid security certificates.
- ❑ OS problems that are sometimes the result of malware include unusual security alerts, slow performance, OS update failure, false antivirus alerts, renamed or missing files, file permission changes, and system/application log errors.

- ❑ Malware may cause unexpected e-mail behavior such as increased spam or hijacked e-mail accounts.
- ❑ On a mobile device, symptoms of infection can include high network traffic, sluggish response time, data-usage limit notifications, a high number of ads, fake security warnings, unexpected application behavior, and leaked personal files/data.

Implementing a Defense Against Malware

- ❑ User Account Control prevents malware from modifying your computer by prompting for your consent.
- ❑ System Protection (System Restore) can be used to return system files to an earlier time if an infection occurs. Make sure the System Restore feature is creating automatic restore points daily.
- ❑ Windows Defender Firewall is enabled by default, but if you install a third-party firewall, Windows Defender Firewall will be turned off. You can edit Windows Defender Firewall settings from the Control Panel to allow or deny access to specific applications and ports.
- ❑ macOS and Linux both have built-in firewall protection. In macOS you configure it via System Preferences | Security & Privacy | Firewall. In Linux you configure it using the **iptables** command at a Terminal window.
- ❑ Antivirus/antimalware programs examine the contents of a drive and RAM, looking for hidden viruses and files that may act as hosts for virus code and malware.
- ❑ Windows has Windows Defender as an antimalware tool, and macOS has XProtect. Linux has no built-in antivirus tools.
- ❑ Always enable the update option in an antivirus program and configure it to automatically connect to the manufacturer's website, check for updates, and install them. These updates will include changes to both the antivirus engine and definition files.
- ❑ Encourage users to acquire applications only from trusted sources, such as the official store app for the operating system.
- ❑ To remove malware, (1) investigate and verify malware symptoms, (2) quarantine infected systems, (3) disable System Restore in Windows, (4) remediate infected systems, (5) schedule scans and run updates, (6) enable System Restore and create a restore point in Windows, and (7) educate end users.

SELF TEST

The following questions will help you measure your understanding of the material presented in this chapter. Read all of the choices carefully, because there might be more than one correct answer. Choose all correct answers for each question.

Security Threats

1. What is the term for malware that is executable code that hides in an executable file and spreads to other executable files?

A. Virus
B. Cryptomining
C. Spyware
D. Social engineering

2. What type of attack sends a large number of requests to a server, overwhelming it so it stops functioning?

A. Trojan horse
B. Ransomware
C. Denial-of-service attack
D. Keystroke logger

3. A hacker discovers and exploits a vulnerability before the software vendor is aware that the vulnerability exists. What type of attack is being described?

A. On-path
B. Brute-force
C. Zero-day
D. Dictionary

4. Which of the following is a term for unsolicited e-mail?

A. Spim
B. Spam
C. DDoS
D. Trojan horse

5. What type of program attempts to guess passwords on a computer?
   A. Keystroke logger
   B. Password cracker
   C. Virus
   D. Spim
6. What type of malware is installed by an administrator and hides from detection by antimalware programs by concealing itself within the OS code or other program code?
   A. Rootkit
   B. Bluesnarfing
   C. Cookies
   D. Phishing
7. This threat installs on a computer without permission and collects information about a user in order to display targeted advertisements.
   A. Spam
   B. Cryptomining
   C. Adware
   D. Spim
8. The symptom of this threat is that your web browser home page changed from the one you selected, pointing to a site advertising some product.
   A. Rootkit
   B. Virus
   C. Spam
   D. Browser hijack
9. This is the general term for any method malware uses to gain access to a computer or network.
   A. Vector
   B. Trojan horse
   C. Worm
   D. Phishing
10. You may install this type of malware because it appears to be a harmless program.
    A. Spam
    B. Worm
    C. Trojan horse
    D. Rootkit

11. What does using secure design practices when constructing website code that collects form data protect against? (Choose two.)

A. SQL injection

B. Cross-site scripting (XSS)

C. Evil twin

D. Whaling

Identifying the Symptoms of Malware Infection

12. Which of these is *not* a common symptom of malware infection?

A. Renamed user profile

B. Slow performance

C. Disabled antivirus/antimalware program

D. Security alert

13. What does an invalid security certificate message mean in a browser?

A. Malware has been detected on your PC.

B. The website you are about to enter does not have a valid security certificate.

C. Malware has been detected on the website you are about to visit.

D. The website you are about to visit is a phishing site.

Implementing a Defense Against Malware

14. What hardware device or software program prevents unwanted traffic from entering a network?

A. Proxy server

B. Firewall

C. Router

D. Switch

15. What two antivirus components are frequently updated?

A. Spyware and rootkits

B. Engine and definitions

C. Engine and spam filter

D. Definition files and phishing filter

16. When a Standard user tries to make a system change, what feature prompts for an Administrator account's password?

A. TPM

B. Spam filter

C. UAC

D. Antimalware

17. What utility that comes with Windows can you use to scan for and remove malware?
A. UAC
B. Windows Defender
C. Pop-up blocker
D. Windows Defender Firewall

18. What security software examines the contents of a drive and RAM, looking for hidden viruses and files that may act as hosts for virus code?
A. Phishing filter
B. Antivirus/antimalware
C. Personal firewall
D. Pop-up blocker

19. What should you do before attempting to remove malware?
A. Sign in as a Standard user
B. Disable System Restore
C. Enable System Restore
D. Educate the end users

20. Why would you want to use Windows Defender Firewall with Advanced Security rather than the standard Windows Defender Firewall?
A. Secure specific port numbers
B. Allow an application through the firewall
C. Check for malware
D. Create rules for inbound and outbound traffic

SELF TEST ANSWERS

Security Threats

1. ☑ **A.** A virus is executable malware that spreads by attaching itself to other executable files.
☒ **B** is incorrect because cryptomining is the process of using other computers' processing power to mine for cryptocurrency without consent. **C** is incorrect because spyware is a type of malware that spies on a user's activities. **D** is incorrect because social engineering is the use of persuasion techniques to discover information that can be used in hacking.

2. ☑ **C.** A denial-of-service (DoS) attack aims to shut down a server by bombarding it with fake requests.
   ☒ **A** is incorrect because a Trojan horse is a type of virus that hides within an apparently harmless program. **B** is incorrect because ransomware locks up a system's files and holds them for ransom. **D** is incorrect because a keystroke logger is a program that logs the user's keystrokes.

3. ☑ **C.** A zero-day attack occurs when the hacker discovers and exploits a vulnerability before the software vendor is aware that the vulnerability exists. It gets its name from the fact that the vendor has zero days to patch the vulnerability before the attack.
   ☒ **A** is incorrect because with an on-path attack, the attacking software (or person) secretly inserts itself between two parties in a secure conversation, gathering data from each. **B** is incorrect because some password crackers fall into the brute-force category, which simply means the program tries a huge number of permutations of possible passwords. **D** is incorrect because a dictionary attack is a password-cracking attempt that systematically tries every word in a dictionary as the password.

4. ☑ **B.** Spam is a term for unsolicited e-mail.
   ☒ **A** is incorrect because spim is unwanted SMS text messages, not e-mail. **C** is incorrect because DDoS is a distributed denial-of-service attack on a server. **D** is incorrect because a Trojan horse is a type of virus that hides within an apparently harmless program.

5. ☑ **B.** Password crackers attempt to guess passwords on a computer.
   ☒ **A** is incorrect because a keystroke logger does not try to "guess" passwords—it tries to steal passwords by capturing keystrokes. **C** is incorrect because a virus is a very general term for malicious code. **D** is incorrect because spim is unwanted SMS text messages.

6. ☑ **A.** A rootkit is malware that hides from detection by antimalware programs by concealing itself within the OS code or other program code.
   ☒ **B** is incorrect because Bluesnarfing is the act of covertly obtaining information broadcast from wireless devices using the Bluetooth standard. **C** is incorrect because cookies are not program code, and they do not allow access to an operating system. **D** is incorrect because phishing is a fraudulent method of obtaining personal and financial information through pop-ups or e-mail messages that purport to be from a legitimate organization.

7. ☑ **C.** Adware is a threat that installs on a computer without permission and collects information about a user in order to display targeted advertisements.
   ☒ **A** and **D** are incorrect because they represent unwanted messages—spam being unwanted e-mail and spim being unwanted instant messaging messages. **B** is incorrect because cryptomining uses the target computer to mine for cryptocurrency without the owner's consent.

8. ☑ **D.** Browser hijack is a change in your web browser home page.
   ☒ **A** is incorrect because a rootkit is a clandestine infection that would not display advertising. **B** is incorrect because a virus relies on stealth to spread itself and would not announce its presence by changing your home page. **C** is incorrect because spam is unwanted e-mail.

9. ☑ **A.** Vector is the general term for how malware gains access to a computer or network.
☒ **B** and **C** are incorrect because Trojan horse and worm are individual examples of vectors. **D** is incorrect because phishing is an attempt to fool a user into entering private information at a fraudulent website.

10. ☑ **C.** A Trojan horse is malware that appears to be a useful, harmless program.
☒ **A** is incorrect because spam is unwanted commercial e-mail. **B** is incorrect because worm is malware that travels via network connections. **D** is incorrect because a rootkit is malware that hides in the OS code.

11. ☑ **A** and **B.** Unsecured forms are vulnerable to SQL injection and cross-site scripting.
☒ **C** is incorrect because an evil twin is a fake Wi-Fi hotspot that a hacker might set up in a public place, hoping that someone will try to connect to it to get free Internet access. **D** is incorrect because whaling is an attack directed at a high-level individual or a group of high-level individuals.

Identifying the Symptoms of Malware Infection

12. ☑ **A.** A renamed user profile was not mentioned in this chapter as a common symptom of malware infection. That is such an obvious, easily noticed change that it would be unlikely that malware would make it, especially because it would serve no real purpose to do so.
☒ **B, C,** and **D** are incorrect because they are all common symptoms of malware infection.

13. ☑ **B.** An invalid security certificate doesn't say anything at all about the content of the site. It only evaluates its certificate.
☒ **A, C,** and **D** are incorrect because none of these are assumptions you can make about a site based on its certificate's validity or invalidity.

Implementing a Defense Against Malware

14. ☑ **B.** A firewall is the hardware device or software program that prevents unwanted traffic from entering a network.
☒ **A** is incorrect because although a proxy server is one of the technologies used by a firewall, it does not fully describe a firewall. **C** is incorrect because a router is a separate device (or software), although it may use one or more of the technologies associated with a firewall. **D** is incorrect because this device or software does not prevent unwanted traffic from entering a network. A switch is a cable-connecting device used within a network.

15. ☑ **B.** The engine and definitions are the two frequently updated antivirus components.
☒ **A** is incorrect because spyware and rootkits are two kinds of threats, not two components of antivirus programs. **C** is incorrect because although the antivirus engine is one of the updated components, the spam filter is not part of antivirus software, even though it may be bundled with antivirus software in a security package. **D** is incorrect because although definition file is part of the correct answer, phishing filter is not part of an antivirus program, but a web browser add-on or feature.

16. ☑ **C.** UAC, or User Account Control, prompts for credentials when a Standard user tries to make a system change.
☒ **A** is incorrect because TPM (Trusted Platform Module) manages disk encryption. **B** is incorrect because a spam filter is not a feature that prompts for an Administrator account's password. **D** is incorrect because antimalware is also not a feature that prompts for an Administrator account's password.

17. ☑ **B.** Windows Defender removes viruses and other malware in Windows.
☒ **A** is incorrect because User Account Control (UAC) prompts for permission when system changes are being made. **C** is incorrect because a pop-up blocker prevents browser pop-ups. **D** is incorrect because Windows Defender Firewall prevents intrusions on ports but does not remove viruses or malware.

18. ☑ **B.** Antivirus/antimalware is security software that examines the contents of a drive and RAM, looking for hidden viruses and files that may act as hosts for virus code.
☒ **A** is incorrect because a phishing filter works within a browser and scans websites for certain social engineering traits. **C** is incorrect because a personal firewall blocks certain types of incoming messages based on information in the packet header but does not look at the contents to determine if it is virus code. **D** is incorrect because a pop-up blocker only works within a browser to prevent unwanted browser windows from opening.

19. ☑ **B.** Before removing malware, disable System Restore in Windows so the virus does not come back via that feature.
☒ **A** is incorrect because a Standard user lacks permission to make system changes. **C** is incorrect because System Restore should be disabled, not enabled. **D** is incorrect because educating the end users is the last step in the malware removal process and should not occur before attempting to remove the malware.

20. ☑ **D.** Windows Defender Firewall with Advanced Security enables you to create rules for inbound and outbound network traffic.
☒ **A** and **B** are incorrect because both of these activities can be done using the standard Windows Defender Firewall. **C** is incorrect because no firewall software checks for malware.

Chapter 23

Scripting

CERTIFICATION OBJECTIVE

- **1102: 4.8** Identify the basics of scripting

Scripting isn't just for developers; IT technicians looking to schedule or automate repetitive tasks can benefit from this skill to save time and reduce human error. You can use scripting languages such as Bash shell scripting (commonly used in Unix and Linux), Microsoft PowerShell (commonly used in Windows), or JavaScript (commonly used in web pages), to name just a few.

Scripting Fundamentals

Scripts can be created using any simple text editor such as *Notepad* in the Windows environment or *vi* or *nano* in Unix and Linux environments. Scripts get interpreted by a *scripting engine* that is designed to run that specific type of script, so they aren't compiled code such as an .exe file. This is why scripts can be created in simple text editors and can stay in plaintext format.

Use Cases for Scripting

Here are a few common uses for scripts:

- Automating repetitive processes, so you don't have to do so much typing
- Restarting machines
- Remapping network drives
- Installing applications
- Automating backups
- Gathering information/data
- Initiating updates

Scripting-Related Risks and Hazards

When you're configuring a single PC, it's important to know what you're doing, but when you're using a script to configure dozens or hundreds of PCs at once, that becomes even more important, because a mistake you make in the script that causes a problem on multiple PCs can be disastrous. Here are some especially important risks to watch out for:

- **Introducing malware** Make very sure that whatever utilities you might be running are from trusted sources and are malware-free.
- **Bad changes to system settings** Make sure there are no errors or typos in your script that create bad system settings changes, or you'll be weeks cleaning up the mess. Even if you don't have any typos, though, you can never be sure that system changes your script makes to multiple PCs will have the same results on each PC. Different hardware, installed apps, and OS versions can all make a difference.
- **Crashes due to mishandling of resources** Badly scripted changes may create crashes to the OS itself, to browsers, and/or to applications. Registry changes can be especially dangerous to make to multiple machines at a time via scripting.

Make sure you understand all these use cases and potential hazards; all these were added as new topics in the latest iteration of the CompTIA A+ exams, so you can assume there will be questions about them.

Script File Types

The type of script you will create depends on factors such as your existing familiarity with a scripting language, existing scripts already in use, the capabilities required in the script to carry out tasks, and the preferred script type used within the organization. For example, JavaScript is used within web pages and is executed by web browsers. Automating administrative tasks in Windows environments is normally done using PowerShell scripts; server-side scripts on web servers might use Python.

exam watch **All these scripting file types are listed in CompTIA A+ exam 1102 Objective 4.8.**

Some scripting languages are case sensitive, such as JavaScript and Shell scripts. PowerShell scripts are not. Table 23-1 lists common script file types.

exam watch **Aside from Table 23-1, the rest of this chapter's information is *not* on the CompTIA A+ exams, so you do not need to study it for test-taking purposes. You may find it useful on the job, though.**

TABLE 23-1 Common Scripting File Types

File Extension	Description
.bat	Batch file; older script type used on DOS and Windows machines.
.ps1	PowerShell script file, modern script type used in Windows environments.
.vbs	Visual Basic Script; older script type used on Windows machines and within older Microsoft web browsers.
.sh	Shell script, used in Unix and Linux environments.
.py	Python script, general-purpose programming language; used often in Windows, Unix, and Linux environments, as well as for server-side web app code.
.js	JavaScript, commonly used to run client-side code within the user web browser.

Scripting Tools

You can create a script in any app that creates plaintext files, including Notepad.

Fancier scripting programs can be acquired, or in some cases they are built into the operating system, such as the Microsoft PowerShell Integrated Scripting Environment (ISE) seen in Figure 23-1.

These tools enhance your script-writing experience by providing

- Color coding of special keyword types
- Built-in help system to ease the pain of learning syntax
- Auto-fill that makes suggestions as you type
- Ability to run the entire script without leaving the editor
- Ability to run selected lines in a script to test them

FIGURE 23-1 Microsoft PowerShell ISE

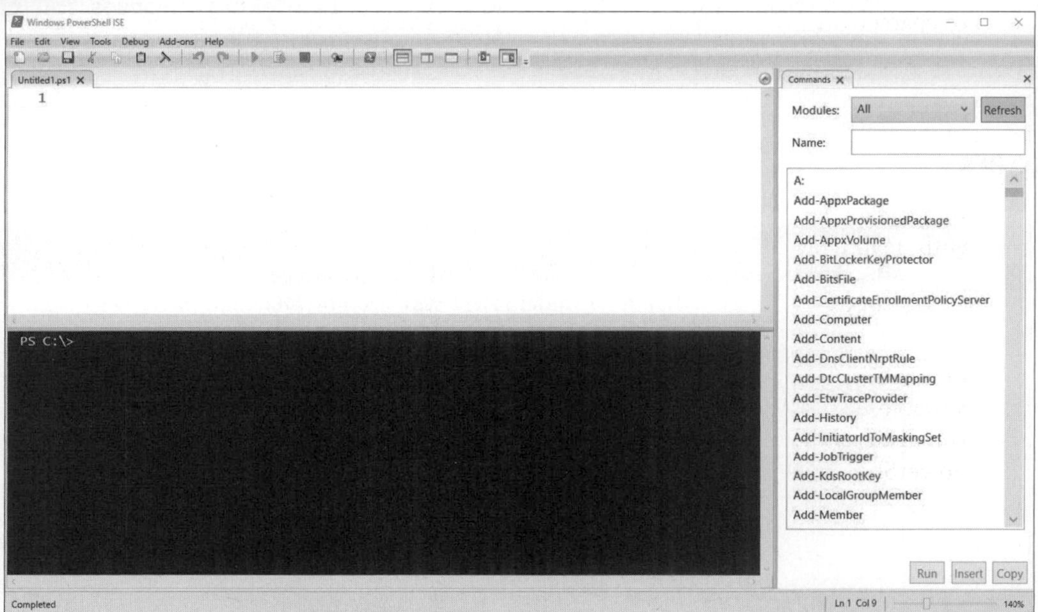

FIGURE 23-2 Microsoft PowerShell GetType()

```
PS C:\> $age=50
PS C:\> $age.GetType()

IsPublic IsSerial Name     BaseType
-------- -------- ----     --------
True     True     Int32    System.ValueType
```

Data Types

The supported data types and related syntax vary between scripting languages, but most scripting languages support common data types such as strings and integers.

Strings

Scripts that deal with user names, filenames, and city names—anything that is a text string—will use some type of string data type. Some scripting language commands work only against certain data types, such as determining the number of characters in a string, as seen in the following JavaScript language where *username* is the name of a variable and *length* is a property, or characteristic, of that variable. Notice the dot separating the variable from the property.

```
username.length
```

Integers

Integers are another common data type. An integer is a positive or negative whole number with no decimal places. The specific minimum and maximum values that can be used with integer values depend on your chosen scripting language.

JavaScript uses a *number* data type; there is no specific *integer* data type. Microsoft PowerShell, on the other hand, does have a specific integer data type with a numeric range of –2,147,483,648 to 2,147,483,647. Figure 23-2, using PowerShell, shows the creation of a variable called *age* being set with a value of *50*. The **.GetType()** method, or action, is being run against that variable and it returns *Int32*, which indicates this is an integer variable. PowerShell variables are always preceded with a dollar sign.

Variables

To facilitate working with scripts, script writers often use custom names for values that change throughout their code; these are *variables*. Operating systems also have built-in variables called *environment variables* that contain values such as the currently logged-on user name, home directory path, version of the operating system, and so on.

FIGURE 23-3 Linux environment variables

```
root@kali:~# env
XDG_SESSION_ID=1
TERM=xterm
SHELL=/bin/bash
SSH_CLIENT=192.168.0.12 29307 22
SSH_TTY=/dev/pts/0
USER=root
MAIL=/var/mail/root
PATH=/usr/local/sbin:/usr/local/bin:/usr/sbin:/usr/bin:/sbin:/bin
PWD=/root
LANG=en_US.UTF-8
SHLVL=1
HOME=/root
LOGNAME=root
```

Environment Variables

You can use environment variables in your scripts as needed. The syntax to accomplish this varies among scripting languages. Figure 23-3 shows how the Linux **env** command returns environment variables.

The same type of result is accomplished in a Windows command prompt (also in a batch file) using the **set** command, as seen in Figure 23-4.

We can view environment variables through PowerShell with the **Get-ChildItem env:** command, as seen in Figure 23-5.

FIGURE 23-4 Using Windows environment variables through a command prompt

```
C:\>set
ALLUSERSPROFILE=C:\ProgramData
APPDATA=C:\Users\danla\AppData\Roaming
CommonProgramFiles=C:\Program Files\Common Files
CommonProgramFiles(x86)=C:\Program Files (x86)\Common Files
CommonProgramW6432=C:\Program Files\Common Files
COMPUTERNAME=LAPTOP-E41MU5AM
ComSpec=C:\WINDOWS\system32\cmd.exe
DriverData=C:\Windows\System32\Drivers\DriverData
HOMEDRIVE=C:
HOMEPATH=\Users\danla
LOCALAPPDATA=C:\Users\danla\AppData\Local
LOGONSERVER=\\LAPTOP-E41MU5AM
NUMBER_OF_PROCESSORS=12
OneDrive=C:\Users\danla\OneDrive
OneDriveConsumer=C:\Users\danla\OneDrive
OS=Windows_NT
```

FIGURE 23-5

Using Windows environment variables through PowerShell

```
PS C:\> Get-ChildItem env:

Name                           Value
----                           -----
ALLUSERSPROFILE                C:\ProgramData
APPDATA                        C:\Users\danla\AppData\Roaming
CommonProgramFiles             C:\Program Files\Common Files
CommonProgramFiles(x86)        C:\Program Files (x86)\Common Files
CommonProgramW6432             C:\Program Files\Common Files
COMPUTERNAME                   LAPTOP-E41MU5AM
ComSpec                        C:\WINDOWS\system32\cmd.exe
DriverData                     C:\Windows\System32\Drivers\DriverData
HOMEDRIVE                      C:
HOMEPATH                       \Users\danla
LOCALAPPDATA                   C:\Users\danla\AppData\Local
LOGONSERVER                    \\LAPTOP-E41MU5AM
NUMBER_OF_PROCESSORS           12
```

Script Variables

Imagine that you are writing a script that will list the running services on a Windows computer. If you need to use that list of running services over and over again in your code, it's much more efficient to get the list of services only once, store it in a variable, and then reuse the variable rather than repeatedly getting the list of services each time it's needed. The following Microsoft PowerShell example stores only running services in a variable named **$running_svcs**; note that the built-in placeholder variable **$_** is being used to process all returned services—also notice the "equals" operator (**-eq**).

```
$running_svcs = Get-Service | Where{$_.status -eq "Running"}
```

Whenever you need to list running services in your script, you can simply refer to the **$running_svcs** variable name instead of issuing the original long command again.

In PowerShell, you could ask a user to enter a cost center code, which would be stored in a variable:

```
$cost_center_code = Read-Host("Please enter a cost center:")
```

In Python, the same thing would look like this:

```
cost_center_code = raw_input("Please enter a cost center:")
```

Common Scripting Elements

Regardless of the scripting language, scripters use certain common elements. Some are related to best practices, such as using comments to document your script. Other items are more functional, such as the conditional execution of commands.

TABLE 23-2 Using Comments in Scripts

Script Type	Example
Batch file (.bat)	REM This is a comment
PowerShell (.ps1)	# This is a comment
Visual Basic Script (.vbs)	' This is a comment
Shell Script (.sh)	# This is a comment
Python (.py)	# This is a comment
JavaScript (.js)	// This is a comment

Comments

Comments in scripts make reading the script much easier, even for the script creator after enough time has passed! They explain exactly what the script does and why it does it. Having that information readily available speeds up troubleshooting and script modifications.

The way to indicate a comment in a script varies among scripting languages. Table 23-2 provides examples of using comments in different scripting languages.

Conditional Execution

Most languages have a method of running a command only if it meets a specific condition. The general format of an *if* statement looks like this:

```
If <condition_to_test>, <code to run if true>, <code to run if false>
```

The specific syntax varies between languages; if you're using Python, it would look something like this:

```
age = raw_input("Enter age:")
if age < 16:
    print "A license cannot be issued."
else :
    print "Submission has been accepted."
```

In PowerShell, the same example would look like the following sample code. Notice the age variable is being declared as an integer with **[int]**, and also notice the **–lt** operator, which stands for "less than":

```
[int]$age=Read-Host("Enter age")
if ($age -lt 16)
{
    "A license cannot be issued."
}
```

```
else
{
    "Submission has been accepted."
}
```

Looping

Loops execute a series of commands zero or more times depending on how they are coded. Sometimes you'll know how many times you need to run the same code, such as checking ten input fields on a web page; you could run the JavaScript command for testing input validity ten times to ensure that all user input is acceptable. Other times you won't know how many times you need to run the same code, such as when processing whatever number of files might exist in a subdirectory. Luckily, most scripting languages provide a multitude of looping options.

Loop Syntax

Most scripting languages support different types of looping constructs. One common loop type is a *while* loop that tests a condition. While the condition is true, the code within the loop executes. The following Microsoft PowerShell example displays a menu of options to the user until the user presses 3 ("Exit this menu"). In some scripting languages "not equal to" is expressed as **!=** or **<>**, but PowerShell uses **–ne** (not equal). The **switch** statement tests the value of what the user entered (stored in the **$user_entered_choice** variable).

```
$user_entered_choice=1
while($user_entered_choice -ne 4)
{
    write-host "Utilities Menu"
    write-host "----------------------"
    write-host
    write-host "1 - List Active Directory user accounts"
    write-host "2 - List Active Directory computer accounts"
    write-host "3 - Exit this menu"
    write-host
    $user_entered_choice=read-host "Enter choice"
    switch($user_entered_choice)
    {
        1{get-aduser -filter *;read-host}
        2{get-adcomputer -filter *;read-host}
        }
        3{cls;break}
    }
    cls
}
```

Active Directory User Logon Scripts

Microsoft Active Directory uses a central network database containing user account definitions, groups, and computers, among other items. Commands can be executed via a script when users log on to a machine (also when they log off), whether that script is a batch file, a VB script, or PowerShell.

Common uses of logon scripts include the following:

- Map network drives
- Set or read environment variables
- Deploy new software or software updates
- Run executable programs

Any type of script will require the invoker to have permissions to run the script itself. Depending on what the script does, additional permissions might be required. For example, a Linux Shell script requires the invoker to have at least Read (r) and Execute (x) permissions. In Figure 23-6, the **ls –l** command lists files with details, the **chmod** command adds the Execute permission for all users, and then the **ls –l** command shows the new permissions.

Microsoft Group Policy in Active Directory enables the centralized configuration of user and computer settings. A user logon script can be specified in Group Policy, as shown in Figure 23-7. The users affected by the group policy object (GPO) will run the logon script.

The following example shows how a batch file (.bat file) could map a drive for a user upon logon using the **username** environment variable:

```
Net Use H: \\Server1\UserHome\%username%
```

We could map a drive letter to any shared folder through a PowerShell logon script (.ps1 file) like this:

```
New-PSDrive -Name "S" -PSProvider "FileSystem" -Root \\Server1\
SharedFiles
```

FIGURE 23-6 Viewing and setting Linux Shell script permissions with the ls command

```
root@kali:~/scripts# ls -l
total 0
-rw-r--r-- 1 root root 0 Jan 21 06:40 script1.sh
root@kali:~/scripts# chmod +x script1.sh
root@kali:~/scripts# ls -l
total 0
-rwxr-xr-x 1 root root 0 Jan 21 06:40 script1.sh
```

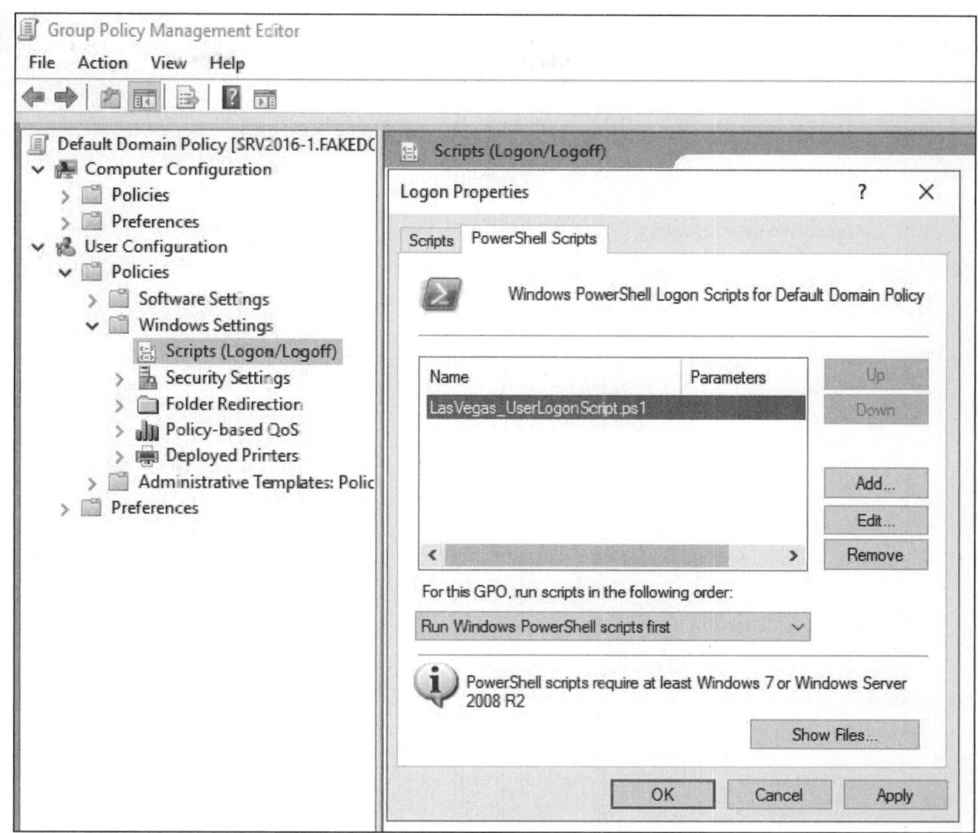

FIGURE 23-7 Specifying a PowerShell logon script in Group Policy

Appendix

About the Online Content

This book comes complete with:

- TotalTester Online customizable practice exam software with more than 400 practice exam questions
- Simulated performance-based questions
- Video training from the author
- Bonus glossary
- Exam Objective Map

System Requirements

The current and previous major versions of the following desktop browsers are recommended and supported: Chrome, Microsoft Edge, Firefox, and Safari. These browsers update frequently, and sometimes an update may cause compatibility issues with the TotalTester Online or other content hosted on the Training Hub. If you run into a problem using one of these browsers, please try using another until the problem is resolved.

Your Total Seminars Training Hub Account

To get access to the online content, you will need to create an account on the Total Seminars Training Hub. Registration is free, and you will be able to track all your online content using your account. You may also opt in if you wish to receive marketing information from McGraw Hill or Total Seminars, but this is not required for you to gain access to the online content.

Privacy Notice

McGraw Hill values your privacy. Please be sure to read the Privacy Notice available during registration to see how the information you have provided will be used. You may view our Corporate Customer Privacy Policy by visiting the McGraw Hill Privacy Center. Visit the **mheducation.com** site and click **Privacy** at the bottom of the page.

Single User License Terms and Conditions

Online access to the digital content included with this book is governed by the McGraw Hill License Agreement outlined next. By using this digital content you agree to the terms of that license.

Access To register and activate your Total Seminars Training Hub account, simply follow these easy steps.

1. Go to this URL: **hub.totalsem.com/mheclaim**
2. To register and create a new Training Hub account, enter your e-mail address, name, and password on the **Register** tab. No further personal information (such as credit card number) is required to create an account.

   If you already have a Total Seminars Training Hub account, enter your e-mail address and password on the **Log in** tab.

3. Enter your Product Key: **2th3-4ckn-s6pc**
4. Click to accept the user license terms.
5. For new users, click the **Register and Claim** button to create your account. For existing users, click the **Log in and Claim** button.

   You will be taken to the Training Hub and have access to the content for this book.

Duration of License Access to your online content through the Total Seminars Training Hub will expire one year from the date the publisher declares the book out of print.

Your purchase of this McGraw Hill product, including its access code, through a retail store is subject to the refund policy of that store.

The Content is a copyrighted work of McGraw Hill, and McGraw Hill reserves all rights in and to the Content. The Work is © 2022 by McGraw Hill.

Restrictions on Transfer The user is receiving only a limited right to use the Content for the user's own internal and personal use, dependent on purchase and continued ownership of this book. The user may not reproduce, forward, modify, create derivative works based upon, transmit, distribute, disseminate, sell, publish, or sublicense the Content or in any way commingle the Content with other third-party content without McGraw Hill's consent.

Limited Warranty The McGraw Hill Content is provided on an "as is" basis. Neither McGraw Hill nor its licensors make any guarantees or warranties of any kind, either express or implied, including, but not limited to, implied warranties of merchantability or fitness for a particular purpose or use as to any McGraw Hill Content or the information therein or any warranties as to the accuracy, completeness, correctness, or results to be obtained from, accessing or using the McGraw Hill Content, or any material referenced in such Content or any information entered into licensee's product by users or other persons and/or any material available on or that can be accessed through the licensee's product (including via any hyperlink or otherwise) or as to non-infringement of third-party rights. Any warranties of any kind, whether express or implied, are disclaimed. Any material or data obtained through use of the McGraw Hill Content is at your own discretion and risk and user understands that it will be solely responsible for any resulting damage to its computer system or loss of data.

Neither McGraw Hill nor its licensors shall be liable to any subscriber or to any user or anyone else for any inaccuracy, delay, interruption in service, error or omission, regardless of cause, or for any damage resulting therefrom.

In no event will McGraw Hill or its licensors be liable for any indirect, special or consequential damages, including but not limited to, lost time, lost money, lost profits or good will, whether in contract, tort, strict liability or otherwise, and whether or not such damages are foreseen or unforeseen with respect to any use of the McGraw Hill Content.

TotalTester Online

TotalTester Online provides you with a simulation of the CompTIA A+ exams 220-1101 and 220-1102. Exams can be taken in Practice Mode or Exam Mode. Practice Mode provides an assistance window with hints, references to the book, explanations of the correct and incorrect answers, and the option to check your answer as you take the test. Exam Mode provides a simulation of the actual exam. The number of questions, the types of questions, and the time allowed are intended to be an accurate representation of the exam environment. The option to customize your quiz allows you to create custom exams from selected domains or chapters, and you can further customize the number of questions and time allowed.

To take a test, follow the instructions provided in the previous section to register and activate your Total Seminars Training Hub account. When you register, you will be taken to the Total Seminars Training Hub. From the Training Hub Home page, select your certification from the Study drop-down menu at the top of the page to drill down to the TotalTester for your book. You can also scroll to it from the list of Your Topics on the Home page, and then click on the TotalTester link to launch the TotalTester. Once you've launched your TotalTester, you can select the option to customize your quiz and begin testing yourself in Practice Mode or Exam Mode. All exams provide an overall grade and a grade broken down by domain.

Other Book Resources

The following sections detail the other resources available with your book. You can access these items by selecting the Resources tab, or by selecting CompTIA A+ Study Guide, 11e (Exams 220-1101 & 220-1102) from the Study drop-down menu at the top of the page or from the list of Your Topics on the Home page. The menu on the right side of the screen outlines all of the available resources.

Performance-Based Questions

In addition to multiple-choice questions, the CompTIA A+ exams include performance-based questions (PBQs), which, according to CompTIA, are designed to test your ability to solve problems in a simulated environment. More information about PBQs is provided on CompTIA's website. You can access the performance-based questions included with this book by navigating to the **Resources** tab and selecting **Performance-Based Questions Quiz**. After you have selected the PBQs, an interactive quiz will launch in your browser.

Video Training from the Author

Video MP4 clips from the author of this book provide detailed examples of key certification objectives in audio/video format. You can access these videos by navigating to the **Resources** tab and selecting **Videos**. The videos are organized by chapter and by exercise and will launch in your Web browser.

Glossary

A bonus glossary for the book has been included for your review. You can access the glossary by navigating to the **Resources** tab and selecting **Glossary**. You can either view the glossary online in your web browser or you can select the download option in the menu to download a PDF.

Exam Objective Map

An Exam Objective Map for the book has been included for your review. The Exam Objective Map shows which chapters cover individual CompTIA A+ exam objectives for both exams 220-1101 and 220-1102. You can access the map by navigating to the **Resources** tab and selecting **Exam Objective Map**. You can either view the Exam Objective Map online in your Web browser or you can select the Download option in the menu to download a PDF.

Technical Support

For questions regarding the TotalTester or operation of the Training Hub, visit **www.totalsem.com** or e-mail **support@totalsem.com**.

For questions regarding book content, visit **www.mheducation.com/customerservice**.

INDEX

A

B

C

D

E

F

I

J

K

L

M

Q

R

U

V

X

Y

Z